CasebookConnect.com

REGISTER NOW to access the Study Center for:

- Hundreds of practice questions
- Selections from popular study aids
- Progress trackers to save you time
- Tutorial videos

Combine this wealth of resources with an **enhanced ebook** and **outlining tool** and you will **SUCCEED** in law school

Use this unique code to connect your casebook today

ccess Code: GLDT835317835696

Go to www.casebookconnect.com and redeem your access code to get started.

PLEASE NOTE: Each access code can only be used once. This access code will expire one year after the discontinuation of the corresponding print title and must be redeemed before then. CCH reserves the right to discontinue this program at any time for any business reason. For further details, please see the Casebook Connect End User License Agreement.

PIN9111149040

18028

TORT LAW

Aspen Casebook Series

TORT LAW

Responsibilities and Redress

FOURTH EDITION

John C.P. Goldberg
Eli Goldston Professor of Law
Harvard Law School

Anthony J. Sebok
Professor of Law
Benjamin N. Cardozo School of Law

Benjamin C. Zipursky
James H. Quinn '49 Chair in Legal Ethics
Professor of Law
Fordham University School of Law

Wolters Kluwer

Published by Wolters Kluwer in New York.

Wolters Kluwer Legal & Regulatory Solutions U.S. serves customers worldwide with CCH, Aspen Publishers, and Kluwer Law International products. (www.WKLegaledu.com)

To contact Customer Service, e-mail customer.service@wolterskluwer.com, call 1-800-234-1660, fax 1-800-901-9075, or mail correspondence to:

Wolters Kluwer
Attn: Order Department
PO Box 990
Frederick, MD 21705

Printed in the United States of America.

1 2 3 4 5 6 7 8 9 0

ISBN 978-1-4548-6820-0

Library of Congress Cataloging-in-Publication Data

Names: Goldberg, John C. P., 1961- author. | Sebok, Anthony James, 1963- author. | Zipursky, Benjamin Charles, 1960- author.
Title: Tort law : responsibilities and redress / John C.P. Goldberg, Eli Goldston Professor of Law, Harvard Law School; Anthony J. Sebok, Professor of Law, Benjamin N. Cardozo School of Law; Benjamin C. Zipursky, James H. Quinn '49 Chair in Legal Ethics, Professor of Law, Fordham University School of Law.
Description: Fourth edition. | New York: Wolters Kluwer, 2016. | Series: Aspen casebook series | Includes bibliographical references and index.
Identifiers: LCCN 2016001698 | ISBN 9781454868200
Subjects: LCSH: Torts — United States. | LCGFT: Casebooks.
Classification: LCC KF1250 .G65 2016 | DDC 346.7303 — dc23
LC record available at http://lccn.loc.gov/2016001698

About Wolters Kluwer Legal & Regulatory Solutions U.S.

Wolters Kluwer Legal & Regulatory Solutions U.S. delivers expert content and solutions in the areas of law, corporate compliance, health compliance, reimbursement, and legal education. Its practical solutions help customers successfully navigate the demands of a changing environment to drive their daily activities, enhance decision quality and inspire confident outcomes.

Serving customers worldwide, its legal and regulatory solutions portfolio includes products under the Aspen Publishers, CCH Incorporated, Kluwer Law International, ftwilliam.com and MediRegs names. They are regarded as exceptional and trusted resources for general legal and practice-specific knowledge, compliance and risk management, dynamic workflow solutions, and expert commentary.

To Julie

—J.C.P.G.

For Max

—A.J.S.

To Antonia

—B.C.Z.

Summary of Contents

Contents

Preface to the Fourth Edition

This edition includes extensive updating in text and notes, along with modest changes in principal case selection. Chapter 4 features new decisions that range from straightforward slip-and-fall cases to complex toxic tort cases. Our hope is that they more clearly convey the doctrinal and evidentiary issues associated with the causation component of negligence. We have also continued to follow the ongoing battle in products liability law between the risk-utility and consumer expectation tests. Toward that end, design defect decisions from 2013 and 2015 have been added to Chapter 12. As always, retired cases from prior editions are available, with accompanying notes, at http://www.aspenlawschool.com/books/goldberg_tortlaw.

Perhaps the most significant changes for the Fourth Edition concern format and pedagogy. In addition to a new, user-friendly design, the book is now sprinkled with sidebars and illustrations designed to enhance comprehension, review, and self-assessment. This edition is also the first to use Wolters Kluwer's Connected Casebook technology. (www.casebookconnect.com) Students who opt for a Connected Casebook will have instant online access to a trove of multiple-choice and essay questions that we have matched to each chapter of the book.

In addition to reiterating our thanks to those acknowledged in prior editions, we would like to express our gratitude to Nicole Pinard at Wolters Kluwer for overseeing this round of revisions, as well as to Andrew Blevins, Geoff Lokke, and Cindy Uh at the Froebe Group for their help in redesigning the book. Ming Cheung, Naomi Gilens, Anna Kurtz, Alex Moses, Colin Reeves, and Michael Rivkin provided excellent research assistance and editorial suggestions. Our work on the Fourth Edition has been generously supported by the Benjamin C. Cardozo School of Law, Fordham University School of Law, and Harvard Law School.

John C. P. Goldberg
Anthony J. Sebok
Benjamin C. Zipursky

Cambridge, MA; New York, NY
January 2016

Preface to the Third Edition

The positive feedback on the Second Edition of *Tort Law*— for which we are most grateful — leaves us mindful of the counsel against fixing things not broken. While we have comprehensively updated the book to reflect important developments since 2008, we have mostly done so in text and notes rather than by replacing principal cases. The few cases that have been removed are available at http://www.aspenlawschool.com/books/goldberg_tortlaw/ with accompanying notes.

While none of the chapters have undergone major surgery, Chapters 9, 12 and 13 contain the most significant revisions. For Chapter 9, we have reorganized and trimmed the materials to make them especially user-friendly for professors who commence their courses with intentional torts. Chapter 12 now more clearly charts the "post-402A" world of products liability that was heralded by the 1998 publication of the Third Restatement's Products Liability provisions and has been marked by the rise to prominence of the risk-utility test for design defect. Chapter 13 updates the treatment of the fast-moving topic of federal preemption of state tort law, and also offers new materials on human rights litigation and the Alien Tort Statute.

The cataclysmic Deepwater Horizon Spill transfixed the nation and the world in the summer of 2010. Its consequences for human health, for the Gulf states' economies, and for the environment are still not fully understood, and may not be for some time. In the meantime, the spill has given lawyers, courts and academics occasion to reconsider the scope and justifications (if any) for the rule against liability for negligence causing economic loss. It has also raised important questions about the interaction between conventional tort litigation and dispute-resolution through entities such as the Gulf Coast Claims Facility. We briefly discuss the spill in a new set of notes in Chapter 2.

The U.S. Supreme Court has continued to maintain an active presence in tort law. Many of the Justices continue to demonstrate receptivity to defendants' preemption arguments. Thus the reprieve for failure-to-warn claims against manufacturers of brand-name drugs provided by *Wyeth v. Levine* (2009) was quickly overshadowed by the elimination of failure-to-warn liability for generic drugs in *Pliva v. Mensing* (2011). Both decisions are reproduced in Chapter 13. Likewise, the Court read the federal Vaccine Act to preempt design defect claims against vaccine manufacturers. (*Bruesewitz v. Wyeth* (2011)). Meanwhile, the Court has influenced tort law in subtler ways that include reading into federal admiralty law a 1:1 cap on the ratio of punitive to compensatory damages (*Exxon Shipping Co. v. Baker* (2008)) and interpreting FELA to operate with a capacious conception of proximate cause (*CSX Transportation v. McBride* (2011)). Each of these developments is discussed in new notes. Finally, in anticipation of the Court taking on a more active role in shaping litigation under the Alien Tort Statute, we have included in Chapter 13 its decision in *Sosa v. Alvarez-Machain* (2004), as well as additional materials pertaining to the debate over that now-controversial federal law.

At the level of common law doctrine, the most important development since 2008 has probably been the publication of the "Physical and Emotional Harm" provisions of the Third Restatement of Torts, which now stand alongside the "Apportionment" and "Products Liability" provisions that were published, respectively, in 2000 and 1998. The Physical and Emotional Harm provisions restate basic negligence law, as well as rules for affirmative duties, premises liability, and infliction of emotional distress (intentional and negligent). They also cover strict liability for abnormally dangerous activities. Other topics — including liability for economic loss, medical malpractice, intentional torts, and property torts — await treatment. (The ALI is currently circulating draft materials on economic loss.) There is much to like in the new Restatement provisions, but also much with which to take issue. We address them in notes throughout the book.

Once again we want to take this opportunity to thank the many professors and students who have generously offered thoughtful advice on how to improve the book. Jonathan Bruno provided indispensable assistance in developing the PowerPoint slides available for use with this edition. http://www.aspenlawschool.com/books/goldberg_tortlaw/ John Devins and Gretchen Otto carefully steered us through the revision process. We remain deeply appreciative of the enthusiastic support that *Tort Law* continues to receive from Mike Gregory, Carol McGeehan, Rick Mixter, George Serafin, and their Wolters Kluwer colleagues. Our work on the Third Edition has been generously supported by the Benjamin N. Cardozo School of Law, Fordham University School of Law, and Harvard Law School.

John C. P. Goldberg
Anthony J. Sebok
Benjamin C. Zipursky

Cambridge, MA; New York, NY
June 2012

Preface to the Second Edition

Much has happened in the world of torts since this book was first published early in 2004. In keeping with the general trend since about 1980, a lot of the action has involved efforts to limit the reach of tort law. Several state legislatures, including those of Georgia, Mississippi, Oklahoma, South Carolina, and West Virginia, joined the now sizable majority that have limited or eliminated joint and several liability for indivisible injuries. Congress failed to pass the mammoth Fairness in Asbestos Injury Resolution (FAIR) Act of 2006, but continued its practice of sporadically intervening to protect certain industries, including gun manufacturers via the 2005 "Protection of Lawful Commerce in Arms Act." Comparable efforts to block "obesity suits" against purveyors of fast food failed in the Senate, although some state legislatures have adopted such laws. The national legislature's efforts to stave off personal injury litigation arising out of 9/11 by capping liability and creating a victim compensation fund appear to have been largely successful. To be sure, the scheme of payouts ultimately devised by special master Kenneth Feinberg has generated considerable commentary and criticism. Still, 97 percent of those eligible for relief from the fund applied for compensation. Suits brought by those who did not apply are about to go to trial. For its part — as mentioned in the notes following Geier (Chapter 13) — the Roberts Court is about to resolve several potentially important suits concerning the extent to which federal statutes and regulations preempt state tort law. Philip Morris USA v. Williams, 127 S. Ct. 1057 (2007) (excerpted in Chapter 13) continued the Court's recent practice of articulating somewhat cryptic due process limits on punitive damage awards. Although talk of a medical malpractice "crisis" seems to be subsiding, activists and scholars are now busily arguing over whether malpractice insurance rates have responded to cyclical market forces or instead to pro-defendant tort reforms.

Yet the story of tort law in the past few years has not been completely one-sided. Large-scale products liability litigation continues. Most notably, thousands of products liability suits were filed alleging that the pain reliever Vioxx caused patients to suffer heart failure and strokes. A tentative settlement involving payouts of nearly $5 billion was recently announced. The settlement is significant as much for its form as its substance: It consists not of agreements between the defendant and individual Vioxx claimants but rather of a contract between the defendant and the key plaintiffs' law firms involved, whereby the latter promise to recommend the settlement to each of their clients. Among the numerous suits against insurers for losses related to the destruction wrought by Hurricane Katrina are many tort claims for bad faith denials of coverage. Claims against churches and other institutions for turning a blind eye to sexual abuse by employees have generated millions of dollars of liability. In less visible ways, state courts have expanded the scope of tort liability, often in the context of holding "background" or "remote" actors liable for injuries caused most immediately by another wrongdoer. Coombes v. Florio, 450 Mass. 182 (2007), a just-issued decision, holds that a treating physician who fails to warn his patient that prescribed medication can cause drowsiness is subject to liability for the death of a bystander who was killed when the driver fell asleep at the wheel. Meanwhile, in Ferdon v. Wisconsin Patients Compensation Fund, 701 N.W.2d 440 (2005), the Wisconsin Supreme Court, joining several other state high courts, went so far as to strike down on state constitutional grounds a medical malpractice reform statute that included caps on noneconomic damages. In Sosa v. Alvarez-Machain, 542 U.S. 692 (2004), decided just after the first edition of this book was published, the Supreme Court perhaps unexpectedly declined an invitation simply to cut off litigation under the Alien Tort Claims Act, instead recognizing the validity in principle of some suits by foreign nationals seeking to hold actors accountable for gross human rights violations. And, after years of dormancy, market share liability met with the approval of courts in Wisconsin and California, and the Southern District of New York.

Our aim in revising the book for this edition has been to introduce incremental rather than sweeping changes. The book's basic structure remains intact, although in various places we have replaced or added new cases and notes to reflect developments of the sort described above, as well the immensely valuable feedback we have received from users of the book. Chapter 9, which covers battery, assault, and false imprisonment, contains the most significant changes, which have been introduced so that the chapter provides better support to professors who begin their classes with intentional torts. Although our judgment is that the changes we have introduced throughout the book constitute improvements, we recognize that some may prefer things the way they were. For this reason, we have made available on the book's website electronic files containing all the main cases that were removed from the First Edition: www.aspenlawschool.com/goldberg2. A table summarizing the major changes between the two editions can be found at the front of the Teacher's Manual for this edition.

We wish first to thank the many law professors and students who generously offered thoughtful advice on how to improve the book. Thanks are also due (again) to Mike Gregory, Carol McGeehan, Rick Mixter, George Serafin, and the other members of the Aspen team for their unflagging support of this project and its authors, as well as Barbara Roth and Troy Froebe for carefully steering us through the revision process. Steven Berneman provided valuable research assistance. Our work on the book has been generously supported by Brooklyn Law School, Benjamin N. Cardozo School of Law, Fordham University School of Law, Harvard Law School, and Vanderbilt Law School.

John C. P. Goldberg
Anthony J. Sebok
Benjamin C. Zipursky

Nashville, New York
February 2008

Preface to the First Edition

This book has been written to help a new generation of law students learn an area of law — Torts — that is at once ancient and contemporary, rule-governed and flexible, well-established and controversial.

American tort law traces back to the law of medieval England, a time and place in which government efforts to secure citizens' security from injury were relatively modest. Today, tort law — itself a complex institution — exists within a vastly more complex regulatory state that devotes substantial effort to promoting safety and to providing for citizens' welfare. We hope to give students a sense of where tort law has come from, and of the roles it plays, and might play, in our modern system of government.

As an evolving body of doctrine shaped in courtrooms around the country, tort law simultaneously empowers and limits individuals in their ability to invoke the legal system, and likewise empowers and limits legal decision-makers such as judges and juries faced with the task of deciding whether to hold one person liable for another's injuries. We aim to help students appreciate both the constraining and the power-conferring aspects of tort law.

Tort has been a part of American law since the nation's founding. Today, however, it is at a crossroads: Lawyers, politicians, and academics disagree sharply about its continued utility and viability. We seek to enable students to see why tort law is basic to our legal system, but also why it has become a source of controversy.

In pursuing these pedagogic goals, we have been guided by five themes:

1. As its title suggests, this book is organized around the general theme of responsibilities and redress. Tort law, in our view, has two fundamental features. First, it articulates and imposes on members of society a set of legal obligations — i.e., responsibilities — to avoid injuring others. Second, it empowers persons to bring suit to establish that they have been injured by another's failure to heed this sort of obligation — i.e., to pursue and obtain redress. Tort is a core part of the first-year curriculum for these reasons: It examines the law's imposition of basic obligations not to injure others, as well as the law's recognition of the right of aggrieved persons to seek redress through the courts for violations of those obligations.

2. We have edited the cases in this book lightly, in a conscious effort to allow readers to experience the "thick" contexts out of which tort law emerges. Put simply, we aim to allow students to read the facts of each case for themselves. We also try to let the judges speak for themselves through their opinions. Our hope is that this approach will help beginning law students appreciate the degree to which judgments about legal responsibilities are sensitive to facts, and to see that common-law principles are not extracted from some "heaven of legal concepts," but instead derive from ordinary

experience. Further, we hope that, by presenting cases edited in this way, we will aid students in developing the capacity to read carefully, an essential tool for good lawyering.

3. The cases and the notes in this book aim to demonstrate to students how the substance of a body of law like torts is heavily influenced by rules of procedure, by the institutions that have been created to handle tort litigation, and by other bodies of law that address some of the same conduct and issues addressed by tort law. Thus, throughout the book, we point out ways in which the demands of trial and appellate processes shape tort doctrine. In various places, we also explore the role played by legislatures in developing, or responding to developments in, tort doctrine. Another of the book's aspirations is to ensure that students appreciate that tort is but one part of the law, and that it can only be adequately understood in relation to other areas of law, including civil procedure, contracts, property, employment law, anti-discrimination law, and constitutional law.

4. Apart from retaining "classic" tort opinions that all law students are expected to know, we have sought as much as possible to use contemporary cases presenting situations that students will be able to recognize. We hope that, by employing these sorts of cases to illuminate the basic concepts of tort law, we will make the subject less archaic and mysterious to novice lawyers, while also helping them to begin to think for themselves about the various choices that courts and lawmakers must make as they carry tort law forward into the future. We also believe that the use of relatively recent cases will help students perceive the relevance of the subject and the significance of the issues that are currently in play in the law of tort.

5. This book adopts a perspective on law that we hope is refreshing. It is, of course, vital that first-year law students come to appreciate that "the law" is not a rule book—that there is play in its joints and deep tensions in its soul. Yet it is equally important that students not be left with the skeptical lesson that law is nothing more than what a particular judge or jury says it is. Thus, in these materials, we strive to help students grasp how the key concepts of tort—concepts such as "reasonable care," "causation," and "intent"—structure and organize legal analysis even as they point it in new directions. A good lawyer, we hope to demonstrate, is one who appreciates both the limits and the flexibility of tort doctrine; one who has a sense of how to make innovative and progressive arguments from within the law. For these reasons, our book has a number of distinctive features. Particularly in its early chapters, it contains a good deal of expository text, in part to help students overcome the steep learning curve encountered in the first weeks of law school. It also contains a number of opinions from intermediate appellate courts, in part because these courts tend to approach cases as presenting problems in the application of law, rather than occasions to rework it. The book also includes some "easy" cases. These opinions can help students avoid basic confusions by providing clear examples of certain torts, or certain concepts. Lastly, the notes following the principal cases strive to be explanatory rather than Delphic. If our own engagement with this subject has taught us anything, it is that tort law, even when presented in a relatively straightforward way, is more than rich enough to captivate students and professors alike.

John C. P. Goldberg
Anthony J. Sebok
Benjamin C. Zipursky

Nashville, Brooklyn, Manhattan
April 2004

Acknowledgments

We owe more debts than we can acknowledge. Thanks to the many faculty and students who over the years have taken the time to review draft materials, to make suggestions for improvements, and to correct our mistakes. Equal thanks to our students for bearing with us as we have field-tested the book manuscript and our revisions to it. Each edition has benefited from careful and insightful comments provided by anonymous reviews arranged by our editors at Aspen/Wolters Kluwer Law and Business.

The book has benefitted from the excellent research assistance of Vijay Bilaga, Lia Brooks, Will Edmonson, Kristina Hill, James Killelea, Erin McMurray, John Rue, Michael Samalin, Lillith Shilton, Elizabeth TeSelle, and Allen Woods. Renee Cote and Curt Berkowitz provided expert editorial assistance in preparing the original manuscript for publication. Jessica Barmack, Melody Davies, Elizabeth Kenny, Carol McGeehan, and Richard Mixer were instrumental in launching this project, helping it take shape, and seeing it through to initial publication. Renee Hawkins generously served double-duty as word processer and editorial advisor. Enid Zafran prepared the Table of Cases and Index. The publication of the first edition was made possible by generous research support from Brooklyn Law School, Fordham University School of Law, and Vanderbilt University Law School.

The following have granted us permission to reproduce their copyrighted works:

Articles, Restatement Provisions, and Jury Instructions

Photographs and Illustration

Clarence Thomas, photograph. Courtesy of the Collection of the Supreme Court of the United States.

Coca-Cola bottling plant, photograph. Copyright © Dick Whittington Studio / Corbis. Reprinted by permission.

"Couldn't Peter claim Mr. McGregor," illustration. Copyright © Shelley Matheis / Cartoonstock. Reprinted by permission.

"Do you have any picture books," illustration. Copyright © Alex Gregory / The New Yorker Collection / The Cartoon Bank. Reprinted by permission.

"I see you signing this liability waiver," illustration. Copyright © Stu Rees. All Rights Reserved. Reprinted by permission.

"I think there's a 'design flow' in these moguls," illustration. Copyright © Jerry King / Cartoonstock. Reprinted by permission.

Ford Pinto defect, illustration. From Douglas Birsch and John H. Fielder, The Ford Pinto Case: A Study in Applied Ethics, Business, and Technology. Copyright © 1994 State University of New York Press. Reprinted by permission.

Guido Calabresi, photograph. Copyright © Robert Benson / Yale Law School. Reprinted by permission.

Headquarters of The American Law Institute, Philadelphia, PA, photograph. Courtesy of Wikipedia.

Henry J. Friendly, photograph. Copyright © Fabian Bachrach. Courtesy of the Harvard Law School Archive. Reprinted by permission.

Judith Kaye, photograph. Copyright © Hollenshead / NYU Photo Bureau. Reprinted by permission.

Learned Hand, photograph. Courtesy of the Harvard Law School Archive. Reprinted by permission.

Map of Atlantic Coast, illustration. Courtesy of Alan Kikuchi Design. Reprinted by permission.

Michigan Avenue Bridge, photograph. Courtesy of Wikipedia.

Oliver W. Holmes, photograph. Courtesy of the Harvard Law School Archive. Reprinted by permission.

Portable floor lift, illustration. Courtesy of the U.S. Department of Health and Human Services Office for Civil Rights.

Richard Posner, photograph. Courtesy of the University of Chicago Law School. Reprinted by permission.

Roger Traynor, photograph. Courtesy of the Berkeley Law Archives. Reprinted by permission.

Sonia Sotomayor, photograph. Courtesy of the Collection of the Supreme Court of the United States.

Stephani Victor, photograph. Courtesy of Wikipedia.

Telephone exchange operators, photograph. Courtesy of Wikipedia.

Trespass writ, photograph. Courtesy of the Harvard Law School Archive. Reprinted by permission.

Vioxx billboard, photograph. Copyright © Bob Daemmrich / Corbis. Reprinted by permission.

William Prosser, photograph. Courtesy of the Berkeley Law Archives. Reprinted by permission.

William S. Andrews, photograph. Courtesy of Wikipedia.

"What with current restrictions on punitive damages," illustration. Copyright © Jack Ziegler / The New Yorker Collection / The Cartoon Bank. Reprinted by permission.

"You wouldn't know this," illustration. Copyright © David Mills / Courtoons. Reprinted by permission.

Notes on the Text

Omissions from judicial opinions reproduced herein are marked with ellipses, except for omitted internal citations, which are not marked unless only part of a citation has been removed. In some opinions we have added paragraph breaks to improve their comprehensibility. For the same reason, we have sometimes deleted headings and subheadings. Numbered footnotes to judicial opinions appear as in the original text. Our additions to the text of judicial opinions are marked with square brackets and/or asterisked and bracketed footnotes. References to scholarly books and articles mentioned in our text and notes can be found in the *References/Further Readings* section at the end of each chapter.

TORT LAW

PART I

OVERVIEW

CHAPTER 1

AN INTRODUCTION TO TORTS

I. WHAT IS A TORT?

Among the courses listed on your schedule, Torts might seem one of the more mysterious. Most entering law students have a rough idea of what a contract or a crime is. The term *tort*, by contrast, tends not to conjure up a clear mental picture or definition.

A brief turn to history may shed some light. Lawyerly usage of the word "tort" dates back to medieval England. There it served primarily as a synonym for "wrong" or "trespass."* Each of these nouns described a category or generic type of misconduct. But what kind? Proceeding still further back in time, we learn that tort derives from the Latin word "*torquere*": to twist. This derivation proves quite illuminating. When a person commits a tort, he acts in a manner that is figuratively "twisted": His acts lack rectitude; they are *wrongful*. Beyond this, a tort is a special sort of wrongful act, one that literally involves a twisting—an *injuring*—of another. And a tort is a special sort of wrong in a second, related sense. When the law identifies misconduct as a tort, it determines that it is the sort of misconduct that entitles the victim to ask a court to assist her in her effort to *set things straight* as between her and the person who has wronged her.

In sum, to commit a tort is to act in a manner that the law deems wrongful toward and injurious to another, such that the other gains a right to bring a lawsuit to obtain relief from the wrongdoer (or *tortfeasor*). The word "torts" in turn refers to a collection of named and relatively well-defined legal wrongs that, when committed, generate a right of action in the victim against the wrongdoer. These include assault, battery, conversion, defamation, defective product sales (products liability), false imprisonment, fraud, intentional infliction of emotional distress, intentional interference with

* Here we mean trespass in its older, broader sense—the sense one finds, for example, in the biblical counsel that we "forgive the trespasses of others."

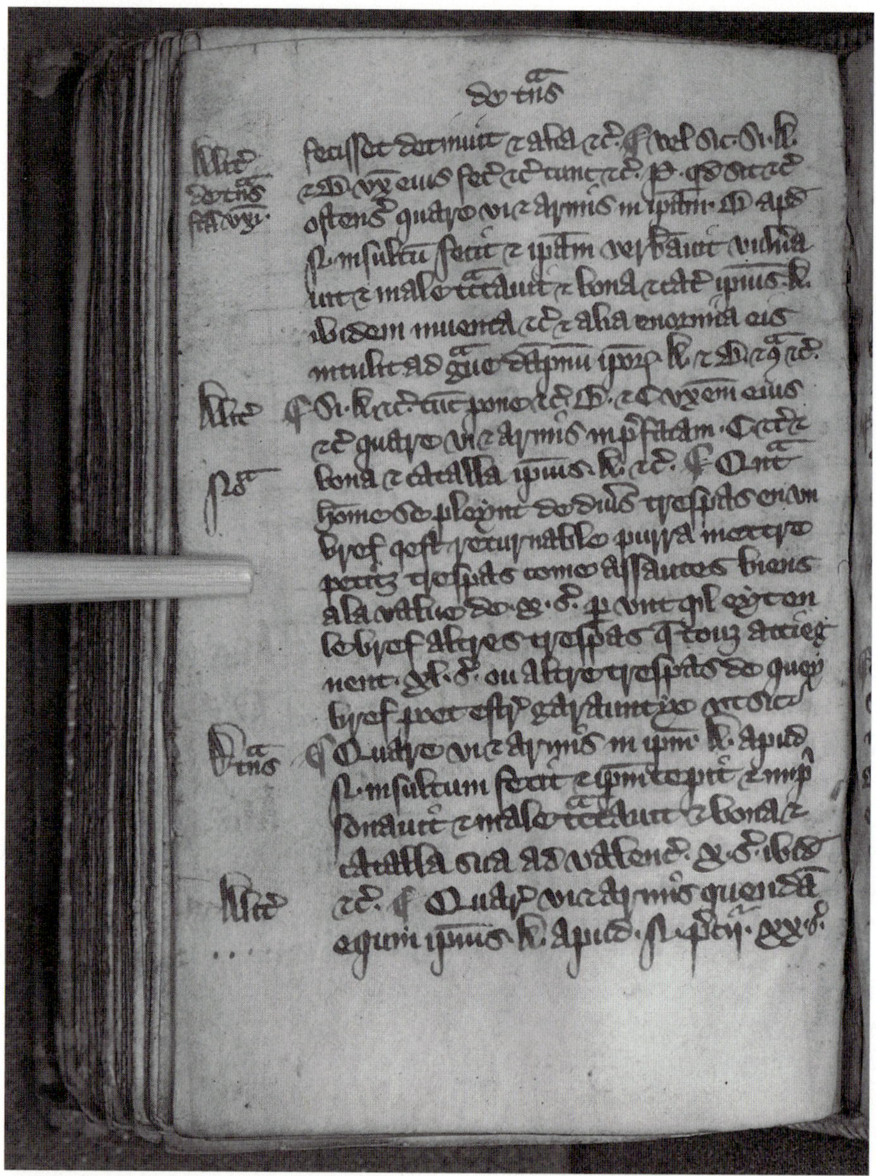

Entry from an English Register of Writs c. 1375-1425: In the royal courts of medieval England, a lawsuit was usually commenced by the filing of a document known as a "writ." To promote uniformity, these writs were recorded in volumes ("registers") such as this one. The phrase "vi et armis," indicating an allegation of wrongdoing involving a forcibly inflicted injury, can be seen in the third line.

contract or economic advantage, invasion of privacy, negligence, nuisance, and trespass to land or chattel. Tort law consists of the rules and principles that define wrongful conduct, delineate the circumstances under which a victim can obtain redress, and designate the form that such redress may take. As this book's title suggests, tort law articulates legal responsibilities or duties that persons owe to one another, and provides victims of conduct breaching those duties with the power to obtain redress against those who have wronged them.

Torts is a first-year course for a number of reasons. Tort suits tend to present legal disputes that are manageable for students untrained in the law. Tort has also become a visible and politically contested part of the American legal landscape. As such it provides a platform for discussion of current policy issues surrounding law. Finally, tort introduces law students to basic legal categories (e.g., civil liability, private rights of action) and basic concepts (e.g., duty, unreasonableness, causation) that will continue to figure prominently in upper-level courses ranging from employment law to securities law to constitutional law. To begin to understand the distinctive domain and concerns of tort law, these materials commence with a judicial opinion concerning a suit that raises a claim for the particular tort of *negligence.*

II. AN EXAMPLE OF A TORT SUIT

The judicial decision you are about to read — *Walter v. Wal-Mart Stores, Inc.* — arose out of an appeal from a $550,000 judgment against Wal-Mart. That judgment was entered by a trial judge at the conclusion of a two-day jury trial held in Knox County, Maine, in 1999. The trial in turn arose out of a suit brought by a woman named Antoinette Walter. Walter sued Wal-Mart because a pharmacist named Henry Lovin, who worked in the pharmacy department at a Wal-Mart store, misread her prescription for cancer medication and gave her the wrong drug, causing her to suffer serious illness.

As you will see, Wal-Mart had relatively little to say in its own defense. In this respect, the case was atypically one-sided. Indeed, the trial judge took the unusual step of announcing that, based on the evidence presented at trial, any reasonable jury would have to conclude that Walter had proven she was the victim of Wal-Mart's negligence. In other words, the judge found that the plaintiff had so clearly proven her case that he was entitled to conclude, without the aid of the jury, that Wal-Mart had acted carelessly toward her so as to injure her. However, the judge's determination that Wal-Mart had committed negligence against Walter still left one open issue for the jury: the amount of compensation she was entitled to receive from Wal-Mart in light of the injury it had wrongly inflicted upon her. On that issue, the jury decided on the figure of $550,000.

The text that follows is an edited version of an opinion issued by the Maine Supreme Court in response to Wal-Mart's appeal of the trial court's entry of judgment against it. As you will see, in appealing, Wal-Mart argued to the Supreme Court that the trial judge erred in concluding that the jury should not even have had a chance to decide for Wal-Mart. It also argued that the amount of the jury's verdict was excessive, and that the trial was defective in other ways. In light of these alleged problems in the trial, Wal-Mart's appeal sought an order from the Maine Supreme Court setting aside the trial court's judgment. Further, Wal-Mart asked the court either to dismiss Walter's tort suit altogether or to order a new trial so that Wal-Mart could raise its defenses without being handicapped by the erroneous rulings allegedly committed by the trial judge.

The seven members of the Maine Supreme Court unanimously concluded that the trial judge did not commit any of the errors alleged by Wal-Mart. In particular, they ruled that the judge was correct in determining that this was an open-and-shut case for Walter. Notice that, in upholding this determination, the court first defines the tort of negligence in terms of constituent parts or "elements." It then explains why the plaintiff's evidence clearly established that these elements were satisfied in this case. Along the way, the Court's opinion also explains why Wal-Mart's main argument against liability was so weak that the trial judge was entitled to reject it without sending that issue to the jury, and why the jury's award of $550,000 was not excessive.

As you read the opinion, pay attention to what Walter had to prove to make out a claim of negligence, and to why the members of the court concluded that she provided ample proof. Also, consider whether the $550,000 award was appropriate and, if so, what it is meant to represent or accomplish. Finally, think about the role that the parties' lawyers played and might have played in resolving this dispute.

Walter v. Wal-Mart Stores, Inc.

748 A.2d 961 (Me. 2000)

Calkins, J.

[¶ 1] Wal-Mart Stores, Inc. appeals from a judgment entered in the Superior Court (Knox County, *Marsano, J.*) following a jury trial awarding damages to Antoinette Walter in the amount of $550,000 for her claim of pharmacist malpractice. . . .

I. Facts

[¶ 2] Walter, an eighty-year-old resident of Rockland, was diagnosed with a type of cancer which attacks the lymphatic system. Dr. Stephen Ross, Walter's treating physician and a board-certified oncologist, termed her condition treatable with the proper medication. Dr. Ross prescribed Chlorambucil, a chemotherapy drug, for Walter. On the prescription slip, he explicitly called for Chlorambucil, the generic name, because he feared that the drug's brand name, Leukeran, could be confused with other drugs with similar trade names.

[¶ 3] Walter took the prescription for Chlorambucil to the pharmacy in the Wal-Mart store in Rockland on May 7, 1997. Henry Lovin, a Maine licensed pharmacist and an employee of Wal-Mart, was on duty at the pharmacy. Instead of giving Walter Chlorambucil, as called for in the prescription, Lovin gave her a different drug with the brand name of Melphalen. The generic name for Melphalen is Alkeran. Lovin did not speak with Walter at the time he filled the prescription, but he provided her with an information sheet which described the effects of Melphalen. Melphalen is also a chemotherapy drug, but it is a substantially more powerful medication than Chlorambucil. Melphalen is typically given in smaller doses over shorter periods of time than is Chlorambucil, and doctors monitor it more closely. Melphalen has a very toxic effect on the body, and it substantially suppresses bone marrow. It has a longer life in the body than Chlorambucil, which means that any side effects from it last longer.

[¶ 4] To the extent that Walter noticed that the information sheet and bottle label read Melphalen, it did not make an impression on her. She assumed that the drug she had been given was the same as Dr. Ross had prescribed, and she began taking the prescribed dosage. Within seven to ten days of starting the drug treatment, Walter began to suffer from nausea and lack of appetite. When she referred to the information sheet, Walter saw that such side effects are common for chemotherapy drugs. She continued to take the Melphalen. During the third week after starting the medication Walter noticed bruises on her arms and legs, and during the fourth week she developed a skin rash on her arms and legs. Although the information sheet warned that bruises and rashes should prompt a call to the doctor, Walter waited a few days before attempting to contact Dr. Ross.

[¶ 5] Dr. Ross testified at trial that his notes indicated that Walter should have had blood tests two weeks after starting medication and that she was to have scheduled an appointment with him within four weeks of beginning the medication. He also testified that because Chlorambucil is slow-acting, he does not insist that his patients have blood tests done in fourteen days but only that they have blood work periodically. Walter testified that she understood she was to have a follow-up appointment with Dr. Ross in four weeks and blood tests sometime before that appointment.

[¶ 6] On the twenty-third day after starting the medication, Walter had blood tests done. She attempted to reach Dr. Ross by phone to tell him about the side effects, but she was unsuccessful until June 3, 1997. On that day Dr. Ross told her that her blood levels were low and to stop taking the medication immediately. He scheduled an appointment for June 5. Walter, however, was rushed to the hospital later in the day on June 3 when she suffered gastrointestinal bleeding. Following her emergency admission, Walter remained in the hospital five weeks and received numerous blood transfusions. She suffered several infections, and a catheter was placed in her chest. The bruising and skin rash continued. For a period of time she was unable to eat because of bleeding gums and an infection in her mouth. Because of her weakened immune system, Walter's visitors could not come within ten feet of her.

[¶ 7] Prior to receiving the Melphalen, Walter lived independently and was active. Following her hospital discharge on July 7, 1997, she was physically weak. She initially had to make daily trips to the hospital and later went less frequently. She had to have additional transfusions after she left the hospital. Melphalen did have the effect of causing her cancer to go into remission. Walter's total medical bills for her treatment came to $71,042.63.

[¶ 8] The two-day jury trial was held in February 1999. Wal-Mart moved for judgment as a matter of law at the close of Walter's case on the grounds that she had failed to present expert testimony on the standard of care by pharmacists, and the motion was denied. At the close of the evidence Walter moved for a judgment as a matter of law, and the court granted Walter's motion concluding that she was entitled to judgment on liability. During Walter's closing argument, Wal-Mart moved for a mistrial arguing that certain comments by Walter's counsel were improper, and the motion was denied. The jury awarded Walter $550,000 in damages. Wal-Mart's post-trial motion for judgment as a matter of law or a new trial was denied.

II. Walter's Motion for Judgment on Liability

. . .

[¶ 10] The effect of the [trial] court's grant of Walter's motion was a determination, as a matter of law, that[:] Wal-Mart had a duty to Walter which it breached; that breach caused Walter harm; and Walter was not negligent—or if she was negligent, her negligence [could not entirely exculpate Wal-Mart]. The only issue left for the jury was the amount of damages caused by Wal-Mart's negligence and whether those damages should be reduced because of any action or inaction by Walter. . . . [Wal-Mart now seeks reversal of the court's ruling. Walter insists that it was proper.]

A. WAL-MART'S REPRESENTATIONS TO THE JURY

[¶ 11] . . . Walter contends that Wal-Mart . . . admitted liability in its [attorney's] opening statement to the jury. . . .[1]

[¶ 13] Wal-Mart's [attorney's] opening statement admitted the error made by its pharmacist in filling the prescription but . . . there was no . . . admission of negligence. Furthermore, the statement taken in its entire context, does not contain an unequivocal admission that the mistake in filling the prescription caused Walter's harm. . . . For these reasons, we cannot conclude that there was [an] . . . admission that Wal-Mart was liable for Walter's damages. . . .

B. WAL-MART'S NEGLIGENCE

[¶ 14] Walter had the burden to prove that Wal-Mart, through its pharmacist employee, owed a duty to Walter that it breached, thereby causing her harm. In Tremblay v. Kimball, 77 A. 405 (Me. 1910), we held that pharmacists owe their customers a duty of ordinary care, but that "ordinary care" for a pharmacist means that

---

1. Wal-Mart's counsel began his opening statement by explaining the process of a lawsuit and why Wal-Mart denied liability in [filing its formal answer to the complaint by which Walter commenced this lawsuit]. He then stated:

> What I'm here to tell you right now is since the filing of the complaint and filing of the answer, Wal-Mart has never denied responsibility for this incident. Never.
>
> Going back to what happened. [Walter's attorney] and I are in substantial agreement in terms of what happened on May 7, 1997, and what has to [sic] occurred since. . . . [We] have a difference of opinion as to what constitutes fair, reasonable and just compensation for Mrs. Walter. That's why we are here. We can't agree. It's as simple as that. We just can't agree on that issue. We need your help. . . .
>
> It's not because we are blaming Mrs. Walter. It's not because we are trying to deflect blame. And it's not because we are trying to sort of make the issues obscure or distracting. We are going to put all the cards on the table. There are no secrets. There are no major disputes as to what occurred. . . .
>
> The hardest issue and the one that is going to be in your laps at the end of tomorrow is what monetary amount represents fair and just compensation for Mrs. Walter? You will be asked to consider medical bills and what she went through during the hospitalization and what she has done [sic] through since then. Wal-Mart is here, and I'm here to ask you as the conscience of the community what that figure is. That's really why we are here. . . .
>
> The evidence in this case will show that . . . on May 7, 1997 . . . Mr. Lovin was given a prescription for Chlorambucil. What came to his mind was Alkeran. And from there the mistake was made. And it was sort of on a path of not being able being [sic] corrected in his mind. He was confident that Chlorambucil was Alkeran. It was a mistake. And it's a mistake for which he's deeply sorry. But that's irrelevant.
>
> The fact is that a mistake was made. That he didn't realize it at the time and wasn't told of the mistake until June 3rd when he received a call from Dr. Ross. . . .

"the highest practicable degree of prudence, thoughtfulness, and vigilance and the most exact and reliable safeguards" must be taken. 77 A. at 408.

[¶ 15] Lovin, the Wal-Mart pharmacist, readily admitted that he made an error in filling Walter's prescription. He testified that he thought that the brand name for Chlorambucil was Alkeran, and he filled the prescription with Alkeran, which is Melphalen. Lovin said that he made a "serious error" that did not "satisfy the proper standard of care for a pharmacist." He admitted that he would have discovered the error if he had followed the standard four-step process utilized to check for errors. He acknowledged that to comply with the standard of pharmacy care he should have checked the stock bottle against the prescription. He further admitted that the standard of practice required that he counsel Walter when she picked up the prescription, at which time he would have showed her the drug and discussed it with her. He testified that he did not counsel her, but if he had done so, he would have discovered the error. He also said that Walter would have no reason to suspect that she was given the wrong drug.

[¶ 16] Pursuant to the standard of "the highest practicable degree of prudence, thoughtfulness, and vigilance and the most exact and reliable safeguards" . . . , Lovin's testimony established that the standard was breached. Even if we were to determine that the standard of practice for pharmacists is the skill and diligence exercised by similar professionals, Lovin's testimony established that standard and the breach of it. None of this evidence was disputed. A jury, acting reasonably, could not have found that Wal-Mart was not negligent.

C. CAUSATION

[¶ 17] In order to establish liability a plaintiff in any negligence action must show that the defendant's negligence was the . . . cause of the plaintiff's harm. Wal-Mart argues that Walter's motion should have been denied because she failed to prove that Wal-Mart's negligence in filling the prescription was the cause of her injury. Causation means "that there be some reasonable connection between the act or omission of the defendant and the damage which the plaintiff has suffered." Wheeler v. White, 714 A.2d 125 [, 127 (Me. 1998)]. . . .

[¶ 18] There was uncontroverted medical evidence that Melphalen, which Wal-Mart provided Walter erroneously, caused damage to her body. . . . Dr. Ross testified that the Melphalen made Walter seriously ill, to the point that he was not sure she would survive, and that her lack of energy after her release from the hospital was the result of the illness caused by the wrong medication. Wal-Mart's expert oncologist also testified that the side effects of Melphalen caused the lengthy hospitalization, and the hospitalization itself likely caused Walter's malaise and depression after her discharge.

[¶ 19] Wal-Mart['s] . . . expert speculated that if a blood test had been done fourteen days after starting the medication it might have shown lowered blood levels and, depending on how low those levels were, Walter's physician might have stopped the medication, and if the medication had been stopped sooner, the harmful effect may have been less. Wal-Mart's expert did not testify that there would have been no damage if a blood test had been done on the fourteenth day. In fact, in his description of Melphalen, he noted it has a long life in the body and that its side effects last longer.[3] . . . No reasonable factfinder could have found that Wal-Mart's negligent act in misfilling the prescription was not a substantial cause in bringing about Walter's suffering. "[W]hen the totality of the evidence adduced in *any particular case* is so overwhelming that it leaves open to a fact-finder, acting rationally, only one conclusion on the issue, the issue is then determined as a matter of law." Laferriere v. Paradis, 293 A.2d 526, 528 (Me. 1972). The trial court did not err in granting judgment as a matter of law to Walter on the issue of causation.

D. COMPARATIVE NEGLIGENCE AND MITIGATION OF DAMAGES

. . . .

[¶ 21] Under Maine's comparative negligence statute, the damages owing to a plaintiff may be reduced when the plaintiff's harm is partly the result of the plaintiff's own fault, and fault is defined as the negligence that would give rise to the defense of contributory negligence. *See* 14 M.R.S.A. § 156 (1980). If the plaintiff's fault is equal to or greater than that of the defendant, the plaintiff cannot recover damages.

. . . .

[¶ 22] [Wal-Mart argued that the trial judge erred by failing to instruct the jury to consider whether Walter was herself at fault for not determining, at the time the medicine was dispensed, that Lovin had improperly filled her prescription. Had such an instruction been given, Wal-Mart argued, the jury might have assigned fault to Walter, which — under Maine's comparative fault statute — would have resulted in a reduction in her damages award or, if her fault was deemed equal to or greater than Lovin's, no recovery at all. Based in part on Lovin's trial testimony that Walter "would have no way of knowing" that she had been given the wrong medication, the Supreme Court concluded that there was no basis for attributing fault to Walter for failing to recognize that she was being sold the wrong drug, and hence no trial court error in declining to give a comparative fault instruction. — EDS.]

. . . .

[¶ 23] [Wal-Mart also appealed on the ground that the trial court erred in failing to instruct the jury to consider assigning fault to Walter based on her failure to promptly contact Dr. Ross after she began to experience side effects from the medication. The Maine Supreme Court concluded that the trial court had — in a different instruction pertaining to the calculation of damages — adequately informed the jury that it could reduce its award to Walter if it found that she had unreasonably delayed in contacting Dr. Ross, and that her delay worsened her injuries. — EDS.]

. . . .

III. WAL-MART'S MOTION FOR JUDGMENT AS A MATTER OF LAW

[¶ 31] Wal-Mart moved for judgment as a matter of law on the ground that Walter failed to present any expert evidence on the pharmacist's standard of care. It points out that Lovin was not designated as an expert. In this case the testimony of an expert was

3. The blood tests alone did not reveal that the wrong medication had been given. Dr. Ross did not discover that she was taking the wrong medication until after she was admitted to the hospital.

not necessary. We have said that where professional negligence and its harmful results "are sufficiently obvious as to lie within common knowledge" no expert testimony is necessary. . . . The negligence of the pharmacist and the harmful results were sufficiently obvious to be within the common knowledge of a lay person. It does not take an expert to know that filling a prescription with the wrong drug and failing to take the steps in place in that pharmacy to check for the wrong drug is negligence.

IV. Wal-Mart's Motion for Mistrial

[¶ 32] Wal-Mart moved for a mistrial because of three comments made by Walter's counsel during closing argument. First, Walter's attorney stated that the pharmacist attempted to accept responsibility but his employer, Wal-Mart, refused to accept responsibility for Walter's injury. Wal-Mart objected, and the objection was sustained. The court admonished counsel that the only issue was damages and told the jury that they were not to be swayed by any bias or predisposition towards one party or the other. [Wal-Mart's second objection is omitted. — Eds.] Third, while referring to the amount of damages the jury could award, during rebuttal, Walter's counsel told the jury it should consider how much money professional basketball players are paid. Wal-Mart objected and the objection was sustained. Wal-Mart argues that the effect of the three comments was to prejudice the jury against Wal-Mart so that it would punish Wal-Mart by the amount of damages.

[¶ 33] We review a refusal to grant a motion for a mistrial for abuse of discretion. *See* Sheltra v. Rochefort, 667 A.2d 868, 871 (Me. 1995). The judge sustained the objections to the comments, told the jurors to ignore the comments, and gave curative instructions. The trial judge did not abuse his discretion. . . .

V. Wal-Mart's Motion for New Trial

[¶ 34] After the verdict Wal-Mart moved for a new trial. . . . Wal-Mart . . . contends that the damages were excessive and the size of the verdict demonstrates that the judge and jury were biased against Wal-Mart.

[¶ 35] "When a court refuses to grant a new trial on the ground of an excessive damage award, the ruling will not be reversed except for clear and manifest abuse of discretion." Gilmore v. Central Maine Power Co., 665 A.2d 666, 670 (Me. 1995). . . .

[¶ 36] Walter's total medical bills and expenses equalled $71,042.63. The jury awarded Walter $550,000 in damages. Presumably, the additional $479,000 of Walter's recovery is in compensation for her pain and suffering. The jury heard several witnesses, including Walter herself, testify about the painful treatment she received in the hospital, the long recovery process, and the continuing difficulties she faces. In light of this evidence, which must be considered favorably to Walter, the jury's award of damages is rational. "Although the verdict may seem large, it reflects the considered opinion of the jury within the range of evidence of sufficient probative character. . . . " [*Michaud v. Steckino*], 390 A.2d [524,] 537 [(Me. 1978)]. (quoting Fotter v. Butler, 145 Me. 266, 273, 75 A.2d 160, 164 (1950)). . . .

Judgment affirmed.

[Concurring opinion omitted. — Eds.]

A. Common Law and Statute

1. *Appellate Courts.* The Maine Supreme Court is comprised of seven justices, one of whom, Justice Calkins, wrote the excerpted opinion that you have just read. As is evident from *Walter*, the court is an appellate court—it decides appeals brought to it by litigants who believe there are legal grounds for challenging adverse lower-court decisions. Because it filed the appeal, Wal-Mart is dubbed the *appellant.* (For the appellate phase of the litigation, Ms. Walter, the plaintiff at the trial level, is deemed the *respondent.*) As indicated by its name, the Maine Supreme Court is the court of last resort for issues governed by Maine law. Thus, the decision in *Walter*—issued in April of 2000—conclusively resolved a lawsuit that had been commenced two years earlier, and that concerned an act of carelessness that took place another year before that.*

2. *Negligence and Judge-Made Law.* We stated above that torts are wrongs that generate injuries for which victims are entitled to seek redress. In *Walter,* the tort alleged is negligence. Much of this book aims to provide insight into that particular tort. For now, we can define it as a failure to heed a duty of reasonable care that causes an injury to a person to whom that duty is owed. Thus, to establish that she was a victim of negligence, Walter had to prove (1) that Wal-Mart owed her a *duty* of reasonable care, (2) that it *breached* that duty, (3) that the breach of duty *caused* her to suffer adverse effects, and (4) that these effects are recognized by the law as an *injury.*

In most U.S. jurisdictions, torts such as negligence are *common law causes of action.* This means that the plaintiff's ability to sue in the first place, and the terms on which she can obtain redress, are established by judicial decisions rather than by a statute passed by a legislature. In *Walter,* for example, the Maine Supreme Court states in ¶ 14 that, "Walter had the burden to prove that Wal-Mart, through its pharmacist employee, owed a duty to Walter that it breached, thereby causing her harm." This description of the tort of *negligence*—which is consistent with the one we provided a moment ago—derives from prior Maine judicial decisions that have defined negligence in terms of the four elements of duty, breach, causation, and harm (injury). The court did not provide a citation to those earlier decisions, perhaps because this basic description of negligence is so well-established as to not warrant the effort. By contrast, the court does cite earlier decisions to help define the elements of breach and causation. *See* ¶ ¶ 14, 17. Likewise, it cites earlier decisions for procedural rules, such as the rule that the trial court's decision not to grant a new trial can only be overturned if it constitutes a clear abuse of discretion. *See* ¶ 35.

3. *The Principle of Stare Decisis.* The court's reliance on earlier decisions to guide its legal analysis was not simply a matter of choice. Rather, the court was obligated to

---

* State and federal courts maintain websites from which opinions may be downloaded. (For Maine decisions, see www.courts.maine.gov.) Publishing companies also reproduce judicial opinions in hardbound volumes that can be found in law libraries, as well as in databases accessible to subscribers. The citation that follows the case-caption at the beginning of Walter v. Wal-Mart—748 A.2d 961—informs you that the decision can be found starting at page 961 of volume 748 of the Atlantic Reporter, Second Series, published by West Publishing Co.

rely on them. This obligation stems from a core principle of the common law called *stare decisis*. *Stare decisis*—which translates as "let the decision stand"—is a complex notion. Here is a rough description of its content:

> A court that is presently required to resolve an issue of law ("the present court") must accept the resolution of that issue that is contained in a prior judicial decision involving other litigants if:
>
> a. the prior decision was rendered by a court with the *authority* to render decisions that are *binding* on the present court;
> b. the issue was *actually resolved* in the prior decision, rather than assumed away;
> c. the resolution of the issue was *necessary* to the prior decision; and
> d. the issue arose in the prior decision in *comparable circumstances* to those of the present decision.

By obliging subsequent courts to follow prior courts' decisions, the principle of *stare decisis* functions to promote a reasonable degree of consistency across decisions within a jurisdiction, and thereby to advance basic values associated with the rule of law, such as predictability and comparable treatment of similarly situated litigants.

The application of *stare decisis* can sometimes be straightforward and sometimes subtle. For example, the citation by the *Walter* court to the 1910 *Tremblay* decision in ¶ 14 for the proposition that pharmacists owe their patients "ordinary care" was routine. Contrast the court's treatment in a footnote (omitted from the above opinion excerpt) of two other court decisions that indicated a willingness to assign some degree of responsibility to patients who failed to prevent or mitigate injuries caused by an erroneous prescription:

> We are aware of two cases from other jurisdictions in which a comparative negligence instruction was given when a pharmacist gave the plaintiff the wrong medication. The facts in one case, however, make it distinguishable from Walter's situation. In Forbes v. Walgreen Co., 566 N.E.2d 90, 91 (Ind. App. 1991), the plaintiff had been taking medication for headaches. When she had the prescription refilled, she noticed that the medication she was given was different in size, shape, and color from what she had been taking, but she took it anyway for several months. The wrong medication did not cause her to be sick, but it was ineffective on her headaches. *See id.* Walter had never taken her medication previously and had no reason to be suspicious of its size, shape, or color. In the other case, the ten percent reduction of plaintiff's damages for comparative negligence was not appealed or discussed. *See Van Hattern v. Kmart Corp.*, 719 N.E.2d 212, 222 (Ill. App. 1999). . . .

Walter v. Wal-Mart Stores, Inc., 748 A.2d 961, 969 n. 5 (Me. 2000).

The first thing to observe is that the Maine court was not obligated to follow these precedents for a very basic reason: They were issued by courts within other states' judicial systems. Each state's tort law forms a distinct body of law. The courts of one state do not have *authority* to issue decisions about substantive tort law that are binding on the courts of another state. Rather, out-of-state precedents such as these are at best *persuasive* authorities—helpful or informative, but not *controlling*.

Second, even if we were to imagine that these earlier decisions had been issued by the Maine Supreme Court itself, the *Walter* court would still have had reasons not to follow them. Thus, the footnote quoted above asserts that the first precedent is *distinguishable*—it was decided on facts sufficiently different from those in *Walter* that one can say without contradiction that the plaintiff in the earlier case failed to mitigate her damages, while Ms. Walter did not. As for the second out-of-state precedent, the court avoided it on the ground that it resolved the issue of the plaintiff's failure to mitigate without analysis, and therefore was not entitled to deference. In other instances, a court might decline to follow a prior decision's resolution of an issue on the ground that the resolution was not *necessary* to the decision—that the earlier court could have resolved the dispute in front of it without ever addressing the issue in question. This idea is sometimes conveyed by saying that the prior resolution was not part of the *holding* of the case, but instead constituted *dictum.*

Finally, note that, even though the principle of *stare decisis* is central to the operation of the common law system, it is not understood by courts—particularly courts of last resort, as is the Maine Supreme Court on issues of Maine law—to state an absolute or inexorable rule that controlling precedents must be followed no matter what. Indeed, courts sometimes conclude that precedents ought to be overruled or abandoned because social or economic circumstances have changed since the time of the original decision, or because the precedent runs counter to important policies or principles, or because they conclude that the initial decision was erroneous at the time it was rendered. As we will see, the question of when departure from otherwise binding precedent is warranted is one of the most difficult issues in common law analysis.

4. *The Varying Role of Statutes.* Tort law need not be judicial in origin. Many European countries have statutes that create and define the general parameters of tort liability. For example, Section 823(1) of the German Civil Code translates in part as follows:

> Anyone who intentionally or negligently injures life, body, health, freedom, ownership or any other right of another in a manner contrary to the law shall be obliged to compensate the other for the loss arising.

A handful of states, including California and Louisiana, whose legal systems reflect the influence of European civil law (as opposed to English common law) have similar provisions. However, because these statutes are written so broadly, they require extensive judicial interpretation as they are applied to concrete cases. As a result, the tort law of those states is in many respects indistinguishable from that of a common law jurisdiction such as Maine.

In European and Anglo-American jurisdictions, statutes can also create what amount to new tort causes of action for specific situations. For example, Massachusetts General Laws, Chapter 93A, is a statute that protects consumers against unfair business practices. In aid of that goal, it states:

> Any person who . . . suffers any loss of money or property . . . as a result of the use . . . by another person . . . of . . . an unfair or deceptive act or practice . . .

[may sue for damages and may also recover reasonable attorneys' fees and litigation costs if successful].

Chapter 93A and its counterparts sometimes permit suits for injuries caused by questionable business practices even though, for one reason or another, the practices do not amount to fraud or some other common-law tort.

In addition to creating new tort causes of action, statutes interact with the common law of tort in other ways. For example, statutes can limit tort remedies that would otherwise be available by setting dollar caps on damage awards. Alternatively, as discussed in Chapter 6, statutes that specify certain standards of conduct — for example, laws that require cars to be driven with their headlights on after dusk and before sunrise — are sometimes treated by the courts as setting the standard of care that will govern the resolution of a tort suit by someone who is injured by a failure to comply with these standards. As noted in *Walter*, the legislature and governor of Maine enacted a statute — 14 M.R.S.A. § 156 — with very important ramifications for tort law. Under that statute, which was originally passed in 1965, if there is some evidence presented at trial that the plaintiff's fault helped bring about her own injuries, the jury will be asked to consider that evidence and to assign a percentage fault to both the plaintiff and the negligent defendant, which assignment will have the effect of reducing or barring any recovery by the plaintiff. The place of statutes in tort law will be a recurring issue in these materials.

5. *The Torts Restatements.* The American Law Institute (ALI) is a private organization founded in the 1920s that is composed of judges, lawyers, and scholars. Its stated mission is to promote clarity and consistency in the application of the law. In aid of this goal, the ALI from time to time publishes treatises covering particular areas of common law such as Contracts, Property, and Torts. These treatises are titled "Restatements." Each Restatement aims to identify "black letter" law: rules and standards on which there is broad consensus among judges from different jurisdictions. Each also provides commentary that elaborates on these rules. Unlike statutes, regulations, and prior judicial decisions within a jurisdiction, a Restatement does not itself have the force of law. However, Restatements have sometimes been enormously influential, and particular provisions often are incorporated into common law by judicial decision.

Each Restatement is shepherded through the ALI by a "Reporter" or set of Reporters. The Reporters, eminent scholars in the relevant field, serve as the primary authors of the Restatements. For this reason, the Restatements tend to reflect a particularly scholarly "take" on the law. The Restatement of Torts has already gone through two versions, and its third iteration is presently under construction. The First Restatement was published in the mid-1930s, with Francis Bohlen acting as Reporter. The Second Torts Restatement was published in the mid-1960s and early 1970s; its Reporter was William Prosser, aided by John Wade. The Third Restatement is being published in installments. Thus far, provisions pertaining to the following topics have been published: "Products Liability" (1998) (James Henderson and Aaron Twerski, Reporters); "Apportionment of Liability" (2000) (Michael Green and William Powers, Reporters);

and "Liability for Physical and Emotional Harm" (2 volumes: 2010 & 2012) (Michael Green, William Powers and Gary Schwartz, Reporters); and "Intentional Torts" (forthcoming) (Kenneth Simons, Ellen Pryor, and Jonathan Cardi, Reporters. We will refer regularly to the Torts Restatements, particularly the Third Restatement, throughout this book.

B. Responsibilities in Tort

Negligence suits like Ms. Walter's aim to establish that another person or entity was legally at fault, and hence legally responsible, for the plaintiff having suffered an injury. Yet, even in an apparently simple case such as this one — which involves a single victim allegedly injured as the result of an in-person interaction with a single careless actor — allegations and attributions of responsibility are not as straightforward as they might first seem. Consider, for example, a seemingly simple question. Why is the caption of this case *Walter v. Wal-Mart Stores, Inc.?* More specifically, why isn't it *Walter v. Lovin?*

1. *Respondeat Superior.* A negligence suit such as Ms. Walter's alleges that a specific individual engaged in conduct that was careless as to her well-being and injured her. Yet, in many instances, a negligence plaintiff will often seek to establish not (or not only) that the careless individual owes her compensation, but instead (or also) that *the entity* for which that individual worked owes her compensation. Ms. Walter, for example, did not seek any compensation from the pharmacist, Henry Lovin, which is why he is not named in court documents as a party to the suit. Instead, she sought compensation from the corporate bank accounts of Wal-Mart, Lovin's employer.

Plaintiffs who sue entities such as corporations often are able to recover from them because of a longstanding substantive rule of tort law called *respondeat superior* (literally, "let the master answer [for the wrongs of the servant]"). Under that rule, an employer is held *vicariously liable* for wrongful acts of its employees committed within the scope of their employment. This responsibility attaches even if the employer (i.e., the firm's managers) were careful in supervising the employee's job performance.

In *Walter* itself the evidence produced at trial revealed that Wal-Mart policy requires all of its pharmacists to follow certain procedures to protect against errors. Thus, each is supposed to check the bottle from which he dispenses medication against the original prescription to ensure that they match. In addition, the pharmacist is always supposed to discuss with the patient the drug he is dispensing to her, which provides another opportunity to catch mistakes. Lovin, however, did neither of these things. Given this policy, and depending on whether Wal-Mart and its store manager took reasonable measures to implement it, one can argue that Wal-Mart *management* was *not* careless in terms of how it set up and operated the pharmacy from which the medication was dispensed to Ms. Walter. Even so, Wal-Mart would still be subject to liability. This is because, under *respondeat superior,* liability attaches to Wal-Mart vicariously, that is, simply because Lovin acted carelessly in performing his job as a Wal-Mart pharmacist, notwithstanding that his actions were perhaps in violation of company policies.

The doctrine of *respondeat superior* is not the only basis for holding corporations, organizations, and government entities liable in tort law, but it is perhaps the primary basis for doing so. (We consider the content and justifications for the doctrine more fully in Chapter 8.) To the extent it does function to impose liability on employers, it does *not* thereby immunize careless employees from liability. In other words, the doctrine functions to add another entity to the roster of potentially responsible parties, not to substitute one for another. Given this fact, it is worth asking one more question about the caption of the *Walter* case: Why doesn't it read *Walter v. Wal-Mart Stores, Inc. & Lovin?* The immediate answer is that Ms. Walter did not bring suit against Lovin. But, given that she could have, that answer simply provokes another question: Why didn't Ms. Walter sue Lovin in addition to suing Wal-Mart? Can you think of any strategic reasons why her lawyer might advise against it?

2. *Multiple Tortfeasors.* *Respondeat superior* adds an important layer to tort attributions of responsibility. Another source of complexity is that tort cases often allege or identify wrongdoing on the part of multiple actors. Reexamine the facts laid out in ¶¶ 2-8 of the majority opinion. Do they identify anyone else (other than Wal-Mart or Lovin) who might be found to have carelessly contributed to Ms. Walter's injury?

What about Walter's physician, Dr. Ross? Did he act with ordinary care in failing to arrange a blood test within two weeks of the commencement of her treatment? Alternatively, or in addition, was it careless of him to respond to her description of her symptoms by arranging for her to come into the office two days later, by which time she had been hospitalized? Suppose this was carelessness and that it did have some role in producing Walter's injuries. How would these suppositions affect your assessment of Wal-Mart's responsibility? Should one or the other be held responsible, or should both? Interestingly, although it was probably open to each of them, neither Walter's attorney nor Wal-Mart's attorney sought to add Dr. Ross as an additional party to the lawsuit, which perhaps would have enabled the jury, at its discretion, to assign some responsibility to him.

It is increasingly common for modern negligence suits to involve claims against and among multiple parties, each of whom is alleged by the others to have been partly or wholly responsible for a given victim's injury. In this respect, at least, *Walter* is helpfully old-fashioned in its simplicity. Much of the discussion of "duty," "cause," and "apportionment" in Chapters 2, 4, 5, and 7 concerns the complexities introduced into negligence law by the presence of multiple potentially responsible parties.

3. *Comparative Responsibility.* There is another group of actors whose conduct must be considered in gauging tort law as a system for articulating and enforcing responsibilities. This group consists of the victims who are bringing the tort suits. To what extent does their own conduct bear on the question of responsibility for their injuries? As noted above, under the Maine comparative fault statute, a party who can be deemed to have been at fault for her own injuries may find that her recovery is reduced or barred because of that fact. Most U.S. jurisdictions apply similar rules. Principles of comparative responsibility are discussed further in Chapter 7.

Check Your Understanding: Revisiting *Walter v. Wal-Mart*

- Explain how the actions of pharmacist Henry Lovin amounted to a tort committed by Lovin against Antoinette Walter. What were the consequences for Walter, Lovin, and Wal-Mart of the Maine courts' determination that Lovin's actions were careless and had caused an injury to Walter?
- If juries are normally supposed to decide the "breach" and "causation" issues raised by a negligence claim, why didn't the jury in Walter v. Wal-Mart decide those issues? Who decided not to submit these issues to the jury, and why was it legally permissible to bypass the jury on those issues?
- The legal rules that define the tort of negligence and the doctrines of *stare decisis* and *respondeat superior* were all critical to the resolution of Walter's lawsuit. Where do these rules come from? By what procedures did they become part of Maine law?

4. *Insurance.* Although it did not figure in *Walter*, there is often one other key player that figures in modern tort suits alleging negligence, namely, an insurance company that has provided *liability insurance* to the defendant. A liability insurance policy is a special kind of contract. In exchange for regular payments (premiums), the insurer agrees to pay for (indemnify) certain liabilities incurred by persons insured under the policy. So, for example, a physician or attorney will typically maintain malpractice insurance to cover liability if she is successfully sued for professional misconduct by a patient or client. Retailers likewise often carry liability insurance for injuries caused to customers and others in the course of their operations. Wal-Mart is so large and wealthy that it "self-insures." Rather than paying premiums to an insurance company, it sets aside a portion of its assets to cover anticipated liabilities. Liability insurance is discussed further in Chapter 8.

Insurance can also relate to tort litigation in another way. Sometimes victims have insurance—so-called first-party insurance—that covers certain costs they might incur, such as health insurance to cover the costs of one's medical care. Walter was in fact covered by Medicare, which is a federal insurance program by which the government pays for certain healthcare services provided to persons over the age of 65. However, under the substantive tort law of Maine, Wal-Mart was barred from arguing that *it* should benefit, by way of a reduced damages award, from the fact that Walter's medical expenses were mostly or entirely covered by Medicare. As we note in Chapter 8, whether juries in tort cases should be given information as to first- and third-party insurance coverage is currently a hotly debated topic.

C. The Role of Lawyers

The legal rules and economic realities that help determine the ability of clients to secure representation and proceed with or fend off tort suits are of central importance to the operation of tort law. Indeed, a practicing tort lawyer would likely tell you that, for purposes of practicing law, a working knowledge of the "nuts and bolts" of getting a case to and through court is of primary importance. The point of such an observation is not that knowledge of tort law is irrelevant to practice. Rather, it is a way of emphasizing that an understanding of tort doctrine can only get the aspiring torts practitioner so far.

Unfortunately, given space constraints, and the complexity of substantive tort doctrine alone, we can here only touch upon basic procedural aspects of tort litigation. Other courses, such as civil procedure and evidence, will provide you with greater knowledge of these topics. *In the discussion that follows, we simplify matters by limiting the discussion to a two-party tort lawsuit in which a plaintiff such as Ms. Walter brings a single tort claim against a defendant such as Wal-Mart.* As cases in later chapters demonstrate, tort cases can involve many parties, as well as various different claims raised by different parties.

1. *Attorneys and Contingent Fees.* Tort actions are lawsuits that are conducted by lawyers who are paid to represent their clients. Lawyers arrange for payment by means of either a contingent fee contract or an hourly rate contract. Under an hourly rate contract, the attorney and client agree to a per-hour rate, the lawyer keeps track of the hours worked on the case, and then the lawyer sends regular bills to the client during the pendency of the litigation. The hourly rate contract is the prevalent form of contract between corporate clients and their counsel.

Contingent fee contracts free the client from any obligation to provide the lawyer with up-front or interim compensation for his labor. In exchange, the lawyer is given the right to obtain a specified percentage of any recovery, often about 33 percent. Under this type of contract, if the tort suit results in no recovery, the client pays nothing by way of fees. However, the client is obligated to pay certain costs — for example, copying costs and court filing fees — regardless of outcome. In the United States, most personal injury plaintiffs secure legal representation through a contingent fee contract.

2. *The Contingent Fee Contract: History.* The shape of modern American tort law has been driven at least in part by significant changes in the regulation of contracts between attorneys and their clients. Early American law, like the English law from which it derived, treated attorneys not so much as private-sector service providers but as public officials. Accordingly, the amount a lawyer could charge his client was determined based on schedules developed and implemented by courts and legislatures. More strikingly, at least to the modern eye, contingent fee contracts, regardless of the percentage charged, were deemed not only void but *criminal.* Any person who financed or otherwise assisted the progress of another's lawsuit in return for a portion of the proceeds of that suit could be prosecuted for the crime of *champerty* and, if found guilty, fined or imprisoned.* Finally, early American law adopted the *loser-pays* rule. Under this rule, the party who loses the suit must pay the legal costs incurred by the prevailing party. As indicated, these sums were set by the courts, but they still threatened to impose a significant burden on the unsuccessful plaintiff (as well as the

* Champerty was closely related to two other crimes: *maintenance* and *barratry.* Maintenance was defined as officious intermeddling in the lawsuit of another. Barratry was broadly defined to include any effort to stir up litigation.

unsuccessful defendant). Each of these features of Revolutionary era law served in some degree to hinder tort litigation.

Early in the 1800s, this regulatory scheme began to break down. In part, this happened because the idea that legislatures and courts should heavily regulate lawyers' fees ran counter to the professional interest of the emerging bar, as well as two core tenets of American political culture: anti-elitism and faith in free markets. The notion that a person should be denied the ability to assert his legal rights simply because he lacked disposable income struck many as fundamentally unjust. Likewise, the notion that the attorney and client should not be free to set the terms of their business relationship increasingly seemed an unwarranted piece of paternalism.

Between 1800 and 1850, state and federal courts began to enforce attorney-client contracts in which clients voluntarily agreed to pay higher-than-statutory fees to their attorneys. Likewise, courts started to rule that contingent fee contracts between lawyers and their clients fell outside the definition of champerty and were therefore enforceable. Eventually, the blanket ban on contingent fee contracts gave way to much more selective bans; contingent fees were decriminalized, except with respect to certain representations. That pattern holds true today: Most states still do not permit lawyers to represent criminal defendants or persons in divorce proceedings on the basis of a contingent fee contract, but do permit them to do so for other representations, including representation in tort suits.

By the early twentieth century, American courts had also shifted away from the loser-pays rule, which meant that the prevailing party was no longer allowed to recover its litigation costs from the other party. For plaintiffs, the rejection of the loser-pays rule arguably reduced the downside risks of litigation and thus may have encouraged the commencement of tort litigation. Because this rule stood in contrast to the English approach, it soon came to be dubbed the "American rule."

3. *Modern Practice.* With some important exceptions, U.S. law today tends not to set caps or otherwise limit the rates charged in contingent fee contracts. In this regard, lawyers are treated no differently than other service providers such as building contractors or repairmen: We rely on the "market" to set fair rates. The market for lawyers has a number of imperfections, however. For example, only in the last 50 years have lawyers been able to advertise widely for clients instead of relying on referrals. There is some evidence that, as the supply of lawyers has increased, and as bans on advertising have been lifted, contingent fees have gone down in response to competition. Today, the rate is likely to be in the vicinity of 33 percent. Beyond this, the degree to which personal injury lawyers compete on price is unclear.

Also, important aspects of the older conception of the lawyer as public official have endured, and provide the basis for judicial regulation of lawyer-client contracts. Every state court system has adopted binding rules of professional conduct that, among other things, prohibit lawyers from collecting clearly excessive fees. Violations of these rules do not necessarily constitute a crime, nor even the tort of legal malpractice. They do, however, subject attorneys to disciplinary actions, including disbarment. The standard for "clearly excessive" fees is obviously vague, and its application depends on factors such as the complexity of the case, the likelihood of success on the merits, etc.*

In common law tort actions in the United States, the American rule against fee shifting continues to predominate. However, federal and state statutes have carved out important exceptions to the rule. You may have noticed, for example, that the Massachusetts Consumer Protection Act, quoted above, provides that a plaintiff who prevails is entitled to attorneys' fees from the defendant. Likewise, federal statutes authorizing persons to sue for certain acts of race, gender, and disability discrimination entitle successful plaintiffs to recover fees from the opposing party. Fee-shifting provisions encourage individuals with meritorious claims to bring suit. Consider, as we proceed through these materials, why legislatures might use them selectively to encourage some types of suits but not others.

Even though the legal validity of contingent fee contracts in tort suits is thus now well established, courts and commentators in the last 30 years have expressed many concerns over their use. These modern critics argue that the pendulum has swung too far in the direction of plaintiffs, and that contingent fees foment litigation by eliminating most of the up-front cost of suing. These criticisms call to mind the picture of "ambulance-chasing" lawyers aggressively promoting litigation regardless of their clients' interests.* Other critics suggest that contingent fee contracts are bad even for

---

* In 1990, England allowed "Conditional Fee Agreements" (CFAs) in suits for personal injuries or human rights violations. Under the terms of a CFA, if the case is lost, the lawyer is not paid. If the case is won, the lawyer is paid the fee that she would normally charge (based on an hourly rate and the time spent on the case) plus an additional "success fee" of up to 100% of the normal fee. In 2000, CFAs were extended to all civil cases, excluding family law cases. One arguable drawback of CFAs is that, since English law still applies the loser-pays rule to civil litigation, a losing party whose opponent obtained representation through a CFA is responsible for both the opposing attorney's legal fees and any success fee that was agreed to under the CFA. In 2013, England modified the application of the loser-pays rule where there is a CFA, so that the success fee is now paid by the winning party. Thus, if the winning party who arranged for a CFA is the plaintiff, the success fee is taken out the damages she recieves. If the winning party who arranged for a CFA is the defendant, the success fee is paid out of pocket by the defendant. (In both cases a party who agrees to a CFA can purchase insurance to cover the cost of the success fee.) However, in order to protect personal injury plaintiffs from paying "too much" of their award to their own lawyer if they win, a success fee in personal injury cases greater than 25% of the plaintiff's damages is now forbidden, excluding damages for future healthcare and economic loss.

In 2013, England also allowed "Damages-Based Agreements" (DBAs). DBAs are only available to plaintiffs. Under a DBA, if the case is lost, the lawyer is not paid, while if the case is won, the lawyer receives a percentage of the damages recovered (a contingency fee). In order to avoid an increase in adverse costs borne by losing defendants as a result of the operation of the English Rule, the losing defendant is responsible for only the portion of the legal fees that the plaintiff's lawyer would have normally earned (based on hourly rate and time spent on the case). If the contingent fee due the lawyer exceeds that amount, the winning plaintiff, rather than the defendant, makes up the shortfall. Again, however, personal injury claims are subject to a 25% cap.

In 2007 the German Constitutional Court ruled that, under certain circumstances, clients and lawyers may have a right to agree to a contingency fee contract, and in 2006 Italy permitted lawyers to charge a contingent fee in civil cases. These countries, like all of Europe, continue to adhere to the loser-pays rule.

* In fairness, we should note that the defense bar is just as frequently accused of manipulating hourly fee arrangements by overstaffing cases and otherwise "overlawyering" cases by pursuing unnecessary motions and needless discovery.

clients with meritorious claims because they encourage lawyers to push for quick settlements that generate very high returns relative to the effort put into the case, rather than to pursue their clients' best interests. Many, however, continue to defend contingent fees both on freedom-of-contract grounds and as necessary to ensure widespread access to justice, particularly in a country reluctant to fund legal services for the poor. Empirical studies seem to indicate that the rate of return on contingent fee contracts is not significantly higher than on hourly contracts.

D. Proceeding Through Court

1. *Complaints and Private Rights of Action.* In tort suits, the sequence of legal events begins at the behest of the injured person, who, if represented by an attorney, will have his lawyer draft a document called a *complaint.* Roughly speaking, we can say that a tort suit is commenced when the complaint is *served on* (i.e., delivered to) the defendant, and filed with the court that will preside over the lawsuit. A typical tort complaint is a modest document. It briefly identifies the most basic allegations contained in the plaintiff's suit, demands a jury trial, and requests that the court order the award of appropriate relief in the event that the defendant is held liable. A copy of the complaint in the *Walter* case is provided in the Appendix.

The role of the plaintiff's complaint in commencing a tort suit attests that tort is in an important sense *private* law rather than public law. Of course, the public might have an interest in a given tort suit. Indeed, the outcome of Ms. Walter's suit might conceivably affect how Wal-Mart, a global retailer, goes about dispensing prescription medications. Still, the matter is private in that tort law operates in the particular manner of empowering a private citizen, rather than a government official, to commence a legal proceeding, at her option. Likewise, the point of the suit, at least in the first instance, is for that citizen to obtain redress from the person who has allegedly wronged her.

2. *Answers and Motions to Dismiss.* Typically, a tort defendant will respond to a complaint by having his attorney file an *answer*— a document that will probably admit certain basic facts alleged in the complaint, while also denying others, as well as denying liability. (Wal-Mart's answer to Walter's complaint is reproduced in the Appendix.) In lieu of an answer, a defendant might instead file a *motion to dismiss* the plaintiff's complaint. A *motion* is a formal request for a ruling from the court, usually made by a party to the lawsuit. As its name suggests, a motion to dismiss requests that the trial judge enter judgment for the defendant at the very outset of the suit, on the basis of nothing more than the paper pleadings. Because there has been no opportunity for the plaintiff to build her case, a heavy burden is placed on the movant/defendant. Essentially, the defendant has to demonstrate that, no matter what evidence the plaintiff may be able to present in support of her tort claim as the suit goes forward, the claim contains some fatal defect that prevents the court from affording any manner of relief to the plaintiff.

By their nature, motions to dismiss will only be granted on issues that can be resolved with minimal or no factfinding. As a result, they are usually— though not exclusively — granted on procedural issues. Thus, motions to dismiss often assert that the plaintiff has commenced her tort suit in a court that has no jurisdiction (no authority) to resolve the dispute. Alternatively, they might assert that the plaintiff has waited too long to commence her action and has thus lost the right to sue. For example, suppose a plaintiff files a complaint alleging that she broke her leg after slipping on a carelessly maintained floor in defendant's restaurant. Suppose further that the complaint demonstrates on its face that the plaintiff served and filed her complaint three years after the slip-and-fall, thereby failing to comply with a statutory rule specifying that such a suit must be commenced within two years of the accident. In such a situation, a court would grant a motion to dismiss the suit on the ground that the suit is time-barred, which renders it impossible for the plaintiff to prevail no matter what evidence she might discover and present at trial. *Cf.* Meiselmann v. McDonald's Restaurants, 759 N.Y.S.2d 506 (App. Div. 2003).

3. *Discovery.* If the suit is not resolved on a motion to dismiss, the lawyers commence the process called *discovery*, whereby they attempt to secure information relevant to the tort suit. Discovery often takes the form of *document requests*, which seek copies of relevant documents in the possession of adversaries or third parties. It also may consist of *interrogatories* — written questions — addressed to the parties to the lawsuit. As indicated in the Appendix, the attorney for Ms. Walter invoked these mechanisms to obtain documents describing Wal-Mart's internal policies for the dispensation of prescription medicines, to identify the particular pharmacist who mishandled her prescription, and to identify persons whom Wal-Mart intended to call as witnesses at trial. Likewise, Wal-Mart's attorney sought to obtain records as to Walter's medical condition before and after her treatment, and records of the expenses she incurred in obtaining medical treatment, including records as to which of those expenses were covered by health insurance.

Another important discovery tool is the *deposition.* A deposition is an interview that is conducted by an attorney for one of the parties in the presence of counsel for the other party. Often a deposition will take place in a conference room at a law firm or at the office of the person being interviewed (the *deponent*). During a deposition, the deponent is under oath, and the questions put to her, as well as her answers, are recorded by a stenographer. Deponents in a tort suit may include anyone who possesses information about the dispute, especially those who may end up serving as testifying witnesses should the case proceed to trial. In *Walter*, for example, Wal-Mart's attorney deposed the plaintiff to get further information about her account of how events unfolded. Among other things, depositions allow counsel to learn more about the strengths and weaknesses of the opponent's case and the likely impact that a given witness will have at trial.

4. *The Jury Trial.* The Seventh Amendment to the United States Constitution grants to each party involved in the litigation of certain suits, including tort suits, the right to demand a jury trial. That right, however, only applies to suits tried in federal courts. Still, most state constitutions provide the same guarantee for suits in state court. (The relevant provision of the Maine Constitution is Article I, Section 20.) Thus, unless the parties agree to forgo that right, if their case goes to trial, they will

litigate it to a jury. If they do agree to waive that right and present evidence to the trial judge without a jury, the proceeding is known as a *bench trial.*

At a jury trial, the attorneys for the parties, overseen by the judge, select a jury of six to twelve men and women drawn from a pool made up of those who have received a notice to report for jury duty. (Individuals receive such notices based on random selections from lists such as lists of registered voters in the relevant locality.) The process of jury selection is beyond the scope of this discussion. Still, it is worth noting that many lawyers regard it as one of the most critical phases of the trial, because it will help determine the jurors' receptivity to the parties' evidence and arguments. Probably most civil juries today are comprised of six jurors. As specified by Maine law, *Walter* was heard by a jury of nine, although one juror was excused because of illness.

After a jury has been selected, the attorneys for the plaintiff and defendant take turns making opening statements that describe in general terms what the dispute is about and the kind of decisions the jurors will be asked to make. Although opening statements often are dramatic, they rarely garner legal analysis of the sort given by the justices of the Maine Supreme Court to the opening statement of Wal-Mart's attorney, Mr. Franco.

Next, the plaintiff's attorney, and then the defendant's attorney, present evidence by calling witnesses to testify and by introducing documents and other forms of physical evidence. In complex cases, the presentation of evidence can take weeks or even months. In a simple case, this process may take only a day or two. In *Walter,* for example, Walter's attorney called four witnesses. The first two were Dr. Morse — a longtime friend of the plaintiff — and Walter herself. Both testified primarily to how the episode affected Walter's health and quality of life. The third witness, Dr. Ross, testified to the medical effects of the misfilled prescription. Finally, Henry Lovin, the Wal-Mart pharmacist, testified as to the circumstances and character of his mistake. The defense offered the testimony only of Dr. Pickus, an oncologist who testified that the drug mistakenly given to Walter had the desired effect of causing her cancer to go into remission. He further opined that the depression experienced by Ms. Walter after being released from the hospital was unlikely to be linked *biologically* to the medication. (As the majority opinion notes in ¶ 18, however, Dr. Pickus also stated that Ms. Walter's depression likely was linked to her hospitalization, which he admitted was caused at least in part by her ingesting the wrong medicine.)

After the evidence is submitted, the attorneys give their closing arguments. Then it is the trial judge's job to instruct the jury on the applicable law. This entails informing the jury of the elements that must be proven before the plaintiff can prevail. The judge will also instruct the jury on any defenses potentially available to the defendant that would prevent or limit the assignment of responsibility to the defendant. For example, in *Walter,* the trial judge instructed the jury on the legal definition of the defense of mitigation of damages.

Once the relevant legal rules are framed by the judge, the jury retires to the jury room to determine on the basis of the evidence presented at trial whether the plaintiff has proved her tort claim and whether the defendant has proved its defenses. The *Walter* jury, for example, was required to determine the extent of the injuries that Ms. Walter suffered as a result of ingesting the wrong medication, and the amount of compensation that Wal-Mart was obligated to pay her for those injuries. Different jurisdictions have different rules, but most do not require unanimity among jurors for the resolution of civil cases such as tort suits. (The rules are different for criminal prosecutions.) Under Maine law, a verdict agreed to by two-thirds of the jurors will be deemed the verdict of the jury. *See* 14 M.R.S. § 1354 (2006). As indicated by the verdict form reproduced in the Appendix, the eight jurors who deliberated over the issues in *Walter* agreed unanimously on the verdict.

The civil jury is virtually unique to American tort law.* England, by contrast, abolished use of the jury for most civil actions in 1933. As we will see, the proper role of judge and jury is a central and contested issue in U.S. tort law. Defenders of the institution maintain that the jury helps ensure that the parties' conduct is evaluated by their peers, keeps law in contact with ordinary citizens' notions of right and wrong, and promotes public participation in the law. Critics maintain that juries make decisions that are arbitrary or systematically biased in favor of "sympathetic" plaintiffs against "unsympathetic" defendants, including corporations. In the remainder of this book, we will have many occasions to consider what is and is not asked of juries by our tort system and whether they are well-suited to live up to those responsibilities.

5. *Questions of Law and Fact.* Courts and commentators sometimes divide the questions raised by lawsuits into two categories: questions of *law* and questions of *fact*. By drawing this distinction, they mean to emphasize that, even when a case is conducted before a jury, some issues — issues of law — are reserved for the judge. For example, the issue of whether the defendant in a negligence suit owed a duty of reasonable care to the plaintiff is said to pose a question of law for the judge rather than a question of fact for the jury. Thus, the trial judge in *Walter* never asked the jury to make a finding as to whether Wal-Mart owed a duty of reasonable care in dispensing prescription medication to Walter. Rather, he relied on Maine precedents to conclude that such a duty was owed.

Dividing questions for the court and questions for the jury by reference to the distinction between law and fact is very common, but can be confusing. This is because many of the questions that are reserved for the jury call on jurors to do more than make factual findings. For example, in a typical negligence suit — and, again, *Walter* was in this regard atypical — the jury will be asked to resolve the issue of whether the defendant fulfilled her duty to exercise the level of care that a reasonably prudent person would have exercised under the circumstances. Doing so will require the jury not only to make factual determinations about what the defendant actually did or failed to do but also to *evaluate* her conduct — that is, determine whether what she did or failed to do amounted to a lack of ordinary prudence. In this sense, many questions of "fact" submitted to juries are actually questions that require both factual findings and normative judgments. These questions are thus sometimes referred to as mixed questions of law and fact.

---

* Jury trials in civil cases are available in many Canadian provinces and also in several Australian states, but are quite rare in both countries.

6. *Judgment as a Matter of Law.* Consistent with the importance attached to the jury by the federal Constitution and its state counterparts, juries are ordinarily given wide berth to determine those issues that are within their province. Moreover, once they have rendered a decision, their determinations are not lightly disturbed. However, a trial judge is sometimes empowered to preempt or second-guess a jury even on issues that are normally reserved for it. One device by which a judge may do so was the device most centrally at issue in the *Walter* appeal — the entry of *judgment as a matter of law.* Precisely because the entry of such a judgment amounts to a circumvention of the jury, a party who makes a motion for judgment as a matter of law bears an onerous burden: The judge may grant such a motion only if she concludes that, in light of the presumed or proven facts, *no reasonable jury faithfully applying governing law could find in favor of the party opposing the motion.* By contrast, such a motion cannot be granted merely because the judge thinks that the evidence more strongly favors the moving party. Thus, Wal-Mart appealed the trial court's judgment in part because it believed that the judge erred in concluding that, based on the evidence presented by Walter at trial, a reasonable jury would be *required* to find for the plaintiff on issues such as breach and causation.

7. *Timing: Entry of Judgment as a Matter of Law Before, During, and After Trial.* All motions for judgment as a matter of law ask the trial judge finally to resolve one or more of the issues in the case. Thus, all require that the moving party meet the onerous standard just described in order for the motion to be granted. These constant features notwithstanding, motions for judgment as a matter of law come in three different varieties, depending on the point in the litigation at which they are brought.

a. Before Trial. After some discovery has taken place, but before a jury has been empaneled, either party may seek entry of judgment as a matter of law on any or all of the legal issues raised by the plaintiff's lawsuit. Such a motion is usually fashioned as a motion for *summary judgment.** Motions for summary judgment are typically brought by a defendant seeking to have some or all of the issues in the case determined in its favor prior to trial, although they can be brought by the plaintiff.

A judge may grant a summary judgment motion only if she makes two findings:

> *First*, she must conclude that, as to one (or more) of the dispositive legal issues in the case, there are no genuine disputes between the parties as to "material" facts — that is, facts relevant to the resolution of that issue (or those issues).

---

* For ease of presentation we are here treating motions for summary judgment as if they are one kind of motion for judgment as a matter of law. Strictly speaking, this is inaccurate. A motion for summary judgment is a distinct type of motion that is authorized by separate rules from those governing motions for judgment as a matter of law. For example, in federal courts, motions for summary judgment are provided for by Federal Rule of Civil Procedure 56, whereas motions for judgment as a matter of law are provided for by Rule 50. Still, the substantive *standard* for granting motions for summary judgment is the same standard that governs judgments as a matter of law. Anderson v. Liberty Lobby, Inc., 477 U.S. 242, 250 (1986).

Second, she must conclude that, in light of these undisputed facts and the applicable law, a reasonable jury could not find for the party opposing the motion.

For example, if a negligence defendant convinces a trial judge that the undisputed facts obtained through discovery that bear on the "breach" element establish that no reasonable juror could deem the conduct of the defendant to have been careless (i.e., a breach of duty), the judge will enter summary judgment for the defendant and the plaintiff's negligence claim will be resolved at that point in the defendant's favor. However, precisely because the question of breach or carelessness is ordinarily for the jury, courts generally express reluctance to grant such a motion.

b. During Trial. The next opportunity for one or both of the parties to make a motion for judgment as a matter of law occurs after the attorneys have presented evidence to the jury but before the jury receives its instructions and retires to deliberate. Such motions are made after the plaintiff has finished presenting all of her evidence and/or at the close of all evidence. Like motions for summary judgment, motions for judgment as a matter of law made at the close of plaintiff's evidence or the close of all evidence can seek complete resolution or partial resolution of the case (i.e., resolution of only certain issues). Also like motions for summary judgment, they are not supposed to be granted lightly.*

Motions for judgments as a matter of law filed at the close of evidence were once commonly described as *directed verdict* motions. Today, however, courts tend to designate them simply as motions for judgment as matter of law. Thus, under the older usage, which is still invoked today by some states' courts, the motions that were filed by Wal-Mart and Walter and discussed by the Maine Supreme Court would have been deemed directed verdict motions because they were made, respectively, at the close of plaintiff's evidence and the close of all evidence. Employing currently predominant usage, however, the Maine Supreme Court in ¶ 8 of its opinion simply refers to them as motions for judgment as a matter of law.

c. After Trial. After the jury has rendered its verdict, a party who is disappointed by it can again seek judgment as a matter of law. In essence, such a motion asks the trial judge to "overrule" the jury on the ground that a reasonable jury could not have ruled as the jury actually did. In federal courts, a post-verdict motion of this sort is treated as simply renewing the motion for judgment as a matter of law that was filed prior to the submission of the case to the jury. (Thus, in federal court, the filing of a motion for judgment as a matter of law at the close of all evidence is a prerequisite to filing a motion for judgment after the verdict has been rendered — if the earlier motion was not filed, there is nothing to renew.) Under older usage, still employed in some jurisdictions, a post-verdict motion for judgment as a matter of law is deemed a motion for *judgment notwithstanding the verdict* (J.N.O.V.).

---

* Because such motions are made after the presentation of some or all of the evidence to the jury, even a trial judge who is inclined to grant such a motion may decide to let the process run its course by having the jury render a verdict. As explained below, the judge can feel comfortable doing this because she will have an opportunity *after* the verdict has been rendered to enter judgment as a matter of law if she believes such a judgment is warranted.

8. *New Trial Orders.* Trial judges enjoy another supervisory power that resembles, yet is distinct from, the power to order judgment as a matter of law. This is the power to set aside the jury's verdict and *order a new trial.* New trial motions, like post-verdict motions for judgment as a matter of law, are made by a party disappointed with the jury's verdict. Moreover, like the power to enter judgment as a matter of law, the new trial power is meant to be exercised sparingly by trial judges. However, the formal threshold for the exercise of this power is somewhat lower. This is because the entry of a new trial order does not resolve any issues in the litigation, whereas entry of judgment as a matter of law is dispositive of some or all of those issues. Instead, when a court grants a motion for a new trial, it is essentially ordering a "do-over."

The grounds on which new trials are sought are numerous and varied. Most commonly, tort defendants who are faced with a jury finding of liability move for a new trial on the ground that the jury's determination in favor of the plaintiff, even viewing the proof presented at trial most favorably to the plaintiff, runs *substantially against the weight of the evidence.* In the alternative, they argue, as did Wal-Mart, that the damages award set by the jury was so large as to evidence "passion and prejudice" against the defendant on the part of the jury, thus warranting a new trial on the issue of damages. Do you find the sum awarded by the jury to Walter reasonable? Unreasonably high? Unreasonably low? Is your assessment influenced by the fact that almost 90 percent of her recovery seems to have been meant to compensate her for intangible harms such as pain, suffering, and depression? Damages are a major topic for consideration in Chapter 8.

The *Walter* opinion informs you that Wal-Mart also unsuccessfully moved for a new trial on other grounds, including alleged misconduct by opposing counsel. What was the alleged misconduct? Does any of it relate to the size of the jury's damage award? Does the Maine Supreme Court's majority opinion deny that this misconduct occurred? If not, why does it decline to award Wal-Mart a new trial?

9. *Reconsidering Walter.* In light of what you have just read about the procedural devices available to trial judges, re-examine ¶8 of the Maine Supreme Court's opinion in *Walter.* Is it more comprehensible than the first time you read it? Among other things, it tells you that, after the presentation of evidence at trial, *both* Walter and Wal-Mart made motions for judgment as a matter of law. In other words, Walter thought that the evidence produced at trial clearly established liability, while Wal-Mart, looking at the same evidence, thought it clearly established that there could be no liability. Here it may be worthwhile briefly to consider each of these positions, starting with the latter.

At the close of plaintiff's evidence, Wal-Mart's attorney argued that his client was entitled to judgment as a matter of law. How could he do that with a straight face? What, according to Wal-Mart, was so obviously defective about the plaintiff's presentation of evidence? As we see in Chapter 3, courts commonly require a plaintiff who is suing for carelessness committed by a member of a profession — that is, malpractice — to present expert testimony as to the standards of care of the profession and as to whether the defendant failed to meet those standards. Why then did the Maine Supreme Court conclude that no such witness was required in this case?

Now consider Walter's motion. We said in the introductory remarks to this section that *Walter* was written to resolve an appeal of a very unusual trial court ruling. In saying that, we were referring to the trial court's decision to *grant* the plaintiff's motion for judgment as a matter of law on the issues of breach, causation, and comparative fault. In fact, this decision is not at all representative of litigation practice as you are likely to encounter it. Perhaps this helps explain why, after the jury returned its verdict, the trial judge *apologized* to the jurors, explaining that it was the first time in his six years on the bench that he had taken these issues into his own hands. Indeed, the judge was no doubt aware that his ruling was not just rare, but doubly rare.

First, it was rare because, as indicated in the earlier discussion of summary judgment, trial judges tend not to enter judgment as a matter of law on fact-intensive issues such as breach and causation. (Recall what the judge needed to conclude in order to grant the plaintiff's motion. As to breach, for example, he had to conclude not merely that a reasonable jury *could* find that Henry Lovin failed to act with reasonable care but that such a jury *would have to* make that finding.) Second, even when trial courts do enter judgments as a matter of law, nine out of ten, if not 99 out of 100, are entered on behalf of *defendants* rather than plaintiffs. This strongly asymmetric pattern is not coincidental. Rather, it reflects two important procedural features of tort cases that we discuss in subsequent chapters: (1) the plaintiff ordinarily bears the *burden of proving* that a tort has occurred, and (2) jurors are ordinarily free to discredit or second-guess witness testimony and other forms of evidence offered by either party. In sum, because there are almost always some grounds for a reasonable juror to doubt the plaintiff's evidence, and because it is the plaintiff who bears the onus of convincing the jury that her account of what the defendant did is probably the correct account, a reasonable jury should almost always be able to conclude that the plaintiff has not done enough to prove her case.

Given this asymmetry, what was it about *Walter* that enabled both the trial court and the Supreme Court to treat it as one of the extraordinary cases in which judgment on several key issues was properly entered for the plaintiff prior to verdict? Are you satisfied with the high court's explanation? Was there anything else about the trial proceedings that might have warranted its conclusion?

10. ***A Final Thought: Litigating Responsibility.*** Materials provided in the Appendix pose additional questions about the procedural, substantive, and tactical issues raised by *Walter*. For now, we conclude the present analysis by considering *Walter* in light of the organizing themes of this book. As we suggested at the outset, tort law is concerned to identify situations in which one person (or entity) can be held responsible for injuring another. It is no surprise, then, that Mr. Silin, Walter's attorney, emphasized notions of responsibility in his opening and closing arguments to the jury. Here is an excerpt from his closing argument:

> . . . This is a case in which all of the parties have tried in many ways to move forward as expeditiously as possible; and to some extent we've been successful, and in other ways we haven't.

> I told you [yesterday] . . . the only real issue in this case is the issue of damages. What are the damages to which Antoinette Walter is entitled to [sic]? What is fair compensation for what she suffered as a result of the negligence of the Wal-Mart Pharmacy store going back to May 7, 1997? I told you that would be the issue.
>
> I also told you that although this should be the only issue, that Wal-Mart Stores, Incorporated nevertheless continued to refuse to accept responsibility and continued to deny the liability. It was okay to substitute these drugs or it doesn't matter, or it was all her fault or all Dr. Ross's fault. We've heard much of that. What we now heard [sic] is that despite all that stuff, His Honor ruled the obvious, which is that there is no question of fact as to whether Wal-Mart was negligent. There is no question of fact as to whether Ms. Walter contributed to her negligence [sic]. She didn't. There is no question she was damaged. . . .

Mr. Franco, the defense lawyer, attempted throughout the litigation to deal with Silin's emphasis on Wal-Mart's failure to accept responsibility for Lovin's mistake. What follows is an excerpt from his opening statement (the last part of which is quoted in the *Walter* opinion):

> . . . Attorney Silin represented to you why he thought we were here, and it's my chance now to tell you why we are here.
>
> First of all, going back to how lawsuits begin and how cases end up in courts such as this, usually a plaintiff, such as Ms. Walter, has a claim against a defendant, in this case Wal-Mart. And there is a filing, a formal complaint. From the time that the complaint is filed the defendant has 30 days in which to answer the complaint. And depending on what information the defendant has in its possession, they either admit or deny the allegations in the complaint.
>
> It's important I think at the outset for you to understand that the complaint made some pretty strong accusations in this case against Wal-Mart, and used some strange words such as negligent[,] careless, reckless conduct. . . . Within the 30-day time period it was my role to deny or admit these allegations. And given the time frame involved, there was a general denial made. It's common practice to do that until the investigation continues.
>
> There was [sic] also allegations of severe pain, physical permanent injuries. There is no way that a defendant, Wal-Mart or anybody in this situation, would be able to know or admit those types of allegation without further investigation and further inquiry in terms of what is alleged.
>
> So I'm not making any apologies on behalf of Wal-Mart or myself for making denials of those allegations. What I'm here to tell you right now is since the filing of the complaint and filing of the answer, Wal-Mart has never denied responsibility for this incident. Never.

The obvious suggestion contained in the excerpted portion of Silin's closing argument is that the jury should take a dim view of "Wal-Mart Stores, Incorporated," not only because its employee's carelessness injured Walter, but also because Wal-Mart persisted in contesting responsibility even though its responsibility was "obvious." In what way was Wal-Mart's decision to litigate liability a culpable failure to "accept responsibility"? Would an offer from Wal-Mart to settle the case prior to trial have constituted an acceptance of responsibility?* Is Franco correct to point out that, in a system of adversarial litigation, we should expect individuals and entities who have been sued to mount a vigorous defense at trial? Or is Silin right to link the ideas of responsibility and acceptance of responsibility? Based on this admittedly limited introduction, do you think that there might be ways in which the institutions and procedures that have been developed for making determinations of responsibility might distort those determinations? If so, are such problems necessary costs of a system of litigation, or can we devise better ways to proceed?

III. TORT LAW IN CONTEXT

A. Tort Contrasted with Other Areas of Law

The preceding discussion offers an examination of how the tort system permits and requires individuals to respond to situations that gave rise to cases like *Walter v. Wal-Mart* in a particular way. Tort, however, is but one area of the law, and many other areas also have relevance to the type of situation that gave rise to *Walter*. Contrasting these other areas of law will help further define the distinctive features of tort law. For purposes of introduction, these contrasts are intentionally overdrawn. At times, the boundary lines between these different areas are fuzzy, and the ideas and methods of one frequently crop up in others.

1. *Criminal Law.* Criminal law is closely related to tort law both historically and conceptually. It, too, is primarily concerned with identifying and sanctioning wrongful conduct. For this reason, "assault" is the name of both a crime and a tort (although the definition of the crime of assault in a given state's law may not match precisely the definition of the tort of assault). Also like tort law, criminal law leaves an important role for the jury in applying the law: The jury typically determines whether the evidence presented by the prosecution is sufficient to establish that the defendant's conduct constituted a given crime.

However, there are also important differences between tort and crime. For one thing, negligence, which is perhaps the most prominent cause of action in modern torts, is less commonly the basis for criminal liability. Thus, Lovin's inadvertent error probably would not provide the basis for a criminal conviction. (So far as we know, he was not criminally prosecuted.) Likewise, a driver who runs over and kills a pedestrian simply because he looked down to adjust his car's stereo probably cannot be found guilty of the crime of negligent homicide. To be sure, criminal law contains provisions that criminalize certain instances of "negligence." Still, the term negligence in the criminal context usually refers to more substantial misconduct than a simple slip or

* Settlement agreements almost always contain language by which the defendant explicitly disavows responsibility, but nonetheless agrees to pay compensation in order to resolve the lawsuit. Obviously, the parties' attorneys were unable to reach a pre-trial settlement in this case. Attorney Silin proposed to settle at a figure about half the size of the jury's eventual award. Franco countered with a substantially lower offer. For more on the dynamics of the *Walter* litigation, see the Appendix.

a momentary lapse. Thus, lawyers sometimes distinguish between "gross" or "criminal" negligence, on the one hand, and "simple" negligence on the other.*

Suppose, however, Lovin had not simply been careless, but had acted for the purpose of poisoning Ms. Walter, or with depraved indifference to her well-being. If that were the case, he would be subject to criminal prosecution, perhaps for the crime of assault. Had such a prosecution been filed, the caption on the court documents would have read *State v. Lovin* or *People v. Lovin.*** This caption would indicate that the action was being commenced not by the victim, but by a government official, such as a district attorney, who represents all the citizens of the jurisdiction. As a result, Walter would have very little formal control over whether such a proceeding were brought, or whether the criminal case were disposed of by a plea agreement or a jury verdict. This in turn indicates that the primary purpose of a criminal prosecution would be for the government, on behalf of the people, to punish the individual wrongdoer, Lovin, and to deter future actors from behaving in a like manner.

Given the potentially harsher nature of criminal punishment—in particular, the prospect of imprisonment—the prosecution would also face a higher set of hurdles in proving its case than did Walter in suing Wal-Mart for negligence. For example, it would have to prove that Lovin's conduct satisfied the elements of the crime of assault *beyond a reasonable doubt.* A tort plaintiff, by contrast, need only prove the elements of her claim by a *preponderance of the evidence,* that is, she must show that it is more likely than not that each element of her claim is satisfied.

Tort differs from crime in another important way: The issue of the victim's responsibility, mentioned in Section II.B above, is usually irrelevant to criminal prosecutions. Put simply, there is no doctrine of comparative fault in criminal law. Even if Walter could have taken reasonable steps to prevent herself from being poisoned in the first place, that failure would, at least as a matter of formal legal rules, be irrelevant to Lovin's criminal culpability.

Another critical difference between tort and the imagined criminal prosecution is that its resolution would not likely include an order from the court specifying redress for Ms. Walter. Although criminal penalties can include payment of restitution to the victims of the crime, such penalties are relatively rarely enforced as compared to jail terms and fines payable to the government. Finally, although criminal law was once part of the common law, today the criminal laws that the district attorney would accuse

---

* It may be tempting to extrapolate from this brief discussion that criminal conduct is simply a subset of tortious conduct (i.e., that crimes are just particularly serious torts). This temptation should be resisted, because certain forms of misconduct can be criminal without being tortious. For example, it is a crime to possess various controlled substances or to attempt to shoot someone, even if the attempt fails. Tort, however, does not recognize liability for mere possession and does not impose liability for attempts unless they generate certain consequences for the victim (e.g., causing him to fear for his physical well-being).

** Modern criminal law, particularly federal criminal law, sometimes permits the imposition of criminal fines payable by corporations and other entities for criminal acts committed by their employees while acting within the scope of employment *and* for the benefit of the entity. It is highly unlikely that Wal-Mart would be at risk of criminal punishment in our imagined case in which Lovin, for his own purposes, deliberately poisons Walter.

Lovin of breaking would not be of judicial creation, but rather would be found in statutes enacted by the legislative branches of the jurisdiction and endorsed by its governor. In all of these respects, criminal law may be described as primarily public, rather than a law of private redress.

Just to avoid confusion, it is worth pointing out that the same acts and events often can give rise to both criminal prosecution and a tort suit. A famous example of this phenomenon involved former football star O.J. Simpson. Simpson was criminally prosecuted for the murder of his ex-wife Nicole Brown Simpson and her acquaintance Ronald Goldman, and acquitted. Notwithstanding the acquittal, the victims' parents brought a tort suit against Simpson, essentially for the tort of battery. The jury in the tort suit found him liable for millions of dollars in damages. Although the "double jeopardy" clause of the Fifth Amendment to the U.S. Constitution forbids a second prosecution for the same crime following an acquittal, it does not preclude a subsequent action in tort. How is it that one person can, on the same facts, be found innocent of murder yet liable for the tort of battery? (Keep in mind the different standards of proof in criminal and civil cases, mentioned above.)

2. *Administrative Regulation.* Throughout the twentieth century, federal and state governments came increasingly to rely on administrative agencies to study and remedy problems that, in prior centuries, were regulated, if at all, exclusively by the common law of tort. For example, at the national level, the Consumer Product Safety Commission (CPSC) now monitors product safety, the Environmental Protection Agency (EPA) addresses issues of harms posed by toxins in air, soil, and water, and the Occupational Safety and Health Administration (OSHA) regulates workplace hazards.

Another agency relevant to modern tort law is the National Highway and Transportation Safety Administration (NHTSA), which sets standards for automobile and road safety. NHTSA, a branch of the U.S. Department of Transportation, was created by a statute passed by the United States Congress and signed into law by President Lyndon Johnson in 1966. The statute authorizes NHTSA, among other things, to prescribe automobile design standards to ensure safety. Relying on this delegation of authority, NHTSA has, for example, required automobile manufacturers to phase in air bags into all new car models and has required anti-lock brakes on certain vehicles. NHTSA is also empowered to request data from manufacturers and to test automobiles and component parts for compliance with its standards. If the agency determines that automobiles and other products fail to meet its standards, it can order the manufacturer(s) to recall the model(s) and correct the defect(s). Manufacturers that fail to abide by these regulations are subject to penalties, including fines payable to the government.

State governments also include numerous regulatory agencies. Indeed, the State of Maine maintains an agency called the Office of Licensing and Registration (OLR). The OLR in turn includes an entity called the Board of Pharmacy. The pharmacy board is empowered to issue licenses, without which it is unlawful to operate as a pharmacist in Maine. It also sets the terms of those licenses through, among other things, regulations concerning procedures that pharmacists must follow. The board in addition employs inspectors who monitor pharmacists to check for compliance with board regulations. Finally, it is empowered to issue certain penalties for violations, including monetary fines, as well as license suspensions and revocations. (By means of the OLR's website, one can search to determine if a particular licensee in any of a number of professions has been subject to disciplinary action.)

As it turns out, the Maine pharmacy board received a report from one of its inspectors concerning Henry Lovin's erroneous filling of Ms. Walter's prescription in February of 1998, several months before the complaint in *Walter* was filed. (It is unclear how Lovin's mistake came to the attention of the inspector. It is possible that Wal-Mart notified her, or that she discovered it in the course of reviewing the pharmacy's files.) The filing of the inspector's report led the board to take action against Lovin, which in turn led to their entry into a "consent agreement," reproduced in the Appendix. Under the terms of this agreement, Lovin admitted his mistake, and accepted penalties that included a $500 fine, a 14-day suspension, and 15 hours of professional education. In this way, the administrative apparatus of the State of Maine responded to Lovin's mistake independently of the litigation by Walter against Wal-Mart.

Administrative law is a vast and complex subject in its own right, so generalizations are hazardous. For present purposes, however, we may here note two broad features of that body of law. First, like criminal and tort law, administrative law seeks to set substantive standards of conduct, for example, standards of how certain chemicals may be discharged into the environment, or whether passenger vehicles must be equipped with certain safety devices. Also like criminal law, but unlike tort law, its primary mechanism for executing or enforcing these standards is via directives and suits initiated by government officials seeking to set standards and impose penalties on violators. As such, administrative regulations typically provide no redress to victims of unlawful conduct. (Lovin's $500 fine was paid to Maine's treasury.) Finally, as with criminal law, even where regulations are in place governing specific conduct, aggrieved private citizens generally have little, if any, control over agency actions. For example, they are usually *not* entitled to demand investigation of, or the issuance of sanctions against, those who have allegedly violated agency regulations. To be sure, concerned citizens and groups may petition agencies to take action, and may participate in the development of administrative standards of conduct, but they have no legal right to force agencies to initiate regulatory action, and instead must rely on the use of political pressure.

Second, in contrast to both tort and criminal law, administrative standards of conduct are set not by judges or lay juries but by officials within the agency, who have expertise concerning the conduct in question. Moreover, regulatory law is often created through the process of notice-and-comment rulemaking. Here, the agency, concerned with a particular problem — say, for example, the problem of trains colliding with cars at railroad grade crossings — announces an intention to regulate the activity and solicits input from any actors who might be affected by the issuance of regulations, as well as the public generally. Based on this input, the agency then issues regulations addressing the conduct in question. In contrast to tort suits, this sort of rulemaking proceeds on an aggregate, forward-looking basis. The agency treats a problem such as grade-crossing accidents as an ongoing social problem, rather than a discrete occasion calling for an inquiry into whether a particular actor was responsible for a particular injury. Thus, it seeks to adopt rules that will, in the aggregate, best achieve a balance between objectives such as safety and efficiency.* Each of these distinctive features of administrative rulemaking — its reliance on experts, its solicitation of information from many sources rather than the parties to a particular dispute, its forward-looking and aggregate orientation — distinguish it to some degree from tort law. Whether these features further suggest that administrative regulation is generally superior to tort law as a response to undesirable conduct is a complex and contested normative question.

3. *Social Welfare Programs and Public Compensation Funds.* Underlying each tort suit is the idea that someone has suffered an injury. Tort law responds to that fact in a particular way: by empowering the alleged victim to bring a claim for redress against the person responsible for the alleged wrongdoing and the resulting injury. Other forms of law might respond to the victim's loss in a way that does not focus on responsibility and redress, but only on the individual victim's need for compensation.

For example, the federal government operates a program popularly known as Medicare. In a nutshell, Medicare collects revenues from taxes on worker's wages and uses them to help cover certain healthcare expenses incurred by designated groups of persons, including persons older than 65. Thus, as indicated earlier, Walter's medical expenses were paid partly or wholly by the federal government under the auspices of the Medicare program. In addition to broadly applicable compensation schemes such as Medicare, Congress has adopted a number of programs designed to assist the victims of particular types of injuries or diseases, including children made ill by vaccines, as well as coal miners who suffer from black lung disease. In 2001, it enacted legislation designed in part to compensate survivors of victims of the September 11 terrorist attack on the World Trade Center and the Pentagon.

In these and other ways, government can in principle provide injury victims relatively easy access to compensation with a minimum of procedure. Certainly nothing approaching the time, effort, and money expended on litigating a tort suit is required in order for a recovery to be secured by an eligible claimant. In part this stems from the fact that, unlike tort law, compensation schemes of this sort make no attempt to identify or deter wrongful conduct, to impose responsibility on a wrongdoer who has injured another, or to provide the victim with individualized redress. Programs such as Medicare and compensation funds are supported by taxes, not by payments from persons deemed responsible for the victims' injuries. In this regard, compensation funds might apply equally to those injured by natural disasters such as earthquakes or hurricanes as to those injured by wrongdoing. The point of such a fund is not to

---

* Agency decisions frequently can take a form similar to judicial proceedings. In such agency *adjudications,* the relevant agency files a complaint against a person or entity alleged to have violated a given regulation, such as the Federal Trade Commission's regulation barring "unfair trade practices." The complaint, however, is not filed with a conventional court, but instead with an administrative law judge, who (without the aid of a jury) hears evidence and issues a ruling as to whether the conduct in question violated the regulation. The extent to which agencies should rely on adjudications to make and enforce policy, rather than notice-and-comment rulemaking, is one of the central debates of modern administrative law.

identify a person or entity responsible for a bad outcome, but to tend to the needs of the victim.

4. *Contract Law.* Consider next how the law might enable the parties themselves to anticipate and respond to problems of the sort that gave rise to *Walter.* The sale of the prescription medicine by Wal-Mart to Ms. Walter was accomplished by means of a contract. It specified, among other things, the price and quantity of the medicine sold to her. In principle, the sales contract might also have addressed the issue of what would happen if Walter were injured because of some problem in the filling of the prescription. For example, Wal-Mart might have included in the fine print on the package containing Walter's medicine the following language: "By purchasing this prescription medicine, purchaser agrees that Wal-Mart shall not be liable for any harm caused as a result of the use of this prescription medicine." Should a court enforce this sort of contractual allocation of the risk of harm? If not, why not? As we see in Chapter 7, courts are often reluctant to enforce contractual provisions that relieve actors of tort liability for injuries, particularly physical injuries, caused by their misconduct.

Like tort law, contract law is private law. It requires an aggrieved party to commence a lawsuit seeking redress against another whose conduct has caused an injury. Likewise, the application of the law to that suit will be the job of judges and juries. However, unlike tort law, a contract suit seeks redress for the failure of the other party to do what he or she has *agreed* to do. Thus, were the facts of *Walter* to have given rise to a contract action, the issue would be to determine what was promised to whom and on what terms. Did Wal-Mart in its contract with Walter promise to take due care to ensure that her prescription was filled correctly? Did it disavow any such promise? If the latter, and if the Maine Supreme Court were to conclude that this contractual disavowal operates to void any tort duties owed by Wal-Mart, Walter would have no claim. (Given these assumptions, Wal-Mart did not break any promise to her because it made no promise whatsoever as to the correctness of the prescription.)

As briefly noted earlier in this chapter, there is a different way in which contract law might figure in this scenario that would involve not a contract between Walter and Wal-Mart, but one between Walter and an insurance company (or between Wal-Mart and an insurance company). To the extent Walter was concerned about the risk of accidental injury, she might have been able to make provision for such injuries by purchasing insurance that would entitle her to reimbursement for any expenses or losses she incurred in the event such an injury came about. First-party insurance of this sort is common today. Examples include health insurance, under which the insurer pays the insured's medical bills, or fire insurance, providing reimbursement for fire damage to the insured's home. First-party insurance, which covers injuries or damage to the insured, her family, or her property, is distinguished from third-party insurance, which protects against losses in the form of liabilities incurred by the insured to others. For example, a homeowner or business might have third-party insurance to cover liabilities incurred when guests or customers suffer injuries on the premises as a result of dangerous conditions on their premises, such as slippery or poorly lit steps.

If Ms. Walter had been insured by a private insurer for injuries caused by others, she could have filed a claim to receive reimbursements for the health care expenses she incurred by virtue of having been poisoned by the wrong medicine. If a dispute arose as to whether she was entitled to such reimbursements, she would eventually have to commence a suit — essentially for breach of contract — to obtain what she believes she was owed under the policy. The critical questions in that suit would be whether or to what extent her injuries were covered under her contract for health insurance.

As the preceding examples emphasize, contract law empowers parties to mold for themselves the terms of their interactions. This flexibility is both a virtue and vice. In principle, and often in practice, contract permits individuals to get exactly what they want out of interactions with others. However, it is sometimes the case in the real world that parties lack the information, judgment, or resources to enter into beneficial contracts. For example, even with the implementation of the 2010 Affordable Care Act, approximately 10 percent of Americans have not contracted for health insurance, some because it is unavailable to them, others because they lack the resources to pay for it, others because they choose (wisely or unwisely) to forgo insurance for other goods and services. Likewise, in the case of a liability limitation provision of the sort imagined above, one would suspect that an ordinary consumer would not be in a position to make a knowing and voluntary decision to waive her right to sue in tort on the basis of fine print on a package. Tort law, in contrast to contract, is not optional in this way. It specifies a set of responsibilities that, absent some legally recognized excuse or justification, actors are not permitted to avoid. When contract ought to prevail — when parties ought to be able to set for themselves the terms of their interaction — is a regularly recurring question in tort and contract law.

B. The Politics of Tort Law

In light of the foregoing discussion, one can begin to get a better sense of the distinctive domain of tort. Tort law is law that provides injured parties with redress from those who have wrongfully injured them. Moreover, it specifies those wrongs at least partly independently of how the parties have structured their relationship. In this way, it is a law of responsibility and redress. Because tort law sets out mandatory responsibilities, it is sometimes in conflict with contract law, although contractual arrangements can also give rise to, and help define, tort liability. Criminal law and administrative regulation often work in conjunction with tort law, although these forms of law, too, can sometimes clash with tort. For example, when administrative standards of conduct demand less care of a certain class of actors than tort law might, those actors often will assert that judges and juries should not be allowed to identify and impose standards that ask more of them than those set by agencies. Finally, tort bears the same sort of complex relationship to compensation funds and private insurance. Liability insurance, for example, often enables victims to recover in tort where they otherwise would not. On the other hand, liability insurance can also reduce incentives for care, and lessen the impact on wrongdoers of tort judgments against them.

Although tort has in one form or another been a part of Anglo-American law for hundreds of years, it was not until the late 1970s that it became a subject of intense political and ideological battles, at least in the United States. To be sure, particular tort rules had from time to time generated criticism and reform. At the turn of the twentieth century, for example, legislatures began modifying or supplanting the tort system as it applied to the industrial workplace because certain tort doctrines made it very difficult for workers to recover from their employers for injuries caused by unsafe working conditions. Still, it is only in the last 30 years that the two major political parties, as well as pundits, have come to adopt general — and polarized — stances toward the tort system.

The explanation for the emergence of tort as a hot-button issue is complex. As we will see, certain changes in mid-twentieth-century law — both procedural and substantive — have expanded the potential reach of tort liability. In addition, with the economic downturns of the 1970s came the recognition that U.S. businesses, even corporate giants such as General Motors, were vulnerable to recessions and global competition, and thus could be hurt by a system that had the potential to saddle them with large liabilities. The 1970s also witnessed the first liability "crisis." Doctors, for example, claimed that they could no longer afford to practice in certain high-risk areas, such as obstetrics, because malpractice insurance premiums had risen dramatically. Likewise, some municipalities shut down recreational facilities and essential services, claiming that tort liability had rendered insurance too expensive. Whether the tort system was the prime culprit, or whether other factors, such as poor returns on insurance companies' investments, played a more important role than tort liability, has been, and still is, hotly contested.

Regrettably, debates about the tort system today tend to degenerate into the overheated, polarized discourse of talk radio and Internet commentary. Critics of the tort system, such as the American Tort Reform Association (ATRA), which was founded in 1986 on behalf of industry to limit tort liability, claim that tort law is crippling the U.S. economy, clogging the courts, and undeservedly enriching the plaintiff's bar. Relying heavily on colorful examples of frivolous lawsuits, ATRA and other political organizations have lobbied vigorously and successfully for the enactment of damage caps, limitations on joint and several liability, and other means of reducing tort awards and deterring the filing of tort suits. *See* www.atra.org; www.overlawyered.com.

In response, or perhaps retort, consumer advocates such as Public Citizen, founded by Ralph Nader, as well as the American Association for Justice (AAJ) (formerly known as the Association of Trial Lawyers of America, or ATLA), have argued that the tort reform movement is a barely disguised effort to shield corporations and other actors from scrutiny and responsibility for harms caused by their irresponsible conduct. In their view, the claims of organizations such as ATRA as to the harmful effects of the tort system are exaggerated, and have been fueled by a misinformation campaign that relies on dubious anecdotes seized upon by a sensation-hungry media and gladly digested by a public desirous of being outraged rather than informed. Just as ATRA has lobbied aggressively for legislation cutting back on tort liability, AAJ has funded candidates and reforms friendly to the maintenance or expansion of the existing tort regime. *See* www.justice.org; www.citizen.org.

"Do you have any picture books that could help a child understand tort reform?"

Apart from political debates over tort law, there has been a longstanding sense among many members of the legal academy that tort law's time has passed. Indeed, with the rise of administrative regulation and public assistance programs, along with the increasing availability of both private insurance and publicly available information about the dangers associated with different activities, many scholars have questioned whether tort law still has an important role to play in the twenty-first century.

It is not our purpose, nor within our abilities, to settle these disputes. Rather, we hope in this book to give the student a better sense of how tort law hangs together as a law of responsibilities and redress. In doing this, of course, we are inevitably taking a certain position with respect to these debates. In our view, tort law should not be dismissed simply as a device by which plaintiffs' lawyers are empowered to manipulate the law and jurors' emotions to feast off business earnings. Yet we also reject a depiction of tort law as mainly a means by which unelected and unaccountable litigants empower themselves to police corporate behavior on behalf of the public good. Finally, while we believe that there is a vital place for expert regulation, as well as a social safety net, we do not share the prevailing academic sense that we as a nation have somehow grown out of the need for a body of law that assigns responsibilities to individuals and entities and provides redress for victims of their misconduct.

Although recent transnational surveys reveal that other nations, such as Germany and Israel, have rates of litigation similar to those of the United States, the U.S.

continues to give greater prominence to tort law than any other industrialized nation. Tort's relative prominence in our law is fueled by several features of our political system. The contingent fee system likely lowers the barriers to lawsuits as compared with a pay-as-you-go model of the sort employed in other countries. Moreover, in contrast to many European countries, the lack of nationalized healthcare and other features of a strong social safety net encourages a greater percentage of injured U.S. citizens and residents to seek relief via tort suits. Finally, tort law reflects our political culture. In some nations, the obligations that one owes to be careful toward another, or to otherwise refrain from injuring another, tend to be viewed as created by, and owed exclusively to, the state. Americans, however, tend to view this class of obligations as part of "civil society" — as obligations owed to one another. Tort law, as we have said, is all about the articulation of the responsibilities that persons (and entities) owe to others, whether it is the obligation of care that a pharmacy owes to its customers, or the responsibility of a driver to drive safely so as to avoid injuring those around him.

C. Some Statistics Concerning the Tort System

It may be helpful to put certain features of the tort system in empirical perspective.* By one measure — namely, the caseload of the federal courts — tort filings increased between 1962 and 2002 almost threefold. However, it is important to view this statistic in context. First, the overall caseload of the federal courts increased even more rapidly. In fact, the *proportion* of tort cases filed in the federal courts dropped in this period from 37 percent to 23 percent. Second, the population of the United States increased by approximately 150 percent during this same period, and the economy more than tripled in size. Third, it is important to keep in mind that the vast majority of tort suits (as can be seen from the selection of cases in this book) are filed in *state* courts, not *federal* courts. Finally, although there are costs associated with filing suit (for example, a plaintiff usually has to go to the trouble of finding a lawyer), these costs are relatively modest, and a plaintiff ordinarily can withdraw the suit without significant adverse consequence. For these reasons, statistics as to filings are of limited value.

The National Center for State Courts (NCSC) has also attempted systematically to classify and measure tort suit filings. According to the NCSC, tort filings, which currently make up no more than 7 percent of all civil filings in state courts, declined about 24 percent between 1998 and 2007.** By contrast, in the same period, contract suit filings increased by 37 percent. However, the percentage of tort filings in any given state

---

* The statistics provided herein are drawn from and available on the following websites: Nat'l Ctr. For State Courts, Court Statistics Project, http://www.courtstatistics.org/civil.aspx (last visited August 10, 2015); Bureau of Justice Statistics Publications (Civil Cases) http://www.bjs.gov/index.cfm?ty=tp&tid=45 (last visited August 10, 2015); http://www-fars.nhtsa.dot.gov/ (last visited Dec. 28, 2011); *see also* Marc Galanter, *The Vanishing Trial: An Examination of Trials and Related Matters in Federal and State Courts*, 1 J. Empir. L. Stud. 459 (2004); James S. Kakalik & Nicholas N. Pace, *Costs and Compensation Paid in Tort Litigation*, The RAND Corporation, R-3391-ICJ (1986).

** A 1986 RAND Institute for Civil Justice study, using NCSC statistics and statistics drawn from other sources, estimated that tort filings in state courts rose between 2.3 percent and 3.9 percent annually in the period 1981–1985.

can vary widely — in 2006 only 2 percent of civil cases filed in North Dakota were torts, whereas in Massachusetts 34 percent of all civil cases filed were torts. By far, automobile accidents make up the largest proportion of tort filings in the state courts — over 50 percent, although this class of claims declined by 23 percent between 1997 and 2006. In the same period, medical malpractice filings, which represent only about 3 percent of all tort filings, declined by 8 percent, whereas products liability claims declined by 4 percent so as to represent 4 percent of all tort filings.

A similar story as to the types of tort claims that tend to be brought can be gleaned from evidence as to the type of tort claims that go to trial. The Bureau of Justice Statistics (BJS) has conducted four surveys of civil trials in the 75 largest counties in the United States between 1992 and 2005. Just as with filings, 50 percent of tort trials arose out of injuries stemming from automobile accidents. The next biggest category of trials — about 17 percent — consisted of those for medical malpractice claims. Trials of suits against property owners by persons injured on the property (such as store customers suing for injuries incurred while in stores) form the third biggest category, at about 15 percent.

Like statistics as to filings, statistics as to trial outcomes must be handled with caution. This is because tort suits that end in a trial are today a rarity. Overwhelmingly, suits are instead abandoned, dismissed in the pre-trial stage of litigation, or — most commonly — resolved by a settlement agreement. The BJS found that there was a 40 percent increase in the number of tort suits that went to trial in the federal courts in 1970–1985, followed by a 79 percent decrease between 1985–2003. The same study that found that the likelihood of a federal tort suit reaching the trial stage decreased from 1:10 in 1985 to 1:50 in 2003. The BJS found that the number of products liability trials in the federal courts has declined significantly. Between 1990–2003 non-asbestos products liability trials in the federal courts declined by approximately 66 percent, and asbestos products liability have declined even more, to the point where there were no asbestos products liability trials in the federal courts in 2002 and 2003. The BJS reports that between 1992 and 2005 tort trials in the states declined by 52 percent. The greatest decline occurred in products liability suits (66 percent fewer trials), whereas the smallest decline occurred in medical malpractice suits (10 percent fewer trials). Current estimates suggest that a mere 3 to 4 percent of tort suits go to a bench or jury trial. Medical malpractice claims are slightly more likely to be resolved by a trial than are other claims.

The causes of the "death" of the civil trial are complicated. In some instances, legislatures have consciously adopted reform measures that encourage the use of arbitration, mediation, and other forms of alternative dispute resolution. More fundamentally, trials can generate huge expenses in the form of attorneys' fees and expert witness fees, and the outcomes are often difficult to predict. As a result, the parties to a lawsuit that is not abandoned or dismissed have a strong incentive to settle the dispute prior to trial.

With respect to those tort claims that are tried by a jury, plaintiffs and defendants each win about half of the time. Again, the medical malpractice figures are different: in 2005 plaintiffs prevailed in only about a fourth (23 percent) of medical malpractice trials. For all tort plaintiffs who prevail at trial, the median compensatory award in

2005 was about $24,000. The median award for the most common tort claim—for injuries arising out of an automobile accident—was about $15,000. By contrast, in medical malpractice and product liability actions in which the plaintiff prevailed, plaintiffs received a median award of $400,000 and $567,000, respectively. Punitive damages are awarded in a very small percentage of tort trials (about 1.5 percent in 2005), in part because plaintiffs are unlikely to pursue punitive damages (they are requested in 5 percent of the tiny percentage of tort cases that go to trial), and juries more often than not decline to award punitive damages even when they are requested (some evidence suggests that punitive damages are awarded in about 30 percent of the cases in which they are requested).

IV. USING THIS BOOK

In thinking about torts it is important to remember that there are many forms of wrongful conduct—hence the many distinct torts denominated at the outset of this chapter. Moreover, conduct can be wrongful in different ways. Certain conduct might be egregiously wrongful and blameworthy: for example, intentional and unjustified infliction of physical harm on another person. Other conduct may be less egregious, as was the case with the careless conduct in *Walter.*

Because negligence has come to dominate the torts landscape in the last 150 years, many introductory torts courses focus primarily on the ins and outs of liability for carelessly caused injuries. This book shares that focus. The various chapters of Part Two thus provide detailed analysis of core issues in negligence, introducing along the way concepts that will be integral to other topics in tort, such as causation.

Part Three examines torts of a different, and in some ways more basic, kind—namely, intentionally caused injuries that generate causes of action for battery, assault, and false imprisonment. In addition, it revisits negligence law as it applies to a special kind of injury, namely harm to one's emotional well-being. Part Four introduces students to actions for interferences with property interests. It also discusses no-fault (or "strict") liability for abnormally dangerous activities and under statutory workers' compensation schemes as a segue into an analysis of products liability.

In Part Five, the book concludes by presenting recent decisions issued by the U.S. Supreme Court that have had, and will in the foreseeable future continue to have, a significant impact on the operation of modern tort law. Finally, the Appendix provides supplemental materials, including litigation documents, concerning the *Walter* case.

REFERENCES/FURTHER READING

Attorneys and Tort Law

Randolph E. Bergstrom, *Courting Danger: Injury and the Law in New York City, 1870-1910* (1992).

Nora Freeman Engstrom, *Sunlight and Settlement Mills*, 86 N.Y.U. L. Rev. 805 (2011).

Nora Freeman Engstrom, *An Alternative Explanation for No-Fault's "Demise,"* 61 DePaul L. Rev. 303 (2012)

Nora Freeman Engstrom, *Attorney Advertising and the Contingency Fee Cost Paradox,* 65 Stan. L. Rev. 633 (2013).

Peter Karsten, *Enabling the Poor to Have Their Day in Court: The Sanctioning of Contingency Fee Contracts, A History to 1940,* 47 DePaul L. Rev. 231, 241 (1998).

Herbert M. Kritzer, *Risks, Reputations, and Rewards: Contingency Fee Legal Practice in the United States* (2004).

John Leubsdorf, *Toward a History of the American Rule on Attorney Fee Recovery,* 47 Law & Contemp. Probs. 9 (1984).

Douglas E. Rosenthal, *Lawyer and Client: Who's in Charge?* (1974).

H. Laurence Ross, *Settled Out of Court: The Social Process of Insurance Claims Adjustment* (1980).

The Jury

Sheri S. Diamond & Jonathan D. Casper, *Understanding Juries* (2000).

Phoebe Ellsworth, *Jury Reform at the End of the Century: Real Agreement, Real Changes,* 32 U. Mich. J.L. Reform 213 (1999).

Michael D. Green, *The Impact of the Civil Jury on American Tort Law,* 38 Pepp. L. Rev. 337 (2011).

Neil Feigensen, *Legal Blame: How Jurors Think and Talk About Accidents* (2000).

Andrew Guthrie Ferguson, *The Jury as Constitutional Identity,* 47 U.C. Davis L. Rev 1105 (2014).

Andrew Guthrie Ferguson, *Jury Instructions as Constitutional Education,* 84 U. Colo. L. Rev. 233 (2013).

Edith Greene, et al., *Jurors' Attitudes About Civil Litigation and the Size of Damage Awards,* 40 Am. U. L. Rev. 805 (1995).

Valerie P. Hans, *Business on Trial: The Civil Jury and Corporate Responsibility* (2000).

Valerie P. Hans & Neil Vidmar, *American Juries: The Verdict* (2007).

Robert E. Litan (ed.), *Verdict: Assessing the Civil Jury System* (1993).

New Zealand Law Commission, *Review of the Judicature Act 1908: Towards A Consolidated Courts Act* 83 (Issues paper 29, 2012) (available at www.lawcom.govt.nz) (last accessed on August 11, 2015).

Lars Noah, *Civil Jury Nullification,* 86 Iowa L. Rev. (2001).

Steven Penney, *Mass Torts, Mass Culture: Canadian Mass Tort Law and Hollywood Narrative Film,* 30 Queen's L. J. 205, 223 (2004).

Jason M. Solomon, *The Political Puzzle of the Civil Jury,* 61 Emory L.J. 1331 (2012).

Neil Vidmar, *The Performance of the American Civil Jury: An Empirical Perspective,* 40 Ariz. L. Rev. 849 (1998).

Developments in the Law — The Civil Jury, 110 Harv. L. Rev. 1408 (1997).

Symposium on the American Civil Jury, 48 DePaul L. Rev. 197 *et seq.* (1998).

Statistics and Modern Debates About Tort Law

Kenneth S. Abraham, *The Liability Century: Insurance and Tort Law from the Progressive Era to 9/11* (2008).

Richard L. Abel, *Questioning the Counter-Majoritarian Thesis: The Case of Torts,* 49 DePaul L. Rev. 533 (1999).

Tom Baker, *The Medical Malpractice Myth* (2005).

Peter A. Bell & Jeffrey O'Connell, *Accidental Justice: The Dilemmas of Tort Law* (1997).

Robert G. Bone, *The Economics of Civil Procedure* (2003) (providing, among other things, statistics on civil litigation).

Frank B. Cross, *Tort Law and the American Economy*, 96 Minn. L. Rev. 28 (2011).

Thomas Eaton & Susette M. Talarico, *A Profile of Tort Litigation in Georgia and Reflections on Tort Reform*, 30 Ga. L. Rev. 627 (1996).

Theodore Eisenberg, *The Need for a National Civil Justice Survey of Incidence and Claiming Behavior*, 37 Fordham Urb. L. J. 17 (2010).

Marc Galanter, *Real World Torts: An Antidote to Anecdote*, 55 Md. L. Rev. 1093 (1996).

John C. P. Goldberg, *Unloved: Tort in the Modern Legal Academy*, 55 Vand. L. Rev. 1501 (2002).

Mark M. Hager, *Civil Compensation and Its Discontents: A Response to Huber*, 42 Stan. L. Rev. 539 (1990).

Valerie Hans & William Lofquist, *Jurors' Judgments of Business Liability in Tort Cases: Implications for the Litigation Explosion Debate*, 26 L. & Soc'y Rev. 85 (1992).

William Haltom & Michael McCann, *Distorting the Law: Politics, Media, and the Litigation Crisis* (2004).

Deborah R. Hensler, et al., *Trends in Tort Litigation: The Story Behind the Statistics*, The RAND Corporation, R-3583-ICJ (1987).

Peter Huber, *Liability: The Legal Revolution and Its Consequences* (1988).

Thomas Koenig & Michael Rustad, *In Defense of Tort Law* (2001).

Douglas A. Kysar, *What Climate Change Can Do About Tort Law*, 41 Envtl. L. 1 (2011).

Deborah Jones Merritt & Kathryn Ann Barry, *Is the Tort System in Crisis? New Empirical Evidence*, 60 Ohio St. L.J. 315 (1999).

Walter K. Olson, *The Rule of Lawyers: How the New Litigation Elite Threatens America's Rule of Law* (2002).

Joseph Sanders & Craig Joyce, *"Off to the Races": The 1980s Tort Crisis and the Law Reform Process*, 27 Hous. L. Rev. 207 (1990).

Michael J. Saks, *Do We Really Know Anything About the Behavior of the Tort Litigation System — And Why Not?*, 140 U. Pa. L. Rev. 1147 (1992).

Peter Schuck (ed.), *Tort Law and the Public Interest* (2001).

Anthony J. Sebok, *Disputes from the Tort Wars: A Review Essay*, 85 Tex. L. Rev. 1465 (2007).

Joanna Shepherd, *Uncovering the Silent Victims of the American Medical Liability System*, 67 Vand. L. Rev. 151 (2014).

Danya Shocair Reda, *The Cost-and-Delay Narrative in Civil Justice Reform: Its Fallacies and Functions*, 90 Or. L. Rev. 1085 (2012).

Charles Silver, *Does Civil Justice Cost Too Much?*, 80 Tex. L. Rev. 2073 (2002).

Symposium: What We Know and Do Not Know About the Impact of Civil Justice on the American Economy and Polity, 80 Tex. L. Rev. 1537 *et seq.* (2002).

PART II

NEGLIGENCE: LIABILITY FOR PHYSICAL HARMS

CHAPTER 2

THE DUTY ELEMENT

I. NEGLIGENCE: A BRIEF OVERVIEW

A. Elements of the Prima Facie Case

Negligence in tort law is a failure to heed a duty of care owed to another that causes injury to that other. Because of its breadth, negligence is today the tort most commonly relied upon by accident victims to obtain redress from an alleged wrongdoer. Suits for injuries caused by careless driving, incompetently rendered professional services, and unsafe premises are usually suits for negligence.

The word "negligence" has not always been used to refer to a particular tort. Indeed, before 1800, it was relatively rare for an English or American court faced with a tort case explicitly to analyze an accident victim's claim as a negligence claim. This is *not* to say that common law prior to 1800 failed to recognize tort liability for accidentally caused injuries. Instead, it is to say that complaints seeking to establish such liability invoked different causes of action that contained somewhat different descriptions of the wrong that had been perpetrated. So, for example, if a British pedestrian in 1750 were run over by a wagon and wanted to sue the driver, his claim against the driver would be for "trespass"—a generic legal wrong that covered any "direct" and "forcible" infliction of injury by an actor upon a victim, whether intentional or careless. Meanwhile, a patient of the same era who claimed to have been injured by the malpractice of his physician would bring an action for "trespass on the case." Whether these differences of categorization reflect substantive differences in doctrine is debated among historians.

Historians also disagree about when one finds the earliest instances in which lawyers and judges invoke the term *negligence* in its modern sense, as the name for a distinct tort. For our purposes, it is enough to note that such usage became increasingly common in the period from 1825 to 1875. By the end of that period, moreover, courts had begun to define negligence in terms similar to those used in contemporary cases.

These formulations typically identify four "elements" that a plaintiff must prove to make out a prima facie claim:*

Negligence: Prima Facie Case

Actor *A* is subject to liability to other person *P* for negligence if:

1. *P* has suffered an *injury*;
2. *A* owed a *duty* to a class of persons including *P* to take care not to cause an injury of the kind suffered by *P*;
3. *A breached* that duty of care;
4. *A*'s breach was an *actual* and *proximate cause* of *P*'s injury.

Students who have read *Walter v. Wal-Mart* (Chapter 1) can get a sense of how this formulation applies to particular claims by plugging into it the facts alleged and proven in that suit:

1. Walter suffered a serious illness (*injury*);
2. Defendant Wal-Mart was obligated to customers of its pharmacy to exercise reasonable care for their physical well-being (*duty*);
3. Wal-Mart, through its employee, failed to exercise reasonable care for Walter's physical well-being when, without appropriate checks, he dispensed the wrong medication to her (*breach of duty*);
4. Wal-Mart's breach functioned as a cause of Walter's illness, which illness was the sort of injury one could expect to be caused by such a breach (*actual* and *proximate cause*).

Our analysis in the next several chapters tracks this account of negligence. After a brief discussion of injury, this chapter concentrates on the duty element. Chapters 3 and 4 turn, respectively, to breach and actual cause. Chapter 5 discusses doctrines, such as proximate cause, that concern how the elements of the prima facie case must align with one another before liability will attach.

B. The Injury Element

Many standard formulations of negligence place "injury" as the last of the tort's four elements. If one thinks of a tort unfolding chronologically, this ordering makes sense: The victim's injury always follows after the injurer's breach of duty. Nonetheless, we have identified injury as the first element of the prima facie case. We do this because it helps better capture the role that injury plays in negligence, and throughout tort law. An injury is the first and most basic condition for a viable tort claim. It is only if the plaintiff can demonstrate that she has suffered the right kind of *adverse effect* that she is entitled to pursue her action for redress from another.

---

* These are the elements that, *at a minimum*, a negligence plaintiff must prove to be eligible for a remedy. Even if the plaintiff can make these out, the defendant may be able to avoid liability on the basis of an affirmative defense. *See* Chapter 7 (discussing defenses). This is the import of the phrase "prima facie case."

Suppose *A* drives carelessly past *B*, narrowly missing her. Suppose also that *A*'s driving is witnessed by a police officer, but that *B* was oblivious to the threat to her well-being and, having since learned about it, is utterly unfazed. *A* can be cited for a traffic violation, but *B* will have no tort claim against *A*. Because *B* has suffered no adverse consequence in connection with *A*'s careless driving, *B* cannot prove an injury, and thus has no grounds for demanding of *A* that *A* provide her with redress.

Even where a person can point to some adverse effect on her, the effect still may not count as an injury in the eyes of negligence law. Imagine that *A* and *B* are standing in a slow-moving supermarket checkout line. *B* is chattering mindlessly on his cell phone, much to *A*'s annoyance. Even though it is intelligible to say that *B*'s conduct has caused *A* to suffer some sort of adverse effect (i.e., temporary annoyance), this will not of itself suffice to establish that *A* has suffered an injury.

So what does count as an injury? Perhaps the most obvious category is *physical harm*. By physical harm we refer to two sub-categories of adverse effects. First, we mean bodily harms, including fatal and non-fatal contusions, lacerations, broken bones, internal organ damage, diseases, and physical illnesses. Second, we refer to damage to, or destruction of, tangible property, including land, structures, and personal possessions. Returning to the case of *A* and *B* mentioned above, if, when *A* drove carelessly past *B*, *A* struck *B*, causing *B* to suffer internal bleeding, or if *A* collided with and damaged *B*'s parked, unoccupied car, *B* will be deemed to have suffered an injury. (Whether *B* can hold *A* responsible for those injuries is a separate question. For now we are concerned only to isolate the kind of adverse effect that satisfies the first, injury element of negligence.)

Loss of wealth can also count as an injury in the law of negligence. Suppose Bank loans money to Company. Soon thereafter, Company files for bankruptcy, and the loan is never repaid. In deciding to make the loan, Bank relied on a financial audit of Company prepared by Company's Accountant. Because of Accountant's carelessness, the audit erroneously deemed Company to be in sound financial condition. Bank has suffered an injury in the form of economic loss and, depending on how the other elements of the negligence tort play out, may be able to prevail on a negligence claim against Accountant.

Although, as we will see in Chapter 10, negligence law at one time declined to treat *emotional distress* as an injury in its own right, today it is recognized as an injury. Thus, if in the careless driving example, *B* was seriously upset because she was aware that *A* almost ran her over, *B* will be deemed to have suffered an injury. Whether she can recover compensation from *B* for that injury will turn on issues of duty, breach and/or proximate cause.

Whether other sorts of effects beyond these will suffice to count as injuries is a sometimes contested matter, as we will see. For now it is enough to note that physical harms, economic loss, and emotional distress are all examples of adverse effects recognized as injuries by the law of negligence.*

---

* Torts other than negligence recognize distinct categories of adverse effects as injuries. For example, as explained in Chapter 9, the torts of assault and battery treat interferences with one's person as injuries even if those interferences do not generate bodily harm or emotional distress. The torts of defamation and invasion of privacy treat loss of reputation and loss of privacy, respectively, as injuries on which tort actions can be founded.

Check Your Understanding

What Counts as an Injury in Negligence?

To get to work each day, a cyclist rides her bicycle to a train station, where she locks it against a railing located above the platform on which passengers stand while waiting for trains. One day, while hurrying to secure her bike, she accidentally drops her heavy lock over the side of the railing, where it falls toward other commuters awaiting their trains. In which of the following scenarios will one of those commuters be able to allege an *injury* for which the cyclist could be held liable if the commuter can also establish the other elements of negligence?

1. The lock strikes the commuter's shoulder, causing permanent nerve damage.
2. The commuter happens to look up and notice the lock falling rapidly toward him. Fearful of being struck, the commuter manages to step out of the way of the falling lock but for some time thereafter remains unnerved by the incident.
3. The lock falls to the ground in front of the commuter as he is about to board a train. Startled but otherwise unfazed, the commuter misses the opportunity to board the train before it departs. Because the commuter must wait for the next train, he is required to stay later at work than he had planned. As a result, he cannot attend his 8-year old daughter's soccer game.

C. Focusing on Physical Harms

Chapters 2 through 8 of this book focus primarily on claims of negligence arising out of one kind of injury, namely *physical harms*. This is not because physical harms are as a group more basic, or more serious, than other injuries. (Most of us probably would prefer to suffer a broken arm than to suffer emotional or economic devastation.) Rather, that focus is driven by several pedagogic considerations.

First, as an empirical matter, negligence claims tend to arise out of physical harms. Suits resulting from car accidents, medical errors, and unsafe premises—which together make up the vast bulk of modern negligence suits—typically allege bodily harm or property damage as the relevant injury. Thus, a focus on physical harms helps provide a realistic sense of the world of negligence outside the classroom.

Second, an emphasis on physical harms is probably the most effective way to put to one side any questions concerning the injury element. When a complaint alleges a broken limb or an illness, there is simply no controversy whether the plaintiff is alleging the sort of effect that counts as an injury—she is. Again, this is not to suggest that claims alleging other sorts of injuries are necessarily less valid than claims for physical harms. Rather, it is to say that physical harms often provide particularly clear examples of injuries.

Third, as explained below, claims in which the injury alleged is emotional distress, intangible economic loss, or some other adverse effect not involving physical harm often raise complex questions of "duty" that are best analyzed in contrast to the issues raised by physical harm cases.

Finally, we note that our organization of negligence law is consistent with that of the Restatement (Third) of Torts, which also isolates negligence claims alleging physical harms for separate treatment from claims alleging other sorts of harms.

Restatement (Third) of Torts: Liability for Physical and Emotional Harm § 4 (2010). Thus, our presentation tracks, and perhaps will help make sense of, what is likely to be a presentation of tort doctrine that will have significant influence on judicial decisions in future tort cases.

II. THE DUTY ELEMENT AND THE GENERAL DUTY OF REASONABLE CARE

On the assumption that the plaintiff alleges and will be able to prove that she has suffered a bodily harm or damage to her property, we now turn our attention to the second element of the prima facie case of negligence: duty. The duty element will occupy us for the rest of this chapter.

As a first pass that will later need refinement, one can say that the duty element requires a negligence plaintiff to establish that the defendant owed her, or a class of persons including her, an obligation to take care not to cause the type of injury that she has suffered.* To put the same point negatively: If an actor was *not* under an obligation to take precautions against causing the sort of injury suffered by the victim to persons such as the victim, she cannot be held liable for failing to take those precautions. Understood on these terms, the duty question is distinct from the subsequent breach question. The latter assumes the existence of a duty of care, and asks whether the defendant did enough to satisfy the duty. Unfortunately, this neat analytic separation of duty from breach can become blurry in particular cases, as we will see.

A. Easy Cases: The Unqualified Duty to Conduct Oneself with Reasonable Care for the Person and Property of Others

Just as a plaintiff who comes into court with evidence of having suffered broken bones or a diagnosed disease will have little trouble satisfying the injury element, so, too, many plaintiffs will have little or no trouble establishing that the defendant owed it to them to take care for their physical well-being. The latter may be termed *easy* duty cases — cases in which neither the litigants nor the court will spend much time on the issue because all are satisfied that the person being sued owed it to the complainant to take reasonable care. Many easy duty cases are ones in which the plaintiff's allegation is that the defendant *carelessly undertook a course of conduct that directly caused the plaintiff physical harm.* As indicated above, that is part of the reason why we limit our focus to physical harms in the opening chapters of the book. More difficult duty cases, by contrast, tend to arise out of allegations that the defendant's carelessness consisted of a *failure to act for the benefit of the plaintiff,* or that the defendant caused *some other kind of injury* besides physical harm. We consider some of these cases in

* This description technically fits only "negative" duties to take care to avoid causing harms. As discussed below in Section III.C, persons are sometimes under "positive" or "affirmative" duties to make reasonable efforts to protect or rescue another.

Section III of this chapter, and others in Chapter 10. As we also note in Section II.B, however, even cases alleging careless affirmative conduct causing physical harm will sometimes give rise to more difficult duty cases.

Easy duty cases are easy in the sense that the existence of a duty owed by the defendant to the plaintiff tends to be taken for granted. Yet these cases bear a second and related feature that distinguishes them from more difficult cases. In the category of easy duty cases, courts are quite comfortable articulating the duty owed by the injurer to the victim in *unqualified* or *general* terms. So, for example, courts are content to say, as did the court in *Walter v. Wal-Mart* (Chapter 1), that a physician or pharmacist owes reasonable care to his patients, without further specifying what reasonable care entails, or when exactly that duty is triggered. Likewise, courts will routinely assert or assume that a car driver owes it to others around him to drive reasonably, without saying anything more about the circumstances in which that duty attaches, or its contours or limitations. By contrast, in the harder-case categories, as we will see, even when courts recognize a duty owed to the plaintiff, they will tend to take pains to *qualify* that duty with various limitations. In these cases — which we explore in Section III — the courts are not content to speak in terms of a general duty of reasonable care, but instead identify relatively specific duties to which the defendant must attend.

B. A Sampling of Easy Duty Cases Drawn from English Law

1. *Reception of English Common Law: Undertaking- and Activity-Based Duties.* The American Revolution notwithstanding, the common law of tort in this country derives from English law. Indeed, after the Revolution, the new states enacted "reception statutes" that explicitly incorporated English law into their law. Not surprisingly, then, many cases falling into the easy duty case category reflect obligations that have been part of the fabric of the common law for centuries. For example, the duty today owed by pharmacists to their customers traces back hundreds of years to the recognition of duties owed by medieval surgeons to take care not to commit malpractice on their patients. Likewise, members of various others trades and callings — veterinarians, innkeepers, ferry operators, and others — have for centuries been held to an unqualified or general obligation to take due care for the physical well-being of their customers and/or their customers' property. In each of these scenarios, the provider of services was treated as having *undertaken* to be careful for the benefit of certain other persons.

Although duties of care often were recognized in old English common law on the basis of well-defined roles and relationships, they also attached to certain activities irrespective of any such connection between wrongdoer and victim, as evidenced by two seventeenth-century decisions issued by the English King's Bench court.* In the famous decision of Weaver v. Ward, 80 Eng. Rep. 284 (1616), the court presumed that

* At the time of *Weaver* and *Mitchil*, the King's Bench — or Queen's Bench, if a woman was sitting on the English throne — was one of the three royal courts that sat in Westminster Hall in London and resolved the legal issues raised by private disputes governed by the common law. The other two were the Exchequer Court and the Court of Common Pleas.

the victim of an accidental shooting could sue the shooter under the writ of "trespass" notwithstanding the absence of any preexisting relationship between them. Likewise, in Mitchil v. Alestree, 86 Eng. Rep. 190 (1676), the court held the owner of a horse could be sued under the writ of trespass on the case for carelessly arranging to have his horse trained in a public park, during which training it ran down the plaintiff, a stranger.

The operation of horse-drawn carriages and ships provides another example of the sort of activity to which a duty to be vigilant of certain other persons' physical well-being attached regardless of whether any such duty was assumed by the driver or owner for the benefit of the victim. In Cotterill v. Starkey, 173 Eng. Rep. 676 (N.P. 1839), the plaintiff, a pedestrian, had been run down by the defendant as he drove his horse-drawn wagon.* The judge presiding over the trial of the case explained the law to the jury as follows:

> [I]t is quite clear that a foot passenger has a right to cross [a public road] and that persons driving carriages along the road are liable if they do not take care so as to avoid driving against the foot passengers who are crossing the road. . . .

Two years earlier, the justices of the English Court of Common Pleas in the case of Vaughan v. Menlove, 132 Eng. Rep. 490 (1837), upheld a claim for liability arising out of a carelessly started fire that spread from defendant's to plaintiff's property. In doing so, they rejected the defendant's argument that he was at liberty to do as he pleased with his own property, regardless of the risks of physical harm it posed to others around him. Said one justice:

> The principle on which . . . [the plaintiff's] action proceeds, is by no means new. It has been urged that the Defendant in such a case takes no duty on himself; but I do not agree in that position: every one takes upon himself the duty of so dealing with his own property as not to injure the property of others.

(Because *Vaughan* includes a discussion of the breach element of negligence that is at least as important as its analysis of duty, a report of the decision is reproduced in Chapter 3.)

2. ***Heaven v. Pender* (1883).** As the foregoing paragraphs suggest, even before the tort of negligence was recognized in its own right, English tort law had identified an array of situations and activities giving rise to a presumptive and unqualified duty to take reasonable care against causing physical harms to others. By the end of the nineteenth century, jurists and lawyers sought to "induce" from these instances a general rule as to when a person can be said to owe such a duty to others. In Heaven v. Pender,

---

* As explained in the preceding footnote, common law tort cases usually were filed in, and resolved by, one of three multi-member courts that sat in Westminster Hall in London. However, at certain times during the year, the justices of these courts traveled throughout England to preside individually over local jury trials. The judges would then reconvene in London to discuss and resolve legal issues that had arisen while they were out "riding circuit." The local proceedings before individual justices were called *nisi prius* proceedings; hence the N.P. notation in the caption of *Cotterill.*

11 Q.B.D. 503 (Eng. C.A. 1883), Justice Brett, a member of England's Court of Appeal,* offered the following observations:

> If a person contracts with another to use ordinary care or skill towards him or his property the obligation need not be considered in the light of a duty; it is an obligation of contract. It is undoubted, however, that there may be the obligation of such a duty from one person to another although there is no contract between them with regard to such duty. Two drivers meeting have no contract with each other, but under certain circumstances they have a reciprocal duty towards each other. So two ships navigating the sea. So a railway company which has contracted with one person to carry another has no contract with the person carried but has a duty towards that person. So the owner or occupier of house or land who permits a person or persons to come to his house or land has no contract with such person or persons, but has a duty towards him or them. . . .
>
> The question[] which we have to solve in this case [is] — what is the proper definition of the relation between two persons . . . which imposes on the one of them a duty towards the other to observe, with regard to the person or property of such other, such ordinary care or skill as may be necessary to prevent injury to his person or property. . . . When two drivers or two ships are approaching each other, such a relation arises between them when they are approaching each other in such a manner that, unless they use ordinary care and skill to avoid it, there will be danger of an injurious collision between them. This relation is established in such circumstances between them, not only if it be proved that they actually know and think of this danger, but whether such proof be made or not. It is established, as it seems to me, because any one of ordinary sense who did think would at once recognise that if he did not use ordinary care and skill under such circumstances there would be such danger. And every one ought by the universally recognised rules of right and wrong, to think so much with regard to the safety of others who may be jeopardised by his conduct; and if, being in such circumstances, he does not think, and in

---

* By 1883, Parliament had reorganized the English judiciary. The courts of Common Pleas, Exchequer, and King's Bench were replaced by a single set of courts still known today as the Queen's Bench Division (or King's Bench Division, should a male ascend to the throne). The Queen's Bench Division hears tort and contract claims, among others. It forms one branch of the "High Court of Justice," which is the name for the civil side of the English court system. Appeals from the Queen's Bench Division are typically heard by a single Court of Appeal, which is the Court that decided *Heaven.* Court of Appeal justices are dubbed "Lord Justices of Appeal." The chief judge responsible for the civil side of the Court of Appeal's docket is titled "Master of the Rolls". (That title refers to a now obsolete responsibility for keeping court records on rolls of parchment paper.) Justice Brett was Master of the Rolls at the time *Heaven* was decided.

In 2009, Parliament created the Supreme Court of the United Kingdom. It serves as the domestic court of last resort for civil litigation. (Prior to the Court's creation, the House of Lords served this function.) Appeal to the Supreme Court is by permission of either the Court of Appeal or the Supreme Court. The Supreme Court will also occasionally hear direct appeals from the Queen's Bench Division.

Great Britain's courts are obligated to interpret domestic law consistently with European Union law and to give effect to the rights contained in the European Convention on Human Rights. Under certain circumstances, a litigant may challenge a decision of the Supreme Court of the United Kingdom in the European Court of Human Rights on the ground that the Supreme Court's application of domestic law violated the litigant's Convention rights.

> consequence neglects, or if he neglects to use ordinary care or skill, and injury ensue, the law, which takes cognisance of and enforces the rules of right and wrong, will force him to give an indemnity for the injury. In the case of a railway company carrying a passenger with whom it has not entered into the contract of carriage the law implies the duty, because it must be obvious that unless ordinary care and skill be used the personal safety of the passenger must be endangered. . . . It follows . . . that there must be some larger proposition which involves and covers both sets of circumstances. The logic of inductive reasoning requires that where two major propositions lead to exactly similar minor premisses there must be a more remote and larger premiss which embraces both of the major propositions. . . .
>
> The proposition which these recognised cases suggest, and which is, therefore, to be deduced from them, is that whenever one person is by circumstances placed in such a position with regard to another that every one of ordinary sense who did think would at once recognise that if he did not use ordinary care and skill in his own conduct with regard to those circumstances he would cause danger of injury to the person or property of the other, a duty arises to use ordinary care and skill to avoid such danger. . . .

Justice Brett's central claim in *Heaven*—that an unqualified duty to take reasonable care not to cause physical harms is owed to another whenever a person "of ordinary sense" would recognize that careless conduct on his part would create "danger of injury to the person or property of the other"—has today been recast by lawyers and judges in the language of *reasonable foreseeability.* In modern legal parlance, drivers are deemed to owe a duty to take care not to cause physical harm to those around them simply because it is a reasonably foreseeable consequence of careless driving that such persons might suffer physical harms.

C. The Evolution of Duty Rules

By identifying "easy" duty cases, the previous section emphasized pockets of duty law that have been relatively stable for centuries. Insofar as this emphasis creates the impression that the duty element is always or even typically governed by a static set of rules, it is misleading, even as applied to claims for physical harms arising out of careless conduct. One of the hallmarks of the common law is that it changes—usually incrementally, but sometimes abruptly and dramatically—as judges apply existing rules to new disputes arising in new circumstances. Indeed, as the remainder of the materials in this chapter will attest, doctrine pertaining to the issue of duty evolved on several fronts throughout the twentieth century, and in some instances changed quite dramatically within a relatively brief period of time. As you read the two main cases in this section, consider what might have prompted the judges who decided them to expand or otherwise alter the rules contained in precedents. Also, consider carefully the content of the new rules that they put in place of the old ones. Do they comport with the notion, emerging from twentieth-century interpretations of *Heaven v. Pender*, that so long as physical harm to a person such as the plaintiff is a reasonably foreseeable consequence of an actor's careless conduct, the actor owes a duty to take care not to cause such harm to the plaintiff?

1. *Winterbottom v. Wright: The Privity Rule.* Historically, the most infamous instance of a rule declining to recognize a duty to regulate one's conduct with care not to cause physical harms to another was the "privity" rule first announced by the English Court of Exchequer in Winterbottom v. Wright, 152 Eng. Rep. 402 (1842) (decided 41 years prior to Heaven v. Pender). Wright built and maintained carriages. He entered into a contract with the English Postmaster General to provide coaches fit for delivering mail. The Postmaster General in turn obtained drivers by contracting with another company that hired Winterbottom as a driver. (Thus, Winterbottom had no contractual relationship with the Postmaster or with Wright, only with the company that hired him.)

Winterbottom suffered permanent harm to his leg when a wheel on the coach he was driving collapsed, causing the coach to crash. He sued Wright, arguing that Wright breached a duty owed to drivers such as him to take reasonable care to ensure the soundness of the coaches being supplied to the Postmaster General. The judges of the Exchequer Court (titled "Barons") rejected this argument. According to the Chief Baron, Lord Abinger, it was necessary to reject emphatically the duty posited by Winterbottom's claim lest the court invite "an infinity of actions."

> Here the action is brought simply because the defendant was a contractor with a third person; and it is contended that thereupon he became liable to every body who might use the carriage.
>
> . . . Unless we confine the operation of such contracts as this to the parties who entered into them, the most absurd and outrageous consequences, to which I can see no limit, would ensue. . . . The plaintiff in this case could not have brought an action on the contract; if he could have done so, what would have been his situation, supposing the Postmaster-General had released the defendant? That would, at all events, have defeated his claim altogether. By permitting this action, we should be working this injustice, that after the defendant had done every thing to the satisfaction of his employer, and after all matters between them had been adjusted, and all accounts settled on the footing of their contract, we should subject them to be ripped open by this action of tort being brought against him.

Likewise, Baron Rolfe opined:

> The breach of the defendant's duty stated in this declaration is his omission to keep the carriage in safe condition. . . . The duty [arose] . . . solely from the contract; and the fallacy consists in the use of that word "duty." If a duty to the Postmaster-General be meant, that is true; but if a duty to the plaintiff be intended, (and in that sense the word is evidently used,) there was none. This is one of those unfortunate cases in which there certainly has been damnum, but is *damnum absque injuria*; it is, no doubt, a hardship upon the plaintiff to be without a remedy, but, by that consideration we ought not to be influenced.* Hard cases, it has been frequently observed, are apt to introduce bad law.

---

* *Damnum absque injuria* ("harm without wrong")—the maxim invoked by Baron Rolfe—describes a loss or harm that, even though a burden on the injured victim, does not support a legal claim against another person.

Does *Winterbottom*'s ruling contradict the principle later induced from other English cases by Justice Brett in *Heaven v. Pender*? Recall that *Heaven*'s principle states, roughly, that a duty of reasonable care attaches whenever it is reasonably foreseeable that careless conduct on one's part risks physical harm to persons such as the plaintiff. Wasn't it reasonably foreseeable to Wright that if he provided an unsound coach to the Postmaster General, a driver hired by the Postmaster could be physically injured? If so, on what ground can *Winterbottom* be distinguished from cases such as *Cotterill v. Starkey* and *Vaughan v. Menlove*?*

Whether consistent with other English case law or not, *Winterbottom*'s rule that a plaintiff who is injured by carelessness on the part of a product manufacturer may not recover in tort absent contractual privity between plaintiff and the manufacturer served to set an important limitation on U.S. and British manufacturers' responsibilities for the next 75 years.

2. Thomas v. Winchester: Imminently Dangerous Products. Even as *Winterbottom* was being imported into American law, it was also being limited. In *Thomas v. Winchester*, 6 N.Y. 397 (1852), the New York Court of Appeals — that state's highest court — permitted the plaintiff, Mrs. Thomas, to proceed against a company that had carelessly mislabeled a bottle of poison as if it were medicine, thereby causing her to be accidentally poisoned. The company argued, under *Winterbottom*, that it owed Mrs. Thomas no duty of care because it sold the mislabeled bottle to a distributor named Aspinwall, who sold it to a pharmacist, who sold it to the plaintiff's husband. The court rejected this argument:

> If, in labeling a poisonous drug with the name of a harmless medicine, for public market, no duty was violated by the defendant, excepting that which he owed to Aspinwall, his immediate vendee, in virtue of his contract of sale, this action cannot be maintained. If A. build a wagon and sell it to B., who sells it to C., and C. hires it to D., who in consequence of the gross negligence of A. in building the wagon is overturned and injured, D. cannot recover damages against A., the builder. A.'s obligation to build the wagon faithfully, arises solely out of his contract with B. The public have nothing to do with it. Misfortune to third persons, not parties to the contract, would not be a natural and necessary consequence of the builder's negligence; and such negligence is not an act imminently dangerous to human life. . . .
>
> This was the ground on which . . . *Winterbottom* . . . was decided. . . . The reason of [that] decision is best stated by Baron Rolfe. A.'s duty to keep the coach in good condition, was a duty to the postmaster general,

---

* Justice Brett was aware of the obstacle that *Winterbottom* posed to his effort in *Heaven* to "induce" a general account of the conditions under which a duty to take reasonable care not to cause physical harm attaches. He suggested that *Winterbottom* was not really a decision about duty at all, but instead denied liability on the ground that the harm suffered by Winterbottom was too "remote" in time and space from the careless acts committed by Wright. Remoteness mattered, according to Brett, in part because it indicated that various other actors were in a position to identify and address the problem in the coach between the time it left Wright's possession and the time it collapsed. Consider the significance of these observations in light of *MacPherson* and *Mussivand infra.*

> with whom he made his contract, and not a duty to the driver employed by the owners of the horses.
>
> But the case in hand stands on a different ground. The defendant was a dealer in poisonous drugs. . . . The death or great bodily harm of some person was the natural and almost inevitable consequence of the sale of [poison] by means of the false label. . . .
>
> No such imminent danger existed in [*Winterbottom*]. . . . [Winchester's] negligence put human life in imminent danger. Can it be said that there was no duty on the part of the defendant, to avoid the creation of that danger by the exercise of greater caution? or that the exercise of that caution was a duty only to his immediate vendee, whose life was not endangered? The defendant's duty arose out of the nature of his business and the danger to others incident to its mismanagement. Nothing but mischief like that which actually happened could have been expected from sending the poison falsely labeled into the market; and the defendant is justly responsible for the probable consequences of the act. The duty of exercising caution in this respect did not arise out of the defendant's contract of sale to Aspinwall. The wrong done by the defendant was in putting the poison, mislabeled, into the hands of Aspinwall as an article of merchandise to be sold and afterwards used as [medicine], by some person then unknown. The owner of a horse and cart who leaves them unattended in the street is liable for any damage which may result from his negligence. . . . The owner of a loaded gun who puts it into the hands of a child by whose indiscretion it is discharged, is liable for the damage occasioned by the discharge. . . .

Which of the following reasons stated by the Court of Appeals provides the best ground for distinguishing *Thomas* from *Winterbottom*: (a) "The death or great bodily harm of some person was the natural and almost inevitable consequence of the sale of [poison] by means of [a] false label"; (b) because drug manufacturers typically sell their products through intermediaries, rather than directly to consumers, whatever injury was likely to result from the mislabeled poison will not befall those in privity with the manufacturer, but will instead affect only third parties; (c) the defendant's negligence put human life in "imminent" danger? Is there a common thread among these grounds? Can you think of others?

3. ***New York Case Law: 1870-1910.*** The New York Court of Appeals decided several other "privity" cases in the period between 1870 and 1910. The five most prominent of these can be briefly summarized as follows. The first two align themselves with *Winterbottom*, whereas the last three follow *Thomas*.

In *Loop v. Litchfield*, 42 N.Y. 351 (1870), the defendant manufactured a piece of machinery that included a cast-iron wheel that spun when in use. As originally manufactured, the wheel was missing a portion of its rim, so the defendant had patched it by riveting some lead to the wheel. The defendant then sold the machinery to Collister. Several years later, Collister leased the frame to Loop, who was fatally injured when the wheel burst at the point of the patch. Loop's estate sued and obtained a jury verdict against the manufacturer. That verdict was overturned by the Court of Appeals for lack of duty under *Winterbottom*'s privity rule.

In *Losee v. Clute*, 51 N.Y. 494 (1873), the defendant manufactured a steam boiler for use in a paper mill that the defendant knew to be located adjacent to other businesses. The mill owner tested and accepted the boiler, which operated without incident for three months, then exploded, causing damage to adjacent property. Citing *Winterbottom*, and stressing that the manufacturer exercised no control over the boiler upon its installation, the Court of Appeals concluded that care in manufacturing was not owed to owners of property adjacent to the mill.

In *Devlin v. Smith*, 89 N.Y. 470 (1882), the plaintiff, a painter, was killed because of the defendant's carelessness in erecting scaffolding on which the painter was standing. The Court of Appeals reversed lower-court judgments for the defendant, invoking *Thomas*. A poorly constructed scaffold was imminently dangerous to human life, the court reasoned. Therefore, the defendant owed a duty of care to third parties who might use the scaffolding.

In *Torgesen v. Schultz*, 192 N.Y. 156 (1908), the plaintiff, a domestic servant, lost an eye after a bottle of carbonated water bottled by the defendant and sold to her employer exploded as she was placing it on ice. As in *Devlin*, the Court of Appeals reversed the trial court's dismissal of the claim on the ground that a bottle of aerated water is an inherently dangerous instrument. In *Statler v. George A. Ray Mfg. Co.*, 195 N.Y. 478 (1909), the court reached the same conclusion with respect to steam-driven coffee urn that exploded and injured the plaintiff.

Check Your Understanding

Precedential Reasoning

Starting with *Vaughan v. Menlove*, the timeline below sets out the English and New York decisions addressing the duty element of negligence summarized in the preceding notes. Imagine that you are a judge on the New York Court of Appeals in 1916, faced with the question of whether an automobile manufacturer that sells its cars through an independent dealer (rather than directly to consumers) owes a duty to consumers to take care to produce cars that are safe for their use. In deciding this question, which prior decisions would you emphasize? Would you reject some of these decisions as wrongly decided or as not applicable in 1916?

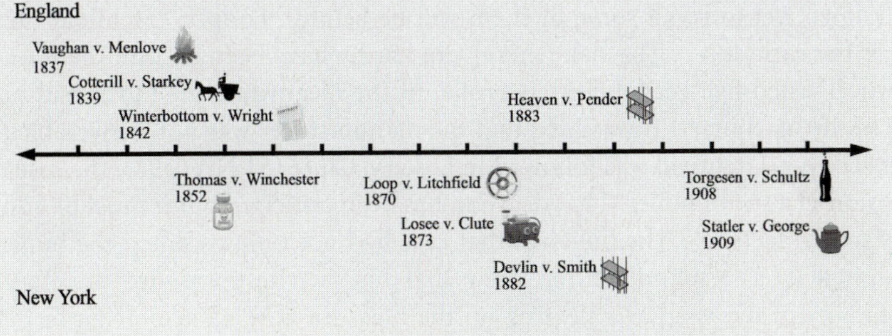

4. *MacPherson v. Buick Motor Co.* (1916) The New York Court of Appeals' struggle with the privity rule in negligence law was largely resolved in the *MacPherson* decision, which follows. Consider Judge Cardozo's treatment of precedent. Consider also the new rule of duty that his opinion articulates.

MacPherson v. Buick Motor Co.

111 N.E. 1050 (N.Y. 1916)

CARDOZO, J. The defendant is a manufacturer of automobiles. It sold an automobile to a retail dealer. The retail dealer resold to the plaintiff. While the plaintiff was in the car, it suddenly collapsed. He was thrown out and injured. One of the wheels was made of defective wood, and its spokes crumbled into fragments. The wheel was not made by the defendant; it was bought from another manufacturer. There is evidence, however, that its defects could have been discovered by reasonable inspection, and that inspection was omitted. There is no claim that the defendant knew of the defect and willfully concealed it. . . . The charge is one, not of fraud, but of negligence. The question to be determined is whether the defendant owed a duty of care and vigilance to any one but the immediate purchaser.

The foundations of this branch of the law, at least in this state, were laid in Thomas v. Winchester (6 N.Y. 397). A poison was falsely labeled. The sale was made to a druggist, who in turn sold to a customer. The customer recovered damages from the seller who affixed the label. "The defendant's negligence," it was said, "put human life in imminent danger." A poison falsely labeled is likely to injure any one who gets it. Because the danger is to be foreseen, there is a duty to avoid the injury. Cases were cited by way of illustration in which manufacturers were not subject to any duty irrespective of contract. The distinction was said to be that their conduct, though negligent, was not likely to result in injury to any one except the purchaser. We are not required to say whether the chance of injury was always as remote as the distinction assumes. Some of the illustrations might be rejected today. The *principle* of the distinction is for present purposes the important thing.

Thomas v. Winchester became quickly a landmark of the law. In the application of its principle there may at times have been uncertainty or even error. There has never in this state been doubt or disavowal of the principle itself. The chief cases are well known, yet to recall some of them will be helpful. Loop v. Litchfield (42 N.Y. 351) is the earliest. . . . The risk [there] can hardly have been an imminent one, for the wheel lasted five years before it broke. In the meanwhile the buyer had made a lease of the machinery. It was held that the manufacturer was not answerable to the lessee. Loop v. Litchfield was followed in Losee v. Clute (51 N.Y. 494), the case of the explosion of a steam boiler. That decision has been criticised but it must be confined to its special facts. . . . The buyer in that case had not only accepted the boiler, but had tested it. The manufacturer knew that his own test was not the final one. The finality of the test has a bearing on the measure of diligence owing to persons other than the purchaser.

These early cases suggest a narrow construction of the rule. Later cases, however, evince a more liberal spirit. First in importance is Devlin v. Smith (89 N.Y. 470). The defendant, a contractor, built a scaffold for a painter. The painter's servants were injured. The contractor was held liable. He knew that the scaffold, if improperly constructed, was a most dangerous trap. He knew that it was to be used by the workmen. He was building it for that very purpose. Building it for their use, he owed them a duty, irrespective of his contract with their master, to build it with care.

From Devlin v. Smith we pass over intermediate cases and turn to . . . Statler v. Ray Mfg. Co. (195 N.Y. 478, 480). . . . We held that the [coffee urn] manufacturer was liable. We said that the urn "was of such a character inherently that, when applied to the purposes for which it was designed, it was liable to become a source of great danger to many people if not carefully and properly constructed."

It may be that Devlin v. Smith and Statler v. Ray Mfg. Co. have extended the rule of Thomas v. Winchester. If so, this court is committed to the extension. The defendant argues that things imminently dangerous to life are poisons, explosives, deadly weapons — things whose normal function it is to injure or destroy. But whatever the rule in Thomas v. Winchester may once have been, it has no longer that restricted meaning. A scaffold is not inherently a destructive instrument. It becomes destructive only if imperfectly constructed. A large coffee urn may have within itself, if negligently made, the potency of danger, yet no one thinks of it as an implement whose normal function is destruction. What is true of the coffee urn is equally true of bottles of aerated water (Torgeson v. Schultz, 192 N.Y. 156). We have mentioned only cases in this court. But the rule has received a like extension in our courts of intermediate appeal. . . . We are not required at this time either to approve or to disapprove the application of the rule that was made in these cases. It is enough that they help to characterize the trend of judicial thought.

Devlin v. Smith was decided in 1882. A year later a very similar case came before the Court of Appeal in England (Heaven v. Pender, L.R. [11 Q.B.D.] 503). We find in the opinion of Brett, M.R., afterwards Lord Esher[,] the same conception of a duty, irrespective of contract, imposed upon the manufacturer by the law itself: "Whenever one person supplies goods, or machinery, or the like, for the purpose of their being used by another person under such circumstances that every one of ordinary sense would, if he thought, recognize at once that unless he used ordinary care and skill with regard to the condition of the thing supplied or the mode of supplying it, there will be danger of injury to the person or property of him for whose use the thing is supplied, and who is to use it, a duty arises to use ordinary care and skill as to the condition or manner of supplying such thing." He then points out that for a neglect of such ordinary care or skill whereby injury happens, the appropriate remedy is an action for negligence. The right to enforce this liability is not to be confined to the immediate buyer. The right, he says, extends to the persons or class of persons for whose use the thing is supplied. It is enough that the goods "would in all probability be used at once . . . before a reasonable opportunity for discovering any defect which might exist," and that the thing supplied is of such a nature "that a neglect of ordinary care or skill as to its condition or the manner of supplying it would probably cause danger to the person or property of the person for whose use it was supplied, and who was about to use it." On the other hand, he would exclude a case "in which the goods are supplied under circumstances in which it would be a chance by whom they would be used or whether they would be used or not, or whether they would be used before there would probably be means of observing any defect," or where the goods are of such a nature that "a want of care or skill as to their condition or the manner of supplying them would not probably produce danger of injury to person or property." What was said by Lord Esher in that case did not command the full assent of his associates. . . . Perhaps it may need some qualification even in our own state. Like most attempts at comprehensive definition, it may involve errors of inclusion and of exclusion. But its tests and standards, at least in their underlying principles, with whatever qualification may be called for as they are applied to varying conditions, are the tests and standards of our law.

We hold, then, that the principle of Thomas v. Winchester is not limited to poisons, explosives, and things of like nature, to things which in their normal operation are implements of destruction. If the nature of a thing is such that it is reasonably certain to place life and limb in peril when negligently made, it is then a thing of danger. Its nature gives warning of the consequences to be expected. If to the element of danger there is added knowledge that the thing will be used by persons other than the purchaser, and used without new tests, then, irrespective of contract, the manufacturer of this thing of danger is under a duty to make it carefully. That is as far as we are required to go for the decision of this case. There must be knowledge of a danger, not merely possible, but probable. It is *possible* to use almost anything in a way that will make it dangerous if defective. That is not enough to charge the manufacturer with a duty independent of his contract. Whether a given thing is dangerous may be sometimes a question for the court and sometimes a question for the jury. There must also be knowledge that in the usual course of events the danger will be shared by others than the buyer. Such knowledge may often be inferred from the nature of the transaction. But it is possible that even knowledge of the danger and of the use will not always be enough. The proximity or remoteness of the relation is a factor to be considered. We are dealing now with the liability of the manufacturer of the finished product, who puts it on the market to be used without inspection by his customers. If he is negligent, where danger is to be foreseen, a liability will follow. We are not required at this time to say that it is legitimate to go back of the manufacturer of the finished product and hold the manufacturers of the component parts. To make their negligence a cause of imminent danger, an independent cause must often intervene; the manufacturer of the finished product must also fail in *his* duty of inspection. It may be that in those circumstances the negligence of the earlier members of the series is too remote to constitute, as to the ultimate user, an actionable wrong. We leave that question open. . . . There is here no break in the chain of cause and effect. In such circumstances, the presence of a known danger, attendant upon a known use, makes vigilance a duty. We have put aside the notion that the duty to safeguard life and limb, when the consequences of negligence may be foreseen, grows out of contract and nothing else. We have put the source of the obligation where it ought to be. We have put its source in the law.

From this survey of the decisions, there thus emerges a definition of the duty of a manufacturer which enables us to measure this defendant's liability. Beyond all question, the nature of an automobile gives warning of probable danger if its construction is defective. This automobile was designed to go fifty miles an hour. Unless its wheels were sound and strong, injury was almost certain. It was as much a thing of danger as a defective engine for a railroad. The defendant knew the danger. It knew also that the car would be used by persons other than the buyer. This was apparent from its size; there were seats for three persons. It was apparent also from the fact that the buyer was a dealer in cars, who bought to resell. The maker of this car supplied it for the use of purchasers from the dealer just as plainly as the contractor in Devlin v. Smith supplied the scaffold for use by the servants of the owner. The dealer was indeed the one person of whom it might be said with some approach to certainty that by him the car would not be used. Yet the defendant would have us say that he was the one person whom it was under a legal duty to protect. The law does not lead us to so inconsequent a conclusion. Precedents drawn from the days of travel by stage coach do not fit the conditions of travel to-day. The principle that the danger must be imminent does not change, but the things subject to the principle do change. They are whatever the needs of life in a developing civilization require them to be. . . .

In England the limits of the rule are still unsettled. Winterbottom v. Wright (10 M. & W. 109) is often cited. . . . [However,] in Heaven v. Pender (*supra*) the defendant, a dock owner, who put up a staging outside a ship, was held liable to the servants of the shipowner. [Judge Cardozo then reviewed other English decisions.] From these cases a consistent principle is with difficulty extracted. The English courts, however, agree with ours in holding that one who invites another to make use of an appliance is bound to the exercise of reasonable care. That at bottom is the underlying principle of Devlin v. Smith. The contractor who builds the scaffold invites the owner's workmen to use it. The manufacturer who sells the automobile to the retail dealer invites the dealer's customers to use it. The invitation is addressed in the one case to determinate persons and in the other to an indeterminate class, but in each case it is equally plain, and in each its consequences must be the same.

There is nothing anomalous in a rule which imposes upon A, who has contracted with B, a duty to C and D and others according as he knows or does not know that the subject-matter of the contract is intended for their use. We may find an analogy in the law which measures the liability of landlords. If A leases to B a tumbledown house he is not liable, in the absence of fraud, to B's guests who enter it and are injured. This is because B is then under the duty to repair it, the lessor has the right to suppose that he will fulfill that duty, and, if he omits to do so, his guests must look to him. But if A leases a building to be used by the lessee at once as a place of public entertainment, the rule is different. There injury to persons other than the lessee is to be foreseen, and foresight of the consequences involves the creation of a duty (Junkermann v. Tilyou R. Co., 213 N.Y. 404, and cases there cited).

. . . Subtle distinctions are drawn by the defendant between things inherently dangerous and things imminently dangerous, but the case does not turn upon these verbal niceties. If danger was to be expected as reasonably certain, there was a duty of vigilance, and this whether you call the danger inherent or imminent. In varying forms that thought was put before the jury. We do not say that the court would not have been justified in ruling as a matter of law that the car was a dangerous thing. If there was any error, it was none of which the defendant can complain.

We think the defendant was not absolved from a duty of inspection because it bought the wheels from a reputable manufacturer. It was not merely a dealer in automobiles. It was a manufacturer of automobiles. It was responsible for the finished product. It was not at liberty to put the finished product on the market without subjecting the component parts to ordinary and simple tests. . . . The obligation to inspect must vary with the nature of the thing to be inspected. The more probable the danger, the greater the need of caution. . . .

. . . The judgment should be affirmed with costs.

Bartlett, Ch. J. (dissenting) . . .

It has heretofore been held in this state that the liability of the vendor of a manufactured article for negligence arising out of the existence of defects therein does not extend to strangers injured in consequence of such defects but is confined to the immediate vendee. The exceptions to this general rule which have thus far been recognized in New York are cases in which the article sold was of such a character that danger to life or limb was involved in the ordinary use thereof; in other words, where the article sold was inherently dangerous. . . . [T]he learned trial judge instructed the jury that an automobile is not an inherently dangerous vehicle. . . .

The doctrine of [*Winterbottom*] was recognized as the law of this state by the leading New York case of Thomas v. Winchester (6 N.Y. 397, 408), which, however, involved an exception to the general rule. . . . Chief Judge Ruggles, who delivered the opinion of the court, distinguished between an act of negligence imminently dangerous to the lives of others and one that is not so, saying: "If A. build a wagon and sell it to B., who sells it to C. and C. hires it to D., who in consequence of the gross negligence of A. in building the wagon is overturned and injured, D. cannot recover damages against A., the builder. A.'s obligation to build the wagon faithfully, arises solely out of his contract with B. The public have nothing to do with it. . . ."

I do not see how we can uphold the judgment in the present case without overruling what has been so often said by this court and other courts of like authority in reference to the absence of any liability for negligence on the part of the original vendor of an ordinary carriage to any one except his immediate vendee. The absence of such liability was the very point actually decided in the English case of Winterbottom v. Wright, and the illustration quoted from the opinion of Chief Judge Ruggles in Thomas v. Winchester assumes that the law on the subject was so plain that the statement would be accepted almost as a matter of course. In the case at bar the defective wheel on an automobile moving only eight miles an hour was not any more dangerous to the occupants of the car than a similarly defective wheel would be to the occupants of a carriage drawn by a horse at the same speed; and yet unless the courts have been all wrong on this question up to the present time there would be no liability to strangers to the original sale in the case of the horse-drawn carriage.

NOTES AND QUESTIONS

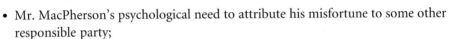

Benjamin N. Cardozo
N.Y. Court of Appeals (1914-32)
U.S. Supreme Court (1932-38)

1. *Benjamin Cardozo.* Although foreshadowed by other decisions, including *Heaven* and *Huset v. J. I. Threshing Machine Co.*, 120 F. 865 (8th Cir. 1903) (deeming a threshing machine to be an imminently dangerous product meriting liability under an exception to *Winterbottom*'s privity rule), *MacPherson* proved to be a landmark. It helped bring about the rejection of the privity rule in the vast majority of state courts, and also helped pave the way toward the development of the modern doctrine of strict products liability, discussed in Chapter 12. *MacPherson* also secured a national reputation for its author, Judge Benjamin Cardozo, who would go on to write many of the leading tort opinions of his time. Cardozo served on the New York Court of Appeals until 1932, and then on the U.S. Supreme Court until his death in 1938.

2. *The Importance of Facts.* James Henderson has argued that Buick's account of the accident in *MacPherson*—that Mr. MacPherson lost control of his car on some loose gravel, which caused him to skid into a telephone pole, which in turn caused his injuries and caused the wheel to break—was probably the right account of what happened. What, then, would explain how the plaintiff's version came to be the basis for the Court of Appeals' decision? According to Henderson, the explanation lies in the interaction of many forces, including:

- Mr. MacPherson's psychological need to attribute his misfortune to some other responsible party;
- the existence of some circumstantial evidence (wheel fragments) that, on first glance, seemed to point toward the broken wheel as a cause rather than a consequence of the accident;
- the willingness of a local lawyer, as well as experts, to maintain that the wheel caused the accident;
- the jury's acceptance of these experts' accounts over those of the defendant (which itself may have turned on considerations such as the experts' demeanor in the courtroom, as well as possible jury sympathy for the plaintiff, or hostility toward the out-of-state, corporate defendant); and
- a tactical decision by Buick not to focus its appeals on the jury's factual findings, and instead to focus on the privity argument.

As against Professor Henderson's analysis, however, it should be noted that the five-member intermediate appellate court that heard the case prior to the Court of Appeals concluded unanimously that a reasonable jury could accept Mr. MacPherson's account of the accident given the evidence presented at trial.

3. *Appellate Opinions: Facts and the Importance of Narrative.* Appellate courts, particularly high courts like the New York Court of Appeals, being far removed

from the actual trial and presentation of evidence, rarely second-guess juries' factual findings. Indeed, they ordinarily will not overturn findings of fact made by trial judges or juries unless they conclude such findings are "clearly erroneous"—a very difficult standard to satisfy. Thus, the Court of Appeals probably believed that they were compelled to decide the legal issues that Buick raised on appeal on the assumption that the accident had been caused by a defect in the wheel that Buick should have detected. (Even Chief Judge Bartlett, who dissented, did not question these aspects of the case.)

Granted the court's limited power to revisit factual questions, reconsider how Cardozo's opinion describes those facts. Notice that he omits the details of the accident and does not mention that the defendant contested this depiction of the facts at trial. Notice also his use of the terms "suddenly" and "thrown out." What sort of mental image of the accident does he create? Suppose Cardozo had mentioned the fact, apparently uncontested at trial, that Mr. MacPherson had owned the car for a year prior to the accident and had frequently driven it, sometimes carrying heavy loads, without incident during that time. Would that have made it harder for him to distinguish certain precedents?

Judge Richard Posner, today a prominent federal judge and legal scholar, has argued that the most effective judicial writing is literary and rhetorical rather than merely analytical and that Cardozo's writing exemplifies this sort of writing. Are there ways in which the *MacPherson* opinion is particularly literary? If so, does that attribute of his analysis affect your own analysis of the legal issues in the suit?

4. *Manufacturer Versus Dealer.* We noted at the outset of this chapter's discussion of the duty element that instances in which one person, through her own affirmative acts, directly causes physical harm to another are usually treated by courts as "easy" duty cases. Does *MacPherson* count as an instance of directly caused harm? Does the answer to this question turn in part on how one describes the dealer's role in the sale of the car to the consumer? What is Cardozo's account of the dealer's role? It was not clear at the time that Mr. MacPherson could have successfully sued the dealer for his personal injuries on a breach of contract theory. In any event, local dealers may not have had the financial wherewithal to pay damages.

5. *Users Versus Bystanders.* Suppose that, when the wheel on Mr. MacPherson's Buick crumbled, it did not cause physical injury to him but instead caused the automobile to veer into and injure a nearby pedestrian walking lawfully along the side of the road. In *Winterbottom*, Lord Abinger maintained that permitting a bystander to sue the manufacturer in negligence would be "absurd and outrageous." Does Cardozo's opinion indicate whether the pedestrian is entitled to recover? Subsequent decisions by other courts allowed bystander recovery on facts such as these. *See, e.g.*, Flies v. Fox Bros. Buick Motor Co., 218 N.W. 855 (Wis. 1928).

6. *Things of Danger?* Does Cardozo launch a frontal assault on the rule of *Winterbottom?* To what degree does the holding of the case turn on the relative dangerousness of an automobile? Would Cardozo apply the same analysis to an injury resulting from the collapse of an ordinary desk chair?

7. Contract, Tort, and Duty. In his *Winterbottom* opinion, Lord Abinger seemed to suppose that the recognition of a tort duty of care running from a manufacturer to foreseeable users of its products would interfere with the manufacturer's "right" to decide, though contractual agreements, the particular obligations that it would bear. In so reasoning, he prioritized freedom of contract over non-contractual obligations. By contrast, in his *MacPherson* opinion, Judge Cardozo emphasized that, although individuals and entities can often define (and therefore limit) their obligations by means of contracts, certain obligations—including the duty to take care to "safeguard life and limb"—have their source "in the law" rather than agreements. For this reason, *MacPherson* has long been regarded as an important rejection of the notion that freedom of contract is paramount among legal principles governing private interactions.

The extent to which duties not to injure should be left to be determined by agreement (contract) or required by law (tort) is a central and recurring question of law and policy in both fields. Today it is quite common for tort obligations to "piggyback" on agreements to provide products and services. For example, the relationship of doctor to patient is often contractual: the patient agrees to pay the doctor in exchange for her services. Yet the activity of delivering medical care comes with various tort duties—most importantly a duty to treat the patient competently—that, for the most part, cannot be waived or avoided by agreement.

8. Duty and Laissez-Faire. By the early part of the twentieth century, many commentators had come to view *Winterbottom* and its privity rule as a leading example of a harshly individualistic "*laissez-faire*" conception of law that privileged the right of business owners to use contracts to limit their potential obligations to those they might injure, particularly consumers and employees. By elevating freedom of contract to a paramount virtue, the critics maintained, courts like the Exchequer Court enabled businesses to avoid responsibility for the mounting toll of injuries associated with the Industrial Revolution. By the same token, Cardozo's *MacPherson* opinion was hailed by these critics as an enlightened decision that recognized changing economic and political realities, including the fact that manufacturers and users of products increasingly interacted with one another through intermediaries.

Because *Winterbottom*'s privity rule was cast by the Exchequer Barons as a "limited duty" rule, it was perhaps inevitable that some progressive critics of nineteenth-century tort law, including most prominently the British legal historian Percy Winfield, concluded that the duty element itself is an inherently regressive component of the negligence tort, one that was inserted by judges who were anxious to limit liability through matter-of-law rulings on the duty issue. Reconsider Cardozo's opinion in light of Winfield's guilt-by-association criticism of the role the duty element plays in the negligence tort. Does Cardozo's opinion suggest that he believed that the duty element is inexorably linked to pro-defendant tort rules?

9. What Is the Holding? What rule of duty is articulated by *MacPherson*? Does Cardozo's opinion embrace *Heaven*'s unqualified duty of care to those who might foreseeably be injured by one's carelessness? If not, what qualifications or limits are built into the duty? Why? What is distinctive about manufacturing and selling products as compared to driving or providing medical services? Consider, in this regard, a modern case that arguably raises some of the same concerns as *MacPherson.*

Mussivand v. David

544 N.E.2d 265 (Ohio 1989)

[Dr. Tofigh Mussivand sued Dr. George David for injuries allegedly stemming from a sexual liaison between David and Dr. Dixie West, who at the time was Mussivand's wife. Mussivand's complaint alleged that David infected West with a sexually transmitted disease, and that she in turn infected him. In his first cause of action, Mussivand alleged that David was negligent toward him by engaging in sex with West without disclosing his infection to her or taking precautions against infecting her. In response, David filed a motion to dismiss the complaint, arguing, among other things, that he owed no duty of care to Mussivand. The trial court granted the motion. The intermediate appellate court reversed, concluding that certain facts, if proven, would establish that David owed a duty to Mussivand. — Eds.]

Syllabus by the Court

1. A person who knows, or should know, that he or she is infected with a venereal disease has the duty to abstain from sexual conduct or, at a minimum, to warn those persons with whom he or she expects to have sexual relations of his or her condition.

2. A spouse is a foreseeable sexual partner and a person who has a venereal disease who fails to inform a married person with whom he or she is engaging in sexual contact of his or her condition is liable to the third-party spouse until the initially infected spouse knows or should have known he or she is infected with a venereal disease.

Resnick, J. This case comes to us on a dismissal of a complaint for failure to state a cause of action. The complaint basically states that appellee contracted a venereal disease due to the acts of the appellant. Therefore we do not know whether the venereal disease was gonorrhea, syphilis, genital herpes, venereal warts or some other sexually transmitted disease. [An unpublished opinion from the lower court reports that the disease complained of was venereal warts. — Eds.] . . .

precedent

It long has been held that one who has a contagious disease must take the necessary steps to prevent the spread of the disease. This standard of care has been imposed by the courts in cases concerning the spread of communicable diseases such as tuberculosis. . . .

A similar standard of care exists for preventing the spread of a venereal disease. In Duke v. Housen (Wyo. 1979), 589 P.2d 334, the plaintiff alleged that her former paramour was grossly negligent when he infected her with gonorrhea. Although her action was barred by the statute of limitations, the court held that "[o]ne who negligently exposes another to an infectious or contagious disease, which such other person thereby contracts, can be held liable in damages for his actions. . . ." (Citations omitted.) *Id.* at 340. . . .

Recently several jurisdictions have allowed tort actions for negligent . . . transmission of genital herpes where the person infected with genital herpes fails to disclose to his or her sexual partner that he or she is infected with such a disease. . . . In other words, people with a venereal disease have a duty to use reasonable care to avoid infecting others with whom they engage in sexual conduct. . . .

. . . [T]he above-cited cases differ from the cause before us in one very important aspect: that is, appellee herein alleges that appellant owed him a duty even though appellee was not appellant's sexual partner and had no direct sexual contact with appellant.

The issue which we must decide in this case, therefore, is what duty, if any, does a person infected with a venereal disease owe to the spouse of his paramour. Determining whether a duty exists is crucial since "[a] person's failure to exercise ordinary care in doing or failing to do something will not amount to actionable negligence unless such person owed to someone injured by such failure a duty to exercise such ordinary care." United States Fire Ins. Co. v. Paramount Fur Service, Inc. (1959), 168 Ohio St. 431, 7 O.O. 2d 267, 156 N.E.2d 121, paragraph three of the syllabus.

. . . The existence of a duty in a negligence action is a question of law for the court to determine. There is no formula for ascertaining whether a duty exists. Duty ". . . is the court's 'expression of the sum total of those considerations of policy which lead the law to say that the particular plaintiff is entitled to protection.' (Prosser, Law of Torts (4th ed. 1971) pp. 325-326.) Any number of considerations may justify the imposition of duty in particular circumstances, including the guidance of history, our continually refined concepts of morals and justice, the convenience of the rule, and social judgment as to where the loss should fall."

The common-law duty of due care is that degree of care which an ordinarily reasonable and prudent person exercises, or is accustomed to exercising, under the same or similar circumstances. A person is to exercise that care necessary to avoid injury to others. (Prosser, *Palsgraf* Revisited (1953), 52 Mich. L. Rev. 1, 15).

A person who has a venereal disease does not have the duty to disclose his condition to everyone. As has been stated, "[i]t should be made clear that this court is not stating here that herpes victims have a specific duty to warn any person of their condition; however, they, like all citizens, are to be guided by those considerations which ordinarily regulate the conduct of human affairs, and they may be sued in this state for negligence in the omission to do something which a reasonable person would do. . . ." Long v. Adams [175 Ga. App. 538, 540 [(1985)], 333 S.E.2d at 855].

We find the reasoning of these other jurisdictions persuasive and accordingly hold that a person who knows, or should know, that he or she is infected with a venereal disease has the duty to abstain from sexual conduct or, at the minimum, to warn those persons with whom he or she expects to have sexual relations of his or her condition.

There is a strong public policy behind imposition of this duty. In general, we are reminded that ". . . [t]he health of the people is an economic asset. The law recognizes its preservation as a matter of importance to the state. To the individual nothing is more valuable than health. The laws of this state have been framed to protect the people, collectively and individually, from the spread of communicable diseases. . . ." [Skillings v. Allen, 143 Minn. 323,] 325-326 [(1919)], 173 N.W. at 664. More specifically, we recognize that venereal diseases are often serious, and, in some instances, there is no known cure for them. Transmission of a venereal disease is generally through sexual contact. The likelihood that one will contract a venereal disease from someone infected with such a disease is often high.

Furthermore, there is statutory support for this duty. R.C. 3701.81 (A) states: "No person, knowingly or having reasonable cause to believe that he is suffering from a dangerous, contagious disease, shall knowingly fail to take reasonable measures to prevent exposing himself to other persons, except when seeking medical aid." . . .

Appellant argues, however, that while he may have had a duty to appellee's wife to disclose his condition, this duty does not extend to appellee. The existence of a duty will depend on the foreseeability of the injury to appellee. *See* Menifee v. Ohio Welding Products, Inc. (1984), 15 Ohio St. 3d 75, 77, 15 OBR 179, 180, 472 N.E.2d 707, 710. "The test for foreseeability is whether a reasonably prudent person would have anticipated that an injury was likely to result from the performance or nonperformance of an act. . . ." *Menifee, supra* [internal citations omitted]. Thus whether appellant owed appellee a duty turns on whether a reasonably prudent person would have anticipated that appellee would be injured by way of appellant's alleged negligence. In this case appellant, allegedly infected with a venereal disease, engaged in sexual relations with a married woman. A reasonably prudent person would anticipate that a wife and husband will engage in sexual relations. In addition, Dr. David is a medical doctor who, more than most people, should be aware of the method of transmitting a venereal disease, its likelihood of spreading through sexual contact, and its potentially devastating effect. If one negligently exposes a married person to a sexually transmissible disease without informing that person of his exposure, it is reasonable to anticipate that the disease may be transmitted to the married person's spouse. Hence liability to a third party for failure to disclose to the original sexual partner turns on whether, under all the circumstances, injury to the third-party spouse was foreseeable. . . .

We do not, however, mean to say that appellant, subsequent to his affair with appellee's wife, will be liable to any and all persons with whom she may have sexual contact. A spouse, however, is a foreseeable sexual partner. Furthermore, the liability of a person with a sexually transmissible disease to a third person, such as a spouse, would be extinguished as soon as the paramour spouse knew or should have known that he or she was exposed to or had contracted a venereal disease. She or he then would become a "conscious and responsible agency which could or should have eliminated the hazard."[Citation omitted.] . . . Whether appellee's wife knew, or should have known, of her exposure to a venereal disease is a question of fact to be decided by the trier of fact. . . .

Appellant also contends that appellee's complaint is barred by R.C. 2305.29, the so-called "anti-heart balm" statute. Appellee's claim, however, clearly is not based on any amatory cause of action, such as . . . alienation of affections, criminal conversation, or seduction. On the contrary, appellee alleges that he has been seriously injured and suffers from an incurable disease as a result of appellant's conduct. The fact that appellee is married to appellant's former paramour does not turn this into an amatory action. Accordingly, appellee's complaint is not barred by R.C. 2305.29.[11] . . .

11. R.C. 2305.29 states in pertinent part:

No person shall be liable in civil damages for . . . alienation of affections, or criminal conversation, and no person shall be liable in civil damages for seduction of any person eighteen years of age or older, who is not incompetent. . . .

[The court affirmed the intermediate appellate court's reinstatement of Mussivand's negligence claim against David. — EDS.]

NOTES AND QUESTIONS

1. *Ohio Syllabi.* Under rules promulgated by the Ohio Supreme Court, the judge who is assigned to write the opinion for the majority of the court must prepare a separate syllabus for the approval of the majority. The syllabus is then treated as specifying the holding that courts must apply in subsequent cases.

2. *Duty: Law and Fact.* The court indicates the question of duty is a question of law for the court to decide, rather than a question for the jury. By this it means that the court must decide, without deference to the jury, whether the defendant was required to act with vigilance for the well-being of a person such as the plaintiff. As we will see, the duty element stands in contrast to the breach and causation elements, both of which are treated as questions primarily for the jury, with the court limited to a supervisory role.

To say that duty is a question of law for the court is *not* to say that the application of duty rules can always be made without reference to factual determinations. Indeed, sometimes findings of fact are necessary to determine whether a given rule of duty applies in a particular case. Here, for example, a factual determination must be made, presumably by the jury, as to whether David *knew or should have known* he was infected at the time of his affair with West. Only if a jury so finds would the duty identified by the court apply.

A question to be revisited throughout our analysis of negligence is why negligence law assigns primary responsibility for the resolution of disputes over the different elements to different actors within the legal system. What is it about the duty issue that renders it appropriate for resolution by judges rather than jurors?

3. *Negligence versus Battery.* Suppose, improbably, that David despised Mussivand, and that his entire reason for taking up with West was to pass along his communicable illness to Mussivand. Such a purposeful transmission of a disease to another can constitute the distinct tort of battery. *See* Chapter 9. David could also be found to have committed a battery if a jury determined that he was *almost certain* that Mussivand would be infected. Thus, assuming that the STD in question was highly infectious, it is possible that, had David actually known of his condition, he could be found by a jury to have committed a battery on Mussivand.

4. *Knowledge versus Reason to Know.* Assume for purposes of analysis that David did *not* actually know he was infected but should have known because he was experiencing symptoms that would reveal to an ordinarily attentive person that he was suffering from an infection. Is it plausible to conclude, as the Ohio Supreme Court does, that David owed a duty to monitor his own health for the benefit of persons such as Mussivand?

5. *Foreseeability and Duty.* Courts faced with duty questions often focus, as did this court, on the issue of whether injury of the type suffered by the plaintiff was

foreseeable to a reasonable person in the position of the defendant. As noted above, the foreseeability inquiry is similar to the one described by Justice Brett in Heaven v. Pender: Would a person of ordinary sense recognize that, if she pursued the conduct at issue without vigilance for the physical well-being of others, her conduct would pose a meaningful risk of physical injury to persons in the position of the plaintiff? Framed this way, the foreseeability test for duty seems easily to cover Mussivand. Surely David could recognize that inattentiveness to his infectiousness while he carried on sexual relations with a woman whom he knew to be married and not separated from her husband posed a nontrivial risk of injury to her husband.

What if, unbeknownst to David, West had another lover (*L*), who, without West's knowledge, also became infected? Would foreseeability analysis entail a duty owed by David to *L*? What if West unknowingly transmitted an STD to her friend *F* by donating blood to be transfused into *F* during an operation? Would the court find a duty owed by David to *F*? Suppose David and West were both single and that each was dating and sexually active with several partners. Could David foresee that, if he failed to protect West against infection, he would put her other partners at risk? Is the *Mussivand* court prepared to recognize such a duty? If not, what has happened to the role of "foreseeability" in determining duty?

6. *Foreseeability in the Third Restatement.* As mentioned in Chapter 1 (notes following *Walter v. Wal-Mart*), the American Law Institute ("ALI") has published since the 1930s several successive "Restatements" of tort law that attempt to identify rules and principles that are accepted by state courts across the country. The task of "restating" the law often calls for a delicate balance between following and reshaping doctrine. However, the Reporters responsible for drafting the recently published provisions on liability for physical and emotional harm contained within the Third Restatement of Torts opted to depart dramatically from case law in opining that

Reflecting on the Restatements

The American Law Institute has overseen the publication of Restatements on a wide array of topics, including Agency, Contracts, Property, Restitution and Torts. Among these, its Torts Restatements have been particularly influential with judges and lawyers. The Restatements have also been criticized on various grounds. For example, in response to the majority's invocation of the Restatement (Third) of Restitution and Unjust Enrichment in *Kansas v. Nebraska*, 135 S. Ct. 1042 (2015), U.S. Supreme Court Justice Antonin Scalia wrote a separate opinion specifically to caution against reliance on the Restatements. "Over time," Scalia claimed, "the Restatements' authors have abandoned the mission of describing the law, and have chosen instead to set forth their aspirations for what the law ought to be." *Id.* at 1064.

foreseeability should be *irrelevant* to the issue of whether a duty is owed by an actor to a potential victim of the actor's carelessness. Restatement (Third) of Torts: Liability for Physical Harm § 7, cmt. j. (2010). According to comment j, foreseeability of harm to persons such as the plaintiff should instead factor exclusively into the determination of the breach element.

Can a document that purports to "restate" the law legitimately take such a radical position? Even if one grants that foreseeability is an elusive concept and that it might also bear on the breach question, does it nonetheless capture something basic about when and why the law is prepared to hold an actor to an obligation to take care not to injure others?

7. Duty and Intervening Acts. Notice the "until" clause that concludes the second paragraph of the *Mussivand* court's syllabus. It limits the scope of David's liability by specifying that his responsibilities were at an end once West knew or had reason to know that she was infected. Why does that conclusion follow? How does this aspect of *Mussivand* related to *MacPherson*'s account of the role of the Buick dealer? Suppose West actually knew she had been infected by David at a time at which she could have taken steps to prevent Mussivand from being infected. Should her knowledge relieve David of his duty to Mussivand to take care against infecting him? Why? Would you reach the same conclusion if, instead of actual knowledge, West only had *reason to know* of her infection? Questions concerning how a third party's intervening misconduct affects the attribution of responsibility to a careless defendant are discussed in Chapters 4, 5, and 7.

If West should have known of her infection, such that Mussivand would have no claim against David, could Mussivand pursue a negligence claim against his wife? (In fact, Mussivand did file a separate claim of negligence against West. The Ohio Supreme Court did not address that claim.) The doctrine of interspousal immunity from tort liability is discussed in Chapter 7.

8. The "Amatory" Torts. At the end of its opinion, the court distinguishes Mussivand's negligence claim against David—which seeks compensation for physical harms—from claims for "criminal conversation" and "alienation of affections."

Criminal conversation is a euphemism for adultery. The tort of that name originally permitted a husband to sue another man for "seducing" his wife. The theory of the case was that the seducer had "damaged" the husband's property, besmirched his honor, and possibly confused the line of succession to his property (given that the paternity of the wife's male children was now thrown into doubt). As such, the action was available only to husbands: Wives were "owned," not owners, and husbands' affairs were not regarded as besmirching wifely honor. Alienation of affections likewise permitted a husband to sue another—stereotypically, his in-laws—for intermeddling in his marriage so as to cause his wife to abandon him. In the 1700s and early 1800s, numerous high profile and high stakes criminal conversation actions were filed in English courts and dutifully reported in scandalous detail by the forerunners of modern tabloid newspapers.

When, in the second half of the nineteenth century legislatures began according married women the status of full legal persons, the question arose as to whether women could now take advantage of the amatory actions. Most courts concluded that it was only fair to let them do so. By so ruling, however, the courts were forced to reconceptualize the claim underlying these torts. No longer was a husband complaining of destruction of his property, honor, or patrimony. Instead, one spouse was complaining that a third party had shattered his or her domestic bliss — albeit with the apparently active participation of the other spouse. Skepticism as to the existence of causation and injury in many of these cases, doubt as to whether the law is well positioned to provide redress for broken hearts, and evidence that the criminal conversation tort was being used collusively by spouses to generate false proofs of infidelity as a basis for securing illegitimate divorces, led Parliament and American legislatures to enact "anti-heart balm" statutes of the sort quoted in footnote 11 of *Mussivand.* Where legislatures have not eliminated these torts, courts often have. *See, e.g.*, Helsel v. Noellsch, 107 S.W.3d 231 (Mo. 2003) (abolishing alienation of affections). Today, amatory torts continue to be recognized in only a handful of states though, where they are recognized, they can sometimes generate notably large verdicts.

III. QUALIFIED DUTIES OF CARE

As noted in Section II.A, modern courts dealing with negligence cases tend to approach the duty element quite differently depending on the type of negligence claim before them. As we have seen, when the plaintiff alleges that the defendant *acted carelessly so as to inflict physical harm on another*, courts tend to be comfortable positing an unqualified duty of reasonable care owed by the defendant to the plaintiff. However, even in this category, as we learn from *MacPherson* and *Mussivand*, courts will sometimes qualify or limit the duty. Moreover, outside of it, courts often resist the embrace of a general or unqualified duty of reasonable care. This section explores three well-established categories of "qualified" or "limited" duty cases. They involve, respectively, cases in which the defendant is alleged to have:

1. unreasonably failed to provide assistance or protection to the plaintiff (*affirmative duty* or *duty-to-rescue* cases);
2. permitted or maintained unreasonably dangerous conditions on property in his or her possession (*premises liability* cases); or
3. acted without reasonable care for the plaintiff's economic prospects (*pure economic loss* cases).

These three categories are *not* the only recognized categories of qualified-duty cases. Indeed, in the second half of Chapter 10 we will encounter another such category: namely, cases in which the plaintiff alleges failure on the part of the defendant to be vigilant of her emotional well-being.

In drawing a line between easy and harder duty cases, we are not drawing a distinction between "duty" and "no duty" cases. In fact, black-letter law identifies many instances in which an actor owes an affirmative duty to another, or is obligated to maintain safe premises for the use of another, or to take reasonable care to avoid causing economic loss to another. Instead, what makes these classes of cases special is, first, that the duty issue will likely be "in play": The court will be looking to the plaintiff for a showing as to why the defendant was obligated to take care with respect to the plaintiff's interests. Often, but not always, the showing will consist of an assertion that the parties stood in some relationship (other than strangers to one another) at the time of the alleged tortious conduct. Thus, claims such as those for negligent causation of pure economic loss, which tend to fail as a matter of law absent some sort of preexisting relationship between the parties, may prevail by virtue of such a relationship. Second, it is to alert you to the fact that, when such duties are recognized, they are likely to be *qualified* by the court rather than treated as creating a broad or unqualified duty of reasonable care.

At the end of this chapter, we will consider two notable decisions rendered by the California Supreme Court in the second half of the twentieth century. The first, Rowland v. Christian, is a premises liability case (category 2 above). The second, Tarasoff v. Regents of the University of California, is an affirmative duty case (category 1 above). We include them to permit students to revisit and extend their understanding of the qualified-duty categories. But we also include them for another reason: They illustrate a distinctive account of the judicial inquiry that takes place, or ought to take place, under the heading of "duty." By concluding with these decisions, we do *not* mean to imply that they provide the last word on duty. (To the contrary, we believe that there are some serious difficulties that attend the approach they adopt.) Rather, we hope that, by engaging them, students will gain a better understanding of different ways in which the duty element can be understood and analyzed.

A. Affirmative Duties to Rescue and Protect

We saw above that the general duty to take care against injuring foreseeable victims governs instances in which an actor's careless conduct causes physical harm to another in a relatively direct manner. Roughly the opposite rule — that is, a general or presumptive rule of "no duty" — applies when the plaintiff's complaint is that the defendant *failed to render assistance* to the plaintiff in a situation in which assistance could have prevented the plaintiff's injury. In the language of the common law, the negligence alleged in these cases takes the form of *nonfeasance* rather than *misfeasance.**

---

* The terms "misfeasance" and "nonfeasance" are notoriously elusive. One source of confusion is that they are sometimes used to characterize the type of (putative) wrong that the defendant has committed, but at other times are used to convey a conclusion about whether the defendant can be held liable for that type of wrong. Suppose that a person standing at the side of a swimming pool does nothing while a user of the pool drowns. A lawyer might describe her wrong as nonfeasance — doing nothing — without meaning to address the further question of whether she can be held liable to the drowning victim for her wrong. The latter question, the lawyer might say, will depend on what role the person occupied relative to the drowning victim. If the person who did nothing was a stranger who happened to be walking by the pool, then her nonfeasance will not give rise to liability. On the other hand, if the person was a lifeguard charged with the task of rescuing pool users, then her nonfeasance might well be actionable.

Unfortunately for the cause of clarity, lawyers also at times use the term "nonfeasance" both to characterize the type of wrong committed and to indicate the further conclusion that, under the circumstances, the wrong will not subject the defendant to liability. In this second usage, to say that

The categories of nonfeasance and misfeasance admit both of clear examples and close calls. A straightforward example of nonfeasance would be the following case. Defendant *D*, taking a stroll in a public park with a swimming hole, happens to come upon stranger *S*, who is flailing in the water. Although he could do so at no risk to himself, *D* declines to throw a nearby life preserver to *S*, who drowns. As *D* played no role in bringing about *S*'s peril, and merely stood by as an inert observer, *D*'s conduct is appropriately described as nonfeasance. At the opposite extreme, suppose *D* is a boat owner who invites *S* onto his boat. *D* drives carelessly, executing a series of turns at excessive speed. As a result, the boat capsizes, pinning *S* underwater and drowning him. Clearly, this is an instance of misfeasance — careless operation of the boat.

The misfeasance-nonfeasance distinction is sometimes equated with a distinction between acting and omitting to act, but that equation has to be handled with care. Suppose *C*, operating his car on a city street at a reasonable speed, sees pedestrian *P* lawfully in a crosswalk in front of him but does nothing to turn or stop the car, thus hitting *P* when he could have avoided doing so. If we consider only the temporal sequence immediately prior to the accident, one can intelligibly say that *C* did not undertake an affirmative act — he did not turn the wheel of the car toward *P*, did not press his foot down on the accelerator, etc. Rather, he merely "omitted" to apply his brakes. Still, few would describe this as an instance of nonfeasance, or as *C* "failing to rescue" or "failing to protect" *P*. Rather, we would assess *C*'s failure to change course or apply his brakes in light of the fact that he had earlier in the sequence commenced driving. In other words, *C*'s omissions were part of *a bundle of acts and omissions* that are best described as *misfeasance* in the form of careless driving. As this example indicates, drawing the line between misfeasance and nonfeasance will often require judgments about which among the various features of a defendant's conduct ought to be taken into account.

However drawn in particular cases, the nonfeasance-misfeasance distinction has important implications for duty analysis. The general duty to take care not to cause foreseeable physical injury or property damage applies only to *mis*feasance (and even then, only to certain forms of misfeasance, such as misfeasance that involves carelessness with respect to the risk of physical harms to others). More or less the opposite presumption — the absence of a duty of care — attaches to instances of nonfeasance, such as that of the indifferent passerby who fails to rescue the drowning man. To say the same thing, a plaintiff must establish special circumstances in order to prevail on a claim of negligent nonfeasance. Again, the presence or absence of a preexisting relationship between plaintiff and defendant is one such special circumstance that will affect duty analysis.

---

the stranger who fails to rescue committed nonfeasance *is* to say that she cannot be held liable for her wrong. (On this second usage, the concept of "actionable nonfeasance" is an oxymoron — to assert that the defendant's wrong was (mere) nonfeasance is already to conclude that it does not give rise to liability.)

In this introductory note, we mean to be using "nonfeasance" in the first sense — to refer to a category or class of putative wrong, not to refer to a category or class of cases in which there will be no tort liability.

Osterlind v. Hill

160 N.E. 301 (Mass. 1928)

Braley, J. This is an action of tort, brought by the plaintiff as administrator of the estate of Albert T. Osterlind to recover damages for the conscious suffering and death of his intestate. There are four counts in the original declaration and five counts in the amended declaration, to each of which the defendant demurred. The first count of the original declaration alleges that, on or about July 4, 1925, the defendant was engaged in the business of letting for hire pleasure boats and canoes to be used on Lake Quannapowitt in the town of Wakefield; that it was the duty of the defendant to have a reasonable regard for the safety of the persons to whom he let boats and canoes; that the defendant, in the early morning of July 4, 1925, in willful, wanton, or reckless disregard of the natural and probable consequences, let for hire, to the intestate and one Ryan, a frail and dangerous canoe, well knowing that the intestate and Ryan were then intoxicated, and were then manifestly unfit to go upon the lake in the canoe; that, in consequence of the defendant's willful, wanton, or reckless disregard of his duties, the intestate and Ryan went out in the canoe, which shortly afterwards was overturned and the intestate, after hanging to it for approximately one-half hour, and making loud calls for assistance, which calls the defendant heard and utterly ignored, was obliged to release his hold, and was drowned; that in consequence of the defendant's willful, wanton, or reckless conduct the intestate endured great conscious mental anguish and great conscious physical suffering from suffocation and drowning. Count 2 differs materially from count 1 only in so far as negligent conduct is alleged as distinguished from willful, wanton, or reckless conduct. . . . The amended declaration adds allegations to the effect that the plaintiff's intestate and Ryan were intoxicated and incapacitated to enter into any valid contract or to exercise any care for their own safety and that the condition of the intestate was involuntary and induced through no fault of his own.

The trial court sustained demurrers to both the original and amended declarations and reported the case for the determination of this court.

. . . The declaration must set forth facts which, if proved, establish the breach of a legal duty owed by the defendant to the intestate. . . .

In the case at bar . . . it is alleged in every count of the original and amended declaration that after the canoe was overturned the intestate hung to the canoe for approximately one-half hour and made loud calls for assistance. On the facts stated in the declaration the intestate was not in a helpless condition. He was able to take steps to protect himself. The defendant [thus] violated no legal duty in renting a canoe to a man in the condition of the intestate. . . .

In view of the absence of any duty to refrain from renting a canoe to a person in the condition of the intestate, the allegations of involuntary intoxication relating as they do to the issues of contributory negligence become immaterial. The allegations of willful, wanton or reckless conduct also add nothing to the plaintiff's case. The failure of the defendant to respond to the intestate's outcries is immaterial. No legal right of the intestate was infringed. The allegation common to both declarations that the canoe was "frail and dangerous" appears to be a general characterization of canoes. It is not alleged that the canoe was out of repair and unsafe.

It follows that the order sustaining each demurrer is affirmed.

Baker v. Fenneman & Brown Properties, LLC

793 N.E.2d 1203 (Ind. App. 2003)

MAY, J. Aaron Baker appeals the trial court's grant of summary judgment to Fenneman & Brown Properties, L.L.C. and Southern Bells of Indiana, Inc., all d/b/a Taco Bell (hereinafter collectively "Taco Bell"). Baker raises one issue, which we restate as whether Taco Bell has a duty to assist a customer who falls to the floor and loses consciousness when the customer's fall was not due to any fault of Taco Bell.

We reverse and remand.

FACTS AND PROCEDURAL HISTORY

On August 26, 1999, Baker entered the Taco Bell store in Newburgh, Indiana, to purchase a soft drink. Upon entering the store, Baker felt nauseous, but he continued to the counter, where he ordered a drink. Baker handed the cashier money for the drink and suddenly fell backward. Baker's head hit the floor, and he was knocked unconscious and began having convulsions.[3]

Baker and Taco Bell disagree regarding whether Taco Bell rendered assistance to Baker. Baker claims that when he regained consciousness, he was staring at the ceiling, he had no idea what was going on, and he did not know where he was. He claims that no Taco Bell employee called for medical assistance or helped him in any way. Taco Bell claims that the cashier walked around the counter to Baker, where she waited for his convulsions to stop, and then she asked Baker if he was okay and if he needed an ambulance. The employee claims Baker said he was fine and he did not need an ambulance, so she walked back around the counter.

What happened next is undisputed. Moments after Baker stood up, he fell again. This time, Baker fell forward and was knocked unconscious. The fall lacerated his chin, knocked out his four front teeth, and cracked the seventh vertebra of his neck. When Baker regained consciousness, he was choking on the blood and teeth in his mouth. Baker stumbled out of the store to a friend, who contacted Baker's fiancé to take him to the hospital.

Baker filed a complaint against Taco Bell, in which he alleged: 1) Taco Bell breached its duty to render assistance to him until he could be cared for by others when Taco Bell employees knew or should have known that he was ill or injured, and 2) Taco Bell's "conduct constituted gross negligence, wanton disregard and wanton recklessness" toward Baker. Baker sought damages for medical bills, lost wages, pain and suffering, and mental anguish.

Taco Bell moved for summary judgment, claiming it owed Baker no duty. Baker responded by arguing Taco Bell had a duty to help him. . . . The trial court granted Taco Bell's motion.

---

3. A doctor determined Baker fell because he experienced "vasovagal syncope." Vasovagal syncope is "[a] form of syncope (fainting) that occurs as a part of a normal physiologic response to stress (often emotional stress). The individual becomes lightheaded, nauseated, flushed, feels warm and then may lose consciousness for several seconds." Medical Dictionary, http://www.medical-dictionary.com/results.php (last visited March 19, 2012).

Standard of Review

When we review a trial court's grant of summary judgment, we apply the same standard the trial court applied: we determine whether a genuine issue of material fact existed and whether the moving party was entitled to judgment as a matter of law. While a trial court's grant of summary judgment is clothed with a presumption of validity and the appellant has the burden of demonstrating the trial court erred, we must assess the trial court's decision carefully to ensure the appellant was not improperly denied his day in court. If the moving party demonstrates that no genuine issue of material fact exists and that it is entitled to summary judgment as a matter of law, then the burden shifts to the nonmovant to designate specific facts that raise a genuine issue for trial.

Discussion and Decision

Baker claims Taco Bell had a duty to assist him and that it breached that duty by failing to provide assistance to him. Taco Bell argues it had no duty to assist Baker because it was not responsible for the instrumentality that caused Baker's initial injury. We believe Baker is correct.

To effectively assert a negligence claim, Baker must establish: (1) that Taco Bell had a duty "to conform [its] conduct to a standard of care arising from [its] relationship with [Baker]," (2) that Taco Bell failed to conform its conduct to that standard of care, and (3) that Baker incurred injuries as a proximate result of Taco Bell's breach of its duty. *See Ind. State Police v. Don's Guns & Galleries*, 674 N.E.2d 565, 568 (Ind. Ct. App. 1996), *trans. denied*, 683 N.E.2d 592 (Ind.1997). The existence of a duty is a question of law for the court to decide. *Id.* To determine whether a duty exists, we must balance three factors: "(1) the relationship between the parties; (2) the reasonable foreseeability of harm to the person injured; and (3) public policy concerns." *Id.*

As a general rule, an individual does not have a duty to aid or protect another person, even if he knows that person needs assistance. *L.S. Ayres v. Hicks*, 220 Ind. 86, 93, 40 N.E.2d 334, 337 (1942), *reh'g denied w/opinion*, 220 Ind. 86, 41 N.E.2d 195 (1942). *See also* Restatement (Second) of Torts § 314 ("The fact that the actor realizes or should realize that action on his part is necessary for another's aid or protection does not of itself impose upon him a duty to take such action.") (hereinafter, "Restatement"). However, both common law and statutory exceptions to that general rule exist. *See, e.g.*, Restatement § 314B (employer has a duty to protect or aid an injured employee); Ind. Code § 35-46-1-4 (neglect of a dependent is a felony).

Baker claims Taco Bell had the duty to assist him described under Section 314A of the Restatement, which provides the following exception to the general rule that one person need not assist another:

> **§ 314A. Special Relations Giving Rise to Duty to Aid or Protect**
>
> (1) A common carrier is under a duty to its passengers to take reasonable action:
>
> (a) to protect them against unreasonable risk of physical harm, and
>
> (b) to give them first aid after it knows or has reason to know that they are ill or injured, and to care for them until they can be cared for by others.

> (2) An innkeeper is under a similar duty to his guests.
>
> (3) A possessor of land who holds it open to the public is under a similar duty to members of the public who enter in response to his invitation.
>
> (4) One who is required by law to take or who voluntarily takes the custody of another under circumstances such as to deprive the other of his normal opportunities for protection is under a similar duty to the other.

The duty that arises under Section 314A exists because of the special relationship between the parties. The relationships listed in the rule are not intended to be exclusive, nevertheless, some courts have restricted the application of § 314A to business invitees. *See, e.g., Gilbertson v. Leininger*, 599 N.W.2d 127, 131 (Minn. 1999) (holding host to an overnight social guest does not have a duty under § 314A). In addition, the exception applies only while the relationship exists, so once the passenger leaves the train or the guest leaves the hotel, the railroad or hotel no longer has a duty to aid or protect an ill or injured individual. Restatement § 314A, cmt. c. *See also Sachs v. TWA Getaway Vacations, Inc.*, 125 F.Supp.2d 1368, 1374 (S.D. Fla. 2000) (holding tour operator had no duty to protect tour participants when on bus not owned by tour operator); *but see Kellner v. Lowney*, 145 N.H. 195, 761 A.2d 421 (2000) (holding motel owner could be liable for injury to boy crossing public highway between two portions of motel property because owner should have foreseen the risk to his guests of crossing the highway to get from hotel rooms to portion of hotel property where religious services were held).

In *L.S. Ayres*, our supreme court considered whether a department store, which was not in any way liable for a boy's initial injury by an escalator, nevertheless could be held liable for aggravation of the injuries caused by its employees' failure to stop the escalator. The court determined

> there may be a legal obligation to take positive or affirmative steps to effect the rescue of a person who is helpless and in a situation of peril, when the one proceeded against is a master or an invitor or when the injury resulted from use of an instrumentality under the control of the defendant. Such an obligation may exist although the accident or original injury was caused by the negligence of the plaintiff or through that of a third person and without any fault on the part of the defendant. Other relationships may impose a like obligation, but it is not necessary to pursue that inquiry further at this time.

40 N.E.2d at 337. The court noted that the boy "was an invitee and he received his initial injury in using an instrumentality provided by" L.S. Ayres and then held L.S. Ayres could be liable for the aggravation of the boy's injury caused by its failure to assist him. *Id.* at 337-38.

Taco Bell claims it had no duty to assist Baker because it was not responsible for Baker's initial illness or injury. It argues that, under *L.S. Ayres*, an Indiana business has a duty to assist a customer only if "the injury resulted from the use of an instrumentality under the control of the defendant." 40 N.E.2d at 337. In essence, Taco Bell argues that Indiana law recognizes only a limited duty under § 314A of the Restatement. Taco Bell's argument fails for a number of reasons.

First, the cases cited by the supreme court in *L.S. Ayres* suggest the court did not intend to limit the application of § 314A to situations where the plaintiff was an invitee *and* the instrumentality causing the injury belonged to the defendant. For example, the court discussed *Depue v. Flatau,* 100 Minn. 299, 111 N.W. 1 (1907), in which a home owner was held liable for aggravation of injuries to a severely ill, fainting, and helpless businessman that the home owner sent away unattended on a cold winter night. There, as here, the initial illness was not the responsibility of the defendant. . . .

Second, when the supreme court had reason later that same year to mention *L.S. Ayres* in another of its opinions, it summarized the holding as follows: "this court recognized a duty to one in peril on the defendant's premises as an invitee even though the peril was created without negligence on the part of the defendant." *Jones v. State,* 220 Ind. 384, 43 N.E.2d 1017, 1018 (1942). That summarization suggests the Supreme Court did not intend, as Taco Bell insists, to limit its holding to situations where a plaintiff could prove both that he was an invitee and that the defendant's instrumentality caused the initial injury.

Third, the Restatement explains:

> The duty to give aid to one who is ill or injured extends to cases where the illness or injury is due to natural causes, to pure accident, to the acts of third person, or to the negligence of the plaintiff himself, as where a passenger has injured himself by clumsily bumping his head against a door.

Restatement § 314A, cmt. *d.* A number of the illustrations provided in the Restatement parallel the fact pattern here and suggest Taco Bell had a duty to assist Baker. For example . . . illustration 7 provides:

> A is a small child sent by his parents for the day to B's kindergarten. In the course of the day A becomes ill with scarlet fever. Although recognizing that A is seriously ill, B does nothing to obtain medical assistance, or to take the child home or remove him to a place where help can be obtained. As a result, A's illness is aggravated in a manner which proper medical attention would have avoided. B is subject to liability to A for the aggravation of his injuries.

Id.

. . . .

Finally, public policy suggests Taco Bell had a duty to provide reasonable care in this situation. When a storeowner opens his property to the public, he does so because he hopes to gain some economic benefit from the public. "Social policy dictates that the storeowner, who is deriving this economic benefit from the presence of the customer, should assume the affirmative duty [to help customers who become ill as] a cost of doing business."[Lloyd v. S.S. Kresge Co., 270 N.W.2d 423, 304 (Wis. App. 1978).]

Taco Bell argues placing this duty on businesses is unreasonable because then, in essence, a business would be required to hire employees who were trained to diagnose and provide medical services. *See* Br. of Appellee at 14 ("A rule requiring first aid to be delivered to any invitee, no matter the type of business and no matter the circumstances that led to the injury, would require an impossible and frightening standard of care for persons employed in the service industry."); *id.* at 15 ("Taco Bell sells tacos.

Taco Bell does not and has never held itself out to be a medical treatment facility. . . . To require Taco Bell to treat these 'patients' would be unfair and unsafe for the 'patient' and the Taco Bell employee alike."). We disagree.

As comment f to Section 314A of the Restatement explains:

> [The business] is not required to take any action beyond that which is reasonable under the circumstances. In the case of an ill or injured person, [the business] will seldom be required to do more than give such first aid as [it] reasonably can, and take reasonable steps to turn the sick man over to a physician, or to those who will look after him and see that medical assistance is obtained. [A business] is not required to give any aid to one who is in the hands of apparently competent persons who have taken charge of him, or whose friends are present and apparently in a position to give him all necessary assistance.

Accordingly, the duty that arises is a duty to "exercise reasonable care under the circumstances." *Id.* cmt. *e.* A high school student employed at Taco Bell would not be expected to provide the type of first aid an emergency room doctor would provide, as such an expectation would not be "reasonable." . . .

Moreover, as a practical matter, we fail to see the logic in Taco Bell's position that it should have no duty to aid in these types of situations. First, we find it unlikely customers would patronize a business that left another customer who was ill or injured lying on the floor of the business simply because the business was not responsible for the customer's illness or injury.

Second, imposing on a business a duty to provide reasonable care even when the business is not responsible for an illness or injury will rarely force a business to act in circumstances in which it should not already have been acting. For example, if, as Taco Bell asserts, a business has no duty to assist if it is not responsible for the instrumentality, then: 1) if a customer falls to the ground, an employee should determine before offering assistance whether the customer slipped on ice, in which case the business has a duty to act, or whether the customer merely passed out from syncope, in which case the business has no duty; or 2) if a customer's face is turning blue, an employee should determine before providing assistance whether the person is choking on a food item from the business, in which case the employee must offer assistance, or whether the person is having a heart attack or choking on a food item purchased from a third party, in which case the employee need not offer assistance. By implementing policies and procedures that allow their employees to assist injured persons only when the business causes the illness or injury, a business might risk liability claims caused by an employee's failure to act, or failure to act promptly, when an illness or injury *was* in fact caused by an instrumentality of the business. Consequently, we are not placing a duty on businesses that they should not have already assumed.

In sum, Indiana case law, the Restatement (Second) of Torts, authority from other jurisdictions, and public policy all suggest Taco Bell had a duty, as a business that invited members of the public to enter its facility, to provide reasonable assistance to Baker even though Taco Bell was not responsible for Baker's illness. Consequently, we hold Taco Bell had a duty to "take reasonable action . . . to give . . . aid" to Baker after he fell and "to care for [him] until [he could] be cared for by others." Restatement § 314A.

Baker asserts Taco Bell provided no assistance. Taco Bell's employee claims she offered Baker assistance, but he refused to accept it. Thus, there is a question of material fact that precludes summary judgment on this issue, and we must reverse and remand for trial.

Reversed and remanded.

NOTES AND QUESTIONS

1. *Misfeasance or Nonfeasance?* Review the notes prior to *Osterlind* that discuss the distinction between misfeasance and nonfeasance. Was the plaintiff in *Osterlind* claiming that Hill should be held liable for negligent misfeasance, negligent nonfeasance, or both? If both, what, according to the court, was the fatal defect in the plaintiff's misfeasance claim? Is it the same defect that the court found in the plaintiff's nonfeasance claim?

2. *"Primitive" Law?* The absence of a general duty to take reasonable steps to rescue has long been a source of academic commentary. Writing in 1908, James Barr Ames opined that the no-duty rule is a vestige of "primitive" law which, in its overriding need for clarity and simplicity, adopted formal, across-the-board rules — such as the blanket rule of no duty to rescue — that rode roughshod over basic principles of ordinary morality. Ames proposed that modern tort law could afford to align itself more closely with morality by recognizing a limited duty to rescue others from imminent physical danger where performing the rescue would cause little or no inconvenience to the rescuer. Defying Ames's expectations, the common law, subject to important exceptions described below, has continued to resist recognition of a duty to undertake even easy rescues. *See* Restatement (Third) of Torts: Liability for Physical and Emotional Harm § 37 (2012).

3. *Liberalism.* Contrary to Ames, others have argued that, even if there is a moral duty to rescue strangers, such a duty should not be recognized in the law. Richard Epstein argues, among other things, that the law would violate basic principles of liberalism if it required more of individuals than simply refraining from injuring others. Epstein also argues that it is impossible to draw a principled line between a duty to rescue someone in imminent peril and a more general duty of beneficence, which, for example, would impose liability on individuals for failing to donate a portion of their earnings to prevent persons from starving to death.

Epstein has drawn responses from various quarters. Steven Heyman has argued that classical liberalism recognized a duty on each citizen to assist government officials in maintaining order and protecting the rights of all citizens. He further claims that this theory found expression in common law, which imposed criminal liability on individuals who failed to take steps to prevent serious crimes. Finally, he suggests that it would be consistent with this tradition to recognize tort liability running parallel to this criminal liability. Against Epstein, Ernest Weinrib has argued that a limited duty to rescue can be distinguished from a more general duty of beneficence.

4. *Duties of Assistance: Criminal Law.* A few states have enacted generally applicable statutes requiring all persons, on pain of fine or even a stint in prison, to render

aid to others in peril. Vermont's Duty to Aid the Endangered Act, Vt. Stat. Ann. Tit. 12, § 519(a), imposes a duty of reasonable assistance on any person who knows that another faces grave physical danger, if assistance can be rendered without peril to the rescuer. Violations are punishable by a fine of up to $100. *See also* Wis. Stat. Ann. § 940.34 (a person who knows that a crime is being committed that exposes its victim(s) to bodily harm has a duty to summon police or intervene when he can do so without danger to himself and without ignoring duties owed to others). Confusingly, these provisions sometimes appear within "good Samaritan statutes" that, as discussed in Note 6, below, *immunize* voluntary rescuers from tort liability for negligence. *See, e.g.*, Vt. Stat. Ann. Tit. 12, § 519(b); Wis. Stat. Ann. § 940.34(3).

General duty-to-rescue statutes are more frequently found outside the United States, particularly in civil law countries such as France, although there is little evidence of enforcement on either side of the Atlantic. This nominal contrast between American and French law was much discussed in 1997, when Princess Diana died in a Paris car crash, and it was thought that paparazzi trailing her car took photographs of the wreck instead of rendering assistance. (The photographers were eventually cleared.) Is any purpose served in enacting underenforced or unenforced statutes of this sort?

In contrast to general duty-to-rescue statutes, some statutes identify particular persons who owe affirmative duties to particular persons. Actors who violate these statutes may be subject to tort liability, essentially on the ground (discussed below in Note 8) that the statute has created or recognized a special relationship that runs between the defendant and plaintiff and supports the recognition of an affirmative duty. *See* Restatement (Third) of Torts: Liability for Physical and Emotional Harm § 38 (2012) (when a statute requires an actor to act for the protection of another, the court may rely on the statute to conclude that an affirmative duty exists).

5. Common Law Exception: Imminent Peril to Plaintiff Caused by Defendant. The rule of no duty to make a reasonable attempt at rescue is subject to a number of important exceptions. A widely, although not universally, recognized exception to the rule arises when the actor knows or should know that he has by his own conduct caused the victim to be physically injured and at imminent risk of further injury, or to be in imminent danger of physical harm. Under such circumstances, the actor has a duty to make reasonable efforts to prevent the victim from suffering further harm or to prevent the risk of harm from being realized. *See* Restatement (Second) of Torts §§ 321-322 (1965). This exception clearly applies in cases in which the defendant injures or imperils the plaintiff through a wrongful act. *See, e.g.*, Heffern v. Perry, 2000 Conn. Super. LEXIS 2708 (2000) (person who buys narcotics for consumption by another has duty to assist that other when he overdoses); Alexander v. Harnick, 237 S.E.2d 221 (Ga. App. 1977) (boat operator who transported guest onto a lake in a boat lacking proper safety equipment can be deemed to have helped create the risk that the guest would drown). According to the Restatement provisions cited above, the "imperilment" exception also applies in some instances in which the defendant innocently injures or imperils the plaintiff. For example, if, through no fault attributable to it, a railroad company's train collides with the victim's truck, causing injuries to the victim that leave him unable to seek medical attention, the railroad's employees thereby incur a duty to make reasonable efforts to secure medical care for the plaintiff. *See* Maldonado v. S. Pac. Transp. Co., 629 P.2d 1001 (Ariz. Ct. App. 1981). *But see* Panagakos v. Walsh, 749 N.E.2d 670 (Mass. 2001) (18-year-old decedent killed while walking home in an intoxicated state after his friends helped him gain illegal entry to a bar; no duty owed by friends to protect the decedent from dangers associated with walking home while drunk).

The Third Restatement of Torts attempts to summarize the rule contained in this cluster of cases as follows: "When an actor's prior conduct, even though not tortious, creates a continuing risk of physical harm of a type characteristic of the conduct, the actor has a duty to exercise reasonable care to prevent or minimize the harm." Restatement (Third) of Torts: Liability for Physical and Emotional Harm § 39 (2012).

How closely is the idea of "imperilment" or "continuing risk" tied to the idea of a duty to render aid in a temporary emergency that is partly of one's own creation? Suppose that *D* is properly using a piece of woodworking equipment in her garage, and that her friend and neighbor *P* is standing nearby, watching her work. Through no fault of *D*'s, a piece of wood unexpectedly flies off the equipment on which *D* is working and strikes *P* in the temple, as a result of which *P* is permanently blinded. Is *D* under a continuing duty to help *P* to avoid risks associated with his loss of sight? Suppose, one year after the accident, *D* encounters *P* as *P* is about to enter a poorly maintained parking lot near their houses that is filled with cracks. *D* says and does nothing to lessen the chance that *P* will trip while walking. If, because of his poor eyesight, *P* trips and injures himself, can he sue *D* on the ground that *D* contributed to his "peril," such that, not withstanding the passage of a year, *D* owed him a duty to take reasonable steps to protect him from the danger posed by the parking lot?

6. Common Law Exception: Voluntary Undertakings. A second exception to the no-duty-to-rescue rule concerns situations in which the defendant has volunteered to protect another from physical injury or property damage, or to rescue another from physical peril. Restatement (Third) of Torts: Liability for Physical and Emotional Harm § 42 (2012). Such a voluntarily assumed duty may arise from a contractual promise or a less formal undertaking. *See* Seeger v. Marketplace, 956 N.Y.S.2d 770 (N.Y. App. Div. 2012) (after the plaintiff fainted while shopping in defendant's store, a store employee used a wheelchair to bring her to her car — the store thereby assumed a duty to act with due care for her well-being and was subject to liability for injuries suffered by the customer when she lost control of and crashed her car in the store's parking lot); Wicker v. Harmony Corp., 784 So. 2d 660 (La. Ct. App. 2001) (contractor who agrees in contract to ensure safety of workers owes duty to take safeguards against plaintiff-employee from being injured on the job); Folsom v. Burger King, 958 P.2d 301 (Wash. 1998) (although defendant security firm had previously entered into a contract with plaintiffs' employer to provide security services, the contract had expired, and the defendant's failure to remove its security equipment upon contract termination is not sufficient to generate an undertaking to protect); Wilmington Gen. Hospital v. Manlove, 174 A.2d 135 (Del. 1961) (hospital that customarily accepted emergency patients effectively undertook to provide care to all such patients). Under this exception, does a trade association that voluntarily circulates safety information about above-ground pools owe a duty to update that information when aware of new risks against which it has not warned? *See* Meneely v. S.R. Smith, Inc., 5 P.3d 49 (Wash. Ct. App. 2000) (such a duty exists).

A related exception to the general rule of no duty holds that, once a rescue is voluntarily undertaken, the rescuer owes a duty to the victim to perform the rescue with reasonable care. *Compare* Hurd v. United States, 134 F. Supp. 2d 745 (D.S.C. 2001) (although under no duty to commence a rescue, the Coast Guard owes a duty under South Carolina law to exercise reasonable care once rescue is commenced) *with* Adams v. City of Fremont, 80 Cal. Rptr. 2d 196 (Ct. App. 1998) (police owe no duty to suicidal man to exercise care in their attempts to prevent his suicide). Suppose *V* volunteers to aid motorist *M*, whose car is stalled on a public road. *V* fails to suggest moving the car to the shoulder or turning on its hazard lights. *P*, another driver, crashes into *M*'s car and suffers injury. May *P* sue *V* for failing to go about his rescue of *M* with due care for *P*'s safety? *See* Redman v. Stone, 667 N.E.2d 526 (Ill. App. 1996) (holding that *V* owed a duty of care to *M* but not to *P*).

7. Good Samaritan Immunities. Recognition of a duty to take reasonable care in voluntarily performing a rescue might deter rescues. In part because of this concern, every state has enacted a "good Samaritan" statute that immunizes certain persons who undertake rescues from liability for negligence — and in some cases, even gross negligence — in rescuing. These statutes tend to be limited in application to "off-duty" professionals, for example, doctors who undertake rescues outside of their ordinary duties. Some also cover volunteer firefighters and "lay" rescuers. *See* Transcare Maryland, Inc. v. Murray, 64 A.3d 887 (Md. 2013) (declining to apply Maryland's good Samaritan statute to a for-profit ambulance service); Hirpa v. IHC Hospitals, Inc., 948 P.2d 785 (Utah 1997) (applying Utah good Samaritan statute and upholding it against constitutional challenge). If the statute in question is not explicit as to the persons it covers, should it be interpreted to protect "official" rescuers performing their official duties, such as police officers while on duty? *See* Praet v. Sayreville, 527 A.2d 486 (N.J. App. Div.), *rev. denied*, 532 A.2d 253 (N.J. 1987) (because the purpose of the good Samaritan statute is to encourage rescue, it should not apply to police and fire personnel, who are already under a duty to perform such rescues). In general, these immunities are not understood as designed to shield emergency medical technicians or emergency room doctors and nurses from ordinary malpractice liability.

8. Common Law Exception: Special Relationships. Probably the most important exceptions to the general rule of no duty to take steps to rescue are grounded in certain kinds of pre-tort special relationships between (1) the defendant and the plaintiff, or (2) the defendant and a third party who injures the plaintiff. The former kind of relationship is discussed in this note. The latter is addressed in connection with the *Tarasoff* decision, Section IV *infra*.

As *Baker* discusses, an affirmative duty can attach by virtue of certain "special relationships" between victim and would-be rescuer. For example, a commercial (or "common") carrier owes a duty to take reasonable steps to protect and rescue passengers while they are in transit, and a property owner owes a comparable duty to invited guests while they are on the premises. For holdings similar to those in *Baker*, *see* Morris v. De La Torre, 113 P.3d 1182 (Cal. App. 2005) (restaurant owner owes a duty to a member of a group of diners who was attacked in the parking lot outside the restaurant to take steps to rescue, such as contacting authorities, at least where feasible and not unduly dangerous) and Heys v. Blevins, 1997 WL 335564 (Ohio. App. 1997) (same). A California appellate decision holds that the operators of an ice rink equipped with an automatic external defibrillator owed rink users no duty to take reasonable steps to alert them to the presence of the device. Thus their failure to provide such notice, which may have contributed to the death of a teenage hockey player who collapsed during a game, was deemed non-actionable. Rotolo v. San Jose Sports & Entertainment, LLC, 59 Cal. Rptr. 3d 770 (Cal. App. 2007), *rev. denied.* (Aug. 15, 2007).

Although a business-customer, innkeeper-guest relationship can generate a duty to take steps to rescue, that duty is conditional on the defendant's either knowing or having reason to know of the plaintiff's peril. In *Estate of K. David Short v. Brookville Crossing 4060 LLC*, 972 N.E.2d 897 (Ind. Ct. App. 2012), a hotel patron collapsed and died outside the motel's side door in the middle of the night. His estate sued the motel, claiming that, under *Baker*, it was obligated to take steps to rescue him. The Court of Appeals granted summary judgment for the defendant, reasoning that the motel's duty under *Baker* was not triggered because, during the overnight period, the motel was staffed by a single employee who was instructed for security reasons to remain at the front desk, and hence the employee did not know, and could not have been expected to discover, that the patron needed assistance.

A separate question exists as to whether a person who enters another's premises without permission, but who is observed to be on the premises and in need of help, is owed a duty of rescue by the owner simply by virtue of the trespasser's presence on the property and his known predicament. *Compare* Winfrey v. GGP Ala Moana LLC, 308 P.3d 891 (Haw. 2013) (even if plaintiff became a trespasser when she entered the defendant mall's ductwork, the mall would owe a duty to take steps to rescue her if she had initially entered the mall "in response to [the mall's] invitation to the public") *with* Rhodes v. Illinois Cent. Gulf R.R., 665 N.E.2d 1260 (Ill. 1996) (commuter-rail operator owes no duty to seek care for trespasser who collapsed on its premises).

Other relationships that can, at least under certain circumstances, generate an affirmative duty to protect or rescue include: school-student (at least for minor students), employer-employee, hospital-patient, and prison-prisoner. *See* Restatement (Third) of Torts: Liability for Physical and Emotional Harm § 40 (2012) (discussing affirmative duties arising out of special relationships between defendant and plaintiff). It is probably accurate to say that courts are generally wary about recognizing new special relationships giving rise to affirmative duties, as the following decisions may suggest. In *Coghlan v. Beta Theta Pi Fraternity*, 987 P.2d 300 (Idaho 1999), the state supreme court ruled that neither a college nor a sorority chapter owes a duty to protect an under-drinking-age student and sorority member from dangers associated with voluntary intoxication. However, *Coghlan* permitted the plaintiff to attempt to prove that agents of each entity voluntarily undertook to protect her. In *Poole v. Janeski*, 611 A.2d 169 (N.J. Super. 1992), the trial court rejected the plaintiff car passenger's argument that the driver and owner of the car owed her a special-relationship duty to protect her from accident-related injuries by taking steps to ensure that she wore her seatbelt.

A few courts have recognized that, at least under some circumstances, an established friendship between defendant and plaintiff will suffice to support a duty to rescue. A famous example is *Farwell v. Keaton*, 240 N.W.2d 217 (Mich. 1976). Farwell, age 18, and Siegrist, age 16, consumed some beer. After attempting to make conversation with two women, they were attacked by the women's friends. Siegrist escaped harm, but Farwell was badly beaten. Siegrist gave Farwell some ice to apply to his head, then the two drove around for about two hours, at which time Farwell lay down in the back of the car. At about midnight, Siegrist drove the car to the driveway of Farwell's grandparents' house, unsuccessfully attempted to rouse Farwell, and then left him there. Farwell's grandparents discovered him the next morning and took him to the hospital, but he died from the beating. The court held that, because the two young men were "companions on a social venture," Siegrist owed Farwell a duty to make reasonable efforts to obtain medical care for him, and, alternatively, that the voluntary-undertaking exception applied, and also warranted the recognition of a duty. Based on this minimal description, is it obvious that *Farwell* is a genuine affirmative duty case?

For two decisions that appear to be in tension with *Farwell*, see *Panagakos* (Note 5 *supra*); Theobald v. Dolcimascola, 690 A.2d 1100 (N.J. App. Div. 1997) (friends of decedent who gathered in decedent's bedroom owed no duty to take steps to prevent decedent from killing himself by playing Russian roulette in their presence; to prevail, decedent's estate must show that they encouraged or otherwise participated in the game).

9. Scope of Duties to Rescue. For those cases in which an exception to the general rule of no duty applies, it is important to stress (as does *Baker*) that the duty owed is a duty to *make reasonable efforts* to rescue. Thus, insofar as rescue efforts would expose a would-be rescuer to a significant risk of serious physical injury, it might be reasonable for the would-be rescuer to refrain from attempting to rescue even when she is under a duty to do so. For example, suppose an employee of an urban subway system notices that a rider has fallen on the tracks and that she needs assistance to get back on the platform so as to avoid being struck by an oncoming train. Even if the employee owes a duty to assist the rider, if the employee reasonably concludes that rendering assistance will create a non-trivial risk of his being struck by the train, a decision not to assist the rider might well be deemed reasonable.

In *Verdugo v. Target Corp.*, 327 P.3d 774 (Cal. 2014), the California Supreme Court, relying in part on state statutes, ruled that a retail store fulfills its duty to assist a patron stricken while on store premises by summoning emergency medical care and by providing basic first aid.* On this basis, it upheld the dismissal of a negligence suit brought by the survivors of a patron who died after suffering sudden cardiac arrest while in the defendant's store. The suit claimed that the defendant was negligent for failing to have on hand an automatic external defibrillator (AED). AEDs, which are commonly found in airports and other public venues, are portable electronic devices through which to administer an electric shock that can restore normal heart rhythms in victims of certain common types of heart attack. In a manner similar to the California court in *Verdugo*, some courts have held that restaurants fulfill their duty to choking

* One of us (Goldberg) served as a consultant to attorneys representing Target Corp., the defendant in *Verdugo*, before the California Supreme Court.

patrons by summoning professional rescuers, and are not liable for the failure of employees to administer abdominal thrusts (a.k.a. the "Heimlich Maneuver"). *See, e.g.*, Lee v. GNLV Corp., 22 P.2d 209 (Nev. 2001); Campbell v. Eitak, Inc., 893 A.2d 749 (Pa. Super. 2006).

Do decisions such as *Verdugo* and *Lee* adopt an unduly narrow view of what is required to satisfy a duty to rescue? Given that courts have tended tightly to control liability for failures to rescue through the duty element, in those cases where there is such a duty, should they leave jurors broad discretion to determine whether a breach has occurred? Or is it part and parcel of recognizing limited duties to rescue that courts should also be relatively aggressive in determining what can count as a failure to fulfill such a duty?

10. Reporting Obligations. Some states have enacted statutes placing a duty on certain individuals who know that a child has suffered injuries, and who have reason to believe those injuries were caused by abuse or neglect, to report their suspicions to authorities. *See, e.g.*, Ham v. Hospital of Morristown, 917 F. Supp. 531 (E.D. Tenn. 1995) (discussing Tennessee's statute, which imposes a duty to report suspected abuse on physicians, teachers, neighbors, and friends of the child(ren) in question). Those who fall within the statute and fail to report suspicions of abuse are subject to a modest fine. What if the report turns out to be erroneous? May the falsely accused parents sue the person who reported the alleged abuse for defamation? The Tennessee statute protects persons who actually report abuse against this risk by requiring a parent complaining of a false report to prove that the reporting party was not merely careless, but acted in "bad faith," that is, out of hostility or malice toward the parent. *See* Bryant-Bruce v. Vanderbilt Univ., 974 F. Supp. 1127 (M.D. Tenn. 1997).

11. Duties to Protect Persons from Third-Party Misconduct. In certain situations, courts have held that a person has a duty to take care to protect another from the threat of being injured by an intervening third-party wrongdoer. The circumstances under which they are (and are not) prepared to identify such duties are discussed further in connection with *Tarasoff*, Part IV *infra*, as well as in Chapters 5 and 7.

Check Your Understanding

Misfeasance and Nonfeasance

In *MacPherson v. Buick* (Chapter 2) the plaintiff alleged that the defendant manufacturer breached its duty of care by *failing to inspect* the wheels on the car that he bought. Did the New York Court of Appeals treat *MacPherson* as a case of misfeasance or nonfeasance? Why? What was the significance of that treatment for the Court's duty analysis?

The traditional rule states that, absent a special relationship, one ordinarily owes no duty to rescue another from a peril that is not of one's own creation. Clearly, there are at least some instances in which this rule does not track ordinary moral judgments about the duties we owe one another. (Would anyone deny that a bystander who happens upon a swimmer struggling to stay afloat in a pool has a moral duty to toss a nearby life preserver to the swimmer?) How large is the gap between this aspect of tort law and morality? What, if anything, can justify the gap?

B. Premises Liability

Owning or possessing land can be described as a form of conduct. Indeed, the terms *owning* and *possessing* are active verbs: They connote that a person is doing something to or with land or chattel. Yet, as contrasted to the acts of providing medical care to a patient, or driving a car, the conduct involved in possessing land seems quite distinct. Much of the time, possession is passive. Moreover, the conditions on one's property, depending on its size and other characteristics, often exist without any immediate participation of the possessor/owner. In part because land ownership is distinctive in these ways, courts have long recognized special duty rules in cases alleging carelessness in the maintenance of real property. However, as noted below, some courts have questioned whether these rules are still warranted in the modern world.

Leffler v. Sharp

891 So. 2d 152 (Miss. 2004)

Cobb, P. J.

¶ 1. On December 4, 2000, Walter Leffler filed suit in the Warren County Circuit Court against Kim Free, individually and d/b/a Quarter Inn (collectively Free) and Harry Sharp, individually, and Sharp Enterprises (collectively Sharp). Leffler sought damages for injuries he received when he fell through the roof of the premises immediately adjacent to the Quarter Inn in Vicksburg, Mississippi. Following discovery and the filing of motions for summary judgment by Free and Sharp, the trial judge determined that Leffler's status upon entering the roof was that of a trespasser. The motions for summary judgment were granted, thereby dismissing all claims against Free and Sharp. Leffler appeals arguing the following issue:

> Whether the trial court erred in finding Leffler to be a trespasser and in granting summary judgment to Free and Sharp on that basis, when there were unresolved issues of fact regarding legal status and duty owed.

Facts

¶ 2. Leffler visited the Quarter Inn, a restaurant and lounge in Vicksburg, Mississippi, while he was in town conducting work on the old Mississippi River bridge. At approximately 10:00 p.m. one evening, Leffler and his co-workers arrived at a casino where they gambled and consumed alcoholic beverages until 11:30 p.m. They left the casino, went to a local sports bar, and continued to consume alcoholic beverages until approximately 2:00 a.m. on February 6, 2000. From the sports bar, they all went to the Quarter Inn. Leffler was a first-time visitor to the Quarter Inn.

¶ 3. While at the Quarter Inn, Leffler noticed an open window leading to the rooftop. (The small window is thirty-two and one-half inches from the floor and when fully opened provides a maximum opening of twenty-four inches in length and thirty-two inches in width.). After Leffler observed individuals on the rooftop, he presumed the area was open to Quarter Inn patrons. Although a locked glass door with "NOT AN EXIT" stenciled on the glass was only four feet away, Leffler entered the roof through the open window. As he was walking on the rooftop, he fell through the roof approximately twenty feet to the ground.

¶4. At the time of the incident, Kim Free owned and managed the Quarter Inn which is located on the second floor of a building owned by Sharp Enterprises, Inc. Harry Sharp is the president of Sharp Enterprises, Inc. Sharp, individually, has no ownership interest in the property which is the subject of this appeal.

¶5. The premises occupied by the Quarter Inn originally included a rooftop terrace, access to which was through a glass door inside the premises. In addition, there were at least two windows which overlooked the rooftop terrace from a common area of the Quarter Inn. Although previous businesses that occupied the present location of the Quarter Inn *may* have utilized the roof area as a part of their business, Free and Sharp assert that the roof was never part of the leased premises. The lease agreement offered as proof included the provision that "[l]essees will not have access to the roof terrace at the rear of 1302 Washington Street."

¶6. Prior to the date of the lease between Sharp and Free, Sharp considered leasing the rooftop area. To determine the safety of the roof, Sharp "consulted with an architect and structural engineer who advised him that the roof was not safe for his intended use." Sharp then informed Free of this defect, and the two individuals, along with Jo Jo Saucier (a lessee of the premises with Free, but not a named party in the trial court or on appeal) discussed what measures should be taken to secure the roof area. The parties then decided that Saucier's husband would weld bars over the window in order to keep people off of the roof. However, neither the bars, nor any other protective measures, were ever placed over the window.

¶7. This appeal involves the dispute over whether Leffler should be classified as an invitee, licensee, or trespasser at the time the injury occurred. It is undisputed that Leffler was an invitee upon his entrance into the Quarter Inn. The status dispute arises, however, when Leffler entered the roof and subsequently fell through it. Although Leffler insists that at the time of his injury he remained an invitee, he does argue in the alternative that his status was at least that of an implied licensee. Leffler also argues for the sake of argument that *if* he is a trespasser, the owner of the premises has a duty to refrain from willfully and wantonly injuring him.

¶8. Free and Sharp argue that upon Leffler's entrance onto the roof, he became a trespasser. As a result, they maintain that there is no showing that they acted willfully and wantonly, resulting in Leffler's injury.

Analysis

¶9. This Court applies a de novo standard of review to a grant of summary judgment by the trial court. The evidence must be viewed in the light most favorable to the party against whom the motion has been made. A motion for summary judgment lies only when there is no genuine issue of material fact, and the moving party is entitled to a judgment as a matter of law. . . .

¶10. Mississippi applies a three-step process to determine premises liability. *Massey v. Tingle*, 867 So.2d 235, 239 (Miss. 2004) (*citing Titus v. Williams*, 844 So.2d 459, 467 (Miss. 2003)). The first step consists of classifying the status of the injured person as an invitee, licensee, or a trespasser. Following this identification, the duty which was owed to the injured party is determined. The third step is to determine whether this duty was breached by the landowner or business operator. The determination of which status a particular plaintiff holds can be a jury question, but where the facts are not in dispute the classification becomes a question of law for the trial judge.

¶ 11. As to the first step, determination of the injured party's status, this Court has held that "[a]s to status, an *invitee* is a person who goes upon the premises of another in answer to the express or implied invitation of the owner or occupant for their mutual advantage. . . . A *licensee* is one who enters upon the property of another for his own convenience, pleasure, or benefit pursuant to the license or implied permission of the owner whereas a *trespasser* is one who enters upon another's premises without license, invitation, or other right." *Corley v. Evans*, 835 So.2d 30, 37 (Miss. 2003) (emphasis added) (*citing Hoffman v. Planters Gin Co.*, 358 So.2d 1008, 1011 (Miss. 1978) (*citing Langford v. Mercurio*, 254 Miss. 788, 183 So.2d 150 (1966)). . . . The Court has added that a trespasser enters another's property "merely for his own purposes, pleasure, or convenience, or out of curiosity, and without any enticement, allurement, inducement or express or implied assurance of safety from the owner or person in charge." *Titus*, 844 So.2d at 459 (*citing White v. Miss. Power & Light Co.*, 196 So.2d 343, 349 (Miss. 1967)).

¶ 12. The second step is to identify the duty owed to the injured party. The owner of the premises "is not an insurer of the invitee's safety, but does owe to an invitee the duty to keep the premises reasonably safe, *and* when not reasonably safe, to warn only where there is hidden danger or peril that is not in plain and open view." *Massey*, 867 So.2d at 239 (*citing Corley* 835 So.2d at 37). Although licensees and trespassers are different classifications, "[l]andowners owe licensees and trespassers the same duty, specifically, to refrain from willfully or wantonly injuring them." *Massey*, 867 So.2d at 239 (*citing Titus*, 844 So.2d at 467).*

¶ 13. Leffler maintains that his status upon his arrival *and* at the time of the accident was that of an invitee of Free, the Quarter Inn, and Sharp, on the premises so that he could have a good time with his co-workers by partaking in services provided by the Quarter Inn. In order to receive classification as an invitee, this Court held that an invitee answers an invitation to enter the owner's premises "for their mutual advantage." *Holliday v. Pizza Inn, Inc.*, 659 So.2d 860, 865 (Miss. 1995). Leffler and the Quarter Inn mutually benefited from the fact that Leffler was allowed to continue the night's fun at the Quarter Inn while the restaurant/lounge could continue making a profit.

¶ 14. Leffler maintains that he remained an invitee at the time of his injury since Free and Sharp "held [the roof] out as a part of the premises by allowing patrons to enter and use the roof terrace." In a deposition, Sharp testified that he and Free

* [This blanket statement notwithstanding, Mississippi law appears to acknowledge an exception under which a duty is owed by a possessor to a licensee to warn the licensee of a concealed danger on the premises of which the possessor has actual knowledge. *See* Vaughn v. Worrell, 828 So.2d 780, 784-785 (Miss. 2002) (presuming the existence of such a duty, as recognized in earlier Mississippi Supreme Court decisions). — EDS.]

discussed what action would best secure the window, thereby keeping patrons off the rooftop. Sharp instructed Free that the roof was not part of the lease and was not to be used by anyone. In order to secure the window, the parties agreed that bars would be welded to the window. Although this safety measure never occurred, the dimensions of the window, being 24 inches by 32 inches, and almost 3 feet above the floor, belie any indication that patrons were invited to go onto the roof. Leffler asserts that because Sharp anticipated that customers might eventually try to utilize the rooftop, a question of fact exists as to whether Free and Sharp knew, or reasonably should have known, that customers were gathering on the roof.

¶ 15. Although Leffler was an invitee at the time he entered the Quarter Inn, he was not an invitee at the time of the injury. An invitee who "goes beyond the bounds of his invitation . . . loses the status of invitee and the rights which accompany that state." *Payne v. Rain Forest Nurseries, Inc.*, 540 So.2d 35, 38 (Miss. 1989) (*citing Dry v. Ford*, 238 Miss. 98, 117 So.2d 456 (1960)). Free and Sharp only extended their invitation to patrons to come inside the establishment. Upon his entrance to the Quarter Inn, Leffler was an invitee, but once he exited the establishment and entered onto the roof terrace, he went "beyond the bounds of his invitation," therefore losing his invitee status. *Id.*

¶ 16. An occupant is an invitee where the owner of the premises and the occupant receive mutual benefits. Neither Free nor Sharp benefited from Leffler's walk on the roof. In addition to mutual benefits, a landowner does not have to insure the invitee's safety, but the landowner must "keep the premises reasonably safe, and when not reasonably safe, to warn only where there is hidden danger. . . ." *Massey*, 867 So.2d. at 239. Free and Sharp kept the Quarter Inn reasonably safe for patrons. Leffler's accident did not happen within the walls of the Quarter Inn, but on a rooftop adjacent to the establishment. Free and Sharp's acts of locking and marking the exit door were done to keep the Quarter Inn safe for patrons. Leffler was not an invitee at the location and time of the accident and, therefore, was not owed the duty given to an invitee.

¶ 17. Leffler argues in the alternative that he was a licensee at the time of the accident. "A licensee, in contrast [to a trespasser], enters the property of another 'pursuant to the license or implied permission of the owner' but enters for the 'convenience, pleasure or *benefit*' *of the licensee.*" *Davis v. Ill. Cent. RR.*, 921 F.2d 616, 618 (5th Cir. 1991) (applying Mississippi law) (emphasis added) (*citing Hoffman v. Planters Gin Co.*, 358 So.2d 1008, 1011 (Miss. 1978)). Leffler entered the roof area for his convenience, pleasure and benefit because the bar was hot, crowded, and loud while the roof terrace was cool, open, and quiet.

¶ 18. In an effort to further clarify the distinction between the status of an injured party, this Court in *Clark v. Moore Memorial United Methodist Church*, 538 So.2d 760, 764 (Miss. 1989), distinguished between the "invitation" required of an invitee and "permission" required for a licensee. The word *invitation* was defined as "conduct which justifies others in believing that the possessor desires them to enter the land," while *permission* was defined as "conduct justifying others in believing that the possessor is willing that they shall enter, if they desire to do so. . . ." *Id.* (*citing* Restatement (Second) of Torts § 332 (1965)). The two terms were further clarified with "[m]ere permission, as distinguished from invitation, is sufficient to make the visitor a licensee . . . but it does not make him an invitee. . . ." *Id.*

¶ 19. Free and Sharp never engaged in conduct signifying to patrons that the roof area was open to patrons. No dispute exists that the window was open on the night in question. However, based upon the definition of *permission*, these facts indicate that they did not intend (or grant permission) for Leffler or other patrons to enter the roof area through the glass door, or through the open window. Although Leffler entered the roof terrace for his own benefit, he lacked permission to enter the roof terrace from Free or Sharp. Leffler did not enjoy the status of a licensee.

¶ 20. Free and Sharp argue that Leffler was a trespasser, citing this Court's reasoning in *Kelley v. Sportsmen's Speedway*, 224 Miss. 632, 80 So.2d 785, 791 (1955): "A trespasser is a person who enters the premises of another without license, invitation, or other right, and *intrudes for some definite purpose of his own, or at his convenience, or merely as an idler with no apparent purpose, other than, perhaps, to satisfy his curiosity*." (emphasis added). Leffler entered the roof area without invitation or permission from Free or Sharp. On his way to the restroom, Leffler had seen two individuals standing outside the window. Returning from the restroom, the two individuals had reentered the Quarter Inn. Wanting to escape the crowd, loud music, heat, and smoke a cigarette, Leffler entered the roof terrace. There was no sign or indication within the Quarter Inn inviting or granting permission to patrons to enter the roof terrace. However, a sign on the glass door warned patrons not to use the door as an exit to the roof terrace.

¶ 21. This Court recently reaffirmed that a trespasser enters another's property "without any enticement, allurement, inducement. . . ." *Massey*, 867 So.2d at 239 (*citing White*, 196 So.2d at 349). Leffler was neither enticed nor allured onto the roof by Free or Sharp. Although the window was open, Free and Sharp did not entice the patrons to step through a high, small, narrow window onto the roof. In addition, neither party has provided evidence that Quarter Inn employees were aware that some patrons had entered the roof area.

¶ 22. The third step in determining premises liability is determination of whether the owner breached a duty. . . . The duty owed to a trespasser is "to refrain from willfully or wantonly injuring [the trespasser]." *Saucier ex rel. Saucier v. Biloxi Reg'l Med. Ctr.*, 708 So.2d 1351, 1357 (Miss. 1998). To constitute willful or wanton injury, "something more is required to impose liability than mere inadvertence or lack of attention; there must be a more or less extreme departure from ordinary standards of care, and conduct must differ in quality, as well as in degree, from ordinary negligence involving a conscious disregard of a known serious danger." *Hoffman v. Planters Gin Co.*, 358 So.2d at 1012-13 (*citing Coleman v. Associated Pipeline Contractors, Inc.*, 444 F.2d 737 (5th Cir. 1971)). Free and Sharp never disregarded or took lightly the condition of the roof terrace. In order to keep patrons off of it, Sharp kept in his possession the only key to the glass door exiting onto the roof in order to ensure that the door remained locked at all times. They not only kept the door locked; they also stenciled in red letters "NOT AN EXIT" on the glass door.

¶ 23. An owner owes trespassers no duty to keep his premises in a safe condition for their use, and as a general rule, he is not held responsible for an injury sustained by a trespasser upon the premises from a defect therein. Although the roof terrace was owned by Sharp Enterprises, the roof was not part of the lease between Free, Sharp, and Sharp Enterprises. The roof was also not a part of the Quarter Inn. Additionally, "[a] landowner need not make it impossible for persons to trespass before he may treat intruders as trespassers." *Adams*, 497 So.2d at 1100. Just as the injured party in *Adams* entered a parking lot without permission, Leffler entered the roof area of the Quarter Inn without invitation or permission. Free and Sharp took reasonable steps to make sure access to the roof was denied by keeping the door locked and stenciling the letters "NOT AN EXIT" on the door. Although this Court is mindful of the fact that Leffler received severe injuries, his status at the time of the incident was that of a trespasser, and the trial court correctly granted summary judgment dismissing his claims against Kim Free, individually, and Quarter Inn, Inc. as well as his claims against Harry Sharp, individually, and Sharp Enterprises, Inc.

Conclusion

¶ 24. . . . The trial court correctly determined that Leffler was a trespasser on the roof terrace. The trial court's grants of summary judgment in favor of Sharp, Sharp Enterprises, Free, and the Quarter Inn are hereby affirmed.

NOTES AND QUESTIONS

1. The Plaintiff-Status Categories and the Duties Owed Invitees and Licensees. The special duty framework for premises liability claims, which links the possessor's duty to the legal status of the plaintiff while on the premises, is a long-standing feature of common law. However, many modern courts have expressed skepticism about the categories, particularly the invitee-licensee distinction. *See* Note 6 *infra*; *see also* Section IV *infra.*

Standard statements of the traditional, tripartite distinction define "invitees" as persons who enter or remain on property at the invitation of the possessor as members of the public or in furtherance of the possessor's business or institutional interests. A customer shopping in a store open to the public is a paradigmatic example of an invitee. Possessors owe to invitees a duty to exercise care to render the premises reasonably safe.

"Licensees," meanwhile, are persons who, for their own purposes, enter or remain on property with the express or implied permission of the possessor. A guest who is in a friend's home for a social event is a paradigmatic example of a licensee. Possessors are usually said to owe licensees a duty to warn of hidden, dangerous conditions on the premises of which the possessor either knows or reasonably should know.

As indicated in the asterisk (*) footnote to the text of *Leffler,* although the Mississippi Supreme Court appears to equate licensees with trespassers (to whom no duty of care is owed), that initial statement is misleading. Licensees and trespassers are treated equivalently only in that neither is owed the general duty of reasonable care that is owed to invitees. They differ, however, in that — as indicated above — possessors are obligated to warn licensees of certain hidden dangers. The Mississippi Court appears to limit this duty to dangers of which a possessor has actual knowledge, whereas most courts that retain the licensee category impose a duty to warn about dangers of which the possessor knows or should know. *See, e.g.*, Stitt v. Holland Abundant Life Fellowship, 614 N.W.2d 88, 91 (Mich. 2000).

2. *Ownership, Possession, and Occupation.* A person need not own the property to be a possessor for purposes of premises liability claims. Thus, a tenant who rents an apartment is a possessor of that property for purposes of tort liability. Indeed, even one who unlawfully occupies land can be a possessor for purposes of liability. Also, one who is entitled to occupy land can be held liable as a possessor even if he or she does not exercise that entitlement. *See* Restatement (Third) of Torts: Liability for Physical and Emotional Harm § 49 (2012).

3. *Hazardous Conditions Versus Hazardous Activities.* It is important to stress that, to the extent special duty rules apply in premises liability cases, they are designed to address dangerous *conditions* on property—traps, holes, uneven or slippery surfaces, etc.—rather than dangerous activities that take place on property. For example, suppose Farmer *F* is driving a large tractor on a path on one edge of his farm. Suppose further that he is driving at an unsafe rate of speed while playing a hand-held electronic game that distracts him from keeping an eye on where he is going. As a result, *F* runs over *P*, who intentionally walks onto the path from a public road. *P* is a trespasser (*see* Note 4), but a court would likely not apply the special duty rules applicable to trespassers bringing premises liability actions, because, in this instance, the injury arose not from a dangerous condition on the land, but from a dangerous activity that happened to take place on the land. *See* Ganna v. Lanoga Corp., 80 P.3d 180 (Wash. App. 2003) (defendant lumber store's employee placed a large beam, unsecured, in the back of plaintiff-customer's pickup truck while it was parked in front of the store; plaintiff was injured when, as he drove off, the beam fell out and he went to retrieve it; plaintiff's claim held not to be a premises liability claim as there was no allegation of a dangerous condition on the property).

4. *Trespassers.* The vast majority of state courts continue to adhere to the rule that no duty of care is owed to trespassers, only a duty to refrain from willfully or wantonly injuring them. The trespasser category is not limited to those entering another's land intending to do wrong, such as a burglar or vandal. A trespasser is anyone who intentionally enters property, or a portion of property, without the possessor's actual or implied permission. Suppose adult hiker *H* unwittingly loses the path of a public trail, proceeds a quarter-mile into woods owned by *O*, and is injured by an unmarked trap lawfully placed by *O* on his property for the purpose of trapping animals. Under the traditional rule, absent special circumstances described in the next note, *H* cannot sue *O* for carelessness in his placement of the traps or for failure to warn of their presence. What might be the justification for such a rule?

Leffler was at one point an invitee of the Quarter Inn. How did he 'lose' that status? For a subsequent application of *Leffler*, consider *Handy v. Nejam*, 111 So.3d 610 (Miss.

2013). In Handy, a teenage guest of a tenant in the defendant's apartment building drowned while using the building's pool. The teenager's estate sued, alleging that the defendant failed to provide required safety equipment. A majority affirmed summary judgment for the defendant, reasoning that, in light of the defendant's posted rule forbidding guests from using the pool unless accompanied by a tenant, the teenager became a trespasser when he entered the pool area unaccompanied by a tenant, and thus was owed no duty of care. Two judges dissented, reasoning that the traditional plaintiff-status categories should be eliminated.

5. Exceptions to the Rule for Trespassers. The general rule of no duty of care applies to adult trespassers. However, a possessor will sometimes owe a limited duty to take steps to warn adult trespassers of a risk of physical harm posed by "artificial" conditions on the land. This duty is triggered only if the possessor knows — or, on the basis of facts already known to her, should know — that trespassers "constantly" intrude upon a "limited" portion of the premises so as to be exposed to the danger. For example, if the owner of a warehouse knows that adults routinely use as a shortcut a path on its property that runs near its loading docks, it can be held liable for failing to warn them of the dangers posed to them when trucks, forklifts, and other vehicles are operating under busy, crowded conditions.

Minors who trespass and are not old enough to appreciate the dangers posed to them by the premises have also historically benefited from an exception to the general no-duty rule. In the early years of the twentieth century, the courts tended to speak in terms of an obligation not to maintain an "attractive nuisance" on one's land — that is, a condition that would pique a child's curiosity but that contained a danger that would not be apparent to such a child, such as an artificial pond or swimming pool. For a modern decision ruling that the attractive nuisance doctrine should be available to children who are licensees and invitees, *see* S.W. v. Towers Boat Club, Inc., 315 P.2d 1257 (Colo. 2013). Given that the doctrine was developed as an exception to the rule that no duty of care is owed to trespassers, how do invitees or licensees — toward whom certain duties are already owed — stand to benefit from its availability? *See id.* at 1263-64 (Eid, J., dissenting) (arguing that the application of attractive nuisance doctrine to nontrespassers does not impose any obligations on possessors distinct from those already owed to invitees and licensees).

Modern courts tend to regard the attractive nuisance formulation as too restrictive, in that it seems to limit liability to those cases in which the plaintiff can prove that it was the dangerous condition that first drew the child onto the property, as opposed to cases in which the child stumbled onto the danger. The typical modern formulation, represented by a provision of the Second Restatement of Torts that the American Law Institute now regards as superseded by the Third Restatement, requires only that the land-possessor have reason to foresee that children might enter the property and be endangered by the condition. *See* Restatement (Second) of Torts § 339 (1965). In addition, many localities have enacted ordinances that protect children against particular dangers. Owners of private swimming pools, for example, are often required by ordinance to erect fences with self-latching gates around swimming pools to prevent

young children from accidentally drowning. Plaintiffs can sometimes invoke such ordinances to establish duty (and, in cases of noncompliance, breach). For two such decisions from the Maryland Supreme Court reaching opposite results, compare *Blackburn Ltd. Partnership v. Paul*, 90 A.3d 464 (Md. 2014) (statute specifying maximum permissible width between gate and fencing around pool is for the protection of young children and thus gives rise to an affirmative duty owed by owner to child trespassers) with *Osterman v. Peters*, 272 A.2d 21 (Md. 1971) (statutory requirement of self-closing, self-latching gate for pool fences was enacted for the benefit of the public and hence does not give rise to an affirmative duty owed by owner to child trespassers).

As discussed below, a few jurisdictions — and now the Third Torts Restatement — no longer rely on attractive nuisance doctrine or its variants because they wholly or largely reject the no-duty rule for trespassers. Restatement (Third) of Torts: Liability for Physical and Emotional Harm § 51, cmt. l (2012).

6. *Licensees Versus Invitees.* Although, as suggested above, there are relatively clear examples of licensees and invitees, the line between them is sometimes blurry. Is a person who goes into a store merely to use a restroom on the premises an invitee or a licensee? *See* Martin v. B.P. Exploration & Oil, 769 So. 2d 261 (Miss. Ct. App. 2000) (plaintiff who stops to use gas station restroom is an invitee if the jury determines that a reasonable person would perceive that the station invited the public to use its restrooms irrespective of purchase).

7. *Rejecting the Invitee-Licensee Distinction.* Even assuming that one can coherently place different plaintiffs into the two categories of licensee and invitee, is their distinctive treatment justified? Church *C* fails to notice, when it should have, that its

front steps are deceptively and dangerously uneven. If churchgoer *A* is injured on her way to services because of the condition of the steps, she may — absent a special immunity, described in Chapter 7 — sue the church for negligence as an invitee. Now suppose that homeowner *H* fails to notice that the steps to the front door of her home are uneven. Suppose further that *H* invites *B* to come to *H*'s house for Bible study. If *B* trips and injures herself as she enters the house, *B*, as a mere licensee, may not recover. Is this disparate treatment of *A* and *B* warranted? *See* Carter v. Kinney, 896 S.W.2d 926 (Mo. 1995) (person invited to defendant's home for Bible study is a licensee, not an invitee). Dissatisfaction with the licensee-invitee distinction has caused approximately half the states to abolish it, so as to create a duty of reasonable care to all those who enter property by permission, while retaining the traditional common law rules for trespassers. *See, e.g.*, Tantimonico v. Allendale Mut. Ins. Co., 637 A.2d 1056, 1062 (R.I. 1994).

8. Rowland v. Christian and the Elimination of the Categories. A few states — fewer than ten — have gone further and abolished all three categories in favor of a general duty of reasonable care for the safety of all persons on the premises, regardless of their status. The leading opinion advocating this approach is *Rowland v. Christian*, 443 P.2d 561 (Cal. 1968). *See* Section IV *infra.*

9. The Restatement (Third) Approach. The Third Restatement of Torts favors a variation on *Rowland.* It would first recognize a general duty to take reasonable care to make premises safe for all persons on the premises, including adult trespassers. However, it would then distinguish "flagrant trespassers," to whom is owed only a duty to refrain from intentionally, willfully, or wantonly causing physical harm. Restatement (Third) of Torts: Liability for Physical and Emotional Harm §§ 51–52 (2012). Commentary adds that "flagrant" means "egregious or atrocious" and is designed to cover, among others, persons who trespass in the course of committing serious crimes such as assault and burglary, or who, for no good reason, knowingly and deliberately violate an owner's right to exclude. *Id.*, § 52, cmt a.

10. Slips and Falls. Perhaps the most common example of a premises liability claim brought by an invitee involves a customer who slips, falls, and injures herself at a retail store or restaurant. If the slip and fall is caused by a foreign substance — for example liquid on the floor of a grocery store aisle — the injury victim traditionally has been required to prove either that the store was responsible for the substance spilling (e.g., because an employee knocked a container off a shelf or improperly stacked certain items such that they were too prone to fall), or that the store had actual or "constructive" notice of the hazard and failed to take reasonable steps to correct it. Restatement (Second) of Torts § 343 (1965).

On the issue of constructive notice, the plaintiff typically is required to offer circumstantial evidence suggesting that the hazard was present for a long enough period of time that the store had a fair opportunity to detect and correct it. For example, a patron who can prove that she slipped on melted ice cream in a well-trafficked part of a grocery store probably has offered sufficient evidence of constructive notice. Courts have wrestled with the question of whether the traditional approach to constructive notice should apply to dangerous conditions created by patrons who use self-service checkout systems. *See, e.g.,* Sheehan v. Roche Bros. Supermarkets, Inc., 863 N.E.2d 1276 (Mass. 2007) (if a business's "mode of operation" predictably generates a certain type of hazard, the store can be deemed careless for not taking reasonable measures to prevent or ameliorate that hazard-type, irrespective of whether the store had actual or constructive notice of a particular instantiation of the hazard-type).

11. Recreational Use Statutes. A staple of the modern "tort reform" movement has been the enactment by states of "recreational use" statutes that are designed to immunize owners of properties that are used for recreational purposes (e.g., land that contains a pond that is used for winter skating) from negligence liability. The breadth of these statutes varies significantly from state to state. California's statute is discussed briefly in the notes following Rowland v. Christian, Section IV *infra.* For a general discussion, see Dan B. Dobbs, *The Law of Torts* § 238, 620-624 (2000).

12. Liability to Non-Entrants. What about injuries caused by conditions on land to persons not on the land? Suppose *C*, cycling down a public street, is knocked off his bike by a difficult-to-see, low-hanging branch from a tree on *D*'s property. Was a duty owed by *D* to *C*? The general rule is that *D* is not liable to take care to protect against harms caused by "natural" conditions, such as trees on the land. The Restatement, however, states that *D is* obligated to take care to ensure that trees on his property do not injure travelers on public roads if the land is being used for commercial purposes and *may* have a duty if the land is being used for non-commercial purposes if the possessor "knows of the risk or if the risk is obvious." Restatement (Third) of Torts: Liability for Physical and Emotional Harm § 53(b)–(c) (2012). The no-duty rule also does not apply when the danger is posed by "artificial" conditions (man-made structures) created by, or known to, the possessor, as well as to risks transported from the land to another location where the risk is realized, injuring the entrant. *Id.* at § 53(a) and cmt b.

13. Municipal Liability. As the owners of thousands of miles of sidewalks, cities are commonly sued for unsafe conditions on property. New York City authorities at one time faced as many as 14,000 claims per year for sidewalk-related injuries, and paid out annually as much as $76 million in damages. In response to the high volume of sidewalk claims, the city enacted in 2003 City Code §§ 7-210 to 7-212, which transferred liability for hazardous conditions on a given stretch of sidewalk to the owner(s) of the property fronted by the stretch of sidewalk. Special provision is made for those who are injured but unable to collect a judgment because of the insolvency of the owner. According to information provided by the Office of the Corporation Counsel for New York City, these provisions have helped reduce the city's liability from $68 million in FY 2003 to $32 million in FY 2011.

14. Acts of Third Parties on the Premises. An important class of negligence claims involves suits against property owners alleging that they failed to take adequate steps to protect tenants or other users of the property from criminal activity on the premises. For example, an office worker who is robbed at gunpoint in an underground parking garage might sue the owner of the office complex, alleging negligence in failing to adequately light or patrol the garage, thus facilitating the robbery. Claims such as these are discussed in Chapter 5.

C. Pure Economic Loss

As noted at the outset of this chapter, negligence law recognizes loss of wealth as a form of injury. Thus, persons who lose existing wealth, or even expected income, may stand to recover from another who has carelessly caused such a loss. Of course, proof of injury is not enough. The plaintiff must further establish that the injury came about as the result of a breach of a duty to take care not to cause such a loss. As it turns out, courts are generally reluctant to recognize duties to look out for another person's economic well-being. Indeed, whereas actors are generally obligated to take reasonable care not to cause foreseeable *tangible property damage*, they have no such general obligation to avoid depriving persons of economic prospects, although they do incur the latter sort of duty in special situations.

The following decision is illustrative of the widespread judicial rejection of a general, unqualified duty to conduct oneself with care not to cause "pure" economic loss to others. The notes that follow the decision further explore those rationales and give illustrations of special situations in which such a duty is recognized. As you read these materials, ask yourself what might justify the sharp line drawn by negligence law between harm to property and loss of revenue.

Aikens v. Debow

541 S.E.2d 576 (W. Va. 2000)*

SCOTT, J. This case arises upon certified question from the Circuit Court of Berkeley County and presents the issue of entitlement to recovery in tort of economic loss not accompanied by bodily injury or property damage, a matter not previously resolved with precision by this Court.

I. FACTUAL AND PROCEDURAL BACKGROUND

Plaintiff Richard Aikens operates a motel and restaurant known as the Martinsburg Econo-Lodge ("Econo-Lodge"), which is located on Route 901 and can be accessed by exiting from Interstate 81 at the Spring Mills Road exit. While the Route 901 overpass bridge permits the shortest, most-convenient means of accessing the Econo-Lodge for south-bound travelers traveling on I-81, the establishment can still be accessed through alternate routing. On September 18, 1996, Defendant Robert Debow, a truck driver and employee of Defendant Craig Paving, Inc., was driving a flatbed truck north on I-81 carrying a trackhoe. Because the trackhoe was too high to pass safely under the Route 901 overpass, an accident resulted which caused substantial damage to the bridge. It was closed for nineteen days to make the necessary repairs.

---

* [Syllabus of the opinion prepared by the Court omitted — EDS.]

Plaintiff instituted the underlying cause of action on May 28, 1997, seeking recovery for the decreased revenues he experienced due to closure of the Route 901 overpass. Asserting that his reduced revenues were proximately caused by the accident, Plaintiff seeks recovery of $9,000 in lost income.

Arguing that as a matter of law Plaintiff could not recover for his economic losses in the absence of direct bodily injury or property damage, Defendants moved for summary judgment. The circuit court denied Defendants' motion for summary judgment, ruling that "there are factual issues in this case pertaining to causation and foreseeability which remain appropriate for jury determination." . . .

Following the circuit court's denial of Defendants' motion for summary judgment, the parties requested and the circuit court agreed to certification of the following issue:*

> Whether a claimant who has sustained no physical damage to his person or property may maintain an action against another for negligent injury to another's property which results consequentially in purely economic loss to the claimant.

The circuit court answered this question in the affirmative. . . . Recognizing that this Court, in addressing certified questions, has "retained the right to address them with some flexibility[,]" we reframe the question presented in the case sub judice. . . . The question, as reformulated, is . . . :

> May a claimant who has sustained purely economic loss as a result of an interruption in commerce caused by negligent injury to the property of a third person recover damages absent either privity of contract or some other special relationship with the alleged tortfeasor?

We answer this question in the negative.

II. Standard of Review

We recognized in syllabus point one of *Light v. Allstate Insurance Co.*, 203 W.Va. 27, 506 S.E.2d 64 (1998), "[a] de novo standard is applied by this Court in addressing the legal issues presented by a certified question from a federal district or appellate court." This same standard . . . applies equally to legal issues presented by circuit courts.

III. The Existence of a Duty

The resolution of any question of tort liability must be premised upon fundamental concepts of the duty owed by the tortfeasor.

---

* ["Certification" is a process by which a lower court invites a higher court to resolve a question of law that, depending on how it is resolved, would be dispositive of the litigation before the lower court. Here the Circuit Court invited the West Virginia Supreme Court to adopt or reject the majority rule of no-duty with respect to negligence causing pure economic loss. Presumably it did so to avoid an unnecessary trial, for if the Supreme Court were to adopt the rule (as it eventually did), the plaintiff's claim would fail as a matter of law. Certification is one way in which an appellate court can review a question of law apart from ordinary appeals, which typically occur only after the full and final resolution of the dispute in lower court(s). — EDS.]

> In order to establish a *prima facie* case of negligence in West Virginia, it must be shown that the defendant has been guilty of some act or omission in violation of a duty owed to the plaintiff. No action for negligence will lie without a duty broken. Syl. Pt. 1, *Parsley v. General Motors Acceptance Corp.*, 167 W.Va. 866, 280 S.E.2d 703 (1981).

Syl. Pt. 4, *Jack v. Fritts*, 457 S.E.2d 431, 432 (W.Va. 1995). Importantly, the determination of whether a defendant in a particular case owes a duty to the plaintiff is not a factual question for the jury; rather, "[t]he determination of whether a plaintiff is owed a duty of care by the defendant must be rendered as a matter of law by the court." *Id.* at at 435. . . .

. . . .

We recognized in *Robertson v. LeMaster*, 301 S.E.2d 563 (W.Va. 1983), that while foreseeability of risk is a primary consideration in determining the scope of a duty an actor owes to another, "[b]eyond the question of foreseeability, the existence of duty also involves policy considerations underlying the core issue of the scope of the legal system's protection[.]" *Id.* at 568. "Such considerations include the likelihood of injury, the magnitude of the burden of guarding against it, and the consequences of placing that burden on the defendant." *Id.*

. . . .

Emphasizing the relationship between foreseeability and duty, we explained in syllabus point three of *Sewell v. Gregory*, 371 S.E.2d 82 (W.Va, 1988):

> The ultimate test of the existence of a duty to use care is found in the foreseeability that harm may result if it is not exercised. The test is, would the ordinary man in the defendant's position, knowing what he knew or should have known, anticipate that harm of the general nature of that suffered was likely to result?

Commentators have similarly evaluated the critical element of duty:

> [T]he obligation to refrain from particular conduct is owed only to those who are foreseeably endangered by the conduct and only with respect to those risks or hazards whose likelihood made the conduct unreasonably dangerous. Duty, in other words, is measured by the scope of the risk which negligent conduct foreseeably entails.

2 F. Harper & F. James, *The Law of Torts* § 18.2 (1956) footnote omitted.

IV. Restrictions on Limitless Expansion of Duty

The appropriate application of these fundamental tort principles has served as a source of great controversy. Justice Benjamin Cardozo, in *Ultramares Corp. v. Touche*, 255 N.Y. 170, 174 N.E. 441 (1931), expressed the danger of expanding the concept of duty in tort to include economic interests and consequent exposure of defendants "to a liability in an indeterminate amount for an indeterminate time to an indeterminate class. The hazards of a business conducted on these terms are so extreme as to enkindle doubt whether a flaw may not exist in the implicating of a duty that exposes to these consequences." *Id.* at 444. . . .

. . . .

The need to restrict the spatial concept of duty to something less than the limits of logical connection was cogently stated as follows in *In re Exxon Valdez*, No. A89-0095-CV, 1994 WL 182856 (D. Alaska March 23, 1994):

> There is no question but that the Exxon Valdez grounding impacted, in one fashion or another, far more people than will ever recover anything in these proceedings. There is an understandable public perception that if one suffers harm which is perceived to be a result of the conduct of another, the harmed person should be compensated. That perception does not always square up with the institutional guidelines (statutes and case law) under which the court must operate. It is the function of both Congress and the courts (principally the courts of appeal and supreme courts) to determine the extent to which public expectations with respect to financial responsibility are to be realized. Legal liability does not always extend to all of the foreseeable consequences of an accident. In the area of harm to one's body, the reach of what is recoverable is very great. Where one's property is injured, the extent of legal liability is considerable, but not to the same extent as with bodily injury. Where pure economic loss is at issue — not connected with any injury to one's body or property, and especially where that economic loss occurs in a marine setting — the reach of legal liability is quite limited except as to commercial fishermen.[2]
>
> . . .
>
> *Were it otherwise, we would have a form of organized anarchy in which no one could count on what rule would apply at any given time or in any given situation.*

Id. at 8-9 (footnote and emphasis added).

. . . . In his dissent [in *Harris v. R.A. Martin, Inc.*, 513 S.E.2d 170 (W.Va. 1988)], Justice Maynard quoted, with approval, the following language from 57A Am. Jur. 2d *Negligence* § 87:

> "A line must be drawn between the competing policy considerations of providing a remedy to everyone who is injured and of extending exposure to tort liability almost without limit. It is always tempting to impose new duties and, concomitantly, liabilities, regardless of the economic and social burden. Thus, the *courts have generally recognized that public policy and social considerations, as well as foreseeability, are important factors in determining whether a duty will be held to exist in a particular situation.*"

513 S.E.2d at 176 (emphasis supplied).

---

2. The Ninth Circuit, in *Union Oil Co. v. Oppen*, 501 F.2d 558 (9th Cir. 1974), found that the routine reliance by commercial fishermen upon an ability to fish in unpolluted waters satisfied the foreseeability requirement and justified an award of economic damages as an exception to the general rule. . . . The rationale for this limited exception for commercial fishermen was explained in *Burgess v. M/V Tamano*, 370 F. Supp. 247 (D. Me. 1973), *aff'd per curiam*, 559 F.2d 1200 (1st Cir. 1977). In *Tamano*, the court reasoned that while fishermen and clammers have no individual property rights to the aquatic life harmed by oil pollution, the fishermen could sue for tortious invasion of a public right, having suffered damages greater in degree than the general public. The court recognized the oil spill as an interference with the "direct exercise of the public right to fish and to dig clams" which was, in fact, a special interest different from that of the general public. *Id.*

The obvious question: Who draws the line demarcating tort liability? Who, in our society, has the burden of defining the existence and extent of the element of "duty" in tort actions? It necessarily falls to the courts to consider all relevant claims of the competing parties; to determine where and upon whom the burden of carrying the risk of injury will fall; and to draw the line, to declare the existence or absence of "duty," in every case, as a matter of law. The temptation is to accede to the arguments of logical connection in every instance of resulting harm while, in fact, the consequences of pure logic would be socially and economically ruinous.

V. Traditional Approach—No Economic Damages in the Absence of Physical Impact

The sole issue presented for our resolution is whether economic loss from an interruption in commerce in the absence of damage to a plaintiff's person or property is recoverable in a tort action. While this Court has never directly addressed this issue, other jurisdictions, almost without exception, have concluded that economic loss alone will not warrant recovery in the absence of some special relationship between the plaintiff and the tortfeasor. In the seminal decision of *Robins Dry Dock & Repair Co. v. Flint*, 275 U.S. 303 (1927), the United States Supreme Court refused to permit recovery from the dry dock owner when plaintiffs [who had leased a ship for temporary use] were denied use of [the] vessel for two weeks because of a third party's act of negligence [that damaged the ship] during the ship's refurbishing. In establishing this long-standing rule of denying recovery in tort for indirect economic injury, Justice Holmes articulated the rationale, based upon English and American precedent, that continues to justify the nonexistence of a legally cognizable or compensable claim for such attenuated injuries even today: "The law does not spread its protection so far." *Id.* at 309. . . .

Where the factual scenario involves a plaintiff's contractual right to use property damaged by a tortfeasor, courts have invoked the Restatement of Torts as a basis for denying causes of action limited to economic damages. In *Philip Morris, Inc. v. Emerson*, 368 S.E.2d 268 (Va. 1988), the plaintiff sought recovery of lost profits to his campground business due to the negligent release of gases from the defendant's property. Citing the well-recognized principle in the Restatement of Torts which recognizes that interference with the ability to contract with third persons is too remote to permit recovery, the court refused to permit recovery of the profits plaintiffs allegedly sustained from his inability to contract with campers for overnight stays. 368 S.E.2d at 282 (citing Restatement (Second) of Tort § 766 (1979)).

In denying economic damages in the absence of physical impact, courts frequently refer to this element of remoteness between the injury and the act of negligence that is the source of such injury. In *Rickards v. Sun Oil Co.*, 41 A.2d 267 (N.J. Sup. 1945), a case remarkably similar to the one under scrutiny by this Court, plaintiff business owners sought to recover "losses from expectant gains" from a defendant whose barge negligently damaged a drawbridge which served as the only means of access to the island on which plaintiffs' business premises were situated. *Id.* at 268. In granting the defendant's motions to strike the complaints, the court held that "[defendant's] negligent action may be a cause of injury to the plaintiffs, but it is not the natural and proximate effect of such negligence and therefore [is] not actionable." *Id.* The court observed:

> The entire doctrine assumes the defendant is not necessarily to be held [liable] for all consequences of his acts. . . . It is fundamental that there must be some reasonable limitation of liability for the commission of the tort. The wrongdoer is not liable in the eyes of the law for all possible consequences. He is thus responsible in damages only for the natural and probable consequence of his negligent act.

41 A.2d at 269 (citation omitted). The court recognized that "[n]o rule embraces within its scope all the resulting consequences of the given act. The effect would be to impose a liability entirely disproportionate to the act committed or to the failure to perform the duty assumed." *Id.*

. . . .

The recognized necessity of imposing a line of demarcation on actionable theories of recovery serves as another rationale for the denial of purely economic damages. In *Stevenson v. East Ohio Gas. Co.*, 73 N.E.2d 200 (Ohio Ct. App. 1946), the Ohio court held that employees of a neighboring company could not recover lost wages incurred after they were evacuated due to an explosion and fire allegedly caused by the defendant's negligence. The *Stevenson* court reasoned as follows:

> While the reason usually given for the refusal to permit recovery in this class of cases is that the damages are "indirect" or are "too remote" it is our opinion that the principal reason that has motivated the courts in denying recovery in this class of cases is that *to permit recovery of damages in such cases would open the door to a mass of litigation which might very well overwhelm the courts so that in the long run while injustice might result in special cases, the ends of justice are conserved. . . .*

Id. at 203 (emphasis added).

. . . .

VI. The Minority View: Recovery of Economic Damages Under Limited Circumstances

A few jurisdictions have permitted recovery of economic damages without damage to person or property under certain limited circumstances. The New Jersey Supreme Court's approach to this concept is recognized as the leading authority for the minority view and represents a departure from a substantial collection of American and British cases. In *People Express Airlines, Inc. v. Consolidated Rail Corp.*, 495 A.2d 107 (N.J. 1985), the New Jersey court permitted economic recovery where a leak of toxic chemicals from a railway car forced a twelve-hour evacuation of a commercial airline office building adjacent to the site of the leak. *Id.* at 115. The plaintiff sought to recover expenses incurred for flight cancellations, lost bookings and revenue, and certain operating expenses. In permitting the action, the court applied a special foreseeability rule, reasoning that the defendant would be liable only for damages proximately caused and requiring that the defendant must have "knowledge or special reason to know of the consequences of the tortious conduct in terms of the persons likely to be victimized and the nature of the damages likely to be suffered. . . ." *Id.*

Narrowly crafting its decision to apply to a limited and particularized group, the New Jersey court held:

> that a defendant owes a duty of care to take reasonable measures to avoid the risk of causing economic damages, aside from physical injury, to particular plaintiffs or plaintiffs comprising an identifiable class with respect to whom defendant knows or has reason to know are likely to suffer such damages from its conduct. A defendant failing to adhere to this duty of care may be found liable for such economic damages proximately caused by its breach of duty.

495 A.2d at 116. In further explaining its rationale for departure from established doctrine, the New Jersey court noted:

> the close proximity of the North Terminal and People Express Airlines to the Conrail freight yard; the obvious nature of the plaintiff's operations and particular foreseeability of economic losses resulting from an accident and evacuation; the defendants' actual or constructive knowledge of the volatile properties of ethylene oxide; and the existence of an emergency response plan prepared by some of the defendants (alluded to in the course of oral argument), which apparently called for the nearby area to be evacuated to avoid the risk of harm in case of an explosion.

Id. at 118. In fashioning its test, the court in *People Express* determined that liability and foreseeability "stand in direct proportion to one another[:] The more particular is the foreseeability that economic loss will be suffered by the plaintiff as a result of defendant's negligence, the more just is it that liability be imposed and recovery allowed." *Id.* at 116.

An analysis of the facts involved in the *People Express* decision supports the conclusion that the New Jersey court traversed a logical path more closely akin to that navigated in cases involving physical damage to property. Subsequent to the Three Mile Island nuclear incident, plaintiffs similarly asserted claims of temporary loss of use of property and "damage to property" as a result of the intrusion of radioactive materials through the ambient air. In resolving their claims in *Commonwealth of Pennsylvania v. General Public Utilities Corp.*, 710 F.2d 117 (3rd Cir. 1983), the United States Court of Appeals for the Third Circuit acknowledged that the complaints did not contain any claim of damages for direct physical damage to any of the plaintiffs' property. *Id.* at 120-21. . . . [However, the Third Circuit permitted] the plaintiffs an opportunity to prove that an invasion by an invisible substance may still constitute a physical damage warranting recovery of economic loss. Similar to the inhabitability problems experienced by the Three Mile Island plaintiffs, the plaintiff's building in *People Express* was rendered uninhabitable by the negligent release of toxic gases. Thus, in *People Express*, the New Jersey court could have reached its decision by reasoning that to render a building uninhabitable by releasing poison gas against it constitutes a direct physical damage to that building.

. . . .

In another case typically referenced as supportive of a minority position on this issue, a California court applied the "special relationship" exception and permitted a restaurant owner to sue for lost profits allegedly caused by a contractor's failure to promptly install and maintain [the air conditioning system of a building in which the restaurant was a tenant]. *J'Aire Corp. v. Gregory*, 598 P.2d 60 (Cal. 1979). The plaintiff introduced evidence that [its] reliance upon the air conditioning function was repeatedly brought to the defendant's attention. In concluding that such action could be maintained, the court explained that "a contractor owes a duty of care to the tenant of a building undergoing construction work to prosecute that work in a manner which does not cause undue injury to the tenant's business, where such injury is reasonably foreseeable." *Id.* at 66. The court's decision to permit recovery was expressly predicated on the existence of a special relationship: "Where a special relationship exists between the parties, a plaintiff may recover for loss of expected economic advantage through the negligent performance of a contract although the parties were not in contractual privity." *Id.* at 63.

. . . .

VII. Conclusion

After thoroughly considering the intricacies of a potential rule permitting the recovery of economic damages absent physical or personal injury, we conclude that an individual who sustains purely economic loss from an interruption in commerce caused by another's negligence may not recover damages in the absence of physical harm to that individual's person or property, a contractual relationship with the alleged tortfeasor, or some other special relationship between the alleged tortfeasor and the individual who sustains purely economic damages sufficient to compel the conclusion that the tortfeasor had a duty to the particular plaintiff and that the injury complained of was clearly foreseeable to the tortfeasor. The existence of a special relationship will be determined largely by the extent to which the particular plaintiff is affected differently from society in general. It may be evident from the defendant's knowledge or specific reason to know of the potential consequences of the wrongdoing, the persons likely to be injured, and the damages likely to be suffered. Such special relationship may be proven through evidence of foreseeability of the nature of the harm to be suffered by the particular plaintiff or an identifiable class and can arise from contractual privity or other close nexus. . . . Any attempt by this Court to more specifically define the parameters of circumstances which may be held to establish a "special relationship" would create more confusion than clarity.

. . . .

Our decision under the limited factual scenario presented in this certified question has no impact upon our prior rulings permitting recovery of purely economic damages in negligence actions where a special relationship exists between the plaintiff and the alleged tortfeasor. Our holding in the case sub judice is, in fact, consistent with the rationale underlying such rulings, and we affirm our previous recognition that where a special and narrowly defined relationship can be established between the tortfeasor and a plaintiff who was deprived of an economic benefit, the tortfeasor can be held liable. . . .

For example, auditors have been held liable to plaintiffs who bought stock in reliance upon a financial statement negligently prepared for a corporation; surveyors and termite inspectors liable to remote purchasers of property; engineers and architects liable to contractors who relied upon plans negligently prepared for property owners who later hired the contractors; attorneys and notaries public liable to beneficiaries of negligently prepare wills; real estate brokers for failure to disclose defects; and telegraph companies liable to individuals who failed to secure a contract due to the negligent transmission of a message. [Citations to cases instantiating each of these special relationships omitted — Eds.]

. . . .

The resolution of this matter of restrictions on tort liability is ultimately a matter of "practical politics." *Palsgraf v. Long Island R.R.*, 162 N.E. 99, 103 (N.Y. 1928)] (Andrews, J., dissenting). The "law arbitrarily declines to trace a series of events beyond a certain point." *Id.* In other words, it is a question of public policy. The purely economic damages sought by a plaintiff may be indistinguishable in terms of societal entitlement from those damages incurred by the restaurant owner in the next block, the antique dealer in the next town, and all the ripple-effect "losses" experienced by each employer and each resident of every town and village surrounding the location of the initial act of negligence. In crafting a rule to address the issue of economic damages, we have attempted to avoid the expression of a judicial definition of duty which would permit the maintenance of a class action as a result of almost every car wreck and other inconvenience that results to our state's citizenry.

In determining questions of duty and extension of duty to particular plaintiffs, the court in *Stevenson* echoed widespread speculation concerning the ripple effects of a negligence claim based upon pure economic loss and observed:

> Cases might well occur where a manufacturer would be obliged to close down his factory because of the inability of his supplier due to a fire loss to make prompt deliveries; the power company with a contract to supply a factory with electricity would be deprived of the profit which it would have made if the operation of the factory had not been interrupted by reason of fire damage; a man who had a contract to paint a building may not be able to proceed with his work; a salesman who would have sold the products of the factory may be deprived of his commissions; the neighborhood restaurant which relies on the trade of the factory employees may suffer a substantial loss. The claims of workmen for loss of wages who were employed in such a factory and cannot continue to work there because of a fire, represent only a small fraction of the claims which would arise if recovery is allowed in this class of cases.

73 N.E.2d at 203-04.

. . . .

. . . This Court's obligation is to draw a line beyond which the law will not extend its protection in tort, and to declare, as a matter of law, that no duty exists beyond that court-created line. It is not a matter of protection of a certain class of defendants; nor is it a matter of championing the causes of a certain class of plaintiffs. It is a question of public policy. Each segment of society will suffer injustice, whether situated as plaintiff or defendant, if there are no finite boundaries to liability and no confines within which the rights of plaintiffs and defendants can be determined. We accept the wise admonition expressed over a century ago, in language both simple and eloquent, proven by the passage of time and the lessons of experience: "There would be no bounds to actions and litigious intricacies, if the ill effects of the negligences of men could be followed down the chain of results to the final effect." *Kahl*[*v. Love*], 37 N.J.L. [5, 8 (N.J. 1874)].

. . . .

[Concurring opinion omitted. — EDS.]

NOTES AND QUESTIONS

1. *What Counts as a Property Interest?* In a footnote, the *Aikens* court notes the willingness of other courts to permit negligence claims against defendants who pollute waters by commercial fishermen, even though the fishermen do not enjoy exclusive possession of fish that swim in public waters. Is the suggestion that physical damage is sufficient to support an award for pure economic loss even when the person who suffers a loss does not "own" the damaged thing outright, but rather has a legal right to use it or to seek to acquire it unimpeded by wrongful interference? Does this same rationale explain the non-application of the no-duty rule in the *J'Aire* decision referenced in *Aikens*? Can this sort of "softening" of the hard edges of the no-duty rule be squared with the holding in the foundational case of *Robins Dry Dock*?

2. *Floodgates.* The *Aikens* opinion emphasizes policy considerations of excessive litigation and liability as the justification for the general no-duty rule. Then-Judge, now

Check Your Understanding

Predicate Injuries and Parasitic Damages

Suppose that Debow had exited I-81 onto Route 901 without incident, but then carelessly lost control of his truck, as a result of which the trackhoe fell off its platform and crashed into the main entrance of Aikens's motel. Suppose further that the motel was thereafter closed for two weeks for repairs, and that Aikens offered compelling evidence of lost revenues suffered during the period of closure. If, given these alternative facts, Aikens had sued Debow, would West Virginia negligence law have called for the dismissal of Aikens's suit?

The clear answer is no. On these facts, Aikens would not be suing for negligence causing *pure economic loss* but instead would be suing for negligence causing *physical harm* in the form of property damage. It is true that, in this suit, too, Aikens would be seeking compensation for economic loss — i.e., lost revenues. But here the lost revenues would be recoverable as damages "parasitic" on the underlying "predicate" injury of property damage. In this alternative scenario, Aikens would not be claiming that Debow breached a duty to take care against causing economic loss. Instead he would be claiming that Debow breached the general *Heaven v. Pender / MacPherson v. Buick* duty to take care against causing physical harm to foreseeable victims. By proving that he was injured as a result of the breach of the latter duty, Aikens would earn the right to recover not just for the cost of repairing the property damage but for all the proven losses he experienced as a result of the tort, including lost revenues.

Justice, Breyer, offered a similar rationale in explaining the role of a comparable no-duty rule in federal admiralty law, which governs liability for maritime accidents. (*Robins Dry Dock* itself was a federal admiralty law decision, as was the opinion in the *Exxon Valdez* case that is cited in *Aikens.*)

> . . . The number of persons suffering foreseeable financial harm in a typical accident is likely to be far greater than those who suffer . . . physical harm. . . . That possibility—a large number of different plaintiffs each with somewhat different claims—in turn threatens to raise significantly the cost of even relatively simple tort actions. Yet the tort action is already a very expensive administrative device for compensating victims of accidents. . . .
>
> [Another] set of considerations focuses on the "disproportionality" between liability and fault. . . . [L]iability for pure financial harm, insofar as it proved vast, cumulative and inherently unknowable in amount, could create incentives that are perverse. . . . Might not unbounded liability for foreseeable financial damage, for example, make auto insurance premiums too expensive for the average driver?

Barber Lines A/S v. M/V Donau Maru, 764 F.2d 50, 54-55 (1st Cir. 1985). Are judges in a good position to make the claims on which the *Aikens* Court and Judge Breyer rely? Suppose it were the case that one could confidently predict non-ruinous levels of liability—should recovery then be permitted? Why should an actor be excused from liability simply because his conduct threatens to generate many lawsuits or a great deal of harm? Today, if a manufacturer physically injures a large number of people by selling a defective product, tort law ordinarily will require it to compensate all of its victims, if it can do so. Why is economic loss different?

3. *Proportionality.* Some commentators have fastened on the vast potential scope of liability for negligently inflicted economic loss as supporting a fairness argument against the recognition of a general duty to take care against causing economic loss. Suppose the careless truck driver in *Aikens* had not hit and damaged the bridge, but instead had collided with a passenger vehicle, killing its driver, a 25-year-old investment banker. Under black letter law, the driver in that case might be liable for millions of dollars in damages corresponding to the expected future earnings of the victim. Would that liability be proportionate to the driver's wrong? If not, why should proportionality justify a special duty rule in pure economic loss cases but not physical harm cases?

4. *A Hierarchy of Interests and Duties.* Others have argued that enforcement of a general duty to take care to avoid causing economic losses would run against basic principles of liberalism (and capitalism). Stephen Perry, for example, has noted that a person's interest in maintaining his wealth is already more vulnerable to interferences through perfectly lawful means such as market competition, boycotts, and true but unfavorable publicity. Negligence law, he suggests, is rendered consistent with the law's assignment of second-class status to this interest by not according it general protection, but instead protecting it only in certain specified situations.

5. *The People Express Decision.* As noted in *Aikens*, a prominent case purporting to reject the majority rule is *People Express Airlines, Inc. v. Consolidated Rail Corp.*, 495

A.2d 107 (N.J. 1985). To what extent does that decision's adoption of the "particularly foreseeable plaintiff" rule depart from the majority no-duty rule? How broad a scope of responsibility does it entail? As explained in Chapter 11, the tort of private nuisance protects the interest of a possessor of land in using its property free from unreasonable, intangible interferences by others. For example, a landowner who uses her land in such a way as to repeatedly generate noxious odors or loud noises that interfere with her neighbor's ability to enjoy his property is subject to liability for a nuisance. Although it is not clear that People Express could have recovered on a nuisance theory given the one-time nature of the gas leak, does the idea of a nuisance help explain or justify the New Jersey court's inclination to permit the imposition of liability?

6. *Accountants' Liability.* Perhaps the most important of the "special relationship" exceptions to the no-duty rule is the duty owed by accountants to take reasonable care in conducting audits of their clients' finances so as not to mislead certain creditors of the client. The scope of this duty, however, varies significantly by jurisdiction.

Ultramares Corp. v. Touche, 174 N.E. 441, 447 (N.Y. 1931), cited in *Aikens*, is a foundational accountant's liability decision. Touche, an accounting firm, was hired by Fred Stern & Co. to review Stern's records and prepare a balance sheet that Touche was to certify as providing an accurate reflection of the company's assets and debts. Touche knew that it had been hired to perform this function so that Stern could present copies of the certified balance sheet to creditors whenever it might need to convince them that the company was in sound financial health and thus in a position to pay back creditors' loans. Touche failed to realize that certain listings of assets in Stern's books were false, a fact that could have been readily discovered if proper accounting procedures were followed. As a result, Touche certified Stern to be in sound financial health when in fact it was insolvent. Plaintiff, a company that had loaned money to Stern in reliance on Touche's audit, sued Touche for negligently causing it to lose the value of the loan when Stern defaulted.

The court, in an opinion by Judge Cardozo (the author of *MacPherson v. Buick*), rejected the idea that accountants owe a broad duty of reasonable care to all those who might foreseeably rely on the results of its audits. However, the opinion also reaffirmed earlier decisions recognizing that such a duty is owed to a third-party creditor if the accountant knew or should have known that the audit was being undertaken specifically in order to facilitate a particular transaction between the audited company and that creditor.

Subsequent courts have expanded the scope of this duty, holding that it is owed to any identifiable third party who might be expected to rely on the accuracy of the audit. *See* Bethlehem Steel Corp. v. Ernst & Whinney, 822 S.W.2d 592 (Tenn. 1991) (surveying different rules for accountants' liability to third-party creditors and adopting the majority rule of Restatement (Second) of Torts § 552).

7. *Other Situations Supporting a Duty to Take Care Not to Cause Economic Loss.* Tort duties to take care not to cause pure economic loss are owed by other actors besides accountants, including attorneys. Suppose *A* hires lawyer *L* to draft a will under which all of *A*'s assets will pass upon her death to her favorite nephew *N*. *L* negligently drafts the will, so that it is invalid, as a result of which the assets go to *A*'s son *S* and not to *N*. May *N* sue *L* for negligently causing *N* to lose claim to the assets? The majority of

courts to consider the question have answered yes. *See, e.g.*, Lucas v. Hamm, 364 P.2d 685 (Cal. 1961). In part, the majority rule has been supported by the notion that only disappointed beneficiaries will have an incentive to sue negligent estate lawyers, since the estate itself usually suffers no economic harm as a result of the lawyer's error. Some state courts treat this kind of claim as sounding in breach of contract, rather than tort, with the claimant having standing to sue as an intended third-party beneficiary of the contract between the donor and the attorney. Increasingly, courts that handle the execution of wills — known as probate courts — will allow interested parties to correct obvious errors in wills, including errors created by attorney malpractice, so as to reduce the need for subsequent malpractice litigation.

The majority rule stated above was rejected by the Texas Supreme Court in *Barcelo v. Elliot*, 923 S.W.2d 575 (Tex. 1996). The *Barcelo* court was concerned that recognition of a duty of care owed to beneficiaries would interfere with the attorney's primary obligation to his client. It also expressed concern over disruption of the disposition of wills, offering the following example: "Suppose . . . that a properly drafted will is simply not executed at the time of the testator's death. The document may express the testator's true intentions, lacking signatures solely because of the attorney's negligent delay. On the other hand, the testator may have postponed execution because of second thoughts regarding the distribution scheme." *Id.* at 578. One of two dissenting judges in *Barcelo* countered that "these are matters subject to proof, as in all other cases. . . . The Court fails to consider that the beneficiaries will in each case bear the burden of establishing that the attorney breached a duty to the testator, which resulted in damages to the beneficiaries. Lawyers, wishing to protect themselves from liability, may document the testator's intentions." *Id.* at 581 (Cornyn, J.).

The Texas Supreme Court revisited attorney liability to nonclients in *McCamish, Martin, Brown & Loeffler v. F.E. Appling Interests*, 991 S.W.2d 787 (Tex. 1999). There, plaintiff, a real estate developer, was locked in a dispute with a bank that had promised to finance certain construction. The dispute was resolved by a settlement agreement under which all debts owed by the developer to the bank were forgiven. To be effective, the debt forgiveness provision had to be formally approved by the bank's board. Defendants, lawyers for the bank, told the developer that the settlement had been approved, when in fact it had not. As a result, the settlement was later deemed ineffective.

Plaintiff sued for negligent misrepresentation. The attorneys argued that *Barcelo* foreclosed attorney liability to nonclients. The court rejected this argument, drawing a sharp distinction between lawyer *malpractice* and negligent *misrepresentation*. Liability for misrepresentations, according to the court, would not pose a danger of unlimited liability, in part because lawyers can control to whom they make such representations.

8. *Economic Loss and the Gulf Oil Spill.* In April 2010, an explosion occurred on the Deepwater Horizon drilling rig, which was located off of the Louisiana coast and was being operated by a subsidiary of BP, plc. As a result of the explosion, 11 workers were killed and 17 injured. In addition, the oil well being drilled began leaking. The leak — images of which were streamed constantly over the

Internet — was not stanched for three months. By then, an estimated 5 million barrels of oil (over 200 million gallons) had entered Gulf waters, the largest oil spill in U.S. history.

With pressure from the White House, BP set aside $20 billion to cover spill-related liabilities. It then delegated the settlement of claims against it to an entity called the Gulf Coast Claims Facility (GCCF) and appointed attorney Kenneth Feinberg to run the GCCF. Feinberg was chosen in part because he had extensive experience settling mass tort claims and had served as the Administrator of the fund set up by Congress in 2001 to compensate victims of the 9/11 terrorist attacks.

The GCCF operated with a relatively streamlined set of procedures through which persons could submit claims for compensation for spill-related damages. If the GCCF deemed the claim valid, it offered a final settlement that, if accepted, required the claimant to waive his or her rights to pursue legal claims against BP and other potential tort defendants. By February 2012, the GCCF had received over 1 million claims filed by more than 500,000 claimants. (Claimants were permitted to file separate claims for emergency and final payments.) It paid out about $6 billion to approximately 200,000 of those claimants.

The GCCF was a private claims facility. There was no obligation to file a claim with it. Indeed, prior to accepting a final payment from the GCCF, persons who alleged injuries caused by the spill could simultaneously pursue remedies in court, as many did. Litigation against BP and other potentially responsible parties was consolidated in federal district court in Louisiana. A tentative settlement of this litigation was announced in March 2012. Under that settlement, all outstanding claims — i.e., all those not waived prior to the settlement in exchange for a final payment from the GCCF — are now being addressed through the settlement. (With its business concluded, the GCCF ceased to operate.) BP subsequently complained that the district judge who presided over the settlement, and the special master appointed by the judge to disperse settlement funds, has authorized payments to persons who are not entitled to them under the terms of the settlement agreement, including persons who have suffered no losses at all. BP's attempt to undo the settlement was rejected by a divided Fifth Circuit Court of Appeals. In re Deepwater Horizon, 739 F.3d 790 (5th Cir.), *cert. denied sub nom.* BP Exploration & Production, Inc. v. Lake Eugenie Land & Develop., Inc., 135 S. Ct. 754 (2014).

The Deepwater Horizon spill caused and probably will continue to cause economic harm to the Gulf Coast region, including harm to thousands of businesses that suffered no property damage. For example, many hotels, restaurants, and other tourist-related businesses located in Florida claim to have suffered a downturn in business only because of tourists' fears about oil contamination, not because of actual contamination. Thus, a central question for the administrator of the GCCF and for the attorneys who negotiated the settlement of pending litigation has been how to value claims for pure economic loss. Should any compensation be offered for such claims? Or should they all be rejected on the ground that they would not be legally viable if pursued in court?

At least some claimants alleging pure economic loss resulting from the Deepwater Horizon spill stood to benefit from statutory liability provisions contained in the federal Oil Pollution Act of 1990 (OPA). Enacted by Congress in the aftermath of another disastrous oil spill — the 1989 *Exxon Valdez* spill in Prince William Sound, Alaska — OPA departs from state tort law in several respects. For example, it adopts a hybrid scheme of fault-based and strict liability. Any owner or operator of a facility that spills oil into navigable waters is liable for damages without proof of fault up to an aggregate amount of $75 million, but this cap is lifted if the spill is proven to have resulted from that party's gross negligence or willful misconduct.

Most saliently for present purposes, OPA abrogates the common law's no-duty rule for pure economic loss, allowing a claimant to recover for lost profits or impaired earnings if such a loss is "due to" property or resource damage that "result[s] from" a spill, irrespective of whether the claimant has a possessory interest in the property or resources. 33 U.S.C. §§ 2702(a); 2702(b)(2)(E). While it is clear that these provisions were meant to expand liability for pure economic loss, it is less clear how far that liability extends. If an amusement park in a landlocked part of Florida claims lost profits because of a general decline in tourism attributable to an oil spill, has it suffered a loss due to resource damage resulting from the spill? What about a seafood restaurant located in Denver, Colorado, that can demonstrate that consumer fears about oil-tainted Gulf seafood have caused it to suffer a loss of business?*

IV. *ROWLAND, TARASOFF,* AND THE MEANING OF DUTY

In this final section, we consider two well-known California Supreme Court decisions that return to the question of whether special duty rules ought to apply to negligence claims alleging: (1) dangerous conditions on land (premises liability); or (2) breaches of affirmative duties to protect or rescue (nonfeasance). We present them in part to permit review and elaboration of previously considered topics, but also to introduce ways of thinking about the duty element of the negligence tort that was particularly prevalent among mid- to late-twentieth-century judges and torts scholars, and remains important today. As you read *Rowland* and *Tarasoff,* consider the conceptual, historical, and political claims that are being made about the meaning and significance of the duty element.

Rowland v. Christian

443 P.2d 561 (Cal. 1968)

Peters, J. Plaintiff appeals from a summary judgment for defendant Nancy Christian in this personal injury action.

---

* One of us (Goldberg) served as a consultant to the GCCF, in which capacity he prepared a report that offered a particular interpretation of the scope of liability for economic loss under OPA. The report, along with criticisms, is reproduced in a volume of the Mississippi College Law Review that is cited in the list of references for this chapter.

In his complaint plaintiff alleged that about November 1, 1963, Miss Christian told the lessors of her apartment that the knob of the cold water faucet on the bathroom basin was cracked and should be replaced; that on November 30, 1963, plaintiff entered the apartment at the invitation of Miss Christian; that he was injured while using the bathroom fixtures, suffering severed tendons and nerves of his right hand; and that he has incurred medical and hospital expenses. He further alleged that the bathroom fixtures were dangerous, that Miss Christian was aware of the dangerous condition, and that his injuries were proximately caused by the negligence of Miss Christian. Plaintiff sought recovery of his medical and hospital expenses, loss of wages, damage to his clothing, and $100,000 general damages. It does not appear from the complaint whether the crack in the faucet handle was obvious to an ordinary inspection or was concealed.

Miss Christian filed an answer containing a general denial except that she alleged that plaintiff was a social guest and admitted the allegations that she had told the lessors that the faucet was defective and that it should be replaced. Miss Christian also alleged contributory negligence and assumption of the risk. In connection with the defenses, she alleged that plaintiff had failed to use his 'eyesight' and knew of the condition of the premises. . . .

. . . .

The summary judgment procedure is drastic and should be used with caution so that it does not become a substitute for an open trial. This court in two recent cases has stated: "Summary judgment is proper only if the affidavits in support of the moving party would be sufficient to sustain a judgment in his favor . . . and doubts as to the propriety of granting the motion should be resolved in favor of the party opposing the motion." (Stationers Corp. v. Dun & Bradstreet, Inc., 62 Cal.2d 412, 417, 42 Cal. Rptr. 449, 452, 398 P.2d 785, 788; Joslin v. Marin Mun. Water Dist., 67 A.C. 127, 142, 60 Cal. Rptr. 377, 429 P.2d 889.). . . .

In the instant case, Miss Christian's affidavit and admissions made by plaintiff show that plaintiff was a social guest and that he suffered injury when the faucet handle broke; they do not show that the faucet handle crack was obvious or even nonconcealed. Without in any way contradicting her affidavit or his own admissions, plaintiff at trial could establish that she was aware of the condition and realized or should have realized that it involved an unreasonable risk of harm to him, that defendant should have expected that he would not discover the danger, that she did not exercise reasonable care to eliminate the danger or warn him of it, and that he did not know or have reason to know of the danger. Plaintiff also could establish, without contradicting Miss Christian's affidavit or his admissions, that the crack was not obvious and was concealed. Under the circumstances, a summary judgment is proper in this case only if, after proof of such facts, a judgment would be required as a matter of law for Miss Christian. The record supports no such conclusion.

Section 1714 of the Civil Code provides: "Every one is responsible, not only for the result of his willful acts, but also for an injury occasioned to another by his want of ordinary care or skill in the management of his property or person, except so far as the latter has, willfully or by want of ordinary care, brought the injury upon himself. . . ."

This code section, which has been unchanged in our law since 1872, states a civil law and not a common law principle. (Fernandez v. Consolidated Fisheries, Inc., 98 Cal. App. 2d 91, 96, 219 P.2d 73.)

Nevertheless, some common law judges and commentators have urged that the principle embodied in this code section serves as the foundation of our negligence law. Thus in a concurring opinion, Brett, M.R. in Heaven v. Pender (1883) 11 Q.B.D. 503, 509, states: "whenever one person is by circumstances placed in such a position with regard to another that every one of ordinary sense who did think would at once recognise that if he did not use ordinary care and skill in his own conduct with regard to those circumstances he would cause danger of injury to the person or property of the other, a duty arises to use ordinary care and skill to avoid such danger."

California cases have occasionally stated a similar view: "All persons are required to use ordinary care to prevent others being injured as the result of their conduct." (Hilyar v. Union Ice Co., 45 Cal.2d 30, 36, 286 P.2d 21; Warner v. Santa Catalina Island Co., 44 Cal.2d 310, 317, 282 P.2d 12; . . . cf. Dillon v. Legg, Cal., 69 Cal. Rptr. 72, 76, 441 P.2d 912, 916.) Although it is true that some exceptions have been made to the general principle that a person is liable for injuries caused by his failure to exercise reasonable care in the circumstances, it is clear that in the absence of statutory provision declaring an exception to the fundamental principle enunciated by section 1714 of the Civil Code, no such exception should be made unless clearly supported by public policy.

A departure from this fundamental principle involves the balancing of a number of considerations; the major ones are the foreseeability of harm to the plaintiff, the degree of certainty that the plaintiff suffered injury, the closeness of the connection between the defendant's conduct and the injury suffered, the moral blame attached to the defendant's conduct, the policy of preventing future harm, the extent of the burden to the defendant and consequences to the community of imposing a duty to exercise care with resulting liability for breach, and the availability, cost, and prevalence of insurance for the risk involved.

One of the areas where this court and other courts have departed from the fundamental concept that a man is liable for injuries caused by his carelessness is with regard to the liability of a possessor of land for injuries to persons who have entered upon that land. It has been suggested that the special rules regarding liability of the possessor of land are due to historical considerations stemming from the high place which land has traditionally held in English and American thought, the dominance and prestige of the landowning class in England during the formative period of the rules governing the possessor's liability, and the heritage of feudalism. (2 Harper and James, The Law of Torts, supra, p. 1432.)

The departure from the fundamental rule of liability for negligence has been accomplished by classifying the plaintiff either as a trespasser, licensee, or invitee and then adopting special rules as to the duty owed by the possessor to each of the classifications. Generally speaking a trespasser is a person who enters or remains upon land of another without a privilege to do so; a licensee is a person like a social guest who is not an invitee and who is privileged to enter or remain upon land by virtue of the possessor's consent, and an invitee is a business visitor who is invited or permitted to enter or remain on the land for a purpose directly or indirectly connected with business dealings between them.

Although the invitor owes the invitee a duty to exercise ordinary care to avoid injuring him, the general rule is that a trespasser and licensee or social guest are obliged to take the premises as they find them insofar as any alleged defective condition thereon may exist, and that the possessor of the land owes them only the duty of refraining from wanton or willful injury. The ordinary justification for the general rule severely restricting the occupier's liability to social guests is based on the theory that the guest should not expect special precautions to be made on his account and that if the host does not inspect and maintain his property the guest should not expect this to be done on his account.

An increasing regard for human safety has led to a retreat from this position, and an exception to the general rule limiting liability has been made as to active operations where an obligation to exercise reasonable care for the protection of the licensee has been imposed on the occupier of land. In an apparent attempt to avoid the general rule limiting liability, courts have broadly defined active operations, sometimes giving the term a strained construction in cases involving dangers known to the occupier.

Thus in Hansen v. Richey, 237 Cal. App. 2d 475, 481, 46 Cal. Rptr. 909, 913, an action for wrongful death of a drowned youth, the court held that liability could be predicated not upon the maintenance of a dangerous swimming pool but upon negligence 'in the active conduct of a party for a large number of youthful guests in the light of knowledge of the dangerous pool.' In Howard v. Howard, 186 Cal. App. 2d 622, 625, 9 Cal. Rptr. 311, where plaintiff was injured by slipping on spilled grease, active negligence was found on the ground that the defendant requested the plaintiff to enter the kitchen by a route which he knew would be dangerous and defective and that the defendant failed to warn her of the dangerous condition. . . .

Another exception to the general rule limiting liability has been recognized for cases where the occupier is aware of the dangerous condition, the condition amounts to a concealed trap, and the guest is unaware of the trap. (See Loftus v. Dehail, 133 Cal. 214, 217-218, 65 P. 379; Anderson v. Anderson, supra, 251 Cal. App. 2d 409, 412, 59 Cal. Rptr. 342; Hansen v. Richey, supra, 237 Cal. App. 2d 475, 489-490, 46 Cal. Rptr. 909. . . .) In none of these cases, however, did the court impose liability on the basis of a concealed trap; in some liability was found on another theory, and in others the court concluded that there was no trap. . . .

The cases dealing with the active negligence and the trap exceptions are indicative of the subtleties and confusion which have resulted from application of the common law principles governing the liability of the possessor of land. Similar confusion and complexity exist as to the definitions of trespasser, licensee, and invitee.

. . . .

The courts of this state have . . . recognized the failings of the common law rules relating to the liability of the owner and occupier of land. In refusing to apply the law of invitees, licensees, and trespassers to determine the liability of an independent contractor hired by the occupier, we pointed out that application of those rules was difficult and often arbitrary. In refusing to apply the common law rules to a known trespasser on an automobile, the common law rules were characterized as "unrealistic, arbitrary, and inelastic," and it was pointed out that exceedingly fine distinctions had been developed resulting in confusion and that many recent cases have in fact applied the general doctrine of negligence embodied in section 1714 of the Civil Code rather than the rigid common law categories test [Quoted authority omitted — Eds.]. . . .

There is another fundamental objection to the approach to the question of the possessor's liability on the basis of the common law distinctions based upon the status of the injured party as a trespasser, licensee, or invitee. Complexity can be borne and confusion remedied where the underlying principles governing liability are based upon proper considerations. Whatever may have been the historical justifications for the common law distinctions, it is clear that those distinctions are not justified in the light of our modern society and that the complexity and confusion which has arisen is not due to difficulty in applying the original common law rules — they are all too easy to apply in their original formulation — but is due to the attempts to apply just rules in our modern society within the ancient terminology.

Without attempting to labor all of the rules relating to the possessor's liability, it is apparent that the classifications of trespasser, licensee, and invitee, the immunities from liability predicated upon those classifications, and the exceptions to those immunities, often do not reflect the major factors which should determine whether immunity should be conferred upon the possessor of land. Some of those factors, including the closeness of the connection between the injury and the defendant's conduct, the moral blame attached to the defendant's conduct, the policy of preventing future harm, and the prevalence and availability of insurance, bear little, if any, relationship to the classifications of trespasser, licensee and invitee and the existing rules conferring immunity.

Although in general there may be a relationship between the remaining factors and the classifications of trespasser, licensee, and invitee, there are many cases in which no such relationship may exist. Thus, although the foreseeability of harm to an invitee would ordinarily seem greater than the foreseeability of harm to a trespasser, in a particular case the opposite may be true. The same may be said of the issue of certainty of injury. The burden to the defendant and consequences to the community of imposing a duty to exercise care with resulting liability for breach may often be greater with respect to trespassers than with respect to invitees, but it by no means follows that this is true in every case. In many situations, the burden will be the same, i.e., the conduct necessary upon the defendant's part to meet the burden of exercising due care as to invitees will also meet his burden with respect to licensees and trespassers. The last of the major factors, the cost of insurance, will, of course, vary depending upon the rules of liability adopted, but there is no persuasive evidence that applying ordinary principles of negligence law to the land occupier's liability will materially reduce the prevalence of insurance due to increased cost or even substantially increase the cost.

Considerations such as these have led some courts in particular situations to reject the rigid common law classifications and to approach the issue of the duty of the occupier on the basis of ordinary principles of negligence. And the common law distinctions after thorough study have been repudiated by the jurisdiction of their birth. (Occupiers' Liability Act, 1957, 5 and 6 Eliz. 2, ch. 31.)*

A man's life or limb does not become less worthy of protection by the law nor a loss less worthy of compensation under the law because he has come upon the land of another without permission or with permission but without a business purpose. Reasonable people do not ordinarily vary their conduct depending upon such matters, and to focus upon the status of the injured party as a trespasser, licensee, or invitee in order to determine the question whether the landowner has a duty of care, is contrary to our modern social mores and humanitarian values. The common law rules obscure rather than illuminate the proper considerations which should govern determination of the question of duty.

It bears repetition that the basic policy of this state set forth by the Legislature in section 1714 of the Civil Code is that everyone is responsible for an injury caused to another by his want of ordinary care or skill in the management of his property. The factors which may in particular cases warrant departure from this fundamental principle do not warrant the wholesale immunities resulting from the common law classifications, and we are satisfied that continued adherence to the common law distinctions can only lead to injustice or, if we are to avoid injustice, further fictions with the resulting complexity and confusion. We decline to follow and perpetuate such rigid classifications. The proper test to be applied to the liability of the possessor of land in accordance with section 1714 of the Civil Code is whether in the management of his property he has acted as a reasonable man in view of the probability of injury to others, and, although the plaintiff's status as a trespasser, licensee, or invitee may in the light of the facts giving rise to such status have some bearing on the question of liability, the status is not determinative.

Once the ancient concepts as to the liability of the occupier of land are stripped away, the status of the plaintiff relegated to its proper place in determining such liability, and ordinary principles of negligence applied, the result in the instant case presents no substantial difficulties. As we have seen, when we view the matters presented on the motion for summary judgment as we must, we must assume defendant Miss Christian was aware that the faucet handle was defective and dangerous, that the defect was not obvious, and that plaintiff was about to come in contact with the defective condition, and under the undisputed facts she neither remedied the condition nor warned plaintiff of it. Where the occupier of land is aware of a concealed condition involving in the absence of precautions an unreasonable risk of harm to those coming in contact with it and is aware that a person on the premises is about to

* [The Occupiers Liability Act eliminated in English law the distinction between invitees and licensees, recognizing a "common duty" to take reasonable care to maintain safe premises that is owed by possessors of land to all "visitors" (i.e., all permitted entrants). The Act did *not* extend this duty to trespassers. A later piece of legislation, the Occupiers' Liability Act of 1984, imposed on possessors a duty to take reasonable measures to protect trespassers against dangers on the possessor's premises if (1) the possessor knows or should know of the danger; (2) the possessor knows or should know that a trespasser is near or may come near the danger; and (3) the danger is one against which an occupier can reasonably be expected to offer trespassers some protection. — EDS.]

come in contact with it, the trier of fact can reasonably conclude that a failure to warn or to repair the condition constitutes negligence. Whether or not a guest has a right to expect that his host will remedy dangerous conditions on his account, he should reasonably be entitled to rely upon a warning of the dangerous condition so that he, like the host, will be in a position to take special precautions when he comes in contact with it.

It may be noted that by carving further exceptions out of the traditional rules relating to the liability to licensees or social guests, other jurisdictions reach the same result, that by continuing to adhere to the strained construction of active negligence or possibly, by applying the trap doctrine the result would be reached on the basis of some California precedents and that the result might even be reached by a continued expansion of the definition of the term 'invitee' to include all persons invited upon the land who may thereby be led to believe that the host will exercise for their protection the ordinary care of a reasonable man. However, to approach the problem in these manners would only add to the confusion, complexity, and fictions which have resulted from the common law distinctions.

The judgment is reversed.

BURKE, J., dissenting (joined by MCCOMB, J.). I dissent. In determining the liability of the occupier or owner of land for injuries, the distinctions between trespassers, licensees and invitees have been developed and applied by the courts over a period of many years. They supply a reasonable and workable approach to the problems involved, and one which provides the degree of stability and predictability so highly prized in the law. The unfortunate alternative, it appears to me, is the route taken by the majority in their opinion in this case; that such issues are to be decided on a case by case basis under the application of the basic law of negligence, bereft of the guiding principles and precedent which the law has heretofore attached by virtue of the relationship of the parties to one another.

Liability for negligence turns upon whether a duty of care is owed, and if so, the extent thereof. Who can doubt that the corner grocery, the large department store, or the financial institution owes a greater duty of care to one whom it has invited to enter its premises as a prospective customer of its wares or services than it owes to a trespasser seeking to enter after the close of business hours and for a nonbusiness or even an antagonistic purpose? I do not think it unreasonable or unfair that a social guest (classified by the law as a licensee, as was plaintiff here) should be obliged to take the premises in the same condition as his host finds them or permits them to be. Surely a homeowner should not be obliged to hover over his guests with warnings of possible dangers to be found in the condition of the home (e.g., waxed floors, slipping rugs, toys in unexpected places, etc.). Yet today's decision appears to open the door to potentially unlimited liability despite the purpose and circumstances motivating the plaintiff in entering the premises of another, and despite the caveat of the majority that the status of the parties may "have some bearing on the question of liability . . . ," whatever the future may show that language to mean.

In my view, it is not a proper function of this court to overturn the learning, wisdom and experience of the past in this field. Sweeping modifications of tort liability law fall more suitably within the domain of the Legislature, before which all affected interests can be heard and which can enact statutes providing uniform standards and guidelines for the future.

. . . .

NOTES AND QUESTIONS

1. *Civil Law and Common Law.* Many continental countries, including France and Germany, have legal systems based on civil law rather than common law principles. In these jurisdictions, legal rules are deemed to derive their authority exclusively from statutory law, and not from judicial precedents. What significance does the *Rowland* majority attribute to Cal. Civ. Code § 1714's pronouncement that "[e]very one is responsible . . . for an injury occasioned to another by his want of ordinary care or skill in the management of his property or person. . . ."? Would the court have reached a different result in the absence of this provision?

2. *Premises Liability: Privileging Property Owners?* If, as *Rowland* seems to suppose, California statutory and common law had long recognized that each person acts under a general duty of reasonable care to avoid causing any sort of harm to others, what, according to the court, explains the recognition in California premises liability decisions prior to 1968 of limited-duty rules such as the rule of no duty to trespassers? What policies or values were being advanced by the enforcement of these "exceptions" to the general duty of care? Is it plausible to suppose that nineteenth- and early-twentieth-century California courts adhered to special duty rules for trespassers and licensees because they were anxious to uphold feudal or aristocratic views of the privileges to which landowners are entitled?

3. *The Rowland Factors.* Examine each of the seven "considerations" or "factors" identified by the *Rowland* court as relevant to the determination of whether an exception to the general duty of care ought to be recognized. What is the court's basis for focusing on these factors? Is each of them appropriately included in the mix? Can you think of others that ought to be considered but are not on the list? *Rowland*'s framing of the duty issue in negligence cases—whether, on balance, policy factors warrant an exemption to the presumptive duty of care that attaches to conduct or possession—has been very influential in and outside of California.

What if some of the factors (e.g., availability of insurance, modest consequences for the community) counsel against granting a no-duty exemption, while others (e.g., improbability of deterrence) favor it? For situations such as these, courts often invoke metaphors of "balancing." What does it mean, really, to balance these sorts of considerations? How is a judge supposed to assign a "weight" to each factor? What information should courts have before them when applying factors such as "consequences for the community," "deterrence," and "availability of insurance"?

Does *Rowland*'s manner of framing the duty question subtly or unsubtly change the duty inquiry? In cases like *Heaven* and *MacPherson*, the duty question concerned whether a person in the position of the defendant was obligated to behave in a certain way toward persons such as the plaintiff. In *Rowland*, the question seems to be whether, on balance, society would be better off if persons such as the defendant were held liable to persons such as the plaintiff? Are these different questions?

4. *Ducking the Problem?* The *Rowland* majority asserts that the traditional rules of duty in premises liability cases are too complex and confusing to be maintained, particularly in light of the values they seem to serve. Does the court's preferred approach provide clearer directives to possessors of property in terms of what sort of maintenance or warnings are now expected of them? Why or why not? Does *Rowland* clarify the law, or does it sweep some of its complexities under the carpet by asking juries to make case-by-case judgments as to what will count as reasonably safe premises?

5. *Judge and Jury.* Procedurally, *Rowland*'s greatest significance is that it eliminates a set of doctrines that had empowered judges to take certain cases away from juries by granting defense motions to dismiss or for summary judgment. (*See* Chapter 1, Section II.D.) After *Rowland*, judges presiding over premises liability claims presumably should never dismiss such suits on no-duty grounds, for it is precisely *Rowland*'s holding that there is always a duty owed by a property possessor to anyone who comes onto her land, no matter what the circumstances of the entry. In principle, then, *Rowland*, like other duty-expanding cases such as *MacPherson*, marks a transfer of power from judge to jury.

6. *Duty Versus Breach.* Notice that *Rowland* does not entirely eliminate from premises liability suits consideration of the plaintiff's status with respect to the defendant's property. Rather, it maintains that status can have "some bearing" on the issue of breach — i.e., the issue of whether the defendant's property was or was not in a reasonably safe condition at the time of the accident. Given the court's decision to banish the traditional common law distinctions from the realm of duty, why did it permit them to re-enter the inquiry under the heading of breach? In what way is the plaintiff's status relevant to an assessment of the dangerousness of defendant's premises? If a homeowner's front steps pose a danger to anyone who uses them (e.g., because they are slippery or uneven), what would permit a jury to declare them to be unreasonably dangerous when an invited guest slips on them, yet reasonably safe when a trespasser slips on them?

7. *Rowland's Egalitarianism.* In one of *Rowland*'s more powerful passages, the majority opinion asserts that "[a] man's life or limb does not become less worthy of protection by the law nor a loss less worthy of compensation under the law because he has come upon the land of another without permission or with permission but without a business purpose." The suggestion is that the traditional rules governing duty in premises liability cases are a product of older, hierarchical societies, whereas the new rule reflects modern, egalitarian principles. Is this suggestion convincing? In order to embrace the older approach, must one deem a trespasser's life and limb as less worthy in a general moral sense? Can one assert that a trespasser is not entitled to expect of a landowner the same amount of care for his well-being as an invited guest without deeming the trespasser's life less worthy?

8. *Scope of the Rowland Duty: Criminal Trespassers and the Legislative Response.* Consider the potential breadth of *Rowland*'s recognition of a general duty of reasonable

care owed to all persons who enter property, whether by permission or not. Suppose a burglar is injured in the process of stealing possessions from defendant's home when a poorly maintained external stairway gives out from under him. Under *Rowland*'s approach, a duty of care was owed, and thus a jury could in principle subject the homeowner to liability to the burglar. Out of concern for such a possibility, the California legislature in 1985 enacted Civil Code Section 847, which immunizes possessors from liability to trespassers injured on the premises in the course of committing certain classes of felonies. As mentioned in Note 9 following *Leffler v. Sharp*, *supra*, the Third Restatement of Torts advocates an approach that, by adopting a no-duty-of-reasonable-care rule for "flagrant trespassers," resembles the regime created in California by the combination of *Rowland* and Section 847.

9. Recreational Uses and Ornelas. Even before *Rowland* was decided, the California legislature had sought to protect certain property owners from premises liability claims. Thus, in 1963, it enacted Civil Code Section 846, a so-called recreational use statute. Under Section 846, a property owner or possessor owes no duty to be careful to keep the premises safe for *recreational use* by others unless the user is a paying customer (e.g., a patron at an amusement park) or the landowner has expressly invited, rather than merely permitted, use of the property by the recreational user. In effect, then, an owner's or possessor's duty to a nonpaying, uninvited-but-permitted recreational user is the same duty owed to a trespasser under the pre-*Rowland* common law rules — i.e., a duty merely to refrain from willfully injuring the user. The central purpose of Section 846 is to protect from liability owners who passively permit some of their lands to be used for activities such as biking, hiking, horse-riding, fishing, and ice-skating.

In *Ornelas v. Randolph*, 847 P.2d 560 (Cal. 1993), the California Supreme Court considered the breadth of "recreational use" immunity created by the statute. Along with several friends, plaintiff, an eight-year-old boy, entered a part of defendant's property on which old farm machinery sat. While plaintiff's friends were playing on some machinery, they dislodged a pipe that fell on and injured the plaintiff. Plaintiff argued that, even if he and his friends were engaged in recreation, the statute should not apply to his claim because it was meant to encourage private landowners to allow recreational activities on their properties, not to grant them a windfall just because a person who is injured on their property happened to be engaged in recreation at the moment of injury. The court rejected this reading of the statute, ruling that it applies to any (uninvited) recreational use of land, regardless of whether the land is suited to recreational use or typically used recreationally.

It seems likely that, under the traditional duty schema, Ornelas, even though he was a trespasser, might have been able to recover from Randolph under the old attractive nuisance doctrine. *See* Note 5 following *Leffler*, *supra*. Is it reasonable to believe that the California legislature meant in 1963 to leave minor plaintiffs like Ornelas worse off in terms of their rights to redress than they were under the law of the late nineteenth century? Professor Keating and his co-author Esper have suggested that *Ornelas* in fact marks a renunciation of the egalitarian and progressive commitments of *Rowland* by a California Supreme Court that, since 1980, has taken a decidedly "conservative" turn.

10. Whither the Revolution? *Rowland* has proved to be an influential decision in California and elsewhere, though more for its progressive tone and its general approach to thinking about duty issues than its elimination of the plaintiff status categories. Between 1968 and 1980, courts in seven other states adopted *Rowland*'s complete abolition of the traditional duty categories. However, since 1980 only one other state has followed suit, while two of the original seven have modified their law to reassert the no-duty rule for adult trespassers. *See* Alexander v. Medical Associates Clinic, 646 N.W.2d 74 (Iowa 2002) (surveying case law and declining to follow *Rowland*: "we remain unconvinced that the rights of property owners have so little value in today's society that those rights should be diminished in favor of persons trespassing on another's land. The common law standard is just as viable today as it was a century ago: a landowner has a duty not to injure a trespasser maliciously or deliberately, and to use reasonable care after the trespasser's presence becomes known to avoid injuring the trespasser.").

Tarasoff v. The Regents of the University of California

551 P.2d 334 (Cal. 1976)

TOBRINER, J. On October 27, 1969, Prosenjit Poddar killed Tatiana Tarasoff. Plaintiffs, Tatiana's parents, allege that two months earlier Poddar confided his intention to kill Tatiana to Dr. Lawrence Moore, a psychologist employed by the Cowell Memorial Hospital at the University of California at Berkeley. They allege that on Moore's request, the campus police briefly detained Poddar, but released him when he appeared rational. They further claim that Dr. Harvey Powelson, Moore's superior, then directed that no further action be taken to detain Poddar. No one warned plaintiffs of Tatiana's peril.

Concluding that these facts set forth causes of action against neither therapists and policemen involved, nor against the Regents of the University of California as their employer, the superior court sustained defendants' demurrers to plaintiffs' second amended complaints without leave to amend.[2] This appeal ensued.

Plaintiffs' complaints predicate liability on two grounds: defendants' failure to warn plaintiffs of the impending danger and their failure to bring about Poddar's confinement pursuant to [California statutory provisions specifying the conditions under which persons can be involuntarily committed for psychological treatment]. Defendants, in turn, assert that they owed no duty of reasonable care to Tatiana and that they are immune from suit under the California Tort Claims Act of 1963.

2. The therapist defendants include Dr. Moore, the psychologist who examined Poddar and decided that Poddar should be committed; Dr. Gold and Dr. Yandell, psychiatrists at Cowell Memorial Hospital who concurred in Moore's decision; and Dr. Powelson, chief of the department of psychiatry, who countermanded Moore's decision and directed that the staff take no action to confine Poddar. The police defendants include Officers Atkinson, Brownrigg and Halleran, who detained Poddar briefly but released him; Chief Beall, who received Moore's letter recommending that Poddar be confined; and Officer Teel, who, along with Officer Atkinson, received Moore's oral communication requesting detention of Poddar.

We shall explain that defendant therapists cannot escape liability merely because Tatiana herself was not their patient. When a therapist determines, or pursuant to the standards of his profession should determine, that his patient presents a serious danger of violence to another, he incurs an obligation to use reasonable care to protect the intended victim against such danger. The discharge of this duty may require the therapist to take one or more of various steps, depending upon the nature of the case. Thus it may call for him to warn the intended victim or others likely to apprise the victim of the danger, to notify the police, or to take whatever other steps are reasonably necessary under the circumstances.

In the case at bar, plaintiffs admit that defendant therapists notified the police, but argue on appeal that the therapists failed to exercise reasonable care to protect Tatiana in that they did not confine Poddar and did not warn Tatiana or others likely to apprise her of the danger. Defendant therapists, however, are public employees. Consequently, [they enjoy statutory immunity for certain "discretionary" acts, including their failure to confine Poddar]. No . . . statutory provision, however, shields them from liability based upon failure to warn Tatiana or others likely to apprise her of the danger. . . .

Plaintiffs therefore can amend their complaints to allege that, regardless of the therapists' unsuccessful attempt to confine Poddar, since they knew that Poddar was at large and dangerous, their failure to warn Tatiana or others likely to apprise her of the danger constituted a breach of the therapists' duty to exercise reasonable care to protect Tatiana.

Plaintiffs, however, plead no relationship between Poddar and the police defendants which would impose upon them any duty to Tatiana, and plaintiffs suggest no other basis for such a duty. Plaintiffs have, therefore, failed to show that the trial court erred in sustaining the demurrer of the police defendants without leave to amend.

1. Plaintiffs' Complaints . . .

Plaintiffs' first cause of action, entitled "Failure to Detain a Dangerous Patient," alleges that on August 20, 1969, Poddar was a voluntary outpatient receiving therapy at Cowell Memorial Hospital. Poddar informed Moore, his therapist, that he was going to kill an unnamed girl, readily identifiable as Tatiana, when she returned home from spending the summer in Brazil. Moore, with the concurrence of Dr. Gold, who had initially examined Poddar, and Dr. Yandell, assistant to the director of the department of psychiatry, decided that Poddar should be committed for observation in a mental hospital. Moore orally notified Officers Atkinson and Teel of the campus police that he would request commitment. He then sent a letter to Police Chief William Beall requesting the assistance of the police department in securing Poddar's confinement.

Officers Atkinson, Brownrigg, and Halleran took Poddar into custody, but, satisfied that Poddar was rational, released him on his promise to stay away from Tatiana. Powelson, director of the department of psychiatry at Cowell Memorial Hospital, then asked the police to return Moore's letter, directed that all copies of the letter and notes that Moore had taken as therapist be destroyed, and "ordered no action to place Prosenjit Poddar in 72-hour treatment and evaluation facility."

Plaintiffs' second cause of action, entitled "Failure to Warn on a Dangerous Patient," incorporates the allegations of the first cause of action, but adds the assertion that defendants negligently permitted Poddar to be released from police custody without "notifying the parents of Tatiana Tarasoff that their daughter was in grave danger from Prosenjit Poddar." Poddar persuaded Tatiana's brother to share an apartment with him near Tatiana's residence; shortly after her return from Brazil, Poddar went to her residence and killed her. . . .

2. *Plaintiffs Can State a Cause of Action Against Defendant Therapists for Negligent Failure to Protect Tatiana*

The second cause of action can be amended to allege that Tatiana's death proximately resulted from defendants' negligent failure to warn Tatiana or others likely to apprise her of her danger. . . . Defendants, however, contend that in the circumstances of the present case they owed no duty of care to Tatiana or her parents and that, in the absence of such duty, they were free to act in careless disregard of Tatiana's life and safety.

In analyzing this issue, we bear in mind that legal duties are not discoverable facts of nature, but merely conclusory expressions that, in cases of a particular type, liability should be imposed for damage done. As stated in Dillon v. Legg (1968) 441 P.2d 912, 916: "The assertion that liability must . . . be denied because defendant bears no 'duty' to plaintiff 'begs the essential question — whether the plaintiff's interests are entitled to legal protection against the defendant's conduct. . . . (Duty) is not sacrosanct in itself, but only an expression of the sum total of those considerations of policy which lead the law to say that the particular plaintiff is entitled to protection.' (Prosser, Law of Torts (3d ed. 1964) at pp. 332-333.)"

In the landmark case of Rowland v. Christian (1968) 443 P.2d 561, Justice Peters recognized that liability should be imposed "for an injury occasioned to another by his want of ordinary care or skill" as expressed in section 1714 of the Civil Code. Thus, Justice Peters, quoting from Heaven v. Pender (1883) 11 Q.B.D. 503, 509 stated: "whenever one person is by circumstances placed in such a position with regard to another . . . that if he did not use ordinary care and skill in his own conduct . . . he would cause danger of injury to the person or property of the other, a duty arises to use ordinary care and skill to avoid such danger."

We depart from "this fundamental principle" only upon the "balancing of a number of considerations"; major ones "are the foreseeability of harm to the plaintiff, the degree of certainty that the plaintiff suffered injury, the closeness of the connection between the defendant's conduct and the injury suffered, the moral blame attached to the defendant's conduct, the policy of preventing future harm, the extent of the burden to the defendant and consequences to the community of imposing a duty to exercise care with resulting liability for breach, and the availability, cost and prevalence of insurance for the risk involved."

The most important of these considerations in establishing duty is foreseeability. As a general principle, a "defendant owes a duty of care to all persons who are foreseeably endangered by his conduct, with respect to all risks which make the conduct unreasonably dangerous." [Quoted authority omitted. — EDS.] As we shall explain, however, when the avoidance of foreseeable harm requires a defendant to control the conduct of another person, or to warn of such conduct, the common law has traditionally imposed liability only if the defendant bears some special relationship to the dangerous person or to the potential victim. Since the relationship between a therapist and his patient satisfies this requirement, we need not here decide whether foreseeability alone is sufficient to create a duty to exercise reasonably [sic] care to protect a potential victim of another's conduct.

Although, as we have stated above, under the common law, as a general rule, one person owed no duty to control the conduct of another,[5] nor to warn those endangered by such conduct, the courts have carved out an exception to this rule in cases in which the defendant stands in some special relationship to either the person whose conduct needs to be controlled or in a relationship to the foreseeable victim of that conduct. Applying this exception to the present case, we note that a relationship of defendant therapists to either Tatiana or Poddar will suffice to establish a duty of care; as explained in section 315 of the Restatement Second of Torts, a duty of care may arise from either "(a) a special relation . . . between the actor and the third person which imposes a duty upon the actor to control the third person's conduct, or (b) a special relation . . . between the actor and the other which gives to the other a right of protection." Although plaintiffs' pleadings assert no special relation between Tatiana and defendant therapists, they establish as between Poddar and defendant therapists the special relation that arises between a patient and his doctor or psychotherapist. Such a relationship may support affirmative duties for the benefit of third persons. Thus, for example, a hospital must exercise reasonable care to control the behavior of a patient which may endanger other persons.[7] A doctor must also warn a patient if the patient's condition or medication renders certain conduct, such as driving a car, dangerous to others.[8]

Although the California decisions that recognize this duty have involved cases in which the defendant stood in a special relationship both to the victim and to the person

---

5. This rule derives from the common law's distinction between misfeasance and nonfeasance, and its reluctance to impose liability for the latter. Morally questionable, the rule owes its survival to "the difficulties of setting any standards of unselfish service to fellow men, and of making any workable rule to cover possible situations where fifty people might fail to rescue . . ." (Prosser, Torts (4th ed. 1971) § 56, p. 341). Because of these practical difficulties, the courts have increased the number of instances in which affirmative duties are imposed not by direct rejection of the common law rule, but by expanding the list of special relationships which will justify departure from that rule.

7. When a "hospital has notice or knowledge of facts from which it might reasonably be concluded that a patient would be likely to harm himself *or others* unless preclusive measures were taken, then the hospital must use reasonable care in the circumstances to prevent such harm." (Vistica v. Presbyterian Hospital (1967) 432 P.2d 193, 196.) (Emphasis added.) A mental hospital may be liable if it negligently permits the escape or release of a dangerous patient (Semler v. Psychiatric Institute of Washington, D.C. (4th Cir. 1976) 44 U.S.L. Week 2439; Underwood v. United States (5th Cir. 1966) 356 F.2d 92; Fair v. United States (5th Cir. 1956) 234 F.2d 288). Greenberg v. Barbour (E.D. Pa. 1971) 322 F. Supp. 745, upheld a cause of action against a hospital staff doctor whose negligent failure to admit a mental patient resulted in that patient assaulting the plaintiff.

8. Kaiser v. Suburban Transp. System (1965) 65 Wash. 2d 461, 398 P.2d 14; *see* Freese v. Lemmon (Iowa 1973) 210 N.W.2d 576 (concurring opn. of Uhlenhopp, J.).

whose conduct created the danger,[9] we do not think that the duty should logically be constricted to such situations. Decisions of other jurisdictions hold that the single relationship of a doctor to his patient is sufficient to support the duty to exercise reasonable care to protect others against dangers emanating from the patient's illness. The courts hold that a doctor is liable to persons infected by his patient if he negligently fails to diagnose a contagious disease, or, having diagnosed the illness, fails to warn members of the patient's family.

Since it involved a dangerous mental patient, the decision in Merchants Nat. Bank & Trust Co. of Fargo v. United States (D.N.D. 1967) 272 F. Supp. 409 comes closer to the issue. The Veterans Administration arranged for the patient to work on a local farm, but did not inform the farmer of the man's background. The farmer consequently permitted the patient to come and go freely during nonworking hours; the patient borrowed a car, drove to his wife's residence and killed her. Notwithstanding the lack of any "special relationship" between the Veterans Administration and the wife, the court found the Veterans Administration liable for the wrongful death of the wife. . . .

Defendants contend, however, that imposition of a duty to exercise reasonable care to protect third persons is unworkable because therapists cannot accurately predict whether or not a patient will resort to violence. In support of this argument amicus representing the American Psychiatric Association and other professional societies cites numerous articles which indicate that therapists, in the present state of the art, are unable reliably to predict violent acts; their forecasts, amicus claims, tend consistently to overpredict violence, and indeed are more often wrong than right. Since predictions of violence are often erroneous, amicus concludes, the courts should not render rulings that predicate the liability of therapists upon the validity of such predictions. . . .

We recognize the difficulty that a therapist encounters in attempting to forecast whether a patient presents a serious danger of violence. Obviously we do not require that the therapist, in making that determination, render a perfect performance; the therapist need only exercise "that reasonable degree of skill, knowledge, and care ordinarily possessed and exercised by members of (that professional specialty) under similar circumstances." Within the broad range of reasonable practice and treatment in which professional opinion and judgment may differ, the therapist is free to exercise his or her own best judgment without liability; proof, aided by hindsight, that he or she judged wrongly is insufficient to establish negligence.

In the instant case, however, the pleadings do not raise any question as to failure of defendant therapists to predict that Poddar presented a serious danger of violence. On

9. Ellis v. D'Angelo (1953) 116 Cal. App. 2d 310, 253 P.2d 675, upheld a cause of action against parents who failed to warn a babysitter of the violent proclivities of their child; Johnson v. State of California (1968) 69 Cal. 2d 782, 73 Cal. Rptr. 240, 447 P.2d 352, upheld a suit against the state for failure to warn foster parents of the dangerous tendencies of their ward; Morgan v. City of Yuba (1964) 230 Cal. App. 2d 938, 41 Cal. Rptr. 508, sustained a cause of action against a sheriff who had promised to warn decedent before releasing a dangerous prisoner, but failed to do so.

the contrary, the present complaints allege that defendant therapists did in fact predict that Poddar would kill, but were negligent in failing to warn.

Amicus contends, however, that even when a therapist does in fact predict that a patient poses a serious danger of violence to others, the therapist should be absolved of any responsibility for failing to act to protect the potential victim. In our view, however, once a therapist does in fact determine, or under applicable professional standards reasonably should have determined, that a patient poses a serious danger of violence to others, he bears a duty to exercise reasonable care to protect the foreseeable victim of that danger. While the discharge of this duty of due care will necessarily vary with the facts of each case,[11] in each instance the adequacy of the therapist's conduct must be measured against the traditional negligence standard of the rendition of reasonable care under the circumstances. . . .

The risk that unnecessary warnings may be given is a reasonable price to pay for the lives of possible victims that may be saved. We would hesitate to hold that the therapist who is aware that his patient expects to attempt to assassinate the President of the United States would not be obligated to warn the authorities because the therapist cannot predict with accuracy that his patient will commit the crime.

Defendants further argue that free and open communication is essential to psychotherapy; that "Unless a patient . . . is assured that . . . information (revealed by him) can and will be held in utmost confidence, he will be reluctant to make the full disclosure upon which diagnosis and treatment . . . depends." (Sen. Com. on Judiciary, comment on Evid. Code, § 1014.) The giving of a warning, defendants contend, constitutes a breach of trust which entails the revelation of confidential communications.

We recognize the public interest in supporting effective treatment of mental illness and in protecting the rights of patients to privacy, and the consequent public importance of safeguarding the confidential character of psychotherapeutic communication. Against this interest, however, we must weigh the public interest in safety from violent assault. The Legislature has undertaken the difficult task of balancing the countervailing concerns. In Evidence Code section 1014, it established a broad rule of privilege to protect confidential communications between patient and psychotherapist. In . . . section 1024, the Legislature created a specific and limited exception to the psychotherapist-patient privilege: "There is no privilege . . . if the psychotherapist has reasonable cause to believe that the patient is in such mental or emotional condition as to be dangerous to himself or to the person or property of another and that disclosure of the communication is necessary to prevent the threatened danger."

We realize that the open and confidential character of psychotherapeutic dialogue encourages patients to express threats of violence, few of which are ever executed.

---

11. Defendant therapists and amicus also argue that warnings must be given only in those cases in which the therapist knows the identity of the victim. We recognize that in some cases it would be unreasonable to require the therapist to interrogate his patient to discover the victim's identity, or to conduct an independent investigation. But there may also be cases in which a moment's reflection will reveal the victim's identity. The matter thus is one which depends upon the circumstances of each case. . . .

Certainly a therapist should not be encouraged routinely to reveal such threats; such disclosures could seriously disrupt the patient's relationship with his therapist and with the persons threatened. To the contrary, the therapist's obligations to his patient require that he not disclose a confidence unless such disclosure is necessary to avert danger to others, and even then that he do so discreetly, and in a fashion that would preserve the privacy of his patient to the fullest extent compatible with the prevention of the threatened danger.

The revelation of a communication under the above circumstances is not a breach of trust or a violation of professional ethics; as stated in the Principles of Medical Ethics of the American Medical Association (1957), section 9: "A physician may not reveal the confidence entrusted to him in the course of medical attendance . . . [u]nless he is required to do so by law or unless it becomes necessary in order to protect the welfare of the individual or of the community." We conclude that the public policy favoring protection of the confidential character of patient-psychotherapist communications must yield to the extent to which disclosure is essential to avert danger to others. The protective privilege ends where the public peril begins.

Our current crowded and computerized society compels the interdependence of its members. In this risk-infested society we can hardly tolerate the further exposure to danger that would result from a concealed knowledge of the therapist that his patient was lethal. If the exercise of reasonable care to protect the threatened victim requires the therapist to warn the endangered party or those who can reasonably be expected to notify him, we see no sufficient societal interest that would protect and justify concealment. The containment of such risks lies in the public interest. For the foregoing reasons, we find that plaintiffs' complaints can be amended to state a cause of action against defendants Moore, Powelson, Gold, and Yandell and against the Regents as their employer, for breach of a duty to exercise reasonable care to protect Tatiana. . . .

Turning now to the police defendants, we conclude that they do not have any such special relationship to either Tatiana or to Poddar sufficient to impose upon such defendants a duty to warn respecting Poddar's violent intentions. Plaintiffs suggest no theory, and plead no facts that give rise to any duty to warn on the part of the police defendants absent such a special relationship. They have thus failed to demonstrate that the trial court erred in denying leave to amend as to the police defendants.

3. *Defendant Therapists Are Not Immune from Liability for Failure to Warn*

[The court next concluded that a state statutory provision granting immunity from tort liability to public employees for their discretionary acts did not bar plaintiffs' claims against the therapist defendants for failure to warn. For a discussion of immunities for the performance of discretionary functions, *see* Chapter 7. However, the Court also concluded that other statutes granted the therapist and police defendants immunity from liability for failure to confine Poddar. — EDS.] . . .

MOSK, J. (concurring and dissenting). I concur in the result in this instance only because the complaints allege that defendant therapists did in fact predict that Poddar would kill and were therefore negligent in failing to warn of that danger. Thus the issue here is very narrow: we are not concerned with whether the therapists, pursuant to the standards of their profession, "should have" predicted potential violence; they allegedly did so in actuality. Under these limited circumstances I agree that a cause of action can be stated. . . .

Clark, J. (dissenting). [Justice Clark first asserted that the duty recognized by the majority was inconsistent with California statutory law protecting the confidentiality of patient-therapist communications. He next turned to the majority's common law analysis. — Eds.] Generally, a person owes no duty to control the conduct of another. Exceptions are recognized only in limited situations where (1) a special relationship exists between the defendant and injured party, or (2) a special relationship exists between defendant and the active wrongdoer, imposing a duty on defendant to control the wrongdoer's conduct. The majority does not contend the first exception is appropriate to this case.

Policy generally determines duty. Principal policy considerations include foreseeability of harm, certainty of the plaintiff's injury, proximity of the defendant's conduct to the plaintiff's injury, moral blame attributable to defendant's conduct, prevention of future harm, burden on the defendant, and consequences to the community.

Overwhelming policy considerations weigh against imposing a duty on psychotherapists to warn a potential victim against harm. While offering virtually no benefit to society, such a duty will frustrate psychiatric treatment, invade fundamental patient rights and increase violence.

The importance of psychiatric treatment and its need for confidentiality have been recognized by this court. . . .

Assurance of confidentiality is important for three reasons.

Deterrence from Treatment

First, without substantial assurance of confidentiality, those requiring treatment will be deterred from seeking assistance. It remains an unfortunate fact in our society that people seeking psychiatric guidance tend to become stigmatized. Apprehension of such stigma — apparently increased by the propensity of people considering treatment to see themselves in the worst possible light — creates a well-recognized reluctance to seek aid. This reluctance is alleviated by the psychiatrist's assurance of confidentiality.

Full Disclosure

Second, the guarantee of confidentiality is essential in eliciting the full disclosure necessary for effective treatment. The psychiatric patient approaches treatment with conscious and unconscious inhibitions against revealing his innermost thoughts. "Every person, however well-motivated, has to overcome resistances to therapeutic exploration. These resistances seek support from every possible source and the possibility of disclosure would easily be employed in the service of resistance."[Quoted authority omitted. — Eds.] Until a patient can trust his psychiatrist not to violate their confidential relationship, "the unconscious psychological control mechanism of repression will prevent the recall of past experiences." (Butler, Psychotherapy and *Griswold*: Is Confidentiality a Privilege or a Right? (1971) 3 Conn. L. Rev. 599, 604.)

SUCCESSFUL TREATMENT

Third, even if the patient fully discloses his thoughts, assurance that the confidential relationship will not be breached is necessary to maintain his trust in his psychiatrist — the very means by which treatment is effected. . . . Patients will be helped only if they can form a trusting relationship with the psychiatrist. All authorities appear to agree that if the trust relationship cannot be developed because of collusive communication between the psychiatrist and others, treatment will be frustrated.

Given the importance of confidentiality to the practice of psychiatry, it becomes clear the duty to warn imposed by the majority will cripple the use and effectiveness of psychiatry. Many people, potentially violent — yet susceptible to treatment — will be deterred from seeking it; those seeking it will be inhibited from making revelations necessary to effective treatment; and, forcing the psychiatrist to violate the patient's trust will destroy the interpersonal relationship by which treatment is effected.

VIOLENCE AND CIVIL COMMITMENT

By imposing a duty to warn, the majority contributes to the danger to society of violence by the mentally ill and greatly increases the risk of civil commitment — the total deprivation of liberty — of those who should not be confined. The impairment of treatment and risk of improper commitment resulting from the new duty to warn will not be limited to a few patients but will extend to a large number of the mentally ill. Although under existing psychiatric procedures only a relatively few receiving treatment will ever present a risk of violence, the number making threats is huge, and it is the latter group — not just the former — whose treatment will be impaired and whose risk of commitment will be increased.

Both the legal and psychiatric communities recognize that the process of determining potential violence in a patient is far from exact, being fraught with complexity and uncertainty. . . .[5] In fact precision has not even been attained in predicting who of those having already committed violent acts will again become violent, a task recognized to be of much simpler proportions.

This predictive uncertainty means that the number of disclosures will necessarily be large. As noted above, psychiatric patients are encouraged to discuss all thoughts of violence, and they often express such thoughts. However, unlike this court, the psychiatrist does not enjoy the benefit of overwhelming hindsight in seeing which few, if

5. A shocking illustration of psychotherapists' inability to predict dangerousness, cited by this court in People v. Burnick, . . . 14 Cal. 3d 306, 326–327, fn.17, is cited and discussed in Ennis, Prisoners of Psychiatry: Mental Patients, Psychiatrists, and the Law (1972): "In a well-known study, psychiatrists predicted that 989 persons were so dangerous that they . . . would have to be kept in maximum security hospitals. . . . Then, because of a United States Supreme Court decision, those persons were transferred to civil hospitals. After a year, the Department of Mental Hygiene reported that one-fifth of them had been discharged to the community, and over half had agreed to remain as voluntary patients. During the year, only 7 of the 989 committed or threatened any act that was sufficiently dangerous to require retransfer to the maximum security hospital. Seven correct predictions out of almost a thousand is not a very impressive record. . . . Other studies, and there are many, have reached the same conclusion: psychiatrists simply cannot predict dangerous behavior." (*Id.* at p. 227.) . . .

any, of his patients will ultimately become violent. Now, confronted by the majority's new duty, the psychiatrist must instantaneously calculate potential violence from each patient on each visit. The difficulties researchers have encountered in accurately predicting violence will be heightened for the practicing psychiatrist dealing for brief periods in his office with heretofore nonviolent patients. And, given the decision not to warn or commit must always be made at the psychiatrist's civil peril, one can expect most doubts will be resolved in favor of the psychiatrist protecting himself.

Neither alternative open to the psychiatrist seeking to protect himself is in the public interest. The warning itself is an impairment of the psychiatrist's ability to treat, depriving many patients of adequate treatment. It is to be expected that after disclosing their threats, a significant number of patients, who would not become violent if treated according to existing practices, will engage in violent conduct as a result of unsuccessful treatment. In short, the majority's duty to warn will not only impair treatment of many who would never become violent but worse, will result in a net increase in violence.

The second alternative open to the psychiatrist is to commit his patient rather than to warn. Even in the absence of threat of civil liability, the doubts of psychiatrists as to the seriousness of patient threats have led psychiatrists to overcommit to mental institutions. This overcommitment has been authoritatively documented in both legal and psychiatric studies. This practice is so prevalent that it has been estimated that "as many as twenty harmless persons are incarcerated for every one who will commit a violent act." (Steadman & Cocozza, Stimulus/Response: We Can't Predict Who Is Dangerous (Jan. 1975) 8 Psych. Today 32, 35.)

Given the incentive to commit created by the majority's duty, this already serious situation will be worsened. . . .

NOTES AND QUESTIONS

1. *More on Tarasoff.* Prosenjit Poddar's presence as a graduate student at Berkeley was quite extraordinary: he grew up in extreme poverty in India, where he and his family were deemed "untouchables." After the killing, Poddar was prosecuted for murder and for the lesser homicide crime of manslaughter. At the criminal trial, Dr. Moore testified on Poddar's behalf, maintaining that Poddar was legally insane at the time of the killing, and also that he suffered from "diminished capacity" (in that he could not appreciate his obligation to obey the law) and hence, if found sane, should be guilty only of manslaughter. The jury found that Poddar was sane, and convicted him of murder, for which crime he was sentenced to prison for a term of five years to life. However, the California Supreme Court reversed the conviction on the ground that the trial court had not given the jury sufficient leeway to find that Poddar had acted with diminished capacity and thus committed manslaughter rather than murder. People v. Poddar, 518 P.2d 342 (Cal. 1974). It was probably during the criminal trial that Tatiana's parents learned that Dr. Moore had ordered Poddar to be confined for observation.

The Supreme Court's 1976 opinion in the tort suit brought by the Tarasoffs, reproduced in part above, nowhere mentions that the court had two years earlier issued an opinion in the very same case ruling that the therapists could be held liable for failing to notify Tatiana or her parents about Poddar. Tarasoff v. Regents of the University of California, 529 P.2d. 553 (Cal. 1974). The 1974 opinion, unlike the 1976 opinion, also held that the police defendants could be held liable. The 1974 opinion was vacated after the court granted the defendants' motion for rehearing.

2. *The Special Obligations of Mental Health Professionals?* To what extent does *Tarasoff*'s holding rest on the superior ability of professional psychiatrists and psychologists to assess accurately the intentions of their patients? Suppose Poddar had confessed his intentions to his lawyer or his best friend. Under the majority's analysis, would either of them be under the same duty to warn Tatiana?

The California Supreme Court has declined to extend *Tarasoff* to clergy. *See* Nally v. Grace Cmty. Church of the Valley, 763 P.2d 948 (Cal. 1988). For decisions likewise declining to extend *Tarasoff, see* Koepke v. Loo, 23 Cal. Rptr. 2d 34 (Cal. App. 1993) (employer and former lover of assailant owes no duty to warn assailant's intended victim); Iseberg v. Gross, 852 N.E.2d 251 (Ill. App. 2006) (partner in real estate business owed no duty to warn other partner that a disgruntled investor had repeatedly threatened to kill the other); James v. Wilson, 95 S.W.3d 875 (Ky. App. 2002) (rejecting, on various grounds, claims of negligence brought on behalf of victims of a school shooting against parents, fellow students, and teachers of the shooters).

3. *Contagious Diseases.* Most states have statutes that require physicians who are aware of a patient having a contagious disease to report that fact to public health officials. The American Bar Association's Model Rules of Professional Conduct permit, but do not require, attorneys to warn nonclients whom they reasonably believe to be at risk of bodily harm or death from a client. A handful of states have adopted this rule in a modified form that requires attorneys to warn. However, violations of disciplinary rules generally do not generate private rights of action for nonclients but instead provide a basis for disciplinary action. Some courts have also recognized a duty on the part of a physician to protect immediate family members, as well as significant others, from contracting infectious diseases diagnosed in the patient. *See* DiMarco v. Lynch Homes-Chester County, 583 A.2d 422 (Pa. 1990) (physicians aware that nurse may have contracted hepatitis from accidental needle-stick owed duty to nurse's boyfriend to convey accurate information about duration of latency period for hepatitis). This duty to warn has sometimes been extended to cases in which the diagnosis suggests a heightened risk not from infection by the patient, but from the source that caused the patient's illness. *See* Bradshaw v. Daniel, 854 S.W.2d 865 (Tenn. 1993) (physician who diagnoses patient with Rocky Mountain spotted fever has duty to warn patient's family members that they may have been exposed to ticks carrying the disease).

4. *Duty and Causation.* Our concern in this chapter is the duty issue, but it is worth noting that many cases involving failure to warn raise difficult issues of causation. Consider, for example, a suit brought by *P*, who contracts an infectious disease from *Q*, a patient of physician *D*. Because *D* may be under legal requirements of confidentiality—and because *D* may be unaware of *P*'s existence—*P* would stand to benefit from the omitted warning only if (1) *D* transmitted a warning to *Q*; (2) *Q* informed *P* of the risk of infection; and (3) *Q* and *P* then altered their behavior to avoid

infection. On what basis can a trier of fact determine whether *Q* would have actually transmitted a warning to *P*, or whether *Q* and *P* would have acted on that information? Such questions are usually left to the jury's discretion, often on the basis of testimony from friends and family as to the patient's or plaintiff's character as a generally responsible person. *Cf.* Reisner v. Regents of the University of California, 31 Cal. App. 4th 1195 (1995) (physician who learns that patient is infected with HIV owes duty to patient's subsequent partner to warn him, via a warning to the patient, of risk of infection; partner must prove that patient would have warned him, and that he and patient would have taken effective steps to avoid infection).

5. *Scope of Tarasoff Duty.* *Tarasoff* holds that a treating therapist need not be *actually aware* that the patient is contemplating an attack on someone, so long as the therapist reasonably should have known of the risk. Other states recognizing similar duties have split on what is required for a duty to attach. *Compare* Schuster v. Altenberg, 424 N.W.2d 159 (Wis. 1988) (duty applies when psychologist should have known of danger) *with* Van Horn v. Chambers, 970 S.W.2d 542 (Tex. 1998) (no duty unless physician actually believes that patient poses danger to another).

To whom does the duty to warn recognized in *Tarasoff* extend? Must the particular victim be known to the treating therapist by name or description? The California Supreme Court in a subsequent decision answered this question affirmatively. *See* Thompson v. County of Alameda, 614 P.2d 728 (Cal. 1980) (county that released a juvenile offender with a known propensity to commit violent assaults to the custody of his mother not liable to parents of minor killed by offender; minor was not "identifiable" as required by *Tarasoff*, and the county had no duty to issue general warnings to mother's neighbors). A subsequent California statute likewise limits *Tarasoff* liability to instances in which a patient "has communicated to the psychotherapist a serious threat of physical violence against a reasonably identifiable victim or victims." Cal. Civ. Code. § 43.92(a). The same statute deems a therapist to have fulfilled her *Tarasoff* duty (where applicable) "by making reasonable efforts to communicate the threat to the victim or victims and to a law enforcement agency." *Id.* § 43.92(b).

Statutes such as New Jersey's "Megan's Law" make it a criminal offense for certain violent sex offenders to fail to provide information to authorities, including their current whereabouts.

6. *Duties to Protect Third Parties from Physical Lapses.* The *Tarasoff* majority supposes that physicians are under a duty to third parties to warn patients with disorders such as epilepsy that they may suddenly become incapacitated while driving, risking injuries to others. However, some prominent courts have rejected such a duty. *See* Medina v. Hochberg, 987 N.E.2d 1206 (Mass. 2013) (a medical professional other than a mental health professional owes no duty to third persons to warn her patient of the risks of dangerous driving associated with an underlying medical condition); Jarmie v. Troncale, 50 A.3d 802 (Conn. 2012) (same); Praesel v. Johnson, 967 S.W.2d 391 (Tex. 1998) (given that a physician has no authority to take away a patient's driver's license, and that the patient is likely aware of risks associated with epilepsy, no duty is owed by the physician to protect a third-party driver killed when the patient suffered a seizure while driving and crashed into plaintiff). Should courts be more willing to impose

liability if the accident stems from the physician's failure to advise of the risks associated with an active course of treatment—for example, the prescription of a particular drug that causes drowsiness? In *Praesel*, the Texas Supreme Court noted an earlier intermediate appellate court decision upholding liability on such facts. *Compare* Coombes v. Florio, 877 N.E.2d 567 (Mass. 2007) (physician owes duty to users of roads to advise elderly patient, to whom physician had prescribed multiple medications, of risk that patient would fall asleep while driving) *and* Taylor v. Smith, 892 So. 2d 887 (Ala. 2004) (director of methadone clinic owes users of the roads a duty to administer treatment to patient with due care for the risk that the treatment will cause the patient to drive badly) *with* Kirk v. Michael Reese Hosp., 513 N.E.2d 387 (Ill. 1987) (finding no duty).

7. Other Forms of Intervening Misconduct. Courts have encountered various scenarios that, like *Tarasoff*, involve the victim of an attack (or other injurious misconduct) claiming that another, more remote actor was also responsible for the attack and the injuries it caused. For example, victims of assaults in parking lots and other enclosed spaces sometimes sue the owners of those spaces for facilitating or failing to prevent the attack. Relatedly, persons injured by drunk drivers have sued bar owners and social hosts for their roles in bringing about the drunk driving. Although claims such as these raise duty issues, they also raise issues of proximate cause. We therefore reserve discussion of them until Chapter 5. Victims of attacks also have brought claims against government officials, such as police officers, for failing to protect them. These sorts of claims raise questions of governmental immunities and are therefore covered in Chapter 7.

8. A High-Water Mark. *Tarasoff* marks one of the last and most aggressive efforts by the California Supreme Court in the period from 1945 to 1980 to reshape and expand the ambit of tort liability. Other notable decisions from this period include: *Greenman v. Yuba Power Products, Inc.* (1963) (introducing the doctrine of strict products liability; see Chapter 12), *Dillon v. Legg* (1968) (expanding liability for negligence causing emotional distress; see Chapter 10), *Li v. Yellow Cab Co.* (1975) (replacing contributory negligence with comparative fault; see Chapter 7), and *Sindell v. Abbott Laboratories* (1980) (introducing the concept of "market share liability"; see Chapter 4). For much of this period, the intellectual leader of the court was legendary jurist Roger Traynor, who served on the bench from 1940 to 1970, and was Chief Judge from 1964 to 1970. So far as you can tell from *Rowland* and *Tarasoff*, what role does the "Traynor Court" see for itself in the area of tort law? What is its conception of the point or purposes of tort law?

During roughly this same period, the U.S. Supreme Court, under the leadership of Chief Justice Earl Warren—himself a former Governor of California—rendered a series of decisions expanding the ambit of individual constitutional rights, including rights to equal protection (most famously in *Brown v. Board of Education* (1954)), free speech, rights against intrusive police conduct, and due process. Because constitutional rights mainly set limits on governmental action, the Warren Court's "activism" primarily took the form of striking down legislation and declaring unlawful certain activities of executive branch officials such as prosecutors and police officers. By contrast, because tort law is largely common law, the California Supreme Court's

Appeals ruled that the alarm company owed no duty of care to the firefighter. Although acknowledging that its ruling allowed a careless actor to escape liability, it maintained that such a conclusion was justified in part for the following reasons:

> . . . [T]he defendant may not be in the best position to prevent a particular class of accidents, and placing liability on it may merely dilute the incentives of other potential defendants. In most cases the best way to avert fire damage is to prevent the fire from starting rather than to douse it with water after it has started. The water company represents a second line of defense, and it has no control over the first. It cannot insist that people not leave oil-soaked rags lying about or that they equip their houses and offices with smoke detectors and fire extinguishers.
>
> How [much weight these arguments should carry] is a matter of fair debate; but they are especially powerful in *this* case. . . . The provider of an alarm service not only has no knowledge of the risk of a fire in its subscribers' premises, and no practical ability to reduce that risk (though we suppose an alarm service like a fire insurer could offer a discount to people who installed smoke detectors in their premises); it also lacks knowledge of the risk of a fire to firemen summoned to extinguish it. That risk depends not only on the characteristics of the particular premises but also on the particular techniques used by each fire department, the training and qualifications of the firemen, and the quality of the department's leadership. The alarm company knows nothing about these things and has no power to influence them.

Id. at 490-491. Notably, *Edwards* was authored by Judge Richard Posner, who, along with Judge Calabresi, is one of the leaders of the "Law and Economics" movement.

REFERENCES/FURTHER READING

Injury

Stephen Perry, *Harm, History and Counterfactuals*, 40 San Diego L. Rev. 1283 (2003).

The Duty Element

W. Jonathan Cardi, *Purging Foreseeability*, 58 Vand. L. Rev. 739 (2005).

John C. P. Goldberg & Benjamin C. Zipursky, *The Moral of* MacPherson, 146 U. Pa. L. Rev. 1733 (1998).

John C. P. Goldberg & Benjamin C. Zipursky, *The Restatement (Third) and the Place of Duty in Negligence Law*, 54 Vand. L. Rev. 657 (2001).

Peter F. Lake, *Common Law Duty in Negligence Law: The Recent Consolidation of a Consensus on the Expansion of the Analysis of Duty and the New Conservative Liability Limiting Use of Policy Considerations*, 34 San Diego L. Rev. 1503 (1997).

David G. Owen, *Figuring Foreseeability*, 44 Wake Forest L. Rev. 1277 (2009).

Michael L. Richmond, *The Development of Duty:* Landgridge *to* Palsgraf, 31 St. Louis U. L.J. 903 (1989).

Benjamin C. Zipursky, *Foreseeability in Breach, Duty, and Proximate Cause*, 44 Wake Forest L. Rev. 1247 (2009).

Winterbottom and *MacPherson*

Frances Bohlen, *Studies in The Law of Torts* 76-81 (1926).

Robert M. Davis, *A Re-examination of the Doctrine of* MacPherson v. Buick *and Its Application and Extension in the State of New York*, 24 Fordham L. Rev. 204 (1955).

Martin P. Golding, *Legal Reasoning* 112-143 (1984).

James A. Henderson, Jr., MacPherson v. Buick Motor Co.: *Simplifying the Facts While Reshaping the Law*, in Robert L. Rabin & Stephen D. Sugarman (eds.), *Tort Stories* 41-71 (2003).

Edward H. Levi, *An Introduction to Legal Reasoning* 8-27 (1949).

Vernon Palmer, *When Privity Entered Tort—An Historical Reexamination of* Winterbottom v. Wright, 27 J. Am. Leg. Hist. 85 (1983).

David W. Peck, *Decision at Law* 38-69 (1961).

William L. Prosser, *The Assault upon the Citadel (Strict Liability to the Consumer)*, 69 Yale L.J. 1099, 1099-1102 (1960).

Michael A. Stein, Priestley v. Fowler (1837) *and the Emerging Tort of Negligence*, 64 B.C. L. Rev. 689 (2003).

Benjamin Cardozo

John C. P. Goldberg, *Book Review: The Life of the Law*, 51 Stan. L. Rev. 1419 (1999).

Andrew L. Kaufman, *Cardozo* (1998).

Richard Polenberg, *The World of Benjamin Cardozo* (1998).

Richard A. Posner, *Cardozo: A Study in Reputation* (1990).

Amatory Torts

Jane Larson, *Women Understand So Little, They Call My Good Nature "Deceit": A Feminist Rethinking of Seduction*, 93 Colum. L. Rev. 374 (1993).

Fernanda G. Nicola, *Intimate Liability: Emotional Harm, Family Law, and Stereotyped Narratives in Interspousal Torts*, 19 Wm. & Mary J. Women & L. 445, (2013).

Lawrence Stone, *Road to Divorce: England 1530–1987*, Ch. 9 (1990).

Duties to Rescue and Protect

James Barr Ames, *Law and Morals*, 22 Harv. L. Rev. 97 (1908).

Richard A. Epstein, *A Theory of Strict Liability*, 2 J. Leg. Stud. 151 (1973).

Steven J. Heyman, *Foundations of the Duty to Rescue*, 47 Vand. L. Rev. 673 (1994).

David A. Hyman, *Rescue Without Law: An Empirical Perspective on Duty to Rescue*, 84 Tex. L. Rev. 653 (2006).

Peter F. Lake, *Boys, Bad Men, and Bad Case-Law: Re-Examining the Historical Foundations of No-Duty-To-Rescue Rules*, 43 N.Y.L. Sch. L. Rev. 385 (1999).

Timothy D. Lytton, *Tort Claims Against Gun Manufacturers for Crime-Related Injuries: Defining a Suitable Role for the Tort System in Regulating the Firearms Industry*, 65 Mo. L. Rev. 1 (2000).

John T. Pardun, *Comment: Good Samaritan Laws: A Global Perspective*, 20 Loy. L.A. Int'l & Comp. L.J. 591 (1998).

Robert L. Rabin, *Enabling Torts*, 49 DePaul L. Rev. 435 (1999).

Anthony J. Sebok, *What's Law Got to Do With It? Duty, Tort Doctrine and the 9/11 Victims Compensation Fund*, 53 DePaul L. Rev. 901 (2003).

Ernest J. Weinrib, *The Case for a Duty to Rescue*, 90 Yale L.J. 247 (1980).

Premises Liability & *Rowland*

Dilan A. Esper & Gregory C. Keating, *Abusing "Duty"*, 79 S. Cal. L. Rev. 265 (2006).

David A. Logan, *When the Restatement Is Not a Restatement: The Curious Case of the "Flagrant Trespasser,"* 37 Wm. Mitchell L. Rev. 1448 (2011).

Robert L. Rabin, Rowland v. Christian, *Hallmark of an Expansionary Era*, in Robert L. Rabin & Stephen D. Sugarman (eds.), *Tort Stories* (2003).

Pure Economic Loss

Peter Benson, *The Basis for Excluding Liability for Economic Loss in Tort Law*, in David G. Owen (ed.), *Philosophical Foundations of Tort Law* 427 (1995).

Mark P. Gergen, *Negligent Misrepresentation as Contract*, 101 Cal. L. Rev. 953 (2013).

Victor P. Goldberg, *Accountable Accountants: Is Third-Party Liability Necessary?*, 17 J. Leg. Stud. 295 (1988).

Ronen Perry, *The Deepwater Horizon Oil Spill and the Limits of Civil Liability*, 86 Wash. L. Rev. 1(2011).

Stephen R. Perry, *Protected Interests in Undertakings in the Law of Negligence*, 17 U. Toronto L.J. 247 (1992).

Robert L. Rabin, *Tort Recovery for Negligently Inflicted Economic Loss: A Reassessment*, 37 Stan. L. Rev. 1513 (1985).

Robert L. Rabin, *Respecting Boundaries and the Economic Loss Rule in Tort*, 48 Ariz. L. Rev. 857 (2006).

Gary T. Schwartz, *Economic Loss in American Tort Law: The Examples of* J'Aire *and of Products Liability*, 23 San Diego L. Rev. 37 (1986).

Anthony J. Sebok, *The Failed Promise of a General Theory of Pure Economic Loss: An Accident of History?*, 61 DePaul L. Rev 615 (2012).

John C. Siliciano, *Negligent Accounting and the Limits of Instrumental Tort Reform*, 86 Mich. L. Rev. 1929 (1988).

Symposium: After Deepwater Horizon, 30 Miss. Coll. L. Rev. 149 *et seq.* (2011) (contributions by Professors Goldberg and Robertson).

Howard Weiner, *Common Law Liability of the Certified Public Accountant for Negligent Misrepresentation*, 20 San Diego L. Rev. 233 (1983).

Tarasoff and the *Traynor* Court

Gary T. Schwartz, *The Beginning and the Possible End of The Rise of Modern American Tort Law*, 26 Ga. L. Rev. 601 (1992).

Symposium: The Future of "The Duty to Protect": Scientific and Legal Perspectives on *Tarasoff*'s Thirtieth Anniversary, 75 U. Cin. L. Rev. 425 *et seq.* (2006).

G. Edward White, *Tort Law in America: An Intellectual History* 139–210 (exp. ed. 2003).

Cheapest Cost Avoider

Guido Calabresi, *The Cost of Accidents* (1971).

Symposium: Calabresi's *The Cost of Accidents: A Generation of Impact on Law and Scholarship*, 64 Md. L. Rev. 1 et seq. (2005).

CHAPTER 3

THE BREACH ELEMENT

I. DUTY, BREACH, AND THE MEANING OF "NEGLIGENCE"

Analytically, duty precedes breach: A judge must first determine if a duty of care was owed by the defendant to persons such as the plaintiff before the question of whether that duty was fulfilled can be put to the jury. So far, we have paid relatively little attention to the latter question of what exactly a defendant is duty-bound to do. For example, once *MacPherson* was decided, auto manufacturers subject to New York law owed a legal duty to users of cars to take reasonable care to protect them against defects such as crumbling wheels. Granted this duty, what course of conduct on the part of auto manufacturers would be sufficient to discharge it? Were they now required to inspect every wheel, or would it be sufficient to check random samples? How would they have to inspect them: visually or under stress tests? What failure of precaution would constitute breach of this duty?

Before proceeding, it is important to note a common terminological confusion that often inhibits clear analysis. We refer to the third element of our formulation of the negligence tort as the "breach" element. This element poses the question of whether the defendant acted with the degree of care that she was duty-bound to exercise. Courts and commentators, however, frequently refer to the breach element by using the terms *negligence* and *negligent*. When they do so, they are *not* referring to the tort of negligence, but to a careless course of conduct. So, for example, a lawyer or judge might say that the failure of a defendant to take appropriate precautions while driving (e.g., by speeding or being inattentive) constitutes "negligent driving." In doing so, the lawyer or court is not addressing whether the driver was under a duty of care to the plaintiff, nor whether the "negligent driving" proximately caused an injury to the plaintiff.

It is critical to keep in mind that negligence in the sense of careless conduct is *not* sufficient to establish that the defendant can be held liable for having committed the tort of negligence. The latter conclusion, as we have seen, also requires a determination as to injury, duty, and cause. Unfortunately, it is easy even for trained lawyers to become confused between these two different senses of negligence. To help avoid confusion, some lawyers and commentators distinguish between *big* "N" *Negligence*, which refers to the tort, and *small* "n" *negligence*, which refers to carelessness. In this book, we use the term *negligence* to refer to the tort. By contrast, we use the terms *breach*, *carelessness*, and *fault* to refer to the tort's third element, which concerns the degree of care that the defendant was supposed to have exercised.

Myers v. Heritage Enters., Inc.

820 N.E.2d 604 (Ill. App. 2004)

MYERSCOUGH, J. Plaintiff, Michael B. Myers, independent executor of the estate of decedent, Mary Prillmayer, appeals the judgment entered in favor of defendant, Heritage Enterprises, Inc., upon the jury's verdict. We reverse and remand.

I. BACKGROUND

In August 2000, Penny Chapman and Carolyn Butler, certified nurse's aides/nursing assistants (CNAs), worked at Heritage Manor, a nursing home owned and operated by defendant. They attempted to transfer decedent, a 78-year-old resident, from her wheelchair to her bed using a device known as a Hoyer lift. During the process, decedent fell approximately 18 inches and hit the bar of the Hoyer lift, fracturing the tibia and fibula on both legs. Decedent died approximately two weeks later, apparently of unrelated causes because there were no allegations that the fall contributed to her death.

The nursing home reported the incident to the Illinois Department of Public Health (IDPH), which investigated the matter. Corey Crouch, a registered nurse who investigates for IDPH, concluded that decedent fell due to no fault of the facility or the staff.

In July 2001, plaintiff brought suit against defendant, alleging . . . violation of the Nursing Home Care Act (Act) (210 ILCS 45/1-101 through 3A-101 (West 2000)). . . . The Act provides that owners and operators of facilities are liable to a resident for injuries caused by the intentional or negligent acts of their employees or agents.

. . . .

Plaintiff . . . alleged that defendant committed the following careless and negligent acts: (1) improperly positioning decedent in the Hoyer-lift sling, (2) failing to observe decedent was not properly seated in the Hoyer-lift sling, (3) failing to provide supervision of the use of the Hoyer lift, (4) failing to properly train its staff in the transfer of patients by use of the Hoyer lift, (5) using obsolete and inadequate equipment for transporting nonambulatory patients, (6) failure of staff to properly position themselves, (7) careless and negligent operation of the Hoyer lift, (8) employing inexperienced staff, and (9) impairing the movement of the Hoyer lift while transferring the patient.*]

At the jury instruction conference prior to trial, plaintiff offered Illinois Pattern Jury Instructions, Civil, Nos. 10.01 and 10.04 (2000) (hereinafter IPI Civil (2000)), the ordinary negligence standard-of-care instructions. Defendant, however, argued that the professional negligence instruction, IPI Civil (2000) No. 105.01, applied to the actions of the CNAs. The trial court reserved ruling on the appropriate jury instruction because defense counsel did not have the exact instruction he intended to tender and the court believed it unfair to ask plaintiff's counsel to respond to an instruction he had been unable to review.

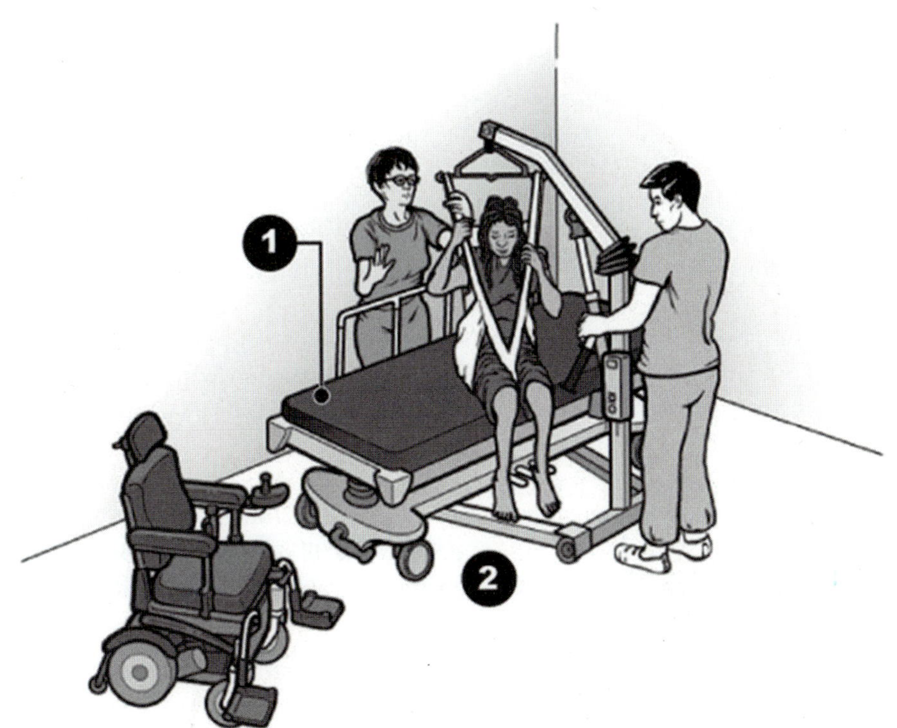

During the trial, plaintiff presented the testimony of, among others, David Jones, an operations manager for Heckman Health Care, and Mary Hendricks, a registered nurse. (Plaintiff had intended to call Donna Bankard, R.N., to testify as to her opinions of the alleged wrongdoings on the part of defendant. In January 2004, the trial court granted defendant's motion to bar Bankard because she had never used a Hoyer lift.) Jones testified that certain new slings and chains were available for Hoyer lifts in August 2000. He also identified the Hoyer instruction manual, which the court admitted into evidence. Hendricks also demonstrated the proper use of the Hoyer lift.

* Diagram added. — EDS. Source: http://www.ada.gov/medcare_mobility_ta/medcare_ta.htm

Defendant called Pamela Sue Brown, holder of a Ph.D. in nursing, who testified as to the nursing standard of care in the use of the Hoyer lift. She reviewed numerous documents, including the pleadings, medical records, discovery documents, IDPH report, IDPH investigation materials, internal investigation materials from the nursing home, incident report, internal transfer policy for use of the Hoyer lift, the operator's manual for the Hoyer lift, discovery depositions, and textbooks on transfer techniques. In her opinion, to a reasonable degree of nursing certainty, the CNAs used an acceptable transfer procedure.

Chapman and Butler, the two CNAs who moved the decedent using the Hoyer lift, also testified about what occurred when decedent fell.

The trial court resumed the jury instruction conference on the third day of trial. Plaintiff again offered IPI Civil (2000) Nos. 10.01 and 10.04, and defendant offered IPI Civil (2000) No. 105.01 in lieu of plaintiff's instructions. Defense counsel stated he originally intended only to tender the first paragraph of IPI Civil (2000) No. 105.01 but believed that the second paragraph — informing the jury it could only decide whether the standard of care had been met from expert testimony — was also appropriate. Plaintiff objected to the professional malpractice instruction because it did not apply to the negligence of the CNAs in the nursing home. The court rejected plaintiff's instructions and instructed the jury on professional negligence.

. . . On January 14, 2003, the jury returned a verdict in favor of defendant.

. . . .

Plaintiff appealed [from a judgment entered on the verdict], arguing [that] the trial court erred in giving the jury a professional negligence instruction for the standard of care of CNAs requiring expert testimony. . . . [Additional basis of appeal omitted — Eds.]

II. Analysis

Plaintiff filed this case as an ordinary negligence action under the Act. The elements of a cause of action for negligence are (1) the existence of a duty owed by defendant to plaintiff, (2) a breach of that duty, and (3) injury proximately caused by that breach.

Over plaintiff's objection, the trial court instructed the jury as follows:

> "In providing professional services to Mary Prillmayer, a certified nurse's aide must possess and apply the knowledge and use the skill and care ordinarily used by a reasonably well-qualified certified nurse's aide under circumstances similar to those shown by the evidence. A failure to do so is professional negligence.
>
> The only way in which you may decide whether a certified nurse's aide possessed and applied the knowledge and used the skill and care which the law required of him is from expert testimony. You must not attempt to determine this question from any personal knowledge you have."

See IPI Civil (2000) No. 105.01.

The court rejected the instructions tendered by plaintiff:

> "When I use the term 'negligence' in these instructions, I mean the failure to do something which a reasonably careful person would do, or the doing of something which a reasonably careful person would not do, under circumstances similar to

> those shown by the evidence. The law does not say how a reasonably careful person would act under those circumstances. That is for you to decide."

See IPI Civil (2000) No. 10.01.

> "It was the duty of the defendant's employees, before and at the time of the occurrence, to use ordinary care for the safety of Mary Prillmayer. This means it was the duty of the defendant's employees to be free from negligence."

See IPI Civil (2000) No. 10.04.

It is within the discretion of the trial court which jury instructions to give to the jury, and the court's decision will not be disturbed absent an abuse of that discretion. . . . Reversal is warranted if the faulty jury instructions misled the jury and resulted in prejudice to the appellant.

Plaintiff argues that the trial court erred in giving the professional negligence instruction because (1) operation of the Hoyer lift does not constitute medical treatment or diagnosis by a professional and, therefore, does not require expert testimony; (2) the CNAs were not parties to the lawsuit, as plaintiff brought the suit under the Act, which imposes liability on facilities for the negligence of its employees; (3) the complaint sounded in negligence and the court instructed the jury on negligence in the issues instruction; (4) several of the allegations of negligence in the complaint did not relate to the actions of defendant's employees, rendering the professional negligence standard particularly inappropriate for those allegations; and (5) the proper standard of care should have been based upon the manufacturer's operational instructions.

Defendant frames the issue as whether the operation of a Hoyer lift to transfer a patient can be evaluated without an expert witness. If not, according to defendant, the proper standard of care is professional negligence.

A determination of the proper standard of care requires an examination of the nature of the action brought. Where, as here, the claim is statutory, an examination of the statute is necessary to determine whether it contemplates a professional standard of care or an ordinary, reasonable standard of care. When determining the legislative intent, a court must first look at the plain meaning of the statutory language.

Plaintiff brought a statutory claim under the Act. Pursuant to the Act, owners and operators of nursing home facilities are liable to residents for injuries caused by the negligent acts of their employees.

The Act guarantees nursing home residents certain rights, including the right not to be subjected to abuse or neglect by nursing home personnel. 210 ILCS 45/2-107 (West 2000); *Harris v. Manor Healthcare Corp.*, 489 N.E.2d 1374, 1377 (Ill. 1986). The Act defines "neglect" as:

> "[A] failure in a facility to provide adequate medical or personal care or maintenance, which failure results in physical or mental injury to a resident or in the deterioration of a resident's physical or mental condition." 210 ILCS 45/1-117 (West 2000).

"Adequate care" has been deemed synonymous with "ordinary care," "due care," or "reasonable care," the terms used to describe the standard of care for negligence.

Harris, 489 N.E.2d at 1381. The Act defines "personal care" to include assistance with movement of the patient. 210 ILCS 45/1-120 (West 2000). Consequently, the plain language of the statute indicates that the appropriate standard of care for liability under the Act is one of ordinary negligence, which does not require expert testimony. See *Eads v. Heritage Enterprises, Inc.*, 757 N.E.2d 107, 113 (Ill. App. 2001) (noting that most of the Act "addresses nonmedical long-term care, which does not require expert testimony"), *aff'd*, 787 N.E.2d 771 (Ill. 2003). . . .

The professional negligence instruction given informed the jury that it could only determine the standard of care by expert testimony:

> "The only way in which you may decide whether a certified nurses's aide possessed and applied the knowledge and used the skill and care which the law required of him is from expert testimony. You must not attempt to determine this question from any personal knowledge you have."

See IPI Civil (2000) No. 105.01. Yet, the professional negligence instruction itself actually permits evidence from sources other than expert testimony:

> "The only way in which you may decide whether (a)(any) defendant possessed and applied the knowledge and used the skill and care which the law required of him is from (expert testimony)(and)(or)(evidence of professional standards or conduct) presented in the trial." IPI Civil (2000) No. 105.01.

The language "evidence of professional standards or conduct" was not included in the instruction.

Further, the act of CNAs moving a nursing home resident does not constitute skilled medical care requiring the professional negligence instruction. A professional is "[a] person who belongs to a learned profession or whose occupation requires a high level of training and proficiency." Black's Law Dictionary 1246 (8th ed. 2004). IDPH requires that nursing assistants meet certain training requirements, including 120 hours of instruction. . . . Successful completion of the program means completion of at least 80 hours of theory and 40 hours of clinical work, completion of IDPH-approved manual skills, and passing the IDPH-established competency test. The Act does not require nursing assistants to obtain a high school diploma. A nursing assistant's duties, as testified to by Chapman and Butler, include bathing, feeding, weighing, dressing, transferring, and communicating with patients, as well as assisting with toileting functions. Given the minimal training requirements and the fact that nursing assistants provide primarily personal care, the nursing assistant position is not a professional position requiring the professional negligence instruction.

Because the proper standard of care was one of ordinary negligence, the trial court should have instructed the jury with IPI Civil (2000) Nos. 10.01 and 10.04, which would have informed the jury that it had to decide how a reasonably careful person would have acted under the circumstances. Under this standard, the parties could have presented evidence to assist the jury in its determination, including expert testimony, IDPH regulations, manufacturer's instructions, or industry standards, although this would not be required.

Defendant argues that even if the trial court gave the wrong instructions, plaintiff suffered no prejudice because he, too, presented expert testimony at trial. Yet, the instructions given to the jury specifically informed it that the only way to determine whether the CNAs used the skill and care required of them was from expert testimony. The jury was told it could not rely on its own knowledge or other evidence. Moreover, the evidence conflicted as to whether the manufacturer's instructions were followed. An assessment of the credibility of the CNAs' testimony was a determination to be made by the jury. If the jury had been instructed that it could determine how a reasonably careful person would have acted under the circumstances, it may have determined that the CNAs were, in fact, negligent, despite Dr. Brown testifying that the CNAs met the standard of care.

Consequently, the trial court abused its discretion by instructing the jury on professional negligence rather than ordinary negligence. The instructions given misled the jury and resulted in prejudice to plaintiff, especially in light of the fact that the court ruled on the proper standard of review on the last day of trial. Therefore, a remand for a new trial is required.

. . . .

Martin v. Evans

711 A.2d 458 (Pa. 1998)

Newman, J. Appellants Weldon R. Evans (Evans) [and] FORC Company request this Court to examine whether the Court of Common Pleas of Allegheny County (trial court) abused its discretion in granting a new trial based on its determination that the verdict was against the weight of the evidence. This personal injury suit arose from an accident in which Evans' tractor-trailer backed into Appellee Anthony Martin (Martin). The parties presented conflicting testimony relating directly to the issue of Evans' negligence, and the jury concluded that Evans was not negligent. Because the verdict rested on a credibility determination, we hold that the trial court usurped the jury's responsibility by disregarding its finding that Evans was not negligent. Accordingly, we reverse and reinstate the jury's verdict.

FORC Company employed Evans as a truck driver. On May 24, 1989, Evans was driving a tractor-trailer that was forty-five feet long, eight feet wide and thirteen feet, six inches tall. He was proceeding southbound on Interstate 79 when he pulled into the Canonsburg rest stop. Along the left-hand side of the parking lot, there were parallel parking spots for trucks. Evans pulled his truck into what he believed to be the last parallel parking spot in that row. Because it was the last spot, he had to angle the cab of the truck to the trailer to maneuver the truck into the space.

Evans left the truck running, and went to the restrooms. When he returned, he looked in back of the truck before he got into the cab and noticed that no one was parked behind him. He recorded the stop in his logbook, which took approximately two minutes, then he prepared to back up. Evans testified that he put the truck into reverse and released both the emergency brake for the cab and the emergency brake for the tractor. When released, the emergency brakes emit a hissing sound that lasts for about two seconds. He activated his four-way flashers, which are similar to an automobile's hazard lights. Then he looked through the side-view mirrors, but because of the angle of the truck and the length of the trailer, he could not see directly behind him. He reversed the truck "[s]lower than you could walk" until he felt a nudge and saw someone waving at him to stop. He stopped the truck and through his right-hand rear view mirror he saw someone fall just to the right, rear of his truck. When he got out of his truck to investigate, Evans saw Martin lying on the ground.

Martin and Rochester Steverson (Steverson) were driving southbound on Interstate 79 on May 24, 1989, when they, too, stopped at the Canonsburg rest area. Their truck was an Isuzu box truck that was about twenty feet long and ten feet wide. The driver of the truck parked approximately seven to ten feet directly behind Evans' tractor-trailer. Martin was either walking or standing between the Isuzu truck and Evans' tractor-trailer when the tractor-trailer began to back into him. He claimed that he tried to get out of the way but was unable to do so. He became pinned between the two vehicles. Once he realized what was happening, Steverson put the Isuzu truck into reverse to free Martin, who fell to the ground. Martin suffered injuries to his right arm and back. As result, Martin brought a negligence action against Evans [and] his employer FORC Company. . . .

A jury trial took place from May 5, 1994 to May 11, 1994. The parties presented conflicting testimony concerning the circumstances surrounding the accident. The trial court instructed the jury on negligence, contributory negligence, and comparative negligence. The court presented the following interrogatories to the jury for its consideration:

Question 1a

Do you find that defendant Weldon R. Evans was negligent?

Yes _____ No _____

If you answered "Yes" to Question 1a, go on to Question 1b. If you answered "No" to Question 1a, the plaintiff cannot recover and you should not answer any further questions and should return to the courtroom.

Question 1b

Was the defendant's negligence a substantial factor in bringing about the plaintiff's harm?

Yes _____ No _____

If you answered "Yes" to Question 1b, go on to Question 2a. If you answered "No" to Question 1b, the plaintiff cannot recover and you should not answer any further questions and should return to the courtroom.

Question 2a

Do you find that plaintiff Anthony Martin was contributorily negligent?

Yes _____ No _____

If you answered "Yes" to Question 2a, go on to Question 2b. If you answered "No" to Question 2a, go on to Question 4.

Question 2b

Was plaintiff's contributory negligence a substantial factor in bringing about his harm?

Yes _____ No _____

If you answered "Yes" to Question 2b, go on to Question 3. If you answered "No" to Question 2b, go on to Question 4.

***

The jury answered "No" to Question 1a, therefore, did not answer the remaining questions. The trial court molded the jury's answer into a verdict in favor of Appellants.

Martin moved for a new trial. The trial court granted the motion on the grounds that the jury's verdict "shocked the Court's sense of justice." Slip Op. at 8. The court reasoned that because Evans sat in his truck for "a couple [of] minutes" before backing up, he was aware that there were blind spots in his mirrors such that he was unable to see directly behind his vehicle, and it was a busy rest area and likely that a pedestrian or vehicle could stand or park directly behind him, the jury's verdict that Evans was not negligent was unacceptable.

Evans appealed to the Superior Court, which concluded in a Memorandum Opinion that the trial court properly granted a new trial, and thus affirmed. This Court granted Evans' Petition for Allowance of Appeal to determine whether the trial court abused its discretion in granting a new trial where the parties presented conflicting testimony that required a credibility determination. We now reverse.

A new trial is warranted when the jury's verdict is so contrary to the evidence that it shocks one's sense of justice. . . .

. . . Negligence is the absence of ordinary care that a reasonably prudent person would exercise in the same or similar circumstances. *Lanni v. Pennsylvania R. Co.*, 371 Pa. 106, 88 A.2d 887 (1952). The mere occurrence of an accident does not establish negligent conduct. Rather, the plaintiff has the burden of establishing, by a preponderance of the evidence, that the defendant engaged in conduct that deviated from the general standard of care expected under the circumstances, and that this deviation proximately caused actual harm.

The trial court instructed the jury with regard to the definition of negligence as follows:

> The legal term, negligence, otherwise known as carelessness, is the absence of ordinary care which a reasonably prudent person would exercise in the circumstances here presented.
>
> Negligent conduct may consist either of an act or an omission to act when there is a duty to do so. In other words, negligence is the failure to do something which a reasonably careful person would do, or the doing of something which a reasonably careful person would not do in light of all the surrounding circumstances established by the evidence in this case. It is for you to determine how a reasonably careful person would act in those circumstances.
>
> Now, I told you in defining negligence that part of that definition was absence of ordinary care.

> I want to define ordinary care for you. Ordinary care is the care a reasonably careful person would use under the circumstances presented in this case. It is the duty of every person to use ordinary care not only for his own safety and the protection of his property, but also to avoid injury to others. What constitutes ordinary care varies according to the particular circumstances and conditions existing then and there. The amount of care required by law must be in keeping with the degree of danger involved. . . .

Thus, the trial court called upon the jury to evaluate the testimony and decide whether Evans exercised ordinary care under the circumstances.

The evidence presented to the jury on the issue of whether Evans was negligent in the operation of his vehicle was contradictory in several respects, including: (1) whether Evans took the necessary precautions prior to moving his tractor-trailer in reverse, specifically, whether he activated his four-way flashers and released the emergency brakes which emit a loud hissing sound; (2) whether Martin or Steverson was driving the Isuzu truck; (3) whether Martin was parked in a legal parking space; and (4) Martin's position when the incident occurred.

Evans testified that when he pulled into the Canonsburg rest area, he parked in what he believed to be the last legal parking space in that particular row. As proof of this, he stated that he had to park at an angle to fit his tractor-trailer into the lines. When he returned from the restrooms, he claimed that no one was parked behind him. He knew that he only had to back up a couple of feet to be able to pull out of the space. After he made a recording in his logbook, he put in the clutch, put the truck into low reverse, activated his four-way flashers, and checked his mirrors. Evans further stated that although he could not see directly behind him at that moment, he kept his eye on the right mirror because he knew he would be able to see out of that side first. According to Evans, he moved his tractor-trailer backwards "[s]lower than you could walk." When he felt a nudge and saw someone waving at him to stop in his rear view mirror, he stopped instantly.

Martin testified that he was driving the Isuzu truck southbound on Interstate 79 on May 24, 1989, despite the fact that he did not have a valid driver's license at that time. He claimed that he saw his brother Neil Martin, who waved to him to pull off at the next rest area. He stated that he pulled into the last parking space and parked approximately ten feet behind the tractor-trailer and turned off the ignition. Then, after about a minute and a half, he exited the truck and walked between the front of his vehicle and the tractor-trailer. He proceeded about two-thirds of the width of the tractor-trailer when he realized that the tractor-trailer was moving towards him. He testified that he did not hear the truck's engine or the release of the emergency brakes, nor did he see any flashing lights from the back of the tractor-trailer. After the tractor-trailer pushed him up against the Isuzu truck, he claimed that Steverson jumped into the truck, started it, and put it in reverse, at which point Martin fell to the ground. Neil Martin corroborated this version of the events.

Steverson, on the other hand, claimed that he, not Martin, had been driving the truck. Steverson testified that he parked the truck approximately ten feet behind the tractor-trailer and turned off the ignition. According to Steverson, Martin got out of the passenger's seat, and walked in front of the Isuzu truck and leaned against it while talking to his brother, Neil, for a couple of minutes. When Steverson realized that the tractor-trailer was moving towards them and that Martin was caught between the two, he started the truck and put it in reverse.

State Police Trooper Dennis Spirk, who arrived at the scene of the accident to investigate, testified that he interviewed Evans, Steverson and Anthony Martin concerning how the accident occurred. When questioned by Trooper Spirk, Evans stated that when he returned from the restrooms he walked around the back of his truck before he got into the cab, and that from the cab he did not see anything behind him. Trooper Spirk stated that Steverson indicated that he was the driver of the smaller truck. In response to questioning, Anthony Martin told Trooper Spirk that he was standing between the two trucks, with his back to the tractor-trailer and facing the truck he had just exited, when the tractor-trailer backed up and hit him.

Credibility determinations are within the sole province of the jury. "A jury is entitled to believe all, part or none of the evidence presented. . . . A jury can believe any part of a witness' testimony that they choose, and may disregard any portion of the testimony that they disbelieve."[Citation to quoted authority omitted — EDS.] Consequently, because of the conflicting versions of the events surrounding the accident, it was the jury's duty to make a credibility determination and to decide whether Evans exercised ordinary care under the circumstances. The jury obviously chose to believe Evans and Steverson, and found that Evans was not negligent.

However, the trial court concluded that "[u]nder all of the facts and circumstances of this case, even when viewed most favorably to the verdict winner, this Court cannot accept the jury's conclusion that Evans was not negligent." In support of its conclusion, the trial court cited evidence supporting the fact that Evans made no effort during the two minutes after he entered his cab and prior to putting his truck in motion, to determine if there was anyone or anything behind his vehicle. This, coupled with the facts that the rest area was busy and there were "blind spots" in the mirrors, caused the trial court to reach its conclusion.

However, the evidence equally supports a finding that Evans exercised ordinary care under the circumstances. Evans testified that he parked in what he believed to be the last legal parking space in the row. In fact, he stated that he had to park his tractor-trailer with the cab at an angle to the trailer because it was the last spot and there was barely enough room for his vehicle. When he returned to his truck, no one was parked behind him. Before backing up, he activated his four-way flashers and released his emergency brakes, which he knew made a loud hissing sound. Then, he proceeded to move the truck backwards "slower than you could walk." Therefore, if the jury were to believe Evans' account of the events, he took the necessary precautions required by the circumstances and proceeded with care.

A resolution of whether Evans was negligent relied upon a credibility determination and the jury's assessment of what constituted ordinary care under the circumstances. Because this assessment was solely within the province of the jury, the trial court was not at liberty to reassess the evidence and make its own credibility determinations simply because it would have reached a different conclusion. Accordingly, we hold that the trial court abused its discretion by disregarding the jury's credibility determination and substituting its own. The verdict was not so contrary to the evidence so as to shock one's sense of justice.

We reverse and reinstate the jury's verdict.

Pingaro v. Rossi

731 A.2d 523 (N.J. Super. App. Div. 1999)

Havey, P.J. A jury awarded $300,000 in damages to plaintiff Ellen Pingaro, a meter reader for . . . New Jersey Natural Gas Company (NJNG), for injuries she sustained as a result of a dog bite she suffered from a German Shepherd owned by defendant Joseph Rossi. . . .

. . . [O]n June 27, 1996, [Pingaro was] performing her meter reading duties for NJNG [on] a route in Beachwood, Ocean County. When she arrived at Rossi's house, her data cap, a hand-held computer, "beeped" a message: "[b]ad dog, knock." The data cap provides the meter reader with the name of the street and location of the meter and at times displays specialized messages pertaining to the customer, such as whether a "bad dog" may be present.

According to plaintiff, she had never been to Rossi's home before. She knocked on Rossi's door but received no answer. She proceeded to the fenced-in backyard, rattled the gate and her keys and yelled "gas company." There was no response. She looked around the backyard for dogs or other animals. After satisfying herself that the yard was clear, she unhooked the gate and walked towards the meter. Immediately upon entering the back yard two dogs approached her. One dog, a large German Shepherd, jumped up, knocked her down and bit her on both arms, legs and head. She subdued the dog by hitting it with her flashlight, exited the yard and called for help. A nearby construction worker summoned an ambulance which took her to Community Medical Center where she received numerous stitches and was released later that afternoon.

[Plaintiff received physical therapy and was unable to work or engage in normal activities for more than a month. She also suffered scars on her arms and on one leg, as well as anxiety, fear, and depression related to the incident. — Eds.] . . .

Rossi testified that the dog which attacked plaintiff was kept fenced in his backyard. The only gate to the backyard was the gate utilized by plaintiff in entering the yard. He stated that a large "Beware of Dog" sign was posted on the gate.

According to Rossi, over the course of ten years he had spoken with several meter readers about his dog and told them they should not enter his yard if no one was home. The meter readers responded that they would comply with his request. Rossi noted that this arrangement had worked for over ten years, and when he was not at home the meter readers would estimate his bill, leave a card for him to mail in or come back at a later date. . . .

Check Your Understanding

Applying the Reasonably Prudent Person Standard

Did the precautions taken by Rossi to prevent meter readers from being attacked by his dog satisfy the "reasonably prudent person" standard as stated in *Martin v. Evans*? Why or why not?

The so-called "dog bite" statute, N.J.S.A. 4:19-16, reads in pertinent part:

> The owner of any dog which shall bite a person while such person is on or in a public place, or lawfully on or in a private place, including the property of the owner of the dog, shall be liable for such damages as may be suffered by the person bitten, regardless of the former viciousness of such dog or the owner's knowledge of such viciousness.

There is no question that plaintiff fulfilled the three elements necessary to establish Rossi's liability under the statute. Rossi was the owner of the dog, the dog bit plaintiff and the bite occurred while plaintiff was lawfully on Rossi's property. Satisfaction of the elements of the statute imposes strict liability upon Rossi for damages sustained by plaintiff. . . .

In order for plaintiff to prevail under the "dog-bite" statute, she need not prove scienter; that is, that Rossi knew of the dog's dangerous propensities.

[The Court proceeded to rule on various other issues raised on appeal. — Eds.]

Jones v. Port Authority of Allegheny County

583 A.2d 512 (Pa. Comm. 1990)

Barry, J. Oscar and Mary Jones, husband and wife . . . appeal an order of the Court of Common Pleas . . . which entered judgment for the defendant, the Port Authority of Allegheny County (PAT), following a jury verdict in favor of PAT and the denial of the Jones' post-trial motions.

Oscar Jones testified that he was injured on a PAT bus. He testified that he had entered the bus and was climbing the stairs to the platform on which the seats were located. Before reaching the platform, the bus pulled out and stopped suddenly. According to Mr. Jones' testimony the doors to the bus had not closed at the time of the accident. He testified that he injured his arm in the incident. PAT posited at trial that the accident never occurred. It took the further position that, if the incident actually happened, there was no negligence on the part of PAT's driver. The jury brought a verdict in favor of PAT. Appellants filed post-trial motions which were denied. This appeal followed.

Appellants make three allegations of error, all of which deal with the trial court's charge to the jury. . . .

Appellants first argue that the trial court erred in refusing to charge the jury that PAT, as a common carrier, owes the highest duty of care to its fare paying passengers. The trial court charged the jury as follows on this question:

> Now, the Port Authority or the Defendant . . . owes a duty to passengers to operate the vehicles in which the passengers are boarding and which they are situated, to use that degree of care which they hold itself out to possess.
>
> Now, this degree of care is different than would be for an ordinary person. An ordinary person doesn't say ["]look [w]e're specialists in transporting you from point A to point B in a safe manner,["] but the Port Authority holds itself out to be an instrumentality that is transporting people and that they possess the skill and the

> knowledge and the training to do this in safety; and this is a duty they owed to Mr. Jones on this particular day in 1986 when he was allegedly injured or as he contends he was injured.
>
> Now, if they breach this duty, if they didn't exercise the degree of care that a reasonably prudent person would who's in the position of the Port Authority, then they would be negligent; . . .

Section 3.05 of the Pennsylvania Suggested Standard Civil Jury Instructions contains the following instruction regarding common carriers.

> The defendant in this case is a common carrier who is required by law to use a higher degree of care for the safety of its passengers than that ordinarily imposed on others and must be judged by a much stricter standard. Although this legal duty does not make the carrier absolutely responsible for the plaintiff's safety in all cases, it does obligate this carrier to exercise the highest degree of diligence and care in the (operation of its vehicle) and the (maintenance of its equipment and facilities). Any failure of the defendant to use such care under all of the circumstances of the particular situation in this case is negligence.

In Burch v. Sears, Roebuck and Co., 320 Pa. Superior Ct. 444, 467 A.2d 615 (1983), the court held that a trial court is to be given broad latitude in the choice of language used in charging a jury. Nevertheless, if the trial court's charge does not adequately explain the principle involved, a new trial must be granted. . . .

The law has long been well settled that a common carrier owes a heightened duty of care to its fare paying passengers. Over a century ago, the Supreme Court held that such a common carrier owed the duty of "extraordinary care." Philadelphia and Reading R.R. Co. v. Boger, 97 Pa. 91, 101 (1881). Cases of a more recent vintage have used the language "highest degree of care" as suggested by the Standard Civil Jury Instructions. . . .

All of the appellate courts of this Commonwealth have made clear that a common carrier owes the "highest duty of care" to its passengers. While the trial court attempted to explain the heightened level of care, we do not believe that attempt was sufficient, when we review the charge in its entirety as we must. . . . Accordingly, a new trial must be granted. . . .

Campbell v. Kovich

731 N.W.2d 112 (Mich. App. 2006)

Per Curiam. Plaintiffs Karie Campbell and David Campbell, individually and as next friends of plaintiffs Allison Campbell and Caitlin Campbell, minors, appeal as of right (1) an order granting summary disposition to defendants Steven Kovich and Julie Kovich and (2) an order granting summary disposition to defendant Ashton Minish. We affirm.

I

Karie was struck in the eye by an unknown, unrecovered object that she alleges was ejected from a lawn mower being operated by Ashton, who was mowing the Koviches' lawn. Plaintiffs' pleadings assert claims of negligence, negligent infliction of emotional distress, and loss of consortium. All defendants moved for summary disposition . . . which the trial court granted. . . .

. . . .

III

. . . [P]laintiffs contend that they presented sufficient evidence to establish that Ashton breached duties he owed in this case. We disagree.

. . . .

The parties cite, and this Court has located, no Michigan authority specifically addressing what degree of care a person mowing a lawn must exercise. In Gore v. Ohio Dep't of Transportation, 774 N.E.2d 817 (Ohio Ct. Cl., 2002), a limousine passenger brought an action against the Ohio Department of Transportation (ODOT) as the employer of an independent contractor that mowed grass on a highway median, alleging that ODOT was liable for injuries she sustained when a piece of rubber thrown from a mower struck her in the head. On ODOT's motion for summary judgment, the court held that ODOT was not liable for the independent contractor's negligence. The court also reasoned that "[r]emoving debris from the mower's path is a routine precaution, which any careful contractor could be expected to take in the exercise of ordinary care." Id. at 817 (emphasis added). Thus, Ohio authority persuasively suggests that inspecting a mower's path is what ordinary care requires.

Adopting the Ohio requirement for ordinary care as our own, there is insufficient evidence that Ashton failed to exercise reasonable care. On September 14, 2004, before mowing the Koviches' lawn, Ashton inspected the lawn for a couple of minutes. Karie admitted that while Ashton was mowing the lawn, he was not doing anything unusual, but was merely pushing the lawn mower, and that he did not appear to be in a hurry and appeared to be watching where he was walking. Before Karie was struck, Ashton was watching the area in front of him, and he did not see anything in front of the lawn mower. Karie also acknowledged in her deposition that Ashton never acknowledged that he had mowed over anything. Under these facts, there is no genuine issue of material fact regarding whether Ashton exercised reasonable care in the operation of the lawn mower.

. . . Ashton was not required to exercise extraordinary care. Ordinarily prudent people, when mowing a lawn, do not go to such extraordinary lengths that they do more than a brief inspection of the lawn before mowing, avoid mowing altogether when other persons are within 75 feet, mow only under close parental supervision, or look anywhere but ahead of where they are going while mowing. The evidence suggests that Ashton exercised ordinary care, but an accident of unclear causation occurred. Viewing the evidence in a light most favorable to plaintiffs, reasonable minds could not disagree that Ashton exercised due care. Accordingly, the trial court did not err in granting summary disposition to Ashton.

. . . .

Affirmed.

Adams v. Bullock

125 N.E. 93 (N.Y. 1919)

Cardozo, J. The defendant runs a trolley line in the city of Dunkirk, employing the overhead wire system. At one point, the road is crossed by a bridge or culvert which carries the tracks of the Nickle Plate and Pennsylvania Railroads. Pedestrians often use the bridge as a short cut between streets, and children play on it. On April 21, 1916, the plaintiff, a boy of 12 years, came across the bridge, swinging a wire about 8 feet long. In swinging it, he brought it in contact with the defendant's trolley wire, which ran beneath the structure. The side of the bridge was protected by a parapet 18 inches wide. Four feet 7 3/4 inches below the top of the parapet, the trolley wire was strung. The plaintiff was shocked and burned when the wires came together. He had a verdict at Trial Term, which has been affirmed at the Appellate Division by a divided court.

We think the verdict cannot stand. The defendant in using an overhead trolley was in the lawful exercise of its franchise. Negligence, therefore, cannot be imputed to it because [it] used that system and not another. There was, of course, a duty to adopt all reasonable precautions to minimize the resulting perils. We think there is no evidence that this duty was ignored. The trolley wire was so placed that no one standing on the bridge or even bending over the parapet could reach it. Only some extraordinary casualty, not fairly within the area of ordinary prevision, could make it a thing of danger. Reasonable care in the use of a destructive agency imports a high degree of vigilance. But no vigilance, however alert, unless fortified by the gift of prophecy, could have predicted the point upon the route where such an accident would occur. It might with equal reason have been expected anywhere else. At any point upon the route a mischievous or thoughtless boy might touch the wire with a metal pole, or fling another wire across it. If unable to reach it from the walk, he might stand upon a wagon or climb upon a tree. No special danger at this bridge warned the defendant that there was need of special measures of precaution. No like accident had occurred before. No custom had been disregarded. We think that ordinary caution did not involve forethought of this extraordinary peril. It has been so ruled in like circumstances by courts in other jurisdictions. [Citations omitted — Eds.] In those cases, the accidents were well within the range of prudent foresight. . . . There is, we may add, a distinction not to be ignored between electric light and trolley wires. The distinction is that the former may be insulated. Chance of harm, though remote, may betoken negligence, if needless. Facility of protection may impose a duty to protect. With trolley wires, the case is different. Insulation is impossible. Guards here and there are of little value. To avert the possibility of this accident and others like it at one point or another on the route, the defendant must have abandoned the overhead system, and put the wires underground. Neither its power nor its duty to make the change is shown. To hold it liable upon the facts exhibited in this record would be to charge it as an insurer.

The judgment should be reversed, and a new trial granted, with cost to abide the event.*

---

* [Prior to 1925, the Court of Appeals was not authorized by New York procedural law to enter a final judgment in a case in which it ruled, as a matter of law, that the plaintiff had failed to prove her

NOTES AND QUESTIONS

1. *Jury and Judge.* We saw in Chapter 2 that judges routinely insist that the duty element raises a question of *law* and that it is hence their province, not jurors', to fashion rules of duty. Judges just as commonly insist that the breach issue raises a question of *fact* that is for the jury. This latter sort of statement, though apt for reasons stated below, is potentially misleading in two ways. First, as *Myers* and *Martin* make clear, jurors are instructed by the judge to apply a particular legal standard in making their breach determinations; they do not have discretion to define breach however they choose. Second, while the application of this standard to particular cases requires jurors to make findings of fact, there is also an evaluative or normative component to the inquiry. In particular, jurors must render a judgment about whether, given the factual findings they have made, the defendant's conduct meets or falls short of the standard of care defined by the judge's instructions. Perhaps, then, when judges assert that breach is a question of fact rather than law, they are best understood as expressing in an emphatic way that it is jurors — rather than judges or policy experts — who ordinarily determine what it means in a given case to act in a reasonably careful manner. The last sentences of the first paragraph of the plaintiff's proffered jury instruction in *Myers* nicely captures this basic political commitment within negligence doctrine: "The law does not say how a reasonably careful person would act under those circumstances. That is for you to decide."

2. *Four Features of the Standard Breach Instruction.* In an extensive study of pattern jury instructions, Patrick Kelley and Laurel Wendt discovered substantial consistency across U.S. jurisdictions, including most notably the following four universal features:

a. The jury is instructed that "negligence" (breach) means a failure to use "ordinary care."
b. "Ordinary care" is defined by reference to a "reasonably careful person" or a "reasonably prudent person," and occasionally by reference to a "reasonable person."
c. The instruction directs that the jury is to consider whether the defendant was negligent *in doing something OR in failing to do something* — the jury is to think both about what a defendant has done and about what the defendant has not done.
d. The jury is required to consider the circumstances in which the defendant acted, and whether the defendant acted with ordinary care given the circumstances.

3. *Rulings as a Matter of Law.* As noted, it is black letter law in every U.S. jurisdiction that breach is an issue for the jury. Yet courts sometimes are willing to preempt or second-guess juries on that issue. Why did the lower court in *Martin* do so?

---

claim(s). Instead, it was required to remand for a new trial, at which the plaintiff in theory could present new evidence. Henry Cohen, *The Powers of the New York Court of Appeals* §§ 160-62, 431-39 (1934). Today, by contrast, a dispositive matter-of-law ruling against the plaintiff by the Court would result in an order finally resolving the case. — EDS.]

Compare *Martin* with *Campbell* and *Adams.* What reasons (if any) seem to support the decisions of the judges in *Campbell* and *Adams* to rule on breach as a matter of law? Are these reasons the same for each decision?

4. *Duty and Breach Revisited.* In standard formulations of negligence, "duty" and "breach" are listed as separate elements. This makes sense: some negligence suits clearly present questions of duty, not breach, whereas others clearly present questions of breach, not duty.

Aikens v. Debow, from Chapter 2, provides an example of a case that cleanly presents a duty issue that stands apart from any breach issue. The truck driver in that case almost certainly drove carelessly. Thus, breach did not present a contested issue. Nonetheless, the court concluded that *no duty* was owed to take care against causing economic loss. *Martin v. Evans,* above, provides an example of a case that cleanly presents a breach issue that stands apart from any duty issue. The truck driver in that case clearly owed a duty to take care not to physically harm those in the immediate vicinity of the truck. There remained nonetheless a question as to whether he breached that duty.

While in many instances the duty and breach elements thus pose distinct questions, it is also true that duty and breach are conceptually linked. After all, as used in negligence law, the word "breach" is shorthand for the phrase "breach of duty." Accordingly, it is easy, in the course of analyzing a breach question, for lawyers to slide into talk of duty. After all, in determining whether a breach has occurred, one naturally looks to isolate the *standard of conduct* by which breach is determined. It is of little help to say that the standard is "due care," because that leads to the question of what care is "due." And this question, in turn, can be understood as a question about duty—that is, the *content* of the duty owed by the defendant to the plaintiff.

Myers simultaneously demonstrates both the distinctiveness of the duty and breach questions and their potential for overlap. There was no question *whether* Heritage owed a duty of care to Myers. It quite clearly did. In this sense, *Myers* is a 'clean' breach case, just like *Martin v. Evans.* And yet *Myers* also invites a further question that emphasizes the connection between duty and breach: namely, the question of how best to characterize the duty of care owed by a nurse's aide to a resident of a nursing home. Is this duty best specified as a duty to use ordinary care? Or is it best specified as a duty to use the care that a professional would have used?

5. *Professional and Ordinary Standards of Care.* Why was the defendant in *Myers* so eager to have the nurses' aides held to a professional standard of care, and the plaintiff so eager to have the ordinary, non-professional negligence instruction? Does it make sense to think that professionals would be held to a standard *lower* than that of a reasonably careful person? As we will see later in this chapter, expert testimony typically plays a much larger role when the defendant's alleged breach consists of a departure from a standard of care owed by professionals to their clients or patients.

6. *Strict Liability.* Is the ruling in *Pingaro* that Rossi, the dog owner, failed to behave with the prudence of a reasonable person even though he erected fencing,

posted a clear warning sign at the only entrance to the premises, and arranged with previous meter readers not to have them enter the premises when there was no one at home to control the dogs? Suppose Rossi had also penned the dogs into an area away from the meter using fencing that he had bought from a reputable store, and that had been represented by the store to be adequate to restrain German Shepherds. Suppose further that, against all odds, the dogs still managed to break loose and attack Pingaro. Would liability still attach under the statute? If so, what can Rossi do to avoid liability for dog bites?

Notice how the dog-bite statute, as applied to attacks on the premises, departs from the rules we encountered in Chapter 2 concerning dangerous conditions located on real property. Even absent such a statute, the common law has long held owners of dogs and other animals strictly liable for injuries caused by them, whether on or off the owner's property. However, in contrast to the standard set by the statute, the common law rule of strict liability applies only to owners who know or have reason to know that the animal in question is prone to be vicious or otherwise abnormally dangerous. (*Pingaro* refers to this as the "scienter" requirement.) Thus, under the common law, so long as the plaintiff can establish that a dog owner knew or should have known his dog was prone to viciousness, the owner cannot escape liability even if he employed all reasonable means to control the animal.* Strict liability for injuries caused by domestic animals and livestock is discussed in Chapter 11.

7. Ordinary Care And Extraordinary Care. As noted by the appellate court in *Jones*, "common carriers" — commercial and governmental operators of boats, buses, planes, and trains — have long been held to owe their passengers greater-than-ordinary care. Implicit in the court's ruling is its sense that, with the proper instruction, the jury might have rendered a verdict for the plaintiffs instead of the defendant. Do you think the bus driver's conduct satisfies the standard of ordinary care but fails the test of extraordinary care?

Many modern courts and commentators have urged that the conduct of common carriers toward their passengers be judged under the ordinary reasonable person standard. *See, e.g.*, Bethel v. New York City Transit Auth., 703 N.E.2d 1214 (N.Y. 1998). *Bethel* reasoned that common carriers are not sufficiently distinct from other actors as to warrant the imposition of a higher standard of care, and that a heightened standard is unnecessary because the reasonable person standard takes into account all relevant factors, including the character of the relationship between defendant and plaintiff. Do you find these rationales convincing? Are there downsides to "flattening" all standards of care into a single standard of reasonableness? In *Rowland v. Christian* (Chapter 2), the California Supreme Court aimed to achieve a similar flattening by getting rid of the plaintiff-status categories for claims arising out of hazardous conditions on land. Eliminating the clutter and seeming arbitrariness of multiple standards

* To say that the dog bite statute and common law impose strict liability (albeit in different forms) is not to say that dog owners have no defenses available to them. For example, owners might be able to eliminate or mitigate liability by establishing that the victim goaded the dog (assumption of risk) or failed to take reasonable care for her own safety (contributory negligence or comparative fault). Defenses are discussed in Chapter 7.

Check Your Understanding

Common Carriers and Extraordinary Care

Courts that require common carriers to exercise extraordinary care do so only with respect to carrier activities closely related to the transportation of passengers. For example, in *Mandal v. Port Authority*, 64 A.3d 239 (N.J. App. Div. 2013), the court held that the carrier was required to use extraordinary care to ensure the safety of boarding areas but only ordinary care in maintaining other parts of its station.

What exactly does it mean to demand "extraordinary care" on the part of an actor? Imagine you were driving a car in a jurisdiction that requires the exercise of extraordinary care by drivers of ordinary passenger cars. Would you behave differently than you would when driving in a jurisdiction that ordinary care? Might a requirement of extraordinary rather than ordinary care make some other practical difference(s)?

of care, or multiple status categories, can achieve a certain kind of intellectual tidiness. In doing so, however, might it also be avoiding, rather than addressing, questions that are highly pertinent to the assignment of responsibility?

8. Unreasonable Versus Reckless Behavior. We saw in Chapter 2 that, in some jurisdictions, owners and occupiers of land owe lesser duties of care to certain persons, such as trespassers. Consider the following instruction, provided in a case in which a train passenger was killed when, after disembarking from a local train at a station, she attempted to cross a set of tracks on foot, at which point she was run down by a different train, owned by Amtrak. Under Massachusetts law, the passenger was deemed a trespasser because she did not cross the tracks at an established crossing. Thus, Amtrak owed her only the lesser duty of not causing her injury through willful or reckless conduct. The trial court instructed the jury as follows on the recklessness standard:

> To prove that Amtrak was reckless in this case, plaintiff must prove that Amtrak intentionally or unreasonably disregarded a risk that presented a high degree of probability that substantial harm would result to another. The risk of death or grave bodily injury must have been known or reasonably apparent to Amtrak, and the harm must have been a probable consequence of Amtrak's election to run that risk or its failure to reasonably recognize it.
>
> To intentionally disregard a risk means to ignore or neglect it deliberately, rather than by accident or mistake.
>
> To unreasonably disregard a risk means to ignore or neglect a risk that a person of ordinary prudence would act to reduce or eliminate.
>
> In this case, plaintiff must also prove that any risk that was intentionally or unreasonably disregarded involved a high probability of substantial harm. This means that plaintiff must prove that substantial harm was more than a foreseeable possibility or likely to occur. Rather, plaintiff must prove that a reasonable person in Amtrak's position would recognize that substantial harm was highly likely to occur. Plaintiff does not, however, have to prove that substantial harm was certain to occur. . . .

> So, to prove recklessness, plaintiff must prove that there was a high probability that a person would be seriously injured or killed crossing the tracks at the Attleboro station and that Amtrak intentionally or unreasonably disregarded that risk.
>
> The mere fact that an accident occurred does not mean that Amtrak was reckless. Moreover, in this case, it would be insufficient for the plaintiff to prove only what is called negligence, which is a failure to use reasonable care. . . . To prevail, the plaintiff must meet a higher standard and prove recklessness, as I defined that term for you today. . . .

Beausoleil v. National R.R. Passenger Corp., 145 F. Supp. 2d 119, 125-126 (D. Mass. 2001). Earlier, Amtrak had moved for summary judgment on the ground that there was insufficient evidence to support a jury finding of recklessness. In rejecting this argument, the court noted that, even though Amtrak had posted warning signs and provided partial fencing, it knew that passengers continued to cross the tracks despite these precautions, and that another passenger had previously been killed under similar circumstances. It had also been warned by a state legislator of the grave dangers posed at this location. Finally, the driver of the train acknowledged in deposition testimony that he knew that passengers who disembarked from other trains routinely crossed the tracks at this station, and that he failed to radio ahead to determine if any trains had just left the station. Beausoleil v. National R.R. Passenger Corp., 138 F. Supp. 2d 189, 205 (D. Mass. 2001).

Does the recklessness instruction, in conjunction with the extraordinary care instruction in *Jones*, help refine the idea of reasonable care? If you were serving as a juror, how might these different formulations affect your deliberations?

9. *Emergencies.* Courts are divided over whether to give specific instructions to juries on certain special instances of breach, for example, breaches that allegedly occur in emergency contexts. Suppose *D* is driving down the highway at a safe distance behind a truck. Several crates suddenly fall off the back of the truck directly in front of *D*. *D* swerves to avoid them and collides with *P*, who is injured and sues *D* for carelessly swerving her car into his. All courts agree that a jury is entitled to take into account that *D* swerved in response to an unforeseen emergency in determining whether *D* behaved like a reasonable person under the circumstances. They differ, however, over whether the jury should receive a general "reasonably careful person under the circumstances" instruction as seen in *Martin*, or whether that instruction should be supplemented with an instruction specifically informing the jury that it may take into account the emergency in assessing the allegedly negligent party's conduct. *See* Dan B. Dobbs, *The Law of Torts* § 131, at 307 (2000) (discussing the debate).

10. *Holmes (Goodman) Versus Cardozo (Pokora).* Some have urged that judges should more frequently issue as-a-matter-of-law rulings on breach. For example, in his book *The Common Law*, future Supreme Court Justice Oliver Wendell Holmes argued as follows:

> [A]ny legal standard must, in theory, be capable of being known. When a man has to pay damages, he is supposed to have broken the law, and he is further supposed to have known what the law was.

> [Accordingly], it is . . . clear that the featureless generality that the defendant was bound to use such care as a prudent man would do under the circumstances, ought to be continually giving place to the specific one, that he was bound to use this or that precaution under these or those circumstances. . . . If . . . courts . . . left every case, without rudder or compass, to the jury, they would simply confess their inability to state a very large part of the law which they required the defendant to know, and would assert, by implication, that nothing could be learned by experience.

Oliver W. Holmes, Jr., *The Common Law* 111-112 (1881).

Later, as a Justice, Holmes had occasion to practice what he preached. In *Baltimore & O. R. Co. v. Goodman*, 275 U.S. 66 (1927), the Court was confronted with a case involving a grade-crossing collision between plaintiff's car and defendant's train. The issue was whether the plaintiff was contributorily negligent — and hence, under the law of the time, barred from recovering any damages — because he failed to come to a complete stop and check for oncoming trains before proceeding across the tracks. Overturning lower court rulings that the issue of contributory fault was for the jury to decide, Holmes, writing for the Court, declared a rule for grade crossing cases specifying that all drivers must, at a minimum, stop at the tracks and look for oncoming trains to avoid being found at fault. Moreover, the Court held, if a driver's view is obstructed at the stopping point, he is further obliged to get out of his car and reconnoiter. While granting that "the question of due care is very generally left to the jury," Holmes reasoned that "we are dealing with a standard of conduct, and where the standard is clear it should be laid down once and for all by the courts." 275 U.S., at 70.

Seven years later, Benjamin Cardozo, the author of *Adams*, now sitting in the Supreme Court seat vacated by Holmes, substantially undid the work of his predecessor. While reaffirming "stop, look, and listen" as a per se rule of reasonable conduct for drivers approaching grade crossings, Cardozo's opinion abandoned *Goodman*'s "get out and reconnoiter" rule. Noting that the latter was not in keeping with normal driving practices and that it creates dangers of its own, Cardozo emphasized "the need for caution in framing standards of behavior that amount to rules of law," particularly where "there is no background of experience out of which the standards have emerged." The courts, he said, should not impose rules that they have "artificially developed." Rather, in the absence of "the guide of customary conduct, what is suitable for the traveler caught in a mesh where the ordinary safeguards fail him is a judgment for the jury." Pokora v. Wabash Ry. Co., 292 U.S. 98, 106 (1934).

11. MacPherson, Pokora, and Adams. Why did Cardozo — who in *MacPherson* dispensed with the judge-imposed privity limit on negligence claims for product-related injuries, and who in *Pokora* spoke eloquently in defense of the jury's discretion on the issue of breach — treat the breach question in *Adams* as one for the court? In support of the court's no-breach-as-a-matter-of-law ruling, Cardozo's very compact opinion cites an array of relevant considerations: the lawfulness of the defendant's franchise, the lack of feasible precautions, conformity with custom, the lack of predictability of the injury, the lack of specificity in the time or place where such an accident could have occurred, the bounds of "prudent foresight," and others. How do all of these considerations enter into the resolution of the breach question?

Reread the final substantive sentence of *Adams*: "To hold [the defendant] liable upon the facts exhibited in this record would be to charge it as an insurer." Is this statement meant to be taken at face value, or is it mere hyperbole? If the former, what would be wrong with holding the defendant liable as an insurer?

Big Think

MacPherson and *Adams*

In his *MacPherson v. Buick* opinion (Chapter 2), Cardozo reasoned that a car manufacturer owes a duty of care to drivers and passengers of its cars in part because they stand out as persons for whom "the consequences of negligence [by the manufacturer] may be foreseen." In his *Adams* opinion, by contrast, Cardozo emphasized that the defendant had no reason to foresee that a user of the bridge might be injured by the defendant's electrified wires in the space below the bridge.

Is Cardozo's claim in *Adams* that the trolley company owed no duty to take care against injuring persons located just a few feet from their tracks and wires? If not — if a duty was owed by the trolley company to persons such as Adams — then what role did foreseeability play in Cardozo's analysis?

The juxtaposition of *MacPherson* and *Adams* illustrates an ongoing struggle experienced by students, professors, lawyers, and judges alike: Can the *duty* question and the *breach* question really be separated? The problem is exacerbated by the fact that foreseeability seems relevant to both. And, while it is true that duty is an issue of law for the court, whereas breach is a mixed question of law and fact for the jury, *Adams* demonstrates that judges are sometimes willing and able to take the breach issue away from the jury when they think the evidence on the issue is completely one-sided.

Cardozo certainly thought that duty and breach posed different questions, though he also recognized ways in which they are connected. He also thought that foreseeability is relevant to both. Overwhelmingly, this remains the view of the courts (and it is the view of the editors of this book).

One way to capture the different roles played by foreseeability in duty and breach is to think about the different levels of generality or abstraction at which one can inquire about the foreseeability of a certain kind of consequence. Returning to *Adams*, consider the following two propositions: (1) the trolley company could foresee that carelessness of one form or another in the operation of its trolley system might result in physical injury to a person in close physical proximity to its operations, and (2) the trolley company could not foresee that a person might be injured by coming into contact with the wires that passed under the Nickle Plate railroad bridge. Are these propositions inconsistent? If not, do they help capture how Cardozo could rule as he did in both *MacPherson* and *Adams*?

II. DEFINING THE PERSON OF ORDINARY PRUDENCE

We noted in Chapter 2 that English courts long ago recognized duties owed by owners and possessors of property to take care in undertaking activities on their property so as not to injure others nearby. As it turns out, the decision cited for that proposition — Vaughan v. Menlove — is more famous for its discussion of breach than of duty.

Vaughan v. Menlove

132 Eng. Rep. 490 (C. P. 1837)

[What follows is a syllabus or summary of the case prepared by a professional case reporter. It begins with the reporter's recitation of the facts and procedural history of the case, and then is followed by his transcription of the judges' opinions, which were issued orally. — EDS.]

The declaration stated, that before and at the time of the grievance and injury, hereinafter mentioned, certain premises, to wit, two cottages . . . in the county of Salop, were . . . in the respective possessions and occupations of certain persons as tenants thereof to the Plaintiff . . . : that the Defendant was then possessed of a certain close near to the said cottages, and of certain buildings of wood and thatch, also near to the said cottages; and that the Defendant was then also possessed of a certain rick or stack of hay before then heaped, stacked, or put together, and then standing, and being in and upon the said close of the Defendant. That on the 1st of August 1835, while the said cottages so were in the occupation of the said tenants, . . . the said rick or stack of hay of the Defendant was liable and likely to . . . break out into a flame . . . ; and by reason of . . . the state and condition of the said rick or stack of hay, the same then was and continued dangerous to the said cottages; of which said several premises the Defendant then had notice; yet the Defendant well knowing the premises, but not regarding his duty in that behalf, . . . wrongfully negligently, and improperly, kept and continued the said rick or stack of hay, so likely and liable to . . . take fire, and in a state and condition dangerous to the said cottages, although he could, and might, and ought to have removed and altered the same, so as to prevent the same from being and continuing so dangerous as aforesaid; and by reason thereof the said cottages for a long time, . . . were in great danger of being consumed by fire. That by reason of the . . . carelessness, negligence, and improper conduct of the Defendant, . . . the said rick or stack of hay of the Defendant, . . . did . . . break out into flame, and by fire and flame thence issuing and arising, the said buildings of the Defendant . . . were set on fire; and thereby . . . fire and flame so occasioned as aforesaid by the igniting and breaking out into flame, . . . was thereupon . . . communicated unto the said cottages in which the Plaintiff was interested . . . , which were thereby then respectively set on fire, and then . . . were consumed, damaged and wholly destroyed, the cottages being of great value, to wit, the value of 500 [pounds].* . . .

At the trial it appeared that the rick in question had been made by the Defendant near the boundary of his own premises; that the hay was in such a state when put together, as to give rise to discussions on the probability of fire; that though there were conflicting opinions on the subject, yet during a period of five weeks, the Defendant was repeatedly warned of his peril; that his stock was insured; and that upon one occasion, being advised to take the rick down to avoid all danger, he said "he would chance it." He made an aperture or chimney through the rick; but in spite,

* [Combustion caused by the release of chemicals from stacked hay that is rotting because of exposure to excessive moisture apparently remains a problem today. *See* www.montana.edu/cpa/news/wwwpb-archives/ag/hayfire.html. — EDS.]

or perhaps in consequence of this precaution, the rick at length burst into flames from the spontaneous heating of its materials; the flames communicated to the Defendant's barn and stables, and thence to the Plaintiff's cottages, which were entirely destroyed.

Patteson J. before whom the cause was tried, told the jury that the question for them to consider, was, whether the fire had been occasioned by gross negligence on the part of the Defendant; adding, that he was bound to proceed with such reasonable caution as a prudent man would have exercised under such circumstances.

A verdict having been found for the Plaintiff, a rule nisi for a new trial was obtained,* on the ground that the jury should have been directed to consider, not, whether the Defendant had been guilty of gross negligence with reference to the standard of ordinary prudence, a standard too uncertain to afford any criterion; but whether he had acted bona fide to the best of his judgment; if he had, he ought not to be responsible for the misfortune of not possessing the highest order of intelligence. . . .

TINDAL, C.J. . . . It is contended . . . that the learned Judge was wrong in leaving this to the jury as a case of gross negligence, and that the question of negligence was so mixed up with reference to what would be the conduct of a man of ordinary prudence that the jury might have thought the latter the rule by which they were to decide; that such a rule would be too uncertain to act upon; and that the question ought to have been whether the Defendant had acted honestly and bona fide to the best of his own judgment. That, however, would leave so vague a line as to afford no rule at all, the degree of judgment belonging to each individual being infinitely various: and though it has been urged that the care which a prudent man would take, is not an intelligible proposition as a rule of law, yet such has always been the rule adopted in cases of bailment, as laid down in Coggs v. Bernard (2 Ld. Raym. 909). Though in some cases a greater degree of care is exacted than in others, yet in "the second sort of bailment, viz. commodatum or lending gratis, the borrower is bound to the strictest care and diligence to keep the goods so as to restore them back again to the lender; because the bailee has a benefit by the use of them, so as if the bailee be guilty of the least neglect he will be answerable; as if a man should lend another a horse to go westward, or for a month; if the bailee put this horse in his stable, and he were stolen from thence, the bailee shall not be answerable for him: but if he or his servant leave the house or stable doors open and the thieves take the opportunity of that, and steal the horse, he will be chargeable, because the neglect gave the thieves the occasion to steal the horse." The care taken by a prudent man has always been the rule laid down; and as to the supposed difficulty of applying it, a jury has always been able to say, whether, taking that rule as their guide, there has been negligence on the occasion in question.

Instead, therefore, of saying that the liability for negligence should be co-extensive with the judgment of each individual, which would be as variable as the length of the foot of each individual, we ought rather to adhere to the rule which requires in all cases a regard to caution such as a man of ordinary prudence would observe. That was in

---

* [The issuance of a "rule nisi" is roughly akin to the modern practice of granting a motion for a new trial on the ground that some error of law may have prejudiced the outcome. — EDS.]

substance the criterion presented to the jury in this case, and therefore the present rule must be discharged. . . .

VAUGHAN, J. . . . It was, if anything, too favourable to the Defendant to leave it to the jury whether he had been guilty of gross negligence; for when the Defendant upon being warned as to the consequences likely to ensue from the condition of the rick, said, "he would chance it," it was manifest he adverted to his interest in the insurance office. The conduct of a prudent man has always been the criterion for the jury in such cases: but it is by no means confined to them. In insurance cases, where a captain has sold his vessel after damage too extensive for repairs, the question has always been, whether he had pursued the course which a prudent man would have pursued under the same circumstance. Here, there was not a single witness whose testimony did not go to establish gross negligence in the Defendant. He had repeated warnings of what was likely to occur, and the whole calamity was occasioned by his procrastination.

Rule discharged.

Appelhans v. McFall

757 N.E.2d 987 (Ill. App. 2001), *app. denied*, 766 N.E.2d 238 (Ill. 2002)

BYRNE, J. . . .

On October 4, 1999, plaintiff, who was 66 years old at the time, was walking north along the eastern edge of McCabe Road in the Township of Nunda when William [McFall], who was five years old, rode his bicycle and struck plaintiff from behind. Plaintiff fell and suffered a fractured hip. At the time of the accident, it was daylight outside, the pavement was clear and dry, and no other pedestrians, automobiles, or bicyclists were present. The roadway in the area was straight and flat.

In count I, plaintiff alleged that William's parents negligently failed to (1) instruct their son on the proper use of his bicycle, or (2) supervise him while he rode his bicycle on a public roadway because they knew or should have known that his youth would prevent him from considering the safety of pedestrians such as plaintiff. Plaintiff alleged that her injuries were proximately caused by the parents' failure to supervise their son or teach him how to use his bicycle properly. In count II, plaintiff generally asserted that William negligently caused the collision.

Defendants filed a motion to dismiss. . . . The trial court granted the motion, concluding that William's youth rendered him incapable of negligence and that plaintiff failed to allege specific facts that would have put William's parents on notice that he might ride his bicycle negligently. This timely appeal followed.

THE TENDER YEARS DOCTRINE

Defendants' motion to dismiss . . . admits all well-pleaded facts in the complaint and all reasonable inferences drawn therefrom. . . . The fact that disposes of this issue is undisputed: William was five years old when he collided with plaintiff.

On appeal, plaintiff contends that we should abandon the well-settled rule that a child is incapable of negligence if he is less than seven years old. She argues that we should adopt the "Massachusetts Rule," under which any child will be found capable of negligence if the fact finder decides that the child failed to exercise a degree of care that is reasonable for similarly situated children.

Section 283A of the Restatement (Second) of Torts (Restatement) mirrors the Massachusetts Rule and provides that "[if] the actor is a child, the standard of conduct to which he must conform to avoid being negligent is that of a reasonable person of like age, intelligence, and experience under like circumstances." Restatement (Second) of Torts § 283A (1965). Comment b to section 283A further provides in relevant part:

> "Some courts have endeavored to lay down fixed rules as to a minimum age below which the child is incapable of being negligent, and a maximum age above which he is to be treated like an adult. Usually these rules have been derived from the old rules of the criminal law, by which a child under the age of seven was considered incapable of crime, and one over fourteen was considered to be as capable as an adult. The prevailing view is that in tort cases no such arbitrary limits can be fixed. Undoubtedly there is a minimum age, probably somewhere in the vicinity of four years, below which negligence can never be found; but with the great variation in the capacities of children and the situations which may arise, it cannot be fixed definitely for all cases." Restatement (Second) of Torts § 283A, Comment b (1965).

In 1886, our supreme court held that an injured child who was seven years and three months old at the time of the accident "was too young, at the time she was injured, to observe any care for her personal safety." Chicago, St. Louis & Pittsburgh R.R. Co. v. Welsh, 118 Ill. 572, 574, 9 N.E. 197 (1886). The court later expressly adopted the tender years doctrine, which states that a child is incapable of . . . negligence if he is less than seven years old. Chicago City Ry. Co. v. Tuohy, 196 Ill. 410, 422, 63 N.E. 997 (1902). . . . The rationale for the tender years doctrine is the belief that a child under the age of seven is incapable of recognizing and appreciating risk and is therefore deemed incapable of negligence as a matter of law. Chu [v. Bowers], 275 Ill. App. 3d 861, 864 [(1995)]. The child's immaturity limits his liability regardless of whether, as a litigant, he is the plaintiff or the defendant.

. . . Plaintiff [argues] that profound societal changes since the adoption of the rule undermine . . . stare decisis. Specifically, plaintiff asserts that the judiciary that crafted the rule did not envision "cable television, video games, the internet, pre-teen gangs, and violent crime." She argues that, in response to these modern-day challenges, children are instructed at an early age that they must exercise good judgment for themselves and others and therefore we may hold them to a reasonable standard of care based upon their age.

In reaffirming its preference for the Massachusetts Rule, the Supreme Court of Minnesota quoted an opinion it drafted in 1936:

> "'Under present-day circumstances a child of [tender years] is permitted to assume many responsibilities. There is much opportunity for him to observe and thus become cognizant of the necessity for exercising some degree of care. Compulsory school attendance, the radio, the movies, and traffic conditions all tend to have this effect. . . . The Illinois rule has no basis in sound reason or logic. It is based upon an outworn historical rule of criminal law which refused to acknowledge any capacity on the part of any child under seven years of age to distinguish between right and

> wrong.'" (Emphasis omitted.) Toetschinger [v. Ihnot], 312 Minn. 59, 65-66 [(1977)], 250 N.W.2d at 208, quoting Eckhardt v. Hanson, 196 Minn. 270, 272, 264 N.W. 776, 777 (1936).

The Minnesota high court recognized that children were sufficiently sophisticated in 1936 to be held to a reasonable standard of care. As society has changed dramatically since the *Eckhardt* court made its observations, children have become even more sophisticated. Because the tender years doctrine is based on the assumption that young children cannot recognize or appreciate risk, the rule is increasingly undermined as society more thoroughly educates them on safety issues. We find *Eckhardt* to be persuasive, and it lends great weight to plaintiff's argument that Illinois children under the age of seven may be negligent.

Plaintiff further contends that the tender years doctrine . . . leads to "ridiculous" results because a child does not "magically" know to exercise due care after his seventh birthday. In *Chu*, the Third District acknowledged that several jurisdictions have accepted this argument and rejected the tender years doctrine accordingly. *Chu*, 275 Ill. App. 3d at 864-65. . . . We agree with plaintiff that the arbitrariness of the rule supports its abandonment. However, we reluctantly conclude that the principle of stare decisis requires this court to reassert the tender years doctrine.

It is well settled that where it is clear that a court has made a mistake in adopting a rule, it should not decline to correct it, even though the rule may have been reasserted and acquiesced in for many years. No person has a vested right in any rule of law entitling him to insist that it shall remain for his benefit. However, when a rule of law has been settled, it should be followed unless a party can show that serious detriment prejudicial to the public interest is likely to arise. The rule of stare decisis is founded upon sound principles in the administration of justice, and a court should not depart from rules long recognized as the law merely because the court believes that it might decide the issue differently if the question were novel.

. . . The modification in the law that plaintiff advocates is . . . far-reaching . . . , and we decline to announce such a sweeping change here. Instead, we invite our supreme court or the legislature to revisit the viability of the tender years doctrine.

When a child is between 7 and 14 years old, the trier of fact must consider the "age, capacity, intelligence, and experience of the child" in light of the rebuttable presumption that a child between the ages of 7 and 14 is incapable of negligence. Savage v. Martin, 256 Ill. App. 3d 272, 281, 195 Ill. Dec. 142, 628 N.E.2d 606 (1993). However, it is well settled in Illinois that a child who is 14 years old or who engages in an adult activity is held to an adult standard of care. Because bicycle riding on a public street is not an adult activity, a bicyclist between the ages of 7 and 14 is held to a reasonable standard of care based upon his age and experience. *Chu*, 275 Ill. App. 3d at 865. Therefore, one could argue that, when a child under the age of 7 engages in an activity that children between the ages of 7 and 14 normally pursue, such as riding a bicycle, the child should be held to the standard of care of a reasonable 7-year-old. However, we do not answer this question here.

. . . We conclude that the trial court correctly dismissed count II of plaintiff's complaint because William was incapable of negligence at the time of the accident.

NEGLIGENT PARENTAL SUPERVISION

Plaintiff next asserts that William's parents were negligent for failing to supervise William or instruct him on the proper use of his bicycle. . . . [T]he parent-child relationship does not automatically render parents liable for the torts of their minor children. [Lott v. Strang, 312 Ill. App. 3d 521, 524 (2000).] Parents may be liable, however, if they do not adequately control or supervise their child. To prove a claim of negligent supervision, a plaintiff must show that (1) the parents were aware of specific instances of prior conduct sufficient to put them on notice that the act complained of was likely to occur and (2) the parents had the opportunity to control the child. *Lott*, 312 Ill. App. 3d at 523-24 . . . ; Restatement (Second) of Torts § 316 (1965).

Here, plaintiff alleged that the parents' mere knowledge of William's age sufficiently informed them that ongoing supervision was necessary. Plaintiff did not assert that the parents knew of a specific prior incident where William negligently struck a pedestrian while he rode his bicycle. Plaintiff essentially contends that parents should be liable for all negligent acts of their children. However, we conclude that holding parents strictly liable for failing to prevent their child's negligence is unreasonable and unsupported by the law. *Cf. Chu*, 275 Ill. App. 3d at 865 ("it is in the nature of children to be careless and thoughtless on occasion, and society must be ever aware of the need to exercise extraordinary caution when children are present").

In *Lott*, the plaintiffs sued the parents of an unemancipated minor who caused a traffic collision while he was allegedly intoxicated. In support of their negligent parental supervision claim, the plaintiffs alleged that the parents knew that their son was likely to drive negligently because he had been at fault in an earlier traffic accident. The . . . Appellate Court affirmed the dismissal, concluding that section 316 of the Restatement does not require parents to "prevent their children from ever entering into a situation where they might commit a negligent act." *Lott*, 312 Ill. App. 3d at 525. . . . The court further noted that the parents had no duty to discipline their child and regulate his conduct on a long-term ongoing basis. Parents are not liable for such broadly defined omissions. *Lott*, 312 Ill. App. 3d at 525. . . .

In this case, plaintiff defines the omission in parenting even more broadly than the alleged parental negligence addressed in *Lott*. Furthermore, plaintiff does not allege that the parents had an opportunity to follow William to ensure that he rode his bicycle safely. We conclude that plaintiff did not allege the two elements of negligent parental supervision. . . .

NOTES AND QUESTIONS

1. *The Objective Standard. Vaughan* is perhaps the leading decision for the proposition that the issue of whether a defendant has lived up to the standard of reasonable care is to be determined by the application of an *objective* standard of care, not a *subjective* one. The objective/subjective distinction with regard to the issue of reasonable care has at least two different ideas packed into it.

The first is a distinction between whether the *conduct of the defendant was reasonably careful* (objective) versus whether *the defendant's attitude was one of trying to be reasonably careful* (subjective). Here, the term *objective* means conduct-based, whereas *subjective* means state-of-mind based. As to this version of the objective/subjective distinction, the standard of reasonable care in negligence law is clearly objective—the primary question is whether the "external" conduct of the defendant was reasonably careful, not whether he maintained an "internal" attitude of concern or care as he went about his business.

A second iteration of the objective/subjective distinction concerns the criteria against which to assess the (external) reasonableness of the defendant's conduct. On the one hand, one could compare the defendant's conduct to how an *ordinary person*, acting reasonably, would have behaved under the circumstances (objective). On the other hand, one could assess the defendant's conduct by considering *how a person with defendant's attributes*, acting reasonably, would have behaved under the circumstances (subjective). Here "objective" is generalized, using a non-individualized norm to set the standard, while "subjective" particularizes or individualizes the standard of care to fit the individual defendant's personal attributes. Again, the black letter law of negligence is that reasonable care is to be determined in the objective, generalized manner, not in a subjective manner that particularizes. However, as we will see, there are some pockets of case law where courts are willing to raise or lower the standard of care, depending on defendant's attributes.

Vaughan holds that the standard of care employed by negligence law is and should be objective in both of the foregoing respects. For what reason(s)? Recall Justice Oliver Wendell Holmes, who (as indicated in the notes following *Adams v. Bullock*) argued in favor of reducing the general ordinary prudence standard to specific rules of conduct. Holmes also penned a memorable defense of *Vaughan*'s objective standard:

> If . . . a man is born hasty and awkward, is always having accidents and hurting himself or his neighbors, no doubt his congenital defects will be allowed for in the courts of Heaven, but his slips are no less troublesome to his neighbors than if they sprang from guilty neglect. His neighbors, accordingly require him, at his proper peril, to come up to their standard. . . .

Oliver W. Holmes, Jr., *The Common Law* 108 (1881). What does Holmes mean by the phrases "guilty neglect" and "proper peril"? What is the point of his contrast between accountability in earthly courts that apply common law and accountability in the "courts of Heaven"?

Oliver W. Holmes, Jr.
Massachusetts Supreme Judicial Court (1899-1902)
U.S. Supreme Court (1902-1932)

Others, including Arthur Ripstein, have argued that, once Menlove undertook an activity posing risk of physical harm to others, those others were entitled to rely on his competence, and hence Menlove is precluded (estopped) from claiming an incapacity to foresee and protect against those harms. Ripstein also suggests that employment of a subjective standard would violate an entitlement of each person to enjoy an equal degree of protection from others' risky conduct. Are there additional (or alternative) arguments, more pragmatic in nature, for the use of the objective standard? What incentives might a subjective standard create for future actors? How compelling are the administrative concerns identified by Chief Judge Tindal?

2. *Inadvertence and Breach.* Menlove's case was not aided by the evidence indicating that he was aware of the risk that the hay rick would ignite, but decided to "chance it." This evidence suggests that Menlove might not even have benefited from the subjective standard for which his lawyers argued. It also raises an important point about the nature of faulty or careless conduct. It is natural to equate negligence with inadvertence. Usually when one is being careless, it is because one is not paying attention to certain risks. However, there are instances of "advertent" negligence (*Vaughan* itself appears to have been one).

Suppose *D* is driving 40 m.p.h. on a seemingly deserted street with a posted speed limit of 25 m.p.h. Suppose further that he is fully aware that he is speeding. *P*, exercising due care, backs his car out of his driveway onto the street. Because *D* is speeding, *D* cannot stop in time to avoid colliding with *P*. The fact that *D* was aware he was speeding does not of itself establish that his conduct was anything other than careless. His awareness does not entail that *D* acted for the purpose of injuring another, or with knowledge to a near certainty that he was going to injure another. Likewise, if the risk of injury to others that attended *D*'s speeding was relatively small, his being aware of that risk may not be sufficient to establish recklessness. Rather, it may be that this is an instance of carelessness in which the defendant happened to appreciate that he was acting carelessly.

3. *Physical Disabilities.* The "objective" standard entails that a given defendant's conduct is to be measured by reference to the abilities ordinarily found in other persons. *Which* other persons are to provide the basis for that comparison varies, depending on the type of incapacity alleged by the defendant, and perhaps the type of conduct in question. A court likely would not hold that a completely blind person who, while walking down a sidewalk, bumps into someone else, has failed to exercise reasonable care *because she did not look where she was going*, even though the ordinary person surely does take such care. In this instance, the basis for comparison is not the ordinary person (who is sighted), but the ordinary blind person. This change in reference point does *not* mean that the blind pedestrian is insulated from all claims of negligence. Rather it means that, to prevail in such a case, the plaintiff must show that the pedestrian failed to take precautions that a prudent blind person would take (e.g., failed to use a cane to sense the presence of others and to alert others to her blindness). *Cf.* Poyner v. Loftus, 694 A.2d 69 (D.C. Ct. App. 1997) (visually impaired pedestrian at fault for not using cane or guide dog that would have prevented his fall); Stephens v. Dulaney, 428 P.2d 27 (N.M. 1967) (plaintiff with no sense of smell must exercise reasonable care in light of that incapacity), *overruled in part on other grounds*, 491 P.2d 1147 (N.M. 1971). Note, however, if a blind person were to attempt to drive a car, he would presumably be found to have acted unreasonably as a matter of law. Is this because he would have failed to act like a sighted person of ordinary prudence? (It is surely unreasonable for a sighted person to drive with her eyes closed.) Or is it consistent with the application of a "reasonable blind person" standard, in that no reasonable blind person would get into a car and drive it?

4. *Heightened Competence.* While expressing doubt that an injury victim should benefit from the "fortuity" of being injured by a person who happens to possess above-average abilities, the Third Restatement of Torts allows that a particular person's superior abilities are "circumstances to be taken into account" in determining whether her conduct conformed to the standard of ordinary prudence. Restatement (Third) of Torts: Liability for Physical and Emotional Harm § 12 (2010). For example, imagine a professional skier who, while skiing recreationally alongside members of the general public, collides with and injures a non-professional skier. If the victim can establish that the professional skier failed to undertake a particular maneuver that would have avoided the collision, the professional skier can be found to have acted. *Cf.* Cervelli v. Graves, 661 P.2d 1032 (Wyo. 1983) (allowing jurors to consider a professional truck driver's heightened driving skill in deciding whether he was negligent). Do you agree with the Restatement's position? Is negligence law inconsistent in refusing to take account of certain inabilities (e.g., an actor's congenital clumsiness) while at the same time taking account of certain special abilities?

5. *Awkward Versus Young. Vaughan* establishes that Holmes's "hasty and awkward" adult is held to an objective standard of reasonable care. *Appelhans* indicates that very young children are not held to that standard. Indeed, in jurisdictions that adopt the tender years doctrine, those children are deemed incapable of being careless as a matter of law. In both instances, the actor in question lacks the capacity to comport with the standard of reasonable care, yet the law treats those incapacities in opposite ways. Is this disparate treatment intelligible?

6. *Older Children and Adult Activities.* With regard to children who are over seven and who are engaged in activities typical of childhood, such as bicycle riding, courts ask the jury to gauge the child's behavior in comparison to that of "other children of the same age, experience, and intelligence." Although this standard is in some ways objective, by factoring in the particular child's experience and intelligence, it points toward a more subjective standard. This rule, however, has exceptions. Most importantly, as the *Appelhans* court notes, minors who engage in "adult" activities, such as driving cars or snowmobiles, are held to the reasonable care standard for competent adults.

7. *Parental Liability: Direct Versus Vicarious.* It is rare for a young child to be the defendant in a negligence action. In part this is because young children tend not to be in a position to provide adequate redress to their victims, except with respect to certain activities covered by an insurance policy taken out by their parents. Moreover, parents are not held *vicariously liable* for their child's faulty conduct in the way that employers can often be held vicariously liable for their employees' careless acts. Thus, a person injured by a child's carelessness who wishes to recover from the child's parents must establish some form of *direct* negligence, that is, carelessness on the part of the parent.

One such form consists of *negligent supervision.* As *Appelhans* explains, the negligent supervision theory is available only in a narrow range of circumstances. For an example of a statute codifying this form of liability, see Tenn. Code. Ann. § 37-10-101-103 (where a minor willfully or maliciously causes personal injury or property damage to another, his parents can be held liable up to the amount of $10,000 if they knew or should have known of the minor's tendency to commit wrongful acts and also failed to exercise reasonable means to restrain him, thereby enabling his tortious conduct); Lavin v. Jordon, 16 S.W.3d 362 (Tenn. 2000) (interpreting and applying these provisions).

Another ground for direct parental liability consists of *negligent entrustment,* whereby a parent carelessly gives a child access to a dangerous instrumentality, such as a gun or a car, that the child is not equipped to handle safely. *See, e.g.,* Rios v. Smith, 744 N.E.2d 1156 (N.Y. 2001) (owner of all-terrain vehicle can be found by a jury to have carelessly entrusted it to his teenage son).

8. The Reasonable Child and Comparative Fault. The issue of the standard of care applicable to children is of considerably more practical importance on the question of comparative fault — that is, fault on the part of the plaintiff contributing to her own injuries. For example, a careless driver who strikes a child pedestrian or cyclist may try to establish that the child acted unreasonably and so contributed to her own injury by darting out into the street. Likewise, parental carelessness is more often "in play" when evidence of such carelessness is being offered not by the plaintiff to establish parental liability, but instead by a defendant seeking to assign a percentage of responsibility and liability to the parents for an injury to their child. Thus, if the tables were turned and the McFalls were bringing an action on behalf of William against Appelhans for carelessly riding *her* bicycle into William as he crossed a street, a court might in that context be more willing to permit the attribution of fault to the senior McFalls for not keeping a close enough eye on William. *See* Chapter 8 (discussing apportionment).

9. Mental Incompetence, Battery, and Negligence. Menlove may have been prone to ignore risks, but there is no suggestion in the opinion that he lacked basic mental competence. How should tort law apply to actors who suffer from a mental disorder that leaves them unable to comprehend the significance of their actions or to control them? Mental incompetence ("insanity") can sometimes serve as a defense to criminal prosecution. However, there is no equivalent to the insanity defense in tort law. Indeed, the black letter rule states that a defendant's insanity does not even defeat the attribution of intent to her in a suit for torts such as battery. (Battery, for present purposes, can be defined as intentionally or knowingly causing harmful contact with another person.) *See Wagner v. State,* Chapter 9.

Some courts have suggested that insanity should sometimes defeat liability for torts such as battery precisely because those torts, unlike the tort of negligence, require the defendant to have acted with a certain subjective mental state — with a *purpose* to cause harmful contact to another person, or *knowing* that such contact would result. On this view, if the jury finds that the defendant in a battery suit was so incapacitated as to be incapable of forming the relevant purpose, or possessing the relevant knowledge, he should not be held liable for battery. Even these courts, however, are prepared to hold a mentally incompetent person liable under *Vaughan*'s objective reasonable person standard. *See* White v. Muniz, 999 P.2d 814 (Col. 2000) (en banc) (if the jury finds that defendant's Alzheimer's disease rendered her incapable of forming an intent to cause harmful contact, she cannot be held liable for battery, although she can be held liable in negligence); Burch v. American Family Mut. Ins. Co., 543 N.W.2d 277 (Wis. 1996) (severely mentally impaired defendant held to reasonable person standard in gauging whether she was careless in causing parked truck to slip into gear). As it turns out, those plaintiffs facing the prospect of suing a mentally incompetent defendant might often prefer to sue for negligence rather than battery, for, as explained in Chapter 8, liability insurance tends not to cover intentional wrongful acts.

What is the justification for holding a person who is incapable of controlling her conduct to the *Vaughan* standard? Does it suggest that legal fault really is quite a different concept than fault as we ordinarily use that term? Or are there special considerations that attend the actions of insane persons that warrant the imposition of what is, in effect, a form of strict liability? If the latter, on what basis can the cases that excuse carelessness by young children be distinguished? *See* Creasy v. Rusk, 730 N.E.2d 659 (Ind. 2000) (identifying policy factors thought by courts to warrant the imposition of the objective standard on insane persons, including (1) the desirability of allocating losses between two innocent parties to the one who caused or occasioned the loss; (2) providing an incentive to family members and other guardians of persons with mental disabilities to control the behavior of those persons; (3) removing inducements for alleged tortfeasors to fake a mental disability in order to escape liability; (4) avoiding administrative problems that are created by requiring courts and juries to identify and assess the significance of an actor's disability; and (5) forcing persons with disabilities to pay for the damage they do if they are to live active lives). In Gould v. American Family Mutual Insurance Co., 543 N.W.2d 282 (Wis. 1996), a paid professional caretaker of an institutionalized and severely mentally disabled patient sought recovery in negligence for injuries inflicted by the patient. Noting the inapplicability of several of the foregoing policy reasons to the acts of an institutionalized patient, the court adopted a rule barring claims of this sort.

10. Fault Versus Comparative Fault. As with negligence litigation involving the conduct of children, the issue of the standard of care to apply to mentally incompetent persons usually arises in assessing a victim's *comparative responsibility* for her injuries. Should there be any difference between the standard of care to which injurers ought to adhere for the protection of potential victims, and the standard of care that victims "owe" to themselves? Commentators frequently deny that there is or ought to be any difference. *See, e.g.*, Dan Dobbs, *The Law of Torts* § 125, at 294 (2000). However, others, including Anita Bernstein, contend that courts are more open to considering subjective factors such as mental disabilities in assessing plaintiffs' comparative fault, and that they are right to do so. Consider the rationales for the application of the objective standard to incompetent persons listed above. Do any of them offer a basis for distinguishing the breach inquiry as it pertains to *comparative fault* from the inquiry as it applies to *fault*?

11. Temporary Insanity and Sudden Incapacity. A leading decision holding the mentally disabled to the objective standard is Breunig v. American Family Ins. Co., 173 N.W.2d 619 (Wis. 1970). In that case, the plaintiff was injured when another driver, Veith, operating under the delusion that she could make her car fly, rammed into plaintiff's truck. Veith's insurer defended on the ground that Veith was schizophrenic, and hence utterly incapable of driving as would a reasonably prudent person.

The Wisconsin Supreme Court declined to exempt persons who satisfy clinical definitions of insanity from the obligation to meet the standard of ordinary prudence. However, *Breunig* allowed that a person who, without forewarning, suffers a bout of "temporary" insanity is not required to meet the standard.

Suppose one can make sound medical distinctions between permanent and temporary forms of insanity. Does *Breunig*'s distinction make sense in light of the reasons justifying the rule of liability for general incapacity specified by *Creasy, supra* Note 9? The differing treatment of "sudden" incapacities is consistent with judicial treatment of sudden physical incapacities. For example, a driver who, without any forewarning, suffers a heart attack that causes him to drive carelessly and injure another, will be held to have not acted unreasonably—at least in this regard—as a matter of law. *See, e.g.*, Goodrich v. Blair, 646 P.2d 890 (Ariz. Ct. App. 1982) (affirming jury instruction on sudden physical incapacity). Sudden incapacity will not defeat a finding of breach, however, when its onset was foreseeable to the actor. *See* Storjohn v. Fay, 519 N.W.2d 521 (Neb. 1994) (epileptic who blacked out while driving, causing injury to plaintiff, cannot claim benefit of sudden incapacity: he knew or should have known that he was subject to losing consciousness without notice and thus was careless as a matter of law for driving at all).

12. The Elderly. If youth is sometimes taken account of in the application of the standard of care, should old age likewise be taken into account? Can an elderly defendant, for example, argue that slower reflexes or lack of attentiveness, which often accompany aging, should be considered? A few courts have recognized such arguments—again, however, primarily in connection with determinations of comparative fault.

13. Gender. Today's "reasonable person" standard historically was stated as the "reasonable man" standard. Professor Schlanger has discussed nineteenth-century cases in which courts differed over whether to apply a distinct standard of reasonableness to women. In one 1873 case, for example, the trial judge instructed the jury to take into account the plaintiff's gender in determining whether she was comparatively at fault in riding her horse. The presumption, apparently, was that this would permit the jury to apply a less demanding standard that would benefit the plaintiff. What if studies show that, on average, women have better reflexes than men? Should the jury take that higher standard into account in determining the reasonableness of a particular woman's driving? Is the use of gender-specific standards appropriate or discriminatory? Martha Minow has argued that feminist theory faces a dilemma on this issue: Women's interests can, in different ways, be served both by recognition of a different standard of care and insistence upon application of a uniform reasonable person standard. Case law interpreting federal statutes barring gender discrimination has sometimes employed a "reasonable woman" standard in connection with determining, for example, whether an employer is responsible for maintaining a harassing or otherwise hostile work environment. *See, e.g.*, Hurley v. Atlantic City Police Dept., 174 F.3d 95 (3d Cir. 1999). Again, theorists have divided over the value of this approach.

14. Reasonableness and Culture. Should negligence law ever recognize a culturally relative standard of care? An analogous issue has arisen in criminal law. In Ha v. Alaska,

892 P.2d 184 (Alaska Ct. App. 1995), Ha, a Vietnamese man, shot and killed another Vietnamese man named Buu, who had attacked and threatened him the night before. When Ha was prosecuted for murder, he sought to establish the justification of self-defense, which, under Alaska law, permits the use of deadly force against another if one *reasonably* believes that its use is necessary to avoid *imminent* death or serious bodily harm. Ha's attorney argued that, in assessing the reasonableness of Ha's perception of imminent harm at the hands of Buu, the jury should consider that death threats are taken very literally in Vietnamese culture. The trial court refused to so instruct the jury, insisting that the perception of imminent harm was to be judged by an objective standard and that Ha had no reasonable basis for perceiving an imminent threat from Buu. The Court of Appeals upheld the trial court on a slightly different rationale, concluding that, even taking into account knowledge of Vietnamese culture, Ha had no basis for perceiving an imminent threat from Buu at the time Ha shot him.

15. Time Frame for Assessing Conduct. Following *Vaughan*, American negligence law focuses on a defendant's conduct, not his or her ostensibly good intentions. But the directive to look at his conduct still leaves many questions open, including the question of the time frame for evaluating it. Should a defendant's conformity to the standard of reasonable care be determined by his or her conduct over a lifetime, a year, a day, or a moment? Negligence law generally permits a plaintiff to prevail (on the breach issue) if she can identify any time-slice in which the conduct fell below reasonable care. It therefore encourages plaintiffs to divide up courses of conduct into discrete episodes or snapshots, rather than connecting them to an individual defendant's record of careful or careless behavior over time. For example, suppose two surgeons, *A* and *B*, are sued for malpractice, each for carelessly leaving an object (e.g., a sponge) inside one of her patients during surgery. For purposes of determining whether one or the other should be held liable, it makes no difference that *A* has a long and sordid history of botching operations, whereas *B*'s record is spotless. The question is whether, *in this instance*, *A* or *B* adhered to the relevant standard of care.* Mark Grady has argued that this snapshot approach to breach introduces a pocket of strict liability into negligence law, simply because even the most careful person can be expected to err once in a while. Grady regards this liability as strict, because it seems to entail that, no matter how careful one is, one cannot avoid sooner or later being careless.

III. INDUSTRY AND PROFESSIONAL CUSTOM

The T.J. Hooper

60 F.2d 737 (2d Cir.), *cert. denied*, 287 U.S. 662 (U.S. 1932)

L. HAND, J. The barges No. 17 and No. 30, belonging to the Northern Barge Company, had lifted cargoes of coal at Norfolk, Virginia, for New York in March, 1928. They were

---

* Evidence of *A*'s or *B*'s record might be admitted as relevant to a factual dispute as to how *A* or *B* actually conducted him- or herself on the occasion in question. However, *B* could not introduce the evidence of his past performance as a reason for the jury to excuse his breach on that occasion.

towed by two tugs of the petitioner [Eastern Transportation Co.], the "Montrose" and the "Hooper," and were lost off the Jersey Coast on March tenth, in an easterly gale. The cargo owners sued the barges under the contracts of carriage; the owner of the barges sued the tugs under the towing contract, both for its own loss and as bailee of the cargoes; the owner of the tug filed a petition to limit its liability. All the suits were joined and heard together, and the judge found that all the vessels were unseaworthy; the tugs, because they did not carry radio receiving sets by which they could have seasonably got warnings of a change in the weather which should have caused them to seek shelter in the Delaware Breakwater en route. He therefore entered an interlocutory decree holding each tug and barge jointly liable to each cargo owner, and each tug for half damages for the loss of its barge. The petitioner appealed, and the barge owner appealed and filed assignments of error.

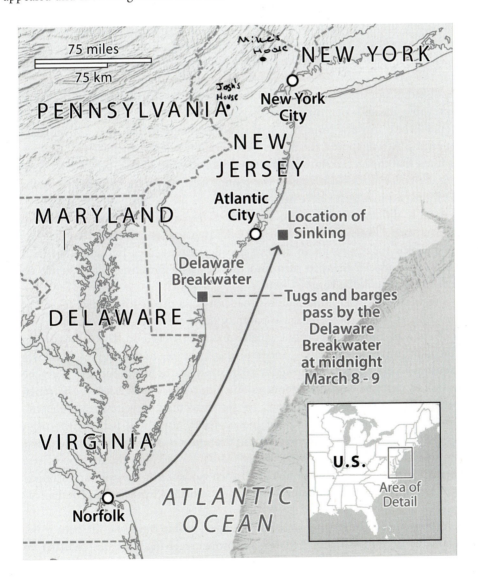

Each tug had three ocean going coal barges in tow, the lost barge being at the end. The "Montrose," which had the No. 17, took an outside course; the "Hooper" with the No. 30, inside. The weather was fair without ominous symptoms, as the tows passed the Delaware Breakwater about midnight of March eighth, and the barges did not get into serious trouble until they were about opposite Atlantic City some sixty or seventy miles to the north. The wind began to freshen in the morning of the ninth and rose to a gale before noon; by afternoon the second barge of the Hooper's tow was out of hand and signalled the tug, which found that not only this barge needed help, but that the No. 30 was aleak. Both barges anchored and the crew of the No. 30 rode out the storm until the afternoon of the tenth, when she sank, her crew having been meanwhile taken off. The No. 17 sprang a leak about the same time; she too anchored at the Montrose's command and sank on the next morning after her crew also had been rescued. The cargoes and the tugs maintain that the barges were not fit for their service; the cargoes and the barges that the tugs should have gone into the Delaware Breakwater, and besides, did not handle their tows properly.

The evidence of the condition of the barges was very extensive, the greater part being taken out of court. As to each, the fact remains that she foundered in weather that she was bound to withstand. . . . As to the cargoes, the charters excused the barges if "reasonable means" were taken to make them seaworthy; and the barge owners amended their answers during the trial to allege that they had used due diligence in that regard. As will appear, the barges were certainly not seaworthy in fact, and we do not think that the record shows affirmatively the exercise of due diligence to examine them. The examinations at least of the pumps were perfunctory; had they been sufficient the loss would not have occurred. . . .

A more difficult issue is as to the tugs. [The critical issue here is whether the tugboats were "unseaworthy" by virtue of not having working radios that would have enabled their captains to receive broadcasted weather forecasts that in turn would have induced them to turn into the Delaware Breakwater, and hence avoid the storm that sunk the barges. — Eds.]

The weather bureau at Arlington broadcasts two predictions daily, at ten in the morning and ten in the evening. Apparently there are other reports floating about, which come at uncertain hours but which can also be picked up. The Arlington report of the morning read as follows: "Moderate north, shifting to east and southeast winds, increasing Friday, fair weather to-night." The substance of this [forecast] . . . reached a tow bound north to New York about noon, and, coupled with a falling [barometer], [convinced] the master [of that tow] to put in to the Delaware Breakwater in the afternoon. The [barometer] had not indeed fallen much and perhaps the tug was over cautious; nevertheless, although the appearances were all fair, he thought discretion the better part of valor. Three other tows followed him, the masters of two of which testified. . . . Courts have not often such evidence of the opinion of impartial experts, formed in the very circumstances and confirmed by their own conduct at the time.

Moreover, the "Montrose" and the "Hooper" would have had the benefit of the evening report from Arlington had they had proper receiving sets. This predicted worse weather. . . . The bare "increase[ing]" of the morning had become "fresh to strong."

To be sure this scarcely foretold a gale of from forty to fifty miles for five hours or more, rising at one time to fifty-six; but if the four tows thought the first report enough, the second ought to have laid any doubts. The master of the "Montrose" himself, when asked what he would have done had he received a substantially similar report, said that he would certainly have put in. The master of the "Hooper" was also asked for his opinion, and said that he would have turned back also, but this admission is somewhat vitiated by the incorporation in the question of the statement that it was a "storm warning," which the witness seized upon in his answer. All this seems to us to support the conclusion of the judge that prudent masters, who had received the second warning, would have found the risk more than the exigency warranted; they would have been amply vindicated by what followed. . . . Taking the situation as a whole, it seems to us that these masters would have taken undue chances, had they got the broadcasts.

They did not, because their private radio receiving sets, which were on board, were not in working order. These belonged to them personally, and were partly a toy, partly a part of the equipment, but neither furnished by the owner, nor supervised by it. It is not fair to say that there was a general custom among coastwise carriers so to equip their tugs. One line alone did it; as for the rest, they relied upon their crews, so far as they can be said to have relied at all. An adequate receiving set suitable for a coat-wise tug can now be got at small cost and is reasonably reliable if kept up; obviously it is a source of great protection to their tows. Twice every day they can receive these predictions, based upon the widest possible information, available to every vessel within two or three hundred miles and more. Such a set is the ears of the tug to catch the spoken word, just as the master's binoculars are her eyes to see a storm signal ashore. Whatever may be said as to other vessels, tugs towing heavy coal laden barges, strung out for half a mile, have little power to maneuvre, and do not, as this case proves, expose themselves to weather which would not turn back stauncher craft. They can have at hand protection against dangers of which they can learn in no other way.

Is it then a final answer that the business had not yet generally adopted receiving sets? There are, no doubt, cases where courts seem to make the general practice of the calling the standard of proper diligence; we have indeed given some currency to the notion ourselves. Indeed in most cases reasonable prudence is in fact common prudence; but strictly it is never its measure; a whole calling may have unduly lagged in the adoption of new and available devices. It never may set its own tests, however persuasive be its usages. Courts must in the end say what is required; there are precautions so imperative that even their universal disregard will not excuse their omission. Wabash R. Co. v. McDaniels, 107 U.S. 454, 459-461; Texas & P. R. Co. v. Behymer, 189 U.S. 468, 470; Shandrew v. Chicago, etc., R. Co., 142 F. 320, 324, 325 (C.C.A. 8); Maynard v. Buck, 100 Mass. 40. But here there was no custom at all as to receiving sets; some had them, some did not; the most that can be urged is that they had not yet become general. Certainly in such a case we need not pause; when some have thought a device necessary, at least we may say that they were right, and the others too slack. . . . We hold the tugs therefore because had they been properly equipped, they would have got the Arlington reports. The injury was a direct consequence of this unseaworthiness.

*Johnson v. Riverdale Anesthesia Associates**

563 S.E.2d 431 (Ga. 2002)

Sears, J. Certiorari was granted in this medical malpractice action in order to consider the Court of Appeals' ruling forbidding the plaintiff from cross-examining the defendants' expert witness as to how he personally would have treated the plaintiffs' decedent. We conclude that because the standard of care in medical malpractice cases is that which is employed by the medical profession generally, and not what one individual physician would do under the same or similar circumstances, how a testifying medical expert personally would have treated a plaintiff or a plaintiff's decedent is not relevant to the issue of whether a defendant physician committed malpractice. Moreover, we conclude that how a testifying medical expert personally would have treated a plaintiff or a plaintiff's decedent cannot be used to impeach the . . . expert's credibility. Therefore, we affirm.

The decedent, Clair Johnson, suffered a severe adverse reaction to anesthesia she received during surgery. The reaction caused Mrs. Johnson's oxygen supply to be interrupted, resulting in massive brain trauma and death. Her husband, Donald Johnson, along with the administratrix of her estate (collectively "Johnson"), sued the anesthesiologist, Dr. Lawhead, and his employer, Riverdale Anesthesia Associates, Inc. (collectively "Anesthesia Associates"), alleging malpractice.

At trial, Johnson alleged that Anesthesia Associates had committed malpractice by failing to "preoxygenate" Mrs. Johnson. Preoxygenation is a procedure where, before surgery, a patient is given a measure of pure oxygen, providing her with a reserve to draw from, should her oxygen supply be interrupted during surgery. The trial court granted Anesthesia Associates' motion in limine to prevent Johnson from cross-examining the defendants' medical expert, Dr. Caplan, about whether he, personally, would have preoxygenated Mrs. Johnson.

After the jury found in favor of Anesthesia Associates, Johnson appealed, claiming the trial court erred by preventing Johnson from cross-examining Dr. Caplan as to whether he would have elected to preoxygenate Mrs. Johnson. The Court of Appeals affirmed, and this Court granted certiorari.

1. The crux of Johnson's complaint against Anesthesia Associates was the contention that the latter violated the applicable standard of care by failing to preoxygenate Mrs. Johnson. Johnson attempted to establish this breach of care through the testimony of an expert witness.[3] Johnson claimed that if preoxygenation had been administered, Mrs. Johnson would have been protected against the low oxygen levels that occurred during surgery and that led to her death. For its part, Anesthesia Associates claimed that because its decision not to preoxygenate Mrs. Johnson was consistent with the applicable standard of care, no malpractice occurred. In support of this argument, Anesthesia Associates presented the testimony of its own medical expert, Dr. Caplan.

---

* [Overruled by *Condra v. Atlanta Orthopaedics Group, infra.*–EDS.]

3. See Slack v. Moorhead, 152 Ga. App. 68 (1979) (except in rare instances, the question of compliance with the required medical standard of care must be presented through expert testimony).

It is axiomatic that in order to establish medical malpractice,

> "the evidence presented by the patient must show a violation of the degree of care and skill required of a physician. Such standard of care is that which, under similar conditions and like circumstances, is ordinarily employed by the medical profession generally." Thus, in medical malpractice actions, "the applicable standard of care is that employed by the medical profession generally and not what one individual doctor thought was advisable and would have done under the circumstances."

[McNabb v. Landis, 223 Ga. App. 894, 896 (1996).]

Accordingly, in cases where expert medical testimony has been presented either to support or to rebut a claim that the applicable standard of care was breached, Georgia case law holds that questions aimed at determining how the expert would have personally elected to treat the patient are irrelevant. The questioning of a medical expert witness should be disallowed as irrelevant when it "pertains to [the expert's] personal views and opinion as to the care and treatment he himself would have rendered." [*Id.*, at 896.] Contrary to Johnson's argument, this is true regardless of whether the expert's personal views are sought through direct testimony or cross-examination; as held by the trial court in this case, a defendant's expert witness is not required to answer questions on cross-examination "as to what course of treatment he personally would have followed."

It follows that the trial court did not abuse its discretion in granting Anesthesia Associates' motion in limine to prohibit Johnson from cross-examining the defendant's expert witness as to whether he personally would have preoxygenated the decedent, because such questioning was irrelevant to the issue of whether Anesthesia Associates breached the applicable standard of care.[8]

2. Questions aimed at determining how a defendant's medical expert personally would have treated a plaintiff or a plaintiff's decedent also are irrelevant for purposes of impeaching the expert. As explained above, a medical expert's personal practices are irrelevant to the issues in controversy in a malpractice case. It is axiomatic that a witness may not be impeached with irrelevant facts or evidence, and cross-examination should be confined to matters that are relevant to the case.

Moreover, when confronted with the same or similar situation, different physicians will, quite naturally, often elect to administer differing treatments, and will exercise their judgments regarding a patient's care differently. However, merely because these procedures and treatments differ, it does not automatically follow that one of them fails to comply with the applicable standard of care.

Georgia precedent holds that " 'testimony showing a mere difference in views between surgeons as to operating techniques, or as to medical judgment exercised,' " is irrelevant in a medical malpractice action when the differing views or techniques are both acceptable and customary within the applicable standard of care. Accordingly,

---

8. The portion of Prevost v. Taylor, 196 Ga. App. 368 (4) (1990), that holds otherwise is hereby overruled.

questions asked on cross-examination as to how a defendant's medical expert "personally would have treated [a patient are] . . . not proper for impeachment."[Cited authority omitted. — EDS.] Therefore, the trial court did not improperly curtail Johnson's ability to impeach the testimony of Anesthesia Associates' medical expert, Dr. Caplan, by granting the defendants' motion in limine.

3. . . . For the reasons explained above, the trial court did not abuse its discretion in this case by prohibiting the cross-examination of the defendants' medical expert as to his personal medical practices, because such information was irrelevant to any issue of fact in controversy.

Judgment affirmed. . . .

CARLEY, J. (dissenting) (joined by Benham and Hunstein, JJ). In a one-sentence footnote, the majority overrules Prevost v. Taylor, 196 Ga. App. 368, 369 (4) (396 S.E.2d 17) (1990), which was not even cited by the Court of Appeals. In my opinion, *Prevost* was simply overlooked by the Court of Appeals and should not be overruled by this Court because the rationale of that decision is so persuasive:

> It is true, as defendant argues, that the issue in a medical professional negligence action is whether the treatment met the standard of care of the profession generally and not what any one individual doctor believes is advisable. However, those cases cited by defendant involved instances where the only testimony presented to support plaintiff's claim is the individual view of one doctor and no testimony was presented as to the standard of care generally practiced by the profession. [Cits.] Here, plaintiff did not present the individual opinion of defendant's expert for the purpose of establishing the acceptable standard of care but offered it to impeach the expert's opinion that the surgery performed by defendant met the standard of care of the profession generally. "Evidence tendered for impeachment purposes need not be of the kind or quality required for proving the facts."[Cits.]

Prevost v. Taylor, *supra* at 369-370 (4).

"The right of a thorough and sifting cross-examination shall belong to every party as to the witnesses called against him." O.C.G.A. § 24-9-64.

> Over one hundred years ago, this Court held that it is the [trial] court's duty to allow a searching and skillful test of the witness' "intelligence, memory, accuracy and veracity(,)"[cit.], and that it is better for cross-examination to be "too free than too much restricted." . . . [Cit.]

Eason v. State, 260 Ga. 445, 446 (1990), *overruled on other grounds*, State v. Lucious, 271 Ga. 361, 365 (1999). "'(W)here the purpose is to impeach or discredit the witness, great latitude should be allowed by the [trial] court in cross-examination . . . [.]' [Cit.]" Corley v. Harris, 171 Ga. App. 688, 689 (1984).

> As a general rule, the liability test to be employed by the court and the jury is the "standard of care" that a reasonably prudent physician would exercise under the same or similar circumstances as the defendant. Therefore, the ultimate test is not whether the expert would perform a medical act and/or teach a medical act in the

> same way or a different way as a particular defendant. *However*, such a line of inquiry *usually is admissible* on the issue of credibility. If, for example, the plaintiff's expert testifies that a defendant deviated from a certain standard of care, said expert's credibility certainly would be severely shaken if, in fact, it can be shown that this expert has performed a medical act in the same or similar manner as the defendant. *If a defense expert has testified that a defendant's medical act conformed with a certain acceptable standard of care, the credibility of said testimony certainly would be severely shaken, if said expert conceded on cross-examination that he personally does not perform and/or teach the medical act in the same manner.* (Emphasis supplied.)

2 Pegalis & Wachsman, American Law of Medical Malpractice 2d § 14:7 (e), p. 492 (1993). The identical circumstances are present in this case. As demonstrated by an offer of proof, the defendants' medical expert would have testified on cross-examination that he would have preoxygenated Mrs. Johnson if she had been his patient. Plaintiffs' counsel also sought to ask Dr. Caplan how he teaches his medical students to treat patients in similar situations. Such testimony is particularly relevant to credibility here, because Dr. Caplan testified on direct examination that there was nothing that could have been done to make it safer for Mrs. Johnson to have the anesthesia.

"'A material abridgement or denial of the substantial right of cross-examination of opposing witnesses is material error and requires the grant of a new trial. (Cits.)'" Hyles v. Cockrill, 169 Ga. App. 132, 140 (1983) (on motion for rehearing), *overruled on other grounds*, Ketchup v. Howard, 247 Ga. App. 54, 61 (2000). Because the trial court did not allow plaintiffs to conduct "a thorough and sifting cross-examination" of the defendant's medical expert, I dissent to the affirmance of the Court of Appeals' judgment.

Condra v. Atlanta Orthopaedic Group

681 S.E.2d 152 (Ga. 2009)

HUNSTEIN, P.J. We granted certiorari to the Court of Appeals in this medical malpractice action to consider (1) whether plaintiffs were properly prohibited from inquiring at trial into the personal practices of defendants' expert witnesses with respect to the medical treatment at issue in the case; and (2) whether the so-called "hindsight" jury instruction was appropriately given under the circumstances presented. The Court of Appeals answered both questions in the affirmative. We now reverse on both issues.

In May 1998, Daphyne Condra sought treatment for back, neck, and arm pain from orthopedist James Chappuis, M.D., who prescribed a 30-day regimen of the anticonvulsive drug Tegretol, followed by another 30-day regimen when her condition had not improved. Shortly after Condra began her second prescription, she began experiencing leg cramping and shortness of breath, leading ultimately to her hospitalization, where she was diagnosed with aplastic anemia, a rare and serious bone marrow disease. Condra and her husband sued Dr. Chappuis and his orthopedic group for medical malpractice, asserting that Tegretol had been an inappropriate drug choice for Condra and that Dr. Chappuis had been negligent in failing to conduct blood count monitoring during Condra's Tegretol therapy to detect any potential adverse reactions.

At trial, Condra's experts and treating hematologists opined that the Tegretol had caused Condra's aplastic anemia and that development of the disease could have been avoided had Dr. Chappuis conducted blood count monitoring during Condra's treatment. Specifically, they testified that conducting an initial "baseline" blood count prior to beginning the medication, followed by subsequent blood tests at regular intervals thereafter, may have alerted her care providers to a drop in white blood cells and in turn led to a discontinuation of the Tegretol and reversal of the development of the aplastic anemia. Condra's expert neurosurgeon further testified that the failure to conduct blood conduct monitoring was a breach of the standard of care.

Defense experts Richard Franco, M.D. and Peter Staats, M.D. acknowledged at trial that much of the medical literature recommends blood count monitoring during Tegretol therapy. They testified further, however, that such monitoring was, though a "reasonable" course of action, not "mandatory or essential"; that failure to conduct such monitoring did not constitute a breach of the standard of care; and that such monitoring, even if it had been conducted, would have been unlikely to detect development of the aplastic anemia at a point at which its development could have been arrested. During pretrial discovery, however, Dr. Franco had deposed that it was his usual practice to conduct blood count monitoring when he prescribed Tegretol. Before trial, the defense moved in limine to prevent plaintiffs from inquiring at trial into these experts' personal practices, and the trial court granted the motion.

Also at trial, the court, over plaintiffs' objection, gave the so-called "hindsight" jury instruction:

> I charge you that in the medical malpractice action the defendant cannot be found negligent on the basis of an assessment of a patient's condition that only later in hindsight proves to be incorrect as long as the initial assessment was made in compliance with reasonable standards of care. In other words, the concept of negligence does not include hindsight. Negligence consists of not foreseeing and guarding against that which is probable and likely to happen, not against that which is only remotely and slightly possible.

. . . . Despite plaintiffs' objections that the charge was inapplicable to their case and that the last sentence thereof is an incorrect statement of the law, the trial court gave this instruction both during the initial jury charge and during a recharge the following day. The jury ultimately returned a defense verdict, and, on appeal, the Court of Appeals affirmed.

1. Regarding the personal practices testimony of defendants' experts, the Court of Appeals upheld the trial court's decision to exclude such testimony by relying on the controlling authority of *Johnson v. Riverdale Anesthesia Assocs.*, 563 S.E. 2d 431 (2002). . . . .

Having considered the matter anew in light of recent statutory developments and the practice of other jurisdictions, we have determined that *Johnson* is no longer viable. Accordingly, we now overrule *Johnson* and hold that evidence regarding an expert witness' personal practices, unless subject to exclusion on other evidentiary grounds, is admissible both as substantive evidence and to impeach the expert's opinion regarding the applicable standard of care.

Our decision in this regard is predicated primarily on the fact that, subsequent to the *Johnson* decision, our Legislature enacted as part of its Tort Reform Act, Ga. L. 2005, p. 1, § 7, a new statute governing admissibility of expert testimony in civil actions. OCGA § 24-9-67.1. This statute places particular emphasis on a proffered medical expert's professional experience and practice in assessing his or her qualification to serve as an expert witness:

> . . . [I]n professional malpractice actions, the opinions of an expert, who is otherwise qualified as to the acceptable standard of conduct of the professional whose conduct is at issue, shall be admissible only if, at the time the act or omission is alleged to have occurred, such expert: . . . had *actual professional knowledge and experience* in the area of practice or specialty in which the opinion is to be given as the result of having been *regularly engaged in:* . . . *[t]he active practice of such area of specialty of his or her profession for at least three of the last five years, with sufficient frequency to establish an appropriate level of knowledge*, as determined by the judge, in performing the procedure, diagnosing the condition, or rendering the treatment which is alleged to have been performed or rendered negligently. . . .

(Emphasis supplied.) OCGA § 24-9-67.1(c)(2)(A). Thus, there can be no dispute as to the relevance, post-Tort Reform Act, of an expert's personal experience and practice to the threshold inquiry into the expert's qualifications.

Given the prominence of the expert's personal practice in this threshold inquiry, it would defy logic to find such experience categorically irrelevant in assessing the credibility of the expert's testimony. "[T]he jury is entitled to fully evaluate the credibility of the testifying expert, and the fact that an expert testifies that the standard of care does not require what that expert personally does in a similar situation may be a critical piece of information for the jury's consideration." *Smethers v. Campion*, 108 P.3d 946, 956 (Az. 2005).

> The relevance and importance of a medical expert's personal choice of a course of treatment is highly probative of the credibility of the expert's opinion concerning the standard of care. A jury is free to disregard the expert's opinion entirely and find that the standard of care is reflected by the course of treatment the expert would have chosen, a highly probable scenario if other evidence admitted in the case supports this proposition. . . . Permitting the expert to be cross-examined on a personal choice regarding course of treatment and why it would be different than the defendant-doctor allows a full examination of the expert's opinion on standard of care and the basis therefor.

(Footnotes omitted.) Overby et al., Trial Practice and Procedure, 51 Mercer L. Rev. 487, 501-502 (Fall 1999). . . .

We find implicit support for this conclusion in the Legislature's exhortation in the expert testimony statute that

> the courts of this state . . . draw from the opinions of the United States Supreme Court in *Daubert v. Merrell Dow Pharmaceuticals, Inc.*, 509 U.S. 579 (1993), [and its progeny].

OCGA § 24-9-67.1(f). Under the *Daubert* line of cases, the trial judge acts as the gatekeeper in determining the admissibility of expert opinion, and the jury is charged with the responsibility of evaluating the credibility of the expert's testimony. *Daubert*, 509 U.S. at 589, 595. Such evaluation is made possible through, among other things, "[v]igorous cross-examination." Id. at 596.

> The right of . . . cross examination . . . is a substantial right, the preservation of which is essential to the proper administration of justice, and extends to all matters within the knowledge of the witness, the disclosure of which is material to the controversy.

News Publishing Co. v. Butler, 22 S.E. 282, [282] (1895). Neither the jury's ability to perform its role as arbiter of the expert's credibility, nor the party's right to a "thorough and sifting cross-examination," OCGA § 24-9-64, is well served by a prohibition on cross-examination of the opposing party's expert regarding personal practices that differ from the standard of care as asserted by that expert.

Also important in our decision to shift course on this issue is the growing body of case law from other jurisdictions supportive of the admissibility of expert personal practices testimony, at least for some purposes. Though not all jurisdictions have followed this trend, admissibility of personal practices testimony appears now to be the prevailing view.

Finally, though defendants assert that allowing expert personal practices testimony is likely to confuse the jury by conflating the standard of care with an expert's personal protocols, we find that such potential for prejudice does not as a general rule outweigh the usefulness of such information in evaluating an expert's credibility. Moreover, any potential confusion created by the admission of such evidence may be remedied through the use of careful jury instructions. Such instructions should, for example, clearly define the legal meaning of standard of care; enunciate the principle that a mere difference in views between physicians does not by itself prove malpractice . . . , and clarify concepts such as burden of proof and credibility of witnesses. In addition, the party whose expert has been cross-examined will have the ability to elicit explanations for why the expert's practices differ from what that expert attested to as the standard of care. Armed with complete information regarding the expert's opinion and personal practices, jurors can make intelligent judgments about the reliability of the expert's testimony.

In this case, the jury was precluded from achieving such an informed judgment. Lacking the benefit of knowledge that defendants' own experts routinely practiced differently from the standard of care to which they had testified, the jury was compelled to make a determination as to the standard of care based on incomplete and potentially misleading information. Under these circumstances, we cannot find the erroneous exclusion of personal practices testimony to have been harmless. The curtailment of plaintiffs' substantial right to a thorough and sifting cross-examination of the defense's experts clearly warrants reversal.

2. On retrial, the use of the hindsight instruction will be limited as set forth in our opinion, issued contemporaneously herewith, in *Smith v. Finch*, 681 S.E.2d 147 (2009). [In *Smith*, the Court approved the use of the first sentence of the "hindsight" instruction in cases with facts warranting its use, but disapproved of the use of the

instruction's second and third sentences on the ground that they could induce jurors to misunderstand the standard of care set by Georgia malpractice law.—EDS.]

Judgment reversed.

Big Think

Stare Decisis Revisited

Condra's overruling of *Johnson* marked the second reversal of course within 20 years by Georgia courts on the issue of whether to allow certain questions to be asked of experts testifying in medical malpractice cases. (*Johnson* had overruled *Prevost v. Taylor*, a 1990 intermediate appellate court decision.) Is this pattern of decisionmaking consistent with the principle of *stare decisis*? Insofar as one might be tempted to look for an explanation of *Condra* in judicial politics, it is worth noting that, between the time of *Johnson* and *Condra*, only one new justice joined the seven-member Georgia Supreme Court, and that justice was appointed by a Republican governor.

The Court in *Condra* relied heavily on the Georgia legislature's post-*Johnson* enactment of a tort reform statute. The primary aim of that statute was to *reduce* medical malpractice liability in order to address a perceived healthcare crisis. (The preamble to the law begins: "The General Assembly finds that there presently exists a crisis affecting the provision and quality of health care services in this state.") Can a statute that was designed to reduce overall malpractice liability fairly be interpreted to support the overruling of a decision (*Johnson*) that itself seemed concerned to limit malpractice liability?

Condra also relies on the U.S. Supreme Court's 1993 *Daubert* decision—which will be discussed in more detail in Chapter 4. *Daubert* aimed to keep "junk science" out of the courtroom by having trial courts scrutinize proposed expert testimony to determine if the testimony has a valid basis in science or experience. *Daubert* concerned the application of evidence law in federal courts rather than state courts. However, as *Condra* notes, the Georgia legislature invoked *Daubert* to help capture the aspirations behind its tort reform statute. How does *Daubert*'s emphasis on the need for courts to guard against "junk science" support *Condra*'s overruling of *Johnson*?

Largey v. Rothman

540 A.2d 504 (N.J. 1988)

PER CURIAM. This medical malpractice case raises an issue of a patient's informed consent to treatment. The jury found that plaintiff Janice Largey had consented to an operative procedure performed by the defendant physician. The single question presented goes to the correctness of the standard by which the jury was instructed to determine whether the defendant, Dr. Rothman, had adequately informed his patient of the risks of that operation.

The trial court told the jury that when informing the plaintiff Janice Largey of the risks of undergoing a certain biopsy procedure, described below, defendant was required to tell her "what reasonable medical practitioners in the same or similar circumstances would have told their patients undertaking the same type of operation." By answer to a specific interrogatory on this point, the jurors responded that defendant had not "fail[ed] to provide Janice Largey with sufficient information so that she could give informed consent" for the operative procedure. On plaintiffs' appeal the Appellate Division affirmed in an unreported opinion, noting that the trial court's charge on informed consent followed the holding in Kaplan v. Haines, 96 N.J. Super. 242, 257 (App. Div. 1967), which this Court affirmed. . . .

Plaintiffs argued below, and repeat the contention here, that the proper standard is one that focuses not on what information a reasonable doctor should impart to the patient (the "professional" standard) but rather on what the physician should disclose to a reasonable patient in order that the patient might make an informed decision (the "prudent patient" or "materiality of risk" standard). The latter is the standard announced in Canterbury v. Spence, 464 F.2d 772 (D.C. Cir.), *cert. den.*, 409 U.S. 1064 (1972). The Appellate Division rejected the *Canterbury* standard, not because it disagreed with that standard but because the court felt itself bound, correctly, by the different standard of *Kaplan*, which represents "the latest word" from this Court.

. . . We now discard *Kaplan*'s "reasonable physician" standard and adopt instead the *Canterbury* "reasonable patient" rule. Hence, we reverse and remand for a new trial.

I

[The New Jersey Supreme Court quotes and adopts the Appellate Division's recitation of the facts. — Eds.]

In the course of a routine physical examination plaintiff's gynecologist, Dr. Glassman, detected a "vague mass" in her right breast. The doctor arranged for mammograms to be taken. The radiologist reported two anomalies to the doctor: an "ill-defined density" in the subareola region and an enlarged lymph node or nodes, measuring four-by-two centimeters, in the right axilla (armpit). The doctor referred plaintiff to defendant, a surgeon. Defendant expressed concern that the anomalies on the mammograms might be cancer and recommended a biopsy. There was a sharp dispute at trial over whether he stated that the biopsy would include the lymph nodes as well as the breast tissue. Plaintiff claims that defendant never mentioned the nodes.

Plaintiff submitted to the biopsy procedure after receiving a confirmatory second opinion from a Dr. Slattery. During the procedure defendant removed a piece of the suspect mass from plaintiff's breast and excised the nodes. The biopsies showed that both specimens were benign. About six weeks after the operation, plaintiff developed a right arm and hand lymphedema, a swelling caused by inadequate drainage in the lymphatic system. The condition resulted from the excision of the lymph nodes. Defendant did not advise plaintiff of this risk. Plaintiff's experts testified that defendant should have informed plaintiff that lymphedema was a risk of the operation. Defendant's experts testified that it was too rare to be discussed with a patient.

Plaintiff and her husband . . . advanced two theories of liability. . . . They claimed that they were never told that the operation would include removal of the nodes and therefore that procedure constituted an unauthorized battery. Alternatively, they claimed that even if they had authorized the node excision, defendant was negligent in failing to warn them of the risk of lymphedema and therefore their consent was uninformed. The jury specifically rejected both claims.

II

The origins of the requirement that a physician obtain the patient's consent before surgery may be traced back at least two centuries. The doctrine is now well-embedded in our law. In Schloendorff v. The Soc'y of the N.Y. Hosp., 105 N.E. 92 ([N.Y.] 1914), Justice Cardozo announced a patient's right to be free of uninvited, unknown surgery, which constitutes a trespass on the patient: "Every human being of adult years and sound mind has a right to determine what shall be done with his own body; and a surgeon who performs an operation without his patient's consent commits an assault, for which he is liable in damages." 105 N.E. at 93. Earlier case law recognized that theories of fraud and misrepresentation would sustain a patient's action in battery for an unauthorized intervention. *See* State v. Housekeeper, 16 A. 382 ([Md.] 1889); W. Keeton, D. Dobbs, R. Keeton, D. Owen, *Prosser and Keeton on The Law of Torts* §§ 18, 32 (5th ed. 1984). . . . Although that cause of action continues to be recognized in New Jersey, *see* Perna v. Pirozzi, 92 N.J. 446, 459-63 (1983) (operation on a patient by a surgeon to whom the patient has not given any consent constitutes a battery), there is no "battery" claim implicated in this appeal because the jury determined as a matter of fact that plaintiff had given consent to the node excision performed by Dr. Rothman.

Although the requirement that a patient give consent before the physician can operate is of long standing, the doctrine of *informed* consent is one of relatively recent development in our jurisprudence. It is essentially a negligence concept, predicated on the duty of a physician to disclose to a patient such information as will enable the patient to make an evaluation of the nature of the treatment and of any attendant substantial risks, as well as of available options in the form of alternative therapies.

An early statement of the "informed consent" rule is found in Salgo v. Leland Stanford, Jr. Univ. Bd. of Trustees, 317 P.2d 170 ([Cal.] Ct. App. 1957), in which the court declared that "[a] physician violates his duty to his patient and subjects himself to liability if he withholds any facts which are necessary to form the basis of an intelligent consent by the patient to the proposed treatment." 317 P.2d at 181. *Salgo* recognized that because each patient presents a "special problem," the physician has a certain amount of discretion in dismissing the element of risk, "consistent, of course, with the full disclosure of facts necessary to an informed consent." *Id.* Further development of the doctrine came shortly thereafter, in Natanson v. Kline, 186 Kan. 393, 350 P.2d 1093, *modified on other grounds*, 354 P.2d 670 ([Kan.] 1960), which represented one of the leading cases on informed consent at that time. In *Natanson* a patient sustained injuries from excessive doses of radioactive cobalt during radiation therapy. Even though the patient had consented to the radiation treatment, she alleged that the physician had not informed her of the nature and consequences of the risks posed by the therapy. Thus, the case sounded in negligence rather than battery. 350 P.2d at 1100-01. The court concluded that when a physician either affirmatively misrepresents the nature of an operation or fails to disclose the probable consequences of the treatment, he may be subjected to a claim of unauthorized treatment. 350 P.2d at 1102. The *Natanson* court established the standard of care to be exercised by a physician in an informed consent case as "limited to those disclosures which a reasonable medical practitioner would make under the same or similar circumstances." 350 P.2d at

1106. At bottom the decision turned on the principle of a patient's right of self-determination:

> Anglo-American law starts with the premise of thorough self-determination. It follows that each man is considered to be master of his own body, and he may, if he be of sound mind, expressly prohibit the performance of lifesaving surgery, or other medical treatment. A doctor might well believe that an operation or form of treatment is desirable or necessary but the law does not permit him to substitute his own judgment for that of the patient by any form of artifice or deception. [350 P.2d at 1104.]

After *Salgo* and *Natanson* the doctrine of informed consent came to be adopted and developed in other jurisdictions, which, until 1972, followed the "traditional" or "professional" standard formulation of the rule. Under that standard, as applied by the majority of the jurisdictions that adopted it, a physician is required to make such disclosure as comports with the prevailing medical standard in the community—that is, the disclosure of those risks that a reasonable physician in the community, of like training, would customarily make in similar circumstances. 2 D. Louisell and H. Williams, *Medical Malpractice* § 22.08 at 22-23 (1987) (hereinafter Louisell and Williams). A minority of the jurisdictions that adhere to the "professional" standard do not relate the test to any kind of community standard but require only such disclosures as would be made by a reasonable medical practitioner under similar circumstances. *Id.* at 22-34. In order to prevail in a case applying the "traditional" or "professional" standard a plaintiff would have to present expert testimony of the community's medical standard for disclosure in respect of the procedure in question and of the defendant physician's failure to have met that standard. *Id.* § 22.09 at 22-35 to -37.

In both the majority and minority formulations the "professional" standard rests on the belief that a physician, and *only* a physician, can effectively estimate both the psychological and physical consequences that a risk inherent in a medical procedure might produce in a patient. The burden imposed on the physician under this standard is to "consider the state of the patient's health, and whether the risks involved are mere remote possibilities or real hazards which occur with appreciable regularity. . . ." Louisell and Williams, *supra*, § 22.08 at 22-34. A second basic justification offered in support of the "professional" standard is that "a general standard of care, as required under the prudent patient rule, would require a physician to waste unnecessary time in reviewing with the patient *every* possible risk, thereby interfering with the flexibility a physician needs in deciding what form of treatment is best for the patient." *Ibid.* (footnotes omitted).

It was the "professional" standard that this Court accepted when, twenty years ago, it made the doctrine of informed consent a component part of our medical malpractice jurisprudence. *See* Kaplan v. Haines, *supra*, 51 N.J. 404, *aff'g* 96 N.J. Super. 242. In falling into step with those other jurisdictions that by then had adopted informed consent, the Court approved the following from the Appellate Division's opinion in *Kaplan*:

> The authorities . . . are in general agreement that the nature and extent of the disclosure, essential to an informed consent, depends upon the medical problem

> as well as the patient. Plaintiff has the burden to prove what a reasonable medical practitioner of the same school and same or similar community, under the same or similar circumstances, would have disclosed to his patient and the issue is one for the jury where, as in the case *sub judice*, a fact issue is raised upon conflicting testimony as to whether the physician made an adequate disclosure. [96 N.J. Super. at 257.]

In 1972 a new standard of disclosure for "informed consent" was established in Canterbury v. Spence, *supra*, 464 F.2d 772. The case raised a question of the defendant physician's duty to warn the patient beforehand of the risk involved in a laminectomy, a surgical procedure the purpose of which was to relieve pain in plaintiff's lower back, and particularly the risk attendant on a myelogram, the diagnostic procedure preceding the surgery. After several surgical interventions and hospitalizations, plaintiff was still, at the time of trial, using crutches to walk, suffering from urinary incontinence and paralysis of the bowels, and wearing a penile clamp. *Id.* at 778.

The *Canterbury* court announced a duty on the part of a physician to "warn of the dangers lurking in the proposed treatment" and to "impart information [that] the patient has every right to expect," as well as a duty of "reasonable disclosure of the choices with respect to proposed therapy and the dangers inherently and potentially involved." *Id.* at 782. The court held that the scope of the duty to disclose

> must be measured by the patient's need, and that need is the information material to the decision. Thus the test for determining whether a particular peril must be divulged is its materiality to the patient's decision: all risks potentially affecting the decision must be unmasked. And to safeguard the patient's interest in achieving his own determination on treatment, the law must itself set the standard for adequate disclosure. [*Id.* at 786-87 (footnotes omitted).]

The breadth of the disclosure of the risks legally to be required is measured, under *Canterbury*, by a standard whose scope is "not subjective as to either the physician or the patient," *id.* at 787; rather, "it remains *objective* with due regard for the patient's informational needs and with suitable leeway for the physician's situation." *Ibid.* (emphasis added). A risk would be deemed "material" when a reasonable patient, in what the physician knows or should know to be the patient's position, would be "likely to attach significance to the risk or cluster of risks" in deciding whether to forego the proposed therapy or to submit to it. *Ibid.*

The foregoing standard for adequate disclosure, known as the "prudent patient" or "materiality of risk" standard, has been adopted in a number of jurisdictions. The jurisdictions that have rejected the "professional" standard in favor of the "prudent patient" rule have given a number of reasons in support of their preference. Those include:

(1) The existence of a discernible custom reflecting a medical consensus is open to serious doubt. The desirable scope of disclosure depends on the given fact situation, which varies from patient to patient, and should not be subject to the whim of the medical community in setting the standard.

(2) Since a physician in obtaining a patient's informed consent to proposed treatment is often obligated to consider non-medical factors, such as a patient's emotional condition, professional custom should not furnish the legal criterion for measuring the physician's obligation to disclose. Whether a physician has conformed to a professional standard should . . . be important [only] where a pure medical judgment is involved, e.g. in ordinary malpractice actions, where the issue generally concerns the quality of treatment provided to the patient.

(3) Closely related to both (1) and (2) is the notion that a professional standard is *totally* subject to the whim of the physicians in the particular community. Under this view a physician is vested with virtually unlimited discretion in establishing the proper scope of disclosure; this is inconsistent with the patient's right of self-determination. As observed by the court in Canterbury v. Spence: "Respect for the patient's right of self-determination . . . demands a standard set by law for physicians rather than one which physicians may or may not impose upon themselves."

(4) The requirement that the patient present expert testimony to establish the professional standard has created problems for patients trying to find physicians willing to breach the "community of silence" by testifying against fellow colleagues. [Louisell and Williams, *supra*, § 22.12 at 22-45 to -47 (footnotes omitted).] Taken together, the reasons supporting adoption of the "prudent patient" standard persuade us that the time has come for us to abandon so much of the decision by which this Court embraced the doctrine of informed consent as accepts the "professional" standard. To that extent Kaplan v. Haines, 51 N.J. 404, *aff'g* 96 N.J. Super. 242, is overruled.

As indicated by the foregoing passages from Louisell and Williams, the policy considerations are clear-cut. At the outset we are entirely unimpressed with the argument, made by those favoring the "professional" standard, that the "prudent patient" rule would compel disclosure of *every* risk (not just *material* risks) to *any* patient (rather than the *reasonable* patient). As *Canterbury* makes clear,

> [t]he topics importantly demanding a communication of information are the inherent and potential hazards of the proposed treatment, the alternatives to that treatment, if any, and the results likely if the patient remains untreated. The factors contributing significance to the dangerousness of a medical technique are, of course, the incidence of injury and the degree of harm threatened. [464 F.2d at 787-88.]

The court in *Canterbury* did not presume to draw a "bright line separating the significant [risks] from the insignificant"; rather, it resorted to a "rule of reason," *id.* at 788, concluding that "[w]henever non-disclosure of particular risk information is open to debate by reasonable-minded men, the issue is one for the finder of facts." *Ibid.* The point assumes significance in this case because defendant argues that the risk of lymphedema from an axillary node biopsy is remote, not material. Plaintiff's experts disagree, contending that she should have been informed of that risk. Thus there will be presented on the retrial a factual issue for the jury's resolution: would the risk of lymphedema influence a prudent patient in reaching a decision on whether to submit to the surgery?

Perhaps the strongest consideration that influences our decision in favor of the "prudent patient" standard lies in the notion that the physician's duty of disclosure "arises from phenomena apart from medical custom and practice": the patient's right of self-determination. *Canterbury, supra*, 464 F.2d at 786-87. The foundation for the physician's duty to disclose in the first place is found in the idea that "it is the prerogative of the patient, not the physician, to determine for himself the direction in which his interests seem to lie." *Id.* at 781. In contrast the arguments for the "professional" standard smack of an anachronistic paternalism that is at odds with any strong conception of a patient's right of self-determination. *Id.* at 781, 784, 789. . . .

III

Finally, we address the issue of [causation]. As with other medical malpractice actions, informed-consent cases require that plaintiff prove not only that the physician failed to comply with the applicable standard for disclosure but also that such failure was the proximate cause of plaintiff's injuries.

Under the "prudent patient" standard "causation must also be shown: *i.e.*, that the prudent person in the patient's position would have decided differently if adequately informed." Perna v. Pirozzi, *supra*, 92 N.J. at 460 n.2 (citing *Canterbury, supra*, 464 F.2d at 791; Louisell and Williams, *supra*, § 2208 at 22-32 to -35). As *Canterbury* observes,

> [t]he patient obviously has no complaint if he would have submitted to the therapy notwithstanding awareness that the risk was one of its perils. On the other hand, the very purpose of the disclosure rule is to protect the patient against consequences which, if known, he would have avoided by foregoing the treatment. The more difficult question is whether the factual issue on causality calls for an objective or a subjective determination. [464 F.2d at 790.]

Canterbury decided its own question in favor of an objective determination. The subjective approach, which the court rejected, inquires whether, if the patient had been informed of the risks that in fact materialized, he or she would have consented to the treatment. The shortcoming of this approach, according to *Canterbury*, is that "it places the physician in jeopardy of the patient's hindsight and bitterness. It places the factfinder in the position of deciding whether a speculative answer to a hypothetical question is to be credited. It calls for a subjective determination solely on testimony of a patient-witness shadowed by the occurrence of the undisclosed risk."[*Id.* at 790-91.]

The court therefore elected to adopt an objective test, as do we. Because we would not presume to attempt an improvement in its articulation of the reasons, we quote once again the *Canterbury* court:

> Better it is, we believe, to resolve the causality issue on an objective basis: in terms of what a prudent person in the patient's position would have decided if suitably informed of all perils bearing significance. If adequate disclosure could reasonably be expected to have caused that person to decline the treatment because of the

> revelation of the kind of risk or danger that resulted in harm, causation is shown, but otherwise not. The patient's testimony is relevant on that score of course but it would not threaten to dominate the findings. And since that testimony would probably be appraised congruently with the factfinder's belief in its reasonableness, the case for a wholly objective standard for passing on causation is strengthened. Such a standard would in any event ease the fact-finding process and better assure the truth as its product. [*Id.* at 791.] . . .

IV

The judgment of the Appellate Division is reversed. The cause is remanded for a new trial consistent with this opinion.

NOTES AND QUESTIONS

1. *Per Se Versus Evidentiary Approaches. T.J. Hooper*, along with the *Behymer* decision it cites, are the leading authorities for the widely accepted rule that, outside of professional negligence, adherence to customary practices does not of itself establish that the defendant acted with reasonable care. Some nineteenth-century and early twentieth-century decisions had endorsed the opposing *per se* approach. *See* Titus v. Bradford, B. & K. R.R. Co., 20 A. 517 (Pa. 1890) ("the unbending test of negligence in methods, machinery and appliances is the ordinary usage of business. No man is held to a higher degree of skill than the fair average of his profession or trade. . . ."). There is some suggestion in these decisions that judges believed that the *per se* rule helped to constrain pro-plaintiff juries.

2. *Is Custom Probative of Reasonableness?* To conclude that customary precaution is not of itself reasonable precaution is not to conclude that evidence of customary precaution is *irrelevant* to the issue of reasonableness. As Holmes, the author of *Behymer*, explained: "What usually is done may be evidence of what ought to be done, but what ought to be done is fixed by a standard of reasonable prudence, whether it was usually complied with or not." 189 U.S. at 470. If, as *T.J. Hooper* suggests, entire industries might lag behind evolving standards of due care, why should one presume that evidence of customary care tells us anything about the standard of reasonable care? *See* Mayhew v. Sullivan Mining Co., 76 Me. 100 (1884) (excluding evidence of custom as irrelevant to the question of reasonable care). In a related vein, Clarence Morris once argued that evidence of custom does not so much tell us what reasonable care is, but instead serves to focus the deliberation of jurors on the practical difficulties defendants may have faced in taking precautions against harming persons such as the plaintiff.

3. *Custom as Sword or Shield.* Should the weight given by courts to custom vary depending on whether it is the plaintiff who seeks to introduce nonconformity with custom as a sword for establishing fault or the defendant who seeks to introduce compliance with custom as a shield against a finding of fault? Alternatively, should it vary depending on whether the plaintiff and defendant were strangers or maintained some sort of preexisting relationship? The Restatement (Third) treats conformity to custom and departure from custom symmetrically; both may be used as evidence by

the factfinder to ascertain whether there was a breach of duty, but neither may be used preclusively. Restatement (Third) of Torts: Liability for Physical and Emotional Harm § 13 (2010). Judge Richard Posner has argued that a *per se* equation of customary and reasonable care ought to apply when the parties were in a relationship, but not when they were strangers, because parties in a relationship can in principle bargain to adopt practices that provide the appropriate level of care. Does *T.J. Hooper* endorse this rationale?

4. *Types of Custom.* Should the rules bearing on custom depend on the type of custom at stake? Steven Hetcher argues that customs develop out of several different circumstances and warrant different legal treatment depending on their type. For example, observance of certain customs enables individuals to coordinate their behavior — such as the custom, now enshrined in American law, that drivers should drive on the right side of the road. Other customs serve an informational role. For example, if a person unfamiliar with carpentry observes experienced carpenters wearing protective goggles, she may infer that there is a risk of eye injury present, and that goggles will help protect against it. Still other customs may have an expressive function, or may be mere vestiges of outdated patterns of conduct. Hetcher argues that the legal treatment of compliance with custom ought to vary according to the type of custom at issue. Which of the foregoing custom-types was in play in *T.J. Hooper?*

5. *Proof of Custom.* How does one prove the existence of a custom? Must adherence be uniform across the entire practice or industry? If not uniform, then what degree of adherence will suffice? Courts typically maintain that a practice must be "widespread" or "common" to count as a custom. *See, e.g.*, Trimarco v. Klein, 436 N.E.2d 502 (N.Y. 1982) (discussing whether usage of shatterproof glass for shower doors had become customary).

6. *Professionals Versus Nonprofessionals.* As *Johnson* attests, prevailing practices play a special role in suits alleging professional malpractice. For example, the standard of care for doctors incorporates the notion of customary care into the very definition of reasonableness: A doctor is required to exercise the same level of care as is considered standard by members of the profession. Thus, in medical cases, proof of compliance with professional custom often *does* establish reasonable care.

7. *Local Versus National Custom.* At one time, courts tended to require medical malpractice plaintiffs to show that the defendant's conduct departed from the custom of other doctors in the same locality. Now courts and statutes tend to speak, as does Georgia law, in terms of "general" custom, or the custom of "similar" localities. In part, this change of rules has been motivated by concern that plaintiffs residing in relatively sparsely populated localities would have a hard time finding a second physician or other expert willing to testify against a treating physician. In addition, the change was spurred by the judicial sense that modern medical training is more standardized, and medical information more readily available today than it once was. Consider how this change as to which customs ought to be considered by the jury might affect the application of the *per se* rule in particular cases. By permitting comparisons and

contrasts with practices in other jurisdictions, does the rule of custom promise at least some plaintiffs a basis for challenging prevailing local customs?

8. Expert Testimony and the Standard of Care. As *Johnson* notes, unless the professional conduct at issue is so unrelated to professional expertise that lay jurors can assess it based on their experience, the plaintiff in a malpractice action must introduce expert testimony to establish that the defendant failed to heed standard of care. (Recall from *Myers, supra*, the high court's conclusion that plaintiff did not need to produce an expert to testify as to the defendant nursing assistants' carelessness because the alleged errors were of a nontechnical nature.) The expert must, moreover, testify in a way that identifies a standard of conduct that the defendant failed to observe. *See, e.g.*, Locke v. Pachtman, 521 N.W.2d 786 (Mich. 1994) (plaintiff's expert failed to identify a standard of care for injections by testifying that hypodermic needles usually break off in a patient only because of the caregiver's improper technique; the expert offered no description of how the defendant should have acted). The identification of an expert who is not only competent to testify, but also will make an effective witness, is among the most significant challenges facing a plaintiff's attorney contemplating the commencement of a malpractice action.

9. Administrative Versus Professional Judgments. In medical malpractice cases, the professional standard of care applies to treatment and other care-related decisions. By contrast, administrative decisions do not fall under the rubric of professional malpractice. *See, e.g.*, Rice v. St. Lukes Roosevelt Hosp. Cent., 739 N.Y.S.2d 384 (App. Div. 2002) (claim for injuries allegedly arising from inadequate hospital security are claims for ordinary negligence, rather than professional malpractice); Doe v. Vanderbilt, 958 S.W.2d 117 (Tenn. Ct. App. 1997) (hospital's decision not to notify patients who received blood transfusions that they may have been exposed to HIV was administrative rather than medical; motion for summary judgment on the ground of compliance with custom denied), *rev'd on other grounds*, 62 S.W.3d 133 (Tenn. 2001).

10. Helling v. Carey. A few decisions have assaulted the *per se* rule head on. A well-known example is *Helling v. Carey*, 519 P.2d 981 (Wash. 1974). Plaintiff, who was nearly blinded by glaucoma, sued her ophthalmologist for failing to administer a "pressure" test, a simple, painless procedure for detecting the disease. The accepted practice among ophthalmologists at the time was to administer this test only to certain high-risk patients (of which class plaintiff was not a member). Hence plaintiff stood to lose her suit under an application of the *per se* rule. The Washington Supreme Court, however, ruled that the ordinary, reasonable person standard ought to control, in part because the decision not to apply the test seemed on its face unreasonable. (Can you think of any reason justifying a failure not to provide a cheap, safe, and efficacious test such as this one?) Even more controversially, the court was so sure of its analysis that it held, as a matter of law, that the ophthalmologist had acted carelessly because the benefits of administering the test so clearly outweighed its costs.

11. Informed Consent. *Largey* indicates another limitation recognized by some courts on the *per se* rule for professional malpractice: It does not apply to claims of malpractice that assert a tortious failure to inform the patient of risks attending medical procedures. About half the states now recognize this exception. What is the strongest basis for *Largey*'s rule that informed consent cases are different?

12. Exceptions to the Rule of Informed Consent. The rule of informed consent admits of exceptions. For example, no informed consent need be obtained to operate on an unconscious patient in need of immediate surgery (although if a guardian or close relative is present or immediately available, it may be necessary to obtain her consent). *See, e.g.*, Miller v. Rhode Island Hosp., 625 A.2d 778 (R.I. 1993) (discussing the scope of the emergency exception and holding that the issue of whether a severely intoxicated emergency-room patient lacked the capacity to consent, such that a surgeon could proceed to operate over his objection, is a question for the jury). Harder cases concern whether a doctor is entitled to refrain from disclosing risks for paternalistic reasons, such as a fear that a particular patient will severely overestimate the risks disclosed and thus make an irrational decision not to opt for the procedure. Courts have suggested that such reasoning runs against the autonomy principle undergirding informed consent analysis. As a matter of informed consent law, must a surgeon disclose that he is HIV positive? *See* Faya v. Almaraz, 620 A.2d 327 (Md. 1993) (disclosure required). Must a physician disclose that she is under a contract with an HMO that provides financial incentives to the physician to avoid, if possible, performing certain tests or procedures? *See* Neade v. Portes, 739 N.E.2d 496 (Ill. 2000) (failure to disclose incentives does not support an independent cause of action, but, if physician testifies as to the propriety of patient's course of treatment at trial, evidence of the nondisclosure of incentives can be admitted to impeach physician's credibility).

13. Medical Malpractice Statutes. In the last 35 years, medical malpractice actions have become increasingly governed by statutes, such as the Georgia Tort Reform Act mentioned in *Condra*, that are designed in large part to limit physicians' liability. These statutes have been enacted in response to perceived crises in medical malpractice insurance markets that are said to threaten to dramatically increase the cost, or reduce the availability, of medical services. (Critics contend that price variations in malpractice premiums are largely a function of fluctuations in the income received by insurance companies from the investment of prior years' premiums, and are not significantly influenced by changes in tort liability.) The provisions of these statutory regimes vary widely and may include rejection of the national standard of care in favor of a similar localities standard; adoption of shorter statutes of limitations, as well as statutes of repose (see Chapter 7); abolition of the collateral source rule (see Chapter 8); damage caps (see Chapter 8); and caps on attorneys' fees. *See* Newton v. Cox, 878 S.W.2d 105 (Tenn. 1994) (discussing Tennessee's medical malpractice statute and upholding its cap on contingent fees). Some statutes also set up administrative schemes, such as medical review boards, through which malpractice claimants must proceed before being eligible to sue in tort. On several occasions in the last decade, federal legislators have introduced in Congress draft legislation that would essentially create a national law of medical malpractice. To date, none have been enacted.

14. MCOs and ERISA. Medical care increasingly is provided through managed care organizations (MCOs). MCOs differ in their particulars, but their basic goal is to find ways of reducing the cost of health care. As more and more health care services are delivered through MCOs, administrators — as opposed to physicians — have gained a larger say over whether patients will be reimbursed for particular procedures. This in turn has raised the issue of whether administrators and the MCOs that employ them can be held liable in tort for carelessly and mistakenly ruling that a particular medical procedure is not necessary or otherwise not covered by the relevant health plan, thus preventing a patient from receiving the benefits of the procedure. There appear to be few instances of such liability. This may be in part because the U.S. Supreme Court has ruled that state tort law, as it pertains to health insurance that is provided through employers, has been substantially supplanted ("preempted") by a federal statute known as the Employee Retirement Income Security Act (ERISA), 29 U.S.C. §§ 1001 *et seq. See* Aetna Health, Inc. v. Davila, 542 U.S. 200 (2004). (Preemption is discussed further in Chapter 13.)

15. Other Professions. The same *per se* rule extends to other professions, including the legal and accounting professions. The textbook example of legal malpractice consists of failing to file suit within the time period set by the relevant statute of limitations, thus causing the client to forfeit her claim. *See, e.g.*, Carpenter v. Cullen, 581 N.W.2d 72 (Neb. 1998) (affirming a $270,000 jury verdict against an attorney who failed to file suit prior to the expiration of the statute of limitations period). However, lawyers can also commit malpractice in other ways, for example, by breaching the duty of confidentiality owed to their clients, by failing to keep them apprised of the progress of their cases, by failing to conduct a diligent examination of documents related to a transaction, or by failing to consult their clients before making critical decisions, such as those pertaining to settlement. Legal malpractice claims, like their medical counterparts, require expert testimony to establish breach of the relevant standard of care, except in cases where the attorney's alleged carelessness is straightforward enough for a layperson to assess. *Cf.* Boyle v. Welsh, 589 N.W.2d 118 (Neb. 1999) (just as the general requirement of expert testimony in medical malpractice suits can be relaxed in certain cases, such as those in which a sponge is left inside a surgical patient, so certain legal malpractice cases will not require expert testimony on the issue of breach).

16. Breach and Cause-in-Fact. As with informed consent cases, legal malpractice claims can present thorny issues of causation and damages. If, for example, the allegation is that Lawyer *L* was negligent in handling the litigation of client *C*'s breach of contract claim, *C* is damaged only insofar as the contract suit was likely to succeed, either in the form of a favorable verdict or a settlement. In other words, as malpractice plaintiff, *C* is required to establish that, but for *L*'s malpractice, she would have prevailed on her underlying contract claim. Thus, in suing *L*, she must prove "a case within a case," that is, the validity of the contract claim, as well as the tort claim against *L* for mishandling the contract claim. This can be a formidable burden.

IV. REASONABLENESS, BALANCING, AND COST-BENEFIT ANALYSIS

We mentioned in the notes to Part I of this chapter that Justice Holmes thought it would be desirable for judges to replace the "featureless generality" of the reasonable person standard with more specific rules as to what constitutes carelessness. We also noted that Holmes's vision has not been realized. Are there other ways to refine and systematize the breach inquiry? Or is reasonableness necessarily bound up with the particular context and type of behavior at issue?

United States v. Carroll Towing Co.

159 F.2d 169 (2d Cir. 1947)

[This suit arose out of events taking place at three piers extending out in a westerly direction into the Hudson River (which runs north-south) from the Manhattan side of the river. The three piers, in order from north to south, were the Public Pier, Pier 52, and Pier 51. On January 4, 1944, four barges were attached to the Public Pier in a "tier" formation, in which the first (easternmost) barge is tied to the end of the pier, the second barge, further out in the river, is tied to the first barge, the third is tied to the second, and so forth. Six barges were attached in the same formation to Pier 52, directly south of the Public Pier. For reasons unknown, someone had attached a line from the fourth (outermost) barge of the tier attached to the Public Pier to the sixth (outermost) barge of the tier attached to Pier 52.

The inner barge in the Pier 52 tier—the one attached to the pier—was named the "Anna C." The Anna C. was owned by Conners Marine Co., was being chartered (leased) by the Pennsylvania Railroad Company, and had on its decks flour owned by the United States Government. Under the terms of the lease between Conners and Pennsylvania Railroad, Conners was obligated to provide a bargee between the hours of 8 A.M. and 4 P.M. (A bargee is charged with looking after the vessel, often living on it.) However, the Anna C.'s bargee was not on board at the relevant times.

At about noon, the harbormaster ordered a tugboat named the Carroll, which was owned by Carroll Towing Co., and was being leased at the time by Grace Line, Inc., to tow away one of the barges in the Public Pier tier. In order to get to that barge, it had to first release the line attaching the outermost barges of the two tiers. Before undertaking that task, the Carroll pulled alongside, and attached itself with a line to the outermost barge of the Pier 52 tier. Two men from the Carroll, one of whom was the harbor-master, proceeded to board each of the barges in the Pier 52 tier and to inspect and adjust the lines holding the tier together, including the two lines holding the Anna C. to Pier 52. With that effort completed, the crew of the Carroll released the line attaching the tug to the outermost barge of the Pier 52 tier, as well as the line connecting the two outermost barges of the respective tiers, then backed away.

Soon thereafter, the entire Pier 52 tier broke away from Pier 52 and floated southward toward Pier 51. The Anna C., the innermost barge, struck a tanker docked at Pier 51. The propeller of the tanker punched a hole in the Anna C.'s hull. Because the hole was below the water line, its presence was not immediately obvious to the crew of the Carroll and others in the area. The Anna C. was pushed to a spot in between Piers 52 and 51, where it soon sunk. Evidence presented to the lower court indicated that, had they been made aware of the hole, both the Carroll and another tug had the opportunity and ability to push the Anna C. to shore after it hit the tanker so as to prevent it from sinking.

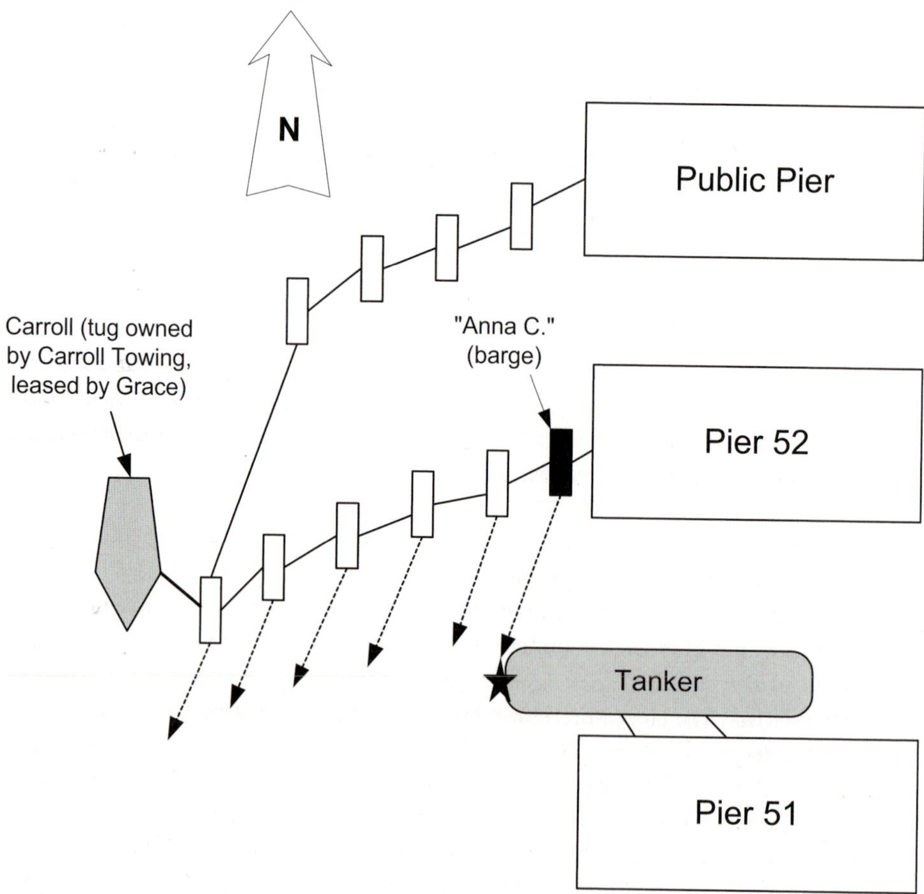

United States v. Carroll Towing Co. 159 F.2d 169 (2d Cir. 1947)

Various claims and counter-claims were filed. In Conners Marine Co. v. Pennsylvania R. Co., 66 F. Supp. 396 (S.D.N.Y. 1946), District Judge Moscowitz found that Carroll Towing and Grace were both equally at fault in inspecting and/or adjusting the lines holding the Anna C. and the rest of the Pier 52 tier. On that basis, he held each of the two liable to Conners for half of the value of the damage to the Anna C.

Carroll and Grace argued that Conners should have to bear some of this liability because Conners was at fault in that it had no bargee on board the Anna C. at the time of the mishap. Unlike most states' negligence law, which at this time applied the all-or-nothing rule of contributory negligence, admiralty law apportioned liability for property damage on a *pro rata* basis among all persons deemed legally responsible for an injury. Thus, to oversimplify, if Conners could not be charged with negligence, the assignment of 50/50 responsibility would stand and Conners could recover all of its damages from Carroll Towing and Grace. By contrast, if Conners were deemed at fault, it would be assigned responsibility for 1/3 of its own losses as one of three at-fault parties. Then it would stand to recover only 2/3 of its damages: 1/3 each from Carroll Towing and Grace.

The District Judge decided that the absence of a bargee should not diminish Conners' recovery. His reasoning, which was the basis of the appeal addressed by the Second Circuit in its *Carroll Towing* opinion, was as follows:

> At the time the lines were shifted by the harbor master and the deckhand on the Anna C, it is believed that the captain of the barge Anna C was absent. The testimony is in conflict with reference to this. The absence of the captain of the Anna C did not in any wise contribute to the accident. He was not required to anticipate negligence of the harbor master, the master and deckhand of the tug Carroll. Under the circumstances here disclosed, the absence of the captain is not in itself negligence.

66 F. Supp. at 398. In support of this holding, Judge Moscowitz cited numerous precedents, including: *The Kathryn B. Guinan*, 176 F. 301 (2d Cir. 1910); *United States Trucking Corporation v. City of New York*, 14 F.2d 528 (E.D.N.Y. 1926); and *The Trenton*, 72 F. 283 (2d Cir. 1896). — Eds.]

L. Hand, J. . . .

[E]ven though we assume that the [Anna C.'s] bargee was responsible for [inspecting and maintaining the lines holding the Anna C. to Pier 52] after the other barges were added outside, there is not the slightest ground for saying that [the Carroll crewmen] would have paid any attention to any protest which he might have made, had he been there. We do not therefore attribute it as in any degree a fault of the "Anna C." that the flotilla broke adrift. Hence she may recover in full against the Carroll Company and the Grace Line for any injury she suffered from the contact with the tanker's propeller, which we shall speak of as the "collision damages." On the other hand, if the bargee had been on board, and had done his duty to his employer, he would have gone below at once, examined the injury, and called for help from the "Carroll" and the Grace Line tug. Moreover, it is clear that these tugs could have kept the barge afloat, until they had safely beached her, and saved her cargo. This would have avoided what we shall call the "sinking damages." Thus, if it was a failure in the Conner [sic] Company's proper care of its own barge, for the bargee to be absent, the company can recover only one third of the "sinking" damages from the Carroll Company and one third from the Grace Line. For this reason the question arises whether a barge owner is slack in the care of his barge if the bargee is absent.

As to the consequences of a bargee's absence from his barge there have been a number of decisions; and we cannot agree that it is never ground for liability even to other vessels who may be injured. As early as 1843, Judge Sprague in *Clapp v. Young*, held a schooner liable which broke adrift from her moorings in a gale in Provincetown Harbor, and ran down another ship. The ground was that the owners of the offending ship had left no one on board, even though it was the custom in that harbor not to do so. Judge Tenney in *Fenno v. The Mary E. Cuff*, treated it as one of several faults against another vessel which was run down, to leave the offending vessel unattended in a storm in Port Jefferson Harbor. Judge Thomas in *The On-the-Level*, held liable for damage to a stake-boat, a barge moored to the stake-boat "south of Liberty Light, off the Jersey shore," because she had been left without a bargee; indeed he declared that the bargee's absence was "gross negligence." In *The Kathryn B. Guinan*, Ward, J., did indeed say that, when a barge was made fast to a pier in the harbor, as distinct from being in open waters, the bargee's absence would not be the basis for the owner's negligence. However, the facts in that case made no such holding necessary; the offending barge in fact had a bargee aboard though he was asleep. In the *Beeko*, Judge Campbell exonerated a power boat which had no watchman on board, which boys had maliciously cast loose from her moorings at the Marine Basin in Brooklyn and which collided with another vessel. Obviously that decision has no bearing on the facts at bar. In *United States Trucking Corporation v. City of New York*, the same judge refused to reduce the recovery of a coal hoister, injured at a foul berth, because the engineer was not on board; he had gone home for the night as was apparently his custom. We reversed the decree, but for another reason. In *The Sadie*, we affirmed Judge Coleman's holding that it was actionable negligence to leave without a bargee on board a barge made fast outside another barge, in the face of storm warnings. The damage was done to the inside barge. In *The P. R. R. No. 216*, we charged with liability a lighter which broke loose from, or was cast off, by a tanker to which she was moored, on the ground that her bargee should not have left her over Sunday. He could not know when the tanker might have to cast her off. We carried this so far in *The East Indian*, as to hold a lighter whose bargee went ashore for breakfast, during which the stevedores cast off some of the lighter's lines. True, the bargee came back after she was free and was then ineffectual in taking control of her before she damaged another vessel; but we held his absence itself a fault, knowing as he must have, that the stevedores were apt to cast off the lighter. *The Conway No. 23* went on the theory that the absence of the bargee had no connection with the damage done to the vessel itself; it assumed liability, if the contrary had been proved. In *The Trenton*, we refused to hold a moored vessel because another outside of her had overcharged her fasts. The bargee had gone away for the night when a storm arose; and our exoneration of the offending vessel did depend upon the theory that it was not negligent for the bargee to be away for the night; but no danger was apparently then to be apprehended. In *Bouker Contracting Co. v. Williamsburgh Power Plant Corporation*, we charged a scow with half damages because her bargee left her without adequate precautions. In O'Donnell Transportation Co. v. M. & J. Tracy, we refused to charge a barge whose bargee had been absent from 9 A.M. to 1:30 P.M., having "left the vessel to go ashore for a time on his own business."

It appears from the foregoing review that there is no general rule to determine when the absence of a bargee or other attendant will make the owner of the barge liable for injuries to other vessels if she breaks away from her moorings. However, in any cases where he would be so liable for injuries to others obviously he must reduce his damages proportionately, if the injury is to his own barge. It becomes apparent why there can be no such general rule, when we consider the grounds for such a liability. Since there are occasions when every vessel will break from her moorings, and since, if she does, she becomes a menace to those about her; the owner's duty, as in other similar situations, to provide against resulting injuries is a function of three variables: (1) The probability that she will break away; (2) the gravity of the resulting injury, if she does; (3) the burden of adequate precautions. Possibly it serves to bring this notion into relief to state it in algebraic terms: if the probability be called *P*; the injury, *L*; and the burden, *B*; liability depends upon whether *B* is less than *L* multiplied by *P*: i.e., whether *B* [is] less than *PL*. Applied to the situation at bar, the likelihood that a barge will break from her fasts and the damage she will do, vary with the place and time; for example, if a storm threatens, the danger is greater; so it is, if she is in a crowded harbor where moored barges are constantly being shifted about. On the other hand, the barge must not be the bargee's prison, even though he lives aboard; he must go ashore at times. We need not say whether, even in such crowded waters as New York Harbor a bargee must be aboard at night at all; it may be that the custom is otherwise, as Ward, J., supposed in *The Kathryn B. Guinan, supra*; and that, if so, the situation is one where custom should control. We leave that question open; but we hold that it is not in all cases a sufficient answer to a bargee's absence without excuse, during working hours, that he has properly made fast his barge to a pier, when he leaves her. In the case at bar the bargee left at five o'clock in the afternoon of January 3rd, and the flotilla broke away at about two o'clock in the afternoon of the following day, twenty-one hours afterwards. The bargee had been away all the time, and we hold that his fabricated story was affirmative evidence that he had no excuse for his absence. At the locus in quo — especially during the short January days and in the full tide of war activity — barges were being constantly "drilled" in and out. Certainly it was not beyond reasonable expectation that, with the inevitable haste and bustle, the work might not be done with adequate care. In such circumstances we hold — and it is all that we do hold — that it was a fair requirement that the Conners Company should have a bargee aboard (unless he had some excuse for his absence), during the working hours of daylight.

[Judge Hand's opinion proceeds to apportion liability among the various parties in light of the ruling on Conners' comparative fault and various other procedural facts about the case, then remands the entire matter for further proceedings in accordance with its dictates. — EDS.]

Hand, *Hooper*, and *Carroll Towing*

Judge Learned Hand was the author of the opinions in both *The T.J. Hooper* and *Carroll Towing*. Does his emphasis in *Carroll Towing* on "*B*,", "*P*," and "*L*" as factors that help determine the care that a reasonably prudent person would take shed light on *T.J. Hooper*'s refusal to give conclusive effect to custom? If a judge were to apply the *Carroll Towing* factors to *T.J. Hooper*, would she be likely to make a finding of breach?

Learned Hand
U.S. District Court,
S.D.N.Y. (1909-24)
U.S. Court of Appeals,
Second Circuit (1924-51)

Rhode Island Hosp. Trust Nat'l Bank v. Zapata Corp.

848 F.2d 291 (1st Cir. 1988)

BREYER, J. The issue that this appeal presents is whether Zapata Corporation has shown that the system used by Rhode Island Hospital Trust National Bank for detecting forged checks — a system used by a majority of American banks — lacks the "ordinary care" that a bank must exercise under the Uniform Commercial Code § 4-406(3) (1977), embodied here in Rhode Island General Laws, § 6A-4-406(3) (1985). The question arises out of the following district court determinations. . . .

1. In early 1985, a Zapata employee stole some blank checks from Zapata. She wrote a large number of forged checks, almost all in amounts of $150 to $800 each, on Zapata's accounts at Rhode Island Hospital Trust National Bank. The Bank, from March through July 1985, received and paid them.

2. Bank statements that the Bank regularly sent Zapata first began to reflect the forged checks in early April 1985. Zapata failed to examine its statements closely until July 1985, when it found the forgeries. It immediately notified the Bank, which then stopped clearing the checks. The Bank had already processed and paid forged checks totaling $109,247.16.

3. The Bank will (and legally must) reimburse Zapata in respect to all checks it cleared before April 25, 1985 (or for at least two weeks after Zapata received the statement that reflected the forgeries). *See* U.C.C. §§ 3-401(1), 4-406(2) (1977).

4. In respect to checks cleared on and after April 25, the Bank need not reimburse Zapata because Zapata failed to "exercise reasonable care and promptness to examine the [bank] statement." U.C.C. § 4-406(1) (1977).

The question before us is whether this last-mentioned conclusion is correct or whether Zapata can recover for the post-April 24 checks on the theory that, even if it was negligent, so was the Bank.

To understand the question, one must examine U.C.C. § 4-406, R.I. Gen. Laws § 6A-4-406. Ordinarily a bank must reimburse an innocent customer for forgeries that it honors, § 6A-3-401(1) (1985), but § 6A-4-406 makes an important exception to the liability rule. The exception operates in respect to a series of forged checks, and it applies once a customer has had a chance to catch the forgeries by examining his bank statements and notifying the bank but has failed to do so.

The statute, in relevant part, reads as follows:

> (1) *When a bank sends to its customer a statement of account* accompanied by items paid in good faith in support of the debit entries or holds the statement and items pursuant to a request or instructions of its customer or otherwise in a reasonable manner makes the statement and items available to the customer, *the customer must exercise reasonable care and promptness to examine the statement* and items *to discover his unauthorized signature* or any alteration on an item *and must notify the bank promptly* after discovery thereof.
>
> (2) *If the bank establishes that the customer failed* with respect to an item *to comply with* the duties imposed on the customer by *subsection (1) the customer is precluded from asserting against the bank.*
>
> (a) *His unauthorized signature* or any alteration on the item if the bank also establishes that it suffered a loss by reason of such failure; *and*
>
> (b) *An unauthorized signature or alteration by the same wrongdoer on any other item paid in good faith by the bank after the* first item and *statement was available to the customer for a reasonable period not exceeding fourteen (14) calendar days* and before the bank receives notification from the customer of any such unauthorized signature or alteration.

§ 6A-4-406(1)-(2) (emphasis added).

The statute goes on to specify an important exception to the exception. It says:

> (3) The preclusion under subsection (2) does not apply if the customer establishes lack of ordinary care on the part of the bank in paying the item(s).

§ 6A-4-406(3). Zapata's specific claim, on this appeal, is that it falls within this "exception to the exception" — that the bank's treatment of the post-April 24 checks lacked "ordinary care." . . .

. . . The statute . . . says that strict bank liability terminates fourteen days after the customer receives the bank's statement unless "*the customer establishes* lack of ordinary care."§ 6A-4-406(3) (emphasis added). . . . And, the U.C.C. commentary makes clear that the statute [places the burden on the customer to prove lack of ordinary care]. . . .

The record convinces us that Zapata failed to carry its burden of establishing "lack of ordinary care" on the part of the Bank. First, the Bank described its ordinary practices as follows: The Bank examines all signatures on checks for more than $1,000. It examines signatures on checks between $100 and $1,000 (those at issue here) if it has reason to suspect a problem, *e.g.*, if a customer has warned it of a possible forgery or if the check was drawn on an account with insufficient funds. It examines the signatures of a randomly chosen one percent of all other checks between $100 and $1,000. But, it does not examine the signatures on other checks between $100 and

$1,000. Through expert testimony, the Bank also established that most other banks in the nation follow this practice and that banking industry experts recommend it. Indeed, Trust National Bank's practices are conservative in this regard, as most banks set $2,500 or more, not $1,000, as the limit beneath which they will not examine each signature.

This testimony made out a *prima facie* case of "ordinary care." U.C.C. § 4-103(3) (1977); R.I. Gen. Laws § 6A-4-103(3) (1985) ("action or nonaction . . . consistent with . . . a general banking usage not disapproved by this [Article or] chapter, prima facie constitutes the exercise of ordinary care"). . . . Of course, Zapata might still try to show that the entire industry's practice is unreasonable, that it reflects lack of "ordinary care." *The T.J. Hooper*, 60 F.2d 737, 740 (2d Cir.), *cert. denied*, 287 U.S. 662, 53 S. Ct. 220, 77 L. Ed. 571 (1932). In doing so, however, "the *prima facie* rule does . . . impose on the party contesting the standards to establish that they are *unreasonable, arbitrary*, or *unfair*." U.C.C. § 4-103 comment 4 (emphasis added).

Second, both bank officials and industry experts pointed out that this industry practice, in general and in the particular case of the Trust National Bank, saved considerable expense, compared with the Bank's pre-1981 practice of examining each check by hand. To be specific, the change saved the Bank about $125,000 annually. Zapata accepts this testimony as accurate.

Third, both a Bank official and an industry expert testified that changing from an "individual signature examination" system to the new "bulk-filing" system led to *no* significant increase in the number of forgeries that went undetected. Philip Schlernitzauer, a Bank vice-president . . . testified that under the prior "individual signature examination" system, some forgeries still slipped through. The Bank's loss was about $10,000 to $15,000 per year. He also determined through a feasibility study that by implementing a "bulk-filing" system in which 99 percent of checks under $1,000 were not individually screened, the loss would remain between $10,000 and $15,000. Dr. Lipis, an executive vice-president of a large consulting firm to the financial industry, testified that among its purposes was the following:

> Well, it improves the ability to return checks back to customers more correctly, simply that the checks do not get misplaced when they are handled; generally [it] can improve the morale within th[e] bank because . . . the signature verification is very tedious, very difficult, and not a function that is liked by anybody who does it. In addition, *it does not impact the amount of forgeries that are produced at the bank.*

Rec. App. 179 (emphasis added).

Zapata points to *no* testimony or other evidence tending to contradict these assertions. An industry-wide practice that saves money without significantly increasing the number of forged checks that the banks erroneously pay is a practice that reflects at least "ordinary care." *Cf.* Vending Chattanooga[, Inc. v. American Nat'l Bank & Trust Co., 730 S.W.2d 624, 628-29 (Tenn. 1987)] (weighing economic feasibility and business practice into definition of "ordinary care" or "reasonable commercial standards").

Fourth, even if one assumes . . . that the new system meant *some* increase in the number of undetected forged checks, Zapata still could not prevail, for it presented *no* evidence tending to show any such increased loss unreasonable in light of the costs that the new practice would save. Instead, it relied simply upon the assertion that costs saved the bank are irrelevant. But, that is not so, for what is reasonable or unreasonable insofar as "ordinary care" or "due care" or "negligence" (and the like) are concerned is often a matter of costs of prevention compared with correlative risks of loss. *See Vending Chattanooga*, 730 S.W.2d at 628-29; United States v. Carroll Towing Co., 159 F.2d 169, 173 (2d Cir. 1947) (Hand, J.) ("duty" defined by calculating probability of injury times gravity of harm to determine "burden of precaution" that is warranted). One does not, for example, coat the base of the Grand Canyon with soft plastic nets to catch those who might fall in, or build cars like armored tanks to reduce injuries in accidents even though the technology exists. . . . In arguing that the Bank provided "no care" in respect to the checks it did not examine, Zapata simply assumed the very conclusion (namely, the unreasonableness of a selective examination *system*) that it sought to prove. Aside from this assumption, its evidentiary cupboard is bare. . . .

We have found a few, more modern cases that arguably support Zapata's view, but they involve practices more obviously unreasonable than those presented here. *See, e.g.*, Hanover Insurance Cos. v. Brotherhood State Bank, 482 F. Supp. 501 (D. Kan. 1979) (no ordinary care where *no* examination of *any size* checks, conspicuous forgeries); Perley v. Glastonbury Bank and Trust Co., 170 Conn. 691, 702-03 (1976) (no ordinary care where *no* authentication of endorsements of *any size* checks). . . . And, in any event, we believe Rhode Island would follow the more significant body of modern case law suggesting analysis along the lines we have undertaken.

For these reasons, the judgment of the district court is *Affirmed.*

NOTES AND QUESTIONS

1. Where Was the Bargee? At the trial of the *Carroll Towing* case, the bargee insisted that he was actually on the Anna C. at the relevant time, but failed to notice that it was taking on water after its collision. The master who presided over the trial found the bargee's testimony utterly incredible. Based on other witnesses' testimony, he concluded that the bargee had not been on the barge on the day in question, and that the bargee had lied to avoid revealing the apparently unimpressive explanation as to why he was not on board. Does the reason for the bargee's absence matter to the analysis of comparative fault? Suppose the bargee had just left the Anna C. one hour prior to the incident in response to an emergency summons from his spouse, who needed medical assistance. Would that change the result? Why? Hand's opinion states that "the barge must not be the bargee's prison, even though he lives aboard; he must go ashore at times." How does this consideration figure into his formula for addressing the fault issue?

2. What Is a General Rule? Why does Hand recite the various precedents on liability for accidents caused in part by the absence of bargees? What lesson or principle do they establish, in his view? In what way do they lead him to consider that the element of carelessness or fault might usefully be described abstractly, as inquiring whether the burden on the company of taking "precautions" (B) is less than the harm that probably will result from not having taken the precautions ($P \times L$)?

3. Reasonableness and Balancing. That the determination of whether a person has behaved reasonably requires consideration of the burdens and expected benefits of taking precautions was not especially novel or controversial when Hand expressed it in 1947. For example, Section 291 of the First Restatement of Torts, published in 1934, following the earlier analysis of Professor Henry Terry, fleshed out the notion of acting as a reasonable person in the following terms:

> Where an act is one which a reasonable man would recognize as involving a risk of harm to another, the risk is unreasonable and the act is negligent if the risk is of such magnitude as to outweigh what the law regards as the utility of the act or of the particular manner in which it is done.

About 75 years prior to the publication of the First Restatement, England's Exchequer Barons had ruled that a waterworks company could not be found to have acted carelessly in failing to take precautions against their pipes cracking during an unprecedented winter freeze. Blythe v. Birmingham Water Works Co., 156 Eng. Rep. 1047 (Exch. 1856). Implicit in the Barons' analysis was the notion that not every precaution is worth taking, and hence not every failure to take a precaution constitutes carelessness.

If judges and lawyers were already alert to the idea that the breach inquiry calls for an assessment of both the burdens and the benefits of taking certain precautions, how much does Hand's algebraic rendition add?

4. Risk/Utility Balancing. The First Restatement's formulation speaks in terms of balancing the risk of harm against the "utility" of the actor's conduct. In so doing, it evokes the doctrine of utilitarianism, formulated most influentially by the English philosopher Jeremy Bentham. Although it comes in many variations, utilitarianism's central claim is that the goal of social arrangements should be to maximize the *aggregate level* of utility or happiness in the world. If many car drivers experience great pleasure from careening down local streets for the fun of it, might their happiness outweigh the displeasure of the few unlucky persons who are injured or killed because the happy drivers were not proceeding more cautiously? The First Restatement's formulation is careful to note that courts should consider "*what the law regards* as the utility of the act." What does that qualification mean? Why did the ALI put it in there?

5. Hand on the Hand "Formula." In other opinions, Hand made quite clear that he himself did not regard his algebraic rendering of reasonable care to be the sort of formula into which a judge could simply place well-defined inputs so as to generate a determinate result. For example, a 1950 decision raised the issue whether a car driver had acted with gross negligence. After noting that the formal legal standard for gross negligence was clear enough, Hand emphasized the difficulties in applying the standard to particular cases, noting that

> the same difficulties inhere in the concept of "ordinary" negligence. It is indeed possible to state an equation for negligence in the form, C equals P times D, in which the C is the care required to avoid risk, D, the possible injuries, and P, the probability that the injuries will occur, if the requisite care is not taken. But of these

> factors care is the only one ever susceptible of quantitative estimate, and often that is not. The injuries are always a variable within limits, which do not admit of even approximate ascertainment; and, although probability might theoretically be estimated, if any statistics were available, they never are; and, besides, probability varies with the severity of the injuries. It follows that all such attempts are illusory, and, if serviceable at all, are so only to center attention upon which one of the factors may be determinative in any given situation. It assists us here to center on the factor of probability, because the difference between "gross" and "ordinary" negligence consists in the higher risks which the putatively wrongful conduct has imposed upon the injured person. The requisite care to avoid the injuries and the possible injuries themselves are the same.

Moisan v. Loftus, 178 F.2d 148, 149 (2d Cir. 1950). Is Hand being appropriately skeptical or too skeptical? Consider *Zapata*, which involves a contract dispute that, because of the wording of the Uniform Commercial Code, raises the issue of whether the bank exercised ordinary care in honoring stolen checks. In the hands of then-Judge Breyer, *Zapata* seems to provide a particularly promising context for application of a fairly rigorous rendition of Hand's algebra. Is this because the case involves "only" money? Or because the parties were in a contractual relationship? Because of other features unusual to the case? Do any of the negligence cases we have seen thus far lend themselves to such analysis in the same way?

6. *Posner on the Hand Formula.* Judge Posner's 1972 article, *A Theory of Negligence*, is primarily responsible for elevating Hand's invocation of algebra into a negligence "formula" that purports to advance the ability of lawyers and academics to analyze questions of breach. It also provided a launching pad for the influential "Law and Economics" movement in the legal academy.

In his article, Posner argued that Hand's formula, whether intended to or not, provided the basis for a more rigorous conception of balancing that asks the factfinder to measure the *dollar cost* of precautions against the *dollar value* of expected harm. Whenever the former is greater than the latter, Posner argued, the precaution ought not to be taken, simply because it is wasteful of society's resources to take a precaution that is more expensive than the harm it is meant to prevent. According to Posner, Hand's use of the $B < P \times L$ formula is a key piece of evidence establishing that the law of negligence is primarily concerned to maximize aggregate social wealth by encouraging actors to take only cost-efficient precautions. Posner further argues that the law has been wise to pursue this goal, because the minimization of waste is a cause that persons with otherwise diverse interests can endorse.

Richard A. Posner
U.S. Court of Appeals, Seventh Circuit (1993–present)

As a judge on the Seventh Circuit Court of Appeals, Posner has had occasion to apply his rendition of the Hand formula in concrete settings. For example, in *McCarty v. Pheasant Run, Inc.*, 826 F.2d 1554 (7th Cir. 1987), the plaintiff was attacked while in her second-floor hotel room. Police later determined that the attacker gained access to the room through a sliding glass door that opened onto a walkway that in turn connected to a stairway that was accessible to the public at ground level. The sliding door had a handle-lock that had not been used. It also featured a chain lock that was in place, but was broken by the intruder.

Plaintiff sued, alleging that the hotel carelessly failed to equip the door with a better lock; ensure that the door was locked when she was first shown to her room; warn her to keep the sliding glass door locked; employ more security guards; and/or block public access to the stairway leading to the second-floor walkway. The jury returned a defense verdict. On appeal, the court, per Judge Posner, affirmed:

> . . . Unreasonable conduct is merely the failure to take precautions that would generate greater benefits in avoiding accidents than the precautions would cost.
>
> . . . Conceptual as well as practical difficulties in monetizing personal injuries may continue to frustrate efforts to measure expected accident costs with the precision that is possible, in principle at least, in measuring the other side of the equation — the cost or burden of precaution. For many years to come juries may be forced to make rough judgments of reasonableness, intuiting rather than measuring the factors in the Hand Formula; and so long as their judgment is reasonable, the trial judge has no right to set it aside, let alone substitute his own judgment.
>
> Having failed to make much effort to show that the mishap could have been prevented by precautions of reasonable cost and efficacy, Mrs. McCarty is in a weak position to complain about the jury verdict. No effort was made to inform the jury what it would have cost to equip every room in the Pheasant Run Lodge with a new lock, and whether the lock would have been jimmy-proof. . . . No effort was made, either, to specify an optimal security force for a resort the size of Pheasant Run. No one considered the fire or other hazards that a second-floor walkway not accessible from ground level would create. A notice in every room telling guests to lock all doors would be cheap, but since most people know better than to leave the door to a hotel room unlocked when they leave the room — and the sliding glass door [opened onto] a walkway, not a balcony — the jury might have thought that the incremental benefits from the notice would be slight. Mrs. McCarty testified that she didn't know there was a door behind the closed drapes, but the jury wasn't required to believe this. Most people on checking into a hotel room, especially at a resort, are curious about the view; and it was still light when Mrs. McCarty checked in at 6:00 P.M. on an October evening.
>
> It is a bedrock principle of negligence law that due care is that care which is optimal given that the potential victim is himself reasonably careful; a careless person cannot by his carelessness raise the standard of care of those he encounters. The jury may have thought it was the hotel's responsibility to provide a working lock but the guest's responsibility to use it. We do not want to press too hard on this point. A possible explanation for the condition of the door as revealed by the police investigation is that Mrs. McCarty on leaving the room for the evening left the door unlocked but with the safety chain fastened, and she might have been reasonable in thinking this a sufficient precaution. But it would not follow that the hotel was negligent, unless it is negligence to have sliding doors accessible to the public, a suggestion the jury was not required to buy. We doubt whether a boilerplate notice about the dangers of unlocked doors would have altered the behavior of the average guest; in any event this too was an issue for the jury.

> Now it is true that in Illinois an innkeeper . . . is required to use a high (not merely the ordinary) standard of care to protect its guests from assaults on the innkeeper's premises. . . .
>
> . . . Ordinarily the innkeeper knows much more about the hazards of his trade than the guest, and can take reasonable (= cost-justified) steps to reduce them, while ordinarily the guest can do little to protect himself against them. Pheasant Run, Inc. knows more about the danger of break-ins to guest rooms at its lodge than the guests do, and more about the alternative methods for preventing such break-ins, as well. Maybe this asymmetry in the parties' position should make the defendant's standard of care higher than it would be in, say, an ordinary collision case. But it does not make the defendant's liability strict. In this case there was evidence of negligence but not so much as to establish liability as a matter of law or . . . to require a new trial. And the rule, based as it seems to be on an asymmetry in the parties' abilities to prevent mishaps, has a certain hollowness in a case such as this, where the victim may have failed to take an elementary precaution — locking the sliding door before leaving the room.

Id. at 1557-1558.

7. *Criticisms of Posner's Rendition of the Hand Formula.* Suppose Posner's interpretation of Hand's formula is adopted. Does it entail that the level of precaution one takes ought to vary according to what sort of person or property might be injured by one's conduct? For example, should *D* spend less effort on care when driving his car in a generally less affluent neighborhood, on the theory that the expected future income of the persons *D* might hurt, as well as the value of property *D* is likely to harm ($P \times L$), will be lower as contrasted to the incomes and properties of persons in more affluent neighborhoods? If so, does this disqualify Posner's interpretation of the Hand formula as fundamentally unjust? What might Posner offer by way of response?

In a related vein, Gregory Keating poses the following hypothetical as a counter-example to the economic interpretation of *Carroll Towing. D* drives on a quiet local road at a speed well above the speed limit solely to secure a good tanning spot on the local beach. *D*'s speeding results in a collision with cyclist *P* that causes *P* a broken leg. Is *D* permitted to argue that the statistical probability of hitting someone was so low that the loss of welfare he stood to experience by not getting his desired spot on the beach outweighs the expected loss to others, such that his speeding was not negligent? Keating suggests that the moral significance that society attaches to particular activities and purposes matters in the fault determination, and cannot adequately be captured by an economic account.

Recall that much conduct that is careless consists of momentary lapses and other forms of inadvertent behavior, as contrasted to calculated decisions, such as Menlove's decision to build his hayrick a certain way. Do balancing notions such as the Hand formula capture the concept of fault at work in cases of *inadvertence?* In what way has one failed to properly balance burdens and benefits by failing to check one's mirrors or signal before changing lanes? By unknowingly driving above the speed limit? By slipping up during the course of surgery or while performing an audit?

8. Lord Reid's "Disproportionate Cost" Test. Some commentators have pointed to the opinion of Lord Reid in the House of Lords decision in *Bolton v. Stone*, [1951] A.C. 850, as providing a more satisfactory account of the balancing that ought to take place in analyzing the breach issue.

In that case, a batsman hit a cricket ball over the fence encircling the cricket pitch. The ball struck Mrs. Stone in the head as she stood in her yard, about 50 feet beyond the wall, causing her serious injury. The residences that included Mrs. Stone's had been constructed 30 years earlier, and, although there was evidence that a ball had left the pitch about once every 5 years, there was no record of a cricket ball ever having caused physical harm to anyone during that time. Nonetheless, Mrs. Stone argued that the club that owned the pitch had been careless for not erecting a higher wall to prevent balls from escaping.

The trial judge ruled that the club had not been negligent. The Court of Appeal reversed by a 2 to 1 decision. On appeal, the House of Lords reinstated the trial court's ruling. In stating his judgment, Lord Reid justified the Lords' decision by invoking a three-tiered mode of analysis, which can be summarized as follows:

1. If, at the time of acting, the risk that the actor's conduct would cause harm of the sort suffered by the plaintiff was exceedingly small, there was no obligation to take precautions against it;
2. If the risk of harm was not far-fetched—"real"—but still very small, the actor was obligated to take precautions against the harm unless the taking of those precautions would have imposed a burden on the actor entirely *disproportionate* to the harm risked;
3. If the risk of harm was "material" or "substantial," the actor was obligated to do everything *possible* to prevent the harm, even if that would entail adopting very expensive precautions to avoid a modest expected loss.

Lord Reid concluded that Mrs. Stone's suit fell under prong (2). Given that balls had occasionally left the pitch, and that there were residences nearby, the risk of someone getting hit was not preposterous, but was still very low. Because the only precautions apparently available to the club were expensive—erecting a higher fence or ceasing to play cricket—the club was under no obligation to take these precautions.

On the assumption that Lord Reid intended prongs (1) and (2) to be reserved for unusual cases, and hence that (3) was meant to cover the vast bulk of suits alleging careless wrongdoing, scholars including Ernest Weinrib and Richard Wright argue that it provides a better account of reasonable care than Posner's Hand formula because it requires an actor whose conduct poses substantial risk of injury to take precautions even when they are not cost-efficient. This, they argue, better captures the intuitive idea that safety (physical well-being) is a more important interest than money or modest restrictions on liberty. Do you agree? Stephen Gilles has suggested that Lord Reid's opinion was an outlier, and that English judges, like their American counterparts, attend to costs of precaution more than prong (3) of Reid's test would permit.

9. *The Third Restatement.* Section 3 of Restatement (Third) construes the reasonable person standard to embrace a version of balancing. It reads:

> § 3. NEGLIGENCE
>
> A person acts negligently if the person does not exercise reasonable care under all the circumstances. Primary factors to consider in ascertaining whether the person's conduct lacks reasonable care are the foreseeable likelihood that the person's conduct will result in harm, the foreseeable severity of any harm that may ensue, and the burden of precautions to eliminate or reduce the risk of harm.

Restatement (Third) of Torts: Liability for Physical and Emotional Harm § 3 (2010).

It is unclear whether the authors of the Third Restatement anticipate that juries will be instructed to balance "costs" and "benefits" instead of, or in addition to, being instructed on the reasonable person standard. Given that the jury usually has broad discretion to make the breach determination, if jurors will not be instructed on balancing, what is the use of framing "breach" in these terms?

10. *The Utility of Formulae.* Review the instances of faulty conduct provided in the cases in this chapter and earlier chapters. In what ways do the formulae offered by the Restatements, Judge Hand, Judge Posner, and/or Lord Reid enhance your ability to grasp what it means for a person to act carelessly?

V. PROVING BREACH: *RES IPSA LOQUITUR*

To say that breach is one of the elements of the plaintiff's prima facie negligence case is to say that the onus of establishing that the defendant acted carelessly is on the plaintiff. Often this onus is described as the plaintiff's "burden of proof." This phrase is somewhat misleading, in that it refers to two different burdens: the burden of *production* and the burden of *persuasion.*

The burden of production is the requirement of providing to the court some evidence in support of an alleged fact or set of facts that the party bearing the burden seeks to establish. So, for example, a negligence plaintiff seeking to establish that a defendant drove carelessly might seek to introduce into evidence a copy of a police report in which the police officer reports having observed the defendant speeding. Evidence offered in satisfaction of the burden of production will often be "circumstantial" rather than in the form of an eyewitness or videotaped account. For example, our imagined plaintiff might have to rely on skid marks at the accident scene, or the extent of damage to the cars involved in the collision, to support an inference that the defendant was driving carelessly. Often a plaintiff in this situation will seek to enlist the testimony of experts who can help establish such an inference based on circumstantial evidence.

The burden of persuasion comes into play only after there is evidence before a judge or jury upon which it must make a decision. As noted in Chapter 1, in criminal

7

prosecutions, the prosecutor bears a high burden of persuasion. With respect to those elements for which she bears the burden, she must establish them *beyond a reasonable doubt.* However, in most civil lawsuits, including most tort suits, the burden of persuasion is phrased in terms of a lower standard, namely, the *preponderance of the evidence* standard. To say that a negligence plaintiff bears the burden of persuasion on an element such as breach therefore entails that the plaintiff must persuade the judge or jury that *it is more likely than not* that the defendant acted as the plaintiff alleges. To say the same thing in reverse, if the plaintiff's evidence establishes that it is equally likely (or less likely than not) that the defendant did or did not engage in the conduct alleged by the plaintiff, then the judge or jury must find for the defendant.*

In sum, the rule that a negligence plaintiff usually bears the burden of proving the breach element requires her to produce enough evidence concerning the defendant's conduct such that a judge or jury can conclude that it is more likely than not that the alleged careless conduct actually occurred. Yet, as we see below, in some situations, a negligence plaintiff will have only two pieces of circumstantial evidence available to her: (1) that the defendant acted *in some undetermined manner* toward the plaintiff, and (2) that, during or subsequent to the interaction, the plaintiff suffered an injury. The question arises: Is this minimal showing ever sufficient to satisfy the plaintiff's burden of proof on breach?

Byrne v. Boadle

159 Eng. Rep. 299 (Exch. 1863)

. . . At the trial before the learned Assessor of the Court of Passage at Liverpool, the evidence adduced on the part of the plaintiff was as follows:

—A witness named Critchley said: "On the 18th July, I was in Scotland Road, on the right side going north, defendant's shop is on that side. When I was opposite to his shop, a barrel of flour fell from a window above in defendant's house and shop, and knocked the plaintiff down. He was carried into an adjoining shop. A horse and cart came opposite the defendant's door. Barrels of flour were in the cart. I do not think the barrel was being lowered by a rope. I cannot say: I did not see the barrel until it struck the plaintiff. It was not swinging when it struck the plaintiff. It struck him on the shoulder and knocked him towards the shop. No one called out until after the accident." The plaintiff said: "On approaching Scotland Place and defendant's shop, I lost all recollection. I felt no blow. I saw nothing to warn me of danger. I was taken home in a cab. I was helpless for a fortnight." (He then described his sufferings.) "I saw the path clear. I did not see any cart opposite defendant's shop." Another witness said: "I saw a barrel falling. I don't know how, but from defendant's." The only other witness was a surgeon, who described the injury which the plaintiff had received. It was admitted that the defendant was a dealer in flour.

F

* Some find it helpful to think of the preponderance standard mathematically. It requires the plaintiff to establish at least a 50.00001 percent probability that her allegations describe what actually happened. By contrast, a "tie"—that is, a 50/50 likelihood—goes to the defendant.

It was submitted, on the part of the defendant, that there was no evidence of negligence for the jury. The learned Assessor was of that opinion, and nonsuited the plaintiff, reserving leave for him to move the Court of Exchequer to enter the verdict for him with 50£. damages, the amount assessed by the jury. . . .

[On appeal, defense counsel argued that the facts established at trial] do not disclose any evidence for the jury of negligence. The plaintiff was bound to give affirmative proof of negligence. But there was not a scintilla of evidence, unless the occurrence is of itself evidence of negligence. There was not even evidence that the barrel was being lowered by a jigger-hoist as alleged in the declaration. [Pollock, C.B. There are certain cases of which it may be said res ipsa loquitur, and this seems one of them. In some cases the Courts have held that the mere fact of the accident having occurred is evidence of negligence, as, for instance, in the case of railway collisions.] On examination of the authorities, that doctrine would seem to be confined to the case of a collision between two trains upon the same line, and both being the property and under the management of the same Company. . . . The law will not presume that a man is guilty of a wrong. It is consistent with the facts proved that the defendant's servants were using the utmost care and the best appliances to lower the barrel with safety. Then why should the fact that accidents of this nature are sometimes caused by negligence raise any presumption against the defendant? There are many accidents from which no presumption of negligence can arise. . . . In a case of this nature, in which the sympathies of a jury are with the plaintiff, it would be dangerous to allow presumption to be substituted for affirmative proof of negligence. . . .

Pollock, C.B. We are all of opinion . . . to enter the verdict for the plaintiff. The learned counsel was quite right in saying that there are many accidents from which no presumption of negligence can arise, but I think it would be wrong to lay down as a rule that in no case can presumption of negligence arise from the fact of an accident. Suppose in this case the barrel had rolled out of the warehouse and fallen on the plaintiff, how could he possibly ascertain from what cause it occurred? It is the duty of persons who keep barrels in a warehouse to take care that they do not roll out, and I think that such a case would, beyond all doubt, afford prima facie evidence of negligence. A barrel could not roll out of a warehouse without some negligence, and to say that a plaintiff who is injured by it must call witnesses from the warehouse to prove negligence seems to me preposterous. So in building or repairing a house, or putting pots on the chimneys, if a person passing along the road is injured by something falling upon him, I think the accident alone would be prima facie evidence of negligence. . . . The present case upon the evidence comes to this, a man is passing in front of the premises of a dealer in flour, and there falls down upon him a barrel of flour. I think it apparent that the barrel was in the custody of the defendant who occupied the premises, and who is responsible for the acts of his servants who had the control of it; and in my opinion the fact of its falling is prima facie evidence of negligence, and the plaintiff who was injured by it is not bound to show that it could not fall without negligence, but if there are any facts inconsistent with negligence it is for the defendant to prove them. . . .

Kambat v. St. Francis Hosp.

678 N.E.2d 456 (N.Y. 1997)

Judith S. Kaye
New York Court of Appeals
(1993-2008)

KAYE, C.J. In this medical malpractice action, an 18-by-18-inch laparotomy pad was discovered in the abdomen of plaintiffs' decedent following a hysterectomy performed by defendant physician at defendant hospital. The question before us is whether plaintiffs were entitled to submit the case to the jury on the theory of res ipsa loquitur. Contrary to the trial court and Appellate Division, we conclude that the jury could have inferred negligence under the doctrine of res ipsa loquitur, and that defendants' evidence of due care and alternative causes of the injury did not remove the doctrine from the case. The trial court's refusal to instruct the jury regarding res ipsa loquitur thus mandates reversal and a new trial.

I

In August 1986, defendant physician Ralph Sperrazza performed an abdominal hysterectomy on decedent, Florence Fenzel, at defendant St. Francis Hospital. Ten laparotomy pads were marked and available for the operation, and Dr. Sperrazza placed several of these pads in decedent's peritoneal cavity, next to the bowel, during the surgery. The patient was unconscious throughout the procedure.

In the months following the operation decedent's condition was at first unremarkable. Eventually, however, she began to complain of stomach pain, and on November 30, 1986 X-rays taken at another hospital revealed a foreign object in her abdomen. On December 5, a laparotomy pad measuring 18-by-18 inches—similar to those used during the hysterectomy—was discovered fully or partially inside decedent's bowel, and it was removed by Dr. Robert Barone. This finding was so unanticipated that a photographer was called to document it. Decedent's condition continued to deteriorate, and she died on December 29, 1986, from infection-related illnesses.

Plaintiffs, decedent's husband and children, commenced this medical malpractice action against Dr. Sperrazza and St. Francis Hospital, alleging that defendants were negligent in leaving the laparotomy pad inside decedent's abdomen. At trial, plaintiffs presented evidence that the pad removed from decedent was the same type and size as those supplied to St. Francis Hospital in 1986 and commonly used during hysterectomies. Plaintiffs also adduced testimony that the pads were provided only to hospitals with operating rooms, where patients would not have access to them.

Plaintiffs called three expert witnesses, who disagreed as to the precise abdominal area where the pad was discovered. Two experts testified that the pad was both partially inside and partially outside decedent's bowel. A third testified that the pad had originally been left outside the bowel, in the peritoneal cavity, where it caused an abscess to develop outside the bowel, which in turn created an artificial opening through which the pad had migrated into the bowel. According to this expert witness, the pad was completely within the decedent's bowel when removed.

In response, defendants introduced evidence that standard procedures were followed during the operation, and that the number of sponges, medical instruments and laparotomy pads used and removed were counted several times, carefully and accurately. Defendants' experts, moreover, opined that the pad had not been left inside decedent but, rather, that she had swallowed it. According to defendants' witnesses, laparotomy pads were frequently left in places accessible to patients in hospitals; decedent suffered from chronic depression; overuse of sleeping pills could suppress the gag reflex and permit her to swallow the pad; and the human gastrointestinal tract would allow the pad to pass to the small bowel. Plaintiffs' expert witnesses, by contrast, agreed that it would be anatomically impossible to swallow the laparotomy pad or for a swallowed pad to reach the bowel.

The trial court denied plaintiffs' request to charge res ipsa loquitur, and the jury returned a defendants' verdict. Plaintiffs moved to set aside the verdict and either enter judgment in their favor or grant a new trial, arguing that the trial court erred in refusing to deliver the requested charge. The court denied the motion, concluding that the lengthy and inconsistent expert testimony demonstrated that resolution of the case was not within a lay jury's experience and, thus, res ipsa loquitur was not applicable. The Appellate Division affirmed Supreme Court's dismissal of the complaint, two Justices dissenting, and we now reverse.

II

Where the actual or specific cause of an accident is unknown, under the doctrine of res ipsa loquitur a jury may in certain circumstances infer negligence merely from the happening of an event and the defendant's relation to it (*see*, Abbott v. Page Airways, 23 N.Y.2d 502, 510; Restatement [Second] of Torts § 328 D, comments *a*, *b*). Res ipsa loquitur "simply recognizes what we know from our everyday experience: that some accidents by their very nature would ordinarily not happen without negligence" (Dermatossian v. New York City Tr. Auth., 67 N.Y.2d 219, 226).

Once a plaintiff's proof establishes the following three conditions, a prima facie case of negligence exists and plaintiff is entitled to have res ipsa loquitur charged to the jury. First, the event must be of a kind that ordinarily does not occur in the absence of someone's negligence; second, it must be caused by an agency or instrumentality within the exclusive control of the defendant; and third, it must not have been due to any voluntary action or contribution on the part of the plaintiff.

Check Your Understanding

Res Ipsa and Proof of "Negligence"

Recall the distinction drawn at the outset of this chapter between big *N* negligence and small *n* negligence. The *Kambat* court states that a plaintiff who meets the three conditions required for a *res ipsa loquitur* instruction has made a showing sufficient to establish a "prima facie case of negligence." Is the court here referring to big *N* negligence (the tort) or to small *n* negligence (the breach element of the tort)? If the latter, what other elements remain to be proven?

To rely on res ipsa loquitur a plaintiff need not conclusively eliminate the possibility of all other causes of the injury. It is enough that the evidence supporting the three conditions afford a rational basis for concluding that "it is more likely than not" that the injury was caused by defendant's negligence (Restatement [Second] of Torts § 328 D, comment *e*). Stated otherwise, all that is required is that the likelihood of other possible causes of the injury "be so reduced that the greater probability lies at defendant's door" (2 Harper and James, Torts § 19.7, at 1086). Res ipsa loquitur thus involves little more than application of the ordinary rules of circumstantial evidence to certain unusual events (*see*, Prosser and Keeton, Torts § 40, at 257 [5th ed.]), and it is appropriately charged when, "upon 'a commonsense appraisal of the probative value' of the circumstantial evidence, . . . [the] inference of negligence is justified" (George Foltis, Inc. v. City of New York, 287 N.Y. 108, 115).

Submission of res ipsa loquitur, moreover, merely permits the jury to infer negligence from the circumstances of the occurrence. The jury is thus allowed—but not compelled—to draw the permissible inference. In those cases where "conflicting inferences may be drawn, choice of inference must be made by the jury" (George Foltis, Inc. v. City of New York, 287 N.Y. at 118, *supra*).

Here, the Appellate Division majority concluded that plaintiffs' proof at trial failed to satisfy any of the three conditions. With regard to the first requirement in particular, the appellate court agreed with the trial court that a lay jury could not determine whether the occurrence was of a kind that ordinarily does not occur in the absence of negligence without evaluating the parties' expert testimony and, therefore, res ipsa loquitur did not apply.

In the typical res ipsa loquitur case, the jury can reasonably draw upon past experience common to the community for the conclusion that the adverse event generally would not occur absent negligent conduct. In medical malpractice cases, however, the common knowledge and everyday experience of lay jurors may be inadequate to support this inference. Courts and commentators across the country have come to varying conclusions as to whether expert testimony can be used to educate the jury as to the likelihood that the occurrence would take place without negligence where a basis of common knowledge is lacking. Courts in this State, as well, have differed as to whether expert testimony can supply the necessary foundation for consideration of res ipsa loquitur by a jury.

Widespread consensus exists, however, that a narrow category of factually simple medical malpractice cases requires no expert to enable the jury reasonably to conclude that the accident would not happen without negligence. Not surprisingly, the oft-cited example is where a surgeon leaves a sponge or foreign object inside the plaintiff's body. As explained by Prosser and Keeton in their classic treatise:

> "There are, however, some medical and surgical errors on which any layman is competent to pass judgment and conclude from common experience that such things do not happen if there has been proper skill and care. *When an operation leaves a sponge or implement in the patient's interior*, . . . the thing speaks for itself

> without the aid of any expert's advice." (Prosser and Keeton, Torts § 40, at 256-257 [5th ed.][emphasis added].)

Manifestly, the lay jury here did not require expert testimony to conclude that an 18-by-18-inch laparotomy pad is not ordinarily discovered inside a patient's abdomen following a hysterectomy in the absence of negligence. Thus, plaintiffs' undisputed proof that this occurred satisfied the first requirement of res ipsa loquitur. We therefore need not resolve today the question whether res ipsa loquitur is applicable in medical malpractice cases in which the jury is incapable of determining whether the first res ipsa loquitur condition has been met without the aid of expert testimony.

Plaintiffs' expert testimony regarding how the presence of the pad led to decedent's ultimate injury and contradicting defendants' alternative theory that decedent swallowed the pad did not render res ipsa loquitur inapplicable. This evidence was probative of the questions of exclusive control and absence of contributory conduct on the part of decedent—the second and third foundational elements of res ipsa loquitur. The debate over the use of expert testimony in res ipsa loquitur cases, however, centers primarily on the first element, since it is with regard to the likelihood that the accident would not happen without negligence that the jury is generally expected to draw upon its common knowledge.

Turning to these remaining res ipsa loquitur conditions, plaintiffs' evidence that similar pads were used during decedent's surgery, that decedent was unconscious throughout the operation, that laparotomy pads are not accessible to patients and that it would be anatomically impossible to swallow such pads sufficed to allow the jury to conclude that defendants had exclusive control of the laparotomy pad "at the time of the alleged act of negligence" (Dermatossian v. New York City Tr. Auth., 67 N.Y.2d at 227, *supra*) and that it did not result from any voluntary action by the patient.

We agree with the Appellate Division dissenters, moreover, that defendants' evidence tending to rebut the three conditions did not disqualify this case from consideration under res ipsa loquitur. Plaintiffs were not obligated to eliminate every alternative explanation for the event. Defendants' evidence that they used due care and expert testimony supporting their competing theory that decedent might have had access to laparotomy pads and inflicted the injury upon herself by swallowing the pad merely raised alternative inferences to be evaluated by the jury in determining liability. The undisputed fact remained in evidence that a laparotomy pad measuring 18 inches square was discovered in decedent's abdomen: "[f]rom this the jury may still be permitted to infer that the defendant's witnesses are not to be believed, that something went wrong with the precautions described, that the full truth has not been told" (Restatement [Second] of Torts § 328 D, comment *n*). Thus, the inference of negligence could reasonably have been drawn "upon 'a commonsense appraisal of the probative value' of the circumstantial evidence," and it was error to refuse plaintiffs' request to charge res ipsa loquitur.

In light of this determination, we need not address plaintiffs' remaining contentions. Accordingly, the orders of the Appellate Division should be reversed, with costs, and a new trial granted as to the first and second causes of action of the complaint.

NOTES AND QUESTIONS

1. *Mode of Proof Versus Cause of Action.* The phrase *res ipsa loquitur*—Latin for "the thing speaks for itself"—is sometimes described by courts as a distinct cause of action; for example, the plaintiff is said to sue on a *res ipsa* theory. Strictly speaking, this usage is inaccurate. *Res ipsa loquitur* is an evidentiary doctrine applicable to certain tort causes of action, including negligence. When applicable in negligence actions, it permits a jury to infer that the plaintiff's injury was caused by defendant's carelessness even when the plaintiff presents no evidence of particular acts or omissions on the part of the defendant that might constitute carelessness.

The question for the court, then, is the preliminary question of whether the case before it is or might be the *type of case* in which the jury will be permitted to draw such an inference. As indicated by *Kambat*, this type of case has traditionally been defined by three features: (1) the injury must happen in a way that ordinarily does not occur absent carelessness on someone's part; (2) the instrumentality causing the injury must have been in the defendant's exclusive control; and (3) the injury must not have arisen from acts or carelessness on the part of the plaintiff.

Under New York law, when a court determines that the doctrine of *res ipsa* might be available to a negligence plaintiff, it will instruct the jury as follows. First, it will ask the jury to determine whether the plaintiff has proven by a preponderance of the evidence that the defendant was in exclusive control of the instrumentality of injury, and that the injury-producing accident is not the sort of accident that ordinarily happens unless the person in exclusive control of the instrumentality failed to exercise ordinary care. Second, it instructs the jury that, if it finds for the plaintiff on these two issues, it "may"—but need not—infer that the defendant was careless. Keyser v. KB Toys, Inc., 82 A.D.3d 713 (N.Y. App. Div. 2011).

Thus, once successfully invoked, *res ipsa* relieves the plaintiff of the burden of producing evidence as to what exactly the defendant did wrong. As *Byrne* and *Kambat* note, and as the New York pattern instruction presumes, it is still open to the defendant to introduce evidence to rebut the inference of carelessness that *res ipsa* permits. In this way, *res ipsa* can be understood in part as an information-forcing rule. It asks the party in the better position to identify what happened to come forth with evidence as to what really did happen.

2. *The Inapplicability of Res Ipsa Loquitur in Standard Cases.* The first element of *res ipsa* precludes its application in the vast majority of negligence cases, even if it turns out that plaintiff has no means of determining or proving whether defendant acted negligently. For example, even though many surgical patients cannot testify to what went wrong in a surgical procedure (because they were anesthetized), the general rule is that they still must provide expert testimony as to the defendant-physician's failure to meet the standards of his profession. This is because surgery, even when properly performed, often fails or produces complications. Therefore, these complications cannot be presumed to be the sort of outcome that only comes about from carelessness on the part of the surgeon or other medical personnel. (If a malpractice complaint avers that a surgeon failed to remove a tumor in its entirety, or failed properly to insert an artificial joint, *res ipsa* will likely be unavailable—these are complex procedures that

often go badly without carelessness on anyone's part.) Accordingly, plaintiff will have to employ the pre-trial discovery process to obtain documents and testimony that will permit plaintiff's expert witnesses to reconstruct what, if anything, went wrong during the procedure.

Similarly, *res ipsa* is inapplicable to more mundane injuries that often occur without anyone's fault. One common example is slips and falls. In *Brown v. Poway Unified Sch. Dist.*, 843 P.2d 624 (Cal. 1993), the plaintiff, a delivery person, was not permitted to invoke *res ipsa* after slipping and falling on a slice of lunchmeat in a hallway in the defendant's building. The California Supreme Court held that, absent a showing that the lunchmeat was present for an unreasonable amount of time, the accident did not speak for itself because "the lunch meat might have been dropped by . . . a visitor, tracked in from the outside or from Brown's own van, transported by an animal, or fallen from an object carried down the hall . . . ." *Id.* at 628.

3. *Medical Events That Tend Not to Happen Without Carelessness.* When *res ipsa* can be invoked in medical malpractice, it is because the plaintiff, like Ms. Fenzel's survivors, can establish that, in the particular case at hand, the injuries suffered are so unlikely to occur without carelessness on the physician's or hospital's part that no proof of specific careless acts need be proffered. As the Court of Appeals indicates, the postoperative presence of medical instruments or materials in a surgical patient's body is the paradigmatic example of such a case. *See also* Umeugo v. Milford Hospital, 2000 Conn. Super. LEXIS 1943 (2000) (*res ipsa* applicable to claim of malpractice against surgeon who performed circumcision; presence of substantial portion of foreskin after procedure indicates the likelihood of carelessness in performing the procedure). By way of contrast, consider *Locke v. Pachtman*, 521 N.W.2d 786 (Mich. 1994), discussed above in the notes on professional custom. There the plaintiff attempted to invoke *res ipsa* by asserting that a broken hypodermic needle is not ordinarily left in a patient's body without carelessness. The Michigan Supreme Court rejected this argument.

Kambat ducked the question of whether *res ipsa* is available even if expert testimony is required to establish that the events leading to the plaintiff's injury would not likely happen without carelessness. Subsequently, however, in *States v. Lourdes Hospital*, 792 N.E.2d 151 (N.Y. 2003), the Court held that *res ipsa* can be invoked in such circumstances. Plaintiff, a surgical patient, complained that the attending anesthesiologist had injured her arm during surgery. In support of this contention, she submitted expert medical opinions stating that her injuries could not have occurred except by careless manipulation of her arm to administer anesthetic. The court held that expert testimony could be used to "educate" the jury as to what sort of injuries tend to come about only through medical error.

4. *Other Accidents.* Since *Byrne*, *res ipsa* has been successfully invoked in many other cases involving injuries caused by objects falling, moving, or exploding. For example, the modern trend is to permit passengers killed in airline crashes for which there is no evidence as to the cause to invoke *res ipsa* as a means of establishing pilot fault. *See* Dan B. Dobbs, *The Law of Torts* § 155, at 374 (2000) (providing examples).

Compare, in this regard, two car accident cases, *Broadnax v. ABF Freight Systems, Inc.*, 1998 U.S. Dist. LEXIS 4662 (N.D. Ill. 1998), *and Martinez v. CO2 Services, Inc.*, 2001 U.S. App. LEXIS 6195 (10th Cir. 2001). In *Broadnax*, the plaintiff's decedent was killed when his car was struck by defendant's truck. Apparently, no evidence existed as to what caused the defendant's driver to strike plaintiff's car. The court permitted plaintiff to invoke *res ipsa*. In *Martinez*, plaintiff's decedent was killed when defendant's tractor-trailer veered across two lanes and struck him. The driver of the truck was later found to have died of cardiac arrest. Given this finding, the court held that *res ipsa* was unavailable, as the accident could have just as easily been caused by the driver suffering an unforeseen heart attack as by any carelessness on his part.

5. *Exclusive Control.* Read literally, the "exclusivity" prong would require plaintiff to establish that the defendant exercised such a degree of physical control over the instrumentality or events that led to plaintiff's injury that it is impossible to suppose any other actor contributed to it. Modern courts, however, have not read the requirement so strictly. In most jurisdictions, it is enough to show that the defendant is likely to be the only one to have undertaken or omitted the relevant acts. When numerous others have access to the place of, or instrumentality causing, the harm, courts are likely not to permit a *res ipsa* argument. *See* Flowers v. Delta Air Lines, Inc., 2001 U.S. Dist. LEXIS 19878 (E.D.N.Y. 2001) (extensive review of New York case law on exclusivity; plaintiff who suffered injury as a result of alleged failure to repair broken chairs at airport terminal cannot invoke *res ipsa*; widespread public access to the chairs indicates that many other persons could have been responsible for their being broken).

Imagine a suit in which the plaintiff alleges that her elderly decedent inexplicably fell out of a train car in the middle of the night. The car is equipped with doors located in the middle of the car that are latched, but can be opened by a passenger. Granted a weak version of the exclusivity requirement, can *res ipsa* be invoked? *See* Harris v. Amtrak, 79 F. Supp. 2d 673 (E.D. Tex. 1999) (denying plaintiff use of *res ipsa* on the ground that defendant lacked exclusive control over the doors).

6. *Multiple Defendants.* Are there situations in which, notwithstanding the exclusive control requirement, a plaintiff can use *res ipsa* to establish carelessness on the part of several defendants? In the famous case of *Ybarra v. Spangard*, 154 P.2d 687 (Cal. 1945), the otherwise healthy plaintiff underwent an appendectomy under general anesthetic. He woke up suffering partial paralysis in his shoulder. The theory of the complaint was that he had been positioned on the operating table in such a way as to damage nerves in his neck and shoulder. His position on the table, however, could have been affected by the acts of several nurses and doctors. Citing the inequity of forcing the plaintiff to prove what happened while he was unconscious, as well as a concern that the defendants in this instance each stood to benefit by remaining silent, the California Supreme Court permitted the plaintiff to invoke *res ipsa* to establish the carelessness of each. Contrast *Samson v. Riesing*, 215 N.W.2d 662 (Wis. 1974), in which a plaintiff who was caused a prolonged illness from ingesting contaminated turkey salad was prevented by the court from invoking *res ipsa* to impose liability on each of eleven mothers who prepared individual batches of the dish for a band fundraiser.

To *Kambat* and *Ybarra*, compare *James v. Wormuth*, 997 N.E.2d 133 (N.Y. 2013). A surgeon who used a surgical guide-wire in performing a lung biopsy lost track of the wire during the procedure, which was otherwise performed successfully. After searching for the wire for 20 minutes, the surgeon decided to end the procedure with the wire still inside the patient's chest. The surgeon later explained to the patient that he left the wire in her chest based on his determination that it would be better for her health to end the procedure rather than continue the search. The patient later complained of debilitating pain, resulting in a second procedure in which the wire was located and removed. The Court of Appeals affirmed dismissal of the patient's malpractice suit, citing plaintiff's failure to offer expert testimony as to whether the surgeon's decision conformed with standard medical practice. The Court further held that *res ipsa* did not apply, both because other medical personnel were involved in the process of inserting the wire and transporting the patient (thus defeating the attribution of exclusive control to the surgeon) and because the alleged malpractice involved an intentional decision to leave an object in a surgical patient rather than inadvertance.

7. Plaintiff's Participation. The third *res ipsa* requirement — that plaintiff establish that she did not voluntarily participate in causing her injury — is arguably just a particular application of the "exclusive control" requirement. If plaintiff played a significant role in bringing about her injury, the likelihood of the defendant's negligence having been the major contributing cause of plaintiff's injury significantly decreases, barring the jury from presuming that defendant's carelessness must have been what brought about plaintiff's injury. Thus, some courts will rebuff a car accident victim's attempt to invoke *res ipsa* if there is evidence of plaintiff having driven carelessly. Needless to say, unconscious surgical patients who suffer injuries during surgery ordinarily will not be found to be contributors to their injuries. In light of the existing requirement of "exclusivity," as well as the fact that modern negligence law takes plaintiff's fault into account in determining liability or damages, some courts have explicitly dropped this requirement. Peplinksi v. Forbes Roofing, Inc., 531 N.W.2d 597 (Wis. 1995).

8. Spoliation of Evidence. If, after an accident, the defendant intentionally (or, in some states, negligently) destroys evidence tending to establish its carelessness as the cause of plaintiff's injury, the plaintiff may have a separate cause of action against the defendant for spoliation of evidence.

REFERENCES/FURTHER READING

The Reasonable Person

Patrick J. Kelley & Laurel A. Wendt, *What Judges Tell Juries About Negligence: A Review of Pattern Jury Instructions*, 77 Chi.-Kent L. Rev. 587 (2002).

Heidi Li Feldman, *Prudence, Benevolence, and Negligence: Virtue Ethics and Tort Law*, 74 Chi.-Kent L. Rev. 1431 (2000).

Benjamin C. Zipursky, *Sleight of Hand*, 48 W. & M. L. Rev. 1999 (2007).

Benjamin C. Zipursky, *Reasonableness In and Out of Negligence Law*, 163 U. Pa. L. Rev. 2131 (2015).

The Objective Standard

Leslie Bender, *A Lawyer's Primer on Feminist Theory and Torts*, 38 J. Leg. Educ. 3 (1988).

Anita Bernstein, *The Communities that Make Standards of Care Possible*, 77 Chi.-Kent L. Rev. 735 (2002).

Anita Bernstein, *Treating Sexual Harassment with Respect*, 111 Harv. L. Rev. 446 (1997).

Mark Grady, *Res Ipsa Loquitur and Compliance Error*, 142 U. Pa. L. Rev. 887 (1994).

Fleming James, *The Qualities of the Reasonable Man in Negligence Cases*, 16 Mo. L. Rev. 1 (1951).

Martha Minow, *Making All the Difference: Inclusion, Exclusion, and American Law* (1990).

Arthur Ripstein, *Equality, Responsibility and the Law* 85-86 (1999).

Carol Sanger, *The Reasonable Woman and the Ordinary Man*, 65 S. Cal. L. Rev. 1411 (1992).

Margo Schlanger, *Gender Matters: Teaching a Reasonable Woman Standard in Personal Injury Law*, 45 St. Louis U. L.J. 759 (2001).

Reasonableness and Custom

Steven Hetcher, *Creating Safe Social Norms in a Dangerous World*, 73 S. Cal. L. Rev. 1 (1999).

Clarence Morris, *Custom and Negligence*, 42 Colum. L. Rev. 1147 (1942).

Richard A. Posner, *Economic Analysis of Law* 168 (4th ed. 1992).

Medical Malpractice

Tom Baker, *The Medical Malpractice Myth* (2005).

Patricia M. Danzon, *Medical Malpractice: Theory Evidence and Public Policy* (1990).

Neal C. Hogan, *Unhealed Wounds, Medical Malpractice in the Twentieth Century* (2003).

David W. Louisell & Harold Williams (eds.), *Medical Malpractice* (1987).

Frank A. Sloan, et al., *Suing for Medical Malpractice* (1993).

Paul C. Weiler, et al., *A Measure of Malpractice: Medical Injury, Malpractice Litigation, and Patient Compensation* (1993).

Learned Hand

Gerald Gunther, *Learned Hand: The Man and the Judge* (1994).

Reasonableness, Balancing, and Cost-Benefit Analysis

Mark Geistfeld, *Reconciling Cost-Benefit Analysis with the Principle that Safety Matters More than Money*, 76 N.Y.U. L. Rev. 114 (2001).

Stephen G. Gilles, *On Determining Negligence: Hand Formula Balancing, the Reasonable Person Standard, and the Jury*, 54 Vand. L. Rev. 813 (2001).

Stephen G. Gilles, *The Emergence of Cost-Benefit Balancing in English Negligence Law*, 77 Chi-Kent L. Rev. 489 (2002).

Stephen G. Gilles, United States v. Carroll Towing Co.: *The Hand Formula's Home Port*, in Robert L. Rabin & Stephen D. Sugarman (eds.), *Tort Stories* 11-39 (2003).

Michael Green, *Negligence = Economic Efficiency: Doubts* >, 75 Tex. L. Rev. 1605 (1997).

Gregory C. Keating, *Pressing Precaution Beyond the Point of Cost-Justification*, 56 Vand. L. Rev. 653 (2003).

Gregory C. Keating, *Reasonableness and Rationality in Negligence Theory*, 48 Stan. L. Rev. 311 (1996).

Patrick J. Kelley, *The Carroll Towing Company Case and the Teaching of Tort Law*, 45 St. Louis U. L.J. 731 (2001).

Geoffrey R. Marczyk & Ellen Wertheimer, *The Bitter Pill of Empiricism: Health Maintenance Organizations, Informed Consent and the Reasonable Psychotherapist Standard of Care*, 46 Vill. L. Rev. 33 (2001).

Richard A. Posner, *A Theory of Negligence*, 1 J. Leg. Stud. 29 (1972).

Henry T. Terry, *Negligence*, 29 Harv. L. Rev. 40 (1915).

Ernest J. Weinrib, *The Idea of Private Law* 147-152 (1995).

Richard W. Wright, *Hand, Posner and the Myth of the* "Hand Formula," 4 Theoretical Inquiries in Law 145 (2003).

Symposium on the Third Restatement of Torts, 54 Vand. L. Rev. 813-940 (2001) (commentary by Professors Gilles, Hetcher, Perry, and Simons).

Benjamin C. Zipursky, *Sleight of Hand*, 48 W. & M. L. Rev. 1999 (2007).

Benjamin C. Zipursky, *Reasonableness In and Out of Negligence Law*, 163 U. Pa. L. Rev. 2131 (2015).

Res Ipsa Loquitur

Mark F. Grady, *Res Ipsa Loquitur and Compliance Error*, 142 U. Pa. L. Rev. 887 (1994).

Saul Levmore, *Gomorrah to* Ybarra *and* Mac: *Overextraction and the Puzzle of Immoderate Group Liability*, 81 Va. L. Rev. 1561 (1995).

Allan H. McCoid, *Negligence Actions Against Multiple Defendants*, 7 Stan. L. Rev. 480 (1955).

CHAPTER 4

THE CAUSATION ELEMENT

I. KEY TERMS AND CONCEPTS

A. Actual and Proximate Cause

Negligence law imposes liability only when careless acts have injurious consequences. Imagine two drivers, *A* and *B*, each of whom carelessly throws a jumbo-sized paper cup half-filled with coffee out of his car window as he drives. Assume that, although they are in different locations, each is driving on a comparably busy public street. The coffee thrown by *A* splatters on the car windshield of nearby driver *Z*, startling *Z*, as a result of which *Z* crashes his car into a lamppost at the side of the road. *B*, by contrast, is luckier. His cup neither hits nor endangers anyone, but falls harmlessly to the ground. Both *A* and *B* were careless in the same way, and both *A* and *B* can be cited for littering, but *A* alone is subject to liability in negligence, because only *A*'s carelessness *caused* injury to another.

Even when a careless act causes injury, liability will tend not to attach if the injury comes about in an entirely haphazard or otherwise attenuated manner. Imagine another driver, *C*, who acts in the same manner as *A* and *B*. Like *B*, driver *C* is lucky and does not hit or endanger anyone with his coffee cup. But *C* happens to do his littering in the sight of *P*, a pedestrian walking on a sidewalk parallel to the road. *C*'s act poses no physical danger to *P*, and *P* does not perceive himself to be in danger. However, *P* does have strong feelings about people who potentially endanger others by throwing coffee cups. Thus, upon seeing *C* toss the cup, *P* instinctively expresses his outrage by stopping in his tracks and lifting his arms over his head. Unfortunately, in doing so, *P* brushes his hand against a hidden bee's nest in an overhanging tree limb. *P* is stung repeatedly. The stings cause him painful welts that require medical treatment.

C's careless act was almost certainly a breach of a duty of care owed to persons such as *P*.* That breach in turn was an actual cause of *P*'s bodily injury — so far as we know, if *C* had not acted carelessly in the presence of *P*, *P* would not have stopped walking, would not have raised his arms, and would not have been stung. Nonetheless, *C* would have a strong argument that he should not be held liable to *P* because the connection between his carelessness and *P*'s injury is too fortuitous. In negligence law, such an argument is typically phrased in terms of the concept of *proximate cause*. Thus, *C* will argue that *even though* his carelessness was an actual cause of *P*'s injury, it was not a proximate cause, and he should therefore not be liable for that injury.

The distinction just drawn between the actual cause question — Was the victim's injury brought about by (among other things) the defendant's carelessness? — and the proximate cause question — Did the actor's carelessness bring about the victim's injury in such a fortuitous manner that it is inappropriate to hold the actor responsible for the injury? — may seem reasonably clear in the context of hypothetical situations. In practice, however, lawyers, judges, and academic commentators routinely confuse the two. This confusion results in part from an unhealthy tendency to use the phrase "proximate cause" — or, alternatively, the phrase "legal cause" — as a shorthand reference for *both* the actual and proximate cause issues. For example, a Florida model jury instruction with the heading "Legal Cause" reads as follows:

> Negligence is a legal cause of . . . [injury] . . . if it directly and in natural and continuous sequence produces or contributes substantially to producing such . . . [injury] . . . , so that it can reasonably be said that, but for the negligence, the . . . [injury] . . . would not have occurred.

Fla. Standard Jury Instr.–Civil § 401.12(a). The phrase "legal cause" in this instruction is synonymous with what this book refers to as the "causation element" — it requires the plaintiff to prove that defendant's carelessness: (1) *actually caused* plaintiff's injury (as indicated by the instruction's use of the phrase "but for"; and (2) did so *proximately* (as indicated by the instruction's use of the phrase "directly and in natural and continuous sequence").

To avoid confusion, we will endeavor to keep the concepts of actual cause and proximate cause as distinct as possible. The present chapter is almost entirely concerned with the issue of actual cause, which is also sometimes labeled as the issue of "cause-in-fact" or "factual cause." Chapter 5 takes up the subject of proximate cause.

---

* Consider a variation on the example of *A* and *Z*, above. *A* tosses his cup and its coffee splatters on *Z*'s windshield, distracting *Z*. However, instead of hitting a tree, *Z* runs over pedestrian *P*. It seems very plausible that such a result was a foreseeable consequence of tossing a half-filled coffee cup out of a moving car in a populated area, and hence that *A* owed and breached a duty to *P* to take care against causing physical harm to *P*.

B. Actual Cause, the Jury, the But-For Test, and "Substantial Factor"

The actual cause inquiry lies at the core of the causation element of the plaintiff's prima facie case. Given the preponderance of the evidence standard of proof (discussed in Chapter 3 in connection with *res ipsa loquitur*), this means that the typical negligence plaintiff must prove that the defendant's breach of duty *probably* functioned as an actual cause of the plaintiff's injury. Like the breach determination, the decision as to whether a plaintiff has met this burden is generally left to the jury, subject to the judge's power to rule on the issue as a matter of law.

Moreover, just as the jury's breach inquiry is usually guided by the legal standard of ordinary care, its actual causation inquiry is usually guided by a particular legal standard. This standard is known as the *but-for* test of causation, also called the "*sine qua non*"* or "counterfactual" test. In U.S. jurisdictions, the but-for test is the predominant test for actual causation. *See, e.g.*, Glover v. Jackson State Univ., 968 So.2d 1267, 1277 (Miss. 2007) ("A defendant's negligence is [a] cause in fact of a plaintiff's damage where the fact finder concludes that, but for the defendant's negligence, the injury would not have occurred.").

The basic content of the but-for test is easy enough to grasp. It calls on the fact-finder to answer the following question: *Would the plaintiff have been injured even if the defendant had acted with the care he was duty-bound to exercise?* If the answer to this question is "no," the but-for test is satisfied and actual causation is established. If the answer is "yes," plaintiff's claim fails the but-for test and, except in certain special cases discussed below, actual causation is not established.

Many courts, following the Second Restatement of Torts, include the phrase "substantial factor" in their descriptions of the test for actual causation. *See* Restatement (Second) of Torts § 431 (1965) (for careless conduct to be a "legal" cause of harm it must be a "substantial factor" in bringing about the harm). This usage is confusing insofar as it suggests that there is a separate test for actual causation known as the "substantial factor test." As explained in notes throughout this chapter, neither the Second Restatement, nor the vast majority of courts that follow it, use the language of "substantial factor" to identify a separate test for actual causation. Rather they use the phrase to explicate or clarify the but-for test, and also to identify a separate *proximate-cause* requirement that further limits negligence liability beyond the limit set by the but-for test.

Because of the confusion generated by "substantial factor" language, the Third Restatement of Torts does not deploy it. Instead, its basic actual cause provision—Section 26—embraces the but-for test as the legal standard for determining actual cause:

> **§ 26 Factual Cause**
>
> Tortious conduct must be a factual cause of harm for liability to be imposed. Conduct is a factual cause of harm when the harm would not have occurred absent the conduct.

---

* "Without which not."—EDS.

Restatement (Third) of Torts: Liability for Physical and Emotional Harm § 26 (2010).*

C. Two Meanings of "Caused"

At the outset of Chapter 3, we warned against confusing the breach element (small "n" negligence) with the entire prima facie case (big "N" Negligence). Because of the imprecision of ordinary English language, it is easy to make a similar mistake in analyzing causation. Consider, for example, a collision of two cars at an intersection that are driven, respectively, by *X*, who is driving with due care, and *Y*, who is driving carelessly. If you were talking to a friend about the accident, it would be perfectly normal to assert that it was *Y* who "caused" the accident. However, if one were to use the word "caused" in a different sense, one could say that *both Y* and *X* caused the accident. To adopt this latter usage is not to deny that *Y*'s careless driving contributed to the accident's occurring. Rather, it is to insist that the accident resulted from both *Y*'s careless driving and *X*'s careful driving. After all, had *X* not been driving carefully when and where she was driving, *Y* would never have had occasion to hit *X*'s car.

This latter usage of "caused" may strike you as odd, yet its apparent oddity results from failure to attend to a distinction between two senses in which the term is commonly used. Speaking as a friend, family member, or interested observer trying to figure out how someone ended up getting hurt, one tends to use a notion of "cause" that imports ideas of responsibility. Thus, when we imagined you saying to a friend that *Y* "caused" the accident that injured *X*, the word "caused" was being used to convey a complex judgment that mixes notions of causation and responsibility. In other words, "caused" functions there as shorthand for a longer statement along the following lines: "Because *Y* was driving carelessly and *X* was not, *Y* is the one who is *responsible for causing* the accident."

By contrast, we can imagine a somewhat different inquiry into causation that is largely divorced from any assessment of moral or legal responsibility. For example, consider how a physicist or highway engineer might go about analyzing the roles played by *X* and *Y* in their car accident. Their analyses might be largely indifferent to issues of blame and responsibility and instead concerned with assessing how the actions of these two actors happened to interact to produce a certain result. From this perspective, it makes perfect sense to assert that the actions of both *X* and *Y* contributed to causing their collision.

When factfinders in negligence cases are asked to focus on the particular question of whether an actor's careless conduct has functioned as an actual cause of an injury to a victim, they are principally being asked to assess causation in the nonblaming sense

* This statement requires one qualification. As explained in Section III of this Chapter, a separate provision in the "Physical and Emotional Harm" portion of the Third Torts Restatement — Section 27 — maintains that the but-for test should not be used as the test for actual causation in the rare scenario in which a defendant's carelessness operates as one of two or more sufficient causes of the plaintiff's injury.

just described. That is, they have already determined or are assuming that the victim has suffered an injury, and that the actor has acted carelessly, and are now trying to figure out whether that carelessness helped to bring about that injury. Of course, this relatively neutral inquiry into causation is but one step in a broader inquiry that aims to determine fault and to assign responsibility. But the limited inquiry conducted within this step itself is focused on determining which of the parties' actions, if any, was necessary for the injury to occur.

D. "A" Cause, Not "The" Cause

Appreciation of the limited nature of the actual causation inquiry may help ward off certain confusions often associated with causation. One common misconception is that actual causation analysis involves a search for *the* (sole) cause of a victim's injury. This conception of the inquiry must be avoided. To attribute a causal relation between a victim's injury and a particular actor's carelessness is *not* to deny that the injury was caused by the conduct of other actors. Rather, it serves to isolate a particular actor as having played a special role in bringing about a victim's injury by virtue of having caused it through a breach of a duty owed to the victim.

Reconsider the car accident in which *Y*'s careless driving functioned as a cause of the collision with *X*. To notice this feature of the incident is *not* to deny that the conduct of innumerable other actors helped to bring about the accident. One could even go so far as to say that *Y*'s parents played a role in causing the accident by giving birth to *Y* years earlier. (Much the same could be said of *X*'s parents, and *X*'s and *Y*'s parents' parents, etc.) Needless to say, even if the accident between *X* and *Y* gives rise to litigation, there will be no inquiry into whether *Y*'s parents should be held *responsible* for contributing to the accident *simply by virtue of giving birth to Y*. But this is not because the parents' conduct played no causal role in bringing about the accident — it did. Rather, it is because there is no remotely plausible basis for holding *Y*'s parents responsible for the accident. (It is preposterous to suppose that they owed any duties to *X* and *Y* in this regard, or breached any such duties simply by giving birth to a child.) The actual causation question is not even raised because the analytically prior issues of duty and breach must be resolved against any claimant who would attempt to hold the parents legally responsible.

For similar reasons, it is important to recognize that a finding of an actual causal link between actor *A*'s carelessness and victim *V*'s injury does *not necessarily entail* the conclusion that *A* is the *only* person whose *carelessness* (or otherwise wrongful conduct) played a role in bringing about *V*'s injury. Suppose that *X* and *Y* would not have collided if another careless driver, *T*, had not entered the intersection at the same time they did. In this scenario, *T*'s carelessness *and* *Y*'s carelessness both played a role in bringing about the collision. Likewise, by virtue of the doctrines of contributory negligence and comparative fault — which we have encountered in previous chapters and discuss more thoroughly in Chapter 7 — the careless conduct of a victim herself may sometimes function as one among two or more careless acts that bring about the victim's injuries.

Check Your Understanding

More Flying Coffee

Consider this variation on the coffee-cup scenarios described at the outset of this chapter.

A is driving on a moderately busy city street when he carelessly throws a half-filled jumbo-sized paper coffee cup out of his moving car. The coffee splatters on the car windshield of nearby driver *Z*, startling *Z*, as a result of which *Z* crashes his car into a lamppost at the side of the road. The lamppost, which was manufactured by *M*, and installed in an appropriate location by city *C*, was meant to "crumple" when struck so as to minimize collision-related injuries. Unfortunately, because of *M*'s careless manufacturing, the lamppost struck by *Z*'s car did not crumple but instead remained rigid. As a result, *Z* suffers a head injury that *Z* would not have suffered had the lamppost crumpled. Is there a plausible argument that *A*'s careless conduct was an actual cause of *Z*'s head injury?

II. PROVING ACTUAL CAUSATION UNDER THE PREPONDERANCE STANDARD

In a garden-variety negligence suit, if there is a "live" issue as to actual causation it is usually one of evidence and proof. In these sorts of cases, because the preponderance of the evidence standard applies to causation, the issue is whether the plaintiff has offered evidence sufficient to permit the factfinder to conclude that defendant's carelessness was *probably* a cause of plaintiff's injury.

As we noted in Chapter 3, proof of the breach element sometimes will come in the form of circumstantial evidence. Thus, the lawyer for a victim of a car collision might call an expert to the witness stand to testify that skid marks at the scene indicate that the defendant was driving at an unreasonable speed just prior to the collision. As the next cases demonstrate, the same holds true with respect to the issue of actual causation. Absent a reliable eyewitness account or an authentic videotape of the events in question, a plaintiff's lawyer typically will have to present circumstantial evidence that is sufficient to permit a reasonable factfinder to infer a probable causal connection between the defendant's carelessness and the plaintiff's injury. Yet, as we will also see, just as courts invoke doctrines such as *res ipsa loquitur* to relieve certain plaintiffs of the burden of producing evidence as to breach, courts will sometimes permit findings of causation notwithstanding an apparent lack of evidence sufficient to meet the preponderance standard.

Muckler v. Buchl

150 N.W.2d 689 (Minn. 1967)

SHERAN, J. . . . . About 8:30 p.m., on August 11, 1962, plaintiff's decedent, a 55-year-old woman, fell down a flight of stairs extending from the landing between the first and second floors down to the first floor of the Minneapolis apartment house in which she had been a tenant for 7 years. She broke her hip in the fall and was taken to a hospital where she died less than 4 months later.

. . . [D]ecedent's husband commenced an action for death by wrongful act against the apartment-house owner. At trial . . . plaintiff claimed the accident was caused by defendant's negligence in having the stairs too dimly lit for safety contrary to a relevant ordinance and to his common-law duty. Pursuant to a verdict in favor of plaintiff, post-trial motions having been denied, judgment for $17,000 was entered. . . .

The issues for decision are these:

(1) Does the evidence justify a finding that the fall which caused injuries resulting in the death of plaintiff's decedent was caused by the negligence of defendant in failing properly to light the stairway in the apartment building where the fall occurred?

[Defendant's other grounds for appeal are omitted. — Eds.]

. . . .

Were it not for our decision in Majerus v. Guelsow, 113 N.W.2d 450 [(Minn. 1962)], we would be hesitant to affirm the jury's implicit finding that decedent was caused to fall because of the darkness of the stairway, there being no direct evidence on the issue.

Just before she fell, decedent was walking down the stairs directly behind a departing guest who had been visiting her in the second-floor apartment occupied by decedent and her husband. The guest gave the following description of the events occurring between the time she left decedent's apartment and the time the critical injury was sustained:

"*Q.* * * * As you went out into the hallway and as the door of the apartment was closed, how can you describe the condition of the light at that time?

* * *

"*The Witness*: It was dark. I could distinguish the handrail and I hung onto that because I could not tell where the steps were.

* * *

"*Q.* I believe there is one flight of steps there from that second floor landing down about five or six steps to a landing between floors; is that your recollection?

* * *

"*A.* Yes, sir.
"*Q.* Right at that landing, between the floors * * * there are two little windows adjacent to the landing; is that right?
"*A.* I believe so.

* * *

"*Mr. Green [plaintiff's attorney]*: Now, you got down to the first floor landing, or the landing between floors, without any particular incident?
"*A.* Yes.
"*Q.* Did you then make the turn to go down the second flight to the landing on the first floor?
"*A.* Yes, sir.
"*Q.* Tell us what happened as you went down that second flight of stairs?

"*A.* I was being very careful. I couldn't tell where the steps were so I had to feel my way down, and then I don't know how far I was from the bottom, probably three or four steps, and I heard something behind me and I imagined it was Mrs. Muckler tripping or falling — I couldn't tell then — so I instinctively put my hand out and there was nothing there, and I heard the scream and the thump and there she was.

"*Q.* At this point where you heard this noise, had Mrs. Muckler been behind you?

"*A.* Yes, she was behind me.

. . . .

"*Q.* Where did Mrs. Muckler then finally wind up?

"*A.* I heard the thump and the scream almost simultaneously and then the doors from the first floor opened so then I could see her.

"*Q.* Where was she?

"*A.* Lying on the floor, on the landing."

If decedent ever said what caused her to fall, the record does not disclose it.

An electrical engineer who measured the light at the place of the accident at a time when, according to the evidence, conditions were substantially the same as those prevailing at the time of the event gave testimony from which the jury could infer that the light at and near the place of the occurrence measured one-tenth of a foot-candle or less — significantly below the two foot-candles required by an ordinance of the city of Minneapolis.

At the time of the accident the stairway was not lighted by artificial illumination. Defendant's agent was in exclusive control of the switch to the lights which could have been used for this purpose.

Except for the inadequacy of the lighting, the evidence shows that there was no defect in the stairway to which the fall could be attributed. A handrail was in place.

Decedent, about 55 years of age, was in good health except for a diabetic condition which under the evidence the jury could have found to be controlled. Also there was evidence from which the jury could have found that decedent did not consume intoxicating liquors on the day of the accident or at any other time. There is no evidence indicating that decedent had fallen while descending the steps of the apartment building on any prior occasion during the 7 years she lived there as a tenant.

The evidence is consistent with the theory that decedent fell on the stairway because of the darkness. But it is also consistent with the possibility that the fall would have occurred no matter what the lighting condition might have been. We can eliminate the diabetic condition as a probable explanation of the occurrence in view of the testimony of competent witnesses that decedent was not suffering observable symptoms before and as she started down the stairway. The possibility that the fall was attributable to intoxication can be eliminated on the basis of testimony to the effect that decedent never used intoxicants. But experience tells us that people sometimes fall on stairways even though fully alert and in the best of health. We cannot say with certitude that this was not one of those instances.

Construing the evidence in the light most favorable to the prevailing party, as we must, we are still working in the field of probability. And the degree of probability of a connection between an alleged cause and a given result needed to sustain an affirmative jury finding cannot be defined with mathematical certainty. The line separating fact situations where an inference of causation is permissible from those in which it is not must, of necessity, reflect the general practical experience of the court called upon to make the demarcation. So considered, it seems reasonable that one attempting to descend a stairway so dark that the steps are barely discernible would be likely to fall because of the darkness. And, the accident having happened, it seems to us more probable that the darkened state of the stairway was the precipitating factor for the accident than otherwise. The minimum standards for lighting for stairways set by Minneapolis ordinance also suggest an experience-tested relationship between lack of adequate lighting on stairs and accidents of the type with which we are here concerned.

Admittedly, the case is a close one. In such a situation, while precedents from other jurisdictions involving an assessment of similar facts are not compelling, we must of necessity be guided by our own prior decisions in comparable situations.

In Majerus v. Guelsow, 113 N.W. 2d 450 [(Minn. 1962)], negligence on the part of the defendant was proved by showing that the stairway which decedent had apparently been using had treads of irregular width and risers of irregular height made more hazardous by the absence of a handrail. The principal question in the case was whether a causal relationship between these defects and a fall by decedent, who was found dead 30 feet from the bottom of the stairs, could be sustained, there being no direct evidence as to what happened. In affirming a jury finding of a causal relationship, the court said (113 N.W.2d 455):

> "From the facts and circumstances shown here, a jury could reasonably infer that the defect in part of the stairway was the cause of the accident which culminated in decedent's death. It is true that there are other possible inferences, such as, foul play resulting in someone pushing him down the stairs, his falling while intoxicated, an injury received before he returned to the apartment; but none of these creates as reasonable an inference as that reached by the jury. The jury found here, based upon evidence as to the time in which alcohol is metabolized and upon the testimony of those who last saw the decedent, that intoxication was *not* a cause of the death."

The decision in Majerus v. Guelsow, supra, is of particular significance because two members of the court dissented upon the grounds that there was nothing in the evidence to establish that defects in the stairway caused the fall and that a finding of causal relationship implicit in the verdict was based on pure speculation and conjecture. . . .

. . . The basic problem in *Majerus*, as here, was to decide whether an event which *could* be an adequate cause of an accident was *in fact* the cause of it. We think the probabilities are as great in the one instance as in the other and therefore resolve our doubts in this borderline situation in favor of affirmance.

. . . .

Butts v. Weisz

2010 WL 703238 (W.D. Pa.), *aff'd* 410 Fed. Appx. 470 (3d Cir. 2010)

CONTI, J.

INTRODUCTION

This case was filed by Levone Butts ("Levone Butts" or "plaintiff"), individually and as executrix of the estate of her deceased husband, Glen Ray Butts ("Glen Butts" or "plaintiff's husband," and together with plaintiff, the "Butts"), against Lloyd Weisz ("Lloyd Weisz") and Georgia Weisz ("Georgia Weisz," and together with Lloyd Weisz, "defendants"). The court has subject-matter jurisdiction over this diversity action pursuant to 28 U.S.C. § 1332. The action arises out of an accident that resulted in the death of Glen Butts. Pending before the court are the parties' cross-motions for summary judgment concerning whether defendants are liable for Glen Butts' death because of their negligence. . . . After considering the joint statement of facts and the other submissions of the parties, viewing all disputed facts in favor of the opposing party, and drawing all reasonable inferences in favor of the opposing party, plaintiff's motion for partial summary judgment will be denied, and defendant's motion for summary judgment will be granted.

BACKGROUND

Levone Butts and her husband, Glen Butts, came to know Lloyd Weisz and Georgia Weisz when the two couples lived in California. Defendants moved to a home located at 164 Miller Farms Road, Edinburg, Pennsylvania; plaintiff and her husband maintained their residence in California.

On August 21, 2006, plaintiff and her husband were guests at the home of Lloyd Weisz and Georgia Weisz. Plaintiff and her husband arrived at the Pittsburgh International Airport at 5:45 p.m. that evening. Defendants picked up plaintiff and her husband and drove them forty-five miles to their home. Plaintiff and her husband had not visited defendants' home in Pennsylvania prior to August 21, 2006. Glenn Butts was eighty-four years old on that date.

Defendants' home is described as a "ranch-style" house. The back door of the house opened into a landing area. A person entering through the back door could proceed straight down a stairwell to the basement, or could turn left and proceed up a single eight-inch stair into the kitchen. There was no door between the landing and basement stairwell. There was a "pocket door" between the landing and the kitchen, but defendants were not aware of this door at the time of the accident. There was an overhead lighting fixture at the top of the basement steps. The light switch for this lighting fixture was not at the top of the basement stairwell, but rather was located outside the landing area above the entryway.

After arriving at defendants' home from the airport, the couples entered the home through the back door; there was ample light in the landing area at the time they entered. Plaintiff's husband and Lloyd Weisz took the Butts' luggage to a guestroom located in the house. Defendants gave the Butts a tour of the home. The tour was brief, however, because plaintiff and her husband were hungry and wanted to eat dinner. Defendants took the Butts out to dinner. In exiting the house the couples passed though the back door, and returned through the same door. Georgia Weisz intentionally turned off the light in the landing area after returning.

After dinner, plaintiff and Georgia Weisz sat in the living room of the home, while plaintiff's husband and Lloyd Weisz went into the den area of the home. Plaintiff's husband entered the living room and stated he was going to "use the little boys' room." He walked through the home's dining room into the kitchen. Plaintiff asserts that the most direct way to the bathroom from her husband's location was through the foyer, although the path he took also leads to the bathroom. Georgia Weisz saw plaintiff's husband enter the kitchen, and was confused why he went that way. Georgia Weisz, however, did not tell him that the other direction was the direct route. Plaintiff's husband did not ask for directions to the bathroom and did not ask that any lights be turned on. Although plaintiff believed her husband was going in the wrong direction, any concern she had was assuaged by Georgia Weisz's failure to redirect him.

Defendants and plaintiff heard a crash from the landing area. They walked to the basement stairwell and found plaintiff's husband unresponsive at the bottom of the steps. No one saw plaintiff's husband fall. Plaintiff attempted to revive her husband, but was unsuccessful. Plaintiff's husband was taken to Jameson Memorial Hospital, arriving at 10:08 p.m. Glen Butts was pronounced dead of blunt head trauma.

At all times when plaintiff's husband passed through the landing area it was amply lit, with the exception of when he fell. The lighting was provided either by natural light or by defendants triggering the light switch. The lighting fixture at the top of the basement stairwell was turned off at the time of the accident.

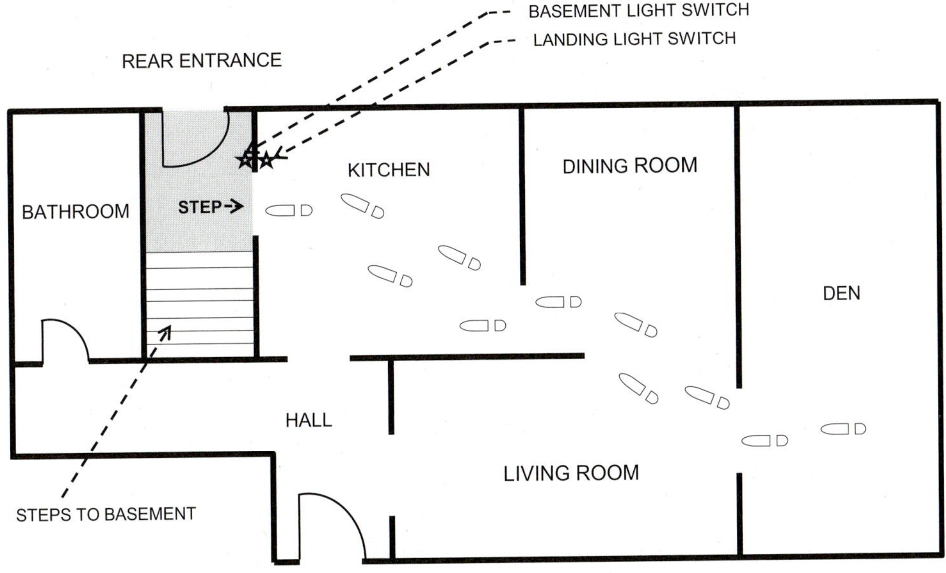

Diagram of Weisz Home (Truncated)

Plaintiff retained an architect expert witness, Robert T. Stevens, Jr., R.A. ("Stevens"). Defendants filed a motion to challenge portions of Stevens' testimony. After hearing argument on May 12, 2009 and June 11, 2009, and taking into the consideration briefs and supplemental briefs, the court on the record ruled that Stevens' testimony would be limited to offering an opinion regarding a normal person's gait, the dangerousness of a single step, and the possible injuries that could result from that danger:

> *The Court*: This is all going to the summary judgment phase of this matter. The question is, at this stage, what can this expert testify to? The consequences of how his testimony would be limited may be a matter that the Court would have to probe and resolve on a motion for summary judgment. But at this stage, . . . the nature of the step, the configuration of the step, the nature of the lighting, how a person would normally walk, . . . those are matters that would be appropriate for Mr. Stevens to opine as to.
>
> He is not going to be able to opine, however, about the reaching for the light switch, because that's just too speculative. We have no idea if the decedent reached for the switch or didn't reach for the switch. So that would be a matter of pure speculation. Whether what is left in terms of the opinion, whether it's sufficient for proving causation under these circumstances, I would have to resolve at a motion for summary judgment.
>
> * * *
>
> 
>
> [*Defendants' Counsel*]: So I understand, Your Honor, at this point your ruling is that Mr. Stevens would be allowed to testify, would be allowed to testify as to the dangerous condition at the top of the stairs, and to his initial — to his first scenario, that it's possible that Mr. Butts missed the step, and then, fell to his left?
>
> *The Court*: Depending on the walking; how someone would walk on that kind of step, and that if someone did fall, they could fall, and going down the steps would be something, too, that could have happened.
>
> But the problem you're going to have, quite frankly, is if there's an equally plausible situation here, I'm not sure that that's sufficient to get past a motion for summary judgment. But I can't resolve that at this stage.
>
> [*Defendants' Counsel*]: But that's something. So, and we discussed it at the last hearing, that my initial argument would, of course, be with regard to duty, but Your Honor would allow me to challenge the causation element, or the facts in support of the causation element of the negligence claim at a motion for summary judgment?
>
> *The Court*: Whether there's sufficient evidence of causation.
>
> [*Defendants' Counsel*]: Okay.
>
> *The Court*: I mean, but Mr. Stevens would be able to testify as to how someone would normally walk, the dangerousness of a single step, and that someone could miss the step and fall consistent with the injuries that were received by the decedent, which resulted in his death.
>
> But he would not be able to testify that he could have also fallen because he was reaching for a light switch which was in a bad location.

Plaintiff also retained a forensic pathologist expert witness, Jonathan Arden, M.D. ("Arden"). Arden opined that "the death of Mr. Butts was caused by blunt impact head injuries received in the fall down the steps." (Pl.'s Ex. N at 2.)

* * *

Discussion

Pennsylvania law is the controlling substantive law in this diversity action. . . .

Glen Butts, a social guest of defendants, was a gratuitous licensee. . . . Pennsylvania courts refer to the Restatement (Second) of Torts § 342 in determining the contours of the duty owed by a landowner to a gratuitous licensee. . . . Section 342 makes a possessor of land liable to a licensee for physical harm caused by dangerous conditions known to the possessor that are not made safe and are not warned of:

> A possesser of land is subject to liability for physical harm caused to licensees by a condition on the land if, but only if,
>
> (a) the possessor knows or has reason to know of the condition and should realize that it involves an unreasonable risk of harm to such licensees and should expect that they will not discover or realize the danger and
>
> (b) he fails to exercise reasonable care to make the condition safe, or to warn the licensees of the condition and risk involved, and
>
> (c) the licensees do not know or have reason to know of the condition and the risk involved.

RESTATEMENT (SECOND) OF TORTS § 342.

. . . [A] landowner can only be subject to liability for physical harm if the harm is caused by the landowner's negligence concerning that condition. "Pennsylvania courts have adopted the Restatement's substantial factor' approach concerning legal causation." *Trude v. Martin*, 660 A.2d 626, 628 (Pa. Super. Ct. 1995); *see* RESTATEMENT (SECOND) OF TORTS § 431. Negligent conduct is said to be a legal cause if it is a substantial factor in bringing about the injury. *Jones v. Montefiore Hosp.*, 431 A.2d 920, 923 (Pa.1981). To be a substantial factor, it need not be the sole factor and need not be quantified as considerable or large, so long as it is significant or recognizable. *Jeter v. Owens–Corning Fiberglass Corp.*, 716 A.2d 633, 636–37 (Pa. Super. Ct. 1998). "'[T]he fact that some other cause concurs with the negligence of the defendant in producing an injury does not relieve defendant from liability unless he can show that such other cause would have produced the injury independently of his negligence.'" *Majors v. Brodhead Hotel*, 205 A.2d 873, 878 (Pa. 1965) (quoting *Carlson v. A. & P. Corrugated Box Corp.*, 72 A.2d 290, 293 (Pa. 1950)).

. . . .

Here, plaintiff failed to adduce sufficient evidence that an alleged breach by defendants caused Glen Butts' death. The evidence presented by plaintiff in responding to defendants' motion for summary judgment with respect to causation, such as evidence of a dangerous single step, the failure to leave on lights, and the failure to warn or alert Glen Butts of potential danger, relates to whether defendants breached a duty owed to Glen Butts. This evidence does not establish a causal link between the alleged breaches of duty and the accident. Plaintiff's expert architect witness, Stevens, offered an opinion about the cause of the accident, i.e., plaintiff's husband was reaching for a light switch, but, upon consideration of defendant's motion to challenge Stevens' opinions, the court held that such testimony is precluded because it was speculative. For purposes of analyzing the pending summary judgment motions, therefore, the court will limit Stevens' testimony as set forth on the record at the June 11, 2009 hearing.

In moving for summary judgment, defendants argue that Stevens' testimony, as limited for trial purposes, is insufficient to establish causation. Defendants cite *Fedorczyk v. Caribbean Cruise Lines, Ltd.*, 82 F.3d 69 (3d Cir.1996), in which Fedorcrzyk, a passenger on a cruise ship, slipped and fell in a bath tub, and sued the ship's operator for negligently causing her injuries. The tub had abrasive strips, but plaintiff did not know whether her feet were on the strips when she slipped. An expert architect witness opined that the strips failed to provide a sufficiently large area of non-slip surface to permit safe use of the tub.

. . . .

. . . . The expert's testimony [in *Fedorczyk*] was admissible to [the] extent he opined that the less adequate the strips the greater the potential to slip, but the Court of Appeals for the Third Circuit recognized that testimony of an increased risk of harm resulting from a party's negligence does not establish that the party's negligence caused the harm. The court relied upon a hypothetical for further explanation:

> . . . . A company provides a stairway in which some of the stairs are defective and some are in fine condition. A person falls on the steps, but does not know which step she fell on. No evidence is introduced that tends to prove she stepped on the defective step. The injured party simply testified that she walked down the steps and fell. We may not reasonably infer that the defective steps probably caused her injury merely because she may have stepped on a defective stair. Without evidence establishing a likelihood that the injured party stepped on the defective stair, a jury would be left to speculate as to the cause of the injury. Simply put, increased risk of harm due to a defendant's negligence, standing alone, does not permit an inference that an injury, more probably than not, was caused by the negligence.

Id. at 75–76. Because the expert's opinion about the cause of the accident was inadmissible, Fedorczyk did not provide direct or circumstantial evidence that the ship operator's negligence caused her injuries. The court granted summary judgment in the ship operator's favor.

The evidence in this case is analogous to that presented in *Fedorczyk*. Stevens' testimony is limited to establishing that the conditions of defendants' rear entry foyer area increased the risk of harm that an individual would fall down the stairwell. Evidence establishing an increased risk of harm, however, is not evidence that those conditions caused Glen Butts' fall. Stevens could not testify that Glen Butts could have been reaching for the light because there was no evidence that happened. In other words, the expert would have to speculate to render an opinion with respect to causation. Like the plaintiff in *Fedorczyk*, plaintiff's husband could have fallen for reasons other than defendants' negligence. Since plaintiff's evidence is not sufficient to raise a genuine issue of material fact with respect to causation, summary judgment must be granted in defendants' favor.

* * *

For the reasons set forth above, defendants' motion for summary judgment is **GRANTED**. . . .

Jones v. LA Fitness Int'l, LLC

2013 WL 3789807 (E.D. Pa. 2013)

Pratter, J. This case brings the court to the Court. Plaintiff Khalif Jones alleges that certain aspects of the basketball court at the LA Fitness International, LLC ("LA Fitness") health club located in Huntingdon Valley, Pennsylvania, constitute dangerous and hazardous property conditions which caused Mr. Jones to injure his elbow while playing basketball. LA Fitness now moves for summary judgment and to preclude the testimony of Plaintiff's liability expert, Steve Bernheim, as inadmissible under Federal Rule of Evidence 702. For the reasons discussed below, the Court will deny both motions.

I. Background

On June 2, 2009, Khalif Jones was playing basketball on an indoor court at the LA Fitness health club located at 2020 County Line Road in Huntingdon Valley. Attempting to block a shot, Mr. Jones jumped beyond the baseline and "suddenly and without warning, fell" into an unpadded section of the back wall of the court, dislocating his elbow. Compl. ¶ 8. As a result, Mr. Jones has suffered severe and permanent injury to the elbow joint, including "right elbow posterior dislocation, lateral epicondylitis, and joint effusion." Compl. ¶ 10.

Mr. Jones initiated this action in the Philadelphia Court of Common Pleas on January 31, 2011. LA Fitness timely removed the case to this Court, on the basis of diversity jurisdiction. In his Complaint, Mr. Jones alleges, *inter alia*, that LA Fitness was negligent . . . in failing to make the basketball court safe for its designated activity and for failing to warn persons of the dangerous and hazardous condition posed by certain aspects of the court, namely that the padding on its back wall was insufficient. Plaintiff's expert is Mr. Steven Bernheim, a sports and recreation consultant, who has further opined that the basketball court was hazardous because (1) it was "undersized"; (2) there was no baseline or end-line painted across the entire width of the court, but only across the twelve-foot length at the bottom of the "key" beneath the basket; (3) there was insufficient clearance between the baseline and the wall. . . . and (5) padding extended only for 16 feet along the back wall below the basket, rather than across the entire wall.

. . . . LA Fitness contends tht Mr. Bernheim's testimony is inadmissible, because he is unqualified to offer a medical or "biomechanical" opinion as to the cause of Mr. Jones's injury, and because he has failed to show that any single alleged defect of the basketball court rendered it inherently unsafe. LA Fitness also argues that, even assuming that the Court admits Mr. Bernheim's testimony, Mr. Jones has failed to offer evidence of "causation" sufficient to withstand a motion for summary judgment, because he has failed to prove that he would *not* have been injured absent the alleged defects.

. . . .

II. Defendant's Motion to Preclude Bernheim Testimony

A. Legal Standard

Federal Rule of Evidence 702 governs the admissibility of expert testimony:

> A witness who is qualified as an expert by knowledge, skill, experience, training, or education may testify in the form of an opinion or otherwise if: (a) the expert's scientific, technical, or other specialized knowledge will help the trier of fact to understand the evidence or to determine a fact in issue; (b) the testimony is based on sufficient facts or data; (c) the testimony is the product of reliable principles and methods; and (d) the expert has reliably applied the principles and methods to the facts of the case.

Fed. R. Evid. 702 (2012).

The Supreme Court in *Daubert v. Merrell Dow Pharm., Inc.,* 509 U.S. 579 (1993), imposed a "gatekeeping" role upon district courts, "in order to 'ensure that any and all scientific testimony or evidence admitted is not only relevant, but reliable.'" *ID Sec. Sys. Canada, Inc. v. Checkpoint Sys., Inc.,* 198 F.Supp.2d 598, 601–02 (E.D. Pa. 2002) (quoting *Daubert,* 509 U.S. at 589 & n. 7). "The adjective 'scientific' implies a grounding in the methods and procedures of science. Similarly, the word 'knowledge' connotes more than subjective belief or unsupported speculation." *Daubert,* 509 U.S. at 590. . . . "*Daubert's* general holding—setting forth the trial judge's general 'gatekeeping' obligation—applies not only to testimony based on 'scientific' knowledge, but also to testimony based on 'technical' and 'other specialized' knowledge." *Kumho Tire Co., Ltd. v. Carmichael,* 526 U.S. 137, 141 (1999).

Rule 702 places "three distinct substantive restrictions on the admission of expert testimony: qualifications, reliability and fit." *Elcock v. Kmart Corp.,* 233 F.3d 734, 741 (3d Cir. 2000) (citing *In re Paoli R.R. Yard PCB Litig.,* 35 F.3d 717, 741–43 (3d Cir. 1994) ("Paoli II")).

. . . .

The first requirement, whether the witness is qualified as an expert, has been interpreted liberally to encompass "a broad range of knowledge, skills, and training." [*ID Sec. Sys. Canada, Inc.*, 198 F. Supp. 2d at 602] (quoting *Paoli II,* 35 F.3d at 741). "Rule 702 requires the witness to have specialized knowledge regarding the area of testimony. The basis of this specialized knowledge can be practical experience as well as academic training and credentials. . . . However, at a minimum, a proffered expert witness must possess skill or knowledge greater than the average layman." *Elcock,* 233 F.3d at 741 (quoting *Waldorf v. Shuta,* 142 F.3d 601, 625 (3d Cir.1998)) (internal punctuation and quotations omitted).

The second prong requires the expert's testimony to be reliable. The Supreme Court has ". . . conclude[d] that a trial court *may* consider one or more of the more specific factors that *Daubert* mentioned when doing so will help determine that testimony's reliability. But . . . the test of reliability is 'flexible,' and *Daubert's* list of specific factors neither necessarily nor exclusively applies to all experts or in every case. Rather, the law grants a district court the same broad latitude when it decides *how* to determine reliability as it enjoys in respect to its ultimate reliability determination." *Kumho Tire,* 526 U.S. at 141 (citation omitted).[2] . . .

The final prong requires that the expert testimony "fit" by assisting the trier of fact. *ID Sec. Sys. Canada, Inc.,* 198 F.Supp.2d at 602–03 (citing *Oddi v. Ford Motor Co.,* 234 F.3d 136, 145 (3d Cir.2000)). "Rule [702], in respect to all such matters, 'establishes a standard of evidentiary reliability.' It 'requires a valid . . . connection to the pertinent inquiry as a precondition to admissibility.'" *Kumho Tire,* 526 U.S. at 149 (quoting *Daubert,* 509 U.S. at 590, 592). But the "fit" standard does not require a plaintiff to "prove [his] case twice." *ID Sec. Sys. Canada, Inc.,* 198 F.Supp.2d at 602 (quoting *Paoli II,* 35 F.3d at 743). Plaintiffs need not "demonstrate to the judge by a preponderance of evidence that the assessments of their experts are *correct,* they only have to demonstrate by a preponderance of evidence that they are reliable." *Id.* (emphasis added). Thus, the test does not require that the opinion have "the best foundation" or be "demonstrably correct," but only that the "particular opinion is based on valid reasoning and reliable methodology." *Id.* (quoting *Oddi,* 234 F.2d at 146).

B. Discussion

LA Fitness first argues that Mr. Bernheim is unqualified to offer an opinion as to the cause of Mr. Jones's injury because he has no medical or "biomechanical" expertise. His background in these areas is immaterial, however, as Mr. Bernheim's opinion is not offered to establish medical causation. Mr. Bernheim's testimony is offered primarily for the purpose of establishing that the basketball court was dangerous because it failed to conform to certain standards within the industry. The Court finds that Mr. Bernheim's background as a consultant and expert in sports risk management and liability renders him qualified to offer an expert opinion as to whether the basketball court in question met certain industry standards, and, if not, in what respects.

Mr. Bernheim testified that, in forming his opinion, he relied on a number of accepted standards and texts, including the basketball rule books of the National Federation of State High School Associations ("NFHS" or "High School Federation"), the National Collegiate Athletic Association ("NCAA"), the National Junior College, the High School Federation Court and Field Diagram Guide, the American Society for Testing and Materials ("ASTM") standards, and the Architectural Graphic Standards

2. The non-exclusive list of factors that *Daubert* and the Court of Appeals for the Third Circuit have declared important for evaluating whether a particular scientific methodology is reliable include: "(1) whether a method consists of a testable hypothesis; (2) whether the method has been subject to peer review; (3) the known or potential rate of error; (4) the existence and maintenance of standards controlling the technique's operation; (5) whether the method is generally accepted; (6) the relationship of the technique to methods which have been established to be reliable; (7) the qualifications of the expert witness testifying based on the methodology; and (8) the non-judicial uses to which the method has been put." *Elcock,* 233 F.3d at 745-46.

("AGS"). Mr. Bernheim testified that he was not aware of any regulations specifically applicable to basketball courts found within health clubs.

.... While the Court recognizes that the cited standards do not expressly specify that they apply to basketball courts located within health or fitness clubs, the Court does not agree [with LA Fitness] that these standards are irrelevant. LA Fitness has not identified any competing standard, regulation, or source of information about the design of basketball courts that contradicts those relied on by Mr. Bernheim. LA Fitness's own expert, Charles Penza, evidently relied on similar texts in formulating his opposing opinion that the LA Fitness court conformed to all available standards and was therefore inherently safe. Therefore, the Court finds that Mr. Bernheim's "methodology" — that is, reviewing generally accepted industry and athletic association standards for basketball courts of various types and comparing them to the design of the court in question — is sufficiently "reliable" to come within the dictates of *Daubert.*

[In his testimony, Bernheim acknowledged that the 3.5-foot space between the basket and the court's back wall satisfied minimum standards suggested by the texts on which he relied, but also noted that the same texts recommend a space of 10-12 feet. In addition, he maintained that the padding on the wall was insufficient because it did not extend across the full width of the court. Finally, Bernheim opined that the court was unreasonably unsafe because some of the lines painted on the court's floor invited players to treat the entire floor — all the way to the wall — as in-bounds. He maintained that, instead, the lines should have been painted so as clearly to mark off some of the space between the basket and the rear wall as out-of-bounds, thereby reducing the risk of players colliding with the wall. — Eds.]

....

While the Court does not find that expert testimony is strictly necessary in this case, where ordinary principles of negligence and the conditions of the premises are well within the jury's comprehension, the Court nonetheless finds that Mr. Bernheim's experience-based testimony regarding various industry standards for basketball courts might assist a jury in determining whether the LA Fitness court conformed to a reasonable standard of care. Of particular note for the Court's conclusion in this case is the likelihood that a jury may well include jurors who do not share equivalent personal experience on a basketball court, and the proposed testimony from Mr. Bernheim can, to borrow from another athletic environment, serve to level the playing field for the jurors.

The Court agrees with LA Fitness, however, that, to the extent Mr. Bernheim's expert report letters and deposition stretch to address the *cause* of Mr. Jones's injury, his testimony is simply too speculative to be admissible at trial. ... Therefore, Mr. Bernheim's trial testimony must be limited to his opinion regarding industry standards and rules for basketball courts, and whether the design and condition of the LA Fitness basketball court met those standards.

III. Defendant's Motion for Summary Judgment

....

Pennsylvania law sets forth the duty that a possessor of land owes to business invitees as follows: "A possessor of land is subject to liability for physical harm caused to his invitees by a condition on the land if, but only if, he (a) knows or by the exercise of reasonable care would discover the condition, and should realize that it involves an unreasonable risk of harm to such invitees, and (b) should expect that they will not discover or realize the danger, or will fail to protect themselves against it, and (c) fails to exercise reasonable care to protect them against the danger." *Gutteridge* [*v. A.P. Green Servs., Inc.*], 804 A.2d [643,] 656 [(Pa. Super. 2002)]. That being said, a possessor of land is *not* liable to an invitee for injuries caused by a "condition on the land whose danger is known or obvious to [the invitee], unless the possessor should anticipate the harm despite such knowledge or obviousness." *Carrender v. Fitterer*, 469 A.2d 120, 125 (Pa. 1983) (citing RESTATEMENT (SECOND) OF TORTS § 343A). . . .

In its initial answer to the complaint, LA Fitness asserted various affirmative defenses, including the doctrine of assumption of risk and/or contributory negligence, and raised issues regarding Mr. Jones's execution of club membership documents releasing LA Fitness from liability for injuries he suffered while using the club facilities. In its motion for summary judgment, however, LA Fitness argues only that Mr. Jones has failed to establish a *prima facie* case for premises liability because he has proffered insufficient evidence that the basketball court was dangerous (*i.e.*, that LA Fitness breached a standard of care) or that his injury was caused by the alleged dangerous conditions. . . .

. . . Mr. Jones, through the testimony of his expert Mr. Bernheim, has established some dispute of material fact as to whether the overall condition or design of the basketball court posed an unreasonable risk of harm to LA Fitness's basketball-playing members. LA Fitness correctly points out that Mr. Bernheim's opinion that the basketball court "could have been safer" does not mean that the court was *per se* dangerous. Nor does the record establish that the basketball court failed to meet a safety standard or regulation cited by either expert. Such a failure is not necessary, however, to show negligence on the part of a defendant, especially where it appears that written standards or regulations specific to facilities such as public health-club basketball courts do not exist.

. . . . Here, in conjunction with consideration of the size of the basketball court and its other attributes, a jury might reasonably find that the few feet of clearance between the baseline and the wall and/or lack of padding along the full length of the end wall posed an unreasonable risk to the players, and failed to conform to a reasonable standard of care, regardless of the court's compliance with minimum industry safety recommendations.

LA Fitness has also argued that, because Mr. Jones is unable to prove that he would *not* have been injured if the end wall of the basketball court had been fully padded, Mr. Jones is therefore unable to establish the "causation" element of his negligence action. Establishing a *prima facie* case of negligence, however, does not require Mr. Jones to prove the negative as posed by LA Fitness. Under Pennsylvania law, a plaintiff must introduce "evidence which provides a reasonable basis for the conclusion that it was more likely than not that the negligent conduct of the defendant was a cause in fact of the injury." *Fedorczyk v. Caribbean Cruise Lines*, 82 F.3d 69, 74 (3d Cir. 1996) (citing W. PAGE KEETON, ET AL., PROSSER AND KEETON ON THE LAW OF TORTS § 41, at 269 (5th ed. 1984)). Exclusivity is not required. At the summary judgment stage, therefore, Mr. Jones must introduce evidence from which a reasonable jury could conclude that there is the requisite causal connection between the condition of the basketball court and his injury.

Mr. Jones has testified that he injured his elbow when his hands collided with an unpadded section of the wall, and his injury was witnessed by several other players on the court, including an LA Fitness trainer named Kenny who treated the dislocated elbow immediately after the injury occurred. LA Fitness has not suggested or offered any evidence to the contrary. The jury in this case will not, therefore, be "left to speculate" as to how Mr. Jones's injury occurred. It is likewise undisputed that the portion of the wall with which Mr. Jones collided was not padded. Finally, Mr. Jones has testified that he played basketball at the Huntingdon Valley location approximately 40 times before the date of the accident, and had collided with the padded portion of the wall previously *without* injuring himself. This is not to say that Mr. Jones has proved that lack of padding was the sole or even the primary cause of his injury; however, a jury might reasonably conclude from this evidence that lack of wall padding was a significant factor in Mr. Jones's injury. Whether Mr. Jones would have suffered the same or similar injury regardless of the size, striping, or padding of the LA Fitness court, whether LA Fitness violated any duty of care by failing to extend wall padding across the full width of the court, and whether Mr. Jones is partially or wholly at fault for his own injuries, are questions of material fact to be determined by the jury.

. . . .

NOTES AND QUESTIONS

1. *Judge Versus Jury.* Ordinarily, the actual causation issue, like the breach issue, is left to the jury, which must assess witness credibility and draw inferences from circumstantial evidence. *Muckler* and *Jones* conform to this rule. In *Butts*, however, the court chose to take the actual causation issue away from the jury. Was the evidence in *Butts* so different from the evidence in *Muckler* and *Jones* as to justify its different outcome?

A negligence claimant who proceeds to trial will typically need to clear several hurdles in order to prevail on the actual causation issue. Assuming that the case goes to a jury, the plaintiff will need to persuade the jury that the defendant's careless conduct *probably* was an actual cause of her injury. To say the same thing, the plaintiff must persuade the jury that it is more probable than not that, but for the defendant's carelessness, the plaintiff would not have been injured. As in both *Butts* and *Jones*, however, it is common for a negligence defendant to argue that the plaintiff should not even be permitted to get to the jury because the evidence she has proffered is too weak to permit a reasonable juror to find for the plaintiff on the actual causation issue (i.e., because the evidence is insufficient to permit a reasonable juror to conclude that, more probably than not, the plaintiff's injury would not have occurred but for the defendant's carelessness). As is indicated in the discussion of civil procedure in the notes following *Walter v. Wal-Mart* in Chapter 1, defendants have opportunities both at trial and after trial to ask the judge to take issues such as actual causation away from the jury because of a failure of proof.

2. What Must Be Proven and What Need Not Be Proven. When actual causation is at issue in a negligence case, the parties will often present evidence that supports plausible alternative accounts of what would have happened had the defendant acted with due care. Defendants will naturally offer accounts according to which the plaintiff's injury would have occurred even if the defendant had acted with care. The plaintiff does *not* need to demonstrate that the defendant's proposed account(s) *could not possibly* have happened. She need only show that her account — according to which defendant's careless conduct was necessary for her injury — is the *more probable account.* Likewise, the plaintiff need not demonstrate that she *could not possibly* have been injured if the defendant had acted with due care. Rather, she need only show that *it is likelier than not* that she would not have been injured had the defendant been careful.

3. Statistics, Individual Cases and the Burden of Production. As explained in connection with the doctrine of *res ipsa loquitur* (Chapter 3), the preponderance of the evidence standard means that a jury may only deem a fact proven if the jurors conclude that it is more likely than not to have occurred. In theory, then, a judge should direct a verdict for the defendant in cases in which there were no eyewitnesses and the circumstantial evidence suggests that the defendant's exercise of reasonable care would have made no difference with respect to the occurrence of the plaintiff's injury.

Consider this example. A sailor is swept overboard during a storm at sea while other crew members are on deck. Assume that it is the duty of the owner of a ship to have life preservers on hand so that other crew members can throw one to a sailor before he drowns. Assume also that, in stormy conditions, the chances of a promptly thrown life preserver saving the life of a sailor in the water is less than 50 percent — say 33 percent. (The wind may blow the preserver astray, or a wave may carry it away, and even if the sailor catches it, he may succumb to the storm before he can be pulled from the sea.) Now suppose the sailor's estate brings a negligence action against the ship owner and can prove only that the sailor fell overboard during a typical storm, that other sailors were on hand to throw him a life preserver, and that the ship was not equipped with life preservers. Must the judge direct a verdict for the defendant? Given that, statistically, the life preserver was not likely to have saved the sailor, is the jury entitled to find that the defendant's breach was a cause-in-fact of the sailor's death?

If the answer to the last question is "no," note the following problem. In a random distribution of sailors who go overboard during storms, one of three will be saved by means of a life preserver. However, no individual plaintiff can show that it was *his decedent* who would likely have survived, since it is 67 percent likely for each individual sailor that he would not have survived. Thus, even though, statistically, one in three would survive but for the boat owner's carelessness, no single plaintiff alleging negligent failure to maintain rescue equipment will ever recover under the preponderance standard. Is this a tolerable result?

Courts are sometimes willing to give jurors room to combine statistical evidence with circumstantial evidence from the case before them to conclude that the defendant's carelessness would have made a difference to the plaintiff, even though the relevant statistics by themselves would seem to suggest that the plaintiff cannot clear the more-probable-than-not hurdle. For example, in *Kallenberg v. Beth Israel Hospital*, 357 N.Y.S.2d 508 (N.Y. App. Div. 1974), *aff'd* 337 N.E.2d 128 (N.Y. 1975), the court upheld a jury verdict against the defendant hospital even though it acknowledged that the plaintiff's own expert had testified that proper treatment would have given the plaintiff "a 20, say 30, maybe 40% chance of survival" (rather than a greater than 50 percent chance of survival). The *Kallenberg* approach does not relieve a plaintiff of the burden of persuading the factfinder that the defendant's conduct was probably necessary for the plaintiff's injury to occur. Rather, it gives juries substantial leeway to infer a probable but-for connection between breach and injury from a combination of statistical and circumstantial evidence. *See* Mortensen v. Memorial Hospital, 483 N.Y.S.2d 264 (App. Div. 1984).

4. *Substantial Factor.* The Pennsylvania court decisions cited in *Butts* call for juries to be instructed that a defendant's carelessness shall be deemed an actual cause of a plaintiff's injury if it is proven by a preponderance of the evidence to have been a "substantial factor" in bringing about the plaintiff's injury. As noted at the outset of this Chapter, the use of this language in jury instructions is quite common, but often a source of confusion because it is not always clear how the idea of "substantial factor" figures in, or relates to, the but-for test.

Probably most courts that employ substantial factor language follow the California Supreme Court in regarding "substantial factor" as a phrase that *refines* or *clarifies* the but-for test, rather than *replacing* it. *See* Mitchell v. Gonzalez, 816 P.2d. 872, 878 (Cal. 1991) (a defendant's carelessness cannot be deemed a substantial factor in bringing about a plaintiff's injury unless it is proven to have been a probable but-for cause of that injury). The California Court in *Mitchell* favored the use of a substantial factor instruction (over a more straightforward instruction on the but-for test) out of concern that jurors are more likely to misconstrue a but-for instruction as asking them to isolate *the* (sole) cause of a plaintiff's injury, rather than asking them to determine whether a defendant's carelessness was *a* cause of the injury. *Id.* at 922. (On the importance of framing the actual causation issue in terms of whether the defendant's carelessness was "a" cause of the plaintiff's injury, see the discussion of Key Terms and Concepts at the start of this chapter.)

Unlike the California Court, some other courts, including the Pennsylvania Supreme Court, have invoked substantial factor language to set a lower, more plaintiff-friendly burden of persuasion on the issue of actual causation than is set by the but-for test. An oft-cited example of this phenomenon is *Hamil v. Bashline*, 392 A.2d 1280 (Pa. 1978). In *Hamil*, the Pennsylvania Supreme Court held that, even if a malpractice victim's estate could not prove that he probably would have survived a fatal heart attack had the defendant physician properly treated him, the estate could still prevail on a showing that the improper treatment, by somewhat increasing the risk that the decedent would not survive, functioned as a "substantial factor" in producing his death. A few other courts have followed *Hamil*, primarily in the medical malpractice context, by holding that a jury can deem an act of medical malpractice to have been a substantial factor in contributing to a patient's injury if it finds that the malpractice probably *increased the risk* of the plaintiff's injury. *See* Herskovits v. Group Health Coop., 664 P.2d 474 (Wash. 1983) (opinion of Dore, J., joined by Rosellini, J.); Van Vleet v. Pfeifle, 289 N.W.2d 781 (N.D. 1980); Ehlinger v. Sipes, 454 N.W.2d 754 (Wis. 1990).

In Note 3, *supra*, we saw that decisions such as *Kallenberg* lower the plaintiff's burden of *production* on actual causation yet maintain the usual burden of *persuasion* (namely, the burden of persuading the factfinder that the defendant's carelessness probably was necessary for the plaintiff to have been injured). By contrast, decisions such as *Hamil* and *Herskovitz* explicitly lower the burden of persuasion, allowing the plaintiff to recover in a case in which the defendant's carelessness increased the risk of the plaintiff being injured, yet the injury probably still would have occurred even if the defendant had been careful. (For example, consider a case in which the evidence shows that a stroke victim was probably going to suffer a stroke regardless of whether her doctor properly diagnosed her condition, but that the misdiagnosis made it somewhat more likely that a stroke would occur.) Is there anything that favors one or the other of these two different ways of easing a negligence plaintiff's path to proving actual causation? A third way of easing the path for plaintiffs on causation — the so-called "loss-of-a-chance" doctrine — has been taken by some courts (again largely in medical malpractice cases). It is discussed below in *Falcon* and the notes that follow it.

Numerous commentators, including the drafters of the Third Restatement, have criticized as unwarranted *Hamil*'s and *Herskovitz*'s employment of "substantial factor" language to lower the plaintiff's burden of persuasion on actual causation. *See, e.g.*, Dan B. Dobbs, The Law of Torts § 178, at 435 (2000). For further discussions of the substantial factor formulation and its relationship to the but-for test and to notions of proximate cause, see the notes following *Boomer* and *Wannall*, *infra*.

5. *Causation and Breaches of Affirmative Duties.* One sometimes finds courts being disposed toward lenience on the issue of causation when dealing with claims grounded in affirmative duties. For example, we observed in a note following the *Tarasoff* case (Chapter 2) that courts sometimes permit juries wide leeway to determine that a given victim would have heeded the warning omitted by the defendant, had it been given. As we see in Chapter 12, when plaintiffs complain that they have been injured because a product manufacturer has failed to warn them of a hidden danger in the product, courts will often adopt a "presumption" that the plaintiff would have heeded the warning had there been one. Likewise, the U.S. Supreme Court has held that when the defendant breaches an affirmative duty to disclose material information, a court may presume that the persons to whom the duty was owed would have changed their conduct had the information been provided. Affiliated Ute Citizens v. United States, 406 U.S. 128, 153-154 (1972). Does attending to the affirmative nature of the defendant's duty in cases such as these help to explain why the courts are sometimes willing to adopt more plaintiff-friendly approaches to cause-in-fact in them? If so, what is special about these sorts of duties that might warrant this judicial disposition toward lenience?

Big Think

Judge and Jury

Why is actual causation deemed a question for juries rather than judges? Are there considerations relevant to the determination of causation that make this element more like breach, and less like duty (the determination of which, as discussed in Chapter 2, is usually up to the judge)? Is our system hypocritical in treating causation as a jury question, given how many opportunities it provides judges to take the causation issue away from the jury? If you were designing the system anew, would you divide the responsibility for resolving causation issues between judge and jury differently? As noted in Chapter 1, these questions generally do not arise in the legal systems of most other industrialized nations, because most have abolished or severely curtailed the use of the civil jury.

Falcon v. Memorial Hospital

462 N.W.2d 44 (Mich. 1990)

Levin, J. The deposition testimony of plaintiff Ruby Falcon's expert witness tended to show that had the defendant physician, S.N. Kelso, Jr., followed the procedures the expert witness claims should have been followed, the patient, Nena J. Falcon, [plaintiff's granddaughter] would have had a 37.5 percent opportunity of surviving the medical accident that was a cause of her death.

The trial court dismissed the complaint because Falcon's evidence did not show that Nena Falcon probably—defined as more than fifty percent—would have survived if the procedure had not been omitted. The Court of Appeals reversed, stating that Falcon need only "establish that the omitted treatment or procedure had the potential for improving the patient's recovery or preventing the patient's death." Falcon v. Memorial Hosp., 443 N.W.2d 431, [435] (Mich. Ct. App. 1989). The Court added that "while a plaintiff must show some probability that the treatment would be successful, that probability need not be greater than fifty percent." We affirm.

I

. . . The defendants contend that because the proofs at a trial of Falcon's claim would not show that it was probable, measured as more than fifty percent, that Nena Falcon would have avoided physical harm had the procedure not been omitted, Falcon cannot show that the asserted negligence of defendants caused her physical harm. They also contend that Falcon cannot maintain an action for wrongful death because such an action can only be maintained where the plaintiff can establish that the act or omission caused death, and, again, Falcon's proofs will fall short because they will show only that there would have been a 37.5 percent opportunity of avoiding death and not a more than fifty percent opportunity had the procedure not been omitted.

II

Some courts disallow recovery for lost opportunity unless the plaintiff can establish that the patient would not have suffered the physical harm but for the defendant's negligence, or, at least, that it is more probable, measured as more than fifty percent, that, but for such negligence, the patient would not have suffered the physical harm.

Under the more probable, measured as more than fifty percent, approach to causation, a plaintiff who establishes that the patient would have had more than a fifty percent opportunity of not suffering physical harm had the defendant not acted negligently, recovers one hundred percent of the damages. The better than even opportunity is compensated as if it were a certainty, although the patient's chances of a better result are significantly less than one hundred percent.[7]

To say that a patient would have had a ninety-nine percent opportunity of survival if given proper treatment, does not mean that the physician's negligence was the cause in fact if the patient would have been among the unfortunate one percent who would have died. A physician's carelessness may, similarly, be the actual cause of physical harm although the patient had only a one percent opportunity of surviving even with flawless medical attention. . . .

III

Other courts have permitted recovery for physical harm on a showing that the lost opportunity was a substantial, albeit fifty percent or less, factor in producing the harm:

> An evolving trend has developed to relax the standard for sufficiency of proof of causation ordinarily required of a plaintiff to provide a basis upon which the jury may consider causation in the "lost chance of survival" cases. McKellips v. St. Francis Hosp., Inc., 741 P.2d 467, 471 (Okla. 1987).

Some courts have held that the plaintiff need only show that the defendant's conduct was a substantial factor in producing the physical harm.[11] Other courts allow recovery for loss of a fifty percent or less opportunity of achieving a better result without clearly articulating a standard of causation.[12] . . .

IV

Nena Falcon, a nineteen-year-old woman, gave birth to a healthy baby, Justice Eugene Falcon, in the early morning hours of March 21, 1973. Moments after delivery, Nena Falcon coughed, gagged, convulsed, became cyanotic, and suffered a complete respiratory and cardiac collapse. Attempts to revive her were unsuccessful. She was pronounced dead soon thereafter.

---

7. The more probable than not approach thus tends to over compensate particular plaintiffs. Professor McCormick stated:

> Should the courts insist, in claims for loss of a single specific advantage, upon a showing that the chances were substantially better than even and upon giving all or nothing? To adopt this attitude seems to result in oscillation between overlavishness and niggardliness. McCormick, Damages, § 31, p.119.

11. Hamil v. Bashline, 481 Pa. 256; 392 A.2d 1280 (1978). . . .

12. Kallenberg v. Beth Israel Hosp., 357 N.Y.S.2d 508 (1974), . . . *aff'd* 337 N.E.2d 128 (1975). . . .

The autopsy report indicated that amniotic fluid embolism, an unpreventable complication that occurs in approximately one out of ten or twenty thousand births, was the cause of death. The survival rate of amniotic fluid embolism is, according to Falcon's expert witness, 37.5 percent if an intravenous line is connected to the patient before the onset of the embolism. In this case, an intravenous line had not been established.

Falcon's theory is that had a physician or nurse anesthetist inserted an intravenous line before administering the spinal anesthetic to assist the physician in dealing with any of several complications, the intravenous line could have been used to infuse life-saving fluids into Nena Falcon's circulatory system, providing her a 37.5 percent opportunity of surviving. By not inserting the intravenous line, the physician deprived her of a 37.5 percent opportunity of surviving the embolism.

V

The question whether a defendant caused an event is not readily answered, and is especially perplexing in circumstances such as those present in the instant case where the defendant's failure to act is largely responsible for the uncertainty regarding causation.

Had the defendants in the instant case inserted an intravenous line, one of two things would have happened, Nena Falcon would have lived, or she would have died. There would be no uncertainty whether the omissions of the defendants caused her death. Falcon's destiny would have been decided by fate and not possibly by her health care providers. The United States Court of Appeals for the Fourth Circuit, observed:

> When a defendant's negligent action or inaction has effectively terminated a person's chance of survival, it does not lie in the defendant's mouth to raise conjectures as to the measure of the chances that he has put beyond the possibility of realization. If there was any substantial possibility of survival and the defendant has destroyed it, he is answerable. Rarely is it possible to demonstrate to an absolute certainty what would have happened in circumstances that the wrongdoer did not allow to come to pass. The law does not in the existing circumstances require the plaintiff to show to a *certainty* that the patient would have lived had she been hospitalized and operated on promptly. Hicks v. United States, 368 F.2d 626, 632 (4th Cir. 1966) [internal citation and footnote omitted — EDS.].

VI

In an ordinary tort action seeking recovery for physical harm, the defendant is a stranger to the plaintiff and the duty imposed by operation of law is imposed independently of any undertaking by the defendant. In an action claiming medical malpractice, however, the patient generally is not a stranger to the defendant. Generally, the patient engaged the services of the defendant physician. The physician undertook to perform services for the patient, and the patient undertook to pay or provide payment for the services.

The scope of the undertakings by a physician or hospital to the patient and by the patient to the physician or hospital is not generally a matter of express agreement.

There is, however, an understanding that the law enforces in the absence of express agreement. The patient expects a physician to do that which is expected of physicians of like training in the community, and the physician expects the patient to pay or provide payment for the services, whether the likelihood of there in fact being any benefit to the patient is only one through fifty percent or is greater than fifty percent.

The defendants assert, in effect, that the scope of their undertaking did not include acts or omissions likely to benefit the patient only to the extent of one through fifty percent — or at least they should not be subject to liability for acts or omissions likely to have caused harm to the extent only of one through fifty percent. They contend that they should be subject to liability only for acts or omissions likely, to the extent of more than fifty percent, to have caused physical harm to the patient. . . .

Patients engage the services of doctors, not only to prevent disease or death, but also to delay death and to defer or ameliorate the suffering associated with disease or death. If the trier of fact were to decide, on the basis of expert testimony, that the undertaking of the defendant physician included the implementation of tasks and procedures that, in the case of Nena Falcon, would have enabled the physician and other medically trained persons, who were present at the time of delivery, to provide her, in the event of the medical accident that occurred, an opportunity to survive the accident, a failure to do so was a breach of the understanding or undertaking.

Nena Falcon, if the testimony of Falcon's expert witness is credited, would have had a 37.5 percent opportunity of surviving had the defendants implemented the procedures Falcon's expert asserts should have been implemented. In reducing Nena Falcon's opportunity of living by failing to insert an intravenous line, her physician caused her harm, although it cannot be said, more probably than not, that he caused her death. A 37.5 percent opportunity of living is hardly the kind of opportunity that any of us would willingly allow our health care providers to ignore. If, as Falcon's expert asserts, the implementation of such procedures was part of the understanding or undertaking, the failure to have implemented the procedures was a breach of the understanding or undertaking. The physician is, and should be, subject to liability for such breach, although Nena Falcon was likely, measured as more than fifty percent, to die as soon as the medical accident occurred and the negligence of the physician eliminated a less than fifty percent opportunity of surviving.

We thus see the injury resulting from medical malpractice as not only, or necessarily, physical harm, but also as including the loss of opportunity of avoiding physical harm. A patient goes to a physician precisely to improve his opportunities of avoiding, ameliorating, or reducing physical harm and pain and suffering.

Women gave birth to children long before there were physicians or hospitals or even midwives. A woman who engages the services of a physician and enters a hospital to have a child does so to reduce pain and suffering and to increase the likelihood of her surviving and the child surviving childbirth in a good state of health even though the likelihood of the woman and child not surviving in good health without such services is far less than fifty percent. That is why women go to physicians. That is what physicians undertake to do. That is what they are paid for. They are, and should be, subject to liability if they fail to measure up to the standard of care.

VII

A number of courts have recognized, as we would, loss of an opportunity for a more favorable result, as distinguished from the unfavorable result, as compensable in medical malpractice actions. Under this approach, damages are recoverable for the loss of opportunity although the opportunity lost was less than even, and thus it is not more probable than not that the unfavorable result would or could have been avoided.

Under this approach, the plaintiff must establish more-probable-than-not causation. He must prove, more probably than not, that the defendant reduced the opportunity of avoiding harm. . . .

The trier of fact should determine whether defendant's negligence was a substantial factor in reducing plaintiff's chances of obtaining a better result.

In DeBurkarte v. Louvar, 393 N.W.2d 131, 135 (Iowa 1986), the Supreme Court of Iowa explained the difference between viewing the injury as a loss of life and viewing it as a loss of opportunity to survive an illness:

> We recognize that the plaintiff's injury may be viewed as a shortening of her life, in which case we would agree with the defendant that the plaintiffs did not produce substantial evidence on causation: there was no evidence the plaintiff's cancer probably spread after September, 1981, preventing her from being cured. [Citation omitted.] On the other hand, as the Restatement [§ 323(a)] indicates, her injury may also be viewed as a lost chance to survive the cancer. The jury could then find from the evidence that the defendant's failure to diagnose and treat the cancer probably caused a substantial reduction in the plaintiff's chance to survive it.

The court concluded: "We believe the better approach is to allow recovery, but *only* for the lost chance of survival." *Id.*, p.136. (Emphasis in original.) . . .

VIII

. . . The harm resulting from defendants' asserted malpractice occurred immediately before Nena Falcon's death when the medical accident occurred and, by reason of the failure to have inserted an intravenous line, it became certain that she would die. At that moment, immediately before her death, Nena Falcon had a cause of action for the harm, the denial of any opportunity of living, that had been caused her. Her claim therefor survived her death because "[a]ll actions and claims survive death." RJA § 2921.

We are persuaded that loss of a 37.5 percent opportunity of living constitutes a loss of a substantial opportunity of avoiding physical harm. We need not now decide what lesser percentage would constitute a substantial loss of opportunity.

IX

In the instant case, while Nena Falcon's cause of action accrued before her death, she did not suffer conscious pain and suffering from the failure to implement the omitted procedures between the moment that the medical accident occurred and the time of her death a few minutes later—she was sedated throughout the entire time period. In this case, 37.5 percent times the damages recoverable for wrongful death would be an appropriate measure of damages. . . .

We would affirm the Court of Appeals reversal of the entry of summary judgment for the defendants, and remand the case for trial.

BOYLE, J. (concurring). I concur in the recognition of "lost opportunity to survive" as injury for which tort law should allow recovery in proportion to the extent of the lost chance of survival, provided that the negligence of the defendant more probably than not caused the loss of opportunity. However, I would emphasize that the Court today is called upon to decide the viability of a claim for "lost opportunity" only where the ultimate harm to the victim is death. Thus, any language in the lead opinion suggesting that a similar cause of action might lie for a lost opportunity of avoiding lesser physical harm is dicta. Whether the social and policy factors which justify compensation for a lost chance of survival would justify recovery for the loss of a chance to avoid some lesser harm is a question for another day.

RILEY, C.J. (dissenting). I would hold that a wrongful death action may not survive a motion for summary disposition where it is uncontested that the plaintiff cannot show that defendant's negligence caused the decedent's death, and will produce evidence only that the decedent would have had an increased chance of survival if the defendant, as in this case, had not negligently failed to insert an intravenous line before or immediately after administering saddle block anesthesia. Where plaintiff cannot show that defendants' omission was probably a cause of the death of Nena Falcon, the degree of certitude which would justify the imposition of liability on defendants is lacking. The recognition of mere chance as a recoverable item of loss fundamentally contradicts the essential notion of causation. By definition, the lost chance theory would compensate plaintiff for a mere possibility that defendants' omission caused the death of Nena Falcon. . . .

. . . .

IV

Even where there is causation in fact, a weighing of social interests requires a limit on how far the consequences of negligence will extend.

> As a practical matter, legal responsibility must be limited to those causes which are so closely connected with the result and of such significance that the law is justified in imposing liability. Some boundaries must be set to liability for the consequences of any act, upon the basis of some social idea of justice or policy. Prosser & Keeton, *Torts*, 5th ed., § 41, p. 264.

Thus, "[b]y adjusting the causation requirement, the court is able to strike a balance between deterring harmful behavior and encouraging useful activity." Abel v. Eli Lilly & Co., 343 N.W.2d 164, [170 n.8] ([Mich.] 1984), *cert. denied*, 469 U.S. 833 (1984). If liability is to be imposed in proportion to any chance at survival, then the medical profession will be subjected to a burden which is not imposed on any other group of defendants. I submit that nothing is to be gained by extracting payment from a defendant who cannot be shown to have caused the adverse result. Such a rule will not serve the deterrence function of tort law. It more likely will encourage the practice of costly defensive medicine in an attempt to avoid practically certain liability in the event of an unfavorable outcome.

The utility of the physician's conduct militates against a relaxation of the causation requirement in medical malpractice cases. "The physician serves a vital function in our society, a function which requires the assumption of a duty to the patient. Yet, his profession affords him only an inexact and often experimental science by which to discharge his duty." [Herskovits v. Group Health Co-op., 664 P.2d 474, 488 (Wash. 1983)] (Brachtenbach, J., dissenting). *See also* Malone, *Ruminations on Cause-in-Fact*, 9 Stan. L. R. 60, 86-87 (1956).

. . . In this case, the question is not who caused Nena Falcon's death; the question, for which we have no answer, is whether any human act or omission caused her death. I do not mean to minimize the tragedy of such events, but only to question the assumption that a human cause may be located.

V

. . . Where the plaintiff can show no more than a possibility that the defendants' conduct was a cause of the harm, I would conclude that the plaintiff has not produced adequate evidence to create a factual issue regarding causation. Inherent in the concept of causation is a degree of certitude which is absolutely lacking in this case. Our case law wisely requires evidence from which it may be inferred that the defendant *probably* caused the ultimate harm before the jury may be allowed to infer that the defendant did cause such harm and should compensate the plaintiff in damages. . . .

NOTES AND QUESTIONS

1. *Duty, Cause, and Injury: Loss of a Chance.* One way of understanding loss-of-a-chance doctrine is as attempting to solve the proof-of-causation problem faced by certain plaintiffs by redefining the injury suffered. Instead of attempting to prove that the defendants breached a duty to take care not to cause *death or bodily harm*, the plaintiff instead is complaining of a breach of a duty to take care *not to reduce her chances for avoiding death or bodily harm.* A concurring opinion in the *Herskovits* decision (discussed in the notes following *Jones*), which suggested this approach, has proved influential with other courts. On this understanding, the injury complained of is the reduction in the victim's chances to escape death or physical injury. In effect, the assertion is that the defendants were required to take care not to deny the plaintiff whatever opportunity for good health his circumstances permitted, even if that opportunity was less-than-50 percent probable to begin with. With the injury thus recharacterized, are any new obstacles posed to the plaintiffs in proving their prima facie case?

2. *Measuring Damages.* If the injury complained of is the loss of a chance to survive, a question arises as to the appropriate measure of damages. A wrongful death plaintiff such as Ruby Falcon — usually a surviving family member of the victim — is entitled to compensation for loss of economic support from the decedent, including compensation for loss of the decedent's companionship. *See* Chapter 6. Under *Falcon*, the wrongful death plaintiff who prevails on a loss-of-a-chance theory will only get a percentage of this compensation corresponding to the percentage chance of which the decedent was deprived. Is that measure of damages obviously correct?

Some judges have suggested that, in loss-of-a-chance cases, the jury should be left, as it ordinarily is in tort cases, to come up with an appropriate damage award unconstrained by the sort of ceiling set in *Falcon.*

3. Falcon's Fate. *Falcon*'s holding proved short-lived in Michigan. M.C.L. § 600.2912a(2), enacted by the Michigan legislature in 1993 in response to *Falcon,* provides:

> In an action alleging medical malpractice, the plaintiff has the burden of proving that he or she suffered an injury that more probably than not was proximately caused by the negligence of the defendant or defendants. In an action alleging medical malpractice, the plaintiff cannot recover for loss of an opportunity to survive or an opportunity to achieve a better result unless the opportunity was greater than 50%.

Notwithstanding the enactment of this statute, the loss-of-a-chance issue returned to the Michigan Supreme Court in *Weymers v. Khera,* 563 N.W.2d 647 (Mich. 1997). There, the Court was faced with the question of whether a malpractice plaintiff who alleged a nonfatal injury should be permitted to use *Falcon*'s loss-of-a-chance doctrine. The alleged malpractice had occurred in the brief window of time after *Falcon* had been decided, but before the effective date of the statute, hence the statute did not determine the resolution of the issue. Nonetheless, the Court declined to extend *Falcon* to medical malpractice suits alleging injuries other than death.

4. Lost Chance Versus Probable Injury Revisited: O'Neal. A fractured Michigan Supreme Court had occasion to apply M.C.L. § 600.2912(a) in *O'Neal v. St. John Hospital & Medical Center,* 791 N.W.2d 853 (Mich. 2010). Plaintiff alleged that the defendants' careless misdiagnosis caused him to suffer a stroke. Plaintiff's experts testified that the misdiagnosis had increased the plaintiff's risk of stroke from 5 to 10 percent to 10 to 20 percent. The jury found for plaintiff. In a 5-2 decision featuring four concurring opinions and a strongly worded dissent, the Supreme Court affirmed.

The majority rejected the dissent's contention that the plaintiff was suing for the loss of a less-than-50 percent chance of avoiding a stroke — a theory of liability barred by the second sentence of § 600.2912(a). Instead, given the statistical evidence indicating that, even with malpractice, a patient such as the plaintiff was unlikely to suffer a stroke, combined with the evidence suggesting that the defendants' malpractice had significantly increased this small risk, it concluded that plaintiff had offered sufficient evidence to permit the jury to find that the stroke probably was caused by the defendants' malpractice. One opinion stressed that the jury could reasonably have concluded that the malpractice had generated a 300 percent increase in the risk of stroke — the 15 percent differential between a 5 percent chance of stroke and a 20 percent chance — and that such an increase sufficed to establish that the stroke probably would not have occurred but for the malpractice. Another opinion reasoned that, because the jury could have found that the malpractice was responsible for 15 percent of the 20 percent chance of stroke that plaintiff faced without proper treatment, it could further have found that the defendants' malpractice was 75 percent likely to have been necessary for the stroke to occur.

Do you agree with the dissent that *O'Neal* is really just a loss-of-chance case? Was the jury entitled to find for the plaintiff on actual causation? Even if O'Neal is not a loss-of-chance case, was the above-described statistical evidence sufficient to permit a reasonable jury to conclude that the defendants' malpractice, more probably than not, was necessary for the plaintiff's stroke to occur?

5. *For Doctors Only?* Loss-of-a-chance doctrine has been formally adopted by an increasing number of state courts in the context of suits for medical malpractice. *See* Matsuyama v. Birnbaum, 452 Mass. 1 (Mass. 2008) (stating that 20 jurisdictions have adopted loss-of-a-chance); Restatement (Third) of Torts: Liability for Physical and Emotional Harm § 26 cmt. n (2010) (reporting "a decided trend toward adopting lost opportunity as cognizable legal harm"). The *Falcon* court seems to have thought that there was something special about claims against physicians that favored the application of loss-of-a-chance doctrine to medical malpractice claims. What is special about them? That they are brought against professionals? If so, should loss of a chance apply to solve the problem of proof faced by many legal malpractice claimants — namely, the claimant's inability to establish by a preponderance of the evidence that she would have prevailed in the "case within the case"? (Some courts in the United Kingdom have taken this approach in legal malpractice.) Or are there special considerations at work that apply to physicians but not attorneys or other professionals? Should loss of a chance be available to any tort plaintiff who may otherwise fail to prove causation?

III. MULTIPLE NECESSARY AND MULTIPLE SUFFICIENT CAUSES

As noted at the outset of this chapter, it is sometimes the case that the search for the careless conduct that produced the victim's injury will turn up more than one actor whose carelessness may have contributed to the occurrence of the injury. In this section we consider how the presence of multiple tortfeasors affects application of the but-for test for actual causation.

McDonald v. Robinson

224 N.W. 820 (Iowa 1929)

Stevens, J. The injuries of which appellee complains were received by her near the northwest corner of the intersection of Fourth Street and Avenue G in the city of Cedar Rapids, and occurred in the following manner: Avenue G lies east and west, and Fourth Street north and south. Appellant Robinson was driving his car westerly along the north side of Avenue G, and Max Padzensky, the son of Dave, who owned the car, was driving his car northerly along the center line of Fourth Street. When near the center of the intersection, the automobiles collided, and as a result, became interlocked. They were thrown out of their course toward the northwest of the intersection. The Padzensky car struck appellee near the corner of the curbing, knocked her down, and she was dragged under the car until it was stopped, 56 feet farther north. After proceeding northward from the corner of the curbing, the cars became separated, and the Robinson car was stopped on the opposite side of the street.

[Plaintiff's] injuries were serious, and, she claims, permanent. The petition alleged that each car was being negligently driven, and that the injury resulted from the concurrent negligence of the two drivers.

The chief ground of error alleged by appellant, to wit, that there is a misjoinder of causes of action and of parties, was raised at every step of the proceeding and in every way known to the profession. All, of course, concede that joint tort-feasors, properly so defined, may be sued jointly, and a joint judgment recovered against them. The point of divergence has its origin in other propositions, on which the courts are somewhat divided. . . .

. . . The real point of controversy between counsel, when carefully analyzed, is as to what wrongful or tortious acts are necessary, to render two or more persons joint tort-feasors. A common intent, purpose, and design on the part of the wrongdoers to do a particular wrong or injury, — as, for example, where a conspiracy is charged, — is not always essential. There is a large class of cases in which joint liability may exist, from which the element of intent and unity of design and purpose is wholly absent. If the acts of two or more persons concur in contributing to and causing an accident, and but for such concurrence the accident would not have happened, the injured person may sue the actors jointly or severally, and recover against one or all, according to the proven or admitted facts of the case.

This rule has the support of the great weight of authority [from other jurisdictions]. . . .

The question here to be decided is, Was there such concurrence of negligent acts on the part of appellant and Max Padzensky which united and concurred to produce the injury complained of, as to render them jointly or severally liable? We think there was. The jury may well have found that both defendants were negligent, and it must have found that, but for the concurrence of such negligence, the injury to appellee could not possibly have happened.

It was said by the New York Court of Appeals in Sweet v. Perkins, 196 N.Y. 482 (90 N.E. 50), that, "Where concurrence in causes is charged, the test is, simply, could the accident have happened without their co-operation?" The injury in this case was indivisible. There was no possible way by which it could be said that the negligence of one or of the other of the defendants was the sole or proximate cause thereof. . . .

The conclusion reached in the court below, that the accident was caused solely by reason of the combined and concurrent negligence of the appellants Robinson and Max Padzensky, and that, but for such combined and concurrent negligent acts, the injury would not have happened, cannot be avoided. . . .

NOTES AND QUESTIONS

1. *"The" Cause Versus "A" Cause Once Again.* The opinion in *McDonald* reminds us again that the question being asked with respect to actual causation is whether a defendant's carelessness was *a* cause of the plaintiff's injury, rather than *the* cause. In a case such as *McDonald*, the plaintiff can establish actual causation with respect to each defendant because the carelessness of each had to occur for the accident to occur: But for *each* actor's carelessness there would have been no accident and no injury to the plaintiff.

2. *Illustrations of Multiple Necessary Conditions.* Careless acts by different actors can function as multiple but-for conditions of a plaintiff's injury even without the literal interlock among the careless actors in *McDonald*. (Reconsider some of the opinions that appear in the duty and breach chapters. Can you identify some that involve multiple tortfeasors?) For example, suppose driver *D* carelessly stops his vehicle in the middle of the road on the far side of a curve to watch the sunset. Taxi driver *T*, who is driving unreasonably fast, comes around the curve, and because he is speeding, cannot avoid colliding with *D*'s car. As a result, *P*, a passenger in *T*'s taxi, suffers injury. If *P* were to sue *D* and/or *T*, and the foregoing facts were established at trial, neither *D* nor *T* could deny that its carelessness was a cause of *P*'s injury: the carelessness of each was required in order for *P* to have been injured. *See* Stemler v. Burke, 344 F.2d 393 (6th Cir. 1965). Likewise, if, after the accident, *P* is rushed to a hospital and then suffers an additional injury via the malpractice of emergency room doctor *E*, then, with respect to that injury, the respective carelessness of *D*, *T*, and *E* each functioned as an actual cause of the injury.

3. *Actual Versus Proximate Cause Again.* To say that the carelessness of each of two or more actors helped to bring about plaintiff's injury is *not necessarily* to say that each should be held responsible or liable for that injury. Some actual causes of a plaintiff's harm, as we will see, will not be deemed *proximate* causes of that harm, in which case no liability attaches to those causes. For example, whether, in the foregoing example, *D* and *T* will be liable for the injury *P* suffered most immediately through *E*'s subsequent malpractice will turn on whether *D*'s and *T*'s respective acts can be deemed to have been proximate causes of that injury. *See* Chapter 5.

4. *Multiple Necessary Conditions Versus Apportionment of Liability.* Even if multiple negligent actors such as *D*, *T*, and *E* are all deemed responsible for having actually and proximately caused a plaintiff's injury, there still remains the question of how to apportion their responsibility: that is, of who among them must pay what percentage of plaintiff's damages. In *McDonald*, the court concluded that "a joint judgment could be recovered against [both defendants]." By saying this, it applied a particular rule of apportionment known as joint and several liability. Joint and several liability is a complex idea. For now, we can say that it entitles a not-at-fault plaintiff such as McDonald to recover up to 100 percent of her damages from any one of two or more defendants who is found liable for her injuries. As a result, McDonald was in this case free to recover all her damages from Robinson, all from Padzensky, or some from each. (However, she was not allowed to recover more than 100 percent in total.) Apportionment is governed by a separate body of rules discussed in Chapter 8.

5. *Breaches of Affirmative Duties.* A breach of an affirmative duty to protect or rescue can count as one of two or more but-for causes of a victim's injury. *See, e.g.*, LeJeune v. Allstate Ins. Co., 365 So. 2d 471 (La. 1978) (jury could find that a deputy sheriff's failure to clear an intersection for a funeral procession was, along with the careless driving of defendant driver, a cause of plaintiff hearse-driver's injuries). Assume that utility company *U* owes pedestrians and drivers a duty to build telephone poles capable of withstanding a modest (say, 10 mph) impact from an ordinary

passenger vehicle without toppling over. Assume further that *U* breached that duty by failing to inspect or test its poles, which turn out not to be capable of meeting the 10 mph standard. Negligent driver *R* crashes into one of *U*'s poles, causing it to fall on *P*, who sues *R* and *U* for negligence. Can *U* be held liable? Under what circumstances? *See* Bernier v. Boston Edison Co., 403 N.E.2d 391 (Mass. 1980) (utility held liable as one cause of plaintiff's injury given evidence that the driver was not going so fast as to render the utility's negligence causally irrelevant).

6. *Plaintiff's Fault as One Among Multiple Necessary Conditions.* In any case in which the factfinder determines that the plaintiff's recovery must be reduced, or her claim denied, because her own fault contributed, along with the defendant's fault, to her injury, the factfinder is treating the plaintiff's faulty conduct as one of (at least) two careless but-for causes of her injury. *See* Chapter 7 (discussing principles of comparative responsibility).

Check Your Understanding

Still More Flying Coffee

Consider the following variations on the coffee-cup scenarios described at the outset of this chapter. Assume for purposes of the following question that *A* and *B* are driving on the same city block at the same time and that both carelessly toss half-filled coffee cups out of their respective car windows while driving. Assume further that actual causation will be determined by applying the but-for test.

1. *A*'s carelessly tossed cup splatters on *Z*'s windshield. In an unlikely twist of fate, *B*'s cup also strikes *Z*'s windshield at the same moment. Seconds later, *Z*'s car strikes the nearby lamppost. What must *Z* establish in order to prove that *A*'s carelessness was an actual cause of her injury? What must *Z* establish in order to prove that *B*'s carelessness was an actual cause of her injury?
2. *A*'s carelessly tossed cup splatters on *Z*'s windshield. Startled from the impact of *A*'s cup, *Z* swerves toward the lamppost. In an unlikely twist of fate, *B*'s cup hits the windshield of a nearby car being driven by *Y*. *Y*, startled from the impact of *B*'s cup, swerves and crashes into *Z*'s car, as a result of which *Z*'s car never reaches the lamppost. *Z* is injured in the crash. What must *Z* establish in order to prove that *A*'s carelessness was an actual cause of her injury? What must *Z* establish in order to prove that *B*'s carelessness was an actual cause of her injury? Is *Z* likely to prevail on a negligence claim against *Y*? If not, is it because *Z* will be unable to prove that *Y* caused her injury?

Ford Motor Co. v. Boomer

736 S.E.2d 724 (Va. 2013)

Millette, Jr., J. These paired appeals arise out of a jury verdict against Honeywell International Incorporated[1] and Ford Motor Company for the wrongful death of James D. Lokey, caused by mesothelioma resulting from exposure to asbestos in

1. Honeywell, the successor-in-interest to Bendix, is referred to herein as Bendix.

dust from Bendix brakes installed in Ford and other vehicles. On appeal, Ford assigns error to: (1) the circuit court's jury instructions as to causation; (2) its admission of plaintiff's expert testimony; (3) the finding of evidence sufficient to show that Ford's failure to warn was the proximate cause of the harm; and (4) the finding of evidence sufficient to show proximate cause despite a more likely alternative. Bendix echoes the first three arguments. For the reasons stated herein, we reverse and remand.

I. Background

Lokey was diagnosed with mesothelioma, a malignant cancer of the pleura of the lungs, in 2005. He passed away in 2007 due to complications related to his disease. Lokey testified at trial via a *de bene esse* deposition taken prior to his death.* His son-in-law, Walter Boomer, is the Administrator of his estate. The relevant facts as presented at trial were as follows:

Lokey served as a Virginia State Trooper for 30 years. Beginning in 1965 or 1966, for approximately seven and a half to eight years, his duties required that he observe vehicle inspections wherein mechanics used compressed air to blow out brake debris (dust) to allow for a visual inspection of the brakes. Lokey testified that, during these years, he observed vehicle inspections in approximately 70 garages a month, for five to six hours a day, ten days each month. Lokey testified to standing within ten feet of the inspectors who were blowing out brake linings with compressed air, and that these blow outs were a fairly common practice in inspections at the time. He also recalled breathing in visible dust in the garages, which to his knowledge had no specialized ventilation systems. He testified that he was not provided protective clothing or masks or warned that breathing brake dust was harmful to his health.

Lokey testified that his rotations included supervising inspections at a Ford dealership and that he was sure he was present when this process was being done on Ford cars. Due to the time period in which he inspected cars, he testified that the vast majority of the cars being inspected at the garages he visited were American-made cars. He also specifically remembered Oldsmobile dealers on his rotation. He testified that the garages he visited in these locations and others did both inspection work and regular mechanical work in adjacent bays, the details of which he was not aware.

Lokey could not identify the type of brake linings being inspected. The Administrator of Lokey's estate presented circumstantial evidence as to the likely manufacturer of the brake linings at trial based on the testimony of a former assistant factory manager for Bendix in charge of "organic products" (including asbestos products). The witness testified that Bendix manufactured asbestos-containing friction products for brakes, including primary brake linings manufactured by Bendix that were approximately fifty percent asbestos material. He also testified that Bendix likely held one hundred percent of the market for Oldsmobile up to the late 1960s or early 1970s, until front disc brakes were phased in. He testified that they also began providing materials for Fords in 1955 and had one hundred percent of the new Ford market share for the 15 years prior to 1983. He also stated that he believed

* A *de bene esse* ("of well being") deposition is one taken of a witness in anticipation that she will be unavailable to testify at trial. — Eds.

they had one hundred percent of the replacement market for brake linings for Oldsmobiles and Fords in the late 1960s.

Dr. John C. Maddox and Dr. Laura Welch, experts for Lokey's estate, testified that chrysotile asbestos, the type of asbestos found in brakes, can cause mesothelioma. They opined that the exposure to dust from Bendix brakes and brakes in new Ford cars were both substantial contributing factors to Lokey's mesothelioma. Maddox and Welch opined that the current medical evidence suggests that there is no safe level of chrysotile asbestos exposure above background levels in the ambient air.

Lokey also testified that he worked as a pipefitter at the Norfolk Naval Shipyard for slightly over a year in the early 1940s. Lokey testified that his own work and the work of those immediately around him involved packing sand into pipes so that the pipes could be bent to fit the ships. He had no personal knowledge of any exposure to asbestos in the shipyard. Lokey admitted, however, that he worked in a large warehouse and was unaware of all the work done and products used in the warehouse, whether asbestos products were present, or whether there was any ventilation.

Dr. David H. Garabrant, expert for the defense, testified that people who work around asbestos-containing brakes are at no higher risk of developing mesothelioma than those who do not, but noted documented evidence of increased risk of mesothelioma for those who worked around shipyards, both directly with asbestos material and also in its vicinity. Dr. Victor Roggli, a pathologist presented by the defense, testified that he found amosite asbestos fibers in Lokey's lung tissue. Following his analysis of Lokey's lung fibers, he opined that Lokey's profile was more consistent with a person who had exposure to amosite asbestos at a shipyard sixty years ago than a person exposed to chrysotile brake products. Dr. Roggli admitted, however, that his investigation did not include the pleura of the lungs and that he opined that each and every exposure to asbestos above background level experienced by an individual is a substantial contributing factor in the development of mesothelioma.

The trial court instructed the jury on negligence and breach of warranty theories. The jury found in favor of the estate as to negligence and awarded damages in the amount of $282,685.69. . . . Bendix and Ford have timely appealed.

II. Discussion

A. Jury Instructions as to Causation

The circuit court instructed the jury on proximate cause but also on five occasions instructed the jury to determine whether Ford's or Bendix' negligence was a "substantial contributing factor" to Lokey's mesothelioma. Defendants challenge the use of the substantial contributing factor language as contrary to prevailing Virginia law as to causation. The determination of whether a jury instruction accurately states the relevant law is a question of law that we review de novo.

The circuit court defined proximate cause in Jury Instruction 19 as follows:

> A proximate cause of an injury, accident, or damage is a cause which in the [sic] natural and continuous sequence produces the accident, injury, or damage. It is a cause without which the accident, injury or damage would not have occurred.

This is a plain-language adaptation of the long-accepted definition of proximate cause set forth by this Court in *Wells v. Whitaker*, 151 S.E.2d 422, 428 (Va. 1966): "The proximate cause of an event is that act or omission which, in natural and continuous sequence, unbroken by an efficient intervening cause, produces that event, and without which that event would not have occurred."

We said in *Wells* that the first element of proximate cause, causation in fact, is "often described as the 'but for' or *sine qua non* rule."[11] *Id.* We explained that "[t]o impose liability upon one person for damages incurred by another, it must be shown that the negligent conduct was a necessary physical antecedent of the damages." *Id.*

The requirement of but-for causation came with a caveat, however: "The 'but for' test is a useful rule of exclusion in all but one situation: where two causes concur to bring about an event and either alone *would have been sufficient* to bring about an identical result." 151 S.E.2d at 428 n. 1 (emphasis added).

In such a scenario, our law provides a means of holding a defendant liable if his or her negligence is one of multiple concurrent causes which proximately caused an injury, when any of the multiple causes would have each have been a sufficient cause. . . .

Causation in a mesothelioma case, however, presents a challenge for the courts beyond even our standard concurring negligence instruction. Mesothelioma is a signature disease: it was uncontroverted at trial that the cause of mesothelioma is exposure to asbestos at some point during an individual's lifetime. The long latency period of the disease, however, makes it exceedingly difficult to pinpoint when the harmful asbestos exposure occurred and, in the presence of multiple exposures, equally difficult to distinguish the causative exposure(s). *See Locke v. Johns–Manville Corp.*, 275 S.E.2d 900, 905 (Va. 1981) (discussing the latency period between the exposure to asbestos, the later onset of the "harm" in mesothelioma cases — the development of the cancer — and, finally, the development of noticeable mesothelioma symptoms). . . .

Further complicating the issue, although numerous individuals were exposed to varying levels of asbestos during its widespread industrial use before safety measures became standard, not all persons exposed developed mesothelioma. It is not currently known why some are more susceptible than others to developing mesothelioma, or why even low levels of exposure may cause mesothelioma in some individuals while others exposed to higher dosages never develop the disease. Thus, in the context of a lifetime of potential asbestos exposures, designating particular exposures as causative presents courts with a unique challenge.

Despite this lack of certainty, we task juries with determining liability in multiple exposure mesothelioma cases. Virginia statutory and case law makes clear that the Commonwealth permits recovery for parties injured by asbestos exposure, including those with mesothelioma, even when a jury must draw inferences from indirect facts to determine whether an exposure was causal. The question before us is whether the

11. We note that there are inconsistencies in the national legal nomenclature as to whether cause-in-fact is considered to be a subset of proximate cause or whether cause-in-fact, in addition to proximate cause (defined as additional legal restrictions as to liability), together create legal cause. We opt for the former nomenclature as it is the more widely used terminology in Virginia as well as the terminology used by the circuit court in this case.

Commonwealth's approach to proximate cause should be modified to allow such recovery in multiple-causation cases and, if so, how. Certainly, if the traditional but-for definition of proximate cause was invoked, the injured party would virtually never be able to recover for damages arising from mesothelioma in the context of multiple exposures, because injured parties would face the difficult if not impossible task of proving that any one single source of exposure, in light of other exposures, was the sole but-for cause of the disease.

The circuit court, in an admirable attempt to offer guidance to the jury as to this point, invoked a supplemental term in its jury instructions: "substantial contributing factor." For example, in Instruction 16, the court stated:

> Before the plaintiff is entitled to recover from either defendant on the negligence theory, he must prove by a preponderance of the evidence each of the following elements against the defendant: Number 1, exposure to asbestos-containing products manufactured and/or sold by defendant was a *substantial contributing factor* in causing plaintiff's injury; Number 2, at the time of Mr. Lokey's exposure, defendants knew or had reason to know that its products could cause injury to persons when the product was being used in a reasonably foreseeable manner; Number 3, defendant failed to adequately warn of such a danger; and Number 4, defendants' failure to adequately warn of the danger was a *substantial contributing factor* in causing plaintiff's injury.

(Emphasis added.) . . .

In the last several decades, with the rise of asbestos-based lawsuits, the "substantial contributing factor" instruction has become prominent in some other jurisdictions. *See, e.g., Lohrmann v. Pittsburgh Corning Corp.*, 782 F.2d 1156, 1162–63 (4th Cir.1986) (upholding Maryland's substantial contributing factor standard in an asbestosis case); *Rutherford v. Owens–Illinois, Inc.*, 941 P.2d 1203, 1219 (Cal. 1997) (approving the substantial contributing factor test in California); *Borg–Warner Corp. v. Flores*, 232 S.W.3d 765, 773–74 (Tex. 2007) (permitting a substantial factor test in a Texas asbestosis case). "Substantial factor" language was also utilized in the Restatement (First) and Restatement (Second) of Torts. The phrase "substantial contributing factor" is not grounded, however, in the jurisprudence of this Court: we have not, in the history of our case law, ever invoked this language.

Considering it now for the first time, we find several problems with the substantial contributing factor instruction. As an initial matter, the circuit court in this case never defined the term "substantial contributing factor" in its jury instructions. It is not clear whether it was meant to alter the proximate cause requirement in some way, such as reducing the cause-in-fact requirement by referring to a "contributing" factor rather than an independent but-for cause. The term substantial contributing factor could be construed to mean any cause that is more than a merely *de minimis* factor. Conversely, the invocation of the term "substantial" could be interpreted to raise the standard for proof of causation beyond a mere preponderance of the evidence to some more elevated standard. In sum, some jurors might construe the term to lower the threshold of proof required for causation while others might interpret it to mean the opposite. We do not believe that substantial contributing factor has a single, common-sense meaning, and we conclude that a reasonable juror could be confused as to the quantum of evidence required to prove causation in the face of both a substantial contributing factor and a proximate cause instruction.

Our concerns are bolstered by the fact that variant definitions have arisen across those jurisdictions invoking substantial contributing factor language in their asbestos litigation. *Compare Lohrmann,* 782 F.2d at 1163 (holding that Maryland's substantial contributing factor standard required a "frequency, regularity and proximity test" to protect asbestos defendants from being held liable on insufficient facts), *with Rutherford,* 941 P.2d at 1219 (defining substantial contributing factor in California to include exposures that increase the plaintiff's "risk" of developing cancer), *and Flores,* 232 S.W.3d at 773–74 (holding that defendant-specific evidence relating to *dose* was necessary to determine whether exposure from a defendant was a substantial factor in causing the disease in Texas).

Moreover, we agree with the explicit rejection of substantial contributing factor language in the recent Restatement (Third) of Torts: Liability for Physical and Emotional Harm (2010). The Restatement (Second) of Torts used substantial factor language, stating that, absent an independent but-for cause, "[i]f two forces are actively operating . . . and each of itself is sufficient to bring about harm to another, [one] actor's negligence may be found to be a substantial factor in bringing it about." Restatement (Second) of Torts § 432 (1965).

The latest revision of the Restatement, however, deliberately abandoned this language, explaining:

> [T]he substantial-factor rubric tends to obscure, rather than to assist, explanation and clarification of the basis of [causation] decisions. The element that must be established, by whatever standard of proof, is the but-for or necessary-condition standard of this Section. Section 27 provides a rule for finding each of two acts that are elements of sufficient competing causal sets to be factual causes without employing the substantial-factor language of the prior Torts Restatements. There is no question of degree for either of these concepts.

Restatement (Third) of Torts § 26, cmt. j. The comment also specifically references the tendency of courts to at times interpret the language as either raising or lowering the factual causation standard, leading to inconsistent and inaccurate statements of law. *Id.* If courts cannot be relied upon to consistently construe the language, we cannot expect lay jurors to accomplish the same task.

The Restatement (Third) of Torts relies instead on the combination of sections 26 and 27:

> **§ 26 Factual Cause**
>
> Tortious conduct must be a factual cause of harm for liability to be imposed. Conduct is a factual cause of harm when the harm would not have occurred absent the conduct. Tortious conduct may also be a factual cause of harm under § 27.
>
> **§ 27 Multiple Sufficient Causes**
>
> If multiple acts occur, each of which under § 26 alone would have been a factual cause of the physical harm at the same time in the absence of the other act(s), each is regarded as a factual cause of the harm.

This model, as explicated in the comments, is quite consistent with our statements in *Wells* regarding concurring causation. The rationale articulated in comment c of § 27 echoes the logic behind our long history of recognizing concurring causes:

> A defendant whose tortious act was fully capable of causing the plaintiff's harm should not escape liability merely because of the fortuity of another sufficient cause. . . . When two tortious multiple sufficient causes exist, to deny liability would make the plaintiff worse off due to multiple tortfeasors than would have been the case if only one of the tortfeasors had existed. Perhaps most significant is the recognition that, while *the but-for standard provided in § 26 is a helpful method for identifying causes, it is not the exclusive means for determining a factual cause. Multiple sufficient causes are also factual causes* because we recognize them as such in our common understanding of causation, even if the but-for standard does not. Thus, the standard for causation in this Section comports with deep-seated intuitions about causation and fairness in attributing responsibility.

Restatement (Third) of Torts § 27, cmt. c. (emphasis added). The multiple sufficient cause analysis allows multiple tortfeasors to be found jointly and severally liable.

The Reporters Note to § 27, comment b, specifically observes that some jurisdictions use the term "concurrent causes" rather than multiple sufficient cause. Indeed, multiple-exposure mesothelioma cases fit quite squarely with our line of concurring cause cases, "where two causes concur to bring about an event and either alone *would have been sufficient* to bring about an identical result." *Wells,* 151 S.E.2d at 428 n. 1 (emphasis added). . . .

Unfortunately, our model jury instruction for concurring negligence invokes only general language that each is a "proximate cause" of the harm, rather than more specifically articulating the standard indicated in *Wells.* The standard that, in this case, exposure to the defendant's product alone must have been *sufficient to have caused the harm* is both an accurate articulation of our concurring cause law and perfectly plain to the average juror. This standard constitutes the cause-in-fact portion of the proximate cause requirement in concurring cause cases. The factfinder is left, having heard the nature of the exposures to each of the products at issue, as well as the medical testimony as to the requisite exposure necessary to cause mesothelioma, to determine whether the exposure attributable to each defendant was more likely than not sufficient to have caused the harm.

While it might be clearly seen in a car accident or converging fires that both acts contributed in some degree to the harm, the nature of mesothelioma leaves greater uncertainty as to which exposure or exposures in fact constituted the triggering event. This is, however, a distinction without a difference: if the jurors, after hearing the testimony and evidence, believe that a negligent exposure was more likely than not *sufficient* to have triggered the harm, then the defendant can be found liable in the same way that a jury can conclude that a driver in a multiple-car collision or the negligent party in one of two converging fires is liable.

Established Virginia law indicates that in order for acts of negligence to constitute concurring causes, it is not necessary that concurring acts occur simultaneously.

Dickenson v. Tabb, 156 S.E.2d 795, 802 (1967). This appears at first glance to be contrary to the language in the latest Restatement:

> **§ 27 Multiple Sufficient Causes**
> If multiple acts occur, each of which under § 26 alone would have been a factual cause of the physical harm *at the same time* in the absence of the other act(s), each is regarded as a factual cause of the harm.

Restatement (Third) of Torts § 27 (emphasis added). We note, however, that the phrase "at the same time" is placed so as to modify "factual cause of the physical harm" rather than "acts occur." We thus read this to be consistent with our precedent. The acts themselves do not have to be concurrent, so long as they are "operating and sufficient to cause the harm contemporaneously." Restatement (Third) of Torts § 27, cmt. e. We have held, as to mesothelioma, that the "harm" occurs not at the time of exposure but at the time when competent medical evidence indicates that the cancer first exists and causes injury. *Locke,* 275 S.E.2d at 905. Recognizing that this date, if possible to isolate, may be decades after an injured party's exposure(s) to asbestos, *id.,* it may often be the case that any exposure sufficient to cause harm that occurred prior to the development of the cancer may constitute one of multiple sufficient causes under the Restatement and a concurring cause in Virginia.

The exposure must have been "a" sufficient cause: if more than one party caused a sufficient exposure, each is responsible. Other sufficient causes, whether innocent or arising from negligence, do not provide a defense. Excluding other exposures from the pool of multiple sufficient causes will require competent medical testimony indicating whether the timing of exposure could possibly have caused the cancer. Defendants with sufficient exposures that occur after the cancer has already developed cannot be held liable.

It must be noted that there is a separate comment under § 27, entitled "Toxic substances and disease," that appears to offer an alternative approach to causation specific to disease. *See* Restatement (Third) of Torts § 27, cmt. g. This approach allows for a finding of causation when multiple exposures combine to reach the threshold necessary to cause a disease, allowing parties who were responsible for some portion of that threshold to be held liable. While it may be the case that this dose-related approach to causation is indeed appropriate for some cancers or diseases, we do not find it to be necessarily appropriate for mesothelioma, in light of the current state of medical knowledge. This comment assumes an identifiable threshold level of exposure triggering a disease. Given the current state of medical knowledge, we find the general approach described in comments a through e of section 27 to be more helpful in mesothelioma and more consistent with our case law.

Here, for the first time, we are called upon to rule explicitly as to the causation standard appropriate for mesothelioma. We find that in concurring causation cases, the "sufficient"-to-have-caused standard as elaborated above is the proper way to define the cause-in-fact element of proximate cause. We note that, while the Commonwealth currently only offers a model jury instruction as to concurrent negligence, concurring causes are not so limited: use of the multiple-sufficient-causes approach remains appropriate whether the concurring causes are all tortious in nature or whether some are innocent.

While we reject defendants' strict interpretation of sole but-for cause argued to the circuit court at trial, we nonetheless conclude that the trial court erred in failing to sustain the defendants' objections to the substantial contributing factor jury instructions. We remand for further proceedings consistent with the multiple sufficient cause analysis.

B. Alternative Causes

Ford alleges that the evidence presented was insufficient to establish that exposure to brake dust from Ford products proximately caused Lokey's mesothelioma when evidence demonstrated a more likely alternative cause (specifically, the earlier alleged exposure to amosite asbestos at the shipyard). Based on our holding above, the plaintiff must show that it is more likely than not that Lokey's alleged exposure to dust from Ford brakes occurred prior to the development of Lokey's cancer and was sufficient to cause his mesothelioma. Given that this approach differs from that taken in the circuit court, we do not find it appropriate to rule on the sufficiency of the evidence at trial at this time.

. . . .

D. Failure to Warn and Proximate Cause

Both defendants allege that the plaintiff failed to present evidence sufficient to show that their failure to warn was the proximate cause of Lokey's mesothelioma. Specifically, they allege the absence of evidence sufficient to show that Lokey's behavior would have changed had the defendants offered sufficient warnings. As a result, defendants argue that plaintiff lacks sufficient evidence to find Ford or Bendix liable. As this issue is both independent of the multiple-sufficient-cause proximate cause analysis addressed in Part II.A, *supra*, and would be dispositive if defendants were correct, we will reach this assignment of error.

In his . . . deposition, Lokey was never asked if his behavior would have been changed had he known that he was inhaling a potentially fatal substance. Lokey, deceased by the time of trial, was obviously unavailable for further questioning. While Virginia does not observe a heeding presumption,[4] we have clearly already ruled on this issue, stating:

> [The injured party], of course, was unable, because of his disability, to tell the jury whether, had a warning been provided, he would have heeded it in the manner suggested by [the expert witness]. Nor could anyone have spoken for [the injured party]. But frequently material facts are not proven by direct evidence. A verdict may be properly based upon reasonable inferences drawn from the facts. If facts are present from which proper inferences may be drawn this is sufficient. Here, from the circumstances that were proven below, and according to the ordinary experience of mankind, the jury was warranted in the conclusion that [the] injury would not have occurred had [a warning] been given.

4. A heeding presumption is "a rebuttable presumption that an injured product user would have followed a warning label had the product manufacturer provided one." Black's Law Dictionary 1305 (9th ed. 2009).

Hoar v. Great E. Resort Mgmt., Inc., 506 S.E.2d 777, 786 (Va. 1998) (internal quotation marks and citations omitted) (final modification in original).

We find this case to be precisely on point. Reasonable jurors are entitled to utilize their own experiences, as well as evidence as to the character of the injured party and the known asbestos dangers at the time the warning should have been given, in order to draw conclusions as to the content of an adequate warning and whether Lokey would have heeded such a warning.

. . . . Lokey's son-in-law testified that Lokey was a "perfectionist," a "by-the-book guy. Everything was to be done correctly." The jury was provided with ample evidence to allow it to conclude that a reasonable person who was concerned for his or her safety and who, like Lokey, was inclined to follow recommended procedures and guidelines, would have heeded a warning had one been given.

. . . .

The jury was . . . left with evidence of the known dangers of asbestos and could reasonably infer that Lokey, if properly informed of these dangers at the time, would have taken precautionary measures. We therefore find no defect in the circuit court's conclusion that there was evidence sufficient for a jury to find that the failure to warn was the proximate cause of the injury.

III. Conclusion

For the foregoing reasons, we reverse and remand for further proceedings.

Wannall v. Honeywell International, Inc.

292 F.R.D. 26 (D.D.C. 2013), *aff'd* 75 F.3d 425 (D.C. Cir. 2014)

Howell, J. This is a products liability case involving allegations that the defendant's automobile brakes, containing chrysotile asbestos fibers, caused the decedent's lung cancer. This case is set for trial on May 20, 2013, and among the thirty pre-trial motions filed is a motion to reconsider the denial of the defendant's motion for summary judgment. The primary basis for that motion is the intervening decision in *Ford Motor Co. v. Boomer,* 736 S.E.2d 724 (Va. 2013), in which the Supreme Court of Virginia abrogated the "substantial contributing factor" test as an appropriate articulation of proximate cause under Virginia tort law. In opposition to the defendant's motion for reconsideration, the plaintiff submitted a revised expert report, which the plaintiff argued creates a genuine issue of material fact for trial on causation. The defendant subsequently moved to strike that declaration on a number of grounds. For the reasons explained below, the Court grants both motions of the defendant to strike the revised expert report and for summary judgment in its favor.

I. Background

An exhaustive recitation of the factual background of this case is not necessary to understand the Court's reasoning on the two motions considered in this opinion. Therefore, the Court will limit its summary of the background to the facts bearing on those two motions.

As referenced above, the decedent died on July 28, 2010 from malignant pleural mesothelioma — a form of lung cancer. The plaintiff claims that the decedent's lung cancer was caused by exposure to chrysotile asbestos fibers contained in automobile brakes manufactured by Bendix Corporation. As the defendant concedes "it is undisputed that . . . [the decedent] performed shade tree automobile repairs, which to some extent included brake repairs." The term "shade tree automobile repairs" refers to the fact that, although he was not licensed as a mechanic, the decedent "did work on automobiles for [himself], [his] family and the neighborhood whenever they asked [him] to do it," which included "changing batteries, changing starter motors, generators, alternators, tires and brakes." The parties dispute the precise extent to which the decedent was exposed to asbestos fibers from Bendix brakes, though the decedent testified in his . . . deposition that he filed and beveled "hundreds and hundreds" of Bendix brake shoes in his lifetime. The decedent further testified that he customarily used Bendix brakes, and he would ask for Bendix brakes by name "because [he] liked their product."

Both before and during his "shade tree mechanic" work, the decedent was also exposed to asbestos when he served in the Navy and when he worked as a trades helper at Fort Belvoir in Fairfax County, Virginia. In fact, the plaintiff not only concedes that the decedent was exposed to asbestos in the Navy, but he also concedes that "[the decedent]'s exposure to asbestos during his Naval service caused his mesothelioma." In light of the decedent's Naval and Fort Belvoir asbestos exposure, there are at least three potential causes of the decedent's cancer: the Naval exposure, the Fort Belvoir exposure, and the Bendix brake exposure.

The decedent and his wife originally filed this lawsuit . . . in D.C. Superior Court against thirty-six separate defendants. The case was removed to this court . . . and transferred to the Eastern District of Pennsylvania (the "MDL Court") by the Judicial Panel on Multidistrict Litigation for coordinated pretrial proceedings.* . . . While this case was pending in the MDL Court, the defendant moved for summary judgment on the plaintiff's claims. . . . In denying that motion, the MDL Court cited the decedent's deposition testimony as well as the testimony of the plaintiff's experts "that [the decedent]'s exposure to Bendix brakes [was] a substantial cause of his mesothelioma." Specifically, the MDL Court cited the testimony of Dr. Steven Markowitz, who opined that the decedent's exposure to Bendix brakes "'was significant and contributed to his over-all exposure, [and] that his mesothelioma was caused by his cumulative exposure to asbestos.'" In the end, the MDL Court denied summary judgment to the defendant because "Plaintiff has raised a genuine issue of fact as to whether Honeywell's products, specifically, were a substantial contributing factor in causing Decedent's injuries." [The case was then transferred back from the MDL Court to this district court — Eds.]

---

* The Judicial Panel on Multidistrict Litigation is authorized to order the transfer of suits that are pending in multiple federal district courts, and that raise common questions of fact, to a single federal district court in order to have the transferee ("MDL") court resolve pretrial issues pertaining to those common questions. If a transferred suit is not resolved in the pre-trial phase, the MDL court is required to return the suit to the district court from which it came for trial. — Eds.

On January 10, 2013 . . . after this case was remanded to this Court, the Virginia Supreme Court decided *Boomer*. . . . The similarity between *Boomer* and the instant case is . . . self-evident. . . . The Virginia Supreme Court, "[c]onsidering it . . . for the first time," rejected the "substantial contributing factor" instruction primarily because "a reasonable juror could be confused as to the quantum of evidence required to prove causation in the face of both a substantial contributing factor and a proximate cause instruction." *Boomer* at 730. Nevertheless, the court also held, in agreement with a prior line of Virginia precedent, that a plaintiff could still recover from a defendant in a multiple-exposure asbestos case if the plaintiff could prove "that a negligent [asbestos] exposure was more likely than not *sufficient* to have triggered the harm." *Id.* at 731 (emphasis in original).

On January 28, 2013—less than three weeks after *Boomer* was decided—the defendant filed a motion to reconsider the denial of its motion for summary judgment in light of *Boomer*. In that motion, the defendant argued that summary judgment is appropriate in light of *Boomer* because the plaintiff "has failed to provide any specific evidence that [the decedent]'s alleged exposure to Bendix brakes . . . was a sufficient cause of his injury." On this same point, the defendant argued that "Plaintiff's own experts contend that [the decedent]'s exposure to Bendix brakes was merely part of his cumulative exposure to asbestos and cause of [the decedent]'s disease." After reviewing the testimony and opinions of the plaintiff's experts—in particular Dr. Markowitz, the plaintiff's primary causation expert—the defendant argued that "Plaintiff has not offered expert evidence to opine that [the decedent]'s alleged lifetime dosage is more likely than not a sufficient cause of his mesothelioma" and "Plaintiff has offered *no* evidence to quantify [the decedent]'s exposure to Bendix brakes."

. . . .

In opposing the defendant's motion for reconsideration, the plaintiff made several arguments, some of which will be discussed in more detail below. Importantly, one of the plaintiff's arguments was that "[e]xpert testimony demonstrates that the exposure to Bendix brake dust described by [the decedent] is sufficient to cause [the decedent]'s mesothelioma." This statement was based on a declaration by Dr. Markowitz, completed on February 8, 2013, after the defendant had filed its motion for reconsideration. In that new declaration, Dr. Markowitz offered four "additional opinions," one of which was that "[the decedent]'s exposure to asbestos from Bendix asbestos-containing brake lining—as well as the non-friction exposures identified in my report of November 22, 2011 [sic] (Naval and Fort Belvoir exposures)—are *each independently sufficient* to cause mesothelioma in and of themselves" (emphasis added). Dr. Markowitz had never before opined that the decedent's exposure to Bendix brakes was independently sufficient to have caused his cancer. The plaintiff, in his opposition, also pointed to the deposition testimony of the plaintiff's pathology expert, Dr. Jerrold Abraham, who opined that "if [the decedent] had only that [Navy exposure], that would have been the only cause. If he had other exposures [*i.e.*, brake exposures] and not that [Navy exposure], those [brake exposures] would have been the only cause."

In response to the submission of the February 8, 2013 Markowitz Declaration, the defendant filed a motion to strike the declaration as both untimely and inconsistent with Dr. Markowitz's prior opinions. Specifically, the defendant argued that (1) the Markowitz Declaration is untimely under Federal Rules of Civil Procedure 26 and 37;

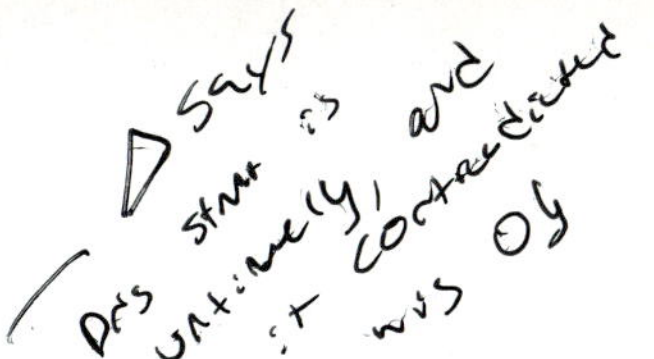

and (2) the Markowitz Declaration constitutes a "sham affidavit" because it contradicts his prior sworn statements. In the alternative, the defendant also contended that the new Markowitz Declaration "does not satisfy the standard under *Boomer*" because it "lacks any support as to the level of exposure [the decedent] allegedly experienced or that this particular level of exposure was sufficient to cause mesothelioma."

. . . .

III. Discussion

[The court granted Bendix's motion to strike the February 8, 2013 Markowitz Declaration on the ground that it was untimely. — Eds.]

. . . .

C. Defendant's Motion for Reconsideration

. . . . The Court concludes that the defendant's motion for reconsideration should be granted, regardless of whether the Markowitz Declaration were a part of the summary judgment record.

. . . .

The Court will begin by revisiting *Boomer* to crystallize exactly what evidence is required to create a genuine issue of material fact regarding causation in a multiple-exposure asbestos case like the instant one. As the Virginia Supreme Court stated, a defendant in such a case may only be found liable "if the jurors, after hearing the testimony and evidence, believe that a negligent exposure was more likely than not sufficient to have triggered the harm." *Boomer,* 736 S.E.2d at 731 (emphasis omitted). . . . Thus, it is clear that, at a minimum, in order to survive summary judgment, a plaintiff must come forth with some medical or scientific evidence that exposure to the defendant's product was sufficient, in and of itself, to trigger the injury.

The *Boomer* court, however, did not stop there. The Virginia Supreme Court also described the kind of expert testimony that is required to establish liability under the "sufficiency" standard. First, *Boomer* stated — not once, but twice — that "experts must opine as to what level of exposure is sufficient to cause mesothelioma, and whether the levels of exposure at issue in this case were sufficient." *Id.* at 733. . . . In stating this, *Boomer* mandated a two-part showing: "[1] what level of exposure is sufficient to cause mesothelioma, and [2] whether the levels of exposure at issue in this case were sufficient." *Id.* at 733. The court further stated that, where a plaintiff has been exposed to multiple sources of asbestos, each of which is potentially sufficient to cause mesothelioma, "[e]xcluding other exposures from the pool of multiple sufficient causes will require competent medical testimony indicating whether the timing of exposure could possibly have caused the cancer." *Id.* at 732. . . .

Having excluded the Markowitz Declaration, the Court will first consider the only other piece of expert testimony, other than the Markowitz Declaration, which the plaintiff cited in opposition to the defendant's motion for reconsideration. That was the deposition testimony of Dr. Jerrold Abraham, in which he opined that "'if [the decedent] had only that [Navy exposure], that would have been the only cause. If he had other exposures [*i.e.,* brake exposures] and not that [Navy exposure], those [brake exposures] would have been the only cause.'" This testimony by Dr. Abraham is insufficient to create a genuine issue of material fact, primarily because it is an opinion about a counterfactual, hypothetical situation not present in this case. As Dr. Abraham stated right before making the statement quoted by the plaintiff: "Well, that's a hypothetical of some other person who had no other exposure. . . ." The bottom line is that Dr. Abraham never opined that the decedent's exposure to Bendix brakes was independently sufficient to trigger his mesothelioma, and thus Dr. Abraham's deposition testimony does not raise a genuine issue of material fact regarding causation under *Boomer.*

The only other evidence that the plaintiff has pointed to in order to create a genuine factual question regarding causation is Dr. Markowitz's prior opinions, contained in his expert report, his March 7, 2011 declaration, and his January 24, 2011 deposition. In fact, plaintiff's counsel asserted at the pretrial conference that "[t]he defendants are setting up a false dichotomy between Markowitz's original pronouncements versus his current pronouncements" because "[t]hey are not mutually exclusive." In fact, plaintiff's counsel went so far as to claim that "[t]he sufficient to have cause[d] position that [Dr. Markowitz] has staked out is effectively a subset of substantially contributed. It's both." To determine the validity of the plaintiff's position, the Court must first provide a brief overview of the various opinions Dr. Markowitz has offered on causation that were not contained in his February 8, 2013 declaration.

In his original, November 22, 2010 expert report, Dr. Markowitz stated the following conclusion regarding the link between the defendant's product and the decedent's injury:

> As you know, most cases of malignant mesothelioma in the United States, especially of the pleura, are caused by prior exposure to asbestos, often occupational in nature. [The decedent] reported such exposure during his work in the Navy, both during the active service and inactive service in the reserves, as well as his work at Fort Belvoir and in performing brake repair replacement over numerous decades. Such exposure is sufficient to cause his malignant mesothelioma.

It is clear that this opinion is insufficient to meet the standard articulated in *Boomer.* Although the final sentence's reference to "[s]uch exposure" is arguably vague, Dr. Markowitz's use of that phrase clearly refers to the multiple exposures that he listed in the previous sentence, which included the decedent's exposures to asbestos in the Navy and at Fort Belvoir. Thus, the Court finds that the only reasonable interpretation of this November 22, 2010 opinion is that Dr. Markowitz believed that *all* of the decedent's cumulative exposures to asbestos, taken together, were sufficient to cause his cancer. That does not satisfy *Boomer* and does not create a genuine issue of material fact on causation.

The plaintiff has also pointed to specific portions of Dr. Markowitz's January 24, 2011 deposition testimony. The first portion of Dr. Markowitz's testimony cited by the plaintiff is as follows:

> Q: All right. And we've just discussed this in the past, but just so we can add it specifically for this case, of those exposures which if any do you believe were responsible for causing [the decedent]'s mesothelioma?

> *A*: Well, I believe that *his exposures were cumulative,* that he had exposures in *each of these settings* that was significant and contributed to his over-all exposure, that *his mesothelioma was caused by his cumulative exposure to asbestos.*

The second portion of the deposition cited by the plaintiff is as follows:

> *Q*: All right. Now, Doctor, we've discussed some of these areas in the past, and I'm just going to jump around very briefly on a couple things to clear up some of my own notes. Do you believe that the[r]e's a threshold for exposure below which asbestos disease, specifically mesothelioma, will not occur?
>
> *A*: No, I don't believe a threshold has been—such a threshold has been established.

Finally, the plaintiff quoted the following from Dr. Markowitz's deposition:

> *Q*: Okay. Does brake dust cause mesothelioma?
>
> . . . .
>
> *A*: To the extent that it includes asbestos fibers and exposure, it would.
>
> *Q*: So—
>
> *A*: It would cause mesothelioma.

None of this testimony, however, creates a genuine factual question regarding causation under *Boomer.* The three opinions quoted can be summarized as follows: (1) the decedent's cumulative exposure to asbestos (including in the Navy and at Fort Belvoir) caused his cancer; (2) no safe level of exposure to asbestos has been established; and (3) at a general level, brake dust containing asbestos causes mesothelioma. None of these opinions single out the decedent's exposure to Bendix brakes and draws a link between *that* exposure and the decedent's cancer. That link, although absent from Dr. Markowitz's deposition testimony, is essential under the *Boomer* sufficiency standard.

Finally, to the extent that the plaintiff has pointed to Dr. Markowitz's March 7, 2011 declaration, that declaration is also clearly insufficient to satisfy the *Boomer* causation standard. In that declaration, Dr. Markowitz opined that "each and every occupational exposure to asbestos-containing products in the Navy, at Fort Belvoir, Virginia and while performing automotive brake work was a substantial contributing factor in causing his malignant mesothelioma and resultant death." It is precisely this sort of opinion that the Virginia Supreme Court rejected. *See Boomer,* 736 S.E.2d at 730 (rejecting the "substantial contributing factor" formulation of proximate causation). . . .

. . . .

In light of the Court's decision to exclude the February 8, 2013 Markowitz Declaration, the preceding holding regarding the plaintiff's other (pre-February 2013) evidence is sufficient to grant the defendant's motion for reconsideration and grant summary judgment to the defendant. Even so, the Court also concludes that the February 8, 2013 Markowitz Declaration would be insufficient to create a genuine issue of material fact regarding causation, even if it had not been excluded.

As discussed above, *Boomer* articulated a two-step showing that is required for a plaintiff to demonstrate liability in a multiple-exposure asbestos cause: "[1] what level of exposure is sufficient to cause mesothelioma, and [2] whether the levels of exposure at issue in this case were sufficient." *Boomer,* 736 S.E.2d at 733. The adequacy of Dr. Markowitz's opinion, therefore, depends upon what the Virginia Supreme Court meant by "level of exposure [that] is sufficient to cause mesothelioma." *See id.* The plaintiff maintains that "level of exposure" does not require "quantification" of exposure. Rather, the plaintiff asserts that, to satisfy *Boomer,* an expert need only opine that the "level of exposure" sufficient to cause mesothelioma is, for example, "any exposure above what is in the background air." The basis for this assertion appears to be that *Boomer* cited with approval a case called *Owens–Corning Fiberglas Corp. v. Watson,* 413 S.E.2d 630 (Va. 1992), which the Court will discuss further below. The plaintiff argued that Dr. Markowitz's opinion satisfies this "level of exposure" requirement by opining that "there's no safe level of exposure to any type of asbestos."

The Court disagrees with the plaintiff's assessment. First, the plaintiff is mistaken regarding the *Boomer* court's citation to the *Watson* case. The *Boomer* court cited that case once for the proposition that "Virginia statutory and case law makes clear that the Commonwealth permits recovery for parties injured by asbestos exposure, including those with mesothelioma, even when a jury must draw inferences from indirect facts to determine whether an exposure was causal." *Boomer,* 736 S.E.2d at 729. In a similar fashion, the *Watson* court held that "the evidence, though circumstantial, was sufficient to support the jury's finding that Watson was exposed to [the defendant's product] and that such exposure was a proximate cause of his death." *Watson,* 413 S.E.2d at 639. None of this has anything to do with the legal standard by which a plaintiff's causation evidence is judged. Rather, *Boomer's* citation to *Watson* addresses the *kind* of evidence that a plaintiff may offer to establish causation in a mesothelioma case. All that *Boomer's* citation to *Watson* means is that a plaintiff may offer circumstantial evidence of exposure in order to establish that a particular exposure was causal, *i.e.,* that a plaintiff was exposed to a particular kind of asbestos prior to developing mesothelioma. Other than observing that "the medical evidence [at trial] revealed that very limited exposure to asbestos fibers can cause mesothelioma," *id.,* the *Watson* court had nothing to say regarding the proper legal standard for determining whether a plaintiff's evidence creates a genuine issue of material fact regarding causation.

Second, the plaintiff's argument draws a false equivalence between (1) the hypothetical opinion that "any exposure [to asbestos] above what is in the background air" is sufficient to cause mesothelioma and (2) Dr. Markowitz's "no safe level" opinion. Specifically, Dr. Markowitz opined for the first time in his February 8, 2013 declaration "that there has not been established a safe level of exposure to asbestos below which individuals are not at risk for developing pleural malignant mesothelioma." This is quite plainly not an opinion regarding "what level of exposure is sufficient to *cause* mesothelioma," *see Boomer,* 736 S.E.2d at 733 (emphasis added). . . .

Dr. Markowitz's opinion about "no safe level" addresses *risk,* not *cause,* and there is a significant distinction between those two concepts. Many substances that we encounter every day raise our risk of developing serious diseases. For example, studies have indicated that consuming alcohol raises one's risk of developing various cancers — particularly cancers of the mouth and throat. Other studies suggest that eating "added sugars" increases one's risk of developing heart disease. Even skipping breakfast has been shown to increase men's risk of developing diabetes by 21%. *See* Rania A. Mekary, *et al., Eating Patterns and Type 2 Diabetes Risk in Men: Breakfast Omission, Eating Frequency, and Snacking,* 95 Am. J. Clinical Nutrition 1182 (2012). This is not the same thing as saying that alcohol causes cancer or eating too much sugar causes heart disease or skipping breakfast causes diabetes. If exposure to a substance is a risk factor for a health outcome, that typically means that exposure to the substance has been associated with that health outcome at a particular level of statistical significance, but correlation does not imply causation. When A is correlated with B, it could be that A causes B, but it could also be that B causes A, or that A and B are both the consequences of a common cause, among other possibilities.

This is only to say that inferring causation is much more complicated than simply observing correlation, and the former should not be confused for the latter. This is *not* to say, however, that exposure to chrysotile asbestos does not cause mesothelioma. The Court lacks the expertise to opine on such matters. The point is that, by merely offering opinions about "risk," neither Dr. Markowitz, nor any of the plaintiff's other experts, has offered an opinion about "what level of exposure is sufficient to *cause* mesothelioma," as required by Virginia law. *See Boomer,* 736 S.E.2d at 733 (emphasis added). Importantly, as discussed below, giving such an opinion may not necessarily require an exact quantification or dosage of chrysotile asbestos that is sufficient to cause mesothelioma. Indeed, *Boomer* implied that "the current state of medical knowledge" has not pinpointed "an identifiable threshold level of exposure [to asbestos] triggering [mesothelioma]," and therefore a "dose-related approach to causation is . . . [not] necessarily appropriate for mesothelioma." *Id.* at 732.

. . . . In short, although *Boomer* does not require evidence about a specific threshold carcinogenic dose of asbestos, it does require expert evidence about the "level of exposure [that] is sufficient to cause mesothelioma," which must constitute more than an opinion about heightened "risk" from exposure to asbestos.

By requiring the presentation of expert evidence regarding a "level of exposure [that] is sufficient to cause mesothelioma," *id., Boomer* also made clear that an expert may not simply take the level of asbestos exposure of a particular plaintiff and opine that such exposure was sufficient to cause the plaintiff's mesothelioma. Instead, the expert must first identify some touchstone "level of exposure [that] is sufficient to cause mesothelioma" and compare that level to the plaintiff's exposure. *See id.* In other words, *Boomer* does not permit a medical expert to offer an *ad hoc* opinion on the sufficiency of a particular exposure, if that opinion is untethered from a scientific benchmark for sufficiency. Yet, that is the opinion that Dr. Markowitz offers in his February 8, 2013 declaration. Dr. Markowitz does not identify any "level of exposure [that] is sufficient to cause mesothelioma," *see id.,* in his February 8, 2013 declaration, but rather only opines that (1) *the decedent's* exposures to asbestos were "each independently sufficient to cause mesothelioma in and of themselves," and (2) "there has not been established a safe level of exposure to asbestos below which individuals are not *at risk* for developing malignant mesothelioma,"(emphasis added). Therefore, even if that declaration were admissible, the medical opinions contained in that declaration would be insufficient to create a genuine issue of material fact regarding causation under *Boomer.*

IV. Conclusion

. . . .

[W]ith or without Dr. Markowitz's February 8, 2013 declaration, the plaintiff cannot create a genuine issue of material fact on the question of factual causation, and therefore the defendant's motion for reconsideration regarding its motion for summary judgment is . . . granted.

NOTES AND QUESTIONS

1. Proof of Actual Causation Revisited: Toxic Torts, General Causation, and Specific Causation. *Boomer* and *Wannall* are examples of suits raising "toxic tort" claims. These claims are characterized by allegations that victims have contracted an illness or disease after having been wrongfully exposed by the defendant to a toxin. Given limitations in scientific and medical knowledge about how certain diseases and illnesses develop, it is often difficult for particular toxic tort plaintiffs to establish actual causation. This problem can be alleviated if the substance in question causes a "signature" illness that appears in connection with exposure to it. (For example, as the court explains, certain lung diseases are known to be caused by asbestos exposure.) In the absence of such a marker, however, medical studies often only suggest — rather than establish as more probable than not — a *general* causal relationship between exposure to a particular substance (e.g, a chemical such as benzene) and a generic disease (e.g., cancer of the liver).

Moreover, even if a plaintiff can establish a general causal linkage between a substance to which she was exposed and her illness, she faces another problem: she must further convince the jury that *her* individual illness is an instance of that general causal linkage. To highlight the contrast between the issue of *general causation* described in the previous paragraph and the issue of whether a particular plaintiff's illness was caused by a given exposure or set of exposures, the latter is often referred to as the issue of *specific causation.* With respect to specific causation, defense counsel will look to establish that factors personal to the plaintiff, such as genetic predispositions, exposure to other environmental factors, and personal health habits (e.g., smoking), acted as the relevant causal agents.

A third problem, apart from proof of general and specific causation, concerns *source identification*: if a plaintiff has been exposed to the same toxic substance through sources (such as working conditions or products) attributable to the carelessness of multiple defendants, she may find it difficult to prove that her exposure to any one source actually caused her injury. This problem is common in asbestos litigation, because plaintiffs often have been exposed to asbestos products manufactured by different companies. Some courts have allowed asbestos plaintiffs facing this sort of situation to prevail by establishing that exposure to each defendant's product would have been sufficient of itself to bring about the plaintiff's disease, even if no one exposure was necessary for that result. (See the discussion of multiple sufficient conditions in Note 5, *infra.*) Courts' willingness to adopt this approach explains why a critical issue in *Wannall* was whether the plaintiff had proven that his exposure to the brake pads was probably sufficient of itself to cause his mesothelioma.

2. Daubert, Experts, and Proof of Causation. Toxic tort plaintiffs will usually have to rely on expert witnesses to make the case that defendant's carelessness operated as an actual cause of their illnesses. As is explained in *Jones v. LA Fitness, supra*, the U.S. Supreme Court's *Daubert* decision directs federal district judges to screen expert witnesses to ensure, as much as possible, that they present jurors with valid hypotheses about issues such as breach and causation. (As also noted in connection with *Jones*, the Federal Rules of Evidence now reflect the *Daubert* approach to expert testimony.) Thus, with respect to actual causation, federal district judges are expected to review the studies on which an expert's testimony will be based to determine if they provide a reliable basis for the expert's assessment of the causal relation between carelessness and injury. If the court determines that there is no reliable basis, the expert is not permitted to testify and the plaintiff's case may well collapse.

As a result of *Daubert*, it is often the case in federal courts that the issue of proof of causation is aired out in the first instance not at trial, but instead at a pre-trial hearing on whether the testimony of the plaintiff's expert is sufficiently well supported to be admitted into evidence at trial. The Third Restatement of Torts has gone to great lengths to aid judges in determining what ought to count as reliable expert testimony on issues of causation. Restatement (Third) of Torts: Liability for Physical and Emotional Harm § 28, comment c (2010).

As noted in *Jones*, the *Daubert* requirement derived from the Supreme Court's interpretation of Rule 702 of the Federal Rules of Evidence, which governs the admissibility of expert testimony in federal courts. Nonetheless, many state courts, in interpreting their states' evidence rules, have followed *Daubert*'s lead. In an important subsequent ruling, the Supreme Court extended the rule of *Daubert* to a wide range of experts, not simply experts opining on medical-scientific evidence. Kumho Tire Co., Ltd. v. Carmichael, 526 U.S. 137 (1999) (applying *Daubert* to an expert testifying on the causes of a tire explosion). Chapter 13 reproduces *Daubert* in part, and provides further discussion of it.

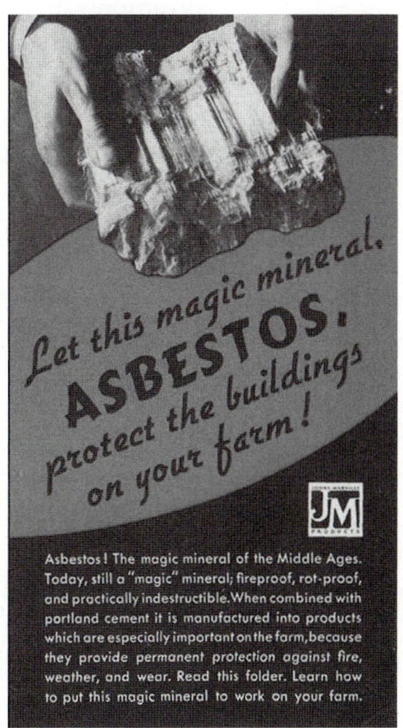

John Mansville Asbestos Advertisement c. 1937

3. Asbestos. Asbestos is a mineral that, when spun into fibers, provides cost-effective insulation against heat and fire. In the middle decades of the twentieth century, asbestos fibers were widely used as insulation in construction materials, industrial machinery, naval vessels, cars, and other consumer products. Research by Dr. Irving Selikoff and his colleagues at the Mount Sinai School of Medicine in the 1960s and 1970s demonstrated that the inhalation of asbestos fibers can cause numerous lung diseases, including mesothelioma (a cancer of the lining of the chest or abdomen), other cancers (especially lung cancer in smokers), asbestosis (a chronic lung disease), and pleural thickening (a condition that makes breathing difficult and has other symptoms).

Because of the extent of asbestos exposure and its toxicity, litigation over injuries caused by asbestos has occurred on a scale that dwarfs tort litigation over any other product or substance. On one estimate, the total liabilities resulting from asbestos litigation, which began in earnest in the 1970s, will be $85 billion. Because of its magnitude, and because of complexities such as those discussed in *Boomer* and *Wannall*, asbestos litigation has left courts to address a wide array of issues in tort law and civil procedure, including proof of causation, the definition of a defective product (*see* Chapter 12), the viability of claims for exposure to a toxin that has not yet resulted in diagnosable injury (*see* Chapter 13), and the application of Federal Rule of Civil Procedure 23, which determines when individual tort claims can be pursued in the form of a class action.

The first asbestos-related lawsuit apparently was filed in 1966. The RAND Corporation has estimated that by 2002 there were 720,000 claims for asbestos-related injuries (for these purposes, a "claim" is an individual's claim against a named defendant; many individuals claimed against more than one defendant for the same injury). By 2002 claims had been brought against 8,400 defendants. The rate of claiming has varied over time. Suits were relatively rare in the 1970s, then increased dramatically in the first half of the 1980s. Filing rates accelerated further in the second half of the 1980s, with claiming reaching a peak around 1990. After another spike at the turn of the millennium, new filings have fallen dramatically. By comparison with earlier high-water marks for claiming, there are relatively few new suits being filed today, although there remain a backlog of filed cases to be resolved through dismissal, settlement, or trial.

The legal environment for asbestos litigation has evolved as well. When the first large wave of asbestos claims arose, trial courts developed new ways to aggregate the thousands of claims they were required to process, and were relatively permissive in allowing claims to go forward even in the face of difficult causation questions of the sort examined in *Boomer* and *Wannall*. Some federal appellate courts set limitations on the use of class actions and other aggregation devices through which both plaintiffs' and defense attorneys had hoped to streamline the litigation of asbestos claims, but by and large the appellate courts were content to let trial courts manage the litigation.

Starting in the late 1990s, the pace and scale of bankruptcies connected to asbestos liabilities began to increase. As a result of litigation settlements, all the available assets of huge companies such as Johns Manville were placed into trusts to permit an orderly distribution of their assets to asbestos victims. Courts at this time became increasingly concerned about the scope of asbestos liability. In two decisions important for asbestos litigation and for mass tort products liability litigation more generally, the U.S. Supreme Court essentially ruled out the use of class actions, reasoning that factual questions about individual plaintiff's claims — including questions about causation — require an individualized determination that must be resolved on a case-by-case basis. *Amchem Products, Inc. v. Windsor*, 521 U.S. 591 (1997); *Ortiz v. Fibreboard Corp.*, 527 U.S. 815 (1999). Meanwhile, plaintiffs began to look past asbestos manufacturers, seeking to impose liability on so-called secondary and tertiary defendants; that is, companies that used asbestos materials in their businesses. While claims of this sort have succeeded, courts have tended to approach them warily.

Although it is quite clear that there is a general linkage between asbestos and the diseases mentioned above, it is often unclear whether a particular plaintiff's disease can be linked to a particular defendant's activities or products. Whereas many courts in the 1970s and 1980s were willing to give plaintiffs some leeway on this issue, increasingly they have demanded more by way of proof. This change in disposition not only reflects concern over the scope of asbestos liability, but also changing scientific understandings. Mesothelioma cases are illustrative. Courts were at one time willing to allow plaintiffs' experts to testify that "any exposure" to asbestos was a substantial factor in generating a given plaintiff's mesothelioma. Their willingness to do so sometimes reflected judicial acceptance of testimony from plaintiffs' experts asserting a probable causal link between even the most minimal asbestos exposure (the inhalation of a single fiber) and a given plaintiff's mesothelioma. Defense lawyers have since introduced substantial scientific evidence against the "single fiber" theory. In turn, courts have shown increasing skepticism toward minimal exposure mesothelioma cases, either by invoking *Daubert* or its state-law equivalents to exclude expert testimony as to the single fiber theory, or by ruling that the plaintiff cannot prove specific causation. *See, e.g.*, Moeller v. Garlock Sealing Techs., LLC, 660 F.3d 950 (6th Cir. 2011); Anderson v. Ford Motor Co., 950 F. Supp. 2d 1217 (D. Utah 2013).

4. Substantial Factor Revisited: Restatement (Second) §§ 431 and 432. As discussed in Note 4 following *Jones v. LA Fitness*, *supra*, some courts frame the test for actual causation in terms of the language of "substantial factor." This phrase has long been a source of controversy and confusion in this area of negligence law, and tort law more generally. It first appeared in the First Restatement of Torts, and then reappeared in two of the main provisions on causation in the Second Restatement, Sections 431 and 432. They read in part as follows:

> **§ 431. Legal Cause; What Constitutes**
>
> [An] actor's negligent conduct is a legal cause of harm to another if (a) his conduct is a substantial factor in bringing about the harm. . . .
>
> **§ 432. Negligent Conduct as Necessary Antecedent of Harm**
>
> (1) Except as stated in Subsection (2), the actor's negligent conduct is not a substantial factor in bringing about harm to another if the harm would have been sustained even if the actor had not been negligent.
>
> (2) If two forces are actively operating, one because of the actor's negligence, the other not because of any misconduct on his part, and each of itself is sufficient to bring about harm to another, the actor's negligence may be found to be a substantial factor in bringing it about.

As we have seen, a few decisions (e.g., *Hamil v. Bashline*) treat the substantial factor test as an alternative test for actual causation that permits plaintiffs alleging malpractice claims to prevail even if they cannot meet the burdens set by the but-for test and the preponderance of the evidence standard. However, a careful reading of the

Restatement provisions above suggests that they were not intended to have this effect. Rather, they were intended to serve two very different goals.

The first, discussed in the next note, was to explain the result in a case involving *multiple sufficient causes*. These cases raise a genuine puzzle as to actual causation because they present instances in which it is intuitive to say that a defendant's carelessness caused plaintiff's injury, yet the but-for test cannot be satisfied. However, because this puzzle only emerges in one special circumstance, the solution achieved by the application of the substantial factor test to these cases does not entail scrapping the but-for test for actual causation in the vast run of cases.

The second goal of these provisions was only indirectly related to the issue of actual causation. Indeed, the aim here was to graft onto the but-for test for actual causation a *proximate cause restriction* that would bar the assignment of responsibility to a defendant whose carelessness functions as a trivial (i.e., non-"substantial") but-for cause of the plaintiff's injury. The nature of this restriction is discussed in Note 6 below.

5. *Substantial Factor (I): § 432(2) and Multiple Sufficient Causes.* Sections 431 and 432 can be reconstructed as follows:

> An actor's carelessness must be a *substantial factor* in bringing about an injury in order to be deemed a legal cause of that injury. Carelessness will be deemed a substantial factor in bringing about an injury only if it constitutes: (i) a *non-trivial necessary condition* for the occurrence of the plaintiff's injury; or (ii) one of two or more simultaneously operating forces that is *each sufficient* to bring about harm to another.

This reconstruction makes clear that Section 431 does not invoke the language of substantial factor to *supplant* the but-for test. After all, a version of the but-for test is incorporated into the substantial factor test by branch (i). Rather, it is invoked primarily so that the alternative test for actual causation stated in branch (ii) can be seen to fall within the umbrella of Section 431's general statement of the requirement of proof of actual causation.

Branch (ii) — which simply restates § 432(2) — reflects a doctrine most commonly attributed to the Minnesota Supreme Court. *See* Anderson v. Minneapolis St. P. & S.S.M. Ry. Co., 179 N.W. 45 (Minn. 1920). In *Anderson*, the plaintiff alleged that the defendant carelessly started a fire that destroyed some of plaintiff's property. Defendant argued, among other things, that the plaintiff's property was destroyed by a separate fire that the defendant had not started, and was of unknown origin. Alternatively, defendant argued that the fire attributable to the defendant had been swallowed up by this other, larger fire before having any effect on the plaintiff's property. The jury returned a verdict for the plaintiff, apparently based on a finding that the two fires had merged, and that *each fire was itself of sufficient magnitude* to have caused the damage. While questioning whether the evidence actually presented this rather exotic scenario, the Minnesota Supreme Court held that, were this such a case, the fire started by the defendant should be treated as a cause of the plaintiff's damage, so long as the defendant's fire could be deemed a "material factor in the destruction of the property," even granted that *neither fire was necessary for the damage to occur*.

Anderson rejected a prior decision rendered by the Wisconsin Supreme Court. *See* Cook v. Minneapolis, St. P. & S.S.M.R. Co., 74 N.W. 561, 566 (Wis. 1898). In *Cook*, the Wisconsin court ruled that the merger of a fire started by the defendant with a second fire of unknown origin that would have been sufficient of itself to damage the plaintiff's property provided grounds for sparing the defendant from liability. In reaching this result, *Cook* distinguished a situation involving the merger of two fires occasioned by independently wrongful acts of two defendants. In such a situation, the court reasoned, "each wrongdoer, in effect, adopts the conduct of [the other wrongdoer]." By contrast, according to *Cook*, for a situation in which a carelessly started fire merges with a fire of natural or unknown origin, "[n]o damage . . . can be traced, with reasonable certainty, to wrongdoing. . . ."

Anderson's rejection of *Cook* is both nuanced and narrow, for it depends critically on issues of timing. If the fire of unknown origin had destroyed the plaintiff's property just moments before the arrival of the fire created by the defendant's carelessness, the defendant would have been deemed entirely free of liability, even if it was true that the defendant's fire would itself have been sufficient to destroy the property. Conversely, if the defendant's carelessly set fire had destroyed the plaintiff's property just moments before the arrival of the fire of unknown origin, *Anderson* would have been treated as a run-of-the-mill causation case, even though the unknown-origin fire would still have been sufficient to destroy the property. On the Minnesota Supreme Court's analysis, therefore, not all cases involving multiple sufficient causes (or what is sometimes called "duplicative causation") trigger the substantial factor test. *It is only when there is temporal concurrence between the force carelessly created by the defendant and the force of unknown origin that the substantial factor test was to be used.* For this reason, cases like *Anderson* are frequently labeled "concurrent causation" cases.

Note that under *Anderson* and all three Restatements, the plaintiff does not have to demonstrate that the "unknown origin" fire was the product of tortious or wrongful conduct. The *innocence* of that force is immaterial to the treatment of the carelessly generated fire as a cause, so long as the latter counts as a "substantial factor."

The *Anderson* court's treatment of the defendant's conduct as a cause of the plaintiff's injury has struck most courts and commentators as intuitively correct. Do you share that intuition? If the plaintiff's property was going to be damaged anyway by another fire, in what sense did the defendant's carelessness cause that damage? Is it because the defendant should not benefit from the "good luck" of having another fire in the vicinity?

6. *Substantial Factor (II): Section 431 and Trivial Necessary Conditions.* The other aspiration underlying the Second Restatement's employment of the language of substantial factor was to deal with the problem of so-called '*de minimis*' or 'trivial' but-for causes. This alternative aspiration is made clear in comment a to Section 431:

> *a. Distinction between substantial cause and cause in the philosophic sense.* In order to be a legal cause of another's harm, it is not enough that the harm would not have occurred had the actor not been negligent. . . . The negligence must also be a substantial factor as well as an actual factor in bringing about the plaintiff's harm. The word "substantial" is used to denote the fact that the defendant's conduct has such an effect in producing the harm as to lead reasonable men to regard it as a cause, using that word in the popular sense in which there always lurks the idea

The issue posited by examples of "doomed" plaintiffs is often thought to present a conundrum as to actual causation. Do you find that characterization satisfactory? Might they be better understood as raising an issue of damages — that is, the amount of compensation that, in fairness, ought to be paid to the victim (or his estate) by the tortfeasor? *See* Chapter 8 (discussing damage measures).

Check Your Understanding

Causation Brainteasers

Consider the following scenario (and some variations thereon) from the Third Torts Restatement. *See* Restatement (Third) of Torts: Liability for Physical and Emotional Harm § 27, illus. 3 (2010). In it, various combinations of persons (*A*, *B*, *C*, *D*, *E*, and *F*) lean against *O*'s car at the parking lot of a roadside rest area that overlooks a steep cliff. Assume that a reasonably prudent person would not lean against the car under these circumstances. Assume further that the car will move only if it is leaned against by a person or combination of persons weighing at least 300 lbs.

1. *A* and *B*, who each weighs 175 lbs., lean against the car simultaneously. The car rolls over the cliff and is destroyed. Against whom can *O* establish a claim of negligence?
2. *A*, *B*, and *C*, who each weighs 175 lbs., lean against the car simultaneously. The car rolls over the cliff and is destroyed. Against whom can O establish a claim of negligence?
3. *A* and *B*, who each weighs 175 lbs., and *D*, who weighs 120 lbs., each lean against the car simultaneously. The car rolls over the cliff and is destroyed. Against whom can *O* establish a claim of negligence?
4. *A*, who weighs 175 lbs., and *D*, *E*, and *F*, who each weighs 120 lbs., each lean against the car simultaneously. The car rolls over the cliff and is destroyed. Against whom can *O* establish a claim of negligence?

IV. CAUSATION AND TORTFEASOR IDENTIFICATION

Chapter 3 discussed the doctrine of *res ipsa loquitur*, which enables certain plaintiffs who face challenges proving breach to proceed with their claims without presenting evidence identifying how exactly the defendant acted carelessly. We consider in this section two instances of doctrinal adjustments on the issue of proof of actual causation that respond to certain situations in which the plaintiff is unable to identify who among multiple potentially responsible parties injured her.

A. Alternative Causation

Summers v. Tice

199 P.2d 1 (Cal. 1948)

CARTER, J. Each of the two defendants appeals from a judgment against them in an action for personal injuries. . . .

Plaintiff's action was against both defendants for an injury to his right eye and face as the result of being struck by bird shot discharged from a shotgun. The case was tried by the court without a jury and the court found that on November 20, 1945, plaintiff and the two defendants were hunting quail on the open range. Each of the defendants was armed with a 12 gauge shotgun loaded with shells containing 7½ size shot. Prior to going hunting plaintiff discussed the hunting procedure with defendants, indicating that they were to exercise care when shooting and to "keep in line." In the course of hunting plaintiff proceeded up a hill, thus placing the hunters at the points of a triangle. The view of defendants with reference to plaintiff was unobstructed and they knew his location. Defendant Tice flushed a quail which rose in flight to a 10-foot elevation and flew between plaintiff and defendants. Both defendants shot at the quail, shooting in plaintiff's direction. At that time defendants were 75 yards from plaintiff. One shot struck plaintiff in his eye and another in his upper lip. Finally it was found by the court that as the direct result of the shooting by defendants the shots struck plaintiff as above mentioned and that defendants were negligent in so shooting and plaintiff was not contributorily negligent.

. . . There is evidence that both defendants, at about the same time or one immediately after the other, shot at a quail and in so doing shot toward plaintiff who was uphill from them, and that they knew his location. That is sufficient from which the trial court could conclude that they acted with respect to plaintiff other than as persons of ordinary prudence. . . .

The problem presented in this case is whether the judgment against both defendants may stand. It is argued by defendants that they are not joint tort feasors, and thus jointly and severally liable, as they were not acting in concert, and that there is not sufficient evidence to show which defendant was guilty of the negligence which caused the injuries — the shooting by Tice or that by Simonson. Tice argues that there is evidence to show that the shot which struck plaintiff came from Simonson's gun because of admissions allegedly made by him to third persons and no evidence that they came from his gun. Further in connection with the latter contention, the court failed to find on plaintiff's allegation in his complaint that he did not know which one was at fault — did not find which defendant was guilty of the negligence which caused the injuries to plaintiff.

Considering the last argument first, we believe it is clear that the court sufficiently found on the issue that defendants were jointly liable and that thus the negligence of both was the cause of the injury or to that legal effect. It found that both defendants were negligent and "[t]hat as a direct and proximate result of the shots fired by *defendants, and each of them*, a birdshot pellet was caused to and did lodge in plaintiff's right eye and that another birdshot pellet was caused to and did lodge in plaintiff's upper lip." In so doing the court evidently did not give credence to the admissions of Simonson to third persons that he fired the shots, which it was justified in doing. It thus determined that the negligence of both defendants was the legal cause of the injury — or that both were responsible. Implicit in such finding is the assumption that the court was unable to ascertain whether the shots were from the gun of one defendant or the other or one shot from each of them. The one shot that entered plaintiff's eye was the major factor in assessing damages and that shot could not have come from the gun of both defendants. It was from one or the other only.

It has been held that where a group of persons are on a hunting party, or otherwise engaged in the use of firearms, and two of them are negligent in firing in the direction of a third person who is injured thereby, both of those so firing are liable for the injury suffered by the third person, although the negligence of only one of them could have caused the injury. (Moore v. Foster, 182 Miss. 15, 180 So. 73 (1938); Oliver v. Miles, 144 Miss. 852, 110 So. 666 (1926); Reyher v. Mayne, 90 Colo. 586 [10 P.2d 1109]; Benson v. Ross, 143 Mich. 452 [106 N.W. 1120, 114 Am. St. Rep. 675].) The same rule has been applied in criminal cases . . . , and both drivers have been held liable for the negligence of one where they engaged in a racing contest causing an injury to a third person. Saisa v. Lilja, 76 F.2d 380. These cases speak of the action of defendants as being in concert as the ground of decision, yet it would seem they are straining that concept and the more reasonable basis appears in Oliver v. Miles, *supra*. There two persons were hunting together. Both shot at some partridges and in so doing shot across the highway injuring plaintiff who was travelling on it. The court stated they were acting in concert and thus both were liable. The court then stated: "We think that . . . each is liable for the resulting injury to the boy, although no one can say definitely who actually shot him. *To hold otherwise would be to exonerate both from liability, although each was negligent, and the injury resulted from such negligence.*"[Emphasis added.] . . . Dean Wigmore has this to say:

> "When two or more persons by their acts are possibly the sole cause of a harm, or when two or more acts of the same person are possibly the sole cause, and the plaintiff has introduced evidence that the one of the two persons, or the one of the same person's two acts, is culpable, then the defendant has the burden of proving that the other person, or his other act, was the sole cause of the harm. (b) . . . The real reason for the rule that each joint tortfeasor is responsible for the whole damage is the practical unfairness of denying the injured person redress simply because he cannot prove how much damage each did, when it is certain that between them they did all; let them be the ones to apportion it among themselves. Since, then, the difficulty of proof is the reason, the rule should apply whenever the harm has plural causes, and not merely when they acted in conscious concert. . . ." (Wigmore, Select Cases on the Law of Torts, § 153.) . . .

When we consider the relative position of the parties and the results that would flow if plaintiff was required to pin the injury on one of the defendants only, a requirement that the burden of proof on that subject be shifted to defendants becomes manifest. They are both wrongdoers — both negligent toward plaintiff. They brought about a situation where the negligence of one of them injured the plaintiff, hence it should rest with them each to absolve himself if he can. The injured party has been placed by defendants in the unfair position of pointing to which defendant caused the harm. If one can escape the other may also and plaintiff is remediless. Ordinarily defendants are in a far better position to offer evidence to determine which one caused the injury. This reasoning has recently found favor in this court. In a quite analogous situation this court held that a patient injured while unconscious on an operating table in a hospital could hold all or any of the persons who had any connection with the operation even though he could not select the particular acts by the particular person which led to his disability. (Ybarra v. Spangard, 25 Cal. 2d 486, 154 P.2d 687.) . . . Similarly in the instant case plaintiff is not able to establish which of defendants caused his injury. . . .

In addition to that, however, it should be pointed out that the same reasons of policy and justice shift the burden to each of defendants to absolve himself if he can — relieving the wronged person of the duty of apportioning the injury to a particular defendant, apply here where we are concerned with whether plaintiff is required to supply evidence for the apportionment of damages. If defendants are independent tort feasors and thus each liable for the damage caused by him alone, and, at least, where the matter of apportionment is incapable of proof, the innocent wronged party should not be deprived of his right to redress. The wrongdoers should be left to work out between themselves any apportionment. . . .

It is urged that plaintiff now has changed the theory of his case in claiming a concert of action; that he did not plead or prove such concert. From what has been said it is clear that there has been no change in theory. The joint liability, as well as the lack of knowledge as to which defendant was liable, was pleaded and the proof developed the case under either theory. We have seen that for the reasons of policy discussed herein, the case is based upon the legal proposition that, under the circumstances here presented, each defendant is liable for the whole damage whether they are deemed to be acting in concert or independently.

The judgment is affirmed.

NOTES AND QUESTIONS

1. *Implications.* The *Summers* rule of "alternative causation" has the immediate effect of taking the onus with respect to proving actual causation off the plaintiff and placing it onto each defendant to *disprove* that his carelessness was a cause of plaintiff's injury. In some jurisdictions, including California at the time *Summers* was decided, a plaintiff who can avail herself of this rule also obtains the benefit of joint and several liability, discussed in Note 4 following *McDonald v. Robinson, supra*. Under this rule, as the court explains, each defendant is subject to liability for the full amount of plaintiff's damages. (Plaintiff is not entitled to recover 200 percent of her actual, proven damages. Rather, she is given the option of seeking the entire amount from either defendant. This can be critically important when, for example, one of the defendants lacks assets or is otherwise unavailable to pay a judgment.)

2. *Burden Shifting or Element Elimination?* How likely is it that a person in the position of the *Summers* defendants will be able to *dis*prove that he caused plaintiff's injury? If the answer is "not at all likely," does this mean that *Summers* is not so much a burden-shifting rule as a rule that simply dispenses with the actual causation component of the causation element? If so, would courts be justified in dispensing with actual causation in other situations in which plaintiffs face seemingly insurmountable problems of proof? Are there special reasons for burden shifting in *Summers*?

3. *Alternative Causation Versus Multiple Necessary Causes. Summers* applies in situations in which one of two (or perhaps more than two) negligent actors acts independently of the other to cause injury to the plaintiff. As such it must be distinguished from three related tort scenarios, discussed in this note and Note 4, below.

The first is that of *multiple actual cause* cases. As discussed above in connection with *McDonald v. Robinson*, multiple cause analysis applies when the independent careless conduct of two (or more) actors each functions as an actual cause of plaintiff's injury. Unlike the rule of *Summers*, this doctrine applies only when each of two or more careless acts by independent actors function as a but-for cause of the injury to the plaintiff. In *Summers*, by contrast, only one actor's careless shooting functioned as a but-for cause of the plaintiff's injury. The other's had no effect whatsoever on the plaintiff.

Are there any theories of negligence that would apply to the facts of *Summers* and that would permit a jury to identify careless acts by Simonson and Tice that each operated as but-for causes of Summers's injury? What about the decision of the shooters to form a "triangle" rather than a straight-line hunting formation?

4. *Aiding and Abetting and Concert of Action.* The other doctrines to be distinguished from alternative causation are *conspiracy* and *concert of action.* Suppose Summers found evidence indicating that Simonson and Tice actually set up the hunting expedition as part of a plan to shoot Summers. If that were the case, Summers would not need the benefit of a burden-shifting rule, because no matter who actually shot Summers, the other would be responsible for "aiding and abetting" the shooting. On these imagined facts, the two shooters would not be acting independently, but rather as part of a planned effort to injure Summers.

Concert of action, like aiding and abetting, treats two tortfeasors as acting jointly, rather than independently. However, it does not require the existence of a plan or undertaking to injure the plaintiff. As *Summers* notes, the classic application of concert-of-action doctrine involves a plaintiff who is struck by one of two speeding cars involved in an illegal drag race. Regardless of which racer's car hits the plaintiff, the two racers are held jointly to have caused plaintiff's injury: their separate acts of careless driving are, in effect, fused into a single coordinated course of conduct. *See, e.g.*, Bierczynski v. Rogers, 239 A.2d 218 (Del. 1968).

5. *Extending Summers.* Is the *Summers* rule applicable only when there are two defendants? *See* Huston v. Konieczny, 556 N.E.2d 505 (Ohio 1990) (plaintiff injured by minor who could have received alcohol from any one of a number of defendants can sue those defendants on alternative causation theory). The Third Restatement of Torts would extend *Summers* to cases involving "multiple" defendants. Restatement (Third) of Torts: Liability for Physical and Emotional Harm § 28(b) (2010). Are there any reasons to draw the line at two?

6. *Other Instances of Burden Shifting.* The *Summers* rule is confined to an unusual situation. Another, more prominent area of tort law in which some courts permit burden shifting on the issue of causation is in products liability suits alleging that the manufacturer of a product failed adequately to warn users of the product of dangers it poses. Here, the causation issue hinges in part on whether the plaintiff

would have heeded the warning that the manufacturer failed to provide. Some courts adopt a presumption that the plaintiff would have heeded the warning, and leave it to the manufacturer to try to prove that the warning would not have been heeded. *See* Chapter 12. Recall Chapter 2's discussion of negligence cases such as *Tarasoff*, in which the allegation is that the defendant acted carelessly by failing to alert the plaintiff of a danger posed by another person. Should these plaintiffs also benefit from a presumption that they would have heeded the warning?

B. Market Share Liability

Sindell v. Abbott Labs.

607 P.2d 924 (Cal.), *cert. denied*, 449 U.S. 912 (1980)

Mosk, J. This case involves a complex problem both timely and significant: may a plaintiff, injured as the result of a drug administered to her mother during pregnancy, who knows the type of drug involved but cannot identify the manufacturer of the precise product, hold liable for her injuries a maker of a drug produced from an identical formula?

Plaintiff Judith Sindell brought an action against eleven drug companies and Does 1 through 100, on behalf of herself and other women similarly situated. The complaint alleges as follows: Between 1941 and 1971, defendants were engaged in the business of manufacturing, promoting, and marketing diethylstilbesterol (DES), a drug which is a synthetic compound of the female hormone estrogen. The drug was administered to plaintiff's mother and the mothers of the class she represents,[1] for the purpose of preventing miscarriage. In 1947, the Food and Drug Administration authorized the marketing of DES as a miscarriage preventative, but only on an experimental basis, with a requirement that the drug contain a warning label to that effect.

DES may cause cancerous vaginal and cervical growths in the daughters exposed to it before birth, because their mothers took the drug during pregnancy. The form of cancer from which these daughters suffer is known as adenocarcinoma, and it manifests itself after a minimum latent period of 10 or 12 years. It is a fast-spreading and deadly disease, and radical surgery is required to prevent it from spreading. DES also causes adenosis, precancerous vaginal and cervical growths which may spread to other areas of the body. The treatment for adenosis is cauterization, surgery, or cryosurgery. Women who suffer from this condition must be monitored by biopsy or colposcopic examination twice a year, a painful and expensive procedure. Thousands of women whose mothers received DES during pregnancy are unaware of the effects of the drug.

In 1971, the Food and Drug Administration ordered defendants to cease marketing and promoting DES for the purpose of preventing miscarriages, and to warn

---

1. The plaintiff class alleged consists of "girls and women who are residents of California and who have been exposed to DES before birth and who may or may not know that fact or the dangers" to which they were exposed. Defendants are also sued as representatives of a class of drug manufacturers which sold DES after 1941.

physicians and the public that the drug should not be used by pregnant women because of the danger to their unborn children.

During the period defendants marketed DES, they knew or should have known that it was a carcinogenic substance, that there was a grave danger after varying periods of latency it would cause cancerous and precancerous growths in the daughters of the mothers who took it, and that it was ineffective to prevent miscarriage. Nevertheless, defendants continued to advertise and market the drug as a miscarriage preventative. They failed to test DES for efficacy and safety; the tests performed by others, upon which they relied, indicated that it was not safe or effective. In violation of the authorization of the Food and Drug Administration, defendants marketed DES on an unlimited basis rather than as an experimental drug, and they failed to warn of its potential danger.

Because of defendants' advertised assurances that DES was safe and effective to prevent miscarriage, plaintiff was exposed to the drug prior to her birth. She became aware of the danger from such exposure within one year of the time she filed her complaint. As a result of the DES ingested by her mother, plaintiff developed a malignant bladder tumor which was removed by surgery. She suffers from adenosis and must constantly be monitored by biopsy or colposcopy to insure early warning of further malignancy.

The first cause of action alleges that defendants were jointly and individually negligent in that they manufactured, marketed and promoted DES as a safe and efficacious drug to prevent miscarriage, without adequate testing or warning, and without monitoring or reporting its effects.

A separate cause of action alleges that defendants are jointly liable regardless of which particular brand of DES was ingested by plaintiff's mother because defendants collaborated in marketing, promoting and testing the drug, relied upon each other's tests, and adhered to an industry-wide safety standard. DES was produced from a common and mutually agreed upon formula as a fungible drug interchangeable with other brands of the same product; defendants knew or should have known that it was customary for doctors to prescribe the drug by its generic rather than its brand name and that pharmacists filled prescriptions from whatever brand of the drug happened to be in stock.

Other causes of action are based upon theories of strict liability, violation of express and implied warranties, false and fraudulent representations, misbranding of drugs in violation of federal law, conspiracy and "lack of consent."

Each cause of action alleges that defendants are jointly liable because they acted in concert, on the basis of express and implied agreements, and in reliance upon and ratification and exploitation of each other's testing and marketing methods.

Plaintiff seeks compensatory damages of $1 million and punitive damages of $10 million for herself. For the members of her class, she prays for equitable relief in the form of an order that defendants warn physicians and others of the danger of DES and the necessity of performing certain tests to determine the presence of disease caused by the drug, and that they establish free clinics in California to perform such tests.

Defendants demurred to the complaint. While the complaint did not expressly allege that plaintiff could not identify the manufacturer of the precise drug ingested by her mother, she stated in her points and authorities in opposition to the demurrers filed by some of the defendants that she was unable to make the identification, and the trial court sustained the demurrers of these defendants without leave to amend on the ground that plaintiff did not and stated she could not identify which defendant had manufactured the drug responsible for her injuries. Thereupon, the court dismissed the action. This appeal involves only five of ten defendants named in the complaint.[4] . . . This case is but one of a number filed throughout the country seeking to hold drug manufacturers liable for injuries allegedly resulting from DES prescribed to the plaintiffs' mothers since 1947. According to a note in the Fordham Law Review, estimates of the number of women who took the drug during pregnancy range from 1 ½ million to 3 million. Hundreds, perhaps thousands, of the daughters of these women suffer from adenocarcinoma, and the incidence of vaginal adenosis among them is 30 to 90 percent. (Comment, *DES and a Proposed Theory of Enterprise Liability* (1978) 46 Fordham L. Rev. 963, 964-967 (hereafter Fordham Comment).) Most of the cases are still pending. With two exceptions, those that have been decided resulted in judgments in favor of the drug company defendants because of the failure of the plaintiffs to identify the manufacturer of the DES prescribed to their mothers. The same result was reached in a recent California case. The present action is another attempt to overcome this obstacle to recovery.

We begin with the proposition that, as a general rule, the imposition of liability depends upon a showing by the plaintiff that his or her injuries were caused by the act of the defendant or by an instrumentality under the defendant's control. . . .

There are, however, exceptions to this rule. Plaintiff's complaint suggests several bases upon which defendants may be held liable for her injuries even though she cannot demonstrate the name of the manufacturer which produced the DES actually taken by her mother. The first of these theories, classically illustrated by Summers v. Tice (1948) 33 Cal. 2d 80, 199 P.2d 1, places the burden of proof of causation upon tortious defendants in certain circumstances. The second basis of liability emerging from the complaint is that defendants acted in concert to cause injury to plaintiff. There is a third and novel approach to the problem, sometimes called the theory of "enterprise liability," but which we prefer to designate by the more accurate term of "industry-wide" liability, which might obviate the necessity for identifying the manufacturer of the injury-causing drug. We shall conclude that these doctrines, as previously interpreted, may not be applied to hold defendants liable under the allegations of this complaint. However, we shall propose and adopt a fourth basis for permitting the action to be tried, grounded upon an extension of the *Summers* doctrine.

I

Plaintiff places primary reliance upon cases which hold that if a party cannot identify which of two or more defendants caused an injury, the burden of proof

4. Abbott Laboratories, Eli Lilly and Company, E.R. Squibb and Sons, The Upjohn Company, and Rexall Drug Company are respondents. The action was dismissed or the appeal abandoned on various grounds as to other defendants named in the complaint; e.g., one defendant demonstrated it had not manufactured DES during the period plaintiff's mother took the drug.

may shift to the defendants to show that they were not responsible for the harm. This principle is sometimes referred to as the "alternative liability" theory.

The celebrated case of Summers v. Tice, *supra*, a unanimous opinion of this court, best exemplifies the rule. In *Summers*, the plaintiff was injured when two hunters negligently shot in his direction. It could not be determined which of them had fired the shot which actually caused the injury to the plaintiff's eye, but both defendants were nevertheless held jointly and severally liable for the whole of the damages. We reasoned that both were wrongdoers, both were negligent toward the plaintiff, and that it would be unfair to require plaintiff to isolate the defendant responsible, because if the one pointed out were to escape liability, the other might also, and the plaintiff-victim would be shorn of any remedy. In these circumstances, we held, the burden of proof shifted to the defendants, "each to absolve himself if he can." We stated that under these or similar circumstances a defendant is ordinarily in a "far better position" to offer evidence to determine whether he or another defendant caused the injury.

In *Summers*, we relied upon Ybarra v. Spangard (1944) 25 Cal. 2d 486, 154 P.2d 687. There, the plaintiff was injured while he was unconscious during the course of surgery. He sought damages against several doctors and a nurse who attended him while he was unconscious. We held that it would be unreasonable to require him to identify the particular defendant who had performed the alleged negligent act because he was unconscious at the time of the injury and the defendants exercised control over the instrumentalities which caused the harm. Therefore, under the doctrine of res ipsa loquitur, an inference of negligence arose that defendants were required to meet by explaining their conduct. . . .

Defendants assert that these principles are inapplicable here. First, they insist that a predicate to shifting the burden of proof under *Summers-Ybarra* is that the defendants must have greater access to information regarding the cause of the injuries than the plaintiff, whereas in the present case the reverse appears. [We disagree.] . . .

. . . Because many years elapsed between the time the drug was taken and the manifestation of plaintiff's injuries she, and many other daughters of mothers who took DES, are unable to [identify the manufacturer of the particular DES that harmed her]. Certainly there can be no implication that plaintiff is at fault in failing to do so — the event occurred while plaintiff was in utero, a generation ago.

On the other hand, it cannot be said with assurance that defendants have the means to make the identification. . . . Nor . . . [is] the absence of evidence on this subject . . . due to the fault of defendants. . . . [T]he difficulty or impossibility of identification results primarily from the passage of time rather than from their allegedly negligent acts of failing to provide adequate warnings. Thus Haft v. Lone Palm Hotel (1970) 3 Cal. 3d 756, 91 Cal. Rptr. 745, 478 P.2d 465, upon which plaintiff relies, is distinguishable.[14] It is important to observe, however, that while defendants do not have

14. In *Haft*, a father and his young son drowned in defendants' swimming pool. There were no witnesses to the accident. Defendants were negligent in failing to provide a lifeguard, as required by law. We held that the absence of evidence of causation was a direct and foreseeable result of the defendants' negligence, and that, therefore, the burden of proof on the issue of causation was upon defendants. . . . There is no proper analogy to *Haft* here. While in *Haft* the presence of a lifeguard on

means superior to plaintiff to identify the maker of the precise drug taken by her mother, they may in some instances be able to prove that they did not manufacture the injury-causing substance. In the present case, for example, one of the original defendants was dismissed from the action upon proof that it did not manufacture DES until after plaintiff was born.

[The] . . . fact [that] defendants do not have greater access to information which might establish the identity of the manufacturer of the DES which injured plaintiff does not per se prevent application of the *Summers* rule.

Nevertheless, . . . [there] is an important difference between the situation involved in *Summers* and the present case. There, all the parties who were or could have been responsible for the harm to the plaintiff were joined as defendants. Here, by contrast, there are approximately 200 drug companies which made DES, any of which might have manufactured the injury-producing drug.

Defendants maintain that, while in *Summers* there was a 50 percent chance that one of the two defendants was responsible for the plaintiff's injuries, here since any one of 200 companies which manufactured DES might have made the product which harmed plaintiff, there is no rational basis upon which to infer that any defendant in this action caused plaintiff's injuries, nor even a reasonable possibility that they were responsible.

These arguments are persuasive if we measure the chance that any one of the defendants supplied the injury-causing drug by the number of possible tortfeasors. In such a context, the possibility that any of the five defendants supplied the DES to plaintiff's mother is so remote that it would be unfair to require each defendant to exonerate itself. There may be a substantial likelihood that none of the five defendants joined in the action made the DES which caused the injury, and that the offending producer not named would escape liability altogether. While we propose, *infra*, an adaptation of the rule in *Summers* which will substantially overcome these difficulties, defendants appear to be correct that the rule, as previously applied, cannot relieve plaintiff of the burden of proving the identity of the manufacturer which made the drug causing her injuries.

II

The second principle upon which plaintiff relies is the so-called "concert of action" theory. . . .

. . . The elements of this doctrine are prescribed in section 876 of the Restatement of Torts. The section provides, "For harm resulting to a third person from the tortious conduct of another, one is subject to liability if he (a) does a tortious act in concert with the other or pursuant to a common design with him, or (b) knows that the other's conduct constitutes a breach of duty and gives substantial assistance or encouragement to the other so to conduct himself, or (c) gives substantial assistance to the other in accomplishing a tortious result and his own conduct, separately considered,

---

the scene would have provided a witness to the accident and probably prevented it, plaintiff asks us to speculate that if the DES taken by her mother had been labeled as an experimental drug, she would have recalled or recorded the name of the manufacturer and passed this information on to her daughter. It cannot be said here that the absence of evidence of causation was a "direct and foreseeable result" of defendants' failure to provide a warning label.

constitutes a breach of duty to the third person." With respect to this doctrine, Prosser states that "those who, in pursuance of a common plan or design to commit a tortious act, actively take part in it, or further it by cooperation or request, or who lend aid or encouragement to the wrongdoer, or ratify and adopt his acts done for their benefit, are equally liable with him. Express agreement is not necessary, and all that is required is that there be a tacit understanding. . . ." (Prosser, *Law of Torts* (4th ed. 1971), sec. 46, p.292.) Plaintiff . . . alleges that defendants' wrongful conduct "is the result of planned and concerted action, express and implied agreements, collaboration in, reliance upon, acquiescence in and ratification, exploitation and adoption of each other's testing, marketing methods, lack of warnings . . . and other acts or omissions . . ." and that "acting individually and in concert, (defendants) promoted, approved, authorized, acquiesced in, and reaped profits from sales" of DES. These allegations, plaintiff claims, state a "tacit understanding" among defendants to commit a tortious act against her.

In our view, this litany of charges is insufficient to allege a cause of action under the rules stated above. The gravamen of the charge . . . is that defendants failed to adequately test the drug or to give sufficient warning of its dangers and that they relied upon the tests performed by one another and took advantage of each other's promotional and marketing techniques. These allegations do not amount to a charge that there was a tacit understanding or a common plan among defendants to fail to conduct adequate tests or give sufficient warnings, and that they substantially aided and encouraged one another in these omissions. . . .

III

A third theory upon which plaintiff relies is the concept of industry-wide liability, or according to the terminology of the parties, "enterprise liability." This theory was suggested in Hall v. E. I. Du Pont de Nemours & Co., Inc. (E.D.N.Y. 1972) 345 F. Supp. 353. In that case, plaintiffs were 13 children injured by the explosion of blasting caps in 12 separate incidents which occurred in 10 different states between 1955 and 1959. The defendants were six blasting cap manufacturers, comprising virtually the entire blasting cap industry in the United States, and their trade association. There were, however, a number of Canadian blasting cap manufacturers which could have supplied the caps. The gravamen of the complaint was that the practice of the industry of omitting a warning on individual blasting caps and of failing to take other safety measures created an unreasonable risk of harm, resulting in the plaintiffs' injuries. The complaint did not identify a particular manufacturer of a cap which caused a particular injury. . . .

We decline to apply this theory in the present case. At least 200 manufacturers produced DES; *Hall*, which involved 6 manufacturers representing the entire blasting cap industry in the United States, cautioned against application of the doctrine espoused therein to a large number of producers. Moreover, in *Hall*, the conclusion that the defendants jointly controlled the risk was based upon allegations that they had delegated some functions relating to safety to a trade association. There are no such allegations here, and we have concluded above that plaintiff has failed to allege liability on a concert of action theory.

Equally important, the drug industry is closely regulated by the Food and Drug Administration, which actively controls the testing and manufacture of drugs and the method by which they are marketed, including the contents of warning labels.[26] To a considerable degree, therefore, the standards followed by drug manufacturers are suggested or compelled by the government. Adherence to those standards cannot, of course, absolve a manufacturer of liability to which it would otherwise be subject. But since the government plays such a pervasive role in formulating the criteria for the testing and marketing of drugs, it would be unfair to impose upon a manufacturer liability for injuries resulting from the use of a drug which it did not supply simply because it followed the standards of the industry.

IV

If we were confined to the theories of *Summers* and *Hall*, we would be constrained to hold that the judgment must be sustained. Should we require that plaintiff identify the manufacturer which supplied the DES used by her mother or that all DES manufacturers be joined in the action, she would effectively be precluded from any recovery. As defendants candidly admit, there is little likelihood that all the manufacturers who made DES at the time in question are still in business or that they are subject to the jurisdiction of the California courts. There are, however, forceful arguments in favor of holding that plaintiff has a cause of action.

In our contemporary complex industrialized society, advances in science and technology create fungible goods which may harm consumers and which cannot be traced to any specific producer. The response of the courts can be either to adhere rigidly to prior doctrine, denying recovery to those injured by such products, or to fashion remedies to meet these changing needs. Just as Justice Traynor in his landmark concurring opinion in Escola v. Coca Cola Bottling Company (1944) 24 Cal. 2d 453, 467-468, 150 P.2d 436, recognized that in an era of mass production and complex marketing methods the traditional standard of negligence was insufficient to govern the obligations of manufacturer to consumer, so should we acknowledge that some adaptation of the rules of causation and liability may be appropriate in these recurring circumstances. . . .

The most persuasive reason for finding plaintiff states a cause of action is that advanced in *Summers*: as between an innocent plaintiff and negligent defendants, the latter should bear the cost of the injury. Here, as in *Summers*, plaintiff is not at fault in failing to provide evidence of causation, and although the absence of such evidence is not attributable to the defendants either, their conduct in marketing a drug the effects of which are delayed for many years played a significant role in creating the unavailability of proof.

From a broader policy standpoint, defendants are better able to bear the cost of injury resulting from the manufacture of a defective product. . . . The manufacturer is in the best position to discover and guard against defects in its products and to warn of

26. Federal regulations may specify the type of tests a manufacturer must perform for certain drugs (21 C.F.R. § 436.206 *et seq.*), the type of packaging used (§ 429.10), the warnings which appear on labels (§ 369.20), and the standards to be followed in the manufacture of a drug (§ 211.22 *et seq.*).

harmful effects; thus, holding it liable for defects and failure to warn of harmful effects will provide an incentive to product safety. These considerations are particularly significant where medication is involved, for the consumer is virtually helpless to protect himself from serious, sometimes permanent, sometimes fatal, injuries caused by deleterious drugs.

Where, as here, all defendants produced a drug from an identical formula and the manufacturer of the DES which caused plaintiff's injuries cannot be identified through no fault of plaintiff, a modification of the rule of *Summers* is warranted. As we have seen, an undiluted *Summers* rationale is inappropriate to shift the burden of proof of causation to defendants because if we measure the chance that any particular manufacturer supplied the injury-causing product by the number of producers of DES, there is a possibility that none of the five defendants in this case produced the offending substance and that the responsible manufacturer, not named in the action, will escape liability.

But we approach the issue of causation from a different perspective: we hold it to be reasonable in the present context to measure the likelihood that any of the defendants supplied the product which allegedly injured plaintiff by the percentage which the DES sold by each of them for the purpose of preventing miscarriage bears to the entire production of the drug sold by all for that purpose. Plaintiff asserts in her briefs that Eli Lilly and Company and 5 or 6 other companies produced 90 percent of the DES marketed. If at trial this is established to be the fact, then there is a corresponding likelihood that this comparative handful of producers manufactured the DES which caused plaintiff's injuries, and only a 10 percent likelihood that the offending producer would escape liability.

If plaintiff joins in the action the manufacturers of a substantial share of the DES which her mother might have taken, the injustice of shifting the burden of proof to defendants to demonstrate that they could not have made the substance which injured plaintiff is significantly diminished. While 75 to 80 percent of the market is suggested as the requirement by the Fordham Comment (at p.996), we hold only that a substantial percentage is required.

The presence in the action of a substantial share of the appropriate market also provides a ready means to apportion damages among the defendants. Each defendant will be held liable for the proportion of the judgment represented by its share of that market unless it demonstrates that it could not have made the product which caused plaintiff's injuries. In the present case, as we have seen, one DES manufacturer was dismissed from the action upon filing a declaration that it had not manufactured DES until after plaintiff was born. Once plaintiff has met her burden of joining the required defendants, they in turn may cross-complaint against other DES manufacturers, not joined in the action, which they can allege might have supplied the injury-causing product.

Under this approach, each manufacturer's liability would approximate its responsibility for the injuries caused by its own products. Some minor discrepancy in the correlation between market share and liability is inevitable; therefore, a defendant may be held liable for a somewhat different percentage of the damage than its share of the appropriate market would justify. It is probably impossible, with the passage of time, to determine market share with mathematical exactitude. But just as a jury cannot be expected to determine the precise relationship between fault and liability in applying the doctrine of comparative fault or partial indemnity, the difficulty of apportioning damages among the defendant producers in exact relation to their market share does not seriously militate against the rule we adopt. As we said in *Summers* with regard to the liability of independent tortfeasors, where a correct division of liability cannot be made "the trier of fact may make it the best it can." (33 Cal. 2d at p.88, 199 P.2d at p.5.) We are not unmindful of the practical problems involved in defining the market and determining market share,[29] but these are largely matters of proof which properly cannot be determined at the pleading stage of these proceedings. Defendants urge that it would be both unfair and contrary to public policy to hold them liable for plaintiff's injuries in the absence of proof that one of them supplied the drug responsible for the damage. Most of their arguments, however, are based upon the assumption that one manufacturer would be held responsible for the products of another or for those of all other manufacturers if plaintiff ultimately prevails. But under the rule we adopt, each manufacturer's liability for an injury would be approximately equivalent to the damages caused by the DES it manufactured.

The judgments are reversed.

RICHARDSON, J. (dissenting) (joined by CLARK AND MANUEL, JJ.) I respectfully dissent. In these consolidated cases the majority adopts a wholly new theory which contains these ingredients: The plaintiffs were not alive at the time of the commission of the tortious acts. They sue a generation later. They are permitted to receive substantial damages from multiple defendants without any proof that any defendant caused or even probably caused plaintiffs' injuries.

Although the majority purports to change only the required burden of proof by shifting it from plaintiffs to defendants, the effect of its holding is to guarantee that plaintiffs will prevail on the causation issue because defendants are no more capable of disproving factual causation than plaintiffs are of proving it. "Market share" liability thus represents a new high water mark in tort law. The ramifications seem almost limitless. . . . In my view, the majority's departure from traditional tort doctrine is unwise. . . .

The "market share" thesis may be paraphrased. Plaintiffs have been hurt by someone who made DES. Because of the lapse of time no one can prove who made it. Perhaps it was not the named defendants who made it, but they did make some. Although DES was apparently safe at the time it was used, it was subsequently proven unsafe as to some daughters of some users. Plaintiffs have suffered injury and defendants are wealthy. There should be a remedy. Strict products liability is unavailable because the element of causation is lacking. Strike that requirement and label what remains "alternative" liability, "industry-wide" liability, or "market share" liability,

29. Defendants assert that there are no figures available to determine market share, that DES was provided for a number of uses other than to prevent miscarriage and it would be difficult to ascertain what proportion of the drug was used as a miscarriage preventative, and that the establishment of a time frame and area for market share would pose problems.

proving thereby that if you hit the square peg hard and often enough the round holes will really become square, although you may splinter the board in the process. . . .

NOTES AND QUESTIONS

1. *Sindell and Summers.* Are *Sindell*'s efforts to distinguish *Summers* merely verbal? What are the court's most significant reasons for concluding that the idea of "alternative" liability does not apply to the plaintiff's claims against DES manufacturers? What are the most important distinctions between market share liability and alternative liability?

2. *Outside California.* Several state courts have adopted a version of market share liability in DES cases. *See, e.g.*, Conley v. Boyle Drug Co., 570 So. 2d 275 (Fla. 1990); Hymowitz v. Eli Lilly & Co., 539 N.E.2d 1069 (N.Y. 1989); Collins v. Eli Lilly & Co., 342 N.W.2d 37 (Wis. 1984); Martin v. Abbott Labs., 689 P.2d 368 (Wash. 1984). Other courts have rejected it. *See* Sutowski v. Eli Lilly & Co., 696 N.E.2d 187 (Ohio 1998) (citing several other jurisdictions that have rejected it). Many have not addressed the question.

Among those states accepting market share liability in DES cases, there are several variations. The New York Court of Appeals' *Hymowitz* decision, cited above, involved numerous cases consolidated for purposes of deciding several questions, including the viability of a market share theory under New York law, as well as statute of limitations issues. As to the latter, the New York legislature had enacted a "savings" statute for DES plaintiffs that revived claims that would otherwise have been time-barred. The Court of Appeals upheld the constitutionality of the savings statute, and went on to endorse market share liability, in part relying on the statute as evidence of special legislative solicitude for DES claimants. Unlike *Sindell, Hymowitz* creates an *irrebuttable* presumption on causation under which each defendant is held liable to each DES plaintiff in proportion to its market share *even if* a given defendant could show that its DES could not have caused a particular plaintiff's injury. *Hymowitz* also specifies that each manufacturer's market share is to be determined by its percentage of the national market for DES, rather than its share of the market in the state or locality in which the plaintiff's mother resided at the time of ingesting DES. (*Sindell* left this question open.) By contrast, in *Conley*, the Florida court held that market share should be calculated at a geographically narrow level, such as the state or preferably the county in which the plaintiff's mother purchased DES. Wisconsin's DES case — *Collins* — treats the defendant pharmaceutical companies as joint tortfeasors, although market share is deemed relevant to the jury's apportionment of responsibility among them.

3. *The Fordham Comment.* As may be apparent from the above excerpt, the California Supreme Court relied heavily on a law student note in the Fordham Law Review. Although it is rare for courts to attribute such significance to a student note (or a faculty article, for that matter), tort law has long been a fruitful area of academic scholarship by law students.

4. *Intergenerational Torts.* One of the most difficult aspects of DES litigation was the fact that the plaintiffs were one generation removed from those who took the

drug—their mothers. The intergenerational problem was only intensified in *Enright v. Eli Lilly & Co.*, 570 N.E.2d 198 (N.Y. 1991), a case brought by *grandchildren* of women who took DES. Should these plaintiffs have a cause of action in negligence for injuries traceable to their grandmothers' ingestion of DES? The Court of Appeals held that the grandchildren could not bring a cause of action sounding in negligence because the manufacturers could not be charged with a duty to be vigilant of the effects of its product on third-generation victims.

5. *Beyond DES?* Many tort claimants face significant proof problems through no fault of their own. Consequently, theories of market share liability have been pleaded by plaintiffs seeking recovery for injuries allegedly caused by asbestos, tobacco, handguns, lead-based paint, latex gloves, blood clotting factors, and many other products. The effort to push market share liability into these other areas has been consistently rejected by courts. The few lower courts that have permitted plaintiffs to proceed have generally been reversed on appeal. There are, however, a handful of decisions in which a high court has endorsed the application of market share liability outside of the DES context. Among the most notable is the Hawaii Supreme Court's decision in *Smith v. Cutter Biological, Inc.*, 823 P.2d 717 (Haw. 1991), which applied the theory to the claims of plaintiffs alleging that they contracted diseases from tainted blood products.

In declining to expand the domain of market share liability, courts have suggested that the DES cases featured an unusual set of conditions that are rarely seen in combination. Among these were (1) the existence of systemic reasons, not bearing on the plaintiffs' diligence, for the absence of evidence on tortfeasor identification; (2) the ability of the plaintiffs to bring before the court a group of defendants that were responsible for almost all sales of the product; (3) the fact that the product in question was entirely generic and fungible in terms of its design specifications, its manufacture, and its propensity to cause the same illness among differently situated victims; and (4) the availability of at least some reliable data on market shares.

Two prominent post-*Sindell* litigations in which principles of market share liability have figured are *In re Methyl Tertiary Butyl Ether (MTBE) Products Liability Litigation*, 379 F. Supp. 2d 348 (S.D.N.Y. 2005) and *Thomas ex rel. Gramling v. Mallett*, 701 N.W.2d 523 (Wisc. 2005). In *MTBE*, suits brought by scores of villages and towns were consolidated before a federal district court in New York City. The suits alleged that a gasoline additive used by the defendant oil companies polluted their groundwater. The plaintiffs, however, could not identify which company's gasoline caused which pollution. Applying state law from several jurisdictions, the district judge determined that the substantive law of several of the relevant jurisdictions would permit the claims to go forward on a market share theory. In 2008, a settlement was reached among the defendants and most of the plaintiffs that called for an aggregate payment of $422 million.

Thomas involved lead-based paint litigation. The plaintiff child alleged mental disabilities resulting from ingestion of lead in rented homes that were painted decades earlier with paint containing lead. Because of the time lag, plaintiffs conceded that they were unable to identify which manufacturer(s)' paint poisoned the plaintiff. Similar arguments had been made in jurisdictions across the country prior to *Thomas*, and in each case appellate courts rejected market share liability on the grounds that different manufacturers' paint products are not fungible, that there is no "signature" injury associated with lead exposure, and that other sources of both lead poisoning (air, water, gasoline) and mental disabilities so cloud the causation and proximate causation inquiries as to render market share liability inappropriate. *See, e.g.*, Skipworth v. Lead Indus. Ass'n, Inc., 690 A.2d 169 (Pa. 1997). Working from its own variation of market share liability for DES — entitled "risk contribution" theory (*see* Collins v. Eli Lilly & Co., 342 N.W.2d 37 (Wis. 1984)), the Wisconsin Supreme Court in *Thomas* held that the plaintiff had stated a cause of action, notwithstanding the product identification problem, and denied summary judgment. The case went to trial in 2007, and the jury returned a verdict for the defendants.

Thomas notwithstanding, subsequent decisions from other courts have continued to reject the use of market share liability in lead paint litigation. In re Lead Paint Litigation, 924 A.2d 484 (N.J. 2007); City of St. Louis v. Benjamin Moore & Co., 226 S.W.3d 110 (Mo. 2007).* A subsequently rendered decision by a federal district court sitting in Wisconsin and applying Wisconsin law ruled that the imposition of liability under *Thomas*'s risk-contribution theory on the corporate successor to a company that had produced paint pigment containing lead would violate the successor's state and federal constitutional right not to be deprived of its property without due process of law. Gibson v. American Cyanamid Co., 719 F. Supp. 2d 1031 (E.D. Wis. 2010).

6. *Causation and Apportionment.* As explained in Chapter 8, in suits against multiple alleged tortfeasors the issue of *causation* — whether the wrongful acts of each of two or more defendants played a role in bringing about a plaintiff's injury — is distinct from the issue of *apportionment* — how liability should be divided among two or more actors found to have tortiously injured the plaintiff. *Sindell*'s adoption of market share liability seems in some respects to collapse that distinction. That is, the California Supreme Court appears to solve the evidentiary problem faced by the plaintiff on the issue of causation by implementing what it takes to be a fair scheme of apportionment. Yet because it was focused on the issue of causation, the court in *Sindell* in fact left open a critical question of apportionment: Would the liability imposed on those DES defendants that failed to *dis*prove causation be *joint and several*, such that the plaintiff could recover from any one defendant the full

---

* An intermediate California appellate court upheld the authority of public officials to bring "public nuisance" actions seeking injunctive relief — namely court-ordered abatement measures to eliminate or reduce the risk of exposures to paints containing lead — against five paint manufacturers. County of Santa Clara v. Atlantic Richfield Co., 137 Cal. App. 4th 292, *rev. denied*, (2006). In 2014, the trial judge hearing the case found three of the defendants jointly and severally liable for causing the nuisance and ordered that a fund be established to pay for the removal of lead paint from certain portions of the interiors of certain houses in California. The court estimated that these abatement measures will cost $1.15 billion. People v. Atlantic Richfield, Co., 2014 WL 1385823 (Cal. Super. 2014). By contrast, the Rhode Island Supreme Court in 2008 rejected as legally unsound a trial court judgment based on public nuisance against several paint manufacturers that included an order requiring the manufacturers to undertake abatement activities around the state. State v. Lead Indust. Ass'n, 951 A.2d 428 (R.I. 2008).

amount owed to her by all defendants?* Eight years later, in *Brown v. Superior Court*, 751 P.2d 470 (Cal. 1988), the California court answered that question with a resounding "no," concluding that market share liability would be several only. The court reasoned that *Sindell*, by imposing liability on each DES manufacturer in approximate proportion to the amount of harm actually caused by its DES, sought to strike an equitable balance between the plaintiff's interest in receiving redress and the defendant's interest in being assigned an appropriate amount of responsibility. Joint and several liability, it concluded, would upset this carefully struck balance. Almost all jurisdictions that relax the product identification requirement in DES cases follow *Brown* in rejecting joint and several liability.

REFERENCES/FURTHER READING

Actual Causation

Arno C. Becht & Frank W. Miller, *The Test of Factual Causation in Negligence and Strict Liability Cases* (1961).

Guido Calabresi, *Concerning Cause and the Law of Torts: An Essay for Harry Kalven, Jr.*, 43 U. Chi. L. Rev. 69 (1975).

Richard Goldberg (ed.), *Perspectives on Causation* (2011).

H. L. A. Hart & Tony Honoré, *Causation in the Law* (2d ed. 1985).

Morton J. Horwitz, *The Doctrine of Objective Causation*, in D. Kairys (ed.), *The Politics of Law: A Progressive Critique* (rev'd ed.) (1990).

Mark Kelman, *The Necessary Myth of Objective Causation Judgments in Liberal Political Theory*, 63 Chi.-Kent L. Rev. 579 (1987).

William M. Landes & Richard A. Posner, *Causation in Tort Law: An Economic Approach*, 12 J. Leg. Stud. 109 (1983).

J. L. Mackie, *The Cement of the Universe: A Study of Causation* (1974).

Michael S. Moore, *Causation and Responsibility: An Essay in Law, Morals and Metaphysics* (2009).

David Robertson, *Causation in the Restatement (Third) of Torts: Three Arguable Mistakes*, 44 Wake Forest L. Rev. 1007 (2009).

David Robertson, *The Common Sense of Cause in Fact*, 75 Tex. L. Rev. 1765 (1997).

David Rosenberg, *The Causal Connection in Mass Exposure Cases: A "Public Law" Vision of the Tort System*, 97 Harv. L. Rev. 851 (1984).

John D. Rue, *Note: Returning to the Roots of the Bramble Bush: The "But For" Test Regains Primacy in Causal Analysis in the American Law Institute's Proposed Restatement (Third) of Torts*, 71 Fordham L. Rev. 2679 (2003).

Joseph Sanders, Michael D. Green, & William C. Powers, Jr., *The Insubstantiality of the "Substantial Factor" Test for Causation*, 73 Mo. L. Rev. 399 (2008).

Jane Stapleton, *Choosing What We Mean By "Causation" in the Law*, 73 Mo. L. Rev. 433 (2008).

---

* By enabling the plaintiff to recover her full damages from one of two or more tortfeasors, joint and several liability puts the onus on the paying tortfeasor to collect contribution for its "overpayment" from the other tortfeasor(s). Thus, the main effect of joint and several liability is to shift from the victim to the paying tortfeasor the risk that one or more co-tortfeasors will be unavailable or insolvent. *See Ravo v. Rogatnick*, Chapter 8.

Sandy Steel, *Proof of Causation in Tort Law* (2015).

Vern R. Walker, *Restoring the Individual Plaintiff to Tort Law by Rejecting "Junk Logic" About Specific Causation*, 56 Ala. L. Rev. 381 (2004).

Richard W. Wright, *Causation in Tort Law*, 73 Cal. L. Rev. 1735 (1985).

Richard W. Wright, *Causation, Responsibility, Risk, Probability, Naked Statistics, and Proof: Pruning the Bramble Bush by Clarifying the Concepts*, 73 Iowa L. Rev. 1001 (1988).

Symposium: *Causation in the Law of Torts*, 63 Chi.-Kent L. Rev. 397 *et seq.* (1987).

Symposium on the Third Restatement of Torts, 54 Vand. L. Rev. 941 *et seq.* (2001) (article and commentaries by Profs. Stapleton, Geistfeld, Kelley, and Wright).

Causation in Rescue Cases

Wex S. Malone, *Ruminations on Cause-in-Fact*, 9 Stan. L. Rev. 60 (1956).

Loss of a Chance

David Fischer, *Tort Recovery for Loss of a Chance*, 36 Wake Forest L. Rev. 605 (2001).

John C. P. Goldberg, *What Clients Are Owed: Some Preliminary Cautions on Loss-of-a-Chance in Legal Malpractice*, 52 Emory L.J. 1201 (2003).

John C. P. Goldberg & Benjamin C. Zipursky, *Concern for Cause: A Comment on the Twerski-Sebok Plan for Administering Negligent Marketing Claims Against Gun Manufacturers*, 32 Conn. L. Rev. 1411 (2000).

Joseph H. King, Jr., *Causation, Valuation and Chance in Personal Injury Torts*, 90 Yale L.J. 1353 (1981).

Andrew R. Klein, *A Model for Enhanced Risk Recovery in Tort*, 56 Wash. & Lee L. Rev. 1173 (1999).

Stephen R. Perry, *Risk, Harm and Responsibility*, in David G. Owen (ed.), *Philosophical Foundations of Tort Law* 321, 330-339 (1995).

Ariel Porat & Eric A. Posner, *Aggregation and Law*, 122 Yale L.J. 2 (2012).

Ariel Porat & Alex Stein, *Tort Liability Under Uncertainty* (2002).

Aaron Twerski & Anthony J. Sebok, *Liability Without Cause? Further Ruminations on Cause-in-Fact as Applied to Handgun Liability*, 32 Conn. L. Rev. 1379 (2000).

Toxic Torts/*Daubert*

Ronald J. Allen, Daubert *and Its Discontents*, 76 Brook. L. Rev. 131 (2010).

Margaret Berger, *Eliminating General Causation: Notes Toward a New Theory of Justice and Toxic Torts*, 97 Colum. L. Rev. 2117 (1997).

David E. Bernstein, *Getting to Causation in Toxic Tort Cases*, 74 Brook. L. Rev. 51 (2008).

Lucinda M. Finley, *Guarding the Gate to the Courthouse: How Trial Judges Are Using Their Evidentiary Screening Function to Remake Tort Causation Rules*, 49 DePaul L. Rev. 335 (1999).

Joseph Sanders, *Applying* Daubert *Inconsistently? Proof of Individual Causation in Toxic Tort and Forensic Cases*, 75 Brook. L. Rev. 1367 (2010).

Joseph Sanders, *The Controversial Comment C: Factual Causation in Toxic-Substance and Disease Cases*, 44 Wake Forest L. Rev. 1029 (2009).

Jane Stapleton, *The Two Explosive Proof-of-Causation Doctrines Central to Asbestos Claims*, 74 Brook. L. Rev. 1011 (2009).

Richard Wright, *Liability for Possible Wrongs: Causation, Statistical Probability, and the Burden of Proof*, 41 Loy. L.A. L. Rev. 1295 (2008).

Asbestos Litigation

Stephen J. Carroll, et al., *Asbestos* Litigation (Rand Institute for Civil Justice, 2005)

Joseph Sanders, *The "Every Exposure" Cases and the Beginning of the Asbestos Endgame*, 88 Tul. L. Rev. 1153 (2014).

Tortfeasor Identification/*Summers, Sindell*

Anita Bernstein, Hymowitz v. Eli Lilly and Co., *Markets of Mothers*, in Robert L. Rabin & Stephen D. Sugarman, *Tort Stories* 151 (2003).

Richard Delgado, *Beyond* Sindell: *Relaxation of Cause-in-Fact Rules for Indeterminate Plaintiffs*, 70 Cal. L. Rev. 881 (1982).

Mark Geistfield, *The Doctrinal Unity of Alternative Liability and Market-Share Liability*, 155 U. Pa. L. Rev. 447 (2006).

Donald Gifford, *Market Share Liability Beyond DES Cases: The Solution to the Dilemma in Lead Paint Litigation?*, 58 S.C. L. Rev. 115 (2006).

Andrew R. Klein, *Beyond DES: Rejecting the Application of Market Share Liability in Blood Products Litigation*, 68 Tul. L. Rev. 883 (1994).

Arthur Ripstein & Benjamin C. Zipursky, *Corrective Justice in an Age of Mass Torts*, in Gerald J. Postema (ed.), *Philosophy and the Law of Torts* 214 (2001).

Allen Rostron, *Beyond Market Share Liability: A Theory of Proportional Share Liability for Nonfungible Products*, 52 U.C.L.A. L. Rev. 151 (2004).

Naomi Scheiner, *Comment: DES and a Proposed Theory of Enterprise Liability*, 46 Fordham L. Rev. 963 (1978).

CHAPTER 5

ALIGNING THE ELEMENTS: PROXIMATE CAUSE AND *PALSGRAF*

This chapter completes the inquiry into the prima facie case of negligence by introducing (1) *proximate cause* and (2) the *relational aspect of breach of duty.*

The first topic — proximate cause — is expressly recognized in the tort doctrine of every jurisdiction, though sometimes under other names, such as "legal cause."* The second — the relational aspect of breach — is not always recognized by scholars or by courts. Our decision to highlight it as a fundamental feature of negligence law rests, in part, on the fact that it lies at the core of the single most famous American negligence case, *Palsgraf v. Long Island Railroad Co.* As this chapter explains, we think there is a commonality between proximate cause and the relational aspect of breach, one which warrants treating them together.

Prior to this chapter, we have treated the elements of the negligence tort — duty, breach, causation, and damages — in isolation from one another. We have done so in an effort to emphasize the distinctive nature of the inquiry under each element. However, as the cases in this chapter help to demonstrate, the prima facie case of negligence cannot be captured without considering how its parts relate to one another. Indeed, negligence law contains a concept or set of concepts that filters out claims by plaintiffs who cannot establish that its components *connect with one another in the right way.* Put differently, the different parts of a negligence claim must be properly aligned with one another if the plaintiff is to have a valid claim.

We briefly encountered the first of these "alignment" concepts at the outset of Chapter 4. As noted there, the proximate cause inquiry — which tends to be treated by courts as a second component of the causation element, standing apart from the actual causation component — presupposes that the plaintiff has proven or can prove that a

---

* The Third Restatement departs dramatically from standard usage by using the phrase "scope of liability" rather than "proximate cause" or "legal cause." Restatement (Third) of Torts: Liability for Physical and Emotional Harm § 29 (2010).

breach of a duty owed to the plaintiff by the defendant was a cause-in-fact of the plaintiff's injury. The further question asked under the heading of proximate cause is whether the breach caused the injury in a natural or expected rather than serendipitous manner. In other words, by virtue of the proximate cause requirement, liability for negligence attaches only if the defendant's breach and the plaintiff's injury are linked to one another in the right sort of way: actual causation does not, by itself, fully capture what makes for a connection of the right sort.

The second "alignment" concept built into the tort of negligence is one that we describe as the relational aspect of breach of duty ("relational breach" for short). As we will see, it requires the plaintiff to demonstrate that the breach of duty about which she is complaining is a breach of a duty *owed to her*, rather than a duty owed only to persons differently situated from her. Whereas proximate cause—which concerns the link between breach and injury—is housed within the causation element of the negligence tort, the relational-breach-of-duty requirement is sometimes housed in the duty element, sometimes in the breach element, and sometimes not in any single element, but left to hover as a requirement over the claim as a whole.

Both proximate cause and relational breach of duty can be difficult to apply. Indeed, each has proved confusing, if not maddening, to students, lawyers, judges, and scholars. In part, the difficulty is inherent in the concepts; they are subtle. Adding to the problem is the tendency among many to muddy the waters further by using these concepts, particularly the concept of proximate cause, to refer not only to the alignment issue mentioned above but also to various other considerations that might affect attributions of responsibility to those whose tortious conduct has caused injury to another. Thus, a central aim of Section I of this chapter is to untangle different senses of "proximate cause," in part so that its primary sense becomes more intelligible. Similarly, we hope in Section II to articulate and clarify what it means to locate within the duty element a "relational aspect." Section III considers linkages between the alignment issues discussed in this chapter and the rules pertaining to affirmative duties discussed in Chapter 2.

I. PROXIMATE CAUSE

The primary question posed under the heading of "proximate cause" is whether there is something about the actual causal connection between a defendant's carelessness and a plaintiff's injury that warrants freeing the defendant from liability for that injury *notwithstanding* the connection. Lawyers and commentators have employed various different concepts and terms to capture the sense(s) in which an attenuated causal connection defeats the attribution to an actor of responsibility for harms caused by an actor's carelessness.

Use of the phrase "proximate cause" traces back at least to Francis Bacon, the great seventeenth-century English politician and scientist, who offered this maxim: *In jure non remota causa, sed proxima, spectatur* ("In law, not the remote cause, but the proximate, is looked to"). Despite its pedigree, the phrase has sometimes been condemned as misleading because the adjective "proximate," if taken literally, suggests that liability should attach for carelessness causing injury only if that carelessness is sufficiently near to an injury in time or space. In fact, notions of spatial or temporal distance, while sometimes relevant to the issue of proximate cause, are not dispositive of it.

Consider the imagined case of the bee-sting plaintiff provided at the beginning of Chapter 4. There, the driver's carelessness was not far removed from the pedestrian's injury either in time or space. Yet we have supposed that it would not be deemed a proximate cause of that damage. Moreover, many injuries complained of in negligence result from careless acts that took place hundreds or even thousands of miles from the locus of the plaintiff's injury (*see MacPherson*, Chapter 2), or that took place years before the plaintiff's injury emerged (*see Sindell*, Chapter 4). Thus, although time and distance certainly can matter in determining whether carelessness counts as a proximate cause of an injury, it is clear that proximate cause is not determined simply by reference to temporal or spatial proximity.

So what is it that makes a given careless act a proximate cause of an injury rather than a remote cause? In the decision that follows, consider the efforts of the Texas Supreme Court to get a handle on this elusive distinction. Notice the array of terms invoked in the different Justices' opinions in the effort to capture what it is about the causal connection in the case before it that defeats or permits the imposition of liability.

Union Pump Co. v. Allbritton

898 S.W.2d 773 (Tex. 1995)

Owen, J. The issue in this case is whether the condition, act, or omission of which a personal injury plaintiff complains was, as a matter of law, too remote to constitute legal causation. Plaintiff brought suit alleging negligence . . . and the trial court granted summary judgment for the defendant. The court of appeals reversed and remanded, holding that the plaintiff raised issues of fact concerning proximate and producing cause. Because we conclude that there was no legal causation as a matter of law, we reverse the judgment of the court of appeals and render judgment that plaintiff take nothing.

On the night of September 4, 1989, a fire occurred at Texaco Chemical Company's facility in Port Arthur, Texas. A pump manufactured by Union Pump Company caught fire and ignited the surrounding area. This particular pump had caught on fire twice before. Sue Allbritton, a trainee employee of Texaco Chemical, had just finished her shift and was about to leave the plant when the fire erupted. She and her supervisor Felipe Subia, Jr., were directed to and did assist in abating the fire.

Approximately two hours later, the fire was extinguished. However, there appeared to be a problem with a nitrogen purge valve, and Subia was instructed to block [off] the valve. Viewing the facts in a light most favorable to Allbritton, there was some evidence that an emergency situation existed at that point in time. Allbritton asked if she could accompany Subia and was allowed to do so. To get to the nitrogen purge valve, Allbritton followed Subia over an aboveground pipe rack, which was approximately two and one-half feet high, rather than going around it. It is undisputed that this was not the safer route, but it was the shorter one. Upon reaching the valve, Subia and Allbritton were notified that it was not necessary to block it off. Instead of returning by the route around the pipe rack, Subia chose to walk across it, and Allbritton followed. Allbritton was injured when she hopped or slipped off the pipe rack. There is evidence that the pipe rack was wet because of the fire and that Allbritton and Subia were still wearing fireman's hip boots and other firefighting gear when the injury occurred. Subia admitted that he chose to walk over the pipe rack rather than taking a safer alternative route because he had a "bad habit" of doing so.

Allbritton sued Union Pump. . . . But for the pump fire, she asserts, she would never have walked over the pipe rack, which was wet with water or firefighting foam. . . . The question before this Court is whether Union Pump established as a matter of law that neither its conduct nor its product was a legal cause of Allbritton's injuries. Stated another way, was Union Pump correct in contending that there was no causative link between the defective pump and Allbritton's injuries as a matter of law?

Negligence requires a showing of proximate cause. . . . Proximate cause consists of both cause in fact and foreseeability. Cause in fact means that the defendant's act or omission was a substantial factor in bringing about the injury which would not otherwise have occurred. . . .

At some point in the causal chain, the defendant's conduct or product may be too remotely connected with the plaintiff's injury to constitute legal causation. As this Court noted in City of Gladewater v. Pike, 727 S.W.2d 514, 518 (Tex. 1987), defining the limits of legal causation "eventually mandates weighing of policy considerations." *See also* Springall v. Fredericksburg Hospital and Clinic, 225 S.W.2d 232, 235 (Tex. Civ. App.—San Antonio 1949, no writ), in which the court of appeals observed:

> [T]he law does not hold one legally responsible for the remote results of his wrongful acts and therefore a line must be drawn between immediate and remote causes. The doctrine of "proximate cause" is employed to determine and fix this line and "is the result of an effort by the courts to avoid, as far as possible the metaphysical and philosophical niceties in the age-old discussion of causation, and to lay down a rule of general application which will, as nearly as may be done by a general rule, apply a practical test, the test of common experience, to human conduct when determining legal rights and legal liability."

Id. at 235 (quoting City of Dallas v. Maxwell, 248 S.W. 667, 670 (Tex. Comm'n App. 1923, holding approved)).

Drawing the line between where legal causation may exist and where, as a matter of law, it cannot, has generated a considerable body of law. Our Court has considered where the limits of legal causation should lie in the factually analogous case of Lear Siegler, Inc. v. Perez, [819 S.W.2d 470 (Tex. 1991)]. The threshold issue was whether causation was negated as a matter of law in an action where negligence and product liability theories were asserted. Perez, an employee of the Texas Highway Department, was driving a truck pulling a flashing arrow sign behind a highway sweeping operation to warn traffic of the highway maintenance. The sign malfunctioned when wires connecting it to the generator became loose, as they had the previous day. Perez got out of the truck to push the wire connections back together, and an oncoming vehicle, whose driver was asleep, struck the sign, which in turn struck Perez. Perez's survivors brought suit against the manufacturer of the sign. In holding that any defect in the sign was not the legal cause of Perez's injuries, we found a comment to the Restatement (Second) of Torts, section 431, instructive on the issue of legal causation:

> In order to be a legal cause of another's harm, it is not enough that the harm would not have occurred had the actor not been negligent. . . . The negligence must also be a substantial factor in bringing about the plaintiff's harm. The word "substantial" is used to denote the fact that the defendant's conduct has such an effect in producing the harm as to lead reasonable men to regard it as a cause, using that word in the popular sense, in which there always lurks the idea of responsibility, rather than in the so-called "philosophic sense," which includes every one of the great number of events without which any happening would not have occurred.

Lear Siegler, 819 S.W.2d at 472 (quoting Restatement (Second) of Torts § 431 cmt. a (1965)).

As this Court explained in *Lear Siegler*, the connection between the defendant and the plaintiff's injuries simply may be too attenuated to constitute legal cause. Legal cause is not established if the defendant's conduct or product does no more than furnish the condition that makes the plaintiff's injury possible. *Id.* . . .

This Court similarly considered the parameters of legal causation in Bell v. Campbell, 434 S.W.2d 117, 122 (Tex. 1968). In *Bell*, two cars collided, and a trailer attached to one of them disengaged and overturned into the opposite lane. A number of people gathered, and three of them were attempting to move the trailer when they were struck by another vehicle. *Id.* at 119. This Court held that the parties to the first accident were not a proximate cause of the plaintiffs' injuries, reasoning:

> All acts and omissions charged against respondents had run their course and were complete. Their negligence did not actively contribute in any way to the injuries involved in this suit. It simply created a condition which attracted [the plaintiffs] to the scene, where they were injured by a third party.

Id. at 122. . . .

Even if the pump fire were in some sense a "philosophic" or "but for" cause of Allbritton's injuries, the forces generated by the fire had come to rest when she fell off the pipe rack. The fire had been extinguished, and Allbritton was walking away from the scene. Viewing the evidence in the light most favorable to Allbritton, the pump fire did no more than create the condition that made Allbritton's injuries possible. We conclude that the circumstances surrounding her injuries are too remotely connected with Union Pump's conduct or pump to constitute a legal cause of her injuries.

Cornyn, J. (concurring). I concur in the Court's judgment, but for different reasons than those given in its opinion. I would hold that although the defective pump was a cause-in-fact of Sue Allbritton's injury, neither Union Pump's negligence nor the defective pump was a legal cause of her injury. Because the Court's opinion conflates foreseeability and other policy issues with its cause-in-fact analysis, I do not join its opinion. . . .

[Justice Cornyn proceeded to undertake an exhaustive review of how cause-in-fact and proximate cause have been analyzed by academics and the Texas courts.—Eds.] . . .

This case does not present a question of cause-in-fact. The pump defect clearly was a "but for" cause of Allbritton's injuries: assuming the truth of Allbritton's allegations, as we must in this summary judgment case, if the pump had not been defective, there would have been no fire, and Allbritton would have gone home uninjured at the end of her shift. . . .

But determining that the defect was the cause-in-fact of Allbritton's injuries does not end the inquiry. We must decide whether the pump defect meets the second prong of . . . proximate cause. . . . In proximate cause, this other element is foreseeability, but it also incorporates policy driven decisions such as when subsequent events will be treated as intervening causes. In this case, the injury to Allbritton was not foreseeable. Allbritton's injuries were the result of a needlessly dangerous shortcut taken after the crisis had subsided.[4] Holding Union Pump liable for Allbritton's failure to use proper care in exiting the area of the fire after the crisis has ended is akin to holding it liable for an auto accident she suffered on the way home, even though the accident probably would not have occurred had she left after her normal shift. Foreseeability allows us to cut off Union Pump's liability at some point; I would do so at the point the crisis had abated or at the point that Allbritton and Subia departed from their usual, safe path. . . .

Spector, J. (dissenting). . . .

The record reflects that at the time Sue Allbritton's injury occurred, the forces generated by the fire in question had *not* come to rest. Rather, the emergency situation was continuing. The whole area of the fire was covered in water and foam; in at least some places, the water was almost knee-deep. Allbritton was still wearing hip boots and other gear, as required to fight the fire. Viewing all the evidence in the light most favorable to Allbritton, I agree with Justice Cornyn that the pump defect was . . . a cause in fact [of Allbritton's injury].

This case is markedly different from the two main cases on which the majority relies: Lear Siegler, Inc. v. Perez, 819 S.W.2d 470 (Tex. 1991), and Bell v. Campbell, 434 S.W.2d 117 (Tex. 1968). In each of those cases, a defendant's negligence simply created a condition that attracted an individual to the scene, where a negligent third party inflicted an injury. Here, in contrast, there was no negligent third party. To whatever extent Allbritton's own negligence may have contributed to her injury, a jury should be allowed to allocate comparative responsibility. . . .

NOTES AND QUESTIONS

1. *Not Lacking for Words.* Explain how the following terms that appear in the majority's opinion relate to one another: "cause," "condition," "cause in fact,"

4. My conclusion might be different had Allbritton taken the shortcut under emergency conditions because it is foreseeable that workers might take extraordinary risks in trying to extinguish a dangerous fire.

"legal cause," "proximate cause," "remote cause," "foreseeability." When the concurring opinion uses some of these terms, does it do so in the same way? What is the significance of the plaintiff's possible carelessness in taking a "shortcut" for the question of whether the defendant's carelessness functioned as a proximate cause of her injuries?

2. *Why Does Fortuity Matter?* Consider the auto-accident hypothetical mentioned in Justice Cornyn's concurrence. Suppose that, through no fault of her own, Allbritton was injured in a car crash while driving home after responding to the fire. Suppose further that she can prove that she would not have been involved in a crash but for the fire generated by Union Pump's carelessness. Why shouldn't Union face liability for her crash-related injuries?

3. *Natural, Direct, Foreseeable.* The *Allbritton* majority's use of foreseeability as a test of sorts for proximate cause is typical among contemporary courts. We will explore applications of that test in the next main case and the notes that follow. Before doing so, it will be instructive to consider two prominent alternative formulations of proximate cause that courts employed in the nineteenth and twentieth centuries but have now generally abandoned, at least in name.

a. *Ryan: Natural and Ordinary.* A prominent nineteenth-century proximate cause decision is *Ryan v. New York Central R.R. Co.*, 35 N.Y. 210 (1866). Defendant owned and operated a railyard. Because of its carelessness, sparks from one of its engines ignited wood in a shed located in the yard. The fire then spread to the plaintiff's house, located about 125-150 feet from the shed. The house was destroyed, as were several others.

The Court of Appeals affirmed entry of judgment for the defendant on plaintiff's negligence claim, reasoning that the defendant's carelessness was not a proximate cause of the house being burned down. According to the Court, while it is a "natural and ordinary" consequence of a fire being set that it will travel from its source to one other structure, it is neither natural nor ordinary for fire to spread further. Because, in this instance, the fire had already traveled from the engine to the shed before spreading to the plaintiff's house, the Court deemed the burning of the plaintiff's house to be a "remote" consequence for which the defendant was not liable. In light of this memorable holding, *Ryan* is sometimes described as adopting the "one-leap rule" for negligence involving the spread of fire.

One way to try to make sense of *Ryan*'s seemingly strained view of fire's limited propensity to spread is to interpret the court as embracing a hyper-literal and extremely narrow conception of "directness." However, the court's reasoning perhaps was fueled less by adherence to an artificially narrow notion of "direct" causation than to a pragmatic anxiety very much in tension with its claim that fire is not wont to "leap" more than once. Said the Court: "To hold that [a property owner] must . . . guarantee the security of his neighbors [from fire damage] on both sides, and to an unlimited extent, would be to create *liability which would be the destruction of all civilized society*" (emphasis added). Less melodramatically, it opined that a more expansive notion of proximate cause would permit the imposition of liability "quite beyond the offense committed."

The unsatisfactory legal reasoning in *Ryan*, as well as the Court's overt invocation of policy and fairness concerns, suggest that, at least at times, the phrase "proximate cause" is used by judges as a way of "dressing up" in legal language arbitrary limits on liability (like the one-leap rule) that are set to prevent the imposition of "disproportionate" liability, or to avoid unduly suppressing useful activity by threat of massive liability. (Of course to observe that courts sometimes use proximate cause in this way is hardly to conclude that the concept can only be used that way, or is always or even commonly used that way.) We will encounter a famous expression of this sort of skepticism about the conceptual content of proximate cause in Judge William Andrews's dissenting opinion in the *Palsgraf* case, reproduced in Section II below.

For its part, the New York Court of Appeals quickly backed away from *Ryan*'s one-leap rule for fire damage. *See* Webb v. Rome W. & O. R.R. Co., 49 N.Y. 420 (1872). Later New York decisions hold that a defendant is liable in negligence for transmitting fire to a plaintiff's property by sparks or by the ignition of materials in its ownership and control, but not for damage caused when the fire spreads to the plaintiff's property by first igniting another property owned by a third party. Homac Corp. v. Sun Oil Co., 180 N.E. 172 (N.Y. 1932).

b. *Polemis: Directness.* Another prominent older formulation of proximate cause emanates, oddly enough, from a 1921 English decision that reviewed an arbitration panel's resolution of a *contract* dispute as to who should bear the cost associated with the destruction of a leased ship. The decision—*In re Arbitration Between Polemis and Furness, Withy & Co. Ltd.*, 3 K.B. 560 (1921)—is now known simply as the Polemis case.

Furness leased a steamship from Polemis. Clause 5 of the lease specified that Furness was obligated to return the boat "in same good order and condition as when delivered to [it], fair wear and tear excepted." However, Clause 21 exempted Furness from liability for damage to the ship caused by, among other things, "*fire on board*. . . ."

The ship carried in one of its cargo holds containers of flammable benzene. Some of these were leaking, which allowed benzene vapor to accumulate in the hold. While the ship was docked, workers employed by Furness were in the process of hoisting containers up to the ship's deck by means of a rope that passed through a winch. In the process, they knocked a wooden plank off the deck into the hold. The fall of the plank "was instantaneously followed by a rush of flames from the . . . hold, and this resulted eventually in the total destruction of the ship."

Polemis initiated an arbitration seeking compensation from Furness equal to the value of the lost ship. The main question raised in the arbitration was whether the fire could fairly be attributed to the negligence of Furness's employees. This was the main question because the arbitrators concluded that the "fire on board" provision of Clause 21 did *not* immunize Furness from liability under Clause 5 for failing to return the boat intact *if* that failure was attributable to the fault of Furness or its employees.

The arbitrators found: (1) Furness's workers had been careless in how they used the rope apparatus; (2) the fire arose from a spark that ignited flammable vapors in the hold emitted by the leaky containers; and (3) the workers *could not reasonably have anticipated that a spark would be produced by the falling of the plank.* Notwithstanding this last finding, the arbitrators concluded that the fire was attributable to the workers' carelessness simply because their carelessness functioned as a cause of it. Thus, they concluded that Furness could not take advantage of the "fire on board" exception to its duty to return the ship in good order. Accordingly, they awarded Polemis nearly £200,000 — a huge sum.

On appeal, Furness's lawyers argued that, even if the arbitrators were correct to read Clause 21 as not immunizing Furness from liability for failure to return an intact ship because of fire damage attributable to Furness's carelessness, they erred in attributing *this* fire to Furness's carelessness. True, the employees' carelessness functioned as an actual cause of the fire. Nonetheless, the unforeseeability of a falling plank causing an explosion — its unexpectedness — entailed that Furness could not be held responsible for it.

The three Kings Bench justices who heard the appeal rejected this argument and upheld the award. In different opinions, each maintained that, because Furness's employees' careless acts *directly caused* the explosion, Furness could not benefit from the "fire on board" exemption of Clause 21. That the workers could not have foreseen that the dropping of the plank to fall would cause an explosion was deemed by the justices to be "irrelevant."

c. *Wagon Mound (No. 1): Foreseeability.* The modern ascension of foreseeability formulations of proximate cause traces back to two English decisions issued in the 1960s that arose out of the same set of events. These decisions are now known as *The Wagon Mound (No. 1)* and *The Wagon Mound (No. 2).*

The ship *Wagon Mound* was moored at a wharf in Sydney Harbor, Australia. Its crew carelessly released a large slick of furnace oil into the harbor. Workers at a nearby dock, known as Morts Dock, were repairing another ship named the *Corrimal.* Their repairs involved the use of welding torches. Upon becoming aware of the oil spill, the supervisor who worked for Morts Dock ordered his workers to suspend their activities. He then inquired of the owner of the wharf at which the *Wagon Mound* was moored whether the oil in the harbor water might ignite. Based on that discussion, he concluded that there was no risk of ignition and ordered his men back to work. The next day, sparks from the welding operations ignited some debris floating in the water, which in turn ignited the oil, resulting in a fire that destroyed Morts Dock and the *Corrimal.*

The first *Wagon Mound* decision primarily concerned an action for negligence brought by the owners of Morts Dock against the owners of the *Wagon Mound.* The trial court in that action, relying in part on the testimony of a "distinguished scientist," concluded that the crew of the *Wagon Mound* could *not* have foreseen that, by spilling large quantities of furnace oil into the harbor, they might cause a fire. Said the trial court: "The raison d'etre of furnace oil is, of course, that it shall burn, but I find the [crew] did not know and could not reasonably be expected to have known that it was capable of being set afire when spread on water." Nonetheless, the trial court went on to conclude that, because the spilled oil made *direct contact* with the dock, thereby mucking it up, the owners of the *Wagon Mound* were liable for the destruction of Morts Dock under *Polemis*'s directness test.

The trial court's decision was reversed on appeal by the Privy Council of the United Kingdom, a London-based court that oversaw the decisions of commonwealth courts, and to which the decisions of Australian courts were at the time appealable. *See* Overseas Tankship (U.K.), Ltd. v. Morts Dock & Eng'g Co., 1 All E.R. 404

(Privy Council 1961). In a lengthy opinion, Viscount Simonds concluded that *Polemis* "should no longer be regarded as good law." Instead, he reasoned, the test for proximate cause should be whether the type of harm suffered by the plaintiff was reasonably foreseeable to the defendants at the time they acted carelessly. In support of this conclusion, Simonds reasoned in part as follows:

> . . . it does not seem consonant with current ideas of justice of morality that, for an act of negligence, however slight or venial, which results in some trivial foreseeable damage, the actor should be liable for all consequences, however unforeseeable and however grave, so long as they can be said to be "direct." It is a principle of civil liability, subject only to qualifications which have no present relevance, that a man must be considered to be responsible for the probable consequences of his act. To demand more of him is too harsh a rule, to demand less is to ignore that civilised order requires the observance of a minimum standard of behaviour.

Elsewhere, Simonds wrote:

> the *Polemis* rule works in a very strange way. After the event even a fool is wise. Yet it is not the hindsight of a fool, but it is the foresight of the reasonable man which alone can determine responsibility. The *Polemis* rule, by substituting "direct" for "reasonably foreseeable" consequence, leads to a conclusion equally illogical and unjust.

In short, given the trial court's conclusion that no reasonable person could have foreseen that the careless spilling of oil posed a risk of fire damage, the defendant could not be held liable for having caused it.

Viscount Simonds' opinion further rejected the idea that liability for the fire damage ought to attach on the ground that the defendant clearly could have foreseen that the oil spill risked *some* adverse effect on the dock — namely, mucking it up with oil. That the defendant could foresee one form of property damage was not, in the court's view, sufficient to hold it responsible for causing an entirely different sort of damage.

d. *Wagon Mound (No. 2).* Five years later, the Privy Council considered the claim of the *Corrimal*'s owner against the owners of the *Wagon Mound.* Overseas Tankship (U.K.) Ltd. v. The Miller Steamship Co., 2 All E.R. 709 (Privy Council 1966) (*Wagon Mound (No. 2)*). In contrast to its first *Wagon Mound* decision, the Privy Council here concluded that the very same fire that destroyed Morts Dock *was* a foreseeable consequence of the furnace-oil spill, and hence the spill should be deemed a proximate cause of damage to the *Corrimal.* The Council justified this about-face on the ground that "the evidence [in *Wagon Mound (No. 2)*] . . . was substantially different from the evidence . . . in *Wagon Mound (No. 1)*." This difference, they opined, resulted from the plaintiffs in the first case being "embarrassed by a difficulty" that did not confront the owner of the *Corrimal.* Can you identify this difficulty? What would have discouraged the owners of Morts Dock from attempting to prove in *Wagon Mound (No. 1)* that the ignition of the oil was foreseeable?

* * *

The *Wagon Mound* decisions signaled the demise of *Polemis'* directness test and brought to prominence the idea that a harm that is an unforeseeable consequence —

even a harm to a foreseeable victim (*i.e.*, a person whom the defendant could readily imagine injuring through some other sequence of events) — is one for which the defendant should not be held liable. Many American courts have likewise settled on a foreseeability test for proximate cause. Still, it would be a mistake to suppose that the adoption of foreseeability tests has spared courts from having to face difficult questions of application. Consider the following contemporary invocation by the British House of Lords of foreseeability as the criterion for proximate cause. Does this decision help clarify what sort of causal sequences will or will not subject a careless actor to liability? If not, are skeptics right to suppose that proximate cause language is often (or always) just empty legal jargon?

Check Your Understanding

Actual and Proximate Cause

In the questions that follow, the terms "actual cause" and "proximate cause" are used as they are described at the outset of this chapter and Chapter 4.

1. Is it possible for a defendant's careless act to be a proximate cause of a plaintiff's injury without being an actual cause? Why or why not?
2. Is it possible for carelessness on the part of two actors, acting independently of each other, each to operate as a proximate cause of a single injury suffered by a plaintiff? Why or why not?
3. *M* carelessly manufactures a toy designed for use by toddlers that is too small, and thus presents a choking hazard. While playing in her house one day, *P*, a toddler, drops the toy into a crack between the floorboards of the hardwood floor in her living room. The toy gets stuck in the crack, and five minutes later, *P* trips over the toy, falls, and breaks her arm. *P*'s parents have brought a negligence claim against *M* on *P*'s behalf. Assume that *P*'s parents will have no difficulty establishing injury, duty, breach, and actual cause. Does *M* have a plausible argument against liability on proximate cause grounds? If you were representing *P*'s parents, how would you attempt to establish that *M*'s carelessness was a proximate cause of *P*'s injury?

Jolley v. Sutton London Borough Council

[2000] 2 Lloyd's Rep. 65 (H.L.)*

. . . .

Lord Steyn. My Lords, on Apr. 8, 1990, in the grounds of a block of council flats owned and occupied by the London Borough of Sutton, Justin Jolley, then a schoolboy aged 14, sustained serious spinal injuries in an accident. It arose when a small abandoned cabin cruiser, which had been left lying in the grounds of the block of flats, fell on Justin

* At the time of this decision, Lord Steyn and his colleagues were known as the Appellate Committee of the House of Lords, or "Law Lords." For centuries, the Law Lords, drawn from Parliament's upper house, served as the highest appellate court in the United Kingdom. As noted in Chapter 2, Parliament in 2009 essentially replaced the Law Lords with a 12-person Supreme Court whose members now have the title of "Justice." The Justices are chosen by a selection commission, subject to the approval of the Lord Chancellor. — Eds.

as he lay underneath it while attempting to repair and paint it. As a result he is now a paraplegic. He claimed damages in tort from the council. At trial the claim was primarily based on a breach of the Occupiers' Liability Acts, 1957 and 1984. After a seven day trial in 1998 Mr. Geoffrey Brice, Q.C., a Deputy High Court Judge, gave judgment for Justin but reduced the damages by 25 per cent by virtue of a finding of contributory negligence. The Judge awarded damages in the sum of £621,710, together with the interest. . . . The council appealed. The Court of Appeal unanimously reversed the judge's conclusions on the merits and entered judgment for the council.

The Uncontroversial Background

The uncontroversial background can be taken from the statement of facts and issues. The council own and occupy the common parts of a block of council flats known as Hayling Court at North Cheam in Surrey. In 1987 a boat was brought on a trailer to the grounds of Hayling Court. It was placed on a grassed area where children played. The boat was abandoned. It was exposed to the elements and became derelict and rotten. It was neither covered nor fenced around. The trailer was by the side of the boat. In December, 1988 the council placed a sticker on the boat which was in a form used for abandoned cars. It read "Danger do not touch this vehicle unless you are the owner" and stated that it would be removed within seven days unless claimed by its owner. Complaints about the boat were made to the council by residents of the block of flats. In the early summer of 1989 when he was 13 Justin and a friend, Karl Warnham, saw the boat when they were walking past the flats. In February, 1990 the two boys returned to the boat, planning to repair it and take it to Cornwall to sail it. Justin was by then 14 years old. They swivelled the boat round, and lifted the front end of the boat onto the trailer so as to be able to get under the boat to repair the hull. The trailer supports made holes in the wooden structure of the boat. Accordingly, the boys pulled the boat off the trailer. In order to repair the holes in the hull, Justin took a car jack and some wood from his home and the boys jacked the front of the abandoned boat up some 2½ feet. In that position the boys painted part of the boat, and attempted to repair holes with wood, nails and glue. On one occasion one of the boys put his foot through the structure. Justin and Karl had worked on the boat on about five occasions over some six weeks from February, 1990 until the date of the accident. On Apr. 8, 1990 Justin and Karl were underneath the jacked up boat working on it. After a while Justin noticed that Karl had crawled out from under the boat. Justin remained. The boat seemed to rock above him. He tried to get out from under the boat but before he could do so it came down onto him and caused him to suffer a broken back and consequent paraplegia. The immediate cause of the collapse was that the boat toppled off the jack and other material upon which it was propped. It was not established that the derelict or rotten condition of the boat was causative of the collapse.

The Judgment at First Instance

In a careful and detailed judgment the judge analysed the evidence and made detailed findings of fact. He then quoted the relevant statutory provisions. Section 2(2) of the Occupiers' Liability Act, 1957 defines the "common duty of care" as:

> . . . a duty to take such care as in all the circumstances of the case is reasonable to see that the visitor will be reasonably safe in using the premises for

> the purposes for which he is invited or permitted by the occupier to be there.

Sub-section (3) provides:

> The circumstances relevant for the present purpose include the degree of care, and of want of care, which would ordinarily be looked for in such a visitor, so that (for example) in proper cases—
>
> (a) an occupier must be prepared for children to be less careful than adults . . .

The judge observed that it has long been established that children are or may be attracted to meddle with objects on premises or property which constitute a danger when meddled with. He stated in very general terms that the occupier is under a duty to protect a child from danger caused by meddling with such an object by taking reasonable steps in the circumstances including, when appropriate, removing the object altogether so as to avoid the prospect of injury. He cited the well known case of *Hughes v. Lord Advocate*, [1963] A.C. 837, as well as a number of other decisions, illustrative of traps or allurements causing harm to children leading to liability by occupiers.

The judge then recorded his conclusions [1998] 1 Lloyd's Rep. 433, pp. 439-440:

> Did the boat present a trap or allurement to the plaintiff and Karl and one which presented a danger of physical injury to them? If so, was this state of affairs reasonably foreseeable to the defendants such that they ought to have taken measures in good time to protect boys such as the plaintiff from such danger? One must keep well in mind that this case is concerned with boys aged 13 and 14. The boat was on a grassed area outside a block of council flats in an area where there were abandoned cars. I have no doubt that the presence of the boat was something which one ought to anticipate would be an attraction to children of differing ages. Younger children might simply play on it and in its rotting condition might suffer injury, perhaps of a quite minor nature. Mr. Palmer stressed that these two boys were not so much playing with the boat as working on it. I do not believe any such distinction assists the defendants. Play can take the form of mimicking adult behaviour. It was reasonably foreseeable that children including those of the age of the plaintiff would meddle with the boat at risk of some physical injury. So far as this type of accident was concerned, it is really only likely to occur if the child was a young teenage boy with strength and ability to raise the boat and prop it up. Abandoned cars were clearly treated by the defendants as a potential source of danger and this abandoned boat must also have fallen into that category. Although the warning DANGER contained on the stickers is not conclusive as to whether a particular object presented a danger it is at least a pointer in that direction.
>
> There was no reason in fact or in law preventing the defendants from removing and disposing of the boat well before the accident (as actually occurred after it). . . . I find that is what the defendants ought to have done, not merely because the boat was an eyesore but because it was a trap or allurement to children.

The judge summed up his conclusion as follows:

> I find that the type of accident and injury which occurred in this case was reasonably foreseeable (albeit that it involved significant meddling with the boat by two young teenage boys and that the injuries proved to be very severe) and that the actions of the plaintiff and/or Karl did not amount to a novus actus. Accordingly, I find the defendants in breach of their duty to the plaintiff as occupiers and (subject to the point on contributory negligence considered below) liable to the plaintiff for the injury, loss and damage which he has sustained.

I have set out these findings of fact at length because the interpretation of the judge's finding became controversial during the hearing of the appeal in the House.

The Judgments of the Court of Appeal

The leading judgment in the Court of Appeal was given by Lord Woolf, M.R. He cited extensively from the decision in the Privy Council in *Overseas Tankship (U.K.) Ltd. v. Morts Dock and Engineering Co. Ltd. (The Wagon Mound)*, [1961] 1 Lloyd's Rep. 1; [1961] A.C. 388 (The Wagon Mound (No. 1)) and *Hughes v. Lord Advocate*, [1963] A.C. 837. Lord Woolf, M.R. then explained his reasons for disagreeing with the judge:

> The Judge attached importance to the presence of the boat as being both an allurement and a trap. While this can be of significance in some cases it is only part of the background to this case. There can be no dispute that, if this boat was left in this position, children would be attracted by it and would play with it. This was conceded. It was also a trap in the sense that it was not immediately apparent that it was in a rotten condition, that is in a condition where it could prove dangerous because a child could find that a plank or planks gave way. It was a combination of these two features that made it the duty of the council to have the boat removed. They failed to do this and in that respect they were negligent. However, these features, the attractiveness of the boat to children and its dangerous condition, were not established to be part of the causes of the accident. The immediate cause of the accident was that the two boys jacked and propped the boat up so that they could work underneath it and did so in a way that meant that the boat was unstable and could and did fall on the plaintiff.
>
> The question which has to be asked is: was this accident in the words of Lord Pearce "of a different type and kind from anything that a defender could have foreseen?" In answering this question it is necessary to have well in mind that the council should have appreciated that it is difficult to anticipate what children will do when playing with a boat of this sort. Boats, like cars, if they were left "abandoned" in an area where children have access, will certainly attract children to play with them. But what the plaintiff was engaged on was an activity very different from normal play.
>
> Even making full allowance for the unpredictability of children's behaviour, I am driven to conclude that it was not reasonably foreseeable that an accident could occur as a result of the boys deciding to work under a propped up boat. Nor could any reasonably similar accident have been foreseen. Ironically the state of the boat was so poor that it made it less likely that it would be repairable or that boys

would embark on doing the necessary repairs. The photographs of the boat and the evidence of Mr. Hall indicate that it was a fairly heavy structure. It would be by no means easy for the boat to be moved or raised. In deciding whether the accident was foreseeable it is important not only to consider the precise accident which occurred but the class of accident.

. . . .

Was the Court of Appeal Entitled to Disturb the Judge's Finding?

. . . [T]he Court of Appeal never squarely addressed the question whether the judge's critical finding was open to him on the evidence. For my part the judge's reasons for that finding are convincing in the context of teenage boys attracted by an obviously abandoned boat. And I do not regard what they did as so very different from normal play. The judge's observation that play can take the form of mimicking adult behaviour is a perceptive one. It is true, of course, that one is not dealing with a challenge to an issue of primary fact. The issue whether an accident of the particular type was reasonably foreseeable is technically a secondary fact but perhaps it is more illuminating to call it an informed opinion by the judge in the light of all the circumstances of the case. In my view it was an opinion which is justified by the particular circumstances of the case. Counsel has not persuaded me that the judge's view was wrong. And I would hold that the Court of Appeal was not entitled to disturb the judge's findings of fact.

. . . .

The Law

Very little needs to be said about the law. The decision in this case has turned on the detailed findings of fact at first instance on the particular circumstances of this case. Two general observations are, however, appropriate. First, in this corner of the law the results of decided cases are inevitably very fact-sensitive. Both Counsel nevertheless at times invited your Lordships to compare the facts of the present case with the facts of other decided cases. That is a sterile exercise. Precedent is a valuable stabilizing influence in our legal system. But, comparing the facts of and outcomes of cases in this branch of the law is a misuse of the only proper use of precedent, viz. to identify the relevant rule to apply to the facts as found.

Secondly, Lord Woolf, M.R. made an observation casting doubt on part of Lord Reid's speech in *Hughes v. Lord Advocate*, [1963] A.C. 837. The defendants left a manhole uncovered and protected only by a tent and paraffin lamp. A child climbed down the hole. When he came out he kicked over one of the lamps. It fell into the hole and caused an explosion. The child was burned. The Court of Session held that there was no liability. The House of Lords reversed the decision of the Court of Session. In the present case Lord Woolf, M.R. cited the following parts of the speech of Lord Reid:

> So we have (first) a duty owed by the workmen, (secondly) the fact that if they had done as they ought to have done there would have been no accident, and (thirdly) the fact that the injuries suffered by the appellant, though perhaps different in

> degree, did not differ in kind from injuries which might have resulted from an accident of a foreseeable nature. *The ground on which this case has been decided against the appellant is that the accident was of an unforeseeable type. Of course, the pursuer has to prove that the defender's fault caused the accident and there could be a case where the intrusion of a new and unexpected factor could be regarded as the cause of the accident rather than the fault of the defender. But that is not this case. The cause of this accident was a known source of danger, the lamp, but it behaved in an unpredictable way.* [Emphasis supplied by Lord Woolf, M.R.]
>
> This accident was caused by a known source of danger, but caused in a way which could not have been foreseen and in my judgment, that affords no defence.

Lord Woolf, M.R. observed that he had difficulty in reconciling these remarks with the approach in *The Wagon Mound (No. 1)*. It is true that in *The Wagon Mound (No. 1)* Viscount Simonds at one stage observed:

> If, as admittedly it is, B's liability (culpability) depends on the reasonable foreseeability of the consequent damage, how is that to be determined except by the foreseeability of the damage which in fact happened — the damage in suit?

But this is to take one sentence in the judgment in *The Wagon Mound (No. 1)* out of context. Viscount Simonds was in no way suggesting that the precise *manner* of which the injury occurred nor its *extent* had to be foreseeable. And Lord Reid was saying no more. The speech of Lord Reid in *Hughes v. Lord Advocate*, [1963] A.C. 837 is in harmony with the other judgments. It is not in conflict with *The Wagon Mound (No. 1)*. The scope of the two modifiers — the precise manner in which the injury came about and its extent — is not definitively answered by either *The Wagon Mound (No. 1)* or *Hughes v. Lord Advocate*. It requires determination in the context of an intense focus on the circumstances of each case.

Conclusion

My Lords, I would restore the wise decision of Mr. Geoffrey Brice, Q.C., the Deputy High Court Judge. I would allow the appeal. I would further remit the case to the Court of Appeal to enable it to consider what course it should adopt on any application in regard to the determination of any issue relating to quantum of damages.

Lord Hoffmann

. . . .

It is . . . agreed that the plaintiff must show that the injury which he suffered fell within the scope of the council's duty and that in cases of physical injury, the scope of the duty is determined by whether or not the injury fell within a description which could be said to have been reasonably foreseeable. *Donoghue v. Stevenson*, [1932] A.C. 562 of course established the general principle that reasonable foreseeability of physical injury to another generates a duty of care. The further proposition that reasonable foreseeability also governs the question of whether the injury comes within the scope of that duty had to wait until . . . *The Wagon Mound (No. 1)* . . . for authoritative recognition. Until then, there was a view that the determination of liability involved a two-stage process. The existence of a duty depended upon whether injury of some kind was foreseeable. Once such a duty had been established, the defendant was liable for any injury which had been "directly caused" by an act in breach of that duty, whether such injury was reasonably foreseeable or not. But the present law is that unless the injury is of a description which was reasonably foreseeable, it is (according to taste) "outside the scope of the duty" or "too remote."

It is also agreed that what must have been foreseen is not the precise injury which occurred but injury of a given description. The foreseeability is not as to the particulars but the genus. And the description is formulated by reference to the nature of the risk which ought to have been foreseen. So, in *Hughes v. Lord Advocate* the foreseeable risk was that a child would be injured by falling in the hole or being burned by a lamp or by a combination of both. The House of Lords decided that the injury which actually materialized fell within this description, notwithstanding that it involved an unanticipated explosion of the lamp and consequent injuries of unexpected severity. . . .

The short point in the present appeal is therefore whether the judge was right in saying in general terms that the risk was that children would "meddle with the boat at the risk of some physical injury" or whether the Court of Appeal were right in saying that the only foreseeable risk was of "children who were drawn to the boat climbing upon it and being injured by the rotten planking giving way beneath them". . . . Was the wider risk, which would include within its description the accident which actually happened, reasonably foreseeable?

. . . .

. . . [Counsel for the borough] says that apart from its rotten planking, the boat was simply a heavy object like any other. It was no more likely to cause injury to the children than any other heavy object they might be able to get hold of. He draws the analogy of a man who negligently leaves a loaded gun where children play with it and one child injures another by dropping it on his toe. The injury does not fall within the scope of the risk created by the fact that it is a gun rather than some other heavy but innocuous object. . . .

I think that in a case like this, analogies from other imaginary facts are seldom helpful. Likewise analogies from real facts in other cases: I entirely agree with my noble and learned friend Lord Steyn in deploring the citation of cases which do nothing to illuminate any principle but are said to constitute analogous facts. In the present case, the rotten condition of the boat had a significance beyond the particular danger it created. It proclaimed the boat and its trailer as abandoned, *res nullius*, there for the taking, to make of them whatever use the rich fantasy life of children might suggest.

. . . [I]t has been repeatedly said in cases about children that their ingenuity in finding unexpected ways of doing mischief to themselves and others should never be underestimated. For these reasons, I think that the judge's broad description of the risk as being that children would "meddle with the boat at the risk of some physical injury" was the correct one to adopt on the facts of this case. The actual injury fell within that description and I would therefore allow the appeal.

. . . .

NOTES AND QUESTIONS

1. *Judge and Jury.* Parliament abolished the jury as a feature of most British civil litigation in 1933, which is why the issue for the House of Lords in *Jolley* was whether to uphold or reverse the trial judge's finding on foreseeability, rather than a jury verdict. In U.S. jurisdictions, by contrast, proximate cause is said to be a question for the jury, although typically jury verdict questionnaires do not isolate cause-in-fact and proximate cause as distinct issues (see, for example, the jury verdict questionnaire in *Martin v. Evans* in Chapter 3). Also, it is important to note that the jury's role in determining proximate cause is subject to the judge's power to decide issues as a matter of law. The question, typically, for trial and appellate judges is whether a jury might reasonably find that the relevant harm or harm-producing event was "foreseeable," or the sort of harm that the prohibition violated by defendant was meant to prevent. The authors' (impressionistic) sense is that judges are, on the whole, less prone to defer to juries on this issue than they are on the issues of breach and cause-in-fact. If so, what might explain such a difference in attitude?

In *CSX Transportation, Inc. v. McBride*, 131 S. Ct. 2630 (2011), the U.S. Supreme Court had occasion to consider the role of jury and judge in defining proximate cause in the context of applying a federal statute known as the Federal Employers Liability Act (FELA). First enacted in the early years of the twentieth century—in part as a response to state courts' restrictive applications of negligence law to work-related injuries suffered by railroad employees—FELA grants to railroad workers a cause of action against their employers for injuries "*resulting in whole or in part* from the negligence of [the railroad or its agents]." 41 U.S.C. § 51 (emphasis added). In *McBride*, the Court addressed whether this language should be understood to incorporate a proximate cause requirement and, if so, how that requirement should be defined and applied.

As a qualifying exercise for a new route assignment, Robert McBride, an engineer employed by CSX, was instructed to operate a train on a run that involved frequent starts and stops. McBride objected that the train was not properly configured for such a run, and that he would therefore be required, while operating the train's lead locomotive, to be continually deploying the train's brakes. McBride's superior instructed him to proceed nonetheless. During the run, McBride found himself constantly using one hand to push a button on the handle that operated the train's brakes. Near the end of his ten-hour shift, McBride accidentally slammed his fatigued hand into the brake handle and immediately experienced excruciating pain. Despite two surgeries and physical therapy, he never regained full use of the hand.

McBride sued CSX under FELA, arguing that CSX was negligent in requiring him to use the improperly configured train and for failing to instruct him how to operate the equipment safely. CSX requested a jury instruction that would have told the jury that it could not impose liability unless it found that CSX's carelessness was a "proximate cause" of McBride's injury (defined as a cause that produces injury through a "natural and probable sequence"). The trial court instead instructed the jury that it should find causation if it concluded that CSX's carelessness "played a part—no matter how small—in bringing about the injury." The jury returned a $275,000 verdict for McBride. (It also deemed him one-third at fault, reducing his recovery by $91,500. *See* Chapter 7's discussion of comparative fault.)

In a 5-4 decision, the Supreme Court ruled that the instruction was proper. While granting that FELA contains a proximate cause requirement, the Court reasoned that an instruction incorporating a common law formulation of proximate cause would be inappropriate because FELA's "in whole or in part" language (quoted above) was designed to ensure that jurors have broad discretion to use "their experience and common sense" on the issue of proximate cause. 131 S. Ct. at 2641. At the same time, the Court acknowledged that trial courts retain the authority to grant matter-of-law judgments when faced with FELA claims involving "far out" causal sequences. *Id.* at 2643. It thus cited approvingly the dismissal of a case in which a railroad's failure to provide a women's lavatory in the railyard in which the plaintiff worked resulted in the plaintiff using a lavatory on a train parked in the yard, then being struck by an object carried by a passenger as she (the employee) exited that train. *Id.*

If the common law rather than FELA applied to McBride's claims, would a jury have been entitled to deem CSX's carelessness a proximate cause of McBride's injuries? Does the answer to this question depend not only on the particular common law formulation applied, but also on a more detailed description of the plaintiff's theory as to what exactly was careless about the railroad's arrangement of the locomotives? Is the answer under FELA similarly dependent?

Although FELA is a federal statute, state courts have jurisdiction to hear claims brought under it. In *Illinois Central Railroad Co. v. Brent*, 133 So.3d 760 (Miss. 2013), a teenager using a pellet gun shot at the defendant's locomotive as it drove by. One pellet struck the plaintiff-engineer in the shoulder, causing permanent injury. Plaintiff sued the defendant railroad under FELA, arguing that it was careless for failing to install adequate air conditioning in the locomotive's cab, which in turn necessitated his opening the cab's window for ventilation, thereby enabling the pellet to strike him. A bare majority of the Mississippi Supreme Court affirmed a jury verdict for the plaintiff. In support of its conclusion that a shooting incident was foreseeable, the Court emphasized that national industry standards call for use of bullet-resistant glass in cab windows because moving trains are frequently targeted by shooters and throwers of objects. Is the result in *Brent* consistent with *McBride*? With common law proximate cause principles?

2. *Proximate Cause and Foreseeability.* In *Ventricelli v. Kinney Sys. Rent A Car, Inc.*, 383 N.E.2d 1149 (N.Y. 1978), the New York Court of Appeals had occasion to apply its foreseeability test for proximate cause. Plaintiff rented an automobile from Kinney. The car had a defective trunk lid that repeatedly flew open so as to obstruct the operator's rear view while the vehicle was moving, despite several returns to the lessor for repair. On the day of the accident, plaintiff had parked the car alongside the curb on a New York City street. While plaintiff and a passenger were attempting to slam the trunk lid shut, the defendant Maldonado's automobile, parked several lengths behind them, unexpectedly jerked forward and severely injured the plaintiff. The jury apportioned fault 80 percent to Kinney and 20 percent to Maldonado. However, the

intermediate appellate court concluded that Kinney's misconduct did not proximately cause plaintiff's injuries. The Court of Appeals affirmed:

> That Kinney's negligence in providing an automobile with a defective trunk lid would result in plaintiff's repeated attempts to close the lid was reasonably foreseeable. Not "foreseeable," however, was the collision between vehicles both parked a brief interval before the accident. Plaintiff was standing in a relatively "safe" place, a parking space, not in an actively traveled lane. He might well have been there independent of any negligence of Kinney, as, for example, if he were loading or unloading the trunk. Under these circumstances, to hold the accident a foreseeable consequence of Kinney's negligence is to stretch the concept of foreseeability beyond acceptable limits.

Id. at 1149. Is the *Ventricelli* majority asserting that the defendant could not reasonably foresee that a user of the rental car might be injured by another driver after getting out of the car to fix the defective trunk lid?

3. *Examples.* Consider the following hypotheticals. Do they shed light on the reasoning in *Allbritton*, *Jolley*, and *Ventricelli*?

a. Driver *D* drives 20 miles over the posted speed limit on a highway for a period of ten minutes without incident. He then exits the highway and proceeds down a local street exercising ordinary prudence. Despite driving prudently, *D* collides with another car on the local street, driven by *P*, thereby injuring *P*. Suppose *P* learns of *D*'s highway speeding and sues on the theory that *D*'s carelessness on the highway caused the accident. Should the court rule that *D*'s speeding was an actual cause of *P*'s injuries? If so, was it a proximate cause? If not, is it because *D* could not foresee that his speeding might lead him to collide with another car?

b. Father *F* returns from target practice and carelessly hands his five-year-old son *S* a small loaded pistol. The gun is no more heavy, sharp, or cumbersome than many toys designed for five-year-olds. *S* accidentally drops the pistol on playmate *P*'s toe, breaking it. Was *F*'s carelessness an actual cause of *P*'s injury? A proximate cause? If not the latter, why not?

c. Restaurant owner *O* places an unlabeled can of what he knows to be rat poison on a shelf directly above a stove used for preparing food. The rat poison is flammable, a fact which *O* had no reason to know. It explodes, injuring chef *C*. Is *O*'s negligence an actual cause of *C*'s injury? A proximate cause? If not the latter, why not?

d. Driver *D*, proceeding carelessly down a residential street, loses control of his car and crashes into the picket fence of *P*'s yard. *D* then drives off. Minutes later, *P*, who was inside his house at the time, discovers the damage and proceeds down the steps to his basement to obtain some tools to repair the fence. In doing so, *P* slips and breaks his arm. Was *D*'s careless driving an actual cause of *P*'s injury? A proximate cause? If not the latter, why not?

4. *Tortious Aspect Causation.* Richard Wright has argued that many cases handled by courts as no-proximate-cause cases are better characterized as cases in which there is a particular kind of problem with *actual causation.* For example, suppose driver *D* fails to

check behind her car and fails to look in her rearview mirror before backing out of her driveway. As a result, she runs over child *P*. It turns out that, because *P* crawled under the back of *D*'s car after *D* entered it, *D*'s use of the rearview mirror and her checking behind the car would not have revealed *P*'s presence. In this example, *D acted carelessly* toward *P* by not looking behind her. Moreover, *D*'s *conduct*—her backing up the car—*was* a cause-in-fact of *P*'s injury: had *D* not backed up, *P* would not have been injured. Still, the *careless aspect* of her conduct—the failure to check and look—was *not* a cause-in-fact of *P*'s injury: even if she had looked and checked, she would not have seen *P*.

According to Wright, examples such as this one indicate that a negligence plaintiff has to establish something more than that (1) *D*'s conduct was careless, and that (2) *D*'s conduct actually caused *P*'s injury. In addition, *P* has to show that (3) the *tortious aspect* of *D*'s conduct played a part in bringing about *P*'s injury. In this view, the precise issue posed by the actual causation inquiry in a negligence case concerns whether the *careless features of the actor's conduct*—the acts or omissions that rendered the conduct unreasonable—operated as a but-for cause of the other's injury. By attending to the tortious aspect of the defendant's conduct, Wright maintains, courts would exclude liability in many of the cases in which they purport to rely on proximate cause grounds.

Do you find this analysis helpful in resolving some of the hypotheticals in Note 3? Is it obvious that "tortious aspect causation" is an inquiry into actual cause and not proximate cause?

5. *The "Scope of the Risk" Formulation.* The "scope of the risk" test—sometimes referred to as the "risk rule"—is probably the leading present-day alternative to foreseeability formulations of proximate cause. Robert Keeton defined it as follows: A careless actor is subject to liability for harm actually caused by his careless conduct if the harm "*is a result within the scope of the risks by reason of which the actor is found to be negligent.*" Under this rule, there would arguably be no liability in any of the examples in Note 3 because none of the risks realized in those cases were of the sort that would prompt one to label the defendant's conduct careless.

In a 1909 article, Joseph Bingham articulated a similar idea, arguing that the primary question posed by proximate cause doctrine is: "Were the . . . consequences which constituted plaintiff's harm within any of the dangers that provoked legal condemnation of defendant's conduct?" Writing in 1927, Leon Green also framed the proximate cause inquiry in similar terms: "[W]as this the sort of hazard protected against by the rule which the [actor] violated?" According to Green, this question cannot be answered simply by employing a test of foreseeability but instead requires a sensitive inquiry into the underlying purposes and policies of the rule in question. In 1939, Warren Seavey likewise maintained that negligence liability is limited by "the reasons for creating liability" and hence requires that the plaintiff's injury be a realization of harms within the risk that rendered the conduct careless.

The Third Restatement adopts a variant of these formulations by framing the proximate cause inquiry in terms of whether the injury suffered by the victim is one of the harms whose risks rendered the actor's conduct careless. *See* Restatement (Third) of Torts: Liability for Physical and Emotional Harm § 29 (2010) ("An actor's liability is limited to those harms that result from the risks that made the actor's conduct tortious.").

As deployed by the courts, the "foreseeability" and "scope of the risk" formulations of proximate cause tend to generate the same outcomes in many if not most cases. Can you think of cases in which they might support different results? Even if the two formulations substantially overlap in their content, is there reason to prefer one to the other? Is one apt to promote greater clarity of analysis?

6. *Expiration of the Risk.* Consider another well-known proximate cause case, *Marshall v. Nugent*, 222 F.2d 604 (1st Cir. 1955). In *Marshall*, a truck driver (call him *T*) negligently crossed over the center line of a road while taking a sharp curve, thereby forcing off the road a car in which plaintiff *M* was a passenger. Luckily, *M* and the other occupants of the car were unhurt. *T* pulled his truck up alongside the car as part of an effort to get it back on to the road. Perhaps at *T*'s suggestion, *M* walked to one end of the curve to warn oncoming traffic of the obstruction formed by the stopped truck. As *M* was getting into position, driver *N* approached the accident scene and, in an effort to avoid colliding with the stopped truck, skidded into a guardrail and struck *M*, severely injuring him. The court held that the question of whether *T*'s initial negligence in driving the truck was a proximate cause of *M* being injured by *N* was for the jury:

> Regarding motor vehicle accidents . . . one should contemplate a variety of risks which are created by negligent driving. . . . In a traffic mix-up due to negligence, before the disturbed waters have become placid and normal again, the unfolding of events between the culpable act and the plaintiff's eventual injury may be bizarre indeed; yet the defendant may be liable for such a result. . . .
>
> Though this particular act of negligence was over and done with when the truck pulled up alongside the stalled [car] without having actually collided with it, still the consequences of such past negligence were in the bosom of time, as yet unrevealed.

The court contrasted a case in which the car in which *M* was riding was successfully restored to the road, but then was involved in a collision with some other car five miles away from the original accident scene. If *M* were injured in that situation, the court reasoned, *T* would be entitled to a judgment as a matter of law that *T*'s negligence was not a proximate cause of *M*'s injuries.

Assume that *Marshall's* distinction between the actual case and the hypothesized case is sound. Does either the foreseeability test or the risk-rule idea capture why the imagined case warrants a finding of no proximate cause? If not, what is it about that scenario that warrants such a finding?

II. THE RELATIONAL ASPECT OF BREACH OF DUTY: *PALSGRAF*

This chapter commenced with a discussion of proximate cause in part because that topic follows quite naturally from the discussion of actual cause in Chapter 4. However, it could have just as easily commenced with a discussion of the other "alignment" concept that is built into the tort of negligence, which we call the "relational aspect of breach of duty." (Analytically, questions of duty and breach precede questions of causation: the inquiry into causation is an inquiry into the causal significance of a breach of duty.) As you read the following decision — arguably the most famous of twentieth-century tort law — consider what exactly the majority finds deficient about the plaintiff's claim, and why the majority insists that this deficiency stands apart from the issue of proximate cause.

Palsgraf v. Long Island Railroad Co.

162 N.E. 99 (N.Y. 1928)

CARDOZO, C.J. Plaintiff was standing on a platform of defendant's railroad after buying a ticket to go to Rockaway Beach. A train stopped at the station, bound for another place. Two men ran forward to catch it. One of the men reached the platform of the car without mishap, though the train was already moving. The other man, carrying a package, jumped aboard the car, but seemed unsteady as if about to fall. A guard on the car, who had held the door open, reached forward to help him in, and another guard on the platform pushed him from behind. In this act, the package was dislodged, and fell upon the rails. It was a package of small size, about fifteen inches long, and was covered by a newspaper. In fact it contained fireworks, but there was nothing in its appearance to give notice of its contents. The fireworks when they fell exploded. The shock of the explosion threw down some scales at the other end of the platform, many feet away. The scales struck the plaintiff, causing injuries for which she sues.

The conduct of the defendant's guard, if a wrong in its relation to the holder of the package, was not a wrong in its relation to the plaintiff, standing far away. Relatively to her it was not negligence at all. Nothing in the situation gave notice that the falling package had in it the potency of peril to persons thus removed. Negligence is not actionable unless it involves the invasion of a legally protected interest, the violation of a right. "Proof of negligence in the air, so to speak, will not do." Pollock, Torts (11th Ed.), p.455; Martin v. Herzog, 228 N.Y. 164, 170; *cf.* Salmond, Torts (6th Ed.), p.24. "Negligence is the absence of care, according to the circumstances." Willes, J., in Vaughan v. Taff Vale Ry. Co., 5 H. & N. 679, 688; 1 Beven, Negligence (4th Ed.), 7; Paul v. Consol. Fireworks Co., 212 N.Y. 117; Adams v. Bullock, 227 N.Y. 208, 211; Parrott v. Wells-Fargo Co., 15 Wall. [U.S.] 524. The plaintiff as she stood upon the platform of the station might claim to be protected against intentional invasion of her bodily security. Such invasion is not charged. She might claim to be protected against unintentional invasion by conduct involving in the thought of reasonable men an unreasonable hazard that such invasion would ensue. These, from the point of view of the law, were the bounds of her immunity, with perhaps some rare exceptions, survivals for the most part of ancient forms of liability, where conduct is held to be at the peril of the actor. If no hazard was apparent to the eye of ordinary vigilance, an act innocent and harmless, at least to outward seeming, with reference to her, did not take to itself the quality of a tort because it happened to be a wrong, though apparently not one involving the risk of bodily insecurity, with reference to some one else.

"In every instance, before negligence can be predicated of a given act, back of the act must be sought and found a duty to the individual complaining, the observance of which would have averted or avoided the injury." McSherry, C.J., in [W. Va.] Central & P. R. Co. v. State, 96 Md. 652, 666. . . . "The ideas of negligence and duty are strictly correlative." (Bowen, L.J., in Thomas v. Quartermaine, 18 Q.B.D. 685, 694. The plaintiff sues in her own right for a wrong personal to her, and not as the vicarious beneficiary of a breach of duty to another.

A different conclusion will involve us, and swiftly too, in a maze of contradictions. A guard stumbles over a package which has been left upon a platform. It seems to be a bundle of newspapers. It turns out to be a can of dynamite. To the eye of ordinary vigilance, the bundle is abandoned waste, which may be kicked or trod on with impunity. Is a passenger at the other end of the platform protected by the law against the unsuspected hazard concealed beneath the waste? If not, is the result to be any different, so far as the distant passenger is concerned, when the guard stumbles over a valise which a truckman or a porter has left upon the walk? The passenger far away, if the victim of a wrong at all, has a cause of action, not derivative, but original and primary. His claim to be protected against invasion of his bodily security is neither greater nor less because the act resulting in the invasion is a wrong to another far removed. In this case, the rights that are said to have been violated, the interests said to have been invaded, are not even of the same order. The man was not injured in his person nor even put in danger. The purpose of the act, as well as its effect, was to make his person safe. If there was a wrong to him at all, which may very well be doubted, it was a wrong to a property interest only, the safety of his package. Out of this wrong to property, which threatened injury to nothing else, there has passed, we are told, to the plaintiff by derivation or succession a right of action for the invasion of an interest of another order, the right to bodily security. The diversity of interests emphasizes the futility of the effort to build the plaintiff's right upon the basis of a wrong to some one else. The gain is one of emphasis, for a like result would follow if the interests were the same. Even then, the orbit of the danger as disclosed to the eye of reasonable vigilance would be the orbit of the duty. One who jostles one's neighbor in a crowd does not invade the rights of others standing at the outer fringe when the unintended contact casts a bomb upon the ground. The wrongdoer as to them is the man who carries the bomb, not the one who explodes it without suspicion of the danger. Life will have to be made over, and human nature transformed, before prevision so extravagant can be accepted as the norm of conduct, the customary standard to which behavior must conform.

The argument for the plaintiff is built upon the shifting meanings of such words as "wrong" and "wrongful," and shares their instability. What the plaintiff must show is "a wrong" to herself, i.e., a violation of her own right, and not merely a wrong to some one else, nor conduct "wrongful" because unsocial, but not "a wrong" to any one. We are told that one who drives at reckless speed through a crowded city street is guilty of a negligent act and therefore of a wrongful one irrespective of the consequences. Negligent the act is, and wrongful in the sense that it is unsocial, but wrongful and unsocial in relation to other travelers, only because the eye of vigilance perceives the risk of damage. If the same act were to be committed on a speedway or a race course, it would lose its wrongful quality. The risk reasonably to be perceived defines the duty to be obeyed, and risk imports relation; it is risk to another or to others within the range of apprehension. This does not mean, of course, that one who launches a destructive force is always relieved of liability if the force, though known to be destructive, pursues an unexpected path. "It was not necessary that the defendant should have had notice of the particular method in which an accident would occur, if the possibility of an accident was clear to the ordinarily prudent eye." Munsey v. Webb, 231 U.S. 150, 156; Condran v. Park & Tilford, 213 N.Y. 341, 345; Robert v. U. S. E. F. [U.S.S.B.E.F.] Corp., 240 N.Y. 474, 477. Some acts, such as shooting are so imminently dangerous to any one who may come within reach of the missile, however unexpectedly, as to impose a duty of prevision not far from that of an insurer. Even today, and much oftener in earlier stages of the law, one acts sometimes at one's peril. Jeremiah Smith, Tort and Absolute Liability, 30 H. L. Rv. 328; Street, Foundations of Legal Liability, vol. 1, pp.77, 78. Under this head, it may be, fall certain cases of what is known as transferred intent, an act willfully dangerous to A resulting by misadventure in injury to B. Talmage v. Smith, 101 Mich. 370, 374. These cases aside, wrong is defined in terms of the natural or probable, at least when unintentional. Parrot v. Wells-Fargo Co. (The Nitro-Glycerine Case), 15 Wall. [U.S.] 524. The range of reasonable apprehension is at times a question for the court, and at times, if varying inferences are possible, a question for the jury. Here, by concession, there was nothing in the situation to suggest to the most cautious mind that the parcel wrapped in newspaper would spread wreckage through the station. If the guard had thrown it down knowingly and willfully, he would not have threatened the plaintiff's safety, so far as appearances could warn him. His conduct would not have involved, even then, an unreasonable probability of invasion of her bodily security. Liability can be no greater where the act is inadvertent.

Negligence, like risk, is thus a term of relation. Negligence in the abstract, apart from things related, is surely not a tort, if indeed it is understandable at all. Bowen, L.J., in Thomas v. Quartermaine, 18 Q.B.D. 685, 694. Negligence is not a tort unless it results in the commission of a wrong, and the commission of a wrong imports the violation of a right, in this case, we are told, the right to be protected against interference with one's bodily security. But bodily security is protected, not against all forms of interference or aggression, but only against some. One who seeks redress at law does not make out a cause of action by showing without more that there has been damage to his person. If the harm was not willful, he must show that the act as to him had possibilities of danger so many and apparent as to entitle him to be protected against the doing of it though the harm was unintended. Affront to personality is still the keynote of the wrong. Confirmation of this view will be found in the history and development of the action on the case. Negligence as a basis of civil liability was unknown to mediaeval law. 8 Holdsworth, History of English Law, p.449; Street, Foundations of Legal Liability, vol. 1, pp.189, 190. For damage to the person, the sole remedy was trespass, and trespass did not lie in the absence of aggression, and that direct and personal. Holdsworth, op. cit. p.453; Street, op. cit. vol. 3, pp.258, 260, vol. 1, pp.71, 74. Liability for other damage, as where a servant without orders from the master does or omits something to the damage of another, is a plant of later growth. Holdsworth, op. cit. 450, 457; Wigmore, Responsibility for Tortious Acts, vol. 3, Essays

in Anglo-American Legal History, 520, 523, 526, 533. When it emerged out of the legal soil, it was thought of as a variant of trespass, an offshoot of the parent stock. This appears in the form of action, which was known as trespass on the case. Holdsworth, op. cit. p.449; *cf.* Scott v. Shepard, 2 Wm. Black. 892; Green, Rationale of Proximate Cause, p.19. The victim does not sue derivatively, or by right of subrogation, to vindicate an interest invaded in the person of another. Thus to view his cause of action is to ignore the fundamental difference between tort and crime. Holland, Jurisprudence (12th Ed.), p.328. He sues for breach of a duty owing to himself.

The law of causation, remote or proximate, is thus foreign to the case before us. The question of liability is always anterior to the question of the measure of the consequences that go with liability. If there is no tort to be redressed, there is no occasion to consider what damage might be recovered if there were a finding of a tort. We may assume, without deciding, that negligence, not at large or in the abstract, but in relation to the plaintiff, would entail liability for any and all consequences, however novel or extraordinary. Bird v. St. Paul [F. & M.] Ins. Co., 224 N.Y. 47, 54; Ehrgott v. Mayor, etc., of [N.Y.], 96 N.Y. 264; Smith v. London & S. W. Ry. Co., L. R. 6 C.P. 14; 1 Beven, Negligence, 106; Street, op. cit. vol. 1, p.90; Green, Rationale of Proximate Cause, pp.88, 118; *cf.* Matter of Polemis, L. R. 1921, 3 K. B. 560; 44 Law Quarterly Review, 142. There is room for argument that a distinction is to be drawn according to the diversity of interests invaded by the act, as where conduct negligent in that it threatens an insignificant invasion of an interest in property results in an unforseeable invasion of an interest of another order, as, e.g., one of bodily security. Perhaps other distinctions may be necessary. We do not go into the question now. The consequences to be followed must first be rooted in a wrong.

The judgment of the Appellate Division and that of the Trial Term should be reversed, and the complaint dismissed, with costs in all courts.

ANDREWS, J. (dissenting).

Assisting a passenger to board a train, the defendant's servant negligently knocked a package from his arms. It fell between the platform and the cars. Of its contents the servant knew and could know nothing. A violent explosion followed. The concussion broke some scales standing a considerable distance away. In falling they injured the plaintiff, an intending passenger.

William S. Andrews New York Court of Appeals (1917-1928)

Upon these facts may she recover the damages she has suffered in an action brought against the master? The result we shall reach depends upon our theory as to the nature of negligence. Is it a relative concept—the breach of some duty owing to a particular person or to particular persons? Or where there is an act which unreasonably threatens the safety of others, is the doer liable for all its proximate consequences, even where they result in injury to one who would generally be thought to be outside the radius of danger? This is not a mere dispute as to words. We might not believe that to the average mind the dropping of the bundle would seem to involve the probability of harm to the plaintiff standing many feet away whatever might be the case as to the owner or to one so near as to be likely to be struck by its fall. If, however, we adopt the second hypothesis we have to inquire only as to the relation between cause and effect. We deal in terms of proximate cause, not of negligence.

Negligence may be defined roughly as an act or omission which unreasonably does or may affect the rights of others, or which unreasonably fails to protect oneself from the dangers resulting from such acts. Here I confine myself to the first branch of the definition. Nor do I comment on the word "unreasonable." For present purposes it sufficiently describes that average of conduct that society requires of its members . . .

But we are told that "there is no negligence unless there is in the particular case a legal duty to take care, and this duty must be one which is owed to the plaintiff himself and not merely to others." Salmond Torts (6th ed.), 24. This, I think too narrow a conception. Where there is the unreasonable act, and some right that may be affected there is negligence whether damage does or does not result. That is immaterial. Should we drive down Broadway at a reckless speed, we are negligent whether we strike an approaching car or miss it by an inch. The act itself is wrongful. It is a wrong not only to those who happen to be within the radius of danger but to all who might have been there—a wrong to the public at large. Such is the language of the street. Such the language of the courts when speaking of contributory negligence. Such again and again their language in speaking of the duty of some defendant and discussing proximate cause in cases where such a discussion is wholly irrelevant on any other theory. Perry v. Rochester Line Co., 219 N.Y. 60. As was said by Mr. Justice Holmes many years ago, "the measure of the defendant's duty in determining whether a wrong has been committed is one thing, the measure of liability when a wrong has been committed is another." Spade v. Lynn & B. R. Co., 172 Mass. 488. . . . Due care is a duty imposed on each one of us to protect society from unnecessary danger, not to protect A, B or C alone.

It may well be that there is no such thing as negligence in the abstract. "Proof of negligence in the air, so to speak, will not do." In an empty world negligence would not exist. It does involve a relationship between man and his fellows, but not merely a relationship between man and those whom he might reasonably expect his act would injure; rather, a relationship between him and those whom he does in fact injure. If his act has a tendency to harm some one, it harms him a mile away as surely as it does those on the scene. We now permit children to recover for the negligent killing of the father. It was never prevented on the theory that no duty was owing to them. A husband may be compensated for the loss of his wife's services. To say that the wrongdoer was negligent as to the husband as well as to the wife is merely an attempt to fit facts to theory. An insurance company paying a fire loss recovers its payment of the negligent incendiary. We speak of subrogation—of suing in the right of the insured. Behind the cloud of words is the fact they hide, that the act, wrongful as to the insured, has also injured the company. Even if it be true that the fault of father, wife or insured will prevent recovery, it is because we consider the original negligence not the proximate cause of the injury. Pollock, Torts (12th Ed.), 463.

In the well-known *Polemis Case* [1921] 3 K.B. 560, Scrutton, L.J., said that the dropping of a plank was negligent for it might injure "workman or cargo or ship." Because of either possibility the owner of the vessel was to be made good for his loss.

The act being wrongful the doer was liable for its proximate results. Criticized and explained as this statement may have been, I think it states the law as it should be and as it is. Smith v. London & S. W. R. Co. R. R. (1870-71) L. R. 6 C.P. 14; Anthony v. Staid, 52 Mass. 290; Wood v. Pa. R. Co., 177 Pa. St. 306; Trashansky v. Hershkovitz, 239 N.Y. 452.

The proposition is this. Every one owes to the world at large the duty of refraining from those acts that may unreasonably threaten the safety of others. Such an act occurs. Not only is he wronged to whom harm might reasonably be expected to result, but he also who is in fact injured, even if he be outside what would generally be thought the danger zone. There needs be duty due the one complaining but this is not a duty to a particular individual because as to him harm might be expected. Harm to some one being the natural result of the act, not only that one alone, but all those in fact injured may complain. We have never, I think, held otherwise. Indeed in the *Di Caprio* case we said that a breach of a general ordinance defining the degree of care to be exercised in one's calling is evidence of negligence as to every one. We did not limit this statement to those who might be expected to be exposed to danger. Unreasonable risk being taken, its consequences are not confined to those who might probably be hurt.

If this be so, we do not have a plaintiff suing by "derivation or succession." Her action is original and primary. Her claim is for a breach of duty to herself— not that she is subrogated to any right of action of the owner of the parcel or of a passenger standing at the scene of the explosion.

The right to recover damages rests on additional considerations. The plaintiff's rights must be injured, and this injury must be caused by the negligence. We build a dam, but are negligent as to its foundations. Breaking, it injures property down stream. We are not liable if all this happened because of some reason other than the insecure foundation. But when injuries do result from our unlawful act we are liable for the consequences. It does not matter that they are unusual, unexpected, unforeseen and unforseeable. But there is one limitation. The damages must be so connected with the negligence that the latter may be said to be the proximate cause of the former.

These two words have never been given an inclusive definition. What is a cause in a legal sense, still more what is a proximate cause, depend in each case upon many considerations, as does the existence of negligence itself. Any philosophical doctrine of causation does not help us. A boy throws a stone into a pond. The ripples spread. The water level rises. The history of that pond is altered to all eternity. It will be altered by other causes also. Yet it will be forever the resultant of all causes combined. Each one will have an influence. How great only omniscience can say. You may speak of a chain, or if you please, a net. An analogy is of little aid. Each cause brings about future events. Without each the future would not be the same. Each is proximate in the sense it is essential. But that is not what we mean by the word. Nor on the other hand do we mean sole cause. There is no such thing.

Should analogy be thought helpful, however, I prefer that of a stream. The spring, starting on its journey, is joined by tributary after tributary. The river, reaching the ocean, comes from a hundred sources. No man may say whence any drop of water is derived. Yet for a time distinction may be possible. Into the clear creek, brown swamp water flows from the left. Later, from the right comes water stained by its clay bed.

The three may remain for a space, sharply divided. But at last, inevitably no trace of separation remains. They are so commingled that all distinction is lost.

As we have said, we cannot trace the effect of an act to the end, if end there is. Again, however, we may trace it part of the way. A murder at Sarajevo may be the necessary antecedent to an assassination in London twenty years hence. An overturned lantern may burn all Chicago. We may follow the fire from the shed to the last building. We rightly say the fire started by the lantern caused its destruction.

A cause, but not the proximate cause. What we do mean by the word "proximate" is that, because of convenience, of public policy, of a rough sense of justice, the law arbitrarily declines to trace a series of events beyond a certain point. This is not logic. It is practical politics. Take our rule as to fires. Sparks from my burning haystack set on fire my house and my neighbor's. I may recover from a negligent railroad. He may not. Yet the wrongful act as directly harmed the one as the other. We may regret that the line was drawn just where it was, but drawn somewhere it had to be. We said the act of the railroad was not the proximate cause of our neighbor's fire. Cause it surely was. The words we used were simply indicative of our notions of public policy. Other courts think differently. But somewhere they reach the point where they cannot say the stream comes from any one source.

Take the illustration given in an unpublished manuscript by a distinguished and helpful writer on the law of torts. A chauffeur negligently collides with another car which is filled with dynamite, although he could not know it. An explosion follows. A, walking on the sidewalk nearby, is killed. B, sitting in a window of a building opposite, is cut by flying glass. C, likewise sitting in a window a block away, is similarly injured. And a further illustration. A nursemaid, ten blocks away, startled by the noise, involuntarily drops a baby from her arms to the walk. We are told that C may not recover while A may. As to B it is a question for court or jury. We will all agree that the baby might not. Because, we are again told, the chauffeur had no reason to believe his conduct involved any risk of injuring either C or the baby. As to them he was not negligent.

But the chauffeur, being negligent in risking the collision, his belief that the scope of the harm he might do would be limited is immaterial. His act unreasonably jeopardized the safety of any one who might be affected by it. C's injury and that of the baby were directly traceable to the collision. Without that, the injury would not have happened. C had the right to sit in his office, secure from such dangers. The baby was entitled to use the sidewalk with reasonable safety.

The true theory is, it seems to me, that the injury to C, if in truth he is to be denied recovery, and the injury to the baby is that their several injuries were not the proximate result of the negligence. And here not what the chauffeur had reason to believe would be the result of his conduct, but what the prudent would foresee, may have a bearing—may have some bearing, for the problem of proximate cause is not to be solved by any one consideration. It is all a question of expediency. There are no fixed rules to govern our judgment. There are simply matters of which we may take account. We have in a somewhat different connection spoken of "the stream of events." We have asked whether that stream was deflected—whether it was forced into new and unexpected channels. This is rather rhetoric than law. There is in truth little to guide us other than common sense.

There are some hints that may help us. The proximate cause, involved as it may be with many other causes, must be, at the least, something without which the event would not happen. The court must ask itself whether there was a natural and continuous sequence between cause and effect. Was the one a substantial factor in producing the other? Was there a direct connection between them, without too many intervening causes? Is the effect of cause on result not too attentuated? Is the cause likely, in the usual judgment of mankind, to produce the result? Or by the exercise of prudent foresight could the result be foreseen? Is the result too remote from the cause, and here we consider remoteness in time and space. Bird v. St. Paul & M. Ins. Co., 224 N.Y. 47, where we passed upon the construction of a contract—but something was also said on this subject. . . . Clearly we must so consider, for the greater the distance either in time or space, the more surely do other causes intervene to affect the result. When a lantern is overturned the firing of a shed is a fairly direct consequence. Many things contribute to the spread of the conflagration—the force of the wind, the direction and width of streets, the character of intervening structures, other factors. We draw an uncertain and wavering line, but draw it we must as best we can.

Once again, it is all a question of fair judgment, always keeping in mind the fact that we endeavor to make a rule in each case that will be practical and in keeping with the general understanding of mankind.

Here another question must be answered. In the case supposed it is said, and said correctly, that the chauffeur is liable for the direct effect of the explosion although he had no reason to suppose it would follow a collision. "The fact that the injury occurred in a different manner than that which might have been expected does not prevent the chauffeur's negligence from being in law the cause of the injury." But the natural results of a negligent act—the results which a prudent man would or should foresee—do have a bearing upon the decision as to proximate cause. We have said so repeatedly. What should be foreseen? No human foresight would suggest that a collision itself might injure one a block away. On the contrary, given an explosion, such a possibility might be reasonably expected. I think the direct connection, the foresight of which the courts speak, assumes prevision of the explosion, for the immediate results of which, at least, the chauffeur is responsible.

It may be said this is unjust. Why? In fairness he should make good every injury flowing from his negligence. Not because of tenderness toward him we say he need not answer for all that follows his wrong. We look back to the catastrophe, the fire kindled by the spark, or the explosion. We trace the consequences—not indefinitely, but to a certain point. And to aid us in fixing that point we ask what might ordinarily be expected to follow the fire or the explosion.

This last suggestion is the factor which must determine the case before us. The act upon which defendant's liability rests is knocking an apparently harmless package onto the platform. The act was negligent. For its proximate consequences the defendant is liable. If its contents were broken, to the owner; if it fell upon and crushed a passenger's foot, then to him. If it exploded and injured one in the immediate vicinity, to him also as to A in the illustration. Mrs. Palsgraf was standing some distance away. How far cannot be told from the record—apparently 25 or 30 feet. Perhaps less. Except for the explosion, she would not have been injured. We are told by the appellant in his brief,

"It cannot be denied that the explosion was the direct cause of the plaintiff's injuries." So it was a substantial factor in producing the result — there was here a natural and continuous sequence — direct connection. The only intervening cause was that instead of blowing her to the ground the concussion smashed the weighing machine which in turn fell upon her. There was no remoteness in time, little in space. And surely, given such an explosion as here it needed no great foresight to predict that the natural result would be to injure one on the platform at no greater distance from its scene than was the plaintiff. Just how no one might be able to predict. Whether by flying fragments, by broken glass, by wreckage of machines or structures no one could say. But injury in some form was most probable.

Under these circumstances I cannot say as a matter of law that the plaintiff's injuries were not the proximate result of the negligence. That is all we have before us. The court refused to so charge. No request was made to submit the matter to the jury as a question of fact, even would that have been proper upon the record before us.

NOTES AND QUESTIONS

1. *Why So Important?* It seems unlikely that *Palsgraf* substantially affected the scope of liability faced by railroads for injuries caused to their passengers. What, then, explains its enduring importance? Can a torts decision be significant even if it does not introduce a radical change in the liability landscape? How?

2. *Cardozo and the ALI.* As a judge, Cardozo bore the reputation of being moralistic, perhaps to a fault. This may partly explain why William Prosser once bothered to report the claim of another scholar that Cardozo had engaged in a minor impropriety in rendering the *Palsgraf* decision. Cardozo was a founding member of the American Law Institute (ALI), the organization of judges, lawyers, and scholars that issues the Restatements. The ALI met to discuss the draft First Restatement of Torts in December of 1927, at which time the intermediate appellate court in New York had just handed down its decision in *Palsgraf.* According to the story circulated by Prosser, even though Cardozo knew he would be asked to rule on the case when it arrived at his court, he attended the ALI meeting and listened intently as members were presented with the facts and debated its proper resolution. Cardozo's biographer, Andrew Kaufman has since discovered that this story is almost certainly false.

3. *Cardozo and the Facts of Palsgraf.* Others have criticized Cardozo for being inattentive to, if not creative with, the facts of the case. For example, some have maintained that Mrs. Palsgraf was quite a bit closer to the explosion than Cardozo suggests when he described her as standing "at the other end of the platform, many feet away." Judge Andrews mentions that the record was unclear, but placed her at about 25 to 30 feet from the point where the package was dropped. Suppose Andrews had the distance right and that Cardozo wrongly implied a greater distance. Would that change the outcome under Cardozo's analysis? *See* Palsgraf v. Long Island R.R. Co., 164 N.E. 564 (N.Y. 1928) (denying motion for reargument) ("If we assume that the plaintiff was nearer the scene of the explosion than the prevailing opinion would suggest, she was

not so near that injury from a falling package, not known to contain explosives, would be within the range of reasonable prevision.").

In a related vein, Judge Noonan has suggested that Cardozo was insensitive to the plight of a working-class woman such as Mrs. Palsgraf, as evidenced by the Court of Appeals' decision to impose the cost of the appeal on her notwithstanding her poverty and the railroad's wealth. In response, Judge Posner has noted that imposition of costs on the losing party, although discretionary with the court, was the norm, and that Mrs. Palsgraf's attorney made no request to deviate from that norm.

4. *Palsgraf Versus MacPherson.* Is there an inconsistency between *MacPherson*'s elimination of the privity rule and *Palsgraf*'s holding? How could Cardozo maintain in the former that a duty was owed irrespective of privity, then turn around and say that the railroad did not breach a duty to a customer with whom it had a contract in the form of a train ticket? *MacPherson* was decided 12 years before *Palsgraf.* Do the different outcomes suggest that Cardozo had grown more conservative or had become concerned about the floodgates he had opened earlier in his career? G. Edward White has suggested as much. Two of us (Goldberg and Zipursky) have argued that the opinions are quite consistent.

5. *Empty Rhetoric?* By far the most common criticism of Cardozo's opinion is that it is empty or circular. For example, although Judge Posner is favorably disposed to the result, he describes Cardozo's opinion as "subtle bluff." By this he means that it is rhetorically effective, but does not actually provide a reason for denying Mrs. Palsgraf's claim. In this, Posner follows Prosser, who famously argued that the main lesson of *Palsgraf* is that efforts to employ legal concepts such as "duty" to resolve difficult cases are hopeless. Proof of this, he claimed, resides in the evident vacuity of Cardozo's duty analysis, as well as Andrews' proximate cause analysis. Gary Schwartz and William Powers, two of the Reporters for the Third Restatement of Torts, took up the mantle of Prosser and Posner by contending that Cardozo's opinion consists of smoke and mirrors. No doubt their attitude helps explains why, as Ernest Weinrib has observed, one of the primary goals of the Third Restatement's provisions on duty and proximate cause has been to excise *Palsgraf* from the modern law of negligence.

Is Cardozo's opinion mere blather or does it contain an argument from legal principle? Critics of the opinion have made much of the fact that the opinion seems to suggest — absurdly — that the railroad owed no duty of care to a paying customer on its premises. Does Cardozo deny that a duty was owed by the railroad to Mrs. Palsgraf? Assuming that he does not, what element did she fail to make out, such that the railroad was entitled to a judgment as a matter of law?

6. *Relational Versus Nonrelational Conceptions of Negligence.* English grammar distinguishes between two kinds of verbs: transitive and intransitive. To use transitive verbs correctly, one must specify or imply a direct object that is *being acted upon.* Intransitive verbs, by contrast, do not take a direct object because they do not describe actions that involve acting upon someone or something. The verb "injures" is an example of a transitive verb. Thus, to write the phrase "*X* injured" without stating or implying *whom or what X* injured is to write a sentence fragment rather than a

complete sentence. An example of an intransitive verb is "littered," as used in the sentence "*X* littered." Obviously, Cardozo and Andrews were not fighting over rules of grammar. Nonetheless, does the distinction between these two types of verbs help capture the meaning of Cardozo's claim that "negligence . . . is a term that imports relation"? Or Andrews' claim that "[d]ue care is a duty imposed on each one of us to protect society from unnecessary danger, not to protect A, B, or C alone"?

7. *Foreseeability, Duty, and Breach.* Cardozo opines that "no hazard [to Mrs. Palsgraf] was apparent to the eye of ordinary vigilance." Later, he states that an injury to Mrs. Palsgraf was, so far as the conductors were concerned, out of the "range of reasonable apprehension." At another point, he proclaims that "[l]ife will have to be made over, and human nature transformed, before prevision so extravagant can be accepted as the norm of conduct." Are these observations addressed to the issue of duty or breach? If breach, what happened to the idea of deferring to the jury (which, in this case, must have found a breach since it imposed liability on the railroad)?

8. *Rights, Wrongs, and Torts.* Cardozo reasons that, because "[n]othing in the situation gave notice that the falling package had in it the potency of peril to persons [far] removed," the defendant's conduct was "not a wrong in its relation to" Mrs. Palsgraf. Even if one assumes that Cardozo is correct in saying this, why does it follow that Mrs. Palsgraf should lose? His answer seems at first blush to rely on a principle that restates the problem, rather than solving it: "What the plaintiff must show is 'a wrong' to herself, i.e., a violation of her own right, and not merely a wrong to some one else, nor conduct 'wrongful' because unsocial, but not 'a wrong' to anyone." *Why must a negligence plaintiff show a wrong to herself?* Consider the following passage from the opinion:

> Affront to personality is still the keynote of the wrong. . . . The victim does not sue derivatively, or by right of subrogation, to vindicate an interest invaded in the person of another. Thus to view his cause of action is to ignore the fundamental difference between tort and crime. . . . [The plaintiff] sues for breach of a duty owing to himself.

What is Cardozo getting at here? Why does Judge Andrews reject this argument?

One of us (Zipursky) has argued that the "relational" aspect of negligence law identified by Cardozo in *Palsgraf* also features prominently in other torts. For example, he notes that under the common law of fraud, even if *P* suffers a loss because of *D*'s knowing misrepresentation, *P* cannot prevail unless she can show that *she herself actually relied* on the content of misrepresentation. If the misrepresentation was not one on which *P* relied, *D*'s utterance of it is not actionable by *P* because its utterance does not constitute a *defrauding of P*, in the same way that the railroad's carelessness was not *carelessness toward Mrs. Palsgraf.* Likewise, even if *P* foreseeably suffers damage to his reputation by virtue of a defamatory statement made by *D*, *P* cannot recover unless the statement was "of and concerning" *P*—that is, a *libeling or slandering of P*. According to Zipursky, each of these doctrines reflects a basic and distinctive feature of tort law, namely, that it empowers a person or entity (*P*) to complain about another's conduct only if that conduct constitutes a wrong to *P*, as opposed to a wrong to someone else, which happens to injure *P*.

9. Bourhill v. Young. Compare to *Palsgraf* the House of Lords' decision in *Bourhill v. Young*, 1942 S.C. (H.L.) 78. Driving his motorcycle, Young approached a stopped tram from behind, heading in a southwesterly direction. He passed the tram on its curb side (which, in England, is the left side as one faces forward). Immediately thereafter he entered an intersection in which he was struck and killed by a car that had been traveling in the opposite direction of the tram and was making a right turn through the intersection. The accident was deemed entirely Young's fault. At the time of the fatal collision, Mrs. Bourhill, who had disembarked from the tram, was on its far (street) side, about 45 feet from the intersection. She did not see and could not have seen the collision. However, she heard it and later saw blood on the street. Bourhill was traumatized as a result, which trauma resulted in physical symptoms.

The House of Lords rejected Bourhill's negligence claim against Young's estate. Lord Thankerton opined that an injury to a person such as Bourhill "must be within that which the cyclist ought to have reasonably contemplated as the area of potential danger which would arise as the result of his negligence," concluding that she was not. Lord Russell likewise maintained that Bourhill's claim fell afoul of the rule that a negligence plaintiff "can recover damages only if she can show that in relation to her [the defendant] acted negligently." Lord Porter emphasized that "[i]t is not enough to say that the cyclist was guilty of negligence toward some one."

10. Palsgraf's Progeny? In *Moore v. Shah*, 458 N.Y.S.2d 33 (App. Div. 1982), a father who donated one of his kidneys to his son sued the son's physician, alleging that there was a need for the donation only because the physician improperly treated the son. The intermediate appellate court rejected the claim as a matter of law, citing *Palsgraf*. Is this a sound application of the relationality requirement? Was the alleged malpractice a wrong only to the son and not a wrong to the father? Why?

In *Zokhrabov v. Park*, 963 N.E.2d 1035 (Ill. App. 2011), a young man used a crosswalk at a train station to reach the station's far (west) platform, at which a southbound commuter train was scheduled to arrive a few minutes later. Tragically, the man failed to notice a northbound Amtrak train traveling through the station at more than 70 m.p.h. The Amtrak train struck and killed the man as he crossed the tracks. The collision in turn propelled a "large part" of the defendant's body into the air. It traveled about 100 feet, onto the southbound platform, where it struck the plaintiff. The plaintiff, who was standing with her back to the Amtrak train as she awaited the arrival of the southbound commuter train, was knocked down by the force of the collision, suffering a broken leg, a broken wrist, and a shoulder injury. She sued the estate of the man for negligence. Although the trial court granted a defense motion for summary judgment, an intermediate appellate court reinstated the suit. It reasoned that a person in the position of the decedent could foresee that another passenger might suffer physical injury if he were carelessly to cross the tracks and be struck by a train. Is this reasoning and result consistent with *Palsgraf*?

11. Palsgraf Versus Wagner. Seven years prior to *Palsgraf*, Cardozo authored the court's opinion in *Wagner v. International Railway Co.*, 133 N.E. 437 (N.Y. 1921). Defendant operated an electric tram. At one point on its route, the tram proceeded up a graded ramp that rose to a height of 25 feet, then took a sharp left turn as the ramp segued into a bridge that spanned another railway's tracks. The bridge itself had a railing, but the ramp leading to the bridge did not. At the point of the sharp left turn, one side of the tram cars extended out over the edge of the ramp.

Plaintiff Arthur Wagner and his cousin Herbert were standing in the doorway of a crowded tram car. The car had doors, but the tram's conductor did not close them. As the tram was navigating the left turn at about 7 m.p.h., "there was a violent lurch," and Herbert was thrown out near the point where the ramp joined the bridge. The tram continued across the bridge, then stopped. By this time, the sun had set. Several other passengers went to look beneath the bridge to see if Herbert was in need of assistance. Arthur, however, walked back along the track a distance of 400 feet. "Reaching the bridge, he had found upon a beam his cousin's hat, but nothing else. About him, there was darkness. He missed his footing, and fell." The trial court held that Arthur could not recover for injuries from his fall *unless* the jury found that the conductor had *invited* him to go upon the bridge, thus actively endangering him. The jury found in favor of the defendant.

The Court of Appeals held this instruction in error, and ordered a new trial. According to Cardozo, the defendant could be held liable even if its conductor had not explicitly invited the plaintiff to participate in a dangerous rescue attempt:

> Danger invites rescue. The cry of distress is the summons to relief. The law does not ignore these reactions of the mind in tracing conduct to its consequences. It recognizes them as normal. It places their effects within the range of the natural and probable. The wrong that imperils life is a wrong to the imperilled victim; it is a wrong also to his rescuer. . . . The state that leaves an opening in a bridge is liable to the child that falls into the stream, but liable also to the parent who plunges to its aid. The railroad company whose train approaches without signal is a wrongdoer toward the traveler surprised between the rails, but a wrongdoer also to the bystander who drags him from the path. . . . The risk of rescue, if only it be not wanton, is born of the occasion. The emergency begets the man. The wrongdoer may not have foreseen the coming of a deliverer. He is accountable as if he had. . . .

Cardozo assumed for purposes of decision that the doctrine of danger-invites-rescue applies to any rescue effort that, like Arthur's, is carried out both reasonably and contemporaneously with the carelessly created peril. He left it to the jury on remand to determine whether Arthur was barred from suing under the doctrine of contributory negligence.

Was Arthur entitled to sue for the railroad's wrong to Herbert? If not, why was Arthur entitled to sue the railroad at all? If so, why did Cardozo later hold that Helen Palsgraf was not entitled to sue for a railroad's wrong to another? What distinguishes the two cases? (Might it help here to recall the special duty principles discussed in Chapter 2, such as attractive nuisance doctrine, as well as the rule that one is obligated to make efforts to rescue persons whom one has imperiled?) In keeping with its hostility to *Palsgraf* and duty analysis generally, the Third Restatement has recast *Wagner*'s rescuer doctrine as a special rule of proximate cause. *See* Restatement (Third) of Torts: Liability for Physical and Emotional Harm § 32 (2010).

12. Andrews' Dissent. *Palsgraf* has become part of the torts canon as much for Judge Andrews' dissent as Cardozo's majority opinion. Why does Andrews claim that

Palsgraf is a case whose outcome turns on proximate cause rather than on the relational aspect of breach of duty? Does Andrews conceive of proximate cause in a manner consistent with the opinions that we studied in Section I of this chapter? Is the dispute between him and Cardozo about whether to analyze the case under duty or proximate cause purely verbal, or is it substantive? Andrews and Cardozo locked horns in other important decisions. *See, e.g.*, People v. Westchester County Natl. Bank, 132 N.E. 241 (N.Y. 1921).

13. The Relational Aspect of Breach of Duty Versus Proximate Cause. Cardozo says that the law of proximate cause has no bearing on the resolution of *Palsgraf*. However, he then states that, if the problem he identifies in Palsgraf's claim were somehow overcome, liability would attach for "any and all consequences" of the railroad's negligence, "however novel or extraordinary." Does this mean that he rejected foreseeability-based or risk-rule conceptions of proximate cause? On what authority?

In his biography of Cardozo, Andrew Kaufman has produced the record of a fascinating pre-*Palsgraf* interchange among Francis Bohlen, Cardozo, Learned Hand, and others, in which Cardozo appears to reject a scope-of-the-risk conception of proximate cause. According to William Powers, New York proximate cause doctrine at the time of *Palsgraf* rejected "scope of the risk" as a limitation on liability. Indeed, Powers concludes that Cardozo invoked the rhetoric of duty as a way of getting to a sound result in *Palsgraf* without overruling existing New York proximate cause doctrine.

Suppose one adopts the modern foreseeable risk/risk rule approach. Would the jury be entitled to conclude that the railroad's breach was a proximate cause of Mrs. Palsgraf's injuries? If not, what additional requirement does *Palsgraf* set beyond the requirement of proximate cause?

14. Androzo (I). Although indisputably a canonical case, *Palsgraf* has sometimes been transformed by subsequent courts into a hybrid that melds certain aspects of the majority opinion — namely, that Mrs. Palsgraf ought not to prevail because harm to her was an unforeseeable consequence of pushing the package-carrying passenger — with certain aspects of the dissent — namely, that the case ought to be resolved by application of proximate cause doctrine. On this view, which has essentially been adopted by the Third Restatement, Cardozo's opinion reaches the right result for the right reason, but misstates the doctrinal "hook" for applying those reasons. Meanwhile, Judge Andrews is understood to have properly framed the question of the case as one of proximate cause, but then reached the wrong result by misunderstanding proximate cause to turn on a blunderbuss inquiry concerning expedience (instead of the narrower scope-of-the-risk question). As Zipursky has noted, "[T]his is an odd way to read any case, especially a central case of our torts canon. . . . [N]either of the famous opinions in the case agrees with — or even presents — the argument most commonly attributed to it."

15. Androzo (II). Influential courts — including the California Supreme Court and later iterations of the New York Court of Appeals — have subsequently melded Cardozo's and Andrews' *Palsgraf* opinions in a different way. According to them,

Andrews was correct to conclude that the question of liability in cases such as *Palsgraf* cannot be resolved by employing a subtle understanding of how the elements of negligence align with one another. Instead, they require an "all things considered" assessment as to whether "expedience" or "policy" suggests that the defendant ought to be let off the hook notwithstanding that its carelessness caused plaintiff's injury. Yet, while these courts agree with Andrews as to the nature of the question being asked, they also "agree" with Cardozo to the following (limited) extent: The question of expedience ought to be asked under the heading of "duty" rather than "proximate cause." Thus, prominent decisions such as *Rowland v. Christian* (Chapter 2) ask roughly the same question that Judge Andrews asked in *Palsgraf.* Yet they do so under the heading of duty rather than proximate cause. While the choice of label for this policy inquiry may seem trivial, notice the important procedural effect of this shift. What Andrews conceived as primarily a mixed question of law and fact for the jury has been converted by these courts into a question of law for the courts.

Petitions of the Kinsman Transit Co.

338 F.2d 708 (2d Cir. 1964), *cert. denied,* 380 U.S. 944 (1965)

Friendly, J. We have here six appeals from an interlocutory decree in admiralty adjudicating liability. The litigation, in the District Court for the Western District of New York, arose out of a series of misadventures on a navigable portion of the Buffalo River during the night of January 21, 1959. The owners of two vessels petitioned for exoneration from or limitation of liability; numerous claimants appeared in these proceedings and also filed libels against the Continental Grain Company and the City of Buffalo, which filed cross-claims. The proceedings were consolidated for trial before Judge Burke. We shall summarize the facts as found by him:

The Buffalo River flows through Buffalo from east to west, with many turns and bends, until it empties into Lake Erie. Its navigable western portion is lined with docks, grain elevators, and industrial installations; during the winter, lake vessels tie up there pending resumption of navigation on the Great Lakes, without power and with only a shipkeeper aboard. About a mile from the mouth, the City of Buffalo maintains a lift bridge at Michigan Avenue. Thaws and rain frequently cause freshets to develop in the upper part of the river and its tributary, Cazenovia Creek; currents then range up to fifteen miles an hour and propel broken ice down the river, which sometimes overflows its banks.

On January 21, 1959, rain and thaw followed a period of freezing weather. The United States Weather Bureau issued appropriate warnings which were published and broadcast. Around 6 P.M. an ice jam that had formed in Cazenovia Creek disintegrated. Another ice jam formed just west of the junction of the creek and the river; it broke loose around 9 P.M.

The *MacGilvray Shiras,* owned by The Kinsman Transit Company, was moored at the dock of the Concrete Elevator, operated by Continental Grain Company, on the south side of the river about three miles upstream of the Michigan Avenue Bridge. She was loaded with grain owned by Continental. The berth, east of the main portion of the dock, was exposed in the sense that about 150′ of the *Shiras*' forward end, pointing upstream, and 70′ of her stern — a total of over half her length — projected beyond the dock. This left between her stem and the bank a space of water seventy-five feet wide where the ice and other debris could float in and accumulate. The position was the more hazardous in that the berth was just below a bend in the river, and the *Shiras* was on the inner bank. None of her anchors had been put out. From about 10 P.M. large chunks of ice and debris began to pile up between the *Shiras*' starboard bow and the bank; the pressure exerted by this mass on her starboard bow was augmented by the force of the current and of floating ice against her port quarter. The mooring lines began to part, and a "deadman," to which the No. 1 mooring cable had been attached, pulled out of the ground — the judge finding that it had not been properly constructed or inspected. About 10:40 P.M. the stern lines parted, and the *Shiras* drifted into the current. During the previous forty minutes, the shipkeeper took no action to ready the anchors by releasing the devil's claws; when he sought to drop them after the *Shiras* broke loose, he released the compressors with the claws still hooked in the chain so that the anchors jammed and could no longer be dropped. The trial judge reasonably found that if the anchors had dropped at that time, the *Shiras* would probably have fetched up at the hairpin bend just below the Concrete Elevator, and that in any case they would considerably have slowed her progress, the significance of which will shortly appear.

Careening stern first down the S-shaped river, the *Shiras*, at about 11 P.M., struck the bow of the *Michael K. Tewksbury*, owned by Midland Steamship Line, Inc. The *Tewksbury* was moored in a relatively protected area flush against the face of a dock on the outer bank just below a hairpin bend so that no opportunity was afforded for ice to build up between her port bow and the dock. Her shipkeeper had left around 5 P.M. and spent the evening watching television with a girl friend and her family. The collision caused the *Tewksbury*'s mooring lines to part; she too drifted stern first down the river, followed by the *Shiras*. The collision caused damage to the Steamer *Druckenmiller* which was moored opposite the *Tewksbury*.

Thus far there was no substantial conflict in the testimony; as to what followed there was. Judge Burke found, and we accept his findings as soundly based, that at about 10:43 P.M., Goetz, the superintendent of the Concrete Elevator, telephoned Kruptavich, another employee of Continental, that the *Shiras* was adrift; Kruptavich called the Coast Guard, which called the city fire station on the river, which in turn warned the crew on the Michigan Avenue Bridge, this last call being made about 10:48 P.M. Not quite twenty minutes later the watchman at the elevator where the *Tewksbury* had been moored phoned the bridge crew to raise the bridge. Although not more than two minutes and ten seconds were needed to elevate the bridge to full height after traffic was stopped, assuming that the motor started promptly, the bridge was just being raised when, at 11:17 P.M., the *Tewksbury* crashed into its center. The bridge crew consisted of an operator and two tenders; a change of shift was scheduled for 11 P.M. The inference is rather strong, despite contrary testimony, that the operator on the earlier shift had not yet returned from a tavern when the telephone call from the fire station was received; that the operator on the second shift did not arrive until shortly before the call from the elevator where the *Tewksbury* had been moored; and that in consequence the bridge was not raised until too late.

The first crash was followed by a second, when the south tower of the bridge fell. The *Tewksbury* grounded and stopped in the wreckage with her forward end resting against the stern of the Steamer Farr, which was moored on the south side of the river just above the bridge. The *Shiras* ended her journey with her stern against the *Tewksbury* and her bow against the north side of the river. So wedged, the two vessels substantially dammed the flow, causing water and ice to back up and flood installations on the banks with consequent damage as far as the Concrete Elevator, nearly three miles upstream. Two of the bridge crew suffered injuries. Later the north tower of the bridge collapsed, damaging adjacent property.

Michigan Ave Bridge

Judge Burke concluded that Continental and the *Shiras* had committed various faults discussed below; . . . that the *Tewksbury* and her owner were entitled to exoneration; and that the City of Buffalo was at fault for failing to raise the Michigan Avenue Bridge. The City was not faulted for the manner in which it had constructed and maintained flood improvements on the river and on Cazenovia Creek, or for failing to dynamite the ice jams. For the damages sustained by the *Tewksbury* and the *Druckenmiller* in the collisions at the Standard Elevator dock, Judge Burke allowed those vessels to recover equally from Continental and from Kinsman. . . . He held the City, Continental and Kinsman equally liable jointly and severally . . . for damages to persons and property sustained by all others as a result of the disaster at the bridge. . . .

The mooring of the *Shiras*, as to which more will be said under the next heading, was the joint work of Kinsman, acting through Captain Davies, her former master, and of Continental. The judge was justified in holding that, with her bow protruding into the river just below a bend and with the eroded bank incapable of taking a long lead line or an anchor chain, the *Shiras* ought to have put out an anchor from her port bow. He was also warranted in finding that Continental was at fault for the inadequately secured "deadman" and the *Shiras* for the shipkeeper's failure to ready the anchors in the interval between 10 P.M. and 10:40 P.M. on January 21. The current and ice conditions on the fateful evening were not so unexpectable as to go beyond the range of foreseeability and hence to come within the principle of inevitable accident; the conditions were of the very sort that had been occurring for years, although not in quite the same degree. . . .

I. The City's Failure to Raise the Bridge

If this were a run of the mine negligence case, the City's argument against liability for not promptly raising the Michigan Avenue Bridge would be impressive: All the vessels moored in the harbor were known to be without power and incapable of controlled movement save with the aid of tugs. The tugs had quit at 4 P.M.; they were not docked in the river, and would not undertake after quitting time to tow a vessel into or out of the inner harbor. Since the breaking loose of a ship was not to be anticipated, it would have been consistent with prudence for the City to relieve the bridge crews of their duties. Neglect by the crews ought not subject the City to liability merely because, out of abundance of caution, it had ordered them to be present when prudence did not so require. . . . [Judge Friendly nonetheless concluded that the conduct of the bridge crew violated applicable federal statutory and regulatory law, and therefore was unreasonable as a matter of law under the doctrine of negligence per se (discussed in Chapter 6, *infra*) — EDS.]

II. THE TIME RELATION OF THE CITY'S FAILURE TO THE PRIOR FAULTS OF THE *SHIRAS* AND CONTINENTAL

. . . Kinsman and Continental contend that the City's failure insulates them from liability for damages to others resulting from the collision at the bridge. . . .

We speedily [reject this contention]. Save for exceptions which are not here pertinent, an actor whose negligence has set a dangerous force in motion is not saved from liability for harm it has caused to innocent persons solely because another has negligently failed to take action that would have avoided this. . . . The contrary argument grows out of the discredited notion that only the last wrongful act can be a cause — a notion as faulty in logic as it is wanting in fairness. The established principle is especially appealing in admiralty which will divide the damages among the negligent actors or non-actors. . . .

III. THE ALLEGEDLY UNEXPECTABLE CHARACTER OF THE EVENTS LEADING TO MUCH OF THE DAMAGE

The very statement of the case suggests the need for considering Palsgraf v. Long Island R.R., 248 N.Y. 339, 162 N.E. 99, 59 A.L.R. 1253 (1928), and the closely related problem of liability for unforeseeable consequences.

In Sinram v. Pennsylvania R.R., 61 F.2d 767, 770 (2d Cir. 1932), which received *Palsgraf* into the admiralty, Judge Learned Hand characterized the issue in that case as "whether, if A. omitted to perform a positive duty to B., C., who had been damaged in consequence, might invoke the breach, though otherwise A. owed him no duty; in short, whether A. was chargeable for the results to others of his breach of duty to B." Thus stated, the query rather answers itself; Hohfeld's analysis tells us that once it is concluded that A. had no duty to C., it is simply a correlative that C. has no right against A. The important question is what was the basis for Chief Judge Cardozo's conclusion that the Long Island Railroad owed no "duty" to Mrs. Palsgraf under the circumstances.

Certainly there is no general principle that a railroad owes no duty to persons on station platforms not in immediate proximity to the tracks, as would have been quickly demonstrated if Mrs. Palsgraf had been injured by the fall of improperly loaded objects from a passing train. Neither is there any principle that railroad guards who jostle a package-carrying passenger owe a duty only to him; if the package had contained bottles, the Long Island would surely have been liable for injury caused to close bystanders by flying glass or spurting liquid. The reason why the Long Island was thought to owe no duty to Mrs. Palsgraf was the lack of any notice that the package contained a substance demanding the exercise of any care toward anyone so far away; Mrs. Palsgraf was not considered to be within the area of apparent hazard created by whatever lack of care the guard had displayed to the anonymous carrier of the unknown fireworks.[5] The key sentences in Chief Judge Cardozo's opinion are these:

> "Here, by concession, there was nothing in the situation to suggest to the most cautious mind that the parcel wrapped in newspaper would spread wreckage through the station. If the guard had thrown it down knowingly and willfully, he would not have threatened the plaintiff's safety, so far as appearances could warn him. Liability can be no greater where the act is inadvertent." 248 N.Y. at 345, 162 N.E. at 101.

We see little similarity between the *Palsgraf* case and the situation before us. The point of *Palsgraf* was that the appearance of the newspaper-wrapped package gave no notice that its dislodgement could do any harm save to itself and those nearby, and this by impact, perhaps with consequent breakage, and not by explosion. In contrast, a ship insecurely moored in a fast flowing river is a known danger not only to herself but to the owners of all other ships and structures down-river, and to persons upon them. No one would dream of saying that a shipowner who "knowingly and willfully" failed to secure his ship at a pier on such a river "would not have threatened" persons and owners of property downstream in some manner.[6] The shipowner and the wharfinger in this case having thus owed a duty of care to all within the reach of the ship's known destructive power, the impossibility of advance identification of the particular person who would be hurt is without legal consequence. Similarly the foreseeable consequences of the City's failure to raise the bridge were not limited to the *Shiras* and the *Tewksbury.* Collision plainly created a danger that the bridge towers might fall onto adjoining property, and the crash of two uncontrolled lake vessels, one 425 feet and the other 525 feet long, into a bridge over a swift ice-ridden stream, with a channel only 177 feet wide, could well result in a partial damming that would flood property upstream. As to the City also, it is useful to consider, by way of contrast, Chief Judge Cardozo's statement that the Long Island would not have been liable to Mrs. Palsgraf had the guard willfully thrown the package down. If the City had deliberately kept the bridge closed in the face of the onrushing vessels, taking the risk that they might not come so far, no one would give house-room to a claim that it "owed no duty" to those who later suffered from the flooding. Unlike Mrs. Palsgraf, they were within the area of hazard. . . .

Since all the claimants here met the *Palsgraf* requirement of being persons to whom the actors owed a "duty of care," we are not obliged to reconsider whether that case

---

5. There was exceedingly little evidence of negligence of any sort. The only lack of care suggested by the majority in the Appellate Division was that instead of endeavoring to assist the passenger, the guards "might better have discouraged and warned him not to board the moving train." 222 App. Div. 166, 167, 225 N.Y.S. 412, 413 (2d Dept. 1927). . . . How much ink would have been saved over the years if the Court of Appeals had reversed Mrs. Palsgraf's judgment on the basis that there was no evidence of negligence at all.

6. The facts here do not oblige us to decide whether the *Shiras* and Continental could successfully invoke *Palsgraf* against claims of owners of shore-side property upstream from the Concrete Elevator or of non-riparian property other than the real and personal property which was sufficiently close to the bridge to have been damaged by the fall of the towers.

furnishes as useful a standard for determining the boundaries of liability in admiralty for negligent conduct as was thought in *Sinram*, when *Palsgraf* was still in its infancy. But this does not dispose of the alternative argument that the manner in which several of the claimants were harmed, particularly by flood damage, was unforeseeable and that recovery for this may not be had — whether the argument is put in the forthright form that unforeseeable damages are not recoverable or is concealed under a formula of lack of "proximate cause."[8]

So far as concerns the City, the argument lacks factual support. Although the obvious risks from not raising the bridge were damage to itself and to the vessels, the danger of a fall of the bridge and of flooding would not have been unforeseeable under the circumstances to anyone who gave them thought. And the same can be said as to the failure of Kinsman's shipkeeper to ready the anchors after the danger had become apparent. The exhibits indicate that the width of the channel between the Concrete Elevator and the bridge is at most points less than two hundred fifty feet. If the *Shiras* caught up on a dock or vessel moored along the shore, the current might well swing her bow across the channel so as to block the ice floes, as indeed could easily have occurred at the Standard Elevator dock where the stern of the *Shiras* struck the *Tewksbury*'s bow. At this point the channel scarcely exceeds two hundred feet, and this was further narrowed by the presence of the *Druckenmiller* moored on the opposite bank. Had the *Tewksbury*'s mooring held, it is thus by no means unlikely that these three ships would have dammed the river. Nor was it unforeseeable that the drawbridge would not be raised since, apart from any other reason, there was no assurance of timely warning. What may have been less foreseeable was that the *Shiras* would get that far down the twisting river, but this is somewhat negated both by the known speed of the current when freshets developed and by the evidence that, on learning of the *Shiras*' departure, Continental's employees and those they informed foresaw precisely that.

Continental's position on the facts is stronger. It was indeed foreseeable that the improper construction and lack of inspection of the "deadman" might cause a ship to break loose and damage persons and property on or near the river — that was what made Continental's conduct negligent. With the aid of hindsight one can also say that a prudent man, carefully pondering the problem, would have realized that the danger of this would be greatest under such water conditions as developed during the night of January 21, 1959, and that if a vessel should break loose under those circumstances, events might transpire as they did. But such post hoc step by step analysis would render "foreseeable" almost anything that has in fact occurred; if the argument relied upon has legal validity, it ought not be circumvented by characterizing as foreseeable what almost no one would in fact have foreseen at the time.

The effect of unforeseeability of damage upon liability for negligence has recently been considered by the Judicial Committee of the Privy Council, Overseas Tankship (U.K.) Ltd. v. Morts Dock & Engineering Co. (*The Wagon Mound*), (1961) 1 All E.R. 404. The Committee there disapproved the proposition, thought to be supported by Re

8. It is worth underscoring that the *ratio decidendi* in *Palsgraf* was that the Long Island was not required to use any care with respect to the package vis-à-vis Mrs. Palsgraf; Chief Judge Cardozo did not reach the issue of "proximate cause" for which the case is often cited.

Polemis and Furness, Withy & Co. Ltd., (1921) 3 K.B. 560 (C.A.), "that unforeseeability is irrelevant if damage is 'direct.'" We have no difficulty with the result of *The Wagon Mound*, in view of the finding, 1 All E.R. at 407, that the appellant had no reason to believe that the floating furnace oil would burn, see also the extended discussion in Miller S.S. Co. v. Overseas Tankship (U.K.) Ltd., *The Wagon Mound No. 2*, (1963) 1 Lloyd's Law List Rep. 402 (Sup. Ct. N.S.W.). On that view the decision simply applies the principle which excludes liability where the injury sprang from a hazard different from that which was improperly risked, see fn.9. Although some language in the judgment goes beyond this, we would find it difficult to understand why one who had failed to use the care required to protect others in the light of expectable forces should be exonerated when the very risks that rendered his conduct negligent produced other and more serious consequences to such persons than were fairly foreseeable when he fell short of what the law demanded. Foreseeability of danger is necessary to render conduct negligent; where as here the damage was caused by just those forces whose existence required the exercise of greater care than was taken — the current, the ice, and the physical mass of the *Shiras*, the incurring of consequences other and greater than foreseen does not make the conduct less culpable or provide a reasoned basis for insulation.[9] The oft encountered argument that failure to limit liability to foreseeable consequences may subject the defendant to a loss wholly out of proportion to his fault seems scarcely consistent with the universally accepted rule that the defendant takes the plaintiff as he finds him and will be responsible for the full extent of the injury even though a latent susceptibility of the plaintiff renders this far more serious than could reasonably have been anticipated.

The weight of authority in this country rejects the limitation of damages to consequences foreseeable at the time of the negligent conduct when the consequences are "direct," and the damage, although other and greater than expectable, is of the same

9. The contrasting situation is illustrated by the familiar instances of the running down of a pedestrian by a safely driven but carelessly loaded car, or of the explosion of unlabeled rat poison, inflammable but not known to be, placed near a coffee burner. Larrimore v. American Nat. Ins. Co., 184 Okl. 614, 89 P.2d 340 (1939). Exoneration of the defendant in such cases rests on the basis that a negligent actor is responsible only for harm the risk of which was increased by the negligent aspect of his conduct. *See* Keeton, *Legal Cause in the Law of Torts*, 1-10 (1963); Hart & Honore, *Causation in the Law*, 157-58 (1959). *Compare* Berry v. Borough of Sugar Notch, 191 Pa. 345, 43 A. 240 (1899).

This principle supports the judgment for the defendant in the recent case of Doughty v. Turner Mfg. Co., (1964) 2 W.L.R. 240 (C.A.). The company maintained a bath of molten cyanide protected by an asbestos cover, reasonably believed to be incapable of causing an explosion if immersed. An employee inadvertently knocked the cover into the bath, but there was no damage from splashing. A minute or two later an explosion occurred as a result of chemical changes in the cover and the plaintiff, who was standing near the bath, was injured by the molten drops. The risk against which defendant was required to use care — splashing of the molten liquid from dropping the supposedly explosion proof cover — did not materialize, and the defendant was found not to have lacked proper care against the risk that did. As said by Lord Justice Diplock, (1964) 2 W.L.R. at 247, "The former risk was well known (that was foreseeable) at the time of the accident; but it did not happen. It was the second risk which happened and caused the plaintiff damage by burning." Moreover, if, as indicated in Lord Pearce's judgment, (1964) 2 W.L.R. at 244, the plaintiff was not within the area of potential splashing, the case parallels *Palsgraf*. . . .

general sort that was risked. . . . Other American courts, purporting to apply a test of foreseeability to damages, extend that concept to such unforeseen lengths as to raise serious doubt whether the concept is meaningful,[10] . . .

We see no reason why an actor engaging in conduct which entails a large risk of small damage and a small risk of other and greater damage, of the same general sort, from the same forces, and to the same class of persons, should be relieved of responsibility for the latter simply because the chance of its occurrence, if viewed alone, may not have been large enough to require the exercise of care. By hypothesis, the risk of the lesser harm was sufficient to render his disregard of it actionable; the existence of a less likely additional risk that the very forces against whose action he was required to guard would produce other and greater damage than could have been reasonably anticipated should inculpate him further rather than limit his liability. This does not mean that the careless actor will always be held for all damages for which the forces that he risked were a cause in fact. Somewhere a point will be reached when courts will agree that the link has become too tenuous—that what is claimed to be consequence is only fortuity. Thus, if the destruction of the Michigan Avenue Bridge had delayed the arrival of a doctor, with consequent loss of a patient's life, few judges would impose liability on any of the parties here, although the agreement in result might not be paralleled by similar unanimity in reasoning; perhaps in the long run one returns to Judge Andrews' statement in *Palsgraf*, 248 N.Y. at 354-355, 162 N.E. at 104 (dissenting opinion). "It is all a question of expediency, . . . of fair judgment, always keeping in mind the fact that we endeavor to make a rule in each case that will be practical and in keeping with the general understanding of mankind." It would be pleasant if greater certainty were possible, see Prosser, Torts, 262, but the many efforts that have been made at defining the locus of the "uncertain and wavering line," 248 N.Y. at 354, 162 N.E. 99, are not very promising; what courts do in such cases makes better sense than what they, or others, say. Where the line will be drawn will vary from age to age; as society has come to rely increasingly on insurance and other methods of loss-sharing, the point may lie further off than a century ago. Here it is surely more equitable that the losses from the operators' negligent failure to raise the Michigan Avenue Bridge should be ratably borne by Buffalo's taxpayers than left with the innocent victims of the flooding; yet the mind is also repelled by a solution that would impose liability solely on the City and exonerate the persons whose negligent acts of commission and omission were the precipitating force of the collision with the bridge and its sequelae. We go only so far as to hold that where, as here, the damages resulted from the same physical forces whose existence required the exercise of greater care than was displayed and were of the same general sort that was expectable, unforeseeability of the exact developments and

10. An instance is In re Guardian Casualty Co., 253 App. Div. 360, 2 N.Y.S.2d 232 (1st Dept.), *aff'd*, 278 N.Y. 674, 16 N.E.2d 397 (1938), where the majority gravely asserted that a foreseeable consequence of driving a taxicab too fast was that a collision with another car would project the cab against a building with such force as to cause a portion of the building to collapse twenty minutes later, when the cab was being removed, and injure a spectator twenty feet away. Surely this is "straining the idea of foreseeability past the breaking point," Bohlen, Book Review, 47 Harv. L. Rev. 556, 557 (1934), at least if the matter be viewed as of the time of the negligent act, as the supposedly symmetrical test of *The Wagon Mound* demands, (1961) 1 All Eng. R. at 415. . . .

of the extent of the loss will not limit liability. Other fact situations can be dealt with when they arise. . . .

The decree is modified so that [Continental, Kinsman and the City of Buffalo can be held jointly liable for, among other things, property damage caused by the flooding resulting from the damming of the river. — Eds.] . . .

Moore, J. (concurring and dissenting): I do not hesitate to concur with Judge Friendly's well-reasoned and well-expressed opinion as to . . . the extent of the liability of the City of Buffalo, Continental and Kinsman for the damages suffered by the City, the *Shiras*, the *Tewksbury*, the *Druckenmiller* and . . . the division of damages.

I cannot agree, however, merely because "society has come to rely increasingly on insurance and other methods of loss-sharing" that the courts should, or have the power to, create a vast judicial insurance company which will adequately compensate all who have suffered damages. Equally disturbing is the suggestion that "Here it is surely more equitable that the losses from the operators' negligent failure to raise the Michigan Avenue Bridge should be ratably borne by Buffalo's taxpayers than left with the innocent victims of the flooding." Under any such principle, negligence suits would become further simplified by requiring a claimant to establish only his own innocence and then offer, in addition to his financial statement, proof of the financial condition of the respective defendants. Judgment would be entered against the defendant which court or jury decided was best able to pay. Nor am I convinced that it should be the responsibility of the Buffalo taxpayers to reimburse the "innocent victims" in their community for damages sustained. In my opinion, before financial liability is imposed, there should be some showing of legal liability.

. . . [N]o bridge builder or bridge operator would envision a bridge as a dam or as a dam potential.

By an extraordinary concatenation of even more extraordinary events, not unlike the humorous and almost-beyond-all-imagination sequences depicted by the famous cartoonist, Rube Goldberg, the *Shiras* with its companions which it picked up en route did combine with the bridge demolition to create a very effective dam across the Buffalo River. Without specification of the nature of the damages, claims in favor of some twenty persons and companies were allowed resulting from the various collisions and from "the damming of the river at the bridge, the backing up of the water and ice upstream, and the overflowing of the banks of the river and flooding of industrial installations along the river banks." (Sup. Finding of Fact #26a.) My dissent is limited to that portion of the opinion which approves the awarding of damages suffered as a result of the flooding of various properties upstream. I am not satisfied with reliance on hindsight or on the assumption that since flooding occurred, therefore, it must have been foreseeable. In fact, the majority hold that the danger "of flooding would not have been unforeseeable under the circumstances to anyone who gave them thought." But believing that "anyone" might be too broad, they resort to that most famous of all legal mythological characters, the reasonably "prudent man." Even he, however, "carefully pondering the problem," is not to be relied upon because they permit him to become prudent "[W]ith the aid of hindsight." . . .

In final analysis the answers to the questions when the link is "too tenuous" and when "consequence is only fortuity" are dependent solely on the particular point of view of the particular judge under the particular circumstances. . . . [T]o me the fortuitous circumstance of the vessels so arranging themselves as to create a dam is much "too tenuous." . . .

NOTES AND QUESTIONS

1. *Palsgraf Revisited.* Judge Friendly's opinion maintains that Continental and Kinsman were each careless *as to* the downstream property owners who suffered flooding damage as a result of the failure to prevent the *MacGilvray Shiras* from careening down the Buffalo River. Is this a faithful application of *Palsgraf*? It also holds the City liable to property owners *upstream* from the Michigan Avenue Bridge, even though footnote 6 suggests that *Palsgraf* would prevent Continental and Kinsman from being held liable to property owners *upstream* from Continental's dock. Is this seemingly disparate treatment of upstream property owners defensible? The same footnote implies that *Palsgraf* might protect Continental and Kinsman from liability to owners of property located away from the banks of the river, unless such properties were at risk of being physically harmed by the fall of the bridge's towers. Is this a faithful application of *Palsgraf*?

2. *Within the Scope of the Risk?* Does Judge Friendly conclude that property damage through flooding was one of the risks that rendered the conduct of Kinsman, Continental, and the city careless? If so, does he mean to say that the risk, properly described, was to property damaged by any means, or property damaged through a specific means, such as flooding or physical impact? Or does he abandon the "scope of the risk" test in favor of some other conception of proximate cause? Does *Kinsman* mark a return to *Polemis* and the directness test?

3. *The Increment of Unforeseeable Harm.* Judge Friendly's opinion maintains that, at least in some circumstances, there is nothing unfair about assigning liability for unforeseeable harms to a defendant found to have acted carelessly. Specifically, he suggests that, since these defendants were already subject to liability for lesser harms foreseeably caused by their negligence, such as damage to the *Tewksbury*, it is perfectly appropriate to add liability for additional, highly improbable but potentially vast harms, such as property damage caused by flooding. The argument seems to be that if an actor is duty-bound to take precautions for the benefit of the plaintiff against certain types of harm, and his breach happens to cause some other kind of harm, there is no reason *not* to hold the defendant liable for this other kind of harm as well. Wasn't this argument rejected by Viscount Simonds in *Wagon Mound (No. 1)*?

4. *The Relevance of Cost-Spreading.* Judge Friendly, invoking Judge Andrews's *Palsgraf* dissent, further suggests that the determination of proximate cause should be driven at least in part by "policy" considerations, such as the ability of different actors to defray the cost of the harms at issue. Is he right in assuming that the city, as opposed to the property owners, was in the best position to defray those costs through,

say, a modest tax increase? What if the property owners could buy flood insurance that would reimburse them for property damage caused by flooding? Wouldn't that be a more efficient way to handle this problem?

5. *Type of Harm Versus Manner of Harm.* *Kinsman* raises some difficult questions for the scope-of-the-risk approach to proximate cause. In particular, the question arises as to whether the *manner* of harm — as opposed to the type of harm — should ever be relevant to the inquiry. Consider the *Guardian Casualty* case mentioned in footnote 10 of the *Kinsman* opinion. How should that case be analyzed under the scope-of-the-risk approach? Does a correct description of the risks posed by driving too fast include the risk of all physical harms caused by impacts flowing from the car's movement? Was the court in *Guardian* correct to conclude that the cab driver ought to be subject to liability to the spectator injured by the debris that fell as the cab was being removed from the building? Should this sort of hard case simply be left to the jury?

Suppose, alternatively, that *S* is a spectator at a stock car race. *O*, the owner of the racetrack, acts carelessly by not providing adequate fencing to protect spectators from debris that can be expected to fly off cars when they collide or break down. It so happens that this race is being televised, in part by means of a large camera mounted on a blimp hovering over the stadium. Unexpectedly, and without fault on the part of the television production company, the camera falls, shattering on the track. *S* is struck and injured by camera shrapnel that would have been blocked by an adequate fence. Was *S*'s injury within the scope of the risk posed by *O*'s carelessness?

6. *Kinsman (II).* In a subsequent case, the Second Circuit determined that the same defendants who were held liable for the losses discussed in *Kinsman* were not liable for economic losses caused to carriers who could not unload wheat from their ships because of the negligent damming of the Buffalo River. According to the court, the connection between the defendants' negligence and these claimants' damages was "too tenuous and remote" to permit recovery. In re Kinsman Transit Co. (*Kinsman (II)*), 388 F.2d 821 (2d Cir. 1968). Is this conclusion defensible in light of the holding of *Kinsman (I)*?

III. SUPERSEDING CAUSE AND AFFIRMATIVE DUTIES

This section provides an occasion to consider the interaction of proximate cause doctrine with substantive duty doctrines encountered in Chapter 2, particularly doctrine pertaining to the recognition of affirmative duties to rescue and protect.

A. Intervening Wrongdoing: Superseding Cause as a Special Case of Proximate Cause

We have seen that a single injury can often result from the wrongful acts of multiple tortfeasors. We have also seen that negligence law is prepared to hold two or more careless actors concurrently responsible for such an injury. For example, in

McDonald v. Robinson (Chapter 4), each of two drivers was held responsible for the injuries caused by their careless driving. More often than not, responsibility in multiple-wrongdoer cases will be concurrent in this sense. However, in a certain kind of negligence case, courts will *sometimes* refuse to assign responsibility to each of two wrongdoers whose wrongs cause a single injury. Instead, they will assign full responsibility to one wrongdoer and no responsibility to the other.

The type of case to which we refer has two basic features. First, the two wrongdoers are acting independently of one another; there is no concert of action or common plan between them. Second, their wrongs are committed in a sequence, such that there is an initial wrongful act that is more remote in time and space from the plaintiff's injury, and a subsequent wrongful act that involves a relatively direct or immediate infliction of injury on the plaintiff. In other words, the allegation is that a background or remote wrongdoer was careless for having "set the stage" for the immediate wrongdoer's wrong. In this scenario, courts will sometimes, though not always, treat the immediate injurer's wrongful injuring of the plaintiff as a *superseding cause*— that is, a cause that precludes imposition of liability upon the remote wrongdoer *even though the remote wrongdoer's act was also a necessary condition of the victim's injury.*

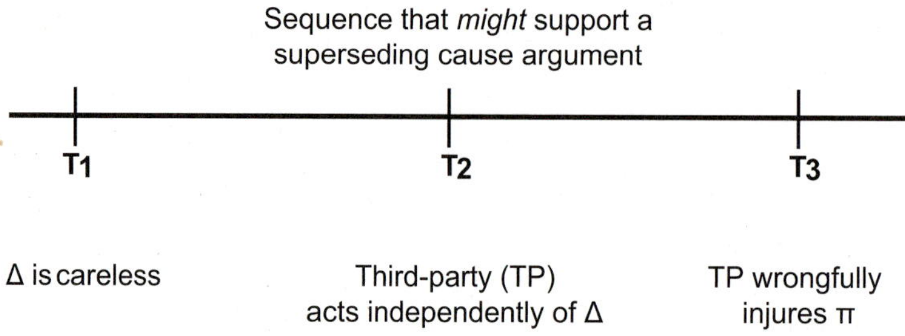

A pair of decisions from the early twentieth century can help isolate the issue of superseding cause as a distinct aspect or instantiation of the notion of proximate cause. In *Pollard v. Oklahoma City Ry. Co.*, 128 P. 300 (Okla. 1912), a contractor working for the defendant railway left strewn about a worksite containers with residual amounts of blasting powder. Millard Justes, a 14-year-old boy who lived near the site, discovered the containers. Over the course of a month, he diligently collected the leftover powder, which he kept in a can stashed near his home. Millard's parents later became aware of the can, and warned him to leave it alone lest he be injured. (Indeed, Millard testified that his father threatened to whip him if he did not discard it.) Their warning notwithstanding, Millard kept the powder. Several weeks later, Millard and Bernie Pollard, a 13-year-old boy, took out some of the powder and both set out to ignite it. The powder exploded, severely injuring Pollard.

Suit on Pollard's behalf was brought against the defendant railway (but not Millard or his parents), alleging that its negligence was an actual and proximate cause of Pollard's injuries. The trial court dismissed the suit, and the Oklahoma Supreme Court affirmed. The Court assumed that the railroad was careless, and that, but for its carelessness, Pollard would not have been injured. It further acknowledged that, under settled Oklahoma law, the mere fact of intervening wrongdoing — in this case, Millard's carelessness or recklessness, which took place after the railroad's carelessness but before Pollard's injury — did not automatically relieve the railroad of liability. Nonetheless, the court held that Millard's intervention was of such a nature as to block the imposition of liability on the railroad.

According to the court, Millard, by taking charge of the powder, and by doing so with his parents' eventual knowledge, had effectively ended the railroad's responsibility. The actions of "several intelligent and responsible human beings intervening between the original negligence and the injury" sufficed to

> . . . show conclusively such independent, intervening, efficient causes as to compel us to say that they in fact were the proximate cause of the injury, and that the original negligence of the company was so remote and the chain of events was so broken that they became independent, and were not the natural or probable consequences of the original or primary cause.

128 P., at 303.

In contrast to *Pollard* stands the nearly contemporaneous decision of the Kansas Supreme Court in *Clark v. E.I. Du Pont de Nemours Powder Co.*, 146 P. 320 (Kan. 1915). An employee of the defendant, an explosives manufacturer, carelessly left on a farm a quart of highly volatile "solidified glycerine." Joe McDowell, a teenager or young adult, had been hired to work on the farm, though not with explosives, about which he had no knowledge. McDowell found the glycerine and, fearing that it might be dangerous, first brought it to his house. After being instructed by his mother to take it away, he buried it in the low stone wall of an abandoned graveyard located on another part of the farm. The glycerine remained there undisturbed for two years before being discovered by the plaintiff's young sons. They were seriously injured when, while playing with the glycerine, it exploded.

Affirming a jury verdict for the plaintiff against defendant, the Kansas Court concluded that McDowell's intervening actions, even if careless with respect to the risk of someone being injured by the glycerine, did not "break" the causal chain running from defendant's carelessness to the boys being injured. It explained:

> No new power of doing mischief was communicated to the solidified glycerine by the acts of young McDowell. The power of doing mischief was inherent in the glycerine all the time. That some terrible accident was likely to happen in letting it out of the close custody of some one skilled in its use was not only natural and probable, but almost inevitable.

146 P., at 322.

Pollard was deemed by the Oklahoma Court to be a case of superseding cause, whereas *Clark* is treated by the Kansas Court as a case of concurrent negligence. Do you agree that the cases differ along this dimension, such that the remote wrongdoer in

Pollard should escape all liability while the remote wrongdoer in *Clark* should not? If so, what is it about the intervening wrongdoing — or the context in which the intervening wrongdoing took place — that distinguishes the cases? To invoke the language of *Clark*, is it correct to say that Millard Justes (in *Pollard*), unlike Joe McDowell (in *Clark*), communicated a "new power of doing mischief"? Why?

NOTES AND QUESTIONS

1. *Effect of Superseding Cause.* When intervening third-party misconduct is deemed a superseding cause, the remote defendant being sued for negligence is relieved of all liability. Conversely, when intervening misconduct is held not to constitute a superseding cause, *both* actors — the remote and the intervening wrongdoer — are subject to liability. *See* Chapter 8 (discussing apportionment of liability among multiple tortfeasors).

2. *Other Examples of Superseding Cause?* In contrast to the duty issue, proximate cause is typically assessed by the jury. Thus, the issue for judges in addressing a superseding cause argument is whether a reasonable juror could find that a third party's intervening wrongful act constitutes a superseding cause. Consider the following hypothetical situations. Should a jury be permitted or required to enter a verdict for any of these defendants?

a. Dockowner *D* carelessly permits a tanker ship owned by *O* and captained by independent contractor *C* to break loose from its moorings. *C* and his crew are on board. Although *C* has ample opportunity to steer the ship to safety, *C* inexplicably ignores standard procedures, instead executing maneuvers that cause the ship to crash and sink. *Cf.* Exxon Co., U.S.A. v. Sofec, Inc., 517 U.S. 830, 833-837 (1996) (noting lower courts' determination that captain's gross negligence constituted a superseding cause relieving dockowner of liability to shipowner).

b. *P* purchases a new car manufactured by *D*. Because of negligence on *D*'s part, the car stalls without warning as *P* crosses a busy intersection. Another driver, *R* decides that it would be "interesting" to see whether his colossal SUV can collide with *P*'s car without sustaining damage. *R* deliberately collides with *P's* car, injuring her.

c. *O* is a police officer on patrol in a busy urban area. *O* hears on his patrol car radio that a car of a certain description may have been involved in an attempted petty theft. *O* spots the car and signals to its driver to pull over. The driver drives away and *O* pursues him at a reasonable speed. To get away from *O*, the driver drives up on a sidewalk and runs down pedestrian *P*. *P* sues *O* and the city that employs him, arguing that, under the department's own rules, no chase should have taken place given the crowded conditions and the minor nature of the driver's alleged offense. *Cf.* Wade v. City of Chicago, 847 N.E.2d 631 (Ill. App. 2006) (affirming judgment for the defendants; even if the officer's pursuit amounted to wanton misconduct, it was not a proximate cause of plaintiff's injury given the driver's decision to drive on the sidewalk).

3. *Intervening Negligence as Superseding Cause.* Although courts often decline to treat intervening wrongful conduct as a superseding cause, when they do treat it as

such, the intervening conduct almost always involves intentional or reckless wrongdoing. However, it is not unheard of for courts to treat intervening *careless* acts as superseding causes. Examples include so-called social host liability cases, which are discussed in the notes following *Fast Eddie's, infra.* Another example is provided by *Roberts v. Benoit*, 605 So. 2d 1032 (La. 1991). The plaintiff was accidentally shot by *C*, who was employed as a cook by defendant sheriff's office (*S*). *C* had been deputized solely to render *C* eligible for supplementary pay. However, in order to be deputized, *C* had to undergo training in the use of firearms, which apparently included "encouragement" to carry a firearm. While drunk and playing with his gun one evening, *C* shot *P*. Granting that *S* breached a duty owed to the plaintiff by its careless training of *C*, the court nonetheless held that *C*'s "foolhardy" conduct amounted to a superseding cause.

In *Martinez v. Lazaroff*, 411 N.Y.S.2d 955 (App. Div. 1978), landlord *L* carelessly failed to provide hot water to tenant *T*'s apartment. To provide warm water for bathing, *T* heated water in a pot, then carried the pot to the bathroom. Along the way, he collided with his infant child *C*, causing *C* to suffer burns. The court ruled that *C*'s suit against *L* was barred because *T*'s carelessness was a superseding cause. Might this result be explicable (although not necessarily defensible) as an indirect means of ruling that *T*'s fault was substantial and in some sense chargeable to *C*, given that the suit, though nominally on *C*'s behalf, was being brought by *T* to recover compensation from *L*?

4. *Subsequent Malpractice and Liability for Enhanced Injuries.* Suppose that drunk driver *D* crashes into the car of *P*, and that *P* suffers a broken leg. As emergency medical technicians transport *P* to the hospital, they carelessly mistreat the injury. As a result, *P*'s leg must be amputated, whereas amputation would not have been required had the EMTs acted carefully. Does the EMTs' carelessness relieve *D* of responsibility for the amputation?

The answer under black letter law is a resounding "no": ordinary medical malpractice committed in the course of treating injuries created by the negligence of a defendant is deemed a foreseeable consequence of that negligence, and not deemed a superseding cause. Restatement (Third) of Torts: Liability for Physical and Emotional Harm § 35 (2010). Suppose *P* is taken to the hospital without incident and is treated and released with instructions to return two weeks later for a follow-up examination. When *P* returns for that examination, the examining physician commits malpractice by using unsterilized instruments, causing *P* to suffer a serious infection. Should *D* be on the hook for having caused the infection?

Returning to the original hypothetical above, suppose that the EMTs are not careless in treating *P*, but that a second drunk driver, *S*, carelessly crashes into the ambulance carrying *P*, which necessitates amputation of *P*'s leg. May a jury conclude that *S*'s post-accident carelessness constitutes a superseding cause of the damages associated with amputation, such that *D* cannot be held liable for those damages? *Cf.* Coates v. Contl. Vinyl Window Co., 2003 WL 21540440 (Mich. App. 2003) (per curiam) (accident caused by a second drunk driver is a superseding cause). If *S*'s carelessness does constitute a superseding cause, is that because it was unforeseeable? Less foreseeable than medical malpractice?

Finally, suppose a third variation on this scenario, in which one of the EMTs treating *P*, without warning, has a psychotic episode that causes him to strangle *P* en route to the hospital. Superseding cause as a matter of law?

5. *An Outmoded Doctrine?* Some commentators maintain that the practical justification for the doctrine of superseding cause has disappeared. Under older negligence law, if the wrongful acts of two or more tortfeasors functioned as but-for causes of a single, indivisible injury, the plaintiff could, under the rule of joint and several liability, recover *all* of his damages from any one of them, even one who was much less culpable than the other(s).* Given this framework, superseding cause doctrine permitted a kind of rough justice by sparing the minimally culpable party from bearing the entirety of the liability. Now, however, with the advent of comparative fault and the move toward apportioned (rather than joint) liability, a jury is permitted to allocate responsibility among multiple wrongdoers on a percentage basis. *See* Chapter 8. Thus — the argument concludes — the need for the crude rule of superseding cause has largely been obviated. Applying federal admiralty law, the U.S. Supreme Court pointedly rejected this argument. *See* Exxon Co., U.S.A. v. Sofec, Inc., 517 U.S. 830, 837 (1996). Apart from the rough justice idea just described, what other justifications might there be for the doctrine?

B. Intervening Wrongdoing, Superseding Cause, and Affirmative Duty

Having introduced the concept of superseding cause, we now turn to a pair of cases that raise the issue of how that concept interacts with concepts of duty encountered in Chapter 2.

Port Authority of New York & New Jersey v. Arcadian Corp.

189 F.3d 305 (3d Cir. 1999)

ROTH, J. This case arises from the February 26, 1993, terrorist detonation of an explosive device under the World Trade Center in New York City, which caused six deaths, many injuries and massive property damage. Plaintiff-appellant, the Port Authority of New York and New Jersey, owner of the World Trade Center, sued defendants, manufacturers of fertilizer products, on theories of negligence and products liability, alleging that the terrorists used defendants' fertilizer products to construct the explosive device.

The District Court, in a thorough and well-reasoned opinion, granted defendants' motion to dismiss for failure to state a claim upon which relief may be granted under Fed.R.Civ.P. 12(b)(6). Plaintiff appealed. We find that it was appropriate, in light of the record, for the District Court to dismiss the action under Rule 12(b)(6). . . . Accordingly, we will affirm the judgment of the District Court.

---

* As explained in Chapter 8, in principle, if one of two or more tortfeasors deemed responsible for a plaintiff's injuries is made to pay the entire cost of those injuries because of the rule of joint and several liability, it is open to the one tortfeasor to seek "contribution" — partial reimbursement — from the other(s). If, however, the other tortfeasors are judgment-proof or otherwise unavailable, the tortfeasor made to pay the plaintiff's damages will be left to bear that cost alone.

I. Factual and Procedural History

A. Factual Background

The Port Authority of New York and New Jersey is the owner of the World Trade Center in New York City. On February 26, 1993, a bomb, which had been fabricated by terrorists out of ammonium nitrate, urea, and nitric acid, exploded in an underground parking garage at the World Trade Center, causing six deaths, many injuries and massive property damage.

The ammonium nitrate, urea, and nitric acid used in the bomb were allegedly sold in New Jersey, and the bomb was allegedly assembled in New Jersey by New Jersey residents. Defendants Hydro-Agri North America, Inc., and Dyno Nobel Inc., formerly known as Ireco, Inc., are alleged to have manufactured, designed, marketed, distributed and/or sold the ammonium nitrate used by the terrorists. Defendant Arcadian Corporation is alleged to have manufactured, designed, marketed, distributed and/or sold the urea used by the terrorists.

The ammonium nitrate and urea, alleged to have been purchased by the terrorists, were sold in prill form, i.e., a white, round, hardened droplet about the size of the tip of a ball point pen. The prills were manufactured to be used as fertilizer. The ammonium nitrate prills can be rendered explosive by the addition of fuel oil or other sensitizing substances; the urea prills can be rendered explosive by the addition of nitric acid and water (forming urea nitrate). The terrorists are alleged to have rendered the prills explosive by adding these substances. Defendants point out that, as conceded in the Amended Complaint, the prills are not explosive in and of themselves.

Plaintiff alleges that defendants knew or should have known that the ammonium nitrate and urea could easily be made into explosives and that terrorists had used them prior to the bombing at the World Trade Center, but nevertheless defendants failed to take appropriate steps to render their products non-detonable. Specifically, plaintiff points to two incidents. First, an explosion of ammonium nitrate over fifty years ago destroyed two ships docked at Texas City, Texas, killing 468 persons and causing extensive damage in the city. Second, more than thirty years ago, anti-war protesters used ammonium nitrate to bomb the Mathematics Research Building at the University of Wisconsin, leading to injuries, death and property damage.

Plaintiff alleges that defendants had the means to reduce the danger of their products. In 1968, Samuel Porter patented a process that rendered ammonium nitrate fertilizers non-detonable. The process called for adding five to ten percent of diammonium phosphate, a high grade of fertilizer, to ammonium nitrate at a nominal additional cost. When the patent was made available to ammonium nitrate manufacturers, one of the explicit purposes was to deter the criminal use of ammonium nitrate in bombs. In 1985, the Porter patent entered the public domain, making the process available to all manufacturers free of license or royalty.

Plaintiff alleges that the danger of these products prompted governments here and abroad to attempt to regulate their manufacture and distribution. Specifically, in response to the University of Wisconsin bombing, several states introduced legislation to require that all ammonium fertilizers be desensitized by a chemical agent (as described in the Porter patent) to reduce, if not eliminate, the explosive properties of ammonium nitrate. The legislative efforts were allegedly well publicized, including within the fertilizer industry, but plaintiff asserts that various fertilizer manufacturers resisted the legislation, leading to its ultimate defeat.

In addition, in 1975, the European Economic Community Council issued a directive that established (1) strict standards for the formulation of solid ammonium nitrate and (2) detonation tests that could be required by member countries to ensure that fertilizer sold in those countries had a low potential for use as explosive. Belgium, Denmark, Germany and the Netherlands prohibited the sale of certain ammonium nitrate fertilizers. France mandated that all ammonium nitrate fertilizer be tested by detonation.

Three years prior to the EEC directive, terrorist bombings in Northern Ireland and the Republic of Ireland prompted the United Kingdom and Ireland to enact regulations that were even more stringent. Those regulations limited the amount of nitrate that could be used in fertilizer products and required the addition of calcium, sulfates, and other materials to reduce their detonability.

Information about urea and the means to desensitize it was allegedly similarly well known, yet not utilized, prior to the World Trade Center bombing. It was allegedly known that the addition of phosphate and other additives to urea prills would decrease or eliminate their use as explosive and energetic materials. Explosives made of urea nitrate were allegedly used in the Middle East, South America, Pakistan and the United States prior to the World Trade Center bombing. In 1992, the sales of urea and ammonium nitrate fertilizer were banned in Peru as a result of the extensive use of urea and ammonium nitrate prills in explosives set off by the Shining Path terrorists.

B. Procedural Background

Plaintiff filed this action . . . in the Superior Court of New Jersey in Essex County. Defendants removed the actions to the United States District Court for the District of New Jersey on the grounds of diversity of citizenship. . . .

The Amended Complaint asserts three grounds for holding defendants liable. Count I, a claim of negligence, asserts that defendants "negligently failed to design, manufacture, market, distribute and/or sell [ammonium nitrate or urea prills] with a formulation" that would either "render them less detonable or non-detonable" or "decrease or eliminate their explosive properties." Count II, a claim in strict [products] liability, asserts that defendants are liable because the ammonium nitrate and urea prills were "unreasonably dangerous and defective when they left the respective control of each of the Defendants." Count III asserts that defendants are liable because they "failed to provide guidelines, instructions, and/or warnings to their distributors, retailers, dealers or other suppliers to confirm that buyers in the general and unrestricted public market have legitimate and lawful purposes for use of Defendants' products."

Defendants filed a Motion to Dismiss pursuant to Fed.R.Civ.P. 12(b)(6). The District Court granted the motion and dismissed the Complaint with prejudice. Plaintiff filed a timely appeal.

II. ANALYSIS

A. Standard of Review

The standard of review of a district court order dismissing a complaint under Fed.R.Civ.P. 12(b)(6) is plenary. *Alexander v. Whitman*, 114 F.3d 1392, 1397 (3d Cir.1997). The court "must determine if plaintiff may be entitled to relief under any reasonable reading of the pleadings, assuming the truth of all the factual allegations in the complaint." *Id.* (citations omitted). "A court may dismiss a complaint only if it is clear that no relief could be granted under any set of facts that could be proven consistent with the allegations." *Id.*

. . .

C. Choice of Law

As an initial matter, the District Court found it was not necessary to make a determination whether New York or New Jersey law applies to the Amended Complaint. Instead, the District Court determined that the Amended Complaint failed to state a claim under the law of either state. . . . Because we agree that dismissal is required under both New Jersey and New York law, we similarly need not decide the choice of law issue.

D. The District Court's Application of Fed.R.Civ.P. 12(b)(6)

. . . .

. . . . Rule 12(b)(6) . . . is designed to screen out cases where "a complaint states a claim based upon a wrong for which there is clearly no remedy, or a claim which the plaintiff is without right or power to assert and for which no relief could possibly be granted. . . ." *Melo-Sonics Corp. v. Cropp*, 342 F.2d 856, 859 (3d Cir.1965) (quoting *Leimer v. State Mutual Life Assurance Co.*, 108 F.2d 302, 305-06 (8th Cir.1940)). We find that the District Court carried out this mandate by taking all the allegations in the Amended Complaint as true and making every favorable inference in favor of plaintiff but deciding nevertheless that no relief could be granted.

Second, we disagree with plaintiff's insistence that the District Court misapplied Rule 12(b)(6) by considering whether plaintiff's claims were sufficient as a matter of "fairness" or "sound policy." Plaintiff argues that such considerations improperly substituted the court's views for those of the jury. Plaintiff, however, misunderstands the role of the courts in developing and administering the tort system. Tort law is essentially concerned with the "allocation of losses" arising out of "socially unreasonable conduct." Prosser & Keeton, The Law of Torts, § 1 at 6. The courts must consider not only the interests of the litigants but also the interests of society in general, including the social and economic costs of any expansion of the outer boundaries of tort liability. *Id.* This consideration necessarily involves considerations of social and public policy. *Id.*

As we will explore more fully below, the legal bounds of duty and of proximate cause are aspects of tort law in which issues of fairness and public policy are particularly relevant. We conclude that the District Court properly considered questions of fairness and policy and made rulings of law on issues of reasonable foreseeability and proximate causation. . . . Because the District Court found as a matter of law that there was no duty and no proximate causation, there was nothing for a jury to consider.

[The Court of Appeals determined that, as between Count I (negligence) and Count II (strict products liability), the plaintiff's burden of proving its prima facie case was *less* onerous for Count II, because a products liability claim, unlike a negligence claim, does not require proof of manufacturer carelessness. It followed, according to the Court, that affirmance of the trial court's dismissal of Count II would entail an affirmance of the dismissal of Count I. Thus, it focused its analysis of duty and proximate cause as they arise under the law strict products liability rather than the law of negligence. For present purposes, the differences between negligence and products liability law are not significant. Products liability law is discussed in Chapter 12. — Eds.]

E. Duty

The District Court properly concluded that the Amended Complaint failed to establish the existence of a duty owed by defendants. Under both New Jersey and New York law, the question of whether a duty is owed is a question of law to be decided by the court.

We find that defendants owed no duty to plaintiff under either New Jersey or New York law. First, the manufacturer of a raw material or component part that is not itself dangerous has no legal duty to prevent a buyer from incorporating the material or the part into another device that is or may be dangerous. By plaintiff's own allegations, defendants' products were not in and of themselves dangerous but were merely the raw materials or components that terrorists used in combination with other ingredients to build a bomb. Second, manufacturers have no duty to prevent a criminal misuse of their products which is entirely foreign to the purpose for which the product was intended.

The New Jersey Supreme Court examined the duties of a component manufacturer in *Zaza v. Marquess & Nell, Inc.*, 675 A.2d 620 (N.J. 1996). In that case, the plaintiff was injured when hot water and carbon overflowed from a quench tank he was attempting to unclog. . . . The defendant, who had manufactured the quench tank, knew from designs that, once integrated into the larger system, the tank would need certain safety devices. Nevertheless, the New Jersey Supreme Court held that the component part manufacturer owed the plaintiff no duty regarding any danger posed by the integrated device, stating that a component part fabricator may only be held "strictly liable for injury caused by a defective component where the defect is in the component part and the part did not undergo substantial change after leaving the manufacturer's hands." *Id.* at 636. The court relied on a tentative draft of the Restatement (Third) of Torts, in which the American Law Institute "concluded that a component part manufacturer generally is not liable unless the component part is defective or the component provider substantially participated in the design of the final product." *Id.* at 629. The court also followed the "majority of courts from other jurisdictions [which] have held that a manufacturer of a component part, which is not dangerous until it is integrated by the owner into a larger system, cannot be held strictly liable to an injured employee for the failure of the owner and/or assembler to install safety devices." *Id.*

In the instant case, there is no allegation that the fertilizer products were dangerous in and of themselves. Under plaintiff's own allegations, the raw ammonium nitrate and urea sold by defendants were not explosive until the terrorists purposefully manipulated and adulterated them by mixing them together with additional chemicals such that they were transformed into energized materials that could be incorporated into an explosive charge. The danger to plaintiff was presented not by the raw materials, but by a bomb that incorporated the raw materials after they had been substantially altered. In addition, defendants had no control over the fertilizer once it was sold and no control over the final assembly of the bomb.

Moreover, under the [New Jersey Products Liability Act—NJPLA], a plaintiff must prove "that the product causing the harm was not reasonably fit, suitable or safe for its *intended purpose*." N.J.S.A. 2A:58C-2 (emphasis added); *see also Zaza*, 675 A.2d at 627 (stating that a "manufacturer has a duty to ensure that the products its places into the stream of commerce are safe when used for their intended purposes"). The "unforeseeable misuse of a product may not give rise to strict liability." *Suter v. San Angelo Foundry and Mach. Co.*, 406 A.2d 140, 144 (N.J. 1979). "A product is not in a defective condition when it is safe for normal consumption and handling." *Id.* (quoting Restatement (Second) of Torts, § 402A cmt. h). Where "the use of the product is beyond its intended or reasonably anticipated scope," an injury resulting from that use is "not . . . probative of whether the product was fit, suitable, and safe." *Id.* There is no allegation here that the fertilizer products were unsafe for their intended purposes, that is, when used as fertilizer.

Plaintiff attempts to argue that defendants should be liable nonetheless because the New Jersey courts have held that a manufacturer's duty also encompasses objectively foreseeable misuses and alterations. *See Oquendo* [*v. Bettcher Indus., Inc.*] 939 F.Supp. [357,] 362 (D.N.J. 1996) ("New Jersey courts have held manufacturers strictly liable for products, despite another's subsequent substantial alterations, where those alterations were objectively foreseeable and likely to cause injuries."). . . .

We conclude, however, that the alteration and misuse of defendants' fertilizer products were not objectively foreseeable. We reject, therefore, plaintiff's attempt to hold defendants liable under this theory. The court in *Oquendo* set forth New Jersey law as follows:

> Objective foreseeability means reasonable foreseeability. The standard "does not affix responsibility for future events that are only theoretically, remotely, or just possibly foreseeable, or even simply subjectively foreseen by a particular manufacturer." . . . Rather it "applies to those future occurrences that, in light of the general experience within the industry when the product was manufactured, objectively and reasonably could have been anticipated."

Oquendo, 939 F.Supp. at 362 (quoting *Brown v. United States Stove Co.*, 484 A.2d 1234, 1241 (N.J. 1984)). Significantly, the fact that plaintiff alleges that defendants were aware of previous instances in which fertilizer products were used in bombs does not suffice to establish objective foreseeability. "Such knowledge . . . tends to show only subjective foreseeability, and . . . subjective foreseeability is irrelevant to the [objective] foreseeability determination." *Id.* at 363.

Plaintiff argued below, and again on appeal, that the issues of objective foreseeability and reasonableness should be left for a jury to decide. We recognize that these issues are indeed generally a matter to be determined by a jury. An exception is to be made, however, where "the inferences are so clear that a court can say as a matter of law that a reasonable manufacturer could not have foreseen the change." [Soler v. Castmaster, 484 A.2d 1225, 1234 (N.J. 1984)] (quoting parenthetically Merriweather v. E.W. Bliss Co., 636 F.2d 42, 45 (3d Cir.1980)) (quoting D'Antona v. Hampton Grinding Wheel Co., 310 A.2d 307 (Pa. 1973)).

The inferences in this case are indeed so clear that we can say as a matter of law that the transformation and integration of the otherwise safe fertilizer products into the type of explosive device used in the World Trade Center bombing was not objectively foreseeable to the defendants at the time of this bombing. We agree with the District Court's conclusion that:

> No jury could reasonably could [sic] conclude that one accidental explosion 50 years ago, one terrorist act in this country almost 30 years ago, and scattered terrorists incidents throughout the world over the course of the last 30 years would make an incident like the World Trade Center bombing anything more than a remote or theoretical possibility.

Port Authority of New York & New Jersey, 991 F.Supp. at 402-03.

. . . . The District Court's conclusion is consistent with the refusal of the New Jersey Supreme Court to impose a duty in cases involving outrageous misuses of a product wholly unrelated to its intended purpose, where such a duty would expose manufacturers to endless liability. *See, e.g., Jurado* [*v. Western Gear Works,*] 619 A.2d [1312,] 1318 [(N.J. 1993)] ("If . . . a plaintiff undertakes to use his power saw as a nail clipper and thereby snips his digits, he will not be heard to complain. . . .") (citation omitted). . . .

We agree with the District Court that imposing a duty on defendants in this case would be unfair. "Ultimately, the determination of the existence of a duty is a question of fairness and public policy. Foreseeability of injury to another is important, but not dispositive. Fairness, not foreseeability alone, is the test." *Kuzmicz v. Ivy Hill Park Apartments, Inc.*, 688 A.2d 1018, 1020 (N.J. 1997). Indeed, it would be grossly unfair to impose a duty on defendants to anticipate and prevent the use of their products as one part of a terrorist's explosive device. Their products were not explosive in and of themselves, without being mixed with other substances and incorporated into a bomb.

Finally, imposing a duty in this case would expand the scope of manufacturers' liability under New Jersey law, a result contrary to the legislative policy of the NJPLA, which "has been interpreted as evincing a legislative policy to limit the expansion of products-liability law." *Zaza*, 675 A.2d at 627 (internal quote marks omitted). We leave such an expansion of duty to the legislature.

Similarly, under New York law, we find that no duty exists that would provide a basis for liability. . . .

. . . *Elsroth v. Johnson & Johnson*, 700 F.Supp. 151 (S.D.N.Y.1988), . . . establishes that a manufacturer cannot be held liable for failing to add a safety device to its product to prevent other substances from being combined with it. In that case, an individual laced Tylenol capsules with cyanide and replaced the deadly product on store shelves, causing a consumer to die after ingesting the capsules. Thus, like the instant case, *Elsroth* concerned a criminal who injured a victim by adulterating the defendant's product. The plaintiff alleged that the manufacturer could have prevented the death by producing the drug in caplet form, which would have made it more difficult for a criminal to adulterate the product. The court rejected this argument, holding that "there exists no common law duty requiring . . . manufacturers to design their product in such a way as to anticipate and frustrate criminal tampering." *Id.* at 164.

This limiting principle is not altered even if the misuse of the product might be foreseeable. In *Elsroth,* the defendant's product had been tampered with in the same way four years earlier. *Id.* at 153. . . . *see also McCarthy v. Sturm, Ruger, and Co.*, 916 F. Supp. 366, 369 (S.D.N.Y. 1996) (holding as a matter of law that defendant, a manufacturer of ammunition, owed no duty to prevent the criminal misuse of ammunition, regardless of its foreseeability).

. . . .

Because no duty exists under the law of either New Jersey or New York, we find that it was appropriate for the District Court to dismiss the Amended Complaint for failure to state a claim upon which relief could be granted.

F. Proximate Causation

The District Court also properly concluded that, under the law of either jurisdiction, defendants' actions or inactions were not the proximate cause of the World Trade Center bombing.

As the District Court explained, the correct legal framework under New Jersey law is set forth in *Zaza:*

> Utilization of [the] term [proximate cause] to draw judicial lines beyond which liability will not be extended is fundamentally . . . an instrument of fairness and policy, although the conclusion is frequently expressed in the confusing language of causation, "foreseeability" and "natural and probable consequences." Many years ago a case in this State hit it on the head when it was said that the determination of proximate cause by a court is to be based "upon mixed considerations of logic, common sense, justice, policy and precedent."

Zaza, 675 A.2d at 635 (quoting *Caputzal v. Lindsay Co.*, 222 A.2d 513, 517 (1966)).

In another case, also cited by the District Court, the New Jersey Supreme Court provided the following guidance:

> A negligent act is not necessarily a substantial factor or proximate cause of an accident simply because it contributed to the occurrence in the sense that absent such an act the accident would not have transpired. Rather, the critical consideration, in the context of multiple factors contributing to the cause of the accident, is whether the faulty act was itself too remotely or insignificantly related to the accident. If it can fairly be regarded as sufficiently remote or insignificant in relation to the eventual accident then, in a legal sense, such fault does not constitute "a cause of

> the accident, . . . [but] simply presents the condition under which the injury was received, ..."

Brown v. United States Stove Co., 484 A.2d 1234, 1243 (N.J. 1984) (citations omitted).

In *Brown*, the court also noted that, with regard to the subsequent alteration of a product, "if the original defect, although not the sole cause of the accident, constituted a contributing or concurrent proximate cause in conjunction with the subsequent alteration, the [original manufacturer] will remain liable." *Id.* at 1242. Furthermore, "[t]he critical factor in determining whether a subsequent substantial alteration of a product or its misuse can be attributed to a manufacturer as a proximate result of an original design defect under the risk-utility standard is 'foreseeability.'" *Id.* at 1240.

Plaintiff argued below and on appeal that the issue of proximate causation is for a jury to decide. The District Court properly recognized, however, that the court may conclude as a matter of law that defendants' actions were not the proximate cause of the plaintiff's injury. "The issue of responsibility for the highly extraordinary consequence is also a matter of law for the court." *Griesenbeck v. Walker*, 488 A.2d 1038, 1043 (N.J. App. Div.1985). . . . The New Jersey courts have on many occasions held that proximate causation did not exist as a matter of law. *See Griesenbeck*, 488 A.2d at 1043; *Jensen v. Schooley's Mountain Inn, Inc.*, 522 A.2d 1043, 1045 (N.J. App. Div.1987); *Brown*, 484 A.2d at 1244; *Caputzal*, 222 A.2d at 518.

Similarly, under New York law, a defendant is not held liable for every conceivable consequence that might somehow be causally related to its conduct. *See Dyer v. Norstar Bank, N.A.*, 588 N.Y.S.2d 499, 499 (App. Div. 1992) ("[C]onceivability is not the equivalent of foreseeability."). . . . As in New Jersey, courts use proximate cause to draw judicial lines to limit liability. *See Ventricelli v. Kinney System Rent A Car, Inc.*, 383 N.E.2d 1149, 1149 (N.Y. 1978) ("What we do mean by the word 'proximate' is, that because of convenience, of public policy, of a rough sense of justice, the law arbitrarily declines to trace a series of events beyond a certain point.").

As the District Court recognized, in New York, as in New Jersey, "questions of whether an intervening act severs the chain of causation depend on the foreseeability of the intervening act and should be determined by the finder of fact." *McCarthy*, 916 F.Supp. at 372 (citation omitted). "However, in appropriate circumstances, the court may resolve the issue as a matter of law. Those cases generally involve independent intervening acts which operate upon but do not flow from the original act." *Id.*

We find the decision of the Tenth Circuit in *Gaines-Tabb v. ICI Explosives, USA, Inc.*, 160 F.3d 613 (10th Cir.1998), to be persuasive on the issue of proximate causation. In that case, the plaintiffs sued the alleged manufacturers of the fertilizer used in the Oklahoma City bombing. The District Court dismissed the complaint . . . and the Tenth Circuit affirmed. Although that case was not decided under New York or New Jersey law, the principles and doctrines applied by the court are similar to those in the instant case. The court noted that causation was generally a question of fact, but that "the question becomes an issue of law when there is no evidence from which a jury could reasonably find the required proximate, causal nexus between the careless act and the resulting injuries." *Id.* at 620 (citation omitted). Applying the relevant state law, the court wrote:

> [W]e hold that as a matter of law it was not foreseeable to defendants that the [ammonium nitrate] that they distributed to the Mid-Kansas Co-op would be put to such a use as to blow up the Murrah Building. Because the conduct of the bomber or bombers was unforeseeable, independent of the acts of defendants, and adequate by itself to bring about plaintiffs' injuries, the criminal activities of the bomber or bombers acted as the supervening cause of plaintiffs' injuries. Because of the lack of proximate cause, plaintiffs have failed to state a claim for negligence.

Id. at 621.

In the instant case, we similarly hold as a matter of law that the World Trade Center bombing was not a natural or probable consequence of any design defect in defendants' products. In addition, the terrorists' actions were superseding and intervening events breaking the chain of causation. Thus, we find that, under the law of either jurisdiction, the District Court was correct in finding the World Trade Center bombing was not proximately caused by defendants. Rather, it was caused by the terrorists' intentional acts to create an explosive device and to cause the harm to the World Trade Center and its occupants. Therefore, the District Court correctly concluded that plaintiff failed to state a claim upon which relief could be granted.

G. Failure to Warn

. . . .

Plaintiff alleges that defendants owed a duty to warn the distributors, wholesalers, retailers, and other suppliers not to sell the fertilizers to customers without confirming "that buyers in the general and unrestricted public market have legitimate and lawful purposes for use of defendants' products.". . . .

. . . . [P]laintiff can cite no authority (and we can find none) under either New Jersey or New York law which supports the existence of a duty to warn middlemen that consumers, after purchasing their products, may alter the products and harm third parties. The District Court properly dismissed the failure to warn claim on this ground. *See also Gaines-Tabb*, 160 F.3d at 625 (holding that plaintiffs failed to state a failure to warn claim under Oklahoma law because "defendants had no duty to warn the suppliers of its product of possible criminal misuse").

In addition, we agree with the District Court that plaintiff is unable to allege facts showing that an adequate warning would have prevented the harm. . . .

. . . .

> In light of the elaborate efforts the terrorists went through to commit their heinous crime, it would defy all logic, common sense, and fairness, the touchstones of proximate causation, to presume that the World Trade Center bombing would have been prevented had Defendants warned their middlemen not to sell to terrorists because terrorists might use the fertilizer to create a bomb. Given the

terrorists' obvious determination, the Court cannot presume that even if the middlemen heeded this warning, the terrorists' plan would have been thwarted.

Port Authority of New York & New Jersey, 991 F.Supp. at 410.

. . . .

III. Conclusion

For the reasons discussed above, we will affirm the District Court's dismissal of the Amended Complaint for failure to state a claim upon which relief may be granted.

Hoeveler, J. (concurring). I concur in the very well developed opinion of Judge Roth. I am, however, constrained to offer an observation which may bear the fruit of protection from further similar disasters. The precedential value of our decision, as well as that of the Tenth Circuit in *Gaines-Tabb v. ICI Explosives, USA, Inc.*, 160 F.3d 613 (10th Cir.1998), rests largely on a slender and temporal reed: lack of foreseeability of the intervening criminal act. Whether experience and failure to use available safeguards will, in time, create new legal duties on the part of the manufacturer remains to be seen. We live in a society in which the disgruntled more and more resort to violence. Appellees' products, so easily convertible to dangerous qualities, need not—with proper treatment—become a part of that violence.

Fast Eddie's v. Hall

688 N.E.2d 1270 (Ind. App. 1997), *transf. denied* 726 N.E.2d 303 (Ind. 1999)

Baker, J. Appellant-defendant Fast Eddie's d/b/a Hyway Tavern, Inc. . . . appeals the trial court's denial of its motions for summary judgment on a complaint filed by the plaintiff-appellee Judy Hall, as executor of the estate of Teresa Hall. . . . Teresa Hall died after one of Fast Eddie's patrons shot and killed her. On appeal, Fast Eddie's argues that it did not owe Hall a common law duty to protect her from another patron's unexpected criminal acts of sexual assault and murder. Additionally, Fast Eddie's argues that its actions were not the proximate cause of Hall's death.

Facts

The facts most favorable to Hall, the non-movant, reveal that on the evening of June 4, 1993, Teresa Hall, Michael Lamb and John Schooley were patrons at Fast Eddie's. Schooley and Lamb arrived together around 7:00 p.m. and began to consume alcoholic beverages. Sometime later in the evening, Hall arrived at the tavern and began to drink and socialize with Schooley. At one point in the evening, after Schooley stepped outside the bar for moment, Lamb began to make advances toward Hall. At about the same time, the on-duty manager, Rita Stephens, noticed that Hall had become heavily intoxicated and was having difficulty sitting up on her bar stool. As a result, Stephens asked Lamb to take Hall out of the tavern. Lamb did as Stephens requested and escorted Hall to Schooley's car and returned to the bar. Schooley then drove Hall to his trailer in Terre Haute. After they arrived, Hall passed out in the passenger's seat of Schooley's car. Schooley then went inside his trailer and passed out on the couch.

Shortly thereafter, Lamb purchased a six-pack of beer from the tavern and drove to his home. After discovering that his wife was not there, he drove to Schooley's trailer. As he approached the trailer, he noticed Hall passed out in the passenger's seat of Schooley's car. Lamb removed Hall's body and placed her in his car. He then drove to the Riley Conservation Club where he shot Hall in the abdomen and head, killing her. When Hall's body was found, her blood alcohol was .23%, her skirt was twisted over her hips and her breasts were partially exposed. Lamb later . . . pled guilty to [Hall's] murder.

On September 30, 1994, Judy Hall, as administrator of the Estate of Teresa Hall, filed a complaint against Fast Eddie's alleging that it was negligent per se for violating IND. CODE § 7.1-5-10-15, Indiana's Dram Shop Act, by serving Lamb and Hall alcoholic beverages when they were visibly intoxicated.* The Estate further argued that Fast Eddie's breached its common law duty of care to provide for Hall's safety by failing to protect her from Lamb's criminal acts of sexual assault and murder.

In response, Fast Eddie's filed a motion for summary judgment in which it argued that it did not violate the Dram Shop Act because it did not serve Lamb or Hall any alcohol on the night of Hall's murder. It further argued that even if Lamb was served, he was not visibly intoxicated. Additionally, Fast Eddie's argued that it did not owe Hall a common law duty to protect her from Lamb's unforeseeable criminal acts of sexual assault and murder because they were not reasonably foreseeable. The trial court, however, denied the motion.

Thereafter, on May 30, 1996, Fast Eddie's filed a second motion for summary judgment in which it argued that its alleged act of serving Lamb and Hall in violation of the Dram Shop Act was not the proximate cause of Hall's death. Specifically, it argued that sexual assault and murder were not the natural and probable consequences of Lamb's alleged intoxication. The trial court, again, denied Fast Eddie's motion. Thereafter, the trial court certified both of Fast Eddie's motions for summary judgment for interlocutory appeal . . . and this court accepted jurisdiction on February 7, 1997.

Discussion and Decision

Fast Eddie's contends that the trial court erroneously denied its motions for summary judgment. Specifically, it argues that it did not have a common law duty to protect Hall from Lamb's unforeseeable criminal acts of sexual assault and murder. Alternatively, it argues that it did not gratuitously assume a common law duty to protect Hall from Lamb by asking Lamb to remove Hall from the tavern. Finally, Fast Eddie's argues that its alleged violation of Indiana's Dram Shop Act was not the proximate cause of Hall's death.

. . . .

* [Under the doctrine of negligence per se, discussed in Chapter 6, if a defendant's conduct is determined to violate a standard of conduct set by a statute (rather than by case-law), the fact of the violation establishes conclusively that the defendant acted carelessly, thus relieving the plaintiff of the usual burden of proving a failure by the defendant to have acted reasonably under the circumstances. — Eds.]

I. Fast Eddie's Common Law Duty

First we address Fast Eddie's contention that it did not owe Hall a common law duty to protect her from Lamb's criminal acts of sexual assault and murder. . . .

This court has previously held that a proprietor of a tavern owes its patrons a duty to exercise reasonable care to protect them from the foreseeable acts of other patrons. However, a proprietor of a tavern is not required to protect its patrons from unexpected criminal acts unless particular facts make it reasonably foreseeable that the criminal act will occur. These include the prior actions of the assailant either on the day the act occurred or on a previous occasion. . . . [A] criminal act is not foreseeable merely because a patron was served beyond the point of intoxication.

. . . .

. . . [T]he Estate offered evidence that Fast Eddies was a "run down . . . kind of dirty" tavern with a reputation for fighting, theft and accidents. It also submitted evidence that Lamb and Hall consumed large amounts of alcohol on the night of Hall's murder and that Hall became physically helpless due to her intoxicated state. Additionally, the Estate submitted evidence that Lamb made advances toward Hall shortly before Schooley took her home and that Rona Slater, a waitress at Fast Eddie's, had personal knowledge that Lamb's "sexual drive increased" when he became intoxicated. Finally, the Estate offered evidence that one or more of the bartenders on duty that evening had knowledge that Lamb carried a gun.

Even accepting all of the Estate's evidence as true, none of it demonstrates that Lamb's sexual assault and murder of Hall were foreseeable. First, it does not follow that because Lamb's sexual drive increased when he was intoxicated and that he showed an interest in Hall, he would intentionally harm Hall absent some evidence which would show his propensity for sexual assault or murder. It also does not follow that because Fast Eddie's had a reputation for violence, that every patron, including Lamb, is violent. Further, even if fighting had occurred at the tavern in the past, the Estate offered no evidence that Lamb had been involved in any of the prior altercations. Finally, Hall's death was not foreseeable merely because Lamb carried a gun. Therefore, the evidence most favorable to Hall supports Fast Eddie's contention that it had no knowledge of Lamb's propensity to commit sexual assault or murder. As a result, Fast Eddie's had no duty to protect Hall from Lamb's intentional criminal acts.

II. Assumption of a Duty

. . . A duty of care may be created by gratuitous or voluntary assumption. . . . Here, the Estate contends that the manager's act of telling Lamb to take Hall out of the tavern, evidences Fast Eddie's intent to assume a duty to provide for Hall's safety.

. . . .

. . . Here, Fast Eddie's only action was to order Lamb to take Hall out of the tavern. . . . [T]his act is not an affirmative step to provide for Hall's safety. Without some affirmative action on the part of a tavern owner or its employees to provide for its patron's safety, we refuse to impute a duty. Were we to do otherwise, we would, in essence, require tavern owners to be the guarantors of each departing patron's safety, which we refuse to do. . . .

III. Proximate Cause of Hall's Assault and Murder

Finally, Fast Eddie's argues that the trial court erroneously denied its motion for summary judgment because its alleged violation of the Dram Shop Act was not the proximate cause of Hall's sexual assault and death. According to the Dram Shop Act, a provider of alcoholic beverages is not liable in a civil action unless:

> (1) the person furnishing the alcoholic beverage had actual knowledge that the person to whom the alcoholic beverage was furnished was visibly intoxicated at the time the alcoholic beverage was furnished; and
> (2) the intoxication of the person to whom the alcoholic beverage was furnished was a *proximate cause* of the death, injury, or damage alleged in the complaint.

I.C. § 7.1-5-10-15.5(b) (emphasis added). Thus, even though a proprietor may have a statutory duty to refrain from providing alcoholic beverages to intoxicated persons, it will not be liable unless the alleged violation is the proximate cause of a patron's death or injury.

Proximate cause is the limitation which courts have placed on the actor's responsibility for the consequences of his act or failure to act. A party's act is the proximate cause of an injury if it is the natural and probable consequence of the act and should have been reasonably foreseen and anticipated in light of the circumstances. However, a willful, malicious criminal act of a third party is an intervening act which breaks the causal chain between the alleged negligence and the resulting harm. Although proximate cause is generally a question of fact, it becomes a question of law where only a single conclusion can be drawn from the facts.

Here, even assuming Fast Eddie's breached its statutory duty under the Dram Shop Act, its breach was not the proximate cause of Hall's sexual assault and death. First, the chain of causation in the instant case is extremely tenuous. Although Lamb initially escorted Hall out of the tavern, he returned to the bar after Schooley drove Hall to his trailer. It was later in the evening, however, when Lamb left the tavern, returned home to discover his wife's absence, decided to proceed to Schooley's home, found Hall passed out in Schooley's car and killed her. The tavern could not have reasonably foreseen this series of events which culminated in Hall's unfortunate death. Additionally, even if the chain of causation were stronger, Lamb's intentional criminal acts were the intervening cause of Hall's death which broke the causal chain between Fast Eddie's negligence and Hall's sexual assault and death. Therefore, Fast Eddie's alleged violation of the statute was not the proximate cause of Hall's sexual assault and death.

Finally, we reject the Estate's contention that Lamb's intoxication was the proximate cause of Hall's death. In support of its contention, the Estate submitted Lamb's deposition testimony that his intoxication caused him to shoot Hall. The Estate concludes that this evidence creates a genuine issue of material fact regarding the proximate cause of Hall's death. We disagree.

Unlike automobile accidents which occur as the result of alcoholic beverage consumption, assault and murder are intentional acts of volition which are the result of an assailant's deliberate design. Here, Hall died because Lamb deliberately decided to kill her. This criminal intent would have been present whether or not Lamb was intoxicated. Thus, despite Lamb's contention, we find as a matter of law that Hall's death was the result of Lamb's deliberate design and volitional act and not his intoxication. . . .

The trial court's denial of summary judgment is reversed.

NOTES AND QUESTIONS

1. *The Per Se Rule Versus the Foreseeability Test.* Some older decisions took the position that any intervening wrongdoing that constitutes a criminal offense is necessarily a superseding cause. For example, in *Watson v. K. & I. Bridge & R. Co.*, 126 S.W. 146 (Ky. 1910), the defendant railroad's carelessness caused a significant amount of gasoline to be spilled, some of which pooled on a residential street. Hours later, the gasoline was ignited by a match thrown by a man named Duerr, who had that same day been fired from his employment with the defendant. An explosion resulted, injuring the plaintiff. The court ruled that the plaintiff could recover from the railroad if the jury were to find that Duerr had merely been careless in tossing the match in the vicinity of gasoline. It also ruled that the plaintiff would be barred from recovering if the jury concluded that Duerr's act was intentional and malicious (and hence the crime of arson), reasoning that an actor "is not bound to anticipate the criminal acts of others. . . ."

The modern tendency has been to abandon the *per se* rule in favor of an inquiry into the foreseeability of the intervening actor's criminal acts. In recognition of this trend, the Kentucky Supreme Court has now abandoned *Watson* in favor of a foreseeability test. *See* Britton v. Wooten, 817 S.W.2d 443 (Ky. 1991) (intervening wrongdoing is a superseding cause only if it is "utterly" or "completely" extraordinary).

Does the concept of unforeseeability capture adequately the considerations that favor treating an intervening wrongful act as a superseding cause? In *Kohn v. Laidlaw Transit, Inc.*, 808 N.E.2d 564 (Ill. App. 2004), the defendant's school bus driver failed to operate a sign attached to the side of the bus that indicates to other drivers that the bus has stopped to let children off. Relying on the absence of the sign, plaintiff drove his car slowly around the stopped bus and hit a child who was crossing the street after disembarking. Plaintiff exited his car to assist the child, who turned out to be unharmed. Several adult bystanders who witnessed and were upset over the collision attacked the plaintiff. Plaintiff sued the bus company on the ground that the driver's carelessness set the stage for the bystanders' attack. Emphasizing the unforeseeability of the latter turn of events, the appellate court upheld summary judgment for defendant in part on superseding cause grounds.

2. *Superseding Cause and Affirmative Duties.* Superseding cause doctrine, like proximate cause doctrine more generally, is concerned with instances in which the path from defendant's careless act to plaintiff's injuries is sufficiently odd or indirect as to warrant the conclusion that, notwithstanding the causal connection between the act and the injury, the injury cannot fairly be deemed something that the defendant has "done to" or "inflicted on" the plaintiff. However, such a conclusion does not necessarily end the inquiry into responsibility. For it is still open to the plaintiff to argue (as

did the plaintiffs in *Arcadian* and *Fast Eddie's*) that, even though the injuring was the intervening actor's "doing" and not the defendant's "doing," the defendant nonetheless breached an *affirmative duty* owed to the plaintiff to protect or rescue her from the intervening wrongdoer's doing. If the court finds such a duty — which, of course, these courts did not — then the issue of superseding cause is rendered moot, *not* because the defendant has now been determined to have inflicted injury on the plaintiff, but instead because the defendant has been found to have owed it to the plaintiff to protect her from infliction of injuries at the hands of others.

The linkage just described between duty and proximate cause rules helps to explain why there is no mention of superseding cause in decisions such as *Tarasoff* (Chapter 2) that quite self-consciously recognize affirmative duties to protect persons such as the plaintiff. In holding that a psychiatrist whose patient has credibly confessed an intention to murder a particular person owes a duty to warn the intended victim, the California Supreme Court quite obviously meant to render some psychiatrists answerable for criminal homicides perpetrated by others.

Relatedly, some judicial decisions may be relying on the (unstated) presence of an affirmative duty to protect when they reject a particular defendant's superseding cause argument. Britton v. Wooten, mentioned in Note 1 *supra*, may provide a good example of this sort of opinion. The court in that case indicated that it was willing to hold a commercial tenant liable even for arson-related damage to the landlord's building, perhaps in part because of its (unstated) belief that the tenant owed its landlord an affirmative duty to protect the property from damage at the hands of others, including vandals.

Conversely, one sometimes finds judicial decisions that seem as if they ought to invoke the doctrine of superseding cause yet are couched exclusively in terms of no-duty rulings. Here, the emphasis on the absence of a duty may be a shorthand means by which the court is expressing its judgment that the plaintiff cannot overcome the superseding cause problem in her claim because she cannot establish that the defendant owed her an affirmative duty to protect her from third-party misconduct.

Consider *Graves v. Warner Bros.*, 656 N.W.2d 195 (Mich. Ct. App. 2002). Warner Brothers produced a popular daytime TV show known for staging confrontations among guests that sometimes led to fistfights in the studio. Indeed, fights were common enough that the show's producers employed security personnel to break them up when they occurred. In this instance, the producers arranged for a man named Schmitz to appear in the studio to meet for the first time a "secret admirer." In doing so, the producers purposely did not tell Schmitz that his admirer was another man (named Amedure). When, during the taping of the show, Amedure's identity and gender were revealed, Schmitz was mortified. Two weeks later Schmitz murdered Amedure. In rejecting a negligence claim on behalf of Amedure against Warner Brothers, the court ruled that, even though it was under an affirmative duty to ensure the safety of guests when in the studio, that duty did not encompass the provision of security outside of the studio.

3. *Scope of Affirmative Duties to Protect.* Even in those cases in which a court explicitly or implicitly deems a defendant to owe an affirmative duty to take care to

protect a victim from wrongful injury at the hands of a third party, there remains the question of whether the duty has been breached or fulfilled, as well as the question of whether the breach, if there was one, actually caused the victim's injury.

In *Commonwealth v. Peterson*, 749 S.E.2d 307 (Va. 2013), surviving family members of students who were victims of a mass shooting at Virginia Tech University brought suit against the state, alleging that campus and state police failed to take reasonable steps that would have prevented the shooting. Several hours prior to the mass shooting, police had been summoned to investigate an incident in which two students were shot while in a Virginia Tech dormitory. Because they suspected that this shooting was an isolated incident, and that the probable assailant had fled the scene, police did not recommend or broadcast a warning that a shooter might be at large on campus. In fact, the shooter was still at large and later shot and killed plaintiff's decedents. Plaintiffs maintained that if the police had used reasonable care in their investigation of the first shooting, a warning would have been issued that would have prevented the subsequent mass shooting.

Plaintiffs prevailed on their claims in the trial court, although each family received only $100,000 because of a statute capping damages recoverable against the state. (On damages and damage caps, *see* Chapter 8.) On appeal, a unanimous Virginia Supreme Court dismissed the suit entirely. Assuming for purposes of analysis that the university owed a duty to take steps to protect its students from the mass shooting, the court ruled that, as a matter of law, the duty was not breached because the police had reason to believe that the first shooting was an isolated incident, and hence were not unreasonable in declining to recommend or issue a warning.

4. *Dram Shop Acts.* The estate of Hall (unsuccessfully) invoked Indiana's Dram Shop Act as a ground for holding Fast Eddie's liable. Dram Shop laws (also referred to as "Civil Damages Laws") were initially enacted in some states in the late 1800s and early 1900s as part of the temperance movement that eventually led to the enactment of Prohibition. *See, e.g.*, N.Y. Laws 1873, c. 646. Their main aim was to benefit dependents who faced dire economic circumstances because their husband and/or father, seduced by the lure of "demon rum," had managed to kill or injure himself while intoxicated. Thus, they specifically enabled dependents to recover compensation for loss of economic support from the tavern or store that had profited from selling alcohol to the injured breadwinner, and sometimes even extended liability to landlords who leased their premises for use by a seller of alcohol. *See* Berthold v. O'Reilly, 74 N.Y. 509 (1878) (upholding the application of New York's Dram Shop law to a landlord). In establishing this form of liability, legislatures broke sharply from common law principles by not treating the victim's decision to drink past the point of sobriety as a superseding cause of the economic losses suffered by his dependents. *See Berthold*, 74 N.Y. at 524 (noting that the common law "looks only to the proximate cause of the mischief," whereas the Dram Shop act imposes liability on "those whose acts contributed, although remotely, to produce it.")

Modern versions of the older Dram Shop laws, like the Indiana statute discussed in *Fast Eddie's*, are usually more concerned to protect third-party victims of drunk drivers than their dependents. Typically, under the terms of these statutes, the victim of a drunk driver can prevail if she proves that her injuries occurred in part because the defendant-establishment served alcohol to a driver who was not of drinking age or who was already visibly intoxicated when served. Is the claim on behalf of Hall really so different from this sort of claim?

5. *Social Host Liability.* Dram Shop laws are limited by their terms to *commercial* sellers of alcohol. Since the 1970s, courts have been faced with common law negligence claims by victims of drunk driving against non-commercial providers, particularly social hosts whose party guests become intoxicated, then drive away from the event and drunkenly crash into another driver or pedestrian. In one of the first high-court decisions on point, *Coulter v. Superior Court*, 577 P.2d 669 (Cal. 1978), the California Supreme Court upheld a "social host liability" claim. However, *Coulter* was promptly overturned by state legislation, and decisions from other courts have generally been reluctant to recognize a duty owed by a social host to third parties to monitor and control adult guests' drinking. *See, e.g.*, Graff v. Beard, 858 S.W.2d 918 (Tex. 1993) (drunk driving is the driver's responsibility; a social host is not expected to supervise the drinking of his or her adult guests).

In *Childs v. Desormeaux*, [2006] 1 S.C.R. 643 (Can.), the Canadian Supreme Court likewise rejected social host liability. The defendants hosted a "BYOB" party at which Desormeaux, their guest, became intoxicated. He drove away from the party while drunk and caused an accident that killed one person and injured several others, including the plaintiff. The Court granted that the risk of drunk driving is well known, yet held for the defendants. According to the Court, the immediate wrong — causing an accident because of driving while intoxicated — was Desormeaux's doing, not the hosts'. Moreover, it reasoned, social hosts are entitled to treat an adult guest as competent, such that they incur no affirmative duty to third parties to monitor and control the guest's drinking: "A person who accepts an invitation to attend a private party does not park his autonomy at the door. The guest remains responsible for his or her conduct." *Id.* at para. 45.

Consistent with the reasoning of *Childs* and other decisions with respect to adult guests, hosts generally *are* subject to liability if the drunk-driving guest is a minor. *See, e.g.*, Biscan v. Brown, 160 S.W.3d 462 (Tenn. 2005) (duty owed by adult host to monitor and control drinking and driving of minor guests). Some courts have held or suggested that hosts who serve or provide alcohol to a guest who is already visibly intoxicated at the time of being served can be held liable if the guest's subsequent drunk driving injures someone. *See, e.g.*, McGuiggan v. New England Tel. & Tel. Co. 496 N.E.2d 141 (Mass. 1986) (dictum) (duty may be owed by host not to risk injury to third parties by knowingly serving a visibly intoxicated guest).

6. *Gun Litigation.* Some victims of shootings perpetrated by persons who acquired their guns illegally have brought negligence claims against gun manufacturers. The theory of liability is that manufacturers have been careless with respect to the well-being of potential victims by deliberately oversupplying guns to retail dealers in states that loosely regulate gun sales, knowing that a significant percentage of these guns will end up being illegally brought into states with tougher gun laws. In the leading opinion on this issue, the New York Court of Appeals rejected this theory

of liability, reasoning that no duty is owed by a gun manufacturer to protect victims against shootings committed with unlawfully possessed firearms. Hamilton v. Beretta U.S.A. Corp., 750 N.E.2d 1055 (N.Y. 2001).

Courts have shown little receptivity to tort claims of this sort. Still, out of concern over the possible effects on the U.S. gun industry of liability arising out suits by individual shooting victims—as well as suits brought on behalf of cities such as Chicago and New Orleans claiming that illegal gun sales have caused them to incur substantial expenditures on emergency services—Congress in 2005 enacted the Protection of Lawful Commerce in Arms Act. 15 U.S.C. §§ 7901-03. With certain exceptions, the Act grants to gun manufacturers and sellers immunity from any claims for damages arising out of a third party's unlawful use of a gun.

7. *Tort Liability for Terrorism (I): The 1993 WTC Attack.* As *Arcadian* attests, courts are now faced with the question of the extent to which victims of terrorist attacks can impose liability on persons other than the terrorists who perpetrated the attacks.

Additional litigation arising out of the 1993 attack on the World Trade Center involved claims by occupants and users of the complex who were killed or injured in the attack against the Port Authority of New York and New Jersey in its capacity as operator of the complex. Plaintiffs presented substantial evidence that the Port Authority had received detailed warnings that the buildings were at risk for just the sort of attack that was perpetrated, yet failed to take precautionary measures. The trial and intermediate appellate courts concluded that the plaintiffs had stated viable claims based on the affirmative duty owed by possessors of land to invitees on their premises. *See* Note 10, *infra*. However, the New York Court of Appeals eventually rejected these claims on the ground that the Port Authority, as a public entity, was protected from liability by governmental immunity. *See* Chapter 7 (discussing immunity defenses). In re World Trade Center Bombing Litig., 957 N.E.2d 733 (N.Y. 2011).

8. *Tort Liability for Terrorism (II): The Anti-Terrorism Act.* Beginning in 1987 Congress has passed federal laws creating a statutory tort for terrorist acts that injure Americans anywhere in the world. These laws are commonly referred to as the "Anti-Terrorism Act" ("ATA"). Banks have been held liable under the ATA for knowingly transferring funds to terrorist groups. *See, e.g.*, Linde v. Arab Bank, PLC, 2015 U.S. Dist. LEXIS 45903 (E.D.N.Y. Apr. 8, 2015). In *Linde*, a jury found that the defendant bank knowingly provided financial services to Hamas by providing financial services to its operatives, to charities controlled by Hamas, and to an organization called the Saudi Committee for the Support of the Intifada Al-Quds, an entity that made payments to beneficiaries identified by Hamas-controlled organizations, including the families of Hamas suicide-bombers and prisoners.

9. *9/11 Tort Litigation and the Victim Compensation Fund.* The course of litigation over the September 11, 2001 attacks on the World Trade Center and the Pentagon was significantly affected by Congress's enactment, within days of the attacks, of legislation capping liability that airlines and others might face for carelessly allowing the attacks to occur. Pub. L. No. 107-71, 115 Stat. 597 (2001). The same statute also created a fund

(financed by general tax revenues) to compensate persons injured in the attacks and survivors of airplane passengers and building occupants who had died. Eligible applicants who opted to obtain compensation from the fund were required to relinquish any tort claims that they might have. Approximately 97 percent of the individuals eligible to claim under the fund did so. Between 2001 and 2004, the fund paid out approximately $7 billion in compensation for the death and injuries of approximately 5,600 persons.

Among those who declined to participate in the fund, several brought negligence claims against the airlines, the owners of the World Trade Center, and the manufacturer of the planes used in the attacks. In a 2003 decision, the trial judge presiding over these claims denied defense motions for summary judgment. The court concluded that the airlines owed an affirmative duty both to their passengers and to the ground victims of 9/11 to take reasonable measures to protect them against injuries resulting from hijackings. In re September 11 Litigation, 280 F. Supp.2d 279 (S.D.N.Y. 2003). These claims settled for undisclosed amounts.

The federal victim compensation fund covered only claims for personal injury. Lawsuits against various defendants for property damage and business interruption, including negligence claims against American and United airlines for failing to take adequate steps to prevent hijackings, have slowly worked their way to resolution. Although the overwhelming majority of these claims have now settled, one suit that remains ongoing as of the date of this volume's publication was brought by the owner of the World Trade Center. A 2013 decision by Judge Alvin Hellerstein — the federal district court judge charged with resolving all 9/11-related litigation — held that the holders of long-term leases for the World Trade Center's buildings had been made whole for their lost leasehold interests by payments from their insurers, and therefore no additional funds ought to be recovered from the airlines or other defendants. *See* World Trade Ctr. Props., LLC v. United Airlines, Inc. (In re September 11 Litig.), 957 F. Supp. 2d 501 (S.D.N.Y. 2013). However, the Second Circuit Court of Appeals reversed this ruling in part, remanding with instructions for the district court to revise its calculations of the diminution in value suffered by the plaintiffs. In re Sept. 11 Litig., 802 F.3d 314 (2d Cir. 2015).

10. Liability of Property Owners for On-Premises Attacks. A prominent line of cases raising potential duty and superseding cause issues concerns the liability of owners and possessors of property for attacks perpetrated on those properties by third parties. A leading early case, now widely followed, holds that landlords are responsible to take reasonable security measures to protect tenants from attacks in common areas such as lobbies and hallways by, for example, providing working locks, adequate lighting, and perhaps in some situations doorpersons or security patrols. Kline v. 1500 Massachusetts Ave. Apt. Corp., 439 F.2d 477 (D.C. Cir. 1970). Likewise, in most jurisdictions, businesses such as motels and stores that are open to the public at least at times operate under an obligation to maintain and monitor their premises (including parking areas) with due care for the possibility of a criminal attack on a customer or other lawful visitor. The prerequisites to and scope of these obligations vary by state. Some impose a duty of care when there is particular reason to foresee a risk of attack on the premises, such as publicly available information indicating relatively high rates of violent crime in the area in which the property is located. *See, e.g.*, Timberwalk Apts. v. Cain, 972 S.W.2d 749 (Tex. 1998). Others employ multi-factor tests to determine whether and to what extent a duty is owed. *See, e.g.*, McClung v. Delta Square Partnership, 937 S.W.2d 891 (Tenn. 1996).

In *Monk v. Temple George Assocs., LLC*, 869 A.2d 179 (Conn. 2005), the plaintiff parked her car in the defendant club's pay lot, then entered the club. While inside, she was confronted by her husband's ex-girlfriend, who had verbally confronted her on a previous occasion. When the plaintiff left the club for her car, the ex-girlfriend followed the plaintiff to the lot and attacked her with a knife. The plaintiff sued the club owner, asserting that it had been careless in failing to provide better lighting and security in the lot. The Connecticut Supreme Court reversed the lower courts' dismissal of the case, remanding it for trial. The court reasoned that attacks in the lot were sufficiently foreseeable to generate an affirmative duty of protection owed by the club to users of its lot, given that the lot was located in an urban area, was frequented by patrons late at night, and included areas that were not observable from the street. It further held that the ex-girlfriend's decision to use the lot as the locus for carrying out her vendetta against the plaintiff did not amount to a superseding cause.

Should the rules for landowner liability differ if the plaintiff-victim is not an invitee or licensee because she was brought, against her will, onto the property by the attacker, as a prelude to his attack. Two fractured Texas Supreme Court decisions reached arguably conflicting results on this question. In *Nixon v. Mr. Property Management Co., Inc.*, 690 S.W.2d 546 (Tex. 1985), the plaintiff, a minor, was dragged by an assailant into an open, vacant, and dilapidated apartment and raped. Plaintiff sued the owners and managers of the building in which the apartment was located, alleging that they were negligent in not securing the doors and windows of the apartment so as to reduce the likelihood that it would be used as a locus for an attack. The trial and intermediate appellate courts granted summary judgment to the defendants. However, the Supreme Court reversed and remanded for trial.

Citing a city ordinance requiring landowners to "keep the doors and windows of a vacant structure . . . securely closed to prevent unauthorized entry," a majority reasoned that the defendants owed and may have breached a duty to persons such as the plaintiff to take reasonable steps to prevent attacks on its property. It further held that, in light of a record of past violent crimes occurring at the same apartment complex, the attack on the plaintiff was foreseeable. Two separate concurring opinions reasoned that the same result ought to have been reached regardless of the ordinance. Three justices dissented, arguing that the assailant's attack should have been deemed a superseding cause of plaintiff's injuries.

Fourteen years later, the same court, now composed of a new set of justices, decided *Mellon Mortgage Co. v. Holder*, 5 S.W.3d 654 (Tex. 1999). The plaintiff was driving in downtown Houston at 3:30 a.m. when she was pulled over by an on-duty police officer. He instructed her to follow him to defendant's parking garage, where he sexually assaulted her. Plaintiff's suit alleged that the defendant had not taken reasonable steps to reduce the likelihood of violent crime occurring on the premises. Reversing an intermediate appellate court ruling, the Supreme Court held that the claim failed as a matter of law.

Invoking *Palsgraf*, a three-justice plurality opinion reasoned that Holder, as someone who was compelled to enter the garage by a law enforcement officer, was an unforeseeable plaintiff, such that any laxness in security at the garage could not constitute carelessness as to her. These justices distinguished *Nixon* on the ground that no comparable city ordinance applied to the defendant's parking garage. One concurring justice reasoned that the owner owed Holder only a duty to refrain from willfully injuring her because, notwithstanding that her presence on the property was involuntary, she was a "trespasser" simply by virtue of being on the property without permission. A fifth justice reasoned that the defendant owed no duty to Holder because there was not enough evidence of prior similar criminal activity in and around the garage to conclude that the defendant should have foreseen the possibility of a sexual assault on the premises. Three justices dissented, arguing that a jury could find that, given the public's access to the garage, plaintiff was on the premises with implicit permission, and therefore a licensee to whom care was owed and not provided. (The court's ninth justice did not participate in the decision.)

Are cases like *Nixon* and *Holder* really "premises liability cases," such that they ought to be analyzed by reference to the plaintiff-status categories? Were those categories meant to handle cases in which the plaintiff does not enter the defendant's property of her own volition? What are the best grounds for distinguishing *Holder* from *Nixon*? Suppose in *Holder* there were a safety ordinance pertaining to parking garages comparable to the ordinance in *Nixon*. Would that fact be enough to bring Holder's claim within *Nixon*'s holding? Assume that each defendant was in a position to foresee the possibility of violent attacks on its property. Is there anything else that might distinguish the attacks, the attackers, or the connection of the attacks to the defendants' respective properties that justifies allowing the claim in *Nixon* but not in *Holder*?

We have seen that courts will sometimes assert that proximate cause and the relational aspect of breach of duty boil down to the issue of whether, or to what degree, the injuring of a person in the position of the plaintiff was foreseeable to a person in the position of the defendant at the time of the allegedly tortious conduct. It is no surprise, then, to discover that many of the *Nixon* and *Holder* opinions are devoted to discussions of records of criminal activity at and around the structures at issue in those cases. How relevant are these records? Is it sensible for the law to conclude that the owner of a structure that happens to have been the locus of a prior sexual assault is by virtue of that fact under a duty to take steps to secure the garage, whereas owners of similar structures that have been the site of petty crimes (or no crimes) are not?

REFERENCES/FURTHER READING

Proximate Cause

Joseph W. Bingham, *Some Suggestions Concerning "Legal Cause" at Common Law (Part II)*, 9 Colum. L. Rev. 136, 154 (1909).

John C. P. Goldberg, *Comment: Rethinking Injury and Proximate Cause*, 40 S.D. L. Rev. 1315 (2003).

Leon Green, *Rationale of Proximate Cause* 195-196 (1927).

Nicholas St. John Green, *Proximate and Remote Cause*, 4 Am. L. Rev. 201 (1870).

Heidi M. Hurd & Michael S. Moore, *Negligence in the Air*, 3 Theoretical Inq. in Law 333 (2002).

Robert E. Keeton, *Legal Cause in the Law of Torts* (1963).

Patrick Kelley, *Proximate Cause in Negligence Law: History, Theory and the Present Darkness*, 69 Wash. U. L.Q. 49 (1991).

Saul Levmore, *The* Wagon Mound *Cases: Foreseeability, Causation and Mrs. Palsgraf*, in Robert L. Rabin & Stephen D. Sugarman (eds.), *Torts Stories* 129 (2003).

Warren A. Seavey, *Mr. Justice Cardozo and the Law of Torts*, 52 Harv. L. Rev. 372 (1939).

Jane Stapleton, *Legal Cause: Cause-in-Fact and the Scope of Liability for Consequences*, 54 Vand. L. Rev. 941 (2001).

Michael L. Wells, *Proximate Cause and the American Law Institute: The False Choice Between the "Direct-Consequences" Test and the "Risk Standard,"* 37 U. Rich. L. Rev. 389 (2003).

Glanville Williams, *The Risk Principle*, 77 L. Q. Rev. 179 (1961).

Benjamin C. Zipursky, *Foreseeability in Duty, Breach, and Proximate Cause*, 44 Wake Forest L. Rev. 1247 (2009).

Palsgraf

Andrew L. Kaufman, *Cardozo* 287-295 (1998).

John C. P. Goldberg & Benjamin C. Zipursky, *The Moral of* MacPherson, 146 U. Pa. L. Rev. 1733, 1812-1824 (1998).

William E. Nelson, *The Legalist Reformation: Law, Politics and Ideology in New York* 1920-1980 (2001).

John T. Noonan, Jr., *Persons and Masks of the Law: Cardozo, Holmes, Jefferson, and Wythe as Makers of the Masks* 144 (1976).

David Owen, *Duty Rules*, 54 Vand. L. Rev. 767 (2001).

Richard A. Posner, *Cardozo: A Study in Reputation* 16-17 (1990).

William Powers, *Thaumotrope*, 77 Tex. L. Rev. 1319 (1999).

William L. Prosser, Palsgraf *Revisited*, 52 Mich. L. Rev. 1 (1953).

Gary T. Schwartz, *Cardozo as Tort Lawmaker*, 49 DePaul L. Rev. 305 (1999).

Ernest J. Weinrib, *The Passing of* Palsgraf?, 54 Vand. L. Rev. 803 (2001).

G. Edward White, *Tort Law in America: An Intellectual History* (2d ed. 2002).

Benjamin C. Zipursky, Palsgraf, *Punitive Damages, and Preemption*, 125 Harv. L. Rev. 1757 (2012).

Benjamin C. Zipursky, *Rights, Wrongs and Recourse in the Law of Torts*, 51 Vand. L. Rev. 1 (1998).

Superseding Cause and Affirmative Duty

Martha Chamallas, *Gaining Some Perspective in Tort Law: A New Take on Third-Party Criminal Attack Cases*, 14 Lewis & Clark L. Rev. 1351 (2010).

John C. P. Goldberg & Benjamin C. Zipursky, *Intervening Wrongdoing in Tort: The Restatement (Third)'s Unfortunate Embrace of Negligent Enabling*, 44 Wake Forest L. Rev. 1211 (2009).

Robert L. Rabin, *Enabling Torts*, 49 DePaul L. Rev. 435 (1999).

CHAPTER 6

STATUTORY SUPPLEMENTS: NEGLIGENCE PER SE, WRONGFUL DEATH ACTS, AND IMPLIED RIGHTS OF ACTION

Statutes and the common law of tort interact in numerous ways. Some statutes supplant tort law. For example, as discussed in Chapter 11, workers' compensation statutes enacted by the states at the beginning of the twentieth century removed most workplace injuries from the ambit of tort law and placed them in an alternative scheme that combines strict liability with scheduled damages. Other statutes eliminate, partially block, or otherwise limit the operation of tort law without providing an alternative scheme of redress. Thus, the *Mussivand* decision in Chapter 2 referred to the outright abolition of "amatory" torts.* Statutes can also expressly create tort or tort-like causes of action by empowering a class of plaintiffs to seek redress for injuries caused by conduct that was not actionable at common law. We provide examples of this sort of statute in Chapter 10, which briefly addresses statutory causes of action for housing and employment discrimination.

In this chapter, we deal with three additional ways in which statutes interact with tort law. First, negligence law can sometimes incorporate standards of behavior contained in criminal or regulatory statutes that, on their face, do not say anything about tort liability. This is accomplished primarily through the doctrine of *negligence per se*. Second, statutes can confer on plaintiffs precisely the power that *Palsgraf* (Chapter 5) denies them as a matter of common law, namely, the power to sue as "vicarious beneficiaries" of rights possessed by others. The most important examples of this sort of statute are the *wrongful death acts* enacted by American legislatures in the nineteenth and early twentieth centuries. Finally, statutes can effectively combine these two functions. That is, in the course of setting standards of conduct, certain statutes

* In Chapter 13, we consider how federal regulatory laws that impose safety requirements on product manufacturers can "preempt" tort claims by persons injured by products. In Chapter 8, we mention caps on damages and other measures used to limit the compensation obtained by successful tort claimants.

implicitly create a "protected class"—a group whose members are deemed by courts to be the beneficiaries of those standards—thereby conferring on those class members the power to seek redress for violations that cause injury to them. Statutes that have this particular effect are said to contain *implied rights of action.*

I. NEGLIGENCE PER SE

Dalal v. City of New York

692 N.Y.S.2d 468 (App. Div. 1999)

Per Curiam. . . . [P]laintiff appeals from a judgment . . . which, upon a jury verdict finding, *inter alia,* that the defendant Alicia Ramdhani-Mack was not negligent, is . . . against him. . . .

ORDERED that the judgment is reversed . . . and a new trial is granted, with costs to abide the event.

The instant action arises out of an automobile accident that occurred at the intersection of Booth Street and 66th Avenue in Queens. The action against the defendant City of New York was discontinued prior to trial. At trial, the plaintiff testified that he stopped at the stop sign controlling traffic on 66th Avenue, and looked both ways for a distance of about one block, without seeing anything, before he proceeded into the intersection. When he was about halfway through the intersection, his vehicle was struck on the driver's side by a vehicle operated by Alicia Ramdhani-Mack (hereinafter the defendant). The plaintiff further testified that he never saw the defendant's car until impact. The defendant testified that she was about 10 to 15 feet away from the intersection when she noticed the plaintiff's vehicle, which was about 14 feet behind the stop sign but moving, and that about 5 to 7 seconds elapsed from the time that she observed the plaintiff's vehicle until the collision. She stated that she attempted to swerve out of the way, but could not avoid the collision. The defendant further testified that although she was nearsighted and required prescription glasses, she was not wearing her glasses at the time of the accident. She claimed she was still able to see while driving. There was no evidence that either driver was speeding. The jury returned a verdict finding that only the plaintiff was negligent, and that his negligence was the sole proximate cause of the accident.

The plaintiff contends that the trial court erred in refusing to charge that the defendant's violation of Vehicle and Traffic Law § 509(3) was negligence per se, and erred in refusing to allow him to cross-examine the defendant on that issue. Vehicle and Traffic Law § 509(3) provides that "no person shall operate any motor vehicle in violation of any restriction contained on his license." The defendant testified at her examination before trial that her New York State driver's license contained a restriction requiring her to wear corrective lenses while driving.

It is well established that an unexcused violation of a statutory standard of care, if unexplained, constitutes negligence per se (*see* Martin v. Herzog, 228 N.Y. 164, 126 N.E. 814 . . .). The defendant's reliance upon the principle that operating a motor vehicle without a license is not negligence per se is misplaced. The absence or possession of a driver's license relates only to the authority for operating the vehicle and not to the manner thereof. However, a restriction placed upon the license requiring the wearing of glasses when driving relates directly to the actual operation of the vehicle. Vehicle and Traffic Law § 509(3) provides that no one shall operate a vehicle in violation of any restriction contained on his or her license, and also relates to the manner in which the vehicle is being operated. Thus, the statute sets up a standard of care, the unexcused violation of which is negligence per se. The trial court erred, therefore, in refusing the plaintiff's request to charge. . . .

In view of the verdict, we cannot conclude that [this and another error] were harmless. The plaintiff is therefore entitled to a new trial.

*Bayne v. Todd Shipyards Corp.**

568 P.2d 771 (Wash. 1977)

Brachtenbach, J. Plaintiff sued for personal injuries sustained while unloading goods being delivered to defendant's premises. Plaintiff was not an employee of the defendant, but rather of the trucking company engaged in the delivery. While unloading those goods, plaintiff fell from a loading platform. Plaintiff contended that the defendant's loading platform lacked a guardrail required by a safety standard regulation promulgated by the Department of Labor and Industries, pursuant to statute. The trial court refused to instruct that violation of that administrative regulation was negligence per se, but did instruct that it was evidence of negligence. . . . [T]he Court of Appeals affirmed a judgment for the defendant. . . . We granted review limited to the sole issue whether violation of an administrative safety regulation is negligence per se or only evidence of negligence. We reverse.

The statute in effect at the time of the injury imposed a duty upon the Director of Labor and Industries to promulgate safety regulations to furnish workers a place of work which is as safe as is reasonable and practicable under the circumstances, surroundings and conditions. RCW 49.16.030, .050. . . .

Pursuant to this authority, the Director of Labor and Industries adopted WAC 296-25-515:

> (1) All elevated walks, runways or platforms, except on loading or unloading sides of platforms, if four feet or more from the floor level, shall be provided with a standard railing on platforms. If height exceeds six feet, a toe-board shall be provided, to prevent material from rolling or falling off. . . .

We have long been committed to the principle that violation of an applicable statute or ordinance is negligence per se. Engelker v. Seattle Elec. Co., 96 P. 1039 ([Wash.] 1908); Portland-Seattle Auto Freight, Inc. v. Jones, 131 P.2d 736 [, 738] ([Wash.] 1942). This is the majority rule. W. Prosser, *Handbook of the Law of Torts* § 36, at 200 (4th ed. 1971).

---

* [Superseded by statute, RCW § 5.40.050 (1986). Subject to certain exceptions, this statute abolished from Washington state law the doctrine of negligence per se. However, it allows a trier of fact to consider statutory or regulatory violations as evidence of carelessness. — Eds.]

However, the courts are divided on the question whether violation of an administrative regulation is evidence of negligence or negligence per se. Prosser, *supra* at 201 n.30. . . .

By our decision in Kness v. Truck Trailer Equip. Co., 501 P.2d 285 ([Wash.] 1972), we already have aligned ourselves with those jurisdictions which hold that under appropriate circumstances violation of an administrative order is negligence per se. In *Kness* a regulation had been adopted limiting the hours of work for a minor. The regulation was based on a rather broad statute authorizing the administrative establishment of standards of wages and conditions of labor for women and minors. In holding violation of the regulation was negligence per se we said:

> In deciding whether violation of a public law or *regulation* shall be considered in determining liability, the Restatement (Second) of Torts § 286 (1965) properly states the rules:
>
> > The court may adopt as the standard of conduct of a reasonable man the requirements of a legislative enactment *or an administrative regulation* whose purpose is found to be exclusively or in part
> >
> > (a) to protect a class of persons which includes the one whose interest is invaded, and
> > (b) to protect the particular interest which is invaded, and
> > (c) to protect that interest against the kind of harm which has resulted, and
> > (d) to protect that interest against the particular hazard from which the harm results.
>
> This court has substantially adhered to these principles in a number of cases: . . .

(Citations omitted. Italics ours.) Kness v. Truck Trailer Equip. Co., *supra* at [289]. . . .

In this case we had a somewhat more specific statutory directive to adopt standards of safety to make safe the place of work of workmen. RCW 49.16.030 and .050.

This is not an instance of violation of some obscure bureaucratic edict. Under the statute in effect when this regulation was adopted, the Director of Labor and Industries was required to hold a public hearing to consider new standards, or changes or modifications of existing standards. Employers and workmen or their representatives could attend such hearing and present testimony. RCW 49.16.080. Written notice of the hearing had to be mailed to *each* employer whose class or establishment was affected. RCW 49.16.090.

We perceive no reason why such a regulation should be of any less force, effect or significance than a municipal ordinance. We are not alone in this result. *See* Porter v. Montgomery Ward & Co., 313 P.2d 854 ([Cal.] 1957); Pierson v. Holly Sugar Corp., 237 P.2d 28 ([Cal. Ct. App.] 1951). . . .

Defendant contends that plaintiff was not within the protected class because he was not an employee of the defendant. The statute requires a safe place of work for workmen. It does not limit it to employees of the defendant employer. A worker who is lawfully on the premises in pursuit of his own employment and at the invitation of the third party, defendant here, is entitled to the benefit of the statute and the regulation. *See* Pierson v. Holly Sugar Corp., *supra*, which so holds, stating that the regulation was a safeguard for the public generally which necessarily included a workman making a delivery who was not an employee of the defendant. Extension of the protection of the regulation to the public generally is not before us.

Finally it is necessary to deal with the defendant's argument that we have a contrary line of cases which were not dealt with in the *Kness* case. Admittedly there has been at least some confusion in our cases concerning the main question. Defendant relies on six cases for its argument that violation of an administrative regulation is only evidence of negligence. Four of those cases are distinguishable and two are in error.

In Engen v. Arnold, 379 P.2d 990 ([Wash.] 1963), the trial court held that violation of safety rules promulgated by the Department of Labor and Industries was contributory negligence as a matter of law. The plaintiff had not elected to be covered by the workmen's compensation act. We held at page 646 that

> [W]hile violation of such rules and regulations may, in a case such as this, afford some evidence of negligence, a violation thereof by one not covered by the Workmen's Compensation Act, even though engaged in an extrahazardous occupation, does not constitute negligence as a matter of law.

We did not hold that in an appropriate case violation would not be negligence per se.

In Vogel v. Alaska S.S. Co., 419 P.2d 141 ([Wash.] 1966), and Cresap v. Pacific Inland Navigation Co., 478 P.2d 223 ([Wash.] 1970), we were concerned with alleged violations of federal safety regulations governing stevedore employers. The defendant there was not such an employer but was the owner of the ship on which the stevedoring work was being done and who had a legal duty to furnish a seaworthy vessel. We held the regulations to be admissible against the shipowner and a violation of them to be evidence of negligence because "they give expression to the minimum standards which must be met in order to render conditions aboard the vessel safe, and hence seaworthy." Vogel v. Alaska S.S. Co., *supra* at 146. . . . That is, the regulations were objective criteria of seaworthiness and though not binding on that defendant were evidence of negligence. Here, the defendant . . . is an employer intended to be governed by the regulation.

Next, defendant cites Nordstrom v. White Metal Rolling & Stamping Corp., 453 P.2d 619 ([Wash.] 1969). That case dealt with standards adopted by a trade association. We held that such voluntary standards are relevant on the standard of care, but not determinative. Such standards simply do not have the force of a statute, ordinance or statutorily authorized administrative regulation.

Thorpe v. Boeing Co., 490 P.2d 448 ([Wash. Ct. App.] 1971), and Loyland v. Stone & Webster Eng'r Corp., 514 P.2d 184 ([Wash. Ct. App.] 1973), held that Department of Labor and Industries safety standards are only evidence of negligence. *Thorpe* erroneously relied upon *Nordstrom* and *Vogel*, failing to draw the distinctions we note here. *Loyland* then relied entirely on *Thorpe*. We do not agree with those cases as they relate to the violation of statutorily authorized administrative regulations.

The judgment is reversed and a new trial ordered.

Hicks, J. (dissenting) (joined by Utter, J.). I dissent. Administrative agencies have a penchant for spawning regulations without end. As a Member of Congress, I served on a subcommittee that had occasion to evaluate regulations promulgated under the Occupational Safety and Health Act (OSHA). While these regulations were generally most appropriate, they were unnecessary, impractical or picayunish (Mickey Mouse) often enough to give me concern as to making violation of any one of them negligence per se in every instance in a damage action.

The court is setting policy in this case and I have no quarrel with that. However, I am more comfortable with the rule that violation of administrative regulations be submitted to the trier of fact as evidence of negligence, as the trial court did in this case, rather than to be submitted as negligence as a matter of law. In my view, when violations of regulations are submitted as evidence of negligence, the trier of fact has a better opportunity to use common sense and reach a more nearly just result between the parties.

Until this case, the state of the law in this jurisdiction did not compel the result the majority reaches. Based on past decisions of this court, I believe the Court of Appeals was correct in both Thorpe v. Boeing Co., 490 P.2d 448 ([Wash. Ct. App.] 1971), and Loyland v. Stone & Webster Eng'r Corp., 514 P.2d 184 ([Wash. Ct. App.] 1973). . . .

In the instant case, WAC 296-25-515 and its supplement No. 13, 7-1-74 do no more than provide an administratively approved standard of safety. By the fiat of this court, the violation of such administratively promulgated standard now becomes negligence as a matter of law in every instance in a damage action. I believe the better course to be to . . . submit the regulation to the trier of fact only as evidence of an approved standard, as the trial court did in this case. . . .

Victor v. Hedges

91 Cal. Rptr. 2d 466 (Ct. App. 1999)

Dau, J. Plaintiff Stephani Victor appeals from the judgment entered in favor of defendants Michael Hedges and Thermtech, Inc. (collectively, "Hedges"), following the grant of defendants' motion for summary judgment, and from the denial of her motion for new trial. Michael Hedges parked his auto on the sidewalk in front of his apartment building. Plaintiff and Hedges were standing on the sidewalk behind the car, when an inattentive motorist drove over the curb and into plaintiff, seriously injuring her. We are required to decide whether a statute prohibiting the parking of a vehicle on a sidewalk may be employed to fix upon Hedges the presumption of negligence in the circumstances of this case and whether reasonable people could conclude that he subjected plaintiff to an unreasonable risk of harm. We hold the statute in question was not designed to prevent the type of occurrence that resulted in plaintiff's injury, and plaintiff has failed to raise a triable issue of fact that an ordinarily prudent person in Hedges's place would have foreseen an unreasonable risk of harm to plaintiff. Accordingly, we affirm.

Factual and Procedural Background

Plaintiff brought an action for damages alleging that . . . defendant Thermtech owned a certain Ford Explorer and defendant Hedges was driving that vehicle with the owner's consent, that defendant Mark Williams was driving a Ford Aerostar van, and that defendants negligently operated and controlled these vehicles so as to cause a collision with plaintiff, who was lawfully upon the sidewalk in the City of Hermosa Beach.

The undisputed facts showed that at approximately 10:00 P.M. Hedges had parked his Ford Explorer on the sidewalk in front of his apartment building, parallel to, and with the driver's side tires three to four feet from, the curb line of Hermosa Avenue in Hermosa Beach. Hedges did this to show plaintiff his new compact disk player, which was located in the rear of the Explorer. Due to construction, northbound traffic along Hermosa Avenue was routed into a single lane along the east curb. There was some gravel on the road, and the surface was rough with bumps and potholes. Immediately before the accident Williams was northbound on Hermosa Avenue, approaching the intersection with First Street, in his Aerostar van. He looked down at the tape deck and, with his right hand, fast forwarded a cassette for approximately two seconds. The steering wheel jostled about an inch each way, Williams's van drifted to the right, and the front and rear passenger side tires hit the First Street curb, causing them to blow out; the van continued in its path. Hedges and plaintiff were standing at the rear of the Explorer, with plaintiff nearer the curb and Hedges to her right, when Williams's van ran into plaintiff and the Explorer about 30 feet from the First Street curb. . . .

Discussion

Plaintiff's claim against Hedges and Thermtech is based on theories of negligence per se and common law negligence. Defendants argued in the court below that a necessary element of plaintiff's case under either theory—proximate cause—could not be established. . . . [W]e will address the negligence per se issue before coming to that of ordinary negligence. We do this, even though the proximate cause argument . . . made by the parties is common to both, for the following reason: If Hedges is not to be presumed negligent, and we will conclude that he is not, the ordinary negligence analysis may proceed uncontaminated by the infraction charge. . . .

B. Negligence Per Se

Plaintiff argues that Hedges must be presumed negligent because he violated Vehicle Code section 22500, subdivision (f), which prohibits parking on a sidewalk.

Section 669, subdivision (a) of the Evidence Code provides: "The failure of a person to exercise due care is presumed if: [¶] (1) He violated a statute . . . [¶] (2) The violation proximately caused death or injury to person or property; [¶] (3) The death or injury resulted from an occurrence of the nature which the statute . . . was designed to prevent; and [¶] (4) The person suffering the death or the injury to his person or property was one of the class of persons for whose protection the statute . . . was adopted." With respect to paragraphs (3) and (4), the Law Revision Commission Comments state: "Whether the death or injury involved in an action resulted from an occurrence of the nature which the statute . . . was designed to prevent . . . and whether the plaintiff was one of the class of persons for whose protection the statute . . . was adopted are questions of law. Nunneley v. Edgar Hotel, 225 P.2d

497 ([Cal.] 1950) (statute requiring parapet of particular height at roofline of vent shaft designed to protect against walking into shaft, not against falling into shaft while sitting on parapet). . . ."

At the time of the accident, section 22500 provided: "No person shall stop, park, or leave standing any vehicle whether attended or unattended, except when necessary to avoid conflict with other traffic or in compliance with the directions of a peace officer or official traffic control device, in any of the following places: . . . [¶] (f) On a sidewalk, except electric carts when authorized by local ordinance, as specified in Section 21114.5."

We are required to determine the nature of the occurrence that section 22500, subdivision (f) was designed to prevent. . . .

Section 22500 designates twelve categories of locations where stopping, standing or parking a vehicle is prohibited. The Legislature specified certain of these with pedestrians obviously in mind. "On a sidewalk" (*id.*, subd. (f)), which the Code defines as "that portion of a highway, other than the roadway, set apart by curbs, barriers, markings or other delineation for pedestrian travel" (§ 555), is one of these. Others are: "[o]n a crosswalk" (§ 22500, subd. (b)); "[b]etween a safety zone and the adjacent right-hand curb" (*id.*, subd. (c)); "[a]longside curb space authorized for the loading and unloading of passengers of a bus engaged as a common carrier in local transportation" (*id.*, subd. (i)); and "[i]n front of that portion of a curb that has been cut down, lowered, or constructed to provide wheelchair accessibility to the sidewalk. . . ." (*Id.*, subd. (*l*).) With the exception of "on a sidewalk" (*id.*, subd. (f)), vehicles normally operate within each of these designated categories, and, for these, the section's prohibition appears designed both to prevent vehicular obstruction of pedestrian traffic and to lessen the danger of vehicle-pedestrian collision. Thus pedestrians finding it necessary to walk around a vehicle that is illegally parked, stopped or left standing may be put at increased risk of injury from unsure footing, from another vehicle in the roadway, or from the sudden movement of the vehicle that had been at rest. Hedges's parked automobile did not obstruct plaintiff's way and increase her risk of injury in this fashion.

Injury to a pedestrian on a sidewalk, resulting from contact with a vehicle that has been parked, stopped or left standing there, can also occur when the vehicle is at rest or when it is again put in motion. The Legislature's 1998 amendment to subdivision (f) appears to reflect an awareness that a vehicle at rest, even if partially on the sidewalk, can cause injury to a passing pedestrian.[10] In this situation, the pedestrian, insufficiently aware of the presence of the vehicle, walks into it, or a portion of it, and is

---

10. Plaintiff argues that the amendment, which was not in effect at the time of the accident in this case, clarifies the Legislature's original intent. The amendment makes more explicit what is meant by "*[o]n* a sidewalk [italics added]." Subdivision (f), as amended, is reproduced here with the language added in italics. "(f) On *any portion of a sidewalk, or with the body of the vehicle extending over any portion of* a sidewalk, except electric carts when authorized by local ordinance, as specified in section 21114.5. *Lights, mirrors, or devices that are required to be mounted upon a vehicle under this code may extend from the body of the vehicle over the sidewalk to a distance of not more than 10 inches.*" (Stats. 1998, ch. 877, § 66.)

injured. That is not what occurred in the case at bar. Here, plaintiff was inspecting the Explorer's compact disk player when she was struck by another vehicle, which ran into her and the Explorer.

We conclude that subdivision (f) of section 22500 was designed to prevent (1) vehicular obstruction of pedestrian traffic on sidewalks, and (2) injury to pedestrians that might occur when a pedestrian (a) walks around the obstructing vehicle and is injured by another hazard, (b) walks into the obstructing vehicle, or (c) is struck when the vehicle, previously at rest on the sidewalk, is put in motion. The section was not designed to prevent the type of occurrence that resulted in plaintiff's injury in this case—being struck on the sidewalk by a vehicle other than the illegally parked vehicle. Accordingly, the court correctly denied to plaintiff the presumption, available under Evidence Code section 669, that defendants failed to exercise due care.

C. Ordinary Negligence

We turn now to the issue of ordinary negligence. . . .

. . . "[N]egligence is conduct which falls below the standard established by law for the protection of others against unreasonable risk of harm." ([Rest. 2d Torts,] § 282.) Only those circumstances which the actor perceives or should perceive at the time of his or her action are to be considered in determining whether the actor should recognize the risks that are involved in his or her conduct. (*Id.*, § 282, com. h.) The actor is required to give his surroundings the attention which the average person in the community would give under like circumstances and such superior attention as the actor himself or herself has. (*Id.*, § 289.) . . .

Plaintiff contends the following undisputed facts are sufficient to defeat defendants' summary judgment motion: Hedges took plaintiff to the sidewalk in front of his apartment at about 10:00 P.M., to see the compact disk player in his car, and stood with plaintiff on the sidewalk within three to four feet of the curb, knowing that the street was undergoing construction, such that traffic was reduced to one lane and the surface of the road had some gravel upon it and was bumpy. In the half-block south of his apartment building Hedges had observed between five and ten dirt mounds; the mounds were six to eight feet in height and four to five feet on the other side of the traffic lane. Hedges acknowledged that due to bumps and potholes in the street, sometimes his car would act a little "squirrelly," causing "momentary [loss of] control of the vehicle for a split second."[12] . . .

The cases relied upon by the parties are focused upon determining whether the defendant's conduct was the cause of the injury. . . . [W]e believe that in the case at bar the proper focus lies elsewhere. "There is a clear distinction . . . between the problem of foreseeability . . . in determining whether the defendant's conduct was the proximate cause of an injury, and the problem of foreseeability in determining whether the

12. We acknowledge that plaintiff points to some additional claimed defects in the road, but the record contains no evidence to show that they were either observed by Hedges or would have been observed by the average person in the community. . . .

defendant was negligent at all. In the latter case the problem is whether or not the defendant's conduct was wrongful toward the plaintiff, while in the former it is whether he should be relieved of responsibility for an admitted wrong because another's wrongful conduct also contributed to the injury." (Richards v. Stanley (1954) 43 Cal. 2d 60, 68-69, 271 P.2d 23.) Where it is contended that the element of foreseeability is determinative of proximate cause, the court "should . . . approach the problem as one of determining the nature of the duty and the scope of the risk of the negligent conduct." (Schwartz v. Helms Bakery Limited (1967) 67 Cal. 2d 232, 240-241, 430 P.2d 68, fn. omitted.) For Hedges to be liable for negligence, his conduct must have fallen below the standard established by law for the protection of those in plaintiff's situation against "unreasonable risk of harm." (Rest. 2d Torts, § 282.) Plaintiff argues that Hedges should have foreseen the likelihood that another vehicle would lose control and come onto the public sidewalk where he and plaintiff were standing, a few feet from the curb. This, says the plaintiff, was negligence because it was near a road made hazardous by construction activity, which Hedges knew about, and it was foreseeable that these conditions could cause a car to lose control and run onto the curb.

In the circumstances of this case these facts do not raise a triable issue that Hedges's conduct was wrongful toward the plaintiff. Reasonable people would not conclude, from these facts, that Hedges's act of taking plaintiff to the sidewalk subjected her to an unreasonable risk of harm. Plaintiff relies solely upon Hedges's knowledge of the following road conditions to establish his negligence: the street was undergoing construction; traffic was reduced to one lane; the road surface was bumpy and had some gravel upon it; and there were dirt mounds four to five feet to the left of the traffic lane. Plaintiff's *expert* declared that these *and other factors*—deficient size of lane of travel, according to applicable manuals and specifications, inadequate delineation of the left side of the roadway, and the asphalt overhang at the gutter—"bias[ed]" the Williams van to the right side of the road, and that the van's drift to the right could be predicted by traffic engineering human factors. But Hedges is not shown to have had the special knowledge of an expert, and his conduct is not judged by that standard. (*See* Rest. 2d Torts, § 289.) Thus, knowledge of the "bias" condition of the roadway, or of what could have been predicted by using traffic engineering human factors, is superior knowledge that Hedges is not chargeable with. There is no evidence in the record that Hedges was aware of any prior accident in this area, and there is no evidence raising a triable issue of fact that an ordinarily prudent person would have understood that he or she was subjecting plaintiff to an unreasonable risk of harm by standing on the public sidewalk at this location. . . .

We conclude that under the undisputed facts here there can be no reasonable difference of opinion as to whether Hedges subjected plaintiff to an unreasonable risk of harm or as to the foreseeability that a driver would become distracted and, due to road conditions that only qualified experts would be able to detect, run up on the sidewalk in the stretch of road in front of Hedges's apartment. We conclude that defendants were entitled to summary judgment. . . .

Did You Know?

An aspiring filmmaker at the time, Stephani Victor lost both her legs in the accident that gave rise to this decision. After enduring eleven surgeries, she became a champion skier, winning numerous national and World Cup titles, as well as a gold medal in the Paralympic Games. She has made a documentary film about her life and is now a motivational speaker.

Sit skier Stephani Victor at the 2013 IPC Alpine World Championships.

NOTES AND QUESTIONS

1. *Negligence Per Se: Fault Versus Evidence of Fault.* As employed by a majority of jurisdictions, the doctrine of negligence per se permits a negligence plaintiff to satisfy the breach element of her cause of action by proving that the defendant violated a certain kind of statutory rule of conduct (or as in *Bayne*, a regulation issued by an administrative agency). By doing so, it relieves the plaintiff of her burden of proving that the defendant violated the common law's ordinary care standard. Conduct in violation of the right sort of statute is *per se* careless in that the state legislature has pronounced it so. Given the pronouncement, there is no need, indeed no room, for further inquiry into whether the defendant acted reasonably under the circumstances.

In *Martin v. Herzog*, 126 N.E. 814 (N.Y. 1920), which is cited by the *Dalal* court, Judge Cardozo provided a typically forceful description of the effect of negligence per se. *Martin* involved the crash of two vehicles. The issue was the plaintiff's alleged contributory negligence in failing to use lights while driving after sunset in violation of a statute requiring their use. The trial court instructed the jury that it could consider the plaintiff's violation of the statute as *evidence* of negligence. Cardozo, for the Court of Appeals, disapproved of the instruction:

> We think the unexcused omission of the statutory signals is more than some evidence of negligence. It *is* negligence in itself. Lights are intended for the guidance and protection of other travelers on the highway. By the very terms of the hypothesis, to omit, willfully or heedlessly, the safeguards prescribed by law for the benefit of another that he may be preserved in life or limb, is to fall short of the standard of diligence to which those who live in organized society are under a duty to conform. . . . In the case at hand, we have an instance of the admitted violation of a statute intended for the protection of travelers on the highway, of whom the defendant at the time was one. Yet the jurors were instructed in effect that they were at liberty in their discretion to treat the omission of lights either as innocent or as culpable. They were allowed to "consider the default as lightly or gravely" as they would (Thomas, J., in the court below). . . . Jurors have no dispensing power by which they may relax the duty that one traveler on the highway owes under the

Suppose Bayne was on the loading platform not for a business purpose, but because he was meeting a friend for lunch. Would he still be considered a member of the protected class? In *Thoma v. Kettler Bros., Inc.*, 632 A.2d 725 (D.C. 1993), the plaintiff, a prospective purchaser of a townhouse, was on the premises by permission and was injured because of a dangerous condition that amounted to a violation of OSHA regulations. The court held that the plaintiff was not an intended beneficiary of the regulations and thus could not invoke them to establish *per se* carelessness on the part of the developer and builder. The court did, however, permit her to introduce the statutory violations as evidence of carelessness.

What if Bayne were technically trespassing because he failed to obtain permission to proceed to the loading dock to meet his friend? Would negligence per se apply? Might the categories of landowner liability discussed in Chapter 2 have any bearing here? If so, does that connection shed any light on the type of inquiry to be made under the "protected class" aspect of negligence per se doctrine?

7. The Right Sort of Accident. Why did the *Victor* court conclude that Victor could not invoke negligence per se? Do you find its interpretation of the statute compelling? Do you see any resemblance between this aspect of the *Victor* court's statutory analysis and the proximate cause inquiry that judges and jurors undertake when resolving negligence claims based on the common law standard of care?

Compare the analysis and result in *Victor* to those of the following four decisions. In *Chevron U.S.A., Inc. v. Forbes*, 783 So. 2d 1215 (Fla. App. 2001), the plaintiff, a patron of the defendant gas station, slipped in a puddle of gas. The plaintiff attempted to invoke negligence per se on the basis of a statute requiring that self-service gas stations be staffed during business hours by an attendant and that attendants promptly clean up spills of gasoline. The court rejected this argument, reasoning that the staffing and clean-up requirement were fire-safety measures, not measures designed to prevent slips and falls.

In *Wawanesa Mut. Ins. Co. v. Matlock*, 60 Cal. App. 4th 583 (Cal. App. 1997), *rev. denied*, 1998 Cal. LEXIS 2048, a lumber company (*L*) lost a good deal of lumber because of a fire caused by a minor (*M*) who dropped a lit cigarette onto a lumber pile. After *L's* property insurer (*PI*) paid for the loss, *PI* sought to recoup the value of its payment from the defendant (*D*), who had provided cigarettes to *M* in violation of a statute barring the provision of cigarettes to minors. The court rejected *PI*'s argument that *D*'s statutory violation constituted *per se* carelessness. The statute, it reasoned, was enacted to prevent young persons from becoming addicted to cigarettes, not to reduce the risk of fire caused by dropping them while lit.

In the famous English case of *Gorris v. Scott*, 1874 L.R. 9 Ex. 125, the ship's owner failed to keep sheep in separate pens in violation of a statute. Because the sheep were not penned, several were lost overboard. The owner sued and attempted to argue negligence per se. The Exchequer Court ruled, however, that the statute was enacted for the purpose of preventing the spread of infectious diseases among animals, not to prevent them from washing overboard.

Finally, consider the last tort-law decision that Cardozo wrote for the New York Court of Appeals before taking a seat on the U.S. Supreme Court: *De Haen v. Rockwood Sprinkler Co.*, 179 N.E. 764 (N.Y. 1932). The plaintiff's decedent was killed when another worker bumped into a radiator that had been placed near the edge of a "hoistway" being used to construct a building, whereupon it fell onto the decedent. The plaintiff successfully invoked negligence per se against the building company on the ground that the company failed to comply with a statute requiring that hoistway openings be fully enclosed on two sides and that the two remaining (open) sides be guarded by a bar at a height of 3 to 4 feet off the floor. Writing for the court, Cardozo affirmed the verdict:

> The chief object of this statute is to protect workmen from the hazard of falling into a shaft. We cannot say, however, that no other hazard was within the zone of apprehension. On two sides of the shaft there must be a solid or comparatively solid fence. Only on the other sides where material is taken on or off may there be a single bar. If there was no thought to give protection against falling missiles or debris, the lawmakers might well have stopped with a requirement that there be a single bar on every side. The fact that they did not stop there is evidence of a broader purpose. True, indeed, it is that on two of the four sides the security is only partial and imperfect. A barrier set in place at a height of four feet will often be of little avail in holding back material or rubbish collected on the floor. Even so, security against the hazard of falling objects will not be lacking altogether. One of the requirements of the statute is that the guard shall be placed at least two feet from the edge. In a barrier so fixed there is warning, if no more. Workmen, who may otherwise be tempted to store material in dangerous proximity to the edge of an open shaft, will be reminded of the danger and will tend to stand afar. The thoughtless will be checked, though the recklessly indifferent will be free to go their way.
>
> The potencies of protection that reside in such a barrier have illustration in the case before us. If the hoistway had been guarded, it is unlikely that the radiators thirty-eight inches high would have been placed as they were within falling distance of the edge. It is still less likely that a worker would heedlessly have brushed against them and so brought about the fall. We do not mean to say that these considerations are decisive. Liability is not established by a showing that as chance would have it a statutory safeguard might have avoided the particular hazard out of which an accident ensued. The hazard out of which the accident ensued must have been the particular hazard or class of hazards that the statutory safeguard in the thought and purpose of the Legislature was intended to correct. None the less, the sequence of events may help to fix the limits of a purpose that would be obscure if viewed alone. A safeguard has been commanded, but without distinct enumeration of the hazards to be avoided. In the revealing light of experience the hazards to be avoided are disclosed to us as the hazards that ensued.

Id. at 765-766.

8. *Excused Violations.* Note that Section 14 of the Third Restatement, cited in Note 5, *supra*, includes the phrase "without excuse." This phrase reflects the fact that courts recognize certain grounds on which actors who have violated statutes are nonetheless spared from being deemed to have acted carelessly simply by virtue of the violation. Section 15 of the Third Restatement identifies five such grounds, which can be summarized as follows: (a) youth or physical incapacity of the defendant; (b) reasonable efforts by the defendant to comply; (c) justified ignorance by the defendant as to the existence of facts rendering the statute applicable; (d) excessive vagueness or ambiguity

in the statutory standard; and (e) compliance posing a greater danger to the defendant or others than non-compliance.

A case illustrative of Section 15(b) is *Busby v. Quail Creek Golf & Country Club*, 885 P.2d 1326 (Okla. 1994). It held that a country club would be excused from being deemed careless for having violated a law against serving alcohol to minors if it could establish that it had no reasonable means of determining that the plaintiff was a minor because she produced a realistic false I.D. and appeared to be over 21. Illustrative of Section 15(e) is *Tedla v. Ellman*, 19 N.E.2d 987 (1939). The plaintiff was walking along the side of a busy road with her back to oncoming traffic in violation of a statute requiring pedestrians to walk so as to face oncoming vehicles. On this basis, the defendant argued that the plaintiff's conduct constituted *per se* contributory fault. The court rejected this argument, concluding that traffic and road conditions on that particular stretch of road were such that the plaintiff had chosen the safer course by violating the statute.

Presumably it is for the court to determine if the excuse proffered by the statutory violator is of a type recognized by the law of negligence and for the jury to determine if the conditions necessary to establish the excuse have been met. Thus, under New York law, jurors in a case such as *Tedla* are instructed to find for the defendant if they determine that, under the circumstances, compliance with the statute "would have placed defendant [or another person] in greater danger than . . . if [the defendant] had not violated the law. . . ." N.Y. Pattern Jury Instr. — Civil: 2:27 (2011).

Dan Dobbs suggests that excuses of the sort recognized in decisions such as *Busby* and *Tedla* effectively convert the doctrine of negligence per se into a device by which the burden of proof on the issue of fault is shifted from the plaintiff to the defendant. The idea is that the plaintiff's being able to point to a violation of a relevant statutory standard of conduct relieves her of the burden of proving fault under the common law's ordinary prudence standard, and places the burden on the defendant to prove an excuse. (Likewise, a defendant in a case such as *Tedla* who seeks to establish comparative fault is relieved of his burden by establishing plaintiff's violation, and the plaintiff is then left to establish a valid excuse.) Dobbs, *supra*, § 140, at 330-331. Note that Dobbs's characterization of the effect of negligence per se is valid only insofar as he is correct to suppose that conduct in violation of an applicable statute is "excused" whenever such conduct is reasonable under the circumstances. At least as a matter of formal law, however, excuses are more narrowly defined. For example, the *Tedla* standard requires a finding not simply that the pedestrian pursued a reasonable course of conduct, where there may have been more than one such course, but that she chose what was in fact the safer course.

9. Interrelation of Negligence Per Se and Common Law Negligence. As demonstrated in *Victor*, if a court concludes that a party seeking to invoke negligence per se is unable to satisfy the pre-requisites for the application of that doctrine — i.e., that the party is a member of the protected class and suffered the sort of injury the statute aimed to prevent — the court does *not* thereby conclude that the party has no negligence action whatsoever. Rather, it determines that the party has not relieved itself of the burden of persuading the judge or jury that a breach occurred under the ordinary care standard. In other words, the court must still undertake standard common law negligence analysis to see whether the party can make out a claim. However, given the resemblance of the doctrinal pre-requisites for negligence per se to the common law requirements of relational breach of duty and proximate cause, the plaintiff's prospects for prevailing on her common law claim will usually be poor. On what ground did the *Victor* court conclude that Victor could not establish liability for ordinary negligence?

10. Regulatory Compliance. Suppose a negligence defendant establishes that her course of conduct *complied* with the requirements of a relevant safety statute. Does the fact of compliance establish conclusively that the defendant has acted with ordinary care, such that judgment as a matter of law should be entered for the defendant? The first-cut answer is no: compliance is not dispositive of the breach issue, even granted that proof of a violation would demonstrate breach as a matter of law. Instead, compliance is typically treated as evidence of ordinary care. *See, e.g.*, Kane v. Hartz Mountain Indus., Inc., 650 A.2d 808 (N.J. App. Div. 1994), *aff'd*, 669 A.2d 816 (N.J. 1996) (compliance with OSHA regulations for worksite safety relevant to, but not dispositive of, the issue of due care). Thus, a driver who skids through a stop sign into an intersection and collides with plaintiff's car can point to the fact that she was driving 25 m.p.h. in a 30 m.p.h. zone as evidence that she was not driving carelessly. Still, it will be open to the plaintiff to argue that, given the presence of particular conditions (e.g., fog, rain, ice), reasonableness required the driver to drive more slowly.

This first-cut answer needs to be qualified, however, because many jurisdictions have adopted statutes under which compliance can defeat or limit liability. Although these rules sometimes apply to claims of negligence, they more typically are invoked in response to "products liability" claims against manufacturers, and are linked to the manufacturer having satisfied a set of safety procedures or protocols set by a legislature or regulatory agency. *See* Chapter 12 *infra*. For example, under statutes enacted by several states, if a manufacturer sells a product that is in compliance with relevant federal safety standards, the fact of compliance will establish conclusively that the product is not "defective." As a result, persons injured while using the product cannot recover from the manufacturer on claims that the product should have been designed to operate more safely or should have carried additional warnings of its dangers.

Big Think

Statutes and Common Law

Under the doctrine of negligence per se, a jury finding that a defendant has violated a certain kind of statute requires a finding that the defendant breached its duty of care. Why should a statutory violation have this significance for the resolution of a suit governed by the common law of torts? Suppose, as in *Dalal* and *Victor*, a legislature enacts a statute that requires specific precautions be taken against certain kinds of accidents yet does not contain a provision granting victims the right to sue a person whose statutory violation causes such an accident. Could one argue that the absence of an explicit statutory provision authorizing claims for damages by victims indicates that the legislature did not intend for violations to serve as a basis for civil liability? How would you respond to such an argument?

II. WRONGFUL DEATH ACTS

The root idea expressed in *Palsgraf* (Chapter 5) is that only one who has been wronged is entitled to sue for injuries caused by that wrong. Thus, *P* is not empowered to sue *D* for conduct that is a wrong only to *T*, even if *D's* wronging of *T* happens to injure *P*. By focusing on the relationality of breach concept, one can begin to comprehend the common law's seemingly strange prohibition of tort claims on behalf of persons killed by the careless acts of others, as well as against tortfeasors who die prior to judgment. That understanding can in turn give us perspective on the statutory regime that has developed as a supplement to the common law.

A. Historical Background

Instances of careless conduct proximately causing death would seem to count as among the most obvious and egregious forms of actionable negligence. Yet, until about 1850, English law almost never authorized causes of action for negligence resulting in death. This surprising gap emerged from a confluence of several common law rules.

1. *Actio Personalis.* Common law observed the maxim *actio personalis moritur cum persona* ("a personal cause of action dies with the person"). The reasoning seems to have been as follows. Suppose plaintiff *P* was the only one wronged by *D*'s negligence. It follows that, if *P* were to die prior to completion of his tort suit against *D*, there would no longer be anyone alive with "standing" to sue *D* for *P*'s injuries.

By parallel reasoning, the common law operated on the rule that the death of a tortfeasor prior to judgment barred tort claims against him simply because the actual perpetrator of the alleged wrong was no longer around to provide redress. In the words of the famous English jurist William Blackstone, the tort action died with the plaintiff or defendant because "neither the [representatives of the deceased] plaintiff have received, nor those of the defendant have committed, in their own personal capacity, any manner of wrong or injury." 3 William Blackstone, *Commentaries on the Law of England* *302 (1765-1769).* It might help to grasp the idea underlying the *actio personalis* maxim to pose the following questions: Why should someone other than the defendant (e.g., his heirs) pay for his wrong? Why should someone other than the wronged plaintiff obtain compensation for that wrong?

2. *Husbands and Loss of Consortium.* One rule of the common law seemed to point toward an exception to the *actio personalis* maxim. This is the rule that permitted suits by husbands for injuries caused to their wives by the wrongful act of another. To these husbands the law made available the action for trespass on the case *per quod*

* These rules did not apply to actions for breach of contract, which were conceived of as actions concerning property rather than the person. One imagines that this variance in treatment encouraged lawyerly manipulation of the categories. For example, claims of medical malpractice causing death were perhaps pleaded as arising in contract (breach of a promise to treat competently) rather than tort.

consortium amisit (literally, a trespass whereby [plaintiff] lost the company of his wife). 3 Blackstone, *supra*, at *140. In modern terminology, the husband whose wife was tortiously injured had an action for *loss of consortium*, by which he could seek compensation from the tortfeasor for the deprivation of the companionship of his wife. In principle, the loss of consortium action applied regardless of whether the deprivation was temporary (i.e., the wife was injured) or permanent (i.e., the wife was killed).

On what basis did the common law recognize an exception to the *actio personalis* maxim for loss of consortium actions seeking compensation for the wrongful injuring of plaintiff's wife? Here one has to appreciate that, by modern Anglo-American standards, English common law was patriarchal and sexist. For these purposes, at least, a husband was treated as owning the "services" of his wife.* The action for loss of consortium thus did not seek compensation for the wife's death, nor for the emotional distress of the husband, but for his loss of the value of her services. Given these premises, it followed that wives could not take advantage of the loss of consortium action. Simply put, they were not regarded in this respect as full-fledged, rights-bearing persons. 3 Blackstone, *supra*, at *142-143.**

3. *Husbands and the Felony Merger Rule.* The consortium action, grounded in this patriarchal conception of ownership, thus empowered one set of persons—husbands—to seek compensation for wrongfully caused death. However, this right was a matter more of theory than practice, because husbands faced a significant practical barrier to bringing such claims, one that arose from a third facet of English common law: the interaction between criminal and tort law.

Under the criminal law of the seventeenth and early eighteenth centuries, all crimes that constituted "felonies" were punishable by forfeiture to the Crown of all the felon's assets. Most felonies also earned the criminal the death penalty. Premeditated killings

* Under the common law doctrine of "coverture," a married woman was not recognized as a separate, rights-bearing person for purposes of civil law. (This treatment did not extend to other areas of law. For example, the intentional killing of a married woman was still treated as a murder.) This subsumption of the wife into the husband meant not only that the husband "owned" her services but also that she lacked the authority to sue in her own name for injuries done to her. Thus, if we imagine an early nineteenth-century suit complaining that someone named Jones had tortiously injured a Mrs. Smith, the case caption for the suit would usually read *Smith et ux. v. Jones.* By use of the phrase "et ux."—an abbreviation of a Latin phrase meaning "and wife"—this formulation indicated that *Mr.* Smith was suing in his own right for loss of consortium (*his* loss of companionship and support, etc.), while also suing to recover for harm suffered by Mrs. Smith (*her* bodily injury, pain and suffering, etc.). Starting in the mid-nineteenth century, U.S. legislatures began enacting statutes granting married women independent legal status.

** Prior to 1600, wives could institute a proceeding called an "appeal," a hybrid criminal-tort action that, contrary to the suggestion of its name, consisted of a suit in its own right, as opposed to a request for higher-court review of a lower-court ruling. By "appealing" a defendant for allegedly killing her spouse, a widow initiated a private criminal prosecution for the felony of homicide. If the prosecution resulted in conviction, the killer would typically be executed. Although the wife was not formally entitled to compensation, the parties to these appeals often "settled" these actions, with the blessing of government prosecutors, by means of a monetary payment to the victim's family. By the 1700s, however, the appeal had fallen into disuse as the Crown increasingly claimed the exclusive power to indict and prosecute criminal offenses.

constituted one class of felonies subject to these penalties. So, too, did killings arising from recklessness and perhaps even negligence on the part of the killer. (Blackstone gives as an example of a felony a worker on a platform throwing down a heavy stone onto a busy city street and killing a pedestrian.) The death penalty and the total forfeiture rule eliminated the practical point of a loss of consortium suit by a husband who might otherwise seek compensation via a tort suit against a person who killed his wife. The execution of the felonious tortfeasor would itself abate any civil action not concluded prior to the criminal punishment. Moreover, given the forfeiture punishment, the defendant's estate would be devoid of assets with which to satisfy a tort judgment. Over time, these *de facto* bars to tort suits complaining of conduct that also constituted a felony became codified into a legal rule called the "felony merger doctrine." That doctrine held that all private rights of action based on felonious conduct were "swallowed up" by the Crown's criminal prosecution and thereby rendered moot. 4 Blackstone, *supra*, at *6.

4. ***Baker v. Bolton.*** By 1800, then, the state of English law was roughly as follows: (1) the death of the victim precluded any tort action on behalf of the victim for his injuries, and (2) although husbands in theory could sue for the wrongful killing of their wives, the felony merger rule barred suits for intentional, reckless, and perhaps some negligent killings. It is possible that this scheme of rules left open room to sue for certain negligent killings not deemed felonies. (In addition, if the standard in actions under the old common law writ of trespass *vi et armis* really was a strict liability standard, certain husbands might also have been able to sue for the innocent killings of their wives.) However, even if these sorts of killings in theory provided a small window for loss of consortium suits by husbands, that window was closed by the 1808 decision of *Baker v. Bolton.* Confronted there with a tort claim by a husband for the negligent killing of his wife, Lord Ellenborough declared summarily that, "[i]n a civil court, the death of a human being [cannot] be complained of as an injury." 1 Campb. 493. *Baker* thus established the hard-and-fast rule that a husband whose wife was accidentally killed could not recover by means of a loss of consortium action. (This even though, if she had been accidentally *injured*, he would be entitled to recover both for her injuries and his loss of consortium.)

B. Lord Campbell's Act and American Statutes

Dissatisfaction in England with the common law bar on tort actions for negligently caused deaths soon mounted. Many bemoaned a system in which a negligence defendant was better off in terms of liability if his careless conduct killed rather than merely wounded the victim.* (Of course, the killer was better off only with respect

---

* Legend has it that, prior to the passage of wrongful death acts, railroad companies designed their cars to ensure that, if there was an accident, the passengers would be killed (nonactionable) rather than merely injured (actionable). This legend transformed into the urban myth that railroad company managers instructed train personnel that, in the event of an accident, they should surreptitiously "finish off" any injured passengers because that would permit the companies to avoid liability.

to tort liability. If the killing was deemed a felony, as most were, he was subject to execution!) They likewise thought it unjust that widows and their children could be driven into destitution by the negligent killing of the husband/father without any recourse against the wrongdoer.

In 1846, Parliament responded by enacting Lord Campbell's Act. The majority of American states soon followed the English lead by enacting their own statutes. These statutes are now generally referred to as *wrongful death statutes*, even though, as we will see, this label creates certain confusions. The statutes were (and still are) diverse in their particulars, but they typically ushered in two broad changes in tort law. First, they allowed tort litigation to proceed after the death of the plaintiff or defendant, with representatives of the deceased party(ies) now taking over the litigation. Second, they empowered certain family members to sue, in Cardozo's words, as "vicarious beneficiaries" of breaches of duties owed only to others.

1. *Survival Actions.* The wrongful death statutes substantially modified both aspects of the *actio personalis* maxim. Thus, tort suits may now proceed after the death of a defendant as claims against the defendant's estate. Moreover, certain tort actions — including negligence actions — that the deceased would have been able to bring against the tortfeasor had he not died can now proceed with an administrator serving as the plaintiff. These latter actions are known as *survival actions.*

Damages recoverable in survival actions have a fairly narrow aim: to provide the decedent's estate with compensation for any harm that the decedent suffered *up to the moment of her death.* By contrast, other harms, including loss of future income, are not compensable in survival actions. The theory is that a dead person *herself* does not suffer from being deprived of future gains: she is no longer around to enjoy them. As such, compensation flowing from these actions is often quite modest, typically being limited to medical expenses incurred prior to death (which may be nonexistent, if death was instantaneous), funeral expenses, and lost earnings between the time of injury and the time of death. However, most states also permit recovery in survival actions for pain and suffering experienced by the decedent prior to death, an element of damages that, where recognized, will often support more substantial damage awards (again, assuming death was not instantaneous).

2. *Wrongful Death Actions.* The same statutes that create survival actions have also authorized *wrongful death* claims by certain family members for at least some of the harms they have suffered by virtue of the wrongful killing of the decedent. "Wrongful" in these statutes is taken to be equivalent of "tortious." Thus, if conduct would have amounted to a tort had the victim been injured, it constitutes "wrongful" death when death rather than injury results. Obviously, by such inclusive wording, the wrongful death statutes laid to rest the felony merger doctrine: An intentional and unjustified killing is "wrongful" and therefore actionable. (Although many states still adhere to the death penalty for especially heinous murders, American criminal law has long rejected the notion that anyone who commits a felony automatically forfeits his assets to the government.)

In contrast to survival actions, wrongful death actions do not seek to impose liability for the *decedent's* losses prior to death. Instead, they compensate immediate family members for the losses that *they have suffered* because of the decedent's death. In this respect, wrongful death claims are "derivative": *R*, close relation of *V*, is given a means to complain of a wrong to *V* that was not a wrong to *R* but nonetheless caused harm to *R*.

3. *New Claims, Not New Wrongs.* The statutes that authorize survival actions by the estates of deceased tort victims and wrongful death actions by surviving family members do *not* purport to recognize new torts. Rather, they authorize new classes of persons to recover upon proof of the commission of a recognized tort against the claimant's decedent. Thus, a surviving family member does not sue for *the tort of wrongful death*—"wrongful death" is not the name of a tort. Instead, she brings a wrongful death claim that is predicated on the defendant's having committed against her decedent a recognized tort such as negligence, assault, battery, and the like.

4. *Wrongful Death Acts: Eligible Claimants and Recoverable Damages.* The question then arises: Actionable by whom and for what? Lord Campbell's Act specified the eligible beneficiaries to be the "wife, husband, parent and[/or] child" of the decedent who was wrongfully killed. Thus, it empowered not only husbands to sue for the loss of their wives' (or children's) support and services, but also wives (and children) to sue for loss of support caused by the wrongful killing of their husbands (and fathers). Evidently, the concern was to compensate two classes of victims: widowers who had lost valuable domestic services, and widows and orphans who had lost their breadwinner. As John Witt has shown, a slight majority of mid-nineteenth-century American statutes declined to empower husbands to sue for wrongful death. Apparently, these American legislatures rejected the patriarchal notion that a husband owned his wife's services, and were primarily concerned to identify a possible source of economic support for economic dependents who had lost their source of income because of the tortious killing of the family "breadwinner." Later, toward the turn of the twentieth century, courts and legislatures added husbands to the list of beneficiaries.

Lord Campbell's Act left it to the jury to specify a wrongful death claimant's damages. In theory, then, the jury was empowered to award compensation not only for the loss to surviving family members of economic support they would have received from the deceased tort victim, but also for their bereavement. However, in keeping with their tendency to exclude claims by husbands, American statutes until recently tended to limit damages exclusively to the *pecuniary losses* suffered by surviving family members, typically measured as the percentage of the decedent's expected future income that would have been devoted to the support of the surviving spouse and/or minor child(ren). This limited conception of damages not only excluded compensation for anguish and loss of companionship caused by the death of a loved one, it also meant that even after husbands were formally empowered to bring wrongful death claims, such claims promised them little compensation, simply because courts tended to assign little or no *economic* value to "wifely" services such as housework.

Consider the following decision on the issue of the type of damages recoverable in survival and wrongful death actions. Does its different treatment of the two make sense?

Nelson v. Dolan

434 N.W.2d 25 (Neb. 1989)

Caporale, J. In this suit joining an action for the wrongful death of Robert James Nelson with . . . [a survival] action on behalf of his estate, the defendant-appellee, Paul J. Dolan, admitted that his negligence proximately caused decedent Nelson's death. The jury thus returned a verdict in favor of the plaintiff-appellant, Phyllis F. Nelson, personal representative of the estate of the aforenamed decedent, and judgment was rendered accordingly in the total sum of $37,968.26. The personal representative nonetheless appeals, asserting as error the district court's sustainment of Dolan's motion in limine preventing her from adducing evidence concerning (1) the mental anguish suffered by the next of kin of the decedent and (2) the mental anguish suffered by the decedent Nelson himself. . . .

I. Offer of Proof

. . . [A] collision occurred in the early morning hours of June 22, 1984, between an automobile operated by Dolan and a motorcycle driven by the 17-year-old decedent Nelson, and on which the latter's friend, Kevin Coffin, was riding as a passenger. Decedent Nelson and Coffin had just left the scene of a fight in Grand Island, Nebraska, and were traveling on a Grand Island street when they noticed behind them an automobile driven by Dolan. In an effort to lose the Dolan automobile, decedent Nelson entered a highway and later turned onto an asphalt road, traveling at 85 miles per hour. Dolan nonetheless continued to follow the motorcycle at a distance of about 50 to 75 feet. In his deposition, Coffin said that "[a]t one point, they got really close. And I got scared, so I turned around and hit the hood of the car with my hand." The automobile was at that time about 1 or 2 feet behind the motorcycle.

After Coffin hit the hood of the Dolan automobile, Dolan backed off, sped up, and hit the motorcycle. Upon impact at a point just outside Grand Island, the two vehicles locked together and, according to an accident reconstructionist, traveled thus locked, with decedent Nelson trying to maintain control, for about 268 feet over a period of approximately 5 seconds until the motorcycle struck a light post, fell, and went under the Dolan automobile. Decedent Nelson's body was found underneath the Dolan automobile, and the personal representative acknowledges that decedent Nelson was crushed by Dolan's automobile and that death was instantaneous.

A psychiatrist offered to testify, in effect, that in his opinion decedent Nelson understood he was going to be run down from the moment the Dolan automobile made contact with the motorcycle and that he "must have been absolutely terrified," knowing or thinking that he was going to die for whatever period of time intervened between the two vehicles' coming together and death.

The personal representative's treating physician offered to testify that he thought she suffered from endogenous depression and acute anxiety caused in part by the loss of the decedent Nelson, who was her son. He treated the condition with medication over a 2-year period and is of the opinion that the condition would continue and should be treated by a psychiatrist.

The personal representative offered to testify that she felt a great loss as the result of her son's death, has found it difficult to sleep since his death, has lost 30 to 40 pounds, is mentally unstable, and has lost her job because of her inability to work.

II. Analysis

The personal representative's contentions require an examination of the types of damages which flow from an actionable death and to whose benefit such damages inure.

A. Wrongful Death Action

While adjudication of the first assignment of error requires only an analysis of the nature of a wrongful death action, the second assignment of error requires an analysis of both the nature of such an action and the nature of an action brought on behalf of a decedent's estate. We concern ourselves first with the wrongful death action.

1. Next of Kin's Damages

The first assignment of error asserts that the district court erred by rejecting the offer of proof concerning the mental anguish suffered by decedent Nelson's next of kin. . . .

The Nebraska wrongful death action is found in Neb. Rev. Stat. §§ 30-809 and 30-810 (Reissue 1985). The first of these statutes provides in relevant part:

> Whenever the death of a person shall be caused by the wrongful act, neglect or default, of any person . . . and the act, neglect or default is such as would, if death had not ensued, have entitled the party injured to maintain an action and recover damages in respect thereof, then . . . the person who . . . would have been liable if death had not ensued, shall be liable to an action for damages, notwithstanding the death of the person injured, and although the death shall have been caused under such circumstances as amount in law to felony.

The second statute reads in relevant part:

> Every such action, as described in section 30-809, shall be . . . brought by and in the name of [the decedent's] personal representatives, for the exclusive benefit of the . . . next of kin. The verdict or judgment should be for the amount of damages which the persons in whose behalf the action is brought have sustained. The avails thereof shall be paid to and distributed among the . . . next of kin in the proportion that the pecuniary loss suffered by each bears to the total pecuniary loss suffered by all such persons.

Thus, the damages recoverable, the disposition of the avails obtained, and the measure of recovery in a wrongful death action are all fixed by statute.

Johnson County v. Carmen, 99 N.W. 502 ([Neb.] 1904), determined that a [predecessor] statute permitting jurors to award such damages, not to exceed $5,000, "as they shall deem a fair and just compensation with reference to the pecuniary injuries, resulting from such death," Gen. Stat. ch. 15, § 2 (1873), did not permit the next of kin to recover for bereavement, mental suffering, or solace. The *Carmen* court ruled that a jury is "limited to giving pecuniary compensation resulting to the next of kin on account of the death of the deceased." 99 N.W. at 503.

A 1919 amendment to the damages language found in the *Carmen* statute produced the damages language now found in § 30-810. In considering that amendment, this court, in Ensor v. Compton, 194 N.W. 458, 459 ([Neb.] 1923), said:

> This amendment was made by the legislature after this court had, by a long line of decisions, held that damages in this class of cases were limited under the statute to money loss or its equivalent. This change, while significant, does not provide a wide open door to all sorts of claims for damages. The loss under the statute is still a pecuniary loss. *Nothing can be allowed on account of mental suffering or bereavement or as a solace on account of such death.* Only such damages can be recovered as are shown by the evidence to have a monetary value. In states having a statute similar to our own, it has generally been construed as permitting recovery of damages for loss of service and companionship under special circumstances where the evidence shows they have a money value. [Citations omitted.] However, recovery for loss of services and companionship by a surviving husband or wife can only be sustained where the evidence shows a reasonable probability that such services and companionship afforded the survivor was of such a character that it would be of advantage to such survivor, and that a disallowance thereof would cause a pecuniary loss to him or her. [Citation omitted.]

(Emphasis supplied.)

In allowing recovery for the economic value of the society, comfort, and companionship lost by the next of kin, the opinion of this court in Selders v. Armentrout, 207 N.W.2d 686 ([Neb.] 1973), noted that the wrongful death damages statute had been interpreted as limiting recovery to pecuniary loss. The *Selders* opinion then went on to explain that damages for loss of society, comfort, and companionship were recoverable because they constituted services which have a financial value to the next of kin.

This court recently reaffirmed . . . that damages on account of mental suffering or bereavement or as a solace to the next of kin on account of the death are not recoverable. . . .

The personal representative concedes the current status of the law but invites us to abandon our prior interpretation and permit the next of kin to recover for her or his mental anguish in an action for wrongful death on the ground that a number of other states so permit. *See, e.g.*, Tommy's Elbow Room, Inc. v. Kavorkian, 727 P.2d 1038 (Alaska 1986); Moore v. Lillebo, 722 S.W.2d 683 (Tex. 1986). . . .

We decline the invitation without undertaking any comparison of the various statutes of other states with our own, for the invitation overlooks the general and dispositive rule that where a statute has been judicially construed and that construction has not evoked an amendment, it will be presumed that the Legislature has acquiesced in the court's determination of its intent. That being so, it cannot now be judicially declared that the Legislature meant something else; thus, the personal representative's first assignment of error fails.

2. Decedent Nelson's Damages

In connection with the second assignment of error, the personal representative first argues that she is entitled to recover in the wrongful death action for the mental anguish decedent Nelson himself experienced prior to his death. In doing so, she ignores the plain language of § 30-810 and thus is once again in error. The statutory language plainly limits a wrongful death recovery to the loss suffered by a decedent's next of kin; it provides no basis upon which to recover a decedent's own damages. . . .

The issue is not unlike that presented in Kroeger v. Safranek, 161 Neb. 182, 72 N.W.2d 831 (1955), a wrongful death action in which . . . the jury . . . [heard evidence that] the person killed suffered "'an excruciating death by electrocution.'" *Id.* at 192, 72 N.W.2d at 840. In reversing a verdict . . . in favor of the plaintiff . . . , this court, quoting from Hindmarsh v. Sulpho Saline Bath Co., 108 Neb. 168, 187 N.W. 806 (1922), said at 192, 72 N.W.2d at 840:

> [I]n the action brought by the personal representative, in behalf of the statutory beneficiaries, to recover damages for the death caused by the wrongful act of the defendant, *the recovery must be measured by the pecuniary loss suffered by those beneficiaries. . . .*
>
> *Thus any pain or suffering endured by the decedent is not an element upon which appellee can herein base any recovery* and it was error for the court to include the allegations in its instructions.

(Emphasis supplied.)

However, the determination that damages for a decedent's preimpact mental anguish cannot be recovered in a wrongful death action does not resolve the second assignment of error; the petition here joins with the wrongful death action a separate action on behalf of the decedent's estate, a procedure which our law permits.

B. Estate Action

Thus, the question becomes whether a decedent's estate may recover for the mental anguish a decedent consciously suffers by the apprehension and fear of impending death prior to sustaining fatal injury.

While we have not heretofore considered this question, we have long permitted a decedent's estate to recover for the conscious physical pain and suffering the decedent endured after a negligently inflicted injury resulting in death. We have also long recognized postinjury mental anguish as an element of damages recoverable in personal injury actions.

Some courts have allowed recovery for conscious preimpact mental anguish suffered by decedents aware of impending death. Most of these cases are federal diversity actions and arise out of airplane crashes.

In one such action, Shu-Tao Lin v. McDonnell Douglas Corp., 742 F.2d 45 (2d Cir. 1984), the decedent was killed when a jet crashed shortly after takeoff. The reviewing court referred with approval to the language of the trial court, 574 F. Supp. 1407, 1416 (S.D.N.Y. 1983), which observed:

> New York provides a cause of action for the pain and suffering of a decedent before his death. In several cases it has been held that a decedent's estate may recover for

> the decedent's pain and suffering endured *after* the injury that led to his death. [Citations omitted.] From this proposition, it is only a short step to the allowing of damages for a decedent's pain and suffering *before* the mortal blow and resulting from the apprehension of impending death.

(Emphasis in original.) The reviewing court then itself reasoned:

> A decedent's representative unquestionably may recover for pain and suffering experienced in a brief interval between injury and death. . . . We see no intrinsic or logical barrier to recovery for the fear experienced during a period in which the decedent is uninjured but aware of an impending death.

742 F.2d at 53.

In Haley v. Pan American World Airways, 746 F.2d 311 (5th Cir. 1984), *reh'g denied*, 751 F.2d 1258, the court interpreting state law concluded that Louisiana would recognize a surviving cause of action for preimpact fear and apprehension of impending death experienced by an airline passenger killed in an airplane crash. In *Haley*, as in our present case, the decedent was killed immediately upon impact. The court based its decision on Louisiana law which permitted recovery for fear suffered during a negligently produced ordeal. . . . [It also] quoted with approval the analysis from its earlier decision in Solomon v. Warren, 540 F.2d 777 (5th Cir. 1976), *cert. denied*, 434 U.S. 801 (1977) (interpreting Florida law):

> While in the garden variety of claims under survival statutes, including the Florida Statute — fatal injuries sustained in automobile accidents and the like — the usual sequence is impact followed by pain and suffering, we are unable to discern any reason based on either law or logic for rejecting a claim because in this case as to at least part of the suffering, this sequence was reversed. We will not disallow the claims for this item of damages on that ground.

Haley at 314-15. . . .

Similarly, in Missouri Pacific R. Co. v. Lane, 720 S.W.2d 830 (Tex. App. 1986), the court affirmed an award for mental anguish suffered by the decedent before a train hit his stalled truck. As to the claim that such damages were not recoverable because decedent died instantly, the court reasoned: "Such an argument fails to consider the terror and consequent mental anguish Lane suffered for the six to eight seconds while he faced imminent death." *Id.* at 833.

Similar results were obtained in [several other decisions]. [Citations omitted. — Eds.] Some courts, however, have denied recovery for preimpact mental anguish. E.g., Nye v. Com., Dept. of Transp., 480 A.2d 318 ([Pa. Super. Ct.] 1984) (no damages available under Pennsylvania statute for conscious preimpact fright); In re Air Crash Disaster Near Chicago, Ill. etc., 507 F. Supp. 21 (N.D. Ill. 1980) (no recovery under Illinois law for fright and terror decedent may have suffered in anticipation of physical injury prior to death in an airplane crash); Fogarty v. Campbell 66 Exp., Inc., 640 F. Supp. 953 (D. Kan. 1986) (no recovery is permitted under Kansas law for negligently induced preimpact mental anguish, not itself resulting in physical injury, notwithstanding that the collision caused physical injury).

Nonetheless, we are persuaded that there exists no sound legal or logical distinction between permitting a decedent's estate to recover as an element of damages for a decedent's conscious postinjury pain and suffering and mental anguish and permitting such an estate to recover for the conscious pre-fatal-injury mental anguish resulting from the apprehension and fear of impending death.

Neb. Rev. Stat. § 25-1401 (Reissue 1985) provides that, among other things, a cause of action for an injury to a personal estate survives the death of the person entitled to the same. Thus, we hold that as an element of a decedent's personal injury action, conscious pre-fatal-injury fear and apprehension of impending death survives a decedent's death and inures to the benefit of such decedent's estate.

Dolan argues that the personal representative's offer of proof fails in any event to establish that the decedent Nelson knew how closely his motorcycle was being followed or otherwise establishes that the decedent Nelson was consciously aware of and feared his impending death. It is true that courts have denied recovery for preimpact mental anguish for lack of evidence that the decedent was aware of his impending death. E.g., Anderson v. Rowe, 73 A.D.2d 1030, 425 N.Y.S.2d 180 (1980); Shatkin v. McDonnell Douglas Corp., 727 F.2d 202 (2d Cir. 1984). . . .

In *Shatkin*, the reviewing court reversed a jury award for preimpact pain and suffering, finding no evidence that the decedent passenger was awake or was aware that anything was wrong; that the pilot or anyone alerted the passengers as to the danger; nor that the airplane tilted and rolled in an unusual manner. However, in Shu-Tao Lin v. McDonnell Douglas Corp., 742 F.2d 45 (2d Cir. 1984), which arose out of the same accident, the same reviewing court distinguished *Shatkin* and concluded that the jury could reasonably find that a passenger seated over the left wing of the airplane (Shatkin's assigned seat was over the right wing) could have seen the left engine and a portion of the wing break off at the beginning of the flight and suffered preimpact mental anguish during the 30 seconds before the crash. . . .

It is fundamental that the nature and amount of damages cannot be sustained by evidence which is speculative and conjectural. The record must provide some basis for the jury to make a reasonable inference that the decedent suffered conscious mental anguish. While it is true that in the present case there is no evidence that decedent Nelson said anything prior to his death revealing an awareness of his impending death, the personal representative's offers of proof nonetheless provide a basis upon which the jury certainly need not, but could, if it wished, find that decedent Nelson apprehended and feared his impending death during the 5 seconds his motorcycle traveled 268 feet locked with Dolan's automobile before he was crushed and thus killed.

We must therefore conclude that the record sustains the personal representative's second assignment of error.

III. Decision

Accordingly, the judgment of the district court is hereby affirmed as to the wrongful death action, and the cause is reversed and remanded for a new trial as to the action on behalf of the decedent's estate.

NOTES AND QUESTIONS

1. The Action for Loss of Consortium in Modern Law. As indicated in the notes preceding *Nelson*, the common law long ago recognized the action for *loss of consortium* for a husband who was temporarily deprived of his wife's services because of injuries caused to his wife by the careless acts of another. Needless to say, the conception of spousal relations underwriting this cause of action, by which the wife was treated as akin to a servant of the husband, has been abandoned. One might have predicted that, with this change in social and legal norms, the action for loss of consortium would disappear, much like the amatory actions such as "criminal conversation" (discussed in the notes following *Mussivand*, Chapter 2). Instead, courts have generally gone the other route by extending the loss of consortium action to wives. In doing so, they have placed the consortium action on a new conceptual footing. It is no longer an action complaining of interference with a quasi-property interest, but instead an action for tortiously caused injury (other than death) that adversely affects the relationship of a husband and wife. As such, it provides compensation for the same kinds of losses that tend to be compensated in wrongful death actions, except that the loss of consortium action provides that compensation in cases involving non-fatal injuries to the tort victim.

In principle, a loss of consortium action is available for any tortious conduct that generates the requisite injury to the spouse and hence to the relationship. Most commonly, however, consortium actions are brought in connection with claims for battery and negligence, as opposed to, say, defamation or fraud. In terms of procedure, actions for loss of consortium are almost always appended to the victim's underlying tort claim, and they are litigated together by the same lawyer who represents the victim.* States have split roughly evenly on whether to permit consortium actions to be brought by parents whose minor children have been tortiously injured, as well as by children whose parents have been tortiously injured. For a decision in which the judges debate the merits of extending loss of consortium actions to children whose parents are tortiously injured, see Berger v. Weber, 303 N.W.2d 424 (Mich. 1981).

2. Loss of Consortium Damages in a Wrongful Death Suit. Loss of consortium *actions* are freestanding causes of action that can be brought by a spouse (and, in some jurisdictions, other close relatives) to recover from a defendant for losses the spouse has suffered because the defendant tortiously *injured* their husband or wife (or child or parent). By contrast, as indicated in *Nelson*, when a family member is tortiously *killed*, survivors seeking compensation for *their* losses do not bring a loss of consortium *cause of action*. Instead, they bring a wrongful death action. Still, as *Nelson* attests, wrongful death actions raise the related issue of whether the survivors can recover damages for loss of services and companionship as one component of their wrongful death award.

---

* Thus, if the complaint in *Smith et ux. v. Jones* (mentioned in a previous footnote) were brought today, the caption would read *Smith and Smith v. Jones*. Obviously, this is not because Mrs. Smith remains dependent on her husband to sue for her injuries. Rather, it is because her underlying negligence claim and Mr. Smith's derivative claim for loss of consortium present mostly the same allegations and facts and hence are more efficiently litigated in one proceeding.

Nelson stresses that a jury award of damages for loss of services and companionship in a wrongful death action is meant to reflect the expected *economic* benefits that surviving family members would have received by virtue of continuing to have the decedent's companionship and support. As explained by the Tennessee Supreme Court, the pecuniary loss associated with the death of a spouse or parent encompasses

> not only tangible services provided by a family member, but also intangible benefits each family member receives from the continued existence of other family members. Such benefits include attention, guidance, care, protection, training, companionship, cooperation, affection, love, and in the case of a spouse, sexual relations.

Jordan v. Baptist Three Rivers Hospital, 984 S.W.2d 593, 602 (Tenn. 1999). Focusing particularly on the issue of the child's loss of a parent, the court further explained:

> A basis for placing an economic value on parental consortium is that the education and training which a child may reasonably expect to receive from a parent are of actual and commercial value to the child. Accordingly, a child sustains a pecuniary injury for the loss of parental education and training when a defendant tortiously causes the death of the child's parent.

Id. at 601.

Conceived as such, damages for loss of services and companionship in wrongful death actions are *not* designed to compensate for a survivor's emotional distress or grief over the death of a loved one, but rather for the reduced quality of life experienced by the surviving family member. *See, e.g.*, Krouse v. Graham, 562 P.2d 1022 (Cal. 1977). As the Texas Supreme Court has explained:

> Mental anguish represents an emotional response to the wrongful death itself. Loss of society, on the other hand, constitutes a loss of positive benefits which flowed to the family from the decedent's having been a part of it. Mental anguish is concerned "not with the benefits [the beneficiaries] have lost, but with the issue of compensating them for their harrowing experience resulting from the death of a loved one." 1 S. Speiser, *Recovery for Wrongful Death 2d* § 3:52 at 327 (1975). Loss of society asks, "what positive benefits have been taken away from the beneficiaries by reason of the wrongful death?" Mental anguish damages ask about the negative side: "what deleterious effect has the death, as such, had upon the claimants?" *Id.*

Moore v. Lillebo, 722 S.W.2d 683, 687-688 (Tex. 1986).

3. Wrongful Death and Emotional Distress Damages. The Nebraska Supreme Court essentially refuses to entertain the question of whether emotional distress damages ought to be compensable in wrongful death actions. As it notes, however, other courts have permitted them.

In *Sanchez v. Schindler*, 651 S.W.2d 249 (Tex. 1983), the Texas Supreme Court overturned its rule of awarding only pecuniary-loss damages in wrongful death actions:

> Sanchez argues the pecuniary loss rule is based on an antiquated concept of the child as an economic asset, and should be rejected. We agree. It is time for this court to revise its interpretation of the Texas Wrongful Death statutes in light of present social realities and expand recovery beyond the antiquated and inequitable

> pecuniary loss rule. If the rule is literally followed, the average child would have a negative worth. Strict adherence to the pecuniary loss rule could lead to the negligent tortfeasor being rewarded for having saved the parents the cost and expense of rearing a child. The real loss sustained by a parent is not the loss of any financial benefit to be gained from the child, but is the loss of love, advice, comfort, companionship and society.

Id. at 251.

Sanchez observed that, at the time, three other jurisdictions permitted recovery for emotional distress damages under statutes similar to Texas's wrongful death act. It also noted that eight other states' legislatures had enacted statutes that had been construed to permit recovery for emotional distress damages. *Id.* at 254. In Girouard v. Skyline Steel, Inc., 158 P.3d 255 (Ariz. App. 2007), an intermediate appellate court, applying Arizona's rule permitting emotional distress damages in wrongful death actions, reversed a trial court ruling that excluded evidence tending to show that the plaintiff's decedent had died in a particularly horrific manner. The evidence was admissible, the appellate court reasoned, because a wrongful death claimant is entitled to compensation for mental anguish over the *manner* of the decedent's death, not merely the fact of the death.

Is it so obviously inequitable to exclude recovery for survivors' grief over the loss of loved ones? Does that conclusion depend on how one understands the purposes of wrongful death acts? Does it depend instead on whether it is actually possible to distinguish between the denial of pleasure — i.e., the positive experience of a loved one's presence — and the suffering of pain — i.e., the negative experience of grief over a loved one's death?

Lord Campbell's Act, now known as the Fatal Accidents Act, was amended numerous times by the English Parliament to keep up with developments in wrongful death in the United Kingdom. In 1982 it was amended to permit a subset of wrongful death plaintiffs to recover for "bereavement damages" — exactly the kind of damages Nelson's mother attempted to recover. In its current form, it allows bereavement damages of £12,980 and extends the availability of those damages to civil partners.

4. *Derivative Causes of Action.* Wrongful death and loss of consortium actions each claim that the plaintiff — usually a relative of the victim of the underlying tort — suffered an injury as a result of an act that was wrongful to someone else, and not wrongful as to the plaintiff herself. In *Nelson*, for example, the defendant Dolan drove carelessly with respect to the physical well-being of Robert Nelson, not Phyllis Nelson. Judge Andrews in his *Palsgraf* dissent (Chapter 5) pointed to the viability of these actions as evidence of modern negligence law's rejection of the relational aspect of breach of duty, and its embrace of the idea that negligence consists of a breach of a duty "owed to the world." In fact, these actions remain in important senses *derivative* of the victim's underlying claim, a point that cuts against Andrews's claim.

The derivative nature of survival and wrongful death claims was most clearly apparent when they were brought under the old rule of contributory negligence. (*See* Chapter 7.) At this time, if a judge or jury determined that the decedent's underlying claim would have been barred because the decedent's own fault was a cause of his injury, this finding not only defeated a survival action on behalf of the victim, but also any claim for wrongful death, *even if the surviving family members were in no way at*

Check Your Understanding

Wrongful Death, Survival Actions, and Loss of Consortium

S and *T* are married and have two young children, *A* and *B*. *T*, *A*, and *B* were aboard a small commercial sightseeing plane when, because of pilot error, the plane crashed into a lake. Tragically, *A* died upon impact. *B* initially survived but became tangled in the wreckage and drowned as the plane sunk to the bottom of the lake. *S* survived but was seriously injured.

Describe the negligence claims that can be brought against the sightseeing company by or on behalf of *S*, *T*, *A*, and *B*. What damages can be recovered in each action?

III. IMPLIED RIGHTS OF ACTION

Wrongful death statutes explicitly empower persons to sue in tort who would otherwise lack the right to sue under common law rules. Other sorts of statutes explicitly create what amounts to tort liability for conduct that, prior to their enactment, was not tortious. For example, Chapter 10 includes cases featuring federal laws that have expressly made certain forms of workplace discrimination actionable, even when such conduct would not be actionable as a common law tort. This section considers a related question about the intersection of statutes and torts: Can a statute create a cause of action even when it says nothing about whether individuals are entitled to sue for violations of it?

In framing this inquiry it is helpful to recall the doctrine of negligence per se. The issue in applying that doctrine is whether a plaintiff suing for the tort of common law negligence can take advantage of a legislative standard of conduct to prove the element of breach. Implicit in such a claim is the idea that the common law, by recognizing the negligence action, has already provided the plaintiff with the vehicle for bringing suit. Suppose, however, a statute regulates a species of conduct to which no common law tort liability attaches, yet also says nothing explicit about whether it is intended to provide causes of actions to those who are injured by violations of the statute. Can a person aggrieved by a violation of the statute assert that it implicitly has conveyed to them a right to sue?

Tex. & Pac. Ry. Co. v. Rigsby

241 U.S. 33 (1916)

Pitney, J. . . . [Rigsby was employed by the railway as a switchman in its yard at Marshall, Texas. There, he] was engaged . . . in taking some "bad order" cars to the shops . . . to be repaired. . . . Rigsby, in the course of his duties, rode upon the top of one of the cars (a box car) in order to set the brakes and stop them and hold them upon the main line. He did this, and while descending from the car . . . he fell, owing to a defect in one of the handholds or grab-irons that formed the rungs of the ladder, and sustained personal injuries. This car had been out of service and waiting on the track spur for some days, perhaps a month. The occurrence took place September 4, 1912.

In an action for damages, based upon the Federal Safety Appliance Acts [of 1893 and 1910], the above facts appeared without dispute. . . . The trial court instructed the jury, as matter of law, that they should return a verdict in favor of plaintiff, the only question submitted to them being the amount of the damages. . . . The resulting judgment was affirmed by the Circuit Court of Appeals.

. . . This action was . . . [based] upon § 2 of the . . . 1910 [act], which declares: "All cars must be equipped with secure sill steps and efficient hand brakes; all cars requiring secure ladders and secure running boards shall be equipped with such ladders and running boards, and all cars having ladders shall also be equipped with secure handholds or grab irons on their roofs at the tops of such ladders." There can be no question that a box car having a handbrake operated from the roof requires also a secure ladder to enable the employee to safely ascend and descend, and that the provision quoted was intended for the especial protection of employees engaged in duties such as that which plaintiff was performing. . . .

. . . A disregard of the command of [a] statute is a wrongful act, and where it results in damage to one of the class for whose especial benefit the statute was enacted, the right to recover the damages from the party in default is implied, according to a doctrine of the common law expressed in 1 Com. Dig., *tit.* Action upon Statute (F), in these words: "So, in every case, where a statute enacts, or prohibits a thing for the benefit of a person, he shall have a remedy upon the same statute for the thing enacted for his advantage, or for the recompense of a wrong done to him contrary to the said law." (*Per* Holt, C.J., Anon., 6 Mod. 26, 27.) This is but an application of the maxim, *Ubi jus ibi remedium. See* 3 Black. Com. 51, 123; Couch v. Steel, 3 El. & Bl. 402, 411; 23 L.J.Q.B. 121, 125. The inference of a private right of action in the present instance is rendered irresistible by the provision of § 8 of the Act of 1893 that an employee injured by any car, etc., in use contrary to the act shall not be deemed to have assumed the risk, and by the language . . . [, discussed below, of] the proviso in § 4 of the 1910 act. . . .

[The court proceeded to consider defendant's argument against the imposition of liability based on § 4 of the 1910 act. Section 4 provided statutorily set fines for each violation of the substantive requirements of the 1910 act. However, it waived those fines if (a) the railroad car in question was at one time properly equipped with the required safety devices; (b) those devices, through no fault of the railroad, had become defective or inoperative in transit; (c) repairs to them could not be effected on the spot; and (d) the car was being taken to the nearest point at which repairs could be effected. Citing its decision in an earlier case, the court's opinion then continued as follows.—Eds.] . . . [A]lthough § 4 . . . relieves the carrier from the statutory penalties while a car is being hauled to the nearest available point for repairs, it [contains a proviso] that it shall not be construed to relieve a carrier from liability in a remedial action for the death or injury of an employee caused by or in connection with the movement of a car with defective equipment.* The question whether the defective condition of the ladder

---

* [The Section 4 proviso referenced in this paragraph and in the preceding one stated that the movement of railcars with nonconforming equipment, even for the purpose of effecting necessary repairs, "shall be at the sole risk of the carrier, and nothing in this section shall be construed to relieve

any liability or duty created by this title . . .". In passing on almost identical language found in the Securities Act of 1933, the Court found the words entirely sufficient to fashion a remedy to rescind a fraudulent sale, secure restitution and even to enforce the right to restitution against a third party holding assets of the vendor. Deckert v. Independence Shares Corp., 311 U.S. 282 (1940). This significant language was used:

> "The power to *enforce* implies the power to make effective the right of recovery afforded by the Act. And the power to make the right of recovery effective implies the power to utilize any of the procedures or actions normally available to the litigant according to the exigencies of the particular case." [*Deckert*, at 288]. . . .

NOTES AND QUESTIONS

1. *Ubi Jus Ibi Remedium.* The foregoing maxim, cited by the *Rigsby* court, translates as "where there is a right, there is a remedy." *Rigsby* seems to presume that whenever a statute sets a standard of conduct a court should permit an individual who is injured by a person's violation of that standard to sue the violator for damages. Is that a plausible presumption? Might a legislature sometimes want to enact rules and regulations that do not give rise to private rights of action? Notice that the *ubi jus* maxim speaks in terms of *rights* demanding remedies, not harms demanding remedies.

Suppose you live in a state with a statute that imposes criminal fines on those who operate industrial plants that emit excessive quantities of airborne pollutants. The statute is silent as to whether it empowers individuals to sue for violations. Should a court infer that the law accords a cause of action against the owner of any plant that is in violation of the statute to all those who suffer asthma traceable to excessive levels of the relevant pollutants? All those whose taxes are increased because of additional burdens on the public health system due to a higher rate of respiratory illness resulting from the pollution?

Might certain kinds of legislation aim to accomplish something other than setting standards of conduct? Each state requires drivers to have valid licenses before driving. Suppose *X* is injured by driver *Y*, who was driving carefully at the time, but never obtained a license. Does *Rigsby* suggest that the licensing law creates a private right of action on *X's* behalf based solely on the statutory violation? (Recall that most states do not permit a plaintiff to invoke a violation of a licensing statute to establish negligence per se.)

2. *Implied Rights of Action Versus Negligence Per Se.* Rigsby does not appear to invoke the doctrine of negligence per se — it does not suggest that the federal Safety Appliance Acts provide a standard of reasonable care that will govern Rigsby's common law tort action.* Rather, it seems to treat the acts as giving rise to a statutory cause of action. Indeed, the action identified by the court apparently imposes strict

---

* At the time *Rigsby* was decided, federal courts were understood to have the power to interpret and apply "general common law." Thus, the *Rigsby* court could have invoked a notion of negligence per se if it had wanted to. As you may have learned in Civil Procedure, the Supreme Court's 1938 decision in *Erie Railroad v. Tompkins* held that the substantive common law of tort is essentially the province of the state courts. Therefore, because a federal court today faced with a common law negligence claim would almost always be applying the common law of a given state, the court could

liability rather than fault-based liability—the court deems "irrelevant" the issue of whether the railroad took reasonable steps to maintain its train car in a safe condition. *Rigsby* was decided in the same year as *MacPherson.* Does the knowledge that railways apparently were sometimes subject to strict liability for injuries caused by defective equipment render more reasonable Cardozo's recognition of a duty on car manufacturers to make reasonable inspections of car wheels?

3. *Jurisdiction and Remedy.* Even more clearly than *Rigsby*, *Borak* locates the source of the plaintiff's cause of action in a statute, here the federal Securities Exchange Act of 1934. Looming large in the court's analysis is Section 27 of the Act, which grants jurisdiction to federal courts to hear and resolve disputes arising under the Act. The court infers from this grant of jurisdiction that courts may supplement explicit statutory provisions with additional remedies, including private rights of action, whenever they deem it necessary to promote the objectives of the statute. Can you imagine situations in which it would not promote justice, or would interfere with the objectives of a statute, to recognize an implied right of action? Or does it follow from *Borak* that courts should always infer the existence of a cause of action when a statute setting standards of conduct is silent on the question?

4. *The Protected Class. Rigsby*'s identification of the class of persons eligible to assert a claim under the Safety Appliance Acts seems to incorporate a traditional notion of common law duty. The acts were clearly intended for the benefit of railroad workers, thus the court identifies them as persons empowered to sue. Does *Borak* invoke a similar notion of duty? How does it define the protected class? Do any of *Borak*'s stated rationales support the idea that a right of action ought to be available not just to a disappointed investor, but to anyone? Wouldn't the broadest possible class provide an even more "effective weapon" for enforcing securities laws?

5. *Federalism.* Any full discussion of the issue of implied rights of action must take into account the complex relationship between federal and state courts, a matter that cannot be pursued in any depth here. One way to highlight some of these issues is to pose the following question: Why was Borak so anxious to assert a claim under the 1934 Act? Assuming that he could prove his allegations, would his suit have been dismissed on the merits by a state court applying state law? As it turns out, probably not. State law then and now treats managers as "fiduciaries" of their shareholders, that is, as requiring them to make every effort to ensure that transactions undertaken by the company are in shareholders' best interests. A shareholder such as Borak who believed that the proposed merger benefited management at the expense of shareholders likely could have brought a state law claim for breach of fiduciary duty.

Thus, in contrast to *Rigsby*, *Borak* probably did not help the plaintiff by supplying a more exacting federal-law standard of liability than was set by state law. Instead, the

---

not permit the plaintiff to invoke a *federal* statute as specifying a legislative standard of care under the doctrine of negligence per se unless it determined that the relevant state's law has incorporated the federal standard by judicial decision or legislation. *See* Crane v. Cedar Rapids & Iowa City Ry., 395 U.S. 164 (1969).

main benefit to Borak was that he avoided a *procedural* requirement imposed by state law. The latter would have required him to post a bond — that is, pledge a substantial sum of money — in order to pursue his claim. The bond requirement had been set to deter frivolous shareholder suits; if a suit turned out to be groundless, the plaintiff would forfeit the amount specified in the bond.

Should the federal courts be in the business of identifying federal statutory causes of action at the behest of plaintiffs whose primary motivation is to avoid this sort of procedural hurdle? Is the idea that the federal courts provide a better brand of justice than state courts? One can certainly identify types of suits for which this was and is likely the case. Consider, for example, the probable receptivity of federal courts, as compared to Southern state courts, to actions brought by African Americans for civil rights violations in the mid-1960s. Does litigation over false proxy statements warrant a similar opening up of the federal courts?

6. *Applying the Brakes.* Within ten years of *Borak*, the U.S. Supreme Court began to show greater reticence in identifying implied rights of action in federal statutes. In *Cort v. Ash*, 422 U.S. 66 (1975), the Court refused to find within a criminal law banning certain campaign contributions by corporations an implied right of action on behalf of shareholders that would empower them to recover for the improper expenditure of corporate funds on campaigns. The Court expressed reluctance to identify a private right of action within general criminal prohibitions. It also identified a four-part test designed to assist courts in determining whether to infer a private right of action from a statute:

> First, is the plaintiff "one of the class for whose especial benefit the statute was enacted," [quoting *Rigsby*] — that is, does the statute create a federal right in favor of the plaintiff? Second, is there any indication of legislative intent, explicit or implicit, either to create such a remedy or to deny one? Third, is it consistent with the underlying purposes of the legislative scheme to imply such a remedy for the plaintiff? And finally, is the cause of action one traditionally relegated to state law, in an area basically the concern of the States, so that it would be inappropriate to infer a cause of action based solely on federal law?

Id. at 78.

Applying this test, the Court concluded that the ban on corporate contributions to political campaigns was designed primarily to clean up the political process for the benefit of the public, rather than a particular class of persons. It further found no hint of congressional intent to create a private right of action, and reasoned that empowering the shareholders to collect damages for illegal payments that had already been made would not advance the regulatory purposes of the statute. Finally, the Court noted that the plaintiffs might be able to pursue state-law causes of action against management for breach of fiduciary duty.

7. *Making a U-Turn.* Although suggesting that federal courts ought to think twice about recognizing implied rights of action, *Cort v. Ash* still operated on the assumption of *Rigsby* and *Borak* that the courts had broad discretion to determine whether, *in their judgment*, it would promote justice or the aims of a statute to identify such a right. Four

years later, the Court abandoned this posture in favor of an approach much more deferential to Congress.

In *Cannon v. University of Chicago*, 441 U.S. 677 (1979), the Court identified, by a 6 to 3 vote, an implied cause of action for victims of discrimination within a federal law prohibiting gender discrimination by universities that receive federal funding. Two of the six votes, however, came by means of the following concurrence, written by then-Justice Rehnquist, 441 U.S., at 717-718.

> Rehnquist, J. (concurring) (with Stewart, J.). Having joined the Court's opinion in this case, my only purpose in writing separately is to make explicit what seems to me already implicit in that opinion. I think the approach of the Court, reflected in its analysis of the problem in this case and [other] cases . . . is quite different from the analysis in earlier cases such as [*Borak*]. The question of the existence of a private right of action is basically one of statutory construction. And while state courts of general jurisdiction still enforcing the common law as well as statutory law may be less constrained than are federal courts enforcing laws enacted by Congress, the latter must surely look to those laws to determine whether there was an intent to create a private right of action under them.
>
> . . . [T]he Court's opinion demonstrates that Congress . . . [has] tended to rely to a large extent on the courts to *decide* whether there should be a private right of action, rather than determining this question for itself. Cases such as [*Borak*] and numerous cases from other federal courts, gave Congress good reason to think that the federal judiciary would undertake this task.
>
> I fully agree with the Court's statement that "[w]hen Congress intends private litigants to have a cause of action to support their statutory rights, the far better course is for it to specify as much when it creates those rights." It seems to me that the factors to which I have here briefly adverted apprise the lawmaking branch of the Federal Government that the ball, so to speak, may well now be in its court. Not only is it "far better" for Congress to so specify when it intends private litigants to have a cause of action, but for this very reason this Court in the future should be extremely reluctant to imply a cause of action absent such specificity on the part of the Legislative Branch.

That same term, in *Touche Ross & Co. v. Redington*, 442 U.S. 560 (1979), Justice Rehnquist wrote an opinion for the Court declining to find a private right of action within Section 17(a) of the Securities Exchange Act of 1934, which mandates that brokerage firms file certain financial reports with the SEC. Treating this provision as setting bookkeeping requirements rather defining wrongful conduct, the Court saw no evidence of congressional intent to create a right of action to those injured by filings containing false statements. The Court also distanced itself from *Borak* and *Cort.* 442 U.S., at 575-579.

> Relying on the factors set forth in Cort v. Ash . . . [respondents, who seek to establish the existence of a cause of action] assert that we . . . must consider whether an implied private remedy is necessary to "effectuate the purpose of the section" and whether the cause of action is one traditionally relegated to state law. . . . It is true that in Cort v. Ash, the Court set forth four factors that it considered "relevant" in

determining whether a private remedy is implicit in a statute not expressly providing one. But the Court did not decide that each of these factors is entitled to equal weight. The central inquiry remains whether Congress intended to create, either expressly or by implication, a private cause of action. Indeed, the first three factors discussed in *Cort*—the language and focus of the statute, its legislative history, and its purpose—are ones traditionally relied upon in determining legislative intent. Here, the statute by its terms grants no private rights to any identifiable class and proscribes no conduct as unlawful. And the parties . . . agree that the legislative history of the 1934 Act simply does not speak to the issue of private remedies under § 17(a). At least in such a case as this, the inquiry ends there: The question whether Congress, either expressly or by implication, intended to create a private right of action, has been definitely answered in the negative.

. . . In *Borak*, the Court found in § 14(a) of the 1934 Act . . . an implied cause of action for damages in favor of shareholders for losses resulting from deceptive proxy solicitations. . . . [Respondents] emphasize language in *Borak* that discusses the remedial purposes of the 1934 Act and § 27 of the Act, which, *inter alia*, grants to federal district courts the exclusive jurisdiction of violations of the Act and suits to enforce any liability or duty created by the Act or the rules and regulations there-under. They argue that Touche Ross has breached its duties under § 17(a) and the rules adopted there-under and that in view of § 27 and of the remedial purposes of the 1934 Act, federal courts should provide a damages remedy for the breach.

The reliance . . . on § 27 is misplaced. Section 27 grants jurisdiction to the federal courts and provides for venue and service of process. It creates no cause of action of its own force and effect; it imposes no liabilities. The source of plaintiffs' rights must be found, if at all, in the substantive provisions of the 1934 Act which they seek to enforce, not in the jurisdictional provision. The Court in *Borak* found a private cause of action implicit in § 14(a). We do not now question the actual holding of that case, but we decline to read the opinion so broadly that virtually every provision of the securities Acts gives rise to an implied private cause of action. The invocation of the "remedial purposes" of the 1934 Act is similarly unavailing. . . . Certainly, the mere fact that § 17(a) was designed to provide protection for brokers' customers does not require the implication of a private damages action in their behalf. To the extent our analysis in today's decision differs from that of the Court in *Borak*, it suffices to say that in a series of cases since *Borak* we have adhered to a stricter standard for the implication of private causes of action, and we follow that stricter standard today. The ultimate question is one of congressional intent, not one of whether this Court thinks that it can improve upon the statutory scheme that Congress enacted. . . .

[. . . . If there is to be a federal damages remedy under these circumstances, Congress must provide it. . . . Obviously, nothing we have said prevents Congress from creating a private right of action on behalf of brokerage firm customers for losses arising from misstatements contained in § 17(a) reports. But if Congress intends those customers to have such a federal right of action, it is well aware of how it may effectuate that intent.]

8. Federal Courts and Limited Jurisdiction. The modern Supreme Court's unwillingness to infer private rights of action proceeds in part from a recognition that federal courts are in a different position vis-à-vis Congress than state courts are with respect to state legislatures. Specifically, federal courts are courts of "limited jurisdiction" — they are only empowered to hear claims when authorized by Congress to do so. By contrast, state courts are often courts of general jurisdiction. As a rule, they can hear any manner of suit, whether grounded in state or federal law. Does it follow that state courts interpreting state regulatory statutes ought to be more inclined to infer rights of action when faced with statutory silence? For a debate among the justices of the Oregon Supreme Court on this issue that includes references to other cases raising the same debate, see *Bob Godfrey Pontiac, Inc. v. Roloff*, 630 P.2d 840 (Or. 1981).

9. Are There Still Federal Implied Rights of Action to Be Found? Decisions such as *Redington* have largely put the federal courts out of the business of inferring rights of action. By placing the ball in Congress's hands, the Supreme Court seems to have indicated that it will not recognize a cause of action unless Congress explicitly indicates an intent to create one. Of course, once Congress has done so, there is little room left for "implied" rights of action: either the statute creates an express cause of action or none will be recognized.

In an important 1988 decision in the area of securities fraud, the Court adopted the expansive and plaintiff-friendly doctrine of "fraud-on-the-market," which allows an investor to recover without proving that she herself relied on a defendant's misrepresentation. Basic v. Levinson, 485 U.S. 224 (1988). Although the Court has declined invitations to overrule *Basic*, *see* Haliburton v. Erica P. John Fund, 131 S. Ct. 2179 (2014), and has not questioned the existence of a private right of action under federal securities laws, it has made clear that it is uninterested in further expanding this form of liability, and arguably has imposed new limits on it. *See* Stoneridge Inv. Partners, LLC v. Scientific-Atlanta, Inc., 552 U.S. 148 (2008); Dura Pharmaceuticals v. Broudo, 544 U.S. 336 (2005).

10. From Statutes to Constitution. Thus far we have considered whether rights of action can be inferred from regulatory statutes that are silent as to whether they mean to empower persons injured by statutory violations to sue for those violations. The same issue has arisen in connection with the "supreme" law of the United States.

Bivens v. Six Unknown Named Agents of Federal Bureau of Narcotics

403 U.S. 388 (1971)

Brennan, J. The Fourth Amendment provides that:

> The right of the people to be secure in their persons, houses, papers, and effects, against unreasonable searches and seizures, shall not be violated. . . .

In Bell v. Hood, 327 U.S. 678 (1946), we reserved the question whether violation of that command by a federal agent acting under color of his authority gives rise to a cause of action for damages consequent upon his unconstitutional conduct. Today we hold that it does.

This case has its origin in an arrest and search carried out on the morning of November 26, 1965. Petitioner's complaint alleged that on that day respondents, agents of the Federal Bureau of Narcotics acting under claim of federal authority, entered his apartment and arrested him for alleged narcotics violations. The agents manacled petitioner in front of his wife and children, and threatened to arrest the entire family. They searched the apartment from stem to stern. Thereafter, petitioner was taken to the federal courthouse in Brooklyn, where he was interrogated, booked, and subjected to a visual strip search.

. . . [The complaint further alleges] that the arrest and search were effected without a warrant, and that unreasonable force was employed in making the arrest; fairly read, it alleges as well that the arrest was made without probable cause. Petitioner claimed to have suffered great humiliation, embarrassment, and mental suffering as a result of the agents' unlawful conduct, and sought $15,000 damages from each of them. The District Court . . . dismissed the complaint on the ground, inter alia, that it failed to state a cause of action. The Court of Appeals . . . affirmed on that basis. . . .

I

Respondents do not argue that petitioner should be entirely without remedy for an unconstitutional invasion of his rights by federal agents. In respondents' view, however, the rights that petitioner asserts — primarily rights of privacy — are creations of state and not of federal law. Accordingly, they argue, petitioner may obtain money damages to redress invasion of these rights only by an action in tort, under state law, in the state courts. In this scheme the Fourth Amendment would serve merely to limit the extent to which the agents could defend the state law tort suit by asserting that their actions were a valid exercise of federal power: if the agents were shown to have violated the Fourth Amendment, such a defense would be lost to them and they would stand before the state law merely as private individuals. . . .

We think that respondents' thesis rests upon an unduly restrictive view of the Fourth Amendment's protection against unreasonable searches and seizures by federal agents. . . . Respondents seek to treat the relationship between a citizen and a federal agent unconstitutionally exercising his authority as no different from the relationship between two private citizens. In so doing, they ignore the fact that power, once granted, does not disappear like a magic gift when it is wrongfully used. An agent acting — albeit unconstitutionally — in the name of the United States possesses a far greater capacity for harm than an individual trespasser exercising no authority other than his own. Accordingly, as our cases make clear, the Fourth Amendment operates as a limitation upon the exercise of federal power regardless of whether the State in whose jurisdiction that power is exercised would prohibit or penalize the identical act if engaged in by a private citizen. It guarantees to citizens of the United States the absolute right to be free from unreasonable searches and seizures carried out by virtue of federal authority. And "where federally protected rights have been invaded, it has been the rule from the beginning that courts will be alert to adjust their remedies so as to grant the necessary relief." Bell v. Hood, 327 U.S., at 684 (footnote omitted). . . .

First. Our cases have long since rejected the notion that the Fourth Amendment proscribes only such conduct as would, if engaged in by private persons, be condemned by state law. . . .

Second. The interests protected by state laws regulating trespass and the invasion of privacy, and those protected by the Fourth Amendment's guarantee against unreasonable searches and seizures, may be inconsistent or even hostile. Thus, [one is permitted by law to] bar the door against an unwelcome private intruder, or call the police if he persists in seeking entrance. The availability of such alternative means for the protection of privacy may lead the State to restrict imposition of liability for any consequent trespass. A private citizen, asserting no authority other than his own, will not normally be liable in trespass if he demands, and is granted, admission to another's house. But one who demands admission under a claim of federal authority stands in a far different position. The mere invocation of federal power by a federal law enforcement official will normally render futile any attempt to resist an unlawful entry or arrest by resort to the local police; and a claim of authority to enter is likely to unlock the door as well. "In such cases there is no safety for the citizen, except in the protection of the judicial tribunals, for rights which have been invaded by the officers of the government, professing to act in its name. There remains to him but the alternative of resistance, which may amount to crime." Nor is it adequate to answer that state law may take into account the different status of one clothed with the authority of the Federal Government. For just as state law may not authorize federal agents to violate the Fourth Amendment, neither may state law undertake to limit the extent to which federal authority can be exercised. The inevitable consequence of this dual limitation on state power is that the federal question becomes not merely a possible defense to the state law action, but an independent claim both necessary and sufficient to make out the plaintiff's cause of action.

Third. That damages may be obtained for injuries consequent upon a violation of the Fourth Amendment by federal officials should hardly seem a surprising proposition. Historically, damages have been regarded as the ordinary remedy for an invasion of personal interests in liberty. Of course, the Fourth Amendment does not in so many words provide for its enforcement by an award of money damages for the consequences of its violation. But "it is . . . well settled that where legal rights have been invaded, and a federal statute provides for a general right to sue for such invasion, federal courts may use any available remedy to make good the wrong done." Bell v. Hood, 327 U.S., at 684 (footnote omitted). The present case involves no special factors counseling hesitation in the absence of affirmative action by Congress. We are not dealing with a question of "federal fiscal policy," as in United States v. Standard Oil Co., 332 U.S. 301, 311 (1947). In that case we refused to infer from the Government-soldier relationship that the United States could recover damages from one who negligently injured a soldier and thereby caused the Government to pay his medical expenses and lose his services during the course of his hospitalization. Noting that Congress was normally quite solicitous where the federal purse was involved, we pointed out that "the United States (was) the party plaintiff to the suit. And the United States has power at any time to create the liability." *Id.*, at 316; *see* United States v. Gilman, 347 U.S. 507 (1954). Nor are we asked in this case to impose liability upon a congressional employee for actions contrary to no constitutional prohibition, but merely said to be in excess of the authority delegated to him by the Congress. Finally, we cannot accept respondents' formulation of the question as whether the availability of money damages is necessary to enforce the Fourth Amendment. For we have here no explicit congressional declaration that persons injured by a federal officer's violation of the Fourth Amendment may not recover money damages from the agents, but must instead be remitted to another remedy, equally effective in the view of Congress. The question is merely whether petitioner, if he can demonstrate an injury consequent upon the violation by federal agents of his Fourth Amendment rights, is entitled to redress his injury through a particular remedial mechanism normally available in the federal courts. "The very essence of civil liberty certainly consists in the right of every individual to claim the protection of the laws, whenever he receives an injury." Marbury v. Madison, 1 Cranch 137, 163, 2 L. Ed. 60 (1803). Having concluded that petitioner's complaint states a cause of action under the Fourth Amendment, we hold that petitioner is entitled to recover money damages for any injuries he has suffered as a result of the agents' violation of the Amendment. . . .

The judgment of the Court of Appeals is reversed. . . .

HARLAN, J. (concurring). . . .

For the reasons set forth below, I am of the opinion that federal courts do have the power to award damages for violation of "constitutionally protected interests" and I agree with the Court that a traditional judicial remedy such as damages is appropriate to the vindication of the personal interests protected by the Fourth Amendment. . . .

. . . [T]he judiciary has a particular responsibility to assure the vindication of constitutional interests such as those embraced by the Fourth Amendment. To be sure, "it must be remembered that legislatures are ultimate guardians of the liberties and welfare of the people in quite as great a degree as the courts." Missouri, Kansas & Texas R. Co. of Texas v. May, 194 U.S. 267, 270 (1904). But it must also be recognized that the Bill of Rights is particularly intended to vindicate the interests of the individual in the face of the popular will as expressed in legislative majorities; at the very least, it strikes me as no more appropriate to await express congressional authorization of traditional judicial relief with regard to these legal interests than with respect to interests protected by federal statutes.

The question then, is, as I see it, whether compensatory relief is "necessary" or "appropriate" to the vindication of the interest asserted. . . . In resolving that question, it seems to me that the range of policy considerations we may take into account is at least as broad as the range of a legislature would consider with respect to an express statutory authorization of a traditional remedy. In this regard I agree with the Court that the appropriateness of according Bivens compensatory relief does not turn simply on the deterrent effect liability will have on federal official conduct. Damages as a traditional form of compensation for invasion of a legally protected interest may be entirely appropriate even if no substantial deterrent effects on future official lawlessness might be thought to result. Bivens, after all, has invoked judicial processes claiming entitlement to compensation for injuries resulting from allegedly lawless official behavior, if those injuries are properly compensable in money damages. I do not think a court of law—vested with the power to accord a remedy—should deny him his relief simply because he cannot show that future lawless conduct will thereby be deterred.

And I think it is clear that Bivens advances a claim of the sort that, if proved, would be properly compensable in damages. The personal interests protected by the Fourth Amendment are those we attempt to capture by the notion of "privacy"; while the Court today properly points out that the type of harm which officials can inflict when they invade protected zones of an individual's life are different from the types of harm private citizens inflict on one another, the experience of judges in dealing with private trespass and false imprisonment claims supports the conclusion that courts of law are capable of making the types of judgment concerning causation and magnitude of injury necessary to accord meaningful compensation for invasion of Fourth Amendment rights. . . .

[I]t is apparent that some form of damages is the only possible remedy for someone in Bivens' alleged position. It will be a rare case indeed in which an individual in Bivens' position will be able to obviate the harm by securing injunctive relief from any court. However desirable a direct remedy against the Government might be as a substitute for individual official liability, the sovereign still remains immune to suit. Finally, assuming Bivens' innocence of the crime charged, the "exclusionary rule" is simply irrelevant.* For people in Bivens' shoes, it is damages or nothing.

The only substantial policy consideration advanced against recognition of a federal cause of action for violation of Fourth Amendment rights by federal officials is the incremental expenditure of judicial resources that will be necessitated by this class of litigation. There is, however, something ultimately self-defeating about this argument. For if, as the Government contends, damages will rarely be realized by plaintiffs in these cases because of jury hostility, the limited resources of the official concerned, etc., then I am not ready to assume that there will be a significant increase in the expenditure of judicial resources on these claims. Few responsible lawyers and plaintiffs are likely to choose the course of litigation if the statistical chances of success are truly de minimis. And I simply cannot agree with my Brother Black that the possibility of "frivolous" claims — if defined simply as claims with no legal merit — warrants closing the courthouse doors to people in Bivens' situation. There are other ways, short of that, of coping with frivolous lawsuits. . . .

. . . [T]he countervailing interests in efficient law enforcement of course argue for a protective zone with respect to many types of Fourth Amendment violations. But, . . . at the very least such a remedy would be available for the most flagrant and patently unjustified sorts of police conduct. Although litigants may not often choose to seek relief, it is important, in a civilized society, that the judicial branch of the Nation's government stand ready to afford a remedy in these circumstances. . . .

Burger, C.J. (dissenting). I dissent from today's holding which judicially creates a damage remedy not provided for by the Constitution and not enacted by Congress. We would more surely preserve the important values of the doctrine of separation of powers — and perhaps get a better result — by recommending a solution to the Congress as the branch of government in which the Constitution has vested the legislative

* [The exclusionary rule states that, subject to certain exceptions, evidence obtained unlawfully — for example, by means of an unconstitutional warrantless search — may not be used in a criminal prosecution to help convict the defendant. — Eds.]

power. Legislation is the business of the Congress, and it has the facilities and competence for that task—as we do not. . . .

[Chief Justice Burger proceeds with a lengthy critique of the exclusionary rule, see *supra* footnote*, arguing that it largely fails to deter official misconduct while permitting some who have committed crimes to escape conviction on technicalities.—EDS.] The problems of both error and deliberate misconduct by law enforcement officials call for a workable remedy. Private damage actions against individual police officers concededly have not adequately met this requirement, and it would be fallacious to assume today's work of the Court in creating a remedy will really accomplish its stated objective. . . . Jurors may well refuse to penalize a police officer at the behest of a person they believe to be a "criminal" and probably will not punish an officer for honest errors of judgment. In any event an actual recovery depends on finding non-exempt assets of the police officer from which a judgment can be satisfied.

I conclude, therefore, that an entirely different remedy is necessary but it is one that in my view is as much beyond judicial power as the step the Court takes today. Congress should develop an administrative or quasi-judicial remedy against the government itself to afford compensation and restitution for persons whose Fourth Amendment rights have been violated. The venerable doctrine of respondeat superior in our tort law provides an entirely appropriate conceptual basis for this remedy. If, for example, a security guard privately employed by a department store commits an assault or other tort on a customer such as an improper search, the victim has a simple and obvious remedy—an action for money damages against the guard's employer, the department store. W. Prosser, *The Law of Torts* § 68, pp.470-480 (3d ed., 1964). Such a statutory scheme would have the added advantage of providing some remedy to the completely innocent persons who are sometimes the victims of illegal police conduct. . . .

A simple structure would suffice. . . . Congress could enact a statute [effecting]:

(a) a waiver of sovereign immunity as to the illegal acts of law enforcement officials committed in the performance of assigned duties;

(b) the creation of a cause of action for damages sustained by any person aggrieved by conduct of governmental agents in violation of the Fourth Amendment or statutes regulating official conduct;

(c) the creation of a tribunal, quasi-judicial in nature . . . to adjudicate all claims under the statute. . . .

BLACK, J. (dissenting). . . . There can be no doubt that Congress could create a federal cause of action for damages for an unreasonable search in violation of the Fourth Amendment. Although Congress has created such a federal cause of action against state officials acting under color of state law,* it has never created such a cause of action

* "Every person who, under color of any statute, ordinance, regulation, custom, or usage, of any State or Territory, subjects, or causes to be subjected, any citizen of the United States or other person within the jurisdiction thereof to the deprivation of any rights, privileges, or immunities secured by the Constitution and laws, shall be liable to the party injured in an action at law, suit in equity, or other proper proceeding for redress." Rev. Stat. § 1979, 42 U.S.C. § 1983.

against federal officials. . . . Congress could, of course, create a remedy against federal officials who violate the Fourth Amendment in the performance of their duties. But the point of this case and the fatal weakness in the Court's judgment is that . . . Congress . . . has [not] enacted legislation creating such a right of action. For us to do so is, in my judgment, an exercise of power that the Constitution does not give us.

Even if we had the legislative power to create a remedy, there are many reasons why we should decline to create a cause of action where none has existed since the formation of our Government. The courts of the United States as well as those of the States are choked with lawsuits. The number of cases on the docket of this Court have reached an unprecedented volume in recent years. A majority of these cases are brought by citizens with substantial complaints — persons who are physically or economically injured by torts or frauds or governmental infringement of their rights; persons who have been unjustly deprived of their liberty or their property; and persons who have not yet received the equal opportunity in education, employment, and pursuit of happiness that was the dream of our forefathers. Unfortunately, there have also been a growing number of frivolous lawsuits, particularly actions for damages against law enforcement officers whose conduct has been judicially sanctioned by state trial and appellate courts and in many instances even by this Court. My fellow Justices on this Court and our brethren throughout the federal judiciary know only too well the time-consuming task of conscientiously poring over hundreds of thousands of pages of factual allegations of misconduct by police, judicial, and corrections officials. Of course, there are instances of legitimate grievances, but legislators might well desire to devote judicial resources to other problems of a more serious nature.

We sit at the top of a judicial system accused by some of nearing the point of collapse. Many criminal defendants do not receive speedy trials and neither society nor the accused are assured of justice when inordinate delays occur. Citizens must wait years to litigate their private civil suits. Substantial changes in correctional and parole systems demand the attention of the lawmakers and the judiciary. If I were a legislator I might well find these and other needs so pressing as to make me believe that the resources of lawyers and judges should be devoted to them rather than to civil damage actions against officers who generally strive to perform within constitutional bounds. There is also a real danger that such suits might deter officials from the proper and honest performance of their duties.

All of these considerations make imperative careful study and weighing of the arguments both for and against the creation of such a remedy under the Fourth Amendment. I would have great difficulty for myself in resolving the competing policies, goals, and priorities in the use of resources, if I thought it were my job to resolve those questions. But that is not my task. . . . Congress has not provided that any federal court can entertain a suit against a federal officer for violations of Fourth Amendment rights occurring in the performance of his duties. A strong inference can be drawn from creation of such actions against state officials that Congress does not desire to permit such suits against federal officials. Should the time come when Congress desires such lawsuits, it has before it a model of valid legislation, 42 U.S.C. § 1983, to create a damage remedy against federal officers. . . .

[Justice Blackmun dissented, largely on the grounds articulated by Justice Black. — Eds.]

NOTES AND QUESTIONS

1. *Rights of Action Against Whom?* *Bivens* renders *individual* federal officers liable for violating a person's Fourth Amendment rights. It does not purport to give rise to a claim against the federal government as employer of those officers. Under the common law doctrine of sovereign immunity (see Chapter 7), federal and state governments were immune from being held vicariously liable for governmental employees' torts under the doctrine of *respondeat superior.* As further explained in Chapter 7, Congress waived much of its common law immunity in 1946 by means of the Federal Tort Claims Act (FTCA). However, at the time of *Bivens,* the FTCA was written so as *not* to waive the government's immunity from liability for injuries caused by *intentional* employee misconduct of the sort alleged by Bivens. In 1974, in response to *Bivens,* Congress amended the FTCA to waive federal governmental immunity for intentional torts committed by "investigative or law enforcement officers" in the course of their official duties. Thus, today, a plaintiff such as Bivens would be able to bring an action against the federal government in its capacity as employer of the agents.

2. *Bivens and § 1983: Constitutional Torts.* As indicated in Justice Black's dissent, long before 1971, Congress had enacted a statute — currently codified as 42 U.S.C. § 1983 — that enables individuals to bring damage actions for violations of constitutional rights committed by *state* or *local government* officials. Thus, if the agents who had carried out the arrest of Bivens had been employed by the State or City of New York, Bivens could have relied on § 1983 to bring claims seeking to impose liability on those agents individually. The Supreme Court has since held that, under certain circumstances, § 1983 can also be invoked to impose liability on municipalities and other local governmental entities for maintaining policies that violate individuals' constitutional rights. However, the statute does not authorize suits for damages against a *state government* (or the federal government) for the enactment and perpetuation of unconstitutional policies. A great deal of civil rights litigation seeking damages has proceeded under § 1983, creating an area of law that (in conjunction with *Bivens* actions) is sometimes referred to as "constitutional torts."

3. *Implied Constitutional Rights of Action after Bivens.* After *Bivens,* the Court recognized implied rights of action against federal officials arising out of other provisions of the Constitution, including the Fifth Amendment's (implicit) Equal Protection principle, as well as the Eighth Amendment's ban on cruel and unusual punishment. Davis v. Passman, 442 U.S. 228 (1979); Carlson v. Green, 446 U.S. 14 (1980). However, as has been the case with statutory implied rights of action, the Court has subsequently shown much greater reticence in recognizing new claims. *See* Bush v. Lucas, 462 U.S. 367 (1983) (federal employee does not have a right of action against his supervisor for violating his First Amendment rights); Wilkie v. Robbins, 551 U.S. 537 (2007) (retaliation by U.S. official against plaintiff for asserting his Fifth Amendment rights, even if wrongful, is not actionable). One of the prime motivations for the Court's increasing reticence in statutory cases — the desire to place the ball in Congress's hands — presumably does not apply to the Constitution, which can be amended only with great difficulty. Instead, the Court in these later cases has pointed to the

availability of other remedies, including administrative procedures, as a reason not to recognize a private right of action. *See* Minneci v. Pollard, 132 S. Ct. 617 (2012) (rejecting an inmate's *Bivens* action for alleged Eighth Amendment violations against officials of a privately managed prison, primarily on the ground that the inmate could have brought a claim for the same conduct under state tort law).

4. *State Constitutions.* Should state courts follow the lead of *Bivens* and recognize private rights of action arising out of state constitutions? *See* Darwart v. Caraway, 58 P.3d 128 (Mont. 2002) (reviewing state court decisions on this issue and determining that about half have recognized *Bivens*-type claims).

REFERENCES/FURTHER READING

Negligence Per Se

Caroline Forell, *Statutory Torts, Statutory Duty Actions, and Negligence Per Se: What's the Difference?*, 77 Or. L. Rev. 497 (1998).

Paul Sherman, *Use of Federal Statutes in State Negligence Per Se Actions*, 13 Whittier L. Rev. 831 (1992).

Wrongful Death Acts

Jacob Lippman, *The Breakdown of Consortium*, 30 Colum. L. Rev. 651 (1930).

John F. Witt, *From Loss of Services to Loss of Support: The Wrongful Death Statutes, The Origins of Modern Tort Law, and the Making of the Nineteenth-Century Family*, 25 Law & Soc. Inquiry 717 (2000).

Claudia Zaher, *When a Woman's Marital Status Determined Her Legal Status: A Research Guide on the Common Law of Coverture*, 94 L. Lib. J. 459 (2002).

Private Rights of Action

Robert H. Ashford, *Implied Causes of Action under Federal Law: Calling the Court Back to* Borak, 79 Nw. U. L. Rev. 227 (1984).

Henry H. Drummonds, *The Dance of Statutes and the Common Law: Employment, Alcohol, and Other Torts*, 36 Willamette L. Rev. 939 (2000).

Caroline Forell, *The Statutory Duty Action in Tort: A Statutory/Common Law Hybrid*, 23 Ind. L. Rev. 781 (1990).

Tamar Frankel, *Implied Rights of Action*, 67 Va. L. Rev. 553 (1981).

Thomas Hazen, *Implied Private Remedies under Federal Statutes: Neither a Death Knell Nor a Moratorium — Civil Rights, Securities Regulation, and Beyond*, 33 Vand. L. Rev. 133 (1980).

Susan J. Stabile, *The Role of Congressional Intent in Determining the Existence of Implied Private Rights of Action*, 71 Notre Dame L. Rev. 861 (1996).

Donald H. Zeigler, *Rights, Rights of Action, and Remedies: An Integrated Approach*, 76 Wash. L. Rev. 67 (2001).

Constitutional Torts

John C. Jeffries, Jr., *Reversing the Order of Battle in Constitutional Torts*, 2009 Sup. Ct. Rev. 115.

John C. Jeffries, *Disaggregating Constitutional Torts*, 110 Yale L.J. 259 (2000).

Daryl J. Levinson, *Rights Essentialism and Remedial Equilibration*, 99 Colum. L. Rev. 857 (1999).

James E. Pfander, *Rethinking* Bivens*: Legitimacy and Constitutional Adjudication*, 98 Geo. L.J. 117 (2009).

Alexander A. Reinert, *Measuring the Success of* Bivens *Litigation and Its Consequences for the Individual Liability Model*, 62 Stan. L. Rev. 809 (2010).

Michael L. Wells, Scott v. Harris *and the Role of the Jury in Constitutional Litigation*, 29 Rev. Litig. 65 (2009).

David Zaring, *Three Models of Constitutional Torts*, 2 J. Tort L. #3 (2008).

CHAPTER 7

DEFENSES

Tort law identifies and enjoins various types of injurious misconduct. The law of negligence, for example, directs persons to refrain from injuring others by acting carelessly toward them. But tort law also identifies certain grounds on which persons who violate these directives are nonetheless spared liability or face only limited liability. Thus, a negligence plaintiff who can prove that she suffered an injury proximately caused by a defendant's carelessness toward her may still lose her suit or may recover only partial compensation. Some tort defenses have to do with the victim's role in bringing about her injury. Others have to do with the actor's status or the circumstances in which the actor acted. Some are provided by common law; others by statute.

If a party defending against a negligence or other tort claim believes that, notwithstanding the ability of the claimant to make out a prima facie case, there are grounds for defeating or limiting liability, it is usually up to that party to identify those grounds early in the proceedings. Doing so is known as raising an *affirmative defense*. Because the onus is on the defending party, a failure to assert a defense usually constitutes a waiver of the defense. For example, if a defendant wishes to invoke a statute of limitations to establish that the plaintiff has forfeited her claim by waiting too long before bringing suit, he normally must raise that argument in his answer to the plaintiff's complaint or in a motion to dismiss. A defendant who fails to do this loses his right to assert the defense, even if the facts support its application to the case.

In addition to having the obligation to plead defenses, the defendant also usually shoulders the burdens of production and persuasion. At times, however, courts will employ the technique of burden shifting that we have seen them employ to assist certain plaintiffs.

I. CONTRIBUTORY NEGLIGENCE AND COMPARATIVE RESPONSIBILITY

A. Contributory Negligence

In the introduction to Chapter 2, we provided a brief excerpt from an 1839 English decision, *Cotterill v. Starkey.* It stated that Starkey, as the driver of a horse-drawn carriage, owed a duty to take reasonable care not to injure pedestrians such as Cotterill. After describing this duty for the jury, and instructing it to deliberate on the question of whether Starkey's running down of Cotterill resulted from a want of due care on Starkey's part, the trial judge presented one other issue to the jury for resolution. This issue concerned the question of Cotterill's fault:

> [D]efendant says that the [accident] arose from the . . . careless and improper conduct of Mrs. Cotterill, which is denied by the plaintiff. You must say whether it arose from plaintiff's fault or not. . . . [You must find for the defendant if you are] satisfied that the matter arose from the . . . careless . . . conduct of Mrs. Cotterill.

The logic of this instruction might seem obvious, but it deserves some reflection. Why should the plaintiff lose just because her carelessness combined with the defendant's carelessness to cause her injury? Is the defendant getting off the hook merely because he happened carelessly to hurt someone who was not careful, as opposed to a careful victim? Why should the defendant benefit from that sort of luck? Notice that, under the judge's formulation, *any* carelessness on the part of the plaintiff that contributes to her injury results in a careless defendant paying nothing and the plaintiff suffering the full burden of the loss. This principle, known as *contributory negligence,* at one time conferred on negligence defendants a complete defense.

1. *Multiple Necessary Causes and Superseding Cause Revisited.* A succinct account of the contributory negligence defense is provided in another early nineteenth-century decision, this one issued by the Massachusetts Supreme Judicial Court. In *Smith v. Smith,* 19 Mass. 621 (1824), the plaintiff (Smith) was driving a wagon containing barrels of cider down a "circuitous" road at night. Defendant (also named Smith) had erected a pile of wood near the road. The plaintiff's horse and wagon struck the wood and the horse was injured. The plaintiff sued for negligence, alleging that defendant had failed to place the wood at a safe distance from the road. The jury was instructed that defendant could not be held liable if the jury found that the plaintiff "had not driven skillfully" and that that lack of skill contributed to the accident. The court upheld a defense verdict. It reasoned that, although a person who carelessly obstructs a highway is "amenable to the public [through a criminal] indictment," he is not to be held liable to an individual plaintiff in tort unless the obstruction "caused" an injury to the plaintiff. When the plaintiff himself was at fault, the court continued, the careless defendant, in the eyes of tort law, is *not* a cause of the injury.

The introduction to Chapter 4 stressed that the actual causation inquiry in negligence law should *not* be framed as a search for *the* (single) person or entity whose carelessness caused an injury, because injuries are always the product of multiple causes. The jury in *Smith* found that the plaintiff could have avoided the collision by driving carefully, hence his carelessness was *a* cause of his own injuries. But to reach this conclusion is by no means to deny that the defendant's carelessness was also a cause of the injuries. Yet the *Smith* court in effect held that, so long as carelessness on the part of the plaintiff is determined to have been *a* cause of his injury, he is totally responsible, notwithstanding that the defendant's carelessness also caused the injury.

It may be that nineteenth-century courts took this position as a result of confusion over how to think about actual causation. More likely, they consciously constructed this affirmative defense by analogy to certain proximate cause doctrines. Recall that, at this time, courts tended to treat certain forms of intervening third-party misconduct as *superseding causes*—i.e., causes that function to block the imposition of liability on more remote wrongdoers even though those remote wrongdoers had also played a role in bringing about the victim's injury. (*See* Chapter 5.) The defense of contributory negligence gave similar effect to fault on the part of the plaintiff. If the plaintiff's carelessness contributed to his injury, then as a matter of law his conduct would be deemed the only *legally relevant* cause of the injury.

Even granted the intelligibility of this analysis, the rule of contributory negligence did not seem to sit comfortably with other facets of proximate cause analysis. Consider a suit by a *careful* plaintiff against two careless defendants, both of whose carelessness combined to cause injury to the plaintiff.

For example, suppose the same facts as *Smith*, except that the driver's horse was not damaged, only the cider barrels he was carrying, which were owned by a person named Jones. Suppose Jones sued both Smiths—Smith the careless stacker of wood, and Smith the careless wagon driver. Could wood-stacker Smith have the claim against him dismissed on the ground that wagon-driver Smith's careless driving functioned as a superseding cause of the property loss suffered by Jones? Perhaps, but certainly by the early years of the twentieth century, courts would more typically deal with this imagined lawsuit by imposing liability on both Smiths, given that the carelessness of each functioned as a cause of the lost cider. (See Chapter 5's discussion of concurrent negligence.) Assume Jones could hold both Smiths liable for negligence on the ground that the carelessness of each was an actual and proximate cause of the damage to Jones's barrels. Would it make sense for the law to allow Jones to hold wood-stacker Smith liable yet at the same time bar wagon-driver Smith's suit against wood-stacker Smith for the very same negligence? Why should wagon-driver's Smith's carelessness have a different legal effect when he is the one suing wood-stacker Smith, rather than being sued as wood-stacker Smith's co-defendant?

2. *Limits: Intentional Torts and Last Clear Chance.* The rule of contributory negligence did not extend to claims alleging recklessness or intentional wrongdoing on the part of the defendant. *See* Restatement (Second) of Torts §§ 481, 503 (1965). Thus, carelessness by the plaintiff was treated as irrelevant in suits for battery of false imprisonment. That rule remains true today, notwithstanding the abandonment of contributory negligence in favor of comparative fault (discussed below).

Even in negligence cases, the harshness of the contributory negligence regime was ameliorated both by informal practices and explicit legal rules. Informally, jurors were often made aware of the harsh implications of a finding of contributory negligence. For example, they may have been apprised by the trial judge's instructions, as were the jurors in *Cotterill*, that they would be required to find for the defendant if they found that the plaintiff's fault played a role in her being injured. Given this awareness, some jurors may have "nullified" the formal law by declining to assign fault to a plaintiff who they thought deserving of compensation.

Did You Know?

Jury Nullification: Criminal and Civil Procedure

The phrase "jury nullification" is typically used to describe cases in which a criminal jury concludes that a defendant is guilty of a crime, yet acquits the defendant to avoid what it perceives to be an unjust application of the law. Some commentators contend that Anglo-American criminal law affirmatively authorizes jurors to nullify. Others maintain that they enjoy no such authority, but instead merely have a raw power to nullify because criminal acquittals are not reviewable on appeal and because jurors are not subject to legal sanction for misapplying the law.

In civil proceedings, any jury verdict can in principle be reexamined by a trial judge or appellate court on proper motion by the losing party. Suppose, for example, in a negligence suit governed by the rule of contributory negligence, a jury finds for the plaintiff even though there is substantial evidence that she was at fault. In such a case, the trial judge would be authorized to grant either a defense motion for judgment notwithstanding the verdict or a motion for a new trial. (See Chapter 1's discussion of civil procedure.) Nonetheless, because rules of civil procedure call for judges to invoke their oversight powers sparingly, with due deference to the jury, there is in practice a certain amount of space within civil litigation for jurors to engage in something akin to nullification.

Apart from this sort of *ad hoc* adjustment, nineteenth-century judges developed special rules to deal with certain cases in which it seemed counterintuitive to permit a defendant to avoid responsibility for an accident that he could have foreseen and avoided, just because the plaintiff's fault also contributed to the injury. Most important among these was the doctrine of *last clear chance*.

A typical last clear chance case would proceed as follows. Imagine that a railroad engineer employed by defendant *D* operates *D*'s train at a carelessly high speed. Plaintiff *P*, a farmer, carelessly drives his truck across a grade crossing so that it gets stuck on the track. Now suppose *P* can prove that, notwithstanding the train's excessive speed, the engineer could have prevented a collision with *P*'s truck by applying the train's brakes, yet for no good reason failed to do so. *D* would not be allowed to raise the affirmative defense of contributory negligence because, even though *P* was careless, *D* had the last clear chance to avoid the accident. (Notice that it is the plaintiff seeking to invoke last clear chance who bears the burden of proving the doctrine's applicability.)

In essence, the doctrine of last clear chance held that if a defendant has the last opportunity to prevent an accident resulting from careless acts of both the defendant and the plaintiff, the defendant will not enjoy the protection of the contributory negligence defense. Does this doctrine rest on an intelligible principle? Why should the temporal order of a defendant's and a plaintiff's respective careless acts make any difference for purposes of assigning responsibility? Is it because the defendant has, in effect, committed a second careless act by not responding appropriately to the plaintiff's carelessness?

3. *Doing Away with Contributory Negligence.* As the twentieth century wore on, dissatisfaction with the regime of contributory negligence mounted. Finally, in the period from about 1970 to 1990, contributory negligence was eliminated and replaced by schemes of comparative responsibility in all but five U.S. jurisdictions (Alabama, District of Columbia, Maryland, North Carolina, and Virginia). Sometimes its adoption was brought about by judicial decision, and sometimes through legislation. As explained below, comparative responsibility regimes differ in many respects. But all of them do away with the idea that *any* degree of carelessness on the part of the plaintiff constitutes a *per se* bar to recovery. As the following notes explain, under many comparative responsibility regimes, a plaintiff's fault can sometimes still function to bar her claim, but only in limited circumstances. More typically, the contribution of the plaintiff's fault to her injury is taken into account by reducing the amount of damages she stands to recover from the defendant.

4. *Terminology: Comparative Fault Versus Comparative Responsibility.* Conventional usage refers to the various schemes that have replaced contributory negligence as "comparative fault" regimes. This usage can occasionally be misleading. For example, in some jurisdictions, the factfinder in a suit alleging injuries arising from a defective product may be asked to apportion liability between an at-fault plaintiff and a defendant even though, because of the doctrine of "strict" products liability (discussed in Chapter 12), the plaintiff is not required to prove that the defendant acted carelessly. In this sort of case, the plaintiff's fault is not being compared to the defendant's fault, for there may have been no fault on the part of the defendant.

For this reason, the locution "comparative responsibility" is perhaps preferable as a label for the rules that allocate responsibility and liability between plaintiff and defendant. In turn, "comparative fault" could be limited to cases in which the comparison at issue concerns the relative degree of *carelessness* chargeable to plaintiff and defendant. Nevertheless, as indicated, it is standard for lawyers and courts to use "comparative fault" as the general or generic term for this branch of tort law.

5. *Terminology: Comparative Fault Versus Apportionment of Liability.* As just indicated, "comparative fault" is now the name most commonly given to the affirmative defense to negligence by which the plaintiff's own carelessness operates to limit (and in some cases defeat) defendant's liability. However, lawyers sometimes use the same phrase to refer not only to this plaintiff-versus-defendant comparison but also to rules governing how liability is to be apportioned between or among co-defendants (i.e., a defendant-versus-defendant comparison).

For example, imagine a variant on the case hypothesized toward the end of Note 1, *supra*, in which a wagon carrying cider barrels crashes and the owner of the cider sues both the wagon driver and the person who stacked wood at the side of the road into which the wagon crashed. Suppose the plaintiff was at fault (e.g., for using substandard barrels where ordinary barrels could have withstood the impact of the crash), and that both defendants were also at fault. Two issues may then arise: (1) the effect of the plaintiff's fault on plaintiff's recovery (the plaintiff-versus-defendants comparison); and (2) the effect of each defendant's fault on the percentage of plaintiff's damages that each of the two defendants must pay (the defendant-versus-defendant comparison).

While it involves a comparison of fault, the defendant-versus-defendant exercise obviously does not concern the question of whether the *plaintiff's* fault provides a defendant with a complete or partial defense to the plaintiff's tort claim. For this reason, it is perhaps less usefully placed under the heading of "comparative fault" and more usefully placed under the distinct heading of "apportionment of liability." The Third Restatement of Torts — unhelpfully to our minds — has taken the opposite tack by using the term "apportionment" to encompass both plaintiff-versus-defendant and the defendant-versus-defendant comparisons. *See* Restatement (Third) of Torts: Apportionment of Liability § 1 (2000).

One downside of the Restatement's approach is that it invites courts and commentators to pose generically the question of whether comparative fault should apply to "intentional tort" cases. Posing the question at this level of generality runs together the plaintiff-versus-defendant issue and the defendant-versus-defendant issue in a context that might seem to call for them to be treated differently. (The question of whether a victim's carelessness should defeat or limit her claim against an intentional tortfeasor is a very different question from whether liability for a victim's injury should be shared as between an intentional tortfeasor and a negligent tortfeasor.) Indeed, courts have generally concluded that "apportionment" between a careless plaintiff and an intentional-tortfeasor defendant is usually *in*appropriate (*i.e.*, that comparative fault is not even a partial defense to an intentional tort), whereas "apportionment" between an intentional tortfeasor and negligent tortfeasor is appropriate. *See* Note 2 following *Hunt v. Ohio Dep't of Rehabilitation & Correction, infra.*

B. Comparative Fault in Action

To move from a scheme of contributory negligence to one of comparative fault is, first and foremost, to reject the rule that a negligence claim must be dismissed upon a finding that some carelessness on the part of the claimant contributed to her injury. However, this negative proposition does not of itself answer the remaining question: How *should* the plaintiff's carelessness affect her claim? Conceptually, there are several possibilities.

One would be to give the plaintiff's fault *no effect*, that is, to treat it as irrelevant to a negligence defendant's liability, which is how it is treated with respect to injuries caused by defendants who commit intentional torts. This option appears never to have earned serious consideration within American law.

Another option would be to adopt the following rule: Responsibility shall be split evenly among the all parties whose fault is found to have contributed to the plaintiff's injury. Under this rule, a careless plaintiff such as the driver in *Smith v. Smith, supra*, would be entitled to recover 50 percent of his damages from a careless defendant simply because there are two at-fault parties among whom to divide legal responsibility. By the same rule, a careless plaintiff who has a claim for a single injury against two careless defendants — for example, imagine that, contrary to the actual facts of the case, the plaintiff in *McDonald v. Robinson* (Chapter 4) was at fault, as were the two defendants — would recover 66.67 percent of her damages, because liability would now be divided evenly among the three at-fault parties responsible for the plaintiff's injuries: plaintiff and the two defendants.

This approach to apportioning fault may strike you as intuitive. If so, that may be because you already encountered it in *Carroll Towing, supra* Chapter 3. *Carroll Towing* was an admiralty case, and admiralty law had long observed the scheme of "divided damages" for claims of property damage, even as the common law of tort applied the rules of contributory negligence. Still, the ancient pedigree of the admiralty rule did not stop the U.S. Supreme Court from reconsidering it.

United States v. Reliable Transfer Co.

421 U.S. 397 (1975)

Stewart, J. [A tanker owned by Reliable Transfer Co. ended up stranded on a sandbar. Reliable Transfer sued the United States for failing to maintain a flashing light that would have helped the ship's captain avoid the sandbar. The district court found that the vessel's grounding was caused 25 percent by the failure of the Coast Guard to maintain the light and 75 percent by the fault of the boat's captain. In so finding, the district court stated:]

> The fault of the vessel was more egregious than the fault of the Coast Guard. . . . Equipped with look-out, chart, searchlight, radiotelephone, and radar, he made use of nothing except his own guesswork judgment. After . . . turning in a loop toward the north so as to pass astern of [another vessel], he should have made sure of his position before setting his new . . . course. The fact that a northwest gale blowing at 45 knots with eight to ten foot seas made it difficult to see, emphasizes the need for caution rather than excusing a turn into the unknown. . . .

The [district] court held, however, that the settled admiralty rule of divided damages required each party to bear one-half of the damages to the vessel.[1]

II.

The precise origins of the divided damages rule are shrouded in the mists of history. . . .

---

1. The operation of the rule was described in *The Sapphire*, 18 Wall. 51, 56:

> It is undoubtedly the rule in admiralty that where both vessels are in fault the sums representing the damage sustained by each must be added together and the aggregate divided between the two. This is in effect deducting the lesser from the greater and dividing the remainder. . . . If one in fault has sustained no injury, it is liable for half the damages sustained by the other, though that other was also in fault.

plaintiff suing a single defendant will have her suit dismissed as a matter of law if the jury assigns more fault to her than to the defendant — that is, anything more than 50 percent of the responsibility for the accident.* Where such a bar is retained, the system is commonly described as a *modified* comparative responsibility regime. This is in contrast to a *pure* system, in which a plaintiff could in principle be found 99 percent at fault for her injuries and yet still recover 1 percent of her damages from an at-fault defendant.

The possible variations on modified comparative fault expand when the plaintiff is suing multiple defendants. Thus, a jurisdiction might adopt the rule that a careless plaintiff is barred from suing if her comparative fault is equal to the total fault of all those whom she is suing. Under this rule, if *P* is suing *D1* and *D2*, and *P* is found to be 40 percent at fault, whereas *D1* is held 50 percent at fault and *D2* 10 percent at fault, *P* would be able to recover from both *D1* and *D2*, and to recover a total of 60 percent of her damages. (How much of that 60 percent she can collect from each will depend on the rules for apportionment of liability, as well as the solvency and amenability to suit of each. *See* Note 8 *infra.*)

6. *Shades of Contributory Negligence?* In light of the fact that most states have adopted modified comparative responsibility regimes, one perhaps should take care not to overstate the significance of the transition from contributory negligence to comparative responsibility. A Nebraska decision illustrates how current law to some extent carries forward the spirit of the old regime.

In *Baldwin v. City of Omaha*, 607 N.W.2d 841 (Neb. 2000), the plaintiff was a college football player who had been hospitalized and medicated for severe mental illness, including a form of psychosis. Weeks after his discharge, he had a psychotic episode, endangering himself and others, which led two female police officers to attempt to subdue him to take him into custody. In the ensuing scuffle, one officer shot Baldwin, leaving him permanently paralyzed.

At a bench trial, Baldwin established to the trial judge's satisfaction that he was injured in part because the officers acted unreasonably in effecting his arrest. In particular, by "utterly failing" to follow standard police procedures for detaining suspects known to be mentally ill (as they knew Baldwin to be), and by thereby provoking a physical confrontation with a suspect whom they also knew to be unusually powerful, they unnecessarily created the need for use of deadly force. However, the defendants established that Baldwin was also negligent, if not reckless, because of his decision — made while he was still taking anti-psychotic medication and therefore not delusional — to discontinue the medication notwithstanding his awareness that doing so might cause him to act in ways dangerous to himself and others. The judge then assigned 55 percent responsibility to Baldwin and 45 percent to the officers.

* Wisconsin was among the leaders in the movement toward comparative fault, adopting it by legislation in 1931. As originally enacted, the statute specified that the plaintiff's claim would be barred if the jury attributed at least 49 percent responsibility to the plaintiff. The legislature moved to the present threshold of greater than 50 percent in 1971, in part because the 49 percent rule was thought to operate harshly given an apparent tendency among Wisconsin juries to divide fault evenly among plaintiffs and defendants. As indicated below, Wisconsin jurors are not informed of the legal consequences of their assignments of responsibility.

In doing so, the judge was aware that the Nebraska legislature had recently adopted a modified comparative fault regime. Like most states, Nebraska had for most of the twentieth century recognized contributory negligence as a complete bar to recovery. However, unlike many states, Nebraska's law lifted this bar if the plaintiff's fault was deemed by a jury to be "slight" in comparison to the defendant's relatively "gross" negligence. (In a case of relatively slight plaintiff's fault, the jury was instructed to reduce the plaintiff's damages by the percentage of fault attributed to the plaintiff.) In 1992, the state legislature replaced this scheme with a modified comparative fault regime under which a claimant's fault serves only to diminish his recovery, except that it bars recovery if the claimant's fault contributes to his injury to an equal or greater degree than the fault of all persons against whom he seeks recovery. 607 N.W.2d at 854. Thus, once the trial judge allocated greater fault to Baldwin, it was compelled to enter judgment for the defendants.

A divided Supreme Court affirmed, concluding that there was credible evidence to support the district court's apportionment of fault. *Id.* at 854. In effect, then, the same result was reached under Nebraska's new comparative fault regime as would have been reached under the old regime that barred claims brought by more-than-slightly-at-fault claimants. Assume that the trial judge's apportionment of fault was reasonable. Why should Baldwin lose his entire claim given that he was only a bit more at fault than the defendants? Would it make more sense to adopt a rule that only bars claims — as opposed to reducing damages — if the plaintiff is substantially more at fault than the defendant(s)?

In light of *Baldwin*, do you suppose that Nebraska's shift from the "more than slightly at fault" rule to the "at least as much at fault as the defendant(s)" rule will significantly decrease the number of claims that are barred outright on the grounds of plaintiff's comparative fault? Is it likely that this decrease has been much more significant in jurisdictions that, unlike Nebraska, recognized no exception to the contributory negligence bar for "slight" fault before shifting to modified comparative fault? Or might it be the case that, even in these jurisdictions, the plaintiffs who ended up being barred from recovery by judges and juries under the old rules of contributory negligence were by and large the same plaintiffs who today would be found "at least as much at fault" as defendants?

7. *Too Much Information?* Tennessee, like Wisconsin and Nebraska, is a modified comparative responsibility jurisdiction. Notice that Tennessee's model comparative fault instruction, reproduced above, as well as question 3 of the special verdict form, inform jurors that if they assign more fault to the plaintiff than the defendant, judgment will be entered for the defendant. Does it make sense to inform the jury of the legal effects that will follow from certain assignations of percentage fault? Most states either require or permit trial judges to inform jurors of these effects in instructions and/or special verdict forms. *See* Russell v. Stricker, 635 N.W.2d 734 (Neb. 2001) (applying Nebraska's comparative fault statute, which requires that the jury be instructed on the legal effects of its assignment of comparative fault). However, some state courts and legislatures have forbidden trial judges from informing jurors of such effects. The concern appears to be that jurors will adjust their calculation of

percentage fault to avoid seemingly harsh legal consequences that would follow from a "true" assignment of percentages. *See, e.g.*, McGowan v. Story, 234 N.W.2d 325, 328-330 (Wis. 1975) (refusing to abrogate the rule against informing juries of the legal effects of apportionment rulings).* Is it undesirable for jurors to adjust apportionments of responsibility in light of the legal consequences that will follow?

In a related vein, notice also that question 4 of Tennessee's model verdict form asks the jury to determine damages *without* regard to its assignment of percentage fault. Is it realistic to ask jurors to determine the dollar amount of damages while ignoring that those damages will be reduced by the percentage fault assigned to the plaintiff?

8. *Comparative Responsibility and Other Apportionment Rules.* Other rules concerning apportionment of damages will influence how a plaintiff's fault affects her recovery. For example, the doctrine of joint and several liability (discussed in a note following *Summers v. Tice* in Chapter 4, and below in Chapter 8) holds that any one of two or more at-fault defendants who cause a single "indivisible" injury can be held liable for 100 percent of plaintiff's damages. Now suppose a case involving a plaintiff adjudged by the jury to be 33 percent at fault for his injuries, and two at-fault defendants who are each deemed 33.5 percent at fault but whose conduct falls within the rule of joint and several liability. Should plaintiff be able to take advantage of joint and several liability, which would entitle him to recover 67 percent of his total damages from a party found to have been only 33.5 percent responsible? Or would that violate the principle of apportioning responsibility in accordance with each party's percentage fault? *See* Ravo v. Rogatnick, Chapter 8 *infra.*

9. *Comparative Fault and Causation.* It is tempting to think of comparative fault as a doctrine that requires the jury to make a finding only as to the unreasonableness of plaintiff's conduct. In fact, the defense requires a finding of fault *and* causation. Two famous New York cases illustrate this point. Both were decided under the old contributory negligence rules, but they nonetheless illuminate analysis under modern comparative fault systems.

The first decision is *Martin v. Herzog*, 126 N.E. 814 (N.Y. 1920), which was mentioned in Chapter 6 under the heading of negligence per se. There, the defendant was driving his car at dusk on the wrong side of the center line and slammed into a buggy driven by the plaintiff's decedent. The buggy was operating without lights in contravention of a New York statute. Writing for the majority, Cardozo held that the defendant driver could rely on the statute to establish that the plaintiff's conduct was *per se* unreasonable. Cardozo noted, however, that establishing the unreasonableness of the plaintiff's conduct was not sufficient to make out the defense of

---

* Some lower federal courts have interpreted Federal Rule of Civil Procedure 49(a), which empowers federal trial judges to submit special verdict forms to juries, as barring judges from informing jurors of the legal effects of assignments of percentage fault. This in turn has raised the question of whether, under *Erie v. Tompkins*, a federal court hearing a tort claim based on the law of a jurisdiction that mandates that juries be instructed as to the effects of their assignments of responsibility, should apply the federal rule or the conflicting state law. *See, e.g.*, Affiliated FM Ins. Co. v. Neosho Const. Co., 192 F.R.D. 662 (D. Kan. 2000) (concluding that rules about informing jurors is procedural rather than substantive, and therefore that the federal rule controls in federal court).

contributory negligence. Rather, the plaintiff's statutory violation would defeat her claim only if *it actually played a role in bringing about the injuries suffered by the decedent.* In other words, a defendant, as part of his burden of proving the affirmative defense of comparative fault, normally has to prove that but for plaintiff's fault the injury would not have happened.*

The second case is *Spier v. Barker*, 323 N.E.2d 164 (N.Y. 1974). There, the defendant drove a truck into plaintiff's car. The plaintiff, who was not wearing a seat belt, was ejected from the car, which rolled over onto her, breaking her leg. Defendant's expert witness testified that the plaintiff likely would not have suffered any serious physical injuries if she had worn her seat belt. The New York Court of Appeals reasoned that plaintiff's failure to use a seat belt could not constitute contributory negligence because there was no evidence that plaintiff's omission was a but-for cause of the *accident.* (It did not, for example, cause her to slide on her seat so as to lose control of her car.) However, the court also held that the jury could consider plaintiff's failure to wear a seat belt in determining whether she failed to take reasonable steps to "mitigate" her damages. Other courts have disagreed with the reasoning of *Spier*, holding that if the factfinder reasonably concludes that the failure to wear a seat belt was a but-for cause of plaintiff's *injuries*, a judge or jury can assign comparative fault to the plaintiff.**

Although in conflict, *Spier* and the decisions that reject it *both* accept that plaintiff's fault must play a causal role in producing the plaintiff's injury before it may be deemed "comparative fault." They disagree over how exactly to specify that role. *Spier* holds that plaintiff's carelessness must contribute to bringing about the accident that injured the plaintiff before it can be deemed comparative fault. Courts that reject *Spier* conclude that, so long as plaintiff's carelessness contributed to bringing about the *injury* that resulted from the accident, it may be treated as comparative fault, even if it did not make its contribution until after the accident.

The fact that *Spier* was decided under the old rule of contributory negligence perhaps influenced that court's analysis. By characterizing the issue as one of "mitigation" rather than contributory negligence, the court circumvented the all-or-nothing rule of contributory negligence, permitting the jury to factor the plaintiff's carelessness into the amount of damages she would recover. Notice that even today, the choice to characterize plaintiff's failure to wear a seat belt as "comparative fault" or "failure to mitigate" is not simply a matter of semantics. For example, in a modified comparative fault regime, the decision to treat such a failure as comparative fault entails that a plaintiff stands to lose her claim outright if the factfinder assigns a high enough percentage fault to that failure, as compared to the defendant's fault.

---

* In *Martin* itself, Cardozo further concluded that the statute not only set the standard of care that plaintiff's decedent had to meet, but also shifted the burden of proof to the plaintiff, requiring her to *disprove* causation by establishing that, even if the buggy had used lights, the accident still would have occurred. Ordinarily, however, the burden of proof will rest on the defendant.

** Still other courts have refused to permit the defendant to raise the issue of the plaintiff's failure to wear a seat belt. Often these are courts in jurisdictions that lack mandatory seat belt laws, thus supporting the inference that individuals are under no legal duty to wear seat belts and hence cannot be found at fault for failing to wear them.

Check Your Understanding

Contributory Negligence and Comparative Fault

While in the course of making deliveries for his employer, driver *D* parked his employer's large truck on the shoulder of a busy six-lane highway so that he could eat the lunch that he had packed for himself without having to exit the highway. Although his truck was not blocking any of the traffic lanes, its left side was only two feet from the right-hand edge of the right-hand lane.

A few minutes after *D* parked the truck, *P*, driving a passenger vehicle, slammed into the left rear corner of the truck and was seriously injured. *D* was uninjured. Although *P* was not intoxicated, he admits that, after having stayed up all night the previous night socializing, and after driving for three hours, he fell asleep at the wheel moments before the collision.

P has brought a negligence action against *D*'s employer. Assume that the total compensable losses suffered by *P* are $1 million. What might *P* expect to recover under each of the following rules?

1. Contributory negligence
2. Divided damages
3. Pure comparative fault
4. Modified comparative fault

II. ASSUMPTION OF RISK

Today, comparative fault provides the primary focal point for defense arguments for reducing or eliminating liability on the ground of the complainant's conduct. There is, however, another set of doctrines pertaining to the complainant's conduct that can affect the ability of the complainant to recover even granted his or her ability to make out a prima facie case. These are the doctrines gathered under the heading of *assumption of risk.* The basic notion is simple enough. Sometimes, a negligent actor will argue that the victim is barred from recovering either because she has agreed to relinquish her right to sue the defendant for its wrongful injuring of her or because she *knowingly and voluntarily* took on the risk that she might be injured *by careless conduct on the part of the defendant(s).* As should be apparent from even this brief description, assumption of risk will frequently raise issues that rest on the boundary line between tort and contract.

A. Express Assumption of Risk

Jones v. Dressel

623 P.2d 370 (Colo. 1981)

Erickson, J. . . . In an action for damages by the plaintiff for personal injuries sustained in an airplane crash, the trial court granted the defendants' motion for partial summary judgment. Summary judgment was based upon the execution of an exculpatory agreement which the court held insulated the defendants from liability for simple negligence involving the crash of an airplane. A claim alleging willful and wanton negligence is at issue in the trial court. The court of appeals affirmed. We affirm the court of appeals.

On November 17, 1973, the plaintiff, William Michael Jones, who was then seventeen years old, signed a contract with the defendant, Free Flight Sport Aviation, Inc. (Free Flight).[1] The contract allowed Jones to use Free Flight's recreational skydiving facilities, which included use of an airplane to ferry skydivers to the parachute jumping site. A covenant not to sue and a clause exempting Free Flight from liability were included in the contract:

> 2A. EXEMPTION FROM LIABILITY. The [plaintiff] exempts and releases the Corporation, its owners, officers, agents, servants, employees, and lessors from any and all liability, claims, demands or actions or causes of action whatsoever arising out of any damage, loss or injury to the [plaintiff] or the [plaintiff's] property while upon the premises or aircraft of the Corporation or while participating in any of the activities contemplated by this Agreement, whether such loss, damage, or injury results from the negligence of the Corporation, its officers, agents, servants, employees, or lessors or from some other cause.

The contract also contained an alternative provision which would have permitted Jones to use Free Flight's facilities at an increased cost, but without releasing Free Flight from liability for negligence.[2]

On December 28, 1973, Jones attained the age of eighteen. Ten months later, on October 19, 1974, he suffered serious personal injuries in an airplane crash which occurred shortly after takeoff from Littleton Airport. Free Flight furnished the airplane as part of its skydiving operation.

On November 21, 1975, nearly two years after attaining his majority, Jones filed suit against Free Flight alleging negligence and willful and wanton misconduct as the cause of the airplane crash. The defendants included the owners and operators of the airplane, the airport, and Free Flight. Based upon the exculpatory agreement, the trial court granted summary judgment in favor of the defendants. The court of appeals affirmed the trial court.

---

1. Even though Jones' mother had ratified the terms of this contract on November 16, 1973, it should be noted that the approval by a parent does not necessarily validate an infant child's contract. *See generally*, Kaufman v. American Youth Hostels, 13 Misc. 2d 8, 174 N.Y.S.2d 580 (1957); Fedor v. Mauwehu Council, Boy Scouts of America, 21 Conn. Sup. 38, 143 A.2d 466 (1958).

2. The record indicates that the alternative provision of the contract was crossed out when Jones signed the contract. However, the record does not establish that Free Flight would have prohibited Jones from participating in skydiving activities if the alternative provision had not been crossed out.

> 2B. ALTERNATE PROVISION. In consideration of the deletion of the provisions, 2A, 3, 4, and 5 herein regarding ASSUMPTION OF RISK, EXEMPTION FROM LIABILITY, COVENANT NOT TO SUE, INDEMNITY AGAINST THIRD PARTY CLAIMS, and CONTINUATION OF OBLIGATIONS, the Participant has paid the additional sum of $50.00 upon execution of this agreement, receipt of which is hereby acknowledged by the Corporation.
>
> 2C. It is understood that acceptance of this ALTERNATIVE PROVISION does not constitute a contract of insurance, but only waives Corporation's contractual defenses which would otherwise be available.

Jones asserts three grounds for reversal of the summary judgment. First, he claims that he disaffirmed the contract with Free Flight within a reasonable time after he attained his majority by filing suit. Second, he asserts that the exculpatory agreement is void as a matter of public policy. Third, he contends that inasmuch as an exculpatory agreement must be strictly construed against the party seeking to avoid liability for negligence, the injuries which he sustained as a result of the airplane crash were beyond the scope of the agreement. . . .

II. Ratification

As a matter of public policy, the courts have protected minors from improvident and imprudent contractual commitments by declaring that the contract of a minor is voidable at the election of the minor after he attains his majority. . . . A minor may disaffirm a contract made during his minority within a reasonable time after attaining his majority or he may, after becoming of legal age, by acts recognizing the contract, ratify it.

. . . What act constitutes ratification or disaffirmance is ordinarily a question of law to be determined by the trial court. We conclude, however, that the trial court properly determined that Jones ratified the contract, as a matter of law, by accepting the benefits of the contract when he used Free Flight's facilities on October 19, 1974. . . .

III. The Contract

Jones' assertion that his contract with Free Flight is void as a matter of public policy, raises two issues: (A) whether the contract with Free Flight is an adhesion contract; and (B) the validity of the exculpatory provisions of the contract. . . .

A. Adhesion Contract

An adhesion contract is a contract drafted unilaterally by a business enterprise and forced upon an unwilling and often unknowing public for services that cannot readily be obtained elsewhere. *See* Chandler v. Aero Mayflower Transit Company, 374 F.2d 129 (1967); A. Ehrenzweig, *Adhesion Contracts in the Conflict of Laws*, 53 Col. L. Rev. 1072. An adhesion contract is generally not bargained for, but is imposed on the public for a necessary service on a take or leave it basis.

. . . [T]his Court [has] stated that even though a contract is a printed form and offered on a "take-it-or-leave-it" basis, those facts alone do not cause it to be an adhesion contract. There must be a showing "that the parties were greatly disparate in bargaining power, that there was no opportunity for negotiation, or that [the] services could not be obtained elsewhere."[Quoted authority omitted. — Eds.] . . .

We conclude that the record in the instant case supports the trial court's determination that the contract between Jones and Free Flight was not an adhesion contract as a matter of law. . . .

We also agree with the court of appeals' conclusion that nothing in the record establishes a disparity in bargaining power, or that the services provided by Free Flight could not be obtained elsewhere.

B. The Exculpatory Provisions

Jones asserts that the exculpatory agreement is void as a matter of public policy. We disagree. The defendants contend that Barker v. Colorado Region, 35 Colo. App. 73, 532 P.2d 372 (1974), is dispositive of the issue of the validity of the exculpatory agreement. In *Barker*, the court of appeals held that an exculpatory clause in a contract relating to recreational activities will be given effect where the intention of the parties is expressed in sufficiently clear and unequivocal language and does not fall within any of the categories where the public interest is directly involved.

Jones, however, claims that summary judgment should not have been granted for three reasons. First, he argues that because exculpatory agreements must be strictly construed against the party seeking exemption, the agreement here does not insulate the defendants from liability for negligence in connection with a crash that occurred prior to the time that Jones made a parachute jump. Second, he claims that Free Flight was acting as a common carrier when it carried Jones, for compensation, to an altitude from which he could make a parachute jump, and that a common carrier by air cannot compel a passenger to release or limit the carrier's legal liability for its own negligence. Third, he contends that Free Flight, which is engaged in the private air charter business and operates under a Part 135 Certificate, is subject to FAA regulations which impose standards of safety upon the pilot of an airplane, and that Free Flight cannot contract away its liability for negligence in the performance of a duty imposed by law or where the public interest requires performance.

The determination of the sufficiency and validity of an exculpatory agreement is a question of law for the court to determine. . . .

An exculpatory agreement, which attempts to insulate a party from liability from his own negligence, must be closely scrutinized, and in no event will such an agreement provide a shield against a claim for willful and wanton negligence. In determining whether an exculpatory agreement is valid, there are four factors which a court must consider: (1) the existence of a duty to the public; (2) the nature of the service performed; (3) whether the contract was fairly entered into; and (4) whether the intention of the parties is expressed in clear and unambiguous language. *See* Rosen v. LTV Recreational Development, Inc., 569 F.2d 1117 (10th Cir. 1978); . . . Threadgill v. Peabody Coal Co., 34 Colo. App. 203, 526 P.2d 676 (1974). . . .

Measured against the four factors which determine the validity of an exculpatory agreement, we conclude that the trial court correctly held, as a matter of law, that the exculpatory agreement was valid. Therefore, the granting of defendants' motion for summary judgment was not error.

The duty to the public factor is not present in this case. In Tunkl v. Regents of University of California, 60 Cal. 2d 92, 383 P.2d 441, 32 Cal. Rptr. 33 (1963), the California Supreme Court stated:

> In placing particular contracts within or without the category of those affected with a public interest, the courts have revealed a rough outline of that type of transaction in which exculpatory provisions will be held invalid. Thus the

> attempted but invalid exemption involves a transaction which exhibits some or all of the following characteristics. It concerns a business of a type generally thought suitable for public regulation. The party seeking exculpation is engaged in performing a service of great importance to the public, which is often a matter of practical necessity for some members of the public. The party holds himself out as willing to perform this service for any member of the public who seeks it, or at least for any member coming within certain established standards. As a result of the essential nature of the service, in the economic setting of the transaction, the party invoking exculpation possesses a decisive advantage of bargaining strength against any member of the public who seeks his services. In exercising a superior bargaining power the party confronts the public with a standardized adhesion contract of exculpation, and makes no provision whereby a purchaser may pay additional reasonable fees and obtain protection against negligence. Finally, as a result of the transaction, the person or property of the purchaser is placed under the control of the seller, subject to the risk of carelessness by the seller or his agents. *Id.* . . . at 444.

In light of the foregoing factors, we conclude that the contract between Jones and Free Flight does not fall within the category of agreements affecting the public interest. . . .

Jones also claims that Free Flight was operating as a common carrier when it accepted funds and provided an aircraft to ferry him to an altitude from which he could make a parachute jump. He is correct in his statement that releases or limitations of liability in airline tickets issued by a common carrier have uniformly been held invalid. Conklin v. Canadian Colonial Airways, Inc., 266 N.Y. 244, 194 N.E. 692 (1935); Curtiss-Wright Flying Service, Inc. v. Glose, 66 F.2d 710 (3d Cir. 1933), *cert. denied*, 290 U.S. 696, 78 L. Ed. 599, 54 S. Ct. 132 (1938). *See* L. Kreindler, I. *Aviation Accident Law* § 3.13 (rev. 1977). He is in error, however, in his contention that Free Flight was operating as a common carrier in the instant case. C.F.R. § 135.1(a)(3). 14 C.F.R. § 1.1 provides:

> "Commercial operator" means a person who, for compensation or hire, engages in the carriage by aircraft in air commerce of persons or property, other than as an air carrier or foreign air carrier or under the authority of Part 375 of this Title. Where it is doubtful that an operation is for "compensation or hire," the test applied is whether the carriage by air is merely incidental to the person's other business or is, in itself, a major enterprise for profit. . . .

Here, the facts are clear that Free Flight was not engaged in "commercial operations" or acting as a common carrier in connection with this skydiving flight. In fact, paragraph four of Jones' complaint alleges that Free Flight was "engaged in the business of operating a service for the general aviation public involving parachuting, soaring, and aerobatics. . . ." Carriage by air was incidental to Free Flight's principal business. . . .

While it is not necessary for a contract to embody all of the characteristics set forth in *Tunkl, supra,* to meet the test, we conclude that an insufficient number of these characteristics are present in the instant case to establish that the contract between Jones and Free Flight affected the public interest. The service provided by Free Flight was not a matter of practical necessity for even some members of the public; because the service provided by Free Flight was not an essential service, it did not possess a decisive advantage of bargaining strength over Jones; and the contract was not an adhesion contract.

Finally, in our consideration of the remaining factors that must be reviewed in considering the validity of an exculpatory agreement, we note that there was no disagreement between the parties that the contract was fairly entered into. Likewise, the agreement expressed the parties' intention in clear and unambiguous language; the contract used the word "negligence" and specifically included injuries sustained "while upon the aircraft of the Corporation."

We conclude that the exculpatory agreement was not void as a matter of public policy, and that there was no genuine issue as to any material fact.

Accordingly, the trial court properly granted a partial summary judgment on the simple negligence issue and we, therefore, affirm the decision of the court of appeals.

"I see you signing this liability waiver, just in case you act on my advice."

Dalury v. S-K-I, Ltd.

670 A.2d 795 (Vt. 1995)

Johnson, J. We reverse the trial court's grant of summary judgment for defendants S-K-I, Ltd. and Killington, Ltd. in a case involving an injury to a skier at a resort operated by defendants. We hold that the exculpatory agreements which defendants require skiers to sign, releasing defendants from all liability resulting from negligence, are void as contrary to public policy.

While skiing at Killington Ski Area, plaintiff Robert Dalury sustained serious injuries when he collided with a metal pole that formed part of the control maze for a ski lift line. Before the season started, Dalury had purchased a midweek season pass and signed a form releasing the ski area from liability. The relevant portion reads:

> Release from Liability and Conditions of Use
>
> 1. I accept and understand that Alpine Skiing is a hazardous sport with many dangers and risks and that injuries are a common and ordinary occurrence of the sport. As a condition of being permitted to use the ski area premises, I freely accept and voluntarily assume the risks of injury or property damage and release Killington Ltd., its employees and agents from any and all liability for personal injury or property damage resulting from negligence, conditions of the premises, operations of the ski area, actions or omissions of employees or agents of the ski area or from my participation in skiing at the area, accepting myself the full responsibility for any and all such damage or injury of any kind which may result.

Plaintiff also signed a photo identification card that contained this same language.

Dalury and his wife filed a complaint against defendants, alleging negligent design, construction, and placement of the maze pole. Defendants moved for summary judgment, arguing that the release of liability barred the negligence action. The trial court, without specifically addressing plaintiffs' contention that the release was contrary to public policy, found that the language of the release clearly absolved defendants of liability for their own negligence.

The trial court based its decision on Douglass v. Skiing Standards, Inc., 142 Vt. 634, 637, 459 A.2d 97, 99 (1983), in which we held that an exculpatory agreement was sufficient to bar a negligence action by a professional freestyle skier who was injured in a skiing competition, and two subsequent decisions of the United States District Court for the District of Vermont. *See* Estate of Geller v. Mount Snow Ltd., No. 89-66, slip op. at 5-6 (D. Vt. May 21, 1991) (summary judgment granted where plaintiff recreational skier signed release on back of ski pass); Barenthein v. Killington Ltd., No. 86-33, slip op. at 7 (D. Vt. June 17, 1987) (summary judgment granted where plaintiff signed equipment rental agreement which contained a release). The trial court did not view the distinction between professional and recreational skiing as significant, and granted summary judgment on the ground that the release was clear and unambiguous.

On appeal, plaintiffs contend that the release was ambiguous as to whose liability was waived and that it is unenforceable as a matter of law because it violates public policy. We agree with defendants that the release was quite clear in its terms. Because we hold the agreement is unenforceable, we proceed to a discussion of the public policy that supports our holding.

I.

This is a case of first impression in Vermont. While we have recognized the existence of a public policy exception to the validity of exculpatory agreements, see Lamoille Grain Co. v. St. Johnsbury & L.C.R.R., 135 Vt. 5, 7, 369 A.2d 1389, 1390 (1976) (public policy forbids a railroad from limiting its duty of care to the public, but this rule does not extend to the railroad's private contractual undertakings), in most of our cases, enforceability has turned on whether the language of the agreement was sufficiently clear to reflect the parties' intent.

Even well-drafted exculpatory agreements, however, may be void because they violate public policy. Restatement (Second) of Torts § 496B comment e (1965). According to the Restatement, an exculpatory agreement should be upheld if it is (1) freely and fairly made, (2) between parties who are in an equal bargaining position, and (3) there is no social interest with which it interferes. § 496B comment b. The critical issue here concerns the social interests that are affected.

Courts and commentators have struggled to develop a useful formula for analyzing the public policy issue. The formula has been the "subject of great debate" during "the whole course of the common law," and it had proven impossible to articulate a precise definition because the "social forces that have led to such characterization are volatile and dynamic." Tunkl v. Regents of Univ. of Cal., 60 Cal. 2d 92, 383 P.2d 441, 444, 32 Cal. Rptr. 33, 36 (1963).

The leading judicial formula for determining whether an exculpatory agreement violates public policy was set forth by Justice Tobriner of the California Supreme Court. *Id.* at 444-46, 32 Cal. Rptr. at 36-38. An agreement is invalid if it exhibits some or all of the following characteristics:

[The court proceeded to quote the same language from *Tunkl* that is quoted above in *Jones v. Dressel.*—Eds.] Applying these factors, the court concluded that a release from liability for future negligence imposed as a condition for admission to a charitable research hospital was invalid. *Id.* at 449, 32 Cal. Rptr. at 41. . . .

[The court reviewed decisions from other states.—Eds.]

Having reviewed . . . various formulations of the public policy exception, we accept them as relevant considerations, but not as rigid factors that, if met, preclude further analysis. Instead, we recognize that no single formula will reach the relevant public policy issues in every factual context. Like the court in Wolf v. Ford, 335 Md. 525, 644 A.2d 522, 527 (Md. 1994), we conclude that ultimately the "determination of what constitutes the public interest must be made considering the totality of the circumstances of any given case against the backdrop of current societal expectations."

II.

Defendants urge us to uphold the exculpatory agreement on the ground that ski resorts do not provide an essential public service. They argue that they owe no duty to plaintiff to permit him to use their private lands for skiing, and that the terms and conditions of entry ought to be left entirely within their control. Because skiing, like

other recreational sports, is not a necessity of life, defendants contend that the sale of a lift ticket is a purely private matter, implicating no public interest. . . . We disagree.

Whether or not defendants provide an essential public service does not resolve the public policy question in the recreational sports context. The defendants' area is a facility open to the public. They advertise and invite skiers and nonskiers of every level of skiing ability to their premises for the price of a ticket. At oral argument, defendants conceded that thousands of people buy lift tickets every day throughout the season. Thousands of people ride lifts, buy services, and ski the trails. Each ticket sale may be, for some purposes, a purely private transaction. But when a substantial number of such sales take place as a result of the seller's general invitation to the public to utilize the facilities and services in question, a legitimate public interest arises.

The major public policy implications are those underlying the law of premises liability. In Vermont, a business owner has a duty "of active care to make sure that its premises are in safe and suitable condition for its customers." Debus v. Grand Union Stores, 159 Vt. 537, 546, 621 A.2d 1288, 1294 (1993). We have recognized this duty of care where the defendant's routine business practice creates a foreseeable hazard for its customers. The business invitee "has a right to assume that the premises, aside from obvious dangers, [are] reasonably safe for the purpose for which he [is] upon them, and that proper precaution [has] been taken to make them so." Garafano v. Neshobe Beach Club, 126 Vt. 566, 572, 238 A.2d 70, 75 (1967). We have already held that a ski area owes its customers the same duty as any other business—to keep its premises reasonably safe.

The policy rationale is to place responsibility for maintenance of the land on those who own or control it, with the ultimate goal of keeping accidents to the minimum level possible. Defendants, not recreational skiers, have the expertise and opportunity to foresee and control hazards, and to guard against the negligence of their agents and employees. They alone can properly maintain and inspect their premises, and train their employees in risk management. They alone can insure against risks and effectively spread the cost of insurance among their thousands of customers. Skiers, on the other hand, are not in a position to discover and correct risks of harm, and they cannot insure against the ski area's negligence.

If defendants were permitted to obtain broad waivers of their liability, an important incentive for ski areas to manage risk would be removed, with the public bearing the cost of the resulting injuries.

For these reasons, we disagree with the decisions of the United States District Court for the District of Vermont, upholding exculpatory agreements similar to the one at issue here. We do not accept the proposition that because ski resorts do not provide an essential public service, such agreements do not affect the public interest. A recognition of the principles underlying the duty to business invitees makes clear the inadequacy of relying upon the essential public service factor in the analysis of public recreation cases. While interference with an essential public service surely affects the public interest, those services do not represent the universe of activities that implicate public concerns.

Moreover, reliance on the private nature of defendants' property would be inconsistent with societal expectations about privately owned facilities that are open to the general public. Indeed, when a facility becomes a place of public accommodation, it "render[s] a 'service which has become of public interest' in the manner of the innkeepers and common carriers of old." Lombard v. Louisiana, 373 U.S. 267, 279, 10 L. Ed. 2d 338, 83 S. Ct. 1122 (1963) (Douglas, J., concurring) (citation omitted) (quoting German Alliance Ins. v. Kansas, 233 U.S. 389, 408, 58 L. Ed. 1011, 34 S. Ct. 612 (1914)). Defendants are not completely unfettered, as they argue, in their ability to set the terms and conditions of admission. Defendants' facility may be privately owned, but that characteristic no longer overcomes a myriad of legitimate public interests. Public accommodations laws that prohibit discrimination against potential users of the facility are just one example of limitations imposed by law that affect the terms and conditions of entry. . . .

Reversed and remanded.

NOTES AND QUESTIONS

1. *Express Assumption of Risk and the Idea of Waiver.* The phrase "assumption of risk" refers to at least two distinct ideas. The first, on display in *Jones* and *Dalury*, is that a plaintiff who is injured by the negligence of another can sometimes be barred from suing the other because she has formally ceded or abandoned the right to redress that tort law would otherwise confer on her. We will refer to this as the idea of "waiving" one's torts rights. When courts invoke "express" assumption of risk, they are usually invoking this notion of waiver.

Alternatively, "assumption of risk" refers to the idea of a plaintiff being barred from suing for negligence because she was aware of a discrete, immediate, and significant risk of injury posed to her by carelessness on the part of the other, yet freely chose to proceed so as to expose herself to that risk. In contrast to the waiver idea, there is no suggestion in this second iteration that the plaintiff has even thought about giving away her right to seek redress for a wrong done to her. Rather, the plaintiff is deemed to lose that right because of the way in which her conduct contributed to her being injured. (Thus, as we will see, there is a close resemblance between this version of assumption of risk doctrine and the doctrine of comparative fault.) When courts invoke "implied" assumption of risk, they often have this latter idea in mind, though, as we will see, they may have other ideas in mind as well.

2. *The Importance of Options.* How important to the *Jones* court was it that the defendant offered the plaintiff the option to pay $50 more to reserve his right to sue for negligently caused injuries? If that option were not available, would the court have found that Jones had waived his tort rights? What exactly does a customer get for $50? A guarantee that the company would pay all damages if it is found to have negligently caused them? An agreement not to contest liability? Would one worry that customers might misunderstand what they are getting for their money? How did the company arrive at $50 as the price for the right to sue?

3. *The Importance of Typeface.* How important is the typeface and font size of a written waiver clause? In *Wang v. Whitetail Mt. Resort*, 933 A.2d 110 (Pa. Super. Ct. 2007), the intermediate appellate court held in a 2 to 1 decision that the plaintiff had knowingly waived her right to sue a ski resort for injuries sustained while "snow tubing" despite the fact that she alleged that the risk she suffered — a negligent instruction by the defendant's employee to walk into the path of an oncoming patron — was

not within her contemplation when she signed the release. Critical to the court's decision was the fact that the "[t]he release at issue was placed prominently in a separately titled paragraph in the middle of a single page document; the release was in a font larger then that used to draft the other portions of the form; finally, the release is highlighted through the use of emboldened capital letters." According to the majority, this feature of the form helped to distinguish the result in *Wang* from a decision by the same court only a year earlier that had reversed a trial judge's grant of a defense motion for summary judgment on the strength of a written waiver. *See* Chepkevich v. Hidden Valley Resort, 911 A.2d 946 (Pa. Super. Ct. 2006).

4. Skydiving Versus Skiing. Do the different outcomes in *Jones* and *Dalury* turn on the different characteristics of skydiving and skiing? What characteristics? Why are those salient to the question of how to interpret, and whether to enforce, contractual waiver provisions? Does the business of operating a ski resort implicate "public policy" concerns in a way that the business of operating a skydiving school does not?

In *Berry v. Greater Park City Co.*, 171 P.3d 442 (Utah 2007), the plaintiff was seriously injured while competing in a "skiercross" race held at defendant's ski resort. A skiercross race involves multiple skiers simultaneously descending a course that features difficult turns and jumps, with each skier trying to complete the course first. Plaintiff sued on claims of negligence and gross negligence (among others), alleging that the defendant had designed the race course in way that made it unreasonably dangerous to racers.

Defendant moved for summary judgment. As to plaintiff's negligence claim, the defendant relied on the release signed by the plaintiff, which purported to waive liability for "injury or death resulting from participating in the [race], regardless of cause, including the negligence of [the defendant and its] employees and agents." *Id.* at 444. As to plaintiff's gross negligence claim, defendant did not rely on the release, but instead argued that a reasonable juror would have to rule for the defendant on the breach issue. The trial court granted the motion as to both claims.

The Utah Supreme Court affirmed judgment for the defendant on the plaintiff's negligence claim, but reversed and remanded on the gross negligence claim. As to the former, it reasoned that the policy considerations disfavoring enforcement of waivers of negligence liability for injuries arising out of recreational skiing do not apply to a kind of skiing that involves only a "limited group of expert, competitive skiers." *Id.* at 448. Skiercross racing, it concluded, is "a form of competition [that] has simply not generated sufficient public interest . . . to generate a call for intervention of state regulatory authority." *Id.* Is this distinction persuasive? Is it consistent with the results and reasoning in *Jones* and *Dalury*?

5. Bailments and Common Carriers. A "bailment" occurs when one person hands over personal property to another for safekeeping. The owner of the property is referred to as the "bailor," and the temporary custodian is deemed the "bailee." Bailees often attempt to relieve themselves from liability for all damage caused to the owner's property during the bailment, even if caused by the bailee's carelessness. A common example is provided by parking garages that, through signs or language on the back of ticket stubs, disclaim liability for "any damage" that befalls cars while parked on the premises. Most courts have refused to permit commercial bailees to exculpate themselves in this manner on the grounds that such provisions are against public policy. As *Jones* and *Dalury* note, the same holds true for attempts by common carriers — commercial operators of boats, buses, planes, taxis, and trains — to exculpate themselves for personal injury and property damage liability. If this is the case, why do some professional bailees and common carriers continue to include exculpatory clauses on signage and ticket stubs?

6. *Defining the Scope of the Waiver.* The waivers in both *Jones* and *Dalury* define the risks waived by reference to activities by either the defendants or the plaintiffs or by location (e.g., "upon premises or aircraft" or "the premises . . . of the ski area"). To what extent do these waivers cover injuries unrelated to the sporting activities that occur on the defendants' premises?

Courts have held that injuries resulting from slips and falls in showers and around swimming pools at health clubs are included in the waivers of liability signed by patrons. *See* Day v. Fantastic Fitness, 378 S.E.2d 166 (Ga. App. 1989); Owen v. Vic Tanny's Enterps., 199 N.E.2d 280 (Ill. App. 1964). By contrast, in *Hawkins v. Capital Fitness, Inc.*, 29 N.E.3d 442 (Ill. App. 2015), the court held that a fitness club patron's suit for injuries caused when a mirror fell off a wall in the club was not precluded by the club's liability waiver. *Hawkins* distinguished *Owen*, reasoning that a patron could not be expected to contemplate the sort of injury suffered by the plaintiff.

Suppose a patron in a health club is injured by the defendant's having mixed cleaning compounds in a manner that produced an explosion. Would this sort of injury be covered by a waiver of claims for injuries occurring on the premises? *See* Larsen v. Vic Tanny Int'l, 474 N.E.2d 729 (Ill. App. 1984) (no waiver). What if Dalury had contracted food poisoning because of improperly prepared food that was served at the snack bar owned and operated by the defendant ski resort? Would that injury have fallen within the scope of the risks identified in the waiver?

7. *Express Assumption of Risk, Breach, and Comparative Fault.* The core holding of *Dalury* is that the trial court erred in granting summary judgment to the ski resort on the basis of the waiver contained in its passes and photo IDs. On remand, Dalury would presumably still have to prove that the placement of the pole was careless and that it proximately caused his injury. Does anything in the court's ruling preclude the defendant from arguing that Dalury was comparatively at fault? In concluding that the resort was not permitted to waive its liability through contract, did the court determine that, as a matter of law, Dalury acted reasonably? If not, how much did Dalury really gain from this ruling?

B. Implied Assumption of Risk

Smollett v. Skayting Dev. Corp.

793 F.2d 547 (3d Cir. 1986)

Hunter, J. On February 15, 1981, Helene Smollett and her husband attended a fundraiser at a skating rink owned by Skayting Development Corporation. Smollett, who was thirty-three years old at that time, is an experienced skater. Although she had not skated for the two years before she went to the appellant's rink, she had skated over fifty times in her life.

When Smollett and her husband entered the rink, they noticed that there were no guardrails. They discussed this with the owner, Les Cooper, who told them that this design was the practice at many new rinks to further safety by avoiding the use of guardrails which could become loose and collapse unexpectedly. Smollett did not take skating lessons although they were offered to everyone at the fundraiser.

The skating area, which had a polyurethane surface, was raised three to five inches higher than the surrounding floor, which was carpeted. Smollett skated for about ninety minutes, until 7:50 p.m., without mishap. The rink was not overcrowded, with fifty to one hundred people skating. There were eight skateguards working that night and at least two were on the skating floor. Several signs reading "skate at your own risk" were posted in the rink. The skaters included many children and inexperienced skaters. At 7:50 p.m. Smollett's husband wished to leave. She told him she would join him after she took two last turns around the rink. On her last lap, Smollett skated behind a young child who fell. To avoid the child and a skater on her left, she swerved to the right onto the carpeted area. She fell and broke her left wrist. Her injury required surgery on the day of the accident and again one year later.

Smollett and her husband filed this suit against the rink. As a defense, Skayting asserted that Smollett had assumed the risk of injury. After a two day jury trial on December 17 and 18, 1984, the jury returned a verdict for Smollett but made no award to her husband. Because the jury found Smollett 50% at fault, her award was reduced from $50,000 to $25,000. The court denied Skayting's motion for judgment notwithstanding the verdict or, in the alternative, for a new trial.

. . .

We hold that it was error to deny the skating rink's motion for judgment notwithstanding the verdict because there was insufficient evidence to find that Smollett had not assumed the risk of injury. The Virgin Islands has enacted a comparative negligence statute, V.I. Code Ann. tit. 5, § 1451 (Supp. 1985) and thereby removed the contributory negligence bar to recovery. Assumption of risk is still available as a complete defense to a negligence claim but it has been limited by enactment of the comparative negligence statute. Assumption of risk, to the extent it incorporates the concept of fault on the part of the actor and, therefore, overlaps with contributory negligence, is no longer available as a defense. However, assumption of risk can still be applied to "non-negligent conduct which constitutes waiver or consent" Keegan v. Anchor Inns, Inc., 606 F.2d 35 (3d Cir. 1979) but which involved no negligence. In such cases the absolute bar to recovery remains.

The evidence in this case shows that Smollett fully understood the risk of harm to herself and voluntarily chose to enter the area of risk. *See Restatement (Second) of Torts* § 496C (1965). She, therefore, implicitly assumed the risk of injury. Smollett admitted that she was aware that there were no guardrails, that the skating area was covered with a smooth surface and was elevated, and that the area around the rink was carpeted. All of these circumstances were clearly visible as was the fact that young and inexperienced skaters were at the rink that day.

Smollett contends that she did not assume the risk because she was not aware of the dangerous condition created by the combination of three circumstances at the rink: 1) lack of guardrails; 2) elevated skating area; 3) difference in coefficient of friction between the skating surface and the surrounding carpeted area. We believe that Smollett was aware of the risk of falling when going from the skating area to the surrounding carpeted area. To reach the rink she had to walk on the carpeted area with her skates and, therefore, she had to be aware that the carpet slowed down the wheels on the skates. She had skated many times before and knew that other skaters might fall down in her path.

We conclude that Smollett assumed the risk of injury. We will reverse the judgment of the district court denying a judgment notwithstanding the verdict and direct the district court to enter judgment for Skayting Development Corporation.

Mansmann, J. (dissenting) . . . I believe that the defendant has not demonstrated that the record lacks a minimum quantum of evidence from which a jury could reasonably have afforded relief. Therefore, I would affirm the judgment of the district court.

I.

Assumption of the risk is an affirmative defense which has traditionally been considered an absolute bar to recovery. Although the Virgin Islands has enacted a contributory negligence statute which permits recovery on a pro rata basis where the plaintiff's negligence does not exceed that of the defendant, V.I. Code Ann. tit. 5, § 1451 (Supp. 1985), the assumption of the risk doctrine is nonetheless an available, although limited, defense. *Keegan v. Anchor Inns, Inc.*, 606 F.2d 35 (3d Cir. 1979). As we noted in *Keegan*, the assumption of the risk doctrine "embraces two distinct concepts-one akin to waiver or consent, the other a species of negligence." *Id.* at 39 n. 5. . . . To the extent that the assumption of risk doctrine involves a negligence theory, the doctrine has been replaced by the Virgin Islands contributory negligence statute. To the extent that the theory involves a consent or waiver principle, it remains a viable defense. . . .

In *Keegan*, we explained that portion of the assumption of the risk theory which continues to operate as an absolute bar to recovery.

> Assumption of risk in its primary and strict sense involves voluntary exposure to an obvious or known danger which negates liability. Under this concept *recovery is barred because the plaintiff is assumed to have relieved the defendant of any duty to protect him.* (emphasis added) (citations omitted).

Id. at 39 n. 5 (quoting *Pritchard*, 350 F.2d at 484). The defendant, who asserts the assumption of the risk defense in its primary sense "has the burden of demonstrating that no duty was owed plaintiff." *Smith v. Seven Springs Farm, Inc.*, 716 F.2d 1002, 1008 (3d Cir. 1983)] (citing Restatement (Second) of Torts § 496G (1965)). "Defendant can sustain its burden by proving that plaintiff knew of the risk, appreciated its character, and voluntarily chose to accept it." *Smith*, 716 F.2d at 1008-09 [internal citation omitted]. The defendant must also demonstrate that the "plaintiff's conduct in knowingly and voluntarily confronting the risk was reasonable." *Smith*, 716 F.2d at 1009 [internal citation omitted].

II.

The defendant here claims that the jury's failure to find assumption of the risk was against the clear weight of the evidence. . . .

The plaintiff admits that she was aware of the separate hazards which contributed to her injuries: the lack of guardrails, the elevation of the skating surface, and the different textures of the carpeted surface and the polyurethaned skating floor. The plaintiff maintains, however, that the defendant is relying impermissibly on the assumption of the risk doctrine in its secondary sense as a theory of negligence. . . .

. . . While the evidence does indicate that the plaintiff knew of the separate hazards, there is no evidence that the plaintiff knew of and appreciated how the various hazards could work in combination. The majority speculates that the plaintiff must have known of the risk because she had walked on the carpeted area with her skates and was aware, therefore, that the carpet slowed her rate of speed. The majority's speculation suggests only that the plaintiff was aware of the separate hazard of the carpeted area. It does not address the issue of the plaintiff's knowledge of the risk created by the combined hazards. . . .

In addition, there is evidence in the record which tends to counter a finding of waiver or consent. The plaintiff and her husband did ask Les Cooper, owner of the defendant skating rink, about the safety of the rink in the absence of guardrails. They were told that the no-guardrail design was used for safety reasons. In light of this representation, I cannot say that all reasonable people would conclude that the combined hazard was so obvious that the plaintiff assumed the risk and that the defendant owed no duty to the plaintiff. . . .

Because there is room for doubt on the questions of the plaintiff's knowledge and understanding and the reasonableness of her conduct, we should not disturb the jury's verdict. I would find that the district court did not err in denying the defendant's motion for a new trial on the basis of the assumption of the risk doctrine.

. . . .

NOTES AND QUESTIONS

1. *Recreational Activities.* Implied assumption of risk — like implied consent to a touching that would otherwise be a battery (*see* Chapter 9) — rests on the idea that one can infer from a plaintiff's conduct that she has made a certain kind of informed choice, such that she loses her right to complain about a danger that has been realized in the form of an injury. Critically, the conditions at the time of choice must attest to a genuinely knowing and voluntary decision to encounter an identified danger. This is why implied assumption of risk finds a natural home in *recreational activities*. Because they tend not to be compulsory and involve an inherent element of physicality, they pose risks of physical harm to which participants, at least under some circumstances, can plausibly be deemed to have voluntarily exposed themselves.

2. *The Industrial Workplace and the "Unholy Trinity."* Other environments, particularly industrial workplaces, are ill-suited to support a notion of implied assumption of risk, simply because employees' choices about the conditions under which they

must work are significantly constrained. Notwithstanding these contraindications, courts in the period from roughly 1850 to 1920 showed themselves quite willing to deem blue-collar workers to have assumed the risk of various job-related dangers. This in turn induced in many commentators a jaundiced view of the entire defense. Indeed, in this period, the doctrine was branded by some to be one prong of an "unholy trinity" of defense-friendly negligence doctrines. (The other two were contributory negligence and the "fellow servant rule," under which an employee injured on the job because of another employee's negligence was barred from invoking the doctrine of *respondeat superior* to recover from the employer.) Employee and scholarly support for the adoption of workers' compensation schemes as a substitute for negligence law was driven to a considerable degree by a desire to eliminate these defenses as obstacles to recovery of compensation for workplace injuries. *See* N.Y. Central R.R. Co. v. White, Chapter 11.

3. *What Must the Plaintiff Appreciate and Choose to Encounter?* Consider the facts identified by the *Smollett* majority as supporting the conclusion that Smollett's negligence claim was defeated on the grounds of her implicit assumption of risk. For the defense to apply, what exactly did she have to understand or appreciate about the situation? Assume that Smollett—as an experienced skater—appreciated the individual risks that the lack of guardrails, the elevation of the skating surface, and the different textures of the carpeted surface and the polyurethane skating floor posed. How would the defendant prove that she appreciated how they operated "in combination"?

4. *Implied Assumption of Risk in an Era of Comparative Fault.* As the *Smollett* judges note, the Virgin Islands' adoption by statute of a comparative fault regime raised a question as to the continued viability of the implied assumption of risk defense. Although the statute does not say anything explicitly on the question, the plaintiff argued that it should be construed to eliminate *every* all-or-nothing plaintiff-conduct defense, regardless of whether the defense rested on plaintiff's unreasonable conduct (comparative fault) or plaintiff's knowing and voluntary encounter of the dangers associated with the defendant's negligence (implied assumption of risk). The idea underlying this argument is that the latter sort of conduct really just is a special instance of the more general category of "unreasonable" or "imprudent" plaintiff conduct and therefore is subsumed under the idea of comparative fault, as opposed to being a distinct defense.

As *Smollett* explains, the federal Court of Appeals for the Third Circuit, which has jurisdiction to resolve questions of substantive Virgin Islands law, had taken an intermediate position on this issue in its earlier *Keegan* decision. *Keegan* concluded that the statutory adoption of comparative fault eliminated the implied assumption of risk defense for any instance in which the plaintiff's conduct could plausibly be described as *both* unreasonable *and* a voluntary encountering of a known and discrete danger. (The unreasonableness of the conduct, in other words, was deemed to take priority over its voluntariness for purposes of determining the significance of that conduct for defendant's liability.) However, under *Keegan*, if the plaintiff's decision to encounter a risk is *reasonable* (which by definition precludes a finding of comparative fault), the defense of implied assumption of risk can still apply. Applying this latter prong of *Keegan*'s holding, the *Smollett* majority concludes that, because the plaintiff's decision to skate despite the missing railing was knowing, voluntary, *and* reasonable, the plaintiff's claim was barred under the doctrine of implied assumption of risk. Do you agree that *Smollett* acted reasonably with respect to her own safety?

Notice one odd effect of *Keegan*'s partial subsumption of implied assumption of risk into comparative fault. Under *Keegan*, plaintiffs who unreasonably choose to encounter certain risks may still obtain partial compensation from the careless defendant because of the operation of comparative fault principles. By contrast, a plaintiff like Smollett, who *reasonably* chooses to encounter a danger, is barred entirely from recovery. How can it be that reasonable plaintiffs fare worse than unreasonable plaintiffs? Wouldn't it make more sense to adopt the mirror image of the Third Circuit's rule? Under this approach, for any instance in which a plaintiff's conduct is both unreasonable and a knowing and voluntary decision to encounter a certain danger, the latter qualities of the plaintiff's conduct should "trump" the former, such that the complete defense of implied assumption of risk will apply rather than the (potentially) partial defense of comparative fault. If this were the rule, plaintiffs who "unreasonably" choose to encounter the relevant dangers will not fare better than plaintiffs who make such choices reasonably—both will be barred from recovery. (This approach lessens a jury's dilemma of "penalizing" a risk-seeker for engaging in rational deliberation before facing an unreasonable risk; the reasonable and the unreasonable risk taker will be treated equally harshly.)*

5. *Implied Assumption of Risk as Comparative Fault.* In part to avoid the oddity of treating reasonable plaintiffs more harshly than unreasonable plaintiffs, many jurisdictions—contrary to the Third Circuit's interpretation of Virgin Islands' law—have ruled by statute or judicial decision that the adoption of comparative fault has *completely eliminated* implied assumption of risk as a distinct defense. Under the law of these jurisdictions, defendants are still free to argue to the jury that the plaintiff was aware of the risk of injury and voluntarily chose to encounter it. However, a defendant who proves such an argument will no longer automatically be entitled to a complete defense. Instead, that proof is factored into the jury's percentage allocation of fault among defendant and plaintiff. (Of course, in a modified comparative fault regime, if the jury finds that the plaintiff's knowing and voluntary assumption of the risk renders the plaintiff more than 50 percent at fault, or more at fault than the defendant, it may still function as a total defense.)

Interestingly, these same jurisdictions have not eliminated *express* assumption of risk. What explains this difference in treatment? What is so important about a writing? If defendant can muster evidence of behavior or conversation that supports the conclusion that the plaintiff knowingly and freely subjected herself to the risk of defendant's carelessness, why shouldn't that evidence have the same legal effect as a writing attesting to the same facts? Or is the notion underlying express assumption of risk

---

* On this approach, instances of unreasonable plaintiff conduct that have nothing to do with knowing and voluntary encounters with danger—for example, unreasonable plaintiff conduct involving inadvertence or inattentiveness—would continue to be handled under the doctrine of comparative fault.

sufficiently distinct from the notion at work in an implied assumption of risk case so as to justify the different treatment?

6. *New York's "Hybrid" Statute.* New York law has retained implied assumption of risk as a distinctive affirmative defense, yet at the same time has converted it into a partial rather than complete defense. This "hybrid" scheme emerged out of judicial interpretations of the somewhat unusual language of New York's comparative fault statute. That statute directs that plaintiff's damages "shall be diminished in the proportion which the culpable conduct attributable to the claimant . . . bears to the culpable conduct which caused the damages." N.Y. C.P.L.R. § 1411. New York's courts have deemed the plaintiff's assumption of risk to count as "culpable conduct." Thus, the statute converts assumption of risk into a partial defense without subsuming it entirely into comparative fault. As a result, a defendant subject to New York law can, if the facts support it, request that the jury be instructed to assign a percentage of responsibility to the plaintiff *either* because the plaintiff carelessly contributed to his own injury or because the plaintiff assumed the risk of the defendant's negligence. *See, e.g.*, McCabe v. Easter, 516 N.Y.S.2d 515 (App. Div. 1987). The New York Court of Appeals has, however, read into Section 1411 a complete bar to recovery for those who are injured by carelessness while participating in sports or recreational activities. Turcotte v. Fell, 502 N.E.2d 964 (N.Y. 1986).

7. *"Primary" Versus "Secondary" Assumption of Risk: Knight v. Jewett.* In her *Smollett* dissent, Judge Mansmann quotes a prior decision distinguishing assumption of risk in its "'primary and strict sense'"—i.e., as a doctrine of consent or waiver according to which the plaintiff is assumed to have "relieved" the defendant of any duty to take care not to injure the plaintiff—from assumption of risk understood as a kind of carelessness or imprudence on the part of the plaintiff. In the subsequent and influential decision of *Knight v. Jewett*, 834 P.2d 696 (Cal. 1992), the California Supreme Court used the nomenclature of "primary" assumption of risk to identify a related but ultimately distinct doctrine.

According to *Knight*, the term "primary" assumption of risk, despite its name, does not refer to an affirmative defense to negligence. Instead, it identifies a special rule of *no duty*, under which participants in a certain kind of activity (typically a recreational sport), simply by virtue of their decision to participate, are owed no duty of reasonable care by other participants. Under this doctrine, one who plays in a pick-up football game or undertakes recreational water skiing is barred from suing another participant even if the other's carelessness causes injury to the victim, at least so long as a judge or jury determines that the carelessness in question formed one of the risks "inherent" in the activity.

There are two crucial differences between *Knight*'s notion of primary assumption of risk as a no-duty doctrine and the traditional defense of implied assumption of risk that was applied in *Smollett*. As a no-duty doctrine, primary assumption of risk poses a question of law for the court rather than a question of fact for the jury, which in turn empowers courts to be more aggressive in excluding the operation of negligence law from certain domains of conduct. Moreover, the question asked under the heading of primary assumption of risk does *not* concern whether the participant in the relevant activity actually (subjectively) appreciated and chose to encounter the relevant dangers. If the plaintiff's participation was voluntary and if the risk realized was one of the risks "inherent" in the activity, the doctrine can apply even if the plaintiff did not know of the relevant dangers or sought not to be subjected to them as she was participating.

For courts that have adopted *Knight*'s nomenclature, "secondary" assumption of risk refers to the affirmative defense discussed in *Smollett.* If the relevant jurisdiction uses the primary-secondary terminology and also adopts the approach evinced in *Smollett* of folding only unreasonable decisions to encounter risks into comparative fault (not reasonable decisions to do so), its courts may speak and write in terms of "reasonable" and "unreasonable" secondary assumptions of risk. Some courts sympathetic with California's approach to negligence have questioned the utility of the terms "primary" and "secondary" assumption of risk in the context of sports-related injuries. *See* Crawn v. Campo, 266 N.J. Super. 599 (App. Div. 1993).

8. *Inherent Risk Statutes.* Many of the states that have eliminated implied assumption of risk as a separate defense by folding it into comparative fault have nonetheless found ways to reintroduce all-or-nothing limitations that resemble the implied assumption of risk defense. For example, several have enacted statutes specifying that all skiers assume the risks that are "inherent" in that sport, including risks associated with the use of ski lifts and tows. *See, e.g.*, N.J.S.A. § 5:13-5. Others have enacted statutes that specify a general assumption of risk defense against negligence claims based on injuries arising out of participation in a sport. *See, e.g.*, 12 Vt. Stat. Ann. § 1037 (a person who takes part in a sport "accepts as a matter of law the dangers that inhere therein insofar as they are obvious and necessary").

The references in these statutes to "inherent" risks is potentially confusing. If, for example, "inherent" means "inevitable" — that is, ineliminable even by the exercise of due care — they are merely restating the common law requirement that a negligence plaintiff cannot prevail without proving that the defendant acted carelessly. Apparently, however, the statutes were intended to bar actions arising out of certain forms of careless conduct on the part of resort owners that are commonly encountered in skiing. What sort of careless acts are these?

In the context of claims against the owners and operators of the venues in which sporting activities take place, it is hard to see what, if any, careless activity on *their* part should be deemed "inherent." Consider again claims against ski resorts. Suppose skier *S* is injured when the ski-lift gondola in which she is riding collapses because of the resort's failure to service the lift. It would be bizarre to say that *S* accepted *that sort* of carelessness as an inherent risk of skiing. Are there *any* risks of owner/operator *carelessness* that *S* might plausibly be deemed to have accepted? Failure to remove difficult-to-see man-made obstacles on the slopes? Jumps or moguls carelessly built into beginner slopes? Other skiers carelessly colliding with them?* In an omitted

* Keep in mind that the focus here is on claims against owners and operators. If the claim is for injuries resulting from being struck by a careless skier, the plaintiff would have to show that the owner/operator was at fault for encouraging, or not taking reasonable measures to control, careless skiing. Presumably this showing could not be made simply by establishing that careless skiing sometimes occurred on the grounds. If an inherent risk statute could be invoked to limit liability

portion of the *Dalury* opinion, the court dismissed the defendant's argument that Vermont's inherent risk statute entailed that Dalury had assumed the risk of running into carelessly placed poles as a matter of law. In doing so, it seemed to question whether the statute could ever be invoked by resort owners:

> The statute places responsibility for the "inherent risks" of any sport on the participant, insofar as such risks are obvious and necessary. A ski area's own negligence, however, is neither an inherent risk nor an obvious and necessary one in the sport of skiing.

670 A.2d at 800.

Inherent risk statutes are more readily applied to claims of negligence brought by one participant in a sport against another. Under the statutes, participants in events such as amateur softball or basketball games are deemed to have accepted the risk of injury caused by certain common forms of careless conduct on the part of fellow participants. Examples might include the careless tossing of a ball or a bat during a friendly softball game. However, if the injury results from recklessness or intentional misconduct on the part of another participant, it may still be actionable. Should the statutes bar claims even by novices who are not aware of risks of careless conduct that more experienced players would find obvious?

"I think there's a 'design flaw' in these moguls."

---

in this scenario, it would arguably be denying liability not on assumption-of-risk grounds, but instead by setting a *per se* rule of careful conduct, to wit: "As a matter of law it shall not be careless for the owner and operator of a ski resort merely to fail to prevent isolated instances of careless skiing from occurring on the premises."

9. Implied Assumption of Risk Versus No Breach. There are at least some instances in which implied assumption of risk rulings seem strongly to resemble no-breach-as-a-matter-of-law rulings. Cardozo provided a famous example of this phenomenon in *Murphy v. Steeplechase Amusement Co.*, 166 N.E. 173 (N.Y. 1929).

Plaintiff, "a vigorous young man," boarded a Coney Island amusement ride known as the "Flopper." It consisted of a conveyer belt moving away from the customer at a very high speed, perhaps as quickly as a gym treadmill set at a rate that would require the user to run rapidly. The belt was surrounded on both sides by padding designed to break customers' falls. The challenge was to step and stay on the belt without losing one's balance. After watching others "flop," plaintiff boarded the ride and fell, breaking his kneecap. He later sued in negligence and obtained a jury verdict of $5,000.

Cardozo's opinion held that, insofar as plaintiff's theory was that the defendant acted carelessly in operating a device that caused its riders to tumble, the claim was barred because the plaintiff had assumed the risk of being injured by that sort of negligence:

> Something more was here, as every one understood, than the slowly-moving escalator that is common in shops and public places. A fall was foreseen as one of the risks of the adventure. There would have been no point to the whole thing, no adventure about it, if the risk had not been there. The very name above the gate, the Flopper, was warning to the timid. If the name was not enough, there was warning more distinct in the experience of others. We are told by the plaintiff's wife that the members of her party stood looking at the sport before joining in it themselves. Some aboard the belt were able, as she viewed them, to sit down with decorum or even to stand and keep their footing; others jumped or fell. The tumbling bodies and the screams and laughter supplied the merriment and fun. "I took a chance," she said when asked whether she thought that a fall might be expected. . . .
>
> *Volenti non fit injuria.** One who takes part in such a sport accepts the dangers that inhere in it so far as they are obvious and necessary, just as a fencer accepts the risk of a thrust by his antagonist or a spectator at a ball game the chance of contact with the ball. . . . The antics of the clown are not the paces of the cloistered cleric. The rough and boisterous joke, the horseplay of the crowd, evokes its own guffaws, but they are not the pleasures of tranquility. The plaintiff was not seeking a retreat for meditation. Visitors were tumbling about the belt to the merriment of

* ["To one who chooses [to encounter a risk] no wrong is done." — Eds.]

> onlookers when he made his choice to join them. He took the chance of a like fate, with whatever damage to his body might ensue from such a fall. The timorous may stay at home.

The suit was then remanded for a new trial on an alternative theory, namely that the padding provided by the defendant to break riders' falls was inadequate.

It seems fair to say, on these facts, that the plaintiff implicitly assumed the risk of falling *by virtue of the normal motion of the conveyer belt.* But isn't this just a roundabout way of saying that, as a matter of law, it is not careless to operate an amusement ride that causes people to fall down onto a padded surface? (Assume for these purposes that the padding was adequate.) Is Cardozo using implied assumption of risk as a stand-in for no breach?

As Kenneth Simons has noted, there is another troubling aspect to Cardozo's analysis in *Murphy*, which is that the above-quoted language fails to engage directly the plaintiff's main allegation of fault. The claim was that the machine contained a defect that caused the belt to *jerk forward* rather than to run smoothly, as it was designed to do. Cardozo and his brethren were apparently highly skeptical that a jerk of this sort could have occurred or did occur.** Assuming, however, that a reasonable jury could find that the jerk did occur, would there be any basis for concluding that the plaintiff implicitly accepted the risk that he would be injured by a mechanical malfunction in the machine?

10. Baseball Stadiums And Other Venues. It is unfortunately not uncommon for patrons at baseball stadiums who sit in seats close to the playing field to be struck and injured by batted or thrown balls or broken bats. Although stadiums provide screening that protects patrons sitting directly behind home plate, the screening does not extend down the first- or third-base lines. Teams warn patrons of these risks through signage and announcements, and also disclaim liability using back-of-ticket waiver provisions. Although a number of injured patrons have sued teams for negligence, these suits have usually been rejected by courts, either on the basis of implied assumption of risk or "primary" assumption of risk (*see* note 7, supra), or on the ground that, as a matter of law, it is reasonable for teams to provide screening only for the area immediately behind home plate, and to otherwise allow patrons unblocked visual access to the playing field. Which of these rationales, if any, is most convincing?

** Notice the actual causation problem posed by Murphy's claim. Given that falls were a common feature of—indeed the very point of—the ride, how would a jury determine that, but for the unexpectedly jerky motion of the belt, the plaintiff would not have fallen in the way that he did?

A 2014 decision by the Missouri Supreme Court earned considerable attention for holding that, while patrons struck by batted or thrown balls during ordinary play do not have a valid cause of action, a negligence action could be pursued by a patron who was struck in the eye by a hot dog that was shot out of an air gun into the stands by the club's mascot as between-innings entertainment. Coomer v. Kansas City Royals Baseball Corp., 437 S.W.3d 184 (Mo. 2014). In December 2015, Major League Baseball's Commissioner recommended, but did not mandate, that teams add additional screening to stadiums. In 2002, in response to a patron's death after being struck by a deflected puck, the National Hockey League required teams to install protective netting behind goal areas.

Big Think

Factoring in the Plaintiff's Contribution

The defenses of comparative fault and implied assumption of risk give negligence defendants a straightforward means through which to argue against liability, or for limited liability, based on the plaintiff's role in causing his or her own injury. However, other components of negligence can also provide defendants with similar opportunities.

For example, certain *limited duty* doctrines — such as the traditional rule holding that a social host owes no duty of care to a licensee with respect to obviously dangerous conditions — may give the defendant an occasion to emphasize a victim's failure to notice a particular danger. As the above discussion of *Murphy* suggests, whether a given defendant's conduct should be deemed a *breach* of the duty of care can also turn in part on judgments about the plaintiff's awareness of the risks associated with the defendant's conduct. And, as noted at the outset of this chapter, courts will sometimes reason that, in light of a plaintiff's intervening careless or reckless actions, the defendant's carelessness should not count as a *proximate cause* of the plaintiff's injury. (See also the dissent in *Allbritton*, in Chapter 5, which accuses the majority in that case of conflating comparative fault and proximate cause.) Finally, at a more diffuse level, it seems likely that judges and jurors will tend to be less well-disposed toward plaintiffs whom they deem to have been insufficiently attentive to their own well-being.

Does negligence law provide defendants with too many opportunities to shift the "blame" to plaintiffs? If so, what might be done to correct for this problem?

11. Assumption of Risk and Consent. In the context of intentional wrongs, such as claims for batteries, the role played by express and implied assumption of risk in negligence law is played by the related defense of express or implied consent. Thus, a batterer can sometimes avoid liability by establishing that his victim consented to being hit, as is the case, for example, if the blow occurred during a licensed boxing match. *See* Chapter 9.

III. STATUTES OF LIMITATIONS AND REPOSE

Plaintiff-conduct defenses are one important category of complete or partial affirmative defenses available to negligence defendants. Other defenses operate as a matter of law for reasons of policy. Perhaps the most mundane yet important of these are the time limits a claimant must observe in order to have his suit heard in court. In general, these limits take two forms. *Statutes of limitations* start the clock running in relation to the occurrence of (a) the alleged tortious conduct and (b) harm to the claimant caused by that conduct. Typically, they specify that a tort claimant must commence her lawsuit within a certain period of time—usually one to three years—of those events. *Statutes of repose*, by contrast, set limits by reference either to the date of the tortious act alone, or to some other date, such as the date on which a particular product is manufactured or purchased. Thus, for example, a statute of repose for products liability actions might say that no tort action may be brought complaining of a product defect more than ten years after the date of the initial sale of the product.

Although statutes of limitations do not always make for interesting law school discussions, they are of the utmost practical importance. If, for example, a given legislature were anxious to restrict certain negligence causes of action, one very effective way to do so would be to adopt a relatively short statute of limitations, as some states have done with respect to medical malpractice actions. As you read the following case consider the policies at stake. How important is it for defendants to have prompt knowledge as to whether they will be sued? Does it matter whether the defendant is an individual or a corporate entity? What other goals are served by setting these limitations on tort actions? What risks to defendants or the judicial process are posed by long delays in bringing suit?

Ranney v. Parawax Co.

582 N.W.2d 152 (Iowa 1998)

TERNUS, J. This case involves the application of the discovery rule and the principle of inquiry notice to a latent injury case arising under Iowa's workers' compensation law. *See* Iowa Code ch. 85 (1993). The district court affirmed the industrial commissioner's summary judgment ruling that the appellant's claim was barred by the two-year statute of limitations for workers' compensation claims. *See id.* § 85.26(1). We affirm.

I. SCOPE OF REVIEW

Judicial review of the industrial commissioner's decisions is governed by the administrative procedure act, Iowa Code chapter 17A. *See id.* § 86.26. The court may reverse if the commissioner's decision is affected by an error of law. *See id.* § 17A.19(8)(*e*). Here, the appellant claims the commissioner erred in his application of the law governing summary judgments. . . .

II. BACKGROUND FACTS AND PROCEEDINGS

The record shows the following facts, when viewed in a light most favorable to the appellant, Joseph W. Ranney III. Ranney worked for the defendant, Parawax Company, Inc., from 1975 through February 1981. During that time he was exposed to toxic materials in the course of his regular duties. In 1985, Ranney became ill and was diagnosed with Hodgkin's disease.

Ranney suspected from the beginning that his condition might be causally connected to his work with toxic chemicals. The physician he first consulted regarding his symptoms made the following statements in a report dated June 26, 1985: "The patient does report working with paint solvents and he associates this work in some manner with these recent episodes. . . . The relationship to the paint solvents is unclear and may suggest an allergic component; however, the unilateral adenopathy and episodic symptoms argue against this." Ranney testified he questioned subsequent treating physicians about a possible connection between his work with chemicals and his disease but none of "the doctors would commit themselves, one way or the other."

Then in 1987, Ranney's wife started law school. Later that year or in 1988, she took a course in which she read cases discussing occupational diseases caused by exposure to chemicals. Ranney and his wife discussed the possibility that his exposure to toxic materials at Parawax caused his condition. Ranney testified he associated his condition to his chemical exposure at that time. It was not until 1991, however, when Ranney asked a new treating physician whether there was a causal link between his work-related exposure and his Hodgkin's disease, that a doctor confirmed Ranney's theory of causation.

This workers' compensation case was filed in 1992 against Ranney's former employer and its workers' compensation carrier, appellee American States Insurance Company. Ranney claimed his Hodgkin's disease was causally connected to his work-related exposure to toxic chemicals. He relied on the discovery rule to extend the two-year statute of limitations applicable to chapter 85 workers' compensation claims.

The industrial commissioner granted a motion for summary judgment filed by American States, ruling that the limitations period had expired before Ranney filed his petition for benefits. The commissioner's ruling was affirmed on judicial review by the district court and this appeal followed. . . .

III. Discussion

The resolution of this case requires the application of three related principles of law: the statute of limitations, the discovery rule and inquiry notice. Parawax has the burden to prove its limitations defense; Ranney has the burden to establish any exception to the ordinary limitations period, such as the applicability of the discovery rule. *See* Estate of Montag v. T H Agric. & Nutrition Co., 509 N.W.2d 469, 470 (Iowa 1993); Sparks v. Metalcraft, Inc., 408 N.W.2d 347, 350 (Iowa 1987).

A. *The statute of limitations and the discovery rule.* A petition for benefits under chapter 85 must be filed "within two years from the date of the occurrence of the injury for which benefits are claimed." Iowa Code § 85.26(1). We have interpreted this statute to mean that the injury occurs when it is discovered. *See* Dillinger v. City of Sioux City, 368 N.W.2d 176, 181 (Iowa 1985). Thus, the two-year limitation period begins to run when "the employee discovers or in the exercise of reasonable diligence should . . . discover[] the nature, seriousness and probable compensable character" of his injury or disease. Orr v. Lewis Cent. Sch. Dist., 298 N.W.2d 256, 261 (Iowa 1980).

As applied here, these principles require that Ranney have actual or imputed knowledge of the nature, seriousness and probable compensable character of his disease in order to commence the limitations period. There is no dispute that Ranney had actual knowledge of the nature and seriousness of his condition more than two years prior to filing his petition for benefits. The controversy here is whether he had imputed knowledge of the probable compensable nature of his disease, i.e., that his disease was caused by his workplace exposure to toxic chemicals. That brings us to the issue of inquiry notice.

B. *Inquiry notice.* Knowledge is imputed to a claimant when he gains information sufficient to alert a reasonable person of the need to investigate. *See* Estate of Montag, 509 N.W.2d at 470. . . . As of that date he is on inquiry notice of all facts that would have been disclosed by a reasonably diligent investigation. We reject Ranney's assertion that inquiry notice does not apply here because he suffered from a latent injury. When Ranney was diagnosed with Hodgkin's disease in 1985, his condition was no longer latent; it was then known. At that point, Ranney was subject to the same duty to investigate as is any other plaintiff who knows he has sustained an injury. Thus, we now turn to an analysis of the inquiry notice rule as applied to the undisputed facts of this case.

The record shows that Ranney suspected from the beginning that his Hodgkin's disease was caused by his work-related exposure to toxic materials. By 1987 or 1988, he learned that chemical exposure can cause disease and that persons suffering from such diseases had successfully sued for damages. He concedes he knew of the *possible* compensable nature of his condition at that time. Ranney claims, however, he was not on inquiry notice until he had facts alerting him to the *probable* compensable nature of his condition. We think that once a claimant knows or should know that his condition is possibly compensable, he has the duty to investigate. *See* Roth v. G.D. Searle Co., 27 F.3d 1303, 1307 (8th Cir. 1994) (holding that inquiry notice began when the plaintiff "knew or should have known of her injuries and their *possible* connection to her IUD") (emphasis added) (applying Iowa law); Jones v. Maine Cent. R.R., 690 F. Supp. 73, 75-77 (D. Me. 1988) (holding, as a matter of law, that statute of limitations commenced when plaintiffs were diagnosed with hearing loss and "thought," "suspected," or "presumed" it resulted from workplace noise). The purpose of the investigation is to ascertain whether the known condition is probably, as opposed to merely possibly, compensable.

Similarly, Ranney also argues that he was not on inquiry notice until 1991 when a physician informed him that his disease was causally connected to his work with toxic chemicals. He relies on the federal district court's decision in Brazzell v. United States, 633 F. Supp. 62 (N.D. Iowa 1985). In *Brazzell*, the court held the statute of limitations under the Federal Tort Claims Act did not begin to run until the plaintiff's doctor made a medical determination of causation. 633 F. Supp. at 69. This court, however, has never so interpreted Iowa's statute of limitations. *See Roth*, 27 F.3d at 1308 ("Under Iowa law, actual knowledge of a causal relationship is not required to begin the running of the statute of limitations."). We have held that "positive medical information is unnecessary if [the claimant] has information *from any source* which puts him *on notice* of [the injury's] probable compensable nature." Robinson v. Department of Transp., 296 N.W.2d 809, 812 (Iowa 1980) (emphasis added); *accord* 7 Arthur Larson, *Larson's Workers' Compensation Law* § 78.41(f), at 15-286 (1998). Thus, the duty to investigate does not depend "on exact knowledge of the nature of the problem that caused the injury." [Franzen v. Deere & Co., 377 N.W.2d 660, 662 (Iowa 1985)]. "Once a person is aware of a problem, he has a duty to investigate." *Sparks*, 408 N.W.2d at 352; *accord Franzen*, 377 N.W.2d at 662 ("It is sufficient that the person be aware that a problem existed."). The purpose of the investigation is to ascertain the exact nature of the problem that caused the injury. . . . Consequently, the lack of an expert opinion supporting causation does not prevent commencement of the statute of limitations under the principle of inquiry notice.

If we adopted Ranney's interpretation of when inquiry notice is triggered, the beginning of the limitations period would be postponed until the *successful completion* of the plaintiff's investigation. Such an application of the discovery rule would be contrary to our holdings in *Estate of Montag* and *Franzen*. As we stated in *Franzen*, "the period of limitations is the outer time limit for making the investigation and bringing the action. The period *begins* at the time the person is on inquiry notice." *Franzen*, 377 N.W.2d at 662 (emphasis added). . . .

We agree with the industrial commissioner that by 1987 or 1988, at the latest, Ranney had enough information to trigger his duty to investigate. *See* Nasim v. Warden, 64 F.3d 951, 956 (4th Cir. 1995) (affirming summary dismissal of complaint on statute-of-limitations grounds because the plaintiff was on inquiry notice that his condition was caused by asbestos exposure when (1) he knew that he was exposed to asbestos, that asbestos presented a health hazard and that he suffered physical and psychological injuries, and (2) he believed that his injury and exposure were linked). As of that date, Ranney was on notice of what a reasonably diligent investigation would have disclosed.

Ranney argues, however, that he conducted a reasonably diligent investigation into the cause of his condition, but was unable to obtain confirmation that his work-related exposure caused his Hodgkin's disease. The undisputed facts establish that Ranney's "investigation" consisted of asking his treating physicians whether there was a causal connection between his chemical exposure and his disease. The undisputed facts also show that his physicians would not commit one way or the other or they told him the cause of Hodgkin's disease was unknown. We hold these facts are insufficient to create a factual issue on the applicability of the discovery rule.

The fact that Ranney's actual investigation was unsuccessful in confirming his suspicions does not toll the statute of limitations. In United States v. Kubrick, 444 U.S. 111 (1979), the plaintiff knew of his injury and its probable cause in 1969, but did not know of the defendant's negligence, an additional factual element of his claim, until 1971 when a physician told him the defendant's treatment was improper. . . . The plaintiff then filed suit. . . . In affirming judgment for the defendant on statute-of-limitations grounds, the United States Supreme Court stated:

> [The plaintiff] may be incompetently advised or the medical community may be divided on the crucial issue of negligence, as the experts proved to be on the trial of this case. But however [the plaintiff] is advised, the putative malpractice plaintiff must determine within the period of limitations whether to sue or not, which is precisely the judgment that other tort claimants must make. If he fails to bring suit because he is incompetently or mistakenly told that he does not have a case, we

> discern no sound reason for visiting the consequences of such error on the defendant by delaying the accrual of the claim until the plaintiff is otherwise informed or himself determines to bring suit, even though more than two years have passed from the plaintiff's discovery of the relevant facts about injury. [*Id.* at 124.] . . .

We think the same reasoning applies here to Ranney's investigation of the probable cause of his Hodgkin's disease. *See* Cochran v. GAF Corp., 542 Pa. 210, 666 A.2d 245, 249 (Pa. 1995) (affirming summary judgment for the defendant despite the plaintiff's claim that he had not discovered the cause of his lung cancer until two years before he filed suit: "It is well settled that the statute of limitations is not tolled by mistake or misunderstanding. Also, a diligent investigation may require one to seek further medical examination as well as competent legal representation.") (citations omitted). By 1988 at the latest, Ranney knew of the possible connection between his disease and his employment; he had two years from that date to complete his investigation and file suit. His inability to find expert support for his theory of causation within that time does not prevent the limitations period from running.

We conclude the commissioner did not err in ruling as a matter of law that Ranney's workers' compensation claim was barred by the statute of limitations. Although this conclusion has the effect of barring a possibly meritorious claim, that is the unfortunate result of any statute of limitations. There must come a time when the interest in preventing stale claims takes precedence over the policy of deciding cases on their merits. That time has arrived in this case.

ANDREASEN, J. (dissenting in part) (joined by Larson, Lavorato, and Snell, JJ.). . . .

The majority opinion suggests that once Ranney knew of his disease and its possible connection with his employment, he had a duty to investigate *and* the two-year statute of limitation period began to run. Apparently, once Ranney was under a duty to investigate (inquiry notice), it made no difference if a reasonable investigation [would have] revealed the cause of his Hodgkin's disease is unknown. This interpretation of the inquiry notice doctrine conflicts with the majority opinion statements that "the purpose of the investigation is to ascertain whether the known condition is probably, as opposed to merely possibly, compensable," and that, when Ranney had enough information to trigger his duty to investigate, "as of that date, Ranney was on notice of what a reasonably diligent investigation would have disclosed."

Ranney is not asking that the statute be tolled until the *successful completion* of his investigation. Inquiry notice did impose a duty on him to investigate. The limitation period should run only if a reasonably diligent investigation would disclose the probable compensable character of his injury. In our previous application of the inquiry notice doctrine, we stated:

> The information they possessed on the date of the accident was plainly sufficient to put them on inquiry notice concerning possible defects in the wagon. They did not investigate at that time. When they later investigated, they found the alleged defects they now rely on. [Franzen v. Deere & Co., 377 N.W.2d 660, 663 (Iowa 1985), quoted in Vachon v. State, 514 N.W.2d 442, 447 (Iowa 1994).]

In United States v. Kubrick, 444 U.S. 111 (1979), the Court in a medical malpractice suit filed in 1992 stated: "It is undisputed in this case that in January 1969 Kubrick was aware of his injury and its *probable* cause." *Kubrick*, 444 U.S. at 119 (emphasis added). The Court was addressing the application of the discovery rule where the plaintiff was ignorant of his legal rights; rather than ignorant of the fact of his injury or its causes. *Id.* at 123. After recognizing reasonably competent doctors would have known the plaintiff should not have been treated with Neomycin, the Court stated:

> Crediting this finding, as we must, Kubrick need only have made inquiry among doctors with average training and experience in such matters to have discovered that he probably had a good cause of action. The difficulty is that it does not appear that Kubrick ever made any inquiry, although meanwhile he had consulted several specialists about his loss of hearing and had been in possession of all the facts about the cause of his injury since January 1969. Furthermore, there is no reason to doubt that Dr. Soma, who in 1971 volunteered his opinion that Kubrick's treatment had been improper, would have had the same opinion had the plaintiff sought his judgment in 1969. [*Id.* at 122-23.]

. . . There is no suggestion in the record that "in the exercise of reasonable diligence" or "in the exercise of a reasonably diligent investigation" Ranney, or a reasonable person, would have acquired actual or implied knowledge of the probable compensable nature of his claim before June 1990, two years prior to the filing of his claim.

Our court's application of the inquiry notice doctrine when a reasonably diligent investigation would not disclose the probable compensable character of the employee's injury, "guts" the basic requirement of the discovery rule that the limitation period begins when the employee discovered or should have discovered the *probable* compensable character of the injury. I would . . . reverse the ruling dismissing the claim under chapter 85. I would then remand to the industrial commissioner for further proceedings under chapter 85. . . .

NOTES AND QUESTIONS

1. *Workers' Compensation.* As explained by the *White* case and notes following it in Chapter 11, claims by employees against their employers for workplace injuries arising from accidents or hazardous conditions at the workplace are generally handled through workers' compensation systems rather than tort law. As *Ranney* indicates, however, the operation of these systems is governed by legal rules that still give rise to questions over which judges retain jurisdiction. Here the court reviews a ruling initially issued by a commissioner within the workers' compensation system who is charged with rendering decisions as to what constitutes a compensable injury within that system.

2. *Varying Limits.* Statutes of limitations vary from jurisdiction to jurisdiction, and, within a given jurisdiction, can vary among different torts. In Kentucky, a plaintiff complaining of personal injury, whether by means of a claim for battery, false imprisonment, or negligence, must commence the claim within one year of the relevant start

date. Ky. Stat. § 413.140(1). However, if the claim is for "intentional infliction of emotional distress" the plaintiff is given five years. Craft v. Rice, 671 S.W.2d 247 (Ky. 1984). In Florida, a plaintiff alleging injury resulting from negligence or battery has four years to bring her claim, unless the action alleges professional malpractice or consists of a claim for wrongful death, in which case the limitations period is two years. Fla. Stat. § 95.11. In Tennessee, the statute of limitations for all claims of personal injury is one year from the relevant start date, although certain defendants, including doctors, also get the benefit of special statutes of repose. Tenn. Code § 28-3-104.

3. *Accrual Rule Versus Discovery Rule.* Courts faced with statutes of limitations in tort cases used to apply the accrual rule to determine the date on which the limitations period commenced. Under the accrual rule, the clock on a negligence claim started to run as soon as two things happened: (1) the defendant acted carelessly and (2) that act caused some harm to the plaintiff. The fact that the plaintiff did not know, and perhaps could not know, of the harm or its connection to the defendant was deemed irrelevant. The emergence of new forms of tort liability, particularly toxic torts, put a great deal of pressure on courts and legislatures to modify the accrual rule. Toxic torts often involve injuries that occur gradually over time, and whose connection to a particular substance is not discovered until many years later. The discovery rule stalls the commencement of the limitations clock until such time as (1) the plaintiff knows, or has reason to know, that she has suffered an injury; and (2) there is sufficient reason to believe that the defendant's conduct is causally linked to that injury such that an inquiry into the connection is warranted and would reveal evidence of such a connection.

A current controversy among courts concerns the application of the discovery rule to suits brought by adults against priests and others for acts of sexual abuse alleged to have occurred decades earlier, when the plaintiffs were minors. Among other issues presented by these claims is whether and how to apply the discovery rule to repressed memories of abuse, or to a plaintiff who remembers the abuse but has only recently linked it to current physical or mental illnesses. *See* Dan B. Dobbs, *The Law of Torts* § 222, at 567-568 (2000).

4. *Statutes of Repose.* Although they generally provide a longer window in which to sue than statutes of limitations, statutes of repose are in some ways even harsher than the old accrual rule. They run from the date on which a specified act or event occurs regardless of whether that act is tortious or has yet produced any harm to any plaintiff. Thus, if the relevant statute of repose specifies that suits claiming injury caused by medical malpractice must be brought within three years of the date on which medical services were provided, and the plaintiff suffers an injury because of malpractice that does not manifest itself until after that period has run, the plaintiff is out of luck. Various special interest groups, most notably product manufacturers, but also architects, engineers, and doctors, have successfully lobbied for statutes of repose in recent years. Dobbs, *supra*, § 219, at 557-558. The typical act or event triggering a statute of repose will be the sale of the product, the completion of the construction project, or the conclusion of a course of medical treatment.

5. *Continuing Torts.* Certain forms of tortious conduct consist not of isolated acts of wrongdoing, but continuing patterns of behavior. A common example of the latter

category is when one landowner uses his land in a manner that pollutes the property of another. Suppose the polluting activity has occurred regularly over the preceding five years and was known to the plaintiff throughout that time. Suppose further that the statute of limitations for bringing a tort action for trespass is two years. Most courts will not treat a suit brought at the end of the five-year period as time-barred, even though the trespass and the harm *began* occurring more than two years prior to the filing of the suit and even though the plaintiff knew this to be the case. In essence, they will permit the plaintiff to proceed on the theory that the defendant committed a single tort that took place over a five-year period. On the other hand, when a court deems a nuisance "permanent" (as opposed to continuous), the statute of limitations for the plaintiff's claim is deemed to begin running when the nuisance first occurred. *See* Bowen v. Kansas City, 646 P.2d 484 (Kan. 1982).

Continuing tort rules do not figure prominently in negligence cases, although they may come into play in medical malpractice cases in which the complaint concerns a long course of treatment. *See* Dobbs, *supra*, § 220, at 561-563. Some courts have concluded that claims of spousal abuse should be subject to the continuing tort rule, such that a battered spouse can complain of injuries stemming from assaults that occurred outside the limitations period. *See, e.g.*, Feltmeier v. Feltmeier, 207 Ill. 2d 263 (2003) (applying continuous tort theory). *But see* Seaton v. Seaton, 971 F. Supp. 1188 (E.D. Tenn. 1997) (applying Tennessee law and refusing to treat a series of assaults as a single, continuing tort; plaintiff may sue only for injuries stemming from the last act of abuse, which fell within the limitations period).

6. *Tolling.* Statutes of limitations themselves, or judicial interpretations of them, sometimes provide for the *tolling* of limitations periods—that is, a pause in the running of the clock. The classic example is the tolling of limitations periods for torts committed against minors. Depending on the statute in question, the clock on such claims might not begin to run until the minor reaches the age of majority. *See, e.g.* N.Y. C.P.L.R. § 213-c (tolling civil actions arising from personal injury for three years after the plaintiff has reached the age of majority *except* in cases of personal injury arising from criminal sexual acts, in which case civil actions are tolled for five years).*

IV. IMMUNITIES AND EXEMPTIONS FROM LIABILITY

An immunity, in tort law, is a complete defense to liability granted to certain entities, as well as to actors in certain relationships. Historically, the three most important immunities recognized by the common law of tort have been intra-family immunity, charitable immunity, and sovereign immunity.

* For a website that tracks statutes of limitations applicable to cases of childhood sexual abuse, see http://sol-reform.com (last visited on September 7, 2015).

Intra-family immunity — specifically, spousal and parental immunity — was designed to prevent family members from suing each other in tort. Traditionally, the rules were defended as outgrowths of the authority of the patriarch over the family, as a means of leaving parents free to discipline children without fear of liability and as a way of preventing collusive litigation between family members. These broad immunities have by now eroded, although special rules limiting liability to other family members often still apply.

In a similar fashion, the doctrine of charitable immunity barred tort actions against charitable organizations, albeit only for their negligent (as opposed to intentional or reckless) wrongs. This immunity was of great significance in the early twentieth century given that most hospitals were run as charitable institutions. Most states have now rejected across-the-board charitable immunity through judicial decision or legislation, although many state legislators have provided charities with other protections, such as damages caps, that are not applicable to other actors.

Historically, the common law doctrine of sovereign immunity was a jurisdictional doctrine: It held that courts have no authority to order the federal or state governments into court at the behest of a private citizen; hence, injured plaintiffs were not permitted to include the federal or state governments as parties to a civil lawsuit. The thought was also that courts, via tort actions, should not be second-guessing or influencing policy decisions of the legislative and executive branches. This blanket immunity did not extend to local or municipal governments, which were not regarded as "sovereigns." Nonetheless, these entities, too, enjoyed certain specific immunities under common law.

The Federal Tort Claims Act (FTCA), enacted by Congress in 1946, along with state statutory counterparts, marked a sea change in the law of sovereign immunity. By means of these statutes, the federal and state governments have given away a good deal of the immunity they enjoyed at common law. However, these waivers of immunity have been partial rather than total, and usually set up special procedural rules designed to provide greater protection from liability for governmental entities than are enjoyed by private actors. As a result, the present contours of government liability at the federal, state, and local levels is quite complex.

In sum, even though modern legislatures and courts have moved away from blanket immunities, specific immunities often remain intact. Moreover, as the last pair of cases reproduced in this section suggest, courts will at times confer liability "exemptions" in the form of no-duty rules that bear a strong resemblance to traditional immunity doctrines. While the cases and materials in this chapter cannot hope to give you a detailed account of immunities and their no-duty cousins, they should give you a basic sense of how these doctrines operate and what sort of rationales, if any, support their continued recognition.

A. Intra-familial and Charitable Immunities

1. *Spousal Immunity.* Under the early common law a married woman had no independent legal identity. All property that she owned was owned and controlled by her husband. Likewise, she had no authority to sue in her own right — instead her

husband had to assert any claims she had on her behalf. This state of affairs changed with the introduction of the Married Women's Property Acts in the nineteenth century. Among other things, they allowed a married woman to maintain suit against her husband to protect her property interests (e.g., the waste of an asset, such as a farm, or the negligent handling of money earned from a trust).

Protecting property interests was a first step, but it generally did not affect personal injury claims. Husbands tended to remain immune from suit by their wives for intentionally or carelessly inflicting personal injuries on them. With respect to physical beatings administered by husbands that would otherwise qualify as batteries, courts justified common law immunity on the ground that domestic relations formed a domain of "private" interaction with which they ought not to interfere. The rationales for recognizing immunity as to negligence claims were different. With respect to one particularly common scenario—namely, a claim by a wife arising out of an automobile accident caused by her husband's careless driving—many courts expressed concern that spouses might collude to defraud the insurer into paying out on the automobile policy it had issued to the husband.

By the 1970s, the majority of states had rejected these sorts of arguments and had thus partially or completely eliminated spousal immunity. *See, e.g.*, Restatement (Second) of Torts § 895F(1) (1979) ("A husband or wife is not immune from tort liability to the other solely by reason of that relationship."). Still, it would be an overstatement to assert that an interspousal tort suit is no different from a tort suit between strangers. For example—as the Restatement acknowledges in Section 895F(2)—generally applicable doctrines such as the defense of "consent" to assaults and batteries may (rightly or wrongly) apply more broadly as between spouses than strangers. The same probably goes for the application of breach and comparative fault doctrines when the suit at hand is alleging that one spouse has been injured by the careless driving of the other. In fact, a number of jurisdictions have so-called guest statutes that, as a matter of formal doctrine, require family members and social guests of a driver to prove that their injuries resulted from the driver's gross negligence or recklessness, rather than simple negligence. *See, e.g.*, Heinze v. Heinze, 274 Neb. 595 (2007) (applying Nebraska's guest statute to bar suit by husband-passenger against wife whose careless driving caused an accident in which he was injured).

Apart from the foregoing issues of law-application, claims by battered spouses raise some potentially difficult questions of doctrine and policy. One is whether such claimants should be allowed to "toll" or suspend relevant statutes of limitations. *See* Section II *supra*. Legislatures usually set short limitations periods for intentional torts. A battered woman may thus find it impracticable to file suit within the relevant period against her husband for fear that the suit will provoke the husband to interfere with her relationship with her children or, if she has not yet left the home, will provoke further violence. Another arises from the question of whether tort claims should be tried together with divorce proceedings. The latter are not typically tried before juries, which would suggest that joinder of a tort claim against a spouse within a divorce proceeding will be possible only if the plaintiff gives up her right to try her tort claim to a jury. If joinder is not permitted, the possibility of "double recovery" arises — the battered spouse might recover damages in her subsequent tort action even though in some jurisdictions the husband's misconduct can serve as a ground for increasing the aggrieved spouse's share of a property settlement in the divorce proceeding.

2. *Parental Immunity.* Parental immunity was a relatively late doctrinal development. The first state to declare that parents were immune from tort suits by their children was Mississippi in 1891. *See* Hewlett v. George, 9 So. 885 (Miss. 1891) (immunizing parent from false imprisonment liability for institutionalizing her minor child), *overruled*, Glaskox v. Glaskox, 614 So.2d 906 (Miss. 1992). Most states have now cut back substantially on this immunity, though many have not abolished it outright, instead preserving pockets of immunity, particularly with respect to negligence claims.

One state's experience with parental immunity may be instructive. The Maryland Supreme Court first adopted the doctrine in *Schneider v. Schneider*, 152 A. 498 (Md. 1930), in which a mother sued her minor son whose careless driving caused her to suffer injuries. That immunity was later generalized to bar all claims by parents against their own children and children against their parents. In the 1950s, the court carved out two principal exceptions, allowing (1) claims by minor children subjected to cruel or outrageous treatment by their parents, and (2) claims by children who had already reached the age of majority at the time of the commission of the tort by the parent.

Thereafter, litigants repeatedly urged the court to join the vast majority of states in at least recognizing claims by minor children against their parents with respect to injuries suffered as a result of the careless operation of a car by the parent. The argument for the recognition of this particular domain of liability rested in large part on the fact that most states had come to require as a condition of driving the purchase of insurance for driving-related liabilities. Compulsory insurance thus promised to "reliev[e] the family of the financial burden of an adverse judgment while at the same time providing a means of recovery for the injured child." Renko v. McLean, 697 A.2d 468, 474 (Md. 1997). Still the court refused to recognize any further exceptions to parental immunity, observing with respect to the issue of liability arising out of the use of cars that the presence of insurance creates a risk that the nominal plaintiff (the injured child) and the nominal defendant (the allegedly careless parent-driver) would collude to generate a fraudulent claim against the insurance company whose money was on the line. *Id.* at 475. The court also expressed concern that jury awards in excess of insurance coverage might contribute significantly to family disharmony, and further opined that many children would already have the benefit of some form of first-party insurance to cover their basic medical expenses. *Id.* at 475-76.

Finally, in 2001, the Maryland legislature, reacting to decisions such as *Renko*, eliminated parent-child immunity with respect to injuries and claims arising out of a parent's use of a motor vehicle. In doing so, however, it tied the award of damages in such actions to available insurance coverage, barring awards in excess of coverage. *See* Allstate Ins. Co. v. Kim, 829 A.2d 611 (Md. 2003) (discussing and applying the statute).

3. *Immunity Versus the Privilege to Discipline.* Even at the height of parental immunity, it did not extend to willful or wanton mistreatments of children. Yet parents

were and still are to some degree authorized to engage in intentional conduct toward their children that might well be tortious if undertaken toward an adult friend or stranger. Most obviously, a parent is permitted intentionally to use a certain amount of physical force (e.g., spanking) or coercion (e.g., confining a child to his room) to discipline a child for bad behavior. The authority of parents to undertake such actions free from the threat of tort liability today tends to be given recognition in the law not via parental immunity doctrine, but instead by virtue of courts' recognition of a privilege of "reasonable parental discipline." Like the privilege to use physical force in self-defense or defense of others, the disciplinary privilege is lost if abused, as when a parent employs excessive force in disciplining her child.

4. *Negligent Parenting.* At what point may a child sue her parent for injuries arising out of a decision that the parent sincerely but unreasonably believed was part of a beneficial program of child-rearing? New York and other states retain immunity for claims that assert negligent "supervision"—a relatively broad category. Thus, in *Nolechek v. Gesuale*, 385 N.E.2d 1268 (1978), the New York Court of Appeals held that a parent who gave a motorcycle to a teenage son with significantly impaired eyesight could not be held liable to the son for injuries he suffered in a crash. Even assuming that the parent who gave the motorcycle was acting in good faith, why should he be immune from liability if a factfinder can fairly conclude that his judgment was objectively unreasonable? A teacher who acts unreasonably toward his students in arranging a physically dangerous school activity may be subject to liability under ordinary negligence principles if one of the students is injured when that danger is realized. Why should a parent be treated differently?

5. *Charitable Immunities.* At the same time that intra-familial immunities were eroding, immunities that protected charitable institutions were also under attack in courts and legislatures. An artifact of the late nineteenth century, this form of immunity blocked the application of *respondeat superior* to charitable organizations. For example, the victim of malpractice committed by a doctor who was employed by a hospital that was owned and operated by a charitable institution could sue the doctor but could not sue the hospital under a *respondeat superior* theory. *See, e.g.*, Schloendorff v. Society of New York Hospital, 105 N.E. 92 (N.Y. 1914), *overruled*, Bing v. Thunig, 143 N.E.2d 3 (N.Y. 1957).

The justifications offered for common law charitable immunity varied. One argument was that immunization operates as an appropriate subsidy for non-profit enterprises. The notion, apparently, was that immunity can function similarly to the granting to non-profit enterprises of tax-exempt status. Can you see a significant difference between these two methods of "subsidizing" the activities of charitable institutions?

Another oft-cited reason for immunity was that one who seeks the benefit of a charitable institution's good works can and should be deemed to have implicitly waived any right to sue if those works are undertaken carelessly so as to cause harm the intended beneficiary. This rationale appears to have been in the mind of the New Jersey Legislature when, in response to the New Jersey Supreme Court's mid-twentieth-century abolition of charitable immunity, it swiftly enacted a statute reinstating that immunity with respect to any suit brought "by a person who was a beneficiary, to whatever degree, of the organization's work." Schultz v. Roman Catholic Archdiocese of Newark, 472 A.2d 531, 537 (N.J. 1984) (applying N.J.S.A. 2A:53A-7-11). Under the New Jersey statute, a stranger to the charity — e.g., the owner of a car hit by a carelessly driven ambulance owned and operated by a charity — can bring a claim against the charity, while a beneficiary — e.g., a patient whose injuries are exacerbated by the same collision caused by the same carelessly driven ambulance — cannot.

Broad charitable immunities have now been abolished in most states. Although perhaps the main significance of this abolition has been the exposure of charitable hospitals to liability for medical malpractice committed by resident physicians, plaintiffs have brought an array of claims against other sorts of charities for other kinds of wrongs. Most notably in recent years, victims of sexual abuse by priests and other religious figures have successfully sued their religious institution employers for negligence in hiring and supervision. In the *Schultz* case, cited above, the New Jersey Supreme Court interpreted New Jersey's charitable immunity statute as *barring* such a claim. However, partly in response to public outcry over church sex abuse scandals, the Legislature amended the statute to permit negligent hiring claims by beneficiaries of a charity who, while minors, were victims of sexual abuse by a charity employee. *See* Hardwicke v. American Boychoir Sch., 902 A.2d 900 (N.J. 2006) (analyzing limits on New Jersey legislature's statutory grant of charitably immunity).

6. *Special Protections for Charities.* Even in states that have abolished charitable immunities, charities sometimes still enjoy special protections from tort liability. For example, some states impose tight damage caps with respect to certain claims against non-profit institutions. *See* Mass. G. L. c. 231 § 85K (capping charitable institutions' liability for injuries caused by "non-commercial" activities in furtherance of such an institution's charitable purpose at $100,000 per claim for medical malpractice claims brought against non-profit healthcare organizations, and at $20,000 per claim for other claims against charitable institutions).

7. *Charitable Immunity and Individual Liability.* Where applicable, charitable immunities protect the assets of the charity, not the individual tortfeasor. In some instances, charitable institutions (such as non-profit hospitals) have contractual agreements with their employees (such as on-staff physicians) to indemnify them for negligence liability incurred in the course of employment. In such situations, even if there is an applicable institutional immunity or damages cap, the institution will not derive any practical benefit from that immunity or cap.

To encourage volunteerism, some states have enacted statutes granting partial or complete immunities to individuals who accidentally injure others in the course of doing volunteer work for charities. For example, a volunteer who knocks someone over in the course of a charity bake sale might be immunized from ordinary negligence liability but still subject to liability for gross negligence, recklessness, or intentional wrongdoing. With certain important exceptions, including for negligent driving, the Volunteer Protection Act, 42 U.S.C. § 14501 *et seq.* (1997), provides immunity from liability for simple (but not gross) negligence to individual volunteers who injure others in the course of volunteering for a charity or governmental entity.

B. Sovereign Immunity

Riley v. United States

486 F.3d 1030 (8th Cir. 2007)

Benton, J. Lucas E. Riley sued the United States under the Federal Tort Claims Act ["FTCA"], 28 U.S.C. §§ 2671-80, for injuries caused by the alleged negligence of the United States Postal Service (USPS). The district court dismissed the complaint based on sovereign immunity. . . . [T]his court affirms.

I.

In February 2002, Riley's car was stopped on Christopher Drive, waiting to turn onto U.S. Highway 63. Mailboxes obscured his view of traffic. Believing the road was clear, Riley started onto the highway. A pickup truck broadsided his vehicle, causing serious injuries.

Before the collision, the county sheriff and a deputy—residents near Christopher Drive—complained to the Postmaster about the location of the mailboxes. The deputy sheriff presented the Postmaster a petition, signed by many residents, requesting they be moved. The Postmaster refused, citing the extra cost. After Riley's injuries, the USPS received letters and another petition. The relocation of the mailboxes was then approved.

Riley sued the United States, alleging that the USPS negligently placed, maintained, and failed to relocate the mailboxes. The district court found sovereign immunity applied, and thus it lacked subject matter jurisdiction. Riley appeals. . . .

II.

The United States is immune from suit unless it consents. . . . "Congress waived the sovereign immunity of the United States by enacting the FTCA, under which the federal government is liable for certain torts its agents commit in the course of their employment." *C.R.S. by D.B.S. v. United States*, 11 F.3d 791, 795 (8th Cir. 1993), *citing* 28 U.S.C. § 2674; *see also* 28 U.S.C. § 1346(b).

The United States is, nevertheless, immune if an exception applies. Under 28 U.S.C. § 2680(a), the FTCA does not waive immunity for "the exercise or performance or the failure to exercise or perform a discretionary function or duty on the part of a federal agency or an employee of the Government, whether or not the discretion involved be abused."

A two-part test determines when the discretionary function exception applies. *See C.R.S.*, 11 F.3d at 795, *citing Berkovitz v. United States*, 486 U.S. 531 (1988). First, the conduct at issue must be discretionary, involving "an element of judgment or choice." *See Berkovitz*, 486 U.S. at 536; *see also United States v. Gaubert*, 499 U.S. 315 (1991) ("the exception covers only acts that are discretionary in nature"). The "second requirement is that the judgment at issue be of the kind that the discretionary function exception was designed to shield." *C.R.S.*, 11 F.3d at 796, *quoting Berkovitz*, 486 U.S. at 536. "Because the exception's purpose is to prevent judicial second-guessing of government decisions based on public policy considerations, it protects only those judgments grounded in social, economic, and political policy." *Id.* at 796, *quoting United States v. S.A. Empresa de Viacao Aerea Rio Grandense (Varig Airlines)*, 467 U.S. 797, 814 (1984); *Appley Brothers v. United States*, 164 F.3d 1164, 1170 (8th Cir. 1999).

The facts here are almost identical to *Lopez v. United States*, 376 F.3d 1055 (10th Cir. 2004) [in which the Court of Appeals concluded that the USPS should benefit from the immunity conferred by the discretionary function exemption in a suit alleging negligence in its placement of mailboxes — Eds.].

[This court agrees with the reasoning of] . . . *Lopez*. . . . First, the USPS's decision on where to locate the mailboxes was discretionary, involving an element of judgment or choice. No federal statute or rule mandated the USPS to locate the mailboxes at any particular place. Guided by the Postal Operations Manual and the Management of Delivery Services Handbook, the USPS determined that curbside delivery (as opposed to sidewalk or central delivery) was most efficient for Christopher Drive. The Postmaster filed a declaration in this case:

> [The] Post Office had chosen to deliver mail via curbside delivery for more than 20 years prior to this accident. . . . [C]urbside delivery was the most efficient mode of delivery for this area. Even with curbside delivery, this particular route is 74 miles long. Delivery to the home sites is not practicable since many homes in this area are set miles back from the highway. Additionally, in my experience many of the roads leading back to the homes are not maintained well enough to effect safe and efficient delivery of the mail.

Further, in 2001, the USPS surveyed this delivery route, "taking into consideration factors including manpower, efficiency, economy, and safety." It then "decided to keep the current mode of delivery." *See C.R.S.*, 11 F.3d at 795 ("Decisions made at the operational level, as well as decisions made at the policy-planning level, can involve the exercise of protected discretion"). . . . Based on these judgments and choices, the USPS's decision about the location of the mailboxes was discretionary.

Riley contends that the USPS had no discretion and was bound by the "Green Book." That Book, incorporated by reference in 23 C.F.R. § 625.4, is published by the American Association of State Highway and Transportation Officials (AASHTO). It addresses sight triangle standards at intersections. The Green Book contains language such as: "After a vehicle has stopped at an intersection, the driver must have sufficient sight distance to make a safe departure through the intersection area."

The Green Book provisions, however, are guidelines and not mandatory. *See Rothrock v. United States*, 62 F.3d 196, 199 (7th Cir. 1995) ("despite the alleged nonconformance with certain AASHTO standards, the [Federal Highway Administration] is charged with balancing a mix of factors such as cost and safety. This is inherently a discretionary judgment involving the balancing of a mix of policy factors"). This case is unlike *Aslakson v. United States*, 790 F.2d 688, 693 (8th Cir. 1986), where the government's policy "clearly required" elevating its power lines if safety considerations "compelled" such action, or *Mandel v. United States*, 793 F.2d 964, 967 (8th Cir. 1986), where the government did not comply with "the previously adopted safety policy."

The Green Book itself says:

> The *guidance* supplied by this text . . . is based on established practices and is supplemented by recent research. This text is also intended to form a comprehensive *reference manual* for *assistance* in administrative, planning, and educational efforts pertaining to design formulation. The fact that new design values are presented herein does not imply that existing streets and highways are unsafe, *nor does it mandate* the initiation of improvement projects. (emphasis added).

The Green Book states that the "intent of this policy is to provide guidance to the designer by referencing a recommended range of values and dimensions. Sufficient flexibility is permitted to encourage independent designs tailored to particular situations." Contrary to Riley's argument, the Green Book further illustrates that the USPS's decision on locating the mailboxes is discretionary.

As to the second part of the *Berkovitz* test, the judgment of where to locate the mailboxes is of the kind that the discretionary function exception was designed to shield. 39 U.S.C. § 403(b) provides:

> It shall be the responsibility of the Postal Service to maintain an efficient system of collection, sorting, and delivery of the mail nationwide . . . and to establish and maintain postal facilities of such character and in such locations, that postal patrons throughout the Nation will, consistent with reasonable economies of postal operations, have ready access to essential postal services.

Balancing personnel, efficiency, economy, and safety, the USPS chose curbside delivery at the U.S. 63-Christopher intersection, as opposed to other locations and modes of delivery. *See id.; see also Lopez*, 376 F.3d at 1061 ("the decision of where to place the mailboxes in question was clearly located on the policy side of the spectrum. Placement of mailboxes entails a calculated decision, based on the weighing of various costs and benefits, and not the mere carrying out of a legislative mandate that can be applied without exercising judgment").

Finally, Riley argues that even if the USPS is protected by the discretionary function exception, this court should make "an exception to the exception" by adopting the "dangerous condition exception" in Missouri's waiver of sovereign immunity as outlined in *Martin v. Missouri Highway and Transp. Dep't*, 981 S.W.2d 577 (Mo. App. 1998). There, the state court, quoting Mo. Rev. Stat. § 537.600, explained that the Missouri Highway and Transportation Commission's immunity was "expressly waived for . . . injuries caused by the dangerous condition of the public entity's property." *Martin*, 981 S.W.2d at 579, 583, 585. Riley concedes, however, that he has "not found Eighth Circuit law approving the application of this doctrine." More importantly, the FTCA has no dangerous condition exception to the discretionary function exception.

The judgment of the district court is affirmed.

NOTES AND QUESTIONS

1. *Respondeat Superior and the FTCA.* The FTCA states that the federal government is subject to liability "if a private person would be liable to the claimant in

accordance with the law of the place where the act or omission occurred." 28 U.S.C. § 1346(b). Notice that the statute attaches liability to the government, rather than its individual employees. (As explained below, individual employees often enjoy immunity from liability for torts committed in the course of their government employment.) Thus, the primary effect of the FTCA is to treat the federal government, for purposes of tort liability, as if it were a private employer. This in turn has the effect of rendering the United States subject to the doctrine of *respondeat superior*, under which it is held vicariously liable for tortious acts by its employees committed within the scope of their employment. *See Taber v. Maine* Chapter 8 *infra* (on *respondeat superior*). However, as Note 3 *infra* indicates, the rules of vicarious liability that apply to the government are slightly different from the rules that apply to private employers under modern common law.

2. *The Paradox of Treating Government as a "Private Person."* Certain activities undertaken by government officials have obvious counterparts in the sphere of private activity, making application of the FTCA's basic directive unproblematic. If a U.S. employee carelessly drives his government-owned car into a pedestrian while acting within the scope of his employment, the government can readily be analogized to a private employer. However, there are other functions performed by government that have no private counterpart, such as maintaining the armed forces, and issuing mandatory, binding regulations backed by threat of fine or other punishment. If there is no private counterpart to such regulation, it would seem to follow that no "private person" can ever be held liable for negligence in the issuance or enforcement of such regulations. So how can the government be held liable under the FTCA?

Noticing this paradox, Justice Robert Jackson argued that the federal government should never be held liable for wrongdoing in connection with its performance of regulatory and other functions that only it performs, no matter what the nature of the particular conduct in question. Feres v. United States, 340 U.S. 135 (1950). However, *Indian Towing, Co. v. United States*, 350 U.S. 61 (1955), abandoned this line of reasoning. In holding that the federal government could be liable for negligently operating a lighthouse, it concluded that the issue posed by the "private person" clause is whether general tort principles contained in the applicable state's law would call for the imposition of liability, even if the activity is one in which only government engages.

3. *Protections Built into the FTCA.* The FTCA marked an historic waiver of immunity previously enjoyed by the federal government for its employees' torts. Still, Congress proceeded with care, as evidenced by the discretionary function exemption and several other provisions of the Act. For example, the Act does not accord claimants the right to a jury trial; judges determine all issues of fact and law. 28 U.S.C. § 2402. Moreover, the act adopts a conception of vicarious liability that is somewhat narrower than the rule at common law because it categorically excludes certain intentional wrongdoings from generating liability, even when those wrongs would permit the imposition of *respondeat superior* liability against a private actor. 28 U.S.C. § 2680(h). Also, when proceeding under the FTCA, claimants cannot obtain punitive damages against the government, even if such damages could be awarded were the defendant a private entity. 28 U.S.C. § 2674.

4. *Discretionary Functions and Discretion.* The mere fact that an activity entails the exercise of some discretion does not necessarily qualify it for the discretionary function exemption. Rather, the exemption is directed at the exercise of a certain kind of discretion having to do with matters of "policy." So, for example, while the activity of surgery often involves discretionary decisions about what instrument to use, or how much anesthesia to administer, the federal government presumably cannot claim that the discretionary function exemption automatically immunizes it from all vicarious liability for malpractice committed by surgeons in its employ. Some courts, however, have concluded that certain medical decisions do qualify under the exemption. For example, *C.R.S. v. United States*, 11 F.3d 791 (8th Cir. 1993), upon which the *Riley* court relied, held that the failure to screen blood used in transfusions for HIV infection constitutes a "policy" decision subject to the discretionary function exemption.

Led by the Supreme Court, courts in recent years have tended to interpret the discretionary function exemption broadly, and thus to immunize the government from liability for a wide range of carelessness on the part of its employees. Perhaps most importantly, *United States v. Gaubert*, 499 U.S. 315 (1991), declined to analyze the discretionary function issue in terms of a categorical distinction between "policy" and "day-to-day" decisions, and instead directed courts to determine whether the conduct in question called for employees to exercise discretion in the pursuit of governmental policy objectives. *Gaubert* also made clear that, at least in some instances, immunity will attach to a policy decision even if the decision in question was made unreflectively, without actual consideration of relevant policy factors. *See also* Aguehounde v. District of Columbia, 666 A.2d 443 (D.C. App. 1995) (decision on timing of traffic signals is a discretionary function even if no judgment was actually exercised in setting their timing).

5. *Why the Exemption?* Keep in mind that a plaintiff proceeding with a claim of negligence against the federal government must prove to a judge's satisfaction that a government employee acted carelessly before obtaining recovery. Given that reasonable people often legitimately disagree over the proper resolution of judgment calls like the proper placement of mailboxes and the proper screening of blood, won't it be the case that most allegations of faulty policymaking will fail on the breach element? Why did Congress feel the need to add a special exemption for discretionary functions? Does *Riley* help capture its concern?

6. *Immunity from Liability to Military Personnel: The Feres Doctrine.* Although, as noted above, its original rationale is no longer endorsed by the Supreme Court, the holding of *Feres v. United States*, 340 U.S. 135 (1950), remains intact. In a nutshell, it found implicit in the FTCA a broad rule barring any suits by military servicemen against the government for injuries arising out of, or incident to, their service. *Feres* is discussed below in the context of a case dealing primarily with vicarious liability. *See* Taber v. Maine, Chapter 8 *infra*.

7. *Personal Immunity of Government Employees.* In contrast to private employees, federal employees have been exempted by a statute known as the Westfall Act from being held individually liable for torts committed in the scope of their employment.

28 U.S.C. § 2679(b). Many states have enacted similar legislation for state employees. Thus, a person injured by the tortious conduct of a government employee acting within the scope of her employment ordinarily *cannot* recover from the employee, but at most may recover only from the government as employer. In this respect, government employees are at least nominally better off than private sector employees, who enjoy no such *de jure* immunity.

The grant of individual immunity contained in the Westfall Act and its state counterparts, when combined with the remaining pockets of sovereign immunity still recognized under the FTCA and its state equivalents, entail that some persons tortiously injured by government employees will be unable to recover any compensation through the tort system for their injuries either from the individual tortfeasor or the government as employer. Victims placed in such a bind have challenged the federal statute granting individual immunity on constitutional grounds, but these challenges have failed. *See, e.g.*, Carr v. United States, 422 F.2d 1007 (4th Cir. 1970).

Under the *Bivens* decision reproduced in Chapter 6, individuals sometimes are empowered by the U.S. Constitution to sue individual federal officers for violating their constitutional rights. In keeping with *Bivens*, the Westfall Act contains an exception that permits the imposition of individual liability (but not governmental liability) for violations of constitutional rights, whether cognizable under *Bivens* or by means of a statutory cause of action. 28 U.S.C. § 2679(b)(2)(A).

8. State and Local Governments; Governmental Versus Proprietary Functions. States, like the federal government, have enacted statutes abolishing common law sovereign immunity. State schemes differ considerably in their particulars. To the extent generalization is possible, one may say that the state schemes tend to resemble the regime applicable to the federal government under the FTCA.

At common law, city and local governments did not enjoy sovereign immunity simply because they were not deemed sovereign entities. However, courts tended to exempt them from liability for *governmental* activities — such as the provision of a police force or a fire department — as opposed to *proprietary* activities — such as the operation of a local utility. In many states, municipal and local government liability rules have also been modified by statute.

The New York Court of Appeals recently applied the governmental/proprietary distinction to claims brought against the Port Authority of New York and New Jersey — an entity created by a compact between those two states for the purpose of operating airports, bridges, tunnels and other key sites, including the World Trade Center (WTC) in New York City. Suits were brought on behalf of several hundred plaintiffs who were injured when, in 1993, terrorists detonated explosives contained in a van parked in a garage beneath the WTC complex. (*See Arcadian*, Chapter 5.) Although most claimants settled, some proceeded to trial. The trials were bifurcated into one consolidated trial on liability, to be followed by individual trials on damages, assuming liability was found. (On bifurcation, *see* Chapter 8's discussion of compensatory damages.)

At the liability phase, substantial evidence was presented that the Port Authority had received detailed and credible warnings that an attack of the sort perpetrated by the terrorists would occur, and that the Port Authority had been given safety recommendations that, if adopted, might have prevented the attack. A jury found the Port Authority liable, and apportioned 68 percent fault to the Port Authority and 32 percent to the terrorists. (On apportionment, *see* Chapter 8.) This verdict was affirmed by a unanimous intermediate appellate court. Individual trials on damages ensued, with one brought on behalf of bombing victim Antonio Ruiz resulting in an award of almost a million dollars.

The Court of Appeals granted leave to the Port Authority to appeal the verdict in favor of Ruiz, including the issue of the Port Authority's liability. Then, in a 4-3 decision, it reversed and dismissed. The majority concluded that, although the interstate compact had explicitly waived whatever common law sovereign immunity the Port Authority might have enjoyed by virtue of being a state entity, the Authority continues to enjoy a different kind of immunity, namely, immunity for liability arising out of the performance of "governmental" functions. It further concluded that the plaintiffs were not suing the Port Authority for careless performance of a "proprietary" duty to maintain safety on the WTC premises, but instead were suing for carelessness in providing police protection:

> While some of plaintiffs' claims may touch upon the proprietary obligations of a landlord, . . . they allude to lapses in adequately examining the risk and nature of terrorist attack and adopting specifically recommended security protocols to deter terrorist intrusion. These actions . . . were a consequence of the Port Authority's mobilization of police resources for the exhaustive study of the risk of terrorist attack, the policy-based planning of effective counterterrorist strategy, and the consequent allocation of such resources. Thus, the ostensible acts or omissions for which plaintiffs seek to hold the Port Authority liable stem directly from its failure to allocate police resources. . . .

In re World Trade Center Bombing Litig., 957 N.E.2d 733, 746 (2011). Compare the majority's reasoning to the reasoning of *Riley*, and to that of the following decision, also issued by the Court of Appeals, which concerns a distinct but perhaps related concept of immunity that is conferred by New York law on *local* governments.

C. Liability Exemptions: No-Duty Rules for Local Government and Private Entities

Riss v. City of New York

240 N.E.2d 860 (N.Y. 1968)

Breitel, J. This appeal presents, in a very sympathetic framework, the issue of the liability of a municipality for failure to provide special protection to a member of the public who was repeatedly threatened with personal harm and eventually suffered dire personal injuries for lack of such protection. The facts are amply described in the dissenting opinion and no useful purpose would be served by repetition. The issue arises upon the affirmance by a divided Appellate Division of a dismissal of the complaint, after both sides had rested but before submission to the jury.

It is necessary immediately to distinguish those liabilities attendant upon governmental activities which have displaced or supplemented traditionally private enterprises, such as are involved in the operation of rapid transit systems, hospitals, and places of public assembly. Once sovereign immunity was abolished by statute the extension of liability on ordinary principles of tort law logically followed. To be equally distinguished are certain activities of government which provide services and facilities for the use of the public, such as highways, public buildings and the like, in the performance of which the municipality or the State may be liable under ordinary principles of tort law. The ground for liability is the provision of the services or facilities for the direct use by members of the public.

In contrast, this case involves the provision of a governmental service to protect the public generally from external hazards and particularly to control the activities of criminal wrongdoers. The amount of protection that may be provided is limited by the resources of the community and by a considered legislative-executive decision as to how those resources may be deployed. For the courts to proclaim a new and general duty of protection in the law of tort, even to those who may be the particular seekers of protection based on specific hazards, could and would inevitably determine how the limited police resources of the community should be allocated and without predictable limits. This is quite different from the predictable allocation of resources and liabilities when public hospitals, rapid transit systems, or even highways are provided.

Before such extension of responsibilities should be dictated by the indirect imposition of tort liabilities, there should be a legislative determination that that should be the scope of public responsibility. . . .

It is notable that the removal of sovereign immunity for tort liability was accomplished after legislative enactment and not by any judicial arrogation of power (Court of Claims Act, § 8). It is equally notable that for many years, since as far back as 1909 in this State, there was by statute municipal liability for losses sustained as a result of riot (General Municipal Law, § 71). Yet even this class of liability has for some years been suspended by legislative action (New York State Defense Emergency Act [L. 1951, ch. 784, § 113, subd. 3; § 121, as last amd. by L. 1968, ch. 115]), a factor of considerable significance.

When one considers the greatly increased amount of crime committed throughout the cities, but especially in certain portions of them, with a repetitive and predictable pattern, it is easy to see the consequences of fixing municipal liability upon a showing of probable need for and request for protection. To be sure these are grave problems at the present time, exciting high priority activity on the part of the national, State and local governments, to which the answers are neither simple, known, or presently within reasonable controls. To foist a presumed cure for these problems by judicial innovation of a new kind of liability in tort would be foolhardy indeed and an assumption of judicial wisdom and power not possessed by the courts. . . .

For all of these reasons, there is no warrant in judicial tradition or in the proper allocation of the powers of government for the courts, in the absence of legislation, to carve out an area of tort liability for police protection to members of the public. Quite distinguishable, of course, is the situation where the police authorities undertake responsibilities to particular members of the public and expose them, without adequate protection, to the risks which then materialize into actual losses.

Accordingly, the order of the Appellate Division affirming the judgment of dismissal should be affirmed.

KEATING, J. (dissenting). Certainly, the record in this case, sound legal analysis, relevant policy considerations and even precedent cannot account for or sustain the result which the majority have here reached. For the result is premised upon a legal rule which long ago should have been abandoned, having lost any justification it might once have had. Despite almost universal condemnation by legal scholars, the rule survives, finding its continuing strength, not in its power to persuade, but in its ability to arouse unwarranted judicial fears of the consequences of overturning it.

Linda Riss, an attractive young woman, was for more than six months terrorized by a rejected suitor well known to the courts of this State, one Burton Pugach. This miscreant, masquerading as a respectable attorney, repeatedly threatened to have Linda killed or maimed if she did not yield to him: "If I can't have you, no one else will have you, and when I get through with you, no one else will want you." In fear for her life, she went to those charged by law with the duty of preserving and safeguarding the lives of the citizens and residents of this State. Linda's repeated and almost pathetic pleas for aid were received with little more than indifference. Whatever help she was given was not commensurate with the identifiable danger. On June 14, 1959 Linda became engaged to another man. At a party held to celebrate the event, she received a phone call warning her that it was her "last chance." Completely distraught, she called the police, begging for help, but was refused. The next day Pugach carried out his dire threats in the very manner he had foretold by having a hired thug throw lye in Linda's face. Linda was blinded in one eye, lost a good portion of her vision in the other, and her face was permanently scarred. After the assault the authorities concluded that there was some basis for Linda's fears, and for the next three and one-half years, she was given around-the-clock protection.

No one questions the proposition that the first duty of government is to assure its citizens the opportunity to live in personal security. And no one who reads the record of Linda's ordeal can reach a conclusion other than that the City of New York, acting through its agents, completely and negligently failed to fulfill this obligation to Linda.

Linda has turned to the courts of this State for redress, asking that the city be held liable in damages for its negligent failure to protect her from harm. With compelling logic, she can point out that, if a stranger, who had absolutely no obligation to aid her, had offered her assistance, and thereafter Burton Pugach was able to injure her as a result of the negligence of the volunteer, the courts would certainly require him to pay damages. (Restatement, 2d, Torts, § 323.) Why then should the city, whose duties are imposed by law and include the prevention of crime (New York City Charter, § 435) and, consequently, extend far beyond that of the Good Samaritan, not be responsible? If a private detective acts carelessly, no one would deny that a jury could find such conduct unacceptable. Why then is the city not required to live up to at least the same minimal standards of professional competence which would be demanded of a private detective?

Linda's reasoning seems so eminently sensible that surely it must come as a shock to her and to every citizen to hear the city argue and to learn that this court decides that the city has no duty to provide police protection to any given individual. What makes the city's position particularly difficult to understand is that, in conformity to the dictates of the law, Linda did not carry any weapon for self-defense (former Penal Law, § 1897). Thus, by a rather bitter irony she was required to rely for protection on the City of New York which now denies all responsibility to her.

It is not a distortion to summarize the essence of the city's case here in the following language: "Because we owe a duty to everybody, we owe it to nobody." Were it not for the fact that this position has been hallowed by much ancient and revered precedent, we would surely dismiss it as preposterous. To say that there is no duty is, of course, to start with the conclusion. The question is whether or not there should be liability for the negligent failure to provide adequate police protection.

The foremost justification repeatedly urged for the existing rule is the claim that the State and the municipalities will be exposed to limitless liability. . . .

The fear of financial disaster is a myth. The same argument was made a generation ago in opposition to proposals that the State waive its defense of "sovereign immunity." The prophecy proved false then, and it would now. The supposed astronomical financial burden does not and would not exist. No municipality has gone bankrupt because it has had to respond in damages when a policeman causes injury through carelessly driving a police car or in the thousands of other situations where, by judicial fiat or legislative enactment, the State and its subdivisions have been held liable for the tortious conduct of their employees. Thus, in the past four or five years, New York City has been presented with an average of some 10,000 claims each year. The figure would sound ominous except for the fact the city has been paying out less than $8,000,000 on tort claims each year and this amount includes all those sidewalk defect and snow and ice cases about which the courts fret so often. (Reports submitted by the Comptroller of the City of New York to the Comptroller of the State of New York pursuant to General Municipal Law, § 50-f.) Court delay has reduced the figure paid somewhat, but not substantially. Certainly this is a slight burden in a budget of more than six billion dollars (less than two tenths of 1%) and of no importance as compared to the injustice of permitting unredressed wrongs to continue to go unrepaired. That Linda Riss should be asked to bear the loss, which should properly fall on the city if we assume, as we must, in the present posture of the case, that her injuries resulted from the city's failure to provide sufficient police to protect Linda is contrary to the most elementary notions of justice.

The statement in the majority opinion that there are no predictable limits to the potential liability for failure to provide adequate police protection as compared to other areas of municipal liability is, of course, untenable. When immunity in other areas of governmental activity was removed, the same lack of predictable limits existed. Yet, disaster did not ensue.

Another variation of the "crushing burden" argument is the contention that, every time a crime is committed, the city will be sued and the claim will be made that it resulted from inadequate police protection. . . . [H]ere too the underlying assumption of the argument is fallacious because it assumes that a strict liability standard is to be

sufficient personnel, the full cost of that choice should become acknowledged in the same way as it has in other areas of municipal tort liability. Perhaps officials will find it less costly to choose the alternative of paying damages than changing their existing practices. That may be well and good, but the price for the refusal to provide for an adequate police force should not be borne by Linda Riss and all the other innocent victims of such decisions.

What has existed until now is that the City of New York and other municipalities have been able to engage in a sort of false bookkeeping in which the real costs of inadequate or incompetent police protection have been hidden by charging the expenditures to the individuals who have sustained often catastrophic losses rather than to the community where it belongs, because the latter had the power to prevent the losses.

Although in modern times the compensatory nature of tort law has generally been the one most emphasized, one of its most important functions has been and is its normative aspect. It sets forth standards of conduct which ought to be followed. The penalty for failing to do so is to pay pecuniary damages. At one time the government was completely immunized from this salutary control. This is much less so now, and the imposition of liability has had healthy side effects. In many areas, it has resulted in the adoption of better and more considered procedures just as workmen's compensation resulted in improved industrial safety practices. To visit liability upon the city here will no doubt have similar constructive effects. No "presumed cure" for the problem of crime is being "foisted" upon the city as the majority opinion charges. The methods of dealing with the problem of crime are left completely to the city's discretion. All that the courts can do is make sure that the costs of the city's and its employees' mistakes are placed where they properly belong. Thus, every reason used to sustain the rule that there is no duty to offer police protection to any individual turns out on close analysis to be of little substance.

. . . [S]tep by step, New York courts are moving to return — albeit with some notable setbacks — toward the day when the government, in carrying out its various functions, will be held equally responsible for the negligent acts of its employees as would a private employer. . . . But although "sovereign immunity," by that name, supposedly died in Bernardine v. City of New York, it has been revived in a new form. It now goes by the name "public duty." . . .

The rule [of no duty] is Judge made and can be judicially modified. By statute, the judicially created doctrine of "sovereign immunity" was destroyed. It was an unrighteous doctrine, carrying as it did the connotation that the government is above the law. Likewise, the law should be purged of all new evasions, which seek to avoid the full implications of the repeal of sovereign immunity.

No doubt in the future we shall have to draw limitations just as we have done in the area of private litigation, and no doubt some of these limitations will be unique to municipal liability because the problems will not have any counterpart in private tort law. But if the lines are to be drawn, let them be delineated on candid considerations of policy and fairness and not on the fictions or relics of the doctrine of "sovereign immunity." Before reaching such questions, however, we must resolve the fundamental issue raised here and recognize that, having undertaken to provide professional police and fire protection, municipalities cannot escape liability for damages caused by their failure to do even a minimally adequate job of it. . . .

. . . [S]ince this is an appeal from a dismissal of the complaint, we must give the plaintiff the benefit of every favorable inference . . . A few examples of the actions of the police should suffice to show the true state of the record. Linda Riss received a telephone call from a person who warned Linda that Pugach was arranging to have her beaten up. A detective learned the identity of the caller. He offered to arrest the caller, but plaintiff rejected that suggestion for the obvious reason that the informant was trying to help Linda. When Linda requested that Pugach be arrested, the detective said he could not do that because she had not yet been hurt. The statement was not so. It was and is a crime to conspire to injure someone. True there was no basis to arrest Pugach then, but that was only because the necessary leg work had not been done. No one went to speak to the informant, who might have furnished additional leads. Linda claimed to be receiving telephone calls almost every day. These calls could have been monitored for a few days to obtain evidence against Pugach. Any number of reasonable alternatives presented themselves. A case against Pugach could have been developed which would have at least put him away for awhile or altered the situation entirely. But, if necessary, some police protection should have been afforded.

Perhaps, on a fuller record after a true trial on the merits, the city's position will not appear so damaging as it does now. But with actual notice of danger and ample opportunity to confirm and take reasonable remedial steps, a jury could find that the persons involved acted unreasonably and negligently. Linda Riss is entitled to have a jury determine the issue of the city's liability. This right should not be terminated by the adoption of a question-begging conclusion that there is no duty owed to her. The order of the Appellate Division should be reversed and a new trial granted.

Did You Know?

Riss's Aftermath

Prior to the events giving rise to Riss's suit against New York City, Burton Pugach was a successful personal injury lawyer. Subsequently, he was disbarred, convicted of conspiring to have Riss maimed, and sentenced to prison for a term of 15–30 years. While in prison, he regularly sent Riss love letters. In 1974, after serving 14 years of his term, Pugach was released on parole. Although under a court order not to contact Riss, Pugach used the occasion of interviews by local television stations to propose marriage to her. Eight months later they were married. Notwithstanding a subsequent infidelity — which led to new criminal charges being brought against Pugach based on his alleged abuse of his lover — Pugach and Riss remained married until her death in 2013. The couple offered an account of their relationship in Berry Stainback, *A Very Different Love Story* (1976). A film documentary about their lives, titled *Crazy Love*, was produced in 2007.

NOTES AND QUESTIONS

1. *The Public Duty Rule. Riss* provides an application of what is sometimes called the "public duty rule." Nominally, this rule does not create an immunity defense, but instead provides a rule that negates the duty element of the plaintiff's prima

facie case. Typically, the rule comes up in cases in which the allegation is that a local governmental entity has acted carelessly in failing to perform, or in performing, an *affirmative duty.*

For example, a plaintiff might sue on a claim that a local government failed to enforce its own building codes, resulting in a dangerous condition that injured the plaintiff. Or a plaintiff whose house has burned down might sue the fire department on the theory that its personnel needlessly delayed in responding or fought the fire in a careless manner. Or a plaintiff who is attacked by a parolee might sue a local parole board on the theory that they mistakenly released the wrong parolee. When they invoke the public duty rule, courts deny liability on the ground that, although government owes certain duties to the public at large, it does not owe those duties to any individual member of the public. Thus, no individual has "standing" to sue for damages caused by the breach of such a duty. What is the best justification for such a rule? Is it convincing?

For an opposite approach to the one adopted in *Riss*, see Torres v. State, 894 P.2d 386 (1995). There, New Mexico police allegedly were careless in not promptly arresting the prime suspect in a triple murder, as a result of which the suspect was able to travel to Los Angeles, where he murdered plaintiffs' decedents. The New Mexico Supreme Court held that "duty" was no obstacle to the plaintiffs' wrongful death claims given that it was foreseeable that, by carelessly permitting the murder suspect to leave town, the police might endanger the lives of others far away. The court remanded the case for a jury to resolve the issues of breach and causation, and, if necessary, to allocate responsibility as between the police and the suspect.

2. *Exceptions to the Public Duty Rule.* Courts have recognized various exceptions to the public duty rule. To a certain extent, these exceptions track the exceptions to the common law rules on duties to rescue. *See* Chapter 2. Thus, some courts will look to see if government actors made a particular undertaking to the plaintiff (i.e., volunteered to assist her), or if they and the plaintiff interacted in a manner that created a "special relationship" between them. Why was the *Riss* majority convinced that, as a matter of law, Linda Riss could not establish the existence of a special relationship between her and New York City police?

The New York Court of Appeals reaffirmed and arguably extended *Riss* in *Kircher v. City of Jamestown*, 543 N.E.2d 443 (1989). There, the plaintiff was abducted in her own car in front of eyewitnesses who gave chase, then came upon a police officer to whom they described the incident as well as the car (including its license plate number). The officer told the witnesses that he would report the incident, but he never did. The plaintiff was brutalized by her kidnapper before later being discovered locked in the trunk of the car. In denying the plaintiff a cause of action against the city, the court held that such a claimant could only establish the requisite duty if there were a special relationship between her and police, and that a special relationship requires:

> (1) an assumption by the municipality, through promises or actions, of an affirmative duty to act on behalf of the party who was injured; (2) knowledge on the part of the municipality's agents that inaction could lead to harm; (3) some form of direct contact between the municipality's agents and the injured

> party; and (4) that party's justifiable reliance on the municipality's affirmative undertaking.

Id. at 446. In a subsequent case, the plaintiff, who suffered a stroke while at work, alleged that his stroke-related injuries were substantially aggravated because a 911 operator was careless in dispatching an ambulance to his workplace after promising that an ambulance would arrive as soon as possible. The Court of Appeals held that *Kircher*'s test for a special relationship was not satisfied and hence that there could be no liability even if the dispatcher had been careless. Laratro v. City of New York, 861 N.E.2d 95 (N.Y. 2006).

In *Florence v. Goldberg*, 375 N.E.2d 763 (1978), the Court of Appeals upheld a jury verdict against the City of New York of $770,000 for injuries suffered by a six-year-old child who was struck by a negligently driven taxi. The theory against the city was that it had a duty to provide a crossing guard at the intersection where the accident occurred, based on both the known danger of the intersection to schoolchildren and the fact that the city had assigned a crossing guard to the intersection. On the day the accident occurred, however, the crossing guard called in sick and no substitute crossing guard was available. Departmental regulations required the precinct captain to be notified if a guard did not show up for work and for that captain to either (1) assign a patrolman to the intersection or (2) notify the principal of the affected school so that the principal could take appropriate steps. The precinct did neither of these things.

The City argued that, under *Riss* and other New York cases, it owed no duty to the child. The Court of Appeals disagreed. By sending a guard to the crossing in earlier weeks, the city had created an expectation by parents upon which they had relied. However, the court also emphasized that the manner by which the city fulfilled its duty was subject to a great deal of deference:

> In passing, we caution, however, that a municipality cannot be held liable solely for its failure to provide adequate public services. The extent of public services afforded by a municipality is, as a practical matter, limited by the resources of the community. Deployment of these resources remains, as it must, a legislative-executive decision which must be made without the benefit of hindsight. . . . Had the city established that a shortage of personnel precluded assignment of a patrolman to cover the intersection of Park Place and Ralph Avenue, notification of this contingency to the school principal or other appropriate action would have been sufficient to relieve the police department and New York City from liability for the failure to supervise the designated school crossing. To place a greater burden upon the police department would be unwarranted.

Florence, 375 N.E.2d at 767-768.

This passage maintains, in essence, that the City of New York would have fulfilled its duty to the children and parents of the public school if, after creating an expectation of protection, it gave notice to the school that it was withdrawing that protection. (Nothing in the record suggests that the school would have been able to replace the protection provided by the police, and nothing in the opinion conditions fulfillment of the city's duty on the ability of the school (and the city's foreknowledge of this ability) to provide substitute crossing guards.) Is a defeasible duty of this sort, which seems capable of being discharged by the city even if does not in the end take reasonable steps to provide the protection it has undertaken to provide, really the most that can be asked of a municipality?

3. *From Public Entities to Public Utilities.* Sovereign immunity and the public duty rule have been developed by courts in light of special concerns that are said to apply when courts review, in the context of tort litigation, the terms on which government undertakes certain actions and provides certain services. Should the same considerations sometimes apply to non-governmental actors that are engaging in the provision of what might plausibly be deemed "public" services? Consider the following opinion, also issued by the New York Court of Appeals. Is it essentially an application of *Riss*?

Strauss v. Belle Realty Co.

482 N.E.2d 34 (N.Y. 1985)

KAYE, J. On July 13, 1977, a failure of defendant Consolidated Edison's power system left most of New York City in darkness. In this action for damages allegedly resulting from the power failure, we are asked to determine whether Con Edison owed a duty of care to a tenant who suffered personal injuries in a common area of an apartment building, where his landlord—but not he—had a contractual relationship with the utility. We conclude that in the case of a blackout of a metropolis of several million residents and visitors, each in some manner necessarily affected by a 25-hour power failure, liability for injuries in a building's common areas should, as a matter of public policy, be limited by the contractual relationship.

. . . .

Plaintiff, Julius Strauss, then 77 years old, resided in an apartment building in Queens. Con Edison provided electricity to his apartment pursuant to agreement with him, and to the common areas of the building under a separate agreement with his landlord, defendant Belle Realty Company. As water to the apartment was supplied by electric pump, plaintiff had no running water for the duration of the blackout. Consequently, on the second day of the power failure, he set out for the basement to obtain water, but fell on the darkened, defective basement stairs, sustaining injuries. In this action against Belle Realty and Con Edison, plaintiff alleged negligence against the landlord, in failing to maintain the stairs or warn of their dangerous condition, and negligence against the utility in the performance of its duty to provide electricity.

Plaintiff moved for partial summary judgment against Con Edison . . . to establish that Con Edison owed a duty of care to plaintiff. . . . Con Edison cross-moved for summary judgment dismissing the complaint, maintaining it had no duty to a noncustomer.

The court . . . denied Con Edison's cross motion to dismiss the complaint, finding a question of fact as to whether it owed plaintiff a duty of care. The Appellate Division reversed and dismissed the complaint against Con Edison. Citing *Moch Co. v. Rensselaer Water Co.* (247 NY 160), the plurality concluded that "Con Ed did not owe a duty to plaintiff in any compensable legal sense" (98 AD2d 424, 428). . . . On public policy grounds, we now affirm the Appellate Division order dismissing the complaint against Con Edison.

A defendant may be held liable for negligence only when it breaches a duty owed to the plaintiff (*Pulka v. Edelman*, 40 NY2d 781, 782). The essential question here is whether Con Edison owed a duty to plaintiff, whose injuries from a fall on a darkened staircase may have conceivably been foreseeable, but with whom there was no contractual relationship for lighting in the building's common areas.

Duty in negligence cases is defined neither by foreseeability of injury (*Pulka v. Edelman, supra*, at p. 785) nor by privity of contract. As this court has long recognized, an obligation rooted in contract may engender a duty owed to those not in privity, for "[there] is nothing anomalous in a rule which imposes upon A, who has contracted with B, a duty to C and D and others according as he knows or does not know that the subject-matter of the contract is intended for their use" (*MacPherson v. Buick Motor Co.*, 217 NY 382, 393). In *Fish v. Waverly Elec. Light & Power Co.* (189 NY 336), for example, an electric company which had contracted with the plaintiff's employer to install ceiling lights had a duty to the plaintiff to exercise reasonable care. And in *Glanzer v. Shepard* (233 NY 236), a public weigher, hired by a seller of beans to certify the weight of a particular shipment, was found liable in negligence to the buyer.

But while the absence of privity does not foreclose recognition of a duty, it is still the responsibility of courts, in fixing the orbit of duty, "to limit the legal consequences of wrongs to a controllable degree" (*Tobin v. Grossman*, 24 NY2d 609, 619; *see also*, *Howard v. Lecher*, 42 NY2d 109), and to protect against crushing exposure to liability (*see*, *Pulka v. Edelman*, 40 NY2d 781, *supra*; *Ultramares Corp. v. Touche*, 255 NY 170). "In fixing the bounds of that duty, not only logic and science, but policy play an important role" (*De Angelis v. Lutheran Med. Center*, 58 NY2d 1053, 1055; *see also*, *Becker v. Schwartz*, 46 NY2d 401, 408). The courts' definition of an orbit of duty based on public policy may at times result in the exclusion of some who might otherwise have recovered for losses or injuries if traditional tort principles had been applied.

Considerations of privity are not entirely irrelevant in implementing policy. Indeed, in determining the liability of utilities for consequential damages for failure to provide service — a liability which could obviously be "enormous," and has been described as "*sui generis*," rather than strictly governed by tort or contract law principles (*see*, Prosser and Keeton, Torts § 92, at 663 [5th ed]) — courts have declined to extend the duty of care to noncustomers. For example, in *Moch Co. v. Rensselaer Water Co.* (247 NY 160, *supra*), a water works company contracted with the City of Rensselaer to satisfy its water requirements. Plaintiff's warehouse burned and plaintiff brought an action against the water company in part based on its alleged negligence in failing to supply sufficient water pressure to the city's hydrants. The court denied recovery, concluding that the proposed enlargement of the zone of duty would unduly extend liability. . . .

. . . .

In the view of the Appellate Division dissenter, *Moch* does not control because the injuries here were foreseeable and plaintiff was a member of a specific, limited, circumscribed class with a close relationship with Con Edison

. . . .

Here, insofar as revealed by the record, the arrangement between Con Edison and Belle Realty was no different from those existing between Con Edison and the millions of other customers it serves. Thus, Con Edison's duty to provide electricity to Belle Realty should not be treated separately from its broader statutory obligation to furnish power to all other applicants for such service in New York City and Westchester County. When plaintiff's relationship with Con Edison is viewed from this perspective, it is no answer to say that a duty is owed because, as a tenant in an apartment building, plaintiff belongs to a narrowly defined class.[2]

. . . .

If liability could be found here, then in logic and fairness the same result must follow in many similar situations. For example, a tenant's guests and invitees, as well as persons making deliveries or repairing equipment in the building, are equally persons who must use the common areas, and for whom they are maintained. Customers of a store and occupants of an office building stand in much the same position with respect to Con Edison as tenants of an apartment building. . . . While limiting recovery to customers in this instance can hardly be said to confer immunity from negligence on Con Edison, permitting recovery to those in plaintiff's circumstances would, in our view, violate the court's responsibility to define an orbit of duty that places controllable limits on liability.

Finally, we reject the suggestion of the dissent that there should be a fact-finding hearing to establish the alleged catastrophic probabilities flowing from the 1977 blackout and prospective blackouts, before any limitation is placed on Con Edison's duty to respond to the public for personal injuries. In exercising the court's traditional responsibility to fix the scope of duty, for application beyond a single incident, we need not blind ourselves to the obvious impact of a city-wide deprivation of electric power, or to the impossibility of fixing a rational boundary once beyond the contractual relationship, or to the societal consequences of rampant liability.

In sum, Con Edison is not answerable to the tenant of an apartment building injured in a common area as a result of Con Edison's negligent failure to provide electric service as required by its agreement with the building owner. Accordingly, the order of the Appellate Division should be affirmed, with costs.

MEYER, J. (dissenting). My disagreement with the majority results not from its consideration of public policy as a factor in determining the scope of Con Ed's duty, but from the fact that in reaching its public policy conclusion it has considered only one

---

2. In deciding that public policy precludes liability to a noncustomer injured in the common areas of an apartment building, we need not decide whether recovery would necessarily also be precluded where a person injured in the home is not the family bill payer but the spouse. In another context, where this court has defined the duty of a public accounting firm for negligent financial statements, we have recognized that the duty runs both to those in contractual privity with the accountant and to those whose bond is so close as to be, in practical effect, indistinguishable from privity, and we have on public policy grounds precluded wider liability to persons damaged by the accountant's negligence. (*See, Credit Alliance Corp. v. Andersen & Co.*, 65 NY2d 536 [decided herewith].)

side of the equation and based its conclusion on nothing more than assumption. I, therefore, respectfully dissent.

As Professors Prosser and Keeton have emphasized (Prosser and Keeton, Torts, at 357-358 [5th ed]), "The statement that there is or is not a duty begs the essential question—whether the plaintiff's interests are entitled to legal protection against the defendant's conduct. . . . It is a shorthand statement of a conclusion, rather than an aid to analysis in itself. . . . But it should be recognized that 'duty' is not sacrosanct in itself, but is only an expression of the sum total of those considerations of policy which lead the law to say that the plaintiff is entitled to protection." . . .

. . . .

There is, of course, legislative intervention in the regulation of gas and electric companies. But the only "legislative" limitation upon the liability of such companies consists of Public Service Commission acceptance and approval of Con Ed's rate schedule, which incorporates the rule, previously enunciated by this court, that liability "be limited to damages arising from the utility's willful misconduct or gross negligence" (*Food Pageant v. Consolidated Edison Co.*, 54 NY2d 167, 172). But, as *Food Pageant and Koch v. Consolidated Edison Co.* (62 NY2d 548, *cert denied*, 105 S.Ct. 1177) establish, what caused the injuries for which compensation is sought in this action was Con Ed's gross negligence.

. . . .

Criteria more extensive than the unsupported prediction of disaster for determining liability are not wanting. . . . Thus, in *Tarasoff v. Regents of Univ.* (17 Cal 3d 425, 434, 551 P2d 334, 342), the Supreme Court of California listed the major factors to be balanced in determining duty as "the foreseeability of harm to the plaintiff, the degree of certainty that the plaintiff suffered injury, the closeness of the connection between the defendant's conduct and the injury suffered, the moral blame attached to the defendant's conduct, the policy of preventing future harm, the extent of the burden to the defendant and consequences to the community of imposing a duty to exercise care with resulting liability for breach, and the availability, cost and prevalence of insurance for the risk involved." Prosser and Keeton (*op. cit., supra*, at 359), on the basis of the *Tarasoff* case and [another case], list similar factors, which are discussed at greater length in section 4 of their treatise. As to the loss distribution factor, they note (*op. cit.*, at 24-25) that, "The defendants in tort cases are to a large extent public utilities, industrial corporations, commercial enterprises, automobile owners, and others who by means of rates, prices, taxes or insurance are best able to distribute to the public at large the risks and losses which are inevitable in a complex civilization. Rather than leave the loss on the shoulders of the individual plaintiff, who may be ruined by it, the courts have tended to find reasons to shift it to the defendants", except where there are "limitations upon the power of a defendant to shift the loss to the public . . . [as] where the liability may extend to an unlimited number of unknown persons, and is incapable of being estimated or insured against in advance."

The majority's blind acceptance of the notion that Consolidated Edison will be crushed if held liable to the present plaintiff and others like him ignores the possibility that through application to the Public Service Commission Con Ed can seek such reduction of the return on stockholders' equity or [an] increase in its rates, or both, as may be necessary to pay the judgments obtained against it. It ignores as well the burden imposed upon the persons physically injured by Con Ed's gross negligence or, as to those forced to seek welfare assistance because their savings have been wiped out by the injury, the State. Doing so in the name of public policy seems particularly perverse, for what it says, in essence, is the more persons injured through a tort-feasor's gross negligence, the less the responsibility for injuries incurred.

I agree that there are situations encompassed by our tort system that require such a result, perverse though it may be, but before granting public utilities absolution beyond that which they already enjoy through the limitation of their liability to acts of gross negligence, I would put the burden upon the utility to establish the necessity for doing so. I am not suggesting that the issue is to be determined by a jury for, as already noted, I do not question that "duty" is a question of law to be determined by the courts. But the law is not without illustrations of preliminary issues involving facts to be determined by a Judge. . . .

All that I am suggesting is that it is Con Ed which claims that its duty does not encompass plaintiff, not because Con Ed was not grossly negligent, but because the effect of that negligence if Con Ed is held liable for it would be to cripple Con Ed as well as the victim's of the negligence. There simply is no basis other than the majority's say so for its assumptions that the impact of a city-wide deprivation of electric power upon the utility is entitled to greater consideration than the impact upon those injured; that a rational boundary cannot be fixed that will include some (apartment tenants injured in common areas, for example), if not all of the injured; that the consequence of imposing some bystander liability will be more adverse to societal interests than will follow from blindly limiting liability for tort to those with whom the tort-feasor has a contractual relationship. Before we grant Con Ed's motion to dismiss, therefore, we should require that a rational basis for such assumptions be established.

Con Ed may well be able to do so, but before its motion is granted at the expense of an unknown number of victims who have suffered injuries the extent and effects of which are also unknown, it should be required to establish that the catastrophic probabilities are great enough to warrant the limitation of duty it seeks.

I would, therefore, deny the summary judgment motions of both sides and remit to Supreme Court for determination of the preliminary fact issues involved.

NOTES AND QUESTIONS

1. *MacPherson to Moch: Back to Privity?* In *Strauss*, the New York Court of Appeals relies heavily on Cardozo's 1928 opinion for the same Court in *Moch Co. v. Rensselaer Water Co.*, 247 N.Y. 160 (1928). There, the defendant water company contracted with the City of Rensselaer to provide sufficient water for the needs of its residents. Because of carelessness, the company failed to pump an adequate supply of water to the City's fire hydrants, as a result of which firefighters were unable to stop a fire that eventually burned down plaintiff Moch's warehouse.

Cardozo, writing for the Court, first concluded that individual citizens such as Moch were not parties to, or intended beneficiaries of, the contract between the City and the water company, and hence Moch had no right to sue for breach of contract.

He then reasoned that, given the absence of any binding promise to Moch to supply water, the company's carelessness toward Moch's property amounted to mere *nonfeasance*, rather than misfeasance. Finally, given that the company's carelessness consisted of nonfeasance, and that none of the standard exceptions to the no-duty-to-rescue rule applied, he concluded that Moch could not sue the company for negligence.

The combined effect of *Moch's* contract and tort rulings was startling. Cardozo, the author of *MacPherson*, had 12 years later issued an opinion that looked a lot like *Winterbottom v. Wright*, which *MacPherson* had rejected. (*See* Chapter 2.) Essentially, it concluded that, absent privity, a party such as Moch could *not* sue for physical harm proximately caused by the carelessness of a utility such as the water company. How could Cardozo (or anyone else) reconcile the dismantling of privity in *MacPherson* with the resurrection of privity in *Moch*?

As indicated, Cardozo thought that the critical distinction between the two cases was that the former involved actionable misfeasance, whereas the latter involved nonfeasance — the mere failure to confer a gratuitous benefit. Essentially, he likened the position of the water company to that of a private citizen who happened to drive his giant tanker truck filled with water past the scene of the fire. Just as the truck owner would not have been legally obligated to Moch to stop and lend his truck to aid the firefighters, so too the company owed Moch no duty.

Most commentators are unconvinced by this distinction, in part because they have found it difficult to see what renders the water company's "failure to act" so dramatically different from the carelessness of Buick in *MacPherson*. (The latter, after all, consisted of a *failure* to inspect and detect a defective wheel.) Indeed, it is probably fair to say that *Moch* is widely regarded as one of Cardozo's least convincing efforts at legal reasoning. This is not to say that commentators uniformly criticize the *result* he reached by means of that reasoning. Like the Court in *Strauss*, many have embraced his conclusion that the liability of utilities for carelessness has to be limited by a special duty rule.

2. *Utilities.* Because water and power companies provide necessary goods and have been thought naturally to form into local monopolies, they have been subject to substantially greater degrees of government regulation than other businesses, such as product manufacturers. For example, federal and state agencies charged with regulating these businesses often mandate that they provide service to all members of the general public and that they do so at particular rates. Rate-setting is accomplished through an elaborate administrative process that involves hearings that often includes consideration of whether rates paid by utility customers should be calculated to include payment of liabilities incurred as a result of utility carelessness. For various reasons, regulators often conclude that it is desirable to limit utilities' liabilities, particularly for economic losses, flowing from an interruption of services. A question lurking beneath the surface of *Strauss* is whether the existence of this alternative scheme of regulation should affect tort analysis. If heavily regulated industries are entitled to a break in terms of tort liability, what should happen if and when they are deregulated?

3. *What Is the Worry?* More information about the events of 1977 might be helpful in analyzing *Strauss*. A strong July storm caused several lightning strikes that hit

power-generating or transmission facilities located north of New York City. These strikes, combined with Consolidated Edison's ("Con Edison's") negligence in responding to them, triggered circuit breakers and other devices that had been installed after an earlier blackout as a means of preventing electrical overloads and equipment damage. Unfortunately, resetting the system was a time-consuming affair, as most of the equipment in question was underground and had to be reset manually.

The result was a citywide blackout that started at about 9:30 P.M. and was not fully rectified for 25 hours. As the Court's opinion indicates, the loss of power cut off lights and water to city residents. It also shut down air conditioners in the midst of a summer heat wave. Thousands were trapped in elevators and subways. Thousands more had to climb and descend innumerable flights of stairs in the dark and heat. Traffic signals were rendered non-operational. Planes lost sight of runways at the city's airports and had to be diverted. During the first night of the blackout, parts of the city were in chaos, with looters causing damage to thousands of businesses and police arresting more than 3,500 suspects. Both the state and federal governments subsequently launched investigations into the causes and consequences of the blackout.

Limited duty and proximate cause rules (discussed in Chapters 2 and 5) provided the Court of Appeals with doctrines by which to cut off Con Edison's liability for a great deal of the economic loss suffered as a result of the blackout, as well as physical harms caused by the intervening criminal acts of looters. Why then, did it feel the need to deny Strauss's claim? What parade of horribles did the majority have in mind?

4. *Should the Breadth of the Tort Matter?* There is something counterintuitive about a judicial ruling that says, in effect, "because this tortfeasor has caused substantial and widespread damage by means of its carelessness, we must find a way to limit its liability." One might have thought that exactly the opposite conclusion ought to be drawn: because of the huge amount of harm generated, the tortfeasor does not deserve the benefit of any special, limited duty rules. Is *Strauss* simply a bow to expedience, in which the court concludes that, for the public good, Con Edison is entitled to a one-time exemption from the normal rules of tort law? If so, is the dissent right to insist that such an exemption should be granted only upon a relatively detailed showing by Con Edison as to the dire consequences of being held responsible to all foreseeable plaintiffs, as opposed to those with whom it had contracted?

5. *Duty, Liability Exemptions, and the Public Duty Rule Revisited.* The majority casts its holding as a no-duty ruling. If we recall from Chapter 2 *Heaven v. Pender's* conception of a duty of care based on the foreseeability of possible harm, the implication seems to be that, as Con Edison goes about the business of providing electricity, it is not obligated (except to those in privity) to take care to prevent unnecessary blackouts and the physical injuries one might expect to attend a blackout. As "foreseeability" provides the default test for duty in cases of misfeasance involving physical harm, the implication would seem to be that Con Edison could not foresee that its carelessness might cause harm to persons such as Strauss. Given that New York City had experienced a blackout just 12 years earlier, in 1965, which in turn led Con Edison to adopt measures to prevent future blackouts, is that a plausible conclusion? Does the majority opinion so conclude? Or is the dissenting judge right to suggest that the substance of the Court's "duty" ruling is not that Strauss failed to establish that

Con Edison was obligated to be vigilant of his physical well being, but instead a ruling that the utility might be entitled to a special affirmative defense that excuses it from liability *notwithstanding* that Strauss can make out all the traditional elements of a negligence cause of action? Does this "affirmative defense" resemble the public duty rule that the New York Court of Appeals invoked in *Riss*?

6. *Calabresi and the Cheapest Cost Avoider.* Does the idea of the cheapest cost avoider—mentioned in the notes following *Rowland v. Christian* in Chapter 2—help make sense of *Strauss*? As between Con Edison, Belle Realty, and Strauss, who was in the better position to minimize the risk of Strauss falling on darkened and defective stairs? If cheapest-cost-avoider analysis suggests that Strauss or Belle Realty were better able to minimize the risk of Strauss falling in the dark, would the same conclusion follow for a person who suffers a heart attack because he was forced during the blackout to ascend numerous flights of stairs in his high-rise apartment building? Who else might have prevented that sort of injury?

7. *Duties, Immunities, and Exemptions.* The discussion in this chapter of the common law doctrines of intra-familial, charitable, and sovereign immunities as well as the public duty rule are often cited as support for the view, discussed in Chapter 2, that the duty element of the negligence tort does not really invite an inquiry into whether the defendant was under an obligation to persons such as the plaintiff to be vigilant as to their physical well being. Instead, it calls for a multifactor inquiry that aims to determine whether society will in some aggregate sense be better off if liability is permitted or blocked. That they are so cited is hardly surprising: When courts invoke these doctrines they typically reference macropolicy considerations that favor protecting the activity in question. Even if this is the kind of reasoning that is going on under the heading of "duty" in this class of cases, is there good reason to suppose that the same reasoning is going on in any case in which a defendant makes and the court recognizes a no-duty argument?

REFERENCES/FURTHER READING

Comparative Fault

Ellen M. Bublick, *Comparative Fault to the Limits*, 56 Vand. L. Rev. 977 (2003).

Paul H. Edelman, *What Are We Comparing in Comparative Negligence?*, 85 Wash. U. L. Rev. 73 (2007).

Gail D. Hollister, *Using Comparative Fault to Replace the All-or-Nothing Lottery Imposed on Intentional Tort Suits in Which Both Plaintiff and Defendant Are at Fault*, 46 Vand. L. Rev. 121 (1993).

Jordan H. Leibman, et al., *The Effect of Lifting the Blindfold from Civil Juries Charged with Apportioning Damages in Modified Comparative Fault Cases: An Empirical Study of the Alternatives*, 35 Am. Bus. L.J. 349 (1998).

Wex S. Malone, *The Formative Era of Contributory Negligence*, 41 Ill. L. Rev. 151 (1946).

Frank L. Maraist, H. Alston Johnson III, Thomas C. Galligan, Jr., & William R. Corbett, *Answering a Fool According to his Folly: Ruminations on Comparative Fault Thirty Years On*, 70 La. L. Rev. 1105 (2010).

William L. Prosser, *Comparative Negligence*, 41 Cal. L. Rev. 1 (1953).

Gary T. Schwartz, *Contributory and Comparative Negligence: A Reappraisal*, 87 Yale L.J. 697 (1978).

William E. Westerbeke, *In Praise of Arbitrariness: The Proposed 83.7% Rule of Modified Comparative Fault*, 59 U. Kan. L. Rev. 991 (2011).

Assumption of Risk

Jennifer Arlen, *Private Contractual Alternatives to Malpractice Liability*, in Rogan Kersh & William Sage (eds.), *Medical Malpractice Liability—Torts and Contracts* (2006).

John L. Diamond, *Assumption of Risk after Comparative Negligence: Integrating Contract Theory into Tort Doctrine*, 52 Ohio St. L.J. 717 (1991).

Dilan A. Esper & Gregory Keating, *Abusing Duty*, 79 S. Cal. L. Rev. 265 (2006).

John C. P. Goldberg & Benjamin C. Zipursky, *Shielding Duty: How Attending to Assumption of Risk, Attractive Nuisance and Other "Quaint" Doctrines Can Improve Judicial Decisionmaking*, 79 S. Cal. L. Rev. 329 (2006).

Kenneth W. Simons, Murphy v. Steeplechase Amusement Co.: *While the Timorous May Stay at Home, The Adventurous Ride the Flopper*, in Robert L. Rabin & Stephen D. Sugarman (eds.), *Tort Stories* 179 (2003).

Kenneth W. Simons, *Reflections on Assumption of Risk*, 50 U.C.L.A. L. Rev. 481 (2002).

Stephen D. Sugarman, *Assumption of Risk*, 31 Val. U. L. Rev. 833 (1997).

Immunities

Jonathan Bruno, *Immunity for 'Discretionary' Functions: A Proposal to Amend the Federal Tort Claims Act*, 49 Harv. J. Leg. 411 (2012).

Erwin Chemerinsky, *Against Sovereign Immunity*, 53 Stan. L. Rev. 1201 (2001).

Joseph W. Glannon, *Liability for "Public Duties" under the Tort Claims Act: The Legislature Reconsiders the Public Duty Rule*, 79 Mass. L. Rev. 17 (1994).

Gail D. Hollister, *Parent-Child Immunity: A Doctrine in Search of a Justification*, 50 Fordham L. Rev. 489 (1982).

Jill R. Horwitz, *The Multiple Common Law Roots of Charitable Immunity: An Essay in Honor of Richard Epstein's Contributions to Tort Law*, 3 J. Tort L. #1 (2010).

Jill R. Horwitz & Joseph Mead, *Letting Good Deeds Go Unpunished: Volunteer Immunity Laws and Tort Deterrence*, 6 J. Emp. Legal Stud. 585 (2009).

Harry D. Krause, *On the Danger of Allowing Marital Fault to Re-emerge in the Guise of Torts*, 73 Notre Dame L. Rev. 1355 (1998).

Timothy D. Lytton, *Holding Bishops Accountable: How Lawsuits Helped the Catholic Church Confront Clergy Sexual Abuse* (2008).

Mark C. Niles, *"Nothing But Mischief": The Federal Tort Claims Act and the Scope of Discretionary Immunity, 54 Admin. L. Rev. 1275 (2002).*

Reva B. Siegal, *"The Rule of Love": Wife Beating as Prerogative and Privacy*, 105 Yale L.J. 2117 (1996).

Carl Tobias, *The Imminent Demise of Interspousal Tort Immunity*, 60 Mont. L. Rev. 101 (1999).

Jennifer Wriggins, *Interspousal Tort Immunity and Insurance "Family Member Exclusions": Shared Assumptions, Relational and Liberal Feminist Challenges*, 17 Wis. Women's L.J. 251 (2002).

Donald N. Zillman, *Protecting Discretion: Judicial Interpretation of the Discretionary Function Exception to the Federal Tort Claims Act*, 47 Me. L. Rev. 365 (1995).

CHAPTER 8

DAMAGES AND APPORTIONMENT

This chapter presents materials concerning the standard form of tort redress: payment of money damages by the tortfeasor to the victim. Section I addresses the legal rules that specify the types and amount of damages a tort plaintiff stands to recover. Sections II-IV concern the extent to which actors other than the individual tortfeasor—including the tortfeasor's employer, co-defendant(s), and liability insurer—may be required to pay some or all of those damages. The chapter concludes with a brief note on problems successful tort plaintiffs may face in enforcing judgments in their favor. Throughout, the focus remains on negligence, although much of the discussion applies to other torts as well.

I. ELEMENTS AND AVAILABILITY OF DAMAGES

A. Compensatory Damages

Smith v. Leech Brain & Co. Ltd.

2 Q.B. 405 (1962)

[William Smith was employed by the defendants at their iron works, which produced "galvanized" articles. The galvanizing process involved dipping items into a large tank filled with extremely hot molten metal. Larger articles were lowered into the tank by means of an overhead crane. The tank was circled by a low brick wall that ran around its circumference about two feet outside the tank's rim. The controls for the crane were located about one foot past this wall.

The location of the controls posed a danger to crane operators, because when items were dipped into the tank, drops of molten metal sometimes spattered out of the tank. To protect operators, the defendants provided a 6.5 × 3-foot sheet of corrugated iron, which was bent over at the top to form a partial roof. Because an operator had to use his hands to manipulate the crane controls, he would deploy this makeshift shield by turning his back to the tank and "sandwiching" the sheet of corrugated iron between his back and the outer side of the low brick wall. Once in this position, the operator would then reach up and operate the crane controls. Because, under this arrangement, the operator's back was to the tank, he could not view the dipping process. Instead, he relied on signals from another employee, standing farther away from the boiling metal, who had a view of the tank.

On August 15, 1950, at 1 A.M., Smith was operating the overhead crane and dipping a large article when he either peered around the makeshift shield to see what he was doing or leaned out to look at the man who was giving him instructions. As a result, he sustained a burn on his lip from a spattering of molten metal. The wound never healed. In fact, Smith developed cancer at the point of the wound, which caused his death.

Smith's widow brought this negligence action. — EDS.] . . .

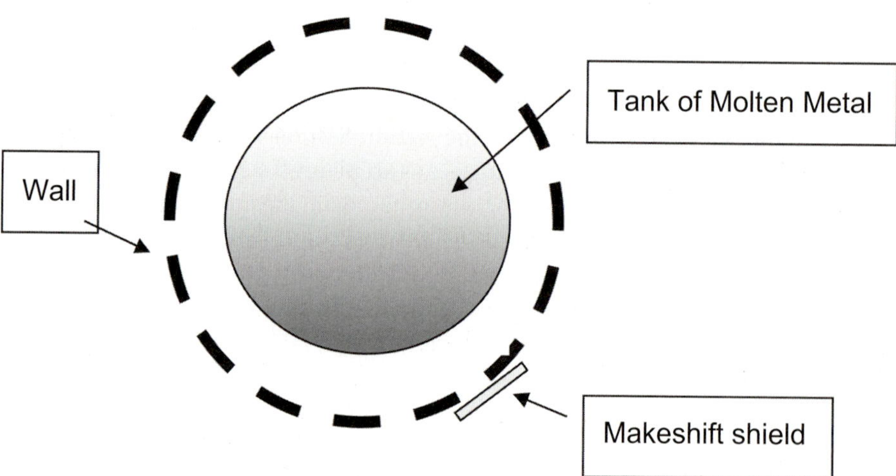

LORD PARKER C.J. . . . On the issue of [fault] I am satisfied that there was a clear and known danger of molten metal flying from the tank when articles were being lowered into it. . . . The dangerous process of lowering was done by remote control, and all that the operator had was the makeshift bit of corrugated iron which was put up and held by the operator himself by leaning against it. Of course, it is only right to say that so long as he stayed behind that shield, it was an adequate protection. But any reasonable employer must reasonably foresee that, men being what they are, the most natural thing in the world is that sooner or later the man will look round. Indeed, the evidence before me is that that is just what was done.

Added to that, in 1950 many galvanisers throughout the country . . . were providing what the defendants, when they altered their works in 1955, provided, namely, a proper shelter akin to a signal box with a window in front whereby the operator could watch what he was doing, and where he was really in complete safety and had no reason to put his head out. . . .

[Judge Parker rejected the contention that Smith was contributorily negligent. — EDS.]

The next question is whether the cancer which the plaintiff's husband had admittedly got, and the death resulting from it, were caused in whole or in part by the burn. The burn was treated at the time with picric acid and probably gauze was put on it. He did not get to hospital for a long time — he thought nothing of it. . . . But ultimately it did not heal, the place where the burn had been began to ulcerate and get larger, and he went to his general practitioner. The general practitioner without a doubt felt that he had epithelioma, a form of cancer on the lower lip. He was sent at once to hospital. This cancer was at once diagnosed, and thereafter he was in and out of hospital, having, first, treatment with radium needles which enable the lip to heal and destroy the primary growth. But even when he got to hospital it was noticed that his glands were swelling, and while no great significance was attached to that in the first instance, it became perfectly clear later that secondary growths were taking place. Thereafter, he had a series of operations, some six or seven, and finally he died in October, 1953.

[Judge Parker reviewed the evidence on actual causation provided by experts at trial. He concluded that the evidence supported the conclusion that the burn was probably an actual cause of the cancer. — EDS.]

The third question is damages. Here I am confronted with the recent decision of the Privy Council in [*Wagon Mound (No. 1)*]. But for that case, it seems to me perfectly clear that, assuming negligence proved, and assuming that the burn caused in whole or in part the cancer and the death, the plaintiff would be entitled to recover. . . .

For my part, I am quite satisfied that the [Privy Council's] Judicial Committee in the *Wagon Mound* case did not have what I may call, loosely, the thin skull cases in mind. It has always been the law of this country that a tortfeasor takes his victim as he finds him. It is unnecessary to do more than refer to the short passage in the decision of Kennedy J. in Dulieu v. White & Sons, where he said: "If a man is negligently run over or otherwise negligently injured in his body, it is no answer to the sufferer's claim for damages that he would have suffered less injury, or no injury at all, if he had not had an unusually thin skull or an unusually weak heart." [(1901) 2 K.B. 669, 679.]

. . . [A]s is well known, the work of the courts for years and years has gone on on that basis. There is not a day that goes by where some trial judge does not adopt that principle, that the tortfeasor takes his victim as he finds him. If the Judicial Committee had any intention of making an inroad into that doctrine, I am quite satisfied that they would have said so.

. . . [In distinguishing] Smith v. London & South Western Railway Company[,][(1870) L.R. 6 C.P. 14.][,] Lord Simonds[' *Wagon Mound (No. 1)* opinion] . . . said: ". . . that the point to which the [*Smith*] court directed its mind was not unforeseeable damage of a different kind from that which was foreseen, but more extensive damage of the same kind." [(1961) A.C. 388, 416.] In other words, Lord Simonds is clearly there drawing a distinction between the question whether a man could reasonably anticipate a type of injury, and the question whether a man could reasonably anticipate the extent of injury of the type which could be foreseen.

. . . .

In those circumstances, it seems to me that this is plainly a case which comes within the old principle. The test is not whether these employers could reasonably have foreseen that a burn would cause cancer and that he would die. The question is whether these employers could reasonably foresee the type of injury he suffered, namely, the burn. What, in the particular case, is the amount of damage which he suffers as a result of that burn, depends upon the characteristics and constitution of the victim.

[Judge Parker then considered the question of damages and concluded that they ought to reflect that the decedent might have developed cancer even if he had not suffered the burn. He awarded the plaintiff £3,064.]

NOTES AND QUESTIONS

1. *The Eggshell Skull Rule. Smith* provides a clear statement of the so-called eggshell (or thin) skull rule, which is also expressed in the maxim that "the tortfeasor takes his victim as he finds him." The idea is that, having wronged and injured another, a tortfeasor cannot be heard to complain that the *amount* of damage caused to that other was much greater than anyone could reasonably have expected because of a hidden physical vulnerability in the plaintiff.

The famous battery case of *Vosburg v. Putney*, 50 N.W. 403 (Wis. 1891) (reproduced in Chapter 9) is perhaps the leading authority in American law for the eggshell skull rule. There, a 12-year-old boy playfully kicked a 14-year-old boy in the shin as they sat in school. Although the kick was of a sort that could not have been expected to cause harm beyond momentary pain and a bruise, the victim suffered a permanent injury because of a pre-existing, hidden vulnerability. The Wisconsin Supreme Court ruled that the defendant could be held liable for the permanent injury. Should the extent of liability vary in accordance with the egregiousness of the wrongdoing? Which is a worse wrong: a schoolboy's purposeful but playful kick of his classmate or an employer's careless failure to provide employees protection against burns?

2. *Wagon Mound and Proximate Cause Revisited.* Recall the holding in *Wagon Mound (No. 1)*, discussed in Chapter 5. It denied recovery to a dock owner whose dock was destroyed by a fire that resulted from defendant shipowner's careless creation of an oil slick. This holding in turn rested on the conclusion that the ignition of the oil slick was not reasonably foreseeable. Yet the shipowner's carelessness apparently did cause *some* foreseeable damage to the dock—it mucked it up with oil. Still, the Privy Council declined to impose liability for the unforeseeable fire-damage harm based on the foreseeability of the mucking harm.

> It is not the act but the consequences on which tortious liability is founded. Just as (as it has been said) there is no such thing as negligence in the air, so there is no such thing as liability in the air. Suppose an action brought by A for damage caused by the carelessness (a neutral word) of B, for example, a fire caused by the careless spillage of oil. It may, of course, become relevant to know what duty B owed to A, but the only liability that is in question is the liability for damage by fire. It is vain to isolate the liability from its context and to say that B is or is not liable, and then to ask for what damage he is liable. For his liability is in respect of that damage and no

> other. If, as admittedly it is, B's liability (culpability) depends on the reasonable foreseeability of the consequent damage, how is that to be determined except by the foreseeability of the damage which in fact happened — the damage in suit? And, if that damage is unforeseeable so as to displace liability at large, how can the liability be restored so as to make compensation payable?
>
> But, it is said, a different position arises if B's careless act has been shown to be negligent and has caused some foreseeable damage to A. Their Lordships have already observed that to hold B liable for consequences however unforeseeable of a careless act, if, but only if, he is at the same time liable for some other damage however trivial, appears to be neither logical nor just. This becomes more clear if it is supposed that similar unforeseeable damage is suffered by A and C but other foreseeable damage, for which B is liable, by A only. A system of law which would hold B liable to A but not to C for the similar damage suffered by each of them could not easily be defended. Fortunately, the attempt is not necessary. For the same fallacy is at the root of the proposition. It is irrelevant to the question whether B is liable for unforeseeable damage that he is liable for foreseeable damage, as irrelevant as would the fact that he had trespassed on Whiteacre be to the question whether he has trespassed on Blackacre. Again, suppose a claim by A for damage by fire by the careless act of B. Of what relevance is it to that claim that he has another claim arising out of the same careless act? It would surely not prejudice his claim if that other claim failed: it cannot assist it if it succeeds. Each of them rests on its own bottom, and will fail if it can be established that the damage could not reasonably be foreseen.

Overseas Tankship (U.K.) Ltd. v. Morts Dock & Eng'g Co., [1961] 1 All E.R. 404, 415.

Given the foregoing analysis, is *Smith* right to conclude that the eggshell skull rule is consistent with the holding of *Wagon Mound No. 1*? Lord Simonds' opinion defends *Wagon Mound No. 1*'s foreseeable-type-of-harm test for proximate cause on the ground that a contrary rule, which would hold a careless actor responsible for an unforeseeable type of harm, would be unfair. If so, how can it be fair to saddle a defendant with unforeseeably large damages resulting from the realization of a risk of a foreseeable type of harm? Is the eggshell skull rule consistent with a scope-of-the-risk conception of proximate cause? *See* Restatement (Third) of Torts: Liability for Physical and Emotional Harm §§ 29, 31 (2010) (adopting a scope-of-the-risk conception of proximate cause and the eggshell skull rule).

3. *Eggshell Psyche?* Consider the relationship between the eggshell skull rule and the duty element, as expressed in a Canadian decision, *Mustapha v. Culligan of Canada, Ltd.* Plaintiff arranged with the defendant company to have the latter provide a water cooler for use by him and his family in their residence. As plaintiff and his wife were placing a not-yet-opened container of water in the cooler, they noticed that it contained a dead fly and part of another dead fly. Plaintiff, who was already compulsive about maintaining a sanitary home, became obsessed with the thought that he and his family had previously consumed contaminated water. As found by the trial judge:

> "[he] could not get the fly in the bottle out of his mind, he had nightmares, he was sleeping only four hours or so a night, he has been unable to drink water since the

Aflague v. Luger, 589 N.W.2d 177 (Neb. App. 1999) (defendant "*may*" be liable for all compensatory damages even though the plaintiff's injury is greater than expected due to the plaintiff's vulnerability).

7. Mitigation of Damages. In *Walter v. Wal-Mart* (Chapter 1), in which the victim sued Wal-Mart for negligently providing her with the wrong prescription medication, the trial judge refused to let the defendant argue that Ms. Walter was comparatively at fault for failing to detect that she had been given the wrong medicine. However, the court also instructed the jury that it could reduce her award on the ground that, by waiting a certain period of time before notifying her treating physician of her symptoms, she permitted the harmful side effects of the medicine to become worse than they would have had she been reasonably attentive to her condition. The notion that a plaintiff may sometimes bear responsibility for the magnitude of her damages—as opposed to the causing of the accident or the injury itself—is sometimes phrased in terms of a plaintiff's "duty" to mitigate damages. Perhaps it would be more accurate to say that a defendant who is liable in negligence may argue that he is not responsible to compensate for certain damages flowing from that negligence on the ground that the plaintiff could and should have taken certain steps to avoid them, but didn't.

The classic example is that of plaintiff *P* who, for no reason, refuses to obtain post-accident medical treatment, as a result of which his injuries are exacerbated. This rule of avoidable consequences applies only to *unreasonable* failures to mitigate. Were *P* to argue, and were the factfinder to determine, that he failed to pursue medical treatment because he was deeply depressed as a result of the accident, *D* presumably should not benefit from the mitigation rule. The same would hold true if *P* refused treatment out of sincerely held and "reasonable" religious beliefs. *See* Munn v. Algee, 924 F.2d 568 (5th Cir. 1991).

8. Pre-accident Mitigation. In *Spier v. Barker*, 323 N.E.2d 164 (N.Y. 1974)—discussed in a Chapter 7 note on comparative fault—the court held that the plaintiff's failure to wear her seat belt was not contributory negligence, but might have been a failure to mitigate. *Spier* is a somewhat unusual application of the avoidable consequences rule, in that the plaintiff's unreasonable failure, if any, occurred prior to the accident caused by the defendant's carelessness, as contrasted to a post-accident failure to seek treatment. Should that difference matter? What sort of pre-accident failures to take precautions against injury should count? As noted in Chapter 7, some courts have deemed evidence of the plaintiff's failure to wear a seat belt inadmissible with respect to damages. Professor Dobbs notes the same split over whether to admit evidence that an injured bicyclist was not wearing a helmet. Dan B. Dobbs, *The Law of Torts* § 205, at 514-516 (2000).

9. Eggshell Skull and Aggravation. Suppose a homeowner's failure to warn her guest of a hidden danger on the premises causes the guest to fall and injure her back. Prior to the fall, the guest was already suffering from chronic back pain. Were the guest to sue the host, the jury would be instructed to award damages reflecting the extent to which the fall worsened or aggravated the guest's chronic condition. Is this rule consistent with the eggshell skull rule? *See* Waits v. United Fire & Casualty Co., 572

N.W.2d 565 (Iowa 1997)) (trial court may properly give both eggshell skull instruction and aggravation instruction because jury might find that the plaintiff's preexisting injury contributed to its being more seriously aggravated by the defendant's negligence than it would have been otherwise).

*Kenton v. Hyatt Hotels Corp.**

693 S.W.2d 83 (Mo. 1985)

[On July 17, 1981, two skywalks located above the lobby of the Hyatt Regency Hotel in Kansas City, Missouri, collapsed onto the hotel's crowded lobby floor. The skywalks were constructed of concrete, steel, glass, and other materials and weighed, in the aggregate, more than 15 tons. Numerous victims and their family members sued various defendants, including Hyatt. A partial settlement was reached whereby Hyatt and other defendants agreed to stipulate to liability at the outset of each victim's trial, thereby leaving the jury to decide only the issue of damages. In exchange for this stipulation, the victims agreed not to present evidence bearing on how the defendants constructed and maintained the skywalks. They also agreed to a cap on the total amount of punitive damages available to them.**

Plaintiff-respondent Kay Kenton was one of the victims of the Hyatt disaster. The trial of her claim resulted in a jury award of $4 million in compensatory damages. Defendant-appellants filed post-verdict motions seeking a new trial on the ground that the jury's award was excessive. The trial judge concluded that the verdict was excessive and entered an order sustaining a motion for a new trial unless the plaintiff filed a remittitur of $250,000.*** Plaintiff-respondent accepted the remittitur. Both sides appealed. — EDS.]

The Court of Appeals . . . affirmed the judgment in all particulars but declined to restore the remittitur ordered by the trial court and transferred the case to this court. . . . We affirm the judgment of the trial court, in all respects, except remittitur; we reverse that part of the trial court's order . . . , and, under the principles of the companion case decided this date, Firestone v. Crown Center Redevelopment Corporation, 693 S.W.2d 99 (1985), remand the cause with directions to . . . reinstate the verdict and enter judgment for plaintiff for the verdict sum of $4,000,000. . . .

* [Superseded in part by statute, Mo. Rev. Stat. § 537.069 (1987). — EDS.]

** The effect of the settlement achieved by Hyatt was thus comparable to the effect of the trial judge's ruling in *Walter v. Wal-Mart* (Chapter 1) that Walter had made out a prima facie case of negligence as a matter of law.

*** Remittitur is a procedural device that can be invoked by trial judges in response to a defendant's motion for a new trial. Specifically, if the judge concludes that the jury's award was excessive in light of the evidence of damages presented at trial, she is empowered to grant plaintiff the option of accepting a lower award — that is, *remitting* a specified portion of the damages found by the jury — instead of re-trying the entire case. Without remittitur, the court would, upon a finding of excessiveness, order a new trial of the entire case.

I.

Appellants' first point is that the trial court erred in admitting evidence concerning events at the hotel on July 17, 1981. They contend: "Such evidence was not relevant to any issue relating to respondent's damages, because appellants admitted that respondent's injuries were caused by the accident. Because the evidence was inflammatory and prejudicial to appellants the jury's verdict was based upon improper passion and prejudice and was greatly enhanced." . . .

[Two witnesses, a fire captain who responded to the disaster, and a TV reporter who happened to be at the hotel to videotape an event there, were permitted by the trial court to testify to the chaos and devastation that followed the collapse. In addition, the trial court let into evidence small portions of videotape taken at the scene, although certain gruesome parts were edited out.]

Respondent's sister, Ann Kenton, who was with her on the evening of the disaster, testified as to her observations of that occurrence. . . . Ann described the sounds she heard coming from people in and around the skywalks after the collapse: "A. It was hysterical, hysteria. There were grown men crying for help and there was nothing I could do for them. There were people crushed everywhere, blood, and I looked in the area where she had been and there was rubble and bodies and I couldn't pick her out of the bodies. And the moans and screams." Ann later found respondent slumped in a chair to the west of the skywalks, and respondent was carried outside and placed on a gurney or a stretcher.

Still photographs of the scene were admitted into evidence, some in color and some in black and white. Ann Kenton identified Exhibit 4K as the area where respondent had been and described it thus: "A. There were people sticking halfway out from under the skywalk, from here up there were grown men screaming for help, moaning and I walked through the blood, or there was blood everywhere. And the rescue people were pulling out whoever was more alive than others, I suppose." None of the admitted photographs show any dead or injured persons.

. . . Appellants argue that the testimony concerning the events of July 17, 1981, was neither probative nor material to the issue of respondent's compensation; it was an attempt to incite the jury with evidence of how she was injured; and that the "slight probative value the testimony may have had concerning the nature of Ms. Kenton's injuries was outweighed completely by the gruesome and highly inflammatory nature of the evidence."

. . . Respondent says that . . . the evidence was not offered or received as bearing on appellants' conduct which was not an issue, but was offered instead for the purpose of showing how respondent was injured, both physically and mentally, as well as her location at the time her injuries were sustained. Begley v. Adaber Realty & Investment Company, 358 S.W.2d 785, 792 (Mo. 1962), held that photographs of ductwork which fell upon plaintiff, taken after it had fallen and had been removed to a parking lot, was admissible to show the type of construction, the presence or absence of straps, and what type of object struck plaintiff. Respondent was similarly entitled to show the force, violence and traumatic circumstances of this tragic occurrence as bearing upon the nature, extent and duration of her injuries. Compare Berry v. Harmon, 329 S.W.2d

784, 794 (Mo. 1959) [reversed and remanded on other grounds], where a photograph vividly showing the damaged interior of the automobile evidencing a terrific impact and showing blood stains on the car top was offered to show the force of the impact, a basis for plaintiff's injuries, and the place where the heads of the occupants were wedged after the evidence was held properly admitted as not being so inflammatory as to indicate any abuse of the court's discretion. . . . Even though photographs are gruesome and depict serious injuries they need not be excluded if they satisfy the rules as to the admission of demonstrative evidence. Chism v. Cowan, 425 S.W.2d 942, 947 (Mo. 1967). . . .

The evidence of respondent's injuries is that she suffered a cervical fracture which produced an initial paralysis of her body. In addition, Dr. Walter Menninger stated that she was subjected to the most severe psychosocial stressor imaginable, Grade 7, and the traumatic event and the crippling effects it produced caused a dramatic and profound psychic trauma which is continuing in nature. Dr. Francisco Gomez, respondent's treating psychiatrist, and Dr. Menninger classified her psychiatric injury as post-traumatic stress disorder, chronic and severe. Dr. Menninger testified further that she exhibited symptoms characteristic of a post-traumatic stress disorder: re-experiencing the trauma by either recurrent recollections, recurrent dreams, or suddenly acting or feeling as if the event was happening; and a numbing of responsiveness or reduced involvement with the external world sometime afterward. Certainly, the jury was entitled to consider the evidence of the scene of the collapse, the utter chaos that prevailed, and the effect upon respondent of being pinned beneath the debris, amidst blood, dead and injured bodies, and the sheer terror of the voices around her, in evaluating her physical and mental injuries for the purpose of fixing her compensation. The evidence was relevant, material, and appropriate. Its probative value far outweighed any prejudicial effect it might have had on the jury. There was no error in admitting the evidence, and Point I is overruled. . . .

III.

[Respondent had completed two years of law school at the time of the accident.] In Point III, appellants contend . . . that the trial court erred in refusing to exclude the testimony of two law school professors that respondent was unable to return to law school or to practice law. . . . Appellants conclude that because of these (claimed) errors the jury considered evidence incompetent in itself and as foundation for economic projections of respondent's future wage loss, and the award was greatly and improperly enhanced by the use of this evidence.

[The professors testified to the rigors of law school, stating, among other things, that law students devote 48 hours per week to preparation for class. One also opined that, in light of respondent's medical records and condition, she could not function as a law student. The second professor testified that respondent perhaps could return as a part-time student. She also stated that, while respondent might be able to practice law part-time after graduation, she was unaware of any part-time positions in the field of law. — Eds.] . . .

[A lawyer who suffered substantial disabilities from polio testified for the appellants. He opined that, with accommodations, respondent could finish law school and practice law. He conceded on cross-examination that respondent's disabilities would narrow her job opportunities. — EDS.]

The trial court properly determined that expert testimony was needed to inform the jury as to the physical and mental rigors of a person attending law school and practicing law. Members of the jury would not ordinarily have knowledge of that subject, and certainly the two professors, being actively engaged in that field would have superior knowledge and expertise thereof by reason of their education and experience. . . .

In addition to stating their knowledge and experience in the practice of law, and in teaching law school courses, both professors reviewed respondent's academic records, medical records, and reports which were in evidence without objection. [One of the professors] had also personally met and interviewed respondent. There was thus a sufficient factual basis for them to give their opinions. They were not . . . giving medical opinions. . . .

This case falls within the category of those allowing the opinion testimony of a non-medical expert witness on the employability of handicapped persons. Such a case is Chrisler v. Holiday Valley, Inc., 580 S.W.2d 309 (Mo. App. 1979), where a diving accident left plaintiff a quadriplegic, with bowel incontinence, sexual disfunction, and a reliance upon assistance to handle almost any activity or function except eating. Medical evidence established the conditions as permanent. The testimony of an employment counsellor, whose job it was to find employment for hard-to-place persons, including those with handicaps, to the effect that plaintiff was permanently unemployable, was held not to have been error. Defendant sought to strike her testimony on the basis that she was not an expert on para- and quadriplegics. The court said, "This misconceives the nature of Mrs. Maly's expertise. She was an expert on employment opportunities, particularly those for hard-to-place people including those with handicaps. It was about those opportunities that she was testifying and she was aware of the requirements for a vast number of jobs. Her slight experience with para- and quadriplegics did not affect her expertise on employment opportunities. . . ." *Chrisler, supra*, at 313. . . .

Appellants also say that the testimony of the two professors permitted respondent's economist, Dr. Ward, to base his opinion as to her projection of economic losses on incompetent evidence. The answer is found in the *Chrisler* case, *supra*, page 313[4], where the court found no error in the economists' expert testimony as based upon the expert testimony of the employment counselor. The jury had the function of evaluating all the evidence of economic loss, both appellants' and respondent's, and the weight to be given thereto. . . .

VI.

Appellants' Point VI contends that the trial court erred in refusing to grant a remittitur of $2,000,000. They contend that as a matter of law the jury's verdict greatly exceeded the upper limits of "fair and reasonable compensation," the proper measure of damages, and that the verdict was, as the trial court itself recognized, the erroneous product of a mistaken evaluation of highly incendiary evidence and [was] improperly disproportionate to awards for comparable or more severe injuries.

Taking respondent's evidence in the light most favorable to her, as this court must do, her loss of income and the reasonably anticipated future loss of income because of the injuries sustained was testified to . . . have been between $1,605,846 as a low, to a high of $2,164,642.

The evidence shows that, to the time of trial, respondent's hospital, medical and therapy expenses incurred amounted to at least $80,000; her future physical therapy and cost of an electronic device (T.E.N.S.) was from $189,759 to $250,000; her homemaking assistance and care, $307,228 to $614,457; her future medical and supplemental insurance, $100,679. This evidence places the low of these items at $677,666, and the high at $1,045,136.

The economic loss, present and future medical, and therapy expenses thus shows a range of between $2,283,512 to $3,209,778.

Respondent's age was 28 years at the time of trial. She has a life expectancy of 51.8 years.

The nature and extent of respondent's injuries, is shown by the following evidence, all shown to have been permanent. She suffered a broken neck with permanent spinal cord damage [with miraculous surgical treatment, she avoided becoming a permanent quadriplegic]; she has spasticity and weakness in all four limbs, inability to walk without crutches, and must wear a knee cage to prevent buckling of the left knee; lack of endurance and easy fatigability; reduced vital capacity and impaired breathing muscles; sensory loss of much of her body below her neck, including female parts. She will not enjoy a normal sexual life or have children normally; she has impaired bladder and bowel function with periods of incontinence. Her bladder condition causes her to retain urine which will eventually produce renal or kidney damage; psychic and emotional trauma diagnosed as chronic and severe post-traumatic stress syndrome, which will require continued psychiatric care; destruction of her athletic lifestyle which will prevent her from ever again playing tennis, skiing, running, jogging, playing softball, racquetball, hiking, backpacking and riding horses; and a commitment to 2 to 4 hours a day to maintain her present limited muscle function.

There was some evidence that respondent's cost of therapy and the T.E.N.S. unit would increase over her lifetime, and her income would also increase should she be employed as a lawyer, these being the effects of inflation.

The jury was entitled to consider the intangibles of the evidence of respondent's past and future pain and suffering, the destruction of her previous lifestyle, along with the evidence of economic loss. All of the matters going to the nature and extent of respondent's injuries were primarily for the jury's consideration because it is in a far better position to appraise them for the assessment of damages which would fairly and reasonably compensate her. . . . In Fowler v. Park Corporation, 673 S.W.2d 749, 758 (Mo. banc 1984), the plaintiff suffered the loss of both legs above the knees. He was 19 years old, with a life expectancy of 50 years. He had not successfully used prosthetic devices; he would need constant care and medical attention, and had doubtful employability. He did not introduce evidence of economic damage other than showing that he stood to lose one million dollars in earnings based upon present wage levels, and the court said that he would obviously be incapable of leading a normal social life. The jury of money, as well as inflation, should be taken into account in setting an appropriate award. *See* Dan B. Dobbs, *The Law of Torts* § 1056, at 1057-1058 (2000).

As Ellen Pryor has noted, lump sum awards can also present a different sort of problem for plaintiffs. Although large awards such as the one received by Kay Kenton might be entirely appropriate in light of her suffering and the lifetime of difficulties she faces, the fact remains that she and other successful tort plaintiffs receive compensation in the form of a single check worth thousands or millions of dollars. This sudden influx of wealth can complicate relations with family and friends, and present many other practical problems for persons not savvy about managing money.

As noted in Chapter 1, tort cases are today almost always resolved prior to trial. When resolution takes the form of a settlement agreement that includes a payment from the defendant (or the defendant's insurer) to the plaintiff, it is open to the parties to structure the settlement so that payment is made over time rather than in a lump sum. British legislation enacted in 2006 empowers judges who award damages meant to compensate for future economic losses to mandate that those damages be paid periodically rather than in a lump sum, even if the parties do not request that the award come in that form.

4. *Workers' Compensation Benefits Compared.* Absent intentional wrongdoing on the part of management, and apart from possible claims by workers against third parties whose actions contributed to workplace dangers, workplace injuries are now ordinarily recompensed through workers' compensation systems. *See* Chapter 11. These systems vary substantially, but they typically limit the injured employee's compensation to medical expenses related to treatment of the workplace injury, plus a fixed percentage of lost wages. The amount of compensation is set by legislative or administrative guidelines that are interpreted by officials employed by the system. These officials' decisions are subject to limited judicial review. Intangible elements of damages such as emotional distress are not separately compensable.

A basic distinction drawn by most systems is between temporary disabilities (e.g., a broken leg that completely heals) and permanent disabilities (e.g., loss of a limb). Those who suffer temporary disabilities are usually entitled to reimbursement for medical expenses and a percentage of lost wages for the period of recovery. Permanent disabilities may be treated differently, depending on whether the victim suffers the loss of a discrete body part (e.g., the loss of a finger, or of hearing in one ear) or suffers a permanent injury or condition that affects the worker's general physical abilities (e.g., a back injury that makes all physical movement difficult).

For discrete injuries, most systems award compensation based on a pre-set schedule. These schedules can make for grisly reading. For example, Neb. Rev. Stat. § 48-121(3) specifies in part that workers suffering discrete injuries shall be compensated as follows:

> For the loss of a thumb, sixty-six and two-thirds percent of daily wages during sixty weeks. For the loss of a first finger . . . sixty-six and two-thirds percent of daily wages during thirty-five weeks. . . . For the loss of a hand, sixty-six and two-thirds percent of daily wages during seventy-five weeks. . . . For the loss of the nose, sixty-six and two-thirds percent of daily wages during fifty weeks.

By contrast, when the injury causes the worker to be partially or totally disabled, she can recover a percentage of her lost wages (often two-thirds) for the length of the disability. (Because workers' compensation benefits are paid out sequentially, rather than in a lump sum, there is usually no need to project future lost income, as is the case in the award of tort damages.) However, these recoveries, too, may be subject to certain ceilings. For example, the Nebraska statute specifies a maximum salary for purposes of calculating permanent disabilities: benefits for a worker suffering a permanent disability who was being paid more than the statutory maximum will be calculated at the amount specified by the statute, rather than the worker's actual salary. Nebraska law also limits recovery for permanent partial disabilities to a maximum of 300 weeks' worth of benefits.

If a worker is killed on the job, surviving family members are not automatically qualified for compensation. Rather, they may receive benefits only if they are economic dependents of the deceased (typically a spouse who relied on the worker's income or a minor child). Qualified dependents are usually entitled to regular payments equal to a fixed percentage of the deceased's lost wages until the period of dependency ends (e.g., the death or remarriage of the widowed spouse, or the minor child's reaching the age of majority). Loss of consortium and emotional distress are, again, not compensable. In the absence of any economic dependents, the employer is often liable only for funeral expenses.

5. *Reproducing Inequality?* Experts who testify as to lost future earnings generally rely on statistics as to how much a person with the same education, background, and traits as the plaintiff could have expected to earn before and after suffering the injuries in question. This means that two careless drivers, each of whom causes identical injuries to his victim, may end up paying very different damage awards depending on the economic prospects of the victim. For example, if Kay Kenton were not a law student, but a bicycle messenger, her recovery for lost wages would have been substantially smaller.

Consider in this regard the situation faced by Kenneth Feinberg, who was appointed by the United States Attorney General to serve as the "Special Master" of the federally created September 11th Victim Compensation Fund of 2001 Pub. L. No. 107-71, 115 Stat. 597 (2001). The purpose of the Fund was to provide compensation to survivors of persons killed in, and to persons physically injured in, the 9/11 terrorist attacks as an alternative to their suing airlines and other actors that may have been negligent in failing to prevent the attacks. To induce potential claimants not to pursue their tort claims, the Fund promised to pay compensation equal to "the extent of the harm to the claimant, including any economic and noneconomic losses." While the federal statute that created the Fund required the Special Master to deduct "collateral sources" (such as life insurance) from any award—a reduction not required by the law of many states, including New York (*see* Note 11 *infra*)—it also left him with broad discretion to calculate "economic and noneconomic losses." Feinberg ruled that, absent "extraordinary circumstances," a claimant's future economic losses would be capped at an amount corresponding to the median income of those whose earnings placed them in the top 2 percent of earners nationally.

9. Remittitur and Additur. The Missouri Supreme Court's abolition of remittitur was unusual, and indeed—as indicated *in Kenton*—was promptly reversed by the state's legislature. What was it about the trial court's use of remittitur in *Kenton* that so bothered the Supreme Court? Notice that the elimination of remittitur did *not* take away the power of trial judges to order new trials in cases in which the judge concludes that the jury's verdict is shockingly large. Rather, it prevented the judge from giving the plaintiff the *option* of accepting a lower damage award *in lieu of* a new trial. Given that the court did not change the formal legal standard against which trial judges assess verdicts for excessiveness, and did not bar them from ordering new trials on grounds of excessiveness, what exactly did it expect to accomplish by abolishing remittitur?

Some jurisdictions empower the trial court to offer the defendant, in lieu of a new trial, the option of paying a specified larger award (again, only upon a finding by the judge that the jury's verdict is shocking—in these instances, shockingly low). This device is known as *additur.* (The same Missouri statute that reinstated remittiturs after *Firestone* and *Kenton* also allows for additurs.) Likewise, it is open to appellate courts to review awards for insufficiency, as opposed to excessiveness.

10. Appellate Review. Appellate court statements as to the standard by which they are to review jury verdicts, as well as the trial judge's initial review of those verdicts, vary. Some indicate that the trial court's ruling upholding or reversing a jury award is entitled to a presumption of correctness, given that the trial judge observed the trial and the jury first hand. Thus, the question is whether the trial court "abused its discretion" in upholding or second-guessing a jury award. *See, e.g.,* Thrailkill v. Patterson, 879 S.W.2d 836 (Tenn. 1994) (applying statute); Kelley v. Montesi, 539 A.2d 1020 (Conn. App. 1988). Others conduct the same sort of deferential review of the jury's verdict as was conducted by the trial court, without reference to the trial court's analysis. Kessel v. Leavitt, 511 S.E.2d 720 (W. Va. 1998).

On the issue of appellate review of damage awards, compare *Kenton* with *Southern v. Lyons,* 696 So. 2d 128 (La. Ct. App. 1997). Plaintiff, a 13-year-old boy, was struck by a boat and seriously injured while swimming in a lake. Defendant Clark was supposed to be supervising plaintiff, but had left him and his friends to play in the water unattended. The jury exonerated the driver of the boat, and found that plaintiff and Clark were each 50 percent responsible for the accident. Given that his injuries were not disabling, and that his mother was responsible for paying his medical expenses, plaintiff's evidence on damages concerned almost entirely the pain and suffering and lost enjoyment of life he had experienced as a result of the accident. It showed that the boat's propeller had torn large gashes in his side, that he remained conscious while being transported to the emergency room, that he underwent two surgeries and a painful skin graft, that he was bed-ridden for a month, and that he suffered permanent scarring that caused him pain, depression, and embarrassment, and limited his activities. In light of this evidence, the jury awarded him about $14,000. (Given the jury's allocation of fault, the trial court entered judgment for plaintiff for $7,000.) On review, the appellate court concluded that the jury's award was shockingly low. It therefore increased that award to about $85,000—a figure it described as representing the smallest quantum of damages that a reasonable jury could have found in light of the evidence. The court also found that the jury's assignment of equal fault to plaintiff and Clark was erroneous, and instead held that plaintiff could be assigned no more than 20 percent of the responsibility for the accident. Accordingly, it entered judgment for $68,000.

11. Compensation for Expenses Not Incurred: The Collateral Source Rule. As noted in Chapter 1, medical and other expenses incurred by injury victims will often be covered at least in part by insurance purchased by the victim or provided to her by her employer or by governmental programs such as Medicare. Thus, in *Walter v. Wal-Mart*, when Antoinette Walter sued Wal-Mart for carelessly poisoning her and offered proof of medical costs amounting to about $70,000, that figure did not represent the amount that she actually paid out of her own assets. Indeed, to the extent these charges were paid, they were paid by Medicare. The *Walter* jury heard no evidence as to who paid what percentage of her medical bills because of the operation of a rule of tort law called the *collateral source rule.* It holds that a tortfeasor is not entitled to present evidence at trial indicating that the victim has received, or stands to receive, compensation for her injuries from some other source.

Various rationales are offered in support of this rule. Some argue that the tortfeasor should not benefit from the "good fortune" of having wrongfully injured a person with insurance or other sources of compensation. Others suggest that, to deduct for insurance proceeds would be to deny the plaintiff the benefit she has secured for herself by obtaining insurance. Still others argue that, as a practical matter, the rule helps counteract the American rule denying successful tort plaintiffs attorneys' fees as part of compensatory damages.

In recent years, as many as half the states have modified or abolished the collateral source rule as it applies to all tort cases or to specific areas of tort, such as medical malpractice. The terms of these statutes vary: Some merely permit the defendant to submit for the factfinder's consideration evidence as to other sources of compensation. Other laws mandate that any recovery by the plaintiff be offset by the value of these other sources. In New York, for example, the legislature has eliminated the collateral source rule in personal injury cases. *See* N.Y. Civ. Prac. L. & Rules § 4545(a) (2009):

> In any action brought to recover damages for personal injury, injury to property or wrongful death, where the plaintiff seeks to recover for the cost of medical care, dental care, custodial care or rehabilitation services, loss of earnings or other economic loss, evidence shall be admissible for consideration by the court to establish that any such past or future cost or expense was or will, with reasonable certainty, be replaced or indemnified, in whole or in part, from any collateral source, except for life insurance and those payments as to which there is a statutory right of reimbursement. If the court finds that any such cost or expense was or will, with reasonable certainty, be replaced or indemnified from any such collateral source, it shall reduce the amount of the award by such finding, minus an amount equal to the premiums paid by the plaintiff for such benefits for the two-year period immediately preceding the accrual of such action and minus an amount equal to the projected future cost to the plaintiff of maintaining such benefits. . . . Any collateral source deduction required by this subdivision shall be made by the

> trial court after the rendering of the jury's verdict. The plaintiff may prove his or her losses and expenses at the trial irrespective of whether such sums will later have to be deducted from the plaintiff's recovery.

What might justify the legislature's decision to carve out from this new rule the value of the insurance premiums that the plaintiff paid two years prior to her injury, as well as the premiums she will have to pay to maintain her insurance benefits in the future?

12. Pain and Suffering Damages and Tort Reform. As noted above, jury awards designed to compensate plaintiffs for pain and suffering and other intangible losses are the subject of intense debate today. Critics of the current system argue that the impossibility of translating pain and suffering into dollar amounts gives jurors carte blanche to award any amount they feel is appropriate in light of their sympathy for the plaintiff and antipathy for the defendant. They also claim that such awards have risen substantially, in real dollar terms, over the last 30 years. Defenders argue that there has been no such increase and that the jury is the appropriate institution to assign values to intangible injuries.

As courts, commentators, interest groups, and legislatures have become increasingly concerned about the size of jury verdicts, legislatures have responded with various measures, including some that directly address compensatory damages. Some legislatures have set flat caps on the compensatory award that a plaintiff can recover in a certain type of tort litigation. A Virginia statute, for example, imposes a $2 million limit on total compensatory damages recoverable in medical malpractice actions based on acts of malpractice that occur between July 1, 2012, and June 30, 2013.* Thus, even if a jury were to determine, based on a reasonable view of the evidence presented, that the plaintiff faces the prospect of $10 million in medical expenses and lost earnings over his lifetime, the trial judge must reduce the award to $2 million. Va. Code. Ann. § 8.01-581.15. Consider who fares worst under Virginia law. Is such a system intolerably regressive? *See* Pulliam v. Coastal Emerg. Servs., Inc., 509 S.E.2d 307 (Va. 1999) (upholding the cap against constitutional challenge).

Other states have enacted legislation placing a cap only on noneconomic losses. *See, e.g.*, Cal. Civ. Code § 3333.2 (imposing a $250,000 cap on noneconomic damages in medical malpractice cases). Still others eschew caps in favor of more robust judicial review. New York law, for example, instructs judges to examine whether a jury award "deviates materially from what would constitute reasonable compensation," a mandate that courts have construed as requiring them to conduct a more searching review of jury awards than under the traditional "shocks the conscience" standard. N.Y. Civ. Prac. L. & Rules § 5501(c) (2007).

In administering the September 11th Fund, mentioned in Note 5 *supra*, Special Master Feinberg concluded that "the fairest and most rational approach" to the "unfathomable task" of compensating victims for their noneconomic losses was to award a uniform amount to the estates of deceased victims and their dependents. Thus for each claim brought on behalf of a person killed in the attacks, the victim's estate

---

* The Virginia law mandates modest annual increases in this cap through 2030–31. Liability for malpractice committed in that time period will be capped at about $3 million.

received $250,000, while the decedent's spouse and dependents (if any) each received an additional $100,000. However, this figure was adjusted upward for claimants facing "extraordinary circumstances," including the loss of multiple family members in the attacks. Do you agree that this was the fairest, most rational approach available for compensating noneconomic loss out of the Fund? (Recall Chapter 6's discussion of the reluctance of courts to award emotional distress damages to wrongful death claimants.) If fairness and rationality called for uniform compensation with respect to noneconomic losses, did it also call for uniform awards with respect to lost earnings?

13. Federal Courts and the Seventh Amendment. The Seventh Amendment to the U.S. Constitution, which governs proceedings in federal but not state courts, guarantees the right to a jury trial, and also mandates that "no fact tried by a jury, shall be otherwise re-examined in any Court of the United States, than according to the rules of the common law." The Supreme Court has held that this "Reexamination Clause" does not prohibit federal *trial* judges from overturning jury verdicts on grounds of excessiveness. Indeed, as we have seen, they have the power to grant new trials upon a finding that the jury's verdict runs counter to the great weight of the evidence, and even to enter post-verdict judgments as a matter of law if no reasonable jury could find as the jury did. These practices, the Court has reasoned, are permissible because they have a long historic pedigree. Thus, although they involve reexamination of jury findings, that reexamination proceeds "according to the rules of the common law."

The Court has taken a different view of the constitutionality of modern state statutes requiring *courts of appeal* to engage in searching review of juries' damage awards. (Recall that when a federal court hears a tort case under its "diversity" jurisdiction, it is obligated to apply substantive state law.) Specifically, it has held that any form of review more robust than deferential "abuse of discretion" review, when undertaken by appellate judges, would violate the Reexamination Clause. Gasperini v. Center for Humanities, Inc., 518 U.S. 415 (1996) (upholding application in federal court of a New York statute mandating appellate review of jury awards, but only on the understanding that the statute called for nothing more rigorous than abuse-of-discretion review).

14. Nominal Damages and Injunctions. A jury is permitted to find that a given defendant has committed a tort against a plaintiff, and that the defendant cannot invoke an affirmative defense, yet still conclude that the plaintiff is not entitled to any compensation. For example, suppose car driver *P* is struck from behind by careless car driver *D*. Suppose further, however, the jury believes that *P* suffered only a trivial scratch to the bumper of her car. Under these circumstances, the jury may enter a verdict awarding *P nominal damages*—usually specified by law as $1. Such an award serves as an acknowledgment of the tort notwithstanding the absence of any compensable losses flowing from it.

In seeking recourse, tort plaintiffs are not necessarily limited to monetary compensation. Alternatively, or in addition, some plaintiffs will be entitled to *injunctive* relief. *See* Chapter 11. Typically, injunctive relief consists of an order from the court mandating that the defendant cease engaging in a particular activity (e.g., discharging pollutants into a stream that runs to plaintiff's land). Failure to comply with the order amounts to contempt of court, which is punishable by fine and/or imprisonment.

Big Think

Compensatory Damages

Why should a tortfeasor's liability be keyed to the extent of the victim's injuries? In what sense is it "fair" or "reasonable" to require a small business owner to pay $1 million to a patron who happens to suffer grave injuries because of a fall caused by unsafe conditions on the premises? Would it be more fair or reasonable to award damages by reference to a defendant's culpability?

Countries including Finland and Denmark pro-rate certain criminal and regulatory penalties, such as fines for speeding, based on the offender's wealth. (To date, fines imposed on very wealthy drivers have run as high as $200,000 for a single incident of speeding.) As discussed below, in U.S. jurisdictions, a tortfeasor's wealth can be taken into account when determining an award of *punitive* damages. While compensatory damages are in principle awarded without regard to wealth, it seems likely that wealth sometimes plays a role, if only subconsciously, in jurors' (and judges') damages assessments. Consider the $550,000 compensatory award in *Walter v. Wal-Mart* (Chapter 1). Is it possible that, if the defendant had been a sole proprietor rather than a huge corporation, the jury's damages award would have been smaller or judicial scrutiny of that award more vigorous?

Suppose a car driver carelessly collides with a bicycle being ridden by a happy, healthy college student. As a result of the accident, the victim suffers permanent brain damage that leaves him unable to communicate with others and in need of constant supervision and care. How should jurors think about compensation for this sort of injury? What is being compensated? If you were a juror, how would you calculate this imagined victim's non-economic damages?

B. Punitive Damages

Although pain and suffering damages have drawn the attention of judges, legislators, and scholars, perhaps no issue has garnered more widespread notice among contemporary observers of tort law than punitive damages. Punitive damages—also called "exemplary" or "vindictive" damages—form a special category of damages in two related respects. First, an award of punitive damages stands apart from damages that compensate a tort victim for lost wages, medical expenses, pain and suffering, and lost quality of life.* Second, these "extra-compensatory" damages are not available to all tort plaintiffs, only to those who can demonstrate that they have been victims of certain "aggravated" forms of mistreatment involving "malice, insult, oppression, [or] wanton or willful violence." Towle v. Blake, 48 N.H. 92 (1868).

Punitive damages have been a part of American law from the time of the nation's founding. Since then, they have episodically become the subject of controversy. In the period from about 1850 to 1900, some judges and scholars disparaged punitive damages as introducing a form of criminal punishment into tort law. Although these critics occasionally expressed concern that punitive awards worked injustices

---

* Many jurisdictions require the plaintiff to establish that she incurred some actual damages before the jury may consider awarding punitive damages.

against particular defendants, the gist of their complaints was conceptual: In their eyes, punitive damages flouted the boundaries separating crime from tort, public law from private law, and punishment from compensation. After this wave of criticism failed to persuade most courts and legislatures to change the common law of punitive damages, a period of relative quiet ensued.* However, in the 1980s, the issue of punitive damages' legitimacy erupted again. In contrast to their nineteenth-century predecessors, contemporary critics argue that punitive awards threaten the vitality of the economy and empower undeserving plaintiffs and their lawyers to extract "windfalls" from corporate defendants. Also in contrast to their predecessors, contemporary critics have had a good deal more success in convincing courts and legislatures to introduce significant new restrictions on the ability of plaintiffs to obtain punitive damages.

The reasons for this shift in the terms of the debate are subtle, and will be explored in more detail in Chapter 13. For now, we note that the debates raise three interrelated questions: (1) Should some tort plaintiffs be permitted to recover an additional quantum of damages beyond the amount that, in principle, compensates for the physical and emotional harms that they have suffered?; (2) If so, which plaintiffs, and why?; and (3) By what criteria should judges and jurors determine the size of this additional quantum of damages? We devote some attention to each of these questions below, and consider question (3) in more detail in Chapter 13.

National By-Products, Inc. v. Searcy House Moving Co.

731 S.W.2d 194 (Ark. 1987)

Dudley, J. The sole issue in this tort case is whether an award of punitive damages should be upheld. We hold there was no substantial evidence to support the award of punitive damages, and reverse the judgment.

On July 11, 1985, Robert Foley was driving a large tractor trailer for appellant National By-Products, Inc. from Batesville south on Highway 167. At the same time, appellee Searcy House Moving Company was moving a house north on the same highway. Appellee could not get the house through a bridge which was just north of Bald Knob, and, while the house was being adjusted on the house moving trailer, traffic was stopped and flagged around in the one lane of traffic still open. Stacy McGee and Lorene Staggs were slowly starting to go through the open lane when appellant Foley, speeding in an over-weight truck smashed into the rear of their car, knocking it eighty feet forward, causing it to hit the house and trailer, and then to hit two bystanders. Appellant National's truck also struck the house and then crashed into another tractor-trailer rig. Lorene Staggs died instantly and Stacy McGee died seven hours later. The estates of Lorene Staggs and Stacy McGee filed

---

* By way of illustration, we note that the index to the 1964 edition of Prosser's *Torts* treatise contains no separate heading for punitive damages, although they are mentioned briefly in the book's opening remarks on the relation of tort to criminal law. The treatise characterizes them as an "anomalous . . . invasion" of criminal principles into tort law, but it does not associate their anomalousness with illegitimacy or impropriety. William L. Prosser, *Handbook of the Law of Torts* § 2, at 9 (3d ed. 1964).

wrongful death actions against Foley and appellant National By-Products, Inc. and appellee moving company. Defendants Foley and National By-Products and defendant moving company filed cross-complaints against each other, each asking compensatory and punitive damages from the other. The cases were tried before a jury which returned compensatory damage awards of $3,000,000 to the estate of Stacy McGee, $1,400,000 to the estate of Lorene Staggs, and $15,000 to appellee moving company. In addition, separate punitive damage awards of $100,000 were given to each estate and to appellee moving company. The judgments in the wrongful death cases were satisfied and appellee moving company agreed to a remittitur of its compensatory damage award from $15,000 to $1,883.14, the stipulated amount of compensatory damages. Therefore, the only damage award involved in this appeal is the $100,000 punitive damage award made in favor of appellee moving company and against appellant National By-Products Company.

Appellant contends that the trial court erred in refusing to grant its motion for a judgment notwithstanding the verdict. The argument is meritorious. An award of punitive damages is justified only where the evidence indicates that the defendant acted wantonly in causing the injury or with such a conscious indifference to the consequences that malice may be inferred. We have previously defined wantonness and conscious indifference to the consequences. In Ellis v. Ferguson, 238 Ark. 776, 385 S.W.2d 154 (1964), we said:

> Wantonness is essentially an attitude of mind and imparts [. . .] such conduct as manifests a "disposition of perversity." Such a disposition or mental state is shown by a person, when, notwithstanding his conscious and timely knowledge of an approach to an unusual danger and of common probability of injury to others, he proceeds into the presence of danger, with indifference to consequences and with absence of all care. . . .
>
> It is not necessary to prove that the defendant deliberately intended to injure the plaintiff. It is enough if it is shown that, indifferent to consequences, the defendant intentionally acted in such a way that the natural and probable consequence of his act was injury to the plaintiff.

In Freeman v. Anderson, 279 Ark. 282, 651 S.W.2d 450 (1983), we quoted with approval from St. Louis, I. M. & S. Ry. Co. v. Dysart, 89 Ark. 261, 116 S.W. 224 (1919):

> The terms "wilfulness, or conscious indifference to consequences from which malice may be inferred," as used in the decisions of this court, means such conduct in the face of discovered peril. In other words, in order to superadd this element of damages by way of punishment, *it must appear that the negligent party knew, or had reason to believe, that his act of negligence was about to inflict injury, and that he continued in his course with a conscious indifference to the consequences,* from which malice may be inferred.

In the case at bar there was proof of gross negligence, but gross negligence is not sufficient to justify punitive damages.

The facts, when viewed most favorably to appellee, reveal that Foley, appellant's driver, was late leaving Batesville and his truck weighed 80,480 pounds, which is

480 pounds over the legal limit. Foley had received six citations in the last year for driving an overweight truck, and appellant had paid all of the citations. One of appellant's employees testified that the company had a disciplinary procedure for drivers who got an excessive number of overweight tickets, and he testified that Foley had an excessive number of such tickets, but admitted that Foley had not been cautioned or disciplined for driving an overweight truck. Appellee's expert witness on accident reconstruction testified that the 480 pounds excess weight on the 80,000 pound rig was a contributing, but insignificant, factor in the accident.

Between Batesville and the place of the accident, Foley exceeded the 55 miles per hour speed limit while going downhill. He got so close to one car that all the driver of the car could see in his rearview mirror was the grill of Foley's tractor. He got extremely close to another car while "tailgating" downhill. Finally, he came around a curve at the crest of a small hill and had 804 feet of clear visibility to the bridge structure where the accident occurred. The house, which was sitting on the trailer, at the bridge, was 17 feet high, 28 feet wide, and 36 feet long, and because of its added height, could be seen from about 900 feet away. Foley either did not apply his brakes, or he applied them but they did not function properly.

Appellee's witnesses said Foley was going 60 to 70 miles per hour and made no effort to stop even though he went past a vehicle with a flashing warning light. They testified his brake lights did not come on, the tires did not skid, there was no smoke from either the brakes or tires, and there were no skid marks. However, appellee's expert brake witness testified that Foley probably did apply his brakes just before the accident, but the brakes were not working properly. While the expert did not testify about standards in the industry, he did testify that the Ryder Truck Company checks truck brakes every 8,000 miles. One of the appellant's employees testified that the company policy was to adjust the trailer brakes once a month, but the brakes on this trailer had not been adjusted for three and one-half months, and the tractor brakes had not been opened for a complete inspection for almost six months, although they were adjusted about 6 weeks before the accident. He further testified that appellant conducted an internal inspection of the brakes every 50,000 miles as recommended by the American Trucking Association and, in addition, the drivers conducted a daily inspection. There was no evidence that appellant had any knowledge that the brakes were faulty.

As Foley sped downhill at 70 miles per hour, he ran into the rear of the decedent's car and then struck appellee's rig and the house.

The foregoing facts do not show that appellant, either by its own policies or through the actions of its agent Foley, intentionally acted in such a way that the natural and probable consequence was to damage appellee's property. Nor do the facts show that appellant knew that some act of negligence was about to cause damage, but still continued to cause that damage. Accordingly, we reverse the judgment for punitive damages. . . .

Reversed.

HAYS, J. (dissenting) (joined by Purtle, J.). The majority's opinion has examined the evidence supporting punitive damages more from the appellant's standpoint than the appellee's. When viewed most favorably to the appellee, and with its fullest probative force, I believe there was substantial evidence to support the trial court's refusal to grant a motion for a directed verdict. Dalrymple v. Fields, 276 Ark. 185, 633 S.W.2d 362 (1982). . . .

We no longer require actual malice as an essential constituent of punitive damages. It is enough if the defendant acted recklessly or wantonly, or with a conscious indifference to the safety and welfare of others using the highways. In Dalrymple v. Fields, *supra*, we said:

> Before punitive damages may be allowed it must be shown that in the absence of proof of malice or willfulness there was a wanton and conscious indifference for the rights and safety of others on the part of the tortfeasor.

While excessive speed may, in many circumstances, be no more than ordinary negligence, actions are not to be viewed in a vacuum, and what may be no more than negligence in one setting can readily be seen as wantonness or conscious indifference in another context. Thus driving 85 m.p.h. on certain stretches of highway may be relatively safe, or it may be negligence, depending on the traffic, weather, etc. But driving only 35 or 40 m.p.h. past a school at dismissal hour or close to a playground crowded with children with an evident indifference to the known tendencies of children could meet even restrictive concepts of wantonness. In Airco, Inc. v. Simmons First National Bank, 276 Ark. 486, 638 S.W.2d 660 (1982), we upheld a monumental award of punitive damages, not on proof that Airco had any intent to injure, but because the injury was the natural and probable consequence of Airco's conduct. It seems a fair analogy to me to say that when one knowingly drives an overloaded 18-wheeler, with defective brakes, on the highway at speeds of 70 m.p.h. by some accounts, oblivious of warning signals and without slowing down and with no apparent effort at stopping, approaching congestion on the highway, a collision is the natural and probable consequence of such conduct. At least, reasonable minds could differ on the issue of conscious indifference and that is enough.

In sum, the proof was that Robert Foley was several hours late leaving Batesville for Little Rock. His truck, an 18-wheeler, was loaded beyond the lawful limit. His truck, by whatever standard one chooses, was equipped with brakes that were not functioning properly. For some miles prior to the point of impact Mr. Foley drove so fast and so close to preceding vehicles that two of those motorists were alarmed by it and described his conduct at trial as speeding and "tailgating." Rounding a curve bearing into a straight, level stretch of highway some 900 feet from the appellee's house-moving rig, Mr. Foley proceeded at a high rate of speed (70 m.p.h. by one account) and with no discernible attempt to reduce his speed (some witnesses testified that his speed actually increased as he neared the impact point), past one vehicle with a warning light flashing, to strike the Staggs-McGee vehicle, knocking it a considerable distance in the air, and resulting in the deaths of the two occupants, before striking another vehicle and the house. Photographs of the scene attest to extraordinary force of the impact.

There was testimony that one of the brake shoes on the truck was not even touching the brake drum, rendering it useless as a braking device. There was testimony that none of the four rear brakes met Department of Transportation specifications. There was other material evidence from which an inference could be drawn that the brakes on the truck were seriously deficient and that fact was known by Foley and was in derogation of the policies of National By-Products, Inc. Lastly, there was proof from which the jury could quite properly have inferred that National By-Products, Inc., in addition to neglecting the safe operation of the truck involved, engaged in practices which promoted the overloading of its trucks beyond the legal limit, by routinely paying weight fines rather than demanding compliance by its drivers.

The proof, I believe, was such that a jury had a right under the law to exemplify the conduct of both defendants by assessing punitive damages. The judgment should be affirmed.

Mathias v. Accor Economy Lodging, Inc.

347 F.3d 672 (7th Cir. 2003)

Posner, J. The plaintiffs brought this diversity suit governed by Illinois law against affiliated entities (which the parties treat as a single entity, as shall we) that own and operate the "Motel 6" chain of hotels and motels. One of these hotels (now a "Red Roof Inn," though still owned by the defendant) is in downtown Chicago. The plaintiffs, a brother and sister, were guests there and were bitten by bedbugs, which are making a comeback in the U.S. as a consequence of more conservative use of pesticides. The plaintiffs claim that in allowing guests to be attacked by bedbugs in a motel that charges upwards of $100 a day for a room and would not like to be mistaken for a flophouse, the defendant was guilty of "willful and wanton conduct" and thus under Illinois law is liable for punitive as well as compensatory damages. The jury agreed and awarded each plaintiff $186,000 in punitive damages though only $5,000 in compensatory damages. The defendant appeals, complaining primarily about the punitive-damages award. . . .

The defendant argues that at worst it is guilty of simple negligence, and if this is right the plaintiffs were not entitled by Illinois law to any award of punitive damages. It also complains that the award was excessive — indeed that any award in excess of $20,000 to each plaintiff would deprive the defendant of its property without due process of law. The first complaint has no possible merit, as the evidence of gross negligence, indeed of recklessness in the strong sense of an unjustifiable failure to avoid a *known* risk, was amply shown. In 1998, EcoLab, the extermination service that the motel used, discovered bedbugs in several rooms in the motel and recommended that it be hired to spray every room, for which it would charge the motel only $500; the motel refused. The next year, bedbugs were again discovered in a room but EcoLab was asked to spray just that room. The motel tried to negotiate "a building sweep [by EcoLab] free of charge," but, not surprisingly, the negotiation failed. By the spring of 2000, the motel's manager "started noticing that there were refunds being given by my desk clerks and reports coming back from the guests that there were ticks in the rooms and bugs in the rooms that were biting." She looked in some of the rooms and discovered bedbugs. The defendant asks us to disregard her testimony as that of a disgruntled ex-employee, but of course her credibility was for the jury, not the defendant, to determine.

from its fraud by escaping detection and (private) prosecution. If a tortfeasor is "caught" only half the time he commits torts, then when he is caught he should be punished twice as heavily in order to make up for the times he gets away.

Finally, if [the defendant's argument is accepted, and] the total stakes in the case were capped at $50,000 (2 × [$5,000 + $20,000]), the plaintiffs might well have had difficulty financing this lawsuit. It is here that the defendant's aggregate net worth of $1.6 billion becomes relevant. A defendant's wealth is not a sufficient basis for awarding punitive damages. That would be discriminatory and would violate the rule of law, as we explained earlier, by making punishment depend on status rather than conduct. Where wealth in the sense of resources enters is in enabling the defendant to mount an extremely aggressive defense against suits such as this and by doing so to make litigating against it very costly, which in turn may make it difficult for the plaintiffs to find a lawyer willing to handle their case, involving as it does only modest stakes, for the usual 33-40 percent contingent fee.

In other words, the defendant is investing in developing a reputation intended to deter plaintiffs. It is difficult otherwise to explain the great stubborness with which it has defended this case, making a host of frivolous evidentiary arguments despite the very modest stakes even when the punitive damages awarded by the jury are included. . . .

All things considered, we cannot say that the award of punitive damages was excessive, albeit the precise number chosen by the jury was arbitrary. It is probably not a coincidence that $5,000 + $186,000 – $191,000/191 – $1,000: i.e., $1,000 per room in the hotel. . . . [In the absence of guidelines attaching specific damage amounts to particular forms of misconduct], it is inevitable that the specific amount of punitive damages awarded whether by a judge or by a jury will be arbitrary. (Which is perhaps why the plaintiffs' lawyer did not suggest a number to the jury.) The judicial function is to police a range, not a point. . . .

NOTES AND QUESTIONS

1. *Placing Punitive Damages in Context.* Jury awards of punitive damages are rare. Studies of recent tort litigation suggest that they are awarded in less than 5 percent of the very few tort suits that go to verdict. For reasons explained below, awards in cases in which the underlying theory of liability is *negligence* are even rarer, making up a small fraction of this already small percentage. Instead, when awarded, punitive damages tend to be given to plaintiffs asserting claims for intentional wrongs that today would fall under the headings of assault, battery, false imprisonment, fraud, and tortious interference with contract. (To say that punitive damages are rare is not necessarily to say that they are unimportant. Indeed, even a handful of punitive awards—particularly awards of enormous magnitude—can have the potential to affect the trial and settlement of many other cases.)

The notes that follow examine the historical and contemporary bases for awarding punitive damages, some of the procedural rules governing the issuance of such awards, and possible theoretical justifications for punitive damages. *It is important to emphasize at the outset that this treatment of the subject is necessarily incomplete.* The U.S. Supreme

Court has added an important constitutional-law overlay onto the common law and statutory law of punitive damages. Because the Court's intervention arguably has been motivated in part by developments in modern products liability law (discussed in Chapter 12), we postpone consideration of it until Chapter 13. In practice, the common law, statutory law, and constitutional law of punitive damages must be considered together.

2. History. In the late eighteenth and early nineteenth centuries, punitive damages were most commonly awarded to victims of torts that involved abuses of power or insults to honor or dignity. The former category is exemplified by *Wilkes v. Wood*, 98 Eng. Rep. 489 (K.B. 1763). There, the court upheld a London jury's imposition of a punitive award of £1000—a large sum for the time—in a claim brought against a member of Parliament who had arranged for the arrest of plaintiff, a newspaper editor, for allegedly defaming King George III. Eighteenth-century "insult" cases included claims for "criminal conversation" brought by husbands against seducers of their wives. (*See* Chapter 2, note following *Mussivand v. David.*) In these cases—the trials of which helped give birth to London's tabloid newspaper industry—juries would occasionally deliver ruinously large verdicts on the order of £10,000 or more. Claims for libel and slander would also sometimes give rise to punitive awards in light of the "insult" to the plaintiff's good name.

In the nineteenth and early twentieth centuries, one finds U.S. decisions upholding jury awards for punitive damages in additional settings. Among the small collection of cases in which they were awarded, one sees them most frequently when employees of railroads and other common carriers mistreated passengers by, for example, forcing them to disembark at locations other than designated stations. *See, e.g.*, Spellman v. Richmond & D. R. Co., 14 S.E. 947 (S.C. 1892) (upholding a punitive award to a passenger against a railroad whose conductor forced him off the train without justification); McLelland v. Burns, 5 Colo. 390 (1880) (upholding an award where a stagecoach driver abandoned his passengers during a snowstorm); *see also* Goddard v. Grand Trunk Ry., 57 Me. 202 (1869) (upholding an award where a railroad brakeman abused and threatened the plaintiff). Punitive damages were also permitted for flagrant intrusions onto, or willful destructions of, property, as well as for instances of deceit or fraud. *See, e.g.*, Duncan v. Stalcup, 18 N.C. 440 (1836) (upholding a punitive award against the defendant for his malicious destruction of plaintiff's dogs, cattle, hogs, and stables); Huffman v. Moore, 115 S.E. 634 (S.C. 1923) (punitive damages appropriate in action for fraudulent sale of used car).

3. Simple Negligence Versus Reckless Indifference. *Mathias* notes the black letter rule that a plaintiff is *ineligible* to receive punitive damages if she can establish *only* that the defendant wronged her by acting carelessly toward her. An equally well-established rule holds that there is a certain subset of negligence suits in which juries retain discretion to award punitive damages. (A jury is never required to award punitive damages.) The Wisconsin Supreme Court described this special subset of negligence cases as instances of "gross and criminal negligence—such negligence as evinces on the part of the defendant a *wanton disregard* of the safety of others, and which in law is equivalent to malice." Pickett v. Crook, 20 Wis. 358 (1866) (emphasis added). In the words of the Second Restatement, a claim of negligence can support a punitive award if the plaintiff establishes that the defendant's unreasonable conduct demonstrates "reckless indifference to the rights of others." Restatement (Second) of Torts § 908(2) (1979).

In this subset of cases, the tort being sued upon is negligence — the defendant's liability for compensatory damages is established on the same terms as any other negligence case. What marks them as special is the plaintiff's ability to prove, in addition, that the defendant's conduct was *so careless* as to constitute a different order of wrongdoing, one that warrants a supplementary form of relief. Thus, there is a conceptual separation between the grounds of liability (unreasonable conduct toward the plaintiff proximately causing injury to her) and the grounds of punitive damages (conduct so unreasonable as to bespeak wanton disregard or deliberate indifference).

The employment of wanton disregard/deliberate indifference as a separate ground for punitive damages dates back at least to the mid-nineteenth century. *See, e.g.*, Brooke v. Clark, 57 Tex. 105 (1882) (upholding, upon rehearing, an award of punitive damages against a doctor for gross malpractice evincing indifference); Whipple v. Walpole, 10 N.H. 130 (1839) (upholding a punitive award upon evidence of defendant's gross negligence in maintaining a bridge, which resulted in the loss of plaintiff's horses). With the advent of the automobile in the early twentieth century, instances of injury resulting from dangerous driving by intoxicated motorists would provide a common instance of the sort of "aggravated" negligence that permits the imposition of punitive damages. *See* Ross v. Clark, 274 P. 639 (Ariz. 1929).

What, if anything, links the sort of conduct described in Note 2 — that is, conduct undertaken for the purpose of harming, oppressing, or insulting identifiable victims — with conduct evincing indifference to the well-being of others?

4. *Recklessness.* According to Section 2 of the Third Restatement of Torts, recklessness is in the first instance distinguished from carelessness by the fact that "the precaution that would eliminate or reduce the risk involves burdens that are so slight relative to the magnitude of the risk" that the failure to take that precaution indicates "indifference to the risk." Restatement (Third) of Torts: Liability for Physical and Emotional Harm § 2(b) (2010). (Section 2 stresses that recklessness can be found with respect to any risk of this description, not just grave or severe risks, such as risk of death or serious bodily injury. *See id.* cmt. f.) However, the presence of this kind of risk is not sufficient. In addition, for acts to be reckless, the actor must "know[ ] of the risk of harm created by the conduct or know[ ] facts that make the risk obvious to another in the person's situation." *Id.* § 2(a). In other words, the actor must not only impose an easily avoidable significant risk of injury on others, but must be *consciously indifferent* to the risk or *wanton* in disregarding it.

5. *Conscious (Deliberate) Indifference.* Because conscious indifference "requires that the [actor] . . . have [actual] knowledge of the danger . . . ," Restatement (Third), *supra*, § 2 cmt. c, it stands in sharp contrast to those forms of negligence that involve inadvertence — momentary lapses, slip-ups, etc. However, an actor's actual awareness of the risk is not sufficient to establish recklessness of this sort.

This is because, as noted in Chapter 3, there are instances of *advertent* (conscious) carelessness that do not rise to the level of recklessness. Restatement (Second) of Torts § 500, cmt. g. ("[T]he actor to be reckless must recognize that his conduct involves a risk substantially greater in amount than that which is necessary to make his conduct negligent.")

To grasp the distinction between "advertent" carelessness and deliberate indifference, it may be helpful to contrast *Mathias* with *Vaughan v. Menlove* (Chapter 3). After being apprised of the risk of fire associated with his method for stacking hay, the defendant Menlove indicated that he would "chance it." Assume that the increased likelihood of fire associated with Menlove's chosen method rendered his conduct unreasonable but was still relatively small. (Incurring even a relatively small increased risk of harm can be unreasonable if it is incurred needlessly.) Given this assumption, one might say of Menlove that he was *consciously careless*. By contrast, the motel owners in *Mathias* had every reason to suppose that their decision not to treat the motel's bedbug infestation would in fact result in their guests being bitten. Thus, it seems natural to say of them that they acted with *conscious indifference* toward the physical well-being of their guests.

6. *Wanton Disregard (herein of Willful Blindness).* Section 500 of the Second Restatement states that a person acts with reckless indifference when his unreasonable conduct poses a grave danger of harm to others and when he has "reason to know of facts which would lead a reasonable man to realize [that those dangers attend his conduct]." Restatement (Second) of Torts § 500 (1965). The drafters of the Third Restatement concluded that this definition was too broad, in that "an actor [could] be found reckless whose only fault consists of the failure to draw an inference that a reasonable person would have drawn." Restatement (Third) of Torts: Liability for Physical and Emotional Harm § 2 cmt. c (2010).

To narrow the definition of wanton disregard, the Third Restatement proposes to apply it to inadvertence where the actor has "knowledge of facts that would make the danger obvious to anyone in the actor's situation." *Id.* It thus would permit a factfinder to deem reckless an actor who was *un*aware of the risks posed by his conduct only if: (1) the facts about the risks are so obvious that an inference can be made that the actor is lying in denying her awareness of the risks; (2) the obviousness of the facts suggest that "the actor — for fear of what might be learned — has, in a studied way, refused to consider the implications of the facts the actor knew" (i.e., willful blindness); or (3) "the actor's denial of actual knowledge of the danger, while sincere, is nevertheless disturbing." The Third Restatement offers as an example of the third circumstance a motorist who, late for an appointment, drives 80 miles per hour on a crowded street, "giving no thought to the risk imposed on others." *Id.* In recognizing this third form of wanton disregard, has the Third Restatement in effect reproduced the Second Restatement's account, which the Third Restatement purports to reject for being too broad?

Return now to *National By-Products.* The majority opinion denies Searcy an award of punitive damages because it concludes that National By-Products and its driver Foley at most acted with extreme negligence, which it labels "gross." It reaches this conclusion in part for a supposed lack of evidence establishing that company management or Foley acted *in the knowledge* that its or his unreasonable conduct posed a grave risk of physical harm to others. Even granting the soundness of this reading of the evidence, couldn't a reasonable jury still have concluded that Foley acted with wanton disregard for the physical well-being of others? For example, couldn't it have found that he drove the way he did because he was by disposition extraordinarily willing to risk harm to others (as well as himself), or because he was almost insanely optimistic about his ability to navigate dangerous traffic situations? Is the majority's apparent refusal to apply the concept of wanton disregard explained by the fact that it confronted the issue of punitive damages in conjunction with Searcy's claim for property damage?* Alternatively, might it be explained by the fact that National By-Products, rather than Foley, would likely be paying those damages? (On the latter point, *see* Note 17 *infra.*) How should the court have ruled in *National By-Products* if it were applying the rules articulated in the Third Restatement?

7. Recklessness and Drunk Driving. As noted above, many jurisdictions allow punitive damages in cases in which the defendant has caused an accident while operating a vehicle with a blood alcohol level above the limit set by criminal statutes. Some defendants have tried to persuade courts to bar the award of punitive damages in these cases on the ground that, unlike the actors in *Mathias,* drunk drivers who are already drunk when they enter their cars do not knowingly choose to engage in highly risky conduct. This argument has been regularly rejected: If the decision to begin drinking is made in the knowledge that driving may soon follow, the whole series of decisions leading up to the erratic driving is deemed reckless. *See* Taylor v. Superior Court, 598 P.2d 854 (Cal. 1979).

Should liability for compensatory or punitive damages attach if an intoxicated driver *who is driving reasonably* collides with and injures the plaintiff? (Keep in mind that many car accidents do not involve erratic or otherwise abnormal driving on anyone's part, and assume that a defendant might with some credibility contend that, even if drunk, he was not driving in an abnormal or erratic manner.) With respect to *compensatory damages,* it is conceivably open to a drunk-yet-competent driver who is involved in an accident to argue that he should not be held liable because his competent driving would suggest that the tortious aspect of his conduct — driving while drunk — played no role in producing the plaintiff's injury. Might a similar argument be invoked to block the imposition of punitive damages? In *Ingram v. Pettit,* 340 So.2d 922 (Fla. 1976), the Florida Supreme Court seemingly rejected such an argument, imposing punitive damages on a drunk driver whose drunkenness appears not to have contributed to the accident resulting in plaintiff's injuries. A dissenting justice responded as follows:

> Sundberg, J. (dissenting) [The majority opinion entails that] [i]n cases where an accident involving an intoxicated driver is concerned, the injured party need only

---

* Of course, Foley's conduct killed two people — Staggs and McGee — but National By-Products apparently paid those punitive damage awards and did not appeal them. Was it appropriate for the jury to provide the *same* punitive damage award ($100,000) to the Searcy House Moving Company as to the estates of Staggs and McGee? Should the punitive damage award to a victim who suffers personal injury because of reckless driving be higher than the award to a victim who suffers only property damage because of the same conduct?

> prove the accident, provide evidence of intoxication and, thereupon, the driver will be subject to assessment of punitive damages. This is strict liability, not only for compensatory damages, but for exemplary damages. . . .
>
> I suggest that the law of torts as it has been carefully developed over the years permits an award of punitive damages in personal injury cases involving vehicles where reckless *conduct* is involved, not reckless *attitude.*
>
> The public policy arguments of the majority are enticing. There can be no question that drunk drivers endanger the lives of citizens of our state. But the Legislature can and has dealt with this problem through enactment of criminal statutes. The Legislature is the appropriate body to assert the public policy of Florida in this regard. That body having done so, it is unnecessary and improvident to [permit the award of punitive damages in such a case]. . . .

Id. at 926-27. What "public policy" arguments might sanction the imposition of punitive damages on a tortfeasor who engages in potentially reckless conduct that does not in fact generate the risks that render the conduct reckless?

8. *Trial Procedure (I): Burden of Proof.* Punitive damages may be awarded only if the evidence is sufficient to permit a reasonable jury to conclude that the defendant not only committed a tort but also acted wantonly, willfully, or recklessly toward the plaintiff. Materials in Chapters 3 and 4 explain that tort law typically employs the "more probable than not" or *preponderance of the evidence* standard in setting the burden of proof. Jurisdictions have split over whether plaintiffs ought to face a greater burden on the threshold question of wantonness, willfulness, or indifference. Many take the position that the plaintiff must present *clear and convincing* evidence—that is, evidence sufficient to permit a reasonable jury to conclude that it is *quite likely* that the defendant acted with the requisite disposition. The adoption of this heightened standard has been achieved by judicial decision and by statute. *See, e.g.*, Travelers Indem. Co. v. Armstrong, 442 N.E.2d 349 (Ind. 1982); Ga. Code Ann. § 51-12-5.1(b).

Although the clear-and-convincing standard is meant to be more onerous than the preponderance standard, it is also meant to be less demanding than the *beyond a reasonable doubt* standard used in criminal law to help protect citizens from being too readily subject to punishment at the behest of government officials. Is the adoption of this intermediate standard defensible? If punitive damages really are part of tort law, why depart from the preponderance standard? If they really are a form of punishment, shouldn't they be adjudicated under the reasonable doubt standard?

9. *Trial Procedure (II): Jury Instructions.* Assuming that the aforementioned threshold showing is made, the issue of punitive damages is, in the first instance, left to the discretion of the jury. The jury is instructed that, upon finding proof of malice, etc., it *may*—but need not—award punitive damages. Jurors are further instructed to consider various factors in determining the amount of any such award. For example, New York's Pattern Jury Instructions provide in part as follows:

> In arriving at your decision as to the amount of punitive damages you should consider the nature and reprehensibility of what [the defendant] did. That

> would include the character of the wrongdoing, as determined by factors such as the following, where applicable: whether [the defendant's] conduct demonstrated an indifference to, or reckless disregard of, the health, safety or rights of others, whether the act or acts constituted outrageous or oppressive intentional misconduct, how long the conduct went on, [the defendant's] awareness of what harm the conduct caused or was likely to cause, any concealment or covering up of the wrongdoing, how often [the defendant] had committed similar acts of this type in the past and the actual and potential harm created by [the defendant's] conduct . . . (including [where applicable] the harm to individuals or entities other than [the plaintiff]. However, although you may consider the harm to individuals or entities other than [the plaintiff] in determining the extent to which [the defendant's] conduct was reprehensible, you may not add a specific amount to your punitive damages award to punish [the defendant] for the harm [the defendant] caused to others.)
>
> The amount of punitive damages that you award must be both reasonable and proportionate to the actual and potential harm suffered by [the plaintiff], and to the compensatory damages you awarded [the plaintiff]. The reprehensibility of [the defendant's] conduct is an important factor in deciding the amount of punitive damages that would be reasonable and proportionate in the view of the harm suffered by [the plaintiff] and the compensatory damages you have awarded. . . .
>
> . . . .
>
> You may also consider [the defendant's] financial condition and the impact your punitive damages award will have on [the defendant]. . . .

N.Y. Pattern Jury Instr.—Civil 2:278 (3d ed. 2011).

With regard to punitive damages, a plaintiff's attorney will attempt to present to jurors a wide range of evidence bearing on defendant's culpability. However, as discussed in Chapter 13, the U.S. Supreme Court has indicated that constitutional principles of due process place certain limits on a plaintiff's discretion to introduce evidence as to the effects of a defendant's misconduct on persons who are not parties to the lawsuit. *See* Philip Morris USA v. Williams, 549 U.S. 346 (2007); State Farm Mutual Auto Insurance Co. v. Campbell, 538 U.S. 408 (2003). In principle, it is likewise open to the defendant to offer evidence tending to show that its conduct was less egregious than it might otherwise appear to have been. By definition, such evidence cannot have been sufficient to prevent the imposition of liability in the first place. If so, why should it be permitted to factor into the jury's determination of the size of a punitive award? *See* Prentiss v. Shaw, 56 Me. 427 (1869) (defendants who were found liable for falsely imprisoning the plaintiff may introduce evidence that they imprisoned the plaintiff only after hearing him express gratification upon hearing the news of President Lincoln's assassination; while plaintiff's "provocation" did not justify the defendants' wrongful act, the jury was entitled to take it into account in determining whether to award punitive damages against them and in what amount).

10. Trial Procedure (III): Bifurcation. Courts have uniformly deemed evidence of a defendant's wealth to be relevant to the jury's determination of the size of any punitive award. As explained in *Mathias*, this is not because wealthy persons or entities deserve greater punishment, but because an actor's wealth may have factored into its decision to behave as it did, and because a larger award may be necessary to send a meaningful "message" to a wealthy individual or entity. To reduce the risk that evidence of the defendant's wealth will shade jurors' judgments on the underlying issue of liability, some states mandate, and other states permit, a trial judge, at the request of a defendant, to bifurcate trial proceedings. *See, e.g.*, N.J.S.A. 2A:15-5.13. In the first phase, the jury is presented with evidence pertaining to the elements of the prima facie case, any relevant defenses, and compensatory damages.* Only if the jury determines that liability for compensatory damages should attach for the underlying tort does the court then preside over a second phase on punitive damages, at which evidence of wealth is introduced. *See* Hodges v. S.C. Toof & Co., 833 S.W.2d 896 (Tenn. 1992) (holding that trial courts "shall," upon a motion of the defendant, separate the punitive damages phase of tort cases from the phase in which liability and compensatory damages are determined, in part out of concern that jurors will be biased by evidence as to certain defendants' wealth).

11. Trial Court and Appellate Review of the Magnitude of Punitive Damage Awards. The degree of scrutiny applied by trial and appellate judges to juries' punitive damage awards is inextricably bound up with an important set of decisions issued by the U.S. Supreme Court. For present purposes, it is sufficient to note that both trial and appellate courts are expected closely to scrutinize such awards for excessiveness. A more detailed examination of the constitutional dimensions of punitive damages law is provided in Chapter 13.

12. Statutory Safe Harbors. In some instances, plaintiffs who might otherwise be eligible to receive punitive damages will be blocked by statutes that bar such an award in particular contexts. For example, by virtue of statutes enacted in some states, if a defendant can establish that its product was produced and sold in conformity with safety standards set by state and federal regulators, then even if a jury could declare the product negligently made or defectively designed, it would nonetheless be barred from awarding punitive damages to a person injured by the product. *See, e.g.*, Poitra v. DaimlerChrysler Corp., 2006 WL 2349981 (D.N.D.) (applying North Dakota's regulatory compliance safe harbor). In the absence of such statutes, a defendant's compliance with applicable regulatory requirements will make a strong, though not dispositive, case for the impropriety of a punitive damages instruction. *See, e.g.*, Nissan Motor Co. v. Maddox, 2015 WL 5626432 (Ky. 2015).

13. Punitive Damages and Punishment. Because they are reserved for instances of "aggravated" misconduct, and because they are awarded apart from ordinary compensatory damages, it is natural (and quite common) to think of punitive damages as inflicting a kind of punishment. Indeed, their name suggests as much. As noted at the outset of this section, some judges and scholars have criticized punitive damages as an

---

* Recall from Section I.A, *supra*, that bifurcation is also sometimes used to separate the presentation of evidence on liability from the presentation of evidence as to the extent of plaintiff's compensatory damages. Some trials are thus *tri*furcated, with separate phases for (1) liability, (2) extent of compensatory damages, and (3) punitive damages.

inappropriate importation of criminal law principles of retribution into the civil law of tort. Consider the materials in Chapter 1 distinguishing criminal and tort law. Granted the existence of various differences between the two bodies of law, do you think tort law is or should be distinguished from criminal law on the ground that the former is solely concerned to compensate victims, whereas the latter is concerned to punish wrongdoers? What conception of tort law is presupposed by the critique of punitive damages as an anomalous feature of that law?

14. *Recourse for a Special Class of Wrongs? Mathias* canvases various rationales for punitive damages. One rationale—sometimes emphasized in eighteenth- and nineteenth-century cases imposing punitive damages for "insult" torts—is that they are appropriately given in recognition of the (perhaps justifiably) greater urge toward private reprisal that tends be felt by victims of egregious mistreatment. *See, e.g.*, Perkins v. Towle, 43 N.H. 220 (1861) (linking the award of punitive damages in cases of insult to the suppression of dueling). Other decisions suggest that punitive awards are an appropriate response to conduct demonstrating a disposition on the part of a tortfeasor to treat harm to a particular individual as simply a cost of doing business. Cashin v. Northern Pac. Ry. Co., 28 P.2d 862, 870 (Mont. 1934) (approving an award of punitive damages where the defendant's employees used explosives in the knowledge that their use would damage the plaintiffs' house because it was cheaper to pay for the damage than to employ alternative construction methods). The concern here is that some well-to-do persons or entities will happily treat compensatory damages as the price to be paid for securing the "right" to injure others.*

Some early critics argued that, to the extent they are awarded because of a defendant's insulting or opportunistic behavior, punitive damages are really a disguised form of compensatory damages that duplicate the portion of the jury's compensatory award designed to compensate the plaintiff for the emotional distress he experienced by virtue of being mistreated. Fay v. Parker, 53 N.H. 342, 380 (1872) (tort law should not recognize a separate category of exemplary damages because they are "the same thing as damages for wounded feelings, as distinguished from damages for an injury to person or property"). Might one accept *Fay*'s insight that punitive damages are in some sense "compensatory" of the plaintiff without drawing the conclusion that they are redundant with damages for emotional distress? If tort compensation is conceived as redress that a victim is entitled to exact from a person who has wronged him, might punitive damages be understood as a special form of recourse appropriately granted to victims of torts who have been subjected to insult on top of injury?

15. *Deterrence of Antisocial Conduct?* Some of the language in *Mathias* is reminiscent of the Supreme Court's *Borak* decision, see Chapter 6, in which the Court based its

---

* To illustrate their concern, nineteenth- and early-twentieth century authorities sometimes pointed to an example drawn from ancient Rome, the law of which required tortfeasors to compensate their victims in pre-set amounts. The example was provided by Lucius Veratius, a Roman citizen who apparently "used to amuse himself by striking those whom he met in the street in the face, and then tendering them the legal amends, which a slave carried after him for that purpose." *Vindictive Damages*, 4 Am. L.J. 61, 75 (1852).

"What with current restrictions on punitive damages, I had no recourse but to shoot the son of a bitch."

willingness to identify implied rights of action within federal securities laws in part on the idea that private suits would assist regulators in enforcing those laws. Thus, Judge Posner suggests that punitive damages can assist in deterring and punishing criminal conduct that would otherwise escape sanction, either because it goes undetected, or because the victim (and her attorney) will not have sufficient incentive to bring suit in light of the psychic and economic costs of litigation (particularly if the defendant is wealthy and inclined to engage in "scorched earth" defense tactics). To what extent can punitive damages be justified as inducing certain tort plaintiffs to play the role of private attorneys general—plaintiffs who sue (and recover) on behalf of the public interest in the enforcement of rules of proper conduct? Would this rationale explain why punitive damages are awarded only in some tort cases? Why they are awarded in response to the particular forms of "aggravated" misconduct currently recognized by courts as supporting such awards?

16. Compensating Others? Splitting Statutes Suppose a given defendant has committed the sort of egregious wrong that warrants harsh sanction. Why should that sanction take the form of money paid *to the plaintiff*? Consider, in light of the foregoing rationales, whether any explains why a tort victim or his survivors should be the one(s) to whom the sanction is paid. Some states have enacted statutes mandating that a certain percentage of any punitive damage award be taken from the plaintiff and contributed to the state's treasury, presumably to be allocated for the public good. *See, e.g.*, Ga. Code Ann. § 51-12-5.1(e)(2) (requiring 75 percent of punitive awards to be paid to the state). Plaintiffs whose awards have been reduced under these statutes have challenged their validity on constitutional grounds, with mixed results. *See, e.g.*, Kirk v. Denver Publg. Co., 818 P.2d 262 (Colo. 1991) (en banc) (striking down Colorado's punitive damages splitting statute).

17. Who Pays? Punitive Damages, Vicarious Liability, and Insurance. Sections II and IV of this chapter respectively examine the doctrine of *respondeat superior*, by which employers are held responsible for certain torts committed by employees, and the role of liability insurance in permitting tortfeasors to defray the costs of judgments entered against them. As a segue to these discussions, consider the role that *respondeat superior* and insurance might have played in *National By-Products* and *Mathias.*

Note first that both decisions are prepared to impose liability for punitive damages not only on the individual employees who perpetrated the torts in question but also on the companies that employed them. For all practical purposes, this entails that the judgments in these cases will be paid out of company bank accounts rather than out of the employees' pockets.

With respect to *compensatory* damages, the basic rule, explored in the next section, is that a plaintiff can seek compensation out of company assets if her injuries result from a tort committed by a company employee in the course of employment. Arkansas seems to take the view that this same standard should control employer liability for punitive damages. Miller v. Blanton, 210 S.W.2d 293 (Ark. 1948). Thus, if the evidence had been deemed sufficient to support an award of punitive damages against Foley, National By-Products would likely have been on the hook, given that his errant driving occurred during the course of his employment. However, many, probably most, jurisdictions require greater managerial involvement before permitting employers to be held liable for punitive damages arising out of employees' tortious acts. In these jurisdictions, firms are held liable for punitive damages only if the tortious conduct was either committed by management-level employees or was committed by lower-level employees whose conduct was then endorsed or "ratified" by management. Dan B. Dobbs, *The Law of Torts* § 381, at 1063 (2000). Might one argue that the *National By-Products* court's refusal to attribute recklessness to Foley was an indirect means of implementing this more restrictive approach to vicarious liability for punitive damages?

The issue of vicarious liability for punitive damages under federal admiralty law was presented to the U.S. Supreme Court in *Exxon Shipping Co. v. Baker*, 554 U.S. 471 (2008). However the Court failed to resolve it, instead splitting 4-4, one Justice having recused himself. It thereby let stand a Ninth Circuit decision that allowed for the imposition on Exxon of vicarious liability for the reckless acts of its employee, Joseph Hazelwood, the captain of the oil tanker *Exxon Valdez.* (Hazelwood, intoxicated, abandoned his post prior to the execution of a critical maneuver. As a result, the tanker ran aground and spilled millions of gallons of oil.) The Ninth Circuit approved instructions by which the jury was permitted to impose vicarious liability for punitive damages as long as it found that Hazelwood was acting in a "managerial capacity," defined as one that calls for the employee to "supervise[] other employees and [have] responsibility for, and authority over, a particular aspect of the corporation's business." It further approved an instruction allowing the jury to reduce the amount of any punitive award against Exxon if it found that "corporate policy makers did not actually participate in or ratify the wrongful conduct . . ." *See* In re Exxon Valdez, 270 F.3d 1215, 1233 (9th Cir. 2001), *rev'd on other grounds*, 554 U.S. 471 (2008).

As to insurance, courts have similarly split over whether insurers should be permitted to issue liability insurance policies — such as medical malpractice policies — that cover punitive damage awards. Courts that have barred such coverage reason that it is against public policy to let perpetrators of egregious wrongs "escape" punishment by purchasing insurance to cover the cost of a punitive award issued in response to that conduct.

Check Your Understanding

Punitive Damages

1. In what sense(s) are punitive damages "non-compensatory," "punitive," or "exemplary"?
2. If mere carelessness does not meet the common-law threshold for allowing a punitive damages award, why are some negligence plaintiffs eligible to recover punitive damages?
3. A landlord operates an apartment building in a high-crime neighborhood. The electronic "buzzer" system that tenants are supposed to use to control access to the building has been broken for months, as a result of which entry to its lobby has been unrestricted. Several tenants have complained to the landlord, but he has not responded. Plaintiff, a tenant in the building, was recently injured as a result of being mugged by an intruder in the lobby. No other attacks had occurred prior to this one. If you were the trial judge presiding over plaintiff's suit against the landlord, would you grant the plaintiff's request to have the jury instructed on punitive damages? Why or why not?

II. VICARIOUS LIABILITY

We have seen many negligence suits in which claims are brought against a company or organization instead of, or in addition to, the individual tortfeasor. As noted briefly in Chapter 1, the ability of plaintiffs to establish the liability of these defendants often — but not always — turns on the doctrine of *vicarious liability*, by which one person or entity is held responsible for the tortious acts of another who is acting on her or its behalf. The following case presents for consideration the scope of the most important form of vicarious liability, namely, *respondeat superior*. Under that doctrine, a "master" (employer) is subject to liability for tortious conduct committed by its "servant" (employee).

Taber v. Maine

67 F.3d 1029 (2d Cir. 1995)

Calabresi, J. Twenty-six years ago, in Ira S. Bushey & Sons, Inc. v. United States, 398 F.2d 167 (2d Cir. 1968), this court held that the United States Government was vicariously liable for damage to a drydock caused by a drunken sailor who was returning to ship from a night's liberty. In his celebrated opinion, Judge Henry Friendly described the basis of respondeat superior as the "deeply rooted sentiment that a business enterprise cannot justly disclaim responsibility for accidents which may fairly be said to be characteristic of its activities." *Id.* at 171. Even though the sailor had become drunk while on liberty and far off base, we noted that drinking on leave was so common a part of naval life that the sailor's drunken return to ship could fairly be deemed to be characteristic of the military enterprise and, hence, that the government should be held liable for the damage that he caused. *See Id.* at 172.

In *Bushey,* we applied admiralty law. Today—in a case that again involves a seaman who had too much to drink—we must apply the law of Guam. This, in turn, points us to California decisions for guidance. As it happens, California had taken the lead in developing the modern law of respondeat superior even before *Bushey.* And, so, rounding out the circle, we now reach the same conclusion as did Judge Friendly, twenty-six years ago. . . .

. . . On the morning of April 13, 1985, Robert S. Maine ("Maine"), a Navy serviceman on active duty at the U.S. Naval Ship Repair Facility on the island of Guam, went on liberty after having completed a grueling 24 hour duty shift. While on liberty he was free to leave the base as he pleased and travel up to 50 miles away. He could also be recalled for duty at any time.

Maine decided to have a good time. By noon, he was relaxing at an on-base beach party and drinking beer with Navy friends. Later that afternoon, he purchased two six-packs of beer at the base PX with his Navy comrade, Karin Conville ("Conville"), and returned with her to his barracks to drink several more cans. At dinnertime, Maine accompanied friends to the enlisted men's club, where he consumed two cocktails with his meal. After dinner, he attended a barracks party in the room of a superior officer, with several other superior officers present. There, Maine drank three or four more beers and—when he left to return to his own barracks at about 11:00 p.m.—Conville and another Navy comrade named Jean Buquet noticed that he seemed to be drunk. At around 11:30 p.m., Maine had difficulty sleeping and decided to drive off base to get something to eat. Feeling tired, he aborted his snack mission and tried to return to base. On the way back, he caused the accident that injured Scott A. Taber ("Taber").

Taber was an enlisted Seabee—a construction worker in the United States Navy—and was stationed at Camp Covington, Guam. At 6:00 p.m. on Friday, April 12th, he too went on liberty. Accordingly, he was free to go off base at any time, to travel anywhere within 50 miles of his base and, unless he was recalled for duty, to do as he pleased until his liberty ended at 6:00 a.m. on the following Monday.

Around 2:00 p.m. on Saturday April 13, Taber's civilian friend, Estelita Stills ("Stills"), met Taber at his base in her car. They planned to spend the weekend together at her house, which was located off the base. Before going there, however, the two drove to her cousins' home for dinner at the nearby U.S. Naval Station. There, Taber enjoyed a meal and, as a friendly gesture in return, helped fix the cousins' car. Shortly before midnight, Stills and Taber left for Stills's house and their weekend of rest and recreation. As fate would have it, they never got there. While they were driving on the public roadway toward Stills's house, Maine crashed into them, injuring Taber severely.

Two years later, Taber started this action for damages under the Federal Tort Claims Act ("FTCA"), 28 U.S.C. §§ 1346(b), 2671, in the United States District Court for the Western District of New York, (David G. Larimer, Judge). Naming both Maine and the United States Government as defendants, Taber complained that he was injured as a result of Maine's negligent driving and that, because Maine was acting within the scope of his Naval employment when he caused the accident, the government was liable on a theory of *respondeat superior*. . . .

Judge Larimer granted summary judgment to the government because "Maine's drunk driving incident on April 13, 1985, was not in the line of duty and therefore the United States is not liable under the doctrine of *respondeat superior*." . . .

The action proceeded against Maine, however. After a bench trial in which Maine appeared pro se, the district court found Maine liable for negligence and assessed Taber's damages at $300,000. A final judgment was entered and Taber appealed. . . .

The FTCA allows civil actions against the government based on the negligent acts or omissions of its employees, see 28 U.S.C. § 1346(b), including those of members of the Armed Services who are acting "in the line of duty." 28 U.S.C. § 2671. The courts have uniformly equated the FTCA's "line of duty" language with the phrase "scope of employment," as that concept is defined by the respondeat superior law of the jurisdiction in which the accident occurred. . . . Because the accident in this case happened in Guam, we must follow Guam's law of respondeat superior. . . .

Where the law of Guam is unclear, the Ninth Circuit, serving as Guam's highest appellate court . . . has instructed courts to look to California law for guidance. . . . It seems clear to us that California law (and by implication the law of Guam) would hold the government vicariously liable for Maine's actions. California was one of the first states in the nation to adopt an expansive reading of the *respondeat superior* doctrine. . . .

This approach to *respondeat superior* is . . . evident in numerous California cases. . . . For example, in Rodgers v. Kemper Construction Co., 50 Cal. App. 3d 608, 124 Cal. Rptr. 143 (4th Dist. 1975), a subcontractor was held vicariously liable for an assault committed by two of its employees who had lounged around drinking for several hours in what was, ironically, called the "dry house" (a rest area/locker room located on the job site). On a Friday night after their work shift had ended, the employees, though free to go home, stayed in the dry house and got drunk. Later they went outside and got in a fight with the plaintiffs. *See id.* at 615, 124 Cal. Rptr. at 146-47.

In finding *respondeat superior* liability, the court stated that "the inquiry should be whether the risk was one 'that may be fairly regarded as typical of or broadly incidental' to the enterprise undertaken by the employer." 50 Cal. App. 3d at 619, 124 Cal. Rptr. at 149 (citations omitted). The court further noted that under California law,

> where social or recreational pursuits on the employer's premises after hours are endorsed by the express or implied permission of the employer and are

regarded as risks of his business, whether they are committed in furthering it or not." Fowler V. Harper, Fleming James, Jr. & Oscar S. Gray, *The Law of Torts* § 26.8 (2d ed., 1986). Judge Friendly made the same point most elegantly in *Bushey.* "The proclivity of seamen to find solicitude by copious resort to the bottle," he wrote, "has been noted in opinions too numerous to warrant citation. Once all this is granted, it is immaterial that [the coastguardsman's] precise action was not to be foreseen." 398 F.2d at 172. After all, the government "cannot justly disclaim responsibility for accidents which may fairly be said to be characteristic of its activities." *Id.* at 171.

We believe the law of Guam reaches the same conclusion. Accordingly, we hold that the government is vicariously liable for Maine's conduct.

[The United States next argued that even if Maine's actions could be attributed to it via *respondeat superior,* it could not be held liable because of the exception to FTCA liability recognized by the U.S. Supreme Court in Feres v. United States, 340 U.S. 135 (1950). *Feres* held that the FTCA does not waive sovereign immunity with regard to claims by members of the armed forces for injuries that "arise out of or are [sustained] in the course of activity incident to service." *Id.* at 146. The Court offered various rationales for this ban, noting, for example, that civil liability to service members might interfere with military organization and discipline, and that servicemen are usually eligible for government benefits available outside the tort system in the event they are injured in the line of duty. After an exhaustive review of *Feres* and subsequent Supreme Court decisions, Judge Calabresi concluded that Taber's claim was *not* barred by the *Feres* exception to the FTCA. Taber's conduct in driving home from a weekend furlough, he reasoned, was so tangentially related to his service that it would not interfere with military operations or government benefits programs. — EDS.] . . .

For the reasons stated above, we reverse the district court's judgment and remand the case to the district court for further proceedings consistent with this opinion.

NOTES AND QUESTIONS

1. *Employee Versus Employer Liability.* It is critical to distinguish the issue of an employee's personal liability from that of his employer's liability. Under the common law of negligence, if an employee drives carelessly while on the job so as to run down a pedestrian, the employee can ordinarily be held liable for the damages caused. (However, the rules of personal liability are different for government employees, *see* Note 14 *infra.*) But establishing the employee's liability does not of itself establish that the employer — a separate "person" or entity in the eyes of the law — should also be held liable. Determining the employer's liability instead requires the application of additional legal principles.

2. *Direct Versus Vicarious Liability.* In general, an employer can be held liable for the tortious acts of its employees on two different theories: *direct* liability and *vicarious* liability. A claim of direct liability asserts that the employer (i.e., managerial personnel) acted wrongfully by failing to screen or supervise its employees, and that this wrongful conduct helped bring about plaintiff's injuries. For example, suppose the manager of a trucking company hires a driver without performing a simple check that would have

revealed that the driver has recently received a string of citations for drunk driving. Now suppose the driver, while intoxicated, crashes into and injures the plaintiff while driving a company truck on company business. Here, any company liability would be direct rather than vicarious because the manager's carelessness helped bring about the crash.

By contrast, an allegation of *respondeat superior* liability asserts that management—and ultimately, the company's owners—are on the hook for a wrong committed by an employee. As *Taber* explains, an employer is liable for the torts of its employees when those torts are committed within the "scope of employment." When *respondeat superior* liability attaches, it does so even to an employer who has carefully screened and monitored its employees. Thus, it is sometimes said that the doctrine creates a form of "strict" or "no-fault" liability.

As indicated in cases and materials in Chapter 7, as well as in *Taber* itself, the main effect of the passage of the Federal Tort Claims Act in 1946 was to expose the federal government to state-law rules of *respondeat superior* liability. As we have seen and will see, however, these rules differ somewhat from the rules that typically attach to private employers.

3. *Direct Liability and Constitutional Torts.* Before examining *respondeat superior* liability in greater detail, it is worth pausing to note an important example of "direct" liability. Under 42 U.S.C. § 1983, city and local governments can be held liable to individuals whose constitutional rights are violated by virtue of conduct pursuant to policies set by those entities. As explained in Chapter 6, individual government officials can be held liable under *Bivens* (federal officials) or Section 1983 (state and local officials) for violating constitutional rights. In addition, however, city and local governments can themselves be held liable for maintaining unconstitutional policies. For example, if a city were to adopt hiring guidelines for municipal employees that resulted in hiring decisions that discriminated against prospective hires on the basis of gender or race, a victim of those policies may be able to obtain redress directly from the city's coffers. *See* Monell v. Department of Social Servs., 436 U.S. 658 (1978) (recognizing direct municipal liability under Section 1983). The idea here is akin to the idea that employers can be held liable for negligent hiring or supervision. A distinct wrong is being perpetrated by the managers of the entity, rather than by lower-level employees in the course of their employment.

4. *Scope of Employment: Purpose Versus Characteristic Activity. Respondeat superior* liability attaches only to employee torts committed within the scope of employment. The meaning of that restriction is, of course, the central issue in *Taber.* Courts in the early twentieth century tended to address the scope issue in terms of the employee's reason for acting: If the careless employee was acting, at least in part, for the purpose of advancing the interests of the employer, the careless act was deemed within the scope of employment. Modern courts, however, have moved away from that test toward the "characteristic activities" analysis employed by Judge Friendly in *Bushey* and by Judge Calabresi in *Taber.*

5. *Scope of Employment: Frolic and Detour.* In an omitted portion of the excerpted opinion, Judge Calabresi opined that, had the situation in *Taber* been reversed, such

that Taber was the negligent driver and Maine the injured plaintiff, the government would not have been subject to vicarious liability:

> There is nothing characteristically military about an employee who, after working-hours are done, goes off to spend a romantic weekend with a companion. Nor is there anything particularly military about having dinner with that companion's family at their home, and helping to fix their car. Finally, there is nothing especially military about returning to the companion's house intending to spend the rest of the weekend engaged in more intimate rest and recreation.

67 F.3d at 1051. In drawing this distinction, Judge Calabresi invoked language from old cases distinguishing between an employee *detour* and an employee *frolic.* A detour consists of a slight deviation from the expected course or route that an employee would take in the course of doing his job. A frolic consists of an employee who so far deviates from his employment obligations that he is deemed to be on his own business. An example of a detour might be a delivery-truck driver who, while en route to a customer, goes three city blocks out of his way on a personal errand and carelessly injures another driver during that diversion. A frolic would be an instance in which the driver played hooky with the truck, using it to take his jet-ski for a day at the beach. *See, e.g., Fiocco v. Carver,* 137 N.E. 309 (N.Y. 1922) (Cardozo, J.) (employer not liable for injuries caused to children when driver deviated from his route, stopped his truck at a street fair, and let a horde of costumed children climb onto the truck).

6. *Scope of Employment: Intentional Torts and State and Federal Law.* Under the older, "purpose" test, courts tended to categorically exclude intentional wrongful acts of employees as being outside the scope of employment. Under the "characteristic activities" test, state courts have held that some but by no means all forms of intentional employee wrongdoing can be attributed to employers. For example, a bar might well be subject to vicarious liability if a bouncer it employs severely beats (without justification) a patron while on the job. However, some intentional acts will be deemed to be too far removed from the business of the employer to provide the basis for vicarious liability. Suppose, for example, the driver of a company's delivery van takes an instant dislike to a customer, as a result of which the driver deliberately backs his van over the customer's dog. Even under the modern approach, a court will be reluctant to hold the company liable under *respondeat superior.* Modern courts have divided over whether schools and churches can be held vicariously liable for sexual assaults by teachers and clergy. *See generally* Dan B. Dobbs, *The Law of Torts* § 335, at 915 (2000).

By means of an explicit statutory command, the FTCA adopts a more restrictive approach to vicarious liability for intentional torts committed by federal employees. Essentially, it excludes such liability unless the intentional tort is committed by an "investigative or law enforcement officer." 28 U.S.C. § 2680(h). *See* Chapter 6. Obviously, this special statutory limitation was not at issue in *Taber,* which involved a claim for careless employee conduct.

7. *Hostile Work Environment.* Federal antidiscrimination statutes provide private rights of actions to employees who are subject to sexual harassment. Harassment

comes in two forms: *quid pro quo* and *hostile work environment.* An example of the former is a situation in which a supervisor makes his supervisee's job advancement contingent on compliance with a request for sex. The latter sort of claim asserts that management has tolerated or endorsed an atmosphere that is pervasively sexist. *See* Chapter 10. Whereas management is usually held vicariously liable for *quid pro quo* harassment, the rule is different for hostile work environment claims. If the employer has in place a reasonable system for preventing and responding to harassment, the plaintiff is not permitted to recover from the employer without demonstrating that she attempted to invoke that system. In effect, then, the employer will only be liable in this class of harassment case on a *direct* theory of liability, that is, if its system for dealing with harassment is found to be unreasonable. *See* Faragher v. City of Boca Raton, 524 U.S. 775 (1998).

8. Rationales. The principle of *respondeat superior* is venerable, running back at least to the law of ancient Rome. As originally cast, it may have been based on the idea that an employee — that is, servant or slave — was not a legally recognized person, but was owned by the master. As such, the master was held to be responsible for the damage caused by his "things." Needless to say, such odious notions no longer provide the rationale for the rule. What rationale does the Second Circuit identify as the most compelling basis for the doctrine? Can you think of others?

Guido Calabresi
Second Circuit Court of Appeals
(1994-present)

9. Friendly Versus Calabresi. Before ascending to the bench from the deanship of Yale Law School, Judge Calabresi established himself as one of the twentieth century's leading torts scholars. His most important contribution to torts scholarship is rooted in the idea that judges and legislatures dealing with the problem of assigning liability for accidents should base their decisions not on "backward-looking" considerations of responsibility, but instead with the "forward-looking" aim of efficiently deterring accidents. They could best accomplish this, he argued, by assigning liability to the actor whom they believe could most easily (cheaply) take precautions that would prevent the same sort of accident from arising in the future. In his words, courts should assign liability to the "cheapest cost avoider" of similar accidents.

Henry J. Friendly
Second Circuit Court of Appeals
(1959-1986)

There is a certain irony in Calabresi's effort to invoke Friendly's opinion in the *Bushey* case. *Bushey* involved a drunken sailor who, for unknown reasons, decided to play with wheels that opened valves controlling the level of water in a drydock, thereby causing property damage to the drydock owner. The trial court invoked Calabresian notions in support of its decision to treat the acts of the drunken sailor as within the scope of employment and hence attributable to the government. In essence, it reasoned that the United States as the shipowner and employer was in the best position to protect against shenanigans by drunken sailors.

Friendly's opinion for the Court of Appeals affirmed the trial court's ruling but expressed skepticism that it was supported by a Calabresian "cheapest cost avoider" rationale:

> [T]he suggestion that imposition of liability here will lead to more intensive screening of employees rests on highly questionable premises. . . . The unsatisfactory quality of the [efficient deterrence] rationale is especially striking on the facts of this case. It could well be that application of the traditional rule [which would have excluded employer liability on the facts of the case] might induce drydock owners . . . to install locks on their valves to avoid similar incidents in the future, while placing the burden on shipowners is much less likely to lead to accident prevention.

398 F.2d at 170-171.

Friendly further cast a skeptical eye toward another commonly cited rationale for *respondeat superior*, namely the idea that attaching liability to the employer permits the legal system to "spread the cost" of injuries from a single injured victim (e.g., the dock-owner) to a large segment of the population (i.e., the customers of a business, who will "pay" for the tort judgment through higher prices, or taxpayers, who fund the federal government and thus pay the tab for its torts). Said Friendly: "[T]he fact that the defendant is better able to afford damages is not alone sufficient to justify legal responsibility. . . ." *Id.* at 171. Having dismissed these rationales, Friendly then invoked the "deeply rooted sentiment" rationale quoted in Judge Calabresi's *Taber* opinion.

10. Employees, Independent Contractors, and Co-workers. As a matter of black letter doctrine, the rule of *respondeat superior* applies to employees, but not to independent contractors. For example, suppose business *B* contracts with bicycle messenger *M* to have *M* deliver documents to local clients, and that *M* carelessly injures someone in the course of making a delivery for *B*. *B* should not be held liable on a theory of *respondeat superior*. Even though *M*'s acts presumably provide a benefit to *B*, they are not acts undertaken *by B*, but instead by an independent entity that has contracted to provide a service to *B*. *Cf.* Bailly v. Rudolf Steiner School, 741 N.Y.S.2d 197 (App. Div. 2002) (school not vicariously liable for negligence of bus company hired to transport students).

In particular situations, the line between an employee and an independent contractor will be elusive. The Third Restatement of the law of agency offers the following guidance in determining whether a person should be deemed an employee of another.

> Numerous factual indicia are relevant to whether an agent is an employee. These include: the extent of control that the agent and the principal have agreed the principal may exercise over details of the work; whether the agent is engaged in a distinct occupation or business; whether the type of work done by the agent is customarily done under a principal's direction or without supervision; the skill required in the agent's occupation; whether the agent or the principal supplies the tools and other instrumentalities required for the work and the place in which to perform it; the length of time during which the agent is engaged by a principal; whether the agent is paid by the job or by the time worked; whether the agent's

> work is part of the principal's regular business; whether the principal and the agent believe that they are creating an employment relationship; and whether the principal is or is not in business. Also relevant is the extent of control that the principal has exercised in practice over the details of the agent's work.

Restatement (Third) of Agency § 7.07, comment f (2006). Needless to say, the distinction between employees (servants) and independent contractors can be critical to the plaintiff's ability to recover. For example, if the putative employer is solvent, whereas the negligent actor is not, the plaintiff will be unable to collect on any judgment if the actor is deemed an independent contractor rather than an employee.

11. Non-Delegable Duties. Common law recognizes limits on the ability of employers to circumvent vicarious liability through the use of independent contractors. Under the *non-delegable duty* doctrine, for example, courts have sometimes prohibited commercial landowners from disavowing carelessness by independent contractors performing work on the premises. *See, e.g.*, Strayer v. Lindeman, 427 N.E.2d 781 (Ohio 1981) (landlord held vicariously liable to tenants for property damage caused by the carelessness of an independent contractor hired to fulfill the landlord's statutory obligation to maintain the premises in good repair). Likewise, they have held general contractors liable for the negligence of independent subcontractors. *See, e.g.*, Brooks v. Hayes, 395 N.W.2d 167 (Wis. 1986).

12. Respondeat Superior and Medical Malpractice. Contrary, perhaps, to public perception, treating physicians at hospitals often are independent contractors rather than hospital employees. For example, some are staff physicians who merely have permission to use a hospital's facilities as they are available. Courts will nonetheless sometimes hold hospitals vicariously liable for injuries caused by careless independent-contractor physicians. Some courts, for example, invoke the "apparent authority" doctrine. Roughly speaking, it allows for an independent contractor to be treated as the agent of a principal when the putative principal endorses or permits arrangements that induce third parties to believe, reasonably, that the contractor is acting as the putative principal's agent. *See, e.g.*, Roessler v. Novak, 858 So. 2d 1158 (Fla. App. 2003). What about a surgical nurse who is formally employed by the hospital but makes a mistake that causes injury to the patient during a surgical procedure that is controlled by the surgeon? Is the hospital liable as employer even though the surgeon had complete authority over the nurse's actions while in the operating room? Is the surgeon vicariously liable? *See, e.g.*, Parker v. Vanderbilt University, 767 S.W.2d 412 (Tenn. Ct. App. 1998) (surgeon not vicariously liable for malpractice of surgical nurses).

13. Joint Liability and Indemnification. Ordinarily, when a private employer is held liable for the tort of its employee under *respondeat superior*, that holding does *not* relieve the employee who tortiously injured the plaintiff of liability. Rather, the employer and employee are held jointly and severally liable to the plaintiff—that is, each is on the hook to the plaintiff, and the plaintiff may decide from whom he wishes to seek compensation. *See infra* Section III (discussing joint and several liability). As a practical matter, however, the plaintiff will almost always seek recovery from the employer, who is more likely to possess the means to pay the judgment. Once the employer pays the judgment, in principle, it has a right to seek either partial or full reimbursement from the employee. Again, however, this right is more notional than real. Employers who have been made to pay judgments for their employees' torts do not typically seek reimbursement for many reasons, including that the employer is itself not likely to be the one footing the bill for the tort claim, but rather the employer's liability insurer. *See* Section IV *infra.*

14. Personal Immunity of Government Employees Revisited. As noted in Chapter 7, federal employees such as Maine have been formally exempted by the Westfall Act from being held individually liable for torts committed in the scope of their employment. 28 U.S.C. § 2679. In other words, a person injured by the tortious conduct of a federal employee acting within the scope of her employment *cannot* recover from the employee, but may only recover from the government as employer. State legislatures have enacted counterparts for state employees.

Recalling this feature of federal law raises an obvious question: Why was Taber permitted to sue Maine individually, along with the federal government? In a portion of the opinion not reproduced, the Court of Appeals informs us that Maine, who represented himself in the litigation, failed to invoke this statutory provision, which would have immunized him from any personal liability to Taber.

15. Related Doctrines: Automobile Owners' Liability. Respondeat superior is a particularly important instance of vicarious liability, one which stems from the employer-employee relationships. Other relationships can sometimes support attributions of vicarious liability. The general partners of a partnership, for example, are vicariously liable for each other's torts. By contrast, as can be seen from *Appelhans* in Chapter 3, parents generally are *not* vicariously liable for the careless acts of their children, although they may sometimes be held *directly liable* if their own carelessness helped bring about the child's negligence, as in cases of negligent supervision (e.g., failing to take any steps to control a child known to have violent or dangerous propensities) or negligent entrustment (e.g., handing a young child a dangerous weapon).

An important exception to this rule concerns the case of parents who permit their children to drive their cars for business or pleasure. In the typical case, the parent/owner permits her teenager to use the car, and the child drives carelessly so as to cause injury to another. In such situations, the parent, *as car owner*, is held liable even if the decision to hand over the car keys to the child was not itself unreasonable. *See, e.g.,* Malchose v. Kalfell, 664 N.W.2d 508 (N.D. 2003) (parents vicariously liable for dependent son's careless driving even though son was away at college at the time of the accident). Some states have extended this rule of car owners' vicarious liability to cover any accidents resulting from careless use of the car by any driver who was given permission by the owner to use the car. *See, e.g.,* N.Y. Veh. & Traf. L. § 388. A federal law known as the Graves Amendment, enacted in 2005, blocks the imposition of vicarious liability (i.e., liability merely on the basis of ownership) on a rental car company for injuries resulting from a renter's operation of a rented car. However, such a company can be held liable directly for negligence on its part. 49 U.S.C. § 30106(a).

Check Your Understanding

Respondeat Superior

Teri works as a delivery driver for a pizza shop. Because she is late for her shift, she runs a red light and crashes into a car lawfully proceeding through the intersection. Although Teri is unharmed, the driver of the other car is seriously injured. The pizza shop's policy is that each driver must deliver at least three pizzas an hour. Teri has discovered that it is difficult to meet this quota without speeding a little here and there during deliveries, and that it is impossible to make all the required deliveries during her shift unless she is on time to work. Is the pizza shop liable for the injuries suffered by the driver of the other car? On what grounds?

III. JOINT LIABILITY AND CONTRIBUTION

We have already touched on the issue of apportionment in connection with causation (Chapter 4) and comparative fault (Chapter 7). However, the topic is sufficiently important and complex to warrant separate treatment. The basic issue is this: When two or more persons are adjudged legally responsible for injuring a plaintiff, how should the courts allocate responsibility and liability between or among them?

Ravo v. Rogatnick

514 N.E.2d 1104 (N.Y. 1987)

Alexander, J. In this medical malpractice action, defendant, Dr. Irwin L. Harris, appeals from an order of the Appellate Division unanimously affirming an amended judgment of Supreme Court, entered on a jury verdict, finding him jointly and severally liable with Dr. Sol Rogatnick for injuries negligently inflicted upon plaintiff, Josephine Ravo, and resulting in brain damage that has rendered her severely and permanently retarded. The issue presented is whether joint and several liability was properly imposed upon defendant under the circumstances of this case where, notwithstanding that the defendants neither acted in concert nor concurrently, a single indivisible injury — brain damage — was negligently inflicted. For the reasons that follow, we affirm.

I.

Uncontroverted expert medical evidence established that plaintiff, Josephine Ravo, who at the time of trial was 14 years of age, was severely and permanently retarded as a result of brain damage she suffered at birth. The evidence demonstrated that the child was born an unusually large baby whose mother suffered from gestational diabetes which contributed to difficulties during delivery. The evidence further established that Dr. Rogatnick, the obstetrician who had charge of the ante partum care of Josephine's mother and who delivered Josephine, failed to ascertain pertinent medical information about the mother, incorrectly estimated the size of the infant, and employed improper surgical procedures during the delivery. It was shown that Dr. Harris, the pediatrician under whose care Josephine came following birth, misdiagnosed and improperly treated the infant's condition after birth. Based upon this evidence, the jury concluded that Dr. Rogatnick committed eight separate acts of medical malpractice, and Dr. Harris committed three separate acts of medical malpractice.

Although Dr. Rogatnick's negligence contributed to Josephine's brain damage, the medical testimony demonstrated that Dr. Harris' negligence was also a substantial contributing cause of the injury. No testimony was adduced, however, from which the jury could delineate which aspects of the injury were caused by the respective negligence of the individual doctors. Indeed, plaintiff's expert, Dr. Charash, . . . concluded that neither he nor anybody else could say with certainty which of the factors caused the brain damage. Similarly, Dr. Perrotta, testifying on behalf of plaintiff, opined that she could not tell whether [Dr. Harris' carelessness] contributed "10 percent, 20 percent, or anything like that" to the injury. Nor, as the Appellate Division found, did Dr. Harris adduce any evidence that could support a jury finding that he caused an identifiable percentage of the infant plaintiff's brain damage. Indeed, Dr. Harris' entire defense appears to have been that he was not responsible for the plaintiff's injury to any degree.

The trial court instructed the jury [on the principles of comparative fault and joint and several liability.] . . .

. . . [T]he jury returned a verdict for plaintiff in the total amount of $2,750,000 attributing 80% of the "fault" to Dr. Rogatnick and 20% of the "fault" to Dr. Harris.

In a postverdict motion, Dr. Harris sought an order directing entry of judgment limiting the plaintiff's recovery against him to $450,000 (20% of the $2,250,000 base recovery—the court having set off $500,000 received by plaintiff in settlement of claims against other defendants) based upon his contention that his liability was not joint and several, but rather was independent and successive. This motion was denied. The Appellate Division . . . affirmed. . . .

II.

When two or more tort-feasors act concurrently or in concert to produce a single injury, they may be held jointly and severally liable (*see*, Suria v. Shiffman, 67 N.Y.2d 87; Bichler v. Lilly & Co., 55 N.Y.2d 571; Derby v. Prewitt, 12 N.Y.2d 100, 105; Sweet v. Perkins, 196 N.Y. 482, 485). This is so because such concerted wrongdoers are considered "joint tort-feasors" and in legal contemplation, there is a joint enterprise and a mutual agency, such that the act of one is the act of all and liability for all that is done is visited upon each (. . . *see generally*, Prosser and Keeton, *Torts* § 46 [5th ed]). On the other hand, where multiple tort-feasors "neither act in concert nor contribute concurrently to the same wrong, they are not joint tort-feasors; rather, their wrongs are independent and successive" (Suria v. Shiffman, 67 N.Y.2d 87, 98, *supra; see*, Melodee Lane Lingerie Co. v. American Dist. Tel. Co., 18 N.Y.2d 57, 66; Derby v. Prewitt, 12 N.Y.2d 100, 105, *supra;* Matter of Parchefsky v. Kroll Bros., 267 N.Y. 410, 413). Under successive and independent liability, of course, the initial tort-feasor may well be liable to the plaintiff for the entire damage proximately resulting from his own wrongful acts (Milks v. McIver, 264 N.Y. 267, 270), including aggravation of injuries by a successive tort-feasor (Milks v. McIver, 264 N.Y. 267, 270, *supra*; Matter of Parchefsky v. Kroll Bros., 267 N.Y. 410, 414, *supra*; Derby v. Prewitt, 12 N.Y.2d 100, 105, *supra*). The successive tort-feasor, however, is liable only for the separate injury or the aggravation his conduct has caused (*see*, Suria v. Shiffman, 67 N.Y.2d 87, 98, *supra*; Derby v. Prewitt, 12 N.Y.2d 100, 106, *supra*; Dubicki v. Maresco, 64 A.D.2d 645, 646; *see also*, Zillman v. Meadowbrook Hosp. Co., 45 A.D.2d 267).

It is sometimes the case that tort-feasors who neither act in concert nor concurrently may nevertheless be considered jointly and severally liable. This may occur in the instance of certain injuries which, because of their nature, are incapable of any reasonable or practicable division or allocation among multiple tort-feasors (*see, e.g.*, Hawkes v. Goll, 281 N.Y. 808, *affg* 256 App. Div. 940; Slater v. Mersereau, 64 N.Y. 138; Wiseman v. 374 Realty Corp., 54 A.D.2d 119; *see also*, Prosser and Keeton, *Torts* § 52, at 347 [5th ed]).

We had occasion to consider such a circumstance in Slater v. Mersereau (64 N.Y. 138, *supra*), where premises belonging to the plaintiff were damaged by rainwater as a result of the negligent workmanship by a general contractor and a subcontractor. We held that where two parties by their separate and independent acts of negligence, cause a single, inseparable injury, each party is responsible for the entire injury: "Although they acted independently of each other, they did act at the same time in causing the damages . . . each contributing towards it, and although the act of each, alone and of itself, might not have caused the entire injury, under the circumstances presented, there is no good reason why each should not be liable for the damages caused by the different acts of all. . . . The water with which each of the parties were instrumental in injuring the plaintiffs was one mass and inseparable, and no distinction can be made between the different sources from whence it flowed, so that it can be claimed that each caused a separate and distinct injury for which each one is separately responsible. . . . [The] contractor and subcontractors were separately negligent, and although such negligence was not concurrent, yet the negligence of both these parties contributed to produce the damages caused at one and the same time" (Slater v. Mersereau, 64 N.Y. 138, 146-147, *supra*).

Our affirmance in Hawkes v. Goll (281 N.Y. 808, *affg* 256 App. Div. 940, *supra*) demonstrates that simultaneous conduct is not necessary to a finding of joint and several liability when there is an indivisible injury. In that case, the decedent was struck by the vehicle driven by the defendant Farrell and was thrown across the roadway, where very shortly thereafter he was again struck, this time by the vehicle driven by the defendant Goll, and dragged some 40 to 50 feet along the highway. He was taken to the hospital where he expired within the hour. The Appellate Division stated (256 App. Div. 940): "As the result of his injuries the plaintiff's intestate died within an hour. There could be no evidence upon which the jury could base a finding of the nature of the injuries inflicted by the first car as distinguished from those inflicted by the second car. The case was submitted to the jury upon the theory that if both defendants were negligent they were jointly and severally liable. While the wrongful acts of the two defendants were not precisely concurrent in point of time, the defendants may nevertheless be joint tort feasors where, as here, their several acts of neglect concurred in producing the injury." . . .

Similarly, here the jury was unable to determine from the evidence adduced at trial the degree to which the defendants' separate acts of negligence contributed to the [brain damage suffered] by Josephine at birth. Certainly, a subsequent tort-feasor is not to be held jointly and severally liable for the acts of the initial tort-feasor with whom he is not acting in concert in every case where it is difficult, because of the nature of the injury, to separate the harm done by each tort-feasor from the others (*see*, Chipman v. Palmer, 77 N.Y. 51; *see generally*, Prosser, *Joint Torts and Several Liability*, 25 Cal. L. Rev. 413). Here, however, the evidence established that plaintiff's brain damage was a single indivisible injury, and defendant failed to submit any evidence upon which the jury could base an apportionment of damage.

Harris argues, however, that since the jury ascribed only 20% of the fault to him, this was in reality an apportionment of damage, demonstrating that the injury was divisible. This argument must fail. Clearly, the court's instruction, and the interrogatory submitted in amplification thereof, called upon the jury to determine the respective responsibility in negligence of the defendants so as to establish a basis for an apportionment between them, by way of contribution, for the total damages awarded to plaintiff (*see*, CPLR 1401; Dole v. Dow Chem. Co., 30 N.Y.2d 143, *supra*). In that respect, the jury's apportionment of fault is unrelated to the nature of defendants' liability (i.e., whether it was joint and several or independent and successive). . . .

Here, the jury determined that the defendants breached duties owed to Josephine Ravo, and that these breaches contributed to her brain injury. The jury's apportionment of fault, however, does not alter the joint and several liability of defendants for the single indivisible injury. Rather, that aspect of the jury's determination of culpability merely defines the amount of contribution defendants may claim from each other, and does not impinge upon plaintiff's right to collect the entire judgment award from either defendant (CPLR 1402). As we stated in Graphic Arts Mut. Ins. Co. v. Bakers Mut. Ins. Co. (45 N.Y.2d 551, 557): "The right . . . to seek equitable apportionment based on relative culpability is not one intended for the benefit of the injured claimant. It is a right affecting the distributive responsibilities of tort-feasors *inter sese*. . . . It is elementary that injured claimants may still choose which joint tort-feasors to include as defendants in an action and, regardless of the concurrent negligence of others, recover the whole of their damages from any of the particular tort-feasors sued (see Kelly v. Long Is. Light. Co., 31 N.Y.2d 25, 30)." This being so, in light of the evidence establishing the indivisibility of the brain injury and the contributing negligence of Dr. Harris, and of the manner in which the case was tried and submitted to the jury, we conclude that joint and several liability was properly imposed.

Accordingly, the order of the Appellate Division should be affirmed.

NOTES AND QUESTIONS

1. *Joint and Several Liability: Indivisible Harms.* As *Ravo* explains, joint and several liability has long been available when two tortfeasors were found to have conspired together or to have acted in concert. At least since the turn of the twentieth century, it has also been regularly applied in situations such as the one in *Ravo*, in which two

negligent actors, acting independently of each other, caused a single *indivisible* harm to the plaintiff, such that there was no way to tell which tortfeasor caused which portion of the harm. *See* Chapter 4 (notes following *McDonald v. Robinson*). Suppose two drivers, *D1* and *D2*, are proceeding in opposite directions, ignore the stop signs at an intersection, and smash into pedestrian *P*. *P* suffers serious injuries to his internal organs, resulting in damages of $1 million. There is no way to figure out how much of that harm resulted from *P* being struck by *D1* and from *P* being struck by *D2*. Under the indivisible injury rule, *D1* and *D2* would be held jointly and severally liable — *P* could ask either *D1* or *D2* to pay the full amount.

2. *Contribution.* Suppose in the foregoing hypothetical that *P* sued *D1* and *D2*, won verdicts against *D1* and *D2*, and then chose to collect the entire judgment of $1 million from *D1*. Does this mean that *D2* gets away with paying nothing, simply because *P* decided to collect from *D1*? Not necessarily. This is because a defendant who is made to pay more than his share of a liability that is jointly owed by another can bring a claim *against that other party*.

This claim does *not* sound in tort or contract (*D2* did not commit a tort against *D1*, nor did *D2* breach any contract with *D1*). Instead, the claim sounds in a body of law called *restitution*. Essentially, the claim is that, because of the operation of the rule of joint and several liability, *D1* has paid too much, and *D2* too little, and therefore in fairness *D2* should transfer some of his wealth to *D1*. As noted in *Ravo*, claims for restitution brought in this special circumstance are called actions for *contribution*. Thus, the rule of joint and several liability, combined with the action for contribution, frees the plaintiff from having to collect from each defendant and in turn *leaves it to the defendants to settle their accounts with one another.**

3. *Actions for Contribution, Cross-Claims, and Impleaders.* Under modern rules of civil procedure, multiple tortfeasors whose torts cause a given injury to the same victim can assert claims for contribution against one another as part of the same lawsuit in which plaintiff brings her claims against the defendants. If a plaintiff has commenced her action against all of the relevant tortfeasors, such that they are all parties to the suit, they can seek contribution from one another by asserting *cross-claims*. Thus, if *P* were to sue *D1* and *D2*, and if *D1* were held liable for *P*'s entire award, *D1* could assert his claim for contribution in the form of cross-claim against *D2*. However, if for some reason *P* initially chooses only to sue *D1*, *D1* has the option of bringing *D2* into the suit for purposes of determining to what extent *D2* will be liable to *D1* for contribution. When one defendant brings a co-defendant into a suit for the purpose of determining whether the co-defendant might be responsible for a share of any liability incurred by

* Historically, an *intentional* tortfeasor subject to joint and several liability for a plaintiff's damages has been barred from seeking contribution from another tortfeasor also responsible for those damages on the ground that one who commits this graver sort of wrong has no basis for asserting that he has "overpaid" and hence no basis for seeking restitution from others. There is today movement among some courts to permit intentional tortfeasors held jointly and severally liable to seek contribution from co-tortfeasors — even merely careless co-tortfeasors — on the ground that intentional wrongs differ merely in degree, rather than in kind, from unintentional wrongs.

the original defendant to the plaintiff, the original defendant is said to have *impleaded* the co-defendant.*

4. *Comparative Responsibility with Joint and Several Liability.* Prior to the adoption of comparative responsibility, the amount that a jointly and severally liable co-defendant would have to contribute to the unlucky defendant who had been chosen by the plaintiff to pay the full judgment was determined on a *pro rata* basis. Thus, to continue the example developed above, if *P* collected her $1 million award from *D1*, and *D1* then sued *D2* for contribution, *D2* would be liable to pay *D1* $500,000—50 percent of the amount *D1* paid to *P*—because *D1* and *D2* were the only two responsible parties. With the adoption of comparative fault, *D2*'s share is no longer determined on a *pro rata* basis, but instead by the jury's percentage apportionment of fault. Thus, for example, if *D1* was found by the jury to be 30 percent at fault, and *D2* 70 percent at fault, yet *D1* was made to pay the full judgment, then *D1* would be entitled to seek contribution in the amount of $700,000 from *D2*.

5. *Comparative Responsibility Without Joint and Several Liability.* With the adoption of comparative responsibility regimes, a question has arisen as to whether the idea of joint and several liability for indivisible harms continues to make sense. After all, comparative responsibility regimes require juries faced with cases such as our imagined intersection collision to assign *percentage* fault to the likes of *D1* and *D2*. If juries can and must *divide responsibility* in this manner, how can it make sense to describe *P*'s injury as *indivisible*, and hence as the sort of injury that requires the special rule of joint and several liability?

Obviously, the *Ravo* court concluded that comparative responsibility and joint and several liability are compatible with one another. Does the court contradict itself by simultaneously asserting that the plaintiff's injury is divisible for purposes of assigning comparative fault, yet indivisible for purposes of applying joint and several liability? Some courts have concluded, in opposition to *Ravo*, that comparative fault is inconsistent with the doctrine of joint and several liability for indivisible injuries. *See, e.g.*, McIntyre v. Balentine, 833 S.W.2d 52 (Tenn. 1992).

6. *What's at Stake?* What is the practical difference between decisions such as *Ravo* and decisions such as *McIntyre*? In either case, *P* is ultimately entitled to recover 100 percent of her damages, and *D1* and *D2* to pay the share of damages apportioned to them by the jury. True, under *Ravo*, the plaintiff can get her $1,000,000 from *D1 or D2*,

---

* Procedural rules authorizing impleaders, such as Rule 14 of the Federal Rules of Civil Procedure, typically authorize a defendant (*D*) to commence an action against a third party (*TP*) if *D* has a colorable claim that *TP* will be liable to *D* in the event that *D* is held liable to plaintiff (*P*). Once impleaded, *TP* becomes a party to the underlying suit by *P* against *D*. *TP* is referred to as the *third-party defendant*. For purposes of its claim against *TP*, *D* is referred to as the *third-party plaintiff*. For example, if Dr. Ravo had initially sued only Dr. Rogatnick, Dr. Rogatnick would likely have been permitted by the court to bring Dr. Harris into the suit, regardless of Ravo's wishes, because there would have been a nonfrivolous basis for asserting that Dr. Harris might be liable to Dr. Rogatnick for all or part of plaintiff's claim against Dr. Rogatnick.

whereas under *McIntyre* she must collect it from *D1 and D2.* Is this a distinction without a difference? What risk is being allocated by the different approaches?

7. Splitting the Difference. *Ravo* and *McIntyre* are "all or nothing" decisions. If it turns out that one defendant is unreachable or insolvent, either the other defendant(s) (under *Ravo*) or the plaintiff (under *McIntyre*) will bear the cost of the missing defendant's share of the damages. An alternative perhaps more in keeping with the "equitable" nature of the law of contribution might be instead to allocate the missing share among all parties found to have contributed to the plaintiff's injuries (including, where applicable, the at-fault plaintiff).

Suppose, for example, a jury faced with our hypothetical intersection collision were to conclude that *P* was 10 percent at fault for her own injuries, *D1* was 50 percent at fault, and D2 was 40 percent at fault. Now suppose *D2* is judgment-proof or otherwise unreachable. The value of *D2*'s "missing" share of liability—$400,000—might be split among *P* and *D1* as the two remaining parties deemed by the jury to have been responsible for *P*'s injuries. Under a *pro rata* version of such a scheme, *P* would recover $700,000 from *D1*—$500,000 based on *D1*'s 50 percent responsibility, plus another $200,000 representing half of *D2*'s missing share. (*P* would thus be forced to bear the other half of *D2*'s share.) Alternatively, a court could divide the value of *D2*'s missing share among *P* and *D1* by reference to the ratio of their percentage responsibilities. Under this approach, *P* would recover $833,333 from *D1*—$500,000 based on *D1*'s 50 percent responsibility, plus another $333,333 representing 5/6ths of *D2*'s missing share. *See, e.g.*, Martignetti v. Haigh-Farr, Inc., 680 N.E.2d 1131 (Mass. 1997) (adopting the latter approach in applying a federal environmental statute that imposes liability for the cost of cleaning up toxic waste sites among parties responsible for creating the site).

8. Joint and Several Liability in Retreat. In addition to focusing on statutes of limitations, as well as compensatory and punitive damage reforms, modern tort reform movements have taken aim at the rule of joint and several liability for indivisible injuries. The result has been that most states have adopted rules eliminating or restricting joint and several liability, at least in some classes of tort cases (e.g., actions for medical malpractice), or for certain damage items (e.g., noneconomic losses). For example, in 1986, Colorado enacted a statute that essentially abolished joint and several liability for cases of indivisible physical harms (although it remains applicable to cases of conspiracy and concert of action):

COLO. REV. STAT. § 13-21-111.5

Civil Liability Cases-Pro Rata Liability of Defendants. . . .

(1) In an action brought as a result of a death or an injury to person or property, no defendant shall be liable for an amount greater than that represented by the degree or percentage of negligence or fault attributable to such defendant that produced the claimed injury, death, damage, or loss, except as provided in subsection (4) of this section. . . .

(4) Joint liability shall be imposed on two or more persons who consciously conspire and deliberately pursue a common plan or design to commit a tortious act. . . .

As plaintiff and his companions stood outside, a bouncer approached. Plaintiff recognized him as the bouncer who was talking to the female when she got pinched. The bouncer said, "I see you guys got your asses kicked." When asked why plaintiff's attacker also had not been removed from the club, the bouncer responded, "[T]he other guy's got juice. . . ."

Plaintiff needed surgery to repair his nose. . . . Plaintiff 's nose contains a scar and a permanent deviation to the right as a result of the incident.

Plaintiff's complaint sought damages from Club 35 and the unnamed intentional tortfeasor, as well as from unnamed employees of the club. The complaint alleged, alternatively, negligent or intentional conduct on the part of Club 35 and its one named and other unnamed employees. Club 35's answer raised defenses that negligent conduct of others caused plaintiff's injuries. . . .

II.

In Blazovic v. Andrich, 124 N.J. 90, 107, 590 A.2d 222 (1991), decided after the trial in this case, the Supreme Court held the Act applies to conduct characterized as intentional. It ruled a jury must be instructed to compare the fault of intentional tortfeasors with that of negligent wrongdoers for the purpose of apportioning liability under the Act. *See* N.J.S.A. 2A:15-5.1. The Court based its ruling on the premise that parties causing an injury should be liable in proportion to their relative fault. Blazovic v. Andrich, *supra*, 124 N.J. at 109-10, 590 A.2d 222.

. . . Blazovic sought compensatory damages for injuries he sustained in a parking lot of the defendant restaurant when he was assaulted by five defendants who had been patrons of the restaurant. The evidence suggested comments made by Blazovic precipitated the assault. *Blazovic* held the fault of all parties, Blazovic, the restaurant, and the five assaultive defendants, who settled with Blazovic prior to trial, should be compared for purposes of the Act.

Blazovic rested his claim against the restaurant proprietor, as plaintiff rests his claim against Club 35, on the holding in Butler v. Acme Markets, Inc., 89 N.J. 270, 275, 445 A.2d 1141 (1982). *Butler* recognized that the "proprietor of premises to which the public is invited for business purposes of the proprietor owes a duty . . . to exercise reasonable care to discover intentionally harmful acts of third parties are being done or are likely to be done, or to give warning adequate to enable patrons to avoid the harm, or otherwise to protect them against the harm." *Id.* [at 280] (quoting Restatement (Second) of Torts § 344, at 223-24 (1965)).

III.

Club 35 asserts the trial court erred when the court rejected its request to instruct the jury to determine the relative percentages of fault of the plaintiff, the fictitiously named and never identified intentional tortfeasor who assaulted plaintiff, and Club 35. It contends *Blazovic* dictates such a result. We disagree. . . .

We turn first to the issue of whether the trial court erred in refusing to instruct the jury to compare the fault of the unnamed intentional tortfeasor in assessing liability. N.J.S.A. 2A:15-5.1 requires comparison of plaintiff's negligence with the negligence, now fault as the result of *Blazovic*, of the person or persons against whom recovery is sought. N.J.S.A. 2A:15-5.2 requires the trier of fact to return a special verdict on "[t]he percentage of negligence of each *party* "with "the total of all percentages of negligence of all the *parties to the suit*" being fixed at 100%. *Id.* (emphasis added).

We conclude the plain and ordinary meaning of the statutory language precludes inclusion of a fictitiously named tortfeasor from the Act's commands for apportioning fault. The plain language of sections 5.1 and 5.2 make the negligence of the person or persons *against whom recovery is sought* and the negligence of each *party* or *parties to the suit* the prerequisites to apportioning fault. A fictitious person is not someone against whom recovery can be sought because the fictitious person rule, *R.* 4:26-4, and due process prevent entry of judgment against a person designated by a fictitious name.

Also, a fictitious person is not a party to a suit. The person plaintiff identifies as a fictitious defendant only becomes a party to the suit when the defendant's true name is substituted in an amended complaint and service is effected. . . . It is at the point of service on the true defendant that a court gains jurisdiction, consonant with due process, and a person becomes a party to a suit. It is at that point when the Act requires the person's conduct be compared for the purposes of apportioning liability and not before.

This result is supported by our holding in Ramos v. Browning Ferris Ind. of So. Jersey, Inc., 194 N.J. Super. 96, 476 A.2d 304 (App. Div. 1984), *rev'd on other grounds*, 103 N.J. 177, 510 A.2d 1152 (1986). There we stated,

> A truer verdict is more likely to be returned where the fact finder's attention is ultimately fixed on the conduct of the parties who will be affected by the verdict. . . . With [the] necessary exception [of assessing the negligence of a settling tortfeasor with that of a non-settling tortfeasor for contribution purposes] there is no more reason to have a fact finder assign a percentage of negligence to someone who is not affected by the verdict than to assign a percentage of negligence to acts of God (such as the snow in this case) or a myriad of other causative factors that may have contributed to the happening of an accident. [*Id.* 194 N.J. Super. at 106, 476 A.2d 304.] . . .

Blazovic does not dictate otherwise. *Blazovic* required fault be apportioned among joint or concurrent tortfeasors regardless of the nature of the fault. It did not specifically rule on whether the Act required apportioning fault of an unnamed party. The Court did, however, suggest resolution of the issue in its response to a concern of an Appellate Division dissent. That concern suggested the liability formula enacted in N.J.S.A. 2A:15-5.3a [excerpted above — EDS.] could limit a plaintiff's recovery where there are multipl[e] liable tortfeasors if an intentional tortfeasor is deemed to have greater than 40% fault and is unable to pay the judgment. The Court responded, "We reject that [concern] because it ignores the principle that the *parties* causing an injury should be liable in proportion to their relative fault." *Id.* 124 N.J. at 110, 590 A.2d 222 (emphasis added). The unnamed intentional tortfeasor, John Doe, is not a party as required by the statute. To sanction inclusion of that tortfeasor in the fault allocation-liability format of the Act would engender a result beyond its plain language. . . .

Furthermore, there are strong policy reasons that dictate against including the absent or unnamed tortfeasor from the fact finder's negligence apportionment.

The amount of plaintiff's judgment and amount of defendant's liability will vary depending upon whether the absent-unnamed person's negligence is considered by the fact finder. Defendant, however, has a greater incentive to join and name additional potential tort-feasors or to see that they are identified. That greater incentive is the percentage-liability formula. That formula proscribes contribution where fault falls below a certain percentage. *See* N.J.S.A. 2A:15-5.3. Thus, defendant has significant incentive in naming and joining multiple tortfeasors so as to create the potential for diminishing defendant's percentage of liability to a level that avoids contribution. Given that incentive, it is appropriate to place upon defendant the burden of finding and naming any additional person since it is to defendant's advantage to spread the risk or defeat the claim. *See* National Farmers Union Prop. and Cas. Co. v. Frackelton, 662 P.2d 1056, 1060 (Colo. 1983).

These policy dictates are particularly poignant here. The evidence recited reflects Club 35 failed to protect plaintiff in the manner the law requires and had the best opportunity to identify the intentional tortfeasor who assaulted plaintiff. Indeed, the evidence suggests the bouncers knew the intentional tortfeasor, yet Club 35 chose to ignore that knowledge and not identify him. Interestingly, Club 35 chose also not to identify its bouncers who were also unnamed defendants, although the bouncers' conduct might have affected the jury's evaluation of Club 35's responsibility. Consequently, and quite apart from our statutory construction, in absence of language demonstrating a contrary legislative purpose, we are satisfied the most equitable result, in light of the circumstances here, is to preclude the unnamed intentional tortfeasor's conduct from the fault comparison for purposes of allocating liability. . . .

IV.

In conclusion we hold the fault of a fictitious person may not be considered when apportioning negligence among parties to the lawsuit. The Act's plain language precludes fault allocation because a fictitious defendant is not a party to the suit and not one against whom recovery is sought. Moreover, we find sound policy reasons applicable to the facts of this case dictate against allocating fault of the unnamed intentional tortfeasor. . . .

The judgment of the trial court is affirmed.

NOTES AND QUESTIONS

1. Apples and Oranges? As this decision notes, the New Jersey Supreme Court, interpreting the state's comparative fault statute, had already held in *Blazovic* that juries should be instructed to allocate percentage "fault" between tortfeasors even if one acted negligently and another acted intentionally. Courts have dealt similarly with cases in which one tortfeasor is being held liable under a strict liability standard whereas another is being held liable under a negligence standard. In these latter cases, the jury is thus being asked to assign a percentage "fault" to a strictly liable tortfeasor. As we noted in Chapter 7, the fact that juries are asked to make percentage assignments of responsibility to intentional and strictly liable tortfeasors suggests that the phrase "comparative fault"—as opposed to "comparative responsibility"—can sometimes be misleading.

2. *"Phantom" Tortfeasors. Bencivenga* refuses to permit the jury to assign fault to the unknown assailant. What is the most compelling justification for its decision? Is it that the unavailability of the assailant is the defendant's fault? If not, why put the onus on the defendant to bear the risk of the assailant's unavailability?

Other state statutes and judicial decisions permit juries to assign fault to non-parties. *See, e.g.*, DeBenedetto v. CLD Consulting Engineers, Inc., 903 A.2d 969 (N.H. 2006) (interpreting New Hampshire's comparative fault statute to require apportionment to absent parties, and citing decisions from several other states adopting the same approach). Some place the burden of proof with respect to a non-party's fault on the defendant and require that the non-party be identified by name. Ind. Code. §§ 34-51-2-7 & 2-15. In these jurisdictions, absent a rule of joint and several liability, the plaintiff cannot collect on the portion of liability assigned to such a non-party. In a modified comparative fault system, should non-parties' fault also be counted in determining, for example, whether plaintiff's fault exceeded that of the defendants?

3. *Immune Tortfeasors.* As is discussed in Chapter 7, various persons who would otherwise be liable in negligence are protected from liability by defenses and immunities, including statutes of limitations and sovereign immunity, as well as particular immunities such as the immunity effectively granted by the exclusive remedy provisions of workers' compensation systems. If actors that are immune from liability are named in the underlying tort suit, yet establish their immunity, should the jury be instructed to assign a percentage fault to these parties if the evidence shows that their carelessness was a cause of the plaintiff's injury? Legislation and judicial decisions vary on this issue, even within a given jurisdiction. *Compare* Dotson v. Blake, 29 S.W.3d 26 (Tenn. 2000) (in suit against multiple tortfeasors, jury should assign a percentage responsibility to any fault attributable to state employees, even though they are immune from liability) *with* Ridings v. Ralph M. Parsons Co., 914 S.W.2d 79 (Tenn. 1996) (in a suit by plaintiff-employee against a third party for injuries suffered at the workplace, the jury should *not* assign a percentage responsibility to the plaintiff's employer, which is immunized from tort liability by workers' compensation law).

4. *Settling Tortfeasors.* What happens when one defendant settles with the plaintiff prior to trial but another chooses to go to trial over the same incident? Should the jury be instructed that it may assign percentage fault to a settling defendant as an absent party to the suit? Assuming the abolition of joint and several liability, how should a remaining defendant's liability be adjusted in light of the settlement? Suppose, for example, *D1*, the settling defendant, pays plaintiff an amount that turns out to equal 30 percent of the damages awarded by the jury. Suppose further that the jury assigns 60 percent responsibility to *D1*, and 40 percent to *D2*. Should *D2* be required to pay only 40 percent of the award in light of the jury's apportionment of fault? Or should *D2* be made to pay 50 percent as one of two responsible tortfeasors? Or some other amount? Rules on allocation of damages in light of settlement are enormously

complicated and vary substantially among jurisdictions. *See* McDermott, Inc. v. AmClyde, 511 U.S. 202 (1994) (discussing alternative rules).

IV. INDEMNIFICATION AND LIABILITY INSURANCE

When one tortfeasor is held jointly and severally liable to compensate a victim for her injuries and then seeks reimbursement from a second tortfeasor who also contributed to the victim's injury but was not made to pay anything, the former brings an action for contribution. As indicated, the action for contribution sounds neither in tort nor contract, but in restitution. The second tortfeasor has been deemed partially responsible for the victim's injury, yet has paid nothing, whereas the first tortfeasor has paid too much. Hence it is equitable to permit the first to obtain reimbursement from the second for a portion of the damages paid out to the victim.

Indemnification is similar to contribution, in that it permits a tortfeasor to look to another person or entity to cover some or all of its liability. However, indemnity is almost always accomplished through contract. By virtue of that contract, a person or entity has *promised* to *indemnify* (reimburse) the tortfeasor for certain liabilities. In tort law, the most important example of a promise to indemnify consists of the issuance of a *liability insurance policy.*

Interinsurance Exch. of the Automobile Club v. Flores

53 Cal. Rptr. 2d 18 (Ct. App. 1996)

Gilbert, J. An insured drives his van to a location to allow his passenger to shoot someone from the van. The driver has a standard auto insurance policy that provides coverage for injuries caused by an accident. Does the policy provide the driver with coverage for injuries to the victim? No.

Rosemary and David Flores (Flores) appeal from the judgment in favor of respondent, Interinsurance Exchange of the Automobile Club of Southern California (Automobile Club) in this declaratory relief action. We affirm. . . .

Facts

. . . An unknown pedestrian punched Eric Michael Sanders in the face while Sanders sat in his van waiting for a traffic light to change. . . . Sanders told Roger Perez of the incident. Perez suggested they return to the scene, locate the assailant and seek retribution. Perez told Sanders he was armed with a handgun before he and others got into the van. Sanders knew that someone was likely to get shot. He drove Perez and the others back to the intersection where Sanders had been punched. David Flores stood on the corner of the intersection. While Sanders drove by, Perez intentionally shot and injured Flores from the van. The van itself did not inflict any injury on Flores, nor was it used to block or pin down Flores.

After his arrest for his involvement in the shooting, Sanders admitted that he knew someone was likely to be shot. In the criminal action Sanders pled [guilty] to the felony of aiding and abetting the shooting of Flores (Pen. Code, § 245, subd. (a)(2)). (People v. Sanders (Super. Ct. Santa Barbara County, 1990, No. 182329).)

Rosemary Flores, individually, and as guardian ad litem for David Flores, filed the underlying civil suit against Sanders and others for conspiracy, battery and negligence. The Floreses' suit alleged, inter alia, that Sanders and Perez "agreed to hunt down, shoot, and either kill or maim the perpetrator of the Sanders attack, using Roger Perez's .22 caliber handgun." These allegations were incorporated into each cause of action in the Floreses' suit.

Sanders owns the van involved and his parents insured it for him under an automobile insurance policy issued by the Automobile Club. The Automobile Club reserved its rights to deny coverage and filed the instant declaratory relief action to determine whether or not it had a duty to defend or indemnify Sanders for liability in the underlying Flores action under the policy.

The trial court denied summary judgment to the Automobile Club and the parties proceeded to trial by the court on the stipulated facts. After trial, the trial court found that the shooting was not an accident, that Sanders acted intentionally in aiding and abetting the shooting and that the injuries inflicted on the Flores family were not covered by the instant policy. In its judgment, the trial court ruled that the Automobile Club is not obligated to indemnify Sanders for liability he may have to the Floreses. This appeal ensued. . . .

Discussion

Interpretation

Interpretation of the insurance policy presents a question of law for this court to decide. (Waller v. Truck Ins. Exchange, Inc. (1995) 11 Cal. 4th 1, 18 [44 Cal. Rptr. 2d 370, 900 P.2d 619]; State Farm Mut. Auto. Ins. Co. v. Partridge (1973) 10 Cal. 3d 94, 100 [109 Cal. Rptr. 811, 514 P.2d 123].) We consider the stipulated facts and the allegations of the Floreses' complaint together with the language of the insurance policy. (Montrose Chemical Corp. v. Superior Court (1993) 6 Cal. 4th 287, 295, 300 [24 Cal. Rptr. 2d 467, 861 P.2d 1153].)

The duty of an insurance company to defend a claim of coverage is broad. . . . Courts first consider whether there may be a potential for coverage under the policy. . . . The insured has the burden to bring the claim within the basic scope of coverage; the insurer must establish the absence of such coverage. . . . Courts will not indulge in a forced construction of the policy's insuring clauses to find coverage. . . . And, courts construe policy terms in their "'ordinary and popular sense.'" (Bank of the West v. Superior Court (1992) 2 Cal. 4th 1254, 1265 [10 Cal. Rptr. 2d 538, 833 P.2d 545]; *Waller, supra*, at p.18. . . .)

Because the Automobile Club reserved its rights, any allegations or judgment of negligence in the underlying civil suit would not preclude the insurance company from asserting there is no coverage here because Sanders expected or intended harm to occur. . . .

Coverage

Use of the Vehicle

In an insurance policy, the phrase "arising out of the use" has broad and comprehensive application. (State Farm Mut. Auto. Ins. Co. v. Partridge, *supra,* 10 Cal. 3d at p.100.) It affords coverage for injuries where the insured vehicle bears "almost *any* causal relation" to the accident at issue, however minimal. (*Id.* at p.100; *see also id.*, at fn.7; *id.* at p.101, fn.8.) Here, Sanders drove to the scene for the purpose of seeking retaliation and left the scene of the shooting by use of the van. The insurer admits that the van "was passing through the intersection" when Perez shot Flores. We agree with the trial court that the Sanders van was being used at all pertinent times within the meaning of the instant policy language.

Occurrence

The instant policy promises to "pay damages for which any person insured is legally liable because of bodily injury . . . *caused by an occurrence* arising out of the ownership, maintenance or use" of the insured vehicle. (Italics added.) "Occurrence" is defined to mean "an *accident* . . . , including injurious exposure to conditions, which results in bodily injury. . . ." (Italics added.) Therefore, the instant policy provides coverage to Sanders only if he accidentally caused the injury to Flores. "[T]he insured has the burden of showing that there has been an 'occurrence' within the terms of the policy." (Waller v. Truck Ins. Exchange, Inc., *supra,* 11 Cal. 4th at p.16. . . .)

When an injury is an unexpected or unintended consequence of the insured's conduct, it may be characterized as an accident for which coverage exists. When the injury suffered is *expected* or *intended,* coverage is denied. When one expects or intends an injury to occur, there is no "accident."

Flores argues that Sanders' acts were not intended or expected because he did not shoot Flores himself or direct that he be shot. Therefore, his conduct was, at most, reckless. (Peterson v. Superior Court (1982) 31 Cal. 3d 147, 158-159 [181 Cal. Rptr. 784, 642 P.2d 1305]; State Farm Mut. Auto. Ins. Co. v. Partridge, *supra,* 10 Cal. 3d at p.101; National American Ins. Co. v. Insurance Co. of North America (1977) 74 Cal. App. 3d 565, 571 [140 Cal. Rptr. 828].) We disagree. The cases cited by appellant are distinguishable.

In *Peterson,* a driver drove with excessive speed after consuming alcohol. In deciding issues not relevant here, our Supreme Court explained that conduct amounting to a conscious disregard for the safety of others does not constitute willful, intentional conduct within the meaning of Insurance Code section 533. (Peterson v. Superior Court, *supra,* 31 Cal. 3d at pp.158-159.) Section 533 states an insurer is not liable for the willful acts of its insured.

In *Partridge,* the insured filed the trigger mechanism of his pistol at home so that the gun would have a "hair trigger action." The insured took the gun into his Bronco truck and placed it either on his lap or on top of the steering wheel. While the insured was driving, he saw a rabbit crossing the road. He drove off the road onto rough terrain to follow the rabbit. When the truck hit a bump, the gun discharged and caused injury to a passenger in the vehicle.

The insurance company filed a declaratory relief action to determine whether its homeowners or its automobile policy provided coverage for the damages caused by the injuries incurred as a result of the accident. The trial court ruled that both policies afforded coverage and our Supreme Court affirmed.

Filing the trigger mechanism and transporting the gun independently concurred to proximately cause the accident. The insured's automobile policy provided coverage because the insured was using the truck at the time the gun accidentally discharged. The homeowners policy also provided coverage, despite an express exclusion for injuries arising out of use of a vehicle, because the insured's negligent filing of the trigger mechanism was an independent, concurrent covered proximate cause of the accidental injury.

Because coverage clauses are broadly construed in favor of the insured and express exclusions are strictly construed against the insurer, an insurer is liable if one of such multiple causes is a covered one. Even though the circumstances in *Partridge* "can only be described as blatant recklessness" ([State Farm Mut. Auto. Ins. Co. v. Partridge, *supra*, 10 Cal. 3d.] at pp.97, 106-107), the concurrent negligent causes of the incident were covered under the policies.

In *National American*, four teenage boys rode in an automobile indiscriminately throwing eggs at other automobiles, homes and people. While the automobile was traveling about 40 miles an hour, one of the boys flipped an egg towards a pedestrian who lost an eye as a result. The most significant factor causing the injury was the speed of the automobile. A jury returned a verdict of liability for negligence against the boy who flipped the egg. The issue in *National American* was not coverage, but causation.

The Court of Appeal stated that substantial evidence supported the findings of the trial court that the injury resulted from negligent conduct which caused an accident involving the use of an automobile. It affirmed the judgment of the trial court and concluded that the judgment comported with policies of law and equity regarding indemnity and defense costs among insurers.

Drunk driving, leaving a loaded hair trigger weapon on one's lap and flipping eggs out of a car at 40 miles an hour all constitute negligent or reckless conduct which may cause injury. As such, they all constitute "accidents" within the meaning of personal injury insurance policies because the injuries are not intended or expected.

Here, however, the underlying complaint and the stipulated facts establish that the instant shooting was no accident. It was planned. Sanders knew Perez was armed with a deadly weapon. He drove Perez to the place where he thought they might find the person who had punched him. Sanders knew that someone was likely to be shot. Sanders therefore intended and expected injury to result from his acts. The Floreses have not borne their burden to show that Sanders' conduct was accidental within the meaning of the instant insurance policy. Accordingly, the Floreses did not establish potential coverage for the shooting incident.

Exclusions

Insurance Code Section 533

Coverage is also excluded because the acts were willful within the meaning of section 533, which provides a statutory exclusion in every insurance policy.

(J. C. Penney Casualty Ins. Co. v. M. K., *supra*, 52 Cal. 3d at p.1019.) Section 533 states, "*An insurer is not liable for* a loss caused by the *wilful act of the insured*; *but* he is *not exonerated by the negligence* of the insured, or of the insured's agents or others." (Italics added.) We determine the Legislature's intent in passing section 533 by considering the words of the statute. Neither the words of section 533 nor its legislative history establishes its meaning.

Because a negligent act may be done "wilfully"—the act is volitional—the term "wilful act" in section 533 means something more than performing a voluntary act which constitutes negligence. (J. C. Penney Casualty Ins. Co. v. M. K., *supra*, 52 Cal. 3d at p.1021.)

Our Supreme Court has explained that ". . . section 533 does not preclude coverage for acts that are negligent or reckless." (J. C. Penney Casualty Ins. Co. v. M. K., *supra*, 52 Cal. 3d at p.1021.) Where application of section 533 becomes an issue, the insurance company must establish that the insured acted with intent to harm or that the insured committed an inherently wrongful act. (52 Cal. 3d at pp.1021-1027.)

But, the general rule of strict construction against the insurer regarding exclusions does not apply to section 533 because it is a statutory exclusion evincing a fundamental public policy. (*See* J. C. Penney Casualty Ins. Co. v. M. K., *supra*, 52 Cal. 3d at pp.1019, 1020, fn.9.) If coverage is excluded under section 533, we may not consider whether there may be coverage under any express exclusions stated in the insurance policy. (52 Cal. 3d pp.1019-1020, fn.8.) Whether there may be coverage due to section 533 depends upon the facts of the case.

There may be coverage under section 533 for an accident caused by drunk driving because drunk driving, per se, is reckless conduct. (*See generally*, Peterson v. Superior Court, *supra*, 31 Cal. 3d at p.159.) There may not be coverage for an act such as child molestation because that act is deemed to be inherently wrongful or harmful in itself. (*See* J. C. Penney Casualty Ins. Co. v. M. K., *supra*, 52 Cal. 3d at pp.1021-1027.)

Although the Supreme Court expressly limited *J. C. Penney* to child molestation, its dictum establishes that under section 533, an insurer bears no liability if the insured acted with intent to harm or committed an inherently wrongful act without legal justification. (*See* J. C. Penney Casualty Ins. Co. v. M. K., *supra*, 52 Cal. 3d at pp.1025, fn.13, 1021-1027; *see also* Fire Ins. Exchange v. Altieri (1991) 235 Cal. App. 3d 1352, 1357-1358. . . .)

Here, Sanders pled nolo contendere to the felony criminal charge of aiding and abetting an assault with a deadly weapon. "The legal effect of such a [nolo] plea, . . . shall be the same as that of a plea of guilty for all purposes." (Pen. Code, § 1016, subd. 3.) Guilty and nolo pleas are admissible in a subsequent civil action, such as the underlying action, as an admission of the crime. Therefore, Sanders admitted committing the crime of aiding and abetting an assault with a deadly weapon.

The admission is not conclusive, per se, and has no collateral estoppel effect. A plea may reflect a compromise or a choice not to undergo prosecution; it does not necessarily establish the underlying factual matters at issue in the civil litigation.

Under section 533, the question here is whether Sanders' admission of the crime of aiding and abetting assault with a deadly weapon, together with the other stipulated or pleaded facts, constitute [sufficient evidence of] acts which are either inherently harmful or which evince an intent to harm.

The stipulated facts establish that Sanders drove Perez back to the intersection where Sanders had been punched in order to retaliate. Sanders knew someone was likely to get shot. When an offense includes the intent to do some act beyond the actus reus of the crime, one who aids and abets the crime *must share the specific intent of its perpetrator.* Although the stipulated facts do not state the crime for which Perez was charged and convicted, they do state that "Roger Perez intentionally shot David Flores with a .22 caliber revolver while Roger Perez was inside the van."

By aiding and abetting the intentional shooting, Sanders is a principal to it and he is equally guilty for that act. . . . Under these facts, we conclude that Sanders harbored intent to harm within the meaning of section 533.

The underlying complaint also supports our conclusion that Sanders evinced an intent to harm another. Each of its causes of action incorporate by reference the allegation that Sanders and Perez "agreed to hunt down, shoot, and either kill or maim the perpetrator of the Sanders' attack, using Roger Perez' .22 caliber handgun."

The Automobile Club has established that it may deny coverage under the implied exclusion set forth in section 533. (Fire Ins. Exchange v. Altieri, *supra*, 235 Cal. App. 3d at pp.1357-1360 [no duty to indemnify for assault even though assailant asserted he did not intend to injure victim]; Reagen's Vacuum Truck Service, Inc. v. Beaver Ins. Co. (1994) 31 Cal. App. 4th 375, 388 [37 Cal. Rptr. 2d 89].) Because coverage is excluded here under section 533, we need not consider whether there may be coverage under the express policy exclusion for bodily injury intentionally caused by or at the direction of an insured.

Conclusion

"The concept of 'fortuity' is basic to insurance law. Insurance typically is designed to protect [against] contingent or unknown risks of harm [citations], not to protect against harm which is certain or expected. [Citation.]" (Chu v. Canadian Indemnity Co., *supra*, 224 Cal. App. 3d at pp.94-95; Waller v. Truck Ins. Exchange, Inc., *supra*, 11 Cal. 4th at pp.16-17.) Sanders expected harm to occur here and he acted deliberately to help bring it about. Under the stipulated facts and allegations in the underlying complaint, the Automobile Club need not defend or indemnify the Floreses' claims against Sanders.

The judgment is affirmed. Each party to bear its own costs.

NOTES AND QUESTIONS

1. *Insurer and Insured.* An insurance policy is a contract. One party to the contract is the insurer. In exchange for a fee ("premium"), the insurer promises to pay certain costs incurred by another person or persons. The person or persons who are entitled to reimbursement for these costs are known as "insureds."

Note that one can be an insured without being a party to the insurance contract. Here, the relevant insured was not the purchaser of the automobile insurance policy, but rather a child of the purchasers of that policy. Depending on the terms of the actual automobile insurance policy, a guest who happened to be in the car and injured in an accident might also have qualified as an insured.

2. First-Party Versus Third-Party Coverage. Policies such as automobile policies often contain two different types of insurance coverage. First, they contain coverage for *first-party* costs, that is, a promise to pay costs incurred directly by one or more of the insureds. First-party coverage typically found in an automobile insurance policy includes collision coverage (a promise to pay for repairs to the insured's vehicle if damaged in an accident) and medical coverage (a promise to pay medical bills incurred by the insured as a result of an accident arising out of use of the insured vehicle).

Second, such policies often provide coverage of certain *third-party* costs, that is, costs that are incurred by some person other than the insured. Here, for example, Flores maintained that the contract between Mr. and Mrs. Sanders and the Automobile Club included a promise from Automobile Club to cover third-party costs that they or their son became obligated to pay as a result of using the car. This sort of promise/coverage is commonly known as *liability insurance*: The insured is covered against the risk of being held liable to a third party.

3. Liability Insurance: The Duties to Indemnify and Defend. In common usage, liability insurance is often equated with the insurer's promise to pay for liabilities incurred by the insured to others. In legal terminology, this is known as a promise to *indemnify* the insured. In the automobile policy at issue in *Flores*, the promise to indemnify read roughly as follows: "Insurer promises to pay damages for which any insured is legally liable because of bodily injury or property damage caused by an occurrence arising out of the use of the insured vehicle."

The promise to indemnify is at the core of any liability insurance policy. However, it is only one of two aspects of the third-party coverage provided in most policies containing liability insurance provisions. The second sort of coverage consists of a promise to pay for and manage the defense of the underlying lawsuit by which the injured party attempts to establish the insured's liability. This promise gives rise to a second duty beyond the duty to indemnify, namely the duty to *defend*. Thus, in *Flores*, the issue was not only whether Automobile Club had to pay for any damages awarded to Flores on his claim that Sanders aided Perez's battery (the duty to indemnify), but also whether it was obligated to defend Sanders against the aiding and abetting claim (the duty to defend). The promise to defend is sometimes described as *litigation insurance*. These notes focus first on the promise to indemnify, then later revisit the promise to defend.

4. Examples of Liability Coverage. Liability insurance is provided through many other types of insurance policies beyond automobile policies. For example, a homeowner's insurance policy might include provisions under which the insurer agrees to indemnify the owner in the event a guest is accidentally injured on the premises and successfully sues the homeowner in tort for those injuries. Businesses commonly maintain liability insurance for personal injuries or property damage accidentally caused to third parties by their products or their employees' carelessness. Professionals such as doctors and lawyers maintain insurance to pay for malpractice liabilities.

5. *History.* Liability insurance is ubiquitous today. However, relative to the history of tort, its emergence is a recent development. Prior to the American Civil War, there was little liability insurance to speak of, in part because there was little demand for it, and in part because it was regarded as against public policy in that it would reduce the incentives of insureds to take care against injuring others. Early examples of liability insurance policies were those issued in the late 1800s to employers to indemnify them for tort liabilities owed to employees injured on the job. By the turn of the twentieth century, insurers were issuing liability policies to many other types of insureds, including manufacturers (for liabilities resulting from injuries caused by their negligently made products), residential and commercial property owners (for injuries on the premises), professionals (for injuries caused by malpractice), and even participants in sports such as golf (for injuries caused to other participants or bystanders).

6. *The Business of Insurance.* To make a profit, insurers must decide, in the context of competing with other insurers, at what level to set premiums and how much coverage to promise in return for those premiums. To make these judgments, insurers rely on actuaries, experts who study statistics as to the frequency of particular kinds of occurrences, the typical costs associated with those occurrences, etc.

For example, an actuary might determine that, for each of the past five years, 1,000 passenger-vehicle drivers in location *L* were involved in accidents that caused an average of $10,000 worth of damage to others per accident. Based on this information, an insurer can, with a reasonable degree of confidence, predict how much it can expect to pay in covered claims by insureds and hence can set premiums to cover these costs, plus overhead, plus a margin for profit.* Notice, however, that the insurer can only take advantage of these statistics if it can "pool" the relevant risks — that is, enter into insurance contracts with a large number of the relevant class of drivers in the relevant location. This is because statistical correlations, if they hold true, only hold true for large numbers. (Think of it in terms of coin flips. If one flips an honestly weighted coin 10,000 times, the ratio of heads to tails will approach 50:50. If, however, one were to flip only 10 times, one might easily come up with heads 8 out of those 10 times.)

Individual insureds, meanwhile, purchase the security of knowing that if they are one of the unlucky drivers who does incur liability to another as a result of driving, they will not have to pay the actual loss out of their own pockets. Of course, if the actuary has done her job well, for most insureds, the risk will never actually come to pass — in hindsight these persons will have "wasted" their money. But it is precisely because hindsight is 20:20, whereas foresight is not, that they made the decision to purchase insurance in the first place.

---

* As it turns out, insurers tend to make their profits not by collecting premiums in excess of payouts and overhead, but from obtaining premiums in advance of making payouts, and thus having in their possession money that they can invest until such time as payouts have to be made. It follows that, as a rule, insurance companies tend to perform poorly when they cannot earn large returns by investing the premium dollars that are in their possession. This feature of the insurance business is noteworthy because insurers often maintain that ever-increasing tort liability is what forces them to raise premiums. Before such claims can be accepted, however, one must discount, among other things, the effect of poor returns on investments on insurers' profitability.

7. *The Duty to Indemnify: Scope.* The scope of the promise to indemnify within a given liability insurance provision is determined primarily by the terms of the insurance contract that:

a. specify who counts as an "insured" under the policy;
b. define "occurrence" and "exclusion"—that is, the sorts of events that do and do not give rise to the duty to indemnify;
c. indicate the type of liabilities flowing from an occurrence for which there is coverage (e.g., bodily injury, property damage, and/or business interruption); and
d. set the dollar-amount ceiling ("coverage amount") for liabilities arising out of a given occurrence, as well as deductible amounts that the insured is responsible to pay.

In *Flores*, the liability insurance provisions of the automobile policy contained an additional restriction on the duty to indemnify: that duty only applies to liabilities for injuries "arising out of the use of the insured vehicle." According to the court, is this a significant restriction on the scope of the liability insurance provided by the policy? Suppose that the same car was sitting in the Sanders' driveway, and that Eric Sanders and Roger Perez were taking turns jumping off its roof onto the driveway. If one of them accidentally crashed into Flores as Flores happened to walk by, would the automobile policy cover that liability?

8. *Duty to Indemnify Versus Duty of Care.* It is important to keep in mind that even though the indemnity provisions of a liability insurance policy have the effect of reimbursing third parties injured by the insured, the insurer's obligation to cover those costs is usually owed exclusively to the insured, not to the injured third party. Thus, with one or two exceptions, states do not require or even permit a tort victim to sue the tortfeasor's insurer directly to obtain compensation.* Rather, the victim must sue the tortfeasor to establish his liability and must leave it up to the tortfeasor to make a claim under the policy. (Of course, the tortfeasor will ordinarily have an interest in doing so.)

Similarly, the victim of a tort typically will not have a freestanding tort cause of action against the tortfeasor's liability insurer. For example, suppose swimming pool owner *D* is insured by *L* Corp. for liabilities associated with accidental bodily injuries suffered by users of the pool. Under the terms of the policy, *L* has the right to inspect *D*'s premises and recommend safety precautions, which *D* in turn is free to accept or reject. Now suppose *P*, a guest invited by *D* to swim at the pool, is injured when she slips off the end of the pool's diving board. *P* brings a negligence claim against *D* for carelessly failing to attach traction strips to the board, but she also tries to sue *L* for failing to recommend such a precaution. Even if *P* has a valid cause of action in negligence against *D*—one that, because of the terms of the policy, results in an obligation on the part of *L* to pay for the damages caused by *D*—*P* will not likely have an independent tort cause of action against *L*. *L*'s obligations as insurer to

---

* Wisconsin law permits a direct action by the tort victim against the tortfeasor's liability insurer.

indemnify *D* for liabilities do not include a duty to take steps to protect those who may suffer injury of the sort covered by the policy issued to *D. See* Goodwin v. Jackson, 484 So. 2d 1041 (Miss. 1986) (parents of child who drowned in insured's pool do not have a tort cause of action against the pool owner's insurer for failing to insist that the pool owner implement proper safety precautions).

9. Exclusion of Intentional Wrongs: Policy Provisions. The central legal issue in *Flores* concerns whether the insured's role in bringing about the shooting of the victim was intentional, on the one hand, or reckless or careless, on the other. The court concluded that Eric Sanders intentionally helped bring about the shooting of Flores. Standard language employed by liability insurers almost always defines "occurrence" to be an event *unintended* by the insured, or *unexpected* from the perspective of the insured. This is just another way of saying, with the *Flores* court, that liability insurance is primarily about fortuities: It is designed to protect against *risks* that may or may not be realized, not harms that the insured intends to bring about. Thus, as a matter of contract law, the plain wording of the typical liability policy will establish that the insurer makes no promise to indemnify for liabilities resulting from intentional injurings. Can you see how the relative paucity of insurance for intentional wrongs, as compared to careless wrongs, might pressure litigants into framing the issues in tort litigation a certain way?

10. Exclusion of Intentional Wrongs: Public Policy. Ordinarily, the public policy exception for intentional wrongs will not need to be litigated or will be litigated as a secondary rationale for a decision, as it was in *Flores.* This is because, as just indicated, most liability policies are written to exclude coverage of intentional misconduct. Suppose, contrary to the facts of *Flores*, the policy had been written so as to clearly cover intentional wrongful use of the car of the sort engaged in by Sanders. Would there be coverage then?

The answer, according to the Court of Appeals, is no, but now because of statute rather than contract. By enacting Section 533 of the state insurance code, the California legislature forbade parties from buying and providing insurance for liabilities resulting from willful misconduct. Although California is unusual in having such a statute, the vast majority of states recognize an equivalent ban on insuring intentional wrongs as a matter of judge-made law. Thus, courts around the country routinely hold that there is an implied public policy exception that excludes coverage of "wilful" or "intentional" wrongful acts no matter what the actual contract says. (It should be noted, however, that there are important differences among the states as to what counts as the sort of "intentional act" for which insurance coverage is precluded.)

The origins of the public policy exception apparently derive from first-party insurance contracts. Courts, for example, long ago held that it was against public policy for *B*, the beneficiary of a life insurance policy, to murder the insured *I*, then collect on the policy. The rationale for these decisions was driven by the moral principle that one ought not to profit from his wrong, as well as a concern not to give people a monetary incentive to commit intentional wrongful acts. Without much discussion, the public policy bar was then carried over to liability insurance policies, apparently on the theory that this, too, would help discourage, or at least not encourage, intentional wrongful conduct.

In general, mandatory rules barring competent adults from making contractual arrangements as to economic matters are quite rare—our legal system leaves them largely free to structure their economic transactions. Do you find the rationales articulated for the public policy exception convincing? Can you think of better ones?

11. The Intentional Acts of Agents and Employees. Intentional wrongs are usually excluded from standard liability policies. Note, however, that a loss that is intentionally or knowingly caused by one actor may still be a fortuity from the perspective of someone else. Mega Corp., for example, might expect that, in any given year, one out of the 1,000 supervisors it employs will commit an act of intentional discrimination against a supervisee on the basis of race, age, or gender. For this reason, although insurers are generally anxious to exclude from coverage any liability arising from intentional acts, one sometimes finds liability policies issued to companies covering certain intentional wrongs by its employees, such as intentional acts of discrimination. A key question in such cases will be whether these policies violate the public policy bar against insuring for intentional wrongs. Courts have split on this issue.

12. The Duty (and Right) to Defend. Thus far, the focus in these notes has been on the obligation of a liability insurer to *indemnify* an insured for liability arising out of a covered event. As noted above, however, liability insurance also includes a promise to defend the underlying lawsuit by the third party against the insured seeking to establish the insured's liability. Unlike the provisions in the insurance policy specifying the duty to indemnify, the provisions describing the duty to defend usually do not contain a dollar cap on the amount the insurer will be obligated to defend. However, the duty to defend is typically accompanied by a corresponding set of *rights* conferred on the insurer, namely, the right to select defense counsel and to control the underlying litigation. This right includes the authority to decide on how to dispose of the case—whether to settle or proceed to trial, how much to settle for, etc. As you might expect, the insurer and the insured may often have different views on these sorts of decisions. For example, an insurer backed by substantial assets might be more willing than an impoverished insured to forgo settlement and take the chance of a jury returning a huge verdict against the insured at trial.

As a rough-and-ready generalization, it is fair to say that insurers are under an obligation to their insureds to act reasonably in responding to settlement offers. If they fail to do so, they run the risk of being held liable to their insureds for a breach of the duty to defend. A famous example of this risk coming to fruition is found in *Crisci v. The Security Insur. Co. of New Haven*, 426 P.2d 173 (Cal. 1967). There, the insurer issued a policy to a landlord that indemnified her for liabilities arising from injuries suffered on the premises up to $10,000 per occurrence. Faced with an obviously strong tort claim brought by an injured tenant against the insured, the insurer chose not to accept an offer to settle the case for the policy limits of $10,000. A jury subsequently rendered a $101,000 verdict against the insured, leaving her to pay $91,000 out of her own pocket, which essentially bankrupted her. The insured then successfully brought an action against the insurer for unreasonably refusing the settlement offer. (A similar action was the basis for *State Farm Mut. Auto Ins. Co. v. Campbell*, discussed in the notes following *BMW v. Gore*, Chapter 13.)

13. Which Comes First: Tort Liability or Coverage under the Insurance Contract? The duty to defend is often described as "broader" than the duty to indemnify. This is because, under standard policies, that duty applies to any lawsuit against the insured that contains *allegations* of a covered liability, even if it turns out subsequently that there is no basis for liability, or that the particular liability established is not covered under the policy.

Suppose, for example, homeowner *D* is covered by a policy issued by insurer *L* for liabilities arising from accidental injuries suffered by others on *D*'s property. Suppose also that plaintiff *P* sues *D* in tort, alleging a physical injury that occurred on *D*'s premises. At that point, *D* will notify *L* of the pending claim, and *L*'s duty to take over the defense of *P*'s claim against *D* will commence. In such a case, questions as to whether *P* actually suffered an injury, whether it occurred on the premises, and whether it occurred by accident, often will not be determined until the judge or jury renders a verdict. However, even if the verdict includes a finding that the injury was not covered, *L* still must pay *D*'s defense costs. (Whether *L* might in some circumstances be relieved of the obligation to defend prior to the conclusion of the *P* v. *D* litigation is a much-debated question.)

Initially, then, the insurer's duty to defend is largely in the hands of the plaintiff's attorney. If the allegations contained in plaintiff's complaint are crafted so as to specify acts or events that may count as an occurrence under the policy, the duty kicks in. However, insurers are not entirely at plaintiffs' attorneys' mercy. For one thing, plaintiffs' attorneys run certain risks if they simply make up allegations that have no grounding in fact. (For example, they can be fined by the court.) In some jurisdictions, moreover, the insurer can ask the court to resolve the issue of coverage *before* proceeding with the underlying tort litigation. This procedure, under which the insurer seeks a *declaratory judgment* as to coverage, was invoked successfully by Automobile Club in *Flores*. In states that permit declaratory judgment actions, the trial court must decide whether to proceed first by resolving the tort suit, then the coverage issue, or by resolving coverage first and tort liability second. Usually, a court will not permit a declaratory judgment action unless the issue of coverage turns on factual and legal issues that can be decided independently of the underlying tort suit.

Can you identify the features of *Flores* that may have encouraged this judge to tackle the declaratory judgment action first, thus enabling Automobile Club to establish in advance of the tort litigation that it owed no obligation to defend or indemnify? Might all the parties, including the plaintiffs, have wanted that question resolved first?

14. The Chicken-Egg Problem. The spread of liability insurance has been integral to the growth in size and significance of tort law as part of the U.S. legal and political system. As Kent Syverud has explained, tort law and liability insurance are "symbiotic" institutions. If there were little or no risk of tort liability, fewer people would buy liability insurance. Likewise, if there were no liability insurance, tort recoveries would be fewer in number and more modest in amount. In this sense, tort law and liability insurance feed off one another.

Syverud elsewhere notes that Americans purchase large amounts of liability insurance by comparison to citizens of other nations. This phenomenon, he hypothesizes, might be part of a cycle that works to the benefit of lawyers and insurers, but causes Americans to overconsume insurance. The cycle runs as follows. Individual insureds are risk-averse; they understandably want to avoid a catastrophic liability. Given a choice between buying a cheaper policy that indemnifies him for up to $100,000 for injuries to a guest on the premises or a slightly more expensive policy providing $1 million in coverage, the risk-averse homeowner will choose the latter. But the very existence of greater coverage might be the thing that encourages a slip-and-fall victim to sue in the first place or to demand greater compensation upon suing. Thus, the decision to buy more insurance results in greater liability, which fuels the demand for more insurance, and so on.

15. Discovery and Insurance Policies. Before 1970, courts were split as to whether, after a tort suit is commenced, a plaintiff's attorney could use the discovery process to obtain information from the defendant as to applicable liability insurance. In that year, the Federal Rules of Civil Procedure were amended to permit such discovery, and most states have followed this rule. Thus, today, the plaintiff often will have a clear idea of how much coverage is available, a figure that can serve as a benchmark for settlement discussions. As part of recent tort reform efforts, some jurisdictions have barred plaintiffs from obtaining information about insurance coverage in certain tort actions. *See, e.g.*, Ala. Code § 6-5-548(d) (barring discovery of the limits of liability coverage in medical malpractice actions).

16. Jury Deliberations: Evidence of Insurance. If the underlying tort case does not settle and instead proceeds to a jury trial, the question arises as to whether the jury can and should be informed of the presence either of liability insurance covering the defendant or first-party insurance such as medical insurance covering the plaintiff. For litigation in federal courts, and many state courts, a rule of evidence exists that, subject to certain exceptions, specifically bars the litigants from presenting evidence that the *defendant* carried liability insurance. *See* Fed. R. Evid. 411. Likewise, as noted earlier in this chapter, about half the states adhere to the *collateral source rule*, which bars admission of evidence that *plaintiff* has been (or will be) compensated, in part or in whole, for her injuries by some other source than the tortfeasor, such as employee benefits or first-party medical insurance.

These rules have been defended on various grounds. One such ground is the belief that jurors might be prejudiced in their thinking about the merits of the underlying tort claim if they know that the defendant will not have to pay the judgment out of his own pocket or that the plaintiff has access to other sources of compensation apart from payment by the defendant. Based on this sort of thinking, many legislatures that have recently set out to "reform" tort law have abolished the collateral source rule for some or all tort claims. A study of 40 tort trials by Shari Diamond and Neil Vidmar found that the jurors' deliberations almost always include discussions of insurance even though little or no evidence on the issue had been presented to them. If this is generally the case, might it make sense to introduce evidence of insurance so that the parties have a chance to educate the jury on the coverage in question?

17. Liability Insurance and Redress. We have suggested that tort is fundamentally about permitting individuals to seek redress for those deemed responsible by the law for injuring them. Is the ability of many tortfeasors to "contract out" of the obligation to pay for injuries they cause consistent with that claim? If the insured tortfeasor is not the one who ends up footing the bill for the harm done to the plaintiff, in what way is he held responsible by the law of tort? Looking at the issue from the opposite end, can one make an argument that the availability of liability insurance often ensures that the tort system operates fairly in attributing responsibility?

V. ENFORCING JUDGMENTS: GETTING TO ASSETS

Even after a tort suit results in a jury verdict (or a judicial judgment if the parties have waived jury trial), there are more procedural steps to complete before the case is deemed resolved at the trial level. (We leave aside issues of appellate procedure—assume that neither party will seek an appeal.) If the verdict is rendered by a jury in favor of the plaintiff, the defendant(s) will almost certainly have moved to set aside the verdict either as a matter of law or on the grounds that a new trial is required. Assuming that the trial judge denies these motions, her next job is to enter judgment in the case. A judgment records the amount of the jury's verdict, the defendant or defendants against whom the judgment is rendered, and the plaintiff or plaintiffs to whom the judgment is owed. Ideally, the judgment will be issued in a separate document, signed by the judge. However, judges sometimes enter judgments orally from the bench.

Although it is necessary for a plaintiff seeking redress from a defendant to obtain a judgment, it is hardly sufficient. Now the plaintiff must collect on it. There are a number of potential obstacles to collection, including obstacles created by other areas of law, such as corporate, property, and bankruptcy law. In the following notes we identify in a very preliminary way how some of these areas of law intersect with tort law. Other courses will provide you with a much richer understanding of these subjects.

1. *Judgment-Proof Defendants.* Most tort plaintiffs seek redress in the form of payment by the tortfeasor. If the tortfeasor lacks available assets by which to satisfy the judgment, the tort victim may be out of luck. The presence or absence of liability insurance coverage often matters enormously. If, for example, driver *D* tortiously injures pedestrian *P*, and *D* has no savings or significant property holdings, *P* still stands to recover if *D*'s careless driving is covered under a liability insurance policy. If not—either because *D* lacked insurance or because his act was intentional and therefore excluded from coverage—*P* may be left without compensation. This latter sort of defendant is sometimes deemed a "judgment-proof" defendant. A few options are still open to plaintiffs who are unlucky enough to have valid claims against judgment-proof defendants. For example, if *D* were gainfully employed, *P* might be able to obtain a court order under which a certain percentage of *D*'s wages are "garnished"—that is, handed over to *P*.

2. *Whose Assets?* Anglo-American law recognizes a number of devices that enable individuals and entities to shield certain assets from being paid over to a tort victim. Perhaps the most important of these is the business corporation. One of the primary purposes of the corporate form is to permit individuals to invest in a business run by others in a manner that limits their potential losses to the amount that they invest. Thus, if a business organized as a corporation incurs tort liability, each shareholder is on the hook for no more than the value of his holdings in the company. Other assets owned by the shareholder — for example, a shareholder's personal bank account or her home — cannot be used to satisfy the corporation's tort liabilities.

This limitation on liability holds not only for shareholders who are "natural" persons, but also for business entities that own shares of other businesses. Chapter 4 discussed asbestos litigation, which often has involved claims by multiple victims against a manufacturing company for injuries caused by asbestos exposure. If the manufacturing company is a wholly owned subsidiary of a larger parent company, the victims will likely only have claims against the manufacturing company, not the parent. This means that, even if the manufacturing company lacks the resources to compensate the plaintiffs, they will not be able to look to the assets of the parent company to make up the deficiency.*

Natural persons and entities can also limit access to their assets by placing control of some of their assets with others. For example, suppose *A* is about to start an accounting business. Although he does not anticipate encountering malpractice liability, he also wants to prepare for the worst. One thing he will likely do is buy malpractice insurance. Another might be to transfer certain assets that he currently owns to others. For example, he might have the deed to his home put in his spouse's name, thereby rendering it the spouse's asset, rather than his. (*But see infra* Note 3.) Certain foreign jurisdictions and some American states have recently begun to offer individuals the opportunity to place assets in a special kind of trust account. These are complex and highly controversial financial devices. When they work, they do so by requiring the owner to give up some of his ability to control the assets — for example, he may have access to the income generated by the assets held in trust but not the principal — in exchange for putting them beyond the reach of creditors.

3. *Limits.* The methods briefly described above give individuals and entities the ability to structure their holdings so as to reduce the availability of their assets to tort victims. However, these methods are subject to a number of important limits. In principle, businesses are not permitted to set up sham or phony corporations for the purpose of avoiding liability. Likewise, courts will nullify transfers of assets that amount to "fraudulent conveyances." Suppose, for example, our imagined accountant *A* learns that he has been sued, or is about to be sued, for malpractice. If *under those circumstances* he tries to transfer his assets so that they will be unavailable to satisfy a judgment against him, a court will likely void those transactions as fraudulent. Finally,

---

* Business entities need not be organized as corporations. For example, they can also be organized (as are many law firms) as partnerships. The rules governing the liability of individual partners for torts vary substantially depending on the type of partnership.

even in the absence of a fraudulent conveyance, particular courts may decline to recognize the validity of particularly aggressive financial devices designed to limit tort victims' access to assets, such as offshore trust accounts. For example, even if a defendant were to assert in court that the bulk of his assets are unavailable because bound up in an offshore trust, the judge might still order the defendant (or the custodian of the trust) to release the assets from the trust. If a defendant were to fail to comply with that order, the judge could hold the tortfeasor in contempt of court, which would in turn authorize his temporary imprisonment.

4. *Corporate Bankruptcy.* For mass torts — torts that involve injuries to hundreds or thousands of persons — there is often a risk that the tortfeasor, even if it is a large and insured corporation, will lack sufficient assets to pay its tort liabilities. For example, because of the toxicity and widespread use of asbestos, Johns Manville and numerous other asbestos manufacturers have incurred liabilities in excess of the company's insurance and assets. In such situations, a corporation may find itself, voluntarily or involuntarily, in bankruptcy proceedings. When that occurs, payment for any debts and liabilities are suspended ("stayed") while the bankruptcy judge attempts to devise an orderly scheme of payment under the rules of federal bankruptcy law. Unfortunately for tort plaintiffs, those laws generally call for the payment of "secured" debts — such as bank loans issued in exchange for a security interest in assets owned by the corporation — before "unsecured" debts, such as tort liabilities. Often by the time secured debts are paid off, there is little or no money left to pay tort liabilities. If so, the debts are permanently "discharged" and the tort claimants are out of luck. Certain liabilities, however, are not dischargeable in bankruptcy, namely those arising out of egregious misconduct. *See In re White,* Chapter 9.

REFERENCES/FURTHER READING

Compensatory Damages

Randall R. Bovbjerg, et al., *Valuing Life and Limb in Tort: Scheduling "Pain and Suffering,"* 83 Nw. U. L. Rev. 908 (1989).

Stephen P. Calandrillo & Dustin E. Buehler, *Eggshell Economics: A Revolutionary Approach to the Eggshell Plaintiff Rule,* 74 Ohio St. L.J. 375 (2013).

Martha Chamallas, *Questioning the Use of Race-Specific and Gender-Specific Data in Tort Litigation: A Constitutional Argument,* 63 Fordham L. Rev. 73 (1994).

Martha Chamallas & Jennifer B. Wriggins, *The Measure of Injury: Race, Gender and Tort Law* (2010).

Kenneth R. Feinberg, et al., *Final Report of the Special Master for the September 11th Victim Compensation Fund of 2001* (2004), http://www.justice.gov/final_report.pdf.

Heidi Li Feldman, *Harm and Money: Against the Insurance Theory of Tort Compensation,* 75 Tex. L. Rev. 1567 (1997).

Mark Geistfeld, *Placing a Price on Pain and Suffering: A Method for Helping Juries Determine Tort Damages for Nonmonetary Injuries,* 83 Cal. L. Rev. 773 (1995).

John C. P. Goldberg, *Two Conceptions of Tort Damages: Fair v. Full Compensation,* 55 DePaul L. Rev. 435 (2006).

Stanley Ingber, *Rethinking Intangible Injuries: A Focus on Remedy*, 73 Cal. L. Rev. 772 (1985).

Louis L. Jaffe, *Damages for Personal Injury: The Impact of Insurance*, 18 Law & Contemp. Probs. 219 (1953).

David Leebron, *Final Moments: Damages for Pain and Suffering Prior to Death*, 64 N.Y.U. L. Rev. 256 (1989).

Edward McCaffery, et al., *Framing the Jury: Cognitive Perspectives on Pain and Suffering Awards*, 81 Va. L. Rev. 1341 (1995).

Clarence Morris, *Liability for Pain and Suffering*, 59 Col. L. Rev. 476 (1959).

Colleen P. Murphy, *Judicial Assessment of Legal Remedies*, 94 Nw. U. L. Rev. 153 (1999).

Ellen S. Pryor, *Rehabilitating Tort Compensation*, 91 Geo. L.J. 659 (2003).

Ellen S. Pryor, *The Tort Law Debate, Efficiency and the Kingdom of the Ill: A Critique of the Insurance Theory of Compensation*, 79 Va. L. Rev. 91 (1993).

Margaret J. Radin, *Compensation and Commensurability*, 43 Duke L.J. 56 (1993).

Alan Schwartz, *Proposals for Products Liability Reform: A Theoretical Synthesis*, 97 Yale L.J. 353 (1988).

Victor E. Schwartz & Leah Lorber, *Twisting the Purpose of Pain and Suffering Awards: Turning Compensation into Punishment*, 54 S.C. L. Rev. 47 (2002).

Warren Seavey, *Torts and Atoms*, 46 Cal. L. Rev. 3 (1958).

Suja Thomas, *Re-Examining the Constitutionality of Remittitur Under the Seventh Amendment*, 64 Ohio St. L.J. 731 (2003).

Neil Vidmar, *Empirical Evidence on the Deep Pockets Hypothesis: Jury Awards for Pain and Suffering in Medical Malpractice Cases*, 43 Duke L.J. 217 (1993).

Albert Yoon, *Damage Caps and Civil Litigation: An Empirical Study of Medical Malpractice Litigation in the South*, 3 Am. L. & Econ. Rev. 199 (2001).

Punitive Damages

Bruce Chapman & Michael Trebilcock, *Punitive Damages: Divergence in Search of a Rationale*, 40 Ala. L. Rev. 741 (1989).

Thomas B. Colby, *Beyond the Multiple Punishment Problem: Punitive Damages as Punishment for Individual, Private Wrongs*, 87 Minn. L. Rev. 583 (2003).

Stephen Daniels & Joanne Martin, *Myth and Reality in Punitive Damages*, 75 Minn. L. Rev. 1 (1990).

Theodore Eisenberg & Michael Heise, *Judge-Jury Difference in Punitive Damage Awards: Who Listens to the Supreme Court?*, 8 J. Emp. Leg. Studies 325 (2011).

Theodore Eisenberg & Martin T. Wells, *The Significant Association Between Punitive and Compensatory Damages in Blockbuster Cases: A Methodological Primer*, 3 J. Emp. Leg. Studies 175 (2006).

Theodore Eisenberg, et al., *Juries, Judges, and Punitive Damages: An Empirical Study*, 87 Cornell L. Rev. 743 (2002).

Dorsey D. Ellis, Jr., *Fairness and Efficiency in the Law of Punitive Damages*, 56 S. Cal. L. Rev. 1 (1982).

Neil R. Feigensen, *Book Review: Can Juries Punish Competently*, 78 Chi.-Kent L. Rev. 239 (2003).

David Friedman, *An Economic Explanation of Punitive Damages*, 40 Ala. L. Rev. 1125, (1989).

Marc Galanter & David Luban, *Poetic Justice: Punitive Damages and Legal Pluralism*, 42 Am. U. L. Rev. 1393 (1993).

Simon Greenleaf, *A Treatise on the Law of Evidence* § 253 (16th ed. 1899).

Jean Hampton, *Correcting Harms Versus Righting Wrongs: The Goal of Retribution*, 39 UCLA L. Rev. 1659 (1992).

Joni Hersch & W. Kip Viscusi, *Saving Lives Through Punitive Damages*, 83 S. Cal. L. Rev. 229 (2010).

Keith N. Hylton, *Punitive Damages and the Economic Theory of Penalties*, 87 Geo. L. J. 421 (1998).

David Owen, *Punitive Damages in Product Liability Litigation*, 74 Mich. L. Rev. 1258 (1976).

David Owen, *The Moral Foundations of Punitive Damages*, 40 Ala. L. Rev. 705 (1989).

A. Mitchell Polinsky & Steven Shavell, *Punitive Damages: An Economic Analysis*, 111 Harv. L. Rev. 869 (1998).

Michael L. Rustad, *Unraveling Punitive Damages: Current Data and Further Inquiry*, 1998 Wis. L. Rev. 15.

Michael Rustad & Thomas Koenig, *The Historical Continuity of Punitive Damages Awards: Reforming the Tort Reformers*, 42 Am. U. L. Rev. 1269 (1993).

Gary T. Schwartz, *The Myth of the Ford Pinto Case*, 43 Rutgers L. Rev. 1013 (1991).

Anthony J. Sebok, *What Did Punitive Damages Do? Why Misunderstanding the History of Punitive Damages Matters Today*, 78 Chi.-Kent L. Rev. 163 (2003).

Anthony J. Sebok, *Punitive Damages: From Myth to Theory*, 92 Iowa L. Rev. 957 (2007).

Theodore Sedgwick, *A Treatise on the Measure of Damages* 515-540 (5th ed. 1869).

Catherine M. Sharkey, *Economic Analysis of Punitive Damages: Theory, Empirics, and Doctrine*, in J. Arlen (ed.), *Research Handbook on the Economics of Tort* (2012).

Catherine M. Sharkey, *Revisiting the Noninsurable Costs of Accidents*, 64 Md. L. Rev. 409 (2005).

Catherine M. Sharkey, *Punitive Damages as Societal Damages*, 113 Yale L.J. 347 (2003).

Cass Sunstein, et al., *Punitive Damages: How Juries Decide* (2002).

W. Kip Viscusi, *Why There Is No Defense of Punitive Damages*, 87 Geo. L.J. 381, 384-387 (1998).

Benjamin C. Zipursky, Palsgraf, *Punitive Damages, and Preemption*, 125 Harv. L. Rev. 1757 (2012).

Benjamin C. Zipursky, *A Theory of Punitive Damages*, 84 Tex. L. Rev. 105 (2005).

Vicarious Liability

William O. Douglas, *Vicarious Liability and Administration of Risk* (Pts. I & II), 38 Yale L.J. 584, 720 (1929).

Young B. Smith, *Frolic and Detour* (Pts. I & II), 23 Colum. L. Rev. 444, 716 (1923).

Michael Wells & Thomas A. Eaton, *Constitutional Remedies* 96-117 (2002).

Joint Liability and Contribution

Restatement (Third) of Torts: *Apportionment of Liability* (1998).

Insurance

Kenneth S. Abraham, *The Liability Century: Insurance and Tort Law from the Progressive Era to 9/11* (2008).

Tom Baker, *Liability Insurance as Tort Regulation: Six Ways that Liability Insurance Shapes Tort Law in Action*, 12 Conn. Ins. L.J. 1 (2005).

Tom Baker, *Medical Malpractice and the Insurance Underwriting Cycle*, 54 DePaul L. Rev. 393 (2005).

Tom Baker, *Risk, Insurance and the Social Construction of Responsibility*, in Tom Baker & Jonathan Simon (eds.), *Embracing Risk: The Changing Culture of Insurance and Responsibility* (2002).

Randall R. Bovbjerg, *Liability and Liability Insurance: Chicken and Egg, Destructive Spiral, or Risk and Reaction*, 72 Tex. L. Rev. 1655 (1994).

Clyde J. Crobaugh & Amos E. Redding, *Casualty Insurance* 394-491 (1929).

Shari Seidman Diamond & Neil Vidmar, *Jury Room Ruminations on Forbidden Topics*, 87 Va. L. Rev. 1857 (2001).

Sean W. Gallagher, *Note: The Public Policy Exclusion and Insurance for Intentional Employment Discrimination*, 92 Mich. L. Rev. 1256 (1994).

Mary C. McNeeley, *The Genealogy of Liability Insurance*, 7 U. Pitt. L. Rev. 169 (1941).

Ellen S. Pryor, *The Stories We Tell: Intentional Harm and the Quest for Insurance Funding*, 75 Tex. L. Rev. 1721 (1997).

Adam F. Scales, *Man, God and the Serbonian Bog: The Evolution of Accidental Death Insurance*, 86 Iowa L. Rev. 173 (2000).

Gary T. Schwartz, *The Ethics and Economics of Liability Insurance*, 75 Cornell L. Rev. 313 (1990).

Kent D. Syverud, *The Duty to Settle*, 76 Va. L. Rev. 1113 (1990).

Kent D. Syverud, *On the Demand for Liability Insurance*, 72 Tex. L. Rev. 1629 (1994).

battery = harm

assult = threat

PART III

BATTERY, ASSAULT, FALSE IMPRISONMENT, AND INFLICTION OF EMOTIONAL DISTRESS

CHAPTER 9

BATTERY, ASSAULT, AND FALSE IMPRISONMENT

I. INTRODUCTION

Part Two of this book provides an in-depth treatment of the tort of negligence as it applies to claims for bodily injury and property damage. Part Three begins with a discussion of torts that are in some ways even more basic and more deeply rooted in our legal history than negligence. These are the torts of *battery*, *assault*, and *false imprisonment*. A straightforward example of a battery is a deliberate punch in the nose. The idea of an assault is captured by a situation in which one person points a gun at another person who is standing nearby and threatens to shoot him. Deliberately locking someone in a room against her will is a straightforward instance of false imprisonment. Precisely because these torts are so basic, many torts professors prefer to start their courses with them. This book is designed to support courses that do so.

The second chapter of Part Three — Chapter 10 — provides materials on another tort, namely, *intentional infliction of emotional distress* (IIED). IIED can be defined, preliminarily, as one person acting abominably or outrageously with the intention of causing another to suffer severe emotional distress. As we will see, although it is a distinct tort, IIED is historically and conceptually linked to battery, assault, and false imprisonment. Indeed, it emerged as part of a judicial effort to fill gaps created by these ancient torts. In turn, the courts' recognition of IIED helped give birth in the twentieth century to a special branch of negligence law often referred to as *negligent infliction of emotional distress* (NIED). This is why Chapter 10 also includes materials on NIED. If your torts class begins with Chapter 9, the discussion of NIED — and perhaps of all the materials in Chapter 10 — may be postponed until after consideration of some of the negligence materials in Part Two.

Before proceeding to our examination of battery, assault, and false imprisonment, it will be helpful to discuss a bit of torts terminology. It is common for lawyers to use the phrase *intentional torts* as a label for a category that includes several distinct causes of action, principally: (1) battery, (2) assault, (3) false imprisonment, (4) IIED, and (5) trespass to property.* The main virtue of this usage is that it emphasizes a basic difference between these torts and the tort of negligence. In contrast to negligence, these torts cannot be committed entirely by accident.** Instead, liability for each requires that the actor being sued acted with an *intent* to accomplish a certain kind of consequence, or with *actual knowledge* that such a consequence would come about. Much of the material in Chapter 9 and the first part of Chapter 10 will be concerned to flesh out what exactly is meant by words like "intent" and "knowledge."

Although now standard, the label "intentional torts" has some downsides. In particular, it seems to suggest that each tort that it covers employs the same notion of intent. As we will see, that is not the case. The intent that is required to commit the tort of trespass to land is different from the intent necessary to commit battery. Moreover, there are other torts that are also distinct from negligence in requiring a certain sort of intentional conduct as a condition of liability, yet are excluded from the intentional torts category. For example, one cannot commit the tort of fraud without acting with intent to deceive another, yet fraud tends not to be grouped with battery, assault, and false imprisonment.

Because of these and other problems, if we were writing on a clean slate, we probably would be inclined to refrain from using the phrase "intentional torts." But the usage is pervasive now, and, as noted above, there are historical and conceptual linkages between several of the torts that now tend to be placed under the intentional torts heading. Thus, we present four of the traditional intentional torts — battery, assault, false imprisonment, and IIED — together in this part of the book. We reserve consideration of trespass to land for Chapter 11 under the separate heading of "Property Torts."

II. BATTERY AND ASSAULT: ELEMENTS

Tort law defines injurious wrongs that one person or entity can commit against another. At the same time it empowers the victim of such a wrong to bring a claim against the wrongdoer as a way of redressing the wrong. Probably there is no clearer example of a legally recognized wrongful injuring — of a tort — than an intentional punch in the nose. A purposeful, harmful striking or touching of one by another is a simple example of *battery*, and the victim of such a touching can often obtain damages

* This usage is quite modern relative to the 800-year history of Anglo-American tort law. It emerged in the late 1800s as judges switched from older nomenclature — in which every tort cause of action was said to be an instance either of "trespass" or "trespass on the case" — to modern usage, under which each nominate tort ("assault," "battery," "fraud," "libel," "negligence," *et al.*) is treated as a cause of action in its own right.

** As discussed in more detail in Part Two and the materials in this chapter, this distinction needs to be handled with care. Negligence often takes the form of inadvertence or heedlessness, but sometimes it can be "advertent." For example, imagine a driver on a lightly traveled road who is aware that he is driving at an unreasonably dangerous rate of speed, yet continues to do so for the enjoyment of it without any intent to harm another or knowledge that he will harm another. If, because of his speeding, the driver unexpectedly runs into and injures another driver, he may be subject to liability for negligence, but not for battery, assault, etc.

against the person who did it. Indeed, the recipient of a purposeful punch can do so even if the punch does not result in a broken nose or other lasting physical harm. This is because the wrongfulness of battery resides in the *intentional touching*, not in the causing of physical harm.

The foregoing description of battery is deliberately loose. The cases that follow will allow us to consider more carefully how the law defines this tort. Before proceeding to those materials, however, it will be useful to outline the distinction between the tort of battery and the separate tort of assault, because legal usage differs somewhat from everyday usage.

In tort law, a battery requires (among other things) an actual touching of the victim, either direct or indirect, by the wrongdoer (or "tortfeasor"). By contrast, an assault occurs when a person intentionally acts so as to cause another to *apprehend* that he is about to suffer a certain kind of contact. Thus, as noted above, if person *D*, while looking person *P* in the eye, points a real gun at *P* with his finger on the trigger, *D* has committed an assault on *P*, whether or not the gun fires or the bullet hits *P*. (However, if the bullet does hit *P*, *D* has committed both an assault and a battery). Conversely, if *D* were to approach *P* from behind and shoot *P* by surprise, there would be no assault because of the absence of any apprehension by *P*. Instead, there would only be a battery.

Battery and assault are thus the names of different torts that identify and respond to different sorts of misconduct and injuries. That the two are often mentioned together, as in the familiar phrase "assault and battery," owes in part to the fact that there is a great deal of conduct—like the actual shooting scenario described in the preceding paragraph—that constitutes both battery and assault. In addition, "assault" and "battery" are the names of crimes as well as torts, and some criminal codes do not draw the line between these two crimes by reference to the distinction between actual contact and apprehension of contact. Even in tort cases—as we see immediately below in *Cecarelli*—judges and lawyers will sometimes use the terms "battery" and "assault" loosely and interchangeably. Finally, as will be discussed below under the heading of "transferred intent," there are certain special instances in which conduct can form an assault-battery hybrid.

A. Battery

1. Harmful *or* Offensive Touching

A more refined but still somewhat skeletal formulation of battery defines it as the infliction of a harmful or offensive contact by an actor upon another with the intent to cause such contact. *See* Restatement (Second) of Torts § 18 (1965). Although most batteries are probably both harmful and offensive, the "or" in this definition indicates that *either* harmfulness or offensiveness in the touching will suffice. The pair of cases below provides one example of a harmful-touching battery and one example of a possible offensive-touching battery. Some basic questions about tort law come to the fore when one examines these "plain vanilla" battery cases. Why have the underlying events given rise to a *tort* suit in addition to, or instead of, a *criminal* prosecution?

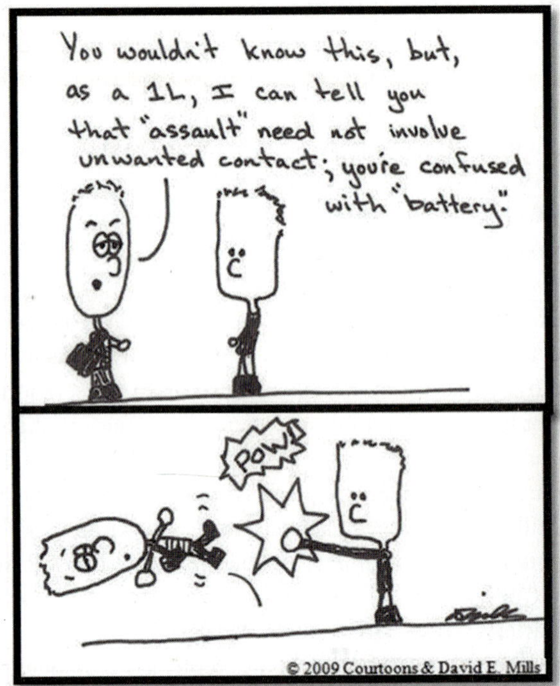

Not assaulting a 1L.

What is the plaintiff hoping to accomplish by bringing the defendant to court? What sort of relief should the plaintiff be able to obtain via his or her lawsuit?

Cecarelli v. Maher

12 Conn. Supp. 240 (Com. Pl. 1943)

Cullinan, J. A willful, apparently unprovoked, and thoroughly unjustifiable assault represents the background of this litigation. The plaintiff, a personable, well-spoken and well-groomed young man, 25 years of age, alleges that the defendant George Maher, in concert with John Heinz and an unknown assailant, beat and assaulted him with intense ferocity to produce most serious physical consequences.

On the evening of August 1, 1943, the plaintiff attended a public dance at Sea Cliff, New Haven, at the conclusion of which three young ladies requested him to drive them to their homes. His willingness to meet this request appears to have provoked the anger and wrath of the defendant and his two companions, who, at a secluded and lonely spot adjacent to the dance hall, set upon him to administer a severe, and painful beating. Fists and dangerous instruments constituted the implements of aggressive warfare.

In consequence, the plaintiff's upper right central and upper right lateral teeth and roots were severed from their sockets; his upper left central, lower right central, and lower right lateral teeth were so destroyed as to necessitate ultimate removal; his upper lip was severely lacerated, requiring sutures and resulting in an involvement of the nasal septum; his nose and left eye were abrased and contused; and his right arm, right shoulder, and right side became exceedingly sore and tender as a result of a vicious kicking process. Thereafter, the plaintiff required emergency hospital treatment and a complete restoration of the dental structures with the replacement of five teeth. In addition, the plaintiff was forced to absent himself from his employment for a complete week, experiencing acute pain for an extended period after his return to work.

The terrifying and violent episode had its basis in the ungovernable tempers of these young men, who, after having had their attentions spurned by three young women, struck fiercely, suddenly, and stealthily at the innocent plaintiff. Both the defendant Maher and his companion Heinz were subsequently arrested and offered guilty pleas to assault charges before the City Court of New Haven. The third assailant is unknown to the plaintiff and his identity has never been disclosed by his colleagues in violence.

This action originally joined both Maher and Heinz as codefendants. Subsequently, the action was withdrawn as to Heinz, and a default judgment has been entered against Maher by reason of his failure to appear. Thus, damages are now to be assessed against Maher alone.

By way of special damage, the plaintiff has lost in wages and has become obligated to expend for dental and medical treatment approximately $315. To this sum may be added $2,000, representing fair and reasonable compensation for his pain, suffering, and permanent injury. Judgment may enter for the plaintiff to recover of the defendant $2,315, together with taxable costs.

Paul v. Holbrook

696 So. 2d 1311 (Fla. App. 1997)

Orfinger, A.J. Meredith A. Paul ("Paul") appeals an order of the trial court granting summary judgment in favor of Professional Medical Products, Inc. ("PMP") and Paul Holbrook ("Holbrook") on Paul's claims against Holbrook and PMP for assault, battery, intentional infliction of emotional distress, negligent infliction of emotional distress and negligent hiring and retention. We affirm the entry of summary judgment in all respects except as to the battery claim against Holbrook. On that single claim, we reverse.

Paul and Holbrook are former employees of PMP. Paul testified that Holbrook was her co-worker and not her supervisor. On various occasions, Paul worked alone with Holbrook. During some of these times, Paul alleges that Holbrook harassed her by asking that she wear revealing clothing and suggesting that they engage in sexual relations. Paul claims that on two occasions, Holbrook came up behind her while she was working and tried to massage her shoulders. On both occasions, Paul immediately pulled away and told Holbrook to leave, which he did. After Paul complained to PMP's management, she and Holbrook never again worked the same shifts and his improper behavior toward her ended.

While Paul takes issue with the trial court's judgment in its entirety, we find merit only in Paul's contention that the trial judge erred in granting summary judgment on her battery claim against Holbrook, finding that Holbrook's contact with Paul amounted to no more than a "casual touching" and concluding that Paul failed to produce evidence establishing intent.

A battery consists of the infliction of a harmful or offensive contact upon another with the intent to cause such contact or the apprehension that such contact is imminent. . . . Restatement (Second) of Torts § 18 (1965); W. Page Keeton, et al., Prosser and Keeton on Torts § 9 (5th ed. 1984). Professor Prosser's treatise explains that the tort of battery exists to protect the integrity of the person. As Prosser & Keeton wrote in section 9:

> Proof of the technical invasion of the integrity of the plaintiff's person by even an entirely harmless, but offensive contact entitles the plaintiff to vindication of the legal right by an award of nominal damages, and the establishment of the tort cause of action entitles the plaintiff also to compensation for the resulting mental disturbance, such as fright, revulsion or humiliation.

Id. (footnotes omitted). Once a contact has been established, its character becomes the focus:

> The element of personal indignity involved always has been given considerable weight. Consequently, the defendant is liable not only for contact[s] which do actual harm, but also for those relatively trivial ones which are merely offensive and insulting. . . .
>
> The time and place, and the circumstances under which the act is done, will necessarily affect its unpermitted character, and so will the relations between the parties. A stranger is not to be expected to tolerate liberties which would be allowed by an intimate friend. But unless the defendant has special reason to believe that more or less will be permitted by the individual plaintiff, the test is what would be offensive to an ordinary person not unduly sensitive to personal dignity.

Id. (footnotes omitted). Offensiveness is an essential element of the tort. The trial court, relying on Gatto v. Publix Supermarket, Inc., 387 So. 2d 377 (Fla. 3d DCA 1980), concluded that, as a matter of law, Holbrook's actions were not offensive. The plaintiff in *Gatto* testified that a store employee, in attempting to retrieve allegedly stolen items from the plaintiff's hands, "came into contact with either part of [his] palm or [his] wrist or [his] arms." 387 So. 2d at 379. The third district concluded that this was not evidence of an offensive contact. But, the act of approaching a co-worker from behind while on the job and attempting to massage her shoulders is, in the circumstances of this case, not capable of such summary treatment. On these facts, offensiveness is a question for the trier of fact to decide.

The trial court also found that Paul failed to produce evidence establishing Holbrook's intent to commit a battery. Proof of intent to commit battery is rarely subject to direct proof, but must be established based on surrounding circumstances. Based on the record before this court, a jury could reasonably infer that Holbrook intended to touch Paul in a matter that would constitute a battery. No evidence of an intention to cause harm is necessary.

The trial court properly granted summary judgment against Paul in all respects except with regard to the battery claim against Holbrook. On that claim, we reverse. In all other respects, we affirm the trial court's judgment.

NOTES AND QUESTIONS

1. *Same Tort, Different Times; Same Wrong?* The judicial opinions in *Cecarelli* and *Paul* rather obviously reflect certain cultural differences between the two eras in which they were written. Yet the same tort of battery was available (or, in Paul's case, may have been available) to enable them to respond to a certain kind of mistreatment. In fact, the action for battery, though sometimes identified by other names, was available to victims of physical attacks in medieval England. What explains the endurance of this tort cause of action, notwithstanding massive economic, political, social and intellectual changes? Given their evident differences, do *Cecarelli* and *Paul* even involve the same wrong? Note that some workplace sexual harassment is now actionable under federal anti-discrimination statutes independently of whether the harassing conduct suffices to constitute a common law battery. *See* Stockett v. Tolin, Chapter 10.

2. *Tort and Crime.* The trial court's opinion in *Cecarelli* mentions that two of the assailants (Maher and Heinz) pleaded guilty to charges of criminal assault. (As noted above, criminal law sometimes uses the term "assault" to cover conduct that tort law defines as "battery.") Under state and federal law, the same conduct can give rise to a criminal prosecution and a civil tort suit. *See* Chapter 1 (Section III, "Tort Law in Context"). Often, however, the civil suit will be stayed (held in abeyance) until the conclusion of the criminal proceedings.

Given that Maher and Heinz were both facing a criminal fine and/or imprisonment, what is the point of having the courts entertain a tort suit against them? It is not difficult to imagine why Cecarelli might want to proceed with such a suit. But why should Connecticut law recognize criminal and civil actions for the same conduct? Would it be better instead to bar tort claims in any instance in which the would-be tort defendant is criminally prosecuted?

3. *Default Judgment.* The *Cecarelli* opinion also mentions that the plaintiff withdrew his claim against Heinz and that he obtained a "default judgment" against Maher. What could explain why Cecarelli withdrew the claim against Heinz?

Default judgments are typically entered by a trial court when the defendant fails entirely to respond to the plaintiff's complaint, and hence without the plaintiff having given any evidence in support of his allegations of wrongdoing. However, before entering a default judgment awarding compensatory damages for personal injuries, a court will usually demand evidence from the plaintiff as to the extent of his or her injuries.

4. *Employer Responsibility for Employee Torts.* Note that in *Paul* the plaintiff brought claims against her fellow employee Holbrook, but also separate claims against their employer, PMP, including claims for battery and negligent hiring. What might be accomplished by bringing the latter claims, assuming they were to have succeeded? Given that Holbrook is the only person alleged to have inappropriately touched Paul, what is the legal basis for claims against PMP?

As it turns out, Paul's battery and negligent hiring claims against PMP stand on different legal grounds. The former is an attempt to hold PMP *vicariously liable*— that is, liable for Holbrook's battery simply because Holbrook committed the battery while acting in his capacity as a PMP employee. As explained in Chapter 1, this particular form of vicarious liability goes under the heading of *respondeat superior*, a Latin phrase that refers to the idea of requiring an employer to answer for wrongs committed by its employee.*

By contrast, a negligent hiring claim is an attempt to hold an employer *directly liable* rather than vicariously liable. In Paul's case, the gist of her negligent hiring claim would have been that, at the time PMP hired Holbrook, it knew or should have known that he posed a danger to other employees, and hence that its decision to hire him was careless as to the physical well-being of persons such as Paul.

5. *Summary Judgment.* As explained in more detail in Chapter 1 (Section II.D, "Proceeding Through Court") a party making a motion for summary judgment is requesting the trial judge to resolve an issue (or issues) that would ordinarily be resolved at trial by a jury. Such a request maintains that a jury trial is unnecessary because there is undisputed evidence pertaining to the issue, and because, given the applicable law, any reasonable juror presented with that evidence would have to decide for the moving party. In *Paul*, both defendants (Holbrook and PMP) moved for summary judgment on the ground that a reasonable jury could only find for them on each of Paul's claims. The trial judge agreed and granted their motions, which entailed the dismissal of Paul's lawsuit prior to trial.

The Florida appellate court concluded that the trial court committed an error of law in granting summary judgment for Holbrook with respect to Paul's battery claim against him. It thus reinstated that one claim and therefore reversed the trial court's dismissal of Paul's lawsuit. Did this ruling entail that Paul would prevail on her battery claim against Holbrook? Notice that the appellate court affirmed the trial court's entry of summary judgment for Holbrook on Paul's other claims against him, as well as for PMP on all of Paul's claims against it. Why?

---

* Note that employers' *respondeat superior* liability more typically attaches when employees commit the tort of negligence. *See, e.g., Walter v. Wal-Mart* (Chapter 1). Indeed, courts will often, but not always, treat employees' intentional torts as falling outside the scope of employment, and hence as not providing a basis for employer vicarious liability. *See* Taber v. Maine, Chapter 8.

6. Elements of Battery. Courts and commentators often find it helpful to define torts in terms of elements or constituent parts. Building on, but also departing somewhat from, the definition provided in Section 18 of the Second Restatement of Torts,* one can describe the elements of battery as follows:

Battery: Prima Facie Case

Actor *A* is subject to liability to other person *P* for battery if:

1. *A* acts,
2. intending to cause a contact with *P*;
3. the contact with *P* that *A* intends is of a harmful or offensive type; and
4. *A*'s act causes *P* to suffer a contact that is harmful or offensive.

This formulation sets out the elements that, *at a minimum*, must be proven by a plaintiff claiming battery in order to be eligible for a remedy. Even if the plaintiff can prove these elements, the defendant may be able to avoid liability on the basis of certain affirmative defenses. This is the import of the phrase "prima facie case."

7. Consent, or Lack Thereof: Defense or Element? All courts agree that consent by the plaintiff to intentional bodily contact by the defendant can affect battery liability. This is hardly surprising—other things being equal, there is a world of difference between consenting to one's hair being shaved off in a salon or barber shop and having it shaved off against one's will. Courts disagree, however, over *where within the analysis of a battery claim* consent should figure.

Some treat lack of consent as an element of the plaintiff's prima facie case, such that the plaintiff must prove nonconsent in order to prevail. *See, e.g.*, Wulf v. Kunnath, 827 N.W.2d 248, 254 (Neb. 2013) (battery is an "infliction of an unconsented injury upon or unconsented contact with another. Consent ordinarily bars recovery, because it 'goes to negative the existence of any tort in the first instance.' It does so by destroying the wrongfulness of the conduct between the consenting parties.") (citations, quoted authority omitted). Others treat consent as an affirmative defense to be pleaded and proved by the defendant. *See, e.g.*, Koffman v. Garnett, *infra*; Janelsins v. Button, 648 A.2d 1039, 1042 (Md. Ct. Spec. App. 1994) (consent is a "complete defense" in a battery action). Still others—possibly the majority—fail clearly to take a stance. *See, e.g.*, Mich. Model Civ. Jury Instrs. 115.02, 115.06 (defining battery as the intentional touching of a person against that person's will but treating consent to participation in a fight as an affirmative defense).

---

* The American Law Institute ("ALI") and its Restatement projects are described in Chapter 1, Note 5 following *Walter v. Wal-Mart.* As explained there, the ALI is presently publishing the Third Restatement of Torts in installments. That project has thus far produced a generic definition of "intent." *See* Restatement (Third) of Torts: Liability for Physical and Emotional Harm § 1 (2010). As of the date of publication of this edition, the Reporters preparing the Third Restatement's intentional tort provisions have circulated draft provisions on battery, assault, and other topics. *See* Restatement (Third) of Torts: Intentional Torts to Persons (Discussion Draft, April 3, 2014). These have not yet been finalized or endorsed by the ALI.

As indicated in the above formulation of the prima facie case of battery, as well as the organization of the current chapter, this book adopts the second approach, generally treating consent as an affirmative defense.

8. *The Act Element.* The first element — the act requirement — is rarely litigated. It builds a minimal volitional component into the tort. One standard example of a non-act in this context would be if *D*, against *C*'s will, were to grab *C*'s hand and use it to slap *P*'s face. *P* would not have a battery claim against *C* even though *C*'s hand made contact with *P*'s body because *C* did not act, much less act with an intent to slap *P*. Likewise, suppose bus passenger *B* is standing on a crowded city bus and holding firmly onto an overhead rail to keep his balance. If the bus unexpectedly comes to a sudden stop, thereby causing *B* to crash into fellow passenger *F*, *B* has not "acted," at least not within the time frame relevant to a potential claim for battery by *F*.*

9. *The Contact Element: Direct and Indirect Contact.* The second element of the above formulation — the intent element — is considered in several cases below. Here we will turn to the third element: contact. Cases like *Cecarelli* and *Paul* provide examples of touchings in the form of relatively direct, flesh-on-flesh (or flesh-on-clothes) contacts. However, a touching need not be flesh-on-flesh, nor directly caused, to give rise to a claim for battery. Most obviously, shootings that cause bodily injury to another can count as batteries, assuming the other elements are met. So too would an attack by a dog that is ordered by the dog's owner. Bernadsky v. Erie R. Co., 70 A. 189 (N.J. Err. & App. 1908) (affirming a jury verdict for the minor plaintiff where the defendant's employee "sicked" his dog on the plaintiff).

10. *What Must Be Touched?* The interest underlying the tort of battery is the interest in controlling others' access to one's body. In protecting that interest, tort law creates a protective zone or space around the body by rendering actionable certain contacts with things closely connected to it. For example, if *D* shoots at *P*, but manages only to make a bullet hole in the sleeve of the shirt that *P* is wearing, *D* has caused a touching of *P* sufficient to generate a claim for battery.

In the well-known case of *Fisher v. Carrousel Motor Hotel, Inc.*, 424 S.W.2d 627 (Tex. 1967), plaintiff, an African American, was standing in a buffet line at defendant's motel while holding an empty plate in his hands. One of defendant's employees snatched the plate away from him, telling Fisher that the restaurant did not serve African Americans. The court upheld a jury award of compensatory and punitive damages for battery on the ground that the employee's snatching of the plate amounted to an offensive touching of Fisher. *Fisher* provides an example of what is sometimes referred to as the doctrine of *extended personality. See* Picard v. Barry Pontiac-Buick, Inc., 654 A.2d 690 (R.I. 1995) (battery can be established by contact with "anything so connected with the body as to be customarily regarded as part of the other's person and therefore as partaking of its inviolability. . . ."). The touching of an

---

* Of course *B* acted when he boarded and took his position on the bus, but those actions are not relevant to an inquiry into whether *B* committed battery against *F* (unless *F* is prepared to show that *B* took the position on the bus that he did as part of an elaborate plan to slam into *F*).

object with which a person happens to be in contact will not always count as a violation of the person of the plaintiff. For example, if *R* were angrily to kick a lamppost against which *S* happened to be leaning, the kick would not likely of itself suffice to establish a touching of *S*.

11. How Physical Must the Touching Be? The notion of contact or touching conveys the idea of physical contact between two objects. However, there are other perhaps less obvious forms of contact. For example, some persons killed by explosions die not because they are crushed by falling objects or hit by shrapnel, but by virtue of an intense shock wave of energy or by massive increases in air pressure (if, for example, the explosion occurs in a confined space). Such persons are treated for purposes of battery law as having been touched. Likewise, if *M* fills *Q*'s house with odorless, colorless, and deadly carbon monoxide gas, *Q* suffers harmful contact by inhaling the poisonous gas.

In *Leichtman v. WLW Jacor Communications, Inc.*, 634 N.E.2d 697 (Ohio App. 1994), the plaintiff, a prominent anti-smoking advocate, alleged that the defendant, a radio personality, invited the plaintiff to the radio station for an interview, then lit up a cigar and repeatedly blew smoke in plaintiff's face for the purpose of causing plaintiff discomfort and embarrassment. Reversing the trial court's dismissal of plaintiff's battery claim, the appellate court reasoned that the plaintiff had adequately alleged an offensive touching, such that he should be entitled to prove his claim to a jury. Although insisting on the plaintiff's right to proceed with the litigation, the court lamented the absence of a simpler, less elaborate, less expensive manner of resolving the dispute. Is your sense that a claim like Leichtman's cries out for resolution outside of the traditional court system? Does your judgment change if one focuses not on the contact he allegedly endured, but on the humiliation and embarrassment that he may have suffered? If the latter injuries provide the gist of Leichtman's complaint, is it really best framed as a complaint about a battery?

Suppose *L* is listening to headphones that are plugged into a stereo system located on a bookshelf six feet behind where *L* is sitting. As a practical joke, *K* sneaks up behind *L*, then sharply increases the volume on the stereo, causing *L* momentary but extreme discomfort from the loud music. Is this a touching of *L* by *K*? Would the result change if *L* had been listening to a portable MP3 player attached to his belt?

12. Purposeful Infliction of Bodily Harm. The portion of the Third Restatement of Torts devoted to "intentional torts to the person"—which, as of the publication date of this edition, has not yet been approved by the American Law Institute—includes a draft provision titled "Purposeful Infliction of Bodily Harm." This provision is offered as a "supplement" to battery, and is meant to capture cases in which an actor acts for the specific intent of causing bodily harm to another through means other than physical contact.* As one illustration, the Reporters give the example of a prison guard who,

* As the Reporter's use of the word "purposeful" is meant to emphasize, the "specific intent" requirement for this separate tort is meant to be narrower than the requirement of "intent" built into the tort of battery. To be liable for purposeful infliction of bodily harm, an actor must intend to harm the victim. The intent requirement for battery is discussed in the next section of this chapter.

for the purpose of making an inmate ill, arranges for the heat to be turned off in the inmate's cell, as a result of which the inmate contracts pneumonia. Would the inmate be unable to make out a claim for battery? Can you think of other examples of intentionally inflicted physical harm that do not fit the definition of battery?

13. Harmful or Offensive Contact. "Harmful" contact is straightforward—it involves contact that causes bodily harms such as bruising or broken bones. The concept of "offensive" contact is somewhat subtler. Crucially, the test for offensiveness is "objective" rather than "subjective." In other words, the issue under the contact element is *not* whether the person touched *actually takes offense* at the contact. (In fact, the victim of a battery usually will feel offended, but such a reaction is not sufficient for a contact to count as offensive in the eyes of the law.) Rather, the contact must *violate prevailing social standards of acceptable touchings.* To be spat upon by a stranger is a quintessential instance of suffering an offensive contact. By contrast, if two strangers, *X* and *Y*, are standing at a public street corner, and *Y* taps *X* on the shoulder to ask for directions, the touching will not be deemed offensive, even if *X* is in fact offended. *Cf.* Wishnaskey v. Huey, 584 N.W.2d 859 (N.D. App. 1998) (defendant lawyer's closing of an office door on the plaintiff (a paralegal), done to push plaintiff out of the office while defendant carried on a conversation with an attorney for whom plaintiff worked, deemed to be not offensive).

The same act of touching might be inoffensive in some contexts, yet offensive in others, depending on who is doing the touching, who is being touched, what the relationship is between them, the setting in which the touching occurs, etc. *Compare* Newsome v. Cooper-Wiss, Inc., 347 S.E.2d 619 (Ga. App. 1986) (a jury may find that an office worker who repeatedly rubbed against his secretary committed an offensive-contact battery) *with* Mangrum v. Republic Indus. Inc., 260 F. Supp. 2d 1229 (N.D. Ga.) (supervisor's hugging plaintiff and patting her bottom cannot support battery claim where plaintiff testified to having participated in similar conduct with supervisor and other employees), *aff'd*, 88 Fed. Appx. 390 (11th Cir. 2003) (Table). Some courts, following the Second Restatement, express the idea of offensiveness in terms of contact that "offends a reasonable sense of personal dignity." Restatement (Second) of Torts § 19 (1965). As noted in *Paul*, Prosser's Hornbook offers as a criterion: "what would be offensive to an ordinary person not unduly sensitive as to his dignity." W. Page Keeton, et al., *Prosser and Keeton on Torts*, § 10, at 42 (5th ed. 1984).

Check Your Understanding

Judge and Jury

If a battery suit goes to trial, who ordinarily decides whether the defendant's touching is of a sort that would be offensive to an ordinary person?

See Mortenson v. City of Oldsmar, 54 F. Supp. 2d 1118, 1126 (M.D. Fla. 1999) (citing *Paul v. Holbrook* for the proposition that the offensiveness of the defendant's kissing of the plaintiff was a factual question to be determined by the jury).

2. Intent

We noted above that battery is grouped by many commentators as one of the intentional torts to emphasize the centrality of intentional or purposive action to the definition of the wrong. A genuinely accidental touching of another person cannot be a battery because of the lack of intentionality on the part of the person doing the touching. Notwithstanding its centrality to battery, intent is an elusive concept. Accurate description and application of the intent element requires careful attention to (1) *what* the law requires an actor to have intended in order to commit battery, and (2) the sort of *evidence* that will suffice to prove that the defendant acted with that intent. The cases below focus mainly on the first of these issues. Before turning to them, we briefly discuss the second issue: proof of intent.

1. *Inferences from Circumstantial Evidence.* In gauging whether an actor has acted toward another person with the requisite intent, judges and juries are required to determine the mental state of the actor at the time of acting. In everyday life, mental states are not directly observable in the way that physical movements and events can be. Thus, even in a straightforward case, a battery plaintiff must rely on circumstantial evidence to establish that the defendant acted with the requisite intent.

In some cases, plaintiffs will have access to evidence "from the horse's mouth." For example, imagine that *A* crashes into and knocks down *B* as they pass one another on the street and that *B* sues *A* for battery. On the witness stand at trial, *A* initially denies that she acted for the purpose of knocking over *B*. However, under withering examination from *B*'s attorney, *A* finally blurts out: "All right, yes, I meant to knock over *B*." Alternatively, suppose that *B* is fortunate enough to discover that *W*, a witness to the incident, is prepared to testify that, moments before the incident, *A* told *W* that she was planning to knock over *B*. In either situation, *B* would seem to have compelling evidence of *A*'s intent from *A* herself.

More typically, an intentional tort plaintiff will have to rely on evidence pertaining to the defendant's outward behavior to support an inference that the defendant acted with the requisite intent. At times, that inference will be relatively easy to draw. Suppose *D*, a champion darts player, is playing an ordinary game of darts in a bar. In typical fashion, *D* is defeating her opponents with an extraordinary display of throwing accuracy. Suppose further that *D* spears *P* with a dart, even though *P* was standing 15 feet away from the dartboard at the time. Finally, suppose that the jury is presented with evidence that *D* and *P* had been seen arguing heatedly earlier that day. Even if *D* were to insist that the dart "slipped" from her hand, a jury would almost certainly be entitled to infer from this evidence that *D* acted for the purpose of spearing *P* with the dart.

Circumstantial evidence can also be used for other purposes besides proving intent. For example, a plaintiff who is subjected to an intentional physical attack can sometimes rely on circumstantial evidence to identify the defendant as the perpetrator. *Compare* Lackie v. Fulks, 2002 WL 1308646 (Mich. App. 2002) (plaintiff, attacked in a bar, did not see his assailant, but circumstantial evidence permitted the jury to conclude that it was the defendant), *app. denied*, 655 N.W.2d 562, *with* O'Connell v. Jacobs, 583 N.Y.S.2d 61 (N.Y. App. Div. 1992) (minor plaintiff who was attacked in her bed but unable to identify her assailant could not prove assault and battery claims brought against one of several older children staying in the house at the time; no evidence indicated who among the older children committed the attack), *aff'd*, 611 N.E.2d 289 (N.Y. 1993).

2. *Burdens of Production and Persuasion.* In tort cases, the onus is ordinarily on the plaintiff to prove that a tort has been committed. Thus, the plaintiff has the burden of supporting her allegations by presenting physical evidence, witness testimony, and the like. In addition, the plaintiff bears the "burden of persuasion." Unlike criminal prosecutions, in which the prosecutor must prove *beyond a reasonable doubt* that the defendant committed the charged crime(s), in tort suits the plaintiff need only prove her allegations by a *preponderance of the evidence.* This means that she must present evidence sufficient to permit the factfinder to conclude that her allegations *are more likely than not* true. To say the same thing, the plaintiff must convince the factfinder that her account of what happened is *probably* what happened.

Thus, when pursuing an intentional tort claim, the plaintiff must, on the issue of intent, produce evidence sufficient to permit the factfinder to conclude that the defendant probably acted with the intent that the law deems necessary for conduct to count as one of the intentional torts. Certainty on the part of the factfinder as to intent (and as to the other elements of these torts) is not required for the plaintiff to prevail.

Vosburg v. Putney

50 N.W. 403 (Wis. 1891)

LYON, J. The action was brought to recover damages for an assault and battery, alleged to have been committed by the defendant upon the plaintiff on February 20, 1889. . . . At the date of the alleged assault the plaintiff was a little more than 14 years of age, and the defendant a little less than 12 years of age. The injury complained of was caused by a kick inflicted by defendant upon the leg of the plaintiff, a little below the knee. The transaction occurred in a school-room in Waukesha, during school hours, both parties being pupils in the school. A former trial of the cause resulted in a verdict and judgment for the plaintiff for $2,800. The defendant appealed from such judgment to this court, and the same was reversed for error, and a new trial awarded. The case has been again tried in the circuit court, and the trial resulted in a verdict for plaintiff for $2,500. . . . On the last trial the jury found a special verdict, as follows:

(1) Had the plaintiff during the month of January, 1889, received an injury just above the knee, which became inflamed, and produced pus? Answer. Yes.
(2) Had such injury on the 20th day of February, 1889, nearly healed at the point of the injury? A. Yes.
(3) Was the plaintiff, before said 20th of February, lame, as the result of such injury? A. No.
(4) Had the *tibia* in the plaintiff's right leg become inflamed or diseased to some extent before he received the blow or kick from the defendant? A. No.

(5) What was the exciting cause of the injury to the plaintiff's leg? A. Kick.
(6) Did the defendant, in touching the plaintiff with his foot, intend to do him any harm? A. No.
(7) At what sum do you assess the damages of the plaintiff? A. Twenty-five hundred dollars. . . .
(8) [J]udgment for plaintiff, for $2,500 damages and costs of suit, was duly entered. The defendant appeals from the judgment.

. . . .

I. The jury having found that the defendant, in touching the plaintiff with his foot, did not intend to do him any harm, counsel for defendant maintain that the plaintiff has no cause of action, and that defendant's motion for judgment on the special verdict should have been granted. In support of this proposition counsel quote from 2 [Simon Greenleaf, *A Treatise on the Law of Evidence*] § 83, the rule that "the intention to do harm is of the essence of an assault." Such is the rule, no doubt, in actions or prosecutions for mere assaults. But this is an action to recover damages for an alleged assault and battery. In such case the rule is correctly stated, in many of the authorities cited by counsel, that plaintiff must show either that the intention was unlawful, or that the defendant is in fault. If the intended act is unlawful, the intention to commit it must necessarily be unlawful. Hence, as applied to this case, if the kicking of the plaintiff by the defendant was an unlawful act, the intention of defendant to kick him was also unlawful. Had the parties been upon the playgrounds of the school, engaged in the usual boyish sports, the defendant being free from malice, wantonness, or negligence, and intending no harm to plaintiff in what he did, we should hesitate to hold the act of the defendant unlawful, or that he could be held liable in this action. Some consideration is due to the implied license of the playgrounds. But it appears that the injury was inflicted in the school, after it had been called to order by the teacher, and after the regular exercises of the school had commenced. Under these circumstances, no implied license to do the act complained of existed, and such act was a violation of the order and decorum of the school, and necessarily unlawful. Hence we are of the opinion that, under the evidence and verdict, the action may be sustained.

II. The plaintiff testified, as a witness in his own behalf, as to the circumstances of the alleged injury inflicted upon him by the defendant, and also in regard to the wound he received in January, near the same knee, mentioned in the special verdict. The defendant claimed that such wound was the proximate cause of the injury to plaintiff's leg, in that it produced a diseased condition of the bone, which disease was in active progress when he received the kick, and that such kick did nothing more than to change the location, and perhaps somewhat hasten the progress, of the disease. The testimony of Dr. Bacon, a witness for plaintiff, (who was plaintiff's attending physician,) elicited on cross-examination, tends to some extent to establish such claim. Dr. Bacon first saw the injured leg on February 25th, and Dr. Philler, also one of plaintiff's witnesses, first saw it March 8th. Dr. Philler was called as a witness after the examination of the plaintiff and Dr. Bacon. On his direct examination he testified as follows: "I heard the testimony of Andrew Vosburg in regard to how he received the kick, February 20th, from his playmate. I heard read the testimony of

Miss More, and heard where he said he received this kick on that day." (Miss More had already testified that she was the teacher of the school, and saw defendant standing in the aisle by his seat, and kicking across the aisle, hitting the plaintiff.) The following question was then propounded to Dr. Philler: "After hearing that testimony, and what you know of the case of the boy, seeing it on the 8th day of March, what, in your opinion, was the exciting cause that produced the inflammation that you saw in that boy's leg on that day?" An objection to this question was overruled, and the witness answered: "The exciting cause was the injury received at that day by the kick on the shin-bone."

It will be observed that the above question to Dr. Philler calls for his opinion as a medical expert, based in part upon the testimony of the plaintiff, as to what was the proximate cause of the injury to plaintiff's leg. The plaintiff testified to two wounds upon his leg, either of which might have been such proximate cause. Without taking both of these wounds into consideration, the expert could give no intelligent or reliable opinion as to which of them caused the injury complained of; yet, in the hypothetical question propounded to him, one of these probable causes was excluded from the consideration of the witness, and he was required to give his opinion upon an imperfect and insufficient hypothesis — one which excluded from his consideration a material fact essential to an intelligent opinion. A consideration by the witness of the wound received by the plaintiff in January being thus prevented, the witness had but one fact upon which to base his opinion, to-wit, the fact that defendant kicked plaintiff on the shin-bone. Based, as it necessarily was, on that fact alone, the opinion of Dr. Philler that the kick caused the injury was inevitable, when, had the proper hypothesis been submitted to him, his opinion might have been different. The answer of Dr. Philler to the hypothetical question put to him may have had, probably did have, a controlling influence with the jury, for they found by their verdict that his opinion was correct. Surely there can be no rule of evidence which will tolerate a hypothetical question to an expert, calling for his opinion in a matter vital to the case, which excludes from his consideration facts already proved by a witness upon whose testimony such hypothetical question is based, when a consideration of such facts by the expert is absolutely essential to enable him to form an intelligent opinion concerning such matter. The objection to the question put to Dr. Philler should have been sustained. The error in permitting the witness to answer the question is material, and necessarily fatal to the judgment.

III. Certain questions were proposed on behalf of defendant to be submitted to the jury, founded upon the theory that only such damages could be recovered as the defendant might reasonably be supposed to have contemplated as likely to result from his kicking the plaintiff. The court refused to submit such questions to the jury. The ruling was correct. The rule of damages in actions for torts was held in Brown v. Railway Co., 54 Wis. 342, 11 N. W. Rep. 356, 911, to be that the wrongdoer is liable for all injuries resulting directly from the wrongful act, whether they could or could not have been foreseen by him. The chief justice and the writer of this opinion dissented from the judgment in that case, chiefly because we were of the opinion that the complaint stated a cause of action *ex contractu*, and not *ex delicto*, and hence that a different rule of damages — the rule here contended for — was applicable. We did not question that the rule in actions for tort was correctly stated. . . . The judgment of the circuit court must be reversed, and the cause will be remanded for a new trial.

Cole v. Hibberd

1994 WL 424103 (Ohio App. 1994)

Young, J. Plaintiff-appellant, Debbie L. Cole, appeals the judgment of the Warren County Common Pleas Court granting summary judgment in favor of defendant-appellee, Sheri L. Hibberd.

Cole filed a personal injury complaint against Hibberd on June 11, 1993, based on an incident that occurred on June 15, 1991. She set forth the operative facts of this action in paragraph two of her complaint: "At said time and place, defendant negligently struck said plaintiff in the lower lumbar area, which negligence directly caused injuries and damages hereinafter set forth." Cole described Hibberd's actions more completely in her deposition taken on August 12, 1993. At the deposition, Cole described the incident as follows:

> The Hibberds had been drinking and Sheri was acting a little rambunctious. While I was standing there leaning over, I had ahold of my daughter with one hand and my niece with the other, I was holding them by the hand, I leaned over to look at her children in her stroller, and she hauled . . . off and kicked me.

Hibberd's attorney asked Cole to describe the incident in more detail, and she responded:

> Well, she kicked me. And I stood up and said, damn it, Sheri, that hurt. She started laughing. And Gary, [Hibberd's husband] Gary called me something fowl [*sic*] and started laughing and thought it was funny. And I told my husband, I said, come on. I was, I was extremely hot about it. She hurt me.

When asked whether she believed Hibberd's action was intentional or accidental, Cole stated:

> I'd say she didn't, she meant to kick me. I mean, she didn't mean to hurt me, she was just horsing around. I guess she thought it wouldn't hurt me. . . .
>
> No, she meant to kick me playingly, but I don't think she meant to hurt me like she did. She basically thought it was funny. I mean, that's how, how she was, really.

R.C. 2305.111 establishes a one-year statute of limitations for claims involving assault and battery. On the other hand, R.C. 2305.10 requires that an action for bodily injury must be brought within two years after the cause arises. Cole filed her complaint more than one year, but less than two years after June 15, 1991, the date Hibberd kicked her.

Hibberd filed a motion for summary judgment contending that her alleged actions constituted a battery which was no longer actionable under R.C. 2305.111 since the complaint was not filed within one year of the incident. The trial court granted Hibberd's motion for summary judgment by entry filed January 14, 1994.

In a single assignment of error, Cole contends that the court erred in concluding that her claim amounted to an action in assault and battery instead of negligence.* Basically, Cole argues that a genuine issue of material fact exists as to whether Hibberd made intentional, offensive contact with Cole. . . .

In Love v. Port Clinton (1988), 37 Ohio St. 3d 98, 99-100, the Ohio Supreme Court stated that "[w]here the essential character of an alleged tort is an intentional, offensive touching, the statute of limitations for assault and battery governs even if the touching is pleaded as an act of negligence. To hold otherwise would defeat the assault and battery statute of limitations."

An individual is liable for battery when he or she acts intending to cause offensive or harmful contact, and such contact results. *Id.* at 99, citing Restatement of the Law 2d, Torts (1965) 25, Section 13. "Offensive contact" is contact that would be offensive to a reasonable sense of personal dignity. *Id.*

Cole insists that Hibberd did not act with an intention to cause harm. However, it is the intentional nature of the contact with the plaintiff that controls the definition, not the intent to cause actual harm or injury. See Restatement of the Law 2d, Torts (1965) 25, Section 13, Comment *c.*

Construing the facts most strongly in favor of Cole, this court concludes that the essential character of her complaint is grounded in the intentional tort of assault and battery. From the evidence presented, reasonable minds can only conclude that Hibberd intended to kick Cole. We also conclude that Hibberd's contact, as testified to by Cole in her deposition, would be considered offensive to a reasonable sense of personal dignity. It is irrelevant to this determination whether or not Hibberd intended to cause injury.

In this case, the statute of limitations for assault and battery applies over the statute of limitations for bodily injury. Accordingly, Cole had only one year from the time of the incident, or until June 15, 1991, to file this lawsuit. The filing of this suit on June 11, 1993, was therefore untimely. . . .

JONES, P.J. (dissenting). Summary judgment was simply inappropriate. A factual question existed with respect to Hibberd's intentions. A jury could, would, and should find that Hibberd's playful "kick in the rear" was not intended to cause offensive or harmful conduct. Hibberd wasn't assaulting her friend Cole any more than one would "assault" a friend by slapping him on the back. Hibberd's "kick" was simply misdirected, striking the coccyx, and a jury could certainly conclude that such was merely negligence. The two-year statute of limitations applies.

---

* [As discussed at length in Part Two of this book, "negligence" is the name of a distinct tort that, unlike battery, does not require proof that the defendant intended some form of contact with the plaintiff. At its core, negligence is about *carelessness* rather than intentionality. An inattentive car driver who accidentally collides his car with another car, thereby injuring the driver of the other car, is subject to liability for negligence, not battery. — EDS.]

NOTES AND QUESTIONS

1. *The Story of Vosburg.* Zigurds Zile has provided an exhaustive account of the proceedings in *Vosburg.* The opinion excerpted above marked the second time that the Wisconsin Supreme Court sent the case back for retrial on a finding of errors in the trial proceedings. (The court's earlier opinion found fault in the trial court's allowance of certain testimony by a medical expert and one of Vosburg's relatives.) The case was tried a third time, resulting in a plaintiff's verdict of about $1,250. That result was upheld in a third Wisconsin Supreme Court decision, issued in 1893 (more than four years after Putney kicked Vosburg). Given the expense associated with the protracted litigation, it seems likely that the entire judgment was consumed by costs and attorneys' fees.

2. *Tortious Because Unlawful?* The *Vosburg* court seemed to attach great weight to the fact that the kick did not occur on the playground, but after class had been called to order. Because it occurred under those circumstances, the court reasoned, the kick was "unlawful." What does "unlawful" mean? Is the court engaging in circular or vacuous reasoning when it states that a defendant acts with the requisite intent to commit battery when he acts with the intent to cause an unlawful contact?

3. *Vosburg, Cole, and Horseplay.* In *Vosburg,* the court observes that, "[h]ad the parties been upon the play-grounds of the school, engaged in the usual boyish sports, the defendant being free from malice, wantonness, or negligence, and intending no harm to plaintiff in what he did, we should hesitate to hold the act of the defendant unlawful, or that he could be held liable in this action." Does this passage amount to an acknowledgment that *Vosburg* involved nothing more than horseplay gone awry? Would that not make *Vosburg* a negligence case, at most? Is *Cole* just *Vosburg* all over again, or are there grounds for concluding that no battery was committed in *Cole* even granted that Putney's kick constituted a battery as to Vosburg?

A number of well-known battery cases have involved unintended and unexpected injuries resulting from horseplay. In each, the defendant was held liable notwithstanding a mismatch between what the defendant intended to happen and what actually happened to the plaintiff. *See* Lambertson v. United States, 528 F.2d 441 (2d Cir. 1976) (applying New York law) (battery found where defendant jokingly jumped on a coworker and began to ride him piggyback, causing coworker to fall onto meat hooks); White v. University of Idaho, 797 P.2d 108 (Idaho 1990) (battery found where defendant touched plaintiff's back in a socially unacceptable manner so as to cause serious physical injury); Caudle v. Betts, 512 So.2d 389 (La. 1987) (battery found where defendant supervisor jokingly administered to employee a slight electric shock, causing an injury that required corrective surgery and left plaintiff with permanent numbness).

An isolated but also well-known counter-example is *Spivey v. Battaglia,* 258 So. 2d 815 (Fla. 1972). Battaglia playfully put his arm around his coworker Spivey's neck and pulled her toward him. He did this even though he apparently knew that she was shy and would not welcome the contact. Unexpectedly, his action caused her to suffer partial facial paralysis. Spivey sued after the statute of limitations for battery had expired but before the negligence limitations period had run. The Florida Supreme Court held that the action sounded in negligence, not battery, and hence was not time-barred. Its rationale was that Battaglia could not have committed a battery because he did not knowingly or intentionally cause Spivey's paralysis. *Id.* at 817.*

As indicated by *Vosburg*, *Cole*, and the other horseplay cases cited above, insofar as *Spivey* supposed that battery requires the defendant to have specifically intended to cause the particular harmful outcome suffered by the plaintiff, it is an outlier. *See also* Frey v. Kouf, 484 N.W.2d 864 (S.D. 1992) (reversing a defense verdict in a battery action because of an erroneous instruction stating that the jury could find for the plaintiff only if it concluded that the defendant threw a beer mug at plaintiff's head with intent to cause the injuries that the plaintiff in fact suffered). How would the *Vosburg* or *Cole* courts have analyzed the facts of *Spivey*?

Imagine a newcomer to the United States who is unfamiliar with prevailing social norms, and who violates those norms by, for example, intentionally and aggressively kissing a stranger in gratitude for a small favor that the stranger had bestowed on the newcomer. Assume that the newcomer meant no harm or offense and did not realize at the time that his conduct was inappropriate. Should the stranger have a claim in battery against the newcomer? Does your answer depend on whether the intended kiss also results in unexpected serious physical injury? How would the *Vosburg* court analyze this case?

4. *The "Eggshell Skull" Rule and the Distinction Between Injury and Damages.* *Vosburg* famously holds that "the wrongdoer is liable for all injuries resulting directly from the wrongful act, whether they could or could not have been foreseen by him." The defendant *takes his plaintiff as he finds him*, courts often say. The basic idea is this: once the plaintiff has proved that the defendant committed a tort upon the plaintiff (and that no applicable defense applies), the defendant is liable to compensate the plaintiff in a manner that approximates making the plaintiff "whole." In some cases — like *Vosburg* — the "make whole" rule supports the imposition of a surprisingly large liability on the defendant merely because the plaintiff suffered from a hidden vulnerability. As long as the defendant's injuring of the plaintiff was an actionable tort, the unforeseeability of the extent of damages flowing from the tort does not provide a ground for limiting liability. What, if anything, is wrong with such a rule? Is it justifiable on the facts of *Vosburg*? More generally? Rules for damages are discussed in Chapter 8.

5. *Cole and Summary Judgment.* In *Cole*, Hibberd's summary judgment motion argued that a reasonable juror faced with the undisputed facts of the case could only

---

* The *Spivey* court's ruling may have been driven more by a desire to ensure plaintiff a remedy than by an adequate account of the intent element of battery. The court also seems to have assumed that Florida law would permit Spivey to proceed with her negligence claim against Battaglia even though workplace injuries caused by a co-employee's negligence were at the time (as they are now) covered by Florida workers' compensation law rather than negligence law. Indeed, Spivey later received workers' compensation benefits from the company, either in addition to or instead of recovering on her tort claim against Battaglia. *See* Spivey v. Battaglia Fruit Co., 287 So. 2d 302 (1973).

conclude that Hibberd committed the tort of battery. Note the irony here: A tort defendant is attempting to *defeat* liability by arguing that the evidence conclusively establishes that she has committed a tort! Does this make any sense?

The trial judge obviously accepted Hibberd's argument, as did a majority of the Ohio appellate court that affirmed the trial court's ruling. The appellate judge who dissented (Judge Jones) seems to take the opposite view, reasoning that a jury "could, would, and should find" that there was no battery committed, only negligence (at most). Does the very fact of the disagreement among the appellate judges suggest that summary judgment was inappropriate? If judges can (reasonably) disagree over whether a battery occurred, couldn't jurors? Why were the trial court and the appellate court majority so eager to decide the statute of limitations issue as a matter of law?

Suppose that Cole had won her appeal and the case was sent back for trial on a claim of negligence. Would Cole have any hope of establishing that Hibberd had injured her by acting *carelessly* toward her physical well-being?

6. *Statutes of Limitation and the Either/Or Problem.* *Cole* and many cases like it from other jurisdictions seem to take as a starting point that, if the defendant's act was a tort at all, then either it was the tort of battery or it was the distinct tort of negligence, but not both. In fact, tort plaintiffs are generally permitted to argue that a defendant acted in a way that amounted to the simultaneous commission of two or more torts.* However, the *Cole* court regarded itself as forced to deal with an either/or issue in order to give effect to the Ohio legislature's decision to set different statutes of limitations for different tort causes of action. In this respect, Ohio law is representative: Most states generally set shorter time limits on the commencement of actions for intentional torts than for other torts, such as negligence, perhaps on the thought that it is generally easier for a potential plaintiff to know that someone has committed a battery against her than to know whether the tort of negligence was committed against her. *See* Chapter 7. Does it make sense for the plaintiff in a case like *Cole* to be held to the shorter statute of limitations?

7. *Interplay of Intent and Offensiveness.* Certain contacts that might otherwise be deemed inoffensive as a matter of law can be rendered offensive if the defendant knows that the plaintiff is unusually averse to being touched in a particular way. *See, e.g.*, Cohen v. Smith, 648 N.E.2d 329 (Ill. Ct. App. 1995) (when patient's religion enjoins her to avoid having her skin touched directly by males, and when hospital has notice of, and agrees to abide by, this restriction, the touching of her skin by a male nurse during surgery can constitute offensive contact battery). In this instance, the offensiveness of the contact is generated in part by the particular intent behind it. The plaintiff is entitled to take offense when the defendant fails to heed what he

---

* However, even if a plaintiff can establish that she was injured by acts on the part of the defendant that amounted to the simultaneous commission of two different torts against the plaintiff, she will still recover only the normal measure of compensatory damages (rather than twice the normal measure). The two torts would be understood as providing alternative grounds for the single damages award.

knows to be her disposition about being touched in certain ways. *See also* Spivey v. Battaglia, Note 3, *supra.*

8. Battery or Negligence? Why It Matters. *Cole* demonstrates one important legal consequence that can flow from conduct being deemed an intentional tort such as battery rather than the distinct tort of negligence, which (loosely speaking) imposes liability for harm caused carelessly rather than intentionally. The difference between the two types of tort can be equally important in other contexts.

- Punitive damages—damages that go beyond the amount necessary to compensate the plaintiff for losses caused by a tort—tend to be more readily available if the plaintiff can prove an intentional tort such as battery. *See* Chapter 8.
- As mentioned in notes following *Paul v. Holbrook,* courts are more likely to regard intentional torts committed by employees as being outside the scope of employment, thereby blocking plaintiffs' ability to hold employers vicariously liable under the doctrine of *respondeat superior. See* Chapter 8.
- Liability insurance policies tend to be written so as to exclude coverage of liabilities arising out of intentional wrongs. *See* Chapter 8.
- Workers' compensation systems, which provide scheduled payments covering medical costs and a portion of lost wages to workers who are injured on the job, bar workers from suing their employers for injuries caused by employer negligence, but allow them to bring claims if they have been injured by an intentional tort for which the employer is responsible. *See* Chapter 11.

Wagner, the decision that follows this note, exemplifies one other important consequence of classifying conduct as a battery rather than negligence: It affects whether an injured person suing a government for injuries inflicted upon her can recover from the government, or whether the government will instead be able to escape liability by arguing that the doctrine of "sovereign immunity" applies. Sovereign immunity is discussed in greater length in Chapter 7. In short, it is the name for the common law principle that a government entity (the United States or each of the 50 states) cannot be held liable for injuries that government employees wrongly inflict upon others in the course of performing their official duties.

By the middle of the twentieth century, every state legislature and the United States Congress had enacted statutes *waiving* their common law right to sovereign immunity. In essence they bound themselves by legislation to being held accountable for tortious injuries inflicted by their employees upon private parties. However, neither the state legislatures nor Congress issued a complete, unconditional waiver; instead, each retained a certain amount of common law immunity. Utah, the defendant in the case below, is typical in retaining immunity for injuries arising out of the intentional torts of government employees.

Wagner therefore displays the same irony seen in *Cole v. Hibberd.* Usually a defendant who is sued for battery hopes to prove that the plaintiff was *not* the victim of a *battery.* Yet in *Wagner,* the State of Utah wishes to prove that its employees were responsible for a battery being committed so that it can take advantage of the rule of retained sovereign immunity for intentional torts.

Wagner v. State

122 P.3d 599 (Utah 2005)

Wilkins A.C.J.

¶ 1. Tracy and Robert Wagner seek review of the court of appeals' ruling that the trial court properly granted a rule 12(b)(6) motion dismissing their suit against the State.* The Wagners' suit, which sought recovery for injuries Mrs. Wagner sustained when a mentally handicapped man attacked her while he was in the custody of state employees, was dismissed at the trial court, and affirmed at the court of appeals, on the ground that the attack constituted a battery, a tort for which the State has retained immunity from suit. The Wagners then petitioned this court for certiorari,** which we granted. We now affirm.

Background

¶ 2. When reviewing a 12(b)(6) motion, we recite the facts in a light most favorable to the non-moving party, though there is no dispute in this case as to the facts.

¶ 3. Tracy Wagner was standing in a customer service line at a K-Mart store in American Fork, Utah, when she was suddenly and inexplicably attacked from behind. The Wagners' alleged that Sam Giese, a mentally disabled patient of the Utah State Development Center ("USDC"), "became violent, took [Mrs. Wagner] by the head and hair, threw her to the ground, and otherwise acted in such a way as to cause serious bodily injury to her."

¶ 4. USDC employees had accompanied Mr. Giese to K-Mart as part of his treatment program and had remained in K-Mart to supervise him. While this particular episode of violence was sudden, it was not altogether unpredictable. Mr. Giese had a history of violent conduct and presented a potential danger to the public if not properly supervised.

¶ 5. Mrs. Wagner and her husband subsequently filed a complaint against USDC and the Utah Department of Human Services, the state agency under which USDC operates, for failing to "properly supervise the activity of" Mr. Giese while he was in its care. Because the defendants to this matter are all governmental entities, they moved to dismiss the complaint under Utah Rule of Civil Procedure 12(b)(6) for failure to state a claim, arguing that Mrs. Wagner's injuries arose out of a battery, a tort for which the

---

* As explained briefly in Chapter 1 in notes following *Walter v. Wal-Mart*, when a defendant files a Rule 12(b)(6) motion to dismiss, it is asserting that, even if all the facts alleged in plaintiff's complaint are true, they do not generate a claim against the defendant under applicable law. In making such a motion, the defendant is hoping to terminate litigation at the very outset, prior to the "discovery" phase of litigation.

** In many court systems, including the federal courts and in this case the Utah state courts, the highest court in the system has broad discretion to choose whether or not to review decisions made by lower courts. A "petition for a writ of certiorari" is a request from a party to a lawsuit that is directed to a high court, which asks it to review a lower court decision for possible error. The high court accepts such a request by granting the petition and thereupon issuing a writ of certiorari to the lower court. (The phrase "writ of certiorari" refers to an order from a high court to a lower court indicating that the former wishes to "apprise itself" of the proceedings in the latter.)

government is immune from suit. Thus, under the Governmental Immunity Act, Utah Code Ann. § 63-30-10(2) (Utah 1997) (repealed 2004), the defendants could not be held liable for injuries arising out of the battery here. The district court agreed with the government and dismissed the Wagners' complaint, holding that because Giese initiated a contact with "deliberate" intent, his attack constituted a battery and the government was immune under the statute.

¶ 6. The Wagners appealed the decision to the court of appeals, arguing that the intentional tort of battery requires proof of both an intent to make a contact and an intent to cause harm thereby, and because Mr. Giese was mentally incompetent to formulate the intent to cause harm, his attack could not constitute a battery as a matter of law. The defendants, on the other hand, maintained that a person need only intend to make a harmful or offensive contact in order for that contact to constitute a battery upon another. A person need not intend to cause harm or appreciate that his contact will cause harm so long as he intends to make a contact, and that contact is harmful.

¶ 7. . . . [T]he court [of appeals] issued a memorandum opinion affirming the district court's order of dismissal. . . .

Analysis

I. Governmental Immunity Act

¶ 10. . . . At the time of the incident in this case, the Governmental Immunity Act read as follows:

> Immunity from suit of all governmental entities is waived for injury proximately caused by a negligent act or omission of an employee committed within the scope of employment except if the injury arises out of . . .:
>
> 2. assault, battery, [or] false imprisonment. . . .

Utah Code Ann. § 63-30-10(2) (Utah 1997) (repealed 2004).

. . . .

¶ 14. The Wagners argue that Mr. Giese's attack could not legally constitute a battery because that intentional tort requires the actor to intend harm or offense through his deliberate contact, an intent Mr. Giese was mentally incompetent to form. The State, on the other hand, argues that the only intent required under the statute is simply the intent to make a contact. The contact must be harmful or offensive by law, but the actor need not intend harm so long as he intended contact.

¶ 15. The outcome of this case, then, turns upon which interpretation of the definition of battery is correct. Accordingly, we turn our attention now to the law of battery as defined in the Restatement [(Second) of Torts].

II. The Restatement Definition of Battery

¶ 16. While there is some variation among the definitions of the tort of battery, *Prosser and Keeton on the Law of Torts* § 8, at 33-34 (W. Page Keeton et al. eds., 5th ed. 1984) (hereinafter Prosser), Utah has adopted the Second Restatement of Torts to define the elements of this intentional tort, including the element of intent. . . . [It] . . . reads:

> An actor is subject to liability to another for battery if
>
> (a) he acts intending to cause a harmful or offensive contact with the person of the other or a third person, or an imminent apprehension of such a contact, and
>
> (b) a harmful contact with the person of the other directly or indirectly results.

Restatement (Second) of Torts § 13 (1965).

¶ 17. The only point of dispute in this case is whether the language of the Restatement requires Mr. Giese to have intended not only to make physical contact with Mrs. Wagner, which the Wagners concede he did, but also to have intended the contact to be harmful or offensive. In other words, is a battery committed only when the actor intends for his contact to harm or offend, or is it sufficient that the actor deliberately make physical contact, which contact is harmful or offensive by law? Determining the answer requires a careful dissection of the elements of battery and the meaning of intent.

¶ 18. We conclude that the plain language of the Restatement, the comments to the Restatement, Prosser and Keeton's exhaustive explanation of the meaning of intent as described in the Restatement, and the majority of case law on the subject in all jurisdictions including Utah, compels us to agree with the State that only intent to make contact is necessary.

¶ 19. In order for a contact to constitute a battery at civil law, two elements must be satisfied. First, the contact must have been deliberate. Second, the contact must have been harmful or offensive at law. We hold that the actor need not intend that his contact be harmful or offensive in order to commit a battery so long as he deliberately made the contact and so long as that contact satisfies our legal test for what is harmful or offensive.

¶ 20. We first address the intent element of battery to explain our holding. Next, we discuss how the limited legal nature of harmful or offensive contact restricts the types of contacts for which actors may be potentially liable.

A. Legal Intent to Commit a Battery

¶ 21. Prosser described intent as "one of the most often misunderstood legal concepts." *Prosser, supra*, § 8, at 33. Because intent is also "one of the most basic, organizing concepts of legal thinking," id., it is crucial that the term is properly defined and understood. We begin our analysis with the language in the Restatement itself.

¶ 22. The Restatement defines a battery as having occurred where "[an actor] acts intending to cause a harmful or offensive contact." Restatement (Second) of Torts § 13. The comments to the definition of battery refer the reader to the definition of intent in section 8A. *Id.* § 13 cmt. c. Section 8A reads:

> The word "intent" is used throughout the Restatement of this Subject to denote that the actor desires to cause *the consequences of his act*, or that he believes that the consequences are substantially certain to result from it.

Id. § 8A (emphasis added).

¶ 23. Although this language might not immediately seem to further inform our analysis, the comments to this section do illustrate the difference between an intentional act and an unintentional one: the existence of intent as to the contact that results from the act. Because much of the confusion surrounding the intent element required in an intentional tort arises from erroneously conflating the act with the consequence intended, we must clarify these basic terms as they are used in our law before we analyze the legal significance of intent as to an act versus intent as to the consequences of that act.

¶ 24. Section 2 of the Restatement (Second) of Torts defines the term "act" as "an external manifestation of the actor's will and does not include any of its results, even the most direct, immediate, and intended." *Id.* § 2. To illustrate this point, the comments clarify that when an actor points a pistol at another person and pulls the trigger, the act is the pulling of the trigger. *Id.* at cmt. c. The consequence of that act is the "impingement of the bullet upon the other's person." *Id.* It would be improper to describe the act as "the shooting," since the shooting is actually the conflation of the act with the consequence. For another example, the act that has taken place when one intentionally strikes another with his fist "is only the movement of the actor's hand and not the contact with the others body immediately established." *Id.* Thus, presuming that the movement was voluntary rather than spastic, whether an actor has committed an intentional or negligent contact with another, and thus a tort sounding in battery or negligence, depends not upon whether he intended to move his hand, but upon whether he intended to make contact thereby.

¶ 25. The example the Restatement sets forth to illustrate this point is that of an actor firing a gun into the Mojave Desert. Restatement (Second) of Torts § 8A cmt. a. In both accidental and intentional shootings, the actor intended to pull the trigger. *Id.* Battery liability, rather than liability sounding in negligence, will attach only when the actor pulled the trigger in order to shoot another person, or knowing that it was substantially likely that pulling the trigger would lead to that result. *Id.* § 8A cmts. a & b. An actor who intentionally fires a bullet, but who does not realize that the bullet would make contact with another person, as when "the bullet hits a person who is present in the desert without the actor's knowledge," is not liable for an intentional tort. *Id.*

¶ 26. A hunter, for example, may intentionally fire his gun in an attempt to shoot a bird, but may accidentally shoot a person whom he had no reason to know was in the vicinity. He intended his act, pulling the trigger, but not the contact between his bullet and the body of another that resulted from that act. Thus, he intended the act but not the consequence. It is the consequential contact with the other person that the actor must either intend or be substantially certain would result, not the act—pulling the trigger—itself. He is therefore not liable for an intentional tort because his intentional act resulted in an unintended contact. On the other hand, the actor is liable for an intentional tort if he pulled the trigger intending that the bullet released thereby would strike someone, or knowing that it was substantially likely to strike someone as a result of his act. *Id.* at cmts. a & b.

¶ 27. Can an actor who acknowledges that he intentionally pulled the trigger, and did so with the intent that the bullet make contact with the person of another, defeat a battery charge if he can show that he did . . . not intend that the contact between the bullet and the body of the person would cause harm or offense to that person? The Wagners argue that such a showing would provide a full defense to a battery charge because the actor lacked the necessary intent to harm.

¶ 28. We agree with the Wagners that not all intentional contacts are actionable as batteries, and that the contact must be harmful or offensive in order to be actionable. We do not agree, however, that, under our civil law, the actor must appreciate that his act is harmful or offensive in order for his contact to constitute a battery. . . .

¶ 29. The plain language of the comments makes clear that the only intent required to commit a battery is the intent to make a contact, not an intent to harm, injure, or offend through that contact. Restatement (Second) of Torts § 13. So long as the actor intended the contact, "it is immaterial that the actor is not inspired by any personal hostility to the other, or a desire to injure him." *Id.* § 13 cmt. c. . . . The linchpin to liability for battery is not a guilty mind, but rather an intent to make a contact the law forbids. . . .

. . . .

¶ 31. . . . [T]he Restatement itself requires neither a "desire to injure" nor a realization that the contact is injurious or offensive. Restatement (Second) of Torts § 13. Instead, the actor need only intend the contact itself, and that contact must fit the legal definition of harmful or offensive.

¶ 32. Prosser echoed the Restatement when he clarified that "[t]he intent with which tort liability is concerned is not necessarily a hostile intent, or a desire to do harm. Rather, it is an intent to bring about a result which will invade the interests of another in a way that the law forbids." *Prosser, supra,* § 8, at 36. While it may be argued that this statement means that the actor must intend that the contact be forbidden, all ambiguity on the point is eviscerated by Prosser's next comment, in which he lists as one type of intentional tort the act of "intentionally invading the rights of another under a mistaken belief of committing no wrong." Id. § 8, at 37.

¶ 33. Though Prosser recognizes that the plaintiff will often recover to the greatest extent "where the [defendant's] motive is a malevolent desire to do harm," he nonetheless ascribes the malevolence to motive, not intent, and labels the less culpable act of innocent invasion of another's rights as an *intentional* invasion. *Id.* These comments only underscore the point repeated throughout both the Restatement and Prosser's analysis that the only intent required is the intent to make a contact to which the recipient has not consented. . . .

. . . .

¶ 36. The Wagners' theory is also in conflict with the majority of case law on the subject in both federal and state courts, including Utah. [Cited authorities omitted — Eds.] While there is a dearth of case law on this precise subject from Utah state courts, our cases that do touch upon the intent element of battery generally support the majority rule to which we subscribe in this decision.

¶ 37. For instance, in Wright v. University of Utah, 876 P.2d 380, 387 (Utah Ct. App. 1994), *cert. denied,* 883 P.2d 1359 (Utah 1994), the court of appeals rejected Mrs. Wright's argument that the autistic university employee who struck her could not have committed a battery because he lacked the mental capacity to form the requisite intent. . . .

¶ 38. Describing Wright's attempt to circumvent the governmental immunity statute by recasting her claim as one sounding in negligence rather than battery as "fruitless, albeit creative," the court looked to analogous federal cases to dismantle her argument. *Id.* at 386-87. . . . [T]he court of appeals concluded that "[n]othing in the [Governmental Immunity] Act or in our case law indicates that the distinction Wright champions was contemplated by the legislature to determine whether immunity exists under section 63-30-10(2). The focus is on the result, not the circumstances leading thereto." *Wright*, 876 P.2d at 387.

¶ 39. We have also implicitly held that mental capacity is not relevant to a liability determination in other cases involving civil battery. In Higgins v. Salt Lake County, 855 P.2d 231, 233 (Utah 1993), the plaintiffs sued Salt Lake County for negligently supervising a mental patient who attacked and repeatedly stabbed their ten-year-old daughter. Though the Higginses did not raise the argument that the attacker's insanity adjudication meant that her attack could not constitute a battery, we found that the battery exception applied. The patient's schizophrenia and marginal intelligence did not persuade us that her actions could not amount to a battery for lack of requisite intent.

¶ 40. The Wagners correctly point out that our decision in Matheson v. Pearson, 619 P.2d 321 (Utah 1980), does not conform to the rule we have applied here. In *Matheson*, a maintenance man sustained injuries when a student threw a piece of candy from an open window at him, striking him in the back. The only way the injured plaintiff could recover against the student for his injuries was if the act sounded in negligence rather than battery, since the statute of limitations on battery had already run by the time the case was filed. We held that battery requires an intent to harm, not just an intent to make contact, and that the adolescent prank did not involve the requisite intent. Thus, the injured maintenance man was able to proceed with his suit on a theory of negligence.

¶ 41. The *Matheson* case, however, was decided before we expressly adopted the Restatement definition of battery, and it has been superceded by more recent case law on the subject of intent. . . . *Matheson* is not a correct interpretation of the Restatement on battery and it is hereby overruled. Instead, we ratify the position taken by the majority of federal and state courts in rejecting the argument that the actor must intend harm or offense through his contact in order for that contact to constitute a battery.

¶ 42. The discussion in Miele v. United States, 800 F.2d 50 (2d Cir. 1986), is informative on this point. There, the Second Circuit held that the family of a child blinded and disfigured when an insane AWOL soldier attacked him with sulphuric acid was barred by the immunity doctrine from recovering against the government, despite the family's argument that the insane soldier could not form the requisite intent to commit a battery. The court held that the attacker's mental capacity was irrelevant to the question of whether the actor committed a battery for two reasons.

¶ 43. First, the government's fault in the attack "does not change depending upon whether the aggressor was sane or insane at the time." *Id.* at 52. "While an insane employee may or may not be less culpable personally for such attacks, the question of whether the injury was perpetrated deliberately or accidentally does not depend upon the employee's sanity." *Id.* Second, under the common law, "one who suffers from deficient mental capacity is not immune from tort liability solely for that reason." *Id.* at 53, (citing W.L. Prosser, *The Law of Torts* § 135 (4th ed. 1971)). The linchpin of an action for battery, then, is simply "the intent to make contact." *Id.* Thus, the Mieles' cause of action against the government arose out of a battery, despite the attacker's mental incompetency.

¶ 44. Though the majority rule is not without its critics, "the fact remains that 'courts in this country almost invariably say in the broadest terms that an insane person is liable for his torts.'" Delahanty [v. Hinckley], 799 F. Supp. [184,] 187 [(D.D.C. 1992)] (quoting Williams [v. Kearbey], 775 P.2d [670,] 673 [(Kan. App. 1989)]). Individuals such as Mr. Giese are included in this category of liable actors because "'mental deficiency does not relieve [them] from liability for conduct which does not conform to the standard of a reasonable man under like circumstances.'" Polmatier [v. Russ], 537 A.2d [468,] 470 [(Conn. 1988)] (quoting Restatement (Second) of Torts § 283B). Indeed, the Restatement provides that, for the sane but mentally deficient, "no allowance is made, and the actor is held to the standard of conduct of a reasonable man who is not mentally deficient, even though it is in fact beyond his capacity to conform to it." Restatement (Second) of Torts § 283B cmt. c.

¶ 45. Otherwise, the law would err on the side of protecting actors who voluntarily make physical contacts with other people, producing injury or offense, from liability for their deliberate action. The result would be that the victims who were subjected to a harmful or offensive physical contact are at the mercy of those who deliberately come into contact with them, and must bear the costs of the injuries inflicted thereby. The practical consequences of such an interpretation would turn the law of our civil liability on its head.

¶ 46. For example, a man who decides to flatter a woman he spots in a crowd with an unpetitioned-for kiss, one of the examples of battery Prosser provides, *Prosser, supra*, § 9, at 41-42, would find no objection under the Wagners' proposed rule so long as his intentional contact was initiated with no intent to injure or offend. He would be held civilly liable for his conduct only if he intended to harm or offend her through his kiss. A woman in such circumstances would not enjoy the presumption of the law in favor of preserving her bodily integrity; instead, her right to be free from physical contact with strangers would depend upon whether she could prove that the stranger hoped to harm or offend her through his contact. So long as he could show that he meant only flattery and the communication of positive feelings towards her in stroking her, kissing her, or hugging her, she must be subjected to it and will find no protection for her bodily integrity in our civil law.

¶ 47. The law would serve to insulate perpetrators of deliberate contact from the consequences their contact inflicts upon their victims. Bodily integrity would be secondary to protecting a perpetrator's right to deliberately touch another person's body without being accountable for the consequences that contact occasioned. The "harmful or offensive" element would, in essence, be viewed from the perspective of the actor, not the objective eye of the law. Under this rule, so long as the actor does not deem his deliberate contact to be harmful or offensive, he may touch others however he wishes without liability under our law of battery. It is clear that the purpose of our civil law on battery was designed to create the opposite incentive.

¶ 48. The objection can be raised that such a theory of liability as we posit today expands liability beyond all reasonable bounds. Perhaps a handshake or other similar gesture will now expose a person to a lawsuit for battery if he happens to unknowingly shake the hand of an unwilling individual. The Restatement, however, and Prosser's analysis thereof, yields this objection wholly without basis.

¶ 49. We must bear in mind that not all physical contacts deliberately initiated constitute batteries, only harmful or offensive ones. Though it is true that the actor need not appreciate that his contact is, nor need he intend it to be, harmful or offensive in order for it to be so and for him to be accountable for the injuries he inflicted by his intentional contact, the contact must in fact be harmful or offensive in order to constitute a battery.

¶ 50. We now explain that the legal test for harmful or offensive contact preserves the Restatement's purpose of protecting the bodily integrity of individuals from invasion while still recognizing the practical realities of our physical world and the inevitable contacts therein. Because "harmful or offensive contact" is determined objectively by the law, only those deliberate contacts that meet the legal test for harmful or offensive will constitute batteries.

B. Harmful or Offensive Contact at Law

¶ 51. . . . [H]armful or offensive contact is not limited to that which is medically injurious or perpetrated with the intent to cause some form of psychological or physical injury. Instead, it includes all physical contacts that the individual either expressly communicates are unwanted, or those contacts to which no reasonable person would consent.

¶ 52. What is not included in this definition are the uncommunicated idiosyncratic preferences of individuals not to be touched in ways considered normal and customary in our culture. . . .

¶ 53. As Prosser notes in his analysis on the subject, "in a crowded world, a certain amount of personal contact is inevitable, and must be accepted. Absent expression to the contrary, consent is assumed to all those ordinary contacts which are customary and reasonably necessary to the common intercourse of life." [*Id.* § 9, at 42.] Among the contacts Prosser noted as part of this common intercourse were: "a tap on the shoulder," "a friendly grasp of the arm," and "a casual jostling to make a passage." *Id.* Thus, the tort of battery seeks to strike a balance between preserving the bodily integrity of others and recognizing and accommodating the realities of our physical world.

. . . .

¶ 57. As already explained, the law of torts, and battery in particular, was designed to protect people from unacceptable invasions of bodily integrity. Taking into account the realities of our physical world, and the physical contacts that are not only inevitable, but are part of our cultural customs, there are limits to the physical contacts from which the law will protect us. The law assumes consent as to all regular and culturally acceptable contacts. Certain contacts from very young children fall into this category primarily because most contacts from very young children are not medically injurious given their relative physical weakness and their standing in our society.

¶ 58. Not so with mentally handicapped adults. Even if the adult had the mental capacity of a small child, the difference in size and strength would make any attempt at an analogy between societal consent to a baby's contact and societal consent to attacks at the hand of such an adult wholly unreasonable. Clearly, society has not simply consented to violent contacts from the mentally handicapped. Under the Restatement, as long as a person, mentally handicapped or not, intended to touch the person of another, and the touch was a harmful or offensive one at law, he has committed a battery, and the price of the injuries he inflicted must be paid out of his, or his caretaker's, pockets.

. . . .

¶ 60. . . . [I]t is not an element of [battery] that the actor appreciate that the contact is unwanted. His mental incompetence may insulate him from criminal liability because the mental handicap may negate the mens rea requirement, but the same level of intent is not required for civil liability to attach.

¶ 61. [I]f we were to adopt the rule urged by the Wagners, we would be contorting the law in order to provide recovery in this isolated instance. Yet, in doing so, we would be contracting the recoveries of all other plaintiffs victimized by insane or mentally handicapped individuals who are suing a non-State entity, and, in the process, limiting the protection of the bodily integrity of everyone.

. . . .

¶ 63. We recognize that, in this instance, the retained immunity doctrine bars the caretakers of such a handicapped person from taking responsibility for the conduct of their charge. It is unfortunate, and perhaps it is improvident of the State to retain immunity in this area. But it is not our role as a judiciary to override the legislature in this matter; it is for us only to interpret and apply the law as it is. We will not limit the recoveries of all other plaintiffs similarly injured by defining the tort of battery in such a way as to make it far more burdensome for plaintiffs to satisfy its elements and recover, nor will we distort the plain language of the Restatement so as to elevate an actor's "right" to deliberately touch others at will over an individual's right to the preservation of her bodily integrity.

Conclusion

¶ 64. Applying the rule we have laid out today to the facts of this case, it is clear that Mr. Giese's attack constituted a battery upon Mrs. Wagner. There is no allegation that his action was the result of an involuntary muscular movement or spasm. Further, the Wagners concede that Mr. Giese affirmatively attacked her; they do not argue that he made muscular movements that inadvertently or accidentally brought him into contact with her.

¶ 65. The fact that the Wagners allege that Mr. Giese could not have intended to harm her, or understood that his attack would inflict injury or offense, is not relevant to the analysis of whether a battery occurred. So long as he intended to make that contact, and so long as that contact was one to which Mrs. Wagner had not given her consent, either expressly or by implication, he committed a battery. Because battery is a tort for which the State has retained immunity, we affirm the court of appeals' decision to dismiss the case for failure to state a claim.

[Concurring opinion omitted — Eds.]

NOTES AND QUESTIONS

1. *Intent to Cause Contact (With a Person)?* The *Wagner* court holds that the only intent required to commit a battery is an intent to cause contact with a person, rather than intent to cause contact of a certain type. This is a relatively capacious conception of intent, in that it allows for a broad array of contacts to count as batteries. Still, it is not without limits. Suppose that Giese was so delusional that, when he attacked Wagner, he actually believed that he was interacting with a tall plant. Would this count as "intent to contact," or does the *Wagner* standard presuppose that the defendant must at least have acted with the intent to contact another human being?

2. *Vosburg and Wagner.* In *Reynolds v. MacFarlane*, 322 P.3d 755 (Utah App. 2014), the plaintiff was standing in the breakroom at his workplace, holding a $10 bill loosely in his hand. The defendant, a coworker, came up from behind and snatched the bill from plaintiff's hand. The defendant jokingly said "that was too easy," then handed the bill back to the plaintiff. The plaintiff proceeded to punch the defendant. Despite the incident, the two interacted on friendly terms later that day and subsequently. However, the plaintiff was disciplined by his employer and later claimed that the bill-snatching incident caused him anxiety. He eventually sued the defendant for battery. The trial court dismissed the suit, but the appellate court, applying *Wagner* and the extended personality doctrine, concluded that the defendant had committed a battery by intentionally grabbing the bill from the plaintiff's hand. It also concluded that the plaintiff was entitled only to an award of nominal damages. (*See* Chapter 8.) Did the appellate court properly apply *Wagner*? Would the defendant's snatching of the bill from the plaintiff be a battery under *Vosburg*?

3. *"Single" Intent, "Dual" Intent, or Something In Between?* The *Wagner* court's decision to adopt an "intent-to-contact" standard seems to have been driven by its sense that any other standard would, in light of Giese's limited mental capacity, require the conclusion that his attack was not a battery. Like *Wagner*, the Third Restatement's draft intentional tort provisions (referenced above) favor an intent-to-contact standard. In these provisions, the intent-to-contact standard is described as a "single intent" standard. According to the Restatement's Reporters, the alternative, "dual intent" standard — which would require the defendant to intend *both* to make contact with another *and* to cause offense or harm by making contact — is not supported by case law and is not sufficiently protective of victims' bodily autonomy. In particular, the Reporters worry that actors who are boorish or clueless about the offensiveness or harmfulness of certain kinds of contact will avoid liability under a dual intent standard by establishing that they lacked any intent to harm or offend. Restatement (Third) of Torts: Intentional Torts to Persons § 101, cmt f (Discussion Draft, April 3, 2014).

Are *Wagner* and the draft Restatement correct in supposing that the only plausible alternative to an intent-to-contact standard is a standard that requires proof that the defendant intended to harm or offend? Or is there an intermediate position between what the Restatement calls "single" and "dual" intent? Recall that *Vosburg* and *Cole* affirmed findings of battery notwithstanding that in each there was a mismatch between the sort of contact the defendant intended and what actually happened to the plaintiff. Did those courts find it necessary to rely on an intent-to-contact standard? If not, what alternative standard did they adopt? If they did adopt an alternative standard, could the *Wagner* court have adopted it and still deemed Giese's attack a battery? On what factual findings?

4. *Intent and Implied Consent.* The Utah Supreme Court concedes that its decision to adopt an intent-to-contact standard threatens to render a good deal of everyday conduct tortious. Can you see why? How does it confront that concern? What does it mean for the court to say that each of us has "implicitly" consented to certain contacts? How has that consent been manifested? (You may want to review what the court in *Vosburg* said about the "implied license" of the playground.) How may implied consent be withdrawn? Actual consent as a defense to battery is considered in more detail in Section III *infra*.

5. *Insanity in Tort and Criminal Law.* *Wagner* holds that a deranged person with a diagnosed, severe mental illness is capable of forming the requisite intent to commit battery. In doing so, *Wagner* states the black letter rule. Some courts, however, have qualified or rejected this rule. *See, e.g.*, White v. Muniz, 999 P.2d 814 (Colo. 2000) (*en banc*) (jury may find that an Alzheimer's sufferer who punched her caregiver committed battery only if it finds that she had the capacity to appreciate that such contact would be harmful or offensive). As the court notes in paragraph 60 of its opinion, this feature of tort law is one that distinguishes it from criminal law, which deems insanity to be a complete defense to charges of criminal assault, murder, etc. Why should tort law be less forgiving of an actor's serious mental illness than criminal law? As suggested in Note 1, *supra*, there probably are some limits to the willingness of courts to deem severely delusional persons liable for battery (raising the hypothetical case of a defendant who does not realize he is making contact with another person).

6. *Degrees of Mental Incapacity.* For claims of batteries brought against very young children, the general rule is that the factfinder (usually the jury) must determine whether the particular minor being sued was capable of forming the requisite intent and acted with such intent. *See, e.g.*, Weisbart v. Flohr, 67 Cal. Rptr. 114 (Ct. App. 1968) (given trial testimony concerning the seven-year-old defendant's capacities and his state of mind when he shot the plaintiff with an arrow, the trial court should have entered judgment for the plaintiff on the ground that the defendant committed battery as a matter of law). Should not the same rule apply for adults with serious mental illnesses? At least one court has suggested so. Edwards v. Stills, 984 S.W.2d 366 (Ark. 1998) (insanity is not generally a defense in tort but can be invoked to defeat liability if the actor's mental incapacity renders him incapable of maintaining the intent necessary to establish liability).

7. *Scope and Rationale of Governmental Immunity for Intentional Wrongs.* The Utah Supreme Court applied the Government Immunity Act as it existed at the

time of the events underlying the litigation — Utah Code Ann. § 63-30-10(2) (Utah 1997) — while noting parenthetically that, by the time its opinion was issued in 2005, the statute had been repealed. The "(repealed)" parenthetical is somewhat misleading, however, because the new immunity statute that replaced the repealed statute contains the same exception. *See* Utah Code Ann. § 63-30d-301(5)(b) (Utah 2004) ("immunity . . . is not waived . . . if the injury arises out of, in connection with, or results from: . . . (b) assault, battery, . . .").

Is there a legitimate rationale for this exception? It is perhaps easy enough to understand why a state would not want to be held liable for a state employee's batteries, because an employee who intentionally strikes someone will frequently be acting in ways that have nothing to do with the performance of her official duties. However, as applied to the facts of *Wagner*, the exception is playing a rather different role. Here the battery was committed by a person in state custody, and the nub of the Wagners' claim against the state is that its employees acted carelessly by failing to use sufficient care to prevent that person from committing battery. Is the Utah Supreme Court right to conclude that it would be exceeding its legitimate authority as a court if it were to interpret the Governmental Immunity Act so as to permit the imposition of liability in cases such as *Wagner*? When faced with essentially the same interpretive question in connection with the Federal Tort Claims Act (FTCA) — a statute that partially waives the federal government's common law sovereign immunity, and on which Utah's governmental immunity statute was modeled — the United States Supreme Court concluded, contrary to *Wagner*, that the FTCA's recognition of continued immunity for injuries arising out of batteries does not extend to a claim alleging that government employees were negligent in failing to prevent a battery from taking place. Sheridan v. U.S., 487 U.S. 392 (1988).

3. Intent and Knowledge to a Substantial Certainty

To say that battery is an intentional tort is to conjure up the image of conduct that is undertaken by a defendant who *means* to make contact with another. *Vosburg*, *Cole*, and *Wagner* seem all to have involved intent of this sort. In each case, the actor alleged to have committed battery meant to cause contact with the plaintiff. However, modern courts and commentators have tended to define the intent element of battery — as well as of assault, false imprisonment, and intentional infliction of emotional distress — so as to capture certain cases that do not on their face involve this sort of purposiveness. The notes that follow describe this aspect of intentional tort doctrine, in which courts recognize liability based on the defendant's *knowledge*, at the time of acting, that her conduct would cause a certain kind of contact.

1. *Garratt v. Dailey.* In *Garratt v. Dailey*, 279 P.2d 1091 (Wash. 1955), the defendant Brian Dailey — who was just shy of six years old — pulled a chair out from under his aunt as she began to sit in it. As a result, she fell and broke her hip. At a bench trial of the aunt's battery claim against Brian, Brian testified that he had moved the chair before realizing that his aunt was about to sit down on it, then hurriedly (and unsuccessfully) tried to move it back under her. Based on this testimony, the judge found for Brian.

On appeal, the Washington Supreme Court reversed and remanded for clarification, relying in part on comment d to Section 13 of the First Torts Restatement. That comment read as follows:

> *Character of actor's intention.* In order that an act may be done with the intention of bringing about a harmful or offensive contact . . . to a particular person . . . the act must be done for the purpose of causing the contact . . . or *with knowledge* on the part of the actor that such contact . . . *is substantially certain* to be produced.

Restatement (First) of Torts § 13, cmt. d, at 29 (1934) (emphasis added). According to the court, on the facts found by the trial judge, Brian could have committed a battery under the "knowledge" prong of comment d's test for intent. Upon remand, the trial court found that Brian was "substantially certain" that his aunt would fall as a result of his moving the chair, and therefore imposed liability. That decision was affirmed by the Washington Supreme Court.* 304 P.2d 681 (Wash. 1956).

Comment d's rule was incorporated, with certain changes, into Section 8A of the Second Torts Restatement. Although the Third Restatement has not yet set out provisions on particular intentional torts, its provisions on "Liability for Physical and Emotional Harm"—which focus primarily on negligence—offer a general definition of the concept intent in line with earlier Restatements. *See* Restatement (Third) of Torts: Liability for Physical and Emotional Harm § 1 (2010) ("A person acts with the intent to produce a consequence if: (a) the person acts with the purpose of producing that consequence; or (b) the person acts knowing that the consequence is substantially certain to result.").

2. *In What Sense(s) Does Knowledge Establish Intent?* Suppose *D* is certain that her actions will cause *P* to suffer the requisite kind of contact. Does *D*'s certainty establish that *D* *intended* to cause that contact? Or is this a distortion of the concept of intent?

Imagine that *D* is driving her car in a crowded urban area when suddenly, and through no fault of her own, her car's brakes completely fail. *D* realizes that, unless she changes course, she is certain to strike the small child lawfully crossing the street in front of her. To avoid that outcome she steers toward the nearest sidewalk, on which is located a crowded sidewalk café. In doing so, she runs into and injures *P*, a patron of the café. Assume that *D* knew to a certainty that by changing direction she would strike and injure *P*. Leaving aside the question of whether *D* was ultimately justified in changing course, is it correct to say that *D* *intended* to cause a harmful or offensive

---

* Although *Garratt* has come to stand as a leading authority for the existence of a separate "knowledge" standard for battery liability, the facts of the case do not seem to have necessitated or even warranted application of that standard. If, as his aunt contended, Brian moved the chair as a prank, he acted for the purpose of causing his aunt to suffer a harmful touching, and no separate knowledge standard is required to establish that he acted with the requisite intent. If, however, Brian had no idea that his aunt was about to sit down in the chair when he moved it, it would seem that he failed to act with the requisite intent even under the knowledge standard. After all, if he didn't know she was about to sit, how could he be *certain* that, by moving it, he would cause her to fall?

touching of *P*? Does the idea of an actor intending an outcome necessarily include some notion that the actor wanted that outcome to come about?

Suppose that, as a philosophical matter, it is a mistake to equate acting in the knowledge that an outcome will result with intending that outcome. Might there nonetheless be justification for the law's recognition of proof of knowledge as sufficient to establish the intent element of torts such as battery and assault? For example, does proof of the defendant's certainty about the outcome allow the factfinder to *infer* that the defendant acted for the purpose of causing the outcome? If so, can the defendant rebut the inference? How? *See* Travis v. Dreis & Krump Mfg. Co., 551 N.W.2d 132 (Mich. 1996) (proof that plaintiff's employer had actual knowledge that injury to the plaintiff was certain to occur as a result of the employer's conduct creates an inference that the employer acted for the purpose of injuring the plaintiff).

Alternatively, is the law entitled to treat a defendant who acts in the knowledge that his conduct will cause an outcome *as if* she had acted for the purpose of causing that contact? *See* Restatement (Second) of Torts § 8A, cmt. b (1965) ("If the actor knows that the consequences are . . . substantially certain . . . to result from his act, and still goes ahead, he is treated by the law *as if* he had in fact desired to produce the result.") (emphasis added). Is this because acting in the near-certain knowledge that one will cause the requisite outcome is as culpable as acting with the intent to cause it?

3. *Knowledge: Subjective or Objective Standard?* The knowledge requirement for intentional torts establishes a *subjective* rather than an *objective* standard. This means that the defendant actually must know to a near certainty that his or her conduct is going to produce the requisite result. Restatement (Third) of Torts: Liability for Physical and Emotional Harm § 1, cmt. c (2010) ("a mere showing that harm is substantially certain to result from the actor's conduct is not sufficient to prove intent; it must also be shown that that actor is aware of this").

Suppose that host *H* serves store-bought food to guest *G*. Unbeknownst to *G*, the food contains nuts, to which *G* is very allergic. *G* eats the food and has a severe allergic reaction. If *H* actually knew that the food contained nuts and that *G* was allergic to them, he has committed a battery. However, if *H* was ignorant of either of these facts, he has not committed a battery — he did not act for the purpose of inducing an allergic reaction in *G*, nor was he certain that his conduct would do so. Perhaps a reasonable person in *H*'s position *should have known* that the food contained nuts and that *G* was allergic to them. If so, *H* may be subject to liability for negligence, not battery.*

State workers' compensation statutes provide scheduled damages to employees who are injured in workplace accidents but, in return, bar negligence suits for such accidents. However, as mentioned in the note prior to *Wagner*, this bar on litigation does not extend to *intentional* torts committed in the workplace. In defining "intentional torts" in this context, the Florida Supreme Court employed an "objective" substantial certainty standard, according to which an employer could be deemed to

---

* We assume that *H* did not serve food to *G* for the purpose of causing some other unwanted touching of *G*; for example, for the purpose of causing him to choke or to burn his tongue. If *H* acted with such a purpose, and then ended up causing the desired injury to *G* by the unexpected means of generating an allergic reaction, he might be held liable for battery.

have committed a battery if a worker were injured as a result of workplace conditions that a reasonable person would recognize as substantially certain to cause injury. Turner v. PCR, Inc., 754 So. 2d 683 (Fla. 2000). In 2010, the Florida legislature responded to *Turner* by amending the state's workers' compensation statute. Under that amendment, an employee can bypass the workers' compensation system and bring a tort suit against an employer for a workplace injury only if the employer "intended" to injure the employee or "engaged in conduct that the employer knew, based on prior similar accidents or explicit warnings specifically identifying a known danger, was virtually certain to result in injury or death to the employee. . . ." R.L. Haines Constr., LLC v. Santamaria, 161 So.3d 528 (Fl. Ct. App. 2014) (suggesting that the amendment was meant to narrow the intentional tort exception to the workers' compensation bar on litigation).

4. *Knowledge Versus Foresight.* Roughly speaking, the tort of negligence requires actors to take care against causing injuries that one can foresee might result from one's careless conduct. It is very important not to confuse the negligence concept of foreseeability with the intentional-tort concept of knowledge. A plaintiff suing for battery does not establish the defendant's intent merely by proving that the defendant *appreciated or should have appreciated* that his actions posed a *risk* of harmful or offensive contact to others. Rather, the plaintiff must establish that the defendant *actually knew* that his actions *would cause* such contact.

German Mut. Ins. Co. v. Yeager, 554 N.W.2d 116 (Minn. Ct. App. 1996), illustrates this point. Yeager, a teenager, demonstrated a homemade bomb to his friends by tossing it over his shoulder, away from where they were sitting. Despite this precaution, shrapnel from the bomb severely injured one of them. Yeager's insurer sought to deny coverage for any tort liability Yeager might incur to his friends on the ground that Yeager's act was "intentional" and thus excluded from coverage under the terms of his insurance policy. The appellate court rejected this argument, noting that while Yeager clearly was *aware* of the *risks* of harm associated with his conduct, he was not substantially certain that someone would be injured by it. Indeed, he quite clearly acted in the belief that no one would get hurt. Thus, his conduct was an instance of carelessness or recklessness, rather than a battery.

5. *Knowledge: Sufficient, Not Necessary.* Proof that the defendant knew his act would cause a harmful or offensive touching is *sufficient* but *not necessary* to satisfy the intent element. It is not necessary because the plaintiff can prove intent by proving that the defendant acted for the purpose of causing such a touching, even if he did not know that his conduct would have that effect, a point illustrated by the following hypothetical.

Suppose that *T* is an inept darts player. While playing darts in a bar, *T* spots his enemy *E* standing near the darts board. *T* throws the dart at *E*, very much hoping it will spear *E* in the leg. *T* is *not certain* that the dart will hit *E*. Indeed, given his ineptitude, he has every reason to believe that the dart will *not* hit *E*. If, nonetheless, the dart miraculously does hit *E*, *T* will have committed a battery because he acted for the purpose of causing a harmful (if improbable) contact with *T* and caused such a contact.

6. *Knowledge and Ongoing Activities.* The knowledge "prong" of the intent element of torts such as battery most obviously applies when the defendant is nearly certain that his conduct will result in the requisite consequence for the plaintiff. Should it also be satisfied if the defendant knows to a certainty that, by virtue of its ongoing conduct, *someone, sooner or later, will be hurt*?

For example, suppose delicatessen owner *O* knows that, in each of the last five years, he has sold 10,000 cups of piping hot coffee in Styrofoam cups. Suppose *O* also knows that, in each of these years, two customers have suffered severe burns because of leaky cups. Now suppose that, in the current year, customer *C* is scalded and sues *O* for battery. In a statistical and predictive sense *O* was perhaps substantially certain that his conduct — selling coffee in the manner that he did — would (eventually) cause a harmful touching to someone. Yet it does not necessarily follow that he has committed battery against *C*. Rather, one could argue that if *O* has wronged *C*, it is because he acted carelessly toward *C*, or perhaps with reckless indifference to *C*'s physical well-being.

The choice between these alternative descriptions of *O*'s conduct can have great practical significance. For example, as mentioned in Chapters 4 and 8, employees who suffer workplace injuries because of dangerous working conditions are usually required by state statute to file a claim for workers' compensation benefits and are barred from suing in tort for negligence. While this arrangement tends to confer certain benefits on workers (including a no-fault liability standard and faster claims processing), it can also result in substantially smaller recoveries. Notably, the same statutes that bar negligence suits for workplace injuries typically *exclude* intentional tort claims. Thus, insofar as an employer's knowledge that its operations will eventually cause injury to some employee suffices to establish intent, a wide range of workplace injuries could fall within the intentional torts exception and hence outside workers' compensation schemes.

Courts have split over whether "statistical" knowledge is sufficient to establish intent. That split is related to the split, discussed above, over whether to treat knowledge as sufficient in its own right to generate liability for battery, or instead to view it as circumstantial evidence of purpose. The latter view, in particular, can help capture why statistical knowledge strikes some courts and commentators as insufficient to prove intent. Simply put, it is very implausible to infer a *purpose* to cause a harmful touching from mere statistical knowledge. For example, there is little, if any, reason to suppose that hypothesized deli owner *O* acted out of a desire to harm his customers. More likely, he regarded these incidents as a matter for regret. To point this out is not to say that *O* acted appropriately, nor to assert that *O* is immune from liability for a tort other than battery, such as negligence. It is only to observe that his willingness to act in a manner that subjects a small number of customers per year to serious burns does not amount to conduct undertaken *for the purpose* of causing harmful touchings of those persons.

B. Assault

Recorded instances of English assault pleas date back at least to the fifteenth century. As explained in the case below, the interest vindicated by the action for assault is that of not being put in apprehension of imminent harmful or offensive contact. Assault, like battery, thus derives from a concern to protect individual bodily integrity. However, assault differs from battery because it gives effect to that right by protecting against certain apprehensions of contact, rather than contact itself.

A prima facie case of assault can be defined as follows:

Assault: Prima Facie Case

Actor *A* is subject to liability to other person *P* for assault if:

1. *A* acts,
2. intending to cause in *P* the apprehension of an imminent harmful or offensive contact with *P;* and
3. *A*'s act causes *P* reasonably to apprehend such a contact.*

One occasionally sees assault described as an "attempted battery," or as a "failed" or "inchoate" battery. These formulations can be misleading. As the cases below demonstrate, a person can be the victim of an assault that is not a battery. Likewise, a battery need not include an assault, as is the case with respect to batteries committed on unconscious plaintiffs, or surreptitious batteries, such as poisonings. Moreover, an assault might arise from an attempt at battery, but it need not. For example, the defendant's purpose may have been all along to scare rather than touch the plaintiff.

An assault is also not properly described as an action for an inchoate—that is, unrealized or incomplete—battery. Rather, an assault is a suit for a fully realized wrong, one that is completed when the requisite apprehension is generated in the victim. In this respect, the law of assault differs fundamentally from the criminal law, which sometimes criminalizes failed efforts to commit other crimes. Suppose, for example, *S* fires a loaded gun equipped with a silencer intending to shoot and kill *V*, but misses his target. *V*, for her part, is completely oblivious to the attempt. By happenstance, *S*'s conduct is observed by a witness who reports *S*'s behavior to the police. *S* can be convicted of attempted murder, but *V* has no action against *S* for assault.

Beach v. Hancock

27 N.H. 223 (1853)

TRESPASS, for an assault.

. . . [I]t appeared that the plaintiff and defendant, being engaged in an angry altercation, the defendant stepped into his office, which was at hand, and brought out a gun, which he aimed at the plaintiff in an excited and threatening manner, the plaintiff being three or four rods distant.** The evidence tended to show that the defendant

* As noted above in connection with the presentation of the prima facie case of battery, some jurisdictions treat lack of consent as an additional element of assault, whereas this book treats lack of consent as an affirmative defense.

** [1 rod = 16.5 feet—EDS.]

snapped the gun twice at the plaintiff, and that the plaintiff did not know whether the gun was loaded or not, and that, in fact, the gun was not loaded.

The court ruled that the pointing of a gun, in an angry and threatening manner, at a person three or four rods distant, who was ignorant whether the gun was loaded or not, was an assault, though it should appear that the gun was not loaded, and that it made no difference whether the gun was snapped or not. . . .

The jury, having found a verdict for the plaintiff, the defendant moved for a new trial. . . .

GILCHRIST, C.J. . . . One of the most important objects to be attained by the enactment of laws and the institutions of civilized society is, each of us shall feel secure against unlawful assaults. Without such security society loses most of its value. Peace and order and domestic happiness, inexpressibly more precious than mere forms of government, cannot be enjoyed without the sense of perfect security. We have a right to live in society without being put in fear of personal harm. But it must be a reasonable fear of which we complain. And it surely is not unreasonable for a person to entertain a fear of personal injury, when a pistol is pointed at him in a threatening manner, when, for aught he knows, it may be loaded, and may occasion his immediate death. The business of the world could not be carried on with comfort, if such things could be done with impunity.

We think the defendant guilty of an assault, and we perceive no reason for taking any exception to the remarks of the court. . . .

Brooker v. Silverthorne

99 S.E. 350 (S.C. 1919)

HYDRICK, J. Defendant appeals from judgment for plaintiff for $2,000 damages for mental anguish and nervous shock alleged to have been caused by abusive and threatening language addressed to plaintiff by defendant over the telephone.

Telephone exchange operators, 1952

Plaintiff alleges: That on October 27, 1916, she was night operator at the telephone exchange at Barnwell. That defendant called the exchange over the telephone and asked for a certain connection, which she promptly tried to get for him, but, upon her failing to do so, he cursed and threatened her in an outrageous manner, saying to her: "You God damned woman! None of you attend to your business." That she tried to reason with him, telling him that she had done all that she could to get the connection he wanted, but he continued to abuse and threaten her, saying to her: "You are a God damned liar. If I were there, I would break your God damned neck." That the language and threat of defendant put her in great fear that he would come to the exchange and further insult her, and that she was so shocked and unnerved that she was made sick and unfit for duty, and had to take medicine to make her sleep.

That for weeks afterwards, when defendant's number would call, she would become so nervous that she could not answer the call. And that her nervous system was so shocked and wrecked that she suffered and continues to suffer in health, mind, and body on account of the abusive and threatening language addressed to her by defendant. . . .

Although it cannot affect the decision, because the truth of the facts alleged is concluded by the verdict, it is nevertheless due to the defendant to say that he denied emphatically using the language attributed to him, and his denial was corroborated by the testimony of his wife and a lineman of the telephone company. Defendant testified, also, that, on hearing that plaintiff was offended, he went to her and told her that he did not intend to say anything to offend her, and did not remember having done so, and asked her what he had said that offended her, and she replied that he had spoken a little harshly to her; that he told her he did not remember having done so, but, if she thought so, he was very sorry, and she seemed to be satisfied with this apology. This conversation was not denied by plaintiff.

Big Think

Appellate Review

The South Carolina Supreme Court acknowledges that it had no grounds for second-guessing the jury's factual findings. This is typical. When appellate courts review trial court rulings, they usually do so by adopting the interpretation of the facts that is most favorable to the appellee. Here, the jury clearly declined to credit Silverthorne's testimony, as well as corroborating testimony from his wife and a telephone lineman. Why, then, does the court bother to mention that testimony? Relatedly, why does the court mention Silverthorne's apology? Does the apology have any relevance to the question of liability for assault? If so, is it relevant in a way that would allow an appellate court to take into account?

The question is whether plaintiff stated or proved a cause of action. That question was decided in the negative in Rankin v. Railroad Co., 58 S.C. 532, 36 S.E. 997. In that case, Mrs. Rankin alleged that the railroad company's agents trespassed upon her premises, and were about to cut down some trees of great value and beauty, and, when she approached them and requested them not to do so, the foreman of the gang "cursed her and ordered her to get away from there, or he would put her in the penitentiary, and threatened to strike her, she being an old woman, and otherwise maltreated and abused her to her great damage." A demurrer to this complaint was sustained. The court considered the complaint as having attempted to set forth two causes of action, one for trespass on the plaintiff's property, and the other for the abusive and threatening language. After showing that no cause of action for trespass was stated, the question whether an action would lie for the abusive and threatening language was considered, and it was held that it would not. . . .

The circuit court rested its conclusions in part upon the following quotations from Cooley on Torts:

> "An act or omission may be wrong in morals, or it may be wrong in law. It is scarcely necessary to say that the two things are not interchangeable. No

suddenly into her lane, and she reacted by steering her van sharply to the right. Vetter's van struck the curb, causing her head to hit the steering wheel and snap back against the seat, after which she fell to the floor of the van. Morgan and Gaither denied that the car veered into Vetter's lane, stating they drove straight away from the intersection and did not see Vetter's collision with the curb.

Vetter filed this action against Morgan and Gaither, alleging their negligent or intentional actions had caused her injuries. The trial court granted summary judgment in favor of Morgan, ruling Vetter could not raise a negligence claim against Morgan for unintended results of his intentional acts. The court concluded that Morgan could not be liable for Gaither's actions because Morgan did not participate in driving the car. The court also concluded Morgan's actions did not constitute assault . . . and dismissed all claims against Morgan. Gaither settled with Vetter, and the trial court approved the settlement. . . .

. . . .

II. Assault

Vetter argues the trial court erred in dismissing her assault claim against Morgan. Assault is defined as "an intentional threat or attempt, coupled with apparent ability, to do bodily harm to another, resulting in immediate apprehension of bodily harm. No bodily contact is necessary." Taiwo [v. Vu], 249 Kan. at 589, 596, 822 P.2d 1024 (quoting PIK Civ. 2d 14.01).

The trial court concluded there was no evidence that Morgan threatened or attempted to harm Vetter, that he had no apparent ability to harm her because her van was locked and the windows were rolled up, and there was no claim of immediate apprehension of bodily harm. Vetter contends all of these conclusions involved questions of fact that should have been resolved by a jury.

There was evidence of a threat. Vetter testified in her deposition that Morgan verbally threatened to take her from her van. Ordinarily, words alone cannot be an assault. However, words can constitute assault if "together with other acts or circumstances they put the other in reasonable apprehension of imminent harmful or offensive contact with his person." Restatement (Second) of Torts § 31 (1964).

The record is sufficient to support an inference that Morgan's threat and the acts and circumstances surrounding it could reasonably put someone in Vetter's position in apprehension of imminent or immediate bodily harm. Morgan's behavior was so extreme that Vetter could reasonably have believed he would immediately try to carry out his threat. It is not necessary that the victim be placed in apprehension of instantaneous harm. It is sufficient if it appears there will be no significant delay. *See* Restatement (Second) of Torts § 29(1), comment b (1964).

The record also supports an inference that Morgan had the apparent ability to harm Vetter. Although Vetter's van was locked and the windows rolled up, the windows could be broken. The two vehicles were only six feet apart, and Morgan was accompanied by two other males. It was late at night, so witnesses and potential rescuers were unlikely. Although Vetter may have had the ability to flee by turning right, backing up, or running the red light, her ability to prevent the threatened harm by flight or self-defense does not preclude an assault. It is enough that Vetter believed that Morgan was

Big Think

Stare Decisis

Suppose that *Brooker* and *Vetter* were issued by the same state high court. Are they reconcilable? Or would *Vetter* amount to an overruling of *Brooker*? In what respect(s)?

capable of immediately inflicting the contact unless prevented by self-defense, flight, or intervention by others.

The trial court erred in concluding there was no evidence that Vetter was placed in apprehension of bodily harm. Whether Morgan's actions constituted an assault was a question of fact for the jury.

[In the remainder of its opinion, the court concluded that a jury could also hold Morgan liable for the tort of negligence if it were to deem his actions unreasonable and if it were to find that his actions played a role in inducing her to veer off the road. The court further held that a jury could deem Morgan responsible for Gaither's alleged swerving of the car toward Vetter on the ground that the two men were acting "in concert" with one another. — Eds.]

NOTES AND QUESTIONS

1. *Apprehension Versus Fear.* A plaintiff can make out a prima facie case of assault without having to establish that she was fearful that she was about to suffer a harmful or offensive contact. It is enough that she was *aware* that such contact might occur. Thus, a plaintiff who testifies to her awareness that the defendant had tried unsuccessfully to dump garbage over her head, or to caress her in an inappropriate but nonviolent manner, need not establish that she was afraid for her physical well-being to make out a prima facie case of assault. Still, these sorts of plaintiffs may sometimes find that their lack of fear will affect the amount of compensatory damages they can expect to recover.

2. *"Mere" Words: Conditional or Indeterminate Threats.* As indicated in *Brooker*, for a threat to constitute an assault, it must be conveyed in a way that creates a reasonable belief in the hearer that the threatened contact is imminent. Thus, as a matter of formal doctrine, it does not constitute assault for *D* credibly to say to *P*: "One of these days, you're gonna get it" or even "If you're not out of town by sunrise, I'm going to find you and beat you to a pulp."

Some courts have generalized from this sort of example to the proposition, mentioned in *Brooker* and *Vetter*, that "words alone" can never constitute an assault. This proposition must be handled with a certain amount of care, given that real-world cases of assault rarely if ever consist of words alone. Instead, they involve words uttered in a context that is created by, among other things, the speaker's tone of voice, accompanying gestures, the physical circumstances in which the statement is uttered, the relationship or lack thereof between defendant and plaintiff, and differentials between the assailant and the victim such as physical size or gender.

Suppose two adult male friends, *D* and *P*, are sitting at a table in the food court of a shopping mall. In the midst of a tense conversation, *D* stands up, pushes away his chair, and says to *P* in an angry tone: "You are driving me nuts! I cannot take this anymore! I am going to have to beat some sense into you right here and right now!" *P* is frightened by *D*'s statement. However, after a few tense seconds, *D* storms off. *P* remains upset over the incident and decides to sue *D* for assault. Is this a case of "mere words"? Are there good reasons for the law to decline to recognize *D*'s conduct as an assault of *P*?

3. *Present Ability and Reasonableness of Apprehension.* Not all apprehensions caused by the intentional act of another count as assaults. Rather, as with respect to offensive-contact batteries, social norms play an important role in determining the circumstances under which an individual is justified in apprehending imminent harmful contact. Thus, some of the cases thought to exemplify the "words alone" maxim are perhaps better explained in terms of a judicial insistence that the victim's apprehension have some objective basis. For example, given the apparent lack of physical proximity between the caller and the operator in *Brooker*, one might conclude that, as a matter of law, the operator was not reasonable in apprehending *imminent* harmful contact. What aspects of the situation in *Vetter* provided the plaintiff with objective grounds for apprehending imminent harmful contact?

In the well-known, if dated, case of *Western Union Tel. Co. v. Hill*, 150 So. 709 (Ala. Ct. App.), *cert. denied*, 150 So. 711 (Ala. 1933), Mrs. Hill entered a telegraph office looking for one Sapp, a Western Union employee, to request of Sapp that he repair a broken clock in her husband's store. Sapp, who had been drinking, reached across a countertop that separated them and stated to Mrs. Hill that, if she would "love and pet him," he would "fix her clock." The appellate court held that the jury could find that, given his height, and the height and width of the counter, Sapp was in a position to reach past the counter's far edge and touch Mrs. Hill. Thus, Sapp's propositioning of Mrs. Hill, when combined with evidence of his "present ability" to act on it, permitted the jury to conclude, first, that he acted with intent to create an apprehension of imminent offensive contact, and, second, that the plaintiff was reasonable to apprehend such contact.

While acknowledging that it expresses a minority position, the draft assault provisions of the Restatement (Third) of Torts employs a subjective standard for apprehension, reasoning that doing so "aligns best with the interests protected by assault" and will not generate excessive liability given other limitations built into the tort. Restatement (Third) of Torts: Intentional Torts to Persons § 103, cmt. d (Discussion Draft, April 3, 2014). Suppose *D*, standing in a field, erroneously believes that he can throw a large rock far enough that it will reach *P*, who is standing 50 yards away. *D* throws the rock toward *P*, intending to scare *P*. Given the rock's trajectory, it would be immediately obvious to an objective observer that the rock had no chance of coming near *P*. Nonetheless, *P*, who is unusually timid, fears that the rock is about to strike him. Should *D* be liable to *P* for assault?

4. *Aiding and Abetting.* Could Vetter successfully sue Gaither, the driver of the car in which Morgan was sitting, for playing a role in the assault? That would depend on whether a jury could find that Gaither "aided or abetted" Morgan's assault, that is,

encouraged, incited, or helped to carry it out. Aiding and abetting closely resembles the idea of "concert of action" mentioned briefly in the notes following *Summers v. Tice* in Chapter 4. Indeed, as indicated at the end of the excerpted *Vetter* opinion, the court held that Morgan could potentially be held liable for Gaither's careless driving, which functioned as a cause of Vetter's crash, on the ground that Morgan and Gaither were co-venturers. Presumably a similar rationale would apply to establish that Gaither aided and abetted Morgan's assault. *See* Halberstam v. Welch, 705 F.2d 472 (D.C. Cir. 1983) (discussing the scope of aiding and abetting liability in tort).

For a decision that provides an interesting application of assault law, while also invoking a seemingly narrow conception of aiding and abetting, see Phelps v. Bross, 73 S.W.3d 651 (Mo. App. 2002). Phelps worked as a "Budweiser girl" who accompanied male golfers during organized golf outings. According to the allegations in Phelps's complaint, at the conclusion of one such outing, her supervisor coerced her into accepting a ride back to her hotel from two golfers, Bross and Church. The two men then drove Phelps to Bross's house, where Church provided Phelps with a beer containing a drug that rendered her unconscious. While Phelps was unconscious, Church sexually assaulted her. When Phelps awoke, she found herself naked in a bed with Bross sitting next to her, fully clothed. Phelps ran from the house and contacted the police. She later sued Bross, among others, for assault and for aiding and abetting Church's battery. The appellate court concluded that, notwithstanding his active participation in the transportation of Phelps to his own house, Bross could not be held to have aided and abetted Church's battery because there was no evidence that he incited, encouraged, or participated in the attack itself. However, the court reversed the trial court's entry of summary judgment on Phelps's assault claim against Bross, concluding that a jury could reasonably find that Bross assaulted Phelps by getting into bed next to her and thereby causing her to fear imminent harmful or offensive contact when she awoke.

In *Rice v. Paladin Enterprises, Inc.*, 128 F.3d 233 (4th Cir. 1997), *cert. denied*, 523 U.S. 1074 (1998), a federal Court of Appeals was faced with a lawsuit against the publisher of a manual, entitled *Hit Man*, that instructs would-be assassins on how to commit and get away with murders. The plaintiffs, survivors of a decedent who was killed by a person who used the book's methods, claimed that the publisher had aided and abetted the killing. The court's opinion was devoted to rejecting the defendant's assertion that the First Amendment creates a blanket immunity from liability for book publishers. The case also poses an interesting question of substantive tort law: Does the publication of an instruction manual not directed to or at any particular person amount to the aiding and abetting of a battery committed in accordance with the manual's instructions?

The concept of civil liability for aiding and abetting has received renewed attention in connection with litigation brought under a federal statute known as the Alien Tort Statute (ATS). The ATS is a jurisdictional rather than a substantive statute. It does not recognize a new cause of action but instead grants federal courts the authority to adjudicate suits by non-U.S. citizens ("aliens") seeking redress for certain torts defined independently of the ATS itself.

In one example of aiding and abetting issues arising in ATS litigation, representatives of Myanmar citizens who allegedly were killed, raped, tortured, dispossessed, and/or conscripted by Myanmar military personnel brought suit in federal court against the Unocal Corporation. The suit alleged that Unocal, a participant in a joint venture responsible for building a gas pipeline in Myanmar, supervised and paid Myanmar soldiers to provide security for the project, and in the process knowingly aided or encouraged the soldiers' human rights abuses. Although a three-judge panel initially ruled that the plaintiffs' complaint stated cognizable claims against Unocal for having aided and abetted human rights abuses in violation of international law, that decision was vacated upon the subsequent granting of Unocal's motion to have the full (*en banc*) court rule on Unocal's motion to dismiss. Doe v. Unocal, 395 F.3d 978 (9th Cir. 2003). The case was then transferred to state court, in which the plaintiffs pursued various state-law claims, including for battery and other intentional torts, under theories of direct and vicarious liability. Unocal's efforts to have those claims dismissed were unsuccessful, but the case settled in 2004 before trial began and before the United States Court of Appeals for the Ninth Circuit, sitting *en banc*, could hear the appeal of the federal suit. 403 F.3d 708 (9th Cir. 2005).

The United States Supreme Court has since cut back substantially on the ATS's reach, ruling that it does not permit claims in federal courts based on misconduct that occurred exclusively or primarily outside of U.S. territory. Kiobel v. Royal Dutch Petroleum Co., 133 S. Ct. 1659 (2013) (affirming dismissal of claims by Nigerian plaintiffs that defendant oil companies aided and abetted the Nigerian government in committing human rights violations).

C. Intent Revisited: Transferred Intent

We have seen examples of battery and assault cases in which it is quite clear that the assailant acted with the requisite purpose or knowledge, and that his act led directly and predictably to the intended outcome. Such was the case in *Cecarelli*, for example. We have also seen cases, such as *Vosburg*, in which there was a mismatch between the harmfulness of the touching intended by the defendant and the harmfulness of the touching that actually occurred. In this section we consider how tort law handles certain other cases involving a mismatch between intent and consequence.

In re White

18 B.R. 246 (Bankr. E.D. Va. 1982)

SHELLEY, BANKR. J. . . .

STATEMENT OF THE FACTS

On September 10, 1977 Walter Calvin White, Jr. (White) shot Ralph Edward Davis (Davis) in the stomach with a handgun. White was arrested for the shooting and on November 29, 1978 the Circuit Court of the City of Richmond found him guilty of maiming Davis and sentenced him to serve five years in the state penitentiary. On February 26, 1980 Davis obtained a default judgment against White in the amount of $50,000.00 in the Circuit Court for the City of Richmond on the ground that White willfully and maliciously wounded Davis. White subsequently filed his petition in bankruptcy and Davis now asks this Court to declare White's debt on account of that judgment nondischargeable in bankruptcy.

On the day of the shooting Davis and his brother, Marvin W. Davis, were washing cars in front of their mother's house on Fairmont Avenue in Richmond, Virginia. At the same time White, a neighbor who lives less than one block away on the same street, was having a conversation with William Tipton (Tipton). In that conversation White and Tipton continued an argument which had begun approximately one week earlier. White had obtained a gun in anticipation of seeing Tipton. White was carrying the pistol in a container on his motorcycle and pulled it out of the container during the course of that argument.

When White pulled the gun Tipton mounted his motorcycle and sped away. White shot at Tipton as Tipton passed within twenty-five feet of Davis. He missed Tipton and the bullet hit Davis in the stomach. White fled the scene.

White testified at the trial that he obtained the gun with the intent of scaring Tipton. He said that he drew the gun after Tipton insulted his mother but that he did not intentionally fire the gun. He claimed the gun went off when he tripped over a rock in the street.

Davis and White did not know each other before the shooting incident. White said he pulled the gun intending to scare Tipton and that it accidently fired. This Court believes that White's testimony that the gun accidently fired when he tripped over a rock is unworthy of belief. White testified that he obtained the gun earlier that week with another meeting with Tipton in mind. Although Davis was located almost a full block from White, the bullet hit him as Tipton passed within twenty-five feet of him. White clearly intended to shoot Tipton; however, he missed and the bullet hit Davis instead.

Conclusions of Law

A debt incurred from an action based upon a willful and malicious injury by the debtor to another person may be nondischargeable in bankruptcy. 11 U.S.C. § 523(a)(6). The word "willful" means deliberate or intentional.*

It is clear . . . that "reckless disregard" is no longer sufficient to make a debt nondischargeable. . . . [However,] the [Bankruptcy] Act does not necessarily restrict the penalty of nondischargeability . . . [to] cases in which the debtor injured the person he intended to injure. ". . . The word 'willful' means 'deliberate or intentional,' a deliberate and intentional act which necessarily leads to injury. Therefore, a wrongful act done intentionally, which necessarily produces harm and is without just cause or excuse, may constitute a willful and malicious injury." *Collier on Bankruptcy*, para. 523.16[1] (15th ed. 1981) (footnotes omitted).

---

* Congress stated in . . . legislative history . . . that "paragraph (6) excepts debts for willful and malicious injury by the debtor to another person or to the property of another person. Under this paragraph, 'willful' means deliberate or intentional. To the extent that Tinker v. Colwell, 193 U.S. 473, 24 S. Ct. 505, 48 L. Ed. 754 (1902), held that a looser standard is intended, and to the extent that other cases have relied on Tinker to apply a 'reckless disregard' standard, they are overruled." H.R. Rep. 95-595, 95th Cong., 1st Sess., 365 (1977), U.S. Code Cong. & Admin. News 1978, pp. 5787, 6320-21.

White committed the wrongful act when he shot at Tipton. The act was intentional and it produced an injury although not to the person White intended to injure. White's actions cannot be excused solely because he missed his intended victim and instead hit someone else. The injury is not required to be directed against the victim, but includes any entity other than the intended victim.

Under the doctrine of transferred intent one who intends a battery is liable for that battery when he unexpectedly hits a stranger instead of the intended victim. W. Prosser, *The Law of Torts*, 33 (4th ed. 1971). If one intentionally commits an assault or battery at another and by mistake strikes a third person, he is guilty of an assault and battery of the third person if "defendant's intention, in such a case, is to strike an unlawful blow, to injure some person by his act, and it is not essential that the injury be to the one intended." Morrow v. Flores, 225 S.W.2d 621, 624, Tex. Civ. App. (1949), *rehearing denied* 1950.

Virginia courts have adopted the doctrine of transferred intent reasoning that ". . . every person is liable for the direct, natural and probable consequence of his acts, and that every one doing an unlawful act is responsible for all of the consequential results of that act." Bannister v. Mitchell, 127 Va. 578, 104 S.E. 800, 801 (1920). There need be no actual intent to injure the particular person who is injured. *Id.* . . .

The evidence here clearly shows that the shooting was a wrongful act intentionally done and that Davis's injuries resulted from that act. White deliberately, intentionally and maliciously fired the gun and injured Davis and the debt resulting from that act is nondischargeable in bankruptcy. . . .

An appropriate order will issue.

NOTES AND QUESTIONS

1. *Transferred Intent (I): Same Victim, Different Intentional Tort.* The doctrine of transferred intent invoked by the *White* court is in reality a collection of doctrines, some of which may be more defensible than others. It will therefore be worthwhile to attempt to disaggregate the various rules that fall under that label.

At times transferred intent is invoked to address a situation in which the defendant intends a victim to suffer one kind of prohibited consequence (e.g., a harmful touching), but ends up causing that victim to suffer a different kind of consequence that is also prohibited (e.g., apprehension of an imminent harmful touching). Consider, for example, the following passage from *Nelson v. Carroll*, a Maryland Supreme Court decision.

In attempting to collect a debt owed to him by one Charles "Pee Wee" Nelson, Albert "Junior" Carroll was about to strike Nelson in the head with a gun when the gun accidentally fired, causing Nelson to be shot. In response to Nelson's battery claim, Carroll argued that he should not be found liable because his intent was merely to "scare" Nelson, not shoot him. The Court rejected this argument.

> The rule is widely recognized that when one commits an assault, and in the course of committing the assault that person comes into contact with the person assaulted,

the intent element of battery may be supplied by the intent element of the assault. Professors Prosser and Keeton explain:

> "Although a contact . . . is . . . essential [to battery], the intent element of the cause of action is satisfied not only if the defendant intends a harmful contact . . . upon the plaintiff . . . *but also if the defendant intends only to cause apprehension that such a contact is imminent (an assault-type consequence).*" (emphasis added) (footnotes omitted).

Prosser & Keeton, The Law of Torts § 9, at 39 (5th ed.1984). *See also* Restatement (Second) of Torts § 13 (1965) ("An actor is subject to liability to another for battery if (a) he acts intending to cause a harmful or offensive contact with the person of the other or a third person, *or an imminent apprehension of such a contact. . . .*" (emphasis added)).

. . . . Therefore, one who intends to frighten another by assaulting him or her, and touches this person in a harmful or offensive manner and claims the touching was inadvertent or accidental, is liable for battery, notwithstanding the contention that the actual touching was never intended. . . .

Nelson v. Carroll, 735 A.2d 1096, 1102-03 (Md. 1999).

In this iteration, the doctrine of transferred intent presumably permits mixing and matching among certain other intentional torts. Thus, if *D* slams a door intending to lock *P* in a room, but *P*'s fingers are crushed in the closing door, *D*'s intent to confine *P* will likely suffice to establish the intent element of *P*'s claim for battery even though *D* never intended to touch *P*. What explains the willingness of tort law to mix and match intents and consequences, and with them, different wrongs?

2. *Transferred Intent (II): Across Victims.* As *White* indicates, courts sometimes also use transferred intent to convey a different idea, namely that victims of certain acts that were intended to injure someone else may sue even though they were not among the persons whom the defendant intended to injure. *Talmage v. Smith*, 59 N.W. 656 (Mich. 1894), is often held out as a leading instance of a court permitting intent to transfer from an intended to an unintended victim. In that case, Smith saw several boys playing on the roof of a shed on his property. He sought to chase them away by hurling a large stick at one of them. The stick instead hit another boy who was on the shed (Talmage) and blinded him in one eye. Smith argued as an affirmative defense that he was entitled to throw the stick at the boys as a reasonable means of defending his property. *See* Section III *infra*. The trial judge instructed the jury that if it found that Smith's action involved excessive rather than reasonable force, it should hold Smith liable regardless of whether he intended to hit Talmage or the other boy. The Michigan Supreme Court upheld this instruction.

Is *Talmage* properly understood as an instance in which the defendant acts with the intent to cause a harmful contact with *A* but ends up causing harmful contact with unintended victim *B*? Or is it an example of an act undertaken with intent to cause harm to any one of several possible victims? (Did Smith really care which boy he hit?) If the latter, does it support the result reached by the bankruptcy judge in *White*? Of course, White's wrongful conduct obviously caused harm to Davis. But did White subject Davis to the sort of purposeful touching characteristic of batteries? Is there a better way to describe the wrong perpetrated by White against Davis? If so, would that description also bar White from discharging his liability to Davis in bankruptcy under the terms of the Bankruptcy Code?

Assume that the bankruptcy judge correctly deemed White's conduct to constitute a battery against Davis. Would the same analysis apply if, upon hearing the gunshot, Davis instinctively (and reasonably) dove to the ground, breaking his arm? What if Tipton, in his haste to avoid being shot, drove his motorcycle into pedestrian *P*, who was crossing the street 50 yards from where White fired his weapon: Could *P* establish a claim of battery against White? If not, why not?

3. *Transferred Intent (III): Across Torts and Victims.* In principle, it is open to courts to combine the foregoing forms of transferred intent to create a third variant, in which the tortfeasor is held liable to actual victim (*AV*) for tort *T1*, even though he acted for the purpose of injuring potential victim (*PV*) in a manner that, had he been successful, would have constituted tort *T2*. Indeed, if the bankruptcy judge credited White's testimony that he shot at Tipton only to scare him, then *White v. Davis* is such a case: White intended to engage in conduct that amounted to an assault of Tipton but ended up being held liable for committing battery against Davis.

4. *Transferred Intent (IV): From Things to Persons.* As noted at the outset of this chapter, commentators often place property torts such as trespass to land and conversion into the category of intentional torts. As a result, they sometimes go so far as to suggest that intent should transfer from these "property torts" to battery and assault. For example, Prosser once suggested that if *D* were knowingly to shoot at a domestic dog, intending to kill it, but ended up shooting person *P* instead, *D*'s intent to commit trespass to "chattel" (i.e., to harm the owned dog) should suffice to provide the necessary intent for *P* to make out a case of battery, even if *D* had no reason to know that *P* was anywhere nearby.

Prosser seems to have based this conclusion primarily on *Corn v. Sheppard*, 229 N.W. 869 (Minn. 1930). There, the defendant sought to avoid liability by arguing that at the time he shot the plaintiff, he was unaware of plaintiff's presence and was instead shooting at a domesticated dog. Noting that the shooting of a domestic animal was unlawful under state statute, and that the discharge of a firearm is an inherently dangerous activity, the court concluded that, "[w]here a person intentionally discharges a firearm for a wrongful purpose and another is hit, he is liable for the injuries inflicted, although he did not intend to hit the other nor even know that any person was within range." *Id.* at 871. Is *Corn* an instance of the sort of broad transferred intent that Prosser describes, or does it impose negligence (or strict) liability on the activity of discharging a firearm?

Compare *Corn* to *Lynn v. Burnette*, 531 S.E. 2d 275 (N.C. Ct. App. 2000). After a confrontation in a parking lot, defendant Burnette fired a gun out of the window of her car at Lynn, who was in his car, striking Lynn in the neck. Lynn sued Burnette after the statute of limitations for battery had run, but prior to the expiration of the limitations period for negligence actions. Burnette admitted in her deposition that she purposely fired in the direction of Lynn's car, but claimed that she was aiming for one of its rear tires and simply missed her target. She thus moved for summary judgment on the ground that the action was time-barred because, in effect, it sought redress for a transferred-intent battery—a harmful touching of a person resulting from an intended trespass to chattel (the intentional shooting at the car).

The court first ruled that the question of what consequences Burnette had intended by firing the gun was settled by her admission, and hence there was no need for a jury to construe what she had in mind when she pulled the trigger. It then concluded, based on Burnette's admission, that Lynn's claim sounded in negligence rather than battery and thus could proceed, apparently rejecting the idea of intent transferring from the tort of trespass to chattels to the tort of battery. Although the court's unwillingness to link trespass and battery in this way was probably sound, its handling of the case in other respects seems problematic, particularly its treatment of the defendant's admission as settling the question of her intent. Shouldn't the factfinder be asked to consider whether Burnette's description of her intent was self-serving? Could not a jury have reasonably concluded that, in shooting at the tire, Burnette acted for the purpose of scaring Lynn, or in the knowledge that she would scare him? If a jury could make that finding, would that change the outcome of the analysis as to whether Burnette committed battery or negligence?

On the problems of transferring intent from property torts to intentional torts, consider the following hypothetical. *D* is invited to a party held on the ground floor of a department store after regular business hours. As he moves among the glamorous crowd, *D* aggressively fondles what he reasonably and sincerely believes to be a mannequin. Much to his horror, he discovers that the "mannequin" is in fact *M*, a model who was hired by the party's organizers to imitate a mannequin. Is it plausible to assert that *D* has committed battery against *M*?

5. *Relational Wrongs and Transferred Intent.* In the *Palsgraf* decision discussed in Chapter 5, Chief Judge Cardozo held that a negligence plaintiff cannot prevail merely by demonstrating careless conduct that happens to injure her. In addition, she must prove that the conduct was careless *as to her.* Does the application of transferred intent in a case such as *White* refute the idea that tort law—or at least intentional tort law—contains a similar requirement? In their *Palsgraf* opinions, both Cardozo and dissenting Judge Andrews discuss transferred intent doctrine in articulating their respective positions on negligence law. If you have read those opinions, consider in light of what you now know whether either's treatment of the doctrine is convincing.

6. *Intentional Torts and Proximate Cause.* Much of Chapter 5 is devoted to explaining the negligence concept of "proximate cause." In a nutshell, it requires a negligence plaintiff to show not only that a defendant's carelessness actually caused her to suffer an injury but also that it caused the injury in the "right way"—i.e., a non-haphazard or non-fortuitous manner. Courts rarely if ever invoke the concept of proximate cause by name when analyzing claims of battery, assault, and the like. Still, there probably are decisions that decline to recognize such claims on grounds that resemble no-proximate-cause grounds.

Consider *Herr v. Booten*, 580 A.2d 1115 (Pa. Super. Ct. 1990). Eric Herr was about to reach the age of 21. He and the defendants—his college roommates and an acquaintance — purchased and consumed large quantities of beer during the day. Later the defendants presented Eric with a bottle of bourbon and induced him to "chug" it. During the ensuing night, Eric died of acute alcohol poisoning. His parents sued the defendants for inducing Eric to drink lethal amounts of alcohol, alleging the torts of negligence and battery. As to the battery claim, the appellate court affirmed the trial court's entry of summary judgment for the defendants, stating that it was "unwilling to view the supplying of an alcoholic beverage to a person as an act intending to cause 'offensive or harmful bodily contact.'" A majority of the court then reversed the trial court's entry of judgment for the defendants on the negligence claim, permitting it to go to the jury primarily on the issues of fault and comparative fault.

What exactly is problematic about the battery claim in *Herr*? The defendants, in providing alcohol to Eric, did not intend to kill him. But it is also quite likely that they *did* intend to cause him to become violently ill. If so, wouldn't the intent element of the tort be satisfied? (Suppose *D* were to force or trick *P* into drinking poison that induced nausea in *P*. *D*'s desire to cause *P* to become sick would presumably suffice to establish the intent element.) If there is not a problem with the intent element, does the difficulty with the claim on behalf of Eric reside instead in the particular way in which the defendants' intentional acts brought about Eric's death — i.e., that their intentional acts did not produce his death "in the right way" *given the role his own actions played*? Perhaps this is what the court was getting at when it reasoned that the defendants' conduct did not amount to an "act that impinges upon th[e] individual's sense of physical dignity or inviolability." If so, then *Herr* arguably is an instance in which a court applies an intentional-tort analogue to the negligence doctrine of "superseding cause," which is the name for a special branch of proximate cause doctrine. *See* Chapter 5.

III. STANDARD DEFENSES TO BATTERY AND ASSAULT

It is sometimes open to parties sued for assault and battery — as well as other torts — to defeat liability notwithstanding the claimant's establishment of a prima facie case. This is because the defendant can establish his entitlement to what the law recognizes as an "affirmative defense" to such a claim. This section focuses on certain important affirmative defenses that are available to those sued for assault and battery. (These same defenses are available to defendants alleged to have committed other intentional torts as well, such as false imprisonment.)

Defenses to assault and battery typically assert that the alleged tortfeasor was *privileged* to act as she did, even though her conduct was prima facie tortious. Privileges recognized by tort law in turn tend to consist of *justifications*, as opposed to *excuses*. To claim a justification for one's conduct is to claim that one was entitled to engage in the conduct, notwithstanding its apparent wrongfulness. So, for example, a person sued for battery who asserts the privilege of self-defense is claiming that she was within her rights to cause intentionally a harmful touching of another because she actually and reasonably believed that doing so was necessary to protect herself from an imminent harmful or inappropriate touching. By contrast, when an actor asserts an excuse, she alleges that something about her condition or circumstances—for example, her diminished mental capacity—entitles her to an exemption from the rules of right conduct. As we have seen already in *Wagner*, tort law is generally reluctant to recognize excuses.

As is the case for claims of negligence (*see* Chapter 7), the burden of pleading and proving affirmative defenses usually rests on the alleged tortfeasor—if he fails to raise them by the appropriate procedures, or to prove them, they will be lost.* However, some states' laws treat what are treated here as defenses as elements of the prima facie case. This is particularly so with the defense of *consent*, to which we turn first. Many states require *plaintiffs* to prove *absence of consent* rather than leaving it to the defendant to prove that the victim consented. Given that torts such as battery concern, at their core, the subjection of another to unwanted touchings, etc., it is perhaps not surprising that the issue of consent is sometimes singled out for this special treatment.

Before considering consent and other defenses available to tortfeasors who have committed assault or battery, it will be helpful to highlight the *unavailability* of another potential defense—*comparative fault*. As explained briefly in Chapter 1, and more extensively in Chapter 7, it is open to a defendant being sued for the tort of *negligence* to argue in defense that the plaintiff's own fault contributed to her being injured. Thus, for example, car driver *D*, who carelessly runs over and injures pedestrian *P*, may attempt to establish that *P* was herself careless by stepping off the curb without checking for traffic. If *D* can establish that *P*'s carelessness, along with *D*'s, played a role in causing *P*'s injuries, then—depending on the rules of the particular jurisdiction and the factfinder's assignment of percentage fault to *D* and *P*—the effect of this showing will be to reduce *P*'s recovery or to bar her suit altogether.

For torts such as assault and battery, the longstanding black letter rule is that comparative fault doctrine has no place. For example, suppose *B* purposely induces *A* to ingest a drink containing poison. Under the majority rule, even if *B* can prove that, had *A* exercised reasonable care, he would have detected the poison (e.g., by taking notice of the poison's powerful bitter odor), *B* cannot invoke comparative fault to reduce *A*'s damages or bar his claim. However, some courts and legislatures have recognized, and some commentators have urged, that comparative fault be recognized as a distinct defense to intentional tort claims. *See* Dan B. Dobbs, *The Law of Torts* § 206, at 517-522 (2000) (discussing the issue). Moreover, it may sometimes be the case that evidence of a victim's carelessness can be offered as relevant to the proof of a defense that actually is recognized in intentional tort law. Thus, evidence that a victim acted with apparent disregard for his physical well-being might, in some circumstances, support an inference that he implicitly consented to being subject to defendant's wrongful conduct.

A. Consent

The doctrine of consent turns on the idea that a plaintiff cannot prevail on her tort claim because she has agreed, under appropriate conditions, to endure a bodily

* For a sample answer that raises affirmative defenses, see Appendix.

contact, or an apprehension of contact, or a confinement, that would otherwise be tortious. As we will see, consent can be communicated *expressly*, through a written or spoken statement, or it can be communicated *implicitly*, through conduct.

Koffman v. Garnett

574 S.E.2d 258 (Va. 2003)

LACY, J. In this case we consider whether the trial court properly dismissed the plaintiffs' second amended motion for judgment for failure to state causes of action for gross negligence, assault, and battery.

Because this case was decided on demurrer, we take as true all material facts properly pleaded in the motion for judgment and all inferences properly drawn from those facts.

In the fall of 2000, Andrew W. Koffman, a 13-year old middle school student at a public school in Botetourt County, began participating on the school's football team. It was Andy's first season playing organized football, and he was positioned as a third-string defensive player. James Garnett was employed by the Botetourt County School Board as an assistant coach for the football team and was responsible for the supervision, training, and instruction of the team's defensive players.

The team lost its first game of the season. Garnett was upset by the defensive players' inadequate tackling in that game and became further displeased by what he perceived as inadequate tackling during the first practice following the loss.

Garnett ordered Andy to hold a football and "stand upright and motionless" so that Garnett could explain the proper tackling technique to the defensive players. Then Garnett, without further warning, thrust his arms around Andy's body, lifted him "off his feet by two feet or more," and "slamm[ed]" him to the ground. Andy weighed 144 pounds, while Garnett weighed approximately 260 pounds. The force of the tackle broke the humerus bone in Andy's left arm. During prior practices, no coach had used physical force to instruct players on rules or techniques of playing football.

In his second amended motion for judgment, Andy, by his father and next friend, Richard Koffman, and Andy's parents, Richard and Rebecca Koffman, individually, (collectively "the Koffmans") alleged that Andy was injured as a result of Garnett's simple and gross negligence and intentional acts of assault and battery. . . . The trial court dismissed the action, finding that . . . the facts alleged were insufficient to state causes of action for gross negligence, assault, or battery because the instruction and playing of football are "inherently dangerous and always potentially violent."

In this appeal, the Koffmans . . . assert that they pled sufficient facts in their second amended motion for judgment to sustain their claims of gross negligence,* assault, and battery.

* [Virginia law immunizes public employees from liability for official acts involving ordinary negligence. Thus, the Koffmans were required to prove at least gross negligence on Garnett's part. — EDS.]

I.

. . . [The Court first concluded that the trial court had erred in ruling as a matter of law that Garnett could not have acted with "gross negligence" toward Koffman. Under Virginia law, public employees cannot be held liable for simple (ordinary) negligence, but can be held liable for "gross" negligence.]

The disparity in size between Garnett and Andy was obvious to Garnett. Because of his authority as a coach, Garnett must have anticipated that Andy would comply with his instructions to stand in a non-defensive, upright, and motionless position. Under these circumstances, Garnett proceeded to aggressively tackle the much smaller, inexperienced student football player, by lifting him more than two feet from the ground and slamming him into the turf. According to the Koffmans' allegations, no coach had tackled any player previously so there was no reason for Andy to expect to be tackled by Garnett, nor was Andy warned of the impending tackle or of the force Garnett would use.

. . . The facts alleged in this case, however, go beyond the circumstances of simply being tackled in the course of participating in organized football. Here Garnett's knowledge of his greater size and experience, his instruction implying that Andy was not to take any action to defend himself from the force of a tackle, the force he used during the tackle, and Garnett's previous practice of not personally using force to demonstrate or teach football technique could lead a reasonable person to conclude that, in this instance, Garnett's actions were imprudent and were taken in utter disregard for the safety of the player involved. Because reasonable persons could disagree on this issue, a jury issue was presented, and the trial court erred in holding that, as a matter of law, the second amended motion for judgment was inadequate to state a claim for gross negligence.

II.

The trial court held that the second amended motion for judgment was insufficient as a matter of law to establish causes of action for the torts of assault and battery. We begin by identifying the elements of these two independent torts. *See* Charles E. Friend, *Personal Injury Law in Virginia* § 6.2.1 (2d ed. 1998). The tort of assault consists of an act intended to cause either harmful or offensive contact with another person or apprehension of such contact, and that creates in that other person's mind a reasonable apprehension of an imminent battery. Restatement (Second) of Torts § 21 (1965); Friend § 6.3.1 at 226; Fowler V. Harper, et al., *The Law of Torts* § 3.5 at 3:18-:19 (3d ed. Cum. Supp. 2003).

The tort of battery is an unwanted touching which is neither consented to, excused, nor justified. Although these two torts "go together like ham and eggs," the difference between them is "that between physical contact and the mere apprehension of it. One may exist without the other." W. Page Keeton, *Prosser and Keeton on Torts* § 10 at 46; *see also* Friend § 6.3.

The Koffmans' second amended motion for judgment does not include an allegation that Andy had any apprehension of an immediate battery. This allegation cannot be supplied by inference because any inference of Andy's apprehension is discredited by the affirmative allegations that Andy had no warning of an imminent forceful tackle by Garnett. The Koffmans argue that a reasonable inference of apprehension can be found "in the very short period of time that it took the coach to lift Andy into the air and throw him violently to the ground." At this point, however, the battery alleged by the Koffmans was in progress. Accordingly, we find that the pleadings were insufficient as a matter of law to establish [an assault].

The second amended motion for judgment is sufficient, however, to establish a . . . battery. The Koffmans pled that Andy consented to physical contact with players "of like age and experience" and that neither Andy nor his parents expected or consented to his "participation in aggressive contact tackling by the adult coaches." Further, the Koffmans pled that, in the past, coaches had not tackled players as a method of instruction. Garnett asserts that, by consenting to play football, Andy consented to be tackled, by either other football players or by the coaches.

Whether Andy consented to be tackled by Garnett in the manner alleged was a matter of fact. Based on the allegations in the Koffmans' second amended motion for judgment, reasonable persons could disagree on whether Andy gave such consent. Thus, we find that the trial court erred in holding that the Koffmans' second amended motion for judgment was insufficient as a matter of law to establish a claim for battery. . . .*

Kinser, J. (concurring in part, dissenting in part). I agree with the majority opinion except with regard to the issue of consent as it pertains to the intentional tort of battery. In my view, the second amended motion for judgment filed by the plaintiffs, Andrew W. Koffman, by his father and next friend, and Richard Koffman and Rebecca Koffman, individually, was insufficient as a matter of law to state a claim for battery.

Absent fraud, consent is generally a defense to an alleged battery. In the context of this case, "[t]aking part in a game manifests a willingness to submit to such bodily contacts or restrictions of liberty as are permitted by its rules or usages." Restatement (Second) of Torts § 50, cmt. b (1965), quoted in Thompson v. McNeill, 53 Ohio St. 3d 102, 559 N.E.2d 705, 708 (1990). . . . However, participating in a particular sport "does not manifest consent to contacts which are prohibited by rules or usages of the game if such rules or usages are designed to protect the participants and not merely to secure the better playing of the game as a test of skill." Restatement (Second) of Torts § 50, cmt. b (1965) quoted in *Thompson*. . . .

The thrust of the plaintiffs' allegations is that they did not consent to "Andy's participation in aggressive contact tackling by the adult coaches" but that they consented only to Andy's engaging "in a contact sport with other children of like age and experience." They further alleged that the coaches had not previously tackled the players when instructing them about the rules and techniques of football.

It is notable, in my opinion, that the plaintiffs admitted in their pleading that Andy's coach was "responsible . . . for the supervision, training and instruction of

* Because we have concluded that a cause of action for an intentional tort was sufficiently pled, on remand, the Koffmans may pursue their claim for punitive damages.

the defensive players." It cannot be disputed that one responsibility of a football coach is to minimize the possibility that players will sustain "something more than slight injury" while playing the sport. Vendrell v. School District No. 26C, Malheur County, 233 Or. 1, 376 P.2d 406, 413 (1962). A football coach cannot be expected "to extract from the game the body clashes that cause bruises, jolts and hard falls." *Id.* Instead, a coach should ensure that players are able to "withstand the shocks, blows and other rough treatment with which they would meet in actual play" by making certain that players are in "sound physical condition," are issued proper protective equipment, and are "taught and shown how to handle [themselves] while in play." *Id.* The instruction on how to handle themselves during a game should include demonstrations of proper tackling techniques. *Id.* By voluntarily participating in football, Andy and his parents necessarily consented to instruction by the coach on such techniques. The alleged battery occurred during that instruction.

The plaintiffs alleged that they were not aware that Andy's coach would use physical force to instruct on the rules and techniques of football since neither he nor the other coaches had done so in the past. Surely, the plaintiffs are not claiming that the scope of their consent changed from day to day depending on the coaches' instruction methods during prior practices. Moreover, they did not allege that they were told that the coaches would not use physical demonstrations to instruct the players.

Additionally, the plaintiffs did not allege that the tackle itself violated any rule or usage of the sport of football. Nor did they plead that Andy could not have been tackled by a larger, physically stronger, and more experienced player either during a game or practice. Tackling and instruction on proper tackling techniques are aspects of the sport of football to which a player consents when making a decision to participate in the sport.

In sum, I conclude that the plaintiffs did not sufficiently plead a claim for battery. We must remember that acts that might give rise to a battery on a city street will not do so in the context of the sport of football. We must also not blur the lines between gross negligence and battery because the latter is an intentional tort. I agree fully that the plaintiffs alleged sufficient facts to proceed with their claim for gross negligence. . . .

NOTES AND QUESTIONS

1. *Express Consent.* To the extent Koffman consented to harmful contact, he did so implicitly, by voluntarily participating on the football team. In many other instances, consent is expressly stated, either in a writing or by oral statement. For example, in a non-emergency room setting, surgical patients will typically be required to complete and sign a form indicating their consent to being subjected to a harmful contact (namely, the surgical procedure itself). These forms usually also require the patient to attest that she has been informed of all relevant risks that attend the surgery. (See the discussion of informed consent claims in Chapter 3.) There is an example of such a form below.

Consent to Operation, Treatment, or Other Procedure

1. (1) Date: ______________ Time: ______________ A.M ______________ P.M.
   (2) I authorize and consent to the performance upon
   ________________ of the following operation, treatment, or procedure.
   NAME OF PATIENT

   ____

   ____

   ____

   to be performed by Dr. ________________ and staff.
2. The nature, advisability, and purpose of the operation, treatment, or other procedure have been explained to me, together with the benefits hoped to result and the material risks. Alternatives to the operation, treatment, or other procedure, if any, and the risks of such alternatives have been explained to me. I understand the explanations that have been given me, and I understand that no guarantee is offered as to the results of the operation, treatment, or other procedure.
3. I authorize and consent to the operation, treatment, or other procedure by the physician and assistants to the physician performing the operation, treatment, or other procedure, by the nursing staff and by other employees of the ABC Medical Center.
4. I authorize and consent to the administration of anesthesia by the anesthesiology staff of ABC Medical Center.
5. I understand that during the course of the operation, treatment, or other procedure unforeseen conditions may be found that make an extension of the original operation, treatment, or other procedure advisable. I authorize and consent to such extension or other operation, treatment, or other procedure as is advisable in the professional judgment of my physician or physicians.
6. I authorize and consent to the disposal, use, retention, or donation by the ABC Medical Center at its discretion of all tissues, materials, and substances that would normally be removed in the course of the operation, treatment, or other procedure.
7. I understand that my physician has determined that I require/may require transfusion of blood and/or blood products. I understand that the blood products may include risks of fever and chills (about 1 in 200), allergic reaction with itching, hives (about 1 in 200), and rare severe allergic reaction (about 1 in 25,000), resulting in death (less than 1 in 1,000,000). In rare instances there may be a chance of infectious blood borne diseases, including Hepatitis B (about 1 in 180,000), Hepatitis C (less than 1 in 1,600,000), HIV/AIDS (about 1 in 1,900,000), as well as other unforeseen risks. I understand that the Red Cross and other blood banks use precautions to minimize these risks by screening the blood/blood products and in blood typing.
8. I have been provided with information regarding transfusions and have had the opportunity to discuss the risks, benefits, alternatives, and risk of no transfusions with my physician. I hereby authorize and consent to the administration of blood/blood products if deemed medically necessary by my physician(s).

________________________________ ___________ ___________A.M. P.M.

SIGNATURE (PATIENT/PATIENT'S LEGALLY AUTHORIZED REPRESENTATIVE — DATE — TIME

____

WITNESS

* * * * * * * * * * * * * * * * * *

I met with ______________ and fully discussed the above-described procedure. Consent cannot be obtained due to an emergency of the following nature:

____

____

____

________________________________ ___________ ___________ A.M. P.M.

PHYSICIAN SIGNATURE — DATE — TIME

2. *Implied Consent.* Voluntary participation in contact sports is a common example of implicit consent to harmful contacts. There are innumerable other settings in which a person can be deemed to have consented to contact that might otherwise be tortious. For example, persons who enter crowded trains and buses will be deemed to have consented to at least some intentionally caused jostlings and other contacts, such as being pushed by another as he tries to cram his way onto the vehicle. We saw above that the Utah Supreme Court in *Wagner* (Section II) further suggested that each of us implicitly consents to a range of everyday contacts just by virtue of being out in the world.

In certain situations, a history of dealings between the parties will support a finding of implicit consent to contacts beyond ordinary, everyday contacts. For example, if two persons have in the past playfully punched or shoved one another in certain situations, that fact may permit an inference of consent to similar contact in a subsequent similar situation. The defense of implied consent thus often requires judges and juries to make judgments turning on factors such as the age, gender, and sophistication of the parties, their relationship, if any, and various other circumstances associated with their interaction.

3. *Actual Consent Versus Objective Indicia of Consent.* Suppose that *D* sincerely believes that *P* has consented to being harmfully touched, when in fact *D* is mistaken because he misunderstood something that *P* said, or because he misread certain non-verbal cues. If *D* causes a harmful touching of *P* and *P* sues for battery, may *D* avoid liability on the ground that he believed that *P* had consented? Or must consent actually have been given?

Courts have typically adopted a third route, which is to bar the imposition of liability on *D* only if, on the basis of the plaintiff's conduct, he *actually* and *reasonably* believed that *P* has consented to the contact. *O'Brien v. Cunard S.S. Co.*, 28 N.E. 266 (Mass. 1891) provides a famous illustration of this doctrine. O'Brien, a young immigrant, was vaccinated on board defendant's ship as it brought her to New York. After suffering an adverse reaction, she sued for battery, alleging that she never consented to the injection. The court concluded that the ship's doctor reasonably inferred that O'Brien consented by virtue of standing in a line of people receiving the vaccination and by holding out her arm as did others in the line. Thus, even if a jury were to believe that O'Brien's actual intent was to refuse the vaccination, the ship's owner would be free from liability because its doctor actually and reasonably inferred consent under the circumstances.

What justifies a rule that would permit an injurer to escape liability on the ground that he reasonably but mistakenly perceived consent on the part of the victim? Why should the risk of error with regard to consent fall on the victim rather than the injurer? According to the Second Restatement, a reasonable but mistaken inference of consent that derives from a source *other than the conduct of the plaintiff* will not suffice to establish a consent defense. *See* Restatement (Second) of Torts § 51, illus. 1 (1965) (surgeon is subject to battery liability given absence of patient consent to a certain procedure even though, because of a mistake by hospital staff, the surgeon reasonably believed that consent had been given).

4. *Implied Consent Versus Hypothetical Consent.* As explained in the preceding notes, a defendant can claim that his touching of the plaintiff was privileged on the basis of plaintiff's implicit actual consent and, in some instances, on the basis of his

reasonable but mistaken perception that plaintiff has consented. Can a defendant go further and argue that he was privileged to commit what would otherwise be a battery of the plaintiff on the ground that the touching was in the plaintiff's best interests, and therefore is one to which the plaintiff "would have" or "should have" consented, even though she did not?

As *Koffman* implicitly demonstrates, the answer is no. Suppose that *D* and *P* are adult friends and that *D* knows that *P*, much to *P*'s own regret, is a timid soul who is inhibited from undertaking various potentially pleasurable activities out of excessive fear of physical injury. As they are walking together one day, *D* suddenly pushes *P* down a steep hill, a fall that causes *P* contusions and a broken finger. Even if a jury were prepared (implausibly) to believe that *D*'s action (by demonstrating to *P* that minor physical injuries are not something about which to be terrified) was in *P*'s best interests, and therefore an act for which *P* might eventually be grateful, *D* has no grounds for claiming privilege. Indeed, battery law's emphasis on actual consent rests precisely on the rejection of this sort of paternalistic justification for touchings. (However, as the next case explains, an intended contact that would otherwise be a battery can sometimes be justified on the distinct and narrower ground that the defendant actually and reasonably believed it to be necessary to save the plaintiff from imminent physical harm.)*

5. *Interaction of Intent and Consent.* In *Mullins v. Parkview Hosp., Inc.*, 865 N.E.2d 608 (Ind. 2007), the plaintiff was admitted to the hospital for a hysterectomy. She told her gynecologist that she wanted privacy during the procedure, and crossed out the portion of the written consent form that read: "I consent to the presence of healthcare learners." Additionally, she received assurances from the anesthesiologist present at her procedure that he would be handling her anesthesia personally. She then signed a consent form that included a provision stating: "I understand that my anaesthesia care will be given to me by the undersigned or a physician privileged to practice anaesthesia." After plaintiff was anaesthetized, a student in a training program entered the operating room with a hospital employee/preceptor. The preceptor asked if the student could intubate Mullins (i.e., place a tube down the patient's trachea). The anesthesiologist assented. In performing the procedure, the student, who had never previously attempted an intubation, lacerated plaintiff's esophagus. That injury necessitated subsequent surgery, followed by a month-long hospital stay.

Plaintiff brought claims of negligence, medical malpractice, and battery against the student, the anesthesiologist, the gynecologist, their practice groups, and the hospital. The trial court granted summary judgment to all defendants. The intermediate appellate court reinstated plaintiff's battery claims against the student, the anesthesiologist, and the gynecologist. The Indiana Supreme court affirmed this ruling as to the

* The inefficacy of "hypothetical consent" relates to another feature of tort law as it bears on the intent element of battery, assault, and other torts. This feature is sometimes expressed as a distinction between the *motives* for which one touches another and the *intent* with which one touches another. In the above hypothetical, *D's* motives arguably were good — he sincerely meant his touching of *P* to confer a benefit on *P*. Still, he acted with intent to touch *P* in a harmful way, and in the eyes of tort law that intent is not somehow undermined or negated by the fact that *D* formed and acted on this intent out of beneficent motives.

anaesthesiologist and the gynecologist, but reversed as to the claim against the student, thereby upholding the trial court's dismissal of that claim. In support of dismissal, the court emphasized that the student had no reason to suspect that plaintiff had insisted on modifying the standard consent form. The court then concluded that, because plaintiff could not show that the student "touched [her] with the intent to cause harm," this battery claim had to fail. *Id.* at 611.

Is this last holding correct? If so, can it be harmonized with *Wagner* and the authorities it cites? Could the Indiana Supreme Court have affirmed the dismissal of the claim against the student on the alternative ground that the student acted in the reasonable but mistaken belief that the patient had consented to have trainees participate in her treatment? Would this justification hold even if the court had ordered the dismissal of the battery claims against the doctors?

6. *Fraud and Coercion.* A tortfeasor cannot benefit from the consent defense if he secures the victim's consent by misrepresentation or other forms of deceit. So, for example, if *D* induces *V* to imbibe a poisonous drink by representing that it is wine, *D* cannot invoke consent as a defense. Some smokers have attempted to argue that they suffered a battery (or, alternatively, a fraud resulting in physical injury) at the hands of cigarette manufacturers by being induced to inhale toxic chemicals on the basis of the manufacturers' misrepresentations, including the failure to disclose the presence of toxic additives such as ammonia. *See* Naegele v. R.J. Reynolds Tobacco Co., 50 P.3d 769 (Cal. 2002) (reversing summary dismissal of claims by an ex-smoker for fraud). In certain instances, the injurer may owe the victim an affirmative duty to disclose information relevant to the victim's decision to consent, such that failure to disclose will constitute fraud. For an interesting and perhaps unusual application of this rule, *see* Neal v. Neal, 873 P.2d 871 (Idaho 1994) (in suit by a wife against an adulterous husband for battery, the jury may find that the husband fraudulently secured the wife's consent to sexual intercourse by failing to disclose to her that he was having an affair).

Consent secured through coercion by the tortfeasor — for example, through physical violence or threats of violence — also will not count as a defense to a suit for battery. Likewise, consent is not a defense if (1) the victim lacks the ability or judgment necessary to give meaningful consent, and (2) a reasonable person in the position of the tortfeasor would perceive this lack of capacity. Lack of capacity may result from youth, mental incompetence, or some other condition or circumstance. *See, e.g.*, Elkington v. Foust, 618 P.2d 37 (Utah 1980) (stepfather not entitled to jury instruction on consent as a defense against a claim for sexual battery of a minor plaintiff).

7. *Subtler Forms of Coercion and Incapacity.* Apparent consent will sometimes be deemed ineffective if the defendant had reason to know that the consent was not freely given. Often in such cases a critical issue will be whether the alleged tortfeasor occupied a position of power or authority in relation to the victim. Thus, a patient who sues her therapist for battery based on a "consensual" sexual encounter between them can argue that the therapist should have known that the patient was not in a position to make a genuinely free choice about having sex with the therapist. For a fractured decision addressing several issues related to consent, see *Reavis v. Slominski*, 551 N.W.2d 528 (Neb. 1996). There, a dentist's receptionist sued her employer for battery after they had

sex at an office party. A few years earlier, while also working as a receptionist for Slominski, Reavis had at times acceded to Slominski's persistent sexual advances. In the instance that took place at the party, Reavis initially resisted, but eventually acceded. Following the encounter, Reavis, guilt-ridden, informed her husband of it and then attempted suicide.

In her suit for battery, Reavis claimed that she acquiesced to sex with Slominski out of fear of losing her job, and because sexual abuse she suffered as a child had habituated her into coping with sexual aggression by acquiescing. The plurality opinion in *Reavis* concluded that expert testimony as to the effects of the past abuse could be admitted on the issue of whether Reavis lacked the capacity genuinely to consent, and whether Slominski, based on their encounters a few years earlier, had reason to know of, and hence was exploiting, this vulnerability when he accosted her at the party. Concurring justices held that the evidence of abuse should not have been admitted but that a jury could find that Reavis's consent was not voluntary because she reasonably feared that she would lose her job if she did not acquiesce. Several dissenters maintained that the evidence on past abuse was irrelevant and that a threat of being fired is, as a matter of law, not sufficiently coercive to vitiate consent to sexual intercourse. (On this last point, note that even if threats to fire employees are not sufficient to vitiate consent in an action for battery, they often are sufficient to generate claims for sexual harassment under federal laws applicable to employers of a certain size. *See* Chapter 10.)

8. Scope of Consent. As *Koffman* indicates, even when a court determines that the victim has expressly or implicitly consented to some harmful or inappropriate contact, the question remains as to whether the contact in question was of the sort to which the plaintiff consented. While a sport's own rules can be relevant to this question, they are not determinative: certain contacts outside the rules will be deemed consensual. For example, even football tackles that earn penalties will rarely provide the basis for a successful battery claim. Conversely, contacts that do not violate any formal rules may still amount to batteries. For an opinion that cites several battery claims arising out of professional sports, see Green v. Pro Football, Inc., 31 F. Supp. 3d 714, 718, 725 (D. Md. 2014). In *Green* the federal district court held that allegations by a professional football player that he suffered a career-ending injury as a result of an opposing team's having adopted a "bounty" system — a scheme whereby players were rewarded for injuring their opponents — stated a claim for battery.

In *Mohr v. Williams*, 104 N.W. 12 (Minn. 1905), the plaintiff voluntarily underwent surgery to improve her hearing in one ear. During the operation, while the plaintiff was unconscious, the surgeon determined that the ear in question was not diseased, but that the plaintiff's other ear was in need of surgical repair, so he proceeded to operate on it. Despite the fact that procedure apparently went well and occurred with the permission of Mohr's family physician, who was in the operating room at the time, Mohr sued the surgeon for battery and prevailed after the court determined that the surgeon had exceeded the scope of Mohr's consent by operating on a different part of the body than the part that she had consented to have touched. Notice how the consent form, Note 1, *supra* deals with this potential source of liability. The negligence case of

Largey v. Rothman from Chapter 3, which primarily concerns the doctrine of informed consent, also raises the issue of whether Ms. Largey, in consenting to a biopsy, had consented to the removal of some of her lymph nodes.

9. Consent to Illegal Activities. As they sometimes do in connection with contractual assumptions of risk, see Chapter 7, courts will in certain situations deem otherwise valid consents void as against public policy. In his capacity as co-Reporter for the Second Restatement, John Wade disapprovingly noted in 1979 that most courts at that time deemed consent *ineffective* if the consented-to conduct amounted to a crime. Thus, if two persons chose to engage in a fistfight that constituted a criminal breach of the peace, either could sue the other for battery. *See* Restatement (Second) of Torts § 892C (1979) (Reporter's note).

In place of this approach, the Restatement maintains that consent to conduct constituting a crime should suffice to establish a defense to a tort claim unless the conduct in question was rendered criminal by the legislature in part to protect the consenting person from his own choices. For example, if *A* and *B* were to participate in an unlicensed boxing match in which *A* severely injured *B*, a court applying Section 892(c) might hold that *B* can sue *A* for battery notwithstanding *B*'s consent to participate in the fight on the ground that the licensing scheme aimed to protect persons such as *B* by reducing the risk of gross mismatches, having competent referees to regulate the contest, etc. *See id.* § 892C, illus. 9.

B. Self-Defense and Defense of Others

When consent operates as an effective defense it does so out of respect for individual autonomy. At least under certain conditions, a competent and informed individual is accorded by tort law a right to choose to experience treatment at the hands of others that, absent the exercise of that choice, would be wrongful. The remaining defenses to be considered in this chapter do not derive from the law's respect for individuals' capacity to choose. Instead, they recognize that there are situations in which an actor is entitled to commit a tort such as battery against another.

Perhaps the most familiar of these entitlements consists of a privilege to use force against another to defend oneself — for example, the privilege to strike another to ward off the other's physical attack. Self-defense in one sense sits quite comfortably within tort doctrine. Essentially, the privilege permits a person to protect the very bodily integrity that is meant to be protected and vindicated by torts such as battery. Yet, in another sense, the fit is potentially awkward. One of the original and most basic functions of tort law is to provide legal redress for victims of wrongs as a substitute for private violence. To the extent tort recognizes a broad privilege of self-defense, it at least runs the risk of sanctioning resort to forcible "self-help." The difficulty of defining lines that will permit victims to protect themselves without sanctioning private violence is reflected in the various doctrines that determine the application of the self-defense privilege. The same difficulties are also apparent (perhaps to an even greater extent) when we encounter in Section III.C the related privilege to use force to protect one's property interests.

Haeussler v. De Loretto

240 P.2d 654 (Cal. App. 1952)

VALLÉE, J. Appeal by plaintiff from a judgment for defendant in an action for damages for assault and battery. The cause was tried by the court without a jury.

The evidence, stated in the light most favorable to the prevailing litigant, discloses that on May 21, 1950, about 10:30 P.M., plaintiff went to the home of defendant, a neighbor, to inquire about his dog which was missing and which frequently had gone to defendant's home. The dog had been the subject of disagreement between the wives of the parties on several previous occasions. When defendant, in response to plaintiff's knock, opened the door, the dog ran out from inside the house. Defendant testified that plaintiff immediately started talking in a loud tone of voice, told him he did not want defendant or his wife to feed the dog or keep it at their house; that plaintiff kept "waving his hands, and while he talked, his face was pretty flushed and he was pretty excited, like he had been drinking, and he kept arguing with me and one word led to another, and I don't know the man, but I do know of him. I know he had trouble with the Teamster's Union and [that another man named] Frowiss and him beat up a couple of friends of mine, and I got a little afraid, and towards the end, after I had asked him to go three times, and he kept waving his hands, I thought he was going to strike me, and I struck him or pushed him, and I went in and closed the door." Plaintiff called the police but no arrest was made nor was any criminal action had.

The court found that plaintiff precipitated the argument; defendant ordered plaintiff to leave his premises; plaintiff advanced threateningly toward defendant; defendant struck him once; two of plaintiff's teeth were loosened, necessitating dental care; defendant used reasonable force in defense of himself and in removing plaintiff from his premises; plaintiff failed to prove by a preponderance of evidence that defendant used or attempted to use wilful and unlawful force upon the person of plaintiff.

The issue of self defense was pleaded by defendant and litigated. The determination of which of the two parties precipitated the fight, and whether defendant acted in self defense, and whether in so doing he used more force than was reasonably necessary under the circumstances, were questions for the trier of fact. One who is involved in an altercation with another has the right to use such force as is necessary to protect himself from bodily injury, and the question of the amount of force justifiable under the circumstances of a particular case is also one for the trier of fact. As the court found that defendant used reasonable force in defense of himself, it necessarily follows the force used was not wilful or unlawful and that plaintiff failed to sustain the burden of proof. Since the conflicts in the evidence were resolved in defendant's favor, and the foregoing narration of the evidence supports the findings, this court may not disturb the judgment.

NOTES AND QUESTIONS

1. *Self-Defense, Provocation, and Imminence.* Self-defense is available to a victim who actually and reasonably believes it is necessary to injure another to avoid *imminent*

injuries to herself such as harmful contact or confinement. A longstanding and fierce debate in criminal law concerns whether a battered spouse, almost always a woman who has been subjugated and repeatedly abused by her husband, may claim self-defense as a justification for homicide even though the killing of the abusive spouse occurred at a moment when that spouse posed no imminent threat. *See* Dan B. Dobbs, *The Law of Torts* § 72, at 165-166 (2000) (discussing the debate).

The privilege of self-defense typically applies when the injury threatened consists of physical harm, inappropriate touching, or confinement. By contrast, it does not apply if the conduct in question threatens only to result in defamation of, or distress to, the victim. Relatedly, the law does not privilege the use of force to respond to nonthreatening provocations, such as tauntings or teasings. In many jurisdictions, a person who immediately precipitates the confrontation in which defensive force is used is barred from invoking the self-defense privilege unless, after precipitating it, the injurer disengages, or manifests an intent to disengage, such that his provocation ceases to provide the main impetus for the confrontation. Gortarez v. Smitty's Super Valu, Inc., 680 P.2d 807 (Ariz. 1984) (if defendant's security guard is found to have unjustifiably induced fight with patron in which patron was injured, the guard cannot claim self-defense).

In *Landry v. Bellanger*, 851 So. 2d 943 (La. 2003), the Louisiana Supreme Court considered the issues of provocation and self-defense in relation to one another. Two acquaintances were drinking in a bar. The victim became increasingly belligerent toward the defendant. Eventually, the defendant asked the plaintiff to step outside, apparently in an effort to avoid a further scene in the bar. When plaintiff continued to harangue the defendant and bumped him, the defendant punched the plaintiff in the face, which caused the plaintiff to fall, resulting in severe injuries. The state's high court rejected earlier Louisiana decisions holding that a victim's initial provocation of a fight functions to bar him from suing the defendant for injuries caused by the fight. It next concluded that although Louisiana does not recognize comparative fault as a defense to a claim of battery, a jury would nonetheless be entitled to apportion responsibility between a batterer and a provoking victim on the ground that a victim's provocation of a fight is not a mere act of carelessness, but instead an "intentional" act. Finally, it held that this particular plaintiff's suit was barred because the defendant's punch was not merely a response to a provocation, but a reasonable effort to defend himself against plaintiff's physical aggression.

2. *Objectivity of the Threat.* An injurer may invoke self-defense only if he actually and reasonably perceives an imminent risk of physical injury to himself. Suppose that *D* mistakenly but reasonably believes that the person walking purposefully and quickly toward him in the darkness is his psychotic and violent enemy *E*, when in fact it is innocent delivery person *P*, who resembles *E*. If *D* punches *P*, *D* can claim the privilege of self-defense as against a battery claim by *P*. Conversely, if *D* recognizes *P* or should recognize *P* for who he actually is, yet punches him, *D* will have no defense, even if he harbored the sincere but unreasonable belief that delivery persons routinely attack people. As with the determination of reasonableness in negligence law, the reasonableness of *D*'s perception of the threat to him is judged in light of the surrounding

circumstances. Thus a jury can give *D* greater leeway to respond forcibly to perceived threats in an emergency situation than in a situation more conducive to the exercise of prudence.

3. *Proportionality and Deadly Force.* As *Haeussler* indicates, the injurer's response must be reasonable not only in being grounded in a reasonable perception of imminent harm but also in consisting of an appropriate or proportional response to the perceived threat. The issue of proportionality arises most starkly when the alleged tortfeasor uses deadly force, that is, force intended or calculated to cause death. As a rule, the use of this degree of force is only justified when the injurer actually and reasonably perceives that the victim is threatening him with imminent death or serious bodily injury. *See* Price v. Gray's Guard Serv., Inc., 298 So. 2d 461 (Fla. Ct. App.) (a security guard who was attacked from behind and being beaten with his own club was privileged to shoot his assailants), *cert. denied*, 305 So. 2d 208 (Fla. 1974). By contrast, a victim who reasonably perceives that he is about to be slapped, or subjected to a nonharmful yet offensive battery, or nonviolent confinement in the manager's office of a department store, will not be able to invoke self-defense to justify the use of *deadly* force.

4. *Conditional Threats.* Suppose *A* approaches *B* from behind as *B* is withdrawing cash from an ATM during daylight hours on a quiet but not deserted street. *A* says to *B*: "Give me your money, and you won't get hurt." May *B* use force against *A*? Deadly force? According to the Second Restatement, *A* is privileged as a matter of law to use *non*-deadly force, and is privileged to use deadly force unless the factfinder determines that *A* actually or reasonably believed that he could in fact secure his personal safety by handing the money to *B*. Restatement (Second) of Torts §§ 63, 65(3) (1965).

5. *Dwellings, Retreat, and "Stand Your Ground" Laws.* Suppose *S*, sleeping upstairs alone in her home, awakens to hear someone coming up the stairs toward her room. Is *S* entitled to reach for the gun in her night table and fire it the moment the person enters her room? The Second Torts Restatement suggests that a person may use deadly force whenever she is being "attacked" in her "dwelling." Restatement (Second) of Torts § 65(2), at 108-09 (1965). Now suppose *A* hears a commotion near the entrance to a barn located on her property 100 feet from her dwelling. If *A* spies a person attempting to break into the barn, may she shoot at him? *See* Goldfuss v. Davidson, 679 N.E.2d 1099 (Ohio 1997) (defendant not entitled to a self-defense instruction on facts similar to these).

The propriety of using deadly force is sometimes bound up with the notion of "safe retreat"—the thought being that, if one actually believes that one can safely retreat from a confrontation that would otherwise justify the use of deadly force (say, by fleeing), one is not justified in using deadly force. Restatement, *supra*, § 65(3), at 109. The Restatement's rule of retreat does not apply, however, to the use of non-deadly force or to the use of deadly force to ward off an intruder's attack in one's dwelling. *Id.* §§ 63(2), 65(2)(a).

A number of states have adopted so-called "Stand Your Ground" laws that expand the privilege to use deadly force. For example, a Florida law eliminates entirely the duty to retreat. Fla. Stat. § 776.012 (a person who reasonably believes that use of force or threat of force against another is necessary to defend herself from the imminent use of unlawful force by the other has no duty to retreat if she is in a place where she has right to be and is not engaged in criminal conduct). Another provision denies a defendant the right to claim self-defense if he or she "initially provokes the use of force or threat of force against himself or herself." Fla. Stat. § 776.041(2). However, this "provocation" exception to the right of self-defense does not apply if: (a) force or threat of force is being used against the provoker after the provoker has withdrawn from the initial engagement; or (b) the force being used against the provoker is "so great" that the provoker reasonably believes that he is in imminent danger of death or serious bodily harm, and that he has "exhausted every [other] reasonable means to escape such danger. . . ." *Id.* Although these provisions form part of the state's criminal code, and are typically invoked by criminal defendants, they also apply to tort actions and have occasionally been invoked in an effort to defeat civil liability. *See, e.g.*, Shehada v. Tavss, 965 F. Supp. 2d 1358, 1377 (S.D. Fla. 2013) (denying summary judgment to city and police officer in suit alleging that officer used excessive force in fatally shooting plaintiffs' decedent).

Florida's Stand Your Ground laws became the object of national attention as a result of the 2012 fatal shooting of Trayvon Martin, an unarmed African-American teenager, by neighborhood watch volunteer George Zimmerman. Zimmerman was charged with the crimes of second-degree murder and manslaughter. Claiming that their client never had an opportunity to retreat, Zimmerman's attorneys disavowed reliance on the Stand Your Ground laws, and instead invoked common law self-defense principles. However, the trial judge instructed jurors that, if they were to conclude that Zimmerman was not engaged in unlawful activity at the time of the incident, and was attacked in a place in which he had a right to be, then he was under no duty to retreat. The judge further instructed jurors that, under Florida law, they could convict Zimmerman only if they were convinced beyond a reasonable doubt that he was *not* legally justified in using deadly force (i.e., only if they were virtually certain that Zimmerman was unreasonable to believe that his use of deadly force against Martin was necessary to avoid imminent death or great bodily harm). The six-person jury acquitted Zimmerman.

With certain exceptions, the Stand Your Ground laws also grant to a defendant an *irrebuttable* presumption that she acted on the basis of a reasonable apprehension of imminent death or seriously bodily harm if her victim: (a) was unlawfully and forcibly entering, or had unlawfully or forcibly entered, a dwelling, residence, or occupied vehicle; and (b) the defendant knew or had reason to believe that an unlawful and forcible entry was occurring or had occurred. *See, e.g.*, Fla. Stat. §§ 776. 013, 776.031. Suppose *P* and his accomplice *A* break into *D*'s house, unaware that *D* is home. *D*, who is out of sight in an upstairs bedroom, overhears *P* in a low voice saying to *A*: "Come on *A*, I'm scared; let's just grab this TV and get out of here before we get caught." *D* calls 911. The dispatcher tells *D* that police will arrive in minutes and instructs *D* to hide in a locked room. Instead, armed with a gun, *D* quietly proceeds to the landing overlooking his first-floor front hallway. There he sees *P* and *A* with their backs to him, carrying his

TV toward the front door. Under the Florida Stand Your Ground law is *D* privileged to shoot *P* and *A* in "self-defense"?

6. *Defense of Others Versus Defensive Use of Others.* The privilege to injure an attacker for the purpose of defending others operates more or less under the same rules that govern the privilege of self-defense. Thus, so long as *D* actually and reasonably believes that injuring *P* is necessary to avoid an imminent injury of the requisite type to one or more third parties, *D* is privileged to use proportionate force against *P* to prevent such injuries. By contrast, the necessity of sparing *oneself* from injury is generally held *insufficient* to excuse the injuring of an innocent third party. So, for example, if *X* were to grab innocent bystander *Y* to shield himself from *Z*'s physical attack, resulting in bodily injury to *Y*, *X* will be held liable to *Y* for battery. Compare the discussion of necessity in connection with trespass to land in Chapter 11 *infra.*

C. Defense and Recapture of Property

Katko v. Briney

183 N.W.2d 657 (Iowa 1971)

Moore, C.J. The primary issue presented here is whether an owner may protect personal property in an unoccupied boarded-up farm house against trespassers and thieves by a spring gun capable of inflicting death or serious injury.

We are not here concerned with a man's right to protect his home and members of his family. Defendants' home was several miles from the scene of the incident to which we refer infra.

Plaintiff's action is for damages resulting from serious injury caused by a shot from a 20-gauge spring shotgun set by defendants in a bedroom of an old farm house which had been uninhabited for several years. Plaintiff and his companion, Marvin McDonough, had broken and entered the house to find and steal old bottles and dated fruit jars which they considered antiques.

At defendants' request plaintiff's action was tried to a jury consisting of residents of the community where defendants' property was located. The jury returned a verdict for plaintiff and against defendants for $20,000 actual and $10,000 punitive damages.

After careful consideration of defendants' motions for judgment notwithstanding the verdict and for new trial, the experienced and capable trial judge overruled them and entered judgment on the verdict. Thus we have this appeal by defendants. . . .

Most of the facts are not disputed. In 1957 defendant Bertha L. Briney inherited her parents' farm land in Mahaska and Monroe Counties. Included was an 80-acre tract in southwest Mahaska County where her grandparents and parents had lived. No one occupied the house thereafter. Her husband, Edward, attempted to care for the land. He kept no farm machinery thereon. The outbuildings became dilapidated.

For about 10 years, 1957 to 1967, there occurred a series of trespassing and housebreaking events with loss of some household items, the breaking of windows and "messing up of the property in general." The latest occurred June 8, 1967, prior to the event on July 16, 1967 herein involved.

Defendants through the years boarded up the windows and doors in an attempt to stop the intrusions. They had posted "no trespass" signs on the land several years before 1967. The nearest one was 35 feet from the house. On June 11, 1967 defendants set "a shotgun trap" in the north bedroom. After Mr. Briney cleaned and oiled his 20-gauge shotgun, the power of which he was well aware, defendants took it to the old house where they secured it to an iron bed with the barrel pointed at the bedroom door. It was rigged with wire from the doorknob to the gun's trigger so it would fire when the door was opened. Briney first pointed the gun so an intruder would be hit in the stomach but at Mrs. Briney's suggestion it was lowered to hit the legs. He admitted he did so "because I was mad and tired of being tormented" but "he did not intend to injure anyone." He gave no explanation of why he used a loaded shell and set it to hit a person already in the house. Tin was nailed over the bedroom window. The spring gun could not be seen from the outside. No warning of its presence was posted.

Plaintiff lived with his wife and worked regularly as a gasoline station attendant in Eddyville, seven miles from the old house. He had observed it for several years while hunting in the area and considered it as being abandoned. He knew it had long been uninhabited. In 1967 the area around the house was covered with high weeds. Prior to July 16, 1967 plaintiff and McDonough had been to the premises and found several old bottles and fruit jars which they took and added to their collection of antiques. On the latter date about 9:30 P.M. they made a second trip to the Briney property. They entered the old house by removing a board from a porch window which was without glass. While McDonough was looking around the kitchen area plaintiff went to another part of the house. As he started to open the north bedroom door the shotgun went off striking him in the right leg above the ankle bone. Much of his leg, including part of the tibia, was blown away. Only by McDonough's assistance was plaintiff able to get out of the house and after crawling some distance was put in his vehicle and rushed to a doctor and then to a hospital. He remained in the hospital 40 days.

Plaintiff's doctor testified he seriously considered amputation but eventually the healing process was successful. Some weeks after his release from the hospital plaintiff returned to work on crutches. He was required to keep the injured leg in a cast for approximately a year and wear a special brace for another year. He continued to suffer pain during this period.

There was undenied medical testimony plaintiff had a permanent deformity, a loss of tissue, and a shortening of the leg.

The record discloses plaintiff to trial time had incurred $710 medical expense, $2056.85 for hospital service, $61.80 for orthopedic service and $750 as loss of earnings. In addition thereto the trial court submitted to the jury the question of damages for pain and suffering and for future disability.

Plaintiff testified he knew he had no right to break and enter the house with intent to steal bottles and fruit jars therefrom. He further testified he had entered a plea of guilty to larceny in the nighttime of property of less than $20 value from a private building. He stated he had been fined $50 and costs and paroled during good behavior from a 60-day jail sentence. Other than minor traffic charges this was plaintiff's first brush with the law. On this civil case appeal it is not our prerogative to review the disposition made of the criminal charge against him.

The main thrust of defendants' defense in the trial court and on this appeal is that "the law permits use of a spring gun in a dwelling or warehouse for the purpose of preventing the unlawful entry of a burglar or thief." . . .

In the statement of issues the trial court stated plaintiff and his companion committed a felony when they broke and entered defendants' house. [In its instructions to the jury, the court stated that property owners are not permitted to use excessive force, including force calculated to cause death or great bodily harm, to protect their property except to prevent the commission of felonies of violence and where human life is in danger. The instructions explained that breaking and entering is not a felony of violence.] . . .

The overwhelming weight of authority, both textbook and case law, supports the trial court's statement of the applicable principles of law. . . .

Restatement of Torts [First], section 85, page 180, states:

> The value of human life and limb, not only to the individual concerned but also to society, so outweighs the interest of a possessor of land in excluding from it those whom he is not willing to admit thereto that a possessor of land has, as is stated in § 79, no privilege to use force intended or likely to cause death or serious harm against another whom the possessor sees about to enter his premises or meddle with his chattel, unless the intrusion threatens death or serious bodily harm to the occupiers or users of the premises. . . . A possessor of land cannot do indirectly and by a mechanical device that which, were he present, he could not do immediately and in person. Therefore, he cannot gain a privilege to install, for the purpose of protecting his land from intrusions harmless to the lives and limbs of the occupiers or users of it, a mechanical device whose only purpose is to inflict death or serious harm upon such as may intrude, by giving notice of his intention to inflict, by mechanical means and indirectly, harm which he could not, even after request, inflict directly were he present.

In Volume 2, Harper and James, *The Law of Torts*, section 27.3, pages 1440, 1441, this is found: "The possessor of land may not arrange his premises intentionally so as to cause death or serious bodily harm to a trespasser. The possessor may of course take some steps to repel a trespass. If he is present he may use force to do so, but only that amount which is reasonably necessary to effect the repulse. Moreover if the trespass threatens harm to property only — even a theft of property — the possessor would not be privileged to use deadly force, he may not arrange his premises so that such force will be inflicted by mechanical means. If he does, he will be liable even to a thief who is injured by such device." . . .

[The court reviewed the holdings of similar cases from Iowa and other jurisdictions holding property owners liable for causing injury by means of excessive force.] In addition to civil liability many jurisdictions hold a land owner criminally liable for serious injuries or homicide caused by spring guns or other set devices.

In Wisconsin, Oregon and England the use of spring guns and similar devices is specifically made unlawful by statute.

The legal principles stated by the trial court in [its] instructions . . . are well established and supported by the authorities cited and quoted *supra*. There is no merit in defendants' objections and exceptions thereto. Defendants' various motions based on the same reasons stated in exceptions to instructions were properly overruled.

Plaintiff's claim and the jury's allowance of punitive damages, under the trial court's instructions relating thereto, were not at any time or in any manner challenged by defendants in the trial court as not allowable. We therefore are not presented with the problem of whether the $10,000 award should be allowed to stand. . . .

LARSON, J. (dissenting). I respectfully dissent, first, because the majority wrongfully assumes that by installing a spring gun in the bedroom of their unoccupied house the defendants intended to shoot any intruder who attempted to enter the room. Under the record presented here, that was a fact question. Unless it is held that there property owners are liable for any injury to a intruder from such a device regardless of the intent with which it is installed, liability under these pleadings must rest upon two definite issues of fact, i.e., did the defendants intend to shoot the invader, and if so, did they employ unnecessary and unreasonable force against him? . . .

[Judge Larson's dissent first maintained that the jury should have been instructed that it could not impose liability unless it found that the defendants had intended to kill or seriously injure an intruder by setting up the spring gun. It further maintained that a reasonable jury could have found that such intent was lacking given Mr. Briney's testimony that the gun was set up to "scare" intruders, and that he (Briney) did not expect the buckshot to go through the bedroom door "quite that hard." The dissent then turned to the issue of punitive damages. — EDS.]

In the case at bar the plaintiff was guilty of serious criminal conduct, which event gave rise to his claim against defendants. Even so, he may be eligible for an award of compensatory damages which so far as the law is concerned redresses him and places him in the position he was prior to sustaining the injury. The windfall he would receive in the form of punitive damages is bothersome to the principle of damages, because it is a response to the conduct of the defendants rather than any reaction to the loss suffered by plaintiff or any measurement of his worthiness for the award.

When such a windfall comes to a criminal as a result of his indulgence in serious criminal conduct, the result is intolerable and indeed shocks the conscience. If we find the law upholds such a result, the criminal would be permitted by operation of law to profit from his own crime. . . .

We cannot in good conscience ignore the conduct of the plaintiff. He does not come into court with clean hands, and attempts to make a claim to punitive damages in part on his own criminal conduct. In such circumstances, to enrich him would be unjust, and compensatory damages in such a case itself would be a sufficient deterrent to the defendant or others who might intend to set such a device. . . .

The admonitory function of the tort law is adequately served where the compensatory damages claimed are high and the granted award itself may act as a severe punishment and a deterrence. In such a case as we have here there is no need to hold out the prospect of punitive damages as an incentive to sue and rectify a minor physical damage such as a redress for lost dignity. Certainly this is not a case where defendants might profit in excess of the amount of reparation they may have to pay. . . .

NOTES AND QUESTIONS

1. *Katko's Aftermath.* According to Geoffrey Palmer, while their appeal to the Iowa Supreme Court was pending, the Brineys sold their farm to pay the judgment to Katko. The case apparently garnered considerable public attention, prompting the publication of strongly opinionated letters on both sides of the issue in Iowa newspapers. Sympathizers with the Brineys raised $7,000 in contributions. The state legislature took up legislation designed by its supporters to enhance the ability of property owners to use deadly force to protect their property, but the legislation was not enacted.

2. *Other Security Measures and Other Victims.* By what means were the Brineys entitled to protect their property? Prior to Katko's attempted robbery, they had boarded up the house and apparently had complained to police about the previous break-ins, but to no effect. Is the majority saying that they had no choice but to accept that they would lose their property to thieves? Suppose the Brineys kept in the farmhouse a large dog that was trained to attack intruders. Would they be subject to liability under the reasoning of *Katko*? In this regard, consider the various opinions issued in *Mech v. Hearst*, 496 A.2d 1099 (Md. Ct. App.), *cert. denied*, 501 A.2d 1323 (Md. 1985), in which the judges differed over whether use of a vicious guard dog to ward off trespassers is always reasonable as a matter of law, or whether, under certain circumstances, a jury might find that a guard dog serves as the equivalent of a spring gun.*

Suppose the person who was shot was not an intruder looking to steal the Brineys' property, but *B*, a 12-year-old boy who broke into the house because he thought it would make a "cool hideout." Or suppose *A*, an adult who was in the market to buy an old farmhouse, was told by a local realtor to "take a look at" a different farmhouse quite near the Brineys', and that *A* entered the Brineys' house in the mistaken belief that he was entitled to force his way in. Does either of these claimants present a stronger claim for recovery than Katko? If so, are we to conclude that the amount of force one may reasonably use to protect property varies according to the nature of the intruder and the reasons for his intrusion? Is one problem with a spring gun that it cannot discriminate between different sorts of intruders and intrusions?

3. *Punitive Damages.* As discussed in detail in Chapter 8, the typical relief accorded to a successful tort plaintiff comes in the form of a compensatory damage payment made by the tortfeasor to the plaintiff. As their name suggests, compensatory damages aim to compensate the plaintiff for losses he has suffered as a result of the tort. Punitive damages, by contrast, consist of damages above and beyond the amount necessary to compensate the plaintiff, thereby providing an additional increment of redress to the victim while also "sending a message" to the tortfeasor that such conduct is unacceptable, as well as a message to others that similar conduct may result in significant penalties. Compensatory damages are available to any tort claimant who

---

* As discussed in *Pingaro v. Rossi*, Chapter 3, some state statutes impose strict liability on dog owners to persons who are attacked while on the owner's property by permission or otherwise lawfully. The issue here pertains only to the right to use reasonable means to repel trespassers.

can prove that he has suffered loss as a proximate result of the tort. These include economic (out-of-pocket) losses, such as medical bills incurred, losses in the form of property damage, and loss of past and future income. They also include noneconomic losses, such as pain and suffering. Punitive damages are only available to claimants who can establish that the tortfeasor committed a malicious or willful wrong, or a wrong that displays reckless disregard for others' well-being. Even then, their award is entirely discretionary with the factfinder.

Because batteries often consist of violent attacks, successful battery plaintiffs typically recover damages reflecting out-of-pocket losses such as medical bills. However, in the case of offensive-contact batteries, out-of-pocket losses may be quite modest. Still, even this sort of battery victim may recover a substantial compensatory award reflecting any pain, embarrassment, or humiliation he experienced. In addition, to the extent a battery plaintiff has been the victim of wilful or wanton misconduct, he will be in a position to seek punitive damages. *See, e.g.*, Jones v. Fisher, 166 N.W.2d 175 (Wis. 1969) (employee who suffered the indignity of being held down by one employer while having her dentures forcibly removed by another is entitled to punitive damages). On the other hand, some batteries — for example, a harmful touching caused intentionally by a defendant in a mistaken but sincere effort at self-defense — might not display sufficient willfulness or wantonness to warrant a punitive award.

In his *Katko* dissent, Judge Larson invokes the doctrine of "unclean hands," an equitable doctrine that is applied by courts faced with requests for injunctive relief as opposed to damages. For example, suppose *H*, the holder of a patent on a particular pain-relieving medicine, requests a court order halting the sale of company *I*'s pain-relief product on the ground that it infringes on *H*'s patent. Now suppose there is evidence that *H* himself had engaged in fraud in the course of securing its patent by knowingly submitting false documentation to the Patent Office. In light of that evidence, the court might decline to exercise its equitable power to issue the requested injunction on the ground that those seeking an injunction must themselves have "clean hands."

Does a similar rationale warrant a ruling that Katko — who was apparently looking to grab a few empty bottles from an unused dwelling — was not entitled to any punitive damages? If it applies to punitive damages, should it also bar him from collecting compensatory damages? Or is there something special about punitive damages that would warrant subjecting a claim for them to a special equitable principle?

4. *Recapture of Property.* As a rule, the privilege to use reasonable force to defend property applies only preventively. However, if the property has, in the owner's absence, momentarily been occupied by an intruder who has no right to be there, the owner may use reasonable force to remove him. Thus, if the Brineys had decided to visit the farmhouse just as Katko arrived, they could have undertaken reasonable efforts to remove him. By contrast, if an owner were forcibly to evict a person who is not entitled to occupy land, yet who enjoys "peaceable," nontransitory possession of it (e.g., a tenant whose lease has expired), the owner runs the risk of criminal penalty, and in some instances tort liability, to the wrongful possessor, even if the amount of force used by the owner is deemed reasonable. *See* Dan B. Dobbs, *The Law of Torts* § 80,

at 181-186 (2000). Here, the aim of the law is to discourage self-help and encourage owners to apply to the courts for relief.

Even in situations of transitory occupation in which the owner is, in principle, permitted to take steps to eject the trespasser, the ejection must be reasonable given the circumstances. For example, absent an imminent threat of bodily harm or death, an owner may not respond to a trespass in a manner that risks imminent and serious bodily harm to the trespasser. In *Whitten v. Cox*, 799 So. 2d 1 (Miss. 2000), the plaintiffs were driving their pickup truck across defendant's land on their way to an adjacent property. The defendant fired his gun at the truck, forced the plaintiffs out of the truck at gunpoint, and handcuffed, physically abused, and threatened to kill them. The Mississippi Supreme Court upheld verdicts for the plaintiffs on claims of battery, assault, and false imprisonment, ruling that the jury was entitled to find that the defendant acted unreasonably in asserting his property rights as he did.

5. Recapture of Chattels. Roughly the same framework applies to efforts to recapture personal possessions (chattels). Thus, once "peaceable" possession of the chattel is enjoyed by another, the owner may not seek to retrieve it through the use of force without risking criminal or tort liability. However, a possessor may use reasonable force against another if the other has obtained only momentary possession of the chattel. Under the Uniform Commercial Code, a person or entity that has sold a good to another on credit, and who under the terms of the sale is entitled to repossess it for lack of timely payments, may repossess the good so long as the repossession does not involve a "breach of the peace." Thus, if car dealer *C* sells a car on credit to buyer *B*, and *B* fails to make required payments, such that *C* is entitled under the sales contract to repossess, *C* may proceed to tow the car away, even if it is parked in the publicly accessible driveway on *B*'s property. *C* may not repossess, however, if doing so involves the use of force against *B* or another, or breaking and entering onto *B*'s property.

While the owner or possessor of a chattel thus enjoys a qualified privilege to recapture it, the privilege does not protect the owner who *mistakenly* seizes property that is not actually hers. Suppose that *A* leaves her expensive and distinctively colored mountain bike in the doorway of a store while she buys a bottle of water. Suppose that moments later she comes out of the store, discovers that the bike is missing, and sees *B* riding nearby on a bike of the same appearance. *A* is privileged to use reasonable force to wrestle the bike away from *B* if it turns out that the bike actually is *A*'s. However, if *A* is mistaken, because *B* just happens to have an identical bike, *B* will be able to sue *A* for battery. This result follows even if *A* was entirely reasonable in believing that the bike on which *B* was riding was *A*'s. The limited privilege to recapture chattel is thus exercised at the possessor's peril.

IV. FALSE IMPRISONMENT

The right to liberty has long been identified as one of the most important rights that Anglo-American law aspires to protect. Liberty has many dimensions, including freedom of thought and conscience, freedom of speech, and freedom to associate with others. But perhaps the most basic component of liberty is physical freedom—freedom of movement. It is no surprise, then, to find that the common law of tort has long accorded redress to those who have been subjected to the indignity of being confined by another. The primary doctrine by which that relief has been provided is through the tort of false imprisonment. Consider how this venerable cause of action applies in the following modern setting.

A. Elements

Fojtik v. Charter Med. Corp.

985 S.W.2d 625 (Tex. Ct. App. 1999)

CHAVEZ, J. Felix Fojtik appeals from . . . summary judgment entered against him on his claim against Charter Medical Corporation. Fojtik had brought a false imprisonment cause of action against Charter arising from his stay at a Charter hospital where he was treated for alcoholism. . . . We affirm the judgment of the trial court. . . .

BACKGROUND FACTS

Fojtik's admission to Charter was preceded by an "intervention," where Dorrill Nabours and Valerie Bullock from Charter, along with a group of Fojtik's family and friends, confronted him and told him that he needed to go through an inpatient treatment at Charter for alcohol abuse. Fojtik's medical records indicate that he told Charter staff he had admitted himself to Charter because those conducting the "intervention" had told him that, if he did not voluntarily admit himself, they would have him committed to the hospital and have him brought in wearing handcuffs.[2] When admitted, Fojtik was angry about being at Charter and refused to be photographed or to agree to permit Charter to contact him after he left the treatment program. While at the hospital Fojtik made several requests for a "pass" permitting him to leave the Charter facility. His initial requests were denied on the ground that he was not "eligible" for a pass until he was further into his stay. Fojtik expressed his opinion that he was getting a "raw deal" because he was "locked up and couldn't get away." Later Fojtik was granted passes for a few hours at a time, and always returned to Charter voluntarily and on time. Fojtik explained that he had vowed to follow all of the rules at Charter. Although nothing in the record explains the reason Fojtik made this "vow," he argues on appeal that he had decided to follow all the rules only because he hoped that obedient behavior might speed his release.

Charter produced summary judgment evidence that Fojtik was free to leave at any time. Charter employees explained that, although they used a system of "passes" and preferred to follow certain procedures when patients left the hospital, if a patient insisted on leaving without following Charter procedures, Charter would permit the

2. Upon a showing that a person is chemically dependent and evidences an imminent, substantial risk of serious harm to himself or to others, a judge or magistrate may order that such person be apprehended and transported to a treatment facility. Tex. Health & Safety Code Ann. §§ 462.042-43 (Vernon 1992 & Supp. 1998).

patient to leave. Charter also refers us to Fojtik's admission documents, which indicate that he consented to inpatient treatment.

Legal Standards

. . . The elements of a false imprisonment cause of action are: (1) willful detention by the defendant, (2) without consent of the detainee, and (3) without authority of law. A detention may be accomplished by violence, by threats, or by any other means that restrain a person from moving from one place to another. Randall's Food Mkts., Inc. v. Johnson, 891 S.W.2d 640, 645 (Tex. 1995).

Where it is alleged that a detention is effected by a threat, the plaintiff must demonstrate that the threat was such as would inspire in the threatened person a just fear of injury to his person, reputation, or property. *Id.* Threats to call the police are not ordinarily sufficient in themselves to effect an unlawful imprisonment. Morales v. Lee, 668 S.W.2d 867, 869 (Tex. App. — San Antonio 1984, no writ) (citing W. Prosser, Torts § 11 (4th ed. 1971)). In determining whether such threats are sufficient to overcome the plaintiff's free will, factors such as the relative size, age, experience, sex, and physical demeanor of the participants may be considered. . . .

Whether Fojtik was Restrained

Although Fojtik was not physically restrained, he alleges that he was detained against his will by threats that, if he did not submit to his detention, he would be forcibly committed and "brought in in handcuffs." Fojtik also contends that Charter used "other means" in addition to threats of commitment in order to restrain him. We first consider whether the evidence raises a question of fact regarding whether Fojtik was restrained by threats.

A review of false imprisonment case law is instructive. In Black v. Kroger, 527 S.W.2d 794 (Tex. App. — Houston [1st Dist.] 1975, writ dism'd) an eighteen year old woman with a tenth grade education and a two-year-old daughter was accused by her employers of stealing. She was led into a small, windowless room lit by bare light bulbs, where the store manager and another man who worked for "Kroger Security" were waiting. She was told repeatedly that they knew she had been stealing, and that if she did not admit to stealing they would handcuff her and take her to jail. She testified that she made a false confession, explaining "I just had it in my head that they were going to put me in jail no matter what I did, and I wasn't going to see my little girl for a long, long time." The court noted the woman's lack of business experience and the harsh and intimidating nature of her questioning. *Black*, 527 S.W.2d at 800. The court held that under these facts the jury could have reasonably concluded that the threats to the woman intimidated her to the point where she was not free to leave and was unreasonably detained. *Id.* at 801.

Skillern & Sons, Inc. v. Stewart, 379 S.W.2d 687 (Tex. Civ. App. — Fort Worth 1964, writ ref'd n.r.e) presents a similar set of facts. A female employee was accused of stealing. She was led by the arm to a room where two men she had never met beat on a desk while telling her "we have the goods on you . . . we know you've been stealing money." She was threatened with imprisonment, and told that she could not leave until she wrote a confession. She managed to leave, but was ordered back, and again told that she would either sign a confession or she would go to jail, but that she could not leave without confessing. When she tried to stand up she was physically pushed back into a chair by her accusers. These facts were held to support a recovery for false imprisonment.

In Safeway Stores, Inc. v. Amburn, 388 S.W.2d 443 (Tex. App. — Fort Worth 1965, no writ) the evidence was held insufficient to support a finding that the plaintiff was falsely imprisoned. In this case as well, an employee was led to a secluded room where others were waiting to accuse him of theft. The employee's path to the door, if he had desired to leave, was not blocked. The only physical contact between the employee and his accusers was a handshake. When the employee denied stealing anything he was accused of lying and threatened with jail. The employee spent thirty to forty minutes with his accusers. The court held that, where there is nothing else particularly overbearing about this kind of meeting, threats of imprisonment are not enough to establish a claim for false imprisonment, and the court reversed the jury's verdict in the plaintiff's favor.

In Randall's Food Markets, Inc. v. Johnson, 891 S.W.2d 640 (Tex. 1995), the plaintiff was a store employee accused of stealing. She was told to either wait in an office or to work on a volunteer project in a particular area. She waited in the office, but left twice and returned each time. The Texas Supreme Court rejected the plaintiff's contention that the store management had impliedly threatened her person, because no one was guarding her and she had in fact left the office twice. Summary judgment in favor of the store on the employee's false imprisonment claim was upheld.

In evaluating Fojtik's claim of false imprisonment, the issue is essentially this: to what extent must plaintiffs insist on their freedom and have it denied to them before they can recover for false imprisonment? Under some circumstances, a combination of the plaintiff's vulnerability and oppressive circumstances permit recovery, even when the plaintiff does not actually resist their detention. Comparing the facts of this case to previous reported cases, however, indicates that this is not one of those cases. None of the factors that are considered in evaluating whether threats are sufficient to overcome the plaintiff's free will, i.e., the relative size, age, experience, sex, and physical demeanor of the participants, weigh in Fojtik's favor. Fojtik was a forty-five-year-old man who had run several businesses. He was not a young, inexperienced woman, like the plaintiff in *Black*. He was not physically restrained, like the plaintiff in *Skillern*. Although he was threatened with the police, there were no other factors adding to the intimidating effect of those threats, and, as in *Amburn*, such threats, standing alone, are not enough to establish false imprisonment. Fojtik left and voluntarily returned, as the plaintiff did in *Johnson*, where the plaintiff's actions were held to negate her false imprisonment theory.

Fojtik contends that his frequent comments at Charter about being "locked up" and his generally uncooperative attitude are evidence that he did not consider himself free to leave. While it may be true that Fojtik considered himself restrained, the issue is not Fojtik's subjective interpretation of his situation, but rather whether he had a "*just* fear of injury." Randall's v. Johnson, 891 S.W.2d at 645. The facts of this case do not raise a fact issue on whether Fojtik had a "just fear" of injury. The record before us indicates that, while Fojtik certainly complained about being at Charter, he never insisted that he be permitted to leave. As discussed above, there is nothing in this case to suggest that Fojtik was a person whose weakness or susceptibility to intimidation might excuse his failure to insist on leaving. . . .

Aside from threats of legal commitment, the "other means" of restraint identified by Fojtik are: (1) constantly telling him that he was an alcoholic and treating him as though he were, and (2) permitting him to leave on temporary passes. Appellant's argument appears to be that these methods lessened his will to insist on being released. We do not believe that such trifling matters as these constitute restraint. Treating Fojtik as an alcoholic did not restrain him; if it contributed to his ongoing presence at the Charter hospital, it did so by persuading Fojtik that he did have a problem with alcohol that should be addressed, not by any actual restraint. The fact that Charter permitted Fojtik to leave on passes undermines his claim for false imprisonment rather than supporting it. . . .

NOTES AND QUESTIONS

1. Elements. By including "lack of consent" and "absence of authority" as "elements," the *Fojtik* court's description of the false imprisonment tort incorporates into the plaintiff's prima facie case what many jurisdictions instead describe and analyze as affirmative defenses. Following Section 35 of the Second Restatement, one could alternatively define false imprisonment as follows:

False Imprisonment: Prima Facie Case

Actor *A* is subject to liability to other person *P* for false imprisonment if:

1. *A* acts,
2. intending to confine *P*;
3. *A*'s act causes *P* to be confined; and
4. *P* is aware of her confinement.

2. Damages Versus Release: Habeas Corpus. Like other torts, false imprisonment can be perpetrated by a private citizen or by a government official. False imprisonment, however, is more closely linked with official misconduct than some other torts because confinements, as opposed to other injuries, often come in the form of detentions at the behest of governmental officials or via government processes such as criminal prosecutions.

The immediate legal remedy sought by most persons who believe that they have been unjustifiably detained by government officials is to obtain not damages, but release. English common law long provided means for individuals being held by executive branch officials to apply to the courts for their release. One particularly important device for doing so has been the writ of *habeas corpus*, whereby a prisoner can ask a judge to order the relevant officials to "produce the body," that is, appear with the prisoner before the court to justify the detention. Absent justification, the judge could order that the prisoner to be released.

Prior to the late eighteenth century, the habeas writ was primarily available only to persons who were being held without judicial proceedings of any kind. By contrast, in modern American law, the habeas writ, which has been codified in federal statutes, now serves to provide prisoners with the ability to raise *collateral* challenges to a criminal conviction obtained in a state court. (The challenge is a "collateral" challenge because it is not raised by appealing a trial-level conviction to a higher court, but instead involves the initiation of a separate lawsuit subsequent to and independent of the original criminal prosecution.) Typically, such a challenge asserts that the prisoner's conviction or confinement violates rights accorded to him by the U.S. Constitution, such as the right to effective assistance of legal counsel or to legal procedures in accordance with due process of law.

3. Civil Rights Laws and False Imprisonment. Apart from obtaining release, a person wrongfully subject to official detention can also sue for damages. Here, she can rely not only on the common law tort of false imprisonment but also on federal civil rights laws. The Fourth and Fifth Amendments to the U.S. Constitution respectively grant individuals the right not to be subjected to unreasonable seizure by government officials and the right to due process of law. In turn — as explained in *Hunt v. State* (Chapter 10) — a federal statute, 42 U.S.C. § 1983, empowers persons who have suffered violations of these (and other) constitutional rights at the hands of state and local officials, as well as certain private citizens, to sue them for damages. The Supreme Court in the *Bivens* decision, discussed in Chapter 6, authorized similar actions against federal officials who deprive individuals of their constitutional rights.

Because these federal remedies tend to provide certain advantages to claimants over common law actions — for example, successful Section 1983 claimants can recover attorneys' fees — suits alleging wrongful detention brought about by state and federal officials such as police officers tend to be framed primarily as federal law civil rights claims, with common law false imprisonment claims tacked on as redundancies. *See, e.g.*, Daley v. Harber, 234 F. Supp. 2d 27 (D. Mass. 2002) (proof that the plaintiff's unjustified arrest was actionable as a civil rights violation under Section 1983 is sufficient to establish as a matter of law that defendant also committed the tort of false imprisonment). When the alleged detention is committed by a private citizen or entity, such as private hospitals and private security personnel, the claim for wrongful detention may still be actionable under Section 1983 if the private actor is deemed to have been acting "under color of law."* Suits complaining of detentions caused by private actors not deemed to be acting under color of law must invoke state-law claims for false imprisonment (and perhaps other torts such as battery).

4. What Counts as Confinement? A confinement occurs when the tortfeasor causes the victim to be within a bounded physical space. Confinement can occur in a relatively

* A private actor may be deemed to have acted under color of law if his conduct toward the plaintiff was undertaken in coordination with government officials or if he enjoyed special authority to detain the plaintiff by virtue of a delegation of authority from the government. *See, e.g.*, Payton v. Rush-Presbyterian-St. Luke's Medical Center, 184 F.3d 623, 628 (7th Cir. 1999) (holding that hospital security guards acted under color of law in detaining the plaintiff because of the authority delegated to them by Illinois law).

small space, such as a closet, or in large spaces, such as a home. However, certain boundaries may be so broad and permissive of free movement as to not count as confinement as a matter of law. *See* Shen v. Leo A. Daly Co., 222 F.3d 472 (8th Cir. 2000) (applying Arkansas law) (employee who was barred from leaving Taiwan by the Taiwanese government because of his employer's willful and unjustified refusal to file certain papers with the government was not "confined" by the employer's misconduct). Likewise, conduct that bars a person from traveling along a particular route, or to a particular destination, will not, absent special circumstances, count as confinement. Smith v. Comair, Inc., 134 F.3d 254 (4th Cir. 1998) (applying Kentucky law) (airline's refusal to allow a connecting passenger to board any flights other than a flight that would return him to the city from which he initially flew does not constitute confinement); Lloyd v. Jefferson, 53 F. Supp. 2d 643 (D. Del. 1999) (applying Delaware law) (no confinement when daughter, who sought to accompany her father as he was being brought into a private entrance of a police station, was barred by an officer from using that entrance and told instead to use a public entrance). Confinement can occur in a non-stationary space. *See* Wilson v. Houston Funeral Home, 50 Cal. Rptr. 2d 169 (Ct. App. 1996) (confinement occurred when deceased's relatives were, against their wishes, driven by a funeral home employee in a company limousine to a bank rather than to the burial site).

The paradigmatic instance of confinement is being placed within a space, such as a jail cell, that renders exit physically impossible. However, confinement can occur even absent the impossibility of departure. If an exit is available to the victim but can only be used by the victim in a manner that poses a risk of physical harm to himself or others, the victim is deemed confined. Likewise, if the victim reasonably perceives that the tortfeasor will seek to prevent her from leaving, she is also confined. *See* Ball v. Wal-Mart, Inc., 102 F. Supp. 2d 44 (D. Mass. 2000) (applying Massachusetts law) (shopper who reasonably believed that the defendant store owner would take steps physically to prevent her from leaving was confined). Other forms of pressure can constitute confinement even if the plaintiff is literally free to move. For example, a threat to detain plaintiff's children or to seize plaintiff's property if plaintiff were to leave can suffice. *See* National Bond & Inv. Co. v. Whithorn, 123 S.W.2d 263 (Ky. App. 1938) (threat by the defendant to seize the plaintiff's automobile deemed to generate confinement). Lesser constraints on exit, including risk of loss of reputation or embarrassment, may also be sufficient. Jacques v. Childs Dining Hall Co., 138 N.E. 843 (Mass. 1923) (customer who was openly accused by waiter of trying to leave without paying her bill was "confined" for the period it took to establish that the accusation was unfounded; in light of the public accusation, the customer's leaving could have been viewed by other diners as an admission of guilt).

By contrast, if the victim can exit with only minimal inconvenience, or if there is no reason to suppose that his effort to exit will be met with resistance, there is no confinement. *See* Caswell v. BJ's Wholesale Co., 5 F. Supp. 2d 312 (E.D. Pa. 1998) (customer who was brought to an office in a store was not confined, even though a store manager stood in the doorway, because there was nothing in the circumstances to suggest that the manager would block her departure). Also, threats of certain consequences not pertaining directly to the confinement, such as subsequent dismissal from employment or prosecution, are often deemed insufficient to establish confinement.

See Foley v. Polaroid Corp., 508 N.E.2d 72 (Mass. 1987) (an at-will employee is not confined in an office simply because he was concerned that, if he left, he would be fired).

5. *Awareness of Confinement.* Section 35 of the Second Restatement and several state high court decisions require the plaintiff to prove that she was aware of her confinement as it happened. These authorities treat false imprisonment in one respect like assault, that is, as requiring apprehension of the condition of being confined. So, a victim who is locked in a room but sleeps for the duration of the confinement, or an infant who is too young to appreciate that she is being confined, cannot maintain a claim for false imprisonment. *See* Sager v. Rochester Gen. Hosp., 647 N.Y.S.2d 408 (Super. Ct. 1996) (five-month-old infant has no claim for false imprisonment absent proof that she was conscious of her confinement). Other authorities have questioned the requirement of awareness or apprehension. *See* Scofield v. Critical Air Medicine, Inc., 52 Cal. Rptr. 2d 915 (Cal. App. 1996) (noting and criticizing the contemporaneous awareness requirement in part on the ground that it would bar recovery by persons who only later learn that their confinement was unlawful).

6. *Willful Versus Accidental Confinement.* To prevail on a claim of false imprisonment, the victim must prove by a preponderance of the evidence that the tortfeasor acted for the purpose of causing her to be confined or with knowledge that she would be confined. Green v. Donroe, 440 A.2d 973 (Conn. 1982) (noting these two liability standards, albeit describing the latter as "extreme recklessness"); Stewart v. Williams, 255 S.E.2d 699 (Ga. 1979) (false imprisonment is an "intentional" tort). Accidental confinements, such as confinements arising out of misunderstandings, are ordinarily not actionable as false imprisonments. *But see* Ortiz v. Hampden County, 449 N.E.2d 1227 (Mass. App. 1983) (rejecting government's motion to dismiss a claim for negligence brought by a plaintiff who was arrested and imprisoned allegedly because a county employee carelessly and mistakenly wrote plaintiff's name on an arrest warrant). If the confinement results in harm such as bodily injury, the person who causes the confinement may be liable in negligence. So, for example, if *A* were carelessly to cause *B* to be trapped in a small, unventilated shed that became so hot as to cause *B* to suffer heatstroke before being freed, *B* may have a negligence claim against *A*.

The Wisconsin Supreme Court has permitted an action for negligent confinement resulting in emotional distress unaccompanied by physical injury. *See* La Fleur v. Mosher, 325 N.W.2d 314 (Wis. 1982) (police officer who took custody of a physically ill teenager for the purpose of returning her to her parent's home, but then forgetfully left her in a locked area of the police station overnight without food, water, or blankets can be held liable for negligent infliction of emotional distress). *But cf.* Garrett v. City of New Berlin, 362 N.W.2d 137 (Wis. 1985) (emphasizing that *La Fleur* was a "narrow" decision, grounded in the special situation of a police officer taking custody of an essentially helpless minor). The California Supreme Court has held that a plaintiff may recover in negligence from a bank that failed to honor a check written out by the plaintiff, which in turn caused the plaintiff's arrest at the behest of the merchant to whom the bounced check was paid. Although the complaint alleged that the arrest had resulted in physical harm, the court seems to have treated the causation of confinement as sufficient to support a claim in negligence, at least given the preexisting relationship of bank and customer. Weaver v. Bank of America Natl. Trust & Sav. Assn., 380 P.2d 644 (Cal. 1963). Harms associated with bank failures to honor checks are today governed by a provision in Article 4 of the Uniform Commercial Code.

7. Causing Confinement: Malicious Prosecution and Abuse of Process. Confinement can be achieved indirectly, by arranging for others to confine the victim. Thus, if a tortfeasor causes a victim to be detained by officials while knowing that there is no basis for such confinement, he can be sued for false imprisonment.

Malicious prosecution and *abuse of process* are two closely related causes of action. The former sometimes permits a claim by a victim who is subjected to an unfounded criminal prosecution against the person(s) who instigated the prosecution. In contrast to false imprisonment claimants, a person suing for malicious prosecution need not establish that she was confined. To recover, the victim must establish, first, that the instigator acted (a) without probable cause to believe that the victim had engaged in the reported misconduct *and* (b) with malice or ill-will toward the victim. Second, she must prove that, but for the instigator's activities, the prosecution would not have gone forward. Finally, she must establish that the prosecution terminated in a manner that establishes or supports the conclusion that she did not engage in the alleged misconduct. Dan B. Dobbs, *The Law of Torts* § 430, at 1215 (2000) (listing elements of malicious prosecution). Thus, a store owner who, out of personal hostility toward the plaintiff, falsely informs police that the plaintiff has stolen goods from his store and thereby subjects the plaintiff to prosecution for shoplifting can be held liable to the victim for malicious prosecution. Mere carelessness in falsely instigating a prosecution ordinarily is not sufficient. Prosecutors themselves, as opposed to instigators of those prosecutions, are generally granted immunity from any tort liability for prosecutions that turn out to be unfounded.

Although the label "malicious prosecution" tends to be reserved for instigations of criminal proceedings against another, comparable causes of action exist for malicious instigation of civil litigation. Actions such as these are sometimes referred to such as *malicious use of process* or *wrongful litigation.* Dobbs, *supra,* § 436, at 1228. The separate tort of *abuse of process* applies to a particular subset of malicious prosecutions and wrongful litigation in which one person invokes the legal system for the particular purpose of extorting, threatening, or harassing the victim, rather than in a good-faith effort to vindicate some interest or right of hers. For example, a person who knowingly launches an utterly unfounded tort suit against another merely to coerce the other into paying her has committed the tort of abuse of process.

8. Damages. Courts sometimes award nominal damages out of recognition of the violation of a wrongfully confined plaintiff's rights independently of any harm suffered, while harms parasitic on the rights violation—bodily injury, lost wages and expenses, loss of reputation, and emotional distress associated with the confinement—are generally compensable. *See* Banks v. Fritsch, 39 S.W.3d 474 (Ky. App. 2001) (perennially absent student who was chained to a tree by a teacher partly in jest is entitled to recover nominal damages for the dignitary harm as well as compensatory damages for subsequent emotional distress). Punitive damages may also be awarded upon the requisite showing of malice or reckless indifference. *See, e.g.*, Edwards v. Stills, 984 S.W.2d 366 (Ark. 1998) (upholding $1.5 million punitive award in suit for false imprisonment and other torts brought by an attorney whose client abducted, bound, and threatened to kill him).

B. The Defense of Investigative Detention and Arrest

As with battery and assault, there are numerous defenses to the tort of false imprisonment. Indeed, the defenses of consent, self-defense, and defense of property may all be asserted, at least on some occasions, to defend against a claim of false imprisonment. Additionally, the defense of investigative detention and arrest may also be asserted to defend against claims of assault or battery. However, its classic utilization is in cases of false imprisonment.

An arrest is a particular kind of detention, one in which a person is held for the purpose of securing his presence at a judicial proceeding or to otherwise aid in the administration of the law. Restatement (Second) of Torts § 112, at 190 (1965). In various circumstances, an actor who arrests another will be privileged against tort liability that he might otherwise incur by virtue of having purposefully and forcibly detained another. The privilege arises not out of a right to defend oneself, others, or property but instead to enable officials and private citizens to advance the cause of law enforcement and the operation of the legal system.

Grant v. Stop-N-Go Market of Texas, Inc.

994 S.W.2d 867 (Tex. Ct. App. 1999)

O'Connor, J. Gerald Grant, the appellant, sued Stop-N-Go Market of Texas, Inc., the appellee, for false imprisonment and defamation. The trial court granted summary judgment in favor of Stop-N-Go. We reverse and remand. . . .

B. False Imprisonment

. . . The elements of false imprisonment are (1) a willful detention, (2) without consent, and (3) without authority of law. [Randall's Food Mkts., Inc. v. Johnson, 891 S.W.2d 640, 644-645 (Tex. 1995).] Stop-N-Go argues it negated the first two elements of Grant's claim because it established Grant was not wilfully detained without his consent. Stop-N-Go argues Grant chose to remain in the store, and he could have left if he so desired. In the alternative, Stop-N-Go argues it negated the third element of a false imprisonment claim because its actions were authorized by law under Chapter 124 of the Civil Practice and Remedies Code.

1. The Summary Judgment Evidence

As evidence to support its motion, Stop-N-Go presented the trial court with an affidavit from Gerald Calhoun, the store manager, and excerpts from Grant's deposition. Grant responded to Stop-N-Go's motion for summary judgment with excerpts from his deposition, Stop-N-Go's responses to interrogatories, the police report, and Stop-N-Go's response to a request for production. . . .

a. Grant's Deposition Testimony

In his deposition, Grant said he went to the Stop-N-Go store with his girlfriend. His girlfriend stayed in the car, which was parked in front of the door to the store. Grant paid for a can of beer, and then decided he wanted to buy some potato chips. He left the bag with the can of beer on the counter, and picked out two bags of potato chips which were marked on sale, two for 99 cents. Grant returned to the clerk and laid both bags of potato chips on the counter along with a one dollar bill.

The store clerk rang up the chips at 69 cents each. Grant told the clerk that the chips were on sale. The store clerk said something to Grant, but Grant did not understand what was said because the clerk spoke with a heavy foreign accent. The store clerk and Grant went back to the chip display. The clerk told Grant that the chips he selected were not on sale, but that another brand was on sale. Although Grant thought the clerk was wrong, he decided to buy the brand that the clerk said was on sale because he was in a hurry.

As the clerk began to total the price for the two bags of chips, Grant noticed someone leaning through the window of his car and apparently talking to his girlfriend. The appellant became concerned for his girlfriend because he did not recognize the person. He went to the door to make sure she was alright. As Grant walked to the door, he picked up the one dollar bill which he had previously laid on the counter. Grant opened the door to the store with his right hand and held the dollar bill in his left hand. After determining that the person leaning on his car was an acquaintance, Grant returned to the counter, paid for the two bags of chips, and began to walk out of the store. As he walked away from the counter, Grant told the clerk that he (the clerk) needed to learn his job better, a reference to the verbal altercation concerning the price of the chips.

Just as Grant reached the door, the store manager, Calhoun, came from the back of the store, grabbed him by the arm, and said words to the effect, "he (the clerk) is doing his job well, let's talk about the cigarettes that you stole." Grant said he was pulled back when Calhoun grabbed his arm. When Calhoun made the accusation against Grant, his voice was loud enough that all the patrons in the store heard what he was saying. Calhoun said words to the effect, "everything was on a surveillance videotape and there is nothing to talk about."

Grant said Calhoun went behind the counter and asked the store clerk three times what it was that Grant had stolen. The clerk did not respond until Calhoun asked if a pack of cigarettes was on the counter, to which the clerk responded affirmatively. Calhoun repeated his accusation that Grant stole a pack of cigarettes and passed them through the door.

Grant tried to explain to Calhoun that he did not steal any cigarettes. Grant said Calhoun told him to shut up. Grant said he got real quiet after Calhoun told him to shut up because he was afraid. After Calhoun grabbed him and accused him of stealing, Grant felt he could not leave. He thought if he did leave, the police would come looking for him.

b. Calhoun's Affidavit

In his affidavit, Calhoun said he was in the back room of the store where a monitor for the store's surveillance camera was located. On the monitor, he saw Grant pick up something from the counter which appeared to him to be a pack of cigarettes. Calhoun said Grant went to the door and stepped at least part way outside, while still holding the object in his hand. Calhoun said a car was parked directly in front of the door to the store. He then saw Grant return to the counter and complete his purchase. However, Calhoun did not see Grant return the item that he picked up from the counter.

Calhoun said he left the back room and approached Grant as he was leaving the store because, after watching the monitor, he believed Grant had passed a pack of cigarettes out the door. He put his hand on Grant's arm to get his attention, and then he asked Grant about the cigarettes he thought were stolen. Calhoun said his hand was only on Grant's arm for a few seconds because, as soon as Grant turned around, Calhoun quit touching his arm.

According to Calhoun's affidavit, Grant denied stealing any cigarettes. Calhoun thought Grant's attitude was hostile and somewhat threatening, and so he decided to call the police to investigate the matter. He said he feared a confrontation with Grant. Calhoun said that when he told Grant he was going to call the police, Grant responded by saying to go ahead and call the police.

The police arrived within 15 to 20 minutes. Calhoun said Grant and the officer viewed the surveillance video. He said Grant told the officer he had picked up a dollar before stepping out the door. Calhoun told the officer he thought the object Grant picked up looked like a pack of cigarettes. According to Calhoun, the officer said he would take Grant in, but Calhoun never asked or directed the officer to do so. Calhoun gave the officer the surveillance video, and then the officer left the store with Grant.

Calhoun said he had no physical contact with Grant other than the initial touching to get Grant's attention. Once he got his attention, Calhoun said he and Grant remained on opposite sides of the counter while they waited for the police. Calhoun said a woman, perhaps Grant's girlfriend, came into the store and waited with Grant. Calhoun said nobody threatened Grant, nobody told Grant he could not leave, nobody prevented Grant from leaving, and nobody told Grant he was under arrest. According to Calhoun, Grant had a clear path to the door, nothing prevented Grant from leaving the store, Grant was never directed to remain in the store, and Grant was not put in or asked to go to a back room.

c. *The Surveillance Videotape*

Grant claims the surveillance videotape is the best evidence to determine the reasonableness of Calhoun's belief that he stole cigarettes and of Calhoun's actions. However, Stop-N-Go did not produce it. Grant presented the trial court with the police report and Stop-N-Go's responses to discovery requests, which all address the location of the videotape.

The police report and the discovery requests are all inconsistent. The police report states the videotape was returned to Stop-N-Go. In a response to interrogatories, Stop-N-Go said the videotape was at the corporate office of the Risk Management Department of National Convenience Stores. However, in a response to a request to produce the surveillance videotape, Stop-N-Go said, "none." During oral argument before this Court, Stop-N-Go said the tape was lost.[1]

d. The Police Report

In the police report, Officer Anderson said when he walked into the Stop-N-Go store, Calhoun and Grant were arguing. Calhoun told the officer Grant stole a pack of cigarettes, and that it would be on the surveillance video. Anderson said he took Grant to the station to view the videotape. After reviewing the tape with Sergeant Hartley, Anderson determined the allegations against Grant were unfounded and released him. Anderson said the videotape was returned to Stop-N-Go.

2. Willful Detention Without Consent

Stop-N-Go relies on Morales v. Lee, 668 S.W.2d 867, 869 (Tex. App.—San Antonio 1984, no writ), to argue that Grant was not willfully detained without his consent as a matter of law.[2] It argues Grant was not detained because he was not restrained from moving from one place to another. . . .

. . . According to Grant, Calhoun told Grant he could not leave and that he (Calhoun) was calling the police. This contradicts Calhoun's affidavit, in which Calhoun said he did not tell Grant that he could not leave. This raises a genuine issue of material fact concerning whether Grant was detained, and whether he consented to stay in the store.

Stop-N-Go also argues that threats of future actions, such as to call the police, are not sufficient to constitute false imprisonment. However, Calhoun did more than threaten to call the police; he actually called the police. Grant said he was afraid of what was going to happen; he had never been in trouble with the police before. He was afraid to try and leave the store because Calhoun had already grabbed him and told him not to leave. *Compare Johnson*, 891 S.W.2d at 645 (finding no detention of employee based on fear of what would happen because no one tried to stop her from leaving, no one guarded her, and she was not threatened). Grant was afraid that if he left, he would be labeled a fugitive from justice, causing even more damage to his reputation.

Under *Johnson*, when we assume these facts are true, we conclude Grant raised fact issues concerning whether he was willfully detained without his consent.

---

1. . . . Grant argues the trial court erred in granting summary judgment because it should have presumed the missing videotape was unfavorable to Stop-N-Go. Stop-N-Go argues Grant was not entitled to this presumption because he has not shown the videotape was intentionally destroyed. Although we need not decide this issue . . . , we note that Grant may be entitled to a jury instruction on this presumption.

2. In *Morales*, the plaintiff was an employee at a doctor's office. The doctor accused the plaintiff of stealing five dollars. When she denied it, he screamed, hollered, threatened her, and then fired her and told her to leave. The plaintiff won on her false imprisonment claim in a jury trial. The appellate court reversed because it found there was no evidence of false imprisonment.*Morales* is distinguishable. It involved a full trial, where all the evidence was developed; here, it was a summary judgment proceeding. In *Morales*, the defendant only threatened to call the police, whereas here, Stop-N-Go actually did call the police.

3. The Shopkeeper's Privilege

In its motion for summary judgment, Stop-N-Go claimed its actions were authorized by law under Civil Practice and Remedies Code section 124.001, the shopkeeper's privilege. If this is true, then Stop-N-Go would have negated the third element of Grant's false imprisonment claim. Grant argues he raised genuine issues of material fact regarding whether Stop-N-Go established this privilege as a matter of law.

Stop-N-Go's only summary judgment evidence was from an interested witness, Calhoun. Calhoun's affidavit explains what Calhoun saw on the surveillance monitor. The videotape is the best evidence of what happened. However, Stop-N-Go has refused to produce the videotape, and each time Stop-N-Go was asked for it, it gave a different reason why it could not be produced.

The shopkeeper's privilege provides that a person who reasonably believes another person has stolen, or is attempting to steal property, is privileged to detain that person in a reasonable manner and for a reasonable time to investigate ownership of the property. Tex. Civ. Prac. & Rem. Code § 124.001; Wal-Mart v. Resendez, 962 S.W.2d 539, 540 (Tex. 1998). Thus, there are three components to the shopkeeper's privilege: (1) a reasonable belief a person has stolen or is attempting to steal; (2) detention for a reasonable time; and (3) detention in a reasonable manner. *Id.* at 540.

Like the court in Wal-Mart Stores, Inc. v. Odem, 929 S.W.2d 513, 520 (Tex. App. — San Antonio 1996, writ denied), we are concerned with a false imprisonment arising out of a detention. *Odem* explained that the shopkeeper's privilege is limited in its application to false imprisonment claims arising from investigative detentions. The test of liability is not based on the store patron's guilt or innocence, but instead on the reasonableness of the store's action under the circumstances; the trier of fact usually determines whether reasonable belief is established. Whether Calhoun was reasonable in believing Grant had committed a theft, or reasonable in detaining Grant, is a question to be determined by the jury.

Stop-N-Go relies on *Resendez* to argue that a ten to 15 minute detention is reasonable as a matter of law. This is a true statement of the law in *Resendez. See* 962 S.W.2d at 540. While *Resendez* held a ten to 15 minute detention was reasonable as a matter of law, it so held, "*without deciding the outer parameters* of a permissible period of time under section 124.001." *Id.* (emphasis added).

Resendez does not support Stop-N-Go's position, because Grant was detained for more than ten to 15 minutes. According to Calhoun, the police arrived 15 to 20 minutes after they were called. Once the police arrived, they viewed the tape at the store, and then they took Grant to the police station and viewed the tape again. Grant said he spent approximately an hour in police custody. Thus, Grant's detention lasted for more than an hour and 20 minutes.

4. Conclusion

Stop-N-Go did not negate any element of Grant's false imprisonment claim as a matter of law, and Grant raised genuine issues of material fact on each element. Therefore, summary judgment on this claim was improper.

[The court next denied summary judgment for the defendant on Grant's defamation claim. It concluded that a jury could find that Calhoun defamed Grant by stating in front of other customers that the store had videotaped Grant stealing cigarettes.]

NOTES AND QUESTIONS

1. *Arrests and Warrants.* Often when a person is detained by a government official such as a police officer, that detention is undertaken pursuant to an arrest warrant. An arrest warrant is a document issued by a judge, or some other official with the appropriate authority, that directs the recipient of the document to arrest an identifiable person (or persons). Restatement (Second) of Torts § 113, at 191 (1965). Typically, warrants are issued only upon the presentation of evidence to the judge (or other official issuing the warrant) that there is probable cause to believe that the person to be arrested has committed a crime. When a government official arrests a person pursuant to a warrant that is actually valid, or in good faith relies on a warrant that appears valid on its face, she is immune from liability for false imprisonment. However, this immunity only applies to actions undertaken within the scope of the warrant. Thus, if officer *O* arrests person *P* under a warrant that authorizes the arrest of different person *D*, *O* does not benefit from any immunity by virtue of the warrant. Likewise, the arresting official may lose the protection provided by the warrant if she acts outside the authority it provides by using excessive force in arrest.

2. *Warrantless Arrests.* Although a warrant thus provides considerable protection from liability for false imprisonment, government officials and private citizens also enjoy a limited privilege to arrest even in the absence of a warrant. (The phrase "citizen's arrest" is a shorthand description of a situation in which such a privilege attaches.) There are two common scenarios in which one private citizen is privileged to arrest another. In the first, a serious criminal offense (usually a felony) has actually been committed. If that is the case, and if the actor who arrests the other acts with "probable cause" — objectively reasonable grounds — to believe that the other committed the offense in question, he is privileged to detain the other. However, even if these conditions are met, the privilege is lost if it turns out that the actor did not act out of a good-faith desire to aid in the administration of the law, but rather used the occasion to harass, extort, or intimidate the detainee.

In the second scenario, the detainee, in the presence of the defendant, is in the process of attempting a serious criminal offence, or commits (or is about to commit) a breach of the peace (e.g., by fighting in public). Under these circumstances, the privilege to arrest will attach, but only if it turns out that the actor was correct in his perceptions. Thus, if *D* detains *C* based on a reasonable but *false* belief that *C* is about to commit a serious crime, *D* cannot invoke the privilege. Restatement (Second) of Torts § 119(c)-(d) & cmt. o.

3. *Investigative Detentions and the Shopkeeper's Privilege.* The U.S. Supreme Court held in *Terry v. Ohio*, 392 U.S. 1 (1968), that the Fourth Amendment permits police officers briefly to detain persons for the purpose of investigating actual or possible criminal activity. Such investigative stops do not require probable cause to believe that

the person has committed a crime, but instead the lower threshold of "reasonable suspicion." Merchants historically enjoyed a much more limited privilege to detain customers to investigate possible thefts. Specifically, they were privileged to detain actual shoplifters, but they exercised that privilege at their peril, because it would not apply if it turned out that they were mistaken, even if their mistake was a reasonable one. *See* Claggett v. State, 670 A.2d 1002 (Md. App.) (reviewing Maryland common law with respect to the privilege to detain a suspected thief, and noting that any such detention is at the shopkeeper's peril), *cert. denied*, 675 A.2d 992 (Md. 1996).

Through common law development and, more typically, legislation of the sort referenced in *Grant*, merchants have been granted the privilege to detain customers believed to have committed or attempted a theft of their property, even if it turns out that the suspect is innocent. These statutes require that store personnel have probable cause or reasonable grounds for believing that the customer has stolen or is about to steal store property. If they have such grounds, they may detain the suspect, but only for a reasonable period of time and in a reasonable manner. In a decision subsequent to *Grant*, another Texas appellate court held that detention of a suspected shoplifter for the period of an hour did not constitute an unreasonably long detention. Dillard Dept. Stores, Inc. v. Silva, 106 S.W.3d 789 (Tex. App. 2003). However, the court in the same case also ruled that a jury was entitled to find that the store had executed the detention in an unreasonable manner because, among other things, its security guard twice placed the suspect on the floor, handcuffed him before taking him to an office, ridiculed him while in custody, and never entertained the victim's request to go out to his car in the parking lot, in which receipts for the allegedly stolen property could be found.

Federal civil rights laws guarantee all persons the right to "make and enforce contracts." 42 U.S.C. § 1981. In certain circumstances, courts have interpreted Section 1981 to provide customers or prospective customers with a federal-law remedy against owners and operators of businesses who refuse to serve them, or otherwise discriminate against them, on the basis of race or national origin. Some of these suits have claimed that store detention policies are discriminatory in that they disproportionately target African Americans and members of other minority groups for investigation and detention. *See, e.g.*, Hampton v. Dillard Dept. Stores, Inc., 247 F.3d 1091 (10th Cir. 2001), *cert. denied*, 534 U.S. 1131 (2002).

Because shoplifting apparently causes the average retail business substantial losses, storeowners have increasingly relied on technology, including hidden surveillance cameras, to guard against theft. These technologies can implicate other interests protected by the law of torts, including the interest in privacy. For example, the issue has arisen as to whether, or under what circumstances, a clothing store can be held liable for secretly videotaping or observing its customers in changing areas. *See generally Annotation: Retailer's Surveillance of Dressing or Fitting Rooms as Invasion of Privacy*, 38 A.L.R. 4th 954 (1985).

4. *Excessive Force: Civil Rights and Battery.* The privilege to arrest, even if otherwise properly invoked, is lost if the arrest is undertaken with excessive force. In contemporary cases, the complaint as to the use of excessive force is typically

presented as a federal civil rights claim under 42 U.S.C. § 1983, although in principle it is also or alternatively brought as a battery claim. The gist of a section 1983 claim is that a government actor's use of excessive force violated the right against being subjected to an unreasonable seizure guaranteed by the Fourth Amendment. As explained in Note 3 following *Fojtik*, claims against private actors for use of excessive force in the course of an arrest may sometimes be brought as federal law civil rights claims. However, if the private actor is deemed not to have been acting "under color of law," the claim must sound in common law torts such as battery.

Whether it is brought as a federal civil rights claim or a common law battery action, the issue in an excessive force claim will be the same: whether the person invoking the privilege to arrest used excessive force in effecting the arrest. In Section 1983 actions, the burden is on the plaintiff to prove excessive force so as to establish that he was subjected to an "unreasonable" seizure in violation of the Constitution. Courts have split over whether, in a common law battery suit against a police officer claiming use of excessive force in arrest, the burden is on the plaintiff to prove excessiveness or on the defendant to prove reasonableness. Edson v. City of Anaheim, 74 Cal. Rptr. 2d 614 (Ct. App. 1998).

5. *Examples of Reasonable Force.* For a decision upholding a store security guard's use of non-deadly force to apprehend a suspected shoplifter, see Watkins v. Sears Roebuck & Co., 735 N.Y.S.2d 75 (App. Div. 2001) (guard who broke suspect's leg in tackling him as he fled store with stereo used reasonable force as a matter of law). As to the justified use of deadly force, see *Edson, supra* Note 4, which upheld a jury's defense verdict on behalf of a police officer. The officer shot a suspect who had led police on a lengthy chase and who, at the end of the chase, had turned toward the officer and reached under his jacket and toward his waistband, leading the officer to believe that the suspect was reaching for a gun.

6. *Statutory Authorization of Deadly Force and Suspects' Constitutional Rights.* In *Tennessee v. Garner*, 471 U.S. 1 (1985), a police officer shot a teenager as he fled from a house that he had attempted to rob. At the time, the teenager was climbing a fence with his back to the officer, and the officer was "reasonably sure" that the teenager was unarmed. Tennessee statutory law permitted a police officer to use deadly force against a fleeing criminal suspect who had ignored a command to stop, even if the sole reason for using such force was to prevent the person from escaping. Reasoning that "[i]t is not better that all felony suspects die than that they escape," the Supreme Court struck down the statute on the ground that its authorization of the use of deadly force against a fleeing suspect who does not present an imminent physical danger to others violates the suspect's right to be free from unreasonable seizure. *Compare* Scott v. Harris, 550 U.S. 372 (2007) (where the driver of a speeding car who is fleeing from arrest for a traffic offense poses a substantial, immediate risk of serious physical injury to others, police officers do not violate the driver's Fourth Amendment right against unreasonable seizure by using their vehicles to force the driver's vehicle off the road, notwithstanding that such a maneuver posed a risk of serious harm to the driver and in fact resulted in his paralysis).

REFERENCES/FURTHER READING

Intent and Substantial Certainty

John Finnis, *Intention in Tort Law*, in David G. Owen (ed.), *Philosophical Foundations of Tort Law* 229 (1995).

David J. Jung & David I. Levine, *Whence Knowledge Intent? Whither Knowledge Intent?*, 20 U.C. Davis L. Rev. 551 (1987).

Walter Probert, *A Case Study of Interpretation in Torts*: Garratt v. Dailey, 19 U. Tol. L. Rev. 73 (1987).

Ellen S. Pryor, *The Stories We Tell: Intentional Harms and the Quest for Insurance Funding*, 75 Tex. L. Rev. 1721 (1997).

Kenneth W. Simons, *Statistical Knowledge Deconstructed*, 92 B.U. L. Rev. 1 (2012).

Kenneth W. Simons, *Rethinking Mental States*, 72 B.U. L. Rev. 463 (1992).

Symposium on the Third Restatement of Torts, 54 Vand. L. Rev. 1133 *et seq.* (2001) (articles and commentary by Profs. Henderson & Twerski, Armour & Sebok).

Apportionment of Responsibility

Ellen Bublick, *Citizen No-Duty Rules: Rape Victims and Comparative Fault*, 99 Colum. L. Rev. 1413 (1999).

Gail D. Hollister, *Using Comparative Fault to Replace the All-or-Nothing Lottery Imposed in Intentional Tort Suits in Which Both Plaintiff and Defendant Are at Fault*, 46 Vand. L. Rev. 121 (1993).

Consent

Larry Alexander, *The Moral Magic of Consent (II)*, 2 Leg. Theory 165 (1996).

Heidi M. Hurd, *The Moral Magic of Consent*, 2 Leg. Theory 121 (1996).

Alan Wertheimer, *What Is Consent? And Is It Important?*, 3 Buff. Crim. L. Rev. 557 (2000).

Symposium, *Five Approaches to Legal Reasoning in the Classroom: Contrasting Perspectives on* O'Brien v. Cunard S.S. Co., 57 Mo. L. Rev. 346 (1992).

Self-Defense

Symposium, *Self-Defense and Relations of Domination: Moral and Legal Perspectives on Battered Women Who Kill*, 57 U. Pitt. L. Rev. 461 *et seq.* (1996) (articles and commentaries by Profs. Richards, Schneider, Armour, Young, Fletcher, Zipursky, Gauthier, Finklestein, Pendleton, Thompson, Ripstein, Sebok, Cohen, Chamallas & Horowitz).

Defense of Property and Detention/Arrest

Regina Austin, *Of False Teeth and Biting Critiques:* Jones v. Fisher *in Context*, 15 Touro L. Rev. 389 (1999).

Anne-Marie Harris, *Shopping While Black: Applying 42 U.S.C. § 1981 to Cases of Consumer Racial Profiling*, 23 Bos. Coll. Third World L.J. 1 (2003).

Geoffrey W. R. Palmer, *The Iowa Spring Gun Case: A Study in American Gothic*, 56 Iowa L. Rev. 1219 (1971).

Richard A. Posner, *Killing or Wounding to Protect a Property Interest*, 14 J.L. & Econ. 201 (1971).

Domestic Violence and Intentional Torts

Martha Chamallas and Jennifer Wriggins, *The Measure of Injury* (2010).
Jennifer Wiggins, *Domestic Violence Torts*, 75 S. Cal. L. Rev. 121 (2001).

Vosburg, Unintended Effects and Transferred Intent

Vincent R. Johnson, *Transferred Intent in American Tort Law*, 87 Marq. L. Rev. 903 (2004).
William L. Prosser, *Transferred Intent*, 45 Tex. L. Rev. 650 (1967).
Osborne M. Reynolds, Jr., *Transferred Intent: Should Its "Curious Survival" Continue?*, 50 Okla. L. Rev. 529 (1997).
Osborne M. Reynolds, Jr., *Tortious Battery*, 37 Okla. L. Rev. 717 (1984).
Symposium on Vosburg v. Putney, 1992 Wis. L. Rev. 853 *et seq.* (articles and comments by Profs. Henderson, Rabin, Hurst & Zile).

CHAPTER 10

INFLICTION OF EMOTIONAL DISTRESS

Chapter 9 focused on legal wrongs that have been part of Anglo-American law since the Middle Ages. By contrast, in this chapter we consider two torts that came to be recognized as causes of action only in the mid-twentieth century.

The first is called *intentional infliction of emotional distress* (IIED). (Some courts refer to it as the tort of *outrage.*) It imposes liability on an actor who, by means of outrageous conduct, intentionally or recklessly causes severe emotional distress to another. In analyzing IIED, we will also have occasion to consider related statutorily based claims for race, age, and gender discrimination.

As its name indicates, the second tort covered in this chapter — *negligent infliction of emotional distress* (NIED) — shifts the focus away from intent-based wrongs to wrongs involving carelessness. Although we have placed our treatment of NIED in this chapter to emphasize its historical and analytic links to assault and IIED, your professor may choose (or may have chosen) to cover it as part of general negligence doctrine.

I. INTENTIONAL INFLICTION OF EMOTIONAL DISTRESS

A. The Emergence of IIED

The hallmark of actions for assault, battery, and false imprisonment is their concern to vindicate "dignitary" interests, such as the interest in controlling others' efforts to gain access to one's body. Given their ancient lineage, it is perhaps not surprising that these torts remain concerned with responding to basic forms of wrongdoing, such as intentional woundings and confinements. Conversely, they do not purport to address the full range of conduct in which one person subjects another to a serious indignity.

Indeed, even the limited range of interests guarded by these torts benefits from only partial protection. For example, while assault permits victims to complain of threats of bodily harm, it only applies to threats of imminent harm.

Even when one takes into account the existence of other longstanding torts, such as actions for libel and slander, significant gaps remain. Consider the famous case of *Wilkinson v. Downton*, [1897] 2 Q.B. 57. There, a man appeared at plaintiff's home and, as a practical joke, falsely informed her that her husband had been "smashed up" in an accident, had suffered two broken legs, and had sent for the plaintiff to rescue him, all of which caused the plaintiff severe and lasting distress. Without specifying the cause of action on which the plaintiff could rely, the trial judge upheld the jury's verdict for the plaintiff. Because there was evidence that the victim had suffered nausea and other physical side effects from the experience, the defendant was held liable because he caused her physical harm by having "wilfully done an act calculated to cause [such] . . . harm. . . ."

For an even more dramatic example, consider *Nickerson v. Hodges*, 84 So. 37 (La. 1920). Carrie Nickerson, a single woman in her early 40s, was privy to a family legend asserting that her relatives had buried a pot of gold on property owned by one John Smith. After visiting a fortune-teller, who gave her what purported to be a map showing the pot's location on Smith's property, Nickerson, with the help of others, spent months digging on the property. (Smith consented to their activities, apparently in the slight hope that they might find something and share it with him.) At some point, Smith's daughter, Minnie, along with two others — William "Bud" Baker and H. R. Hayes — formulated a plan to "assist" the explorers in their quest.

> Accordingly they obtained an old copper kettle or bucket, filled it with rocks and wet dirt, and buried it [in the area where Nickerson was searching]. . . . [A] note was written by Hayes . . . directing whoever should find the pot not to open it for three days, and to notify all the heirs. This note was wrapped in tin, [and] placed [in between the pot's two lids]. . . . [A]ccording to these three defendants, [their plan] was . . . [for the discovery of the pot] to be an April fool; but . . . the proper opportunity for the "find" did not present itself until April 14th. On that day Miss Nickerson and her associates were searching and digging near the point where the pot had been buried, when one Grady Hayes, a brother of H. R. Hayes, following directions from the latter, and apparently helping the explorers to hunt for the gold, dug up the pot and gave the alarm. All of those in the vicinity, of course, rushed to the spot, those who were "in" on the secret being apparently as much excited as the rest, and, after some discussion, it was decided to remove the [upper] lid. When this was done, the note was discovered, and H. R. Hayes advised Miss Nickerson that he thought it proper that its directions should be carried out, and that the bank at Cotton Valley, a few miles distant, was the best place to deposit the "gold" for safe-keeping, until the delays could run and the heirs be notified, as requested. Following this suggestion, the pot was placed in a gunny sack, tied up, and taken to the bank for deposit. . . .
>
> As might have been supposed, it did not take long for the news to spread that Miss Nickerson and her associates in the search for fortune, had found a pot of gold,

> and the discussion and interest in the matter became so general that defendant A. J. Hodges, vice president of the bank, went over from his place of business in Cotton Valley to the bank, and he and [Gatling, the bank's cashier] . . . decided to examine the pot, so that, in event it did contain gold, proper precautions to guard the bank might be taken. . . . These two undid the wire sufficiently to peep into the pot, and discovered that it apparently contained only dirt. They then replaced the lid and held their tongues until the reappearance of Miss Nickerson. However, the secret leaked out from other sources, that the whole matter was a joke, and this information too, became pretty well distributed.
>
> After depositing the pot in the bank, Miss Nickerson went to Minden, La., and induced Judge R. C. Drew to agree to accompany her to Cotton Valley on the following Monday (the deposit at the bank having been made on Saturday) for the purpose of seeing that the ceremonies surrounding the opening of the treasure were properly conducted. . . . Some half a dozen other relatives . . . were notified, and either accompanied or preceded Miss Nickerson to Cotton Valley.
>
> With the stage thus set, the parties all appeared at the bank on Monday morning at about 11 o'clock, and among the number were H. R. Hayes, one of the defendants, who seems to have been one of the guiding spirits in the scheme, and one Bushong, the latter, we infer, from intimations thrown out by witnesses in the record, being at the time either an avowed or supposed suitor of Miss Nickerson's. Judge Drew, as the spokesman for the party, approached Gatling and informed him that it was desired that the pot be produced for the purpose of opening and examining the contents for the benefit of those thus assembled. The testimony of the witnesses varies a little as to just when the storm began; some say, as soon as the sack was brought out. Miss Nickerson discovered that the string was tied near the top, instead of down low around the pot, and immediately commenced to shout that she had been robbed; others insist that she was calm until the package was opened and the mocking earth and stones met her view. Be that as it may, she flew into a rage, threw the lid of the pot at Gatling, and for some reason, not clearly explained, turned the force of her wrath upon Hayes to such an extent that he appealed for protection, and Bushong, with another, held her arms to prevent further violence.
>
> Miss Nickerson . . . some 20 years before had been an inmate of an insane asylum, to the knowledge of those who had thus deceived her. She was energetic and self-supporting in her chosen line of employment [as a salesperson] . . . until [this episode took place]. The conspirators, no doubt, merely intended what they did as a practical joke, and had no willful intention of doing the lady any injury. However, the results were quite serious indeed, and the mental suffering and humiliation must have been quite unbearable, to say nothing of the disappointment and conviction, which she carried to her grave some two years later, that she had been robbed.

Id. at 37-39.

Before she died Nickerson instituted suit against H. R. Hayes, William Baker, and Minnie Smith, among others, seeking compensation for expenses, lost wages, mental and physical suffering, and humiliation. (As noted by the court, she died prior to trial, leaving her legal heirs to proceed with the suit.) After the jury returned a defense verdict, the Louisiana Supreme Court reversed and ordered payment to Nickerson's survivors in the amount of $500. The court indicated that, had Nickerson still been alive, a substantially larger sum would have been appropriate to compensate her for the "wrong thus done." As was the case in *Wilkinson*, the court nowhere in its opinion purported to identify the cause of action that provided redress for this wrong.

In 1936, Calvert Magruder published an influential article that attempted to fill the doctrinal void evidenced by decisions such as *Wilkinson* and *Nickerson*. Magruder began his analysis by noting the then-black letter rule (discussed more extensively in Section II *infra*) that causation of emotional distress, *independent of any other harm or setback*, did not count as an "injury" in the eyes of tort law and hence was (almost) never *of itself* actionable. He then surveyed an array of cases in which plaintiffs had recovered substantial damage awards on claims of assault, battery, false imprisonment, and defamation even though the predicate injuries of which they complained were minimal. (For example, he identified cases in which battery plaintiffs had won damages for physically harmless but offensive contacts, and in which false imprisonment plaintiffs had similarly obtained damage awards for brief and not-unpleasant confinements.) Although each of these claims had been framed in terms of one of these other torts, Magruder argued that they in fact formed a class unto themselves — a class that was defined by two features.

First, in each case, the interest whose invasion nominally gave rise to the tort (e.g., the interest in bodily integrity or freedom from confinement) was *not* the interest primarily being vindicated by the jury's damage award. Instead, given the minimal nature of the predicate injury of which the plaintiffs had complained, these awards, on his view, had to be understood as mainly compensating the victim for his emotional distress. Second, Magruder argued that judges had been led in these cases to sidestep the black letter rule against recovery for freestanding emotional distress because of the sheer outrageousness of the defendants' conduct.

In short, courts had, without fully realizing it, come to articulate a new tort cause of action. Under it, an actor could be held liable for conduct (a) that is *outrageous* (Magruder's phrase was "beyond all bounds of decency"); (b) that is undertaken for the *purpose* of causing the victim *emotional distress* so severe that it could be expected to affect adversely his physical health; and (c) that *causes* such distress (even if that distress does not actually generate the expected physical harm).

The cause of action outlined by Magruder has in one sense taken firm root in U.S. tort law. Indeed, the "outrage" or "IIED" tort is now widely if not universally recognized. However, there is another sense in which the action still remains at the periphery of tort practice. Although they are today often pleaded, IIED claims appear *rarely to succeed*. The two cases excerpted below are in this respect unrepresentative: In each, the plaintiff prevails. Compare their facts to those of the cases discussed in the notes that follow them. Taken together, do the principal and note cases reveal a pattern as to who recovers and who does not? Do they give you a sense of why courts have been willing to recognize this new cause of action as a general matter, yet reluctant to permit particular plaintiffs to prevail on it?

B. Elements

Dickens v. Puryear

276 S.E.2d 325 (N.C. 1981)

EXUM, J. Plaintiff's complaint is cast as a claim for intentional infliction of mental distress. It was filed more than one year but less than three years after the incidents complained of occurred.... Defendants' motions for summary judgment were allowed on the ground that plaintiff's claim was for assault and battery; therefore it was barred by the one-year statute of limitations applicable to assault and battery.

... We hold that ... plaintiff's claim is not altogether barred by the one-year statute because plaintiff's factual showing indicates plaintiff may be able to prove a claim for intentional infliction of mental distress, a claim which is governed by the three-year statute of limitations....

... For a time preceding the incidents in question plaintiff Dickens, a thirty-one year old man, shared sex, alcohol and marijuana with defendants' daughter, a seventeen year old high school student. On 2 April 1975 defendants, husband and wife, lured plaintiff into rural Johnston County, North Carolina. Upon plaintiff's arrival defendant Earl Puryear, after identifying himself, called out to defendant Ann Puryear who emerged from beside a nearby building and, crying, stated that she "didn't want to see that SOB." Ann Puryear then left the scene. Thereafter Earl Puryear pointed a pistol between plaintiff's eyes and shouted "Ya'll come on out." Four men wearing ski masks and armed with nightsticks then approached from behind plaintiff and beat him into semi-consciousness. They handcuffed plaintiff to a piece of farm machinery and resumed striking him with nightsticks. Defendant Earl Puryear, while brandishing a knife and cutting plaintiff's hair, threatened plaintiff with castration. During four or five interruptions of the beatings defendant Earl Puryear and the others, within plaintiff's hearing, discussed and took votes on whether plaintiff should be killed or castrated. Finally, after some two hours and the conclusion of a final conference, the beatings ceased. Defendant Earl Puryear told plaintiff to go home, pull his telephone off the wall, pack his clothes, and leave the state of North Carolina; otherwise he would be killed. Plaintiff was then set free.*

Plaintiff filed his complaint on 31 March 1978. It alleges that defendants on the occasion just described intentionally inflicted mental distress upon him. He further alleges that as a result of defendants' acts plaintiff has suffered "severe and permanent mental and emotional distress, and physical injury to his nerves and nervous system." He alleges that he is unable to sleep, afraid to go out in the dark, afraid to meet strangers, afraid he may be killed, suffering from chronic diarrhea and a gum disorder, unable effectively to perform his job, and that he has lost $1000 per month income....

II

... Defendants contend, and the Court of Appeals agreed, that this is an action grounded in assault and battery. Although plaintiff pleads the tort of intentional

* [Earl Puryear was later convicted for the crime of conspiracy to commit simple assault. — EDS.]

infliction of mental distress, the Court of Appeals concluded that the complaint's factual allegations and the factual showing at the hearing on summary judgment support only a claim for assault and battery. The claim was, therefore, barred by the one-year period of limitations applicable to assault and battery. Plaintiff, on the other hand, argues that the factual showing on the motion supports a claim for intentional infliction of mental distress[,] a claim which is governed by the three-year period of limitations.[8] At least, plaintiff argues, his factual showing is such that it cannot be said as a matter of law that he will be unable to prove such a claim at trial. . . .

A

. . . The interest protected by the action for battery is freedom from intentional and unpermitted contact with one's person; the interest protected by the action for assault is freedom from apprehension of a harmful or offensive contact with one's person. McCracken v. Sloan, 40 N.C. App. 214, 252 S.E.2d 250 (1979); *see also* Prosser, *Law of Torts* §§ 9, 10 (4th ed. 1971) (hereinafter "Prosser"). The apprehension created must be one of an immediate harmful or offensive contact, as distinguished from contact in the future. . . .

[A]s noted by Prosser, § 10, p.40, "(t)hreats for the future . . . are simply not present breaches of the peace, and so never have fallen within the narrow boundaries of (assault)." Thus threats for the future are actionable, if at all, not as assaults but as intentional inflictions of mental distress.

The tort of intentional infliction of mental distress is recognized in North Carolina. Stanback v. Stanback, 297 N.C. 181, 254 S.E.2d 611 (1979). "[L]iability arises under this tort when a defendant's 'conduct exceeds all bounds usually tolerated by decent society' and the conduct 'causes mental distress of a very serious kind.'" *Id.* at 196, 254 S.E.2d at 622, quoting Prosser, § 12, p.56. In *Stanback* plaintiff alleged that defendant breached a separation agreement between the parties. She further alleged . . . "that defendant's conduct in breaching the contract was 'wilful, malicious, calculated, deliberate and purposeful' . . . (and) that 'she has suffered great mental anguish and anxiety . . . ' as a result of defendant's conduct in breaching the agreement . . . (and) that defendant acted recklessly and irresponsibly and 'with full knowledge of the consequences which would result. . . .'" *Id.* at 198, 254 S.E.2d at 622-23. We held . . . that these allegations were "sufficient to state a claim for what has become essentially the tort of intentional infliction of serious emotional distress. Plaintiff has

8. Although defendants argue that even the tort of intentional infliction of mental distress is governed by the one-year statute of limitations, we are satisfied that it is not. The one-year statute, G.S. 1-54(3), applies to "libel, slander, assault, battery, or false imprisonment." As we go to some length in the opinion to demonstrate, the tort of intentional infliction of mental distress is none of these things. Thus the rule of statutory construction embodied in the maxim, *expressio unius est exclusio alterius*, meaning the expression of one thing is the exclusion of another, applies. No statute of limitations addresses the tort of intentional infliction of mental distress by name. It must, therefore, be governed by the more general three-year statute of limitations, G.S. 1-52(5), which applies to "any other injury to the person or rights of another, not arising on contract and not hereafter enumerated." . . .

alleged that defendant intentionally inflicted mental distress." *Id.* at 196, 254 S.E.2d at 621-22.

The tort alluded to in *Stanback* is defined in the Restatement [(Second) of Torts Section] 46 [(1965)] as follows:

> One who by extreme and outrageous conduct intentionally or recklessly causes severe emotional distress to another is subject to liability for such emotional distress, and if bodily harm to the other results from it, for such bodily harm.

The holding in *Stanback* was in accord with the Restatement definition of . . . intentional infliction of mental distress. We now reaffirm this holding. . . .

. . . This tort imports an act which is done with the intention of causing emotional distress or with reckless indifference to the likelihood that emotional distress may result. A defendant is liable for this tort when he "desires to inflict severe emotional distress . . . (or) knows that such distress is certain, or substantially certain, to result from his conduct . . . (or) where he acts recklessly . . . in deliberate disregard of a high degree of probability that the emotional distress will follow" and the mental distress does in fact result. Restatement § 46, Comment i, p.77. "The authorities seem to agree that if the tort is wilful and not merely negligent, the wrongdoer is liable for such physical injuries as may proximately result, whether he could have foreseen them or not." Kimberly v. Howland, 55 S.E.[778,] 780 [(N.C. 1906)].

[The court reviewed earlier North Carolina cases, which suggested that except in cases of assault, the state's tort law does not permit recovery for fright alone, but does permit recovery for tortiously caused physical injury, such as a heart attack, resulting from fright. It distinguished those cases as concerned to define the necessary elements of a claim for *negligent* rather than intentional infliction of emotional distress. See *infra* Section II for a discussion of NIED and physical harm. — EDS.]

Stanback, in effect, was the first formal recognition by this Court of the relatively recent tort of intentional infliction of mental distress. This tort, under the authorities already cited, consists of: (1) extreme and outrageous conduct, (2) which is intended to cause and does cause (3) severe emotional distress to another. The tort may also exist where defendant's actions indicate a reckless indifference to the likelihood that they will cause severe emotional distress. Recovery may be had for the emotional distress so caused and for any other bodily harm which proximately results from the distress itself. . . .

C

The question [raised by the defendants' summary judgment motion] is . . . whether the evidentiary showing demonstrates as a matter of law that plaintiff's only claim, if any, is for assault and battery. If plaintiff, as a matter of law, has no claim for intentional infliction of mental distress but has a claim, if at all, only for assault and battery, then plaintiff cannot surmount the affirmative defense of the one-year statute of limitations and defendants are entitled to summary judgment. . . .

Although plaintiff labels his claim one for intentional infliction of mental distress, we agree with the Court of Appeals that "(t)he nature of the action is not determined by what either party calls it. . . ." Hayes v. Ricard, 244 N.C. 313, 320, 93 S.E.2d 540,

545-46 (1956). The nature of the action is determined "by the issues arising on the pleading and by the relief sought," *id.*, and by the facts which, at trial, are proved or which, on motion for summary judgment, are forecast by the evidentiary showing.

Here much of the factual showing at the hearing related to assaults and batteries committed by defendants against plaintiff. The physical beatings and the cutting of plaintiff's hair constituted batteries. The threats of castration and death, being threats which created apprehension of immediate harmful or offensive contact, were assaults. Plaintiff's recovery for injuries, mental or physical, caused by these actions would be barred by the one-year statute of limitations.

The evidentiary showing on the summary judgment motion does, however, indicate that defendant Earl Puryear threatened plaintiff with death in the future unless plaintiff went home, pulled his telephone off the wall, packed his clothes, and left the state. The Court of Appeals characterized this threat as being "an immediate threat of harmful and offensive contact. It was a present threat of harm to plaintiff. . . ." 45 N.C. App. at 700, 263 S.E.2d at 859. The Court of Appeals thus concluded that this threat was also an assault barred by the one-year statute of limitations.

We disagree with the Court of Appeals' characterization of this threat. The threat was not one of imminent, or immediate, harm. It was a threat for the future apparently intended to and which allegedly did inflict serious mental distress; therefore it is actionable, if at all, as an intentional infliction of mental distress.

The threat, of course, cannot be considered separately from the entire episode of which it was only a part. The assaults and batteries, construing the record in the light most favorable to the plaintiff, were apparently designed to give added impetus to the ultimate conditional threat of future harm. Although plaintiff's recovery for injury, mental or physical, directly caused by the assaults and batteries is barred by the statute of limitations, these assaults and batteries may be considered in determining the outrageous character of the ultimate threat and the extent of plaintiff's mental or emotional distress caused by it.[11]

Having concluded, therefore, that the factual showing on the motions for summary judgment was sufficient to indicate that plaintiff may be able to prove at trial a claim for intentional infliction of mental distress, we hold that summary judgment for defendants based upon the one-year statute of limitations was error and we remand the matter for further proceedings against defendant Earl Puryear. . . .

---

11. We note in this regard plaintiff's statement in his deposition that "(i)t is not entirely (the future threat) which caused me all of my emotional upset and disturbance that I have complained about. It was the ordeal from beginning to end." If plaintiff is able to prove a claim for intentional infliction of mental distress it will then be the difficult, but necessary, task of the trier of fact to ascertain the damages flowing from the conditional threat of future harm. Although the assaults and batteries serve to color and give impetus to the future threat and its impact on plaintiff's emotional condition, plaintiff may not recover damages flowing directly from the assaults and batteries themselves.

NOTES AND QUESTIONS

1. *IIED and the Restatements.* The ALI first endorsed the IIED cause of action in a 1948 Supplement to the First Restatement, which contained the following provision:

> § 46. One who, without a privilege to do so, intentionally causes severe emotional distress to another is liable (a) for such emotional distress, and (b) for bodily harm resulting from it.

The "without . . . privilege" clause tracked language that the Reporter, William Prosser, had used in an article published shortly after Magruder's that also purported to locate the new IIED tort within the interstices of existing case law. Prosser introduced this clause in part to block use of the tort against creditors who induced severe emotional distress in others simply by insisting on their legal right ("privilege") to foreclose on property securing defaulted loans. It was replaced in 1965 by the requirement of "extreme and outrageous conduct" when Section 46 was published as part of the Second Restatement. Apparently, the ALI thought that the change of language would more effectively limit the potential scope of the new tort.

William L. Prosser (1898-1972) Principal Reporter, Second Restatement of Torts

The language of Section 46(1) of the Second Restatement, quoted in *Dickens*, is essentially replicated in the Third Restatement:

> An actor who by extreme and outrageous conduct intentionally or recklessly causes severe emotional harm to another is subject to liability for that emotional harm and, if the emotional harm causes bodily harm, also for the bodily harm.

Restatement (Third) of Torts: Liability for Physical and Emotional Harm § 46 (2012).

2. *Assault and IIED: Conditional Threats Revisited.* As *Dickens* makes clear, IIED has been recognized by courts in part to deal with a special class of cases that closely resemble assault, yet do not meet the definition of that tort because the defendant intentionally induces in the plaintiff an apprehension of harmful contact that will take place in the indefinite future, rather than imminently.

One of the most prominent early American decisions adopting the new tort of IIED involved this sort of threat. In *State Rubbish Collectors Assn. v. Siliznoff*, 240 P.2d 282 (Cal. 1952), Siliznoff, an independent hauler, obtained a contract to haul garbage from a brewery. The brewery previously had used another hauler who belonged to the association. Two association officers prevailed on Siliznoff to join and to abide by its rules, which would have required him to compensate the prior hauler for having taken over the brewery account. Siliznoff balked, inquiring what the consequences would be if he did not, whereupon the officials informed him that he would be beaten up and his truck destroyed. During the course of a two-hour nighttime meeting, the association's officers extracted a verbal promise from Siliznoff that he would join the association and abide by its rules. Siliznoff never signed the agreement, however, and, although association members did not carry out their threat, they did sue him for breach of his promise to join and pay compensation(!). Siliznoff successfully defended against this contract claim by pleading duress, and won a jury verdict of $8,750 in compensatory and punitive damages on a counterclaim for assault (although the trial court reduced the award to $4,750).

Writing for the California Supreme Court, Justice Roger Traynor upheld the award for the plaintiff. Agreeing with the defendants that their threats failed to constitute an assault because they were conditional, and because they referred to actions that would take place at some indefinite future time, the court nonetheless concluded that Siliznoff had established a valid tort claim. Following the formulation of the 1948 Restatement supplement, Traynor reasoned that it was sufficient for the plaintiff to establish that the defendants "intentionally subject[ed][him] to the mental suffering incident to serious threats to his physical well-being. . . ." *Id.* at 284.

3. *Statutes of Limitations: Substitute or Supplement?* Suppose that Puryear had not issued the threat on which the *Dickens* court fastened in determining that the plaintiff had pleaded a valid claim of IIED. Could Dickens have still availed himself of the longer statute of limitations by arguing that the rest of Puryear's conduct, even though it amounted to an assault, battery, and false imprisonment, also amounted to IIED? Following Section 47 of the Second Restatement, some courts have answered that question with a no. In these jurisdictions, when the defendant's conduct would be actionable as another tort such as battery, the statute of limitations for those other torts will control. *See* K.G. v. R.T.R., 918 S.W.2d 795, 799-800 (Mo. 1996) (IIED was intended to supplement, not supplant, existing torts; a claimant who is distressed as a result of acts constituting a battery must seek compensation for that distress within the time limits set for battery actions).

Some courts have not been as clear about the relation of IIED to torts such as battery. A notable example arose out of the suit brought by Paula Jones against President Bill Clinton. According to Jones's complaint, in 1991, then-governor Clinton arranged for an Arkansas state trooper to bring Jones, a state employee, up to his hotel room. There, he allegedly pulled her next to him, rubbed her leg, and attempted to kiss her neck. Jones further alleged that when she extricated herself and sat on a sofa across the room, the governor lowered his pants, exposed himself, and instructed her to kiss his penis. When Jones indicated that she wanted to leave, Governor Clinton relented, warning Jones that the matter should be kept between them.

In 1994, one day prior to the third anniversary of the date on which the alleged events took place, Jones filed suit. The suit raised various federal claims for civil rights violations and employment discrimination, but also state law claims, including one for IIED.* President Clinton's lawyers moved to dismiss on the ground that the conduct alleged by Jones in connection with her IIED claim in fact supported claims for battery and/or false imprisonment, which are subject to a one-year limitations period. The trial judge rejected this argument, concluding that the facts alleged by Jones made out a colorable claim of IIED. Jones v. Clinton, 974 F. Supp. 712 (E.D. Ark. 1997). The judge

---

* President Clinton's lawyers initially argued that the suit should be stayed during the term of his presidency. The Supreme Court, however, ruled that a sitting president enjoys no special privilege to delay litigation that does not concern actions connected with his office. Clinton v. Jones, 580 U.S. 681 (1997).

did not explain, however, whether she reached this conclusion because Jones had alleged conduct *apart* from the conduct that would have established a claim for battery or false imprisonment (e.g., the alleged solicitation of oral sex), or because Jones was authorized to sue for IIED even with respect to conduct that also constituted a battery or false imprisonment.

4. *Aggravated Torts?* Outside the statute of limitations context, courts sometimes permit plaintiffs to point to the same conduct to prove that they have been the victims of a more "traditional" tort and IIED. For example, in *Miller v. National Broadcasting Co.*, 187 Cal. App. 3d 1463 (Ct. App. 1986), the defendant's television crew followed paramedics into the plaintiff's home without her permission and there filmed for broadcast the paramedics' unsuccessful attempt to resuscitate the plaintiff's husband, who had suffered a heart attack. The appellate court affirmed the trial court's denial of the defendant's summary judgment motion on claims for trespass, invasion of privacy, and IIED, even though the operative facts of the IIED claim seem to have been identical to those of the trespass and privacy claims.

Arguably, in cases such as *Miller*, the court's recognition of an IIED claim serves to indicate that the defendant has committed an "aggravated" (i.e., especially culpable) version of these other torts. Recognition of an IIED action in these contexts thus resembles a finding of malice or reckless indifference of the sort that justifies the imposition of punitive damages. *See* Chapter 8; *see also Miller, supra.* (noting that defendant's conduct evidenced not just a trespass and an invasion of privacy, but also a callous disregard for plaintiff's rights). Consider in this regard *Burgess v. Taylor*, 44 S.W.3d 806 (Ky. Ct. App. 2001). Plaintiff was deeply attached to her two horses, but couldn't adequately maintain them on her property. Although she retained ownership, she arranged for them to live on defendants' farm after defendants professed to be fellow horse-lovers. Shortly thereafter, defendants sold the horses for slaughter, then attempted to cover up their actions. The intermediate appellate court upheld plaintiff's claim for IIED even though the action could and probably should have been framed as a claim for the tort of conversion—unlawful destruction of personal property. In effect, the outrageousness of the defendants' conduct marked this as an instance of particularly malicious or aggravated conversion.

Littlefield v. McGuffey

954 F.2d 1337 (7th Cir. 1992)

Wood, J. Susanne Littlefield sued Malcolm McGuffey, also known as Wally Mack among other persona, claiming he denied her rental housing because her boyfriend, the father of her daughter, was not of the same race as she. She sought relief under the Equal Opportunity in Housing provision of the Civil Rights Act of 1866 and the Fair Housing Act as amended by the Fair Housing Amendments Act of 1988: 42 U.S.C.A. §§ 1982, 3604, 3613, and 3617.* In addition she . . . raised a claim for intentional

* [42 U.S.C. § 1982 bans intentional discrimination by governmental or private actors against non-white citizens in connection with the ownership, purchase, sale, or lease of property. The Fair

infliction of emotional distress under Illinois common law. The jury found Mr. McGuffey liable and awarded $50,000 in compensatory damages and $100,000 in punitive damages.

McGuffey thereupon moved for a judgment notwithstanding the verdict and, alternatively, for a new trial. Judge Williams denied both motions. She then entered judgment on the verdict [and] awarded attorney's fees. . . . Littlefield v. Mack, 750 F. Supp. 1395, 1404 (N.D. Ill. 1990). Defendant McGuffey appeals [these decisions]. For the reasons stated below we affirm.

Background

On September 14, 1988, Ms. Littlefield, who was then 23 years old, met Malcolm McGuffey at one of his apartment buildings. After viewing the advertised apartment she completed a rental application form and gave him a $280 check as a security deposit, leaving the name of the payee blank at McGuffey's request. Later, McGuffey filled in the name of the payee with the fictitious "Santa Maria Realty," claiming at trial to have chosen that name because it had been close to Columbus Day. He endorsed the check first as "Santa Maria Realty" then as "Osvaldo Kennardo," another persona of his. At their meeting McGuffey and Ms. Littlefield had agreed she, her younger sister Sandra, and her daughter Shaunte would occupy the two-bedroom apartment and that McGuffey would purchase and install a carpet with Ms. Littlefield paying the cost of installation. McGuffey gave Ms. Littlefield a key to the apartment, and between then and September 27 she, members of her family, and friends cleaned and painted the apartment and moved various belongings into it.

On September 27, 1988, Bruce Collins, accompanied by Shaunte, the two-year old daughter of Collins and Littlefield, took a check to McGuffey to pay for the carpet installation. When McGuffey realized Mr. Collins was not the same race as Ms. Littlefield but was the father of her daughter, he became quite agitated and exclaimed "the old man" had rented the apartment to someone else. At trial McGuffey admitted he sometimes referred to himself as "the old man."

After Collins left, McGuffey called Ms. Littlefield at work and told her she could not rent the apartment because "the boss" (another of McGuffey's persona) had rented it to someone else. He also told her he had changed the locks and had put her belongings out on the porch. This was but the first of many phone calls McGuffey made to Ms. Littlefield. That evening he called her at home, identified himself as Walley Luther, and, mimicking a stereotypical black manner of speaking, told her he wanted to move in with her and "six black guys, . . . quit work and take welfare . . . and drugs with [her] . . . and swap wives with Bruce." He called her at least two more times that night and several other times that week with similar, degrading messages.

Ms. Littlefield was not the only recipient of McGuffey's harassing, insulting and racist phone calls. Her sister, Kathleen Gutierrez, was called many times over the next week or so. McGuffey told her he was a member of the Ku Klux Klan and regularly asked how her sister, Susanne, "could have [gone] to bed with a nigger and how she

---

Housing Act also bans such acts, but in addition regulates a wider range of conduct pertaining to housing. — Eds.]

could . . . have a nigger baby." On one occasion McGuffey attempted to lure Ms. Gutierrez outside on the pretext that she had to move her car because the church lot where it was parked was being caulked.

The phone calls did not suffice. In early November McGuffey tracked down Ms. Littlefield's new residence and left a note, written on a napkin taped to her door, threatening the life of Bruce Collins and repeating racist slurs. When she arrived home that evening, Ms. Littlefield found her sister, Sandra, hiding behind the door, clutching a broom.

Ms. Littlefield and her witnesses . . . testified to all these events and more. Additionally, Ms. Littlefield testified to numerous episodes of severe emotional distress. She became hysterical upon receiving McGuffey's call at work, went to the restroom, and cried; the rest of the day she suffered from stomach upset and diarrhea. She experienced numerous episodes of disquiet and fright, being particularly fretful because she feared for her daughter's safety. Ms. Littlefield also testified that when she came home at night with Shaunte, she would run from her car to her apartment, clutching her daughter in one arm, with her keys in one hand and a can of mace in the other.

McGuffey denied Ms. Littlefield's allegations, claiming he had not refused her rental housing on the basis of race and that he had not harassed her. He asserted, instead, he had learned from various businesses and prior landlords that she was a poor credit risk and had a history as an undesirable tenant. He presented no witnesses, however, that confirmed having given him the negative rental-history or credit information. On the other hand, Ms. Littlefield presented witnesses [who] generally testified [that] the credit information McGuffey claimed to have acquired would not be given out and that, anyway, Ms. Littlefield's credit history was respectable. The testimony of Brice Fawcett, Ms. Littlefield's former landlord, was notably damaging for the defendant. He contradicted everything McGuffey claimed to have been told by him; he stated Ms. Littlefield had been a good tenant; and he testified McGuffey did not interview him until October 1, four days after McGuffey evicted Ms. Littlefield. As the district court observed, "Mr. McGuffey's story therefore depended almost entirely on his own credibility, and he was, to put it mildly, a witness with credibility problems." *Littlefield*, 750 F. Supp. at 1398.

Analysis

. . . Mr. McGuffey raises [various] issues, [including]: (1) whether the district court erred in admitting or refusing to admit certain items of evidence, . . . (4) whether there was sufficient evidence to support the damage awards, and (5) whether the award of attorney's fees was excessive. . . .

Admission of Evidence

McGuffey claims the trial court made three errors regarding admission of evidence that singly and collectively denied him a fair trial. . . .

On the merits we review claims of reversible error in a trial court's decision to admit or exclude evidence only for abuse of discretion, giving the judge great deference. . . .

[The court rejected McGuffey's first claim of error. — Eds.]

McGuffey further asserts it was error for the district court to admit Ms. Littlefield's testimony about episodes of fear and anxiety not accompanied by medically significant, physical manifestations. This claim of error fails because in Illinois physical manifestation of emotional distress is not an element of the tort of intentional infliction of emotional distress.

Under Illinois common law the tort comprises three elements.

> First, the conduct involved must be truly extreme and outrageous. Second, the actor must either intend that his conduct inflict severe emotional distress, or know that there is at least a high probability that his conduct will cause severe emotional distress. Third, the conduct must in fact cause severe emotional distress.

McGrath v. Fahey, 126 Ill. 2d 78, 127 Ill. Dec. 724, 533 N.E.2d 806, 809 (1988) (citing Public Finance Corp. v. Davis, 66 Ill. 2d 85, 4 Ill. Dec. 652, 360 N.E.2d 765 (1976)). These are the only elements enunciated by the court. Medically significant, physical manifestation of emotional distress is not among them. . . .

[Discussion of McGuffey's third claim of error omitted. — EDS.]

Jury Instructions

. . . A court of review should "proceed cautiously when asked to set aside a jury's verdict and order a new trial, bound to consume substantial judicial resources, on the ground that the instructions contained erroneous or confusing passages." Needham v. White Laboratories, Inc., 847 F.2d 355, 360 (7th Cir. 1988). . . .

First, McGuffey finds fault with Plaintiff's Instruction No. 21 regarding her state-law claim of intentional infliction of emotional distress. He raises numerous allegations, the essence of which is that there was insufficient evidence of past, present, or future damages to justify giving the challenged instruction.

. . . There is sufficient evidence in the record to support giving the challenged instruction. A perusal of the facts recited above shows Ms. Littlefield presented evidence of her having suffered severe emotional distress. Additionally, there was some evidence of that distress continuing through the time of trial. Thus, the district court was not without justification for giving the instruction with respect to past, present, and future damages. . . .

Next, McGuffey claims the court erred in giving, over his objection, an instruction that did not state the Fair Housing Act ("FHA") capped punitive-damage awards at $1,000. At the time McGuffey racially discriminated against Ms. Littlefield, as well as at the time she initiated her action against him, the Fair Housing Act contained [a $1,000 cap] on punitive-damage awards. 42 U.S.C.A. § 3612 (West 1977). In contrast, no similar statutory limitation existed (or now exists) on punitive damages awarded under 42 U.S.C. § 1982.[3] By the time the case went to trial, however, the Fair Housing

3. Under Illinois common law, punitive damages are not available in an action for intentional infliction of emotional distress because outrageous conduct is an element of the action. [Thus, an IIED plaintiff's compensatory award is deemed by Illinois law to be sufficiently punitive in itself. — EDS.] Knierim v. Izzo, 22 Ill. 2d 73, 174 N.E.2d 157, 165 (1961).

Amendment Act of 1988, codified at 42 U.S.C. §§ 3601-3619, had gone into effect. It removed the cap on punitive-damage awards. . . .

McGuffey's specific claim of error—the claim that the FHA's damage-limitation should have been stated in the jury instruction, although there was an accompanying § 1982 claim—fails. This is because the district court was correct when it instructed the jury on the law in effect at the time of decision rather than on the prior law.

It is a long-held, general principle "that a court is to apply the law in effect at the time it renders its decision, unless doing so would result in manifest injustice or there is statutory direction or legislative history to the contrary." Bradley v. Richmond School Board, 416 U.S. 696, 711, 94 S. Ct. 2006, 2016, 40 L. Ed. 2d 476 (1974) (Award of attorney's fees permitted for services rendered before effective date of statute where the statute became effective after trial court decision but before resolution of direct appeal.).

Applying the new § 3613 to McGuffey is not a manifest injustice and is not contrary to statutory direction or legislative history. . . . [N]o material injustice was worked on the defendant by the trial court's applying the law in effect at the time of decision. Moreover, McGuffey points to no statutory directive or legislative history that clearly demonstrates removal of the cap applies only to causes of action arising after the effective date of the amendments. We are not convinced by McGuffey's argument that the statute's general delay in its effective date until 180 days after enactment constitutes a statutory direction sufficient to overcome application of the principle enunciated in *Bradley*. The trial court properly refused McGuffey's proposed instruction. . . .

Sufficient Evidence

. . . McGuffey's next two claims of error are that there is insufficient evidence to support the jury's verdict awarding, on the one hand, $50,000 in compensatory damages and, on the other, $100,000 in punitive damages. A damage award will not be vacated "for excessiveness unless it is 'monstrously excessive' or there is 'no rational connection between the evidence on damages and the verdict.'" Matlock v. Barnes, 932 F.2d 658, 667 (7th Cir.), *cert. denied*, 502 U.S. 909, 112 S. Ct. 304, 116 L. Ed. 2d 247 (1991) (quoting Abernathy v. Superior Hardwoods, Inc., 704 F.2d 963, 972 (7th Cir. 1983)). . . .

McGuffey claims . . . [that] the amount of the award was the result of the jury's being carried away by passion and prejudice, due in large part to Ms. Littlefield's testimony about her emotional feelings.

But it is precisely the testimony about her emotional feelings and response to his terror tactics which supports the award for the claims of intentional infliction of emotional distress and racial discrimination. For example, Ms. Littlefield testified that after Mr. McGuffey called her at work to tell her she could not move into the apartment, she became scared, went to the washroom, cried for a half hour, and left work for the day without explaining to her boss why because she was too embarrassed. She also testified that in late October or early November 1988, after moving into an apartment with her daughter and sister, a terrifying note was discovered taped to her door. The note read: "By THE Time you read this message Kiss your Niger [sic] friend goodbye Bitch hand he's dead!!!" Plaintiff's Exhibit A. Plaintiff's handwriting expert testified the note had been written by McGuffey, but the defendant's expert was equivocal. All death threats are heinous and would support a finding of intentional infliction of emotional distress. This one all the more because it employs the most venomous and loathsome of racist epithets.

In addition, Ms. Littlefield testified she purchased cleaning, repair, and painting supplies, that she, members of her family, and friends cleaned and painted the apartment she was never allowed to occupy, and that she moved numerous personal items into it. This testimony belies McGuffey's appellate argument that Ms. Littlefield suffered no out-of-pocket loss.

Lastly, the jury's award is not out of line with other, similar awards. In Webb v. City of Chester, Ill., 813 F.2d 824 (7th Cir. 1987), we approved an award that included $20,250 as compensation specifically for embarrassment and humiliation where a police officer successfully asserted a claim of sexually discriminatory discharge. In *Webb* we also noted awards had passed appellate review where they "ranged from a low of $500 to a high of over $50,000." *Id.* at 837. At least one Illinois appellate court has approved a compensatory-damage award of $138,450 in an action that included a claim for intentional infliction of emotional distress. . . .

We, therefore, affirm the jury's compensatory-damage award.

McGuffey's other complaint is about the amount of the punitive-damage award. . . .

. . . [W]e, like the district court, conclude there is sufficient evidence to support the jury's punitive-damage award. . . . Initially, McGuffey rejected Ms. Littlefield as a tenant because of the race of her boyfriend and their daughter. McGuffey's subsequent acts of harassment and intimidation were entirely gratuitous and did not begin until *after* his initial act of racial discrimination. These later acts, as Judge Williams noted, included the following: (a) he immediately removed her belongings from the apartment, exposing them to theft and vandalism and her to public ridicule and humiliation; (b) he made numerous, blatantly racist, harassing phone calls to Ms. Littlefield; (c) he made similar racist, harassing phone calls to members of Ms. Littlefield's family who did not live with her; (d) he went to her sister's home and physically intimidated her; and (e) there is, of course, the death threat to Bruce Collins posted on Ms. Littlefield's door. Not only is the evidence sufficient to support the award of punitive damages, it also supports the award of compensatory damages for the federal and state law claims. . . .

Attorney's Fees

In his final claim of error McGuffey asserts the fees awarded Ms. Littlefield's attorneys should be reduced to reflect what he claims are the reasonable hours spent on the litigation. . . . A district court's rulings on attorney's fees will rarely be reversed on appeal, and then only for abuse of discretion. . . .

McGuffey, nonetheless, asks us to reduce the fee awarded from approximately $140,000 to nearly $50,000 by scrutinizing and excising some 473 individual time-charges, the largest of which is for 9.5 hours and the smallest of which is for 0.1 hours. This we shall not do. . . .

McGuffey also argues the amount of the fees awarded is disproportionately large compared to the damages awarded: approximately $140,000 versus $150,000. The size of a damage award, however, is not the gauge of a plaintiff's victory. Rather, value is gauged more broadly . . . Ms. Littlefield prevailed on her federal law claims, receiving both compensatory and punitive damages. The latter certainly will punish McGuffey and, one hopes, deter him from further violations. The award is also likely to deter others. Therefore, we find the attorney's fees awarded are not unreasonable, and the award stands. . . .

Hunt v. State

69 A.3d 360 (Del. 2013)

Berger, J. This appeal involves alleged torts and a civil rights violation, arising from a police officer's interrogation of a young child at school. The Superior Court granted summary judgment to the State and all other remaining defendants. Viewing the record in the light most favorable to the child, we hold that there is sufficient evidence to support all claims except the battery claim. Accordingly, we affirm in part and reverse in part.

Factual and Procedural Background

On January 30, 2008, David McDowell, Vice Principal of the Richard A. Shields Elementary School, asked Delaware State Trooper David Pritchett to come to the school and talk to a small group of students about bullying. At the time, Pritchett was on a four month assignment as the School Resource Officer (SRO) for the Cape Henlopen School District. Under the Agreement Between the Cape Henlopen School District and the Delaware State Police, an SRO is tasked with "creating and maintaining a safe, secure, and orderly environment for students, teachers, and staff." The SRO "represents a proactive strategy designed to bring crime prevention and intervention into the school." The agreement states that the SRO is to be assigned to the high school, but Pritchett said that he was the SRO for all schools in the district.

In any event, Pritchett gave a talk about bullying to four or five fifth grade students who were under "in-school suspension." McDowell was present during the entire presentation. The next day, McDowell was told that there had been another bullying incident involving an autistic student whose money had been taken from him on the school bus. One of the fifth graders serving in-school suspension told McDowell that "AB," another fifth grade student, sat behind the autistic student on the school bus, and took the money. McDowell then told AB's mother about the incident, and asked her permission to have Pritchett talk to AB about it. AB's mother consented, and McDowell again asked Pritchett to come to the school.

When Pritchett arrived, McDowell told him what had happened, including how he learned that AB had taken the money. McDowell asked Pritchett to question AB, and the two men went to the reading lab, where AB was waiting. McDowell was called away on a school emergency, leaving Pritchett alone with AB. Pritchett got AB to admit that he had the money (one dollar), but AB claimed that another student had taken the money from the autistic student. AB said that he did not know that other student's name, but that the student was seated with AB on the school bus.

Without discussing the matter with McDowell, Pritchett followed up on AB's claim that another student had taken the money. He did so despite being virtually certain that AB was the perpetrator. Pritchett obtained the school bus seating chart from a secretary, and determined that Anthony J. Hunt's seat was next to AB's. He then instructed the secretary to call Hunt to the office. Pritchett greeted Hunt in the hall outside the office and walked him to the reading lab, where AB was seated. While walking, Pritchett claims that he told Hunt that "[t]here's a boy in here that's claiming that you . . . took a dollar. I know that you didn't do that. You're not in any trouble. I just need you to be brave and come in here." Pritchett also claims to have instructed Hunt, "When I tell you — when I tell the story of what's happened and I look at you, you just say no, you didn't do it. . . ."

Once inside the reading lab room with AB and Hunt, Pritchett questioned Hunt about the bullying incident. Pritchett closed the door, and told the boys what would happen to them if they lied. According to Hunt, Pritchett used a mean voice and told him 11 or 12 times that Pritchett had the authority to arrest Hunt and place him in jail if he did not tell the truth. Pritchett also explained that bad children are sent to the Stevenson House, where people are mean and children are treated like criminals. Pritchett said that if Hunt were sent to the Stevenson House, his siblings would be upset and would not be able to see him. Hunt started to cry. As soon as Hunt appeared visibly shaken, Pritchett turned to AB and stated "this is crazy now, [AB]. Look at him [referring to Hunt]. He's over there, his eyes are — you know, you can tell he looks like he's about ready to cry." AB finally admitted to taking the money from the autistic student. After the confession, Pritchett claims to have told Hunt that he did "a great job." Pritchett says that he asked Hunt if he wanted Pritchett to call his parents, but Hunt said, "No." Pritchett also testified that he told Hunt "it takes a man to stand up to a bully like this is here." Hunt did not recall any such comments.

When he got home from school, Hunt told his mother, Lisa DeSombre, what had happened. Hunt withdrew from school and was home schooled for the rest of that school year. Hunt returned to public school approximately 18 months after the incident. DeSombre filed suit on her son's behalf, as well as individually, against the Cape Henlopen School District, the Board of Education of Cape Henlopen School District, and David McDowell (collectively, District Defendants), and the State of  Delaware, the Department of Safety and Homeland Security, the Division of the Delaware State Police, and Trooper Pritchett (collectively, Pritchett). Hunt's claims against the District Defendants have been resolved. Pritchett successfully moved for summary judgment. This appeal followed.

. . . .

Section 1983 Claim

Federal law, specifically 42 U.S.C. § 1983, "imposes civil liability upon any person who, acting under the color of state law, deprives another individual of any rights, privileges, or immunities secured by the Constitution or laws of the United States." To prevail on his § 1983 claim, Hunt must establish that: (1) he was deprived of a federal right, and (2) Pritchett was acting under color of state law. In addition, Hunt must establish that Pritchett's conduct is not protected by qualified immunity. To overcome qualified immunity, Hunt must demonstrate that Pritchett's conduct violated a "clearly established" right. That means it must be "clear to a reasonable [official] that his conduct was unlawful in the situation he confronted." [*Saucier v. Katz*, 533 U.S. 194, 202 (2001) (citation omitted).] The determination "must be undertaken in light of the specific context of the case, not as a broad general proposition[.]" [*Id.* at 201.]

The Fourth Amendment guarantees the right to be free from unreasonable seizures. "[W]henever a police officer accosts an individual and restrains his freedom to walk away, he has 'seized' that person." [*Terry v. Ohio*, 392 U.S. 1, 8 (1968).] A seizure occurs for Fourth Amendment purposes when "a reasonable person would have believed that he was not free to leave." [*Id.* at 16.]. . . . Several appellate courts, including the Third Circuit Court of Appeals, have held that seizures in public schools are valid if reasonable, "giving special consideration to the goals and responsibilities of our public schools," especially with regard to disciplinary matters. [*Shuman v. Penn Manor School District*, 422 F.3d 141, 148 (3d Cir. 2005).] A child's age is one of the circumstances to be considered in evaluating the reasonableness of a seizure.

Viewing the record in the light most favorable to Hunt, the facts support a finding that he was seized for Fourth Amendment purposes. He was called to the Vice Principal's office and was escorted there by a teacher's aide. Outside the office, Pritchett met Hunt and walked with him into the reading lab. Pritchett was in uniform, carrying a gun, handcuffs, and other indicia of police authority. Pritchett then met with AB and Hunt in the reading lab for close to one hour. For some period of time, the door to the reading lab was closed. Hunt was eight years old. Pritchett never told Hunt that he could leave the reading lab, and Pritchett admitted that he did not expect Hunt to leave. Based on these facts, a reasonable child would not believe he was free to leave the room.

The next issue is whether Pritchett's seizure was reasonable. McDowell informed Pritchett that he knew AB had taken the money, and Pritchett stated that he was 99% sure Hunt was not involved in the incident. Neither Pritchett nor any school official contacted Hunt's parents to ask permission to conduct the interrogation. Pritchett has no training on how to question elementary school children, and, according to the State Police contract with the school district, Pritchett was to perform SRO duties only at the high schools. McDowell never asked Pritchett to question Hunt, and Pritchett never requested that permission.

When Pritchett brought Hunt into the reading lab, Pritchett claims to have told Hunt that he knew Hunt did not take the money. If Pritchett knew that Hunt had nothing to do with the incident, his reason for questioning Hunt becomes suspect. One could reasonably infer that Pritchett brought Hunt to the reading lab not to find out whether Hunt was involved in the theft, but to use Hunt to elicit AB's confession. AB could see that Hunt was younger than he, and AB watched as Pritchett intimidated Hunt by threatening arrest, and describing the unpleasant detention facility where Hunt might be housed. When Pritchett achieved his goal, by getting Hunt to start depression, traumatically induced neurosis or psychosis, or phobia, and/or was prescribed medication;

(4) Evidence regarding the duration and intensity of the claimant's physiological symptoms, psychological symptoms, and medical treatment;

(5) Other evidence that the defendant's conduct caused the plaintiff to suffer significant impairment in his or her daily functioning; and

(6) In certain instances, the extreme and outrageous character of the defendant's conduct is itself important evidence of serious mental injury.

The court added that this evidence may be presented by plaintiff's "own testimony, the testimony of lay witnesses acquainted with the plaintiff such as family, friends, and colleagues, or by the testimony of medical experts." *Id.* at 210.

6. *Intent-Driven or Harm-Based Tort?* By bringing order to what struck them and others as an ad hoc collection of cases, Magruder and Prosser performed the valuable service of providing an analytic structure that lawyers and judges could use to assess the merits of claims for wrongs of the sort seen in *Wilkinson, Nickerson, Dickens,* and *Littlefield.* Still, their insistence of proof of severe emotional distress as part of the plaintiff's prima facie case arguably points to a tension within their renditions of this cause of action.

As explained above, the common thread that Magruder and Prosser saw in the cases was that the defendant had acted in an outrageous manner for the purpose of causing severe emotional distress in the plaintiff. This description seems to emphasize two different features of the cases: the egregious way in which the defendant *mistreated* the plaintiff, but also the *emotional impact* that the plaintiff stood to suffer and did suffer from the mistreatment. The former emphasis arguably suggests that IIED belongs in the realm of torts such as assault and battery. On this view, the wrong done to Nickerson was the wrong of humiliating her. Likewise, the wrong done to Littlefield was that of discriminating against and harassing her because of her (and her boyfriend's) race. The wrong done to Hunt was callously using him as a means for getting a third party to confess. On a view that instead emphasizes the harm suffered by the victim, IIED more closely resembles actions such as negligence. In this rendition, the wrong done to Nickerson, Littlefield, and Hunt was that of acting toward the plaintiffs in a manner calculated to cause them serious harm.

Admittedly, the difference between these two characterizations is subtle — they will end up covering a lot of the same ground simply because severe emotional distress is a common reaction to being badly mistreated. Nonetheless, it might be important. Conceived as an intent-based wrong, IIED in principle perhaps ought to permit victims such as Nickerson, Littlefield, and Hunt to recover *even if the defendant's conduct, for whatever reason, does not happen to cause the victim to suffer severe distress.* Conceived as a harm-based wrong, IIED will permit victims to recover only if their emotional reaction to their mistreatment is "extreme." As we have seen, victims of batteries and assaults are permitted to proceed with claims against intentional wrongdoers notwithstanding the absence of severe harm. Why should the rule be any different for IIED victims (many of whom will have been subjected to more egregious misconduct than victims of these other torts)? If the concern is to avoid "opening the floodgates," isn't it enough to maintain, as courts generally have done, a narrow definition of outrageousness?

7. Punitive Damages: Common Law and Statute. The rule of Illinois law cited in footnote 3 of *Littlefield*—which sets a *per se* bar on the award of punitive damages for IIED claims—appears to be unusual. Most states' courts will permit juries to award punitive damages based on proof of the elements of IIED.

As *Littlefield* notes, Congress amended the Fair Housing Act in 1988 by eliminating the $1,000 cap on punitive damage awards to successful FHA claimants. Because the 1988 amendments had not been enacted at the time of McGuffey's discriminatory acts, he argued that it was unfair to subject him to a penalty of which he had no notice. The *Littlefield* court obviously was unimpressed with this argument, in part because it regarded Littlefield's separate claim under 42 U.S.C. § 1982 as providing an independent ground for the jury's punitive award.

In 1994, the U.S. Supreme Court considered the retroactive effect of the punitive damages provisions of another piece of federal antidiscrimination legislation: the Civil Rights Act of 1991. That act for the first time allowed juries to award compensatory and punitive damages to victims of employment discrimination on the basis of race, gender, or religion. The Court concluded that these provisions could not be applied retroactively because it would unfairly saddle employers with substantial additional liability of which they had no notice. Landgraf v. USI Film Prods., 511 U.S. 244 (1994). Although *Landgraf* did not interpret the FHA—which, unlike the laws amended by the Civil Rights Act, already provided for limited punitive damages prior to its amendment—its reluctance to apply new punitive damages provisions retroactively arguably runs counter to *Littlefield*'s analysis.

8. Reckless IIED. One feature that distinguishes IIED from the other torts with which it is sometimes grouped is that an IIED defendant can be held liable for being reckless as to the risk of causing the victim severe emotional distress (as opposed to intending such distress or knowing to a near certainty that such distress will occur). Recklessness may be defined for these purposes as a failure to heed a very obvious and very significant risk of serious injury. Do the plaintiff's allegations in *Hunt* provide a good example of reckless infliction of emotional distress? Have we encountered other examples in the preceding IIED materials?

Note that, just as an intentional touching that would not otherwise be offensive can be rendered offensive if the actor who causes the touching knows that it will offend the victim, so, too, conduct that might not otherwise be deemed extreme and outrageous may become so if it involves purposeful preying on—or even reckless disregard for—a plaintiff's known vulnerability. *See, e.g.*, Gordon v. Frost, 388 S.E.2d 362 (Ga. Ct. App. 1989) (upholding jury finding of outrageousness against a pharmacist who caused a patient to be arrested for fraud in reckless disregard for what he knew from repeated interactions to be her vulnerable emotional condition).

9. Recklessness, Transferred Intent, and Bystander Claims. Although courts faced with IIED claims have traditionally invoked "Section 46" of the Second Restatement for its definition of the tort, that Section in fact contains two separate provisions.

based on age, gender, race, and disabilities. These and other factors have begun to give rise to employment-related IIED suits, the likes of which Magruder and Prosser probably never envisioned. Largely excluded from the ambit of negligence law through the adoption of workers' compensation schemes at the beginning of the twentieth century, the workplace is perhaps once again becoming a fertile source of tort claims.* Consider in the following cases how federal laws that render certain forms of employment discrimination actionable interact with the IIED tort.

Wilson v. Monarch Paper Co.

939 F.2d 1138 (5th Cir. 1991)

Jolly, J. In this employment discrimination case, Monarch Paper Company . . . appeals a $3,400,000 jury verdict finding it liable for age discrimination . . . under the Age Discrimination in Employment Act (ADEA), 29 U.S.C. § 621, and for intentional infliction of emotional distress under Texas state law. . . . Upon review of the entire record, we affirm.

I

Because Monarch is challenging the sufficiency of the evidence, the facts are recited in the light most favorable to the jury's verdict. In 1970, at age 48, Richard E. Wilson was hired by Monarch Paper Company. Monarch is an incorporated division of Unisource Corporation, and Unisource is an incorporated group of Alco Standard Corporation. Wilson served as manager of the Corpus Christi division until November 1, 1977, when he was moved to the corporate staff in Houston to serve as "Corporate Director of Physical Distribution." During that time, he routinely received merit raises and performance bonuses. In 1980, Wilson received the additional title of "Vice President." In 1981, Wilson was given the additional title of "Assistant to John Blankenship," Monarch's President at the time.

While he was Director of Physical Distribution, Wilson received most of his assignments from Blankenship. Blankenship always seemed pleased with Wilson's performance and Wilson was never reprimanded or counseled about his performance. Blankenship provided Wilson with objective performance criteria at the beginning of each year, and Wilson's bonuses at the end of the year were based on his good

* As indicated by the next two cases in this section, courts entertaining employment discrimination suits expressly authorized by federal statutes are often asked to rule on "pendent" state law tort claims arising out of the same facts alleged in plaintiffs' federal law claims. In ruling on these employment-related state law tort claims, a court must determine whether any or all such claims have been removed from the tort system by the relevant state's workers' compensation legislation. *Compare* Livitsanos v. Superior Court, 828 P.2d 1195 (Cal. 1992) (suit alleging IIED can be brought by employee against employer for employment-caused distress if the employer's conduct (1) contravenes fundamental public policy or (2) exceeds the inherent risks of employment) *with* Green v. Wyman-Gordon Co., 664 N.E.2d 808 (Mass. 1996) (IIED claim brought by employee against employer based on conduct arising out of, and in the course of, employment is barred by the exclusivity provisions of the Massachusetts Workers' Compensation laws: The plaintiff may only receive disability benefits as per those laws).

performance under that objective criteria. In 1981, Wilson was placed in charge of the completion of an office warehouse building in Dallas, the largest construction project Monarch had ever undertaken. Wilson successfully completed that project within budget.

In 1981, Wilson saw a portion of Monarch's long-range plans that indicated that Monarch was presently advancing younger persons in all levels of Monarch management. Tom Davis, who was hired as Employee Relations Manager of Monarch in 1979, testified that from the time he started to work at Monarch, he heard repeated references by the division managers (including Larry Clark, who later became the Executive Vice President of Monarch) to the age of employees on the corporate staff, including Wilson.

In October 1981, Blankenship became Chairman of Monarch and Unisource brought in a new, 42-year-old president from outside the company, Hamilton Bisbee. An announcement was made that Larry Clark would be assuming expanded responsibilities in physical distribution. According to the defendants, one of Blankenship's final acts as President was to direct Clark (who was in his mid-forties at the time) to assume expanded responsibility for both the operational and physical distribution aspects of Monarch.

When Bisbee arrived at Monarch in November 1981, Wilson was still deeply involved in the Dallas construction project. Richard Gozon, who was 43 years old and the President of Unisource, outlined Blankenship's new responsibilities as Chairman of the company and requested that Blankenship, Bisbee, Wilson, and John Hartley of Unisource "continue to work very closely together on the completion of the Dallas project." Bisbee, however, refused to speak to Wilson or to "interface" with him. This "silent treatment" was apparently tactical; Bisbee later told another Monarch employee, Bill Shehan, "if I ever stop talking to you, you're dead." Shehan also testified that at a meeting in Philadelphia at about the time Bisbee became President of Monarch, Gozon told Bisbee, "I'm not telling you that you have to fire Dick Wilson. I'm telling you that he cannot make any more money."

As soon as the Dallas building project was completed, Bisbee and Gozon intensified an effort designed to get rid of Wilson. On March 8, 1982, Gozon asked for Bisbee's recommendations on how to remove Wilson from the Monarch organization. On March 9, 1982, Bisbee responded with his recommendation that Wilson be terminated, and that any salary continuance to Wilson be discontinued should Wilson elect to pursue an adversarial role toward Monarch. Gozon then asked the Unisource Employee Relations Manager, John Snelgrove, to meet with Wilson with the goal of attempting to convince Wilson to quit.

During the same time frame, . . . Bisbee and Clark began dismantling Wilson's job by removing his responsibilities and assigning them to other employees. Clark was also seen entering Wilson's office after hours and removing files.

Blankenship [died in June of 1982]. . . . Immediately [there]after . . . Bisbee and Snelgrove gave Wilson three options: (1) he could take a sales job in Corpus Christi at half his pay; (2) he could be terminated with three months' severance pay; or (3) he could accept a job as warehouse supervisor in the Houston warehouse at the same

Likewise, that the same persons — Tolin, Rayle and Fenster — essentially managed and supervised the different entities, and that the companies had common officers and boards of directors, is evidence of the kind of common management that supports the second prong of the interrelated test.

45. [The court noted that the Limelite entities maintained centralized control of labor relations though a single personnel department.]

46. The final factor to be considered in assessing applicability of the interrelated enterprise theory is the degree of common ownership or financial control over the entities. In this case, the evidence on that point strongly supports the theory's application. Frank Tolin controls all the companies and serves as an officer and director with each of them.

47. Defendants, then, taken together, are so integrated and interrelated as to constitute a single employer with 15 employees under Title VII. Therefore, they fall within the Court's jurisdiction. At all events, we observe again that Limelite Video alone had 19 employees who worked 20 or more weeks during 1987, which is sufficient to satisfy Title VII's jurisdictional requirements as to Video itself.

48. "Courts recognize two forms of sexual harassment: quid pro quo sexual harassment and hostile work environment sexual harassment." Steele v. Offshore Shipbuilding, Inc., 867 F.2d 1311, 1315 (11th Cir. 1989) (citing [Meritor Savings Bank v.] Vinson, 477 U.S. [57, 65-66, 106 S. Ct. 2399, 2404-2405 (1986)]. . . . "Quid pro quo sexual harassment occurs when an employer alters an employee's job conditions as a result of the employee's refusal to submit to sexual demands." *Id.* (citing *Vinson*, 477 U.S. at 65, 106 S. Ct. at 2404 . . .). Hostile environment sexual harassment occurs when an employer's conduct "has the purpose or effect of unreasonably interfering with an individual's work performance or creating an intimidating, hostile, or offensive environment." *Steele*, 867 F.2d at 1315 (citing *Vinson*, 477 U.S. at 67, 106 S. Ct. at 2405 (quoting 29 C.F.R. § 1604.11(a)(3) (1987)). . . . "[W]here sexual harassment is 'sufficiently pervasive so as to alter the conditions of employment and create an abusive working environment,' a Title VII claim is made out 'irrespective of whether the complainant suffers tangible job detriment.'" Phillips v. Smalley Maintenance Services, Inc., 711 F.2d 1524, 1529 (11th Cir. 1983) [authority quoted within quote omitted — Eds.].

49. In order to prove a hostile environment sexual harassment case, a plaintiff must demonstrate:

- **a.** that she belongs to a protected group, i.e., that she is a woman;
- **b.** that she was subject to unwelcome sexual harassment;
- **c.** that the harassment complained of was based upon sex, i.e., that the actor did not similarly harass male employees; and
- **d.** that the harassment involved affected a "term, condition or privilege" of employment.

Henson v. City of Dundee, 682 F.2d 897, 903-04 (11th Cir. 1982). Unwelcomeness means that an employee did not solicit or invite the alleged behavior. *Id.* at 903. . . .

51. At the outset, "[f]or sexual harassment to be actionable, it must be sufficiently severe or pervasive 'to alter the conditions of [the victim's] employment and create an abusive working environment.'" *Meritor Savings Bank, supra* (citation

omitted). . . . The requirement that the sexual harassment be pervasive both permits and may require the introduction of evidence of Tolin's similar harassment of other women. . . .

52. Defendant Tolin, individually and as a managing agent for the corporate defendants, blatantly and repeatedly harassed Plaintiff and many other women who worked for him. His conduct included both constant sexually explicit, degrading, and vulgar language and repeated acts of physical abuse. His offensive sexual behavior was relentless, and can only be characterized as crossing all bounds of common decency. According to Plaintiff, she tolerated Tolin's advances because she wanted to keep her job. Finally, toward the end of Plaintiff's tenure, Tolin spelled out for her the quid pro quo terms of her continued employment: "F—me or you're fired!" On this record, then, Plaintiff has plainly established quid pro quo sexual harassment, [and] hostile environment sexual harassment. . . .

53. Stockett is accordingly entitled to back pay from the date of termination of her employment with Defendant corporations (4/22/87) up to the date of trial (2/20/90) totalling 147 weeks. Therefore, at her rate of $16,380/year base pay, Stockett is entitled to back pay in the amount of $46,305, less $4,401 that she earned from other employment, for a total back pay award of $41,904.

54. Additionally, because of the working conditions detailed at the Tolin studios, reinstatement would be ineffective as a make-whole remedy, and Stockett is entitled to "front pay." Because of Stockett's testimony that she could not and would not return to the production industry in general, nor to the Tolin companies in particular, reinstatement would be a wholly ineffectual remedy. Front pay will therefore be awarded to make Plaintiff whole, but will be limited to one year, a reasonable time in which Plaintiff could have obtained comparable employment. . . .

55. Inasmuch as Tolin was managing agent and principal of each of the corporations, and since the evidence of a pervasively hostile work environment was well known to the principal officers, agents, and employees of the Defendant companies, each of the corporations . . . is responsible for . . . harassment by Tolin.

56. As an individual defendant, Tolin, as an agent for a corporate employer, is directly liable for his actions that violate Title VII. . . .

58. Plaintiff also asserts . . . claims for . . . battery, invasion of privacy, intentional infliction of emotional distress, and false imprisonment. . . . On the ample record presented, Plaintiff is entitled to prevail on her state-law claims.

59. [The court's description of the torts pleaded by Stockett is omitted. —Eds.] . . . Florida recognizes the tort of intentional infliction of emotional distress. . . .[4]

---

4. . . . [C]ourts . . . consistently have held that the allegations sufficient to state a claim for sexual harassment are sufficient to state a claim for emotional distress, and have generally found what one court called "a common thread—a continued course of sexual advances, followed by refusals and ultimately, retaliation." Shaffer v. National Can Corp., 565 F. Supp. 909, 915 (E.D. Pa. 1983). As phrased in Fawcett v. IDS Financial Services, 41 FEP Cases 589, 593, 1986 WL 9877 (W.D. Pa. 1986) . . .:

> Other district courts have held that cases in which a supervisor has conducted a continued course of sexual advances and harassment, followed by refusals by the employee, and retaliation by the supervisor in the form of denying promotions or making the atmosphere of the

61. We find that Stockett is entitled to recover for the tortious behavior of Tolin. Tolin's groping and kissing of Stockett constituted both an offensive and unwelcome touching (i.e., battery) and an invasion of her physical solitude (invasion of privacy). Tolin's battery of Plaintiff—the repeated and offensive touching of the most private parts of Plaintiff's body—constitutes an intrusion into her physical solitude. Similarly, the act of entering the ladies bathroom constitutes an invasion of her privacy. In addition, the act of pinning Plaintiff against the wall and refusing to allow her to escape, even though only done for a short period of time, was false imprisonment. Further, the evidence establishes repeated physical attacks, as well as repeated verbal licentiousness. Tolin's conduct toward Stockett can only be characterized as being wanton, willful, and in total disregard of her rights. An ordinary prudent person, viewing his cumulative behavior, would be compelled to find this to be outrageous. The sum total of Tolin's conduct therefore also constituted an intentional infliction of emotional distress.

62. Under Florida law, Plaintiff is entitled to a sum that will reasonably compensate her for . . . pain, suffering and mental anguish [that she has already suffered or can reasonably be expected to suffer as a result of the defendant's conduct]. . . . We conclude that, as to the state torts of battery, invasion of privacy, false imprisonment, and intentional infliction of emotional distress, Plaintiff is entitled to compensatory damages in the aggregate amount of $250,000. . . .

Stockett suffered from severe emotional distress during the entire time she worked at Limelite because of the sexually hostile atmosphere and Tolin's advances toward her. She continues to suffer distress, a loss of self esteem, and other lingering effects of her experience, and she will continue to suffer such distress in the future. On this record, we are satisfied that these damages are not fanciful or fleeting in nature. . . . Stockett is entitled to compensation for past mental anguish and loss of capacity for enjoyment of life; for future psychological care; and for future mental anguish and loss of capacity for enjoyment of life. . . .

65. Plaintiff is . . . entitled to recover punitive damages. . . . While a punitive damages award is a drastic and often disfavored remedy, under controlling Florida law the particularly extensive and egregious conduct evident here warrants [it]. . . .

71. Under controlling Florida law, we conclude that Tolin's relentless pursuit of Plaintiff and others warrants special remediation by this Court. The Court will impose punitive damages in this case. In doing so, this Court is guided by the following:

> work place oppressive, involved conduct that is sufficiently outrageous to state a cause of action for intentional infliction of emotional distress.

Also relevant to the determination is the persistence with which the Defendant, Tolin, conducted himself. As the court observed in Cummings v. Walsh Construction Co., 561 F. Supp. 872 (S.D. Ga. 1983), in denying a motion for summary judgment on an emotional-distress count:

> While it is true that Professor Prosser states that a solicitation for sex to an unwilling woman has been held not to lead to liability, [Prosser], at 55, he states, at page 56, that prolonged or repeated invitation, when raised to the point of "hounding" the invitee, can lead to liability.
>
> 561 F. Supp. at 882.

a. The "overwhelming" public policy of the State of Florida is against sexual harassment. [Cited authority omitted.]

b. Tolin evidenced extreme insensitivity to the inappropriateness of his behavior, its effect on his victims and, for that matter, on the reputation of his studio and industry. . . . The willfulness of his conduct was exemplified by his continuous assertions that "the business belonged to him" and that he "could do what he wanted."

c. There is potential for great harm to be caused by Tolin's behavior, and similar behavior by others. We are mindful that many of the women who are involved in the production and film industries are young and inexperienced. . . .

d. Tolin made oppressive and invasive demands on Plaintiff and blatantly attempted to extort sex from her as a condition of employment.

e. The cost to Stockett of performing the role of a "private attorney general" is real. It is worth repeating that a sexual harassment plaintiff, more so than perhaps any litigant besides a rape victim, is herself on trial. No corner of Ms. Stockett's life or psyche was beyond the attempted reach of the Defendants' inquiry. She pursued this action knowing that the most embarrassing and intimate details of her life likely would be discussed in a public courtroom. If sexual harassment is to be eradicated—particularly the degrading and pervasive conduct well-documented on this record—the sacrifice called for in terms of the victim's privacy and dignity must be recognized and her service rewarded for bringing the wrongdoer to account.

f. The great wealth of Tolin, and his observation that $20 million dollars is but a small fraction of his wealth must also be considered. This boast, which Defendant contends was meant only to impress his competitors, will be a yardstick against which others will measure any punitive damage award. He is known, indeed self-proclaimed, to be fabulously wealthy. Under Florida law, if a punitive damage award against Tolin is to have either a special or general deterrent effect, it will have to be sufficiently large to be punitive at all.

g. We also consider the pervasiveness of the sexually hostile atmosphere and the frequency with which Tolin accosted Plaintiff and so many other women on the premises, and the thoroughly egregious, wanton nature of Tolin's conduct. Video, Studios, and DPC each knowingly allowed Tolin to carry on his activities as he served as principal officer and agent of each of them. . . .

73. Furthermore, it is axiomatic that a corporation can act only through its agents. Thus, when the agent of a corporation who causes the harm is the managing agent or primary owner of the corporation, punitive damages may be assessed against the corporation for the acts of the managing agent.

Therefore, based on the evidence and arguments presented, it is

ORDERED AND ADJUDGED that Plaintiff, Michelle Ann Stockett, shall recover from the Defendants, Frank Tolin, Limelite Studios, Inc., Limelite Video, Inc. and Directors Production Company, jointly and severally, judgment for damages in the aggregate amount of $308,284 [$41,904 in back pay, $16,380 in front pay, and $250,000 in tort damages.]. . . . Additionally, it is

ORDERED AND ADJUDGED that Plaintiff shall have judgement for punitive damages in the amount of $1.00 against Directors Production Company, $5,000 against Limelite Studios, Inc., $50,000 against Limelite Video, Inc., and $1 million against Frank Tolin, for a total of $1,055,001 in punitive damages. . . . Finally, it is further

ORDERED AND ADJUDGED that Plaintiff, as a prevailing plaintiff in a Title VII action, is entitled to recover reasonable attorney's fees. . . .

NOTES AND QUESTIONS

1. *The ADEA and Title VII: Procedures.* The Age Discrimination in Employment Act (ADEA) and Title VII are but two of several important federal statutes regulating the terms and conditions of employment. Others include statutes that set the terms under which unions and management negotiate wages and working conditions, that bar discrimination on grounds of disability, and that mandate that employers of a certain size grant employees maternity and medical leaves.

As the foregoing cases attest, both Title VII and the ADEA expressly generate private rights of action for victims of certain forms of employment discrimination. However, they do so in a manner that involves an administrative law overlay. Title VII grants employees of businesses of the requisite size the right to sue, but they must first file charges with a federal agency, the Equal Employment Opportunity Commission (EEOC). The EEOC, in turn, must notify the employer of the charge of discrimination and investigate the matter within a specified period of time. In addition, the agency must decide whether it will commence its own lawsuit against the employer. Only after these steps have been taken may the plaintiff proceed to commence her claim. By this means, the statute is designed to promote prompt and relatively informal resolution of charges of employment discrimination.

With certain important variations, the ADEA likewise empowers individuals to sue after first filing notice with the EEOC. One such variation is that a Title VII plaintiff may proceed with her individual suit even if the EEOC decides to sue in its own right, whereas an ADEA plaintiff may not.

2. *Employment Discrimination: Dignitary or Economic Injury?* When Title VII was enacted in 1964, it described the redress available to litigants who commenced employment discrimination suits in terms of *equitable* rather than legal remedies. In particular, it stated that upon a finding by the court that the employer had engaged in intentional discrimination in violation of its substantive provisions, the court was authorized to (1) enjoin the conduct in question, and (2) order other equitable relief as it deemed appropriate.

The object of these remedies was often described by courts in terms familiar to tort students — that of making the plaintiff "whole." However, the goal here was *not* that of fully compensating the plaintiff for having been mistreated, but instead that of providing her with *the terms of employment she would have enjoyed* but for the defendant's discrimination. Thus, in the case of plaintiffs such as Stockett, who were effectively forced out of their jobs by discriminatory acts, the courts were to award *back pay* (wages and benefits the employee would have received between the time of termination and the time of trial). In addition, they could either order the employee's reinstatement (where feasible), or award *front pay* (wages and benefits that the employee would stand to earn going forward, until such time as she could reasonably be expected to find comparable work). As originally enacted, Title VII did not permit an award to the plaintiff of emotional distress or punitive damages. Hence the importance of Stockett's assertion of separate common law tort claims: They provided the basis for the award to Stockett of emotional distress and punitive damages.

In 1991, Congress amended Title VII in ways that have rendered private actions brought under the statute more akin to tort actions. Thus, employees can now recover compensatory and punitive damages directly under the statute, although these awards are subject to statutory caps that vary with the size of the employer. These amendments also for the first time directed that individual Title VII claims shall be tried before a jury, rather than the trial judge. As a result, Title VII plaintiffs are now, like typical dignitary tort plaintiffs, in a position to recover emotional distress and punitive damages as determined by juries, although those damages are subject to statutory caps.*

The ADEA, consistent with the original terms of Title VII, empowers courts to grant appropriate equitable relief to victims of age discrimination in employment. As evidenced by *Wilson*, the ADEA, unlike Title VII, has always permitted jury trials, as well as "liquidated" (i.e., double) damages for "willful violations" of the act. It does not authorize awards for emotional distress or punitive damages.

3. *Discrimination and IIED.* *Wilson* and *Stockett* hold that IIED (and other torts) can provide certain ADEA and Title VII plaintiffs with the ability to convert claims of discrimination into claims of "outrageous" discrimination that, depending on the contours of state law, may warrant large compensatory and punitive awards. Given the ADEA's refusal to permit recovery of such damages, and given that even the amended Title VII sets caps on emotional distress and punitive awards, is there anything problematic about the interaction in this context of state tort law and federal antidiscrimination law? Or do they work in a complementary fashion? Do you agree with the *Wilson* court's assessment that the particular discriminatory acts undertaken by Wilson's supervisors against him rise to the level of outrageous discrimination, as opposed to ordinary discrimination?

4. *Harris: Economic Versus Dignitary Injury Revisited.* *Stockett* cites the Supreme Court's 1986 *Meritor Savings Bank* decision for the rule that a Title VII plaintiff complaining of gender discrimination may prevail by proving either *quid quo pro* harassment or *hostile work environment* harassment. In *Harris v. Forklift Systems, Inc.*, 510 U.S. 17 (1993), the Court elaborated on the requirements for proving the latter form of harassment. Harris, a manager at the company, alleged various wrongful

---

* *Stockett* was issued after the enactment of the 1991 amendments. Apparently, however, the trial judge decided not to apply them "retroactively" to Tolin's discriminatory conduct, which took place before their enactment. (On the retroactivity of the amendments, see Note 7 following *Hunt v. State.*) Given this decision, Stockett's Title VII claims had to be tried by the judge, without a jury. Moreover, as indicated in the text, Stockett could only hope to recover emotional distress and punitive damages by asserting parallel state law tort claims. The parties were entitled to try the latter claims before a jury but opted to have the judge resolve Stockett's federal and state law claims by means of a single bench trial.

entitled to compensation for various losses that flowed from it, including the pain and suffering she experienced as a result of her illness. However, those losses were compensable only because they were *consequent to* (or *parasitic on*) the *predicate* injury of bodily harm. Walter's bodily harm — her illness — was the injury that rendered Wal-Mart's conduct actionable in the first place.*

By contrast to claims such as Walter's, a claim for NIED *does* assert that the defendant committed the wrong of failing to be sufficiently vigilant of the plaintiff's emotional well-being. For these sorts of claims, emotional distress is the injury that the defendant is supposed to have taken care not to cause. In such cases, the relationship between compensation for bodily harms and for emotional distress is inverted. (Indeed, a true NIED claimant can recover compensation for having suffered a miscarriage or a heart attack if she can show that this sort of physical injury was consequent to the emotional distress that she suffered because the defendant failed to attend to a duty to be vigilant of her mental well-being.)

As we will now see, the idea that tort law ought to provide a remedy to persons who are carelessly caused by others to suffer "only" emotional distress, and the corresponding idea that actors are sometimes under obligations to be vigilant against causing distress to others, was very late in coming to American tort law. In fact, one can argue that it is only in the second half of the twentieth century that one finds courts regularly recognizing "true" NIED claims.

A. From "No Injury" to the "Zone of Danger"

Wyman v. Leavitt

71 Me. 227 (1880)

[This suit involved two separate claims against a subcontractor alleging that the subcontractor acted carelessly by blasting rocks in an area adjacent to the land on which the Wymans lived, as a result of which rocks were thrown upon the property. One claim, brought by Mr. Wyman in his capacity as owner of the property, sought compensation for damage to the land. The second claim, brought on behalf of Mrs. Wyman, alleged that she suffered anxiety as a result of the blasting. At trial, Mrs. Wyman testified that she was in fear for her own safety, as well as that of their child. On that claim, the jury awarded $264 in damages. The defendant appealed. — Eds.]

Virgin, J. . . . As a general proposition, damages are recoverable when they are the natural and reasonable result of the defendant's unlawful act — that is when they are such a consequence as in the ordinary course of things, would flow from such an act. This is the broad rule, covering all the elements of damages, some of which do

* A claimant who proves she has been the victim of an assault, battery, or false imprisonment at the hands of the defendant will likewise be entitled to recover compensation for her distress over that mistreatment. The common law has also long permitted defamation plaintiffs to recover for distress associated with tortiously caused injury to reputation.

not enter into every case. The rule though correct as a general abstract statement has its limitations in particular cases. . . . Personal injury usually consists in pain inflicted both bodily and mental. When bodily pain is caused, mental follows as a necessary consequence, especially when the former is so severe as to create apprehension and anxiety. And not only the suffering experienced before the trial, but such as is reasonably certain to continue afterward, as the result of the injury, rightfully enters into the assessment of damages.

In [an action of] trespass for assault and battery, the jury may consider not only the mental suffering which accompanies and is a part of the bodily pain, but that other mental condition of the injured person which arises from the insult of the defendant's blows. . . . Or for an assault alone, when maliciously done, though no actual personal injury be inflicted. . . . So in various other torts to property alone when the tort-feasor is actuated by wantonness or malice, or a willful disregard of others' rights therein, injury to the feelings of the plaintiff, resulting from such conduct of the defendant, may properly be considered by the jury in fixing the amount of their verdict.

But we have been unable to find any decided case, which holds that mental suffering alone, unattended by any injury to the person, caused by simple actionable negligence, can sustain an action. And the fact that no such case exists, and that no elementary writer asserts such a doctrine, is a strong argument against it. On the contrary it has been held that a verdict, founded upon fright and mental suffering, caused by risk and peril, would in the absence of personal injury, be contrary to law. So it is said (in Lynch v. Knight, 9 Ho. L. 577, 598,) that, "mental pain and anxiety, the law cannot value, and does not pretend to redress when the unlawful act complained of causes that alone." Again, in Johnson v. Wells, 6 Nev. 224 (3 Am. R. 245), after a very elaborate examination, it was held that pain of mind aside and distinct from bodily suffering, cannot be considered in estimating damages in an action against a common carrier of passengers. If the law were otherwise, it would seem that not only every passenger on a train that was personally injured, but every one that was frightened by a collision or by the trains leaving the track, could maintain an action against the company. . . . We are of the opinion, therefore, that Mrs. Wyman's testimony relating to her fears, as to her own personal safety, was erroneously admitted. Whether a fright of sufficient severity to cause a physical disease would support an action, we need not now inquire. . . .

Robb v. Pennsylvania R.R. Co.

210 A.2d 709 (Del. 1965)

Herrmann, J. The question before us for decision is this: May the plaintiff recover for the physical consequences of fright caused by the negligence of the defendant, the plaintiff being within the immediate zone of physical danger created by such negligence, although there was no contemporaneous bodily impact?

Considering the record in the light most favorable to the plaintiff, the facts may be thus summarized:

. . . On March 11, 1961, the plaintiff was driving an automobile up the lane toward her home when the vehicle stalled at [a] railroad grade crossing. A rut about a foot deep had been negligently permitted by the defendant to form at the crossing. The rear out of the rule and permit recovery for serious physical injuries resulting from the accompanying fright. Token impact sufficient to satisfy the rule has been held to be a slight bump against the seat, Homans v. Boston Elevated R. Co., supra; dust in the eyes, Porter v. Del., L. & W.R. Co., 73 N.J.L. 405, 63 A. 860 (1906); [and] inhalation of smoke, Morton v. Stack, 122 Ohio St. 115, 170 N.E. 869 (1930). . . .

This leaves the public policy or expediency ground to support the impact rule. We think that ground untenable.

It is the duty of the courts to afford a remedy and redress for every substantial wrong. Part of our basic law is the mandate that "every man for an injury done him in his . . . person . . . shall have remedy by the due course of law. . . ." Del. Const. Art. 1, Sec. 9, Del. C. Ann. Neither volume of cases, nor danger of fraudulent claims, nor difficulty of proof, will relieve the courts of their obligation in this regard. None of these problems are insuperable. Statistics fail to show that there has been a "flood" of such cases in those jurisdictions in which recovery is allowed . . .; but if there be increased litigation, the courts must willingly cope with the task. As to the danger of illusory and fictional claims, this is not a new problem; our courts deal constantly with claims for pain and suffering based upon subjective symptoms only; and the courts and the medical profession have been found equal to the danger. Fraudulent claims may be feigned in a slight-impact case as well as in a no-impact case. Likewise, the problems of adequacy of proof, for the avoidance of speculative and conjectural damages, are common to personal injury cases generally and are surmountable, being satisfactorily solved by our courts in case after case.

We are unwilling to accept a rule, or an expediency argument in support thereof, which results in the denial of a logical legal right and remedy in all cases because in some a fictitious injury may be urged or a difficult problem of the proof or disproof of speculative damage may be presented. Justice is not best served, we think, when compensation is denied to one who has suffered injury through the negligence of another merely because of the possibility of encouraging fictitious claims or speculative damages in other cases. Public policy requires the courts, with the aid of the legal and medical professions, to find ways and means to solve satisfactorily the problems thus presented — not expedient ways to avoid them. . . .

We hold, therefore, that where negligence proximately caused fright, in one within the immediate area of physical danger from that negligence, which in turn produced physical consequences such as would be elements of damage if a bodily injury had been suffered, the injured party is entitled to recover under an application of the prevailing principles of law as to negligence and proximate causation. Otherwise stated, where results, which are regarded as proper elements of recovery as a consequence of physical injury, are proximately caused by fright due to negligence, recovery by one in the immediate zone of physical risk should be permitted. . . .

We conclude, therefore, that the Superior Court erred in the instant case in holding that the plaintiff's right to recover is barred by the impact rule. The plaintiff claims physical injuries resulting from fright proximately caused by the negligence of the defendant. She should have the opportunity to prove such injuries and to recover therefor if she succeeds. The summary judgment granted in favor of the defendant must be reversed and the cause remanded for further proceedings.

Consolidated Rail Corp. v. Gottshall

512 U.S. 532 (1994)

THOMAS, J. These cases require us to determine the proper standard for evaluating claims for negligent infliction of emotional distress that are brought under the Federal Employers' Liability Act. . . .

I

Respondents James Gottshall and Alan Carlisle each brought suit under the Federal Employers' Liability Act (FELA), . . . 45 U.S.C. §§ 51-60, against their former employer, petitioner Consolidated Rail Corporation (Conrail). . . .

A

Gottshall was a member of a Conrail work crew assigned to replace a stretch of defective track on an extremely hot and humid day. The crew was under time pressure, and so the men were discouraged from taking scheduled breaks. They were, however, allowed to obtain water as needed. Two and one-half hours into the job, a worker named Richard Johns, a longtime friend of Gottshall, collapsed. Gottshall and several others rushed to help Johns, who was pale and sweating profusely. They were able to revive him by administering a cold compress. Michael Norvick, the crew supervisor, then ordered the men to stop assisting Johns and to return to work. Five minutes later, Gottshall again went to Johns' aid after seeing his friend stand up and collapse. Realizing that Johns was having a heart attack, Gottshall began cardiopulmonary resuscitation. He continued the process for 40 minutes.

Meanwhile, Norvick attempted to summon assistance, but found that his radio was inoperative; unbeknownst to him, Conrail had temporarily taken the nearest base station off the air for repairs. Norvick drove off to get help, but by the time he returned with paramedics, Johns had died. The paramedics covered the body with a sheet, ordered that it remain undisturbed until the coroner could examine it, and directed the crew not to leave until the coroner had arrived. Norvick ordered the men back to work, within sight of Johns' covered body. The coroner, who arrived several hours later, reported that Johns had died from a heart attack brought on by the combined factors of heat, humidity, and heavy exertion.

The entire experience left Gottshall extremely agitated and distraught. Over the next several days, during which he continued to work in hot and humid weather conditions, Gottshall began to feel ill. He became preoccupied with the events surrounding Johns' death, and worried that he would die under similar circumstances. Shortly after Johns' funeral, Gottshall was admitted to a psychiatric institution, where he was diagnosed as suffering from major depression and post-traumatic stress disorder. During the three weeks he spent at the institution, Gottshall experienced nausea, insomnia, cold sweats, and repetitive nightmares concerning Johns' death. He lost a great deal of weight and suffered from suicidal preoccupations and anxiety. Gottshall has continued to receive psychological treatment since his discharge from the hospital.

Gottshall sued Conrail under FELA [alleging] . . . that Conrail's negligence had created the circumstances under which he had been forced to observe and participate in the events surrounding Johns' death. The District Court granted Conrail's motion for summary judgment. . . .

A divided panel of the United States Court of Appeals for the Third Circuit reversed. . . . Gottshall v. Consolidated Rail Corp., 988 F.2d 355 (1993). . . .

The panel majority concluded that there were genuine issues of material fact concerning whether Gottshall's injuries were foreseeable by Conrail, whether Conrail had acted unreasonably, and whether Conrail's conduct had caused cognizable injury to Gottshall. The court therefore remanded for trial. *Id.*, at 383. . . .

B

Respondent Carlisle began working as a train dispatcher for Conrail in 1976. In this position, he was responsible for ensuring the safe and timely movement of passengers and cargo. Aging railstock and outdated equipment made Carlisle's job difficult. Reductions in Conrail's work force required Carlisle to take on additional duties and to work long hours. Carlisle and his fellow dispatchers frequently complained about safety concerns, the high level of stress in their jobs, and poor working conditions. In 1988, Carlisle became trainmaster in the South Philadelphia yards. With this promotion came added responsibilities that forced him to work erratic hours. Carlisle began to experience insomnia, headaches, depression, and weight loss. After an extended period during which he was required to work 12- to 15-hour shifts for weeks at a time, Carlisle suffered a nervous breakdown.

Carlisle sued Conrail . . . for negligent infliction of emotional distress. He alleged that Conrail had breached its duty to provide him with a safe workplace by forcing him to work under unreasonably stressful conditions, and that this breach had resulted in foreseeable stress-related health problems. At trial, Carlisle called . . . experts who testified that his breakdown and ensuing severe depression were caused at least in part by the strain of his job. The jury awarded Carlisle $386,500. . . .

The Third Circuit affirmed. . . . [It concluded] that "when it is reasonably foreseeable that extended exposure to dangerous and stressful working conditions will cause injury to the worker, the employer may be held to be liable under the FELA for the employee's resulting injuries." [Carlisle v. Consolidated Rail Corp., 990 F.2d 90, 97 (3d Cir. 1993).] The Third Circuit held that Carlisle had produced sufficient evidence that his injury had been foreseeable to Conrail. The court also found sufficient evidence that Conrail had breached its duty to provide Carlisle with a safe workplace by making his employment too demanding, and that this breach had caused Carlisle's injury. . . .

II

A

. . . Section 1 of FELA provides that "[e]very common carrier by railroad . . . shall be liable in damages to any person suffering injury while he is employed by such carrier . . . for such injury or death resulting in whole or in part from the negligence of any of the officers, agents, or employees of such carrier." 45 U.S.C. § 51. Our task today is determining under what circumstances emotional distress may constitute "injury" resulting from "negligence" for purposes of the statute. As we previously have recognized when considering § 51, when Congress enacted FELA in 1908, its "attention was focused primarily upon injuries and death resulting from accidents on interstate railroads."[Cited decision omitted.] Cognizant of the physical dangers of railroading that resulted in the death or maiming of thousands of workers every year, Congress crafted a federal remedy that shifted part of the "'human overhead'" of doing business from employees to their employers. Tiller v. Atlantic Coast Line R. Co., 318 U.S. 54, 58, 63 S. Ct. 444, 446-447, 87 L. Ed. 610 (1943). *See also* Wilkerson v. McCarthy, 336 U.S. 53, 68, 69 S. Ct. 413, 420, 93 L. Ed. 497 (1949) (Douglas, J., concurring) (FELA "was designed to put on the railroad industry some of the cost for the legs, eyes, arms, and lives which it consumed in its operations"). In order to further FELA's humanitarian purposes, Congress did away with several common-law tort defenses that had effectively barred recovery by injured workers. . . .

We have liberally construed FELA to further Congress' remedial goal. . . .

That FELA is to be liberally construed, however, . . . "does not make the employer the insurer of the safety of his employees while they are on duty. The basis of his liability is his negligence, not the fact that injuries occur." Ellis v. Union Pacific R. Co., 329 U.S. 649, 653, 67 S. Ct. 598, 600, 91 L. Ed. 572 (1947). And while "[w]hat constitutes negligence for the statute's purposes is a federal question," Urie [v. Thompson], 337 U.S. [163], . . . 174 [(1949)], 69 S. Ct., at 1027, we have made clear that this federal question generally turns on principles of common law: "[T]he Federal Employers' Liability Act is founded on common-law concepts of negligence and injury, subject to such qualifications as Congress has imported into those terms," *id.*, at 182, 69 S. Ct., at 1030-1031. Those qualifications, discussed above, are the modification or abrogation of several common-law defenses to liability, including contributory negligence and assumption of risk. Only to the extent of these explicit statutory alterations is FELA "an avowed departure from the rules of the common law." Sinkler v. Missouri Pacific R. Co., 356 U.S. 326, 329, 78 S. Ct. 758, 762, 2 L. Ed. 2d 799 (1958). Thus, although common-law principles are not necessarily dispositive of questions arising under FELA, unless they are expressly rejected in the text of the statute, they are entitled to great weight in our analysis. Because FELA is silent on the issue of negligent infliction of emotional distress, common-law principles must play a significant role in our decision.

B

We turn, therefore, to consider the right of recovery pursued by respondents in light of the common law. The term "negligent infliction of emotional distress" is largely self-explanatory, but a definitional point should be clarified at the outset. The injury we contemplate when considering negligent infliction of emotional distress is mental or emotional injury, *cf. id.*, at 568, 107 S. Ct., at 1417, apart from the tort law concepts of pain and suffering. Although pain and suffering technically are mental harms, these terms traditionally "have been used to describe sensations stemming directly from a physical injury or condition." Pearson, Liability to Bystanders for Negligently Inflicted Emotional Harm — A Comment on the Nature of Arbitrary Rules, 34 U. Fla. L. Rev. 477, 485, n.45 (1982). The injury we deal with here is mental or emotional harm (such as fright or anxiety) that is caused by the negligence of another and that is not directly brought about by a physical injury, but that may manifest itself in physical symptoms.

Nearly all of the States have recognized a right to recover for negligent infliction of emotional distress, as we have defined it. No jurisdiction, however, allows recovery for all emotional harms, no matter how intangible or trivial, that might be causally linked to the negligence of another. Indeed, significant limitations, taking the form of "tests" or "rules," are placed by the common law on the right to recover for negligently inflicted emotional distress. . . .

Behind these limitations lie a variety of policy considerations, many of them based on the fundamental differences between emotional and physical injuries. "Because the etiology of emotional disturbance is usually not as readily apparent as that of a broken bone following an automobile accident, courts have been concerned . . . that recognition of a cause of action for [emotional] injury when not related to any physical trauma may inundate judicial resources with a flood of relatively trivial claims, many of which may be imagined or falsified, and that liability may be imposed for highly remote consequences of a negligent act." Maloney v. Conroy, 208 Conn. 392, 397-398, 545 A.2d 1059, 1061 (1988). The last concern has been particularly significant. Emotional injuries may occur far removed in time and space from the negligent conduct that triggered them. Moreover, in contrast to the situation with physical injury, there are no necessary finite limits on the number of persons who might suffer emotional injury as a result of a given negligent act. The incidence and severity of emotional injuries are also more difficult to predict than those of typical physical injuries because they depend on psychological factors that ordinarily are not apparent to potential tortfeasors.

For all of these reasons, courts have . . . placed substantial limitations on the class of plaintiffs that may recover for emotional injuries and on the injuries that may be compensable. . . . Some courts phrase the limitations in terms of proximate causation. . . . Other courts speak of the limitations in terms of duty; the defendant owes only a certain class of plaintiffs a duty to avoid inflicting emotional harm. . . . We shall refer to the common-law limitations as outlining the duty of defendants with regard to negligent infliction of emotional distress.

Three major limiting tests for evaluating claims alleging negligent infliction of emotional distress have developed in the common law. The first of these has come to be known as the "physical impact" test. . . . At the time Congress enacted FELA in 1908, most of the major industrial States had embraced this test. Under the physical impact test, a plaintiff seeking damages for emotional injury stemming from a negligent act must have contemporaneously sustained a physical impact (no matter how slight) or injury due to the defendant's conduct. Most jurisdictions have abandoned this test, but at least five States continue to adhere to it.

The second test has come to be referred to as the "zone of danger" test. It came into use at roughly the same time as the physical impact test, and had been adopted by several jurisdictions at the time FELA was enacted. . . . [T]he zone of danger test limits recovery for emotional injury to those plaintiffs who sustain a physical impact as a result of a defendant's negligent conduct, or who are placed in immediate risk of physical harm by that conduct. . . . The zone of danger test currently is followed in 14 jurisdictions. . . .

[The third test permits recovery by relatives of a physical-injury victim who are traumatized by contemporaneously observing the victim being injured by the carelessness of the defendant. This test is discussed below in Section II.C of this Chapter. — EDS.]

III

A

Having laid out the relevant legal framework, we turn to the questions presented. As an initial matter, we agree with the Third Circuit that claims for damages for negligent infliction of emotional distress are cognizable under FELA. . . . We see no reason why emotional injury should not be held to be encompassed within that term, especially given that "severe emotional injuries can be just as debilitating as physical injuries." *Gottshall*, 988 F.2d, at 361. We therefore hold that, as part of its "duty to use reasonable care in furnishing its employees with a safe place to work," [Atchison, Topeka & Santa Fe Ry. v.] Buell, 480 U.S. [557,] 558 [(1987)], 107 S. Ct., at 1412, a railroad has a duty under FELA to avoid subjecting its workers to negligently inflicted emotional injury. This latter duty, however, is not self-defining. . . .

B

When setting out its view of the proper scope of recovery for negligently inflicted emotional distress under FELA, the Third Circuit explicitly refused to adopt any of the common-law tests described above; indeed, the court in *Gottshall* went so far as to state that "doctrinal common law distinctions are to be discarded when they bar recovery on meritorious FELA claims." 988 F.2d, at 369. . . . By the time . . . [it decided *Carlisle*, the court had] refined its test to two questions — whether there was convincing evidence of the genuineness of the emotional injury claim (with "genuine" meaning authentic and serious), and if there was, whether the injury was foreseeable. If these questions could be answered affirmatively by the court, there was "no bar to recovery under the FELA." 990 F.2d, at 98.

The Third Circuit's standard is fatally flawed in a number of respects. First, . . . [b]y treating the common-law tests as mere arbitrary restrictions to be disregarded if they stand in the way of recovery on "meritorious" FELA claims, the Third Circuit put the cart before the horse: The common law must inform the availability of a right to recover under FELA for negligently inflicted emotional distress, so the "merit" of a FELA claim of this type cannot be ascertained without reference to the common law.

Perhaps the court below believed that its focus on the perceived genuineness of the claimed emotional injury adequately addressed the concerns of the common-law courts in dealing with emotional injury claims. But the potential for fraudulent and trivial claims — the concern identified by the Third Circuit — is only one of the difficulties created by allowing actions for negligently inflicted emotional distress. A more significant problem is the prospect that allowing such suits can lead to unpredictable and nearly infinite liability for defendants. The common law consistently has sought to place limits on this potential liability by restricting the class of plaintiffs who may recover and the types of harm for which plaintiffs may recover. This concern underlying the common-law tests has nothing to do with the potential for fraudulent claims; on the contrary, it is based upon the recognized possibility of *genuine* claims from the essentially infinite number of persons, in an infinite variety of situations, who might suffer real emotional harm as a result of a single instance of negligent conduct.

Second, we question the viability of the genuineness test on its own terms. . . . [T]esting for the "genuineness" of an injury alone cannot appreciably diminish the possibility of infinite liability. Such a fact-specific test, moreover, would be bound to lead to haphazard results. Judges would be forced to make highly subjective determinations concerning the authenticity of claims for emotional injury, which are far less susceptible to objective medical proof than are their physical counterparts. To the extent the genuineness test could limit potential liability, it could do so only inconsistently. . . .

Third, to the extent the Third Circuit relied on the concept of foreseeability as a meaningful limitation on liability, we believe that reliance to be misplaced. If one takes a broad enough view, *all* consequences of a negligent act, no matter how far removed in time or space, may be foreseen. Conditioning liability on foreseeability, therefore, is hardly a condition at all. "Every injury has ramifying consequences, like the ripplings of the waters, without end. The problem for the law is to limit the legal consequences of wrongs to a controllable degree." Tobin [v. Grossman], 24 N.Y.2d, at 619, 301 N.Y.S.2d, at 560, 249 N.E.2d, at 424. . . .

This is true as a practical matter in the FELA context as well, even though the statute limits recovery to railroad workers. If emotional injury to Gottshall was foreseeable to Conrail, such injury to the other seven members of his work crew was also foreseeable. Because one need not witness an accident to suffer emotional injury therefrom, however, the potential liability would not necessarily have to end there; any Conrail employees who heard or read about the events surrounding Johns' death could also foreseeably have suffered emotional injury as a result. Of course, not all of these workers would have been as traumatized by the tragedy as was Gottshall, but many could have been. Under the Third Circuit's standard, Conrail thus could face the potential of unpredictable liability to a large number of employees far removed from the scene of the allegedly negligent conduct that led to Johns' death.[12] Finally, the Third Circuit in *Carlisle* erred in upholding "a claim under the FELA for negligent infliction of emotional distress arising from work-related stress." 990 F.2d, at 97-98. We find no support in the common law for this unprecedented holding, which would impose a duty to avoid creating a stressful work environment, and thereby dramatically expand employers' FELA liability to cover the stresses and strains of everyday employment. Indeed, [this] . . . ruling would tend to make railroads the insurers of the emotional well-being and mental health of their employees. We have made clear, however, that FELA is not an insurance statute. . . .

12. The Third Circuit did require that the emotional injury be "reasonably" foreseeable, but under the circumstances, that qualifier seems to add little. Suffice it to say that if Gottshall's emotional injury stemming from Johns' death was reasonably foreseeable to Conrail, nearly any injury could also be reasonably foreseeable.

C

. . . We [conclude] . . . that the zone of danger test best reconciles the concerns of the common law with the principles underlying our FELA jurisprudence.

As we did in Monessen [S. W. Ry. v. Morgan, 486 U.S. 330 (1988)], we begin with the state of the common law in 1908, when FELA was enacted. . . . [T]he right to recover for negligently inflicted emotional distress was well established in many jurisdictions in 1908. Although at that time, [most U.S. courts] favored the physical impact test . . ., the zone of danger test had been adopted by a significant number of jurisdictions. Moreover, because it was recognized as being a progressive rule of liability that was less restrictive than the physical impact test, the zone of danger test would have been more consistent than the physical impact test with FELA's broad remedial goals. Considering the question "in the appropriate historical context," *Monessen, supra*, 486 U.S., at 337, 108 S. Ct., at 1843, then, it is reasonable to conclude that Congress intended the scope of the duty to avoid inflicting emotional distress under FELA to be coextensive with that established under the zone of danger test. That is, an emotional injury constitutes "injury" resulting from the employer's "negligence" for purposes of FELA only if it would be compensable under the terms of the zone of danger test.

Current usage only confirms this historical pedigree. The zone of danger test . . . remains to this day a well-established "common-law concep[t] of negligence," [cited authority omitted], that is suitable to inform our determination of the federal question of what constitutes negligence for purposes of FELA.

The zone of danger test also is consistent with FELA's central focus on physical perils. . . . FELA was intended to provide compensation for the injuries and deaths caused by the physical dangers of railroad work by allowing employees or their estates to assert damages claims. By imposing liability, FELA presumably also was meant to encourage employers to improve safety measures in order to avoid those claims. . . . But while the statute may have been primarily focused on physical injury, it refers simply to "injury," which may encompass both physical and emotional injury. We believe that allowing recovery for negligently inflicted emotional injury as provided for under the zone of danger test best harmonizes these considerations. . . .

Respondents decry the zone of danger test as arbitrarily excluding valid claims for emotional injury. But "[c]haracterizing a rule limiting liability as 'unprincipled' or 'arbitrary' is often the result of overemphasizing the policy considerations favoring imposition of liability, while at the same time failing to acknowledge any countervailing policies and the necessary compromise between competing and inconsistent policies informing the rule." Cameron v. Pepin, 610 A.2d 279, 283 (Me. 1992). Our FELA cases require that we look to the common law when considering the right to recover asserted by respondents, and the common law restricts recovery for negligent infliction of emotional distress on several policy grounds: the potential for a flood of trivial suits, the possibility of fraudulent claims that are difficult for judges and juries to detect, and the specter of unlimited and unpredictable liability. Although some of these grounds have been criticized by commentators, they all continue to give caution to courts. We believe the concerns that underlie the common-law tests, and particularly the fear of unlimited liability, to be well-founded. . . .

IV

Because the Third Circuit applied an erroneous standard for evaluating claims for negligent infliction of emotional distress brought under FELA, we reverse the judgments below. In *Gottshall,* we remand for reconsideration under the zone of danger test announced today. Gottshall asserts before this Court that he would in fact meet the requirements of the zone of danger test, while Conrail disagrees. The question was not adequately briefed or argued before us, however, and we believe it best to allow the Third Circuit to consider the question in the first instance in light of relevant common-law precedent.

In *Carlisle,* however, we remand with instructions to enter judgment for Conrail. Carlisle's work-stress-related claim plainly does not fall within the common law's conception of the zone of danger, and Carlisle makes no argument that it does. Without any support in the common law for such a claim, we will not take the radical step of reading FELA as compensating for stress arising in the ordinary course of employment. In short, the core of Carlisle's complaint was that he "had been given too much — not too dangerous — work to do. That is not our idea of an FELA claim." *Lancaster, supra,* at 813.

The judgments of the Court of Appeals are reversed, and the cases are remanded for further proceedings consistent with this opinion.

[Concurrence of Justice Souter omitted. — Eds.]

Ginsburg, J., (dissenting) (joined by Blackmun and Stevens, JJ.) . . .

. . . In view of the broad language of [FELA], and this Court's repeated reminders that [it] is to be liberally construed, I cannot regard as faithful to the legislation and our case law under it the restrictive test announced in the Court's opinion. . . .

III

. . . The Court offers three justifications for its adoption of the "zone of danger" test. First, the Court suggests that the "zone" test is most firmly rooted in "the common law." The Court mentions that several jurisdictions had adopted the zone of danger test by 1908, *ante,* at 2406, and n.8 (citing cases from eight States), and that the test "currently is followed in 14 jurisdictions." *Ante,* at 2406. But that very exposition tells us that the "zone" test never held sway in a majority of States. . . .

The Court further maintains that the zone of danger test is preferable because it is "consistent with FELA's central focus on physical perils." *Ante,* at 2410. But, as already underscored, see *supra,* at 2413, the FELA's language "is as broad as could be framed. . . . On its face, every injury suffered [on the job] by any employee . . . by reason of the carrier's negligence was made compensable." *Urie,* 337 U.S., at 181, 69 S. Ct., at 1030. . . .

The Court's principal reason for restricting the FELA's coverage of emotional distress claims is its fear of "infinite liability" to an "infinite number of persons." The universe of potential FELA plaintiffs, however, is hardly "infinite." The statute does not govern the public at large. Only persons "suffering injury . . . while employed" by a railroad may recover . . ., and to do so, the complainant must show that the injury resulted from the railroad's negligence. 45 U.S.C. § 51. The Court expresses concern that the approach Gottshall and Carlisle advocate would require "[j]udges . . . to make highly subjective determinations concerning the authenticity of claims for emotional injury, which are far less susceptible to objective medical proof than are their physical counterparts." *Ante*, at 2409. One solution to this problem . . . would be to require such "objective medical proof" and to exclude, as too insubstantial to count as "injury," claims lacking this proof.

IV

. . . Instead of the restrictive "zone" test that leaves severely harmed workers remediless, however negligent their employers, the appropriate FELA claim threshold should be keyed to the genuineness and gravity of the worker's injury. . . .

NOTES AND QUESTIONS

1. *Predicate Injuries: Bodily Harm Versus Property Damage.* Every U.S. court has long accepted *Wyman*'s observation that a jury may award compensation for (adequately proven) pain and suffering *parasitic* on a physical injury caused by the defendant's failure to take care not to cause bodily harm. Recall from Chapter 2 that the "general" duty of care recognized by decisions such as *Heaven v. Pender* includes a duty to take care against damaging tangible property owned or possessed by another. Why, then, does the *Wyman* court seem unwilling to permit Wyman to recover for her emotional distress as a loss consequent to the predicate injury of property damage? Here, she faced two problems. First, her husband appears to have been the sole owner of the land. Second, most courts are unwilling to treat negligent causation of tangible property damage as sufficient in itself to support a parasitic award of emotional distress damages to the property owner or possessor. *See* Erlich v. Menezes, 981 P.2d 978 (Cal. 1999); Stahli v. McGlynn, 366 N.Y.S.2d 209 (N.Y. App. Div. 1975). Intentional causation of property damage, however, may sometimes permit such recovery. *See, e.g.*, Blache v. Jones, 521 So. 2d 530 (La. Ct. App. 1988).

The rule as to negligence might be different if the property damaged by the defendant's carelessness has sentimental rather than just commercial value. For example, suppose Leavitt's careless blasting proximately caused the death of Wyman's beloved pet dog, which she owned outright. Should she be able to recover emotional distress damages as parasitic on the injury to her "property"? Compare the majority and dissenting opinions in *Rabideau v. City of Racine*, 627 N.W.2d 795 (Wis. 2001); *see also* Tenn. Code Ann. § 44-17-403 (2001) (permitting a pet owner up to $5,000 in emotional distress damages for certain wrongful killings of a pet).

2. *Injury Revisited.* Decisions such as *Wyman* are sometimes described as holding that a defendant owes *no duty* to others to take reasonable care not to cause them emotional distress. Although late-nineteenth-century courts may have at times expressed themselves in this way, such a description is misleading insofar as it suggests that the perceived problem with a claim such as Mrs. Wyman's resided in her inability to satisfy the duty element. In fact, courts at this time tended to deny liability on other

grounds. Indeed, in quoting with approval the analysis of *Lynch v. Knight*, the *Wyman* court seems to concede, at least for purposes of analysis, that the defendant's conduct breached an obligation owed to Wyman (i.e., was "unlawful") so as to cause her to suffer an adverse effect.

The problem with her claim, instead, resided in the particular adverse effect of which she was complaining. According to the court, mental suffering alone, although undoubtedly a setback to Wyman, did not count as the sort of setback that constitutes an *injury* required by the first element of the negligence cause of action. (To help grasp this point, you may wish to refer to the brief analysis of the injury element provided at the outset of Chapter 2.) Without an injury of which to complain, Wyman was in exactly the same position as a person who, although *at risk* of being hit by flying debris because of Leavitt's carelessness, was not struck by any debris, and was at all times completely oblivious to the danger. *Cf.* Canning v. Inhabitants of Williamstown, 55 Mass. 451 (1848) (neither peril nor fright constitutes an injury within the meaning of a statute permitting a person "injured" because of poor road conditions to recover damages from the person or party responsible for maintaining the road).

Suppose that the perceived absence of injury provides the basis for the *Wyman* court's holding. Is the court guilty of an inconsistency when it acknowledges that Wyman *could prevail* if she could somehow prove that Leavitt conducted blasting *for the purpose* of causing her to apprehend that she was about to be struck by rocks? How is it that fear of being physically injured can at one and the same time constitute an injury that will support a claim of assault, yet not constitute an injury that will support a claim of negligence?

3. *Gender Bias?* Some scholars, most prominently Martha Chamallas, have argued that the rule denying recovery for emotional distress owes its origins to the gender biases of nineteenth-century judges. It is no coincidence, they maintain, that the law developed special and restrictive rules for these claims, because such claims tended to be brought by female plaintiffs and sought relief for invasion of the sort of nonmaterial interest that male judges traditionally regarded as unmanly and unworthy of legal protection. *See* Spade v. Lynn & B.R. Co., 168 Mass. 285 (1897) (female trolley passenger suffered nervous shock as a result of a commotion caused by a conductor's negligence; rule against recovery for negligently inflicted nervous shock justified on the ground that actors cannot be held hostage to the "peculiar sensitiveness" of others). Chamallas further notes that even as decisions such as *Robb* have whittled away at the blanket no-duty rule, they have refused to go so far as to embrace a *Heaven*-like general duty to avoid causing emotional injury. This asymmetry, she claims, reveals a continuing bias in the law.

4. *NIED Versus Ordinary Negligence: Impacts as Bodily Harms.* As noted in *Robb*, by the turn of the twentieth century, courts had begun to cabin the rule articulated in decisions such as *Wyman*. One common technique was to expand what would suffice to establish the requisite "predicate" physical injury. Under the *impact rule*, recovery for disturbance of emotional tranquility could be had if the defendant made even the most minimal physical contact with the plaintiff's person. By this means, courts moved certain "emotional distress" claims into the category of physical harm cases by, in

effect, borrowing a page from battery law, under which any touching, no matter how slight, is sufficient. *See, e.g.*, Morton v. Stack, 170 N.E. 869 (Ohio 1930) (child trapped in burning building because of landlord's failure to provide a fire escape can recover for being traumatized; inhalation of smoke treated as sufficient to generate an impact).

While the impact rule was perhaps well intentioned as a corrective to the blanket rule denying claims for negligently inflicted emotional distress, the fix it provided was largely ad hoc. (Consider why the minimal touching requirements of battery law might be out of place in the context of negligence.) Perhaps the poster child for its unprincipled nature was the decision in *Mitchell v. Rochester Ry. Co.*, 45 N.E. 354 (N.Y. 1896), which held that a pregnant woman who suffered a miscarriage as a result of being descended upon, but not touched, by a team of horses, could not recover. In light of decisions such as *Mitchell*, courts came to view the impact rule with considerable skepticism and have by and large replaced it with alternative rules permitting recovery. Courts have not always clearly stated whether these new rules are meant to supersede or supplement the impact rule (i.e., they have not explicitly stated that impact remains sufficient to permit recovery, even if not necessary). However, most hold or assume that trivial touchings are *not* sufficient to count as the sort of predicate injury that will support the award of emotional distress compensation as parasitic damages. *See, e.g.*, Metro-North Commuter R.R. Co. v. Buckley, 521 U.S. 424 (1997) (reproduced in Chapter 13) (declining to treat inhalation of asbestos particles as sufficient to constitute a predicate physical injury under the Federal Employers Liability Act).

5. *Extending Liability for Physical Harm.* While some courts were seizing on the impact rule as a means of mitigating the perceived harshness of the rule articulated in decisions such as *Wyman*, others pursued an alternative path. These courts focused not on *how the emotional distress came about* (i.e., whether it occurred contemporaneously with, or subsequent to, a bodily contact) but instead on *its effects* on the plaintiff. In particular, courts and commentators came to argue that a plaintiff who could establish that she had suffered a discrete bodily harm or diagnosable illness because of having been exposed to a sudden "shock" should be deemed to be suing not for emotional distress but for the consequent physical harm or illness. By this means, the plaintiff in *Mitchell*, for example, could be understood to be suing for negligent driving that caused a miscarriage, a claim no different in kind from Antoinette Walter's claim to have been made physically ill by Wal-Mart's careless mishandling of her prescription.

Many commentators argued that a rule confining recovery to victims who could prove a physical harm flowing from their distress was superior to the impact rule on at least two counts. First, it is arguably consistent with decisions such as *Wyman* because it does *not* deem interference with the victim's interest in emotional tranquility as itself an injury. Second, by recognizing claims brought by those who suffered significant adverse physical effects as a result of distress, it seems likely to provide redress for persons who are among the most severely traumatized, whereas the impact rule worked in favor of the arbitrary class of persons who happen to have been touched. Still, before courts could proceed down this road, they had to overcome an important doctrinal barrier, one set not by the injury element, but by the requirement of proximate cause.

6. *The Problem of Remoteness.* The proximate cause problem arose because of a basic difference between a claim such as Antoinette Walter's, on the one hand, and a claim of the sort seen in *Mitchell*, on the other. In *Walter*, the distress experienced by the plaintiff followed as a consequence of her being poisoned — the distress played no significant role in her becoming ill in the first place. In *Mitchell*, by contrast, the defendant's careless driving brought about a miscarriage only via the medium of the plaintiff's emotional response to that carelessness. Many of the same courts that refused to recognize emotional distress as an injury unto itself treated this difference as providing a compelling reason not to impose liability even in cases such as *Mitchell*, in which carelessly caused distress produced physical harms. Claims such as Mitchell's were, in essence, claims for "remote" harm, that is, harm not *proximately caused* by the carelessness of the defendant. In their view, it was the plaintiff's responsibility to control her reactions to the defendant's carelessness. To the extent she was "unable" or "unwilling" to do so, any consequent emotional distress was deemed to be her doing, rather than the defendant's.

For the foregoing reasons, proximate cause doctrine, at least as much as injury doctrine, blocked liability for physical harms arising out of carelessly caused emotional traumas. By the same token, as courts began to expand liability in this area, they did so at first *not* by treating disturbance of emotional tranquility as an injury, but instead by liberalizing proximate cause doctrine as it applied to claims of consequential physical harms. Specifically, they abandoned the idea that the causal connection between defendant's breach and plaintiff's injury was always too remote simply because the injury was linked to the breach through the plaintiff's emotional response to it.

With the abandonment of this *per se* rule of remoteness, potential liability for careless acts expanded *within* the domain of liability for carelessly caused *physical harms*. This explains why, when it came time for William Prosser to "restate" the law of negligence in 1965, he declined to treat decisions such as *Robb* as recognizing a cause of action for negligent infliction of emotional distress. Instead, he described them as claims for carelessness causing *physical harms* via an emotional traumatization of the plaintiff. *See* Restatement (Second) of Torts § 313(1) (1965) (noting that recoveries in cases such as *Robb* do not vindicate the victim's interest in emotional tranquility, but instead permit recovery for physical harms caused by emotional distress).

7. *From Remote to Proximate: The Special Salience of Shock.* *Robb* partakes of the expansionist strategy just described in Note 6. Yet it also emphasizes that it is not enough for the plaintiff to establish that she suffered consequential physical harm as a result of emotional distress caused by the defendant's carelessness. In addition, the court requires her distress to have come about in a particular way, or to be of a particular kind. Specifically, she must have experienced that distress as a result of *being imminently endangered* by the defendant's careless conduct. Thus, if we imagine that Robb's car stalled 20 yards from the railroad crossing, she would apparently not be entitled to recover, even if she could prove that she was actually afraid for her life and that she suffered the same illness as a result of that fear.

Given that *Robb*, like the Second Restatement, seems to treat claims such as Robb's as claims for physical harms, what is the point of requiring her to have been (objectively) endangered? If she actually perceived a danger, and if she can prove that that trauma caused her to become physically ill, what is gained by denying her recovery simply because her fear was unfounded? For that matter, once we conceive of this class of negligence claims as falling within the class of claims for negligence causing physical harm, why should *fear of bodily injury* be privileged as a special form of distress that can (if it produces consequent physical harm) lay the basis for a claim in negligence? Why not other fears? Why not distress that has nothing to do with fear? Suppose, for example, Robb was sitting in her car 30 yards from the grade crossing, but was severely traumatized because she witnessed the negligent killing of another driver whose car became stuck on the crossing. Why shouldn't she be entitled to recover for her illness notwithstanding that she was outside the "zone of danger"?

Again, history sheds some light here. It seems that the zone of danger requirement is in part an effort to express in more contemporary language an older idea of "nervous shock." As noted above, the effort to move past the impact rule crystallized around cases such as *Mitchell*, in which the plaintiff suffered an injury or illness after being exposed to a sudden threat of physical harm. These cases apparently struck many courts and commentators as presenting the most compelling grounds for rejecting the old proximate cause limitation on liability for physical harm caused through emotional distress because this particular sort of shock was thought to be transmitted immediately and directly through the plaintiff's nervous system. In their view, a plaintiff who apprehends being killed or seriously harmed—particularly a female plaintiff—suffered an instantaneous fraying of the nerves. In these cases, the defendant could be held liable for having caused physical harm in a direct, unmediated way by physically damaging the plaintiff's nervous system.

Representative of this mindset is the decision in *Lindley v. Knowlton*, 179 Cal. 298 (1918). There, a mother whose children were attacked by her neighbor's pet chimpanzee was permitted to recover for lasting trauma associated with fending off the attack. Quoting an earlier California decision, Sloane v. Southern Cal. Ry. Co., 111 Cal. 668, 680 (1896), the Court explained:

> The nerves and the nerve centers of the body are a part of the physical system, and are not only susceptible of lesion from external causes, but are also liable to be weakened and destroyed from causes primarily acting on the mind. If these nerves or the entire nervous system is thus affected, there is a physical injury produced. . . .

Robb does not explicitly link its zone-of-danger requirement to a biological thesis of the sort propounded in *Lindley*. Still, it seems to share *Lindley*'s view that there is something particularly salient about having been distressed by virtue of having been imminently endangered.

8. *From Harm to Symptoms: The Emergence of True NIED Claims.* Most jurisdictions have today at least gone so far as to embrace *Robb*'s holding recognizing a negligence action for plaintiffs who suffer physical harms as a result of having been placed in imminent physical peril by another's carelessness. But this still leaves open the question of the doctrinal and theoretical basis on which they have done so. The choice of basis in turn has important implications for the scope of responsibility and liability in this area.

B. Special Relationships and Undertakings to Be Vigilant of Another's Emotional Well-Being

Even as late-nineteenth-century courts were asserting, with *Lynch v. Knight* (quoted in *Wyman*), that "mental pain or anxiety the law cannot value, and does not pretend to redress," they were also recognizing exceptions to this rule. Thus, as was noted in the introduction to the materials on intentional infliction of emotional distress, courts would occasionally permit recovery for what appeared to be pure claims of distress against defendants who caused it through abominable misconduct. In addition, courts recognized a few pockets of liability even for carelessly caused emotional distress.

In one common scenario, a telegraph company, *T*, would promise sender *S* to deliver promptly a telegram to recipient *R*. The telegram was meant to inform *R* that *R*'s close relative had passed away and that the relative's funeral was imminent. *T*, however, would carelessly fail to deliver the telegram, causing *R* to miss the funeral. Many courts permitted *R* to recover for the distress associated with missing the funeral. Of these, some treated *R*'s claims as sounding in contract. (These courts deemed *R* a "third-party beneficiary" to the contract between *S* and *T*.) Other courts treated such claims as tort actions in which the duty to attend to the recipient's emotional well-being was deemed to arise out of the implicit undertaking on the part of *T* to deliver an important and emotionally freighted message to *R* in a prompt fashion. *See, e.g.*, Mentzer v. Western Union Tel. Co., 62 N.W. 1 (Iowa 1895) (adopting both rationales).

In a related vein, courts have long recognized a duty to take reasonable care not to cause distress to family members when undertaking to dispose appropriately of the corpse of their decedent, regardless of whether those family members were the ones who contracted for funeral services. *See* Christensen v. Superior Court, 820 P.2d 181 (Cal. 1991) (recognizing a negligence cause of action for relatives of decedents distressed over defendants' mishandling of their decedents' corpses).

Finally, one other class of plaintiffs was frequently permitted to sue for negligence causing them emotional distress. These consisted of passengers—often young women—who sued common carriers for causing them, or even failing to protect them from, severe distress experienced in transit. *See, e.g.*, Wilson v. Northern Pac. R. Co., 32 P. 468 (Wash. 1893) (imposing liability on a common carrier in favor of a passenger who suffered distress after being erroneously caused to exit the train on which she was riding and then made to pay an additional fare). Similar claims were sometimes recognized by guests against inns and hotels.

Can one identify a set of principles that make sense of the courts' willingness to impose duties to be vigilant of others' emotional well-being in these sorts of cases? Consider the following passage from *Fitzsimmons v. Olinger Mortuary Ass'n.*, 17 P.2d 535, 536-537 (Colo. 1932), quoted in *Christensen, supra*:

> "One who prepares a human body for burial and conducts a funeral usually deals with the living in their most difficult and delicate moments. . . . The exhibition of callousness or indifference, the offer of insult and indignity, can, of course, inflict no injury on the dead, but they can visit agony akin to torture on the living. So true is this that the chief asset of a mortician and the most conspicuous element of his

> advertisement is his consideration for the afflicted. A decent respect for their feelings is implied in every contract for his services."

Christensen, 820 P.2d at 196. Do the other contracts or undertakings mentioned above carry with them a similar sort of obligation of "decent respect" for the feelings of certain others? If so, is this because of characteristics unique to the businesses of telegraph operators, morticians, and common carriers? Consider in this regard the following modern decision.

Beul v. ASSE Int'l, Inc.

233 F.3d 441 (7th Cir. 2000)

Posner, J. In this . . . suit for negligence, governed (so far as the substantive issues are concerned) by Wisconsin law, the jury returned a verdict finding that plaintiff Kristin Beul's damages were $1,100,000 and that she was 41 percent responsible for them; in accordance with the verdict, judgment was entered against defendant ASSE International for $649,000 (59 percent of $1.1 million). . . .

The defendant is a nonprofit corporation that operates international student exchange programs. For a fee of $2,000 it placed Kristin, a 16-year-old German girl who wanted to spend a year in the United States, with the Bruce family of Fort Atkinson, Wisconsin. The family, which consisted of Richard Bruce, age 40, his wife, and their 13-year-old daughter, had been selected by Marianne Breber, the defendant's Area Representative in the part of the state that includes Fort Atkinson. Breber is described in the briefs as a "volunteer," not an employee; the only payment she receives from ASSE is reimbursement of her expenses. Nothing in the appeal, however, turns either on her "volunteer" status or on ASSE's nonprofit status. Charities are not immune from tort liability in Wisconsin, . . . and ASSE does not deny that if Breber was negligent it is liable for her negligence under the doctrine of *respondeat superior*, even though she was not an employee of ASSE. The doctrine is nowadays usually described as making an employer liable for the torts of his employees committed within the scope of their employment, but strictly speaking the liability is that of a "master" for the torts of his "servant" and it extends to situations in which the servant is not an employee, provided that he is acting in a similar role, albeit as a volunteer. . . .

There is also no argument that the contract between ASSE and Kristin's parents is the exclusive source of ASSE's legal duties to Kristin. Negligence in the performance of a contract that foreseeably results in personal injury, including as here emotional distress, is actionable under tort law. . . . As we pointed out in Rardin v. T & D Machine Handling, Inc., 890 F.2d 24, 29 (7th Cir. 1989), "tort law is a field largely shaped by the special considerations involved in personal-injury cases, as contract law is not. Tort doctrines are, therefore, prima facie more suitable for the governance of such cases than contract doctrines are" even when victim and injurer are linked by contract.

As the sponsor of a foreign exchange student, ASSE was subject to regulations of the United States Information Agency that require sponsors to train their agents, "monitor the progress and welfare of the exchange visit," and require a "regular schedule of personal contact with the student and host family." 22 C.F.R. §§ 514.10(e)(2), 514.25 (d)(1), (4) (now §§ 62.10(e)(2), 62.25(d)(1), (4)). These regulations are intended for the protection of the visitor, see "Exchange Visitor Program," 58 Fed. Reg. 15,180, 15,190 (1993) (statement of USIA accompanying promulgation of 26 C.F.R. § 514.25), and the jury was therefore properly instructed, under standard tort principles not challenged by ASSE, that it could consider the violation of them as evidence of negligence. There is no argument that the regulations create a private federal right of suit that would allow the plaintiffs to sue ASSE under the federal-question jurisdiction of the federal courts . . ., or that Wisconsin is legally obligated to use the regulations to define the duty of care of a sponsor sued under state tort law. . . . But the district court was entitled to conclude that a state court would look to the regulations for evidence of the sponsor's duty of care. Courts in tort cases commonly take their cues from statutes or regulations intended to protect the safety of the class to which the tort plaintiff belongs.

ASSE is also a member of a private association of sponsors of foreign exchange students, the Council on Standards for International Educational Travel, which requires members to "maintain thorough, accurate, and continual communication with host families and school authorities." A jury could reasonably consider the Council's statement as additional evidence of the standard of care applicable to sponsors and it could also accept the plaintiff's argument that due care required Breber to try to develop rapport with Kristin so that Kristin would trust and confide in her and so that Breber could pick up any signals of something amiss that Kristin might be embarrassed to mention unless pressed.

Kristin Beul arrived in Wisconsin from Germany on September 7, 1995, and was met at the airport by Richard Bruce and his daughter. Marianne Breber did not go to the airport to meet Kristin. In fact, apart from a brief orientation meeting at a shopping mall in September with Kristin and one other foreign exchange student, at which Breber gave Kristin her phone number, she didn't meet with Kristin until January 21 of the following year—under unusual circumstances, as we'll see. She did call the Bruce home a few times during this period and spoke briefly with Kristin once or twice, but she made no effort to make sure that Kristin was alone when they spoke. She would ask in these calls how Kristin was doing and Kristin would reply that everything was fine. Breber did not talk to Mrs. Bruce, who would have told her that she was concerned that her husband seemed to be developing an inappropriate relationship with Kristin.

Kristin had led a sheltered life in Germany. She had had no sexual experiences at all and in fact had had only two dates in her lifetime. On November 17, 1995, Richard Bruce, who weighed almost 300 pounds and who was alone at home at the time except for Kristin, came into the loft area in which she slept and raped her.

This was the start of a protracted sexual relationship. In the months that followed, Bruce frequently would call the high school that Kristin was attending and report her ill. Then, with Mrs. Bruce off at work and the Bruce's daughter at school, Bruce would have sex with Kristin. By February 22, Kristin had been absent 27 days from school. Bruce brandished a gun and told Kristin that he would kill himself if she told anyone what they were doing together.

Curiously, in January Bruce and Kristin called Marianne Breber and told her that Mrs. Bruce appeared to be jealous of the time that her husband was spending with

Kristin. Bruce invited Breber to dinner on January 21. Breber did not meet privately with either Kristin or Mrs. Bruce on that occasion, and she observed nothing untoward. In February, however, Mrs. Bruce told Breber that she and her husband were getting divorced, and Breber forthwith found another host family to take in Kristin. Kristin didn't want to leave the Bruce home, but on February 22 Breber arrived there with a sheriff's deputy to remove Kristin. The deputy asked Kristin in the presence of Richard Bruce and his daughter whether there was any inappropriate sexual activity between Richard and Kristin, and Kristin answered "no." The same day Breber, upon calling Kristin's school to tell them that Kristin would be out for a few days in connection with her change of residence, learned for the first time of Kristin's many absences.

Kristin lived with Breber for a few days between host families, but Breber didn't use the occasion to inquire about any possible sexual relationship between Kristin and Bruce. Breber told the new host family that Kristin was not to contact Bruce for a month, but she did not tell Bruce not to have any contact with Kristin. They continued to correspond and talk on the phone. Kristin had decided that she was in love with Bruce and considered herself engaged to him.

In April, Mrs. Bruce discovered some of Kristin's love letters and alerted the authorities. A sheriff's deputy interviewed Bruce. The next day Bruce, who had committed a misdemeanor by having sex with a 16 year old, Wis. Stat. § 948.09, killed himself, leaving a note expressing fear of jail. It is undisputed that the events culminating in Bruce's suicide inflicted serious psychological harm on Kristin; the jury's assessment of her damages is not claimed to be excessive.

The defendant argues that it was entitled to judgment as a matter of law, or alternatively to a new trial because of trial error. The first argument divides into three: there was insufficient proof of a causal relationship between the defendant's negligence in failing to keep closer tabs on Kristin Beul and her sexual involvement with Bruce culminating in his suicide; Bruce's criminal activity was the sole, or superseding, cause of her harm; and the harm was too "remote" in a legal sense from the defendant's failure of due care to support liability.

Since Kristin was determined to conceal her relationship with Bruce, the defendant argues, no amount of care by Breber would have warded off the harm that befell Kristin; she would have stonewalled, however pertinacious Breber had been in her questioning. This is conceivable, and if true would let ASSE off the hook; if there was no causal relation between the defendant's negligence and the plaintiff's harm, there was no tort.

But it is improbable, and the jury was certainly not required to buy the argument. Suppose Breber had inquired from the school how Kristin was doing—a natural question to ask about a foreigner plunged into an American high school. She would have learned of the numerous absences, would (if minimally alert) have inquired about them from Kristin, and would have learned that Kristin had been "ill" and that Richard Bruce had been home and taken care of her. At that point the secret would have started to unravel.

As for the argument that Bruce's misconduct was so egregious as to let ASSE off the hook, it is true that the doctrine of "superseding cause" can excuse a negligent defendant. Suicide by a sane person, unless clearly foreseeable by the tortfeasor, for example a psychiatrist treating a depressed person, is a traditional example of the operation of the doctrine. . . . So if Bruce's boss had refused him a raise and Bruce had responded by killing himself, the boss even if somehow negligent in failing to give him the raise would not be considered the legal cause of the death. Or if through the carelessness of the driver a truck spilled a toxic substance and a passerby scraped it up and poisoned his mother-in-law with it, the driver would not be liable to the mother-in-law's estate; the son-in-law's criminal act would be deemed a superseding cause.

Animating the doctrine is the idea that it is unreasonable to make a person liable for such improbable consequences of negligent activity as could hardly figure in his deciding how careful he should be. The doctrine is not applied, therefore, when the duty of care claimed to have been violated is precisely a duty to protect against ordinarily unforeseeable conduct, as in our earlier example of a psychiatrist treating depression. The existence of the duty presupposes a probable, therefore a foreseeable, consequence of its breach. (All that "foreseeable" means in tort law is probable ex ante, that is, before the injury that is the basis of the tort suit.) Thus a hospital that fails to maintain a careful watch over patients known to be suicidal is not excused by the doctrine of superseding cause from liability for a suicide, . . . any more than a zoo can escape liability for allowing a tiger to escape and maul people on the ground that the tiger is the superseding cause of the mauling.

So Kristin's high school would not have been liable for the consequences of Bruce's sexual activity with Kristin even if the school should have reported her frequent absences to Breber; the criminal activities with their bizarre suicide sequel were not foreseeable by the school. But part of ASSE's duty and Breber's function was to protect foreign girls and boys from sexual hanky-panky initiated by members of host families. Especially when a teenage girl is brought to live with strangers in a foreign country, the risk of inappropriate sexual activity is not so slight that the organization charged by the girl's parents with the safety of their daughter can be excused as a matter of law from making a responsible effort to minimize the risk. Sexual abuse by stepfathers is not uncommon, see, e.g., Diana E.H. Russell, "*The Prevalance and Seriousness of Incestuous Abuse: Stepfathers vs. Biological Fathers*," 8 Child Abuse & Neglect 15 (1984), and the husband in a host family has an analogous relationship to a teenage visitor living with the family.

It is true (we turn now to the issue of remoteness) that when through the negligence of an alarm company, to which ASSE in its role as protector of foreign students from the sexual attentions of members of host families might perhaps be analogized, a fire or burglary is not averted or controlled in time, the company is generally not liable for the consequences; the consequences are deemed too remote. E.g., Edwards v. Honeywell, Inc., 50 F.3d 484, 491 (7th Cir. 1995). . . . There are two related considerations. One is that so many factors outside the alarm company's control determine the likelihood and consequences (whether in property loss or personal injury) of a failure of its alarm to summon prompt aid on a particular occasion that the company is bound to lack the information that it needs to determine what level of care to take to prevent a failure of its system. . . . A harm is not foreseeable in the contemplation of the law if the injurer lacked the information he needed to determine whether he must use special care to avert the harm. The second point is that the alarm company is not the primary accident avoider but merely a backup, and the principal responsibility for avoiding disaster lies with the victim.

The points are related because both involve the difficulty a backup or secondary protector against disaster has in figuring out the consequence of a lapse on its part. Neither point supports ASSE, which was standing in the shoes of the parents of a young girl living in a stranger's home far from her homeland and could reasonably be expected to exercise the kind of care that the parents themselves would exercise if they could to protect their 16-year-old daughter from the sexual pitfalls that lie about a girl of that age in those circumstances. ASSE assumed a primary role in the protection of the girl. . . .

The defendant . . . complains about the following instruction to the jury: "You're instructed that the law of Wisconsin does not allow a child under the age of 18 to consent to an act of intercourse." This was a reference to the state's statutory rape law, but it was not elaborated further. The jury was instructed to consider the instructions as a whole and another instruction was that it was to consider Kristin's comparative fault. The jury assessed that fault at 41 percent, so obviously it did not think the age-of-consent instruction prevented it from considering Kristin's responsibility for the harm that befell her as a consequence of her sexual relationship with Bruce.

But should the jury have been told what the age of consent is in Wisconsin and, if so, was the information conveyed to the jury in the right way? The answer to the first question is yes. The age of consent fixed by a state represents a legislative judgment about the maturity of girls in matters of sex. Eighteen is a pretty high age of consent by today's standards and of course the law was not fixed by reference to German girls; but it is nonetheless a reminder that teenage children are not considered fully responsible in sexual matters, and this was something relevant to the jury's consideration of Kristin's share of responsibility for the disaster. The criminal law is frequently used to set a standard of care for civil tort cases . . . and that was essentially the use made of it here. It would have been error to instruct the jury that because Kristin was below the age of consent her comparative fault must be reckoned at zero. That would have given too much force to the criminal statute in this civil case, for the statute cannot be considered a legislative judgment that minors are utterly incapable of avoiding becoming ensnared in sexual relationships. A comparative-fault rule, moreover, requires gradations of victim responsibility that are alien to the normal criminal prohibition. Victim fault is not a defense, either partial or complete, to criminal liability. It is not a defense to a charge of rape that, for example, the victim was dressed provocatively, or drunk, or otherwise careless in the circumstances in which the rape occurred.

It would have been better, though, if the jury had been told how it should take the age of consent into account in their deliberations. It should have been told that in deciding how much responsibility to assign to Kristin for the events that gave rise to the harm for which she was suing, it could consider that the state had made a judgment that girls below the age of 18 should be protected by the criminal law from sexual activity even if they agree to it. As it was, the jury was left to tease out the relation between the age-of-consent instruction and the comparative-fault instruction for itself. But we cannot think that it was other than a harmless error. Indeed, we are surprised that the jury assigned so large a responsibility to this young foreign girl virtually abandoned by the agency that was standing in for her parents. The jury verdict was rather favorable to the defendant than otherwise.

Affirmed.

NOTES AND QUESTIONS

1. *Beul and NIED.* Judge Posner does not explicitly describe *Beul* as addressing a claim for negligent infliction of emotional distress. What exactly is the theory of Beul's negligence suit? Is the claim that ASSE owed it to her to take care to prevent her from suffering the physical or dignitary harms associated with Bruce's initial sexual assault? Or is the claim that ASSE breached a duty to prevent any inappropriate physical contact between Bruce and Kristin?

In its opinion denying ASSE's motion for judgment as a matter of law, the district court described Beul's suit as seeking compensation for the psychological harm associated with her emotionally tangled "relationship" with Bruce. Beul v. ASSE Int'l, Inc., 65 F. Supp. 2d 963, 964 (E.D. Wis. 1999). The district court also described Bruce's initial assault less dramatically than does Judge Posner. We note this difference in characterization not to suggest that Bruce's act was less culpable than Posner's opinion suggests, but as indicative of the trial court's view that the crux of Beul's claim did not concern Bruce's assault *per se*, but rather his having coerced her into a disastrous relationship, and her complicated emotional response to its revelation and Bruce's subsequent suicide.*

Assume that the appropriate description of the gist of Beul's negligence claim is as a claim for NIED. On what basis is Judge Posner prepared to identify the requisite undertaking on the part of ASSE to look out for Kristin's emotional well-being? Notice his assertion that Kristin's school owed her no duty to protect her emotional well-being in connection with her interactions with her host family. Is it plausible to draw such a sharp distinction between ASSE and the school?

2. *Zone of Danger and Special Relationships/Undertakings.* The Third Torts Restatement explicitly embraces the notion that negligence law recognizes essentially two categories of liability for carelessness that *directly* cause emotional distress: zone-of-danger cases and cases involving certain special relationships or undertakings:

> An actor whose negligent conduct causes serious emotional harm to another is subject to liability to the other if the conduct:
>
> (a) places the other in danger of immediate bodily harm and the emotional harm results from the danger; or
>
> (b) occurs in the course of specified categories of activities, undertakings, or relationships in which negligent conduct is especially likely to cause serious emotional harm.

* This interpretation of the nature of Beul's claim is also supported by the trial court's findings that a background check by ASSE would have revealed nothing untoward in the Bruces' past. Beul v. ASSE Int'l, Inc., 55 F. Supp. 2d 942, 945, 949-950 (E.D. Wis. 1999). Admittedly, the trial judge did fault Breber for failing to advise Kristen on how she might attempt to handle the sexual advances of a host parent, which in turn might suggest a focus on the possible causal link between Breber's carelessness and the harm caused by Bruce's initial assault. However, that failure is listed as one of several that left Kristin to cope with the trauma of her ongoing interactions with Bruce and his subsequent suicide. 65 F. Supp. 2d at 965.

Restatement (Third) of Torts: Liability for Physical and Emotional Harm § 47 (2012). In addition, as is discussed below, the Restatement recognizes some liability for distress caused *indirectly* to bystanders.

3. Undertakings, Contracts, and Emotional Distress Damages. Judge Cardozo's landmark 1915 opinion in *MacPherson v. Buick* (see Chapter 2) firmly established that a contractual relationship is not a prerequisite to the existence of a tort duty of care. *Beul*, like some of its nineteenth-century predecessors, poses a different issue bearing on the relation of tort and contract. Suppose there is a contract between defendant and plaintiff, and the plaintiff is injured by the defendant as a result of the defendant inadequately performing—that is, breaching—the contract. May the plaintiff sue in contract, tort, or both?

The short answer is the one given in *Beul*: A contractual relationship between defendant and plaintiff *usually* does not of itself prevent the plaintiff from suing in tort, particularly if the suit alleges that the defendant's performance or failure of performance was careless and caused *physical harm* to the plaintiff. For example, as discussed in Chapter 12, when a consumer contracts to purchase a product from a company, the consumer usually is not thereby barred from suing in tort for physical injuries caused by a defect in the product. However, with respect to certain contracts and certain types of injuries, particularly intangible economic injuries, courts are more willing to treat the contractual relationship as strictly contractual, without any tort overlay. These typically include business transactions (e.g., the sale and purchase of goods or services between two firms), as well as sales of real property. In these cases, even if one party negligently fails to attend to her end of the contractual bargain so as to injure another, a tort action generally will not lie, and the aggrieved party's *only* remedy lies in a suit for breach of contract.

The line between "merely" contractual relationships and contractual relationships that can support tort duties of care has important implications for claimants seeking to recover for emotional distress injuries. When contract law provides the exclusive source of the plaintiff's right to sue the defendant, the plaintiff usually cannot recover emotional distress damages that flow from the other party's breach of contract, even if that breach was the product of carelessness and the distress was foreseeable to the defendant. *See, e.g.*, Erlich v. Menezes, 981 P.2d 978 (Cal. 1999) (contractor who negligently built a shoddy house for the plaintiffs in breach of contract is not liable for emotional distress caused to the plaintiffs by the breach); Wehringer v. Standard Sec. Life Ins. Co., 440 N.E.2d 1331 (N.Y. 1982) (no right to recover for emotional distress resulting from breach of a merely contractual duty). By contrast, as we learn from *Beul*, when a contractual relationship is also deemed to support tort duties of care, a plaintiff may be able to recover on a claim for pure emotional distress.

4. Which Special Relationships and Undertakings? Which relationships or undertakings will support an NIED claim of the sort contemplated by § 47(b) of the Third Restatement? Courts' reasoning in this area resembles the reasoning they deploy in determining whether a "special relationship" supports an affirmative duty to protect or rescue (*see* Chapter 2). Professional setting, the plaintiff's reliance on the defendant, the plaintiff's vulnerability to emotional distress, and a variety of other contextual features frequently are emphasized. As suggested by § 47(b), the inquiry is often trying to gauge whether the defendant's relationship to plaintiff included within it an implicit undertaking by the defendant to be attentive to the plaintiff's emotional well-being.

Hedgepeth v. Whitman Walker Clinic, 22 A.3d 789 (D.C. 2011), is illustrative. An employee of the defendant clinic erroneously recorded the plaintiff, a patient of the clinic, as having tested HIV-positive. After receiving the false diagnosis, plaintiff suffered severe and lasting depression, developed an eating disorder, began to use illegal drugs heavily, and became alienated from his family. Five years later, another set of tests revealed that in fact plaintiff was HIV negative.

Hedgepeth's suit against the clinic and the doctor who reported the erroneously recorded lab result was dismissed by the trial court and by a panel of the D.C. Court of Appeals. Both concluded that D.C. law recognized only zone-of-danger NIED claims. However, the suit was reinstated by the Court of Appeals sitting *en banc*. It ruled that a person owes a duty to take care against causing emotional distress to another if (1) that person, explicitly or implicitly, has undertaken an obligation to the other that implicates the other's emotional well-being, and (2) if it is "especially likely" that careless performance of the undertaking will cause serious emotional harm to the other. *Id.* at 810-11.

Consider also *Broadnax v. Gonzalez*, 809 N.E.2d 645 (N.Y. 2004), in which the plaintiff sued her obstetrician and nurse-midwife for failing to recognize the necessity of a caesarean section, resulting in a stillborn child. Overturning a 20-year-old precedent, the court concluded that the doctor-patient relationship generated a duty to take care not to cause the plaintiff distress by mishandling the birth of her child. In a footnote, it added that the defendants owed no such duty to the expectant father, though the father could recover for loss of his wife's services and companionship through an action for loss of consortium. *Id.* at 420 n. 3. (On loss of consortium, see Chapter 6.) Does it make sense for the law to validate the mother's but not the father's NIED claim? Does the concept of duty really help justify the law's different treatment of the two?

5. Affirmative Duties and NIED. To the extent *Beul* deems ASSE to have been obligated to take care with respect to Kristin Beul's emotional well-being, it seems to recognize not just a "negative" duty of taking care to avoid causing such distress, but an affirmative duty to protect her psychological well-being from risks of harm posed by others. Can you think of alternative scenarios in which a court should recognize an affirmative duty to take steps to rescue or protect persons from suffering emotional distress? *Compare* Rowell v. Holt, 850 So. 2d 474 (Fla. 2003) *with* Lauer v. City of New York, 733 N.E.2d 184 (N.Y. 2000). In *Rowell*, the plaintiff was falsely arrested. At his arraignment, the plaintiff handed his lawyer documentary proof of his innocence. However, the lawyer carelessly delayed presenting the proof to a judge for ten days, during which time the plaintiff remained in prison. The Florida Supreme Court permitted the client to recover from his lawyer for the distress he experienced by virtue of being imprisoned.

In *Lauer*, a medical examiner (ME) employed by New York State conducted an autopsy on the plaintiff's infant son and concluded in his report that he died from blows to the head. The plaintiff thereby became the chief suspect in the police investigation of his son's death. Several weeks after issuing the report, the ME conducted a follow-up autopsy and concluded that the son died of a birth defect. However, the ME did not issue an amended report or transmit his new findings to the police. Police continued to investigate the plaintiff for more than a year, as a result of which his wife divorced him, his friends and neighbours ostracized him, and he suffered acute anguish and anxiety. Finally, a journalist uncovered the exonerating information in the ME's second report. On these facts, the New York Court of Appeals declined to recognize a duty owed by the ME to the plaintiff to release the exonerating evidence so as to spare the plaintiff the trauma associated with being falsely identified as the killer of his son. Its stated concern was that recognition of such liability would interfere too greatly with the operation of the ME's office.

6. *Undertakings to Persons Other Than Plaintiff.* As is apparent from the materials in this subsection, tort law treats certain relationships or interactions as generating a duty to be vigilant of others' emotional well-being. Is the converse true? That is, can certain actors plausibly argue that obligations already owed to persons other than the plaintiff ought to *preclude* the recognition of a duty to take care not to cause distress to the plaintiff? Suppose motorist *M* is involved in an accident with other driver *P*. Suppose further that an employee of *M*'s liability insurer *L* takes a "hard line" position in settlement negotiations with *P*, as a result of which the negotiations are heated and protracted, dragging on for two years before generating a settlement. May *P* sue *L* for NIED? *Cf.* Krupnick v. Hartford Accident & Indemnity Co., 28 Cal. App. 4th 185 (Ct. App. 1994) (motorist's insurer owes no duty to conduct settlement negotiations with reasonable care for the emotional well-being of plaintiffs injured by the insured driver).

The possibility that recognition of a claim for NIED will create a conflict among duties has figured prominently in suits against therapists who specialize in helping emotionally disturbed patients "recover" memories of early childhood abuse. Suppose therapist *T* is treating *Q*, the daughter of *F*. During therapy, *Q* becomes convinced that *F* sexually abused her, confronts him with these allegations, and severs all ties with him. *F*, distraught, sues *T*, claiming that this form of therapy is not medically sound and therefore negligent. Does *T* owe *F* a duty to conduct *Q*'s therapy with due care for *F*'s emotional well-being? In *Doe v. McKay*, 700 N.E.2d 1018 (Ill. 1998), the Illinois Supreme Court answered in the negative, noting that recognition of a duty to the parent might interfere with the therapist's duty to act in the best interests of her client. For its part, the Wisconsin Supreme Court was unimpressed with this argument. Sawyer v. Midelfort, 595 N.W.2d 423 (Wis. 1999).

7. *Employment and Undertakings.* Implicit in the Supreme Court's analysis in *Gottshall* is the assumption that a standard employment relationship does not ordinarily carry with it an undertaking on the part of the employer to take reasonable care against causing severe emotional distress to its employees. (If there were such an undertaking, presumably Gottshall's and Carlisle's claim could proceed by analogy to the old undertaking cases and their modern counterparts, such as *Beul.*) Is this an obviously sound assumption? What, generally, might distinguish the employment relationship from the relationship of Kristin Beul to ASSE, or a train passenger to the train's operator? *Compare* Conaway v. Control Data Corp., 955 F.2d 358 (5th Cir. 1992) (noting that Texas law does not recognize a duty owed by employers to

employees to take care not to cause them distress by virtue of employment-related decisions; even a careless termination, for example, does not give rise to claim for NIED), *cert. denied*, 506 U.S. 864 (1992). Even granted the soundness of the Court's conclusion, can one argue that Gottshall's complaint alleged a viable cause of action other than NIED?

Check Your Understanding

Review Session

Judge Posner's *Beul* opinion covers numerous topics in addition to the elements of an NIED claim. (Depending on the structure of your Torts course, you may or may not have covered them.) Identify and review his discussion of the following doctrines: (1) *respondeat superior*; (2) charitable immunity; (3) privity of contract; (4) negligence per se; (5) private rights of action; (6) customary care and ordinary care; (7) superseding cause; and (8) comparative fault. Was it necessary to discuss each of these topics in order to resolve ASSE's appeal? Which (if any) of these discussions contain questionable or contentious applications of tort doctrine?

C. Bystander NIED

NIED liability is still subject to more significant constraints than liability for negligence causing physical harms. Indeed, courts have generally been cautious about extending NIED theories outside of "zone of danger" and "undertaking" cases. The most prominent exception to this tendency involves the imposition of "bystander" liability — that is, liability to certain persons who witness another being injured or killed by the carelessness of the defendant. The next three cases all involve bystander claims. Consider carefully the differences among the approaches adopted by the three opinions.

Waube v. Warrington

258 N.W. 497 (Wis. 1935)

WICKHEM, J. [Susie Waube was looking out the window of her house watching her daughter Dolores cross the road in front of it when she witnessed defendant Amber Warrington negligently run over and kill Dolores.* According to the complaint, Susie was already frail at the time, and died two weeks later in part because of her anguish. Plaintiff, Susie's husband, brought a survival action against Amber Warrington, Amber's husband (the owner of the car), and the car's insurer. The survival action proceeded on the theory that, had Susie not died, she would have been able to recover compensation for her anguish via a cause of action for negligent infliction of emotional

* [Overruled by Bowen v. Lumbermens Mut. Cas. Co., 517 N.W.2d 432, 442-43 (Wis. 1994) — EDS.]

distress. The trial court granted the defendant's motion for dismissal, and the Court of Appeals reversed the trial court. — EDS.]

. . . [T]he question presented is whether the mother of a child who, although not put in peril or fear of physical impact, sustains the shock of witnessing the negligent killing of her child, may recover for physical injuries caused by such fright or shock.

The problem must be approached at the outset from the view-point of the duty of defendant and the right of plaintiff, and not from the viewpoint of proximate cause. The right of the mother to recover must be based, first, upon the establishment of a duty on the part of defendant so to conduct herself with respect to the child as not to subject the mother to an unreasonable risk of shock or fright, and, second, upon the recognition of a legally protected right or interest on the part of the mother to be free from shock or fright occasioned by the peril of her child. It is not enough to find a breach of duty to the child, follow the consequences of such breach as far as the law of proximate cause will permit them to go, and then sustain a recovery for the mother if a physical injury to her by reason of shock or fright is held not too remote.

Upon this point we adopt and follow the doctrine of Palsgraf v. Long Island R. R. Co., 248 N.Y. 339, 162 N.E. 99. . . .

> Negligence is not actionable unless it involves the invasion of a legally protected interest, the violation of a right. . . . The plaintiff sues in her own right for a wrong personal to her, and not as the vicarious beneficiary of a breach of duty to another. . . . The passenger far away, if the victim of a wrong at all, has a cause of action, not derivative, but original and primary. His claim to be protected against invasion of his bodily security is neither greater nor less because the act resulting in the invasion is a wrong to another far removed.

. . . [Wisconsin case law holds that] . . . in order to give rise to a right of action grounded on negligent conduct, the emotional distress or shock must be occasioned by fear of personal injury to the person sustaining the shock, and not fear of injury to his property or to the person of another.

Thus it may be said that the doctrine most favorable to plaintiff is not sufficiently broad to entitle him to recover. The question presented is whether there should be an extension of the rule to cases where defendant's conduct involves merely an unreasonable risk of causing harm to the child or spouse of the person sustaining injuries through fright or shock. . . .

The only case squarely dealing with this problem is Hambrook v. Stokes Bros. [1925], 1 K.B. 141. [There, the defendant's employee parked the defendant's truck at the top of a hill without taking reasonable care to ensure that it would not roll away. When it did, it ran over the plaintiff's daughter as she walked to school. The plaintiff was nearby, but not herself endangered. She soon thereafter learned that a young girl had been run over by the truck, went to the hospital, and found her injured daughter there. According to the court, plaintiff "sustained a severe shock and consequent physical injuries from which she died." — EDS.] Viewing the matter from the standpoint of proximate cause rather than duty, the court held that . . . defendant ought to have anticipated that if the unattended truck ran down this narrow street it might terrify some woman to such an extent, through fear of some immediate bodily injury to herself, that she would receive a mental shock with resultant physical injuries, and that defendant ought also to have anticipated that such a shock might result from the peril to the child of such a woman.

While the majority, mistakenly, as it seems to us, approach this problem from the standpoint of proximate cause, the dissenting opinion of Sargant, L.J., approaches it from the standpoint of duty. The dissenting opinion concedes that since it was defendant's duty to exercise due care in the management of his vehicle so as to avoid physical injury to those on or near the highway, this duty cannot be limited to physical injuries caused by actual physical impact. The dissenting opinion, however, states that . . . "it would be a considerable and unwarranted extension of the duty of owners of vehicles towards others in or near the highway, if it were held to include an obligation not to do anything to render them liable to harm through nervous shock caused by the sight or apprehension of damage to third persons." The dissenting opinion concludes that there is no sound reason for erecting an exception in favor of the mother of a child, and points out that once the defendant's duty is held to extend to those outside the field of physical peril, a doctrine is stated to which no rational boundaries can be erected. . . .

. . . Fundamentally, defendant's duty was to use ordinary care to avoid physical injury to those who would be put in physical peril, as that term is commonly understood, by conduct on his part falling short of that standard. It is one thing to say that as to those who are put in peril of physical impact, impact is immaterial if physical injury is caused by shock arising from the peril. It is the foundation of cases holding to this liberal ruling, that the person affrighted or sustaining shock was actually put in peril of physical impact, and under these conditions it was considered immaterial that the physical impact did not materialize. It is quite another thing to say that those who are out of the field of physical danger through impact shall have a legally protected right to be free from emotional distress occasioned by the peril of others, when that distress results in physical impairment. The answer to this question cannot be reached solely by logic, nor is it clear that it can be entirely disposed of by a consideration of what the defendant ought reasonably to have anticipated as a consequence of his wrong. The answer must be reached by balancing the social interests involved in order to ascertain how far defendant's duty and plaintiff's right may justly and expediently be extended. It is our conclusion that they can neither justly nor expediently be extended to any recovery for physical injuries sustained by one out of the range of ordinary physical peril as a result of the shock of witnessing another's danger. Such consequences are so unusual and extraordinary, viewed after the event, that a user of the highway may be said not to subject others to an unreasonable risk of them by the careless management of his vehicle. Furthermore, the liability imposed by such a doctrine is wholly out of proportion to the culpability of the negligent tort-feasor, would put an unreasonable burden upon users of the highway, open the way to fraudulent claims, and enter a field that has no sensible or just stopping point.

It was recognized by the court in the *Hambrook Case* that had the mother there merely been told of the injury to her child, instead of having been virtually a witness to the transaction, there would have been no liability. The court thus selected at least one arbitrary boundary for the extension. . . . [I]f the mother may recover, why not a child whose shock was occasioned by the peril of the mother? It is not necessary to multiply these illustrations. They can be made as numerous as the varying degrees of human relationship, and they shade into each other in such a way as to leave no definite or clear-cut stopping place for the suggested doctrine, short of a recovery for every person who has sustained physical injuries as a result of shock or emotional distress by reason of seeing or hearing of the peril or injury of another. No court has gone this far, and we think no court should go this far. It is our view that fairness and justice, as well as expediency, require the defendant's duty to be defined as heretofore stated. . . . Human wrong-doing is seldom limited in its injurious effects to the immediate actors in a particular event. More frequently than not, a chain of results is set up that visits evil consequences far and wide. While from the standpoint of good morals and good citizenship the wrong-doer may be said to violate a duty to those who suffer from the wrong, the law finds it necessary, for reasons heretofore considered, to attach practical and just limits to the legal consequences of the wrongful act. . . .

Order reversed, and cause remanded with directions to sustain the demurrer.

Dillon v. Legg

441 P.2d 912 (Cal. 1968)

TOBRINER, J. That the courts should allow recovery to a mother who suffers emotional trauma and physical injury from witnessing the infliction of death or injury to her child for which the tortfeasor is liable in negligence would appear to be a compelling proposition. As Prosser points out, "All ordinary human feelings are in favor of her [the mother's] action against the negligent defendant. If a duty to her requires that she herself be in some recognizable danger, then it has properly been said that when a child is endangered, it is not beyond contemplation that its mother will be somewhere in the vicinity, and will suffer serious shock." (Prosser, *Law of Torts* (3d ed. 1964) p.353.)

Nevertheless, past American decisions have barred the mother's recovery. Refusing the mother the right to take her case to the jury, these courts ground their position on an alleged absence of a required "duty" of due care of the tortfeasor to the mother. . . .

We have concluded that [the grounds offered for these decisions are inadequate to justify] the frustration of the natural justice upon which the mother's claim rests. . . .

. . . [P]laintiff's first cause of action alleged that . . . defendant's negligent operation of his vehicle caused it to "collide with the deceased Erin Lee Dillon [as she lawfully crossed a street] resulting in injuries to decedent which proximately resulted in her death." (Complaint, p.3.) Plaintiff, as the mother of the decedent, brought an action for compensation for the loss.

Plaintiff's second cause of action alleged that she, Margery M. Dillon, "was in close proximity to the . . . collision and personally witnessed said collision." She further alleged that "because of the negligence of defendants . . . and as a proximate cause [*sic*] thereof plaintiff . . . sustained great emotional disturbance and shock and injury to her nervous system" which caused her great physical and mental pain and suffering.

[Plaintiff's third cause of action asserted a claim for negligent infliction of emotional distress on behalf of Erin's sister Cheryl, who was alleged to have been standing near Erin when Erin was struck down. — EDS.]

damages are allowed for "mental suffering," a type of injury, on the whole, less amenable to objective proof than the physical injury involved here; the mental injury can be in aggravation of, or "parasitic to," an established tort. In fact, fear for another, even in the absence of resulting physical injury, can be part of these parasitic damages. The danger of plaintiffs' fraudulent collection of damages for nonexistent injury is at least as great in these examples as in the instant case.

In sum, the application of tort law can never be a matter of mathematical precision. In terms of characterizing conduct as tortious and matching a money award to the injury suffered as well as in fixing the extent of injury, the process cannot be perfect. Undoubtedly, ever since the ancient case of the tavernkeeper's wife who successfully avoided the hatchet cast by an irate customer (I de S et ux v. W de S, Y.B. 22 Edw. iii, f.99, pl.60 (1348)), defendants have argued that plaintiffs' claims of injury from emotional trauma might well be fraudulent. Yet we cannot let the difficulties of adjudication frustrate the principle that there be a remedy for every substantial wrong.

2. *The alleged inability to fix definitions for recovery on the different facts of future cases does not justify the denial of recovery on the specific facts of the instant case; in any event, proper guidelines can indicate the extent of liability for such future cases.*

In order to limit the otherwise potentially infinite liability which would follow every negligent act, the law of torts holds defendant amenable only for injuries to others which to defendant at the time were reasonably foreseeable.

In the absence of "overriding policy considerations . . . foreseeability of risk [is] of . . . primary importance in establishing the element of duty." (Grafton v. Mollica (1965) 231 Cal. App. 2d 860, 865 [42 Cal. Rptr. 306]. . . . As a classic opinion states: "The risk reasonably to be perceived defines the duty to be obeyed." (Palsgraf v. Long Island R.R. Co. (1928) 248 N.Y. 339, 344 [162 N.E. 99, 59 A.L.R. 253].) Defendant owes a duty, in the sense of a potential liability for damages, only with respect to those risks or hazards whose likelihood made the conduct unreasonably dangerous, and hence negligent, in the first instance. (*See* Keeton, *Legal Cause in the Law of Torts* (1963) 18-20; Seavey, *Mr. Justice Cardozo and the Law of Torts* (1939) 52 Harv. L. Rev. 372; Seavey, *Principles of Torts* (1942) 56 Harv. L. Rev. 72.) . . .[5]

Since the chief element in determining whether defendant owes a duty or an obligation to plaintiff is the foreseeability of the risk, that factor will be of prime concern in

---

that a plaintiff threatened with an injurious impact may recover for bodily harm resulting from shock without impact, it is easy to agree with Atkin, L.J. ([Hambrook v. Stokes Bros., [1925] 1 K.B. 141, 158-159]), that to hinge recovery on the speculative issue whether the parent was shocked through fear for herself or for her children 'would be discreditable to any system of jurisprudence.'"

5. The concept of the zone of danger cannot properly be restricted to the area of those exposed to *physical* injury; it must encompass the area of those exposed to *emotional* injury. The courts, today, hold that no distinction can be drawn between physical injury and emotional injury flowing from the physical injury; indeed, in the light of modern medical knowledge, any such distinction would be indefensible. As a result, in awarding recovery for emotional shock upon witnessing another's injury or death, we cannot draw a line between the plaintiff who is in the zone of danger of physical impact and the plaintiff who is in the zone of danger of emotional impact. The recovery of the one, within the guidelines set forth *infra*, is as much compelled as that of the other.

every case. Because it is inherently intertwined with foreseeability such duty or obligation must necessarily be adjudicated only upon a case-by-case basis. We cannot now predetermine defendant's obligation in every situation by a fixed category; no immutable rule can establish the extent of that obligation for every circumstance of the future. We can, however, define guidelines which will aid in the resolution of such an issue as the instant one.

We note, first, that we deal here with a case in which plaintiff suffered a shock which resulted in physical injury and we confine our ruling to that case. In determining, in such a case, whether defendant should reasonably foresee the injury to plaintiff, or, in other terminology, whether defendant owes plaintiff a duty of due care, the courts will take into account such factors as the following: (1) Whether plaintiff was located near the scene of the accident as contrasted with one who was a distance away from it. (2) Whether the shock resulted from a direct emotional impact upon plaintiff from the sensory and contemporaneous observance of the accident, as contrasted with learning of the accident from others after its occurrence. (3) Whether plaintiff and the victim were closely related, as contrasted with an absence of any relationship or the presence of only a distant relationship.

The evaluation of these factors will indicate the *degree* of the defendant's foreseeability: obviously defendant is more likely to foresee that a mother who observes an accident affecting her child will suffer harm than to foretell that a stranger witness will do so. Similarly, the degree of foreseeability of the third person's injury is far greater in the case of his contemporaneous observance of the accident than that in which he subsequently learns of it. The defendant is more likely to foresee that shock to the nearby, witnessing mother will cause physical harm than to anticipate that someone distant from the accident will suffer more than a temporary emotional reaction. All these elements, of course, shade into each other; the fixing of obligation, intimately tied into the facts, depends upon each case.

In light of these factors the court will determine whether the accident and harm was *reasonably* foreseeable. Such reasonable foreseeability does not turn on whether the particular defendant as an individual would have in actuality foreseen the exact accident and loss; it contemplates that courts, on a case-to-case basis, analyzing all the circumstances, will decide what the ordinary man under such circumstances should reasonably have foreseen. The courts thus mark out the areas of liability, excluding the remote and unexpected.

In the instant case, the presence of all the above factors indicates that plaintiff has alleged a sufficient prima facie case. Surely the negligent driver who causes the death of a young child may reasonably expect that the mother will not be far distant and will upon witnessing the accident suffer emotional trauma. As Dean Prosser has stated: "when a child is endangered, it is not beyond contemplation that its mother will be somewhere in the vicinity, and will suffer serious shock." (Prosser, *The Law of Torts*, *supra*, at p. 353. *See also* 2 Harper & James, *The Law of Torts*, *supra*, at p. 1039.)

We are not now called upon to decide whether, in the absence or reduced weight of some of the above factors, we would conclude that the accident and injury were not reasonably foreseeable and that therefore defendant owed no duty of due care to effect of the defendant's conduct would throw us into "the fantastic realm of infinite liability." Yet the majority opinion in the present case simply omits to either mention or discuss the injustice to California defendants flowing from such a disproportionate extension of their liability — an injustice which plainly constituted a "prime hypothesis" for rejection of the liability sought to be imposed by the plaintiffs in *Waube* and in *Amaya.*

Additionally, the majority fail to explain their bare assertion (*ante,* p. 733) that contributory negligence of Erin will defeat any recovery by plaintiff mother and sister. The familiar and heretofore unquestioned principle is that the relationships of parent and child or of husband and wife *in themselves furnish no basis* for imputation of contributory negligence. Is this principle now abrogated in California? If so, it is a ruling extending far beyond the confines of the particular issue now before us, and reaches potentially every negligence action in which the plaintiffs are members of the same family. . . .

Thing v. La Chusa

771 P.2d 814 (Cal. 1989)

Eagleson, J. The narrow issue presented by the parties in this case is whether the Court of Appeal correctly held that a mother who did not witness an accident in which an automobile struck and injured her child may recover damages from the negligent driver for the emotional distress she suffered when she arrived at the accident scene. The more important question this issue poses for the court, however, is whether the "guidelines" enunciated by this court in Dillon v. Legg . . . are adequate, or if they should be refined to create greater certainty in this area of the law. . . .

. . . [We] conclude that the societal benefits of certainty in the law, as well as traditional concepts of tort law, dictate limitation of bystander recovery of damages for emotional distress. In the absence of physical injury or impact to the plaintiff himself, damages for emotional distress should be recoverable only if the plaintiff: (1) is closely related to the injury victim, (2) is present at the scene of the injury-producing event at the time it occurs and is then aware that it is causing injury to the victim and, (3) as a result suffers emotional distress beyond that which would be anticipated in a disinterested witness.

I. Background

On December 8, 1980, John Thing, a minor, was injured when struck by an automobile operated by defendant James V. La Chusa. His mother, plaintiff Maria Thing, was nearby, but neither saw nor heard the accident. She became aware of the injury to her son when told by a daughter that John had been struck by a car. She rushed to the scene where she saw her bloody and unconscious child, who she believed was dead, lying in the roadway. Maria sued defendants, alleging that she suffered great emotional disturbance, shock, and injury to her nervous system as a result of these events, and that the injury to John and emotional distress she suffered were proximately caused by defendants' negligence.

The trial court granted defendants' motion for summary judgment, ruling that, as a matter of law, Maria could not establish a claim for negligent infliction of emotional distress because she did not contemporaneously and sensorily perceive the accident. Although prior decisions applying the guidelines suggested by this court in Dillon v. Legg, *supra*, 68 Cal. 2d 728, compelled the ruling of the trial court, the Court of Appeal reversed the judgment dismissing Maria's claim after considering the decision of this court in Ochoa v. Superior Court (1985) 39 Cal. 3d 159 [216 Cal. Rptr. 661, 703 P.2d 1]. The Court of Appeal reasoned that . . . contemporaneous awareness of a sudden occurrence causing injury to her child was not a prerequisite to recovery under *Dillon.*

We granted review to consider whether *Ochoa* supports the holding of the Court of Appeal. We here also further define and circumscribe the circumstances in which the right to such recovery exists. To do so it is once again necessary to return to basic principles of tort law. . . .

III. Limitations in Negligence Actions

[The court reviewed the progression in California law from *Amaya* to *Dillon.*—Eds.] . . .

The *Dillon* court anticipated and accepted uncertainty in the short term in application of its holding, but was confident that the boundaries of this NIED action could be drawn in future cases. . . . Underscoring the questionable validity of that assumption, however, was the obvious and unaddressed problem that the injured party, the negligent tortfeasor, their insurers, and their attorneys had no means short of suit by which to determine if a duty such as to impose liability for damages would be found in cases other than those that were "on all fours" with *Dillon.* Thus, the only thing that was foreseeable from the *Dillon* decision was the uncertainty that continues to this time as to the parameters of the third party NIED action.

IV. Post-*Dillon* Extension

The expectation of the *Dillon* majority that the parameters of the tort would be further defined in future cases has not been fulfilled. Instead, subsequent decisions of the Courts of Appeal and this court, have created more uncertainty. And, just as the "zone of danger" limitation was abandoned in *Dillon* as an arbitrary restriction on recovery, the *Dillon* guidelines have been relaxed on grounds that they, too, created arbitrary limitations on recovery. Little consideration has been given in post-*Dillon* decisions to the importance of avoiding the limitless exposure to liability that the pure foreseeability test of "duty" would create and towards which these decisions have moved. . . .

[The court reviewed post-*Dillon* decisions relaxing the requirement of "sensory and contemporaneous observance" by permitting bystanders to recover if they recognized that the victim was about to be injured, or if they came upon the victim almost immediately after she was injured. These decisions culminated in *Ochoa, supra.* The defendants operated a juvenile facility in which plaintiff's teenage son was incarcerated. Because they carelessly failed to provide appropriate medical treatment to the son, he contracted and died of pneumonia. For several days, Mrs. Ochoa visited her son at the facility, watched his condition deteriorate, and unsuccessfully pleaded with staff

. . . Ochoa v. Superior Court, *supra*, 39 Cal. 3d 159, 165, footnote 6, offers additional guidance, justifying what we acknowledge must be arbitrary lines to similarly limit the class of potential plaintiffs if emotional injury absent physical harm is to continue to be a recoverable item of damages in a negligence action. The impact of personally observing the injury-producing event in most, although concededly not all, cases distinguishes the plaintiff's resultant emotional distress from the emotion felt when one learns of the injury or death of a loved one from another, or observes pain and suffering but not the traumatic cause of the injury. Greater certainty and a more reasonable limit on the exposure to liability for negligent conduct is possible by limiting the right to recover for negligently caused emotional distress to plaintiffs who personally and contemporaneously perceive the injury-producing event and its traumatic consequences.

Similar reasoning justifies limiting recovery to persons closely related by blood or marriage since, in common experience, it is more likely that they will suffer a greater degree of emotional distress than a disinterested witness to negligently caused pain and suffering or death. Such limitations are indisputably arbitrary since it is foreseeable that in some cases unrelated persons have a relationship to the victim or are so affected by the traumatic event that they suffer equivalent emotional distress. As we have observed, however, drawing arbitrary lines is unavoidable if we are to limit liability and establish meaningful rules for application by litigants and lower courts.

No policy supports extension of the right to recover for NIED to a larger class of plaintiffs. Emotional distress is an intangible condition experienced by most persons, even absent negligence, at some time during their lives. Close relatives suffer serious, even debilitating, emotional reactions to the injury, death, serious illness, and evident suffering of loved ones. These reactions occur regardless of the cause of the loved one's illness, injury, or death. That relatives will have severe emotional distress is an unavoidable aspect of the "human condition." The emotional distress for which monetary damages may be recovered, however, ought not to be that form of acute emotional distress or the transient emotional reaction to the occasional gruesome or horrible incident to which every person may potentially be exposed in an industrial and sometimes violent society. Regardless of the depth of feeling or the resultant physical or mental illness that results from witnessing violent events, persons unrelated to those injured or killed may not now recover for such emotional upheaval even if negligently caused. Close relatives who witness the accidental injury or death of a loved one and suffer emotional trauma may not recover when the loved one's conduct was the cause of that emotional trauma. The overwhelming majority of "emotional distress" which we endure, therefore, is not compensable.

. . . In identifying those persons and the circumstances in which the defendant will be held to redress the injury, it is appropriate to restrict recovery to those persons who

---

issue of a parental claim for loss of filial consortium. The intangible character of the loss, which can never really be compensated by money damages; the difficulty of measuring damages; the dangers of double recovery or multiple claims and of extensive liability — all these considerations apply similarly to both cases." (Baxter v. Superior Court (1977) 19 Cal. 3d 461, 464 [138 Cal. Rptr. 315, 563 P.2d 871].)

will suffer an emotional impact beyond the impact that can be anticipated whenever one learns that a relative is injured, or dies, or the emotion felt by a "disinterested" witness. The class of potential plaintiffs should be limited to those who because of their relationship suffer the greatest emotional distress. When the right to recover is limited in this manner, the liability bears a reasonable relationship to the culpability of the negligent defendant. . . .

We conclude, therefore, that a plaintiff may recover damages for emotional distress caused by observing the negligently inflicted injury of a third person if, but only if, said plaintiff: (1) is closely related to the injury victim;[10] (2) is present at the scene of the injury-producing event at the time it occurs and is then aware that it is causing injury to the victim; and (3) as a result suffers serious emotional distress — a reaction beyond that which would be anticipated in a disinterested witness and which is not an abnormal response to the circumstances.[12] These factors were present in *Ochoa* and each of this court's prior decisions upholding recovery for NIED.

. . . The merely negligent actor does not owe a duty the law will recognize to make monetary amends to all persons who may have suffered emotional distress on viewing or learning about the injurious consequences of his conduct. . . . Experience has shown that, contrary to the expectation of the *Dillon* majority, and with apology to Bernard Witkin, there are clear judicial days on which a court can foresee forever and thus determine liability but none on which that foresight alone provides a socially and judicially acceptable limit on recovery of damages for that injury.

VI

The undisputed facts establish that plaintiff was not present at the scene of the accident in which her son was injured. She did not observe defendant's conduct and was not aware that her son was being injured. She could not, therefore, establish a right to recover for the emotional distress she suffered when she subsequently learned of the accident and observed its consequences. The order granting summary judgment was proper.

The judgment of the Court of Appeal is reversed. . . .

[KAUFMAN, J., concurred in the result, arguing that the court should return to *Amaya*'s zone of danger rule.]

[MOSK, J., dissented, arguing that the majority's decision marked an unwarranted departure from *Dillon* and subsequent precedents.]

---

10. . . . Absent exceptional circumstances, recovery should be limited to relatives residing in the same household, or parents, siblings, children, and grandparents of the victim.

12. As explained by the Hawaii Supreme Court, "serious mental distress may be found where a reasonable [person] normally constituted, would be unable to adequately cope with the mental distress engendered by the circumstances of the case." (Rodrigues v. State (1970) 52 Hawaii 156, 173 [472 P.2d 509, 519-520].)

BROUSSARD, J., (dissenting). . . .

Under the majority's strict requirement, a mother who arrives moments after an accident caused by another's negligence will not be permitted recovery. No matter that the mother would see her six-year-old son immediately after he was electrocuted, lying in a puddle of water in a dying state, gagging and choking in his own vomit, as in Hathaway v. Superior Court (1980) 112 Cal. App. 3d 728 [169 Cal. Rptr. 435]. No matter that the mother would be following her daughters' car and would come upon the wreckage of the car "before the dust had settled" to find the mangled bodies of her daughters, who were dead or dying, as in Parsons v. Superior Court (1978) 81 Cal. App. 3d 506, 509 [146 Cal. Rptr. 495]. . . .

II.

Of course I share the majority's policy concern that tortfeasors not face *unlimited* liability for their negligent acts. As stated above, the *Dillon* court recognized foreseeability as a general limit on tort liability. . . .

To determine whether defendants owed plaintiff a duty of care in this case, I think it is fruitful to reexamine the second *Dillon* guideline in light of Rowland v. Christian (1968) 69 Cal. 2d 108 [70 Cal. Rptr. 97, 443 P.2d 561, 32 A.L.R.3d 496], our leading case defining a defendant's duty of care. In *Rowland*, decided just two months after *Dillon*, we held that in the absence of a statutory exception to the legislative mandate that all persons are liable for injuries caused by failure to exercise due care (Civ. Code, § 1714, subd. (a)), "no such exception should be made unless clearly supported by public policy. [Citations.][para.] A departure from this fundamental principle involves the balancing of a number of considerations; the major ones are the foreseeability of harm to the plaintiff, the degree of certainty that the plaintiff suffered injury, the closeness of the connection between the defendant's conduct and the injury suffered, the moral blame attached to the defendant's conduct, the policy of preventing future harm, the extent of the burden to the defendant and consequences to the community of imposing a duty to exercise care with resulting liability for breach, and the availability, cost, and prevalence of insurance for the risk involved." (*Rowland, supra*, 69 Cal. 2d at pp. 112-113. . . .)

While our cases defining a bystander's cause of action for negligent infliction of emotional distress consistently emphasize the first of the *Rowland* factors—foreseeability of harm to plaintiff—discussion of the others has been limited. The second, fourth, and fifth factors may be disposed of quickly: certainty of injury is usually a jury question, particularly since we no longer require physical manifestations of mental distress (Hedlund v. Superior Court (1983) 34 Cal. 3d 695, 706, fn. 8 [194 Cal. Rptr. 805, 669 P.2d 41, 41 A.L.R.4th 1063]); moral blame almost always militates in favor of recovery; and the policy of preventing future harm favors the plaintiff, but only slightly since, in most cases, any *Dillon* claim is simply added to the primary victim's complaint. The third, sixth and seventh factors, however, merit more discussion.

This court has emphasized the importance of the third *Rowland* factor—nexus between defendant's conduct and the risk of injury—in establishing limitations on recovery. In J'Aire Corp. v. Gregory (1979) 24 Cal. 3d 799, 808 [157 Cal. Rptr. 407, 598 P.2d 60], we stated that case law "[places] a limit on recovery by focusing judicial attention on the foreseeability of the injury and the nexus between the defendant's conduct and the plaintiff's injury." There, we limited recovery for the tort of negligent interference with economic advantage "to instances where the *risk of harm is* foreseeable and is *closely connected with the defendant's conduct,* where damages are not wholly speculative and the injury is not part of the plaintiff's ordinary business risk." (*Ibid.,* italics added.)

The sixth and seventh *Rowland* factors — the burden on the defendant and the community, and the cost and availability of insurance — also merit further evaluation. Amici curiae contend that recovery in this case would mark an unwarranted expansion of *Dillon,* resulting in a new category of plaintiffs, fewer settlements, higher administrative costs and premiums, delays in payment, increased litigation, and higher awards. Amici insist that *Dillon's* second guideline should be applied strictly, as a prerequisite for recovery. . . .

The authorities upon which amici rely do not persuade me that *Dillon* has significantly contributed to any substantial increase in litigation and insurance premiums. Nor do I find any indication that other jurisdictions are retreating from *Dillon.* . . . As the *Dillon* court responded to the contention that otherwise meritorious claims should be barred out of fear of increases in the number of suits and of fraudulent claims: "'[We] should be sorry to adopt a rule which would bar all such claims on grounds of policy alone, and in order to prevent the possible success of unrighteous or groundless actions. Such a course involves the denial of redress in meritorious cases, and it necessarily implies a certain degree of distrust, which [we] do not share, in the capacity of legal tribunals to get at the truth in this class of claim.'" (*Dillon, supra,* 68 Cal. 2d at p. 744, quoting Hambrook v. Stokes Bros. (1925) 1 K.B. 141, quoting Dulieu v. White and Sons (1901) 2 K.B. 669, 681, opn. by Kennedy, J. . . .)

I also do not believe courts lack the means to prevent unmeritorious cases from going to trial. As the case at bar demonstrates, trial courts are well aware of their duty to determine before trial whether the defendant could have owed the plaintiff a duty of care under the facts. . . .

Check Your Understanding

Assume the following variation of the facts in *Dillon*: Erin, the daughter who was struck, was not crossing the street "lawfully" but was running across the street to retrieve a ball. Further, assume that a jury finds Erin and Legg both to have been at fault for the accident. According to the court, how would that finding affect Margery's recovery for NIED? By what reasoning?

NOTES AND QUESTIONS

1. *Waube and Palsgraf.* Is *Waube* a fair application of *Palsgraf* (Chapter 5)? If the defendant driver's conduct was careless, and if it caused genuine distress to Waube, why shouldn't the law impose liability? What does it mean to say that the driver

committed a wrong "from the standpoint of good morals and good citizenship" yet that Waube was not the victim of a tort committed by the driver? Suppose Waube's daughter was riding a bicycle at the time of the accident, and the negligent driver, in colliding with the daughter, caused a part of the bike to fly off so as to strike and physically harm Waube. Would there be a duty problem with a claim seeking compensation for that injury? A proximate cause problem? If the answer to these questions is no, what is so different about claims for bystander emotional distress? Does the result in *Waube*—later abrogated by the Wisconsin Supreme Court—suggest that a "Cardozoan" approach to tort law is essentially "conservative" in terms of not permitting the expansion of negligence liability? Can you construct an argument that, without rejecting *Palsgraf*, produces a different result in *Waube*?

2. *Bystander Claims for Physical Harm Versus NIED.* Like *Robb*, *Dillon* speaks in terms of permitting recovery for *physical harms* resulting to a plaintiff from distress caused by the defendant's careless conduct. Nonetheless, it has come to stand for the authorization of recovery even absent consequent physical injury (at least so long as there is sufficient proof of the sort of "severe" distress now required by *Thing*). Thus, like *Robb*, which was decided as a physical harm case, *Dillon* has been received by subsequent courts as a decision articulating the rules for NIED recovery.

3. *The California Revolution.* *Dillon v. Legg* was decided in 1968, which was also the year that the California Supreme Court abolished the status categories for premises liability claims in *Rowland v. Christian* (reproduced in Chapter 2). The two decisions not only substantially expanded tort liability, they brought to bear longstanding academic skepticism about the duty element in a manner that promised to revolutionize the law of negligence. Quoting Prosser, *Dillon* emphasizes that the invocation of a legal no-duty rule to resolve a case always "begs the essential question. . . ." What is the essential question? How does *Dillon* define the duty inquiry? What are the elements of negligence, according to *Dillon?* How does that formulation differ from the traditional formulation? Does the court's conception of negligence resemble Judge Andrews' conception (stated in his *Palsgraf* dissent) of negligence as grounded in a "duty to the world"?

4. *Dillon and Palsgraf.* Suppose *Dillon* is rightly read as siding with Judge Andrews' *Palsgraf* dissent in holding that a negligence plaintiff need not show a wrong to her, merely a wrong to someone resulting in injury to her. If so, is dissenting Justice Burke justified in being puzzled as to the effect the majority is prepared to give to a finding that Erin was contributorily negligent? Why should Erin's negligence defeat Mrs. Dillon's claim? Shouldn't it instead be treated as one of two careless acts by persons other than Mrs. Dillon, each of which functioned as a cause of her emotional distress?

5. *Uses of History.* In an omitted portion of *Dillon*, the court relies on Prosser, who in turn relied on the British historian Percy Winfield, for the claim that the duty element was originally no part of the tort of negligence, but was tacked on by judges such as the Exchequer Barons of *Winterbottom v. Wright* (*see* Chapter 2), who were anxious to find a way to limit the imposition of tort liability on emerging industry. Suppose Winfield's historical claims are correct. In what ways should they inform the

analysis of a contemporary negligence case? What does the *Dillon* court's invocation of this history tell us about how it conceives of the nature and purpose of negligence law?

2. *The Zone of Danger and Arbitrariness.* *Dillon* scores rhetorical points by stressing the "hopeless artificiality" of rules that would permit Cheryl, who was in the zone of danger, to recover for her emotional distress, but would bar recovery by Margery Dillon, standing a few feet farther away. Is this line so arbitrary? Assuming that Cheryl were entitled to recover damages under the zone of danger rule, for what losses would she be compensated? Negligence law draws "arbitrary" lines in other contexts. Imagine two careless drivers, *A* and *B*. *A* strikes and injures pedestrian *P*. *B* narrowly misses pedestrian *Q*, who happens at the time to have his back turned and to be listening to a portable MP3 player, and thus is oblivious to the peril. If *P* sues *A*, *A* must pay *P*'s damages. *Q*, however, has no cause of action against *B*. Is this an intolerably arbitrary result, in that *A* and *B* did the same bad thing yet only *A* is made to pay? Would the *Dillon* court permit recovery by *Q*?

3. *Progressive or Paternalistic?* The *Dillon* court, along with Prosser and Magruder, decry the denial of redress to persons such as Margery Dillon. Such a rule, they suggest, offends "natural justice" and "discredit[s]" our legal system. What exactly are they so indignant about? On what grounds do they assert that cases such as *Dillon* present especially compelling claims for compensation?

4. *The Dillon Factors.* *Dillon* offers "guidelines" to help lower courts determine when bystanders may recover for negligence causing emotional distress. It says that these factors aid in the determination of whether the distress was reasonably foreseeable to the defendant. Do the factors set out by the court actually bear on foreseeability? Is distress to a close friend of a person killed by careless driving less foreseeable to the driver than distress to a relative? What about distress to a relative who learns about the death an hour after it occurs?

5. *Every Tort = Two Torts?* Assume that *Dillon*'s holding is grounded in the sense that negligence law would be callous insofar as it does not permit compensation for the "secondary" harms consisting of the grief caused to others when a victim is wrongfully killed (or injured). If that is the concern, should every instance of negligence causing serious injury warrant two lawsuits: one by the victim for his injuries, the second by those grieving over the fate or plight of the victim? If not, why not?

6. *From Dillon to Thing.* *Dillon* was handed down during the tumultuous summer of 1968, which, in the eyes of some, marked the beginning of the end of the counterculture movement of the 1960s. By 1989, the nation was, generally speaking, in a more conservative mood, and the composition of the California Supreme Court reflected that transition. Equally or more saliently, the courts had begun to encounter phenomena such as liability insurance crises, and were now receiving *amicus* briefs from organizations such as the "Association for California Tort Reform" (founded in 1979). Note, in this regard, the *Thing* court's emphasis on the "social cost" of imposing liability. Does that sort of consideration figure at all in *Dillon*?

killed when her car crashed into the truck. The plaintiff testified in his deposition that, because of the relative size of the vehicles and their speed, he was not fearful for his physical safety. Instead, he became very upset when he exited his truck and viewed the deceased defendant in her car. Adopting the position that NIED claims should be analyzed no differently than claims for negligence causing physical harm, the court ruled that the truck driver's action could proceed on the theory that the defendant, by running a red light, carelessly risked foreseeable distress to others who might observe her injuring or killing herself.

If *Camper*'s purported collapsing of the line between physical harm and emotional distress cases is taken at face value, it would seem to follow that all persons subject to the decision now must exercise reasonable care not to conduct themselves in a way that might foreseeably cause serious distress to others. For example, a homeowner who carelessly lacerates his arm or falls off a ladder while doing yard work could presumably be sued by a stranger who happened to witness the aftermath of the accident. It may be, however, that the Court did not mean the case to stand for such a broad proposition. In a subsequent case, for example, it seemed to circumscribe the *Camper* duty. Ramsey v. Beavers, 931 S.W.2d 527 (Tenn. 1996).

The oddity of the rule suggested by *Camper* may suggest a fallacy in the chain of inferences that led from *Dillon*'s "overruling" of *Amaya* to the adoption of a general duty to take care against causing emotional distress to others. Indeed, it hardly follows that by refusing to employ the zone of danger test to block the peculiarly salient claim of a close relative who observes her loved one being killed before her eyes, *Dillon* entails that emotional distress ought to be actionable whenever it is caused by careless conduct. Several courts, including the California Supreme Court, seem to have recognized this point, although they often have expressed it in confusing language. For example, in *Burgess v. Superior Court*, 831 P.2d 1197 (Cal. 1992), the court held that bystander cases form a limited exception to the general rules applicable to "direct" claims of NIED, that is, claims arising out of undertakings or physical endangerment.* A similar idea has been expressed in different language by the Texas Supreme Court, which has held that bystander claims operate under separate rules because they are the only "true" NIED claims, whereas other claims — including death telegram and undertaking claims that other states would treat as "direct" NIED claims — are permitted to proceed because they arise out of "independent" duties, that is, duties, other than the duty to take care against causing the plaintiff emotional distress. Boyles v. Kerr, 855 S.W.2d 593 (Tex. 1993).

---

* *Burgess* involved a malpractice claim by a mother against her obstetrician for carelessness in delivering her baby, which caused severe birth defects in the baby, and trauma to the plaintiff-mother. Because the mother was not herself endangered by the defendant's carelessness, and because she was unconscious during the delivery, the defendant argued that she was barred from recovering for NIED under *Thing.* The court held that *Thing* was inapplicable because this was an instance of "direct" infliction of emotional distress, rather than a bystander claim, and because an obstetrician is chargeable with a duty to look after the emotional well-being of the mother and baby, given that both are his patients in the period up to and including birth. (*See* Note 4 following *Beul, supra.*)

REFERENCES/FURTHER READING

Francis H. Bohlen, *The Right to Recover for Injury Resulting from Negligence Without Impact*, 41 Am. L. Reg. 141 (1902), *reprinted in* Francis H. Bohlen, *Studies in the Law of Torts* 252-290 (1926).

Martha Chamallas, *Removing Emotional Harm from the Core of Tort Law*, 54 Vand. L. Rev. 751 (2001).

Martha Chamallas with Linda K. Kerber, *Women, Mothers, and the Law of Fright: A History*, 88 Mich. L. Rev. 814 (1990).

David Crump, *Evaluating Independent Torts Based upon "Intentional" or "Negligent" Infliction of Emotional Distress: How Can We Keep the Baby from Dissolving in the Bath Water?*, 34 Ariz. L. Rev. 439 (1992).

Julie A. Davies, *Direct Actions for Emotional Harm: Is Compromise Possible?*, 67 Wash. L. Rev. 1 (1992).

Richard Delgado, *Words That Wound: A Tort Action for Racial Insults, Epithets, and Name-Calling*, 17 Harv. C.R.-C.L. L. Rev. 133 (1982).

John L. Diamond, Dillon v. Legg *Revisited: Toward a Unified Theory of Compensating Bystanders and Relatives for Intangible Injuries*, 35 Hastings L.J. 477 (1984).

Dennis P. Duffy, *Intentional Infliction of Emotional Distress and Employment at Will: The Case Against "Tortification" of Labor and Employment Law*, 74 B.U. L. Rev. 387 (1994).

Avlana K. Eisenberg, *Criminal Infliction of Emotional Distress*, 113 Mich. L. Rev. 607 (2015).

Daniel Givelber, *The Right to Minimum Social Decency and the Limits of Evenhandedness: Intentional Infliction of Emotional Distress by Outrageous Conduct*, 82 Colum. L. Rev. 42 (1982).

Erica R. Goldberg, *Emotional Duties*, 47 Conn. L. Rev. 809 (2015).

John C. P. Goldberg & Benjamin C. Zipursky, *Unrealized Torts*, 88 Va. L. Rev. 1625 (2002).

Herbert F. Goodrich, *Emotional Disturbance as Legal Damage*, 20 Mich. L. Rev. 497 (1922).

Leon Green, *"Fright" Cases*, 27 Ill. L. Rev. 761 (1933).

Betsy J. Grey, *The Future of Emotional Harm*, 83 Fordham L. Rev. 2605 (2015).

Fowler V. Harper & Mary Coate McNeeley, *A Re-Examination of the Basis for Liability for Emotional Distress*, 1938 Wis. L. Rev. 426 (1938).

Gregory C. Keating, *Is Negligent Infliction of Emotional Distress a Freestanding Tort?*, 44 Wake Forest L. Rev. 1131 (2009).

Charles Lawrence, *If He Hollers Let Him Go: Regulating Racist Speech on Campus*, 1990 Duke L.J. 431.

Calvert Magruder, *Mental and Emotional Disturbance in the Law of Torts*, 49 Harv. L. Rev. 1033 (1936).

M. H. Matthews, *Negligent Infliction of Emotional Distress: A View of the Proposed Restatement (Third) Provisions from England*, 44 Wake Forest L. Rev. 1177 (2009).

Virginia E. Nolan & Edmund Ursin, *Negligent Infliction of Emotional Distress: Coherence Emerging from Chaos*, 33 Hastings L.J. 583 (1982).

Richard N. Pearson, *Liability to Bystanders for Negligently Inflicted Emotional Harm — A Comment on the Nature of Arbitrary Rules*, 34 U. Fla. L. Rev. 477 (1982).

Robert C. Post, *The Constitutional Concept of Public Discourse: Outrageous Opinion, Democratic Deliberation, and* Hustler Magazine v. Falwell, 103 Harv. L. Rev. 601 (1990).

William L. Prosser, *Insult and Outrage*, 44 Cal. L. Rev. 40 (1956).

William L. Prosser, *Intentional Infliction of Mental Suffering: A New Tort*, 37 Mich. L. Rev. 874 (1939).

CHAPTER 11

PROPERTY TORTS AND ULTRAHAZARDOUS ACTIVITIES

I. INTRODUCTION

Insofar as modern tort law has concerned itself with accidents, it has tended to do so under the rubric of negligence, which requires for the imposition of liability a failure on the part of the alleged tortfeasor to act with the care that a person of ordinary prudence would exercise. Still, it would be a mistake to say that the Anglo-American law of accidents just is negligence law.

At a minimum, this sort of blanket statement is misleading because, as we have seen, negligence itself comes in many shades. What constitutes carelessness, or adequate proof of carelessness, varies significantly depending on, among other things: (a) the actor whose conduct is being assessed (is she a child? a professional?), (b) the capacity in which she was acting when undertaking the conduct (driver? landowner? rescuer?), (c) the nature of the conduct (misfeasance? nonfeasance?), (d) the kind of injury suffered by the victim (physical? emotional? economic?), and (e) the applicability of special doctrines such as *res ipsa loquitur* and negligence per se. In addition, courts have in certain domains explicitly permitted an injury victim to recover from another without proof that he acted carelessly, let alone recklessly or with intent to injure. Some scholars have even argued that, prior to the nineteenth century, liability routinely attached without regard to fault. While this contention is perhaps exaggerated, there is no question that liability without fault has been, and remains, an important feature of U.S. tort law.

The most common label used by judges and lawyers to describe liability that attaches without proven or presumed carelessness, recklessness, or intentional wrongdoing is *strict liability*. Reliance on this phrase is unfortunate. First, it suggests that actors can be held responsible for injuries entirely without regard to what they do or don't do—as if an injury victim could randomly pick a name from a directory and then instruct a court to order that person to pay for the victim's losses. While it is the case that the torts covered in this part permit liability to attach even to reasonable actions, they nonetheless tend to require the defendant to have acted in a manner that can fairly be described as wrongful in some other sense.

Second, some tort causes of action today that are taken to fall within the category of strict liability turn out to share important features of negligence law, a commonality that has generated a good deal of terminological confusion. Products liability law, for example, has often been described as imposing strict liability, yet its standards for the imposition of liability at least sometimes seem to contain some notion of fault, though perhaps not the same one that is found in negligence cases. Conversely, there are several forms of tort liability that have not traditionally been placed within the category of strict liability but that are actionable without proof of fault, recklessness, or intent. These include torts vindicating certain property rights, such as trespass and conversion.

To avoid some of these confusions, we shall use the phrase "liability without fault" in place of strict liability. Within the ambit of the common law of tort,* such liability arguably applies in at least three different settings: (1) conduct that interferes with a person's interest in the possession, use, or enjoyment of land or personal possessions, (2) "ultrahazardous" (or "abnormally dangerous") activities, in particular the use of explosives and the keeping of wild animals; and (3) the manufacture, design, and sale of defective products by manufacturers and certain other commercial actors. This chapter discusses cases falling within the first two categories. Chapter 12 turns to the important and politically contentious subject of products liability.

Before we undertake to examine these areas in detail, it is worth pausing to reflect on some of the considerations that underlie the choice between fault-based and no-fault liability regimes. We therefore begin with two older decisions addressing that issue. The first is a nineteenth-century decision that helped to define the tort of negligence as it emerged out of the old English common law, which did not recognize a tort by that name (although it did recognize, under other names, instances of liability that today would fall within the ambit of negligence). The second is an early twentieth-century decision in which the U.S. Supreme Court considered and rejected constitutional challenges to the displacement of the common law of negligence by a statutory scheme of liability without fault.

Brown v. Kendall

60 Mass. 292 (1850)

This was an action of trespass for assault and battery, originally commenced against George K. Kendall, the defendant, who died pending the suit, and his executrix was summoned in.

---

* Liability without fault has also been imposed by statutory and administrative schemes that have supplanted the common law of negligence as it applied to particular activities. Workers' compensation systems—which reimburse workers injured on the job for healthcare costs and lost wages without inquiring into the employer's fault—provide the most familiar examples of these sorts of schemes.

It appeared in evidence, on the trial . . . that two dogs, belonging to the plaintiff and the defendant, respectively, were fighting in the presence of their masters; that the defendant took a stick about four feet long, and commenced beating the dogs in order to separate them; that the plaintiff was looking on, at the distance of about a rod, and that he advanced a step or two towards the dogs. In their struggle, the dogs approached the place where the plaintiff was standing. The defendant retreated backwards from before the dogs, striking them as he retreated; and as he approached the plaintiff, with his back towards him, in raising his stick over his shoulder, in order to strike the dogs, he accidentally hit the plaintiff in the eye, inflicting upon him a severe injury.

. . . .

The defendant requested the judge to instruct the jury, that "if both the plaintiff and defendant at the time of the blow were using ordinary care, or if at that time the defendant was using ordinary care and the plaintiff was not, or if at that time both plaintiff and defendant were not using ordinary care, then the plaintiff could not recover."

. . . .

The judge declined to give the instructions, as above requested, but left the case to the jury under the following instructions:

> If the defendant, in beating the dogs, was doing a necessary act, or one which it was his duty under the circumstances of the case to do, and was doing it in a proper way; then he was not responsible in this action, provided he was using ordinary care at the time of the blow. If it was not a necessary act; if he was not in duty bound to attempt to part the dogs, but might with propriety interfere or not as he chose; the defendant was responsible for the consequences of the blow, unless it appeared that he was in the exercise of extraordinary care, so that the accident was inevitable, using the word inevitable not in a strict but a popular sense.
>
> If, however, the plaintiff, when he met with the injury, was not in the exercise of ordinary care, he cannot recover, and this rule applies, whether the interference of the defendant in the fight of the dogs was necessary or not. If the jury believe, that it was the duty of the defendant to interfere, then the burden of proving negligence on the part of the defendant, and ordinary care on the part of the plaintiff, is on the plaintiff. If the jury believe, that the act of interference in the fight was unnecessary, then the burden of proving extraordinary care on the part of the defendant, or want of ordinary care on the part of the plaintiff, is on defendant.

The jury under these instructions returned a verdict for the plaintiff; whereupon the defendant alleged exceptions.

Shaw, C. J. . . .

. . . The whole case proceeds on the assumption, that the damage sustained by the plaintiff, from the stick held by the defendant, was inadvertent and unintentional; and the case involves the question how far, and under what qualifications, the party by whose unconscious act the damage was done is responsible for it. We use the term "unintentional" rather than involuntary, because in some of the cases, it is stated, that the act of holding and using a weapon or instrument, the movement of which is the immediate cause of hurt to another, is a voluntary act, although its particular effect in hitting and hurting another is not within the purpose or intention of the party doing the act.

It appears to us, that some of the confusion in the cases on this subject has grown out of the long-vexed question, under the rule of the common law, whether a party's remedy, where he has one, should be sought in an action of [trespass on the case], or of trespass. This is very distinguishable from the question, whether in a given case, any action will lie. The result of these cases is, that if the damage complained of is the immediate effect of the act of the defendant, trespass . . . lies; if consequential only, and not immediate, [trespass on the] case is the proper remedy. . . .

In these discussions, it is frequently stated by judges, that when one receives injury from the direct act of another, trespass will lie. But we think this is said in reference to the question, whether trespass and not case will lie, assuming that the facts are such, that some action will lie. These *dicta* are no authority, we think, for holding, that damage received by a direct act of force from another will be sufficient to maintain an action of trespass, whether the act was lawful or unlawful, and neither wilful, intentional, or careless. In the principal case cited, *Leame* v. *Bray*, the damage arose from the act of the defendant, in driving on the wrong side of the road, in a dark night, which was clearly negligent if not unlawful. In the course of the argument of that case, (p. 595,) Lawrence, J., said: "There certainly are cases in the books, where, the injury being direct and immediate, trespass has been holden to lie, though the injury was not intentional." . . . [That] proposition may be true, because though the injury was unintentional, the act may have been unlawful or negligent, and the cases cited by him are perfectly consistent with that supposition. . . .

We think, as the result of all the authorities, the rule is correctly stated by Mr. Greenleaf, that the plaintiff must come prepared with evidence to show either that the *intention* was unlawful, or that the defendant was *in fault;* for if the injury was unavoidable, and the conduct of the defendant was free from blame, he will not be liable. 2 Greenl. Ev. §§ 85 to 92; Wakeman v. Robinson, 1 Bing. 213. If, in the prosecution of a lawful act, a casualty purely accidental arises, no action can be supported for an injury arising therefrom. In applying these rules to the present case, we can perceive no reason why the instructions asked for by the defendant ought not to have been given. . . .

In using this term, ordinary care, it may be proper to state, that what constitutes ordinary care will vary with the circumstances of cases. In general, it means that kind and degree of care, which prudent and cautious men would use, such as is required by the exigency of the case, and such as is necessary to guard against probable danger. A man, who should have occasion to discharge a gun, on an open and extensive marsh, or in a forest, would be required to use less circumspection and care, than if he were to do the same thing in an inhabited town, village, or city. To make an accident, or casualty, or as the law sometimes states it, inevitable accident, it must be such an accident as the defendant could not have avoided by the use of the kind and degree of care necessary to the exigency, and in the circumstances in which he was placed.

We are not aware of any circumstances in this case, requiring a distinction between acts which it was lawful and proper to do, and acts of legal duty. . . . We can have no doubt that the act of the defendant in attempting to part the fighting dogs, one of which was his own, and for the injurious acts of which he might be responsible, was a lawful and proper act, which he might do by proper and safe means. If, then, in doing this act, using due care and all proper precautions necessary to the exigency of the case, to avoid hurt to others, in raising his stick for that purpose, he accidentally hit the plaintiff in his eye, and wounded him, this was the result of pure accident, or was involuntary and unavoidable, and therefore the action would not lie. Or if the defendant was chargeable with some negligence, and if the plaintiff was also chargeable with negligence, we think the plaintiff cannot recover without showing that the damage was caused wholly by the act of the defendant, and that the plaintiff's own negligence did not contribute as an efficient cause to produce it.

. . . .

. . . [The trial judge's instructions] were not conformable to law. If the act of hitting the plaintiff was unintentional, on the part of the defendant, and done in the doing of a lawful act, then the defendant was not liable, unless it was done in the want of exercise of due care, adapted to the exigency of the case, and therefore such want of due care became part of the plaintiff's case, and the burden of proof was on the plaintiff to establish it.

Perhaps the learned judge, by the use of the term extraordinary care, in the above charge, explained as it is by the context, may have intended nothing more than that increased degree of care and diligence, which the exigency of particular circumstances might require, and which men of ordinary care and prudence would use under like circumstances, to guard against danger. If such was the meaning of this part of the charge, then it does not differ from our views, as above explained. But we are of opinion, that the other part of the charge, that the burden of proof was on the defendant, was incorrect. Those facts which are essential to enable the plaintiff to recover, he takes the burden of proving. . . . [W]hether directly proved, or inferred from circumstances, if it appears that the defendant was doing a lawful act, and unintentionally hit and hurt the plaintiff, then unless it also appears to the satisfaction of the jury, that the defendant is chargeable with some fault, negligence, carelessness, or want of prudence, the plaintiff fails to sustain the burden of proof, and is not entitled to recover.

New trial ordered.

NOTES AND QUESTIONS

1. *Trespass and Trespass on the Case.* In medieval English usage, the term "trespass" had a very broad meaning, referring to the generic idea of a transgression by one against another. When royal courts in the 1200s first began entertaining suits for damages arising out of injuries, they named the procedural device by which such suits were commenced the "writ of trespass *vi et armis.*" This writ — literally a piece of parchment that victims' lawyers would purchase from an office of the royal government called the Chancery — directed the sheriff in the locality in which the defendant resided to bring the defendant before a judge to explain (if he could) why the allegations made against him in the writ were false or otherwise defective. The "*vi et armis*"

formulation ("with force and arms") indicated that the writ was in principle available to anyone alleging that another person had *directly* and *forcibly* caused him harm. Thus, it covered a range of conduct, including acts that would today be actionable as assault, battery, false imprisonment, negligence, and other torts, and perhaps in some instances imposed liability where today there would be none.*

In the mid- to late-1300s, the royal courts expanded their jurisdiction to encompass claims for certain injuries caused without force. These included actions against surgeons for incompetent provision of medical services, against farriers for incompetent treatment of horses, and against innkeepers for failing to take care to keep guests and their possessions safe. Because these actions carried something of the flavor of traditional trespass actions, yet did not complain of forcible injurings, they were placed under the heading of a new writ, called "trespass on the case." The latter phrase conveyed the idea that a plaintiff could proceed in the royal courts if the facts stated in the writ looked and felt enough to the judges like the core instance of forcible injuring covered by the writ of trespass *vi et armis*.

2. Relevance of Fault to "Trespass." Suits brought under the trespass-on-the-case writ typically contained a statement of facts that aimed to convince the courts that what happened to the claimant was sufficiently like conduct that would give rise to a claim via the writ of trespass *vi et armis* to be actionable, and therefore tended to emphasize fault or wrongdoing on the part of the defendant. For example, a suit against a farrier (horseshoer) who improperly shod and injured a plaintiff's horse would allege professional incompetence.

By contrast, the claims stated in the older writ of trespass *vi et armis* were very sparse, alleging in a sentence or two that the defendant had forcibly and directly injured the plaintiff, without any mention of wrongdoing or fault on the part of the defendant. Some historians have argued that the absence of any allegations of wrongdoing in trespass writs indicates that liability under the writ was "strict" — that, so long as the harm was directly and forcibly inflicted on the plaintiff by the defendant, the defendant was liable, regardless of whether the defendant acted with reasonable or even extraordinary care. Other historians have disputed this claim, arguing that it was always open to juries to find for a trespass defendant on the ground that the defendant had acted reasonably. The trial court in *Brown* seems to have adopted an intermediate position by instructing the jury that, at least if Kendall was under no obligation to intervene in the dog fight, then he would be liable for striking Brown unless he acted with extraordinary care.

Writing for the Massachusetts Supreme Court in *Brown*, Chief Justice Lemuel Shaw, one of the most influential jurists of the mid-nineteenth century, summarily rejected the notion that the writ of trespass *vi et armis* contemplated or permitted no-fault liability. Anglo-American tort law, he claimed, has always required a plaintiff complaining of accidentally caused injury to make a showing of fault before recovering. Regardless of their accuracy, Shaw's historical claims in Brown v. Kendall would soon come to stand for the idea that accident-based tort liability is and has always been fault-

* Note that Brown's claim is initially described by the court as "an action of trespass for assault and battery." Here, the terms "assault and battery" are not used as we use them in Chapter 9, but instead indicate that Brown had alleged a trespass (transgression) involving bodily injury as opposed, say, to property damage.

based rather than strict, an idea that gained considerable currency among jurists in the late nineteenth century.

Brown's influence owes in part to Oliver Wendell Holmes, Jr. (See the notes following *Vaughan v. Menlove* in Chapter 3.) In his 1881 book *The Common Law*, Holmes praised Shaw and *Brown* and offered several arguments in favor of the claim that tort liability in modern Anglo-American law had never recognized—and ought not to recognize—"strict" liability that attaches simply by virtue of a causal connection between the defendant's act and the plaintiff's injury.

At the level of policy, Holmes argued, tort litigation is an expensive and otherwise burdensome mechanism for transferring assets from one person (the victim who initially bears the loss) to another (the defendant who is held liable). If government is going to impose this sort of burden on its citizens, he reasoned, it needs good grounds to do so, and the mere fact of the defendant's causal connection to the loss is not sufficient. Holmes continued:

> The undertaking to redistribute losses [from the plaintiff to the defendant through the award of tort damages] simply on the ground that they resulted from the defendant's act would not only be open to [objections raised previously], but . . . to the still graver one of offending the sense of justice. Unless my act is of a nature to threaten others, unless under the circumstances a prudent man would have foreseen the possibility of harm, it is no more justifiable to make me indemnify my neighbor against the consequences, than to make me do the same thing if I had fallen upon him in a fit, or to compel me to insure him against lightning.

Oliver W. Holmes, Jr., *The Common Law* 96 (1881). What features of a system of liability without fault would render it offensive to "the sense of justice"? Assume that Brown was in no way at fault for being struck by Kendall. As between Brown, who did nothing to hurt himself, and Kendall, who wielded the stick, why would it be unjust to demand that Kendall bear the loss?

3. *Harvey v. Dunlop.* Another opinion cited by Holmes in support of the idea that strict liability is foreign to Anglo-American tort law is *Harvey v. Dunlop*, [1843] Hill & Den. 193 (N.Y. Sup. Ct.). There the defendant, a six-year-old boy, threw a stone at the plaintiff's five-year-old daughter, blinding her in one eye. Affirming a jury verdict for the defendant, Chief Justice Nelson reasoned as follows:

> No case or principle can be found, or if found can be maintained, subjecting an individual to liability for an act done without fault on his part; and this was substantially the doctrine of the charge. All the cases concede that an injury arising from inevitable accident, or, which in law or reason is the same thing, from an act that ordinary human care and foresight are unable to guard against, is but the misfortune of the sufferer, and lays no foundation for legal responsibility. Thus it is laid down that, "If one man has received a corporal injury from the voluntary act of another, an action of trespass lies, provided there was a neglect or want of due caution in the person who did the injury, although there was no design to injure." (Bac. Abr. tit. Trespass, D.) But if not imputable to the neglect of the party by whom it was done, or to his want of caution, an action of trespass does not lie, although the consequences of a voluntary act. It was said by Dallas, C.J., in Wakeman v.

> Robinson (1 Bingh., 213), "if the accident happened entirely without default on the part of the defendant, or blame imputable to him, the action does not lie"; and the same principle is recognized in Bullock v. Babcock, (3 Wend., 391).
>
> . . . [The jury reasonably concluded] that the misfortune happened without fault on either side, and that it was one of those unhappy accidents to which children of the tender age of these parties are not unfrequently exposed in their little innocent plays and amusements—a result rather to be deplored than punished.

Although terse, *Harvey* is densely packed with statements supporting variations on the idea that fault or carelessness is required before tort liability will be imposed on an actor who accidentally injures another. Consider each of the following statements (emphases have been added to each). Are they equivalent to one another? If not, are some more plausible than others as generalizations about the common law of tort? Are some more persuasive than others as a matter of policy or principle?

a. "No case or principle can be found, or if found can be maintained, subjecting an individual to liability, for *an act done without fault on his part. . . .*"
b. "All the cases concede that an injury arising *from inevitable accident* . . . is but the misfortune of the sufferer, and lays no foundation for legal responsibility."
c. "*[A]n act that ordinary human care and foresight are unable to guard against,* is but the misfortune of the sufferer, and lays no foundation for legal responsibility."
d. "*But if not imputable to the neglect of the party by whom it was done, or to his want of caution,* an action [under the writ] of trespass does not lie, although the consequences of a voluntary act."
e. "[I]f the accident happened *entirely without default on the part of the defendant, or blame imputable to him,* the action does not lie . . ."
f. If a case presents a "*misfortune [that] happened without fault on either side,* and . . . *was one of those unhappy accidents to which children* of the tender age of these parties *are not unfrequently exposed* in their little innocent plays and amusements" then it is best treated as a result "to be deplored [rather] than punished."

Notice that proposition f. contains an early statement of the "tender years doctrine" applied in *Appelhans v. McFall* (Chapter 3).

4. *The Ordinary Care Standard (I).* Along with *Vaughan v. Menlove* (Chapter 3), *Brown v. Kendall* helped to place the objective reasonable person at the center of Anglo-American tort law insofar as it applies to conduct that does not involve intentional or knowing infliction of harm. Under this standard, an accident victim cannot recover from a person who played a role in bringing about the accident unless the person caused the accident *by failing to exercise ordinary care.* Thus, when Shaw ordered a new trial in *Brown,* he directed the trial judge to instruct the jury that it must determine whether Kendall acted with the care that a person of ordinary prudence would have exercised under the circumstances. Of what would such care consist? Does it matter that the situation may have been one requiring immediate and violent action?

5. *The Ordinary Care Standard (II).* The trial judge seemed to suppose that the degree of care owed to Brown varied with the justification for Kendall's action. Thus, he instructed the jury that, if Kendall had been acting out of necessity or was otherwise "duty bound" to act, Kendall should be held to the standard of ordinary care. However, if Kendall's actions were not in fulfillment of a duty, but instead a matter of choice, then Kendall should be held to the standard of extraordinary care.

Chief Justice Shaw suggests that the trial judge's instruction on extraordinary care was perhaps not intended to set a separate, higher standard of conduct, but instead may have been an inartful effort to suggest to the jury that the ordinary care standard can, under certain circumstances, require an actor to take substantial (extraordinary) precautions to avoid injuring another person. Do you agree with Shaw's interpretation?

As is noted in Chapter 3, some courts impose a duty of extraordinary care on common carriers such as railroads and bus companies. (*See* Jones v. Port Authority of Allegheny County.) Typically they have done so on the theory that the public relies on carriers for an essential service. What, if anything, could explain why the trial judge thought that a person who chooses to break up a dogfight should be subject to the same higher-than-usual standard of care that is applied to defendants who operate railroads?

6. *From Standard of Care to Burden of Proof.* Suppose we grant that ordinary care is the standard against which to gauge the defendant's conduct for purposes of assessing Kendall's conduct. Does it follow, as Shaw maintains, that the plaintiff has the burden of establishing that the defendant acted without ordinary care? Why not place the burden on the defendant to present evidence establishing that he acted carefully? What is the practical significance of Shaw's decision to place the burden of proof on the plaintiff?

7. *Contributory Negligence.* Despite their disagreements, the lawyers and judges involved in *Brown* all agree that, if the jury were to determine that the plaintiff Brown was himself careless, then he cannot sue Kendall, even if Kendall is also found to have acted at fault. (How might Brown have been at fault here?) This is just a way of expressing the old rule of contributory negligence, i.e., that a plaintiff whose carelessness is found to contribute in some way to his being injured may not bring a negligence action. *See* Chapter 7.

N.Y. Central R.R. Co. v. White

243 U.S. 188 (1917)

Pitney, J. A proceeding was commenced by [Mrs. White] before the Workmen's Compensation Commission of the State of New York, established by the Workmen's Compensation Law of that state, to recover compensation from the New York Central & Hudson River Railroad Company for the death of her husband, Jacob White, who lost his life September 2, 1914, through an accidental injury arising out of and in the course of his employment under that company. The Commission awarded compensation in accordance with the terms of the law; its award was affirmed, without opinion, by the appellate division of the supreme court for the third judicial department, whose order was affirmed by the court of appeals, without opinion. . . .

The fault may be that of the employer himself, or — most frequently — that of another for whose conduct he is made responsible according to the maxim *respondeat superior.* In the latter case the employer may be entirely blameless, may have exercised the utmost human foresight to safeguard the employee; yet, if the alter ego, while acting within the scope of his duties, be negligent, — in disobedience, it may be, of the employer's positive and specific command, — the employer is answerable for the consequences. It cannot be that the rule embodied in the maxim is unalterable by legislation.

. . . .

[The Court next observed that legislatures have the power to limit or even eliminate certain negligence defenses, such as contributory negligence and implied assumption of risk. — Eds.]

. . . .

. . . [I]t [is not] necessary, for the purposes of the present case, to say [whether] a State might . . . [violate the Fourteenth Amendment's guarantee of] "due process of law" . . . [by] suddenly set[ting] aside all common-law rules respecting liability as between employer and employee, without providing a reasonably just substitute. . . . [I]t perhaps may be doubted whether the State could abolish all rights of action, on the one hand, or all defenses, on the other, without setting up something adequate in their stead. No such question is here presented, and we intimate no opinion upon it. The statute under consideration sets aside one body of rules only to establish another system in its place. If the employee is no longer able to recover as much as before in case of being injured through the employer's negligence, he is entitled to moderate compensation in all cases of injury, and has a certain and speedy remedy without the difficulty and expense of establishing negligence or proving the amount of the damages. Instead of assuming the entire consequences of all ordinary risks of the occupation, he assumes the consequences, in excess of the scheduled compensation, of risks ordinary and extraordinary. On the other hand, if the employer is left without defense respecting the question of fault, he at the same time is assured that the recovery is limited, and that it goes directly to the relief of the designated beneficiary. And just as the employee's assumption of ordinary risks at common law presumably was taken into account in fixing the rate of wages, so the fixed responsibility of the employer, and the modified assumption of risk by the employee under the new system, presumably will be reflected in the wage scale. The act evidently is intended as a just settlement of a difficult problem, affecting one of the most important of social relations, and it is to be judged in its entirety. We have said enough to demonstrate that, in such an adjustment, the particular rules of the common law affecting the subject matter are not placed by the Fourteenth Amendment beyond the reach of the lawmaking power of the State; and thus we are brought to the question whether the method of compensation that is established as a substitute transcends the limits of permissible state action. . . .

. . . .

. . . The pecuniary loss resulting from the employee's death or disablement must fall somewhere. It results from something done in the course of an operation from which the employer expects to derive a profit. In excluding the question of fault as a cause of the injury, the act in effect disregards the proximate cause and looks to one more remote,—the primary cause, as it may be deemed,—and that is, the employment itself. For this, both parties are responsible, since they voluntarily engage in it as coadventurers, with personal injury to the employee as a probable and foreseen result. In ignoring any possible negligence of the employee producing or contributing to the injury, the lawmaker reasonably may have been influenced by the belief that, in modern industry, the utmost diligence in the employer's service is in some degree inconsistent with adequate care on the part of the employee for his own safety; that the more intently he devotes himself to the work, the less he can take precautions for his own security. And it is evident that the consequences of a disabling or fatal injury are precisely the same to the parties immediately affected, and to the community, whether the proximate cause be culpable or innocent. Viewing the entire matter, it cannot be pronounced arbitrary and unreasonable for the State to impose upon the employer the absolute duty of making a moderate and definite compensation in money to every disabled employee, or, in case of his death, to those who were entitled to look to him for support, in lieu of the common-law liability confined to cases of negligence.

This, of course, is not to say that any scale of compensation, however insignificant, on the one hand, or onerous, on the other, would be supportable. In this case, no criticism is made on the ground that the compensation prescribed by the statute in question is unreasonable in amount, either in general or in the particular case. Any question of that kind may be met when it arises.

. . . .

We have not overlooked the criticism that the act imposes no rule of conduct upon the employer with respect to the conditions of labor in the various industries embraced within its terms, prescribes no duty with regard to where the workmen shall work, the character of the machinery, tools, or appliances, the rules or regulations to be established, or the safety devices to be maintained. This statute does not concern itself with measures of prevention, which presumably are embraced in other laws. But the interest of the public is not confined to these. One of the grounds of its concern with the continued life and earning power of the individual is its interest in the prevention of pauperism, with its concomitants of vice and crime. And, in our opinion, laws regulating the responsibility of employers for the injury or death of employees, arising out of the employment, bear so close a relation to the protection of the lives and safety of those concerned that they properly may be regarded as coming within the category of police regulations. . . .

Judgment affirmed.

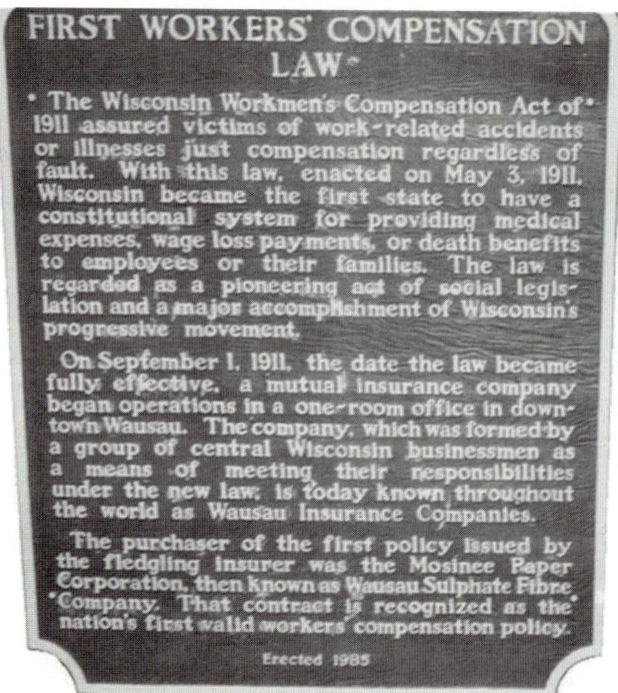

Highway Marker Commemorating Wisconsin's First Workers' Compensation Law

NOTES AND QUESTIONS

1. Workers' Compensation Laws. In the early decades of the twentieth century, many state governments, including New York's, enacted schemes that compensate workers for workplace injuries outside of the tort system. Today, these schemes continue to apply to a wide array of private-sector employees, as well as to government employees. *See, e.g.*, 5 U.S.C. §§ 8101 *et seq.* (Federal Employees' Compensation Act (FECA)).

The initial displacement of negligence law as it applied to suits against employers for workplace injuries was fueled in part by the sense that negligence doctrine at the turn of the twentieth century was highly unfavorable to injured workers and their dependents. For one thing, workers often could not take advantage of *respondeat superior. See* Chapter 8. If an employee's injury was caused by the carelessness of another employee — a "fellow servant" — the injured employee could only sue his co-worker, not the employer. Moreover, some courts presiding over suits arising from workplace injuries gave broad rein to defenses such as assumption of risk and contributory negligence. *See* Chapter 7. Thus, a worker might be found to have assumed the risk of being injured by workplace dangers simply by showing up to work. Finally, given the norm of high-risk work and the absence of modern safety equipment, it was not always easy to establish that the employer had failed to maintain a reasonably safe workplace.

Railroad workers — a group particularly vulnerable to workplace injury — received relief from some of these burdens at the turn of the twentieth century when Congress passed the Federal Safety Appliance Acts, *see* Tex. & Pac. Ry. Co. v. Rigsby (Chapter 6), as well as the Federal Employers' Liability Act (FELA), 45 U.S.C. §§ 51 *et seq.* FELA, which has now superseded the Safety Appliance Acts, created national statutory tort law by enabling railroad workers to sue their employers for injuries on the job caused by the employer's negligence. The big advantage of FELA to workers over common law is that it eliminated the defenses of contributory negligence and assumption of risk. (FELA is discussed further in the *Gottshall* and *Buckley* decisions, reproduced in Chapters 10 and 13, respectively.)

By contrast to FELA, workers' compensation statutes were predominantly enacted by state legislatures and are designed to cover workers in a wide variety of industries and businesses. Also in contrast to FELA, these statutes departed more radically from the common law of negligence, thus giving rise to constitutional arguments by employers of the sort discussed in *White.* As with FELA, the defenses of contributory negligence and assumption of risk were eliminated. In addition, however, employers were now held *strictly liable* for workplace injuries. This has meant that an injured worker is no longer required to prove fault on the part of anyone in order to obtain benefits, only that he incurred an injury in the course of his employment. Finally, employees often can recover benefits for occupational diseases without having to run the tort gauntlet of proving exactly what caused their illnesses.

For their part, employers secured an important benefit through the enactment of worker's compensation laws. Under these laws, employees injured as a result of a workplace accident *are barred from suing their employers in negligence.** Thus, they can no longer obtain compensatory damage awards set by a jury. Instead—as explained in a note following *Kenton v. Hyatt Hotels Corp.* (Chapter 8)—they receive payments in accordance with certain formulae. For example, an employee who loses a limb on the job receives a payment according to a schedule or chart that attaches a fixed monetary value to that sort of injury. Likewise, an employee who is injured and totally disabled typically receives a percentage of lost wages for a set period of time (usually a certain number of months or years) plus medical expenses.

The advantage of workers' compensation systems is that they deliver relatively prompt and predictable payments to employees injured in workplace accidents, and therefore promise predictable costs to employers, while diverting fewer resources to lawyers and litigation. However, these systems have come under criticism from both labor and management. Scheduled payments under workers' compensation schemes have not kept pace with increases in jury awards. Survivors of workers killed on the job, in particular, receive small sums of money as compared to successful wrongful death plaintiffs. The administrative costs of workers' compensation systems are lower than those of the tort system, but lawyers still are often needed to hash out disputes.

---

* Under most workers' compensation laws, employees who are the victims of *intentional torts* such as battery and false imprisonment at the hands of fellow workers are permitted to invoke the tort system against those workers. However, as explained in Chapter 8, the doctrine of *respondeat superior* often does not extend to individual employees' intentional torts, in which case the injured employee will likely have no recourse against her employer. As further explained in Chapter 9, courts have occasionally (and contentiously) invoked an expanded notion of intent to permit employees to bring claims of battery against employers whose managers have "knowingly" exposed employees to a risk of bodily harm.

Employers, meanwhile, complain that employees are increasingly able to circumvent the workers' compensation system by, for example, alleging a "knowing or intentional" wrong on the part of the employer. *See* Chapter 9.

Finally, note that workers' compensation laws bar only negligence actions for workplace injuries by employees *against their employers.* This bar does not extend to other actors whose tortious conduct played a role in causing injurious accidents in the workplace. Thus, for example, if a worker is injured while using a machine installed on a shop floor, the workers' compensation system will bar him from suing his employer for negligence, but does not bar him from pursuing a products liability claim against the machine's manufacturer. (Of course, injured workers may face other hurdles in trying to recover in tort from persons other than their employer.)

2. *Common Law and the Constitution.* Law students are taught that U.S. law consists of a hierarchy composed of common law, legislation, and constitutional law, in which legislation "trumps" common law and constitutional law "trumps" legislation. The holding of *White* is mostly consistent with this picture, given its reaffirmation of state legislatures' authority to replace the common law of negligence with at least some versions of no-fault workers' compensation schemes.* Does *White* indicate that any and all manner of legislative reform of the common law is permissible? Suppose a state legislature were simply to abolish the common law of negligence while putting nothing in its place. Would this modification of the common law be constitutional? State high courts have sometimes invoked provisions in state constitutions to strike down state legislation restricting the reach of the common law of tort through devices such as damages caps. *See, e.g.,* Ferdon v. Wisc. Patients Comp. Fund, 701 N.W.2d 440 (Wisc. 2005). On the other hand, many state and federal courts have ruled that Congress and state legislatures have broad authority to reform the common law of tort.

Although the bulk of tort reform statutes are enacted by state legislatures, Congress has from time to time weighed in. *See, e.g.,* 49 U.S.C. § 28103 (2007) (capping Amtrak's total liability for a single train accident at $200,000,000); 15 U.S.C. §§ 7901 *et seq.* (2005) (liability may not be imposed on gun manufacturers and sellers for injuries caused in the first instance by a third party's unlawful use of an otherwise lawfully sold gun).

3. *Justice and the Constitution.* In the excerpt from *The Common Law* reproduced in the notes following *Brown v. Kendall,* Holmes argues that liability without fault offends basic principles of justice by forcing *A* to pay for *B*'s loss even though *A* did nothing wrong. Is the gist of *White* that state legislatures are free to adopt *unjust* laws if they choose to? Does *White* concede that workers' compensation schemes entail an injustice as against employers? Employees? If not, what in the Court's view reconciles these departures from the idea of fault-based liability with notions of justice?

4. *Holmes and Strict Liability Revisited.* By the time of decisions such as *White,* Holmes was a member of the U.S. Supreme Court. In that capacity, he signed on to a

---

* Discussions of some basic features of workers' compensation schemes are provided in notes in Chapter 7 (following *Ranney*) and Chapter 8 (following *Kenton*).

series of decisions upholding no-fault workers' compensation statutes against constitutional challenges. Indeed, in one such instance, he concurred in a decision upholding a scheme that entitled certain workers to no-fault recovery of *full* compensation (rather than scheduled damages):

> There is some argument made for the general proposition that immunity from liability when not in fault is a right inherent in free government. . . . But if it is thought to be public policy to put certain voluntary conduct at the peril of those pursuing it, whether in the interest of safety or upon economic or other grounds, I know of nothing to hinder. . . . Indeed the criterion which is thought to be free from constitutional objection, the criterion of fault, is the application of an external standard, the conduct of a prudent man in the known circumstances, that is, in doubtful cases, the opinion of the jury, which the defendant has to satisfy at his peril, and which he may miss after giving the matter his best thought.

Arizona Copper Co. v. Hammer, 250 U.S. 400, 431 (1919) (Holmes, J., concurring). Are you convinced by Holmes's argument that tort law's reliance on the objective reasonable person standard indicates that it has adopted liability without consideration of fault?

5. Ives and Substantive Due Process. The New York Court of Appeals' decision in Ives v. South Buffalo Ry. Co., 94 N.E. 431 (N.Y. 1911), mentioned in *White*, struck down the predecessor to the statute upheld in *White*. *Ives* concluded that the earlier version of the act, which was substantially the same as the statute upheld in *White*, violated federal and state constitutional provisions protecting citizens against being deprived of liberty or property without due process of law, and barring government from taking private property without providing just compensation. In support of those conclusions, it reasoned in part as follows:

> One of the inalienable rights of every citizen is to hold and enjoy his property until it is taken from him by due process of law. When our Constitutions were adopted it was the law of the land that no man who was without fault or negligence could be held liable in damages for injuries sustained by another. That is still the law, except as to the employers enumerated in the new statute. . . .
>
> . . . .
>
> . . . It would probably conduce to the welfare of all concerned if there could be a more equal distribution of wealth. Many persons have much more property than they can use to advantage and many more find it impossible to get the means for a comfortable existence. If the legislature can say to an employer, "you must compensate your employee for an injury not caused by you or by your fault," why can it not go further and say to the man of wealth, "you have more property than you need and your neighbor is so poor that he can barely subsist; in the interest of natural justice you must divide with your neighbor so that he and his dependents shall not become a charge upon the state?" . . .
>
> In its final and simple analysis [the statute entails] taking the property of A and giving it to B, and that cannot be done under our Constitutions. . . .
>
> . . . .

94 N.E. at 439-440. Is the imposition of liability without fault necessarily the same thing as taking the assets of *A* and giving them to *B*?

Within a few years of its issuance, *Ives* had not only been effectively overruled by decisions such as *White*, it had become a poster child for the evils of "substantive due process"—a slogan invoked to condemn judges' reliance on ambiguous constitutional provisions such as due process clauses to block legislation seeking to regulate markets, ameliorate harsh working conditions, and redistribute income. As you have learned or will learn in Constitutional Law, in the 1930s the U.S. Supreme Court issued a series of decisions in which it backed away from the idea that the federal Constitution contains significant constraints on social and economic legislation, thus helping to clear the way for the New Deal and the modern administrative state.

II. PROPERTY TORTS

A. Trespass to Land: Prima Facie Case

Perhaps the oldest and least controversial instances of tort liability without fault (in the sense of carelessness) involve the tort of trespass to land. A trespass to land involves a certain kind of interference with rights conferred under the terms of property law onto possessors of land. Specifically, a trespass involves an actor *physically* invading—or causing a physical invasion of, or remaining present on—land lawfully possessed by another. Under the common law of trespass, it is immaterial to the issue of liability whether the actor who causes such an invasion took reasonable care to prevent it. All that matters, at least prima facie, is whether the actor set out to make or remain in contact with the land in question, and whether the actor did in fact make or remain in such contact. As the following case illustrates, liability in trespass thus may fall even on those who conduct themselves reasonably.

Burns Philp Food, Inc. v. Cavalea Cont'l Freight, Inc.

135 F.3d 526 (7th Cir. 1998)

Easterbrook, J. Nabisco broke up a tract of industrial real estate in Chicago. Cavalea Continental Freight bought several parcels and Burns Philp Food the remainder. In 1986 real estate records were changed to reflect these transactions, but something went awry. . . . [As a result, Burns Philp mistakenly paid property taxes on land owned by Cavalea. It notified Cavalea of the mistake in 1993.] Instead of resolving matters amicably, these neighbors have acted like the Hatfields and McCoys. Cavalea refused to pay a dime, leading Burns Philp to sue [in restitution to obtain reimbursement for the tax payments]. Cavalea filed a counterclaim accusing Burns Philp of building a fence that encroached onto its parcel. . . . The district judge held a bench trial . . . and entered a judgment from which, predictably, both sides have appealed.

[The court first held that Burns Philp could recover for taxes unwittingly paid on behalf of Cavalea for the five years immediately prior to the filing of the suit.—Eds.]

Now for Cavalea's counterclaim. Burns Philp constructed a fence on what it thought was the border between its property and Cavalea's. Whoever surveyed the land to fix the border for the fence did a lousy job. The border is 205 feet long. One end of the fence was located several feet inside Burns Philp's lot and the other was 20 feet into Cavalea's. Burns Philp thus occupied about 2,000 square feet of land that belonged to Cavalea. After . . . a survey [was conducted] in 1995, Cavalea learned that some of its land was on the other side of the fence. It did not notify Burns Philp of the problem until November 1995, when it filed the counterclaim seeking damages for trespass and an injunction requiring Burns Philp to remove the fence. Burns Philp responded by denying liability; it did not verify the accuracy of Cavalea's survey or move the fence back to the property line. In December 1996 Cavalea ripped out the fence and appurtenances without Burns Philp's leave and placed a large container right at the property line, interfering with the use of Burns Philp's loading dock. Burns Philp now concedes that Cavalea was entitled to do these things. But the district judge held that Cavalea is not entitled to damages, because it did not notify Burns Philp that the fence had been erected on its land. Trespass is a strict liability tort . . . ; Restatement (2d) of Torts § 158 (1982), and an obligation to notify the intruder is inconsistent with the idea of strict liability. Nonetheless, the district judge stated:

> [The notice requirement] may be difficult to rationalize in terms of the traditional law of trespass, but it's not difficult for me to rationalize in terms of elemental justice, and that's the way I come out.

In diversity litigation, however, state law prevails over notions of "elemental justice." The only question for decision is whether Illinois conditions damages on the landowner's notice to the trespasser. (Cavalea contends that the counterclaim filed in 1995 gave whatever notice state law requires, a possibility the district judge did not discuss, but we need not pursue that prospect.)

Burns Philp locates a notice-to-trespassers requirement in cases holding that a landowner who has consented to entry may not complain about trespass until the consent has been revoked. The proposition is unremarkable. Trespass is entry without consent; while the consent lasts there can be no trespass, and therefore no legal remedy. How can this assist Burns Philp? Cavalea did not consent to the construction of a fence on its land. Had it done so, a change of mind would not necessarily require demolition of the fence — the original consent may grant a license that can be revoked only with compensation. But Burns Philp did not seek anyone's consent to build the fence. It thought that the fence was on its land, and no one knew otherwise until 1995. Knowledge of a fence's existence is not equivalent to consent — not, at least, when the landowner does not suspect that the border has been crossed. Paths that cut diagonals across parcels with known borders and similarly obvious intrusions, where failure to protest might imply consent, pose different questions. Burns Philp built its fence under a claim of right; it did not seek an express license (or an easement) and did not obtain an implied one; it does not assert that principles of adverse possession entitle it to maintain the fence. Cavalea accordingly is entitled to damages — if it suffered monetary loss.

Cavalea offered evidence that it used the land along its border with Burns Philp to store trailers and freight containers, and that it could have stored 102 additional trailers or containers had the fence been located correctly. It charges shippers and truckers $25 per day to store loaded containers, 75 cents a day for empty truck trailers, and 55 cents a day for empty containers. Proposing that all 102 places would have been used all of the time, Cavalea demanded nearly $1 million in damages, which would make this the most valuable twentieth of an acre in Chicago. Burns Philp responds that its employees consistently noticed empty places at Cavalea's facility even before the fence was removed, and it argues that access to the extra land accordingly would not have added to Cavalea's receipts. Because it concluded that Cavalea could not maintain an action for trespass, the district judge did not resolve this dispute. It is not our place to play factfinder . . . , but we hope that it will prove possible for the new district judge (see Circuit Rule 36) to wrap things up after reviewing the existing record without taking additional evidence. . . .

The judgment is vacated and the case remanded for two purposes: to limit damages for unjust enrichment to the five-year period preceding suit, and to calculate and award the damages (if any) that Cavalea sustained from the trespass.

NOTES AND QUESTIONS

1. *Why Litigation?* Judge Easterbrook plainly expresses his annoyance that the parties in *Burns Philp* had sued one another "instead of resolving matters amicably." Is there something special about this case, as opposed to other disputes we have seen, that would suggest the parties acted inappropriately in resorting to the courts? What steps might their attorneys have taken to encourage resolution of the matter without litigation?

2. *Elemental Justice.* What did the district judge mean when he suggested that "elemental justice" warranted the notice requirement advocated by Burns Philp? Judge Easterbrook rejects this idea, noting that a federal court exercising jurisdiction over a tort case on the basis of diversity of citizenship between the parties is obligated to follow state law.* Of course, Judge Easterbrook's analysis leaves open the possibility that a state court interpreting state tort law could invoke elemental justice in support of a notice requirement. Do you agree that notice of the sort at issue here is required by basic principles of fairness? Is it unjust to force Burns Philp to pay damages for erecting a fence on another's land, even though it had good reason to believe that the land was its own?

3. *Strict Liability and Intentionality.* The court cites the Second Restatement of Torts for the proposition that trespass is a strict liability tort. While that description is

---

* As you may have learned in Civil Procedure, this rule was introduced by the Supreme Court's decision in *Erie R.R. v. Tompkins*, 304 U.S. 64 (1938). The scope and significance of the *Erie* rule is a complicated matter. For present purposes, it is enough to note that, when parties are able to have their suit heard in federal rather than state court because of the federal statute that grants federal courts jurisdiction to hear disputes between citizens of different states—so-called diversity jurisdiction—the federal court must apply substantive state law rather than invent federal common law of its own.

accurate in one respect, there is another respect in which trespass can also accurately be described as containing an intent element. As we have seen, trespass requires that one person act so as to cause a certain kind of interference with a property possessor's rights of exclusive possession and control. Implicit in this formulation is the idea that the defendant's interfering act must have been *intentionally undertaken.*

The "intentional" and "strict liability" aspects of the tort of trespass are not self-contradictory, even if they may at times appear to be. While the touching of land must have been intentional, there need not be any intention to do harm to the plaintiff, or to invade property that the actor knows to be owned or possessed by someone else, just as there need not be any unreasonable conduct. Rather, it is enough if (a) the defendant intentionally "invades" or occupies a swath of land (by walking on it, driving across it, throwing things onto it, digging it up, flooding it, building on it, etc.), and (b) the plaintiff owns or possesses the swath in question. On the other hand, a defendant who undertakes no voluntary or intentional act with respect to a piece of land cannot have committed a trespass.

For example, if *D* unintentionally loses control of his car and crashes it into a residence or commercial establishment, he has not committed a trespass—he had no intention to make contact with the property in question—even though he may have committed negligence. *Cf.* Restatement (Second) of Torts § 166, illus. 2 (1977) (driver overcome by paralytic stroke not liable in trespass to owner of lawn damaged by car); Hammontree v. Jenner, 97 Cal. Rptr. 739 (Ct. App. 1971) (declining to apply liability without fault to hold driver liable for property damages caused when a driver lost control of his car as a result of an unexpected seizure).

In *Scribner v. Summers*, 84 F.3d 554 (2d Cir. 1996), the plaintiff property owner could not sell his land because it had been contaminated by hazardous waste that had flowed onto the land from defendant's adjacent property. Defendant knew that by washing its furnaces, it was sending water contaminated with hazardous materials down a swale toward plaintiff's property. If the washing was intentional, the drainage was virtually certain, and the leakage from the swale highly foreseeable, may one conclude that the defendant trespassed onto plaintiff's land? *See* Chapter 9 (discussing the relationship between knowledge and intentionality).

Big Think

Battery, Negligence, and Trespass to Land

To commit a battery, one must arguably (among other things) intend to touch another person in a manner regarded as inappropriate. To commit negligence, one must (among other things) act unreasonably. Neither an intention to engage in inappropriate contact nor carelessness is required to commit the tort of trespass to land. Does this make trespass a tort that is easier to commit than battery or negligence? Is trespass 'too easy' to commit? If, as was suggested in *Katko v. Briney* (Chapter 9), the right to bodily integrity takes precedence over the right to exclude others from one's land, why should a battery or negligence plaintiff be required to make more of a showing than a trespass plaintiff?

4. *Breaking the Close.* As explained in the notes following *Brown v. Kendall, supra*, in medieval English usage, the term "trespass" had a very broad meaning, referring to the generic idea of a transgression by one against another. Thus when royal courts first began entertaining suits for damages arising out of injuries, they named the procedural device by which such suits would be commenced the "writ of trespass *vi et armis*." As also noted above, the "*vi et armis*" formulation indicated that trespass writ was in principle available to anyone alleging that another person had *directly* and *forcibly* caused him harm, thus covering a range of conduct and harms, including acts that would today be actionable as assault, battery, negligence, or other torts. To identify instances in which the writ was being invoked specifically to complain of alleged interferences with property rights, the plaintiff's claim was described as an action for "trespass *quare clausum fregit*." This variation on the general trespass writ instructed a sheriff to produce the defendant in court to answer the charge that he had "broken the close" — i.e., invaded plaintiff's property.

5. *Nature of the Interference.* Will *any* physical invasion onto another's property suffice to establish a trespass, no matter how minimal? Historically, the answer has been yes. The Case of the Thorns (Hulle v. Orynge), decided in 1466, presents a famous example of judicial concern for seemingly trivial claims of interference. The defendant in that case was held to have trespassed by trimming hedges on his property, which caused some thorns to fall onto his neighbor's land. According to the opinion of one of the judges: "Even though it was lawful for him to cut the thorns, it was not lawful to allow them to fall into another person's soil, for he was to cut them in such a way that they did not damage others."

Very minimal interferences continue be treated as actionable in modern trespass law. For example, a cable company or an Internet service provider must obtain consent from those whose property has to be traversed with wires or other equipment in order to provide service to customers. If such consent is not obtained, the property owners will have trespass claims, even if the equipment takes up a miniscule amount of space. *Cf.* Loretto v. Teleprompter Manhattan CATV Corp., 458 U.S. 419 (1982) (regulations authorizing the attachment of small pieces of equipment to buildings without the consent of building owners constitutes a "taking" of property by government in violation of the Fifth Amendment; owners are entitled to just compensation from the government for the invasion).

What is the point of rendering such minimal interferences actionable? In related contexts, tort observes the maxim *de minimis non curat lex* ("the law does not concern itself with trivial matters"). Why should trespass be different? Some scholars have argued that the explanation is purely historical. English property law, they maintain, tended to leave property boundaries very poorly defined. Thus, courts positively welcomed the commencement of even trivial trespass actions to give them occasion to undertake the important business of more clearly defining the parties' property lines.

6. *Invasions On, Below, and Above the Surface.* According to the Second Restatement, "a trespass may be committed on, beneath, or above the surface of the earth." Restatement (Second) of Torts § 159 (1965). Many contemporary cases are brought by a plaintiff whose land has been contaminated by underground leakage of gas or toxic

waste. *See, e.g.*, Hill v. Sw. Energy Co., No. 4:12-CV-500-DPM, 2013 WL 5423847, at *4 (E.D. Ark. Sept. 26, 2013) (allegation that defendant's fracking waste fluid migrated to subsurface strata of plaintiffs' real property supports claim for trespass); JBG/Twinbrook Metro Ltd. Partnership v. Wheeler, 697 A.2d 898 (Md. 1997) (subsurface gas leakage supports claim for trespass). Under the maxim *cujus est solum ejus est usque ad coelum*, a property owner was deemed to own the space directly above his land all the way "up to the heavens." The arrival in the twentieth century of routine airplane travel rendered strict observance of this maxim untenable. In the 1920s, Congress enacted legislation essentially annexing the skies for public use, subject to government regulation. United States v. Causby, 328 U.S. 256 (1946). However, a property owner may still be able to complain of an above-surface trespass caused by particularly low-flying aircraft, by a drone, or, for that matter, by rocks being hurled across his property even if they do not land on it.

7. *Failure to Leave or Remove.* A trespass can occur by a refusal to leave another's land just as it can by entry onto land. One who is invited to enter another's land has consent to be there and is not a trespasser. But the failure to leave when the consent has been withdrawn, or its duration has expired, can provide the basis for a trespass claim. Similarly, the failure to remove an object from another's land is a trespass, even if the initial placement of the object was not tortious. *See, e.g.*, Rogers v. Board of Road Commissioners, 30 N.W.2d 358 (Mich. 1948) (plaintiff/widow permitted to bring a trespass action for the death of her husband, which occurred when he collided with a snow fence erected by the defendant county on their property: The plaintiff's and decedent's consent to the fence remaining on the property had terminated at the end of the winter season).

8. *Who May Complain of a Trespass?* Property torts adhere to the "proper plaintiff" requirement that figured prominently in Judge Cardozo's articulation of the tort of negligence in *Palsgraf v. Long Island Railroad*. *See* Chapter 5. Thus, a plaintiff cannot prevail on a claim of trespass to land unless the plaintiff herself owns or otherwise is lawfully in possession of the land trespassed upon. Lal v. CBS, Inc., 726 F.2d 97 (3d Cir. 1984). Courts have, however, stretched the idea of a possessory interest to include members of the property owners' household. Restatement (Second) of Torts § 162 (1965).

9. *Injury, Harm, and Damages.* Decisions reproduced in Chapter 9 demonstrate that torts such as assault, battery, and false imprisonment are actionable without physical injury to the victim. For example, a nonharmful but offensive touching can provide the basis for a battery claim. The tort of trespass shares this feature—there is no requirement that the invasion in question damage or render less valuable the plaintiff's property, although the absence of such harm will affect the damages that the plaintiff will receive. Some nonharmful trespasses that do not generate a significant compensatory award may nonetheless generate substantial punitive damages, although only if the defendant's trespass is found to be willful, malicious, or committed with reckless disregard for plaintiff's rights. *See* Chapter 6.

A striking example of this sort of trespass case is provided by *Jacque v. Steenberg Homes*, Inc., 563 N.W.2d 154 (Wis. 1997). After unsuccessfully attempting to obtain permission to drive a large truck carrying a mobile home across plaintiff's farm, defendant did so anyway. However, because the land was covered in snow, it suffered no adverse effects. The jury awarded the plaintiffs nominal compensatory damages of $1, but also $100,000 in punitive damages.

On appeal, the Wisconsin Supreme Court upheld the award, reasoning in part as follows:

> . . . This court has long recognized "[e]very person['s] constitutional right to the exclusive enjoyment of his own property for any purpose which does not invade the rights of another person." Diana Shooting Club v. Lamoreux, 114 Wis. 44, 59, 89 N.W. 880 (1902). . . .
>
> Yet a right is hollow if the legal system provides insufficient means to protect it. Felix Cohen offers the following analysis summarizing the relationship between the individual and the state regarding property rights:
>
> > [T]hat is property to which the following label can be attached:
> > To the world:
> > Keep off X unless you have my permission, which I may grant or withhold.
> > Signed: Private Citizen
> > Endorsed: The state
>
> Felix S. Cohen, *Dialogue on Private Property*, IX Rutgers Law Review 357, 374 (1954). Harvey and Lois Jacque have the right to tell Steenberg Homes and any other trespasser, "No, you cannot cross our land." But that right has no practical meaning unless protected by the State. . . . [A nominal] award does not constitute state protection.
>
> . . . Because a legal right is involved, the law recognizes that actual harm occurs in every trespass. . . . Thus, in the case of intentional trespass to land, the nominal damage award represents the recognition that, although immeasurable in mere dollars, actual harm has occurred. . . .
>
> . . . Private landowners should feel confident that wrongdoers who trespass upon their land will be appropriately punished. When landowners have confidence in the legal system, they are less likely to resort to "self-help" remedies. . . . [O]ne can easily imagine a frustrated landowner taking the law into his or her own hands when faced with a brazen trespasser, like Steenberg, who refuses to heed no trespass warnings.
>
> . . . If punitive damages are not allowed in a situation like this, what punishment will prohibit the intentional trespass to land? Moreover, what is to stop Steenberg Homes from concluding, in the future, that delivering its mobile homes via an intentional trespass . . . is not more profitable than obeying the law? . . .

Id. at 160-161.

Does *Jacque* go overboard in its description of the strength and importance of property rights or its condemnation of the defendant's conduct? Recall, if you have read it, *Katko v. Briney*—the "spring gun" case from Chapter 9. If defense of the right to property against intentional invasion is as important as the Wisconsin court suggests, why doesn't the law permit owners to set dangerous traps for trespassers?

Notice that *Jacque* postdates the U.S. Supreme Court's decision in *BMW of North America, Inc. v. Gore* (Chapter 13). In purporting to apply *Gore*'s test for determining whether a punitive damage award is so large as to amount to an unconstitutional deprivation of *defendant's* property (i.e., its assets), the Wisconsin Supreme Court concluded that the award was not excessive. Is the affirmance of a punitive damages award that is 100,000 times the size of the jury's compensatory award a faithful application of *Gore*?

10. Injuries Parasitic on the Invasion. While physical damage to property is not required to support a claim for trespass, such harm, should it result, is ordinarily compensable in a trespass action. Should the same rule apply to personal injuries? Consider *Kopka v. Bell Tel. Co.* 91 A.2d 232 (Pa. 1952). Plaintiff, a farmer, suffered back and leg injuries when he stumbled on a hole in the ground on his property. The digging of the hole had been commissioned by defendant Bell, which was installing new telephone poles in the area. However the actual digging was done by defendant Sedwick, an independent contractor. Neither Sedwick nor Bell had permission or authority to dig on Kopka's land.

The jury returned a verdict exonerating Sedwick but imposing liability on Bell in the amount of $11,000. A divided Pennsylvania Supreme Court affirmed the two verdicts but ordered that the award against Bell be reduced to $7,000, given that Kopka had produced only scanty evidence of lasting physical harm.

According to the majority, Bell could *not* be held liable on a claim of negligence because *respondeat superior* does not apply to independent contractors and because the jury had in any case determined that Sedwick did not act carelessly. Nonetheless, it held that Bell could be held liable for trespass because it "authorized" Sedwick to dig the hole and because Kopka's physical injuries were caused by the hole having been dug. Does this result make sense? Even if Sedwick did not commit negligence as against Kopka, wasn't he as much of a trespasser as Bell? If so, how could the Court affirm the jury's no-liability ruling as to Sedwick?* Notice that, under the rule of *Kopka*, a special subset of physical injury claimants can, in contrast to claimants suing for negligence, recover even without a showing of carelessness by the defendant, though of course only if the claimant can establish that her injury was the product of a trespass. Essentially the same position is taken in the Restatement of Torts. Restatement (Second) of Torts § 162 (1965).

Kopka's result raises several questions. First, given that the basis for liability in this special sort of case is trespass rather than negligence, should the defense of comparative fault apply? The *Kopka* majority seems to have supposed that contributory

---

* A possible clue is provided by the court's emphasis on the fact that Bell "authorized or directed" Sedwick to trespass on Kopka's land, as well as the fact that Kopka chose to sue Bell and did not sue Sedwick. (Bell brought Sedwick into the suit as a third-party defendant.) As an independent contractor, Sedwick probably could have demanded that Bell, as the principal, indemnify him for any liability to third parties resulting from his faithful execution of Bell's instructions. The Supreme Court's affirmance of the jury's verdict in effect achieved this result—no liability for Sedwick, full liability for Bell—albeit by means of affirming a questionable jury ruling that Sedwick committed no wrong against Kopka, as opposed to the doctrinally sounder ground that Bell was required to indemnify Sedwick for any liability he incurred by virtue of the wrong he committed at Bell's direction.

negligence — the rule in place at the time the case was decided — would apply, such that Kopka would have been barred from recovering from Bell if the evidence revealed that his own negligence played a role in bringing about his injury.

Second, who has "standing" to invoke *Kopka*'s rule? Suppose that *P* is trespassing by walking along a dirt road located on farmland owned by *O*. Suppose also that *D*, another trespasser, is driving on the road *with reasonable care* but nonetheless strikes *P*. Assume that *P* cannot prevail on a negligence claim against *D* because *D* was driving with reasonable care. Should *P* recover from *D* on the ground that *D*'s driving constituted a trespass as against *O*?

Third, should principles of proximate cause apply to a trespass action seeking compensation for physical harm? In *Beavers v. West Penn Power Co.*, 436 F.2d 869 (3d Cir. 1971) (applying Pennsylvania law), the plaintiff, ten years old, was killed when he came into contact with the defendant's power lines. The plaintiff sued in trespass, and the federal district judge instructed the jury to find for the plaintiff if they found that the defendant's erection of power lines trespassed in the space above the plaintiff's home, regardless of whether the power lines had been negligently constructed or maintained. The Third Circuit upheld the instruction, noting that, as a trespasser, the defendant would be strictly liable for all personal injuries caused by the trespass, whether "proximate or indirect." Can this be right? Suppose in *Kopka* the plaintiff had gone out to observe the hole in his yard, returned safely to his kitchen, then injured his hand with a kitchen knife because he was still fuming over the fact that the hole had been dug without his permission. Would liability in trespass attach?

11. Injunctions and Self-Help. Damages are the most typical remedy obtained by property owners who suffer trespasses. However, other forms of relief may be available to them. Depending on the equities of the situation, property owners may be able to obtain a court order enjoining *ongoing* trespassory activity. *See, e.g.*, Anntco v. Shrewsbury Bank & Trust Co., 230 N.E.2d 795 (Mass. 1967) (upholding the issuance of an injunction against the continuous discharge of water by defendant onto plaintiff's property); *see also* Restatement (Second) of Torts §§ 933-951 (1979) (discussing the factors to be considered in determining the propriety of granting injunctive relief in response to trespasses). In the case of buildings and other permanent structures that have been constructed wholly or partly on another's land, the issuance of an injunction ordering the removal of the structure may result in considerable hardship to the defendant. Different jurisdictions seemingly take different views on the relative significance of the hardship faced by the defendant in deciding whether to grant such an order. *Compare* Brink v. Summers, 227 N.E.2d 476 (Mass. 1967) (courts will order the removal of permanent trespassory structures notwithstanding the hardship such an order may impose, and even as against innocent trespassers), *with* Hanson v. Estell, 997 P.2d 426 (Wash. App. Div. 2000) (affirming the trial court's refusal to order the relocation of a barn that encroached slightly on the claimants' property in light of the negligible harm caused by the encroachment and the considerable expense associated with moving the barn).

The *Katko* decision in Chapter 9 indicates that possessors of land may sometimes employ self-help to defend their property rights, but only insofar as such efforts are reasonable. Seizure, destruction, or damaging of trespassory objects or structures can, depending on the circumstances, be deemed reasonable if done for the purpose of preventing invasion. In such cases, the possessor enjoys a privilege that will defeat any tort claim brought by the owner of the object or structure complaining of its seizure or destruction. (For more on tort claims for damage to personal property, see the notes following the next case.) For example, landowners may be permitted to remove limbs of neighbors' trees encroaching onto their property. Indeed, they may be required to do so to avoid forfeiting any claim to damages. Granberry v. Jones, 216 S.W.2d 721 (Tenn. 1949) (a homeowner who had long permitted the defendant's hedge to encroach onto his property is entitled to trim so much of the hedge as is on his property, but may not recover for damages allegedly caused to his house by the hedge).

This limited right of reasonable self-help is presumably what entitled Cavalea to rip out the fence that Burns Philp had unwittingly constructed on Cavalea's property (at least after having given notice of the trespass to Burns Philp in its counterclaim). Given the limited nature of the privilege, a landowner who engages in self-help runs the risk of being found to have acted unreasonably in destroying or seizing an object or structure that trespasses on its property. *See* Sears v. Summit, Inc., 616 P.2d 765 (Wyo. 1980) (landowner held not entitled to commandeer construction equipment located on his property for the purpose of forcing the trespassing construction crew to pay him compensation).

B. Trespass and Necessity

By now you have perhaps encountered canonical tort decisions such as *MacPherson v. Buick* (Chapter 2), *Vaughan v. Menlove* (Chapter 3), and/or *Vosburg v. Putney* (Chapter 9). The next main case — *Vincent v. Lake Erie Transportation Co.* — is of a similar stature. However, unlike the foregoing, *Vincent* is at least as famous for presenting a difficult theoretical puzzle as for stating an important rule of modern tort law. In this regard, its notoriety is akin to that of *Palsgraf v. Long Island Railroad Co.* (Chapter 5). The puzzle presented in *Vincent* is whether (and if so why) an actor can be held liable for invading another's property notwithstanding that the invasion was undertaken out of *necessity.*

Imagine a cab driver who, in order to escape imminent death or serious injury at the hands of a passenger who turns out to be an armed robber, dives out of his cab and thereby permits it to run off the road and injure a pedestrian. If the pedestrian were to sue the driver for negligence, the suit would probably flounder on the breach element — courts will be inclined to say that the driver's conduct was reasonable given the exigency of the situation. *See* Cordas v. Peerless Transp. Co., 27 N.Y.S.2d 178 (City Ct. 1941) (granting defense motion to dismiss on facts similar to those hypothesized). As we will see, *Vincent* reaches a different result. The obvious question to ask is why.

Before we turn to *Vincent,* it will be useful to mention a decision issued two years before it. In *Ploof v. Putnam,* 71 A. 188 (Vt. 1908), the defendant owned an island in Lake Champlain that included a boat dock. Plaintiff was sailing on the lake with his wife and two children when a sudden, violent storm arose that placed the boat and its occupants in danger. According to plaintiff's complaint, he moored the boat at defendant's dock to save himself, his family, and his boat. However, defendant's employee unmoored the boat, which was wrecked on the shore with resultant injuries to the plaintiff and his family members.

Ploof sued, alleging that the employee's pushing away of the boat was a "trespass" (in the old sense of a direct and forcible injury) and also negligence. The defendant responded with a demurrer — essentially a motion to dismiss the complaint for failing to state a valid claim. The trial court denied the motion, and that decision was appealed to the state supreme court, which unanimously affirmed that denial. In reaching this result, the latter court reasoned as follows:

> There are many cases in the books which hold that necessity, and an inability to control movements inaugurated in the proper exercise of a strict right, will justify entries upon land and interferences with personal property that would otherwise have been trespasses. A reference to a few of these will be sufficient to illustrate the doctrine. In Miller v. Fandrye, Poph. 161, trespass was brought for chasing sheep, and the defendant pleaded that the sheep were trespassing upon his land, and that he with a little dog chased them out, and that, as soon as the sheep were off his land, he called in the dog. It was argued that, although the defendant might lawfully drive the sheep from his own ground with a dog, he had no right to pursue them into the next ground; but the court considered that the defendant might drive the sheep from his land with a dog, and that the nature of a dog is such that he cannot be withdrawn in an instant, and that, as the defendant had done his best to recall the dog, trespass would not lie. . . . A traveler on a highway who finds it obstructed from a sudden and temporary cause may pass upon the adjoining land without becoming a trespasser because of the necessity. An entry upon land to save goods which are in danger of being lost or destroyed by water or fire is not a trespass. . . .
>
> This doctrine of necessity applies with special force to the preservation of human life. One assaulted and in peril of his life may run through the close of another to escape from his assailant. One may sacrifice the personal property of another to save his life or the lives of his fellows. In Mouse's Case, 12 Co. 63, the defendant was sued for [destroying] the plaintiff's casket and its contents. It appeared that the ferryman of Gravesend took 47 passengers into his barge to pass to London, among whom were the plaintiff and defendant; and the barge being upon the water a great tempest happened, and a strong wind, so that the barge and all the passengers were in danger of being lost if certain ponderous things were not cast out, and the defendant thereupon cast out the plaintiff's casket. It was resolved that in case of necessity, to save the lives of the passengers, it was lawful for the defendant, being a passenger, to cast the plaintiff's casket out of the barge; that, if the ferryman surcharge the barge, the owner shall have his remedy upon the surcharge against the ferryman, but that if there be no surcharge, and the danger accrue only by the act of God, as by tempest, without fault of the ferryman, every one ought to bear his loss to safeguard the life of a man.

The Supreme Court remanded the case for trial, which resulted in a jury verdict for the plaintiff of $650. As you read *Vincent*, keep in mind *Ploof*'s discussion of the relevance of necessity to the imposition of tort liability.

Vincent v. Lake Erie Transp. Co.

124 N.W. 221 (Minn. 1910)

O'Brien, J. The Steamship Reynolds, owned by the defendant, was for the purpose of discharging her cargo on November 27, 1905, moored to plaintiff's dock in Duluth. While the unloading of the boat was taking place a storm from the northeast developed, which at about 10 o'clock P.M., when the unloading was completed, had so grown in violence that the wind was then moving at 50 miles per hour and continued to increase during the night. There is some evidence that one, and perhaps two, boats were able to enter the harbor that night, but it is plain that navigation was practically suspended from the hour mentioned until the morning of the 29th, when the storm abated, and during that time no master would have been justified in attempting to navigate his vessel, if he could avoid doing so. After the discharge of the cargo the Reynolds signaled for a tug to tow her from the dock, but none could be obtained because of the severity of the storm. If the lines holding the ship to the dock had been cast off, she would doubtless have drifted away; but, instead, the lines were kept fast, and as soon as one parted or chafed it was replaced, sometimes with a larger one. The vessel lay upon the outside of the dock, her bow to the east, the wind and waves striking her starboard quarter with such force that she was constantly being lifted and thrown against the dock, resulting in its damage, as found by the jury, to the amount of $500.

We are satisfied that the character of the storm was such that it would have been highly imprudent for the master of the Reynolds to have attempted to leave the dock or to have permitted his vessel to drift a way from it. One witness testified upon the trial that the vessel could have been warped into a slip, and that, if the attempt to bring the ship into the slip had failed, the worst that could have happened would be that the vessel would have been blown ashore upon a soft and muddy bank. The witness was not present in Duluth at the time of the storm, and, while he may have been right in his conclusions, those in charge of the dock and the vessel at the time of the storm were not required to use the highest human intelligence, nor were they required to resort to every possible experiment which could be suggested for the preservation of their property. Nothing more was demanded of them than ordinary prudence and care, and the record in this case fully sustains the contention of the appellant that, in holding the vessel fast to the dock, those in charge of her exercised good judgment and prudent seamanship. . . .

The appellant contends by ample assignments of error that, because its conduct during the storm was rendered necessary by prudence and good seamanship under conditions over which it had no control, it cannot be held liable for any injury resulting to the property of others, and claims that the jury should have been so instructed. An analysis of the charge given by the trial court is not necessary, as in our opinion the only question for the jury was the amount of damages which the plaintiffs were entitled to recover, and no complaint is made upon that score.

The* situation was one in which the ordinary rules regulating property rights were suspended by forces beyond human control, and if, without the direct intervention of

* [Our presentation of the court's opinion in *Vincent* reproduces, in relevant part, the text as it appears in the official Minnesota Reports (and West's Northwestern Reporter). For reasons explained in Note 2, *infra*, we are of the view that an error probably occurred during the original

2. *Scrivener's Error?* The phrase "scrivener's error" refers to a typographical error in the text of official documents such as statutes and official court reports. If a court determines that such an error has occurred, it is entitled to correct the text after the fact. *See, e.g.*, United States Nat'l Bank v. Independent Ins. Agents of America, Inc., 508 U.S. 439 (1993) (re-punctuating a federal statute upon a finding that its existing punctuation resulted from a clerical error). As noted above in an asterisked footnote, we conjecture that such an error can be found in the official text of *Vincent*. Moreover, we think the error is significant, in that its correction can shed light on the court's reasoning.

The apparent error is in the fourth paragraph of the excerpted opinion. Its first sentence, in our view, should start with the word "If" before the word "The." This conjecture is based on the remaining text of the paragraph, as well as the ultimate rationale adopted by the majority opinion. Notice, for example, that the second clause of the first sentence begins "*and if*." The use of the conjunction "and" to commence this clause seems to presuppose the presence of an initial "If." Notice also that the second and third sentences respectively begin with "If" and "Again if." Their wording suggests that the first three sentences were meant to form a parallel construction, in which the first sentence was to provide an abstract statement of the principle that would have applied *if* the events in *Vincent* were truly beyond human control, whereas the second and third would provide concrete illustrations of that principle. This inference is in turn reinforced by the "But here" phrase that commences the paragraph's fourth and final sentence. Use of that phrase suggests that the last sentence was meant to stand in opposition to each of the three preceding sentences, which it cannot do unless the first sentence is deemed to start with an "If."

With the missing text in place, the gist of the paragraph comes into much sharper relief. As written, the paragraph seems initially to suggest that the court regarded *Vincent* as a case in which property rights were suspended because natural forces had taken over the situation. Such a suggestion runs directly counter to the entire point of the paragraph, and the opinion as a whole, which concludes that Vincent's property rights were not suspended.

3. *Tort or Contract?* At least for a time, the defendant's ship had permission to be moored at Vincent's dock. Indeed, that permission was presumably obtained through a contract by which the defendant paid for the privilege to use the dock for a specified period of time. Might *Vincent* best be understood, then, not as a tort case, but as a contract case in which the court fills in a missing term as to the conditions under which Vincent's consent to entry expired? Suppose the court were to determine that the parties had implicitly agreed that Vincent was entitled to revoke consent after the ship was unloaded *regardless* of the risks faced by the ship upon casting off. Would the amount of damage to the dock be the appropriate measure of compensation to Vincent for not having the benefit of Lake Erie living up to such an unconditional commitment?

4. *Tort or Restitution?* Although *Vincent* was treated by the court as a tort case, some scholars have argued that its outcome turns on principles drawn from another area of law, namely the law of *restitution* or *unjust enrichment*. The basic idea of

restitution is that, at least in some circumstances, when one person confers a benefit onto another, the beneficiary owes it to the other to pay for the benefit. Thus, in contrast to tort, the obligation to pay restitution can arise even if no wrong has been done that is in need of rectification. The *Vincent* majority's cable hypothetical example, in the penultimate paragraph, lends some credibility to this reading of *Vincent.* What benefit was voluntarily conferred by the plaintiff to the defendant? What is the value of that benefit?

5. *Private Necessity and Incomplete Privilege.* *Vincent* is most commonly analyzed today as standing for the proposition that *private necessity supplies an incomplete privilege* to commit trespass. *See, e.g.,* Dan B. Dobbs, *The Law of Torts* § 107, at 248-250 (2000). The "privilege" part of this phrase refers to the fact that the defendant is held to have been entitled to override the property owner's right to exclude—the owner lacks the authority he would otherwise possess to take reasonable steps to eject a trespasser. The privilege is "incomplete" because, as in *Vincent,* the defendant is still liable for compensatory damages that result from his exercise of the privilege.

The incomplete privilege of private necessity is to be contrasted with the complete privilege of *public necessity,* whereby, at least in the midst of an emergency, a private citizen is entitled to use or destroy another's property in order to avert a greater harm to the public without suffering any sanction. However, the destruction or harming of private property in the name of public necessity typically will be effected by government officials. So, for example, a fire department official might order the burning of a private citizen's property to help divert a fire away from a heavily populated area. *See, e.g.,* Brewer v. State, 341 P.3d 1107 (Alaska 2014). The clause of the Fifth Amendment to the U.S. Constitution that prohibits the government from "taking" private property without "just compensation" entails that in some, but by no means all of these instances, officials will be obligated to compensate the owner for her losses out of funds from the public fisc. Dobbs, *supra,* § 109, at 253-54.

6. *Vincent and Ploof.* *Vincent* relies in part on the Vermont Supreme Court's holding in *Ploof v. Putnam,* described above. Did *Ploof* really need to invoke necessity to salvage the plaintiff's cause of action against the dockowner? What role does necessity play in establishing liability in *Ploof*?

An earlier decision may perhaps shed light on these questions. In *Cincinnati, N.O. & T.P. Ry. Co. v. Marrs' Adm'x,* 85 S.W. 188 (Ky. Ct. App. 1905), Marrs, who was heavily intoxicated, disembarked from the defendant's train late at night and proceeded to fall asleep in the defendant's trainyard between two tracks. The defendant's employees later roused Marrs and told him to leave. An hour later, while operating an engine in the yard, the employees ran over and killed Marrs, who had fallen asleep again, this time on a track. The jury awarded Marrs's widow $4,500, and the defendant appealed. In rejecting the appeal, the court reasoned in part as follows:

> There was no relation of passenger and carrier between Marrs and appellant, and therefore his entrance into the private switchyard of the corporation made him a trespasser; and, if those in charge of the switch engine had run it over him when he

his exclusion and it was undisputed that Nationwide owned the AOA system. [The other causes of action were dismissed. — EDS.]

In his appeal to the United States Court of Appeals for the Second Circuit, Thyroff sought reinstatement of his conversion cause of action, along with other relief. Nationwide countered that a conversion claim cannot be based on the misappropriation of electronic records and data because New York does not recognize a cause of action for the conversion of intangible property. The Second Circuit determined that the issue was unresolved in New York and therefore certified the following question of law to this Court: is a claim for the conversion of electronic data cognizable under New York law?[2]

II

"The hand of history lies heavy upon the tort of conversion" (Prosser, *The Nature of Conversion*, 42 Cornell LQ 168, 169 [1957]). The "ancient doctrine" has gone through a great deal of evolution over time (Franks, *Analyzing the Urge to Merge: Conversion of Intangible Property and the Merger Doctrine in the Wake of Kremen v. Cohen*, 42 Hous. L. Rev. 489, 495 and n. 32 [Summer 2005]), dating back to the Norman Conquest of England in 1066 (see Ames, *The History of Trover*, 11 Harv. L. Rev. 277, 278 [1897][hereinafter Ames]).

Before the English royal government undertook the prosecution of crime, redress for the tortious or criminal misappropriation of chattels was limited to private actions, such as "the recuperatory appeals of robbery or larceny" available to persons whose property had been stolen (*id.* at 278). In general, these appeals took two forms. If a thief was immediately apprehended while in possession of the stolen goods, the wrongdoer "was straightaway put to death [by the court], without a hearing, and the [victim] recovered his goods" (*id.*). In other cases, rightful ownership of the property was usually determined by a "wager of battle" — a physical altercation or duel between the victim and the thief (*see* Black's Law Dictionary 1544 [8th ed. 2004]), with the victor taking title to the goods (*see* Ames, 11 Harv. L. Rev. at 279). Because this "remedy" could lead to a thief killing or maiming the chattel's owner and taking legal ownership of the stolen property, it was "widely detested" by the populace (Black's Law Dictionary 1544).

Over time, the practice of trial by jury was instituted and wager of battle steadily lost favor (*see* Ames, 11 Harv. L. Rev. at 279-280). Contributing to its demise at the end of the 12th century was the advent of criminal prosecutions by the Crown. But successful prosecution by the government could result in forfeiture of the stolen chattels to the King rather than the return of property to its rightful owner — an unwelcome prospect for the victim of a theft.

The appeals of robbery and larceny also failed to provide an adequate remedy because a victim could not seek monetary damages from the thief-the only remedy was return of the stolen property. By 1252, a new cause of action — *trespass de bonis*

2. . . . Because Thyroff's conversion claim was dismissed pursuant to Federal Rules of Civil Procedure rule 12(b)(6) and a reviewing court must construe all facts and inferences in Thyroff's favor, we presume that he is the owner of the data for the purpose of resolving the certified question.

asportatis[5] —was introduced. It allowed a plaintiff to obtain pecuniary damages for certain misappropriations of property and, following a favorable jury verdict, the sale of the defendant's property to pay a plaintiff the value of the stolen goods. If, however, the defendant offered to return the property to its rightful owner, the owner had to accept it and "recovery was limited to the damages he had sustained through his loss of possession, or through harm to the chattel, which were usually considerably less than its value" (Prosser, *The Nature of Conversion*, 42 Cornell LQ at 170).

In the late 15th century, the common law was extended to "fill the gap left by the action of trespass" (Prosser and Keeton, Torts § 15, at 89 [5th ed.]) by providing a more comprehensive remedy in cases where a defendant's interference with property rights was so serious that it went beyond mere trespass to a conversion of the property (*see* Prosser, 42 Cornell LQ at 169). Known as "trover," this cause of action was aimed at a person who had found goods and refused to return them to the title owner, and was premised on the theory that:

> the defendant, by 'converting' the chattel to his own use, had appropriated the plaintiff's rights, for which he was required to make compensation. The plaintiff was therefore not required to accept the chattel when it was tendered back to him; and he recovered as his damages the full value of the chattel at the time and place of the conversion. . . . The effect was that the defendant was compelled, because of his wrongful appropriation, to buy the chattel at a forced sale, of which the action of trover was the judicial instrument (*id.* at 170).

An action for trover originally could not be invoked by a person who did not lose personal property or have a right to immediate possession of the property (*see* Restatement [Second] of Torts § 222A, Comments a, b; Ames, 11 Harv. L. Rev. at 277). Because of the advantages that trover afforded over older forms of relief, its use was stretched to cover additional misappropriations, including thefts (*see* Prosser, 42 Cornell LQ at 169; Restatement [Second] of Torts § 222A, Comment a).

Trover gave way slowly to the tort of conversion, which was created to address "some interferences with chattels for which the action of trover would not lie," such as a claim dealing with a right of future possession (Restatement [Second] of Torts § 222A, Comment b). The technical differences between trover and conversion eventually disappeared. The Restatement (Second) of Torts now defines conversion as an intentional act of "dominion or control over a chattel which so seriously interferes with the right of another to control it that the actor may justly be required to pay the other the full value of the chattel" (*id.* § 222A [1]).

III

As history reveals, the common law has evolved to broaden the remedies available for the misappropriation of personal property. As the concept of summary execution and wager of battle became incompatible with emerging societal values, the law changed. Similarly, the courts became willing to consider new species of personal property eligible for conversion actions.

5. A Latin phrase meaning "trespass for carrying goods away" (Black's Law Dictionary 1542).

conceive of any reason in law or logic why this process of virtual creation should be treated any differently from production by pen on paper or quill on parchment. A document stored on a computer hard drive has the same value as a paper document kept in a file cabinet.

The merger rule reflected the concept that intangible property interests could be converted only by exercising dominion over the paper document that represented that interest (*see* Pierpoint v. Hoyt, 260 N.Y. at 29, 182 N.E. 235). Now, however, it is customary that stock ownership exclusively exists in electronic format. Because shares of stock can be transferred by mere computer entries, a thief can use a computer to access a person's financial accounts and transfer the shares to an account controlled by the thief. Similarly, electronic documents and records stored on a computer can also be converted by simply pressing the delete button (*cf.* Kremen v. Cohen, 337 F.3d at 1034 ["It would be a curious jurisprudence that turned on the existence of a paper document rather than an electronic one. Torching a company's file room would then be conversion while hacking into its mainframe and deleting its data would not" (emphasis omitted)]).

Furthermore, it generally is not the physical nature of a document that determines its worth, it is the information memorialized in the document that has intrinsic value. A manuscript of a novel has the same value whether it is saved in a computer's memory or printed on paper. So too, the information that Thyroff allegedly stored on his leased computers in the form of electronic records of customer contacts and related data has value to him regardless of whether the format in which the information was stored was tangible or intangible. In the absence of a significant difference in the value of the information, the protections of the law should apply equally to both forms — physical and virtual.

In light of these considerations, we believe that the tort of conversion must keep pace with the contemporary realities of widespread computer use. We therefore answer the certified question in the affirmative and hold that the type of data that Nationwide allegedly took possession of — electronic records that were stored on a computer and were indistinguishable from printed documents — is subject to a claim of conversion in New York. Because this is the only type of intangible property at issue in this case, we do not consider whether any of the myriad other forms of virtual information should be protected by the tort.

Accordingly, the certified question should be answered in the affirmative.

NOTES AND QUESTIONS

1. Personal Property. "Under the traditional common law rule, only *tangible* personal property could be converted." Dan B. Dobbs, *The Law of Torts* § 63, 130-31 (2000) (emphasis added). Thus, historically, conversion actions were not available for the appropriation of another's land, nor for the appropriation of "inchoate" rights such as the right of a person to collect payment on an acknowledged debt.

While remaining cautious and incremental, modern courts have tended to expand the reach of conversion law beyond the traditional rule, sometimes permitting actions for exercises of dominion over intangibles such as electricity, negotiable instruments, shares of stock, and even intellectual property. Courts have used the merger rule discussed in *Thyroff* as a means of facilitating this expansion while nevertheless keeping some limits on the reach of the tort. Section 242 of the Restatement (Second) of Torts articulates the rationale for the merger rule, and expands it to cover interferences with the sort of possessory rights that would normally be merged with a document (e.g., ownership of shares of stock, which usually are embodied in a paper certificate) even if in a given case no tangible document was actually seized or destroyed. Does the merger rule provide an appropriate framework for deciding whether plaintiffs situated like *Thyroff* should have a remedy? If not, how else might the court have analyzed the issue before it? Was there any basis for permitting the plaintiff to recover under the traditional rule requiring interference with possessory rights in tangible property?

For another instance of a court recognizing an action for conversion with respect to intangible property, see *Kremen v. Cohen*, 337 F.3d 1024 (9th Cir. 2003), cited in *Thyroff.* In *Kremen*, a scam artist (Cohen) convinced a company called Network Solutions that the Internet domain name "sex.com" had been abandoned by its registered owner (Kremen). Cohen's misappropriation earned him a great deal of money, and although Kremen obtained a judgment against Cohen that included an order that Cohen disgorge his profits to Kremen, Cohen secreted the assets and fled the United States.

Meanwhile, Kremen sought recovery for his losses from Network Solutions on the theory that the company, in its capacity as bailee of Kremen's intangible property, had committed conversion by transferring the property to Cohen. Applying California law, the Ninth Circuit Court of Appeals held that Kremen's complaint stated a valid cause of action. While questioning the continued usefulness of the merger doctrine, it held that the Domain Name System — an electronic database holding domain names — counted as a "document" into which Kremen's intangible rights had merged. *Id.* at 1034.

2. Conversion and Fault. As noted in *Thyroff*, the Second Restatement defines conversion as the sort of "intentional exercise of dominion or control over a chattel" that completely (or nearly completely) deprives the owner of the property's usefulness or economic value. Clear instances of conversions include criminal thefts, such as the stealing of another's car or wallet, or criminal destructions of property, such as the intentional killing of another's farm animal. But conversions need not be criminal or even morally culpable.

In *Ranson v. Kitner*, 31 Ill. App. 241 (1889), the defendant shot at and killed an animal that he believed to be a wolf, but which turned out to be the plaintiff's dog. When the plaintiff sued for conversion, the defendant argued that he could not be found liable because he had no intent to injure anyone's property; rather he had intended the (apparently lawful) act of shooting a wild animal. The court rejected this argument, concluding that the defendant's mistake as to the unowned condition of the animal, even if a reasonable mistake, was no excuse. In *Kremen v. Cohen*, discussed in the previous note, the Ninth Circuit observed that the application of the merger doctrine to Kremen's domain name meant that Network Solutions was strictly liable for intentionally transferring the domain name owned by Kremen to Cohen. *Kremen*, 337 F.3d at 1036.

(collectively KSTP) for trespass. . . . The district court . . . granted KSTP's summary judgment motion on the trespass claim.

Issues

I. Did the district court err in granting KSTP's motion for summary judgment on the homeowners' trespass claim? . . .

Analysis

A trespass is committed when a person enters the land of another without consent. Consent may be implied from the conduct of the parties, but silence alone will not support an inference of consent. Consent may be geographically or temporally restricted.

The district court concluded that KSTP was entitled to summary judgment on the Copelands' trespass claim because Johnson did not exceed the geographic boundaries of the Copelands' consent and the Copelands did not expressly limit their consent to Johnson's educational or vocational goals. We read the case law differently. For reasons we will more fully discuss, we hold that KSTP is not entitled to summary judgment on either basis.

Minnesota case law establishes that an entrant may become a trespasser by moving beyond the possessor's invitation or permission. See State v. Brooks-Scanlon Lumber Co., 128 Minn. 300, 302, 150 N.W. 912, 913 (1915) (when consent given to cut mature trees, cutting of immature trees exceeded scope of consent and constituted trespass); Rieger v. Zackoski, 321 N.W.2d 16, 20 (Minn. 1982) (court correctly instructed jury that lawful entrant may become trespasser by moving beyond scope of possessor's invitation). Although trespass in *Brooks-Scanlon* related to tangible objects, the decision nonetheless demonstrates that the scope of consent can be exceeded even though the entrant remains within the geographic limits of the consent. . . .

In support of its motion for summary judgment, KSTP cites Baugh v. CBS, Inc., for the proposition that the scope of consent can be exceeded only when physical boundaries are crossed. See 828 F. Supp. 745, 756 (N.D. Cal. 1993). *Baugh* is, however, factually distinguishable. In Baugh, the homeowner granted the broadcaster permission to videotape events at her house so long as they were not shown on television. *Id.* at 752. The homeowner brought a trespass action when the videotape was subsequently broadcast. *Id.* at 756. The court held that the scope of consent was not exceeded because the plaintiff agreed to the initial videotaping and the homeowner's cause of action was not trespass. *Baugh* has limited applicability to this case because the Copelands did not consent to any videotaping.

Courts in other jurisdictions have recognized trespass as a remedy when broadcasters use secret cameras for newsgathering. Newsgathering does not create a license to trespass or to intrude by electronic means into the precincts of another's home or office. Dietemann v. Time, Inc., 449 F.2d 245, 249 (9th Cir. 1971).

Whether a possessor of land has given consent for entry is, when disputed, a factual issue. The district court determined that the Copelands did not present any evidence indicating that the scope of consent was limited to educational purposes. The record, however, indicates that consent was given only to allow a veterinary student to accompany Dr. Ulland. Viewing the evidence in the light most favorable to the Copelands[], there is sufficient evidence to withstand summary judgment. . . .

NOTES AND QUESTIONS

1. *Aspects of Consent.* As with respect to torts such as assault and battery, the issue of consent in trespass law has several dimensions. First, consent comes in two basic forms: *express* and *implied.* Which form of consent did the defendant invoke in *Copeland*?

Second, assuming consent has been granted explicitly or implicitly, it immunizes only those trespasses that fall within the scope of consent, either spatially or temporally. For example, the consent of the dockowner in *Vincent v. Lake Erie* included a temporal limitation. Thus, once the consent expired, the shipowner's decision to remain at the dock arguably converted a permitted entry into a trespass.

Third, consent to enter can be limited by reference to the *purposes* for which entry has been authorized. Thus, a homeowner who consents to have a cable TV repairman on the premises to install or repair his cable connection does not thereby consent to have the repairman spend the afternoon sunning himself in the yard or swimming in the homeowner's pool.

Fourth, the capacity of consent to operate as a defense will depend upon *the communicative context* in which the consent is signaled. As indicated by the court's opinion in *Burns Philp,* Section II.A *supra,* reasonable mistake as to whether a particular patch of land is owned by another generally will not suffice to excuse a trespass. The Second Restatement adopts the same position with respect to the effect of mistake as to consent. *See* Restatement (Second) of Torts §§ 164, 244 (1965) (reasonable but erroneous belief that entrant has permission to enter provides no defense to claim for trespass to land or chattel, or to claim for conversion). However, Section 164 adds an important qualification to this rule by immunizing a defendant from trespass liability for instances in which the defendant's reasonable but mistaken belief as to permission to enter is "induced by the conduct of the possessor," as opposed to being induced by a third-party or some other feature of the situation. *Id.*; *see also* Restatement (Second) of Torts § 892, illus. 2 (1979) (defendant who reasonably but mistakenly infers from plaintiff-land owner's gesture that plaintiff has permitted defendant's entry onto the land is not liable for trespass). This qualification aligns the law of property torts with battery law insofar as the latter immunizes from liability a defendant who touches another in the mistaken but reasonable belief that the other has in fact signaled his consent to being touched. *See* Chapter 9.

Finally, even when consent is given, there will sometimes be an issue as to whether that consent has been given *knowingly and voluntarily.* In the distinct context of medical procedures, consent will only be deemed valid in some jurisdictions if obtained after disclosure of all material information. *See* Chapter 3. Is the court in *Copeland* suggesting that the plaintiffs' consent to entry was similarly invalid because the homeowners did not have enough information about the entry to which they were consenting? In this setting, is it plausible to believe that the lack of information about the presence of the video camera vitiated the plaintiffs' consent to entry? Or is there slight, and the complaint, if it could be called a complaint, of the invalid lady, and can be looked upon as evidence, was of so trifling a character, that, upon the maxim *de minimis non curat lex*,* we arrive at the conclusion that the Defendant's acts would not have given rise to any proceedings either at law or in equity. Here then arises the objection to the acquisition by the Defendant of any easement. . . . [Given that the operation of the kitchen had only a *de minimis* impact on the plaintiff's property prior to the construction of the consulting room, the plaintiff would have had no grounds during that period to seek an injunction against, or damages based on, the defendant's activities. Thus, the fact that the defendant has, until now, been at liberty to use the mortars cannot be regarded as evidence that the plaintiff had acquiesced in their use so as to forfeit his right to complain about them now. — EDS.]

It is said that if this principle is applied in cases like the present, and were carried out to its logical consequences, it would result in the most serious practical inconveniences, for a man might go — say into the midst of the tanneries of *Bermondsey*, or into any other locality devoted to a particular trade or manufacture of a noisy or unsavoury character, and, by building a private residence upon a vacant piece of land, put a stop to such trade or manufacture altogether. The case also is put of a blacksmith's forge built away from all habitations, but to which, in course of time, habitations approach. We do not think that either of these hypothetical cases presents any real difficulty. As regards the first, it may be answered that whether anything is a nuisance or not is a question to be determined, not merely by an abstract consideration of the thing itself, but in reference to its circumstances; what would be a nuisance in *Belgrave Square* would not necessarily be so in *Bermondsey*; and where a locality is devoted to a particular trade or manufacture carried on by the traders or manufacturers in a particular and established manner not constituting a public nuisance, Judges and juries would be justified in finding, and may be trusted to find, that the trade or manufacture so carried on in that locality is not a private or actionable wrong. As regards the blacksmith's forge, that is really an *idem per idem* case with the present. It would be on the one hand in a very high degree unreasonable and undesirable that there should be a right of action for acts which are not in the present condition of the adjoining land, and possibly never will be any annoyance or inconvenience to either its owner or occupier; and it would be on the other hand in an equally degree unjust, and, from a public point of view, inexpedient that the use and value of the adjoining land should, for all time and under all circumstances, be restricted and diminished by reason of the continuance of acts incapable of physical interruption, and which the law gives no power to prevent. The smith in the case supposed might protect himself by taking a sufficient curtilage to ensure what he does from being at any time an annoyance to his neighbour, but the neighbour himself would be powerless in the matter. Individual cases of hardship may occur in the strict carrying out of the principle upon which we found our judgment, but the negation of the principle would lead even more to individual hardship, and would at the same time produce a prejudicial effect upon the development of land for residential purposes. The Master of the Rolls in the Court below took substantially the same view of the matter as ourselves and granted the relief

---

* ["The law does not concern itself with trivial matters." — EDS.]

which the Plaintiff prayed for [namely, an injunction against the continued operation of the mortars — Eds.], and we are of opinion that his order is right and should be affirmed, and that this appeal should be dismissed with costs.

NOTES AND QUESTIONS

1. More on Sturges. A.W.B. Simpson reports that Bridgman unsuccessfully tried to appease Sturges by, among other things, limiting the hours during which the mortars were used. He further reports that the injunction that was affirmed by the Court of Appeal ordered Bridgman to cease using the mortars for so long as they remained located on the wall shared with Sturges. After the litigation, Bridgman continued to operate the business for several years, apparently in compliance with the injunction.

2. Types of Nuisance. Because the term "nuisance" is used colloquially to refer to various sorts of annoyance, it is worth emphasizing that in tort law the term is restricted to ongoing interferences with another's right to use and enjoy *real property.* The receipt of repeated and unwanted phone calls from a telemarketer is a "nuisance" in the colloquial sense, but it is not a nuisance in the tort sense. Many activities have been adjudged to cause sufficient interference with the use and enjoyment of property so as to amount to nuisances, at least under certain circumstances. These include a noisy racetrack, low-flying air traffic, an incessantly howling dog, the emission of pollutants, the operation of an animal farm in a nonrural setting, use of bright lights in a residential neighborhood, and the erection of structures that block another's access to air or light.

3. Nuisance Versus Trespass. As mentioned above, there are both similarities and differences between trespass to land and nuisance as torts. The most salient similarities include the following: (a) both involve interferences with an interest in land; (b) both require as a condition of actionability that the plaintiff have a possessory interest in the relevant property; (c) both frequently involve requests for injunctive relief in addition to, or apart from, claims for damages; (d) neither requires proof of physical damage; (e) neither requires proof that the defendant acted for the purpose of interfering with someone else's property rights; and (f) neither requires that defendant's conduct fall below the threshold of reasonableness.

As to differences, nuisance requires the defendant's conduct to have caused *unreasonable* interference with another's use and enjoyment of land, whereas trespass exists even for trivial physical invasions. In this respect, liability for trespass is more "strict" than liability in nuisance. Liability in trespass is also more one-sided, in that there is little, if any, consideration given to the value of trespassory activity in determining whether a trespass has occurred. In nuisance, by contrast, the defendant's interest in pursuing the putatively offending activity often enters into the analysis of whether a nuisance exists. Although courts might sometimes deem a transitory interference as a nuisance, the much more common nuisance scenario involves a *continuing* interference, wearas trespass will be satisfied by a one-off event. On the other hand, trespass requires that the invasive act be an intentional using of the property in question, whereas nuisance does not.

7. *Zoning.* Cities and municipalities today enact elaborate zoning ordinances that set out to distribute systematically different forms of land use (industrial, retail, residential, etc.) in order to provide landowners with notice of what they may do and what they may expect others in their vicinity to do. Should the advent of zoning eliminate the need for a common law of nuisance? Trickett v. Ochs, 838 A.2d 66 (Vt. 2003) (evidence that the defendant's use of property conforms with applicable zoning laws is relevant to, but not dispositive of, the question of whether the use constitutes a nuisance).

8. *Coasean Analysis.* Nobel prize–winning economist Ronald Coase relied in part on Sturges to develop a set of claims that he articulated most famously in a 1960 article entitled *The Problem of Social Cost.* This note describes the basic features of Coasean analysis, using *Sturges* to help illustrate its key points.

a. Reciprocal Causation and Entitlements. Coase began with the observation that standard analyses of nuisance cases tended to have a unidirectional focus: They inquire whether there is some reason for making an injurer (*D*) pay compensation to a victim (*P*) for *P*'s losses. Analyses of this sort invoking doctrinal reasoning might attempt to resolve this question by parsing precedents to determine whether P had a valid claim against D. Economic analyses might alternatively pose the question of whether it would promote the efficient use of resources to impose liability on *D.* Regardless of their differences, both forms of analysis assume that the liability flows in one direction: *from* the one whose activity interferes with another's use of his property (*D*) to the one whose use of his property is interfered with (*P*).

In Coase's view, standard analyses are in the foregoing respect fundamentally flawed. All torts, he maintained, are *reciprocal*— they consist of interactions between at least two actors whose activities interfere with each other. Recall the facts of *Sturges.* As framed by the court, the question was whether the confectioner's interference with the doctor's practice was sufficiently serious to constitute a nuisance. Yet, according to Coase, as an analytic matter, one might just as well ask whether the doctor's insistence on quiet was an interference with the business of the confectioner. To treat the confectioner as the party who has "interfered" with the doctor's activity, and hence as eligible for legal sanctioning, is unjustifiably to presume a baseline by which the doctor enjoys a prima facie *entitlement* to engage in the activity, whereas the confectioner does not. Yet the crux of the legal problem posed by a case such as *Sturges* is, presumably, to figure out *who should be* entitled to engage in what sort of activity. Thus, to begin the analysis by characterizing the defendant as a person who has interfered with the activities of the plaintiff is to beg the critical question. One must instead begin with the assumption that each person is at liberty to act in the manner that he wishes, then ask whether there is some reason for the law to assign a right to engage in the activity to one of the two.

b. The Irrelevance of Entitlements in the Absence of Transaction Costs: The Coase Theorem. The economic theory of legal rules that was conventionally accepted when Coase entered the field had two prongs. The first (often tacit) presumption was evaluative — economists presumed that the best outcome was one in which resources were allocated such that they realized their most efficient or wealth-enhancing use. The second seemed to follow swiftly from the first: Legal rules should be designed so as to confer the legal entitlement to a resource to those who are able to use the resource in the most efficient manner (i.e., to generate the most wealth for the least cost).

Accepting the first prong of economic analysis, Coase famously rejected the second by advancing what has become known as the "Coase Theorem." Specifically, he argued that in a world in which parties could enter private transactions *costlessly* — that is, instantly, effortlessly, with full information, etc. — resources would find their way to their most efficient use *regardless of to whom they are initially allocated by the law.* This surprising result follows from the supposition that it will always be to the advantage of a party who is unable to make maximally efficient use of a resource to sell that resource to a party who is able to make such use of it. In short, even when the law "misallocates" the entitlement to use a given resource by granting it to someone who can't make the best use of it, that entitlement will naturally "migrate" (by means of voluntary transactions) to the party who can make the most efficient use of the resource.

A variation on *Sturges* will illustrate the point. Suppose that the confectioner's use of mortars during the doctor's consulting hours earns the confectioner \$100 in profits, yet costs the doctor \$150 in lost profits. Now suppose that the doctor is granted a legal entitlement to use his property free of this interference. In this situation, the confectioner cannot make it worthwhile to the doctor to forgo consulting unless he can pay the doctor more than he stands to lose from not consulting. However, since the confectioner makes less than \$150 from operating his machines, it would be economically irrational for him to make such a payment. So the property ends up being devoted to its more efficient use.

But now turn the example around. Suppose that the confectioner is deemed by the law to be the one with the property right, and yet the relative profits are the same as indicated above. In this situation, the doctor, if acting rationally, will pay the confectioner to cease using his mortars. After all, it costs the doctor \$150 in profits that he would otherwise obtain, so he can pay the confectioner anything under \$150 and still make a profit. Likewise, the confectioner will, if acting rationally, accept some amount over \$100 to cease using his equipment. Thus, even if the legal rules are set up to give the confectioner the initial entitlement to the relevant resource (the right to use the space adjacent to the wall), a mutually acceptable transaction should be possible by which the resource is allocated to its highest-value use (consulting). Under these circumstances, the question of to whom to allocate the entitlement to act turns out to be uninteresting: Considerations of efficiency give us no reason to confer the entitlement on one or the other party.

c. The Irrelevance of Distribution: Kaldor-Hicks Efficiency. To say that the choice of entitlement will, in the absence of transaction costs, have no differential effect on the attainment of the efficient result is not to say that it won't have *any* effects. In particular, alternative entitlement rules will have very different *distributional* effects. If the rule is adopted entitling the doctor to consult, the confectioner will lose out on \$100 worth of business, while the doctor will retain the full value of the \$150 he obtains from consulting. However, if the alternative rule is adopted, the doctor will have to pay the confectioner for the right to consult, which means that the confectioner will earn his \$100 plus a bit more, while the doctor will retain only what is left of the \$150 after he pays the confectioner.

Still, while this distributional difference might matter to those interested in analyzing a problem such as the one posed in Sturges as a problem of *justice*, it does not matter (at least in the first instance) to efficiency analysis. In economic analysis, the concern is not *who* gets a bigger or smaller slice of the total pie of aggregate social wealth, but how to fashion rules to ensure that the pie is as big as it can be. Indeed, followers of Coase typically rely upon the so-called *Kaldor-Hicks* conception of efficiency, which quite deliberately defines efficiency without regard to distributional issues. Under Kaldor-Hicks, a reallocation of resources is efficient if it generates a net gain in societal wealth, such that the beneficiaries of the extra wealth *could* fully compensate all those who lose wealth as a result of the reallocation, *regardless* of whether such compensation is actually paid. Thus, on the assumptions given above, the Kaldor-Hicks efficient solution to the problem is to have the doctor consult because the profits generated by consulting are sufficiently great that the doctor could fully compensate the confectioner for the losses he suffers by not being permitted to use his machines. Whether the rule should be adopted that requires the doctor *actually* to pay that compensation is a different question. Indeed, as we saw above, on the assumption of no transaction costs, the Coasean analyst is completely *indifferent* as to whether such a rule is adopted, since either rule will result in the property being put to its highest use.

d. The Payoff: Reintroducing Transaction Costs. As explained above, Coase's chief theoretical insight is that legal rules will have no influence on the relative efficiency of resource allocations when parties can enter into transactions with one another effortlessly, when they have perfect information, and when there are no other impediments to agreement. But, as he understood, the world of no transaction costs is a fantasy world. Bargaining takes time and effort, and is often conducted under conditions of limited information by actors who are not fully "rational." Moreover, even if all these problems are put aside, there often remains a substantial impediment to agreement, namely, the distributional question of how to divide up the economic pie. For example, we posited above that absent a court-granted entitlement to the doctor to use the consulting room, the doctor will seek to purchase that entitlement from the confectioner. Yet we also noted that the amount the doctor will rationally pay, and that the confectioner will rationally accept, falls somewhere between \$100 and \$150. The parties might well find it hard to settle on a number, since the doctor wants to pay as little as possible over $100 and the confectioner wants to be paid as much as possible up to $150.

Why, then, is the Coase Theorem at all significant, given the omnipresence of transaction costs? Does their existence render Coasean analysis irrelevant? Quite the opposite. As Coase explained, once transaction costs are reintroduced, we finally arrive at an *economic* explanation as to why the choice of legal rules bearing on entitlements *does* matter after all. They matter precisely because parties cannot enter transactions with one another costlessly. And so the lesson of the Coase Theorem in the end turns out *not* to be that legal rules are unimportant to efficiency. Rather, it suggests that they are important to the efficient allocation of resources *because* transactions are costly. It follows, according to Coase, that legal rules should not (generally) be designed with the goal of directly steering resources to their most efficient uses. They should instead be designed to avoid or overcome situations in which parties face high transactions costs — significant impediments to bargaining. In short, law is most likely to promote efficient use of resources when it "greases the wheels" of consensual transactions, which in turn permits resources to migrate to their most efficient uses.

Coase's insight is deeper than it might perhaps at first blush seem, because transaction costs present a more substantial obstacle to making the most efficient use of resources than one might suspect. In our *Sturges*-inspired illustrations, we have been assuming, artificially, that courts will be able to identify which of two possible uses of a given piece of property will be the higher-value use, such that they are left to determine only how to resolve the dispute before them in a way that is most likely to get the property in the hands of the person who will put the property to that use. In the real world it is often impossible to gain this sort of knowledge unless fair market transactions take place, through which actors can determine and demonstrate how much they actually value the right to own and use a property. In this sense, transactions (if conducted voluntarily, rationally, and with good information) both push toward efficiency and produce critical information about value.

Perhaps the most important lesson to take away from Coasean analysis is that a judge faced with a dispute over conflicting uses of property — or at least disputes of the sort in which there is no obvious wrongdoer — might do well not to conceive of her job as deciding the first-order question of who can make better use of the property, but instead should ask herself which resolution of the case will facilitate subsequent transactions on terms that will permit interested parties to determine who in fact values the property more highly. (For this reason, as we will see in a moment, a central implication of Coasean thinking for standard "A v. B" nuisance cases concerns *not* the decision as to *who* ought to be given the right to use the property but rather *how* — by what sort of legal rule — that right should be enforced.) The more general point, applicable not just to nuisance cases, but to all manner of civil disputes involving ongoing rather than one-off interactions, is that a given judicial decision, even if it finally resolves a particular dispute at a particular moment in time, will not necessarily be the last word, given that is usually open to actors to negotiate and transact in light of the decision. Therefore, in these sorts of situations, judges will want to consider how their decisions will affect and be affected by the ability of parties to transact.

e. Limitations. We have chosen this occasion to engage in a lengthy excursus on Coasean thinking for two reasons. First, its historical and natural home is the law of nuisance, precisely because nuisance cases can sometimes exemplify a form of no-fault liability. It may be that neither party is really doing anything wrong and that instead the two just happen to be engaging in lawful but incompatible activities. In such cases, there may be good reason to focus on the sorts of questions about transactions costs and efficiencies emphasized by Coase. Of course in many other instances it will be equally or more appropriate to ask different questions, such as the question of whether the defendant has wrongfully interfered with the plaintiff's use and enjoyment of her property.

Second, Coasean analysis now plays an important role in the academic analysis of tort law, and not just in the realm of nuisance. Most notably, Judge Calabresi has independently developed a similar set of claims in writing about how to reform accident law so as to render it a more effective means of deterring undesirably risky conduct. Whereas Coase in effect urged lawyers to think about how tort law might be enlisted to enable parties to engage in value-creating private transactions, Calabresi has urged courts and legislatures to think about how to craft liability rules that will incentivize persons or entities who are likely to be in the best position to deter efficiently certain kinds of accidents actually to take appropriate precautions to prevent such accidents. More ambitiously, some scholars have claimed that Coasean analysis is the only useful way, or normatively the most desirable way, to analyze problems of tort law. Others have asserted that judges have historically (if unwittingly) tended to reach the result in tort cases that Coasean analysis would call for. Even if these more ambitious claims are overstated, there is still plenty of insight to be had in asking the sorts of efficiency-related questions posed by Coase, Calabresi and others with respect to tort law.

Penland v. Redwood Sanitary Sewer Serv. Dist.

965 P.2d 433 (Or. Ct. App. 1998)

HASELTON, J. . . .

To "reset the scene," we reproduce the summary of undisputed facts . . . :

> [Defendant] District operates sewage-related facilities, including a sewage treatment plant, in rural Josephine County. As part of the sewage treatment process, the District reduces incoming raw sewage to sludge, or biosolids, a bacteria-laden condensed form of sewage, by draining the liquids from the solids. Before 1988, the District trucked the sludge to various sites for land application, which involved spreading the sludge over a large area for agricultural and disposal purposes.
>
> In 1988, the District's manager, Weber, who was charged with day-to-day oversight of its operations, instituted a small-scale pilot composting operation at the treatment plant. In July 1990, the District instituted composting on a permanent basis.
>
> In the initial stages of the composting process, sludge is solidified by being poured into an outdoor levee, or "drying ring," which is exposed to the open

air. After about two weeks, the material loses enough moisture to be mixed with organic material for composting. The reduced sludge, or biosolids, is then mixed with organic materials, such as wood, animal bedding, including animal waste, and yard waste, provided by local residents and businesses. The bacteria in the sludge break down the mixture. In order for the bacteria to decompose the sludge, the mixture must be exposed to air. Thus, the mixture is placed in a large pile, approximately nine feet high, 20 feet wide, and 100 hundred feet long, and exposed to the open air. The composted material is first piled over a perforated pipe for aeration. After two to three weeks, the pile is removed from the pipe and is turned every two weeks for aeration. There are normally seven piles at one time, each in a different stage of the composting process. Defendant uses heavy equipment to move the piles as they decompose and to load the finished product.

After approximately 90 days, the material becomes finished compost, which defendant sells to the public as mulch or soil amendment. The product, called Jo-Gro, contains no nutrients for fertilizing but is valuable for retaining moisture in soils.

If the sludge mixture is not aerated, it becomes anaerobic and, as a result, generates hydrogen sulfide. Hydrogen sulfide can cause headaches, nausea, and throat problems, and its odor is akin to that of rotten eggs. Hydrogen sulfide is generally released whenever a compost pile or the sludge pool is disturbed, but some level of hydrogen sulfide is always present as a result of the composting operation.

Plaintiffs are landowners and homeowners who live in rural Josephine County near the plant and composting operation. Many lived in the neighborhood before the District instituted the permanent composting operation. The closest plaintiffs, the Penlands, live about 180 feet from the property where the composting activities take place. Plaintiffs and other neighbors began to notice odor, noise, and dust, which they associated with the composting operation, in October 1991. Beginning in February 1992, plaintiffs and others complained to the District that, because of the odor and noise they ascribed to the plant, they were unable to enjoy outdoor activities, such as gardening, sitting on their porches, and barbequing. In response to those complaints, the District undertook several measures, including placing sound deflection panels on the electric wood grinder. Plaintiffs apparently found those measures to be ineffective and their complaints continued. . . .

[In the summer of 1994, after receiving the recommendation of an advisory committee, the District's board of directors voted] to continue the composting operation at the sewage plant while implementing 21 of the ad hoc committee's recommended mitigation measures. Those measures included using a quieter loader, constructing vegetation screens, adding sound mufflers to equipment, eliminating construction lumber demolition, applying a commercial deodorizer, mixing the sludge more rapidly and efficiently, using fly bait, and adding dust-reducing spray misters.

In August 1994, plaintiffs filed this action, seeking to enjoin the continuation of the composting operation. Plaintiffs alleged that that operation created a nuisance in that it created excessive odor, noise, and dust and interfered with the reasonable use of their properties.

146 Or. App. at 227-29, 934 P.2d 434 (footnote omitted).

to provide crowd control monitors, and failed to keep the invitees at the mandated safe distance.

During the fireworks display, one of the 5-inch mortars was knocked into a horizontal position. From this position an aerial shell inside was ignited and discharged. The shell flew 500 feet in a trajectory parallel to the earth and exploded near the crowd of onlookers. Plaintiffs Danny and Marion Klein were injured by the explosion. Mr. Klein's clothing was set on fire, and he suffered facial burns and serious injury to his eyes.

The parties provide conflicting explanations of the cause of the improper horizontal discharge of the shell. Pyrodyne argues that the accident was caused by a 5-inch shell detonating in its above-ground mortar tube without ever leaving the ground. Pyrodyne asserts that this detonation caused another mortar tube to be knocked over, ignited, and shot off horizontally. In contrast, the Kleins contend that the misdirected shell resulted because Pyrodyne's employees improperly set up the display. They further note that because all of the evidence exploded, there is no means of proving the cause of the misfire.

The Kleins brought suit against Pyrodyne under theories of products liability and strict liability. Pyrodyne filed a motion for summary judgment, which the trial court granted as to the products liability claim. The trial court denied Pyrodyne's summary judgment motion regarding the Kleins' strict liability claim, holding that Pyrodyne was strictly liable without fault and ordering summary judgment in favor of the Kleins on the issue of liability. Pyrodyne appealed the order of partial summary judgment to the Court of Appeals, which certified the case to this court. Pyrodyne is appealing solely as to the trial court's holding that strict liability is the appropriate standard of liability for pyrotechnicians. A strict liability claim against pyrotechnicians for damages caused by fireworks displays presents a case of first impression in Washington.

I. Fireworks Displays as Abnormally Dangerous Activities

. . . The modern doctrine of strict liability for abnormally dangerous activities derives from Fletcher v. Rylands, 159 Eng. Rep. 737 (1865), rev'd, 1 L.R.-Ex. 265, [1866] All E.R. 1, 6, *aff'd sub nom.* Rylands v. Fletcher, 3 L.R.-H.L. 330, [1868] All E.R. 1, 12, in which the defendant's reservoir flooded mine shafts on the plaintiff's adjoining land. Rylands v. Fletcher has come to stand for the rule that "the defendant will be liable when he damages another by a thing or activity unduly dangerous and inappropriate to the place where it is maintained, in the light of the character of that place and its surroundings." W. Keeton, D. Dobbs, R. Keeton & D. Owen, *Prosser and Keeton on Torts* § 78, at 547-48 (5th ed. 1984).

The basic principle of Rylands v. Fletcher has been accepted by the Restatement (Second) of Torts (1977). *See generally Prosser and Keeton* § 78, at 551 (explaining that the relevant Restatement sections differ in some respects from the *Rylands* doctrine). Section 519 of the Restatement provides that any party carrying on an "abnormally dangerous activity" is strictly liable for ensuing damages. The test for what constitutes such an activity is stated in section 520 of the Restatement. Both Restatement sections have been adopted by this court, and determination of whether an activity is an "abnormally dangerous activity" is a question of law.

Section 520 of the Restatement lists six factors that are to be considered in determining whether an activity is "abnormally dangerous." The factors are as follows:

(a) existence of a high degree of risk of some harm to the person, land or chattels of others;
(b) likelihood that the harm that results from it will be great;
(c) inability to eliminate the risk by the exercise of reasonable care;
(d) extent to which the activity is not a matter of common usage;
(e) inappropriateness of the activity to the place where it is carried on; and
(f) extent to which its value to the community is outweighed by its dangerous attributes.

Restatement (Second) of Torts § 520 (1977). As we previously recognized in Langan v. Valicopters, Inc., supra, 88 Wash. 2d at 861-62, 567 P.2d 218 (citing Tent. Draft No. 10, 1964, of comment (f) to section 520), the comments to section 520 explain how these factors should be evaluated:

> Any one of them is not necessarily sufficient of itself in a particular case, and ordinarily several of them will be required for strict liability. On the other hand, it is not necessary that each of them be present, especially if others weigh heavily. Because of the interplay of these various factors, it is not possible to reduce abnormally dangerous activities to any definition. The essential question is whether the risk created is so unusual, either because of its magnitude or because of the circumstances surrounding it, as to justify the imposition of strict liability for the harm that results from it, even though it is carried on with all reasonable care.

Restatement (Second) of Torts § 520, comment *f* (1977). Examination of these factors persuades us that fireworks displays are abnormally dangerous activities justifying the imposition of strict liability.

We find that the factors stated in clauses (a), (b), and (c) are all present in the case of fireworks displays. Any time a person ignites aerial shells or rockets with the intention of sending them aloft to explode in the presence of large crowds of people, a high risk of serious personal injury or property damage is created. That risk arises because of the possibility that a shell or rocket will malfunction or be misdirected. Furthermore, no matter how much care pyrotechnicians exercise, they cannot entirely eliminate the high risk inherent in setting off powerful explosives such as fireworks near crowds.

The dangerousness of fireworks displays is evidenced by the elaborate scheme of administrative regulations with which pyrotechnicians must comply. Pyrotechnicians must be licensed to conduct public displays of special fireworks. WAC 212-17-220. To obtain such a license, the pyrotechnician must take and pass a written examination administered by the director of fire protection, and must submit evidence of qualifications and experience, including "participation in the firing of at least six public displays as an assistant, at least one of which shall have been in the current or preceding year." WAC 212-17-225. The pyrotechnician's application for a license must be investigated by the director of fire protection, who must confirm that the applicant is competent and experienced. WAC 212-17-230. Licensed pyrotechnicians are charged with ensuring that the display is set up in accordance with all rules and regulations. WAC 212-17-

8. From Non-Natural to Ultrahazardous to Abnormally Dangerous. The drafters of the first torts Restatement synthesized a number of different pockets of strict liability, including Lord Cairns' concept of non-natural activities, into a new category dubbed *ultrahazardous* activities. This suggestive label was replaced in the Restatement (Second) with the related concept of *abnormally dangerous* activities.

The Third Restatement of Torts continues to use the "abnormally dangerous" formulation, though it offers a sparer definition of what constitutes an abnormally dangerous activity than does Section 520 of the Second Restatement. According to the Third Restatement, an activity is abnormally dangerous if it "(1) . . . creates a foreseeable and highly significant risk of physical harm even when reasonable care is exercised by all actors; and (2) [is] not one of common usage." Restatement (Third) of Torts: Liability for Physical and Emotional Harm § 20(b) (2010). Which of these formulations sheds the clearest light on the sorts of activities that warrant liability without fault, either as interpretations of "non-natural" or on their own?

Whatever its shortcomings, the "abnormally dangerous" label has at least one virtue: Its use of the word "abnormal" emphasizes the very limited array of activites to which the *Rylands* rule of strict liability applies. Understandably, plaintiffs' lawyers have repeatedly attempted to expand the domain of the rule, but with little success. The Reporters' notes to Section 20 of the Third Restatement suggest that many of the instances in which an activity will qualify as abnormally dangerous will be ones involving uncommon and very risky uses of land, including especially the use of explosives for construction and other purposes.

9. Bystanders Versus Participants. "The rules of strict liability [for abnormally dangerous activities] are designed largely to protect innocent third parties or innocent bystanders." Restatement (Third) of Torts: Liability for Physical and Emotional Harm § 24, cmt. a (2010). Thus, "while certain jurisdictions impose strict liability on airlines when an airplane crash causes ground damage, claims by injured passengers against the airline are governed by negligence law." *Id.* Likewise,

> if [a zoo] animal escapes from [its] cage, leaves the zoo, and injures a person living in the neighborhood, that person has a strict-liability claim against the zoo. But if the plaintiff is a patron of the zoo, exposed to wild animals because of the benefits the plaintiff secures by visiting the zoo, the plaintiff is beyond the scope of the defendant's strict liability. Similarly, if the plaintiff is a veterinarian or a groomer who accepts an animal such as a dog from the defendant, the plaintiff is . . . beyond the scope of strict liability, even if the dog can be deemed abnormally dangerous."

Id.; *see also* Berry v. Greater Park City Co., 171 P.3d 442, 450 (Utah 2007) (as a participant in a ski race, plaintiff cannot sue the owner of the site of the race on the theory that the race constituted an abnormally dangerous activity). Does limiting the reach of strict liability to bystanders make sense in light of the rationales for recognizing this form of liability?

One consequence of limiting strict liability for ultrahazardous activities to bystanders is that it seemingly renders irrelevant the issue of whether a plaintiff can expressly or implicitly assume the risk associated with an ultrahazardous activity. *See*

Restatement (Third), *supra*, § 25, cmt. e. For example, by (implicitly) treating the plaintiff as a bystander to, rather than a participant in, the activity of setting off a public fireworks display, the court in *Pyrodyne* probably foreclosed a defense argument that the plaintiff had assumed the risk of the sort of accident that befell him. Contrast *Pullen v. West*, 92 P.3d 584 (Kan. 2004), which rejected as a matter of law an abnormally dangerous activities claim brought by a guest injured while lighting powerful fireworks supplied by his host.

10. Causation, Proximate Cause, Defenses, and Apportionment. As indicated by the *Pyrodyne* court's analysis of the effect on the defendant's liability of possible "intervening" negligence on the part of the fireworks' manufacturer, even in situations in which the plaintiff is entitled to recover in tort on a no-fault basis, the courts engage in causation analysis of a sort more or less identical to the forms of analysis seen in Chapters 4 and 5. Thus, a plaintiff suing for injuries allegedly flowing from the use of explosives must demonstrate that the blasting was an actual and proximate cause of her injuries.

A famous example of a case in which blasting was held to be an actual cause, but not a proximate cause, of property damage, is *Foster v. Preston Mill Co.*, 268 P.2d 645 (Wash. 1954). There, defendant's blasting operation frightened a mother mink that resided on a mink farm two miles from the blast sight, inducing her to kill her kittens, causing her owner substantial economic loss. The defendant was held not liable because of the fortuity of the causal link between his hazardous conduct and the injury suffered by the plaintiff.

Although liability for ultrahazardous activities is "strict," some of the defenses canvassed in Chapter 7 that apply to negligence actions will be relevant in this context as well. These include statute of limitations and governmental immunity defenses, as well as the plaintiff-conduct-based defense of comparative fault. Given the abandonment of all-or-nothing contributory negligence in most jurisdictions, and the general inclination toward permitting jurors to apportion liability equitably among multiple tortfeasors (even tortfeasors being held liable on different theories — *see* Chapter 8), the trend probably is toward recognizing all forms of comparative fault, whether advertent or inadvertent, as forming the basis for a partial defense to claims seeking to impose liability based on ultrahazardous activities. *See* Maddy v. Vulcan Materials Co., 737 F. Supp. 1528 (D. Kan. 1990) (applying Kansas law and presuming the applicability of comparative fault principles); Restatement (Third) of Torts: Liability for Physical and Emotional Harm § 25 (2010) (endorsing the application of comparative fault to abnormally dangerous activities).

11. Abnormal Danger and Non-Reciprocal Risk. An influential attempt to analyze the concept of ultrahazardous or abnormally dangerous activity was provided by George Fletcher in his 1971 article, *Fairness and Utility in Tort Law.* Fletcher argued that, broadly speaking, risks come in two different categories. First, risks can be "reciprocal," in the sense that persons are exposing each other to roughly similar risks of injury. Such is the case, Fletcher supposed, as between drivers of cars — as they go about driving normally, they generate roughly comparable risks of injury to one another. According to Fletcher, fault ought to be the standard of liability for reciprocal risks, because each member of society tolerates (or assumes) a baseline of risk reciprocal to that which he generates. In turn, it is only exceptional risks — the risks associated, for example, with *careless* driving — that should generate tort liability in reciprocal risk situations.

Fletcher's second category consists of "non-reciprocal" risks. These are risks that are generated by unconventional activities, that is, risks of harm that are unilaterally imposed by one actor upon others. While fault is the fair liability standard for activities that, when undertaken in the usual manner, generate reciprocal risks, fairness requires the different rule of strict liability for non-reciprocal risks. Otherwise, Fletcher argued, the unilateral risk creator will enjoy the right to impose risks on others even though those others enjoy no equivalent right.

Does Fletcher's distinction between reciprocal and non-reciprocal risks help make sense of *Rylands*? Have the negligence cases we have encountered typically involved careless conduct that, if undertaken with ordinary care, would generate risks reciprocal to those the victim was imposing on the actor engaged in the conduct?

12. Conditional Fault. As an alternative basis for its holding, the *Pyrodyne* court relies on an insurance statute that, on its face at least, seems not to address the standard of liability to which Pyrodyne will be held. Yet the issue of the ability of an actor to absorb the costs of its hazardous activity figures prominently in many analyses of liability without fault, including Judge Robert Keeton's important article, *Conditional Fault in the Law of Torts.*

Keeton argued that the distinction between negligence liability and liability without fault can be better understood as involving a distinction between two "types" of fault. Fault of the first type — what we typically deem "negligent" conduct — involves activity that violates norms of behavior even granted that the actor who engages in the behavior has made provision for the payment of any damages his behavior causes. Thus, we tend to regard careless driving as exemplifying fault of the first type. A careless driver's conduct is condemned even if he has purchased insurance sufficient to provide reasonable compensation to those he injures. By contrast, liability "without fault" is in reality a second type of fault, dubbed by Keeton "conditional fault." Conditional fault describes risky conduct that we are nonetheless prepared to treat as permissible if the actor who undertakes it stands ready to provide reasonable compensation to those injured by such conduct. Thus, according to Keeton, we say of highly risky activities such as blasting that it is permissible, but only on the condition that those who engage in it are prepared to compensate those who are injured by it.

Do you find Keeton's distinction between types of fault plausible? Does it help make sense of the majority's reading of the Washington insurance statute? How well does the category of conditional fault mesh with the multifactor test of Section 520 of the Second Restatement? Note that the *Klein* court invoked Washington's mandatory insurance statute to support the claim that the state had intended to impose strict liability on pyrotechnical activity, since coverage extended to injuries resulting from *any* pyrotechnical activity, not just negligent pyrotechnical activity. States often require actors to obtain no-fault insurance to cover first-party injuries (as with automobile no-fault plans). It is much less common for a state to impose no-fault insurance to pay for third party injuries — these are typically paid by insurance only in the event of a finding of negligence.

REFERENCES/FURTHER READING

Workers' Compensation and Strict Liability

Ernst Freund, *Constitutional Status of Workmen's Compensation*, 6 Ill. L. Rev. 432, 433, 435-436 (1912).

Gregory C. Keating, *The Theory of Enterprise Liability and Common Law Strict Liability*, 54 Vand. L. Rev. 1285 (2001).

David Rosenberg, *The Hidden Holmes: His Theory of Torts in History* (1995).

Eugene Wambaugh, *Workmen's Compensation Acts: Their Theory and Their Constitutionality*, 25 Harv. L. Rev. 129 (1912).

Trespass and Conversion

Richard A. Epstein, *The Roman Law of Cyberconversion*, 2005 Mich. St. L. Rev. 103.

Orin S. Kerr, *Norms of Computer Trespass*, 116 Colum. L. Rev. (forthcoming 2016).

Greg Lastowka, *Decoding Cyberproperty*, 40 Ind. L. Rev. 23 (2007).

Catherine M. Sharkey, *Trespass Torts and Self-Help for an Electronic Age*, 44 Tulsa L. Rev. 677 (2009).

Michael R. Siebecker, *Cookies and the Common Law: Are Internet Advertisers Trespassing on Our Computers?*, 76 S. Cal. L. Rev. 893 (2003).

Vincent and Necessity

Alan Brudner, *A Theory of Necessity*, 7 Oxford J. Leg. Stud. 339 (1987).

George C. Christie, *The Defense of Necessity Considered from the Legal and Moral Points of View*, 48 Duke L.J. 975 (1999).

Jules L. Coleman, *Risks and Wrongs* 371-372 (1992).

Richard Epstein, *A Theory of Strict Liability*, 2 J. Leg. Stud. 151 (1973).

Richard Epstein, *The Ubiquity of the Benefit Principle*, 67 S. Cal. L. Rev. 1369 (1994).

Stephen D. Sugarman, Vincent v. Lake Erie Transportation Co.: *Liability for Harm Caused by Necessity*, in Robert L. Rabin & Stephen D. Sugarman, *Tort Stories* 259 (2003).

Ernest J. Weinrib, *The Idea of Private Law* 196-203 (1995).

Symposium on *Vincent v. Lake Erie Transportation Co.*, Issues in Legal Scholarship No. 7, http://www.bepress.com/ils/iss7 (numerous authors).

Nuisance

Guido Calabresi, *Some Thoughts on Risk Distribution and the Law of Torts*, 70 Yale L.J. 499 (1961).

Guido Calabresi & A. Douglas Melamed, *Property Rules, Liability Rules and Inalienability: One View of the Cathedral*, 85 Harv. L. Rev. 1089 (1972).

Ronald Coase, *The Problem of Social Cost*, 3 J.L. & Econ. 1 (1960).

Donald G. Gifford, *Public Nuisance as a Mass Products Liability Tort*, 71 U. Cin. L. Rev. 741 (2003).

Douglas Laycock, *The Neglected Defense Of Undue Hardship (And The Doctrinal Train Wreck In* Boomer v. Atlantic Cement), 4 J. Tort Law 1 (2012).

John Copeland Nagle, *Moral Nuisances*, 50 Emory L.J. 265 (2001).

Gideon Parchomovsky & Peter Siegelman, *Selling Mayberry: Communities and Individuals in Law and Economics*, 92 Cal. L. Rev. 75 (2004).

Symposium, *Property Rules, Liability Rules and Inalienability: A Twenty-Five Year Retrospective*, 106 Yale L.J. 2083 *et seq.* (1997).

Ultrahazardous Activities

David Abraham, *Liberty and Property: Lord Bramwell and the Political Economy of Liberal Jurisprudence*, 38 Am. J. Leg. Hist. 288 (1994).

Kenneth S. Abraham, Rylands v. Fletcher: *Tort Law's Conscience*, in Robert L. Rabin & Stephen D. Sugarman, *Tort Stories* 207 (2003).

Francis H. Bohlen, *The Rule in* Rylands v. Fletcher, 59 U. Pa. L. Rev. 298 (1911).

Gerald W. Boston, *Strict Liability for Abnormally Dangerous Activity: The Negligence Barrier*, 36 San Diego L. Rev. 597 (1999).

Danielle Keats Citron, *Reservoirs of Danger: The Evolution of Public and Private Law at the Dawn of the Information Age*, 80 S. Cal. L. Rev. 241 (2007).

George Fletcher, *Fairness and Utility in Tort Law*, 85 Harv. L. Rev. 537 (1972).

William K. Jones, *Strict Liability for Hazardous Enterprise*, 92 Colum. L. Rev. 1705 (1992).

Robert Keeton, *Conditional Fault in the Law of Torts*, 72 Harv. L. Rev. 401 (1959).

Thomas W. Merrill & David M. Schizer, *The Shale Oil and Gas Revolution, Hydraulic Fracturing, and Water Contamination: A Regulatory Strategy*, 98 Minn. L. Rev. 145 (2013).

Gary T. Schwartz, Rylands v. Fletcher, *Negligence and Strict Liability*, in Peter Cane & Jane Stapleton, *The Law of Obligations: Essays in Celebration of John Fleming* 201 (1998).

Jed H. Shugerman, Note: *The Floodgates of Strict Liability: Bursting Reservoirs and the Adoption of* Fletcher v. Rylands *in the Gilded Age*, 110 Yale L.J. 333 (2000).

Jed H. Shugerman, *A Watershed Moment: Reversals of Tort Theory in the Nineteenth Century*, 2 J. Tort L. 2 (2008).

A.W.B. Simpson, *Legal Liability for Bursting Reservoirs: The Historical Context of* Rylands v. Fletcher, 13 J. Leg. Stud. 209 (1984).

Glanville Williams, *Liability for Animals* (1939).

CHAPTER 12

PRODUCTS LIABILITY

I. INTRODUCTION

Products liability claims stand at the center of modern tort law. Today when one encounters high-stakes, cutting-edge litigation in tort, it tends to involve claims for injuries caused by defective products. For this reason, products liability is also perhaps the most politically controversial branch of tort. This chapter introduces you to its basic features.

Suits seeking redress for injuries caused by products are hardly novel. Chapter 2, for example, mentions the New York Court of Appeals' decision in the 1852 case of *Thomas v. Winchester*, in which the plaintiff was poisoned by a mislabeled medicine and was permitted to sue the manufacturer. For most of the modern history of tort—roughly 1850 to 1970—actions of this sort fell within one of two existing doctrinal categories. First, they might sound in negligence, as did Mrs. Thomas's claim, as well as the claim of Mr. MacPherson against the Buick Motor Co. Alternatively, some consumers injured by products sued for breach of an express or implied *warranty*: a contractual promise that the product was safe for ordinary use. Today, by contrast, suits for product-related injuries are typically grounded in a separate body of law called *strict products liability* or just *products liability*. The change in label signifies that claims for injuries caused by defective products are now governed by a body of law that generates its own principles of responsibility, distinct from those at work in the law of negligence and warranty.

If one were to pick a date for the emergence of products liability law as a distinct branch of tort law, it would probably be 1963, the year in which the California Supreme Court decided *Greenman v. Yuba Power Products, Inc.* In *Greenman*, a unanimous court led by Justice Roger Traynor permitted a man injured while using a defective power tool to recover from the manufacturer on a theory of liability that relied neither on proof of fault nor on warranty. *Greenman* dubbed this action to be one of "strict liability" in tort for a defective product. Within two years, the American Law Institute issued Section 402A of the Second Restatement of Torts. Relying primarily on California doctrine, Section 402A did not so much "restate" an existing law of products liability as recommend its adoption. Lawyers and courts across the country quickly latched onto Section 402A as providing a superior approach to claims alleging injuries caused by product defects. Within a decade of *Greenman*, a majority of jurisdictions in the United States had adopted causes of action in strict products liability. Today all but a handful of states employ some version of products liability law.

To say that products liability has been widely adopted as a distinct theory of liability is not to say that it has proved uncontroversial. Quite the opposite—it has generated intense debate throughout its brief life. The main *theoretical* concern associated with the recognition of this separate department of tort law can be stated succinctly: If, with some notable exceptions, accidents have tended to be addressed in Anglo-American tort law under the rubric of negligence, and if, as cases such as *Greenman* insist, products liability is really a form of liability without fault, what can explain why victims of this class of accidents are entitled to the benefit of not having to prove fault? Various thoughtful answers have been proposed to this question. For example, some have insisted that products liability is faithful to a historical baseline of strict liability for accidentally caused harms and that negligence is the upstart in the field that is in need of justification. Others, by contrast, insist that negligence is the default rule for liability arising out of accidents but that there is no difficulty reconciling products liability law with that default because the "strictness" of products liability is illusory—in reality it is a form of fault-based liability. Still others insist that products liability is strict and that it is incompatible with the law's baseline commitment to fault as a threshold for liability, and therefore suspect or illegitimate.

In our view, it is mistake to privilege either "strict liability" or "negligence" as the core principle of our tort law, in part because it is a mistake to suppose that either of those concepts has a single or constant meaning. As explained in Chapter 11, notwithstanding the central importance to tort law of negligence-based concepts, there remain important areas in which one or another version of liability without fault applies, including claims arising out of interferences with property rights, ultrahazardous activities, and workplace accidents. Likewise, as the materials in Part Two surely demonstrate, negligence liability itself is multifaceted, reflecting an array of duties that differ substantially in terms of what they demand of various actors. For these and other reasons, we are disinclined to suppose that tort law privileges any one theory of responsibility as paradigmatic. Thus, there is no reason to believe that products liability law—even assuming it differs substantially from other tort law—has come into the world with either a special claim of privilege or a special stigma attached to it.

More affirmatively, we are of the view that products liability is controversial in part because, as a later entrant into the world of torts, it has emerged as a doctrinal hybrid that contains cross-currents reflecting various aspects of tort law and policy. From negligence law, there is an emphasis on manufacturers' duties of vigilance, and on the proper balance among precaution and harm. From property torts, one sees a concern for consumers' legitimate expectations for their physical safety. From the law of ultra-hazardous activities, there is attention to the idea that certain forms of large-scale production pose unavoidable hazards that may call for different rules of liability. From workers' compensation, one detects the distinctively modernist sense of the propriety of risk- and loss-spreading and the concern for an uneven playing field between the individual and the large commercial enterprise. And, as elsewhere in torts, one sees these concerns being given expression in doctrines bearing on everything from rules of evidence to standards of liability.

In explicating the law of products liability, this chapter focuses primarily (but not exclusively) on the law of California. It does so because the California courts have tended to pave the way in this area, because California law provides a representative cross-section of issues, and because it provides a contemporary opportunity to examine the development of doctrine within a precedent-based system. The goal is primarily to lay out basic concepts and to see how they apply in a variety of settings. But, in doing so, we also explore the broader debates that this area has spawned on issues of practical, political, and theoretical importance.

A. Precursors

Escola v. Coca-Cola Bottling Co. of Fresno, excerpted below, is a simple but memorable case. Like some other notable concurring opinions — including, for example, Justice Louis Brandeis's concurring opinion on the importance of free speech rights in *Whitney v. California*, 274 U.S. 357 (1927) — Justice Traynor's *Escola* opinion is far more famous and important than the majority's. Indeed, as *Greenman* will attest, it is Traynor's opinion that has rendered *Escola* a legal landmark. If *Greenman* is the case that made strict products liability the law, *Escola* is the case that best presents its rationales.

Escola v. Coca Cola Bottling Co. of Fresno

150 P.2d 436 (Cal. 1944)

Gibson, C.J. Plaintiff, a waitress in a restaurant, was injured when a bottle of Coca Cola broke in her hand. She alleged that defendant company, which had bottled and delivered the alleged defective bottle to her employer, was negligent in selling "bottles containing said beverage which on account of excessive pressure of gas or by reason of some defect in the bottle was dangerous . . . and likely to explode." This appeal is from a judgment upon a jury verdict in favor of plaintiff.

Defendant's driver delivered several cases of Coca Cola to the restaurant, placing them on the floor, one on top of the other, under and behind the counter, where they remained at least thirty-six hours. Immediately before the accident, plaintiff picked up the top case and set it upon a nearby ice cream cabinet in front of and about three feet from the refrigerator. She then proceeded to take the bottles from the case with her right hand, one at a time, and put them into the refrigerator. Plaintiff testified that after she had placed three bottles in the refrigerator and had moved the fourth bottle about

18 inches from the case "it exploded in my hand." The bottle broke into two jagged pieces and inflicted a deep five-inch cut, severing blood vessels, nerves and muscles of the thumb and palm of the hand. Plaintiff further testified that when the bottle exploded, "It made a sound similar to an electric light bulb that would have dropped. It made a loud pop." Plaintiff's employer testified, "I was about twenty feet from where it actually happened and I heard the explosion." A fellow employee, on the opposite side of the counter, testified that plaintiff "had the bottle, I should judge, waist high, and I know that it didn't bang either the case or the door or another bottle . . . when it popped. It sounded just like a fruit jar would blow up. . . ." The witness further testified that the contents of the bottle "flew all over herself and myself and the walls and one thing and another."

The top portion of the bottle, with the cap, remained in plaintiff's hand, and the lower portion fell to the floor but did not break. The broken bottle was not produced at the trial, the pieces having been thrown away by an employee of the restaurant shortly after the accident. Plaintiff, however, described the broken pieces, and a diagram of the bottle was made showing the location of the "fracture line" where the bottle broke in two.

One of defendant's drivers, called as a witness by plaintiff, testified that he had seen other bottles of Coca Cola in the past explode and had found broken bottles in the warehouse when he took the cases out, but that he did not know what made them blow up.

Plaintiff then rested her case, having announced to the court that being unable to show any specific acts of negligence she relied completely on the doctrine of res ipsa loquitur.

Defendant contends that the doctrine of res ipsa loquitur does not apply in this case, and that the evidence is insufficient to support the judgment.

Many jurisdictions have applied the doctrine in cases involving exploding bottles of carbonated beverages. Other courts for varying reasons have refused to apply the doctrine in such cases. . . .

Res ipsa loquitur does not apply unless (1) defendant had exclusive control of the thing causing the injury and (2) the accident is of such a nature that it ordinarily would not occur in the absence of negligence by the defendant.

Many authorities state that the happening of the accident does not speak for itself where it took place some time after defendant had relinquished control of the instrumentality causing the injury. Under the more logical view, however, the doctrine may be applied upon the theory that defendant had control at the time of the alleged negligent act, although not at the time of the accident, *provided* plaintiff first proves that the condition of the instrumentality had not been changed after it left the defendant's possession. As said in Dunn v. Hoffman Beverage Co., 126 N.J.L. 556, 20 A.2d 352, 354, "defendant is not charged with the duty of showing affirmatively that something happened to the bottle after it left its control or management; . . . to get to the jury the plaintiff must show that there was due care during that period." Plaintiff must also prove that she handled the bottle carefully. . . .

Upon an examination of the record, the evidence appears sufficient to support a reasonable inference that the bottle here involved was not damaged by any extraneous force after delivery to the restaurant by defendant. It follows, therefore, that the bottle was in some manner defective at the time defendant relinquished control, because sound and properly prepared bottles of carbonated liquids do not ordinarily explode when carefully handled.

The next question, then, is whether plaintiff may rely upon the doctrine of res ipsa loquitur to supply an inference that defendant's negligence was responsible for the defective condition of the bottle at the time it was delivered to the restaurant. Under the general rules pertaining to the doctrine, as set forth above, it must appear that bottles of carbonated liquid are not ordinarily defective without negligence by the bottling company. . . .

An explosion such as took place here might have been caused by an excessive internal pressure in a sound bottle, by a defect in the glass of a bottle containing a safe pressure, or by a combination of these two possible causes. The question is whether under the evidence there was a probability that defendant was negligent in any of these respects. If so, the doctrine of res ipsa loquitur applies. . . .

A chemical engineer for the Owens-Illinois Glass Company and its Pacific Coast subsidiary, maker of Coca Cola bottles, explained how glass is manufactured and the methods used in testing and inspecting bottles. He testified that his company is the largest manufacturer of glass containers in the United States, and that it uses the standard methods for testing bottles recommended by the glass containers association. A pressure test is made by taking a sample from each mold every three hours—approximately one out of every 600 bottles—and subjecting the sample to an internal pressure of 450 pounds per square inch, which is sustained for one minute. (The normal pressure in Coca Cola bottles is less than 50 pounds per square inch.) The sample bottles are also subjected to the standard thermal shock test. The witness stated that these tests are "pretty near" infallible.

It thus appears that there is available to the industry a commonly-used method of testing bottles for defects not apparent to the eye, which is almost infallible. Since Coca Cola bottles are subjected to these tests by the manufacturer, it is not likely that they contain defects when delivered to the bottler which are not discoverable by visual inspection. Both new and used bottles are filled and distributed by defendant. The used bottles are not again subjected to the tests referred to above, and it may be inferred that defects not discoverable by visual inspection do not develop in bottles after they are manufactured. Obviously, if such defects do occur in used bottles there is a duty upon the bottler to make appropriate tests before they are refilled, and if such tests are not commercially practicable the bottles should not be re-used. This would seem to be particularly true where a charged liquid is placed in the bottle. It follows that a defect which would make the bottle unsound could be discovered by reasonable and practicable tests.

Although it is not clear in this case whether the explosion was caused by an excessive charge or a defect in the glass there is a sufficient showing that neither cause would ordinarily have been present if due care had been used. Further, defendant had exclusive control over both the charging and inspection of the bottles. Accordingly, all the requirements necessary to entitle plaintiff to rely on the doctrine of res ipsa loquitur to supply an inference of negligence are present.

It is true that defendant presented evidence tending to show that it exercised considerable precaution by carefully regulating and checking the pressure in the bottles

A Coca-Cola Bottling Plant (located in Wyandotte, Michigan), c. 1940

and by making visual inspections for defects in the glass at several stages during the bottling process. It is well settled, however, that when a defendant produces evidence to rebut the inference of negligence which arises upon application of the doctrine of res ipsa loquitur, it is ordinarily a question of fact for the jury to determine whether the inference has been dispelled.

The judgment is affirmed.

TRAYNOR, J. (concurring). I concur in the judgment, but I believe the manufacturer's negligence should no longer be singled out as the basis of a plaintiff's right to recover in cases like the present one. In my opinion it should now be recognized that a manufacturer incurs an absolute liability when an article that he has placed on the market, knowing that it is to be used without inspection, proves to have a defect that causes injury to human beings. MacPherson v. Buick Motor Co., 217 N.Y. 382, 111 N.E. 1050 . . . established the principle, recognized by this court, that irrespective of privity of contract, the manufacturer is responsible for an injury caused by such an article to any person who comes in lawful contact with it. In these cases the source of the manufacturer's liability was his negligence in the manufacturing process or in the inspection of component parts supplied by others. Even if there is no negligence, however, public policy demands that responsibility be fixed wherever it will most effectively reduce the hazards to life and health inherent in defective products that reach the market. It is evident that the manufacturer can anticipate some hazards and guard against the recurrence of others, as the public cannot. Those who suffer injury from defective products are unprepared to meet its consequences. The cost of an injury and the loss of time or health may be an overwhelming misfortune to the person injured, and a needless one, for the risk of injury can be insured by the manufacturer and distributed among the public as a cost of doing business. It is to the public interest to discourage the marketing of products having defects that are a menace to the public. If such products nevertheless find their way into the market it is to the public interest to place the responsibility for whatever injury they may cause upon the manufacturer, who, even if he is not negligent in the manufacture of the product, is responsible for its reaching the market. However intermittently such injuries may occur and however haphazardly they may strike, the risk of their occurrence is a constant risk and a general one. Against such a risk there should be general and constant protection and the manufacturer is best situated to afford such protection.

The injury from a defective product does not become a matter of indifference because the defect arises from causes other than the negligence of the manufacturer, such as negligence of a submanufacturer of a component part whose defects could not be revealed by inspection, or unknown causes that even by the device of res ipsa loquitur cannot be classified as negligence of the manufacturer. The inference of negligence may be dispelled by an affirmative showing of proper care. If the evidence against the fact inferred is "clear, positive, uncontradicted, and of such a nature that it can not rationally be disbelieved, the court must instruct the jury that the nonexistence of the fact has been established as a matter of law." An injured person, however, is not ordinarily in a position to refute such evidence or identify the cause of the defect, for he can hardly be familiar with the manufacturing process as the manufacturer himself is. In leaving it to the jury to decide whether the inference has been dispelled, regardless of the evidence against it, the negligence rule approaches the rule of strict liability. It is needlessly circuitous to make negligence the basis of recovery and impose what is in reality liability without negligence. If public policy demands that a manufacturer of goods be responsible for their quality regardless of negligence there is no reason not to fix that responsibility openly.

In the case of foodstuffs, the public policy of the state is formulated in a criminal statute. [Indeed, various provisions of] the Health and Safety Code [impose penalties for the sale of "adulterated" food — food that is itself unwholesome or injurious to health, or that is delivered in a container so as to be injurious to health]. The criminal liability under the statute attaches without proof of fault, so that the manufacturer is under the duty of ascertaining whether an article manufactured by him is safe. . . . Statutes of this kind result in a strict liability of the manufacturer in tort to the member of the public injured.

The statute may well be applicable to a bottle whose defects cause it to explode. In any event it is significant that the statute imposes criminal liability without fault, reflecting the public policy of protecting the public from dangerous products placed on the market, irrespective of negligence in their manufacture. While the Legislature imposes criminal liability only with regard to food products and their containers, there are many other sources of danger. It is to the public interest to prevent injury to the public from any defective goods by the imposition of civil liability generally.

The retailer, even though not equipped to test a product, is under an absolute liability to his customer, for the implied warranties of fitness for proposed use and merchantable quality include a warranty of safety of the product. This warranty is not necessarily a contractual one. The courts recognize, however, that the retailer cannot bear the burden of this warranty, and allow him to recoup any losses by means of the warranty of safety attending the wholesaler's or manufacturer's sale to him. Such a procedure, however, is needlessly circuitous and engenders wasteful litigation. Much would be gained if the injured person could base his action directly on the manufacturer's warranty.

The liability of the manufacturer to an immediate buyer injured by a defective product follows without proof of negligence from the implied warranty of safety attending the sale. Ordinarily, however, the immediate buyer is a dealer who does not intend to use the product himself, and if the warranty of safety is to serve the purpose of protecting health and safety it must give rights to others than the

Roger J. Traynor
California Supreme Court
(1940-64)

dealer. . . . While the defendant's negligence in the *MacPherson* case made it unnecessary for the court to base liability on warranty, Judge Cardozo's reasoning recognized the injured person as the real party in interest and effectively disposed of the theory that the liability of the manufacturer incurred by his warranty should apply only to the immediate purchaser. It thus paves the way for a standard of liability that would make the manufacturer guarantee the safety of his product even when there is no negligence.

This court and many others have extended protection according to such a standard to consumers of food products, taking the view that the right of a consumer injured by unwholesome food does not depend "upon the intricacies of the law of sales" and that the warranty of the manufacturer to the consumer in absence of privity of contract rests on public policy. Dangers to life and health inhere in other consumers' goods that are defective and there is no reason to differentiate them from the dangers of defective food products.

In the food products cases the courts have resorted to various fictions to rationalize the extension of the manufacturer's warranty to the consumer: that a warranty runs with the chattel; that the cause of action of the dealer is assigned to the consumer; that the consumer is a third party beneficiary of the manufacturer's contract with the dealer. They have also held the manufacturer liable on a mere fiction of negligence: "Practically he must know it [the product] is fit, or take the consequences, if it proves destructive." Parks v. C. C. Yost Pie Co., 93 Kan. 334, 144 P. 202, 203. . . . Such fictions are not necessary to fix the manufacturer's liability under a warranty if the warranty is severed from the contract of sale between the dealer and the consumer and based on the law of torts (Decker & Sons v. Capps, *supra*; Prosser, *Torts*, p.689) as a strict liability. . . .

As handicrafts have been replaced by mass production with its great markets and transportation facilities, the close relationship between the producer and consumer of a product has been altered. Manufacturing processes, frequently valuable secrets, are ordinarily either inaccessible to or beyond the ken of the general public. The consumer no longer has means or skill enough to investigate for himself the soundness of a product, even when it is not contained in a sealed package, and his erst-while vigilance has been lulled by the steady efforts of manufacturers to build up confidence by advertising and marketing devices such as trademarks. Consumers no longer approach products warily but accept them on faith, relying on the reputation of the manufacturer or the trade mark. Manufacturers have sought to justify that faith by increasingly high standards of inspection and a readiness to make good on defective products by way of replacements and refunds. The manufacturer's obligation to the consumer must keep pace with the changing relationship between them; it cannot be escaped because the marketing of a product has become so complicated as to require one or more intermediaries. Certainly there is greater reason to impose liability on the manufacturer than on the retailer who is but a conduit of a product that he is not himself able to test.

The manufacturer's liability should, of course, be defined in terms of the safety of the product in normal and proper use, and should not extend to injuries that cannot be traced to the product as it reached the market.

NOTES AND QUESTIONS

1. *Res Ipsa Revisited.* The jury and the trial court in *Escola* did not seem to balk at reaching a verdict for plaintiff under the rubric of negligence through an application of *res ipsa loquitur* (*see* Chapter 3). A majority of the California Supreme Court similarly seemed capable of affirming the judgment on a negligence theory. Is the majority's application of *res ipsa* plausible? Under the majority's reasoning, should a negligence claim against the manufacturer of the bottle, Owens-Illinois Glass Company have been allowed to go to the jury, had it been sued? (Recall the trial testimony of the Owens-Illinois engineer, who asserted that the company's tests were "pretty near" infallible.) Why did Justice Traynor think it was necessary to create a new cause of action if *res ipsa* sufficed?

2. *Are Products Different?* Assume that the defendant in *Escola* really did use reasonable care. How, then, would the situation here differ from that of *Brown v. Kendall* (Chapter 11)? In *Brown*, a man raised a stick to separate fighting dogs and thereby struck and injured the plaintiff. The court ruled that the man could not be held liable without proof that he had acted carelessly. Absent proof of fault, the *Brown* court reasoned, the plaintiff's injury was but an unfortunate tragedy, not an occasion for a victim to obtain redress. If we assume that Coca-Cola acted carefully, isn't Escola's injury likewise a tragic occurrence for which the defendant cannot be held responsible? Should it be enough that it was the company's bottle that caused the injury?

3. *Justifying Defect-Based Liability.* The first two paragraphs of Justice Traynor's concurrence set forth several mutually reinforcing justifications for a new conception of liability for injuries caused by defective products. These include (a) a suggestion that manufacturers owe to consumers a particularly demanding obligation to be vigilant of product safety (an obligation-based rationale); (b) an argument that manufacturers are best situated to take precautions, and therefore should be given strong incentives to take such precautions (a deterrence rationale); (c) an argument that manufacturers are best situated to spread the costs of accidental injuries caused by their products (a compensation-insurance rationale); (d) an observation that responsibility for injury stems from having marketed a product that caused injury, regardless of negligence (a causation-strict liability rationale); (e) an argument that victims' entitlement to compensation should not depend on the nature of the conduct that caused it (a compensation-equality rationale); (f) an analysis of disparities in power in litigation concerning evidence and procedure (a litigation-structure rationale); (g) an assertion that, if two ways of structuring the law lead to the same result, the more open and direct structure is preferable (a judicial-candor rationale).

It is worthwhile to identify the text in the opinion that corresponds to each of these rationales. Which among them is most persuasive? Which seem most important to Justice Traynor? Why does he put forward all of them, rather than simply the ones he views as most important? Are there any rationales that he should have mentioned that he did not? Do these rationales overlap with those put forward for liability without fault in the property tort and ultrahazardous activity cases presented in Chapter 11?

4. *Negligence, Defect-Based Liability, and Absolute Liability.* The phrase "strict liability" has multiple meanings or implications, and it must therefore be handled with

care. In the first instance, Justice Traynor uses the adjective "strict" negatively, to emphasize that a plaintiff such as Escola should not have to prove carelessness on the part of the defendant. And yet by limiting liability to injuries caused by *defective* products, he also qualifies the strictness of his proposed new products liability regime. Certainly, one could imagine a stricter form of liability: it would require a plaintiff to prove only that she was actually injured by a product, regardless of whether the product contained a defect. In the context of products liability, lawyers and scholars sometimes refer to this latter, stricter form of strict liability as "absolute liability."* What in Traynor's analysis supports *defect-based* liability rather than *absolute liability*?

5. *Unprecedented?* Thanks in part to its invocation in Justice Traynor's concurrence, Judge Cardozo's *MacPherson* opinion is today commonly heralded as setting modern tort law on a course that led naturally to the adoption of strict products liability. Yet *MacPherson* itself, as Traynor acknowledges, was a negligence decision. Why does Traynor believe it provides any support whatsoever to the plaintiff in *Escola*? How can he cite *MacPherson* when his whole point is to urge liability *without negligence*?

Note 3, *supra*, identifies many of the policy arguments put forward by Justice Traynor. Yet, to say that reasons of policy or principle support a particular doctrine is not to address whether extant legal authorities justify its adoption. Although they are not reproduced in the above excerpt, numerous sources are cited by Justice Traynor in his concurrence. These include negligence cases, criminal statutes, and warranty cases. Among those that appear or are referenced in the above excerpt, which sources of authority seem most supportive of his efforts at doctrinal innovation? Does he interweave the different authorities effectively?

6. *Food Impurities Versus Product Defects.* As Justice Traynor notes, numerous courts had, prior to *Escola*, recognized warranty-based causes of action for persons injured by ingesting "impure" or otherwise defective food products. A typical case, cited by Traynor, is *Parks v. G. C. Yost Pie Co.*, 144 P. 202 (Kan. 1914), in which a widow recovered damages from a manufacturer whose ptomaine-poisoned pie killed her husband. Another of the many food liability cases cited by Justice Traynor was a well-known New York decision authored by Judge Cardozo. *Ryan v. Progressive Grocery Stores*, 175 N.E. 105 (N.Y. 1931), permitted the plaintiff to recover on an implied warranty theory for injuries to his mouth caused by a pin contained in a loaf of bread sold by defendant. Is there any reason why foodstuffs — and in *Escola*, a soft-drink bottle — should have been among the first sorts of products in which strict liability would apply? Did it aid Traynor's cause that he was able to write his opinion in a case in which the defective "product" was a bottled beverage?

7. *Henningsen.* The warranty roots of modern products liability law received their most important and influential treatment in a New Jersey Supreme Court decision. In *Henningsen v. Bloomfield Motors, Inc.*, 161 A.2d 69 (N.J. 1960), Helen Henningsen

* The phrase "absolute liability" carries different meanings in other contexts. For example, it is sometimes used to refer to the imposition of liability based on the violation of a certain kind of statute (such as a child labor statute) that precludes the defendant from raising generally applicable affirmative defenses. D.L. v. Huebner, 329 N.W.2d 890, 917 (Wis. 1983).

was driving a ten-day-old Plymouth sedan when its steering wheel suddenly spun in her hands, causing the car to crash into a wall. Mrs. Henningsen and her husband Claus, who had purchased the car, sued the car dealer (Bloomfield Motors) and the car's manufacturer (Chrysler). The Henningsens brought causes of action in both negligence and warranty, but the trial court dismissed the negligence claim for lack of sufficient evidence of breach, and sent the case to trial on warranty claims alone. The jury returned verdicts for the plaintiffs against both defendants.

On appeal, Chrysler emphasized provisions in the contract of sale that limited its liability for breach of warranty to the cost of replacing any defective parts, and that disclaimed any other liabilities. These contractual provisions, it argued, precluded recovery of tort compensation for Mrs. Henningsen's injuries on either an *express* or *implied* warranty theory. In addition, it argued that any warranties that accompanied the product were not for the benefit of persons other than the actual purchaser (Mr. Henningsen).

The New Jersey court declared the contract's disclaimer of liability for personal injuries void as against public policy. In support of this holding, it noted that the limitation was provided in fine print in a standard-form contract drafted and used by each of the "Big Three" U.S. auto makers (General Motors, Ford, and Chrysler), and hence that consumers were not likely to have any meaningful choice as to whether to accept it. The court also rejected the privity argument, reasoning as follows:

> There is no doubt that under early common-law concepts of contractual liability only those persons who were parties to the bargain could sue for a breach of it. In more recent times a noticeable disposition has appeared in a number of jurisdictions to break through the narrow barrier of privity when dealing with sales of goods in order to give realistic recognition to a universally accepted fact. The fact is that the dealer and the ordinary buyer do not, and are not expected to, buy goods, whether they be foodstuffs or automobiles, exclusively for their own consumption or use. Makers and manufacturers know this and advertise and market their products on that assumption; witness, the "family" car, the baby foods, etc. The limitations of privity in contracts for the sale of goods developed their place in the law when marketing conditions were simple, when maker and buyer frequently met face to face on an equal bargaining plane and when many of the products were relatively uncomplicated and conducive to inspection by a buyer competent to evaluate their quality. With the advent of mass marketing, the manufacturer became remote from the purchaser, sales were accomplished through intermediaries, and the demand for the product was created by advertising media. In such an economy it became obvious that the consumer was the person being cultivated. Manifestly, the connotation of "consumer" was broader than that of "buyer." He signified such a person who, in the reasonable contemplation of the parties to the sale, might be expected to use the product. Thus, where the commodities sold are such that if defectively manufactured they will be dangerous to life or limb, then society's interests can only be protected by eliminating the requirement of privity between the maker and his dealers and the reasonably expected ultimate consumer. In that way the burden of losses consequent upon use of

> defective articles is borne by those who are in a position to either control the danger or make an equitable distribution of the losses when they do occur.

161 A.2d at 80-81.

The *Escola* majority avoided issues of privity by working within the domain of negligence law. *Henningsen*, by contrast, had to solve the privity problem from within the law of warranty. It did so, first, by ruling that an implied warranty of fitness "runs with" a product, and thus passes through an intermediate seller to the ultimate consumer. Second, and equally important, it held that a manufacturer and consumer were barred by law from agreeing to waive this implied warranty. As between *Escola* and *Henningsen*, which sort of "stretch" seems more plausible to you? Which one is more likely to help accident victims in the long run? Is there something intuitive about grounding products liability claims in an implicit promise from the manufacturer that the product will perform more or less as expected?

8. Modern Warranty Law. Following *Henningsen*, a majority of jurisdictions abandoned the privity requirement in implied warranty actions. Today, under Article 2-314 of the Uniform Commercial Code (UCC), which has been adopted in one form or another by every state, all goods come with an implied warranty of *merchantability*, that is, a promise that the goods are safe and fit for ordinary use. Such warranties can be waived, but only by conspicuous and specific language agreed to by the buyer at the time of sale. U.C.C. § 2-316(2). (Some states have adopted versions of Section 2-316 that void even conspicuous and specific waivers of implied warranties, at least with respect to personal injury claimants.) Breaches of the implied warranty of merchantability that result in physical harms generate in the victim a claim for consequential damages for the losses associated with those harms. Contractual terms purporting to cap or otherwise limit such damages are generally deemed void as unconscionable. U.C.C. §§ 2-715, 2-719. The reach of the implied warranty of merchantability differs across jurisdictions. Some extend it past the purchaser to her immediate family members. Others go so far as to render the warranty enforceable by any foreseeable user of the product. *See* U.C.C. § 2-318 A-C (offering alternative provisions as to the class of persons protected by warranty).

In spite of sellers' (limited) ability to waive warranties, as well as limits in some jurisdictions on the class of persons who are entitled to complain of breaches of warranty, modern warranty law is capable of providing legal redress to many persons who suffer bodily harm because of a product not fit for ordinary use. In general, however, modern products liability law, in which issues of waiver and privity do not arise, has tended to push warranty theories of recovery to the side. There are some important exceptions to this tendency. For example, as we will see, there are some jurisdictions in which warranty-based liability for product-related physical injuries is in some respects broader than liability under tort doctrine. In these jurisdictions, at least, the question of whether to provide separate warranty and tort causes of action for injuries caused by products, or whether all such actions should be unified under a single heading, remains very much alive.

B. The Emergence of Strict Products Liability

Greenman v. Yuba Power Prods., Inc.

377 P.2d 897 (Cal. 1963)

Traynor, J. Plaintiff brought this action for damages against the retailer and the manufacturer of a Shopsmith, a combination power tool that could be used as a saw, drill, and wood lathe. He saw a Shopsmith demonstrated by the retailer and studied a brochure prepared by the manufacturer. He decided he wanted a Shopsmith for his home workshop, and his wife bought and gave him one for Christmas in 1955. In 1957 he bought the necessary attachments to use the Shopsmith as a lathe for turning a large piece of wood he wished to make into a chalice. After he had worked on the piece of wood several times without difficulty, it suddenly flew out of the machine and struck him on the forehead, inflicting serious injuries. About ten and a half months later, he gave the retailer and the manufacturer written notice of claimed breaches of warranties and filed a complaint against them alleging such breaches and negligence.

After a trial before a jury, the court ruled that there was no evidence that the retailer was negligent or had breached any express warranty and that the manufacturer was not liable for the breach of any implied warranty. Accordingly, it submitted to the jury only the cause of action alleging breach of implied warranties against the retailer and the causes of action alleging negligence and breach of express warranties against the manufacturer. The jury returned a verdict for the retailer against plaintiff and for plaintiff against the manufacturer in the amount of $65,000. The trial court denied the manufacturer's motion for a new trial and entered judgment on the verdict. The manufacturer and plaintiff appeal. . . .

Plaintiff introduced substantial evidence that his injuries were caused by defective design and construction of the Shopsmith. His expert witnesses testified that inadequate set screws were used to hold parts of the machine together so that normal vibration caused the tailstock of the lathe to move away from the piece of wood being turned permitting it to fly out of the lathe. They also testified that there were other more positive ways of fastening the parts of the machine together, the use of which would have prevented the accident. The jury could therefore reasonably have concluded that the manufacturer negligently constructed the Shopsmith. The jury could also reasonably have concluded that statements in the manufacturer's brochure were untrue, that they constituted express warranties,[1] and that plaintiff's injuries were caused by their breach.

---

1. In this respect the trial court limited the jury to a consideration of two statements in the manufacturer's brochure. (1) "WHEN SHOPSMITH IS IN HORIZONTAL POSITION—Rugged construction of frame provides rigid support from end to end. Heavy centerless-ground steel tubing insures perfect alignment of components." (2) "SHOPSMITH maintains its accuracy because every component has positive locks that hold adjustments through rough or precision work."

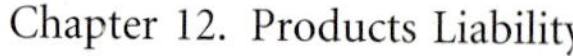

The Complete 5-in-1 Power Tool

Woodworking's wonderful with a SHOPSMITH—a welcome relief from the pressures of a work-a-day world! This unique multi-purpose tool gives you the joy of creative relaxation—saves money on all sorts of remodeling, cabinetry and furniture making—simple or intricate.

The only truly 5-in-1 power shop, SHOPSMITH converts from saw to sander, to lathe, to vertical drill press or horizontal drill. Selective speed dial gives correct speed and power . . . for every job, any wood.

SHOPSMITH costs two-thirds less than equivalent single-purpose tools—yet fits easily in a bicycle's parking space.

See this fine, multi-purpose, power-tool at your local dealer or Montgomery Ward. For literature, write: Dept. SNG-4.

9" Circular Saw
12" Sander
34" Lathe
Unlimited Horizontal Drill
16½" Vertical Drill Press

SPECIAL HARDWARE WEEK OFFER
Expires May 7th

SHOPSMITH Mark 5, complete with ¾ hp motor and bench..........$299.50
4" Jointer........regularly.......... 58.50
VALUE $358.00

Now complete for only $299⁵⁰

YUBA POWER PRODUCTS, INC.
800 EVANS ST., CINCINNATI 4, OHIO

A Subsidiary of **YUBA CONSOLIDATED INDUSTRIES, INC.**

Manufacturer of SAWSMITH Radial Arm Saw • CHOREMASTER Garden Tillers.

YUBA

Yuba Shopsmith Advertisement c.1960

The manufacturer contends, however, that plaintiff did not give it notice of breach of warranty within a reasonable time and that therefore his cause of action for breach of warranty is barred by section 1769 of the Civil Code. Since it cannot be determined whether the verdict against it was based on the negligence or warranty cause of action or both, the manufacturer concludes that the error in presenting the warranty cause of action to the jury was prejudicial.

Section 1769 of the Civil Code provides: "In the absence of express or implied agreement of the parties, acceptance of the goods by the buyer shall not discharge the seller from liability in damages or other legal remedy for breach of any promise or warranty in the contract to sell or the sale. But, if, after acceptance of the goods, the buyer fails to give notice to the seller of the breach of any promise or warranty within a reasonable time after the buyer knows, or ought to know of such breach, the seller shall not be liable therefor."

Δ's Argument

Like other provisions of the uniform sales act (Civ. Code, §§ 1721-1800), section 1769 deals with the rights of the parties to a contract of sale or a sale. It does not provide that notice must be given of the breach of a warranty that arises independently of a contract of sale between the parties. Such warranties are not imposed by the sales act, but are the product of common-law decisions that have recognized them in a variety of situations. It is true that in many of these situations the court has invoked the sales act definitions of warranties in defining the defendant's liability, but it has done so, not because the statutes so required, but because they provided appropriate standards for the court to adopt under the circumstances presented.

The notice requirement of section 1769, however, is not an appropriate one for the court to adopt in actions by injured consumers against manufacturers with whom they have not dealt. "As between the immediate parties to the sale (the notice requirement) is a sound commercial rule, designed to protect the seller against unduly delayed claims for damages. As applied to personal injuries, and notice to a remote seller, it becomes a booby-trap for the unwary. The injured consumer is seldom 'steeped in the business practice which justifies the rule,' (James, *Product Liability*, 34 Texas L. Rev. 44, 192, 197) and at least until he has had legal advice it will not occur to him to give notice to one with whom he has had no dealings." (Prosser, *Strict Liability to the Consumer*, 69 Yale L.J. 1099, 1130, footnotes omitted.) It is true that in [three of our prior decisions, this] court assumed that notice of breach of warranty must be given in an action by a consumer against a manufacturer. Since in those cases, however, the court did not consider the question whether a distinction exists between a warranty based on a contract between the parties and one imposed on a manufacturer not in privity with the consumer, the decisions are not [binding in this case]. We conclude, therefore, that even if plaintiff did not give timely notice of breach of warranty to the manufacturer, his cause of action based on the representations contained in the brochure was not barred.

Moreover, to impose strict liability on the manufacturer under the circumstances of this case, it was not necessary for plaintiff to establish an express warranty as defined in section 1732 of the Civil Code. A manufacturer is strictly liable in tort when an article he places on the market, knowing that it is to be used without inspection for defects, proves to have a defect that causes injury to a human being. Recognized first in the case of unwholesome food products, such liability has now been extended to a variety of other products that create as great or greater hazards if defective. [Citing state and federal cases involving products including a grinding wheel, bottle, vaccine, surgical pin, automobile, skirt, tire, home permanent, hair dye, and plane. — EDS.]

Although in these cases strict liability has usually been based on the theory of an express or implied warranty running from the manufacturer to the plaintiff, the abandonment of the requirement of a contract between them, the recognition that the liability is not assumed by agreement but imposed by law, and the refusal to permit the manufacturer to define the scope of its own responsibility for defective products (Henningsen v. Bloomfield Motors, Inc., 32 N.J. 358, 161 A.2d 69, 84-96 . . .) make clear that the liability is not one governed by the law of contract warranties but by the law of strict liability in tort. Accordingly, rules defining and governing warranties that were developed to meet the needs of commercial transactions cannot properly be invoked to govern the manufacturer's liability to those injured by their defective products unless those rules also serve the purposes for which such liability is imposed.

We need not recanvass the reasons for imposing strict liability on the manufacturer. They have been fully articulated in the cases cited above. (*See also* 2 Harper and James, *Torts*, §§ 28.15-28,16, pp.1569-1574; Prosser, *Strict Liability to the Consumer*, 69 Yale L.J. 1099; Escola v. Coca Cola Bottling Co., 24 Cal. 2d 453, 461, 150 P.2d 436, concurring opinion.) The purpose of such liability is to insure that the costs of injuries resulting from defective products are borne by the manufacturers that put such products on the market rather than by the injured persons who are powerless to protect themselves. Sales warranties serve this purpose fitfully at best. In the present case, for example, plaintiff was able to plead and prove an express warranty only because he read and relied on the representations of the Shopsmith's ruggedness contained in the manufacturer's brochure. Implicit in the machine's presence on the market, however, was a representation that it would safely do the jobs for which it was built. Under these circumstances, it should not be controlling whether plaintiff selected the machine because of the statements in the brochure, or because of the machine's own appearance of excellence that belied the defect lurking beneath the surface, or because he merely assumed that it would safely do the jobs it was built to do. It should not be controlling whether the details of the sales from manufacturer to retailer and from retailer to plaintiff's wife were such that one or more of the implied warranties of the sales act arose. "The remedies of injured consumers ought not to be made to depend upon the intricacies of the law of sales." (Ketterer v. Armour & Co., D.C., 200 F. 322, 323; Klein v. Duchess Sandwich Co., 14 Cal. 2d 272, 282, 93 P.2d 799.) To establish the manufacturer's liability it was sufficient that plaintiff proved that he was injured while using the Shopsmith in a way it was intended to be used as a result of a defect in design and manufacture of which plaintiff was not aware that made the Shopsmith unsafe for its intended use. . . .

The judgment is affirmed.

NOTES AND QUESTIONS

1. *Beyond Negligence and Warranty.* How does *Greenman*'s holding differ from the holdings in *Escola* and *Henningsen*? Would a *res ipsa loquitur* theory have succeeded

in *Greenman*? Why not? Justice Traynor describes California warranty law's notice requirement as a "trap." Is that because product consumers, unlike merchants buying goods for commercial use or sale, would frequently have no occasion to discover a breach of warranty within the time frame contemplated by warranty law? If so, could the California Supreme Court have solved this problem by reading into warranty law something like the 'discovery rule' for the onset of statute of limitations periods (*see* Chapter 7)? Suppose this "fix" would have salvaged Greenman's implied warranty claim. Did Justice Traynor have other reasons for insisting that the claim against Yuba should sound in tort, not contract?

2. *From Escola to Greenman.* Compare the rationales provided in *Greenman* with those stated by Justice Traynor in his *Escola* concurrence. Which rationales, if any, are omitted in *Greenman?* Are any new ones added?

3. *Defect.* Justice Traynor uses the terms *defect, defectively designed or constructed, defective condition*, and numerous other cognates of "defect" in describing the gist of Greenman's complaint about the Shopsmith. Do these terms address the issue of carelessness? Or breach of express or implied warranty? Do they concern all three? Is it possible for a product to contain a defect without the seller of the product having acted carelessly in marketing it? Is it possible for the product to be defectively designed without a seller having acted carelessly?

4. *Retailer Liability: Vandermark.* In Vandermark v. Ford Motor Co., 391 P.2d 168, 171-172 (Cal. 1964), the California Supreme Court extended *Greenman*, applying defect-based liability to the *retailer* of a product (Maywood Bell, a car dealer), not simply the manufacturer:

> Retailers like manufacturers are engaged in the business of distributing goods to the public. They are an integral part of the overall producing and marketing enterprise that should bear the cost of injuries resulting from defective products. In some cases the retailer may be the only member of that enterprise reasonably available to the injured plaintiff. In other cases the retailer himself may play a substantial part in insuring that the product is safe or may be in a position to exert pressure on the manufacturer to that end; the retailer's strict liability thus serves as an added incentive to safety. Strict liability on the manufacturer and retailer alike affords maximum protection to the injured plaintiff and works no injustice to the defendants, for they can adjust the costs of such protection between them in the course of their continuing business relationship. Accordingly, as a retailer engaged in the business of distributing goods to the public, Maywood Bell is strictly liable in tort for personal injuries caused by defects in cars sold by it.
>
> Since Maywood Bell is strictly liable in tort, the fact that it restricted its contractual liability to Vandermark is immaterial. Regardless of the obligations it assumed by contract, it is subject to strict liability in tort because it is in the business of selling automobiles, one of which proved to be defective and caused injury to human beings. . . .

As is discussed in materials below, the modern rules of products liability law apply to *sellers* of the products at issue. Retailers and manufacturers both qualify as sellers, as do others in the chain of distribution. Reconsider the majority and concurring opinions in *Escola.* Would the *res ipsa* theory of the majority apply equally well to a car dealer such as Maywood Bell? Which of Justice Traynor's stated rationales in his *Escola* concurrence apply to a retailer? Which (if any) do not?

5. *Defect = Negligence?* As we will see, some scholars have suggested that products liability law is, in the end, just a variation on negligence law that provides the plaintiff with the advantage of being able to prove carelessness by identifying a fault in the defendant's product rather than in the defendant's production or distribution methods. Does *Vandermark* support this supposition?

6. *Risk Spreading: Manufacturers Versus Retailers.* Maywood Bell was a smaller enterprise than Ford Motor Company. As such, it presumably possessed a lesser ability to spread the costs of product-related injuries. Is it obvious that a modestly sized retail operation can more readily secure liability insurance than an individual consumer can secure health insurance? As a rule, will retailers always be relatively less well suited to spread risk than manufacturers? Suppose a present-day Greenman purchased his Yuba Shopsmith at a Wal-Mart store. Wouldn't this reverse the size differential of *Vandermark*?

7. *From Product Users to Bystanders.* When the New York Court of Appeals in *MacPherson v. Buick* eliminated the privity rule (*see* Chapter 2), it extended the duty of care owed by car manufacturers at least to foreseeable users of those cars, including the car's passengers. Recall, however, that the court declined to indicate whether the duty of care further extended to nonusers such as pedestrians and other bystanders. In *Elmore v. American Motors Corp.*, 451 P.2d 84 (Cal. 1969), the California Supreme Court was faced with the same issue in the context of delineating the emerging cause of action for products liability. One of the plaintiffs was the driver (and owner) of an automobile with a defective drive shaft. The defect caused the owner's car to crash into a vehicle from the oncoming lane. The other plaintiff, whose action is discussed below, was the injured driver of the oncoming vehicle.

> In [*Greenman*], we pointed out that the purpose of strict liability upon the manufacturer in tort is to insure that "the costs of injuries resulting from defective products are borne by the manufacturers that put such products on the market rather than by the injured persons who are powerless to protect themselves." We further pointed out that the rejection of the view that such liability was governed by contract warranties rather than tort rules was shown by cases which had recognized that the liability is not assumed by agreement but imposed by law and which had refused to permit the manufacturer to define its own responsibility for defective products. Similarly, in Vandermark v. Ford Motor Co. . . . we held that, since the retailer is strictly liable in tort, the fact that it restricted its contractual liability was immaterial.
>
> These cases make it clear that the doctrine of strict liability may not be restricted on a theory of privity of contract. Since the doctrine applies even where the manufacturer has attempted to limit liability, they further make it clear that the doctrine may not be limited on the theory that no representation of safety is made to the bystander.

> The liability has been based upon the existence of a defective product which caused injury to a human being, and in both *Greenman* and *Vandermark* we did not limit the rules stated to consumers and users but instead used language applicable to human beings generally.
>
> It has been pointed out that an injury to a bystander "is often a perfectly foreseeable risk of the maker's enterprise, and the considerations for imposing such risks on the maker without regard to his fault do not stop with those who undertake to use the chattel. [A restriction on the recovery by bystanders] is only the distorted shadow of a vanishing privity which is itself a reflection of the habit of viewing the problem as a commercial one between traders, rather than as part of the accident problem." (2 Harper and James, *The Law of Torts* (1956) p.1572, fn.6.)
>
> If anything, bystanders should be entitled to greater protection than the consumer or user where injury to bystanders from the defect is reasonably foreseeable. Consumers and users, at least, have the opportunity to inspect for defects and to limit their purchases to articles manufactured by reputable manufacturers and sold by reputable retailers, where as the bystander ordinarily has no such opportunities. In short, the bystander is in greater need of protection from defective products which are dangerous, and if any distinction should be made between bystanders and users, it should be made, contrary to the position of defendants, to extend greater liability in favor of the bystanders.
>
> An automobile with a defectively connected drive shaft constitutes a substantial hazard on the highway not only to the driver and passenger of the car but also to pedestrians and other drivers. The public policy which protects the driver and passenger of the car should also protect the bystander, and where a driver or passenger of another car is injured due to defects in the manufacture of an automobile and without any fault of their own, they may recover from the manufacturer of the defective automobile.

Id. at 88-89. Can the idea of a negligence/warranty hybrid, pioneered in *Greenman* by Traynor (who signed on to *Elmore*) bear the weight put on it by *Elmore*? Is the *Elmore* court on solid ground when it states that, as compared to a product user, a bystander is likely to be more vulnerable and in greater need of the protection afforded by the deterrence effects of liability and by an available deep pocket? Is it important that a bystander, unlike a purchaser or user of the product, does not even benefit from the product, or from the lower cost that might be associated with a less safe product?

Those jurisdictions that have directly addressed the *Elmore* question overwhelmingly have permitted bystanders to recover on a products liability theory, for reasons similar to those articulated by the court. On this question, courts seem to maintain a sense—one that traces back to *MacPherson*—that any vestiges of the old privity doctrine must be eliminated.

8. Restatement (Second) Section 402A. In 1965, on the heels of *Greenman*, the American Law Institute added a new section to the Second Restatement of Torts that endorsed recognition of a distinct cause of action for injuries caused by defective products. This provision—Section 402A—proved to be extraordinarily influential. During the 1960s and 1970s, state courts overwhelmingly adopted some variant of Section 402A either judicially or legislatively. Indeed, it is fair to say that, at least for the period from 1965 to 2000, Section 402A set the terms of analysis in product liability cases. Its "black letter" reads as follows:

§ 402A Special Liability of Seller of Product for Physical Harm to User or Consumer

(1) One who sells any product in a defective condition unreasonably dangerous to the user or consumer or to his property is subject to liability for physical harm thereby caused to the ultimate user or consumer, or to his property, if

(a) the seller is engaged in the business of selling such a product, and

(b) it is expected to and does reach the user or consumer without substantial change in the condition in which it is sold.

(2) The rule stated in Subsection (1) applies although

(a) the seller has exercised all possible care in the preparation and sale of his product, and

(b) the user or consumer has not bought the product from or entered into any contractual relation with the seller.

As will become apparent in several decisions reproduced below, this text was accompanied by substantial commentary from the Reporter, William Prosser, that addressed an array of issues and that provided a fairly detailed legal framework for treatment of products liability actions. Still, the fact that Section 402A's adoption occurred just at the time that products liability law was getting underway helped to render it influential, but also meant that it could not help but fail to anticipate and provide guidance on important developments in the field. For this reason, the courts and legislatures that adopted Section 402A have also embellished and revised it.

9. *The Third Restatement of Torts.* In 1998, the ALI published a new set of provisions on products liability as one part of the Third Restatement of Torts, an ongoing project that is being completed in phases. Some states have adopted some of these provisions, while others have declined to do so. As is discussed in greater detail below, the Third Restatement's products liability provisions expand on and depart from Section 402A of the Second Restatement in certain ways. Its most basic provision, however, reaffirms the idea that a commercial seller is subject to liability for causing injury through the sale of a defective product.

§ 1. Liability of Commercial Seller or Distributor for Harm Caused by Defective Products

One engaged in the business of selling or otherwise distributing products who sells or distributes a defective product is subject to liability for harm to persons or property caused by the defect.

Restatement (Third) of Torts: Products Liability § 1 (1998).

II. BASICS OF A PRODUCTS LIABILITY CLAIM

Neither the Second nor the Third Restatement expressly breaks down products liability claims by reference to the elements that constitute a prima facie case. Some jurisdictions offer such formulations, but these vary, at least superficially. We offer the following reconstruction of the elements of a products liability claim as an aid to analysis, not as an effort to mimic standard judicial usage:

Products Liability: Prima Facie Case

Actor *A* is subject to liability to person *P* in products liability if:

1. *P* has suffered an *injury;*
2. *A sold* a *product;*
3. *A* is a commercial *seller of such products;*
4. at the time it was sold by *A*, the product was in a *defective condition;* and
5. the defect functioned as an actual and proximate *cause* of *P*'s injury

It may be instructive to compare this list of elements to the elements of a prima facie case of negligence. The injury and causation elements—1 and 5, respectively—are plainly parallel to those of negligence. These concepts are examined later in the chapter. Nominally, at least, the duty and the breach elements are also plainly absent. In their place, we see three new elements: (2) the sale of a product; (3) by a seller; (4) in a defective condition.

A. What Counts as an Injury?

Before turning to consider the doctrinally novel aspects of products liability causes of action, it is worth pausing to emphasize an obvious point that might nonetheless cause confusion if ignored. When complainants file products liability actions, they overwhelmingly do so to obtain redress for physical harm caused by product defects. This pattern is not entirely coincidental. As a rough-and-ready rule, products liability doctrine, like negligence law, is much more reticent in recognizing claims for other sorts of injuries allegedly flowing from product defects, such as intangible economic loss.

A particularly important question as to the injury element concerns whether the owner of a product can invoke products liability law to recover for a defect that causes damage to, or the destruction of, the *product itself.* The general rule, subject to exceptions that vary by jurisdiction, is that the owner cannot, and is instead left to the protections he was able to obtain in the contract of sale via express or implied warranties. This is sometimes dubbed the "economic loss" rule. *See, e.g.,* East River S.S. Corp. v. Transamerica Delaval, Inc., 476 U.S. 858 (1986) (shipowner complaining of damage to turbines caused by a defect in them must proceed in contract rather than admiralty/tort). By contrast, tangible property damage caused by a product defect to property *other than the product itself* is ordinarily actionable in products liability.

Thus, a consumer injured by a defective lawnmower purchased at a local hardware store can sue the store under a products liability theory because it sold the lawnmower. That consumer can also sue the manufacturer of the lawnmower, who likely sold the lawnmower either directly to the local hardware store or through a distributor or distributors. If it was through distributors, the distributors are also "sellers" subject to products liability law. Indeed, while we normally think of the classic antecedents of products liability as eliminating privity, it is important to see that products liability law creates causes of action against various actors within a distributive chain. *See generally* Restatement (Third) of Torts: Products Liability § 20 ("Definition of 'One Who Sells or Otherwise Distributes'") (1998).

1. *Sellers and Strict Liability.* Because products liability applies to sellers, it often attaches liability to a person or entity that played no role in the design, manufacture, or inspection of the product. For this reason alone, many successful products liability actions really do impose a form of liability without fault. The Ford dealer who sells a new model of car with a flaw in the design of the transmission system will be held liable if the jury finds the car defective (and that the defect proximately caused harm to a victim). Whether the dealer knew or could have known of the flaw, was entitled to rely on Ford's general reputation for quality, or had any ability to inspect or test the model for defects, is irrelevant. As we will see, liability for defectively designed products also attaches to manufacturers. But when it does, it is not as obviously a form of liability without fault, if it is that at all. Indeed, the issue of the "strictness" of liability for design defects is the subject of intensive debate. Yet for large numbers of bread-and-butter cases in which sellers have little or no direct control over product quality, the phrase "strict liability" fits well. (Perhaps unsurprisingly, trade groups comprised of retailers have recently achieved some success obtaining legislative reforms that scale back their liability under such circumstances.)

2. *Sellers and the Law of Warranty.* Because of the fact that liability is placed on *sellers*, products liability law has an enduring — and often legally important — relation to contract law and other forms of commercial law. Several states in fact locate their products liability law, in part, within their versions of the Uniform Commercial Code (UCC). Even those few jurisdictions that lack a tort of strict products liability have fairly close analogues within their contract law. *See, e.g.*, N.C.G.S. § 25-2-314 (implied warranty of merchantability attaches to products). In addition, many states have overlapping statutory law that provides what are essentially products liability actions under consumer protection laws or deceptive trade practices statutes. Such laws provided much of the impetus for state-government initiated tobacco products liability litigation that took place in the 1990s.

3. *Distribution Chains and Indemnification.* Distribution chains are often long, wide, and complicated by a variety of legal and commercial variables. For example, suppose a McDonald's franchise in a town in Illinois sells a "Happy Meal" to a family with a small child, and a component of the toy that comes with the Happy Meal injures the child. The distributional chain might include the franchise, McDonald's, the distributor that sold the toy to McDonald's, the manufacturer of the toy, and the

manufacturer of the component of the toy that injured the child. There likely will be contracts among these companies that include indemnification clauses—provisions that permit one to sue another to recover costs expended in litigation and liability for injuries stemming from the products supplied. In fact, the capacity for members of such a distributive chain to insure themselves, and to negotiate with one another over indemnification, is among the reasons that our system does not consider strict liability for (not-at-fault) sellers to be inherently inequitable.

4. *Sellers, Not Buyers.* Early in Chapter 2 we saw that, thanks to decisions such as *MacPherson*, negligence law permits not just buyers of products, but also users of products, to sue sellers in negligence for product-related injuries. Products liability applies at least as broadly. Thus, despite its emphasis on "sellers," products liability law *does not* require the plaintiff to be a buyer of the product. Indeed, as indicated by *Elmore* (discussed in Note 7 following *Greenman*), the plaintiff need not even be a *user* of the product; a bystander who is struck by a car because of a defect in the car is eligible to invoke products liability law. On this issue, jurisdictions tend to speak in the language of "easy duty" negligence cases, requiring only that the plaintiff be within a class of persons foreseeably put at risk of physical harm by the defective product.

5. *In the Business of.* A person or entity who sells a product does not automatically qualify as a "seller" of that product for purposes of products liability law. She must also be "in the business of selling (or marketing)" such products. Thus, a lawyer who contracts to purchase a new car, but then contracts to sell it to his neighbor before ever using it, would not qualify as a "seller" for products liability law. Similarly, the owner of pizza parlor that sells a car that she had just purchased and had never used would not count as a "seller" of the car (although, of course, she would count as a seller of pizzas and soft drinks).

6. *What Constitutes Selling.* It is enough to establish that an actor has "sold" a product if the actor took steps to place the product on the market or figured in the distributional chain through which the product is placed on the market. Thus, a sale can occur even if the actor did not transfer legal title to the product and even if he did not enter a bargain in which ownership was transferred for consideration. So, for example, an automobile company or dealer cannot avoid products liability law by leasing the product rather than by selling it. Likewise, a distributor cannot avoid products liability law by organizing its transactions so that it never actually holds title to the products. Courts will look to the underlying reality of the transaction and ask whether the defendant has placed the product in the stream of commerce. *See, e.g.*, Baker v. Promack Prods. West, Inc., 692 S.W.2d 844 (Tenn. 1985) (applying strict liability to lessors).

Similarly, an actual transfer or sale is not necessary to trigger products liability law, if the nature of the plaintiff's contact with the product is sufficiently close to the normal domain of the marketplace. Thus, just as a shopping mall owner would be liable to a visitor injured by an unsafe condition in the mall under an "invitee" theory even if the plaintiff did not actually come to the mall with the intention of purchasing anything, so a car manufacturer would be liable under a products liability theory for a plaintiff injured by a defect in a "demonstrator" car or a "loaner" — actual sale or transfer is not necessary.

7. *Time of Sale Versus Time of Accident.* As noted above, the inquiry into a product's defectiveness focuses on the condition of the product at the time it leaves the defendant's control. Under common law strict products liability rules, the fact that the product was resold prior to causing an injury does not of itself defeat liability. However, as indicated in Chapter 7, certain products benefit from legislatively enacted statutes of repose that block liability for injuries caused by a defective product on account of the product's age.

8. *Sales Versus Service.* In a number of contexts, a business or professional engaged in a service will utilize or sell a product to a consumer as part of the service. For example, a surgeon who inserts a plastic hip joint into a patient in a meaningful sense delivers the hip joint to the patient. Still, as noted above, if the courts deem the defendant to be engaged primarily in a service, rather than a sale, they will not treat the defendant as a seller of the product for products liability law. *See, e.g.*, Ayyash v. Henry Ford Health Sys., 533 N.W.2d 353 (Mich. App. 1995) (declining to apply strict products liability law to a hospital that implanted a defective jaw implant and relying upon the sales/service distinction), *app. denied*, 549 N.W.2d 561 (Mich. 1996).

9. *Component Parts.* If a component part — such as a bicycle tire — is defective, and because of the defect the larger product of which it is a part injures the plaintiff, the seller and manufacturer of the component part will be liable. However, there are numerous cases in which the component manufacturer is able to demonstrate that there was nothing intrinsically defective in *its* product; the problem was simply that the larger product did not function optimally with that particular component — for example, the bicycle manufacturer should have chosen a different wheel rim to match the tire in question. The component part manufacturer or supplier in this setting frequently will avoid liability. *See, e.g.*, Artiglio v. General Elec. Co., 71 Cal. Rptr. 2d 817 (Cal. App. 1998) (manufacturer of silicone for silicone breast implants not subject to strict liability for defective breast implants); In re TMJ Implants Prods. Liab. Litig., 97 F.3d 1050 (8th Cir. 1996) (limiting liability of suppliers of Teflon to be used in jaw implants). However, when the plaintiff is able to establish that defendant had an ongoing relationship with the manufacturer of the larger part, and/or the defendant had adequate awareness of and involvement with the design or manufacture of the product in which its part was being integrated, the question of whether the component manufacturer will face liability becomes much closer. *See* Restatement (Third), *supra*, § 5(b) (a seller or distributor of a component may be liable if it "substantially participates in the integration of the component into the design of the product" and "the integration of the component causes the product to be defective").

10. *Liability for Injuries Caused by Replacement Parts.* The California Supreme Court rejected an aggressive version of the converse argument in *O'Neil v. Crane Co.*, 266 P.3d 987 (Cal. 2012). There, plaintiffs who had been injured by asbestos gaskets and pump linings sued the manufacturer of the pumps and valves containing those products. However, because the defendant did not manufacture the linings or gaskets

(which were replacements of earlier parts), did not place those components within its own products, and did not have any causal connection with them, the Court held it could not be held liable for injuries caused by them, even if it may have been foreseeable that asbestos-laden gaskets and linings manufactured by others would be used in conjunction with its own products.

D. The Key to Products Liability: Defect

Products liability is "strict" in the sense of focusing on the condition of the product at the time of sale, rather than focusing on the prudence with which the seller acted. But it is not "absolute." A commercial seller is not subject to liability merely because its product injures someone. In addition, the injury must have been caused by a defect in the product that existed at the time of sale or marketing. The legal definition of "defect" (or "defectiveness") is thus at the center of this branch of tort law.

The centrality of the concept of defect notwithstanding, the California Supreme Court in its 1972 decision in *Cronin v. J.B.E. Olson Corp.*, 501 P.2d 1153, refused to define the term "defective." Instead, *Cronin* held that jurors should determine whether a product was defective without any instruction from trial courts identifying or organizing the considerations that might be relevant to that determination.

This aspect of *Cronin* proved short-lived. U.S. courts, including the California Supreme Court, have since identified three different categories of defect: *manufacturing defects, design defects*, and *warning (or instructional) defects*. In addition, at least with respect to two of these categories—design defect and failure to warn—they have since adopted one or more tests for determining what constitutes a defect. In the remainder of this section, we will outline in a rough way the main differences among the three categories. The next section discusses at some length the different ways in which post-*Cronin* courts have sought to define the idea of a "design defect."

Manufacturing Defect

A particular product (e.g., Ms. Smith's 2011 Toyota Camry) has a manufacturing defect if it diverges from the manufacturer's own specifications for the product. *Escola*'s flawed soda bottle is a good example of a manufacturing defect: Coca-Cola designed and filled its bottles in a manner designed to *prevent* them from exploding; the bottle that injured Escola contained a flaw that it was not supposed to contain. Although the phrase "manufacturing defect" appropriately calls to mind an isolated "lemon" that comes off the assembly line in a substandard condition, it can apply more broadly. Thus, an item need not be mass-produced to count as a product with a manufacturing defect. "Jean-Claude's Frozen Quiches" might be prepared lovingly and individually in Jean-Claude's small bakery, but if one of his pies contains a metal pin, it would still count as a product with a manufacturing defect. Second, the defect will be charged to the manufacturer so long as it emerges while the product is in its control or possession. If an automobile suffers a bent axle as it is being rolled off the manufacturer's car carrier and onto the dealer's lot, it will be deemed to have a manufacturing defect even though the problem developed after the product was assembled.

Design Defect

In contrast to manufacturing defects, design defects inhere in an entire line of products. The idea is that there is a flaw in the plan or specifications for the product. The flaw (or flaws) alleged may be small or technical, or may go to the essence of the product. Thus, for example, the allegation in *Greenman* that the set screws were too small to hold certain items in the Shopsmith was an allegation of a somewhat technical design defect. By contrast, one of the central allegations in litigation over surgical gloves made of latex is that the very idea of using latex as the primary material for such gloves is unacceptably risky given the severe allergic responses that some persons exposed to latex may suffer. This too is a design defect claim. There are many levels in between these two extremes. Plaintiffs commonly assert several design defects or several reasons that together support the finding of design defect.

The issue of what criteria should be used by the factfinder to ascertain whether a design is defective is probably the most controversial and hotly debated question within products liability doctrine. Indeed, the next section is devoted almost entirely to this question. But several factors tend to play at least some role in most or all jurisdictions. These include: the significance of the risks of physical injury posed by the particular design; how ordinary consumers would expect the product to function; and whether there is a feasible, safer, and affordable alternative design. The task of fashioning these and other factors into an operative legal test has turned out to be a singularly important question in products liability law, with California and the American Law Institute playing leading roles in the debate.

Failure to Warn or Instruct

The term *defect* and the phrase "defective condition" are well suited to the sort of flaw found in an exploding bottle or a power tool built with screws that are too small to render it safe for normal use. The same cannot be said of the phrases "warning defects" or "failure to warn." Nonetheless, these phrases are used in the law to describe a distinct category of product defect. A product is defective for failure to warn when safety requires that the product be sold with a warning but the product is sold without a warning (or without an adequate warning). A mislabeled product—paint thinner labeled as vodka, for example—would count as a product that is defective because of its misrepresentation as to the contents of the bottle. So, too, would a bottle of medication that is accompanied by dosage instructions incorrectly directing the user to consume an amount that is ten times larger than the proper dosage. Another classic failure to warn case might involve a microwave oven that fails to warn that heating metal objects inside it can cause an explosion or a fire. In all these cases, there is some information, instruction or warning (different from any information, instruction or warning that was actually provided) that should have been included, and was not. The "defect" is the omission of the language.

Despite the fact that the word "defect" applies awkwardly to these cases, failure to warn claims are as firmly grounded in the law of products liability as are claims for manufacturing and design defects. As such, they generally require proof of the same basic elements as these other claims, are subject to the same defenses, and extend to the same sorts of actors. Moreover, as with manufacturing and design defects, one focuses on the product as sold or distributed, not on the conduct of the defendant. Failure to warn is examined in Section IV of this chapter.

The tripartite division among kinds of defect has become a central feature of U.S. products liability law, and it is a goal of this chapter to clarify these divisions. Nevertheless, it is worth keeping in mind that the early products liability cases that you read in Section I of this chapter drew no such divisions, and that U.S. products liability law did not generally do so until the 1970s. Likewise, products liability law in other nations does not necessarily utilize these categories. Thus, even though these categorizations will and should become part of your thinking about products liability law, one should keep in mind that they are no less a doctrinal construction than the various doctrines encountered in the law of negligence and battery, and that there are other ways to "slice the bologna."

In real-world products liability cases, it is common for a plaintiff to assert claims that fall within two or all three of the foregoing categories. Part of the skill involved in lawyering these cases involves selecting a plausible categorization, or refuting such a selection. The following case presents allegations and discussions of all three types of defect. The notes that follow provide greater detail on manufacturing defects (and other issues that arise in the case). Sections III and IV of this chapter provide greater detail on design defects and failure to warn.

Gower v. Savage Arms, Inc.

166 F. Supp. 2d 240 (E.D. Pa. 2001)

McLaughlin, J. The plaintiffs, John and Debra Gower, seek to hold Savage Arms, Inc. and Savage Sports Corporation liable . . . under a theory of "successor liability" for injuries John Gower sustained when his hunting rifle discharged inadvertently, shooting him in the foot. Gower alleges that the rifle was defective as follows. First, it was designed so that it could not be unloaded with the safety engaged (the "unloading defect"). Second, it was designed without a detent system, which would have made the safety mechanism more user-friendly ("the detent defect"). Third, it was manufactured with a metal ridge that impaired the functioning of the safety mechanism (the "manufacturing defect"). Fourth, it was not accompanied by adequate warnings. . . .

The Court grants the defendants' motion with respect to . . . the "unloading defect" [and] insufficient warnings, claims. The Court denies the defendants' motion for summary judgment with respect to successor liability. The Court further denies the defendants' motion for summary judgment with respect to the strict liability claims concerning the "detent defect" and the manufacturing defect . . . without prejudice to renew these arguments after the Court has reached a decision on the pending motion to exclude the testimony of plaintiffs' expert, James Mason.

I. Facts in the Light Most Favorable to the Plaintiffs

A. The Incident

The plaintiffs claim damages for injuries sustained in a hunting accident in 1997. On December 15, 1997, John Gower was hunting with his two brothers, Clark and Craig, and with his brother-in-law, Robert Swan, at Long Pond, Pennsylvania. They spent much of the day hunting for deer in the woods. At approximately 4:30 p.m., after a

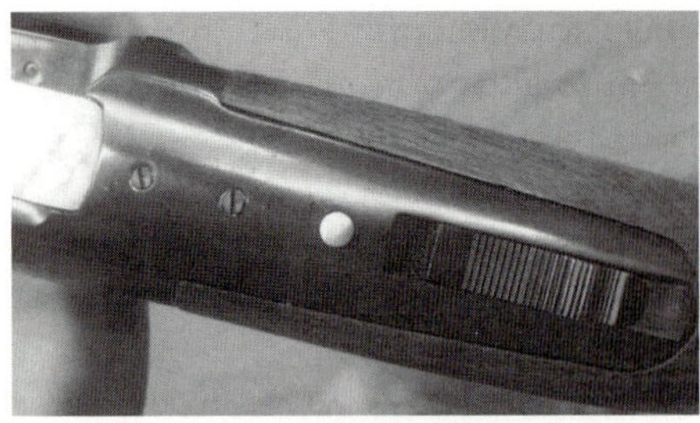

Safety Mechanism on Savage 99C Lever Action Rifle (viewed from above)

day of hunting, the plaintiff left the woods and headed toward the truck in which they had driven to Long Pond. As he emerged from the woods, he turned around for one more visual sweep of the woods and field. Gower was preparing to unload his gun when the gun discharged, shooting him in the foot.

Gower was wearing thick gloves, and his fingers were inside the trigger guard when the gun discharged. At the time of the discharge the plaintiff had not taken the gun off the "safe" position. The rifle was designed so as not to fire when in the "safe" position.

B. The Rifle

The rifle at issue in this lawsuit is a Savage Model 99C lever action repeating center fire rifle, serial number E850706. It was manufactured in or around 1987 by Savage Industries, Inc. The plaintiff, John Gower, purchased the rifle in October, 1989 from the Quarry Sporting Goods Store. . . .

According to the uncontradicted testimony of Savage Industries' Inspections Supervisor Mark Kwiecien, who is now a Quality Assurance Coordinator for Savage Arms, all guns shipped out by Savage Industries in 1987 were shipped in boxes containing safety manuals. It is also uncontradicted that John Gower purchased the gun without its box and did not receive a safety manual with the gun. As confirmed by expert inspections after the incident and conceded by both parties at oral argument, the rifle was not working properly at the time of the accident. The safety mechanism could only be placed in the "safe" position with more than the usually required force.

C. Corporate History

The rifle at issue in this law-suit was manufactured by Savage Industries, Inc. in 1987. In February 1988, Savage Industries filed for bankruptcy. Around this time, the owners of Savage Industries set up a company, named Savage Arms. In May, 1989 Savage Industries filed a motion in Bankruptcy Court to sell its remaining assets. In July of 1989, Savage Industries sold four of its eleven product lines, including the Model 99 product line, together with associated tooling, machinery, trademarks, trade-names, patents, trade secrets, and goodwill, to Savage Arms.

[Although successor companies are sometimes not obligated for torts committed by their predecessors, the court held that a jury could find, under a doctrine called the "product line" exception, that Savage Arms was liable for injuries caused by a defective rifle manufactured by Savage Industries, Inc. — Eds.] . . .

. . . .

III. Discussion

. . . .

C. Strict Liability

The Pennsylvania Supreme Court has adopted Section 402A of the Restatement (Second) of Torts. . . . In order to succeed in a claim brought under 402A, the plaintiffs must show (1) that the product was defective, (2) that the defect existed at the time the product left the manufacturer's hands, and (3) that the defect caused the plaintiff's injury.

1. The Alleged Defects

The plaintiffs allege the following four defects: (1) the gun was not accompanied by warnings; (2) the gun was defectively designed in that it cannot be unloaded while in the "safe" position (the "unloading defect"); (3) the gun was defectively designed in that it did not incorporate a detent system, which would have made the safety mechanism more "user-friendly" (the "detent defect"); and (4) the gun was defectively manufactured with a metal ridge that caused the gun's safety mechanism to fail over time (the "manufacturing defect").

a. Insufficient Warnings

The Pennsylvania courts have recognized a cause of action under [Restatement (Second) §] 402A for insufficient warnings. For an insufficient warnings claim, the plaintiffs must establish the same three elements required under 402A for design defect claims, including causation.

The Court grants the defendant's motion for summary judgment with respect to the plaintiffs' insufficient warnings claim, because the plaintiffs have failed to present any evidence that the lack of instructions caused Gower's injury. In Sherk v. Daisy-Heddon, 498 Pa. 594, 450 A.2d 615 (1982), the Court held that the manufacturer of a BB gun was not liable for injuries sustained when the plaintiff fired the gun at a friend:

> Where, as here, the lethal propensity of a gun was known or should have been known to the user, liability cannot be imposed upon the manufacturer merely because the manufacturer allegedly has failed to warn of that propensity.

Id. at 618. The Court reasoned that insufficient warnings could not be the cause of the injury, because the plaintiff had independent knowledge of the gun's dangerous propensities.

John Gower had extensive training in the use and safety of firearms while in the United States military. In his deposition, John Gower testified that he was familiar with the Ten Commandments of Firearm Safety, one of which states: "Never point your gun at anything you don't want to shoot." Gower also testified that he made a practice of complying with the No. 1 Commandment, which reads: "Don't rely on your gun's safety. Treat every gun as if it were loaded and ready to fire." The Court finds that Gower was aware of the dangers inherent in the use of a gun and that the holding of *Sherk* is applicable.

In addition, the plaintiffs have not provided any evidence that the gun was lacking instructions when it left the manufacturer's hands. Mark Kwiecien has testified that every rifle left the manufacturing plant with a manual. Gower has testified that he did not receive a manual when he purchased the gun from Quarry Sporting Goods off the rack (i.e. not in its original box). Gower has not produced any evidence, however, to contradict Kwiecien's statement that all guns were shipped with manuals. According to comment "n" to Section 388 of the Restatement (Second) of Torts, a supplier's duty to warn is discharged by providing information to third parties upon whom it can reasonably rely to communicate the information to the ultimate users of the product. . . .

b. *The "Unloading Defect"*

The plaintiffs allege that the Model 99 rifle is defectively designed in that the shooter must take the firearm off safety in order to unload the chamber. John Gower claims not to have been unloading the gun when it discharged, however. Therefore, the fact that the gun could not be unloaded while in the "safe" position is not causally related to Gower's injury. . . .

c. *The "Detent Defect"*

The plaintiffs' expert, James Mason, alleges that "lack of positive detents on the safety slide will leave an operator with the impression that the safety is 'on' when indeed the gun is ready to fire." According to James Mason's expert report, a safety mechanism with a detent system would make it easier for a user to tell whether the safety had been engaged, because the position of the safety would be more clearly visible and because the mechanism would make an audible clicking noise when placed into the "safe" position. A detent system would also prevent the safety from slipping into the "fire" position.

[The only evidence before the court on the issue of a defect in the design of the gun was the report of plaintiff's expert.] The Court notes that, in his report, James Mason described the "exemplar trigger system" as "adequate" and found only that the detent would make the rifle more "user friendly." On this basis, it seems unlikely that Mason's report would support a finding that the gun without the detent is [defective in design]. Nonetheless, the Court declines to rest its decision on this basis for two reasons.

First, the defendant, who bears the burden of proof for this threshold determination as to whether the product is [defective in design] has provided no evidence that would enable the Court to make this determination.

Second, the Court is unwilling to rely solely on Mason's report in making this determination without first deciding the defendants' pending *Daubert* motion regarding Mason. Mason's report does not clearly distinguish between the "detent defect" and the "manufacturing defect" or between the factual bases for his views on either one. Due to this lack of clarity in the writing of the report, the Court is unwilling to make a decision at this stage without holding a hearing in which Mason can more clearly explain the bases for and the meaning of his report. . . .

The Court, therefore, denies the defendant's summary judgment motion with respect to the "detent defect" claim without prejudice to the defendant to renew the motion after the Court's decision on the *Daubert* motion.

d. *The "Manufacturing Defect"*

The plaintiffs allege that there was a manufacturing defect in the rifle in the form of a metal ridge that affected the functioning of the safety mechanism:

> The subject safety button has a shallow ridge on the bottom of its rear radius that contacts the rising radius of the slot. This contact limits (to about .133-inch) the free, unobstructed movement of the button to the rear when applying the safety. This defective condition was present at the time of manufacture.

For purposes of summary judgment, the question of whether the ridge rendered the gun defective is not difficult to answer. In Dambacher v. Mallis, 336 Pa. Super. 22, 485 A.2d 408 (1984), the court stated: "In a manufacturing defect case, the question whether the product is defective is relatively simple. Since the allegation is that something went awry in the manufacturing process, so that, for example, the product lacked a component it should have had, the finder of fact need only compare the product that caused the injury with other products that were manufactured according to specifications." *Id.* at 426. Mason undertook such a comparison and found that the subject rifle had the above-mentioned metal ridge, whereas an exemplar rifle of the same model did not.

. . . For the above reason, the Court denies the defendant's summary judgment motion with respect to the "manufacturing defect" claim without prejudice to the defendant to renew the motion after the Court's decision on the *Daubert* motion.

. . . .

NOTES AND QUESTIONS

1. *Gower's Subsequent History.* A subsequent unpublished opinion reveals later developments in *Gower.* As the court anticipated, the testimony of Mason, plaintiff's expert witness on the issue of design defect, was deemed inadmissible, and summary judgment was granted on the design defect claim. For this and other reasons the only issue left for trial was Gower's manufacturing defect claim.

2. *Proving Manufacturing Defect.* Fortunately for Gower, he appears to have faced a relatively straightforward task in proving that the gun contained a manufacturing defect. The dangerous feature of the rifle was visually identified by an expert, and the demonstration that it was a manufacturing defect was accomplished by comparing it to a prototype in which the defective feature did not exist. Proving a manufacturing defect is often not so easy, as the plaintiff in *Escola* learned. (Recall that she was unable to prove what went wrong with the bottle.) This helps explain why Escola's lawyer was drawn to *res ipsa loquitur,* as was the majority of the California Supreme Court.

Does the advent of strict liability eliminate the need for a doctrine like *res ipsa?* The short answer is no. While the concept of manufacturing defect eliminates the need to identify unreasonable conduct on the part of the defendant, it substitutes its own question: What exactly was defective about the product? Particularly in cases in which the harmful product has been severely damaged or destroyed or is missing, proof problems can be daunting. In such cases, products liability plaintiffs, in a manner akin to negligence plaintiffs who benefit from *res ipsa loquitur,* will usually be given a fair bit of leeway to rely on circumstantial evidence to prove the existence of a manufacturing defect, as Section 3 of the Restatement (Third)'s provisions on products liability indicates:

> **§ 3. Circumstantial Evidence Supporting Inference of Product Defect**
>
> It may be inferred that the harm sustained by the plaintiff was caused by a product defect existing at the time of sale or distribution, without proof of a specific defect, when the incident that harmed the plaintiff:

(a) was of a kind that ordinarily occurs as a result of a product defect; and

(b) was not, in the particular case, solely the result of causes other than product defect existing at the time of sale or distribution.

The Reporters note that Section 3 will most commonly apply to claims of manufacturing defect rather than design defect or failure to warn. *Compare* Speller v. Sears, Roebuck & Co., 790 N.E.2d 252 (N.Y. 2003) (permitting plaintiffs alleging that a wiring defect in a refrigerator manufactured by the defendant caused a fire that killed their decedent to prove both defect and causation by circumstantial evidence) *with* Myrlak v. Port Auth. of N.Y. & N.J., 723 A.2d 45 (N.J. 1999) (declining to apply Section 3 to a suit alleging injuries caused by defectively manufactured chair).

3. *Time of Sale.* A critical issue raised by Gower's manufacturing defect claim was whether the defect existed at the time of sale. The plaintiff, of course, alleged that the "ridge" that limited the movement of the safety button was present at that time, whereas the defendants argued that it was not. Normally, it is the plaintiff's burden to prove that the defect existed at the time of sale. However, this factual issue is so important and so often closely argued that several jurisdictions have passed legislation that set forth specific burdens of proof and production on this timing issue. Note that, as to the warning defect, the defendants were able successfully to argue that the "defect" (assuming there was one) did not exist at the time of sale.

4. *Actual and Proximate Causation.* As *Gower* suggests, actual causation is as central to products liability claims as it is to negligence claims. As in negligence cases, actual causation issues in products liability cases are ordinarily determined using the but-for test and raise the same fact-intensive issues for the factfinder. However, just as certain negligence cases such as *Summers v. Tice* (Chapter 4) have posed conceptually difficult issues pertaining to actual causation, certain "cutting-edge" causation doctrines have also developed primarily within products liability law. One such example is *market share liability*, adopted by the California Supreme Court for cases involving injuries caused by the drug DES in *Sindell v. Abbott Labs* (Chapter 4).

Moreover, as in negligence, the issue of proof of causation can, in certain kinds of products liability cases, be quite difficult. Indeed, as noted in Chapter 4, the field of "toxic torts"—which mainly involves products liability claims—has required lawyers to master complex bodies of evidence involving epidemiological studies and the use of statistics, and has pushed courts and scholars to refine tort principles and doctrines so as to arrive at satisfactory rules for proof of causation. The significance of these issues of proof of causation to modern negligence law, and by implication to modern products liability law, is attested to by the careful and elaborate attention devoted to them in the Third Torts Restatement. *See* Restatement (Third) of Torts: Liability for Physical and Emotional Harm § 28, cmt. c (2010). Discussion of the U.S. Supreme Court's decisions in the *Daubert* and *Metro-North* cases—*see* Chapter 13—provides occasion to examine these issues in greater depth.

Proximate cause principles comparable to those that apply in negligence are also applied by courts to products liability claims. Thus, certain injuries caused only fortuitously by a product defect will fail for lack of proximate cause. Indeed, the New York Court of Appeals' *Ventricelli* decision (discussed in Note 2 following *Jolley* in Chapter 5)—which declined to impose liability for injuries caused to the driver of a rental car with a defective trunk lid on proximate cause grounds—involved a products liability claim. The doctrine of superseding cause also is recognized in products liability cases. Suppose *V* is injured only because *T*, out of a desire to injure *V*, tricks *V* into driving a new car with brakes that *T* knows to be defective. In a products liability suit by *V* against *M*, the manufacturer, *M* could argue the issue of superseding cause to the jury.

5. *Loss of Consortium.* An omitted portion of *Gower* addressed the issue of whether the plaintiff's wife could proceed with a loss of consortium claim derivative of Gower's underlying products liability claim. As a general rule, such claims stand on the same footing in products liability actions as they do in negligence actions. Similarly, if a defective product proximately causes a death, it will give rise to a survival action on behalf of the decedent and a wrongful death on behalf of statutory beneficiaries such as immediate family members under the same terms as if the death had been caused by negligence. *See* Chapter 6.

6. *Successor Liability.* The specter of successor liability for "product lines" is obviously important for litigators representing plaintiffs or defendants in products liability actions. But it is also important for corporate lawyers contemplating the possible merger of two business entities, or the sale or purchase of a product line. Detailed doctrine exists both in and out of products liability law regarding when a successor corporation may be held liable for the predecessor corporation's torts. As *Gower* indicates, because of the "product line" doctrine, causes of action sounding in products liability enjoy a unique ability to prevail as against successor entities. Why should products liability law—which is generally less forgiving of defendants in its standards of liability—also have the capacity to stretch beyond sellers to product line owners? Is this a logical extension of products liability doctrine, or counterintuitive?

7. *Other Causes of Action.* The fact that products liability claims are recognized for personal injury actions based on product dangers does not mean that they are the only causes of action a plaintiff can or will bring in such actions. Instead, the victim's lawyer is likely to file a complaint that might include causes of action for negligence, breach of implied warranty, breach of express warranty, and misrepresentation, as well as applicable state and federal statutory claims. Before learning what facts the defendant will allege and what defenses he will assert, the plaintiff will want to be in the best position possible to sustain her lawsuit by diversifying the causes of action on which she will rely, subject to the (minimal) requirement that each has a colorable basis given her attorney's diligent (if early) review of the facts.

8. *Relationship to Negligence.* Given the resemblance of a negligence complaint such as MacPherson's against Buick to a products liability claim of the sort raised by Gower, it is likely that many, if not most, complaints containing products liability

claims will also include claims for negligence in the design and/or manufacture of the product and for negligent failure to warn. It is natural to wonder whether these two sets of claims are essentially redundant, a problem felt particularly keenly with respect to design defect claims, in which the standard for defect sometimes closely resembles negligence law's reasonable person standard.

As a matter of black letter law, the rule is that these two bodies of law describe distinct causes of action. However, to the extent a plaintiff can recover in products liability for injuries caused by a defective product, he cannot recover again for the same injuries caused by the same product in negligence. Moreover, as was emphasized by Justice Traynor's *Escola* and *Greenman* opinions, products liability law in principle ought to free plaintiffs from relying on negligence by removing the burden of having to prove lack of reasonable care. The extent to which the shift to products liability has actually opened up a wider swath of liability than would have existed under a continuing regime of negligence law is very difficult to assess. Some lawyers and jurists have argued that, at least at times, plaintiffs may obtain strategic advantages by framing a claim in negligence rather than in strict products liability. In particular, they suggest that by focusing the jury's attention on the issue of fault, the building of a negligence case is more likely to foster a sense among jurors that a genuine wrong has been done and that compensation is therefore owed.

Check Your Understanding

The "Strictness" of Strict Products Liability

Explain why each of the following statements is misleading:

1. Under strict products liability, a manufacturer is subject to liability for any injury caused by its product, irrespective of the care it exercised in manufacturing the product.
2. The doctrine of strict products liability subjects manufacturers to liability for injuries caused by their defective products.
3. Under strict products liability, a commercial seller is liable to persons who are injured while using its defective product.

III. DESIGN DEFECT

Although many areas of products liability have been the subject of intensive debate, the issue of how to define a "design defect" has proved to be singularly controversial. In part, the debate is political. The issue here is how easy or difficult it should be for plaintiffs to recover on a claim that a manufacturer has designed and produced a line of products with features that pose excessive risks of physical injury to product users. In equal part, it is theoretical, reflecting a significant gap left open by scholarship and judicial decisions written at the birth of products liability law. When leading figures like Justice Traynor and Prosser first fashioned the doctrine of strict products liability, they probably had foremost in mind relatively simple defects, most of which were probably *manufacturing defects*— flaws in individual products, such as the overpressured and/or weakened bottle that injured Escola, the car that veered sharply as Mrs. Henningsen drove it, or a particular pie containing a toxin or foreign object. (*Greenman*, however, probably involved what today would be deemed a claim for design defect.) Plaintiffs who recovered in such cases did so because something in one unit of a mass-produced product deviated in a dangerous way from the product's design. The question, as they saw it, was whether to permit recovery for injuries caused by a product not up to its own specifications, in the absence of any evidence that the defendant failed to use reasonable care to guard against the creation of that flaw.

While the concept of a flaw or defect is almost internally self-defining for manufacturing defects, it is not for design defects. In the former case, a reference to the manufacturer's own standards will provide the criteria for determining defectiveness; a product containing a danger that results from a departure from its intended design can be said to contain a manufacturing defect. There is no ready equivalent to this "internal" standard in the design defect context. Indeed, the very question posed by this type of case is: Should the product have been *designed* differently? For these cases, "defect" or "flaw" connotes deviation from some *external* standard(s).

As noted above, the position initially staked out by the California Supreme Court in its *Cronin* decision was to refuse to identify a standard, and instead to leave the defect issue to the discretion of the jury. *See* Cronin v. J.B.E. Olson Corp., 501 P.2d 1153 (Cal. 1972) (In Bank). Subsequent decisions, however, have rejected this approach and aspired to articulate a standard for design defect. Yet while courts and commentators in the years following *Cronin* generally agreed on the desirability of articulating *some* standard to guide thinking about what constitutes a "design defect," they have disagreed (often strenuously) over what that standard should be. As a result, one can find in case law several different and at least partially conflicting tests. These different approaches are surveyed in Section III.B, *infra*.

For now, it is enough to note that the majority of contemporary courts tend most frequently to deploy one particular test, commonly referred to as the *risk-utility* test. As discussed below, a version of this same test is also embraced by the products liability provisions of the Third Torts Restatement. The following New York decision provides an illustration of a court applying a risk-utility test to a relatively straightforward claim of design defect.

A. The Risk-Utility Test

Chow v. Reckitt & Colman, Inc.

950 N.E.2d 113 (N.Y. 2011)

Lippman, C.J. Plaintiff, Yun Tung Chow, and his wife brought this products liability action against the defendant entities responsible for the manufacture, distribution and package design of a product sold under the brand name Lewis Red Devil Lye (RDL). Defendants moved for summary judgment, and Supreme Court granted the motion.

inherent in marketing" it (*Denny v. Ford Motor Co.*, 662 N.E.2d 730[, 735] [N.Y. 1995] [internal quotation marks and citation omitted] [listing seven factors identified as relevant to the risk-utility analysis: "(1) the product's utility to the public as a whole, (2) its utility to the individual user, (3) the likelihood that the product will cause injury, (4) the availability of a safer design, (5) the possibility of designing and manufacturing the product so that it is safer but remains functional and reasonably priced, (6) the degree of awareness of the product's potential danger that can reasonably be attributed to the injured user, and (7) the manufacturer's ability to spread the cost of any safety-related design changes" (*id.*)]).

Defendants here may ultimately prevail on the merits by showing that RDL's utility outweighs its inherent danger and by demonstrating through expert testimony that it was not feasible to design a safer, similarly effective and reasonably priced alternative product. On this motion, however, merely stating in an attorney's affirmation that RDL is dangerous, that everyone knows it is dangerous, and that precise warnings of its danger were given and not followed was insufficient to entitle defendants to summary judgment as a matter of law. Defendants were required to demonstrate that RDL was reasonably safe for its intended use, but they offered no such evidence.

Accordingly, the Appellate Division order should be reversed, with costs, and the motion of defendants-respondents for summary judgment denied.

Smith, J. (concurring) (joined by Read, J.). I join the Court's unanimous opinion. I write separately to point out that our decision is the result not of the merit of plaintiff's case, but of a feature of New York procedural law.

As the Court's opinion says, the issue on plaintiffs design defect claim is whether lye is reasonably safe for its intended use. This is an issue on which plaintiff will have the burden of proof at trial . . . To do this, plaintiff will have to show that the product can be designed in such a way "that it is safer but remains functional" [*Voss*, 450 N.E.2d at 209]—i.e., that a safer version of the product would be of equivalent utility.

Here, plaintiffs tried to meet that burden in an expert's affidavit opposing defendants' summary judgment motion, but fell short. The expert proposed several products that he called "safer" alternatives to lye, but he did not show that any alternative capable of preventing plaintiff's accident would perform as well as lye at a reasonable cost. Describing his principal proposal—a 3% to 5% solution of lye—the expert admitted that it would take "somewhat longer to do the job" of unclogging drains, and did not say how much longer.

If a record identical to the present one were developed at trial, plaintiff would fail to meet his burden of proof and the court would be required to direct a verdict for defendants. One might think, therefore, that the record would entitle defendants to summary judgment. But one who thought that would be wrong under New York law, because the initial burden to make an evidentiary showing on summary judgment rests on the moving party. . . .

Thus the inadequacy of plaintiff's expert's affidavit is irrelevant here, as the Court's opinion points out, because defendants, in support of their summary judgment motion, produced no evidence of the absence of a safer but functionally equivalent alternative to lye. Defendants relied simply on a statement in an attorney's affirmation that "the product at issue . . . cannot be designed differently without making it into an entirely different product" (emphasis omitted). The burden of making the necessary evidentiary showing might not have been hard to meet: an affidavit from someone knowledgeable in the industry — either a retained expert or an employee of one of the defendants — could have done it. But the burden was not met.

The federal courts have a different rule, which would probably lead to a different result in this case. [Under that rule, the moving party can satisfy its burden by pointing out that there is absence of evidence to support the nonmoving party's case. — Eds.]. . . . If I were writing on a clean slate, I might prefer [the federal] rule to ours, but we are not, and I am not urging a change in our law. I am urging, however, that parties moving for summary judgment in the future be alert to the burden that New York law places on a moving party.

NOTES AND QUESTIONS

1. *The Wade Factors.* In *Chow*, the New York Court of Appeals quotes its own prior statements from its *Denny* decision as to the content of the risk-utility test. *Denny* in turn quoted from a famous article on design defect liability authored by John Wade, Co-Reporter on the Second Restatement of Torts. Because of their provenance, the factors mentioned in *Chow* and *Denny* are sometimes referred to as "the Wade factors." Do the Wade factors support the result in *Chow*? Why? How might the defendant have argued to the contrary?

2. *Proof of Defect and Summary Judgment.* Judge Smith's concurrence suggests that, with respect to the burden of production faced by parties moving for summary judgment, the Federal Rules of Civil Procedure are superior to New York's rules. Do you agree?

3. *Failure to Warn Versus Design Defect.* As *Gower* demonstrates, products liability claimants may pursue multiple theories of defect simultaneously. In *Chow*, the plaintiff sought to recover both on design defect and failure-to-warn theories, but the latter was rejected by the trial court at the summary judgment stage. Is it obvious from the opinion that this ruling was correct? Is there a way that Chow might have kept alive his failure-to-warn claim?

4. *Warranty and Design Defect.* The law of implied warranty served as one of the sources for modern products liability law, and it continues in some states to serve as an independent ground of liability for injuries caused by products. (*See* Note 7 following *Escola, supra.*) New York is one such state. Should Chow be permitted a separate breach of warranty action against the defendant? Does the product in question breach an implied warranty of fitness for its intended purpose? Do the answers to these questions have any bearing on whether there should be a viable design defect claim?

5. *Affirmative Defenses: Comparative Fault, Assumption of Risk, and "Product Misuse."* Chapter 7 discussed in the context of negligence law two defenses to liability based on the plaintiff's contribution to his own injuries: comparative fault (formerly contributory negligence) and implied assumption of risk. Today, comparative fault is

widely recognized as an affirmative defense to products liability claims, as is implied assumption of risk in those jurisdictions that still recognize it as a distinct defense. However, this was not always so.

Products liability emerged at a time when the plaintiff's fault, if found to have contributed to his injuries, automatically barred his negligence claim. Given the potentially drastic effects of this regime, as well as the consumer-protection rationales relied upon by the likes of Justice Traynor, it is perhaps no surprise to find that early products liability decisions declined to recognize contributory negligence as a defense. Some courts that rejected the defense maintained that the problem was not only one of politics and policy, but was also conceptual. Because products liability is *not* premised on negligence but on defect, they reasoned, there was nothing against which to compare the plaintiff's fault—the jury would be faced with the task of comparing apples and oranges.

With the shift to regimes of comparative fault, courts have revisited and, by and large, rejected the foregoing reasons against recognition of plaintiff's fault as a partial (or even complete) bar to recovery. As in negligence, the plaintiff's careless conduct must function as a cause of the accident to count as a defense. Thus, today, in most jurisdictions, if there is evidence of causally relevant unreasonable conduct on the part of the plaintiff, the jury will be asked to assign a percentage of responsibility both to the defendant and to the plaintiff. *See* Daly v. General Motors Corp., 575 P.2d 1162 (Cal. 1978); Restatement (Third) of Torts: Products Liability § 17(b) (1998) (generally applicable rules of comparative fault apply in products liability). Under the rules of *modified* comparative responsibility regimes, a plaintiff whose fault passes a certain threshold relative to the defendant's will be barred from recovering.

As discussed in Chapter 7, many courts have folded *implied* assumption of risk into the defense of comparative fault. However, some states, in reaction to worries about excessive liability and frivolous claims, have preserved or reinvigorated this traditional all-or-nothing defense. *See, e.g.*, Green v. Allendale Planting Co., 954 So. 2d 1032 (Miss. 2007) (applying a Mississippi statute that bars plaintiffs from recovering in products liability if, at the time of use, they appreciated the risks of the product that injured them). Given that a major goal of decisions such as *Henningsen* and *Greenman* was to prevent sellers from inducing consumers to waive their rights to complain about product defects that cause personal injuries, one must assume that *express* assumption of risk has little role to play in this area.

Finally, in a minority of jurisdictions, "product misuse" stands as a distinct defense unique to products liability law that serves as a complete bar to recovery. This practice is frowned upon by the Third Restatement. *See* Restatement (Third), *supra*, § 17, cmt. c ("Product misuse, alteration, and modification, whether by a third party or the plaintiff, are not discrete doctrines within products liability law.").

In *Chow*, the defendant maintained that the plaintiff was responsible for his own injuries. Assuming that, on remand, he can make out a prima facie case, should Chow's fault reduce or bar his recovery?

6. *Design Defect and Summary Judgment.* Earlier in this chapter we offered a schematic description of a products liability plaintiff's prima facie case, indicating

that the plaintiff bears the burden of persuading the factfinder that the defendant's product was defective (among other things). New York, like most states, follows this approach. In *Chow*, however, the New York Court of Appeals requires a defendant seeking summary judgment to make a "showing that [its product's] utility outweighs its inherent danger and [demonstrating] through expert testimony that it was not feasible to design a safer, similarly effective and reasonably priced alternative product." Is it fair (in the summary judgment context) to require a defendant to offer evidence sufficient to allow a reasonable factfinder to conclude that its product was satisfactorily designed under the risk-utility test even though it is the plaintiff who alleges the defect?

7. *Judge and Jury.* Wade maintained that his seven-factor risk-utility test (see Note 1, *supra*) could not accurately be conveyed in a workable jury instruction and thus should be used only to aid judicial review of the legal sufficiency of the plaintiff's case. For jurors, he crafted a proposed instruction that called for them to inquire whether a product's design rendered it "so likely to be harmful . . . that a reasonable prudent manufacturer . . . who had actual knowledge of its harmful character would not place it on the market." John Wade, *On the Nature of Strict Liability for Products*, 44 Miss. L.J. 825, 839-40 (1973).

The New York Pattern Jury Instruction on design defect states as follows:

> *A product is defectively designed if a reasonable person who knew or should have known of the product's potential for causing injury and of the feasible alternative design[s] would have concluded that the product should not have been marketed in that condition.* Whether the product should have been marketed in that condition depends upon a balancing of the risks involved in using the product against (1) the product's usefulness and its costs, and (2) the risks, usefulness and costs of the alternative design[s] as compared to the product the defendant did market.
>
> It is not necessary to find that the defendant . . . knew of the product's potential for causing injury in order for you to decide that it was defectively designed. *It is sufficient that a reasonable person who did in fact know of the product's potential for causing injury would have concluded that the product should not have been marketed in that condition.*

N.Y. Pattern Jury Instr.—Civil 2:278 (2012) (emphasis added). Is this instruction a clear articulation of Wade's suggested approach? Could one devise an intelligible jury instruction that contains all seven Wade factors? If so, would that be a desirable instruction? Are some of the factors appropriately considered by a judge and not by a jury?

8. *The Hand Formula and The Wade Factors.* Note the use of the phrase "reasonable person" in N.Y. Pattern Jury Instr.—Civil 2:278. Does its inclusion in this instruction, which is supposed to convey to a jury the gist of the Wade factors, indicate that the Wade factors simply recapitulate the elements of Learned Hand's "formula" for determining what counts as carelessness? (*See* Chapter 3.) If not, what is the difference between (1) a negligence claim alleging that a defendant carelessly designed its product, and (2) a products liability claim alleging that the risks of a product's design outweigh its utility? Is it significant that New York's design defect instruction allows for liability if

a reasonable person "who did *in fact know* of the product's potential for causing injury" would have declined to market the product?

9. The Significance of Available Alternative Designs: Wade Factors Versus Restatement (Third). Note that the third and fourth factors of the Wade test ask judges to consider the availability of substitute products, as well as the feasibility and reasonableness of adopting an alternative design. What is the difference, if any, between these two ideas? Why is it important to consider whether there exists a reasonable alternative design? Is a product's safety necessarily a relative issue? Does this requirement follow from the negligence roots of products liability? If there is no reasonable alternative design, does that mean the product cannot be defective? What sorts of alternative design might be presented by the plaintiff in *Chow*?

One of the most controversial aspects of the Restatement (Third) of Products Liability is its assertion that, for the vast run of design defect cases, the availability of an alternative design should not merely count as a factor in risk-utility analysis, but should constitute a necessary element of the plaintiff's prima facie case. *See* Restatement (Third) of Torts: Products Liability § 2(b) (1998) (a product "is defective in design when the foreseeable risks of harm posed by the product could have been reduced or avoided by the adoption of a reasonable alternative design"); *id.* cmt. d (noting that subsection 2(b) sets a "requirement . . . that the plaintiff show a reasonable alternative design"). Both the descriptive and normative versions of this assertion have prompted voluminous critical commentary from lawyers, academics, and judges.

10. Focus on the Consumer: Factor Six. The sixth factor of *Chow's* rendition of the Wade test invites courts to consider, along with the other factors, the degree to which a product's users can be expected to appreciate its risks and thus take steps to reduce them. In this regard, consider the example of automobile airbags. Although of considerable utility, airbags pose a risk of injury to children and smaller adults who sit in the front passenger seat, because the rapid inflation of the airbag into what would be the chest of an average adult can hit a shorter person in the head and break her neck. Insofar as consumers can be expected to be aware of this risk, perhaps in part through prominent warnings provided by manufacturers, and insofar as consumers can adjust accordingly (e.g., by having children sit in rear seats), there is less reason to deem automobiles with airbags of this sort to be defectively designed. Note, however, that, as it is cast in the Wade test, consumer awareness is only one factor. Hence a product can still be deemed defectively designed even if awareness of its dangers can be attributed to consumers.

Taken together, do factor six and comparative fault (see Note 5, *supra*) unfairly give defense lawyers two bites at the apple (i.e., two opportunities to emphasize the plaintiff's contribution to her product-related injury)? As discussed in Section III.B, *infra*, the extent to which consumers' potential awareness of a product's risks should figure in design defect determinations has long been a source of debate. At one time, courts were inclined to hold that designs posing obvious risks could not be deemed defective. Against this backdrop, the Wade test's treatment of consumer awareness as a factor, rather than a dispositive consideration, was meant to permit determinations that a product design's dangers, even if obvious, are still unjustifiable (given, for example, the availability of a safer and cost-effective alternative design). Does the majority in *Chow* suggest that RDL is a product that might be deemed defective notwithstanding the awareness of its dangers that can be attributed to consumers?

11. Relevance of Regulatory Compliance to Design Defect. Chapter 6 canvassed the doctrine of "negligence per se." Roughly, it holds that a negligence plaintiff who can prove that her injury resulted from the defendant's violation of a safety statute or regulation is entitled to rely on the violation as conclusively establishing the "breach" element of her claim. As was also noted, the doctrine is "asymmetrical," in that a negligence defendant *cannot* usually point to its compliance with a safety statute or regulation as conclusively establishing that it acted reasonably, though evidence of compliance is relevant to the jury's determination of breach.

Defendants have long sought to eliminate this asymmetry by establishing as a matter of common law doctrine a "regulatory compliance defense" to claims of negligence. They generally have not succeeded in persuading courts to recognize this defense. However, some states have enacted statutes that recognize a partial or complete defense to products liability claims (and sometimes negligence claims) based on proof of the defendant's compliance with relevant state or federal safety laws. For example, a Michigan statute provides that Food and Drug Administration (FDA) approval of a manufacturer's drug bars a plaintiff who suffers harmful side effects when using the drug from recovering in tort on a claim of products liability or negligence. *See* Rowe v. Hoffman-La Roche, Inc., 917 A.2d 767 (N.J. 2007) (applying Michigan law).* Somewhat less drastically, a Tennessee statute specifies that compliance by a manufacturer with applicable federal or state safety statutes and regulations creates a rebuttable presumption that the product is not unreasonably dangerous. Tenn. Code Ann. § 29-28-104. A North Dakota statute, meanwhile, bars plaintiffs from recovering punitive damages (but not compensatory damages) from a product manufacturer if the product was made and sold in compliance with relevant federal safety regulations. N.D.C.C. § 32-03.2-11(6).

B. The Contest Between the Consumer Expectations Test and the Risk-Utility Test

Most state courts today will in most cases employ a version of the risk-utility test for determining whether a product is defectively designed. However, they may differ among themselves as to how they understand and apply that test. To complicate

* The Michigan law also provides that this regulatory compliance defense is lost if the plaintiff can prove that the defendant obtained FDA approval by means of *misrepresentations* to the agency. The Supreme Court at one time agreed to hear a case in which a products liability defendant argued that, in light of the Court's decision in *Buckman Co. v. Plaintiffs' Legal Committee*, 531 U.S 341 (2001), this fraud exemption is "preempted" by federal law because it interferes with the FDA's discretion to determine how best to handle the submission of information by regulated entities. However, the Court was unable to reach a decision, instead splitting 4-4 on the preemption question, with the Chief Justice recusing himself. Warner-Lambert Co., LLC v. Kent, 552 U.S. 440 (2008). The doctrine of preemption is discussed in Chapter 13.

matters further, some states that treat risk-utility as the dominant test also recognize that certain kinds of cases call for the application of a different test, known as the *consumer expectations test.* Still other states claim to rely exclusively on this alternative test or to treat the consumer expectations test and the risk-utility test as standing on an equal footing with each other.

In this section, we introduce you to the consumer expectations test, as well as disputes among courts and commentators as to when, if ever, it is appropriate for courts to use one, the other, or both. Like many other disputes in legal doctrine, the "battle" between the consumer expectations test and the risk-utility test has gone through different phases.

1. *The Consumer Expectations Test: Origins and Basic Content (c. 1964-1972).* The consumer expectations test actually predates the risk-utility test and indeed predates the widespread acceptance of the distinction between manufacturing defects and design defects. It derives, in part, from a comment to Section 402A of the Second Restatement, which elaborated on the idea of "defect" by stating that a product, to be defective, "must be dangerous to an extent beyond that which would be contemplated by the ordinary consumer who purchases it, with the ordinary knowledge common to the community of its characteristics." Restatement (Second) of Torts § 402A, cmt. i (1965). As this language suggests, the core idea of the consumer expectations test is that a product is defective in design if aspects of its design render it more dangerous than an ordinary consumer would expect it to be.

Part of the appeal of the consumer expectations test is that, notwithstanding the differences between manufacturing and design defect claims, it seems to handle paradigmatic cases in both categories pretty well. Thus, one might naturally say of products containing manufacturing defects that they disappoint ordinary consumer expectations. In *Escola,* for example, the exploding bottle was more dangerous than an ordinary consumer would expect. Likewise, an automobile whose gas tank location causes it to burst into flames when rear-ended at a moderate speed would count as defectively designed under this test—an ordinary consumer would expect a new automobile to withstand such a collision and certainly not to explode. The same conclusion might apply to a ski binding, the design of which prevents it from releasing even under severe stress; a large roasting pan designed to hold a heavy turkey that is built with small handles that make it difficult to hold the pan steady as it is removed from the oven; a shower door with glass that, when subjected to a moderate force, shatters into razor-sharp shards; and a throat lozenge prepared with ingredients that cause convulsions in a significant minority of the population. In all these cases, *the concept of a flaw or a defect can be given content by comparing the actual product to a prototype in the mind of the ordinary consumer.* In this regard, the consumer expectations test, although a feature of tort law, reveals its roots in the law of contract and warranty, which is primarily concerned to protect the expectations of the contracting parties (here the consumer).

2. *Consumer Expectations and Risk-Utility: Coexistence (c. 1972-1994).* As indicated, Section 402A, which served as a template for many state courts when they first fashioned their products liability law, used language that seemed to support the

adoption of the consumer expectations test. Moreover, risk-utility analysis, with its emphasis on balancing costs and benefits, was seen by many as threatening to push the new law of strict products liability back toward negligence. And judges and plaintiffs' lawyers found the consumer expectations test congenial because it allowed jurors a good deal of leeway to determine whether a given product was defective.

In at least two kinds of scenarios, however, plaintiffs found the concept of "consumer expectations" an obstacle to recovery, and courts regarded the obstacle as indefensible. In one scenario, typified by *Barker v. Lull Eng'g Co.*, 573 P.2d 443 (Cal. 1978), the product is of a kind with which consumers lack familiarity and therefore arguably have no settled expectations as to its safety. (The product at issue in *Barker* was a front-end loader used at construction sites; the plaintiff alleged that it was designed in a way that allowed it too easily to tip over when positioned on sloped ground.) In the other sort of case, there is a good argument to be made that the product should have been designed more safely, even though the product's danger was relatively obvious and hence not more dangerous than ordinary consumers would expect. *See* Ray v. BIC Corp., 925 S.W.2d 527 (Tenn. 1996) (alleging that a disposable cigarette lighter was defective for not being child-resistant even granted that adult consumers would readily appreciate that lighters pose a fire hazard); Cepeda v. Cumberland Eng'g Co., 386 A.2d 816 (N.J. 1978) (although use of the defendant's machine without a detachable safety mechanism posed an obvious danger, the machine could be deemed defective under the risk-utility test for not being designed to operate only with the mechanism attached), *modified on other grounds*, Suter v. San Angelo Foundry & Mach. Co., 406 A.2d 140 (N.J. 1979).

In light of both kinds of cases, *plaintiffs' lawyers* put forward the risk-utility test as an alternative to the consumer expectations test. In *Barker*, for example, the plaintiff argued that, even if an ordinary user would not expect the defendant's loader to remain stable on an incline, the design was defective under the risk-utility test because an alternative design would have provided such stability at a reasonable cost and with no loss of functionality. In keeping with the liability-expanding spirit of the 1970s, courts like the California Supreme Court in *Barker* were sometimes willing to allow a plaintiff to recover if he or she could establish a defect under *either* test.

Beginning around 1980, in response to broad changes in the political mood of the country, as well as the growth of products liability law in general and design defect litigation in particular, lawyers for repeat-player defendants (such as automobile manufacturers) seized on the risk-utility test for reasons very different than had plaintiffs and courts in the 1970s. Specifically, defendants mounted risk-utility arguments *against* findings of defect by focusing on the costs and lost utility associated with alternative product designs. At the same time, they worked to persuade many legislatures and courts (including the U.S. Supreme Court) to adopt more rigorous standards for the admissibility of expert testimony in products liability cases. (*See* Daubert v. Merrell Dow Pharmaceuticals, Inc., Chapter 13.)

As a result of these developments, by the mid-1980s plaintiffs' lawyers increasingly found themselves advocating for the consumer expectations test on the ground that it was less likely to require or encourage jurors and trial judges to defer to expert testimony as to the downsides of alternative product designs. Meanwhile, defense lawyers pressed courts to rely *exclusively* on the risk-utility test for design defect, and to reject the consumer expectations test as giving judges and jurors too much leeway to second-guess design decisions without an adequate understanding of the cost-benefit trade-offs associated with those decisions.

3. *Soule's Solution.* The California Supreme Court confronted the latter argument as made by lawyers for General Motors in the landmark case of *Soule v. General Motors Corp.*, 882 P.2d 298 (Cal. 1994). The plaintiff's ankles were broken when her Chevrolet Camaro was hit in a low-impact, drivers' side collision that drove the "toe-plate" of the car up into her feet at an odd angle. The plaintiff argued that the Camaro's vulnerability to an ankle-breaking episode of this sort made its design more dangerous than an ordinary consumer would expect. However, General Motors argued that the jury should be required to use a risk-utility test to ascertain whether the Camaro was defectively designed. The trial judge permitted the jury to use the consumer expectations test, and the plaintiff prevailed.

On appeal, the California Supreme Court declined to embrace risk-utility to the complete exclusion of consumer expectations. However, it re-ordered their relationship in a way that favors use of the former over the latter. In particular, rather than re-affirming its prior decision in *Barker* to treat the two tests as equally available options for all design defect cases, it instead held that the risk-utility test should be used for any case in which the question of how to design the product involves technical issues beyond jurors' common knowledge. Conversely, in cases involving design issues that are a matter of everyday experience — and hence do not call for jurors to defer to engineers and other experts — the consumer expectations test alone should apply.*

Because the California Supreme Court made clear that it expected most design defect cases to raise issues that go beyond common knowledge and hence will call for the use of the risk-utility test, *Soule* was a clear "win" for products liability defendants. However, *Soule* did not go so far as to eliminate the consumer expectations test. Moreover, it retained one element of California risk-utility doctrine that is relatively plaintiff friendly: upholding *Barker*'s decision to place on defendants the burden of persuading the factfinder that a design's utility outweighs its costs.

4. *Risk-Utility Ascendant: The Third Restatement (c. 1994-present).* The Reporters for the products liability portion of the Third Torts Restatement — James Henderson and Aaron Twerski — forcefully asserted that, by the mid-1990s, American jurisdictions had reached a broad doctrinal consensus that *only* the risk-utility test should be used. Further still, they insisted that this consensus was sound as a matter of policy.

---

* *Soule* was also a victory for Soule herself. Despite ruling that the trial court had erred in allowing Soule to invoke the consumer expectations test to establish that the design of her Camaro was defective, the California Supreme Court nonetheless affirmed the plaintiff's verdict on the ground that the error was "harmless," in that there was sufficient evidence to establish defect under the risk-utility test.

Thus—subject to its recognition of the possibility that a design defect can on rare occasions be inferred from the mere happening of an accident (*see* Note 1 following *Hickox, infra*)—the Restatement's products liability provisions recommend unequivocally that design defect be defined exclusively by reference to the risk-utility test. *See* Restatement (Third) of Torts: Products Liability § 2 (1998). Section 2(b) accordingly defines design defect as follows:

> **§ 2. Categories of Product Defect**
>
> . . . A product . . .
>
> (b) is defective in design when the foreseeable risks of harm posed by the product could have been reduced or avoided by the adoption of a reasonable alternative design by the seller or other distributor, or a predecessor in the commercial chain of distribution, and the omission of the alternative design renders the product not reasonably safe. . . .
>
> **Comment: . . .**
>
> d. . . . Subsection (b) adopts a reasonableness ("risk-utility balancing") test. . . . [T]he test is whether a reasonable alternative design would, at a reasonable cost, have reduced the foreseeable risks of harm posed by the product and, if so, whether the omission of [that] design . . . rendered the product not reasonably safe. . . .

The Reporters' normative and descriptive claims about the dominance of risk-utility analysis provoked a great deal of controversy in the American Law Institute, and a great deal of controversy remains, not only among lawyers and academics, but also in the courts. *See, e.g.*, Potter v. Chicago Pneumatic Tool Co., 694 A.2d 1319 (Conn. 1997) (discussing and criticizing Section 2(b) and adopting a consumer expectations test suitable to sophisticated products).

Note that Section 2(b) departs from *Soule* by placing the burden of proving defectiveness (by means of proof of a reasonable alternative design) squarely on the plaintiff. Restatement (Third), *supra*, § 2, cmt. d (1998) ("plaintiff must prove that . . . a reasonable alternative [design] was, or reasonably could have been, available at the time of sale or distribution."). This feature of the Third Restatement has been as controversial as its decision to treat risk-utility as the single test for design defect in almost all cases. *See* Vautour v. Body Masters Sports Indus., Inc., 784 A.2d 1178 (N.H. 2001) (rejecting the proof of reasonable alternative design requirement); Dan B. Dobbs, *The Law of Torts* § 361, at 996-1002 (2000) (reviewing the debate).

The following decisions—from the District of Columbia and Texas, respectively—indicate that, even though risk-utility is now for many jurisdictions the default test for design defect, the back-and-forth between the two tests is not yet over. The first decision arguably suggests that the consumer expectations test can play a significant role even from within a doctrinal framework similar to the one articulated by the California Supreme Court in *Soule*. The second, meanwhile, exemplifies modern courts' increasing reliance on the risk-utility test as part of a broader retooling of products liability law aimed at curbing perceived excesses in liability and damages.

burden of proof are the traditional and appropriate means of attacking shaky but admissible evidence.") (quoting *Daubert v. Merrell Dow Pharm., Inc.*, 509 U.S. 579, 596 (1993)).

1.

Wilson faults Dr. Paul for failing to conduct his own tests, but there is no requirement that an expert perform tests, particularly where the expert relies on published data generated by another expert in the pertinent field. As noted above, Dr. Paul's testimony relied in part on the published results of tests conducted by an industry association.

. . . .

2.

Wilson also faults Dr. Paul for failing to provide an adequate explanation of his reasoning. Wilson is correct that courts should exclude expert testimony that consists of mere assertions. But Dr. Paul did not merely assert that the angle of the throat guard was a defect that caused Mr. Hickox's injuries; rather, Dr. Paul explained his reasoning, step by step. Using freeze frames of the video of the incident, Dr. Paul stated his opinion that the angle of the throat guard caused the mask to trap the ball before deflecting it, concentrating the energy of the ball at the point of impact. Dr. Paul further explained how the impact of the ball hitting the throat guard created a wedging action that pushed the wire portion of the mask against Mr. Hickox's jaw bone, causing injury.

It is true, as Wilson emphasizes, that Dr. Paul did not fully explain every aspect of his reasoning. In expert testimony, however, as "[i]n administrative proceedings . . . [and] ordinary life, 'explanations come to an end somewhere.'" *Liskowitz v. Astrue*, 559 F.3d 736, 743 (7th Cir. 2009) (quoting Ludwig Wittgenstein, *Philosophical Investigations* § 1 (G.E.M. Anscombe trans. 1968)). Any remaining gaps in Dr. Paul's explanation of his reasoning did not require exclusion of Dr. Paul's testimony but rather were the proper subject of cross-examination and closing argument.

3.

. . . . [Wilson invokes prior cases from] this court . . . holding that an expert testifying to the standard of care in a negligence case could not testify solely to a personal opinion about what should have been done, but rather also had to demonstrate knowledge of the applicable national standard of care and testify as to whether that standard was met. Some of Dr. Paul's testimony related to standard of care, and it may well be true that Dr. Paul's testimony was not sufficient to establish a national standard of care. Wilson, however, was found liable on strict-liability theories that do not require proof of a national standard of care, and Dr. Paul's testimony was admissible on issues pertinent to those theories.

. . . .

B.

. . . .

An assumption-of-risk instruction is warranted in a design-defect case if the defendant offers evidence that the plaintiff knew about the specific alleged defect and the associated danger. Simply showing that Mr. Hickox knew the general risks of baseball umpiring was inadequate. Wilson needed evidence that Mr. Hickox knew that the throat guard's acute, forward angle had a tendency to concentrate energy and increase the risk of injury. Because Wilson failed to present such evidence, the trial court did not err by declining to give an assumption-of-risk instruction.

C.

Wilson argues that there was insufficient evidence to support judgment against it on any of the products-liability claims. We view the evidence in the light most favorable to the Hickoxes and will reverse only if no reasonable person could have rendered a verdict in the Hickoxes' favor. A motion for judgment notwithstanding the verdict should be granted only in extreme cases. As Wilson acknowledges, a finding that the evidence was sufficient on any one of the claims found by the jury will support the judgment in this case in its entirety. Because we find sufficient evidence to support the design-defect claim, we address only that claim.

There are two tests commonly used to determine whether a product's design was defective: the consumer-expectation test and the risk-utility test. In challenging the sufficiency of the evidence to support the jury's finding of a design defect, Wilson appears to analyze the evidence under the risk-utility test. In the circumstances of this case, however, we conclude that the evidence should properly be analyzed under the consumer-expectation test.

Wilson explicitly assented at trial to jury instructions that required the jury to make findings under a consumer-expectation test. Specifically, the jury was told that "[a] design is defective if the product fails to perform as safely as an ordinary customer would expect when [the product is] used in an intended or reasonably foreseeable manner." This formulation is essentially equivalent to the consumer-expectation test as defined by this court and others. *See Warner Fruehauf* [*Trailer Co.*], 654 A.2d [1272,] 1276 & n. 9 [(D.C. 1995)] ("[A] product is unreasonably dangerous when it fails to perform in the manner reasonably to be expected by the ordinary consumer."); *see also, e.g., Caterpillar Tractor Co. v. Beck*, 593 P.2d 871, 884 (Alaska 1979) (design defect if product "failed to perform as safely as an ordinary consumer would expect when used in an intended or reasonably foreseeable manner") (internal quotation marks omitted).[5]

---

5. The trial court and the parties derived this jury instruction from Standardized Civil Jury Instructions for the District of Columbia, No. 23.09, at 23–9 (2012 rev. ed.). The comment to that instruction indicates that either the consumer-expectation test or the risk-utility test may apply in this jurisdiction, "depending on the factual situation." *Id.* at 23–10 (citing *Warner Fruehauf*, 654 A.2d at 1276 n. 9). In *Warner Fruehauf*, this court applied the risk-utility test, finding that test appropriate for the type of product at issue in that case, a truck lift-gate. Although *Warner Fruehauf* raises the possibility that the consumer-expectation test might apply in other circumstances, this court has not applied the consumer-expectation test in any case. It therefore is an open question whether the consumer-expectation test is applicable in the District of Columbia. Whatever the answer to that question may be, Wilson did not object in the trial court to the consumer-expectation instruction, and does not appear to argue on appeal that giving the instruction was legal error.

slippery, and subject to tripping hazards. But the evidence showed that a wider rail would have increased the cost and weight of the trailer and would have presented a more inviting danger to users. We held, as a matter of law, that the risk, which was fully obvious to all, did not outweigh the trailer's utility, and that the trailer was not unreasonably dangerous.

On the other hand, in *Uniroyal Goodrich Tire Co. v. Martinez,* we held that there was a factual dispute for the jury to decide. [977 S.W.2d at 331.] There, Martinez was injured when a 16″ tire he was attempting to mount on a 16.5″ rim exploded. That such mismatches occur frequently and easily was well known in the industry — hence the warnings and recommended safety precautions. Martinez himself knew of the danger, but testified that he mistakenly believed, because the old tire was 16″, that the rim was also 16″. He might have avoided injury from an explosive mismatch between the tire and the rim if he had available (and used) a tire-mounting machine, a safety cage or an extension hose while inflating the tire. Nonetheless, because even experienced operators like Martinez could mistakenly believe they were in compliance with the warning against mounting a 16″ tire on a 16.5″ rim, there remained a latent risk that a person unaware he was mounting a 16″ tire on a mismatched 16.5″ rim would fail to appreciate the concomitantly increased danger posed by an unsecured tire. The Court concluded that whether there was a safer alternative design for the tire that would have decreased the likelihood of an explosion was a question for the jury. In the case at hand, a person on the ground can readily see that lifting the outriggers on a lift, while the platform bearing his colleague remains 40′ in the air, puts that colleague at serious risk of a potentially deadly fall. The ground-based lift-user cannot mistakenly believe that his actions are safe, as Martinez mistakenly believed based on the misapprehension that the tire and rim matched.

In the case before us, the evidence of the AWP–40S's utility is undisputed. The lift is designed to be small, lightweight, portable, and relatively inexpensive. To accommodate a wide variety of working environments, the lift uses outriggers with manual leveling jacks to stabilize the lift once it is positioned. This allows the lift to be used on surfaces that are not completely flat, such as the gradually sloped floor in this case, without having to sacrifice stability. Furthermore, the lift is designed so that the outriggers are removable in order to keep the lift as narrow as possible when being moved. This allows the AWP–40S to fit through standard door frames, therein expanding the range of uses for the machine. As previously explained, the lift also incorporates a mechanical interlock to make sure that all four outriggers are installed and the leveling jacks are firmly pressed against a given workspace. Until the outriggers are properly set, the lift cannot be operated. This maximizes the utility of the lift while still ensuring that it is used safely.

The risk is that a user will ignore the instructions in the user manual, the signs on the lift itself, and the danger, obvious to even a casual observer, that the lift will tip if the outriggers are removed when a person is on a fully elevated platform. So obvious is the risk of danger from misuse of the lift that the evidence does not reflect a single other accident involving a fully extended 40′ lift. Church employees testified that they sometimes released the outriggers with the platform elevated, but only if the worker could jump down to avoid injury. The plaintiffs introduced evidence of three similar accidents,[39] but in none is there an indication that the platform was fully elevated. Genie's witness testified that there may been eight or ten other instances "of not doing it right" when using the lift, but again, none bear any indication that they, too, involved a fully elevated platform. The undisputed evidence is that Genie has sold more than 100,000 AWP model lifts all over the world, which have been used millions of times. But the record does not reflect a single misuse as egregious as that in this case.

The five factors to be considered in determining whether a product's risk outweighs its utility, with which we began this discussion, conclusively establish that the AWP–40S is not, on this record, unreasonably dangerous. The first is whether the gravity and likelihood of injury outweighs the lift's utility. While misuse of the lift can result in the most serious injury, as this case illustrates, the likelihood of its occurrence is all but nonexistent. In *Martinez,* the likelihood of injury was greater, and more importantly, even an experienced user might not appreciate the danger in a particular circumstance. Here, the danger was patent. The second factor asks whether there is a substitute that would meet the same need and not be unsafe or unreasonably expensive. There is no evidence of one. The third factor is whether there is a safer alternative design. As we have already explained at length, there is only slight evidence of such a design. The fourth factor is whether the danger of misuse is obvious and readily avoidable. The risk of tip-over is both. One need only look at the machine to appreciate this truth. And the lift's history of use in the world further confirms this fact. The last factor considers ordinary consumers' expectations. Again, the danger of misuse is obvious, even to someone not trained in handling the AWP–40S. These factors require the conclusion that the AWP–40S is not unreasonably dangerous.

We agree with the dissent that it is completely irrelevant what we would have done had we been jurors in the case, although it seems odd that the dissenting Justices would feel constrained to repeat three times that they probably would have sided with Genie. The dissent acknowledges that the AWP–40S cannot be unreasonably dangerous absent evidence that the gravity and likelihood of injury outweighs its utility, but then it concludes that a single accident is enough to show likelihood. The evidence here shows that while it is very likely that users of the lift will not read or follow the user manual or the warning signs on the machine, and likely that they will try to release the outriggers and move the lift with someone on a partially elevated platform, the chance that anyone would attempt to do so with the platform fully elevated is only one in millions. The risk of misuse in this case cannot in any sense be said to be likely.

As we said in *Caterpillar,* "[t]he law of products liability does not guarantee that a product will be risk free," only that it will not be unreasonably dangerous. [911 S.W.2d at 381-82.] There is no evidence in the record before us that the AWP–40S is unreasonably dangerous.

---

39. . . . [W]e are aware of but one other case — across the entire United States — in which a similar Genie lift was intentionally destabilized while elevated and fell. *See Cohalan v. Genie Indus., Inc., 276 F.R.D. 161, 162 (S.D.N.Y.2011)* ("At the time the lift fell over, it was being wheeled around the warehouse by a colleague of Mr. Cohalan's, and the outriggers with which the lift was equipped in order to prevent tip-over were not set up.").

was much lower when the lifts tipped over. And more importantly, Genie asserts that the evidence of those three accidents did not indicate a "likelihood" of such accidents because the evidence also established that Genie has sold "hundreds of thousands" of these lifts worldwide, and they have been used without incident "literally 'millions' of times." Genie contends that the evidence thus conclusively establishes that the relevant risk is "very slight."

. . . .

. . . . Under *Hernandez* and *Martinez,* the Court's matter-of-law conclusion here that the lift is not unreasonably dangerous because the jury heard evidence of only a few similar accidents is simply wrong. Although the number of similar accidents that the jury heard about was small compared to the "millions" of uneventful uses of the lift worldwide, we have held that such evidence does not conclusively establish that the relevant risk is "very slight."

In addition, the Court's reliance on the relatively small number of similar accidents ignores the evidence that the jury heard about how and why this accident occurred. Here, as in *Martinez* and *Hernandez,* the record contains other evidence of the circumstances surrounding the accident, which would permit a reasonable juror to conclude that the relevant risk was high even if the number of actual accidents was relatively low.

. . . .

[Witness] testimony, combined with the evidence of at least three similar accidents involving the same lift design, would permit a reasonable juror to conclude, or at least draw the reasonable inference, that:

- Adams did not intentionally destabilize the lift knowing that it was "fully elevated," but instead assumed that the platform was at a lower and less dangerous level;
- Despite the warning and apparently obvious dangers, Adams believed it was safe to destabilize and move the lift, at least with the platform at a lower level, because he and others regularly did so without incident;
- Despite the warning and apparently obvious dangers, this is a common assumption, particularly in light of how often untrained non-professionals use the lift, and as a result, the use and movement of the lift when it is destabilized is a regular or common occurrence;
- Workers like Boggan and Matak, who do not use the lift very often, will follow the lead of workers like Adams, who do, and will try to move the lift when it is occupied despite the warning and apparently obvious dangers;
- The lift is not safe when it is moved or destabilized, even when the platform is at a lower level, because a fall when the platform is at any level can cause serious injuries and death;
- The fact that the lift can be, and commonly is, destabilized and moved at a lower level without incident makes the lift even more dangerous because it gives users a false sense that it is safe to move the lift with the platform at a lower level, which can lead to the kinds of assumptions and accidents that occurred here;

- Despite the warning and apparently obvious dangers, it is foreseeable and likely that operators are going to destabilize and move the lift when the platform is extended and occupied; and
- It is therefore likely that some users of this product will sustain serious injuries and deaths due to the misuse of the lift, despite the warning and apparent obvious dangers.

Based on this evidence, I conclude that reasonable jurors could have different views regarding "the user's anticipated awareness of the dangers inherent in the product," the "avoidability" of those dangers "because of general public knowledge of the obvious condition of the product, or of the existence of suitable warnings or instructions," the "expectations of the ordinary consumer," and thus the "gravity and likelihood of injury" from the product's use. *Timpte,* 286 S.W.3d at 311 (quoting *Grinnell,* 951 S.W.2d at 432). I would thus hold that the record contains at least some evidence on which a reasonable juror could conclude that the relevant risk of the Genie lift outweighs its utility.

. . . .

The Court relies heavily on *Timpte,* in which we held that a product's risks did not outweigh its utility as a matter of law. The plaintiff in *Timpte,* Gish, was injured when a gust of wind blew him off of the top of a dual-hopper trailer, onto which he had climbed to grab a malfunctioning silo downspout. . . .

. . . . [W]hat is present in this case that was not present in *Timpte* is evidence that ordinary users would commonly misuse the product despite the warning and apparently obvious dangers. We mentioned in *Timpte* that Gish had climbed up on the trailer "on several other occasions when the downspout would not lower," but we made no reference to any evidence that anyone other than Gish had ever done so. *Id.* at 308. While the evidence in *Timpte* thus could establish only that the risk was "extremely low" and "very slight," *id.* at 313–14, the evidence of other users' common misuse of the Genie lift could establish that the risk was relatively high, given the availability of a safer alternative design, or at least permit a reasonable juror to conclude it was.

This case, therefore, is more analogous to *Martinez,* in which the plaintiff was seriously injured when he attempted to install a 16–inch tire on a 16.5–inch rim. 977 S.W.2d at 332. He did this in spite of the fact that the tire bore a "prominent warning label containing yellow and red highlights and a pictograph of a worker being thrown into the air by an exploding tire." *Id.* As here, the product's label prohibited the specific conduct the plaintiff was engaged in at the time of his injury and warned that such conduct could result in serious injury or death. . . .

The issue was the same in *Martinez* as it is here: "whether a manufacturer who knew of a safer alternative product design is liable in strict products liability for injuries caused by the use of its product that the user could have avoided by following the product's warnings." *Id.* at 331. We concluded that the answer was yes, observing that the defendant acknowledged at trial "that warnings are an imperfect means to remedy a product defect," just as Curtin did in this case. *Id.* at 336. We agreed with the Restatement that warnings and safer alternative designs are merely "factors, among others, for plaintiffs sought a writ of mandate: a special interlocutory appeal in which the appellant (usually styled the "petitioner") alleges that a lower court has committed such a gross error of law as to be acting outside the scope of its authority, and by which the petitioner seeks a "mandate" (a command) from the appellate court instructing the lower court to reverse its erroneous ruling. In their petition, plaintiffs argued that the trial judge in the coordinated proceeding committed a gross error by rejecting the contention that there was an ordinary consumer expectation among workers that they would not sustain injury simply by wearing—or being around those who were wearing—latex gloves for the purpose of protecting themselves from contact with infectious agents. According to the plaintiffs, the product was "a simple one that can give rise to simple consumer expectations of safety that have nothing to do with the chemical composition of the material from which the product is manufactured, or any other design characteristics for which specialized knowledge is required for understanding or taking appropriate precautions." *Id.* at 357.

The Court of Appeals confidently rejected this argument:

> [T]he protective or barrier function of the latex gloves, on which the Plaintiffs' safety argument is mainly premised, is not their only characteristic. These gloves are made of a particular material through a particular manufacturing process. The effect of this material and these processes may well be to create in their users many degrees of allergic reactions. Understanding and assessing responsibility for such allergic reactions is a matter that is driven by the science of the manufacturing and preparation procedures, as well as the medical aspects of an individual's allergic reactions to various substances.
>
> Plaintiffs' theory of design defect, therefore, is a complex one. When we re-formulate the Plaintiffs' underlying consumer expectations statements to comport with their actual arguments in these proceedings, we see that their simple formulation of an expectation that they would not be harmed by the use of this product is totally inaccurate. Rather, their arguments posit that exposure to the natural substance of latex may make their dormant, incipient, or developing allergies worse than they would otherwise have been. We find it an inevitable conclusion that before the issues of design defect can be adequately litigated and resolved, expert testimony will be essential to assist the finder of fact in understanding the pros and cons of Plaintiffs' arguments.

Id.

Did the *Morson* court decide the issue correctly under *Soule*? Why were plaintiffs concerned enough to seek a writ of mandate? Because the issue was brought to the appellate court by means of this special procedure, rather than an ordinary post-trial appeal, the court could have denied the writ without reaching the merits simply by concluding that any error alleged by the petition was an ordinary legal error that should be pursued on appeal, rather than the sort of extraordinary error that warrants the issuance of a writ of mandate. Why, then, did the court go out of its way to deny the writ on the merits? Do you think that litigation under the risk-utility test will appropriately determine whether the latex gloves in question should be deemed to have contained a design defect? Do you think this form of analysis is a fair way to ascertain whether the manufacturers of the gloves should be held liable?

Morson is directly opposed to a contemporaneous decision of the Wisconsin Supreme Court, mentioned in Note 3 above. In *Green v. Smith & Nephew AHP, Inc.*, 629 N.W.2d 727 (Wis. 2001), the trial court had employed the consumer expectations test and had declined to instruct the jury that the injuries alleged by the plaintiff had to have been foreseeable to the defendant at the time of manufacture. A majority of Wisconsin Supreme Court Judges affirmed the jury's verdict for the plaintiff, expressly declaring that Wisconsin law favors the consumer expectations test across the board, even for sophisticated products. In the process, the court expressly rejected the Third Restatement's embrace of risk-utility, its demand of foreseeability, and its requirement of proof of a reasonable alternative design.

5. *The Menu of Design Defect Definitions.* Some jurisdictions today, for example South Carolina, now use the risk-utility test for all design defect cases. Others, like Wisconsin, have adopted a consumer expectations test as the exclusive test for defect. (*Green, supra* note 3). Many retain a two-pronged test for design defect, which calls for application of the risk-utility test to design questions that exceed common knowledge, while reserving the consumer expectation test for product designs about which ordinary consumers have expectations that merit deference. As if the foregoing array of tests and standards were not enough, the New York Court of Appeals has indicated that even if its products liability law demands application of the risk-utility test and only that test, the consumer expectations test might still have a role to play through a separate cause of action for breach of implied warranty. *See* Denny v. Ford Motor Co., 662 N.E. 2d 730 (N.Y. 1995). In *Denny*—a case involving the rollover of a passenger vehicle—the court held that many plaintiffs with product-related personal injury claims may proceed either in tort under the risk-utility test or under an implied warranty theory governed by the consumer expectations test.

6. *Manifestly Unreasonable Designs.* Suppose a product contains a significant danger but cannot be redesigned to avoid that danger. Is it ever open to a judge or jury to declare that the product is of so little utility that it cannot be sold without subjecting the seller to liability for injuries caused by its dangerous features?

Courts have occasionally rendered decisions suggesting as much. For example, the New Jersey Supreme Court rendered a famous decision in which it indicated that it was willing to declare all above-ground swimming pools ineliminably defective for posing an inherent and unavoidable risk of bodily harm to those who dive headfirst into them. O'Brien v. Muskin Corp., 463 A.2d 298 (N.J. 1983).* Other candidates for unavoidably unsafe products that have been mentioned by courts and commentators include asbestos, tobacco, handguns, and metal-tipped lawn darts for use by children. The Third Restatement grudgingly acknowledges that such products might exist. *See* Restatement (Third) of Torts: Products Liability § 2, cmt. e (1998) (suggesting that a toy gun

* *O'Brien* generated a prompt legislative response. *See* N.J.S. 2A:58C-3a(2) (1987) (blocking liability for products containing "inherent" dangers that are known or knowable to the ordinary consumer).

designed for use with hard rubber pellets to create a sense of "realism" might be deemed manifestly unreasonable even though no other design could more safely provide such realism).

7. Design Defects and Punitive Damages. As discussed in Chapters 9 and 13, punitive damages are extra-compensatory—they provide a plaintiff who recovers them something more than compensation for the losses she experienced as a result of the tort. Under common law rules, such damages can only be awarded upon proof that the defendant's tort was willful, wanton, or committed with reckless disregard for the rights of others. Even where there is such proof, their award is at the factfinder's discretion.

In the vast majority of products liability suits, there will be no occasion for a punitive damages award. After all, proof that the plaintiff was injured by a defective product is hardly proof of willful, wanton, or reckless misconduct. However, there have been notable products liability cases in which punitive damages were awarded, typically on the basis of a finding that the manufacturer intentionally misled consumers about the safety of its product or was callously indifferent to the dangers the product posed.

An early and still controversial example of punitive damages being awarded on a claim of design defect is *Grimshaw v. Ford Motor Co.*, 174 Cal. Rptr. 348 (Ct. App. 1981), widely known as the "Ford Pinto" case. Thirteen-year-old Richard Grimshaw suffered disfiguring burns when the car he was riding in, a Ford Pinto, was involved in a collision and burst into flames. The plaintiff alleged that the Pinto was defectively designed because its gas tank was incorporated into the car's chassis in such a way as to make it susceptible to explode in response to relatively minor rear-end collisions. In support of this contention, the plaintiff introduced evidence that Ford had performed an internal assessment of the alternative designs that could have protected the unshielded gas tank. The plaintiff maintained that Ford had chosen to forgo such designs because each would have added between $4 and $15 to the car's sticker price, as well as extra weight, and that Ford was determined to keep the Pinto at a weight of 2000 lbs. and a price of $2000. It further introduced testimony of a former Ford engineer who described the process by which Ford "had engaged in cost-benefit analyses" in deciding whether to change the fuel tank design once it became aware of the risk that it could rupture at low-speed collisions.*

The jury found that the Pinto was defectively designed under California law, and it awarded Grimshaw $550,000 in compensatory damages. It also awarded $125 million in punitive damages, which the trial judge reduced to $3.5 million. Ford appealed the *Grimshaw* case, primarily to challenge the reduced punitive award. The Court of Appeal for the Fourth Appellate District upheld it.

Ford raised many issues on appeal. However, its central argument was that a jury should not be permitted to infer common law malice or reckless disregard from the

---

* This is not to say that the Pinto's *overall* safety record was equally problematic. While the Pinto was unduly susceptible to fire and explosion as a result of rear-end collisions, the overall risk of a fatal accident for Pinto users was apparently lower than for users of subcompact cars designed and manufactured by competitors, including Datsun and Volkswagen.

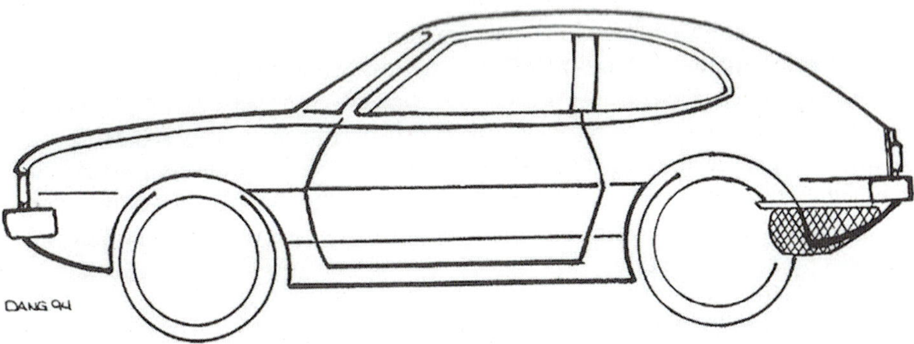

FIGURE 1
This diagram shows the placement of the fuel tank in the Ford Pinto.

mere fact that a design deemed by the jury to be defective was adopted by the manufacturer after consideration of different alternatives with different risks and benefits. *Every* design choice, Ford argued, is the result of deliberation over costs and benefits, including safety. Thus, to allow punitive damages merely on the basis of the manufacturer's having considered and rejected safer designs would be to make punitive damages available in practically any design defect case. The *Grimshaw* court rejected Ford's contentions. In so ruling, it noted that the plaintiff was not arguing that Ford should be punished merely for engaging in cost-benefit analysis. Rather, punishment was warranted, according to the plaintiff, because Ford undertook that analysis on terms that suggested a wanton failure to take seriously the potential "costs" (in terms of injuries) associated with its product.

Ford made a number of arguments in addition to the argument that design choices found to be defective under the rules of products liability can never be viewed as reckless or wanton acts. These arguments concerned larger issues of policy, in particular the problems of "multiple punishment" and "overdeterrence." Both of these arguments turn on the fact that manufacturers of mass-produced products may sometimes face the prospect of a succession of suits and a succession of jury verdicts imposing huge punitive damages awards.* The court rejected these arguments, and responded with a series of policy arguments of its own:

---

* In general, there are no substantive or procedural rules that bar the same manufacturer from being subjected to multiple punitive damage awards for the same conduct (e.g., producing a defectively designed car model) in multiple proceedings in one or many jurisdictions. For example, the federal constitutional prohibition on "double jeopardy" does not apply to civil proceedings. Thus, the jury's award of punitive damages in *Grimshaw* would have no effect on the ability of a jury in another suit — whether brought in California or any other state — alleging injuries to another person caused by the Pinto's defective gas tank. However, the U.S. Supreme Court has held that, for any case involving a claim for punitive damages, the U.S. Constitution's guarantee of "due process of law" limits the ability of a plaintiff's lawyer to invoke evidence that a defendant's conduct has injured persons other than the plaintiff. *See* Chapter 13.

> . . . [I]n commerce-related torts, the manufacturer may find it more profitable to treat compensatory damages as a part of the cost of doing business rather than to remedy the defect. Deterrence of such "objectionable corporate policies" serves one of the principal purposes of [California law]. Governmental safety standards and the criminal law have failed to provide adequate consumer protection against the manufacture and distribution of defective products. Punitive damages thus remain as the most effective remedy for consumer protection against defectively designed mass produced articles. . . .

Id. at 382-383 (citations omitted).

Whether the allowance of punitive damages in products liability cases has in fact led to unpredictable and unbounded liability predicated on jurors' second-guessing of corporate cost-benefit analysis is very much a contested issue today. Despite the impression created by occasional awards of eye-popping magnitude (the vast bulk of which are reduced on appeal), punitive damages are rarely awarded, and when they are awarded, it is usually in cases involving allegations of fraud, battery, and other "intentional" torts, not products liability. Yet anecdotal evidence and some empirical research suggest that punitive damages are frequently requested in products liability complaints. Thus, it may be that punitive damages, even though rare, have a "shadow effect." In short, because of the unpredictability of when punitive damages will be awarded and in what amount, defendants may feel pressure to settle cases that they would have taken to trial or to settle for higher amounts than the compensatory damages demanded by the plaintiffs would have justified, out of fear of that their case may fall within the 3 to 4 percent of products liability cases in which punitive damages are awarded. Some of the issues associated with the award of punitive damages for injuries caused by conduct evincing "reckless disregard" are discussed in Chapters 8 and 13.

8. *Punitive Damages and Corporate Intentionality.* Consider Ford's argument that juries should not be entrusted with the task of distinguishing between the production of a defectively designed product and the *malicious* or *reckless* production of a defectively designed product. Design decisions in large manufacturing operations are rarely the result of a single person exercising broad discretion. Instead, like other corporate acts, they are collaborative among key personnel who work for the corporation. How should the factfinder determine the attitude of a corporation? One might look to the individual employees responsible for the conduct to which one attributes the attitude, but that may not capture the whole picture. (After all, it may be the case that no single actor within the production process possessed all the information that was possessed by the corporation as a whole.) If the plaintiff cannot point to any single actor's malicious or reckless attitude, should she be barred from obtaining punitive damages? Or is it appropriate to ascribe such attitudes to the corporation itself? In ordinary discourse, it is quite common to ascribe dispositions such as "greed" or "environmental irresponsibility" to a collective entity such as a corporation. Are there philosophical or policy-based objections to adopting similar usage in the language of products liability law?

C. Standards of Defectiveness for Prescription Drugs

Chapter 4's treatment of actual causation in negligence included *Sindell v. Abbott Labs.*, 607 P.2d 924 (Cal. 1980). *Sindell* permitted a plaintiff alleging injurious *in utero* exposure to the prescription drug DES to rely on "market share liability" to overcome her inability to identify which of several manufacturers sold the drug that injured her. In ruling on this issue, the California court did not address the analytically prior question of what standard ought to apply to determine whether or not DES was defectively designed. However, it later addressed that issue in Brown v. Superior Court, 751 P.2d 470 (Cal. 1988).

The plaintiffs in *Brown* sought redress for alleged DES-related injuries on several theories, including design defect and failure-to-warn claims. Noting that *Sindell* had merely presumed, rather than endorsed, the application of products liability theories to injuries caused by prescription drugs, the *Brown* court took the occasion to address those theories. In stark contrast to *Sindell*, *Brown* adopted a relatively defendant-friendly approach to liability, issuing the following rule (here paraphrased rather than quoted):

1. A plaintiff alleging injuries caused by use of a *prescription drug*
2. sold by the seller with adequate *warnings* of health risks
   a. that are posed by the drug's use, and
   b. of which the seller *knew or should have known* at the time of sale,
3. may *not* invoke *either* the consumer expectations test or the risk-utility test to impose liability on the seller.

Citing various sources, including, most importantly, comment k to Section 402A of the Second Restatement (discussed below), *Brown* concluded that the public interest would be best served by requiring personal injury claimants suing for injuries caused by prescription drugs to proceed exclusively on theories of manufacturing defect, negligence, warranty, or misrepresentation, or a failure-to-warn theory differing only subtly from negligence:

> If drug manufacturers were subject to strict liability, they might be reluctant to undertake research programs to develop some pharmaceuticals that would prove beneficial or to distribute others that are available to be marketed, because of the fear of large adverse monetary judgments. Further, the additional expense of insuring against such liability—assuming insurance would be available—and of research programs to reveal possible dangers not detectable by available scientific methods could place the cost of medication beyond the reach of those who need it most.
>
> Dean Prosser summed up the justification for exempting prescription drugs from strict liability as follows:
>
>> The argument that industries producing potentially dangerous products should make good the harm, distribute it by liability insurance, and add the cost to the price of the product, encounters reason for pause, when we consider that two of the greatest medical boons to the human race, penicillin and cortisone, both

(a) Second Restatement § 402 A

In dealing with products other than prescription drugs, this court has recognized a manufacturer's liability in tort for design defects. Liability arises when an article a manufacturer has placed in the market, knowing that it is to be used without inspection for defects, proves to have a defect which causes an injury to a human being rightfully using the product. We have also adopted and applied the test set out in the Second Restatement § 402 A. . . .

[Nebraska law thus ordinarily applies] the consumer expectations test for strict liability. *See, e.g.*, Haag v. Bongers, 256 Neb. 170, 589 N.W.2d 318 (1999). . . . Prescription drugs, however, have been treated differently both by this court and by the Second Restatement.

(i) Comment k. Exception for Unavoidably Unsafe Products

Under the Second Restatement, prescription drugs are treated specially under § 402A, comment *k.* Comment *k.* at 353-54 provides an exception from strict liability when a product is deemed to be "unavoidably unsafe" and states:

> There are some products which, in the present state of human knowledge, are quite incapable of being made safe for their intended and ordinary use. These are especially common in the field of drugs. An outstanding example is the vaccine for the Pasteur treatment of rabies, which not uncommonly leads to very serious and damaging consequences when it is injected. Since the disease itself invariably leads to a dreadful death, both the marketing and use of the vaccine are fully justified, notwithstanding the unavoidable high degree of risk which they involve. Such a product, properly prepared, and accompanied by proper directions and warning, is not defective, nor is it *unreasonably* dangerous. The same is true of many other drugs, vaccines, and the like, many of which for this very reason cannot legally be sold except to physicians, or under the prescription of a physician. It is also true in particular of many new or experimental drugs as to which, because of lack of time and opportunity for sufficient medical experience, there can be no assurance of safety, or perhaps even of purity of ingredients, but such experience as there is justifies the marketing and use of the drug notwithstanding a medically recognizable risk. The seller of such products, again with the qualification that they are properly prepared and marketed, and proper warning is given, where the situation calls for it, is not to be held to strict liability for unfortunate consequences attending their use, merely because he has undertaken to supply the public with an apparently useful and desirable product, attended with a known but apparently reasonable risk.

Application of comment *k.* has been justified under the law in some jurisdictions as a way to strike a balance between a manufacturer's responsibility and the encouragement of research and development of new products. Under certain instances, it is in the public interest to allow products to be marketed which are unsafe, because the benefits of the product justify its risks.

We applied § 402A, comment *k.* to a products liability action involving a prescription drug in McDaniel v. McNeil Laboratories, Inc. . . . In *McDaniel*, a woman was rendered permanently comatose after being given doses of a prescription drug, Innovar, during surgery. At the time of her surgery, Innovar and the warnings and information contained in the package inserts had been approved for use by the FDA. . . . On appeal, we placed emphasis on FDA approval of the drug, and citing to § 402 A, comment *k.*, we held:

> An unavoidably unsafe drug which has been approved for marketing by the United States Food and Drug Administration, properly prepared, compounded, packaged, and distributed, and accompanied by proper approved directions and warnings, as a matter of law, is not defective nor unreasonably dangerous, in the absence of proof of inaccurate, incomplete, misleading, or fraudulent information furnished by the manufacturer in connection with such federal approval or later revisions thereof.

McDaniel, 196 Neb. at 201, 241 N.W.2d at 828. Under the evidence presented, we determined that it was not error for the trial court to refuse to submit the issue of strict liability or warranty, either express or implied, to the jury.

(ii) Interpretation of Comment k. in Other Jurisdictions

Comment *k.*, however, has been interpreted in a variety of ways in other jurisdictions, and there has been a wide range of disagreement regarding its application.

Only a few jurisdictions have interpreted comment *k.* in a manner that strictly excepts all prescription drugs from strict liability. Under the minority view, a drug that is properly manufactured and accompanied by an adequate warning of the risks known to the manufacturer at the time of sale is not defectively designed as a matter of law. Brown v. Superior Court (Abbott Laboratories), 44 Cal. 3d 1049, 245 Cal. Rptr. 412, 751 P.2d 470 (1988). . . . These jurisdictions are commonly described by legal commentators as providing manufacturers with a "blanket immunity" from strict liability for design defects in prescription drugs. Our decision in *McDaniel, supra,* generally falls under this category of interpretation of comment *k.*

(iii) Cases Applying Risk-Utility Analysis Under Comment k.

[The categorical approach of *Brown* and *McDaniel* has been widely criticized.] . . . One court has stated:

> We believe that a more selective application [of comment *k.*] will encourage, rather than discourage, improvements in prescription products. Comment *k* was designed in part to protect new and experimental drugs. . . . "Comment k states: 'There are some products which, in the present state of human knowledge, are quite incapable of being made safe for their intended and ordinary use.' Obviously, for this to be true, the design must be as safe as the best available testing and research permits." . . . Thus, a product which is as safe as current testing and research permits should be protected. The reverse is also true; a product which is not as safe as current technology can make it should not be protected. (Citation omitted.)

Adams v. G.D. Searle & Co., Inc., 576 So. 2d 728, 732 (Fla. App. 1991).

As of this writing, no state court has faced the issue of whether to adopt § 6(c). A few federal courts have discussed this section, but only to the extent of either predicting whether the applicable state court would adopt § 6(c) or declining to apply it in the absence of state precedent.

[Scholars have offered] several criticisms of § 6(c), which will be briefly summarized. First, [they argue,] it does not accurately restate the law. It has been repeatedly stated that there is no support in the case law for the application of a reasonable physician standard in which strict liability for a design defect will apply only when a product is not useful for any class of persons. Rather, as illustrated by the discussion of the treatment of comment *k.* under the Second Restatement in other jurisdictions, the majority of courts apply some form of risk-utility balancing that focuses on a variety of factors, including the existence of a reasonable alternative design. . . .

Second, the reasonable physician test is criticized as being artificial and difficult to apply. The test requires fact finders to presume that physicians have as much or more of an awareness about a prescription drug product as the manufacturer. The test also ignores concerns of commentators that physicians tend to prescribe drugs they are familiar with or for which they have received advertising material, even when studies indicate that better alternatives are available.

A third criticism of particular applicability to Freeman's case is that the test lacks flexibility and treats drugs of unequal utility equally. For example, a drug used for cosmetic purposes but which causes serious side effects has less utility than a drug which treats a deadly disease, yet also has serious side effects. In each case, the drugs would likely be useful to a class of patients under the reasonable physician standard for some class of persons. Consequently, each would be exempted from design defect liability. But under a standard that considers reasonable alternative design, the cosmetic drug could be subject to liability if a safer yet equally effective design was available. . . .

Fourth, the test allows a consumer's claim to be defeated simply by a statement from the defense's expert witness that the drug at issue had some benefit for any single class of people. Thus, it is argued that application of § 6(c) will likely shield pharmaceutical companies from a wide variety of suits that could have been brought under comment *k.* of the Second Restatement. . . . Thus, even though the rule is reformulated, any application of § 6(c) will essentially provide the same blanket immunity from liability for design defects in prescription drugs as did the application of comment *k.* in the few states that interpreted it as such.

We conclude that § 6(c) has no basis in the case law. We view § 6(c) as too strict of a rule, under which recovery would be nearly impossible. Accordingly, we do not adopt § 6(c) of the Third Restatement. . . .

We conclude that § 402 A, comment *k.*, of the Second Restatement should be applied on a case-by-case basis and as an affirmative defense in cases involving prescription drug products. Under this rule, an application of the comment does not provide a blanket immunity from strict liability for prescription drugs. Rather, the plaintiff is required to plead the consumer expectations test, as he or she would be required to do in any products liability case. The defendant may then raise comment *k.* as an affirmative defense. The comment will apply to except the prescription drug product from strict liability when it is shown that (1) the product is properly manufactured and contains adequate warnings, (2) its benefits justify its risks, and (3) the product was at the time of manufacture and distribution incapable of being made more safe.

In this case, because the application of comment *k.* is an affirmative defense, Freeman was only required to plead that the Accutane she took was unreasonably dangerous under a consumer expectations test. Freeman alleged that Accutane was unreasonably dangerous for use, that it was not fit for its intended purpose, that the risks inherent in the design outweighed the benefits of its use, and that Accutane was more dangerous to Freeman than was anticipated due to undisclosed side effects. As facts supporting her allegations, Freeman alleged that Accutane is sold as an acne medication and that the side effects of Accutane present life-threatening conditions. Thus, Freeman alleged facts that the Accutane was dangerous to an extent beyond that which would be contemplated by the ordinary consumer who purchases it, with the ordinary knowledge common to the community as to its characteristics. Accordingly, we conclude that Freeman has stated a theory of recovery based on a design defect. . . .

3. Failure to Warn

[The court considered Freeman's claim that Hoffman failed adequately to warn her, via her physician, of Accutane's dangers. The court's treatment of this claim is discussed in Part V of this chapter. — Eds.] . . .

4. Implied and Express Warranty

Freeman also alleges in her petition theories of recovery for breach of implied warranty on the basis that Accutane was not fit for its intended purpose and for breach of express warranty on the basis that Hoffman expressly warranted that Accutane was of merchantable quality.

(a) Implied Warranty

[The court concluded that implied-warranty claims for personal injuries caused by products are subsumed into products liability claims. — Eds.] . . .

(b) Express Warranty

We treat Freeman's express warranty claim differently. Express warranty is grounded in terms of an express promise made as part of a pending purchase. Thus, unlike implied warranties, there is a clearer contractual difference between a theory of recovery based on express warranty and a tort theory of recovery based on a product defect. Thus, we are not convinced that we should endeavor to merge those theories of recovery. Accordingly, we address whether Freeman has stated a theory of recovery for breach of express warranty.

Neb. U.C.C. § 2-313 (Reissue 1992) requires that in order to create an express warranty, the seller must make an affirmation of fact or promise to the buyer which relates to the goods and becomes part of the basis of the bargain. The comments indicate that express warranties rest on "dickered" aspects of the individual bargain. See *id.*, comment 1.

> the latter should bear the loss. The same rationale would apply to the marketing of a product which contains an ingredient which the manufacturer knows or should know "by the application of reasonable developed human skill and foresight" is dangerous. But, in the view of this court, that is where the reason for the rule ceases and the rule of "strict" liability itself should stop. To exact an obligation to warn the user of unknown and unknowable allergies, sensitivities and idiosyncrasies would be for the courts to recast the manufacturer in the role of an insurer beyond any reasonable application of the rationale expressed above.

(272 Cal. App. 2d at pp.650-651, 77 Cal. Rptr. 709.) . . .

. . . [In deciding Brown v. Superior Court, (1988) 44 Cal. 3d 1049, 245 Cal. Rptr. 412, 751 P.2d 470, we concluded] that a manufacturer is not strictly liable for injuries caused by a prescription drug so long as it was properly prepared and accompanied by warnings of its dangerous propensities that were either known or reasonably scientifically knowable at the time of distribution. . . .

. . . [D]ecisions of the Courts of Appeal persuade us that California is well settled into the majority view that knowledge, actual or constructive, is a requisite for strict liability for failure to warn. . . . *Brown, supra,* 44 Cal. 3d 1049, 245 Cal. Rptr. 412, 751 P.2d 470, if not directly, at least by implication, reaffirms that position.

However, even if we are implying too much from the language in *Brown*, the fact remains that we are now squarely faced with the issue of knowledge and knowability in strict liability for failure to warn in other than the drug context. Whatever the ambiguity of *Brown*, we hereby adopt the requirement, as propounded by the Restatement Second of Torts and acknowledged by the lower courts of this state and the majority of jurisdictions, that knowledge or knowability is a component of strict liability for failure to warn.

One of the guiding principles of the strict liability doctrine was to relieve a plaintiff of the evidentiary burdens inherent in a negligence cause of action. . . . The proponents of the minority rule, including the Court of Appeal in this case, argue that the knowability requirement, and admission of state-of-the-art evidence, improperly infuse negligence concepts into strict liability cases by directing the trier of fact's attention to the conduct of the manufacturer or distributor rather than to the condition of the product. Similar claims have been made as to other aspects of strict liability, sometimes resulting in limitations on the doctrine and sometimes not. In *Cronin*, for example, we concluded that the "unreasonably dangerous" element, which the Restatement Second of Torts had introduced into the definition of a defective product, should not be incorporated into a plaintiff's burden of proof in a product liability action because it "rings of negligence." . . .

However, the claim that a particular component "rings of" or "sounds in" negligence has not precluded its acceptance in the context of strict liability. . . . [For example,] . . . in Daly v. General Motors Corp., *supra*, 20 Cal. 3d 725, 144 Cal. Rptr. 380, 575 P.2d 1162, that the principles of comparative negligence apply to actions founded on strict products liability. . . .

[Likewise,] . . . in Barker [v. Lull Engineering Co.], this court rejected the claim that the risk/benefit test was unacceptable because it introduced an element which "rings of negligence" into the determination of design defect. . . .

As these cases illustrate, the strict liability doctrine has incorporated some well-settled rules from the law of negligence and has survived judicial challenges asserting that such incorporation violates the fundamental principles of the doctrine. It may also be true that the "warning defect" theory is "rooted in negligence" to a greater extent than are the manufacturing- or design-defect theories. The "warning defect" relates to a failure extraneous to the product itself. Thus, while a manufacturing or design defect *can be* evaluated without reference to the conduct of the manufacturer, the giving of a warning cannot. The latter necessarily requires the communicating of something to someone. How can one warn of something that is unknowable? If every product that has no warning were defective per se and for that reason subject to strict liability, the mere fact of injury by an unlabelled product would automatically permit recovery. That is not, and has never been, the purpose and goal of the failure-to-warn theory of strict liability. Further, if a warning automatically precluded liability in every case, a manufacturer or distributor could easily escape liability with overly broad, and thus practically useless, warnings.

. . . Furthermore, despite its roots in negligence, failure to warn in strict liability differs markedly from failure to warn in the negligence context. Negligence law in a failure-to-warn case requires a plaintiff to prove that a manufacturer or distributor did not warn of a particular risk for reasons which fell below the acceptable standard of care, i.e., what a reasonably prudent manufacturer would have known and warned about. Strict liability is not concerned with the standard of due care or the reasonableness of a manufacturer's conduct. The rules of strict liability require a plaintiff to prove only that the defendant did not adequately warn of a particular risk that was known or knowable in light of the generally recognized and prevailing best scientific and medical knowledge available at the time of manufacture and distribution.[13] Thus, in strict liability, as opposed to negligence, the reasonableness of the defendant's failure to warn is immaterial.

Stated another way, a reasonably prudent manufacturer might reasonably decide that the risk of harm was such as not to require a warning as, for example, if the manufacturer's own testing showed a result contrary to that of others in the scientific community. Such a manufacturer might escape liability under negligence principles. In contrast, under strict liability principles the manufacturer has no such leeway; the manufacturer is liable if it failed to give warning of dangers that were known to the scientific community at the time it manufactured or distributed the product. Whatever may be reasonable from the point of view of the manufacturer, the user of the product must be given the option either to refrain from using the product at all or to use it in such a way as to minimize the degree of danger. . . . Thus, the fact that a manufacturer acted as a reasonably prudent manufacturer in deciding not to warn, while perhaps

13. The parties do not dispute the accepted definition of *scienter* in the failure to warn context, namely, actual or constructive knowledge. As noted in comment j of section 402A of the Restatement Second of Torts, constructive knowledge is knowledge which is obtainable "by the application of reasonable, developed human skill and foresight." As we have explained, however, the element of *scienter* is not necessarily determinative of the duty to warn or of the liability that flows from the failure to warn. Thus, a manufacturer with knowledge, actual or constructive, might have acted reasonably in failing to warn and might escape liability for negligence; the manufacturer's reasonable conduct, however, would not relieve the manufacturer of liability on a strict liability theory.

absolving the manufacturer of liability under the negligence theory, will not preclude liability under strict liability principles if the trier of fact concludes that, based on the information scientifically available to the manufacturer, the manufacturer's failure to warn rendered the product unsafe to its users.

The foregoing examination of the failure-to-warn theory of strict liability in California compels the conclusion that knowability is relevant to imposition of liability under that theory. Our conclusion not only accords with precedent but also with the considerations of policy that underlie the doctrine of strict liability.

We recognize that an important goal of strict liability is to spread the risks and costs of injury to those most able to bear them.[4] However, it was never the intention of the drafters of the doctrine to make the manufacturer or distributor the insurer of the safety of their products. It was never their intention to impose *absolute* liability.

Conclusion

Therefore, in answer to the question raised in our order granting review, a defendant in a strict products liability action based upon an alleged failure to warn of a risk of harm may present evidence of the state of the art, i.e., evidence that the particular risk was neither known nor knowable by the application of scientific knowledge available at the time of manufacture and/or distribution. The judgment of the Court of Appeal is affirmed with directions that the matter be remanded to the trial court for proceedings in accord with our decision herein.

Broussard, J. (concurring). I concur in the majority opinion, but write separately simply to emphasize the narrow scope of the opinion's holding. As the majority opinion properly recognizes, the issue presented by this case is whether so-called "state-of-the-art" evidence is admissible in a strict products liability action *when the plaintiff contends that a product is defective because it failed to contain an adequate warning of the risk that caused the injury.* I agree with the majority that when the plaintiff proceeds *on an absence-of-warning theory,* the defendant is entitled to present evidence that the risk in question was scientifically unknown at the time the product was manufactured and distributed. A warning, by its nature, presupposes that the risk to be warned against is capable of being known, and a rule which permits the trier of fact to find a product defective simply because it lacked a warning of a scientifically unknown risk would go a long way to making a manufacturer an insurer of any injuries caused by its product.

---

4. The suggestion that losses arising from unknowable risks and hazards should be spread among all users to the product, as are losses from predictable injuries or negligent conduct, is generally regarded as not feasible. Not the least of the problems is insurability. (*See* Henderson, *Coping with Time Dimension in Products Liability* (1981) 69 Cal. L. Rev. 919, 948-949; Wade, *On the Effect in Product Liability of Knowledge Unavailable Prior to Marketing* (1983) 58 N.Y.U. L. Rev. 734.) Dean Wade stated the dilemma, but provided no solution: "How does one spread the potential loss of an unknowable hazard? How can insurance premiums be figured for this purpose? Indeed, will insurance be available at all? Spreading the loss is essentially a compensation device rather than a tort concept. Providing compensation should not be the sole basis for imposing tort liability, and this seems more emphatically so in the situation where the defendant is no more able to insure against unknown risks than is the plaintiff." (58 N.Y.U. L. Rev. at p. 755.)

The majority's holding in this case, however, does not mean that state-of-the-art evidence is admissible in all strict products liability cases. Although the majority finds no need to reach the issue here, in my view it is both prudent and appropriate to make it clear that state-of-the-art evidence would not necessarily be relevant when, for example, a plaintiff in a strict products liability action relies solely on the so-called "consumer expectation" prong of the design defect standard. . . .

Under the consumer expectation standard, when a product proves to be unexpectedly unsafe when used as intended by the manufacturer, an injured plaintiff is entitled to recover for the resulting injuries . . . without regard to whether the manufacturer knew or could have known at the time of manufacture or distribution of the specific safety problem that was inherent in its product. Thus, when the plaintiff in a strict products liability action relies solely on a consumer expectation theory, state-of-the-art evidence may not be relevant or admissible.

In this case, however, plaintiff sought to rely, inter alia, on the absence of a warning to prove that the product was defective. Under these circumstances, I agree with the majority that state-of-the-art evidence was admissible.

[Opinion of Mosk, J., concurring and dissenting, omitted. — EDS.]

NOTES AND QUESTIONS

1. Carlin: Updating Brown after Anderson. The California Supreme Court subsequently issued a decision reaffirming *Anderson*'s distinction between theories of strict liability and negligence liability for failure to warn. Notably, it did so in a case concerning the marketing of a prescription drug, even though in the interim the court had held in Brown v. Superior Court, *supra*, that strict *design defect* liability has no application to prescription drugs.

In *Carlin v. Superior Court*, 920 P.2d 1347 (Cal. 1996), the plaintiff alleged that she suffered severe side effects from the medication Halcion. She sued its manufacturer, the Upjohn Company, for failing to warn of these side effects. Upjohn argued that *Brown*'s refusal to permit a plaintiff to proceed with a design defect claim for injuries caused by prescription drugs entailed that only negligence-based liability ought to be recognized when the claim is for failure to warn. The majority of a sharply divided court disagreed, seeing "no reason to depart from our conclusion in *Anderson* that the manufacturer should bear the costs, in terms of preventable injury or death, of its own failure to provide adequate warnings of known or reasonably scientifically knowable risks." *Id.* at 1354. *Carlin* reiterated *Anderson*'s observation that "[w]hatever may be reasonable from the point of view of the manufacturer, the user of the product must be given the option either to refrain from using the product at all or to use it in such a way as to minimize the degree of danger." *Id.* at 1348 (quoting *Anderson*, 810 P.2d, at 559). *Carlin* also rejected Upjohn's argument that its compliance with federal FDA regulations should suffice to establish the adequacy of its warnings for purposes of California products liability law:

> . . . The fact that the pharmaceutical drug industry is highly regulated does not distinguish it from numerous other industries. Moreover, as the dissenting opinion

> concedes, the FDA's approval of a particular warning is not determinative of liability. Nor have our courts adopted the approach of the narrow line of cases cited by the dissenting opinion which would insulate manufacturers for failure to warn if they merely gave FDA-approved warnings. . . .

Id. at 1353 n.4.

2. *How Thin a Line?* Rhetoric aside, is there really a meaningful line to be drawn between strict liability and negligence in the failure to warn context? In attempting to draw that line, *Anderson* states:

> Negligence law in a failure-to-warn case requires a plaintiff to prove that a manufacturer or distributor did not warn of a particular risk for reasons which fell below the acceptable standard of care, i.e., what a reasonably prudent manufacturer would have known and warned about. Strict liability is not concerned with the standard of due care or the reasonableness of a manufacturer's conduct. *The rules of strict liability require a plaintiff to prove only that the defendant did not adequately warn of a particular risk that was known or knowable in light of the generally recognized and prevailing best scientific and medical knowledge available at the time of manufacture and distribution.* Thus, in strict liability, as opposed to negligence, the reasonableness of the defendant's failure to warn is immaterial. [Emphasis added.]

Unfortunately, the italicized sentence is either false, or at best elliptical, as the court in effect concedes a few sentences later:

> Thus, the fact that a manufacturer acted as a reasonably prudent manufacturer in deciding not to warn, while perhaps absolving the manufacturer of liability under the negligence theory, will not preclude liability under strict liability principles if the trier of fact concludes that, based on the information scientifically available to the manufacturer, *the manufacturer's failure to warn rendered the product unsafe to its users.* [Emphasis added.]

In other words, strict liability for failure to warn requires proof that the defendant failed adequately to warn of a risk not just when the risk was known or knowable but also when the failure to warn of that risk *renders the product unsafe* to its users. Thus, in evaluating the width of the line between negligence and strict liability in the failure-to-warn context, one must ask: Are there known or knowable dangers such that the failure to warn of them would render a product unsafe to its users, yet of which a reasonably prudent manufacturer would not warn? Even if this category is small, why else might it matter to make a strict products liability action for failure to warn available to plaintiffs?

3. *Obvious Dangers and Patent Defects.* Black letter failure-to-warn law states that the failure to warn of *obvious* dangers is not actionable. In *Maneely v. General Motors Corp.*, 108 F.3d 1176 (9th Cir. 1997), the plaintiffs were sleeping in the back of a pickup truck as it drove down a highway. When the driver fell asleep, the pickup crashed, causing the plaintiffs to be thrown against the walls of the pickup truck's bed, resulting in paralyzing injuries. Although the obviousness of a risk is generally a question of fact, the court affirmed a grant of summary judgment for GM, reasoning that, as matter of

California law, GM had no obligation to warn of the "obvious" risks of forcible impact associated with riding in the bed of a pickup truck.

As noted in Section III.B, *supra*, courts in the 1970s initially were drawn to the risk-utility test for design defect in part because they wanted to allow for liability even when the danger posed by a product's design is relatively obvious. This feature of design defect law remains in place today; in most jurisdictions a patent danger can warrant a finding of design defect if, for example, the danger can be readily avoided without any loss of functionality. (The obviousness of the danger, however, might support a finding of comparative fault.) In contrast to the law of design defect, failure-to-warn law, as just noted, rejects the idea that commercial sellers have any obligation to warn of dangers that are obvious. What, if anything, might explain this difference?

4. *Failure to Warn and Design Defect.* Comment j to Section 402A states in part: "Where warning is given, the seller may reasonably assume that it will be read and heeded; and a product bearing such a warning, which is safe for use if it is followed, is not in defective condition, nor is it unreasonably dangerous." Read literally, comment j thus appears to immunize sellers from liability for any design defect, no matter how dangerous, so long as they have warned and/or instructed users on how to use the product safely. The Third Restatement follows several commentators and courts in rejecting this idea:

> In general, when a safer design can reasonably be implemented and risks can reasonably be designed out of a product, adoption of the safer design is required over a warning that leaves a significant residuum of such risks. . . . Warnings are not . . . a substitute for the provision of a reasonably safe design.

Restatement (Third) of Torts: Products Liability § 2, cmt. l (1998); *see also* Glover v. Bic Corp., 6 F.3d 1318 (9th Cir. 1993) (applying Oregon law).

5. *Which Dangers Require a Warning?* A seller need not warn of every known or knowable danger that is not obvious. Whether a warning is required, as Note 2, *supra*, indicates, involves whether "the omission of the instructions or warnings renders the product not reasonably safe." Restatement (Third) of Torts: Products Liability § 2(c) (1998). Whether a product is not reasonably safe because of the absence of adequate warnings or instructions is normally for the jury to decide. Given this standard, how should manufacturers go about identifying those dangers of which they should warn? How should lawyers advise client-sellers as to which warnings and instructions are necessary?

A particularly thorny contemporary issue in this area involves whether warnings are required about possible allergic reactions to a product or some ingredient or constituent element of a product. In *Livingston v. Marie Callender's, Inc.*, 85 Cal. Rptr. 2d 528 (Ct. App. 1999), the plaintiff suffered an allergic reaction to monosodium glutamate (MSG) in the defendant's soup. The defendant argued that there was no duty to warn of possible allergic reaction to MSG. Invoking the Second and Third Restatements, the court ruled that the issue was for the jury:

> Restatement Second of Torts, section 402A, comment j states: "Directions or warning. In order to prevent the product from being unreasonably dangerous,

> the seller may be required to give directions or warning, on the container, as to its use. The seller may reasonably assume that those with common allergies, as for example to eggs or strawberries, will be aware of them, and he is not required to warn against them. *Where, however, the product contains an ingredient to which a substantial number of the population are allergic, and the ingredient is one whose danger is not generally known, or if known is one which the consumer would reasonably not expect to find in the product, the seller is required to give warning against it, if he has knowledge, or by the application of reasonable, developed human skill and foresight should have knowledge, of the presence of the ingredient and the danger.* Likewise in the case of poisonous drugs, or those unduly dangerous for other reasons, warning as to use may be required." (Italics added.) The recently adopted Restatement Third of Torts: Products Liability, section 2, comment k, similarly states: "Cases of adverse allergic or idiosyncratic reactions involve a special subset of products that may be defective because of inadequate warnings. . . . [¶] The general rule in cases involving allergic reactions is that a warning is required when the harm-causing ingredient is one to which a substantial number of persons are allergic." Further, . . . comment k notes: "The ingredient that causes the allergic reaction must be one whose danger or whose presence in the product is not generally known to consumers. . . . When the presence of the allergenic ingredient would not be anticipated by a reasonable user or consumer, warnings concerning its presence are required."

Id. at 532-533.

6. *Proliferation = Dilution?* The Reporters for the Third Restatement's provisions on products liability have argued that the ease with which many jurisdictions permit plaintiffs to recover for failure to warn is having the perverse effect of reducing the efficacy of warnings. Because the issuance of further warnings is relatively cheap, manufacturers, they suppose, are inclined to attempt to ward off liability by warning of virtually any conceivable danger that might be associated with their product, no matter how remote. This proliferation of warnings in turn creates a culture in which consumers become dismissive of warnings because of their overuse. Thus, by too easily permitting failure-to-warn claims in the name of consumer safety, the law ends up diminishing safety.

7. *Adequacy of Warning.* A manufacturer's inclusion of a warning with the product, and its inclusion of instructions as to certain precautions, will not necessarily relieve the manufacturer of liability for ensuing injuries *even under a failure-to-warn theory.* This is because warnings and instructions must be *adequate* to notify the consumer of the existence and nature of the hazard at issue. The issue of adequacy is normally for the jury. Although there are cases in which warnings are clearly inadequate—imagine a manufacturer that purports to alert consumers of a severe, nonobvious risk of a product in a small-font footnote buried in the product's owners' manual—adequacy is ordinarily highly context-specific, requiring a judgment that cannot be reduced to hard and fast rules. *See* Restatement (Third) of Torts: Products Liability § 2, cmt. i (1998) ("No easy guideline exists for courts to adopt in assessing the

adequacy of product warnings and instructions. In making their assessments, courts must focus on many factors, such as content and comprehensibility, intensity of expression, and the characteristics of expected user groups."). Thus, for purposes of litigation as well as client counseling, consideration will have to be given to the placement and prominence of the warning on the product itself and/or in accompanying packaging or instructional materials; the nature of the risk(s) posed by the product; the extent to which the risk and its consequences, if realized, are defined and communicated by the warning; the precautions that can or should be taken in light of the warning; whether the warning is given in conjunction with other information that might cause confusion or a downplaying of the danger; and what the seller knows or should know about likely reactions to the warnings.

Some of the nuances of the "adequacy" issue are illustrated by *Schwoerer v. Union Oil Co.*, 17 Cal. Rptr. 2d 227 (Ct. App. 1993). The plaintiff sued the manufacturers and distributors of a solvent that he had inhaled and touched while working with it. As a result, he alleged that he suffered multiple physical ailments, including permanent liver damage. The trial court granted summary judgment for the defendants, but the Court of Appeals reversed, finding that the adequacy of the warnings issued by the defendants was an issue of fact on which reasonable factfinders could disagree. It was undisputed that the defendants provided "material safety data sheets" (MSDS) to the plaintiff's employer and that these contained warnings stating, among other things, that persons using the solvent should wear impermeable gloves, boots, aprons, and should also wear a gas mask or other breathing apparatus in situations in which significant inhalation might occur. The sheets further indicated that contact with the solvent could produce skin irritation, rashes, and dermatitis; that inhalation could cause respiratory tract irritation, dizziness, fatigue, nausea, and asphyxiation; and that chronic overexposure to the solvent might have effects of an unspecified nature on the central nervous system.

For purposes of summary judgment, it was assumed that the plaintiff did not receive this information from his employer and was not equipped with protective clothing or goggles. On appeal, the central issue was whether the warnings were adequate as a matter of law, such that the issue should be taken away from the factfinder. The Court of Appeals concluded that they were not, reasoning as follows:

> It cannot be disputed that liver damage is far more apt to have a devastating effect on one so afflicted than is dermatitis, as to which the MSDS do warn. Since, for our purposes, defendants are assumed to have known of this devastating potential yet failed to warn against it, defendants have not shown the warnings provided in the MSDS are adequate as a matter of law.

Id. at 232. Assume that the plaintiff did receive the information described above. Was *Schwoerer* rightly decided? Was it enough, on this assumption, that the plaintiff was put on notice that he was dealing with materials that were clearly not benign? That there was a possible connection between inhalation and unspecified dangers to the central nervous system?

> *see Kellogg v. Wyeth,* 762 F.Supp.2d 694, 700 (D.Vt.2010) (asserting that Vermont has neither adopted nor rejected the learned intermediary doctrine), New Mexico, *see Rimbert v. Eli Lilly & Co.,* 577 F.Supp.2d 1174, 1214–1224 (D.N.M.2008) (predicting that the Supreme Court of New Mexico would not adopt the learned intermediary doctrine), and, of course, West Virginia.

Tyree, 56 F. Supp.3d at 834 n.3.

With this sketch of the learned intermediary doctrine in mind, consider now the issues mentioned at the outset of this section as to the burden plaintiffs do or should face in proving causation within a failure-to-warn claim.

Motus v. Pfizer Inc.

196 F. Supp. 2d 984 (C.D. Cal. 2001), *aff'd,* 2004 U.S. App. LEXIS 1944 (9th Cir.)

Matz, J.

I. Introduction

Six days after Dr. Gerald Trostler prescribed Zoloft to Victor Motus, Mr. Motus took his life. His widow, Flora Motus, sued Zoloft's manufacturer, Pfizer Inc., for failing to adequately warn that Zoloft can cause those who ingest it to commit suicide. She alleges five claims: (1) "wrongful death/negligence"; (2) strict liability; (3) "survival action"; (4) fraud; and (5) breach of warranty. Each of Ms. Motus's claims is premised on the allegation that Pfizer's "package insert and marketing materials do not warn . . . that [Zoloft] can cause some people to think and act in violent or suicidal ways." First Amended Complaint ("FAC") ¶ 20. She alleges that Pfizer's failure to warn of this risk caused her husband to commit suicide.

Pfizer now moves for summary judgment on the ground that Ms. Motus cannot prove that its alleged failure to warn or inadequate warning caused her injury. Pfizer argues that Ms. Motus has no evidence that Dr. Trostler would have acted differently had adequate warnings been provided. The Court agrees with Pfizer, and accordingly grants it summary judgment on all claims.

II. Factual Background

A. Dr. Trostler Prescribes Zoloft to Victor Motus

Mr. Motus first saw Dr. Trostler on July 16, 1998 because he was having trouble controlling his diabetes and cholesterol. Mr. Motus did not mention any symptoms of anxiety or depression during his first visit, nor during his next three visits to Dr. Trostler on July 27, August 25, and October 13. Mr. Motus visited Dr. Trostler for the last time on November 6, 1998. During that visit, Mr. Motus appeared "unhappy," "depressed," and "frustrated," and he "had a lot on his mind that he wanted to share" with Dr. Trostler. Mr. Motus told Dr. Trostler that his savings of $150,000 were gone, that he was losing $5,000 to $10,000 per week on a bad investment, that he could not sleep, that he was the president of a school district, that he had a political problem and that he had some numbness in his hands. Mr. Motus also told Dr. Trostler that he was contemplating bankruptcy.

As a result of these revelations, Dr. Trostler concluded that Mr. Motus was moderately depressed. Dr. Trostler did not think that Mr. Motus was suicidal or sufficiently depressed to warrant sending Mr. Motus to a mental health professional. Dr. Trostler prescribed Mr. Motus 25 milligrams of Zoloft for seven days, followed by 50 milligrams of Zoloft for fourteen days.

To fill this prescription, Dr. Trostler gave Mr. Motus a sample packet of Zoloft, which he had received from a Pfizer representative. The sample packet did not have any warning printed on it. Dr. Trostler opined that the box containing the sample packets probably did contain a package insert (i.e., an insert that contains information about the drug, including warnings), or that each sample packet originally came with the package insert attached, but he could not recall removing the package insert from the packets or whether one package insert came in the box of samples.

Dr. Trostler did not provide Mr. Motus with a package insert or any other written information concerning Zoloft, and he could not recall whether he had any promotional materials for Zoloft in his office at the time he prescribed Zoloft for Mr. Motus. Dr. Trostler did not warn Mr. Motus that taking Zoloft could cause him to have suicidal thoughts or experience akathisia [a condition that may entail muscle twitches, agitation, and restlessness]. He did not discuss with Mr. Motus any contraindications of taking Zoloft, and was not aware of any contraindications that would have suggested Mr. Motus was not a good candidate for Zoloft. During Dr. Trostler's deposition, Plaintiff's lawyer asked: "If you had been told that Zoloft can cause an increased risk in suicide during the first few weeks of drug treatment, is that the kind of information you would pass on to your patients?" Dr. Trostler responded, "Yes." Dr. Trostler told Mr. Motus to call him if his condition worsened or if he experienced any side effects, and he also had Mr. Motus schedule a follow-up appointment for November 26 (i.e., twenty days later). Before Mr. Motus took his life, Dr. Trostler did not speak to Mr. Motus or any member of Mr. Motus's family and he did not know whether Mr. Motus experienced adverse reactions to Zoloft, such as confusion, akathisia, or suicidal thoughts. Six days later, on November 12, 1998, Mr. Motus committed suicide by shooting himself.

B. How Did Dr. Trostler Learn About Zoloft?

Dr. Trostler could not recall reviewing any information from Pfizer before deciding to prescribe Zoloft to Mr. Motus, although he "may have" relied on some unspecified written information from an "article or seminar." He stated that his familiarity with Zoloft was "probably multi-source," and included "reading articles" and attending "drug company meetings." By "drug company meetings," Dr. Trostler meant physician meetings such as seminars, lectures or conferences, where information was delivered by various people, including drug company representatives. Dr. Trostler stated that the articles he read were "occasional articles that appear[ed] in journals to which I subscribe," such as the New England Journal of Medicine and the Annals of Internal Medicine. Dr. Trostler stated that he also received "hundreds of journals that come to the office unsolicited." Plaintiff argues that Dr. Trostler obtained information from sources other than the package insert, such as "PDR's" (Physician's Desk Reference), "Dear Doctor" letters and promotional activities of sales people. There is no evidence

2d 162, 920 P.2d 1347 (1996). California follows the learned intermediary doctrine, which states that in the case of prescription drugs, the duty to warn "runs to the physician, not to the patient." *Id.* at 1116, 56 Cal. Rptr. 2d 162, 920 P.2d 1347 (citations omitted). Thus, a manufacturer discharges its duty to warn if it provides adequate warnings to the physician about any known or reasonably knowable dangerous side effects, regardless of whether the warning reaches the patient.

A plaintiff asserting causes of action based on a failure to warn must prove not only that no warning was provided or the warning was inadequate, but also that the inadequacy or absence of the warning caused the plaintiff's injury.

Pfizer tacitly concedes for purposes of this summary judgment motion that its warning about the risk of suicide was inadequate. It moves for summary judgment on the ground that Ms. Motus cannot demonstrate that the inadequate warning was the proximate cause of her injury, because she has failed to demonstrate that the inclusion of an adequate warning would have altered Dr. Trostler's decision to prescribe Zoloft to Mr. Motus. If it is not genuinely disputable that Dr. Trostler would have prescribed Zoloft to Mr. Motus even if Pfizer had provided an adequate warning about the risk of suicide, then Ms. Motus cannot prove proximate cause, and Pfizer is entitled to summary judgment.

C. The Burden of Proof and the Rebuttable Presumption

Both sides agree that under California law [on actual causation] Plaintiff must prove that Pfizer's alleged failure to warn or inadequate warning was a "substantial factor" in bringing about Mr. Motus's death. . . . The threshold issue here is whether she can do so by invoking the rebuttable presumption, adopted by some states, that had there been an adequate warning, the doctor would have heeded it. Courts have premised the adoption of this presumption on the following language in comment j of section 402A of the Restatement (Second) of Torts:

> Where warning is given, the seller may reasonably assume that it will be read and heeded; and a product bearing such a warning, which is safe for use if followed, is not in defective condition, nor is it unreasonably dangerous.

Under the rebuttable presumption, once the plaintiff establishes that the manufacturer provided inadequate warnings, the burden shifts to the defendant to show that an adequate warning would not have affected the doctor's conduct in prescribing the drug. If the defendant fails to make that showing, "the presumption satisfies the plaintiff's burden of demonstrating that the inadequate warning was the proximate cause of the ingestion of the drug." [Quoted authority omitted. — Eds.] The rebuttable presumption is simply a burden-shifting device that makes it easier for a plaintiff to prove causation.

By contrast, in states that have not adopted the rebuttable presumption, the plaintiff in a prescription drug case bears the full burden of proving through affirmative evidence that the inadequate warning was the proximate cause of the injury, or, in other words, that an adequate warning to the prescribing physician would have altered the physician's conduct. . . .

In this case, if the presumption applies, Pfizer must come forward with evidence affirmatively demonstrating that an adequate warning would not have affected Dr. Trostler's decision to prescribe Zoloft to Mr. Motus. If the rebuttable presumption does not apply, Pfizer may prevail by showing that Plaintiff lacks evidence establishing that an adequate warning would have affected Dr. Trostler's decision to prescribe Zoloft. Pfizer need not produce its own evidence; pointing to an absence of evidence on Plaintiff's part is sufficient.

D. Does California Apply the Rebuttable Presumption?

"A federal court sitting in diversity must follow the law directed by the Supreme Court of the state whose law is found to be applicable, and if there is no direct decision by the highest court of that state, the federal court should determine what it believes that state's highest court would find if the issue were before it." Plummer v. Lederle Laboratories, 819 F.2d 349, 355 (2d Cir. 1987) (citation omitted).

Plaintiff asserts that California has adopted the presumption, and that it applies to this case. . . .

As Defendant argues in its supplemental brief, California appellate courts — citing comment j to section 402A of the Restatement (Second) of Torts — have reasoned that when an adequate warning is provided to the plaintiff, the defendant *manufacturer* "may assume that it will be read and heeded." Plaintiff has cited no California case using comment j to shift either the burden of proof as to causation or the burden of going forward to a defendant in a failure-to-warn case.

Moreover, even if California *had* adopted the rebuttable presumption in failure-to-warn cases generally, California courts would not necessarily apply that presumption in the prescription drug context, which raises distinct policy concerns. . . . [In] *Brown v. Superior Court of City and County of San Francisco*, 751 P.2d 470 (1988) . . . the California Supreme Court . . . noted:

> [There is] an important distinction between prescription drugs and other products such as construction machinery . . ., a lawnmower . . ., or perfume . . ., the producers of which were held strictly liable. In the latter cases, the product is used to make work easier or to provide pleasure, while in the former it may be necessary to alleviate pain or to sustain life. Moreover, unlike other important medical products (wheelchairs, for example), harm to some users from prescription drugs is unavoidable. Because of these distinctions, the broader public interest in the availability of drugs must be considered in deciding the appropriate standard of liability for injuries resulting from their use.

Id. at 1063, 245 Cal. Rptr. 412, 751 P.2d 470. . . .

[*Brown*'s admonition notwithstanding,] [t]he Court recognizes the difficulty in predicting how the California Supreme Court would rule on the issue whether prescription drug manufacturers should be subject to the application of the rebuttable presumption. In *Carlin*, for example, the California Supreme Court held that manufacturers of prescription drugs can be held strictly liable for failing to warn of risks that are scientifically knowable, but which were not actually known to the drug manufacturer at the time it manufactured the drug. In reaching this conclusion, the *Carlin*

Court minimized the differences between strict liability rules in the prescription drug context and in the non-prescription drug context. . . . If in fact California had adopted the rebuttable presumption in a failure-to-warn case involving a product other than a prescription drug, this language in *Carlin* might be some indication that the California Supreme Court would also adopt the rebuttable presumption in the prescription drug failure-to-warn context.

But in fact, no California court *has* adopted or applied that presumption, and several California courts have decided whether proximate cause has been or can be established in prescription drug and medical device failure-to-warn cases without mentioning the rebuttable presumption. For example, in Plenger v. Alza Corp., 11 Cal. App. 4th 349, 13 Cal. Rptr. 2d 811 (1992), the plaintiffs sued an IUD manufacturer after their wife and mother died as a result of an infection caused by her use of an IUD. The plaintiffs alleged that the warnings the manufacturer gave the decedent's doctor were inadequate. . . . The court granted summary judgment to the defendant on the ground that the risk of infection and death was so well known in the medical profession that the failure to warn the physician of that risk could not be the legal cause of the decedent's death. If the rebuttable presumption had been applied in *Plenger*, the court would have assumed that the doctor would have heeded an adequate warning about the risk of infection and death from the implantation of IUDs, and so the defendant would have had the burden to demonstrate with affirmative evidence that the doctor still would have implanted the IUD even if an adequate warning had been provided. . . .

Perhaps the most persuasive California case on this point is Ramirez v. Plough, Inc., 6 Cal. 4th 539, 25 Cal. Rptr. 2d 97, 863 P.2d 167 (1993), a failure-to-warn case involving a non-prescription drug. In *Ramirez*, an infant sued a drug manufacturer, alleging that he contracted Reyes Syndrome as a result of ingesting non-prescription aspirin. The product label, which was entirely in English, contained a warning that aspirin has been associated with Reyes Syndrome and stated that the dosage for a child under two should be "as directed by doctor." *Id.* at 543-44, 25 Cal. Rptr. 2d 97, 863 P.2d 167. The plaintiff's mother, who was literate only in Spanish, did not consult a doctor before giving him aspirin. The mother did not ask anyone to translate the label or package insert into Spanish, even though other members of her household could have done so.

The primary question in *Ramirez* was whether the drug manufacturer had a duty to provide warnings in Spanish. The Court concluded it did not. After losing on this ground, the plaintiff asserted an alternative ground of liability: that, lack of Spanish warnings aside, the English label provided defective warnings. The Court rejected this argument because the plaintiff's mother "neither read nor obtained translation of the product labeling. Thus, there is no conceivable causal connection between the representations or omissions that accompanied the product and plaintiff's injury." The Court did not apply or even mention any rebuttable presumption that the plaintiff's mother would have read and heeded an adequate warning. *Ramirez* is strong evidence that the Court would not apply the rebuttable presumption in this case, involving a prescription drug.

Given that other no other court applying California law in this context has adopted the presumption, and several courts have failed to do so when the presumption could have been critical, this Court will not apply it here.

E. There Is No Evidence That Adequate Warnings Would Have Changed Dr. Trostler's Conduct

Given the Court's conclusion that the "rebuttable presumption" is not applicable, Pfizer may prevail in its motion for summary judgment if Ms. Motus has failed to adduce evidence that Dr. Trostler would have acted differently had Pfizer provided an adequate warning about the risk of suicide associated with the ingestion of Zoloft. Ms. Motus has introduced no such evidence.

Mr. Motus did not disclose any contraindications to Dr. Trostler suggesting that he was not a good candidate for Zoloft. . . .

Mr. Motus did not exhibit symptoms that became progressively worse over a period of time. *Cf.* McEwen v. Ortho Pharmaceutical Corp., 270 Or. 375, 528 P.2d 522, 539 (1974) (substantial evidence supported finding that adequate warnings would have changed doctor's decision to permit plaintiff to continue using birth control pills because plaintiff had cumulative symptoms that developed over a period of time). . . . Under *McEwen* . . . Motus may have been able to create a genuine issue if, for example, Dr. Trostler became aware that Mr. Motus experienced adverse reactions to Zoloft such as confusion, akathisia, or suicidal thoughts. But Mr. Motus ingested Zoloft for, at most, only six days and Dr. Trostler testified in his deposition that he did not speak to Mr. Motus or any member of his family after he prescribed Zoloft to Mr. Motus.

Nor has Ms. Motus produced evidence that the risk of suicide associated with Zoloft is so high that it would have affected Dr. Trostler's (or any reasonable physician's) decision to prescribe Zoloft to a moderately depressed patient. "The burden [is] on the plaintiff to demonstrate that the additional non-disclosed risk was sufficiently high that it would have changed the treating physician's decision to prescribe the product for the plaintiff." Thomas [v. Hoffman-LaRoche, Inc.], 949 F.2d [806,] 815 ([5th Cir.] 1992) (plaintiff who suffered seizures after taking Accutane failed to prove that an inadequate warning caused her injuries because the risk of seizures from Accutane is so low that it could not have affected the doctor's decision to prescribe the medication); *see also* Willett v. Baxter Int'l, Inc., 929 F.2d 1094, 1099 (5th Cir. 1991) (unlikely that doctor would have changed his mind to implant artificial heart valves where the risk undisclosed by the warnings — a .03 percent per annum rate of failure due to soot pockets — was minimal and "plaintiff failed to present any specific evidence that this . . . risk would have changed [the doctor's] decision"). . . .

Next, Plaintiff has presented no evidence that Dr. Trostler relied on statements from Pfizer in making his decision to prescribe Zoloft to Mr. Motus. Dr. Trostler's recollection of how he learned about Zoloft is vague. But he did state unequivocally that in making that decision, he did not rely either on any statements Pfizer representatives made to him nor any written materials they may have provided to him. Indeed, Dr. Trostler stated that he did not read the package insert or PDR entry for Zoloft until after Mr. Motus committed suicide. It follows that the inclusion of adequate warnings in that information would not have affected his decision. . . .

Ms. Motus argues that Dr. Trostler's credibility is a jury question. Plaintiff is correct that some courts permit a plaintiff to get past the summary judgment phase even when a prescribing doctor makes unequivocal statements demonstrating that adequate warnings would not have changed his or her decision to prescribe a drug. . . .

The Court [rejects this argument]. If Dr. Trostler's testimony on this point were "equivocal or uncertain," or if there was evidence placing his credibility in question, the Court might agree that it should "reserve the issue of credibility for the jury's determination."[Quoted authority omitted.] Here, there is no such equivocal evidence in the record, nor evidence undermining Dr. Trostler's veracity. Indeed, Plaintiff never asked Dr. Trostler what could have been (depending on the answer) the following dispositive question: "Dr. Trostler, if even without reading the package insert you had become aware that Pfizer itself had disclosed that [whatever is the precise warning regarding suicide that plaintiff considers necessary], would you have prescribed Zoloft to Mr. Motus?" Plaintiff's lawyer did ask Dr. Trostler: "If you had been told that Zoloft can cause an increased risk in suicide during the first few weeks of drug treatment, is that the kind of information you would pass on to your patients?" Dr. Trostler responded, "Yes." Plaintiff argues that this response creates a genuine issue as to whether Dr. Trostler would have changed his behavior had Pfizer provided adequate warnings. The Court does not agree. Given that this case is about the sufficiency of the warnings accompanying Zoloft, the appropriate question would have been: "If Zoloft's package insert had contained a warning that Zoloft can cause an increased risk in suicide during the first few weeks of drug treatment, would you have prescribed Zoloft to Mr. Motus?" But Plaintiff's lawyer did not ask this question, and at the hearing, in response to the Court's inquiry why not, he displayed commendable candor in acknowledging that he, and probably defense counsel as well, were afraid of how Dr. Trostler might respond. The testimony Dr. Trostler did give does not establish that if that warning had been provided, he would not have prescribed Zoloft or would have told Mr. Motus something other than what he did say.

On this record Plaintiff has failed to create a question of fact for the jury, especially given that it would appear to be against Dr. Trostler's professional interest to testify as he did. (It is hardly a testament to his diligence that he did not read the package insert before prescribing Zoloft to Mr. Motus.) . . .

. . . .

G. Overpromotion

In her complaint, Plaintiff alleges that Pfizer overpromoted Zoloft: "Pfizer aggressively distributed and marketed Zoloft, encouraging all types of physicians (including those who have no specialized training or expertise in the mental health field such as Dr. Trostler) to dispense and prescribe Zoloft, not only for depression, but also for other maladies." Plaintiff alleges that this alleged overpromotion "has nullified what warnings Pfizer has given regarding this drug." On the basis of these allegations, Plaintiff argues that Pfizer's "overpromotion" caused Dr. Trostler to prescribe Zoloft despite his awareness of the alleged risk that Zoloft can cause patients to commit suicide.

An overpromotion theory is one way that a plaintiff in a failure-to-warn case can overcome the manufacturer's argument either (1) that it provided adequate warnings or (2) that the doctor's decision to prescribe a drug despite his awareness of its dangers was an intervening cause sufficient to vitiate the manufacturer's liability. *See* Stevens v. Parke, Davis & Co., 9 Cal. 3d 51, 65, 107 Cal. Rptr. 45, 507 P.2d 653 (1973) ("[A]n adequate warning to the [medical] profession may be eroded or even nullified by overpromotion of the drug through a vigorous sales program which may have the effect of persuading the prescribing doctor to disregard the warnings given.") . . .

The logic of an overpromotion theory is that the manufacturer's aggressive marketing caused a physician to discount a known risk when prescribing a drug to a patient. Because this Court's ruling is based only on the ground that Plaintiff failed to prove that Dr. Trostler would not have prescribed Zoloft if an adequate warning had been provided, not on his awareness of claims that SSRI drugs were linked to increased suicide, there is no need to address whether Pfizer's alleged overpromotion contaminated Dr. Trotsler's decision. [In any event,] . . . it would appear that Plaintiff could not demonstrate that Pfizer's alleged overpromotion caused Dr. Trostler to prescribe Zoloft to Mr. Motus.

IV. Conclusion

Ms. Motus points to no evidence establishing that Dr. Trostler would have acted differently had Pfizer provided an adequate warning about the alleged risk that Zoloft causes those who ingest it to commit suicide. She is therefore unable to create a genuine issue as to whether Pfizer's alleged failure to provide an adequate warning caused her injuries. All of Plaintiff's claims are premised to some extent on the allegation that Pfizer's failure to warn caused her injuries. Accordingly, Defendant is entitled to summary judgment.

NOTES AND QUESTIONS

1. *Actual Causation.* Like manufacturing defect and design defect claims, failure-to-warn actions require the plaintiff to prove that the defect (the absence of an adequate warning) actually caused the plaintiff's injury. Unlike the other two sorts of defect cases, however, the application of cause-in-fact to failure-to-warn cases necessarily raises the speculative question of whether someone would have selected a different course of conduct if different, or greater, information or warnings had been provided. As noted above, failure-to-warn claims in this respect involve an issue similar to the causation issue in informed consent cases (*see* Chapter 3), as well as fraud.

Previous sections of this chapter have indicated that, at its inception, products liability law was expressly designed to ease a plaintiff's burden in suing a product seller for a product-related injury. It is therefore not surprising that courts developed doctrinal devices—such as the heeding presumption mentioned (but not applied) in *Motus*—that, in effect, put a thumb on the plaintiff's side of the scale in failure-to-warn cases. However, we have also seen a number of courts displaying hostility to the proliferation of products liability claims, which might suggest diminished receptiveness to devices aiding plaintiffs, particularly when it relates to an issue as central as causation. Do you find the federal district judge's application of California law right eye. The explosion occurred while he was recharging the battery, during which procedure he failed to use various safety precautions that would have prevented the explosion. The plaintiff's lawyers argued at trial that the battery maker ought to have warned of all the dangers of recharging and ought to have instructed users on proper precautions. (The battery itself did have a warning, but the warning was not detailed and was in any case covered in dust.) Although D.C. law incorporates a heeding presumption, East Penn rebutted the heeding presumption by presenting Pineda's admission, in his deposition, that he did not read the label on the battery. One might have supposed that his admission would spell defeat for his claim, but it did not. Upholding a jury verdict for plaintiff, the court concluded that the jury was entitled to find that if a better set of warnings had been provided, some of Pineda's co-workers might have read them and conveyed the information to Pineda, which might have caused him to use different precautions.

Most likely, jurors and judges involved in these cases understandably sympathized with the plaintiffs and their families. Is there anything wrong with decisions such as *Ayers* or *Pineda*? Are they the sort of decision contemplated by Justice Traynor's *Escola* concurrence?

REFERENCES/FURTHER READING

History and Overview

Mark Geistfeld, Escola v. Coca Cola Bottling Co., *Strict Products Liability Unbound*, in Robert L. Rabin & Stephen D. Sugarman, *Tort Stories* 259 (2003).

Oscar S. Gray, *Reflections on the Historical Context of Section 402A*, 10 Touro L. Rev. 75 (1993).

James R. Hackney, Jr., *The Intellectual Origins of American Strict Products Liability: A Case Study in American Pragmatic Instrumentalism*, 39 Am. J. Leg. Hist. 443 (1995).

James A. Henderson, Jr. & Theodore Eisenberg, *The Quiet Revolution in Products Liability: An Empirical Study of Legal Change*, 37 UCLA L. Rev. 479 (1990).

James A. Henderson, Jr. & Aaron D. Twerski, *Closing the American Products Liability Frontier: The Rejection of Liability Without Defect*, 66 N.Y.U. L. Rev. 1263 (1991).

Gregory C. Keating, *The Theory of Enterprise Liability and Common Law Strict Liability*, 54 Vand. L. Rev. 1285 (2001).

David G. Owen, *The Graying of Products Liability Law: Paths Taken and Untaken in the New Restatement*, 61 Tenn. L. Rev. 1241 (1994).

George L. Priest, *The Invention of Enterprise Liability: A Critical History of the Intellectual Foundations of Modern Tort Law*, 14 J. Leg. Stud. 461 (1985).

George L. Priest, *Strict Products Liability: The Original Intent*, 10 Cardozo L. Rev. 2301 (1989).

William L. Prosser, *The Fall of the Citadel (Strict Liability to the Consumer)*, 50 Minn. L. Rev. 791 (1966).

William L. Prosser, *The Assault upon the Citadel (Strict Liability to the Consumer)*, 69 Yale L.J. 1099 (1960).

William L. Prosser, *The Implied Warranty of Merchantable Quality*, 27 Minn. L. Rev. 117 (1943).

Marshall S. Shapo, *Products Liability: The Next Act*, 26 Hofstra L. Rev. 761 (1998).

G. Edward White, *Tort Law: An Intellectual History* (exp. ed. 2003).

Underpinnings: Contours and Rationales

John B. Attanasio, *The Principle of Aggregate Autonomy and the Calabresian Approach to Products Liability*, 74 Va. L. Rev. 677 (1988).

Richard Ausness, *Conspiracy Theories: Is There a Place for Civil Conspiracy in Products Liability Litigation?* 74 Tenn. L. Rev. 383 (2007).

Leslie Bender, *Feminist (Re)Torts: Thoughts on the Liability Crisis, Mass Torts, Power, and Responsibilities*, 1990 Duke L.J. 848 (1990).

Anita Bernstein, *Product Dynamism in the Law*, in Floyd Rudmin & Marsha Richins (eds.), *Meaning, Measure and Morality of Materialism* (1992).

Carl Bogus, *War on the Common Law: The Struggle at the Center of Products Liability*, 60 Mo. L. Rev. 1 (1995).

Guido Calabresi & Jon T. Hirschoff, *Toward a Test for Strict Liability in Torts*, 81 Yale L.J. 1055 (1972).

Alan Calnan, *A Consumer-Use Approach to Products Liability*, 33 U. Mem. L. Rev. 755 (2003).

Steven P. Croley & Jon D. Hanson, *Rescuing the Revolution: The Revised Case for Enterprise Liability*, 91 Mich. L. Rev. 683 (1993).

Richard A. Epstein, *Products Liability: The Search for the Middle Ground*, 56 N.C. L. Rev. 643 (1978).

Adam Feeney, *Note: In Search of a Remedy: Do State Laws Exempting Sellers from Strict Product Liability Adequately Protect Consumers Harmed by Defective Chinese-Manufactured Products?* 34 J. Corp. L. 567 (2009).

Mark Geistfeld, *Principles of Products Liability* (2005).

Mark Geistfeld, *The Political Economy of Neo-Contractual Proposals for Products Liability Reform*, 72 Tex. L. Rev. 803 (1994).

Mark Geistfeld, *Implementing Enterprise Liability: A Comment on Henderson and Twerski*, 67 N.Y.U. L. Rev. 1157 (1992).

John C.P. Goldberg and Benjamin C. Zipursky, *The Easy Case for Products Liability Law: A Response to Professors Polinsky and Shavell*, 123 Harv. L. Rev. 1919 (2010).

Peter Huber, *Safety and the Second Best: The Hazards of Public Risk Management in the Courts*, 85 Colum. L. Rev. 277 (1985).

Fleming James, Jr., *Products Liability* (Pts. I & II), 34 Tex. L. Rev. 44, 192 (1955).

Gregory C. Keating, *The Idea of Fairness in the Law of Enterprise Liability*, 95 Mich. L. Rev. 1266 (1997).

William M. Landes & Richard A. Posner, *A Positive Economic Analysis of Products Liability*, 14 J. Leg. Stud. 535 (1985).

David G. Owen, *Rethinking the Policies of Strict Products Liability*, 33 Vand. L. Rev. 681 (1980).

A. Mitchell Polinsky & Steven Shavell, *The Uneasy Case for Product Liability*, 123 Harv. L. Rev. 1437 (2010).

A. Mitchell Polinsky & Steven Shavell, *A Skeptical Attitude About Product Liability Is Justified: A Reply to Professors Goldberg and Zipursky*, 123 Harv. L. Rev. 1949 (2010).

Alan Schwartz, *The Case Against Strict Liability*, 60 Fordham L. Rev. 819 (1992).

Gary T. Schwartz, *Foreword: Understanding Products Liability*, 67 Cal. L. Rev. 435 (1979).

Marshall S. Shapo, *A Representational Theory of Consumer Protection: Doctrine, Function and Legal Liability for Product Disappointment*, 60 Va. L. Rev. 1109 (1974).

Roger Traynor, *The Ways and Meanings of Defective Products and Strict Liability*, 32 Tenn. L. Rev. 363 (1965).

PART V

TORTS AT THE SUPREME COURT

Act (*see Riley*, Chapter 7), and the Federal Employers' Liability Act, or FELA (*see Gottshall*, Chapter 10). They also include areas governed by federal common law, particularly admiralty law (*see Carroll Towing*, Chapter 3, *Kinsman*, Chapter 5, and *Reliable Transfer*, Chapter 7). In applying these bodies of law, as well as in resolving cases brought under the federal courts' diversity jurisdiction, titans of the federal bench, such as Holmes (in his years on the Supreme Court) and Hand, Calabresi, and Posner, have played a role in crafting important pieces of federal tort law and have influenced the shape of state tort law.

Second, we have gone out of our way to point out another respect in which "federal" tort law can be said to exist. If tort law is understood as the means by which private individuals who are wrongfully injured by others seek rectification for those wrongs, then private rights of action afforded by federal statutes outlawing sexual harassment, employment discrimination, civil rights violations, securities fraud, and electronic invasions of privacy are in a sense "torts." By making available and defining the contours of these statutory causes of action in cases such as *Borak* and *Bivens* (Chapter 6), and *Hunt* and *Harris* (Chapter 10), the Court has played an important role in the world of torts, writ large.

These qualifications notwithstanding, the 1990s marked the beginning of a phase in which the Supreme Court has sought more aggressively to shape the legal environment in which tort law operates:

- In two short and seemingly technical opinions on the law of evidence—*Daubert v. Merrell Dow Pharmaceuticals, Inc.*, 509 U.S. 579 (1993), and *Kumho Tire Co. v. Carmichael*, 526 U.S. 137 (1999)—the Court changed the ground rules for litigating toxic tort claims and products liability suits more generally.
- In a series of decisions centering around *BMW of North America, Inc. v. Gore*, 517 U.S. 559 (1996), the Justices have fashioned an increasingly elaborate set of federal constitutional limits on punitive damage awards.
- In *Metro-North Commuter R.R. Co. v. Buckley*, 521 U.S. 424 (1997), the Court revisited the scope of liability for emotional distress under FELA, and, in the process, offered an influential answer to the question of what counts as an "injury" sufficient to support a tort claim. (Notably, it asked and answered this question in a suit arising out of a worker's prolonged exposure to asbestos, a known toxin that has produced by far the largest amount of litigation and liability in the history of American tort law.)
- In a wobbly course of decisions that includes *Wyeth v. Levine*, 555 U.S. 555 (2009) and *Pliva v. Mensing*, 131 S. Ct. 2567 (2011), the Court has displayed an increasing willingness to find that federal safety laws "preempt" state tort law—that is, render state tort law void because it threatens to impose greater safety obligations than do federal directives and thereby interfere with them. In this manner, a Court that is often accused of undermining congressional power in the name of states' rights has demonstrated considerable willingness to permit federal law to displace states' decisions about the content of the obligations citizens owe one another.

There is no simple explanation to the Court's re-entry into tort law. Clearly, tort's expansion and front-page visibility have played a role. Equally clearly, cries over "junk" science, "obscene" punitive damage verdicts, "extortionate" settlements, and "drummed-up" litigation have registered, at least to some degree, with some of the Justices.

Still, epithets like "judicial activism" do not seem to offer much by way of explanatory value. (For example, *Daubert*, *Wyeth*, and *Pliva* can all be understood as displaying fidelity and deference to the work of the federal legislative and/or executive branches.) Nor can one point to a solid block of "conservative" Justices caught in the thrall of modern tort reform movements. As you will see, the decisions excerpted below have instead been issued by shifting coalitions of Justices of varying political leanings. By setting forth several of the Court's leading "tort" decisions, we hope to permit you to begin to formulate your own answers to these important questions.

II. TORTS AND EVIDENCE: GUIDELINES FOR EXPERT TESTIMONY IN PERSONAL INJURY CASES

The 1960s and 1970s saw a rapid development in certain aspects of tort law, most noticeably a trend toward more expansive forms of products liability. *See* Chapter 12. Equally important, however, were related changes in procedural and evidentiary law. By the middle of the twentieth century, an array of legal scholars and judges had critiqued traditional rules preventing the admission of various forms of evidence at trial as setting arbitrary and unnecessarily restrictive limitations on the ability of litigants to prove and defend lawsuits. Confident that judges and juries, aided by the process of adversarial litigation, are capable of separating fact from fiction, these jurists advocated for a more permissive set of evidence rules. Eventually, in 1975, Congress responded by enacting the Federal Rules of Evidence, which effected a broad liberalization of the rules applicable to suits brought in federal court. Many state courts and legislatures followed suit, often using the Federal Rules as their model.

In the following decision — *Daubert* — the Supreme Court considered the effect of Congress's enactment of a particular rule of evidence — Rule 702 — which authorizes parties to enlist expert witnesses to testify on their clients' behalf. Specifically, the question was whether Rule 702 had incorporated "the *Frye* test," a doctrine which, prior to the adoption of the rules, had been employed by federal courts to determine whether to admit expert testimony on matters of *scientific knowledge*. The *Frye* test derived its name from a lower federal court decision, Frye v. United States, 293 F. 1013 (D.C. Ct. App. 1923), in which the court barred an expert from testifying to the results of a primitive and scientifically controversial lie detector test that he had conducted in connection with a criminal prosecution. In support of this result, *Frye* reasoned that an expert should not be permitted to present jurors with a scientific hypothesis or theory relevant to the resolution of a lawsuit unless the methodology on which the expert relies is "generally accepted" in the scientific community. From the time *Frye* was decided, defendants consistently advocated its use as necessary to prevent jurors from being swayed by putative experts who indulge in speculative "junk" science.

Prior to *Daubert*, the lower federal courts had split on the issue of whether *Frye* had survived the adoption of the Federal Rules. Some held that it had. Others held that it had not, in part because the rule does not mention *Frye* and in part because the rules as a whole were intended to liberalize the admission of evidence. The Supreme Court in *Daubert* accepted the latter position, and held that the *Frye* test has no place within the Federal Rules. Indeed, Justice Blackmun, who wrote the opinion for the Court, quite clearly thought that he was giving force to the "liberal" spirit of the Federal Rules. By rejecting *Frye*, he seemed to believe, the Court was embracing a system that would let jurors decide difficult scientific issues on which experts disagreed. Still, notwithstanding its general tenor, Justice Blackmun's opinion concludes on a note of caution, suggesting that even though district courts should not employ the *Frye* test, they should continue to play *some* role in determining whether a purported scientific expert really can claim to be bringing scientific expertise to bear on a particular issue. It then offered some guidelines, distinct from the *Frye* test, to help trial judges perform this "gatekeeping" role.

In one of those unpredictable twists characteristic of our precedent-based system, *Daubert* has since come to stand for a position quite opposed to the one that Justice Blackmun's opinion intended. Indeed, *Daubert* and its progeny — including subsequent federal court decisions, congressional modifications of Rule 702, and comparable changes in many states' evidence law — have bolstered the idea that trial judges must play an *aggressive* role in barring testimony from plaintiffs' experts who offer novel or speculative theories on issues such as actual causation or reasonable alternative product designs. As a result, the allocation of authority between judge and jury to resolve factual disputes in tort cases has shifted toward judges. Moreover, the general tenor of tort litigation has shifted from the pro-plaintiff orientation of the 1960s and 70s to one more favorable to defendants. Indeed, tort plaintiffs today find themselves increasingly having to go to the trouble and (often considerable) expense of establishing the bona fides of experts who will be called to testify on issues such as design defect and cause-in-fact.

Daubert v. Merrell Dow Pharmaceuticals, Inc.

509 U.S. 579 (1993)

Blackmun, J. In this case we are called upon to determine the standard for admitting expert scientific testimony in a federal trial.

I

Petitioners Jason Daubert and Eric Schuller are minor children born with serious birth defects. They and their parents sued respondent in California state court, alleging that the birth defects had been caused by the mothers' ingestion of Bendectin, a prescription antinausea drug marketed by respondent. Respondent removed the suits to federal court on diversity grounds.

After extensive discovery, respondent moved for summary judgment, contending that Bendectin does not cause birth defects in humans and that petitioners would be unable to come forward with any admissible evidence that it does. In support of its motion, respondent submitted an affidavit of Steven H. Lamm, physician and epidemiologist, who is a well-credentialed expert on the risks from exposure to various chemical substances. Doctor Lamm stated that he had reviewed all the literature on Bendectin and human birth defects—more than 30 published studies involving over 130,000 patients. No study had found Bendectin to be a human teratogen (i.e., a substance capable of causing malformations in fetuses). On the basis of this review, Doctor Lamm concluded that maternal use of Bendectin during the first trimester of pregnancy has not been shown to be a risk factor for human birth defects.

Petitioners did not (and do not) contest this characterization of the published record regarding Bendectin. Instead, they responded to respondent's motion with the testimony of eight experts of their own, each of whom also possessed impressive credentials. These experts had concluded that Bendectin can cause birth defects. Their conclusions were based upon "in vitro" (test tube) and "in vivo" (live) animal studies that found a link between Bendectin and malformations; pharmacological studies of the chemical structure of Bendectin that purported to show similarities between the structure of the drug and that of other substances known to cause birth defects; and the "reanalysis" of previously published epidemiological (human statistical) studies.

The District Court granted respondent's motion for summary judgment. The court stated that scientific evidence is admissible only if the principle upon which it is based is "'sufficiently established to have general acceptance in the field to which it belongs.'" 727 F. Supp. 570, 572 (S.D. Cal. 1989), quoting United States v. Kilgus, 571 F.2d 508, 510 (CA9 1978). The court concluded that petitioners' evidence did not meet this standard. Given the vast body of epidemiological data concerning Bendectin, the court held, expert opinion which is not based on epidemiological evidence is not admissible to establish causation. Thus, the animal-cell studies, live-animal studies, and chemical-structure analyses on which petitioners had relied could not raise by themselves a reasonably disputable jury issue regarding causation. Petitioners' epidemiological analyses, based as they were on recalculations of data in previously published studies that had found no causal link between the drug and birth defects, were ruled to be inadmissible because they had not been published or subjected to peer review.

The United States Court of Appeals for the Ninth Circuit affirmed. 951 F.2d 1128 (1991). Citing Frye v. United States, 54 App. D.C. 46, 47, 293 F. 1013, 1014 (1923), the court stated that expert opinion based on a scientific technique is inadmissible unless the technique is "generally accepted" as reliable in the relevant scientific community. The court declared that expert opinion based on a methodology that diverges "significantly from the procedures accepted by recognized authorities in the field . . . cannot be shown to be 'generally accepted as a reliable technique.'" *Id.*, at 1130, quoting United States v. Solomon, 753 F.2d 1522, 1526 (CA9 1985).

. . . Contending that reanalysis is generally accepted by the scientific community only when it is subjected to verification and scrutiny by others in the field, the Court of Appeals rejected petitioners' reanalyses as "unpublished, not subjected to the normal peer review process and generated solely for use in litigation.". . . .

We granted certiorari, in light of sharp divisions among the courts regarding the proper standard for the admission of expert testimony.

II

A

. . . .

The *Frye* test has its origin in a short and citation-free 1923 decision concerning the admissibility of evidence derived from a systolic blood pressure deception test, a crude precursor to the polygraph machine. In what has become a famous (perhaps infamous) passage, the then Court of Appeals for the District of Columbia described the device and its operation and declared:

> "Just when a scientific principle or discovery crosses the line between the experimental and demonstrable stages is difficult to define. Somewhere in this twilight zone the evidential force of the principle must be recognized, and while courts will go a long way in admitting expert testimony deduced from a well-recognized scientific principle or discovery, *the thing from which the deduction is made must be sufficiently established to have gained general acceptance in the particular field in which it belongs.*" 54 App. D.C., at 47, 293 F., at 1014 (emphasis added).

Because the deception test had "not yet gained such standing and scientific recognition among physiological and psychological authorities as would justify the courts in admitting expert testimony deduced from the discovery, development, and experiments thus far made," evidence of its results was ruled inadmissible. *Ibid.*

The merits of the *Frye* test have been much debated, and scholarship on its proper scope and application is legion. Petitioners' primary attack, however, is not on the content but on the continuing authority of the rule. They contend that the *Frye* test was superseded by the adoption of the Federal Rules of Evidence. We agree.

We interpret the legislatively enacted Federal Rules of Evidence as we would any statute. Rule 402 provides the baseline:

> All relevant evidence is admissible, except as otherwise provided by the Constitution of the United States, by Act of Congress, by these rules, or by other rules prescribed by the Supreme Court pursuant to statutory authority. Evidence which is not relevant is not admissible.

"Relevant evidence" is defined as that which has "any tendency to make the existence of any fact that is of consequence to the determination of the action more probable or less probable than it would be without the evidence." Rule 401. The Rule's basic standard of relevance thus is a liberal one.

Frye, of course, predated the Rules by half a century. . . .

Here there is a specific Rule that speaks to the contested issue. Rule 702, governing expert testimony, provides:

> If scientific, technical, or other specialized knowledge will assist the trier of fact to understand the evidence or to determine a fact in issue, a witness qualified as an

> expert by knowledge, skill, experience, training, or education, may testify thereto in the form of an opinion or otherwise.

Nothing in the text of this Rule establishes "general acceptance" as an absolute prerequisite to admissibility. Nor does respondent present any clear indication that Rule 702 or the Rules as a whole were intended to incorporate a "general acceptance" standard. The drafting history makes no mention of *Frye*, and a rigid "general acceptance" requirement would be at odds with the "liberal thrust" of the Federal Rules and their "general approach of relaxing the traditional barriers to 'opinion' testimony." [Quoted authority omitted.] Given the Rules' permissive backdrop and their inclusion of a specific rule on expert testimony that does not mention "general acceptance," the assertion that the Rules somehow assimilated *Frye* is unconvincing. *Frye* made "general acceptance" the exclusive test for admitting expert scientific testimony. That austere standard, absent from, and incompatible with, the Federal Rules of Evidence, should not be applied in federal trials.

B

That the *Frye* test was displaced by the Rules of Evidence does not mean, however, that the Rules themselves place no limits on the admissibility of purportedly scientific evidence. Nor is the trial judge disabled from screening such evidence. To the contrary, under the Rules the trial judge must ensure that any and all scientific testimony or evidence admitted is not only relevant, but reliable.

The primary locus of this obligation is Rule 702, which clearly contemplates some degree of regulation of the subjects and theories about which an expert may testify. "*If scientific*, technical, or other specialized *knowledge will assist the trier of fact* to understand the evidence or to determine a fact in issue" an expert "may testify *thereto.*" (Emphasis added.) The subject of an expert's testimony must be "scientific . . . knowledge."[8] The adjective "scientific" implies a grounding in the methods and procedures of science. Similarly, the word "knowledge" connotes more than subjective belief or unsupported speculation. The term "applies to any body of known facts or to any body of ideas inferred from such facts or accepted as truths on good grounds." Webster's Third New International Dictionary 1252 (1986). Of course, it would be unreasonable to conclude that the subject of scientific testimony must be "known" to a certainty; arguably, there are no certainties in science. *See, e.g.*, Brief for Nicolaas Bloembergen et al. as *Amici Curiae* 9 ("Indeed, scientists do not assert that they know what is immutably 'true' — they are committed to searching for new, temporary, theories to explain, as best they can, phenomena"); Brief for American Association for the Advancement of Science et al. as *Amici Curiae* 7-8 ("Science is not an encyclopedic body of knowledge about the universe. Instead, it represents a *process* for proposing and refining theoretical explanations about the world that are subject to further testing and refinement" (emphasis in original)). But, in order to qualify as "scientific knowledge," an inference or assertion must be derived by the scientific method.

8. Rule 702 also applies to "technical, or other specialized knowledge." Our discussion is limited to the scientific context because that is the nature of the expertise offered here.

That conduct is sufficiently reprehensible to give rise to tort liability, and even a modest award of exemplary damages does not establish the high degree of culpability that warrants a substantial punitive damages award. Because this case exhibits none of the circumstances ordinarily associated with egregiously improper conduct, we are persuaded that BMW's conduct was not sufficiently reprehensible to warrant imposition of a $2 million exemplary damages award.

Ratio

The second and perhaps most commonly cited indicium of an unreasonable or excessive punitive damages award is its ratio to the actual harm inflicted on the plaintiff. The principle that exemplary damages must bear a "reasonable relationship" to compensatory damages has a long pedigree. Scholars have identified a number of early English statutes authorizing the award of multiple damages for particular wrongs. Some 65 different enactments during the period between 1275 and 1753 provided for double, treble, or quadruple damages. Our decisions in both *Haslip* and *TXO* endorsed the proposition that a comparison between the compensatory award and the punitive award is significant.

In *Haslip* we concluded that even though a punitive damages award of "more than 4 times the amount of compensatory damages" might be "close to the line," it did not "cross the line into the area of constitutional impropriety." 499 U.S. at 23-24. *TXO*, following dicta in *Haslip*, refined this analysis by confirming that the proper inquiry is "'whether there is a reasonable relationship between the punitive damages award and *the harm likely to result* from the defendant's conduct as well as the harm that actually has occurred.'" *TXO*, 509 U.S. at 460 (emphasis in original), quoting *Haslip*, 499 U.S. at 21. Thus, in upholding the $10 million award in *TXO*, we relied on the difference between that figure and the harm to the victim that would have ensued if the tortious plan had succeeded. That difference suggested that the relevant ratio was not more than 10 to 1.

The $2 million in punitive damages awarded to Dr. Gore by the Alabama Supreme Court is 500 times the amount of his actual harm as determined by the jury. Moreover, there is no suggestion that Dr. Gore or any other BMW purchaser was threatened with any additional potential harm by BMW's nondisclosure policy. The disparity in this case is thus dramatically greater than those considered in *Haslip* and *TXO*.

Of course, we have consistently rejected the notion that the constitutional line is marked by a simple mathematical formula, even one that compares actual *and potential* damages to the punitive award. Indeed, low awards of compensatory damages may properly support a higher ratio than high compensatory awards, if, for example, a particularly egregious act has resulted in only a small amount of economic damages. A higher ratio may also be justified in cases in which the injury is hard to detect or the monetary value of noneconomic harm might have been difficult to determine. It is appropriate, therefore, to reiterate our rejection of a categorical approach. Once again, "we return to what we said . . . in *Haslip:* 'We need not, and indeed we cannot, draw a mathematical bright line between the constitutionally acceptable and the constitutionally unacceptable that would fit every case. We can say, however, that [a] general concer[n] of reasonableness . . . properly enter[s] into the constitutional calculus.'" *Id.*, at 458 (quoting *Haslip*, 499 U.S. at 18). In most cases, the ratio will be within a constitutionally acceptable range, and remittitur will not be justified on this basis. When the ratio is a breathtaking 500 to 1, however, the award must surely "raise a suspicious judicial eyebrow." *TXO*, 509 U.S. at 481 (O'Connor, J., dissenting).

Sanctions for Comparable Misconduct

Comparing the punitive damages award and the civil or criminal penalties that could be imposed for comparable misconduct provides a third indicium of excessiveness. As Justice O'Connor has correctly observed, a reviewing court engaged in determining whether an award of punitive damages is excessive should "accord 'substantial deference' to legislative judgments concerning appropriate sanctions for the conduct at issue." Browning-Ferris Industries of Vt., Inc. v. Kelco Disposal, Inc., 492 U.S. at 301 (opinion concurring in part and dissenting in part). . . . In this case the $2 million economic sanction imposed on BMW is substantially greater than the statutory fines available in Alabama and elsewhere for similar malfeasance.

The maximum civil penalty authorized by the Alabama Legislature for a violation of its Deceptive Trade Practices Act is $2,000; other States authorize more severe sanctions, with the maxima ranging from $5,000 to $10,000. Significantly, some statutes draw a distinction between first offenders and recidivists; thus, in New York the penalty is $50 for a first offense and $250 for subsequent offenses. None of these statutes would provide an out-of-state distributor with fair notice that the first violation—or, indeed the first 14 violations—of its provisions might subject an offender to a multimillion dollar penalty. . . .

The judgment is reversed, and the case is remanded for further proceedings not inconsistent with this opinion.

Breyer, J. (concurring) (joined by O'Connor and Souter, JJ.). . . .

. . . .

. . . The standards the Alabama courts applied here . . . provided no significant constraints or protection against arbitrary results.

First, the Alabama statute that permits punitive damages does not itself contain a standard that readily distinguishes between conduct warranting very small, and conduct warranting very large, punitive damages awards. That statute permits punitive damages in cases of "oppression, fraud, wantonness, or malice." Ala. Code § 6-11-20(a) (1993). But the statute goes on to define those terms broadly, to encompass far more than the egregious conduct that those terms, at first reading, might seem to imply. . . . The statute . . . authorizes punitive damages for the most serious kinds of misrepresentations, say, tricking the elderly out of their life savings, for much less serious conduct, such as the failure to disclose repainting a car, at issue here, and for a vast range of conduct in between.

Second, the Alabama courts, in this case, have applied the "factors" intended to constrain punitive damages awards in a way that belies that purpose. Green Oil Co. v. Hornsby, 539 So. 2d 218 (Ala. 1989), sets forth seven factors that appellate courts use to

NOTES AND QUESTIONS

1. *On Remand.* When the *Gore* case returned to the Alabama Supreme Court, it ordered a new trial unless Dr. Gore would accept a remittitur of all but $50,000 of the jury's award of punitive damages. 701 So. 2d, at 515. The plaintiff accepted that amount. How did the Alabama Court determine that $50,000 set the maximum permissible award under the Constitution?

2. *Leatherman and State Farm.* In two post-*Gore* decisions, the Court continued to emphasize the need for trial and appellate judges to exercise substantial control over punitive damage awards. First, it held that federal appellate courts are obligated to undertake *de novo* review of the jury's punitive award (i.e., should not defer to the trial court's ruling as to whether a particular award was constitutionally excessive). Cooper Indus., Inc. v. Leatherman Tool Group, *Inc.*, 532 U.S. 424 (2001). Note the contrast with *Gasperini* (mentioned in Chapter 8 in the notes following *Kenton*), in which the Court held that federal appellate courts may *not* engage in hard-look review of compensatory damage awards.

The second decision, *State Farm Mutual Automobile Insurance Co. v. Campbell*, 538 U.S. 408 (2003), involved a suit by a car owner (and his spouse) against his liability insurer for willfully mishandling the defense of a negligence suit that resulted in a large judgment against the owner. (For a brief discussion of the insurer's role in defending tort suits, see Chapter 8, Section IV.) The jury awarded the insured car owner $1 million in compensatory damages. At the punitive phase of the trial, the owner's attorneys introduced evidence that the insurer's conduct toward the owner was part of a nationwide scheme for denying policyholders the coverage that was owed to them under a variety of different types of insurance policies. On the basis of that evidence, the jury issued a $145 million punitive award, which was upheld on appeal by Utah's high court. Relying on *Gore*, the Supreme Court struck the award on the ground that due process bars plaintiffs from relying on evidence of misconduct that does not pertain directly to the mistreatment of the plaintiff himself.

Writing for a six-Justice majority, Justice Kennedy also offered refinements (arguably in dicta) to the "ratio" prong of the *Gore* test. Pulling together statements from *Haslip* and *Gore*, his opinion asserted that: (1) "few awards exceeding a single-digit ratio between punitive and compensatory damages, to a significant degree, will satisfy due process"; (2) a "4-to-1 ratio" often will be "close to the line of constitutional impropriety"; (3) higher ratios may be appropriate when "a particularly egregious act has resulted in only a small amount of economic damages," where "the injury is hard to detect," or where "the monetary value of noneconomic harm might have been difficult to determine"; and (4) lower ratios, perhaps as low as 1-to-1, may "reach the outermost limit of the due process guarantee" when "compensatory damages are substantial." Having said all this, *State Farm* also reiterated that the Court was not prepared to draw "bright line" rules, and that the "precise award in any case . . . must be based upon the facts and circumstances of the defendant's conduct and the harm to the plaintiff."

3. *Calculating the Ratio. State Farm* described the *Gore* test's second factor as requiring an assessment of the ratio between the amount of punitive damages awarded

and the amount of damages awarded for the "actual *or potential* harm" suffered by the plaintiff. This in turn has invited litigation in lower courts over how to calculate the potential harm associated with a defendant's misconduct. *See, e.g.*, Simon v. San Paolo U.S. Holding Co., 113 P.2d 63 (Cal. 2005) (rejecting plaintiff's contention that it lost $400 million in potential profits as a result of defendant's fraud, and instead assessing plaintiff's losses at $50,000 for purposes of applying the ratio prong of *Gore*).

4. *Is There a "Ratio Rule"? (Part I).* The *State Farm* decision described in Note 2, *supra*, was received enthusiastically by the defense bar and American industry, who understood the Court to be setting out a "hard cap" that limited punitive damages to at least no more than nine or ten times the underlying compensatory award. Some courts explicitly reversed their own views on the constitutionality of punitive damages with ratios higher than "single digits" in light of *State Farm. See, e.g.*, Romo v. Ford Motor Co., 113 Cal. App. 4th 738 (Cal. Ct. App. 2003). In *Romo* a jury in a products liability case involving the rollover of an SUV awarded $5 million in compensatory damages and $290 million in punitive damages. Reasoning that *State Farm* explicitly forbids juries from using punitive damages to punish the defendant for wrongs it inflicted on anyone other than the plaintiff, and noting *State Farm*'s emphasis on single-digit ratios, the Fifth Appellate District Court determined that a roughly 5:1 ratio was appropriate given the "extreme reprehensibility" of Ford's conduct.

5. *Non-Constitutional "Hard Look" Appellate Review.* Should the federal courts of appeal see in *Gore, Leatherman*, and *State Farm* a policy favoring more aggressive appellate review of punitive damages awards, separate and apart from constitutionally mandated limits? For an argument that they should, *see* Payne v. Jones, 711 F.3d 85 (2d Cir. 2013).

6. *State-Law Limits.* Justice Ginsburg noted in an appendix to her *Gore* dissent that state legislatures had already taken various steps to control jury awards of punitive damages. A few have gone so far as to abolish punitive damages as a matter of common law, permitting them only when specifically authorized by statute. N.H. Rev. Stat. Ann. § 507:16. Others set dollar caps on punitive awards (or caps in the form of a maximum ratio to compensatory damages), or require a substantial portion of any punitive award to be paid to the state. Still others set heightened standards of proof. With this degree of legislative activity, Justice Ginsburg argued, the Court was venturing into an area where its efforts were not needed. Is that a convincing rationale for declining to recognize a right against having to pay excessive punitive damages?

Philip Morris USA v. Williams

127 S. Ct. 1057 (2007)

Breyer, J. The question we address today concerns a large state-court punitive damages award. We are asked whether the Constitution's Due Process Clause permits a jury to base that award in part upon its desire to *punish* the defendant for harming persons who are not before the court (*e.g.*, victims whom the parties do not represent). We hold that such an award would amount to a taking of "property" from the defendant without due process.

opportunity to present every available defense." *Lindsey* v. *Normet*, 405 U.S. 56, 66 (1972). Yet a defendant threatened with punishment for injuring a nonparty victim has no opportunity to defend against the charge, by showing, for example in a case such as this, that the other victim was not entitled to damages because he or she knew that smoking was dangerous or did not rely upon the defendant's statements to the contrary.

For another, to permit punishment for injuring a nonparty victim would add a near standardless dimension to the punitive damages equation. How many such victims are there? How seriously were they injured? Under what circumstances did injury occur? The trial will not likely answer such questions as to nonparty victims. The jury will be left to speculate. And the fundamental due process concerns to which our punitive damages cases refer — risks of arbitrariness, uncertainty and lack of notice — will be magnified.

Finally, we can find no authority supporting the use of punitive damages awards for the purpose of punishing a defendant for harming others. We have said that it may be appropriate to consider the reasonableness of a punitive damages award in light of the *potential* harm the defendant's conduct could have caused. But we have made clear that the potential harm at issue was harm potentially caused *the plaintiff*. See *State Farm*, *supra*, at 424 ("We have been reluctant to identify concrete constitutional limits on the ratio between harm, or potential harm, *to the plaintiff* and the punitive damages award" (emphasis added)). We did use the term "error-free" (in *BMW*) to describe a lower court punitive damages calculation that likely included harm to others in the equation. But context makes clear that the term "error-free" in the *BMW* footnote referred to errors relevant to the case at hand. Although elsewhere in *BMW* we noted that there was no suggestion that the plaintiff "or any other BMW purchaser was threatened with any additional potential harm" by the defendant's conduct, we did not purport to decide the question of harm to others. Rather, the opinion appears to have left the question open.

Respondent argues that she is free to show harm to other victims because it is relevant to a different part of the punitive damages constitutional equation, namely, reprehensibility. That is to say, harm to others shows more reprehensible conduct. Philip Morris, in turn, does not deny that a plaintiff may show harm to others in order to demonstrate reprehensibility. Nor do we. Evidence of actual harm to nonparties can help to show that the conduct that harmed the plaintiff also posed a substantial risk of harm to the general public, and so was particularly reprehensible — although counsel may argue in a particular case that conduct resulting in no harm to others nonetheless posed a grave risk to the public, or the converse. Yet for the reasons given above, a jury may not go further than this and use a punitive damages verdict to punish a defendant directly on account of harms it is alleged to have visited on nonparties.

Given the risks of unfairness that we have mentioned, it is constitutionally important for a court to provide assurance that the jury will ask the right question, not the wrong one. And given the risks of arbitrariness, the concern for adequate notice, and the risk that punitive damages awards can, in practice, impose one State's (or one jury's) policies (*e.g.*, banning cigarettes) upon other States — all of which accompany awards that, today, may be many times the size of such awards in the 18th and 19th centuries — it is particularly important that States avoid procedure that unnecessarily deprives juries of proper legal guidance. We therefore conclude that the Due Process Clause requires States to provide assurance that juries are not asking the wrong question, *i.e.*, seeking, not simply to determine reprehensibility, but also to punish for harm caused strangers.

IV.

. . . .

The instruction that Philip Morris said the trial court should have given distinguishes between using harm to others as part of the "reasonable relationship" equation (which it would allow) and using it directly as a basis for punishment. The instruction asked the trial court to tell the jury that "you *may* consider the extent of harm suffered by others *in determining what [the] reasonable relationship is*" between Philip Morris' punishable misconduct and harm caused to Jesse Williams, "*[but] you are not to punish the defendant for the impact of its alleged misconduct on other persons, who may bring lawsuits of their own* in which other juries can resolve their claims. . . ." App. 280a (emphasis added). And as the Oregon Supreme Court explicitly recognized, Philip Morris argued that the Constitution "prohibits the state, acting through a civil jury, from using punitive damages to punish a defendant for harm to nonparties." 127 P.3d 1165, 1175 (2006).

The [Oregon Supreme Court] rejected that claim. In doing so, it pointed out (1) that this Court in *State Farm* had held only that a jury could not base its award upon "dissimilar" acts of a defendant. 127 P.3d at 1175-1176. It added (2) that "if a jury cannot punish for the conduct, then it is difficult to see why it may consider it at all." 127 P.3d at 1175, n. 3. And it stated (3) that "it is unclear to us how a jury could 'consider' harm to others, yet withhold that consideration from the punishment calculus." *Ibid.*

The Oregon court's first statement is correct. We did not previously hold explicitly that a jury may not punish for the harm caused others. But we do so hold now. We do not agree with the Oregon court's second statement. We have explained why we believe the Due Process Clause prohibits a State's inflicting punishment for harm caused strangers to the litigation. At the same time we recognize that conduct that risks harm to many is likely more reprehensible than conduct that risks harm to only a few. And a jury consequently may take this fact into account in determining reprehensibility. Cf., *e.g.*, *Witte* v. *United States*, 515 U.S. 389 (1995) (recidivism statutes taking into account a criminal defendant's other misconduct do not impose an "'additional penalty for the earlier crimes,' but instead . . . 'a stiffened penalty for the latest crime, which is considered to be an aggravated offense because a repetitive one'" (quoting *Gryger* v. *Burke*, 334 U.S. 728, 732 (1948))).

The Oregon court's third statement raises a practical problem. How can we know whether a jury, in taking account of harm caused others under the rubric of reprehensibility, also seeks to *punish* the defendant for having caused injury to others? Our answer is that state courts cannot authorize procedures that create an unreasonable and unnecessary risk of any such confusion occurring. In particular, we believe that where the risk of that misunderstanding is a significant one — because, for instance, of the sort of evidence that was introduced at trial or the kinds of argument the plaintiff made to the jury — a court, upon request, must protect against that risk. Although the States have some flexibility to determine what *kind* of procedures they will implement, federal constitutional law obligates them to provide *some* form of protection in appropriate cases.

V.

As the preceding discussion makes clear, we believe that the Oregon Supreme Court applied the wrong constitutional standard when considering Philip Morris' appeal. We remand this case so that the Oregon Supreme Court can apply the standard we have set forth. Because the application of this standard may lead to the need for a new trial, or a change in the level of the punitive damages award, we shall not consider whether the award is constitutionally "grossly excessive." We vacate the Oregon Supreme Court's judgment and remand the case for further proceedings not inconsistent with this opinion.

It is so ordered.

Stevens, J. (dissenting) (joined by Thomas, J. and Ginsburg, J.).

The Due Process Clause of the Fourteenth Amendment imposes both substantive and procedural constraints on the power of the States to impose punitive damages on tortfeasors. I remain firmly convinced that the cases announcing those constraints were correctly decided. In my view the Oregon Supreme Court faithfully applied the reasoning in those opinions to the egregious facts disclosed by this record. . . .

Of greater importance to me, however, is the Court's imposition of a novel limit on the State's power to impose punishment in civil litigation. Unlike the Court, I see no reason why an interest in punishing a wrongdoer "for harming persons who are not before the court" should not be taken into consideration when assessing the appropriate sanction for reprehensible conduct.

Whereas compensatory damages are measured by the harm the defendant has caused the plaintiff, punitive damages are a sanction for the public harm the defendant's conduct has caused or threatened. There is little difference between the justification for a criminal sanction, such as a fine or a term of imprisonment, and an award of punitive damages. In our early history either type of sanction might have been imposed in litigation prosecuted by a private citizen. And while in neither context would the sanction typically include a pecuniary award measured by the harm that the conduct had caused to any third parties, in both contexts the harm to third parties would surely be a relevant factor to consider in evaluating the reprehensibility of the defendant's wrongdoing. We have never held otherwise.

In the case before us, evidence attesting to the possible harm the defendant's extensive deceitful conduct caused other Oregonians was properly presented to the jury. No evidence was offered to establish an appropriate measure of damages to compensate such third parties for their injuries, and no one argued that the punitive damages award would serve any such purpose. To award compensatory damages to remedy such third-party harm might well constitute a taking of property from the defendant without due process. . . . But a punitive damages award, instead of serving a compensatory purpose, serves the entirely different purposes of retribution and deterrence that underlie every criminal sanction. This justification for punitive damages has even greater salience when, as in this case, see Ore. Rev. Stat. § 31.735(1) (2003), the award is payable in whole or in part to the State rather than to the private litigant.

While apparently recognizing the novelty of its holding, the majority relies on a distinction between taking third-party harm into account in order to assess the reprehensibility of the defendant's conduct — which is permitted — from doing so in order to punish the defendant "directly" — which is forbidden. . . . This nuance eludes me. When a jury increases a punitive damages award because injuries to third parties enhanced the reprehensibility of the defendant's conduct, the jury is by definition punishing the defendant — directly — for third-party harm. A murderer who kills his victim by throwing a bomb that injures dozens of bystanders should be punished more severely than one who harms no one other than his intended victim. Similarly, there is no reason why the measure of the appropriate punishment for engaging in a campaign of deceit in distributing a poisonous and addictive substance to thousands of cigarette smokers statewide should not include consideration of the harm to those "bystanders" as well as the harm to the individual plaintiff. The Court endorses a contrary conclusion without providing us with any reasoned justification.

. . . Judicial restraint counsels us to "exercise the utmost care whenever we are asked to break new ground in this field." *Ibid.* Today the majority ignores that sound advice when it announces its new rule of substantive law.

. . . .

[Justice Thomas' dissent omitted — EDS.]

GINSBURG, J. (dissenting) (joined by Scalia, J. and Thomas, J.) The purpose of punitive damages, it can hardly be denied, is not to compensate, but to punish. Punish for what? Not for harm actually caused "strangers to the litigation," the Court states, but for the *reprehensibility* of defendant's conduct. . . .

The right question regarding reprehensibility, the Court acknowledges, would train on "the harm that Philip Morris was prepared to inflict on the smoking public at large." (quoting 127 P.3d at 1175). See also 127 P.3d at 1177 ("The jury, *in assessing the reprehensibility of Philip Morris's actions,* could consider evidence of similar harm to other Oregonians caused (or threatened) by the same conduct." (emphasis added)). The Court identifies no evidence introduced and no charge delivered inconsistent with that inquiry.

. . . .

For the reasons stated, and in light of the abundant evidence of "the potential harm [Philip Morris'] conduct could have caused" (emphasis deleted) . . . I would affirm the decision of the Oregon Supreme Court.

NOTES AND QUESTIONS

1. *Williams: Second Remand and Third Certiorari Grant.* The United States Supreme Court's remand order in *Williams* provided the Supreme Court of Oregon with another opportunity to opine on the dispute between Mayola Williams and Philip

Morris. Wasting little time, a unanimous Oregon Supreme Court once more affirmed the jury's punitive damages award. Sidestepping the Due Process problem identified by the U.S. Supreme Court, the state court held that Philip Morris had failed properly to preserve under the rules of Oregon procedural law its objection to the punitive damages instruction that the U.S. Supreme Court had deemed deficient. Williams v. Philip Morris Inc., 176 P.3d 1255, 1260 (Or. 2008).

Undaunted, Philip Morris for a third time in the history of the case petitioned the U.S. Supreme Court for certiorari, and the Court for a third time granted the company's petition, this time focusing on whether the Oregon high court was entitled to rely on state-law procedural rules to avoid deciding whether the punitive award in *Williams* resulted from a violation of Due Process requirements. Philip Morris USA Inc. v. Williams, 553 U.S. 1093 (2008) (granting certiorari). The Court heard oral argument in December 2008. Eventually, however, the Justices let go of the *Williams* case, allowing the verdict and the Oregon Supreme Court's 2008 decision to stand by dismissing its third grant of certiorari for having been "improvidently granted." *See* Philip Morris USA v. Williams, 556 U.S. 178 (2009).

2. *Twice More at the Oregon Supreme Court.* Philip Morris has had mixed success in two subsequent appearances before the Oregon Supreme Court raising issues pertaining to punitive damages. The first was *Estate of Schwarz v. Philip Morris, Inc.*, 246 P.3d 479 (Or. 2010), which involved another smoker's wrongful death suit. That suit resulted in a punitive damages verdict of $150 million, although the verdict was later reduced by the trial judge to $100 million. In *Schwarz*, unlike in *Williams*, Philip Morris was deemed to have preserved its objection to the trial judge's jury instructions on punitive damages and non-party harm. The Oregon Supreme unanimously ruled that the instructions that were given unacceptably risked the confusion that the U.S. Supreme Court had cautioned against in its 2007 *Williams* decision, and therefore vacated the award and remanded for a new trial on punitive damages.

Second, post-judgment litigation in *Williams v. Philip Morris* itself returned to the Oregon Supreme Court on a question separate from the due process concerns with the jury's punitive damages award that had been previously litigated. Williams v. RJ Reynolds Tobacco Co., 271 P.3d 103 (Or. 2011).* This time, the issue on appeal was the application of Oregon's "splitting" statute, Or. Rev. Stat. § 31.735(1)(b). Under that statute, 60 percent of any claimant's punitive damage award is payable to a state fund for the assistance of crime victims. (For a brief discussion of punitive damages and splitting statutes, see Chapter 8.)

After losing its challenges to the jury's punitive damages award, Philip Morris eventually paid "the Williams estate over $61 million in full satisfaction of the award of economic and noneconomic damages, and in full satisfaction of the estate's interest in 40 percent of the punitive damages award allocated to the Williams estate under Or. Rev. Stat. § 31.735, plus costs and interest on those awards." 271 P.3d, at 106. Philip Morris contended, however, that it was not obligated to pay the remaining 60

* The case caption differs because the Oregon courts' dealings with the legal question at issue in this case have proceeded on a different track than the issues that went before the U.S. Supreme Court.

percent of the award to the State of Oregon because the state had released its claims to any portion of a punitive damages award arising in the context of tobacco litigation.

Philip Morris's release argument relied upon the fact that Oregon was a party to an agreement between state attorneys general and the major tobacco companies known as the Master Settlement Agreement (MSA). (The MSA is discussed briefly in Note 9, *infra.*)

The MSA did indeed include a broad release clause. However, because the MSA was an agreement to settle claims brought by the states themselves for costs they had incurred in dealing with smoking-related illnesses rather than to settle personal injury claims brought by individual smokers, a question remained as to whether an allocation to a state of a smoker's punitive damages would fall within the terms of its release. (Interestingly, Williams's estate appears to have sided with the State of Oregon in arguing that the state had not released its claim, but also argued that *if* the state were deemed to have released its claim, then the 60 percent of the jury's punitive award should revert to the estate.) Reasoning that the state's claim under Oregon's splitting statute is an entitlement that applies by operation of the statute whenever punitive damages are awarded — and not a tobacco-related claim of the state's, which could have been deemed relinquished — the Oregon Supreme Court ruled that the MSA did *not* release the state's statutory share of the punitive damages award in *Williams.*

3. *What Now?* The U.S. Supreme Court in *Williams* requires trial courts to give instructions that will encourage the jury to consider "harm to others" for only some purposes and not others. Imagine being asked to draft such an instruction. How would you word it? Chapter 8 reproduces in part New York's pattern instruction on punitive damages. Is it worded in way that complies with the due process requirements identified in *Williams*?

4. *Is There a "Ratio Rule"? (Part II).* The U.S. Supreme Court declined Philip Morris's invitation to examine for excessiveness plaintiffs' punitive damages award, which was 78 times the jury's compensatory award. Justice Stevens, who had joined in the majority in *State Farm,* indicated by his dissent that he thought the award in *Williams* was not excessive. Does this mean that at least one member of the Court has changed his mind about the existence of a "ratio rule"? Can you think of any other reasons why Justice Stevens may have thought that the ratio (145:1) in *State Farm* suggested that the award was excessive but that the ratio (78:1) in *Williams* did not?

5. *Mathias Revisited.* In the *Mathias* case from Chapter 8, the Seventh Circuit upheld a $186,000 punitive award on top of a $5,000 compensatory award against the corporate owner of a motel that rented rooms in the knowledge that they were infested with bedbugs. Mathias v. Accor Economy Lodging, Inc., 347 F.3d 672 (7th Cir. 2003). *Mathias* was decided after *Gore* and *State Farm* but before *Williams.* It concluded that the award did not violate the Court's guidelines on constitutional excessiveness.

Writing for the circuit court, Judge Posner contrasted the punitive award against the motel owner, which was 37.5 times the compensatory award, with the awards in cases such as *State Farm* and the suit arising from the *Exxon Valdez* oil spill, in which "huge" compensatory damages were provided. In those cases, he reasoned, the Supreme Court has forbidden punitive damages with multiples higher than single digits. *Mathias*, however, presented a different type of case because the actual injury to the plaintiffs was very small, and was as much an indignity as it was an economic or physical loss:

> . . . [O]ne function of punitive-damages awards is to relieve the pressures on an overloaded system of criminal justice by providing a civil alternative to criminal prosecution of minor crimes. An example is deliberately spitting in a person's face, a criminal assault but because minor readily deterrable by the levying of what amounts to a civil fine through a suit for damages for the tort of battery. Compensatory damages would not do the trick in such a case, and this for three reasons: because they are difficult to determine in the case of acts that inflict largely dignatory harms; because in the spitting case they would be too slight to give the victim an incentive to sue, and he might decide instead to respond with violence . . . and because to limit the plaintiff to compensatory damages would enable the defendant to commit the offensive act with impunity provided that he was willing to pay.

347 F.3d, at 676-677.

Is *Mathias* correct to place the wrong committed by the motel managers in the same category as intentionally spitting in someone's face? Surely a wrong was committed, and the decision to expose the plaintiffs to bedbugs produced great anger, distress, and probably embarrassment on their part. But was the attitude of the managers such that one could infer that they wished to offend the dignity of their customers? Does it help clarify analysis to describe the injury arising from the tort as "dignitary"? *Mathias* also reasoned that a punitive award that is large in relation to a compensatory award may be necessary to create adequate incentives to sue (and thus to make sure that the wrongdoer does not profit from his wrongdoing), particularly when the losses caused by the defendant's misconduct come in the form of small increments of harm experienced by many victims. As Judge Posner noted, the $191,000 awarded by the *Mathias* jury had a certain arithmetic logic to it — it equaled $1,000 times the total number of rooms in the hotel.

Recall that, in the end, the Alabama Supreme Court implemented *Gore* by ordering the punitive damages in the case reduced to $50,000, and that there were 14 Alabama residents who had been defrauded by BMW, including Dr. Gore. Would this 12.5: 1 ratio have been accepted by the *State Farm* court? Can Judge Posner claim that he has faithfully followed *Gore* and *State Farm*?

6. *Ratios and Federal Common Law.* In *Exxon Shipping Co. v. Baker*, 554 U.S. 471 (2008), the Supreme Court had occasion to consider punitive damages as a matter of common law rather than constitutional law. Suits brought under federal maritime law by commercial fishermen and others for losses caused by the disastrous 1989 *Exxon Valdez* oil spill resulted in a jury verdict that awarded $507 million in compensatory damages. In addition, the jury awarded $5,000 in punitive damages against the ship's captain, Joseph Hazelwood, and $5 billion in punitive damages against Exxon. On appeal, the latter award was reduced to $2.5 billion.

As mentioned in Chapter 8 (notes on punitive damages), in *Baker* an equally divided Court let stand lower court rulings that an employer's vicarious liability can extend to liability for punitive damages even without employer "ratification" of the employee's tortious actions. However, by a 5-3 vote, the Court also concluded that federal maritime law should be interpreted to set a 1:1 ratio as a "fair upper limit" on punitive awards. *Id.* at 513. In defending its relatively aggressive decision, the majority emphasized that the Court has greater leeway to fashion rules of federal common law than constitutional law, in part because the former can be changed by ordinary federal legislation. It also relied on empirical studies that purport to find in reported decisions from roughly 1990 to 2000 a median ratio of punitive to compensatory damages of about 0.65: 1. *Id.* at 498, 512-13.

7. Tobacco Litigation: Theories of Liability. *Williams* was decided against the backdrop of an ongoing and complex history of suits against tobacco companies for smoking-related injuries. Indeed, as Robert Rabin has insightfully commented, since the 1950s there have been three "waves" of tort litigation against companies that manufacture and sell tobacco products, particularly cigarettes. *See* Robert L. Rabin, Essay, *A Sociolegal History of the Tobacco* Litigation, 44 Stan. L. Rev. 853 (1992); Robert L. Rabin, *The Third Wave of Tobacco Tort Litigation,* in Robert L. Rabin & Stephen D. Sugarman (eds.), Regulating Tobacco, 176-206 (2001).

In the first wave (lasting, roughly, from 1954 and 1965), individual smokers sued manufacturers on *negligence* and *warranty* theories. In the second (lasting, roughly, from 1983 to 1992), smokers brought individual actions primarily under theories of *strict products liability.* In the third, which has been under way since 1993, plaintiffs have changed the focus of their complaints. Instead of suing for harms allegedly caused by defects in tobacco products, they allege (as did the plaintiff in *Williams*) that tobacco sellers committed the tort of *fraud* in the course of developing and marketing tobacco products.

The first wave of litigation emerged in response a steady stream of articles in the 1950s and 1960s linking smoking to lung cancer. Invoking negligence law, some plaintiffs argued that manufacturers had been careless in failing to make cigarettes safer or in failing to offer warnings as to the health risks of smoking. Breach of warranty claims came in two variations. Implied warranty theories maintained that tobacco products were not of merchantable quality or reasonably fit for ordinary use. Express warranty claims asserted that tobacco companies had explicitly guaranteed that ordinary use of the product would not harm smokers.

None of these theories proved successful. As to negligence, courts tended to enter judgments for the companies on the ground that diseases such as cancer were not reasonably foreseeable at the time of manufacture and sale. *See, e.g.,* Lartigue v. R.J. Reynolds Tobacco Co., 317 F.2d 19 (5th Cir. 1963). Warranty claims were rejected on the ground that the alleged unwholesomeness of a product line, rather than an anomalous defect in a given pack of cigarettes, could not be deemed a breach of warranty. *See, e.g.,* Green v. American Tobacco Co., 409 F.2d 3 (5th Cir. 1969) (en banc).

As the first wave of tobacco litigation drew to a close, tobacco companies were being subjected to increased governmental regulation. A critical event was the release in

1964 of the U.S. Surgeon General's report, in which the federal government officially acknowledged the health hazards posed by smoking. In 1965 and 1969, Congress passed the Cigarette Acts. The 1965 Act required warnings on all cigarette packaging that read "Caution: Cigarette Smoking May Be Hazardous to Your Health." In 1969, Congress changed "May Be" to "Is."

The second wave of tobacco litigation was a product of successes achieved by plaintiffs and their lawyers in pursuing "mass tort" claims against defendants such as asbestos manufacturers and other pro-plaintiff developments in products liability law. Indeed, one of the most well-known cases from this era — *Cipollone v. Liggett Group, Inc.*, 693 F. Supp. 208 (D.N.J. 1988) — was developed and litigated by a team of veteran asbestos attorneys who had gained expertise through that litigation on the link between lung cancer and cigarette smoking. Two other important developments offered new hope to tobacco litigants. The first was informational. Since the 1960s more evidence had emerged suggesting that the tobacco industry had long been aware of the possibility of a connection between smoking and cancer, which undercut the notion that cancer and other diseases were unforeseeable consequences of smoking. The second development concerned changes in products liability doctrine. As noted in Chapter 12, in the 1970s and 1980s a series of important products liability decisions had purported to modify or abandon "consumer expectations" as the test for whether a product may be deemed defectively designed, and adopted the risk-utility test as a complementary or alternative standard. Because the risk-utility test focuses less on what the consumer might know about the dangers of a product, and more on the social costs and benefits associated with a product's use, its adoption suggested that, in principle, a manufacturer might sometimes be held liable even if the dangers posed by a product were inherent and widely known.

Despite these promising developments, plaintiffs still failed to hold the tobacco companies liable, mostly because of a new hurdle — the problem of plaintiff responsibility. For example, in *Cipollone* itself, the plaintiff was able to convince the jury that the defendant had been negligent in failing to warn of the health risks of smoking and that in doing so had "cause[d] some or all of Mrs. Cipollone's smoking." However, the jury also found that Cipollone had "voluntarily and unreasonably encountered a known danger." On that basis, it found Cipollone 80 percent at fault, which barred recovery under New Jersey's modified comparative fault scheme.

Cipollone also helped mark the transition from the second to the third wave, in which tobacco plaintiffs have begun to enjoy more success. This is because, before ultimately abandoning her claim for lack of funds, Cipollone's lawyers had persuaded the U.S. Supreme Court to review lower court rulings that granted very broad preemptive effect to the Cigarette Labeling Acts. *See* Cipollone v. Liggett Group, Inc., 505 U.S. 504 (1992). According to these rulings, Congress, by enacting federal cigarette labeling requirements, had deliberately supplanted all state tort law claims against manufacturers for smoking-related illnesses. (For more on this argument, see the discussion of preemption in Section V of this chapter.) The Court held that Congress's 1969 Labeling Act was intended to preempt *some* tort claims — namely, failure-to-warn claims predicated on the theory that the manufacturers should have included stronger warnings of health risks on cigarette packages and in cigarette advertising than the warnings mandated by the Act. However, the Court also ruled that the Act was not intended to preempt other tort claims, including express warranty or fraud claims. This last holding, in particular, suggested a possible doctrinal "hook" for future tobacco litigation.

Still, this hook would have been of limited use to third-wave plaintiffs and their lawyers had not a breadth of new evidence emerged concerning the conduct of the tobacco companies, some of which came to light through the actions of tobacco company insiders, acting as whistleblowers. This new information as to the industry's knowledge of nicotine's addictive qualities helped open potential new avenues for tort plaintiffs. In particular, it promised to begin eroding the industry's seemingly impenetrable comparative fault/assumption of risk defense. First- and second-wave cases had generally proceeded on the premise that smokers had made an informed and voluntary choice to take up and continue smoking. By graphically demonstrating a disconnect between the public and private communications of industry insiders on the issue of tobacco's health risks, the documents suggested that the companies had not merely marketed a dangerous product, but had done so while covering up dangers about which they knew. This in turn suggested that claims of fraud, which the Supreme Court in *Cipollone* had left open almost as an afterthought, began to look promising, since smokers could argue that their decision to smoke was based on their reliance on the tobacco companies' false assurances of the safety of their product. Thus, in the last decade, tort suits brought against tobacco companies routinely include fraud claims such as in *Williams.*

8. Tobacco Litigation: Class Actions. Whereas in the first and second waves of tobacco litigation, suits were brought on an individual basis, in the third wave lawyers have attempted to combine individual claims by means of the class action device. *See, e.g.,* Castano v. American Tobacco Co., 160 F.R.D. 544 (E.D. La. 1995), *rev'd* 84 F.3d 734 (5th Cir. 1996). The *Castano* suit, purportedly brought on behalf of 45 million smokers nationwide, alleged a class-wide injury of addiction, and alleged that the tobacco industry had committed either fraud or negligent misrepresentation when it failed to warn smokers of the risk of addiction from nicotine. Ultimately, the Fifth Circuit concluded that the *Castano* class was too large and too varied to allow the case to proceed as a class action, though it kept open the possibility that smaller plaintiff classes could be certified at the state level. The court noted two problems with the proposed nationwide class. First, the diversity of state laws, especially as they relate to fraud, would make it impossible to define common questions of law for a single trial. Second, the claims on behalf of class members would likely present more individualized than common-to-the-class issues of fact: a suit based in large part on allegations of fraud, the court reasoned, would bring to the fore for each class member the question of whether he or she had actually and reasonably relied on the defendants' misrepresentations.

After the Fifth Circuit's denial of class certification, several plaintiffs filed "son of *Castano*" cases in state courts, almost all of which have failed. However, there have been some important exceptions, including an immense collection of cases being litigated in Florida, as well as a handful of "light cigarettes" class actions around the country.

In the Florida litigation, the plaintiffs sued the tobacco industry on theories of products liability and fraud. In 1996, a Florida intermediate court of appeals upheld the certification of a class of up to 700,000 Florida smokers allegedly suffering from tobacco-related diseases. R.J. Reynolds Tobacco Co. v. Engle, 672 So. 2d 39 (Fla. Dist. Ct. App. 1996). The Florida Supreme Court at the time declined to review this decision. On remand from the intermediate appellate court, the trial court held a single trial on the following issues that it deemed common to all class members' claims: whether the industry had engaged in deceptive conduct; whether cigarettes as designed and marketed were unreasonably unsafe; whether, in general, there is a causal link between the diseases alleged by the plaintiffs and smoking; and whether punitive damages were warranted. The jury answered "yes" to each question and found that the plaintiff class, as a whole, was entitled to $144.8 billion in punitive damages.

On appeal, the same appellate court that had previously upheld the certification of a class consisting of all Florida smokers had a change of heart and decertified the class it had previously certified. Liggett Group Inc. v. Engle, 853 So. 2d 434 (Fla. App. 2003). However, the decertification was then reversed by the Florida Supreme Court. Engle v. Liggett Group, Inc., 945 So. 2d 1246 (Fla. 2006). Though clearly a victory for the plaintiffs, the Florida Supreme Court's decision also in some ways benefited the *Engle* defendants. The decision reinstated the class action and upheld the jury's finding that the defendants had engaged in fraudulent conduct. It also reversed the punitive damages award for the class and ordered "mini-trials" for each class member to determine which individual class members actually were harmed by the defendants' deceit and, among those who were, the punitive damages each should individually receive. These mini-trials—an estimated 8,000—began soon after the Florida Supreme Court's remand and are still working their way through state and federal courts. *See, e.g.*, Graham v. R.J. Reynolds Tobacco Co., 782 F.3d 1261 (11th Cir. 2015); Philip Morris USA, Inc. v. Douglas, 110 So. 3d 419 (Fla. 2013) (determining under different bodies of law the preclusive effects of the *Engle* trial).

In the "light cigarettes" cases, plaintiffs have also attempted to use the class action mechanism to obtain large damages awards. The theory of these cases is that the decision to market a specific type of cigarette—the so-called light or low-tar cigarette—was a fraudulent act because the defendants knew that these cigarettes did not provide any health benefits compared to regular or "full-tar" cigarettes, yet their advertising campaigns were designed to give the opposite impression. In part to avoid strictures on the use of class actions in personal injury cases that have been imposed by the U.S. Supreme Court and other courts, these actions seek recovery only for the pecuniary loss associated with customers paying more for light cigarettes than they would have paid had the defendants not made false health claims. Most of these suits have been dismissed, but a few have survived. *See* Aspinall v. Philip Morris, Inc., 813 N.E.2d 476 (Mass. 2004).

9. Tobacco Litigation: The Master Settlement Agreement. Perhaps the biggest impact of the third wave of tobacco litigation resulted not from tort litigation commenced by smokers, but from the settlement of lawsuits brought by state officials seeking reimbursement for costs allegedly incurred by governments in treating their citizens' tobacco-related illnesses. In 1994, the State of Mississippi filed a "restitution" action against the largest tobacco companies. The suit contended that the state should recover damages from the companies because, when the states paid for their citizens' tobacco-related healthcare, the states were really paying for a cost that should have been borne by the tobacco companies, thereby "unjustly enriching" the tobacco companies by billions of dollars. Within a year, scores of other states filed similar lawsuits using the same unjust enrichment theory. While these suits were filed as claims for restitution, which does not necessarily require allegations of fraud, the arguments for unjust enrichment made by the states critically relied on the claim that smokers were deceived by the tobacco companies.

The Mississippi lawsuit was settled in July 1997 on terms that called for the companies to pay the state $3.3 billion over 25 years. Florida next settled its suit with the industry in August 1997 for $11.3 billion, then Texas settled its suit in January 1998 for $15.3 billion, and finally Minnesota settled for $6.1 billion on the eve of a jury verdict. On the basis of this trend, the attorneys general from 46 states (including the four that already settled) negotiated in 1998 a global settlement now known as the "Master Settlement Agreement" (MSA). The MSA requires the companies to pay the states $206 billion over a multi-year period in reimbursement for healthcare costs incurred by the states. While not technically class actions, the state reimbursement suits in some respects performed the function of a class action, given that they allowed a small group of lawyers to bring a claim based on a common course of conduct that affected masses of victims in a single (or a handful of) proceeding(s).

IV. TORTS WITHOUT INJURIES? UNRIPENED PHYSICAL HARM AND MEDICAL MONITORING CLAIMS

Chapter 10 included the *Gottshall* decision, in which the U.S. Supreme Court held that a railroad worker who cannot prove that he has suffered bodily harm as a result of his employer's carelessness can still recover under the Federal Employers' Liability Act (FELA) for negligently caused emotional distress, but only if that distress arises because the employer carelessly placed him in immediate danger of bodily harm. Left open was the question of what, exactly, counts as "bodily harm" and "immediate danger of bodily harm." The question soon arose as to whether inhalation of large quantities of a known toxin can count as a bodily harm in and of itself, or the sort of endangering that would support a claim for negligently inflicted emotional distress. A second and related issue concerned whether a railroad employee who, because of employer negligence, inhales a known toxin, might recover for the cost of medical monitoring to gauge the effects of such an exposure on the plaintiff's long-term health.

As it turns out, the Supreme Court, in the *Buckley* decision excerpted below, confronted these questions in a very special context—that of litigation arising out a worker's on-the-job exposure to airborne asbestos fibers. This context is sufficiently important for understanding *Buckley*, and for understanding modern tort law more generally, that it is worth brief exploration. (Asbestos-related liability figures in the

Boomer and *Wannall* decisions (Chapter 4), and in the California Supreme Court's analysis of liability for failure to warn in its *Anderson* decision (Chapter 12).

Asbestos, a natural fiber that functions as an effective heat insulator, had for decades been used in the construction of buildings, industrial boilers, ship engines, and vehicle braking systems. In the construction process, *millions* of workers were exposed over extended periods to high concentrations of asbestos fibers. Inhalation of these fibers can cause asbestosis, a nonmalignant condition causing minor-to-severe breathing impairments. It can also cause lung cancer and mesothelioma, a lethal form of cancer in the lining of the lung. At least some of these dangers were known at a relatively early date by prominent manufacturers such as Johns Manville.

The physical devastation wrought by asbestos generated a genuine litigation crisis. Manufacturers and distributors of asbestos were confronted with tens of thousands of products liability claims brought by workers and others exposed to asbestos. In response, scores of companies that produced or used asbestos threatened or entered bankruptcy. The lack of adequate funds raised the prospect of an unseemly "race to the courthouse," in which plaintiffs recovered not on the basis of the relative seriousness of their injuries or needs, but simply because they happened to manifest their illnesses sooner than others. Meanwhile, the court system, already swamped with growing criminal dockets, was in danger of being overwhelmed with asbestos-related suits.

In response, lawyers and federal district judges sought ways to resolve asbestos claims on a mass scale. In the 1980s and 1990s, they primarily did so by means of the procedural device known as the class action, which is authorized by Federal Rule of Civil Procedure 23 and state-law counterparts. By means of a class action, a single named plaintiff, or a small group of named plaintiffs, litigates a suit on behalf of a large group of similarly situated persons. In principle, if a class action goes forward and is resolved through settlement or verdict, all members of the class are bound by that resolution, whether favorable or unfavorable. (If the representative plaintiff prevails, for example, each class member receives some part of the award, even though none participated in the actual litigation.)

Although many viewed the class action device as the best hope for bringing order and fairness to asbestos litigation, others saw asbestos class actions as untenable extensions of a procedural tool that had been created with less sprawling cases in mind. In particular, the litigation raised red flags concerning both the diversity among the claimants and the role of the lawyers representing them. Asbestos victims' suits sought compensation for a wide array of physical injuries ranging from the trivial to the fatal, as well as emotional and economic harms of the sort discussed below in *Buckley*. Their exposure to asbestos occurred in different circumstances and involved inhalation of varying amounts of asbestos. In addition, a victim's own conduct—in particular, her smoking habits—could complicate the inquiry into the causal significance of her asbestos exposure. Moreover, for different plaintiffs, determinations of issues such as injury, causation, and comparative fault perhaps would need to be adjudicated under different states' laws, depending in part on the place of manufacture and exposure. Finally, lawyers representing large classes of asbestos victims faced potential conflicts of interest because, for example, their resolution of claims on terms favorable to some clients (e.g., those currently manifesting serious illnesses) might work to the disadvantage of other clients (e.g., those who could be expected to manifest illnesses at some future date).

Animated by these and other concerns, a pair of U.S. Supreme Court decisions interpreting Rule 23—*Amchem Prods., Inc. v. Windsor*, 521 U.S. 591 (1997) and *Ortiz v. Fibreboard Corp.*, 527 U.S. 815 (1999)—largely blocked the use of class actions in asbestos and other mass products liability litigation, leaving courts and lawyers scrambling to find alternative ways of handling asbestos claims on a mass or aggregate basis.

The years after *Ortiz* and *Amchem* saw additional asbestos-related bankruptcies, an expansion of asbestos litigation to reach additional companies not conventionally regarded as part of the asbestos industry (e.g., corporations and school districts that own premises on which asbestos-containing products were used), and continued delays in the provision of compensation to plaintiffs. Efforts to design and enforce private administrative-type compensation systems for asbestos claims, moreover, have not abated. Instead, they largely have gravitated from the vehicle of class actions to that of corporate reorganization plans under a special provision of the federal Bankruptcy Code for the handling of asbestos-related claims. *See* 11 U.S.C. § 524(g).

Several of the Justices have publicly urged Congress to craft a legislative solution to the asbestos "mess." Congress has tried—numerous times. For example, the 2003 Asbestos Victims Fairness Compensation Act, S. 1125, proposed the creation of a $114 billion trust fund for asbestos claimants and the simultaneous termination of asbestos litigation by injured persons. The bill stalled in the Senate in the fall of 2003. Although the idea behind the Act was later revived with proposed funding of over $140 billion, legislative enthusiasm petered out by 2006, apparently a result of brute political forces as well as difficult design issues concerning the classes of persons eligible for compensation, how the burdens of funding would be allocated, and how potentially responsible parties (manufacturers, insurers, government) would be protected against the prospect of subsequent tort litigation.

In these circumstances, it is impossible to suppose that the Justices' analyses of the "injury" issue in *Buckley* were not influenced by the larger context of modern asbestos litigation. Indeed, the majority opinion, written by Justice Breyer, explicitly refers to that context in support of its conclusions. Yet, while the questions about injury addressed in *Buckley* were of a piece with the larger problems of asbestos litigation, they also arose in a context that was, in another respect, quite isolated. Ordinarily, when employees suffering from work-related illnesses seek compensation for those illnesses from their employers, they will receive only the modest, scheduled amounts authorized under state workers' compensation statutes. However, in enacting FELA, Congress long ago ordained that the members of a single industry—railroads—would remain subject to negligence liability in their capacity as employers. Thus, *Buckley* provides the unusual sight of an employer, rather than a manufacturer or distributor, being sued in tort for carelessly injuring a worker by exposing him to asbestos.

In sum, *Buckley* is a fascinating opinion because, on the one hand, it raises a set of theoretical, almost esoteric, questions in an odd pocket of federal negligence law. On the other hand, it raises those questions against the backdrop of a cluster of pressing practical and political problems generated by the most massive and unruly body of tort litigation ever encountered by U.S. courts.

Metro-North Commuter R.R. Co. v. Buckley

521 U.S. 424 (1997)

Breyer, J. The basic question in this case is whether a railroad worker negligently exposed to a carcinogen (here, asbestos) but without symptoms of any disease can recover under the Federal Employers' Liability Act (FELA), 35 Stat. 65, as amended, 45 U.S.C. § 51 *et seq.*, for negligently inflicted emotional distress. We conclude that the worker before us here cannot recover unless, and until, he manifests symptoms of a disease. . . .

I

Respondent, Michael Buckley, works as a pipefitter for Metro-North, a railroad. For three years (1985-1988) his job exposed him to asbestos for about one hour per working day. During that time Buckley would remove insulation from pipes, often covering himself with insulation dust that contained asbestos. Since 1987, when he attended an "asbestos awareness" class, Buckley has feared that he would develop cancer—and with some cause, for his two expert witnesses testified that, even after taking account of his now-discarded 15-year habit of smoking up to a pack of cigarettes per day, the exposure created an *added* risk of death due to cancer, or to other asbestos-related diseases of either 1% to 5% (in the view of one of plaintiff's experts), or 1% to 3% (in the view of another). Since 1989, Buckley has received periodic medical check-ups for cancer and asbestosis. So far, those check-ups have not revealed any evidence of cancer or any other asbestos-related disease.

Buckley sued Metro-North under the FELA, a statute that permits a railroad worker to recover for an "injury . . . resulting . . . from" his employer's "negligence." 45 U.S.C. § 51. He sought damages for his emotional distress and to cover the cost of future medical check-ups. His employer conceded negligence, but it did not concede that Buckley had actually suffered emotional distress, and it argued that the FELA did not permit a worker like Buckley, who had suffered no physical harm, to recover for injuries of either sort. After hearing Buckley's case, the District Court dismissed the action. The court found that Buckley did not "offer sufficient evidence to allow a jury to find that he suffered a real emotional injury." App. 623. And, in any event, Buckley suffered no "physical impact"; hence any emotional injury fell outside the limited set of circumstances in which, according to this Court, the FELA permits recovery. *Id.*, at 620; *see* Consolidated Rail Corporation v. Gottshall, 512 U.S. 532, 114 S. Ct. 2396, 129 L. Ed. 2d 427 (1994). The District Court did not discuss Buckley's further claim for the costs of medical monitoring.

Buckley appealed, and the Second Circuit reversed. 79 F.3d 1337 (1996). Buckley's evidence, it said, showed that his contact with the insulation dust (containing asbestos) was "massive, lengthy, and tangible," *id.*, at 1345, and that the contact "would cause fear in a reasonable person," *id.*, at 1344. Under these circumstances, the court held, the contact was what this Court in *Gottshall* had called a "physical impact"—a "physical impact" that, when present, permits a FELA plaintiff to recover for accompanying emotional distress. The Second Circuit also found in certain of Buckley's workplace statements sufficient expression of worry to permit sending his emotional distress claim to a jury. Finally, the court held that Buckley could recover for the costs of medical check-ups because the FELA permits recovery of all reasonably incurred extra medical monitoring costs whenever a "reasonable physician would prescribe . . . a monitoring regime different than the one that would have been prescribed in the absence of" a particular negligently caused exposure to a toxic substance. *Id.*, at 1347 (internal quotation marks omitted).

We granted certiorari to review the Second Circuit's holdings in light of *Gottshall.*

II

The critical question before us in respect to Buckley's "emotional distress" claim is whether the physical contact with insulation dust that accompanied his emotional distress amounts to a "physical impact" as this Court used that term in *Gottshall.* [Justice Breyer proceeded to review *Gottshall*'s analysis, including its holding that FELA permits recovery on a claim of NIED for]

> "those plaintiffs who *sustain a physical impact* as a result of a defendant's negligent conduct, or who are placed in immediate risk of physical harm by that conduct." *Id.*, at 547-548 (emphasis added).

The case before us, as we have said, focuses on the italicized words "physical impact." The Second Circuit interpreted those words as including a simple physical contact with a substance that might cause a disease at a future time, so long as the contact was of a kind that would "cause fear in a reasonable person." 79 F.3d at 1344. In our view, however, the "physical impact" to which *Gottshall* referred does not include a simple physical contact with a substance that might cause a disease at a substantially later time—where that substance, or related circumstance, threatens no harm other than that disease-related risk.

First, *Gottshall* cited many state cases in support of its adoption of the "zone of danger" test quoted above. And in each case where recovery for emotional distress was permitted, the case involved a threatened physical contact that caused, or might have caused, immediate traumatic harm.

Second, *Gottshall*'s language, read in light of this precedent, seems similarly limited. *Gottshall,* 512 U.S. 532 at 555 ("zone of danger test . . . is consistent with FELA's central focus on physical perils"); *id.*, at 556 (quoting Lancaster v. Norfolk & Western R. Co., 773 F.2d 807, 813 (CA7 1985), *cert. denied,* 480 U.S. 945 (1987)) (FELA seeks to protect workers "'from physical invasions or menaces'").

Taken together, language and cited precedent indicate that the words "physical impact" do not encompass every form of "physical contact." And, in particular, they do not include a contact that amounts to no more than an exposure—an exposure, such as that before us, to a substance that poses some future risk of disease and which contact causes emotional distress only because the worker learns that he may become ill after a substantial period of time.

Third, common-law precedent does not favor the plaintiff. Common law courts do permit a plaintiff who suffers from a disease to recover for related negligently caused emotional distress, and some courts permit a plaintiff who exhibits a physical symptom of exposure to recover. But with only a few exceptions, common law courts have denied recovery to those who, like Buckley, are disease and symptom free.

Fourth, the general policy reasons to which *Gottshall* referred — in its explanation of why common law courts have restricted recovery for emotional harm to cases falling within rather narrowly defined categories — militate against an expansive definition of "physical impact" here. Those reasons include: (a) special "difficulty for judges and juries" in separating valid, important claims from those that are invalid or "trivial," *Gottshall*, 512 U.S. at 557; (b) a threat of "unlimited and unpredictable liability," *ibid.*; and (c) the "potential for a flood" of comparatively unimportant, or "trivial," claims, *ibid.*

To separate meritorious and important claims from invalid or trivial claims does not seem easier here than in other cases in which a plaintiff might seek recovery for typical negligently caused emotional distress. The facts before us illustrate the problem. The District Court, when concluding that Buckley had failed to present "sufficient evidence to allow a jury to find . . . a real emotional injury," pointed out that, apart from Buckley's own testimony, there was virtually no evidence of distress. App. 623-625. Indeed, Buckley continued to work with insulating material "even though . . . he could have transferred" elsewhere, he "continued to smoke cigarettes" despite doctors' warnings, and his doctor did not refer him "either to a psychologist or to a social worker." *Id.*, at 624. The Court of Appeals reversed because it found certain objective corroborating evidence, namely "workers' complaints to supervisors and investigative bodies." 79 F.3d at 1346. Both kinds of "objective" evidence — the confirming and disconfirming evidence — seem only indirectly related to the question at issue, the existence and seriousness of Buckley's claimed emotional distress. Yet, given the difficulty of separating valid from invalid emotional injury claims, the evidence before us may typify the kind of evidence to which parties and the courts would have to look. . . .

More important, the physical contact at issue here — a simple (though extensive) contact with a carcinogenic substance — does not seem to offer much help in separating valid from invalid emotional distress claims. That is because contacts, even extensive contacts, with serious carcinogens are common. *See, e.g.*, Nicholson, Perkel & Selikoff, *Occupational Exposure to Asbestos: Population at Risk and Projected Mortality — 1980-2030*, 3 Am. J. Indust. Med. 259 (1982) (estimating that 21 million Americans have been exposed to work-related asbestos); U.S. Dept. of Health and Human Services, 1 Seventh Annual Report on Carcinogens 71 (1994) (3 million workers exposed to benzene, a majority of Americans exposed outside the workplace); Pirkle, et al., *Exposure of the U.S. Population to Environmental Tobacco Smoke*, 275 JAMA 1233, 1237 (1996) (reporting that 43% of American children lived in a home with at least one smoker, and 37% of adult nonsmokers lived in a home with at least one smoker or reported environmental tobacco smoke at work). They may occur without causing serious emotional distress, but sometimes they do cause distress, and reasonably so, for cancer is both an unusually threatening and unusually frightening disease. *See* Statistical Abstract of United States 94 (1996) (23.5 percent of Americans who died in 1994 died of cancer);

American Cancer Society, Cancer Facts & Figures—1997, p.1 (half of all men and one third of all women will develop cancer). The relevant problem, however, remains one of evaluating a claimed emotional reaction to an *increased* risk of dying. An external circumstance—exposure—makes some emotional distress more likely. But how can one determine from the external circumstance of exposure whether, or when, a claimed strong emotional reaction to an *increased* mortality risk (say from 23% to 28%) is reasonable and genuine, rather than overstated—particularly when the relevant statistics themselves are controversial and uncertain (as is usually the case), and particularly since neither those exposed nor judges or juries are experts in statistics? The evaluation problem seems a serious one.

The large number of those exposed and the uncertainties that may surround recovery also suggest what *Gottshall* called the problem of "unlimited and unpredictable liability." Does such liability mean, for example, that the costs associated with a rule of liability would become so great that, given the nature of the harm, it would seem unreasonable to require the public to pay the higher prices that may result? The same characteristics further suggest what *Gottshall* called the problem of a "flood" of cases that, if not "trivial," are comparatively less important. In a world of limited resources, would a rule permitting immediate large-scale recoveries for widespread emotional distress caused by fear of future disease diminish the likelihood of recovery by those who later suffer from the disease?

We do not raise these questions to answer them (for we do not have the answers), but rather to show that general policy concerns of a kind that have led common law courts to deny recovery for certain classes of negligently caused harms are present in this case as well. That being so, we cannot find in *Gottshall's* underlying rationale any basis for departing from *Gottshall's* language and precedent or from the current common-law consensus. That is to say, we cannot find in *Gottshall's* language, cited precedent, other common law-precedent, or related concerns of policy, a legal basis for adopting the emotional-distress recovery rule adopted by the Court of Appeals.

Buckley raises several important arguments in reply. He points out, for example, that common law courts do permit recovery for emotional distress where a plaintiff has physical symptoms; and he argues that his evidence of exposure and enhanced mortality risk is as strong a proof as an accompanying physical symptom that his emotional distress is genuine.

This argument, however, while important, overlooks the fact that the common law in this area does not examine the genuineness of emotional harm case by case. Rather, it has developed recovery-permitting categories the contours of which more distantly reflect this, and other, abstract general policy concerns. . . . The relevant question here concerns the validity of a rule that seeks to redefine such a category. It would not be easy to redefine "physical impact" in terms of a rule that turned on, say, the "massive, lengthy, [or] tangible" nature of a contact that amounted to an exposure, whether to contaminated water, or to germ-laden air, or to carcinogen-containing substances, such as insulation dust containing asbestos. . . .

Finally, Buckley argues that the "humanitarian" nature of the FELA warrants a holding in his favor. We do not doubt that the FELA's purpose militates in favor of recovery for a serious and negligently caused emotional harm. *Cf. Gottshall*, 512 U.S. at

550. But just as courts must interpret that law to take proper account of the harms suffered by a sympathetic individual plaintiff, so they must consider the general impact, on workers as well as employers, of the general liability rules they would thereby create. Here the relevant question concerns not simply recovery in an individual case, but the consequences and effects of *a rule of law that would permit that recovery.* And if the common law concludes that a legal rule permitting recovery here, from a tort law perspective, and despite benefits in *some* individual cases, would on balance cause more harm than good, and if we find that judgment reasonable, we cannot find that conclusion inconsistent with the FELA's humanitarian purpose.

III

Buckley also sought recovery for a different kind of "injury," namely the economic cost of the extra medical check-ups that he expects to incur as a result of his exposure to asbestos-laden insulation dust. The District Court, when it dismissed the action, did not discuss this aspect of Buckley's case. But the Second Circuit, when reversing the District Court, held that "a reasonable jury could award" Buckley the "costs" of "medical monitoring" in this case. 79 F.3d at 1347. We agreed to decide whether the court correctly found that the FELA permitted a plaintiff without symptoms or disease to recover this economic loss.

The parties do not dispute—and we assume—that an exposed plaintiff can recover related reasonable medical monitoring costs if and when he develops symptoms. As the Second Circuit pointed out, a plaintiff injured through negligence can recover related reasonable medical expenses as an element of damages. No one has argued that any different principle would apply in the case of a plaintiff whose "injury" consists of a disease, a symptom, or those sorts of emotional distress that fall within the FELA's definition of "injury." . . .

Other portions of the Second Circuit's opinion, however, indicate that it may have rested this portion of its decision upon a broader ground, namely that medical monitoring costs themselves represent a separate negligently caused economic "injury," 45 U.S.C. § 51, for which a negligently exposed FELA plaintiff (including a plaintiff without disease or symptoms) may recover to the extent that the medical monitoring costs that a reasonable physician would prescribe for the plaintiff exceed the medical monitoring costs that "would have been prescribed in the absence of [the] exposure." 79 F.3d at 1347 (citation omitted). This portion of the opinion . . . suggests the existence of an ordinary, but separate, tort law cause of action permitting (as tort law ordinarily permits) the recovery of medical cost damages in the form of a lump sum [damages award]. . . . As so characterized, the Second Circuit's holding, in our view, went beyond the bounds of currently "evolving common law." *Gottshall,* at 558 (Souter, J., concurring).

Guided by the parties' briefs, we have canvassed the state-law cases that have considered whether the negligent causation of this kind of harm (i.e., causing a plaintiff, through negligent exposure to a toxic substance, to incur medical monitoring costs) by itself constitutes a sufficient basis for a tort recovery. . . . [S]everal important State Supreme Court cases have permitted recovery. Ayers v. Jackson, 106 N.J. 557, 525 A.2d 287 (1987); Hansen v. Mountain Fuel Supply Co., 858 P.2d 970 (Utah 1993);

Potter v. Firestone Tire & Rubber Co., 6 Cal. 4th 965, 863 P.2d 795 (1993); *see also* Burns v. Jaquays Mining Corp., 156 Ariz. 375, 752 P.2d 28 (Ct. App. 1987).

We find it sufficient to note, for present purposes, that the cases authorizing recovery for medical monitoring in the absence of physical injury do not endorse a full-blown, traditional tort law cause of action for lump-sum damages — of the sort that the Court of Appeals seems to have endorsed here. Rather, those courts, while recognizing that medical monitoring costs can amount to a harm that justifies a tort remedy, have suggested, or imposed, special limitations on that remedy. *Compare Ayers, supra,* at 608, 525 A.2d at 314 (recommending in future cases creation of "a court-supervised fund to administer medical-surveillance payments"); *Hansen, supra,* at 982 (suggesting insurance mechanism or court-supervised fund as proper remedy); *Potter, supra,* 1010, n.28, 863 P.2d at 825, n.28 (suggesting that a lump-sum damages award would be inappropriate); *Burns, supra,* 381, 752 P.2d at 34 (holding that lump-sum damages are not appropriate) *with,* e.g., Honeycutt v. Walden, 294 Ark. 440, 743 S.W.2d 809 (1988) (damages award for future medical expenses made necessary by physical injury are awarded as lump-sum payment); Rice v. Hill, 315 Pa. 166, 172 A. 289 (1934) (same); and Restatement (Second) of Torts § 920A(2) (1977) (ordinarily fact that plaintiff is insured is irrelevant to amount of tort recovery). We believe that the note of caution, the limitations, and the expressed uneasiness with a traditional lump-sum damages remedy are important, for they suggest a judicial recognition of some of the policy concerns that have been pointed out to us here — concerns of a sort that *Gottshall* identified.

Since, for example, the particular, say cancer-related, costs at issue are the *extra* monitoring costs, over and above those otherwise recommended, their identification will sometimes pose special "difficulties for judges and juries." *Gottshall,* 512 U.S. at 557. Those difficulties in part can reflect uncertainty among medical professionals about just which tests are most usefully administered and when. And in part those difficulties can reflect the fact that scientists will not always see a medical need to provide systematic *scientific* answers to the relevant *legal* question, namely whether an exposure calls for *extra* monitoring. Buckley's sole expert . . . was equivocal about the need for *extra* monitoring, and the defense had not yet put on its case.

Moreover, tens of millions of individuals may have suffered exposure to substances that might justify some form of substance-exposure-related medical monitoring. . . . And that fact, along with uncertainty as to the amount of liability, could threaten both a "flood" of less important cases (potentially absorbing resources better left available to those more seriously harmed) and the systemic harms that can accompany "unlimited and unpredictable liability" (say, for example, vast testing liability adversely affecting the allocation of scarce medical resources). The dissent assumes that medical monitoring is not a "costly" remedy. But Buckley here sought damages worth $950 annually for 36 years; by comparison, of all claims settled by the Center for Claims Resolution, a group representing asbestos manufacturers, from 1988 until 1993, the average settlement for plaintiffs *injured* by asbestos was about $12,500, and the settlement for non-malignant plaintiffs among this group averaged $8,810. . . .

We do not deny important competing considerations — of a kind that may have led some courts to provide a form of liability. Buckley argues, for example, that it is inequitable to place the economic burden of such care on the negligently exposed plaintiff rather than on the negligent defendant. He points out that providing preventive care to individuals who would otherwise go without can help to mitigate potentially serious future health effects of diseases by detecting them in early stages; again, whether or not this is such a situation, we may assume that such situations occur. And he adds that, despite scientific uncertainties, the difficulty of separating justified from unjustified claims may be less serious than where emotional distress is the harm at issue.

We do not deny that Justice Ginsburg paints a sympathetic picture of Buckley and his co-workers; this picture has force because Buckley *is* sympathetic and he *has* suffered wrong at the hands of a negligent employer. But we are more troubled than is the dissent by the potential systemic effects of creating a new, full-blown, tort law cause of action — for example, the effects upon interests of other potential plaintiffs who are not before the court and who depend on a tort system that can distinguish between reliable and serious claims on the one hand, and unreliable and relatively trivial claims on the other. The reality is that competing interests are at stake — and those interests sometimes can be reconciled in ways other than simply through the creation of a full-blown, traditional, tort law cause of action.

We have not tried to balance these, or other, competing considerations here. We point them out to help explain why we consider the limitations and cautions to be important — and integral — parts of the state-court decisions that permit asymptomatic plaintiffs a separate tort claim for medical monitoring costs. That being so, we do not find sufficient support in the common law for the unqualified rule of lump-sum damages recovery that is, at least arguably, before us here. And given the mix of competing general policy considerations, plaintiff's policy-based arguments do not convince us that the FELA contains a tort liability rule of that *unqualified* kind.

This limited conclusion disposes of the matter before us. We need not, and do not, express any view here about the extent to which the FELA might, or might not, accommodate medical cost recovery rules more finely tailored than the rule we have considered.

IV

For the reasons stated, we reverse the determination of the Second Circuit, and we remand the case for further proceedings consistent with this opinion.

Ginsburg, J. (concurring and dissenting) (joined by Stevens, J.). . . .

Buckley's extensive contact with asbestos particles in Grand Central's tunnels, as I comprehend his situation, constituted "physical impact" as that term was used in *Gottshall.* Nevertheless, I concur in the Court's judgment with respect to Buckley's emotional distress claim. In my view, that claim fails because Buckley did not present objective evidence of severe emotional distress. Buckley testified at trial that he was angry at Metro-North and fearful of developing an asbestos-related disease. However, he sought no professional help to ease his distress, and presented no medical testimony concerning his mental health. Under these circumstances, Buckley's emotional distress claim fails as a matter of law. *Cf. Gottshall,* 512 U.S. at 563-564, 566-567 (Ginsburg, J., dissenting) (describing as "unquestionably genuine and severe" emotional distress suffered by one respondent who had a nervous breakdown, and another who was hospitalized, lost weight, and had, *inter alia*, suicidal preoccupations, anxiety, insomnia, cold sweats, and nausea).

. . . .

II

. . . .

It is not apparent why (or even whether) the Court reverses the Second Circuit's determination on Buckley's second claim. The Court of Appeals held that a medical monitoring claim is solidly grounded, and this Court does not hold otherwise. Hypothesizing that Buckley demands lump-sum damages and nothing else, the Court ruminates on the appropriate remedy without answering the anterior question: Does the plaintiff have a claim for relief? Buckley has shown that Metro-North negligently exposed him to "extremely high levels of asbestos," 79 F.3d at 1341, and that this exposure warrants "medical monitoring in order to detect and treat [asbestos-related] diseases as they may arise." *Id.*, at 1346. Buckley's expert medical witness estimated the annual costs of proper monitoring at $950. We do not know from the Court's opinion what more a plaintiff must show to qualify for relief.

A

In my view, the Second Circuit rightly held that a railworker negligently exposed to asbestos states a claim for relief under the FELA; recovery in such cases, again as the Court of Appeals held, should reflect the difference in cost between the medical tests a reasonable physician would prescribe for unexposed persons and the monitoring regime a reasonable physician would advise for persons exposed in the way Michael Buckley and his co-workers were.

Recognizing such a claim would align the FELA with the "evolving common law." *Gottshall*, 512 U.S. at 558 (Souter, J., concurring). "[A medical monitoring] action has been increasingly recognized by state courts as necessary given the latent nature of many diseases caused by exposure to hazardous materials and the traditional common law tort doctrine requirement that an injury be manifest." Daigle v. Shell Oil Co., 972 F.2d 1527, 1533 (CA10 1992). . . . As the Court understates, several state high courts have upheld medical monitoring cost recovery. In a path-marking opinion, the United States Court of Appeals for the Third Circuit, interpreting Pennsylvania law, recognized a right to compensation for monitoring "necessary in order to diagnose properly the warning signs of disease." *See Paoli I*, 916 F.2d at 851; *see also Paoli II*, 35 F.3d at 785-788. Similarly, a number of Federal District Courts interpreting state law, and several state courts of first and second instance, have sustained medical monitoring claims. This Court, responsible for developing FELA law, finds little value in these decisions.

These courts have answered the question this Court passes by: What are the elements of a compensable medical monitoring claim? The Third Circuit, for example, has enumerated: A plaintiff can recover the costs of medical monitoring if (1) he establishes that he was significantly exposed to a proven hazardous substance through

It is scarcely surprising that the Second Circuit did not consider relief through a court-supervised fund. So far as the record before us shows, no party argued in the District Court, the Second Circuit, or even this Court, that medical monitoring expenses may be recoverable, but not through a lump sum, only through a court fund. The question aired below was the prime one the Court obscures: Does Buckley's medical monitoring claim warrant any relief? . . .

The Court today reverses the Second Circuit's determination that Buckley has stated a claim for relief, but remands the case for further proceedings. If I comprehend the Court's enigmatic decision correctly, Buckley may replead a claim for relief and recover for medical monitoring, but he must receive that relief in a form other than a lump sum. Unaccountably, the Court resists the straightforward statement that would enlighten courts in this and similar cases: A claim for medical monitoring is cognizable under the FELA; it is a claim entirely in step with "'evolving common law.'" I therefore dissent from the Court's judgment to the extent it relates to medical monitoring.

NOTES AND QUESTIONS

1. *Ayers.* The Court in *Buckley* makes clear that, so far as FELA liability is concerned, a *de minimis* physical impact will not count as the sort of predicate injury that will support an award of compensatory damages for emotional distress associated with that impact. At what point does an impact become a physical harm? The Court confronted this question in another FELA case, *Norfolk & West. Ry. Co. v. Ayers*, 538 U.S. 135 (2003). In *Ayers*, the claimants sought to recover for emotional distress, including for fear of cancer. However, unlike Buckley, these claimants alleged that they suffered from *asbestosis*, a disease involving the scarring of lung tissue by asbestos fibers. Asbestosis is almost never fatal, and apparently is not causally related to the development of other asbestosis-related diseases, such as lung cancers. Instead, it produces symptoms ranging from mild to severe shortness of breath, coughing, and fatigue.

Justice Ginsburg, writing for a five-person majority, concluded that asbestosis constitutes a predicate physical harm that supports recovery for emotional distress damages "related" to the disease, including damages for plaintiff's fear of contracting cancer in the future. The dissenters agreed that asbestosis constitutes a predicate physical harm but argued that fear-of-cancer damages should not be awarded parasitically on that injury, because the plaintiff's distress *was not over asbestosis itself* but over the prospect that the same exposure to asbestos that caused the plaintiff to develop asbestosis might someday cause him to develop cancer.

2. *Zone of Danger Revisited.* The *Buckley* majority obviously concluded that Buckley could not establish that he had been physically endangered by exposure to asbestos fibers; otherwise, he could have prevailed under the holding of *Gottshall.* This observation provides an occasion to reconsider the "zone of danger" rule discussed in Chapter 10. What is so significant about the risk of imminent bodily harm, as opposed to long-term health risks? As noted in Chapter 10, courts at the turn of the twentieth century may have been under the impression that "near misses" have a physical effect

on the nervous system that distress over less immediate harms does not. Is there an alternative explanation, more normative and less biologically dependent, that can explain why Buckley should not recover for his fear of future injury?

Two of us (Goldberg and Zipursky) have argued that the zone of danger test is best understood as one instantiation of a more general requirement that negligent infliction of emotional distress (NIED) claimants prove that the defendants' carelessness placed them in a situation that generated the sort of extreme stress that reasonable people should not be required to endure. These are situations, they suggest, "in which a reasonable person cannot be expected to keep a stiff upper lip; she cannot be expected to avoid responding by tumbling into severe emotional distress, that is, situations in which the mountain is a mountain, not a molehill." Instances of being exposed to imminent bodily harm provide important examples of such situations, but they are not the only ones. For example, suppose a defendant were carelessly to expose his neighbor to radioactive materials, thereby rendering the neighbor and each member of his family 20 times more likely than the general population to develop a very rare form of cancer by the age of 60. In this view, liability ought to attach for the distress associated with having been exposed to the sort of threat that would cast a pall over the life of even a person of ordinary resilience.

Could the same be said for Buckley? While most of us would undoubtedly regard any increase in the percentage likelihood of contracting lung cancer to be highly undesirable, can one say of a small marginal increase in the risk of cancer (Justice Breyer posits a shift from 23 to 28 percent) that it is itself sufficient to generate the sort of pall that would entitle a person of ordinary fortitude to experience severe distress?

3. Medical Monitoring: Right and Remedy. In her separate opinion, Justice Ginsburg expresses puzzlement over the majority's treatment of Buckley's claim to be entitled to compensation by virtue of the fact that Metro-North's carelessness caused him to incur reasonable expenses for medical tests that he would not otherwise have had to incur. The majority seems to acknowledge the validity of this sort of claim, yet links its validity to the form of the remedy sought by Buckley. (According to the majority, whereas Buckley's medical monitoring claim failed as a matter of law insofar as it sought lump-sum damages, it might be viable if instead it sought an order enjoining Metro-North to pay for his medical monitoring.)

Can you think of an explanation as to why the majority might have linked right and remedy in this way? Is Buckley's medical monitoring claim a claim for negligence causing pure economic loss? (*See Aikens*, Chapter 2.) Is there another way to characterize what Metro-North did to Buckley and how its conduct might translate into an obligation to make reasonable efforts to assist him in detecting the onset of cancer in the future?

4. Medical Monitoring Claims as Claims for Completed Torts. As noted in *Buckley*, a number of state courts allow claims for medical monitoring. Some treat these claims as falling within the traditional framework for negligence claims, with the injury element (*see* Chapter 2) being satisfied by proof of: (a) exposure to a known toxin, (b) physiological changes traceable to the exposure, and (c) a heightened risk of future serious illness or disease from the exposure.

For example, *Donovan v. Philip Morris USA, Inc.*, 914 N.E.2d 891 (Mass. 2009), outlined the elements that ex-smokers would need to establish to obtain coverage of future monitoring expenses from the manufacturer of cigarettes they smoked:

> (1) [t]he defendant's negligence (2) caused (3) the plaintiff to become exposed to a hazardous substance that produced, at least, subcellular changes that substantially increased the risk of serious disease, illness, or injury (4) for which an effective medical test for reliable early detection exists, (5) and early detection, combined with prompt and effective treatment, will significantly decrease the risk of death or the severity of the disease, illness or injury, and (6) such diagnostic medical examinations are reasonably (and periodically) necessary, conformably with the standard of care, and (7) the present value of the reasonable cost of such tests and care, as of the date of the filing of the complaint.

Id. at 902. The court added that proof of these elements will ordinarily require competent expert testimony. Suppose a claimant can make out these elements and can also demonstrate that she has suffered emotional distress over her heightened risk of illness. Should she be able to recover damages for her distress as parasitic on her recovery of medical monitoring expenses? *Donovan* seems to indicate that such recovery is not permitted. *Id.* at 903.

Donovan noted that the attribution of a ripened negligence claim to medical monitoring claimants raises potential procedural conundrums. For example, if such a claim is successfully pursued, but the claimant later develops the disease for which she obtained monitoring, has the claimant forfeited her ability to sue for the disease on the ground of the "single controversy rule," which ordinarily requires a litigant to bring all related claims against an opposing party in a single proceeding? (*Donovan* answered this question in the negative.)

V. TORT LAW AND THE ADMINISTRATIVE STATE: PREEMPTION

The Supremacy Clause of Article VI of the United States Constitution provides that "*the Laws of the United States . . . shall be the Supreme Law of the Land; and the Judges in every state shall be bound thereby, any Thing in the Constitution or Laws of any State to the Contrary notwithstanding.*" By virtue of this clause, federal statutes, as well as agency regulations validly issued under them, *preempt* conflicting state laws (that is, so long as the federal laws themselves fall within Congress's constitutional powers and do not violate individuals' constitutional rights). For example, a federal statute imposing specific limits on the emission of air pollutants by automobiles would preempt—render null and void—any state statute that purports to impose less stringent limits.

Federal preemption of state law extends not only to state statutes and regulations but also to tort law. Thus, insofar as federal law *relieves* certain actors of obligations to take care not to injure others, state tort law that would impose liability for a breach of those obligations is preempted. Suppose that Congress, in an effort to reduce transportation costs, authorizes all trains traveling in interstate commerce to drive at speeds of up to 45 mph regardless of weather and track conditions, time of day, etc. With such a federal law in place, a negligence suit brought by a person whose car was struck by a train could not be predicated on the theory that the train's operator failed to act reasonably *because he was driving at 45 mph.* To be clear, the imagined statute would *not* free train owners and operators from *all* obligations under state tort law. It would, however, preempt claims predicated on duties that are inconsistent with the rights granted to them by the statute. (Train owners and operators would continue, for example, to be under obligation to use reasonable care to ensure that their equipment is in good working order. Likewise, they would remain subject to liability for injuries caused by other forms of driver carelessness, such as falling asleep at the controls and thereby failing to heed a stop signal.)

Until the mid-twentieth century, the potential for conflict between federal law and state tort law was relatively modest, simply because the federal government played a much smaller regulatory role in the first 150 years of the country's existence. With the post-New Deal emergence of the modern administrative state, the situation has changed dramatically. Congress and an array of federal agencies now regulate vast fields of activity, including the emission of industrial pollutants, the manufacture and marketing of goods, and the use of highways, railways, and airports, etc. As a result, the occasions for federal-state conflict, and hence for instances of federal preemption of state tort law, are today much more plentiful. Moreover, because a finding of preemption essentially grants immunity from tort liability for any claim deemed preempted, it is not surprising to find defendants increasingly turning to the federal courts, including the Supreme Court, to achieve a form of nationwide "tort reform" through the application of preemption doctrine.

And so the Court has found itself considering, among other questions, whether federal water pollution control schemes preempt individuals from bringing nuisance and trespass actions against polluters, *see* International Paper Co. v. Ouellette, 479 U.S. 481 (1987); whether federally mandated warnings on cigarette packages preempt failure-to-warn, breach-of-warranty, and fraud suits brought by smokers against tobacco companies, *see* Cipollone v. Liggett Group, Inc., 505 U.S. 504 (1992); whether regulations as to the design of railroad grade crossings preempt negligence actions against railroads for failure to render such crossings reasonably safe, *see* CSX Transp., Inc. v. Easterwood, 507 U.S. 658 (1993); and whether laws requiring Food and Drug Administration (FDA) approval of certain medical devices preempt products liability actions alleging defects in those products, *see* Medtronic, Inc. v. Lohr, 518 U.S. 470 (1996). Lower federal courts have faced an even larger array of preemption claims.

Preemption can be either *express* or *implied.* Express preemption occurs when Congress includes within a regulatory statute a clause or provision that specifically declares that the statute is intended to preempt the operation of conflicting state law. Even absent such a provision, courts will sometimes infer an implicit intent on the part of Congress to give preemptive effect to a federal statute and/or regulatory regime.

Implied preemption comes in several forms, though it is not always easy to distinguish them. "Conflict" or "impossibility" preemption occurs when a particular federal law or regulation is so directly opposed to a state law that the two bodies of law simultaneously authorize and prohibit the same conduct. Even when compliance with state and federal law is not literally impossible, congressional intent to preempt may still be inferred if the application of state tort law to a particular activity would interfere substantially with the attainment of the objectives or purposes of a federal regulatory scheme. This form of preemption is sometimes called "frustration of purpose" or "obstacle" preemption. Yet another version of implied preemption comes into play when Congress legislates so exhaustively with respect to a given domain of activity as to evince an intent for "federal law to occupy [the] field exclusively." English v. General Elec. Co., 496 U.S. 72, 78-79 (1990).

In 2000, the Supreme Court issued a decision that proved to be a harbinger of what has become a wave of high stakes litigation over federal preemption of state tort law. *Geier v. American Honda Motor Co.*, 529 U.S. 861 (2000), involved claims arising out of a car accident in which the driver, Alexis Geier, was injured. Geier asserted that her 1987 Honda Accord was defectively designed because it lacked a driver-side airbag that would have prevented her injuries. Honda defended on the ground that a vehicle safety standard promulgated by the federal Department of Transportation (DOT), known as "FMVSS 208," preempted state products liability law for two reasons. First, the federal statute under which FMVSS 208 was promulgated contained an express preemption provision voiding state safety requirements conflicting with federal requirements. Second, state tort law stood to frustrate the purposes of the federal regulatory regime because FMVSS 208 aimed to give auto manufacturers leeway to equip some but not all of their 1987 vehicles with airbags and other passive restraints.

Despite concluding that the federal statute's express preemption clause did not extend to state tort law (only to state regulatory law), a bare majority of the Court also concluded that Geier's suit was preempted under the "frustration of purpose" prong of implied preemption analysis. Writing for the majority, Justice Breyer looked closely at the DOT's explanation of the objectives behind FMVSS 208, observing that the agency affirmatively desired to permit manufacturers to equip their cars with a variety of different safety devices: "a mix of devices would help develop data on comparative effectiveness, would allow the industry time to overcome the safety problems and the high production costs associated with airbags, and would facilitate the development of alternative, cheaper, and safer passive restraint systems." *Id.* at 879.

A decade later, Justice Breyer wrote an opinion for the Court *rejecting* a facially similar preemption argument. In *Williamson v. Mazda Motor Co. of America*, 562 U.S. 323 (2011), the plaintiff sued Mazda on a claim that its installation of a lap-only seat belt for the rear outer seat of certain minivans (as opposed to a lap-and-shoulder belt) rendered the vans defectively designed. As did Honda in *Geier*, Mazda invoked FMVSS 208 in support of a preemption argument. The Court concluded, however, that Williamson's claim was not preempted because the DOT's phase-in program did not have as one of its "significant" objectives the allowance of discretion to manufacturers on whether to install lap-and-shoulder belts.

Williamson notwithstanding, it would be a mistake to underestimate the importance of *Geier* in contemporary products liability law. Indeed, much of its significance resides not in its specific holding, but in its discussion of the weight that courts should give to the views of federal administrative agencies on the preemptive effect of their own agency regulations. This issue has taken on great importance in recent years.

In a unanimous decision, *Sprietsma v. Mercury Marine*, 537 U.S. 51 (2002), the Court held that neither the Federal Boat Safety Act of 1971 nor the Coast Guard's decision to refrain from exercising its authority under the Act to issue a regulation requiring propeller guards on outboard motors preempted a suit alleging that a particular motor was defectively designed because it lacked a guard. In so holding, however, the Court paid deference to the Coast Guard's statements that it did not regard its refusal to issue a regulation on propeller guards as having preemptive effect. By contrast, in *Bates v. Dow Agrosciences, LLC*, 544 U.S. 431 (2005), the Court declined to defer to agency statements about whether a federal statute should be interpreted as preempting state tort and consumer fraud law claims. In *Bates*, the Environmental Protection Agency agreed with the defendant that the Federal Insecticide, Fungicide, and Rodenticide Act (FIFRA) preempted Texas law with regard to injuries caused to crops because of alleged defects in a pesticide. *Per* Justice Stevens, the Court disagreed, remarking that "Dow and the United States exaggerate the disruptive effects of using common-law suits to enforce the prohibition on misbranding." *Id.* at 451.

Starting in 2005, a number of federal agencies published "preambles" to their issuance of new rules. These preambles sometimes included strong statements as to the preemptive effect of the rules being issued. Among the most aggressive of these was the statement published by the FDA during George W. Bush's presidency. 71 Fed. Reg. 3922 (2006). It asserted that the Food, Drug, and Cosmetic Act establishes both a "floor" and a "ceiling," such that "FDA approval of labeling . . . preempts conflicting or contrary State law." *Id.*, at 3934–35. Given that the U.S. Supreme Court sometimes defers to the interpretations by federal administrative agencies under *Chevron U.S.A., Inc. v. Natural Res. Def. Council, Inc.*, 467 U.S. 837 (1984), manufacturers believed that the FDA preamble paved the way for a broad-based preemption attack on state failure-to-warn law as applied to prescription drugs. The prospect of a broad preemption decision on prescription drugs seemed even likelier after the Supreme Court ruled 8-1 in *Riegel v. Medtronic, Inc.*, 552 U.S. 312 (2008), that many claims against manufacturers of defective medical devices are preempted. In *Wyeth v. Levine*, reprinted below, the Court addressed the question of whether state failure-to-warn claims against manufacturers of brand-name pharmaceutical products are preempted when the manufacturer complies with FDA labeling requirements.

Wyeth v. Levine

555 U.S. 555 (2009)

Stevens, J. Directly injecting the drug Phenergan into a patient's vein creates a significant risk of catastrophic consequences. A Vermont jury found that petitioner Wyeth, the manufacturer of the drug, had failed to provide an adequate warning of that risk and awarded damages to respondent Diana Levine to compensate her for the amputation of her arm. The warnings on Phenergan's label had been deemed sufficient by the federal Food and Drug Administration (FDA) when it approved Wyeth's new drug application in 1955 and when it later approved changes in the drug's labeling. The question we must decide is whether the FDA's approvals provide Wyeth with a complete defense to Levine's tort claims. We conclude that they do not.

between FDA regulations and Levine's state-law claims because those regulations permit strengthened warnings without FDA approval on an interim basis and the record contained evidence of at least 20 reports of amputations similar to Levine's since the 1960's. The court also found that state tort liability in this case would not obstruct the FDA's work because the agency had paid no more than passing attention to the question whether to warn against IV-push administration of Phenergan. In addition, the court noted that state law serves a compensatory function distinct from federal regulation.

The Vermont Supreme Court affirmed. . . . In dissent, Chief Justice Reiber argued that the jury's verdict conflicted with federal law because it was inconsistent with the FDA's conclusion that intravenous administration of Phenergan was safe and effective.

The importance of the pre-emption issue, coupled with the fact that the FDA has changed its position on state tort law and now endorses the views expressed in Chief Justice Reiber's dissent, persuaded us to grant Wyeth's petition for certiorari. The question presented by the petition is whether the FDA's drug labeling judgments "preempt state law product liability claims premised on the theory that different labeling judgments were necessary to make drugs reasonably safe for use."

II

Wyeth makes two separate pre-emption arguments: first, that it would have been impossible for it to comply with the state-law duty to modify Phenergan's labeling without violating federal law, . . . and second, that recognition of Levine's state tort action creates an unacceptable "obstacle to the accomplishment and execution of the full purposes and objectives of Congress," *Hines v. Davidowitz,* 312 U.S. 52, 90 (1941), because it substitutes a lay jury's decision about drug labeling for the expert judgment of the FDA. As a preface to our evaluation of these arguments, we identify two factual propositions decided during the trial court proceedings, emphasize two legal principles that guide our analysis, and review the history of the controlling federal statute.

. . . . That the inadequate label was both a but-for and proximate cause of Levine's injury is supported by the record and no longer challenged by Wyeth.[2]

The trial court proceedings further established that the critical defect in Phenergan's label was the lack of an adequate warning about the risks of IV-push administration. Levine also offered evidence that the IV-push method should be contraindicated and that Phenergan should never be administered intravenously, even by the IV-drip method. Perhaps for this reason, the dissent incorrectly assumes that the state-law duty at issue is the duty to contraindicate the IV-push method. But, as the Vermont Supreme Court explained, the jury verdict established only that Phenergan's warning was insufficient. It did not mandate a particular replacement warning, nor did it require contraindicating IV-push administration: "There may have been any number of ways for [Wyeth] to strengthen the Phenergan warning without completely

2. The dissent nonetheless suggests that physician malpractice was the exclusive cause of Levine's injury. The dissent's frustration with the jury's verdict does not put the merits of Levine's tort claim before us, nor does it change the question we must decide — whether federal law pre-empts Levine's state-law claims.

eliminating IV-push administration." 944 A.2d, at 189, n. 2. We therefore need not decide whether a state rule proscribing intravenous administration would be pre-empted. The narrower question presented is whether federal law pre-empts Levine's claim that Phenergan's label did not contain an adequate warning about using the IV-push method of administration.

Our answer to that question must be guided by two cornerstones of our pre-emption jurisprudence. First, "the purpose of Congress is the ultimate touchstone in every pre-emption case." *Medtronic, Inc. v. Lohr,* 518 U.S. 470, 485 (1996) (internal quotation marks omitted). . . . Second, "[i]n all pre-emption cases, and particularly in those in which Congress has 'legislated . . . in a field which the States have traditionally occupied,' . . . we 'start with the assumption that the historic police powers of the States were not to be superseded by the Federal Act unless that was the clear and manifest purpose of Congress.'" *Lohr,* 518 U.S., at 485 (quoting *Rice v. Santa Fe Elevator Corp.*, 331 U.S. 218, 230 (1947)).

In order to identify the "purpose of Congress," it is appropriate to briefly review the history of federal regulation of drugs and drug labeling. . . . In the 1930's, Congress became increasingly concerned about unsafe drugs and fraudulent marketing, and it enacted the Federal Food, Drug, and Cosmetic Act (FDCA), ch. 675, 52 Stat. 1040, as amended, 21 U.S.C. § 301 *et seq.* The Act's most substantial innovation was its provision for premarket approval of new drugs. It required every manufacturer to submit a new drug application, including reports of investigations and specimens of proposed labeling, to the FDA for review. Until its application became effective, a manufacturer was prohibited from distributing a drug. The FDA could reject an application if it determined that the drug was not safe for use as labeled, though if the agency failed to act, an application became effective 60 days after the filing. FDCA, § 505(c), 52 Stat. 1052.

In 1962, Congress amended the FDCA and shifted the burden of proof from the FDA to the manufacturer. Before 1962, the agency had to prove harm to keep a drug out of the market, but the amendments required the manufacturer to demonstrate that its drug was "safe for use under the conditions prescribed, recommended, or suggested in the proposed labeling" before it could distribute the drug. §§ 102(d), 104(b), 76 Stat. 781, 784. In addition, the amendments required the manufacturer to prove the drug's effectiveness by introducing "substantial evidence that the drug will have the effect it purports or is represented to have under the conditions of use prescribed, recommended, or suggested in the proposed labeling." § 102(d), *id.*, at 781.

As it enlarged the FDA's powers to "protect the public health" and "assure the safety, effectiveness, and reliability of drugs," *id.*, at 780, Congress took care to preserve state law. The 1962 amendments added a saving clause, indicating that a provision of state law would only be invalidated upon a "direct and positive conflict" with the FDCA. § 202, *id.*, at 793. Consistent with that provision, state common-law suits "continued unabated despite . . . FDA regulation." *Riegel v. Medtronic, Inc.*, 552 U.S. 312[, 340] (2008) (Ginsburg, J., dissenting). . . . And when Congress enacted an express pre-emption provision for medical devices in 1976, see § 521, 90 Stat. 574 (codified at 21 U.S.C. § 360k(a)), it declined to enact such a provision for prescription drugs.

approved a change to Phenergan's label, we will not conclude that it was impossible for Wyeth to comply with both federal and state requirements.

. . . .

. . . [T]he trial court found "no evidence in this record that either the FDA or the manufacturer gave more than passing attention to the issue of" IV-push versus IV-drip administration. The Vermont Supreme Court likewise concluded that the FDA had not made an affirmative decision to preserve the IV-push method or intended to prohibit Wyeth from strengthening its warning about IV-push administration. Moreover, Wyeth does not argue that it supplied the FDA with an evaluation or analysis concerning the specific dangers posed by the IV-push method. We accordingly cannot credit Wyeth's contention that the FDA would have prevented it from adding a stronger warning about the IV-push method of intravenous administration.[6]

Impossibility pre-emption is a demanding defense. On the record before us, Wyeth has failed to demonstrate that it was impossible for it to comply with both federal and state requirements. The CBE regulation permitted Wyeth to unilaterally strengthen its warning, and the mere fact that the FDA approved Phenergan's label does not establish that it would have prohibited such a change.

IV

Wyeth also argues that requiring it to comply with a state-law duty to provide a stronger warning about IV-push administration would obstruct the purposes and objectives of federal drug labeling regulation. Levine's tort claims, it maintains, are pre-empted because they interfere with "Congress's purpose to entrust an expert agency to make drug labeling decisions that strike a balance between competing objectives." We find no merit in this argument, which relies on an untenable interpretation of congressional intent and an overbroad view of an agency's power to pre-empt state law.

Wyeth contends that the FDCA establishes both a floor and a ceiling for drug regulation: Once the FDA has approved a drug's label, a state-law verdict may not deem the label inadequate, regardless of whether there is any evidence that the FDA has considered the stronger warning at issue. The most glaring problem with this argument is that all evidence of Congress' purposes is to the contrary. Building on its 1906 Act, Congress enacted the FDCA to bolster consumer protection against harmful products. . . . Congress did not provide a federal remedy for consumers harmed by unsafe or ineffective drugs in the 1938 statute or in any subsequent amendment. Evidently, it determined that widely available state rights of action provided

---

6. The dissent's suggestion that the FDA intended to prohibit Wyeth from strengthening its warning does not fairly reflect the record. The dissent creatively paraphrases a few FDA orders — for instance by conflating warnings about IV-push administration and intra-arterial injection — to suggest greater agency attention to the question, and it undertakes a study of Phenergan's labeling that is more elaborate than any FDA order. But even the dissent's account does not support the conclusion that the FDA would have prohibited Wyeth from adding a stronger warning pursuant to the CBE regulation.

appropriate relief for injured consumers.[7] It may also have recognized that state-law remedies further consumer protection by motivating manufacturers to produce safe and effective drugs and to give adequate warnings.

If Congress thought state-law suits posed an obstacle to its objectives, it surely would have enacted an express pre-emption provision at some point during the FDCA's 70–year history. But despite its 1976 enactment of an express pre-emption provision for medical devices, see § 521, 90 Stat. 574 (codified at 21 U.S.C. § 360k(a)), Congress has not enacted such a provision for prescription drugs.[8] Its silence on the issue, coupled with its certain awareness of the prevalence of state tort litigation, is powerful evidence that Congress did not intend FDA oversight to be the exclusive means of ensuring drug safety and effectiveness. . . .

. . . Wyeth nonetheless maintains that, because the FDCA requires the FDA to determine that a drug is safe and effective under the conditions set forth in its labeling, the agency must be presumed to have performed a precise balancing of risks and benefits and to have established a specific labeling standard that leaves no room for different state-law judgments. In advancing this argument, Wyeth relies not on any statement by Congress, but instead on the preamble to a 2006 FDA regulation governing the content and format of prescription drug labels. . . . 71 Fed. Reg. 3922 (2006). . . . In that preamble, the FDA declared that the FDCA establishes "both a 'floor' and a 'ceiling,'" so that "FDA approval of labeling . . . preempts conflicting or contrary State law." *Id.*, at 3934–3935. It further stated that certain state-law actions, such as those involving failure-to-warn claims, "threaten FDA's statutorily prescribed role as the expert Federal agency responsible for evaluating and regulating drugs." *Id.*, at 3935.

This Court has recognized that an agency regulation with the force of law can pre-empt conflicting state requirements. See, *e.g.*, *Geier v. American Honda Motor Co.*, 529 U.S. 861 (2000); *Hillsborough County v. Automated Medical Laboratories, Inc.*, 471 U.S. 707, 713 (1985). In such cases, the Court has performed its own conflict determination, relying on the substance of state and federal law and not on agency proclamations of pre-emption. We are faced with no such regulation in this case, but rather with an agency's mere assertion that state law is an obstacle to achieving its statutory objectives. Because Congress has not authorized the FDA to pre-empt state law directly, cf. 21 U.S.C. § 360k (authorizing the FDA to determine the scope of the Medical Devices

---

7. Although the first version of the bill that became the FDCA would have provided a federal cause of action for damages for injured consumers, see H.R. 6110, 73d Cong., 1st Sess., § 25 (1933) (as introduced), witnesses testified that such a right of action was unnecessary because common-law claims were already available under state law. See Hearings on S.1944 before a Subcommittee of the Senate Committee on Commerce, 73d Cong., 2d Sess., 400 (1933) (statement of W.A. Hines); see *id.*, at 403 (statement of J.A. Ladds) ("This act should not attempt to modify or restate the common law with respect to personal injuries").

8. In 1997, Congress pre-empted certain state requirements concerning over-the-counter medications and cosmetics but expressly preserved product liability actions. See 21 U.S.C. §§ 379r(e), 379s(d) ("Nothing in this section shall be construed to modify or otherwise affect any action or the liability of any person under the product liability law of any State").

pronouncements of pre-emption, as they reveal the longstanding coexistence of state and federal law and the FDA's traditional recognition of state-law remedies—a recognition in place each time the agency reviewed Wyeth's Phenergan label.

In short, Wyeth has not persuaded us that failure-to-warn claims like Levine's obstruct the federal regulation of drug labeling. Congress has repeatedly declined to pre-empt state law, and the FDA's recently adopted position that state tort suits interfere with its statutory mandate is entitled to no weight. Although we recognize that some state-law claims might well frustrate the achievement of congressional objectives, this is not such a case.

V

We conclude that it is not impossible for Wyeth to comply with its state and federal law obligations and that Levine's common-law claims do not stand as an obstacle to the accomplishment of Congress' purposes in the FDCA. Accordingly, the judgment of the Vermont Supreme Court is affirmed.

BREYER, J. (concurring). I write separately to emphasize the Court's statement that "we have no occasion in this case to consider the pre-emptive effect of a specific agency regulation bearing the force of law." The FDA may seek to determine whether and when state tort law acts as a help or a hindrance to achieving the safe drug-related medical care that Congress sought. . . . It may seek to embody those determinations in lawful specific regulations describing, for example, when labeling requirements serve as a ceiling as well as a floor. And it is possible that such determinations would have pre-emptive effect. . . . I agree with the Court, however, that such a regulation is not at issue in this case.

THOMAS, J. (concurring in the judgment). I agree with the Court that the fact that the Food and Drug Administration (FDA) approved the label for petitioner Wyeth's drug Phenergan does not pre-empt the state-law judgment before the Court. . . . It . . . was possible for Wyeth to label and market Phenergan in compliance with federal law while also providing additional warning information on its label beyond that previously approved by the FDA. . . .

I write separately, however, because I cannot join the majority's implicit endorsement of far-reaching implied pre-emption doctrines. In particular, I have become increasingly skeptical of this Court's "purposes and objectives" pre-emption jurisprudence. Under this approach, the Court routinely invalidates state laws based on perceived conflicts with broad federal policy objectives, legislative history, or generalized notions of congressional purposes that are not embodied within the text of federal law. Because implied pre-emption doctrines that wander far from the statutory text are inconsistent with the Constitution, I concur only in the judgment. . . .

III

The origins of this Court's "purposes and objectives" pre-emption jurisprudence . . . and its broad application in cases like *Geier*, illustrate that this brand of the Court's pre-emption jurisprudence facilitates freewheeling, extratextual, and broad evaluations of the "purposes and objectives" embodied within federal law. This, in turn, leads to decisions giving improperly broad pre-emptive effect to judicially manufactured policies, rather than to the statutory text enacted by Congress pursuant to the Constitution and the agency actions authorized thereby. Because such a sweeping approach to pre-emption leads to the illegitimate—and thus, unconstitutional—invalidation of state laws, I can no longer assent to a doctrine that pre-empts state laws merely because they "stan[d] as an obstacle to the accomplishment and execution of the full purposes and objectives" of federal law . . . as perceived by this Court. I therefore respectfully concur only in the judgment.

Alito, J. (joined by Roberts, C.J. and Scalia, J.) (dissenting). This case illustrates that tragic facts make bad law. The Court holds that a state tort jury, rather than the Food and Drug Administration (FDA), is ultimately responsible for regulating warning labels for prescription drugs. That result cannot be reconciled with *Geier v. American Honda Motor Co.*, 529 U.S. 861 (2000), or general principles of conflict pre-emption. I respectfully dissent.

I

The Court frames the question presented as a "narro[w]" one—namely, whether Wyeth has a duty to provide "an adequate warning about using the IV-push method" to administer Phenergan. But that ignores the antecedent question of who—the FDA or a jury in Vermont—has the authority and responsibility for determining the "adequacy" of Phenergan's warnings. Moreover, it is unclear how a "stronger" warning could have helped respondent; after all, the physician's assistant who treated her disregarded at least six separate warnings that are already on Phenergan's labeling, so respondent would be hard pressed to prove that a seventh would have made a difference.

More to the point, the question presented by this case is not a "narrow" one, and it does not concern whether Phenergan's label should bear a "stronger" warning. Rather, the real issue is whether a state tort jury can countermand the FDA's considered judgment that Phenergan's FDA-mandated warning label renders its intravenous (IV) use "safe." Indeed, respondent's amended complaint alleged that Phenergan is "not reasonably safe for intravenous administration"; respondent's attorney told the jury that Phenergan's label should say, "'Do not use this drug intravenously,'"; respondent's expert told the jury, "I think the drug should be labeled 'Not for IV use,'"; and during his closing argument, respondent's attorney told the jury, "Thank God we don't rely on the FDA to . . . make the safe[ty] decision. You will make the decision. . . . The FDA doesn't make the decision, you do."[2]

Federal law, however, *does* rely on the FDA to make safety determinations like the one it made here. The FDA has long known about the risks associated with IV push in general and its use to administer Phenergan in particular. Whether wisely or not, the

---

2. Moreover, in the trial judge's final charge, he told the jury that "the critical factual issue which you must decide" is whether Phenergan's FDA-mandated label reflects a proper balance between "the risks and benefits of intravenous administration and the potential for injury to patients.". . . .

Wyeth met to discuss Phenergan's warning label. At that meeting, the FDA specifically proposed "that Phenergan Injection should not be used in Tubex & reg;." 2 Record 583, 586 (Plaintiff's Trial Exh. 17, Internal Correspondence from W.E. Langeland to File (Sept. 5, 1975) (hereinafter 1975 Memo)). "Tubex" is a syringe system used exclusively for IV push. See App. 43. An FDA official explained that the agency's concerns arose from medical-malpractice lawsuits involving IV push of the drug, see 1975 Memo 586, and that the FDA was aware of "5 cases involving amputation where the drug had been administered by Tubex together with several additional cases involving necrosis," *id.,* at 586–587. Rather than contraindicating Phenergan for IV push, however, the agency and Wyeth agreed "that there was a need for better instruction regarding the problems of intraarterial injection." *Id.,* at 587.

The next year, the FDA convened an advisory committee to study, among other things, the risks associated with the Tubex system and IV push. App. 294. At the conclusion of its study, the committee recommended an additional IV-push-specific warning for Phenergan's label, but did not recommend eliminating IV push from the drug label altogether. In response to the committee's recommendations, the FDA instructed Wyeth to make several changes to strengthen Phenergan's label, including the addition of upper case warnings related to IV push. See *id.,* at 279–280, 282–283.

In 1987, the FDA directed Wyeth to amend its label to include the following text:

> "'[1] When used intravenously, [Phenergan] should be given in a concentration no greater than 25 mg/ml and at a rate not to exceed 25 mg/minute. [2] Injection through a properly running intravenous infusion may enhance the possibility of detecting arterial placement.'" *Id.,* at 311–312.

The first of the two quoted sentences refers specifically to IV push; as respondent's medical expert testified at trial, the label's recommended rate of administration (not to exceed 25 mg per minute) refers to "IV push, as opposed to say being in a bag and dripped over a couple of hours." *Id.,* at 52. The second of the two quoted sentences refers to IV drip. See *id.,* at 15–16 (emphasizing that a "running IV" is the same thing as "IV drip").

In its 1987 labeling order, the FDA cited voluminous materials to "suppor[t]" its new and stronger warnings related to IV push and the preferability of IV drip. One of those articles specifically discussed the relative advantages and disadvantages of IV drip compared to IV push, as well as the costs and benefits of administering Phenergan via IV push. The FDA also cited published case reports from the 1960's of gangrene caused by the intra-arterial injection of Phenergan, and the FDA instructed Wyeth to amend Phenergan's label in accordance with the latest medical research. The FDA also studied drugs similar to Phenergan and cited numerous cautionary articles — one of which urged the agency to consider contraindicating such drugs for IV use altogether.

In "support" of its labeling order, the FDA also cited numerous articles that singled out the inner crook of the elbow — known as the "antecubital fossa" in the medical community — which is both a commonly used injection site, see *id.,* at 70 (noting that respondent's injection was pushed into "the antecubital space"), and a universally recognized high-risk area for inadvertent intra-arterial injections. . . . Based on this and other research, the FDA ordered Wyeth to include a specific warning related to the use of the antecubital space for IV push.[11]

. . . .

When respondent was injured in 2000, Phenergan's label specifically addressed IV push in several passages (sometimes in lieu of and sometimes in addition to those discussed above). For example, the label warned of the risks of intra-arterial injection associated with "aspiration," which is a technique used only in conjunction with IV push. The label also cautioned against the use of "syringes with rigid plungers," which are used only to administer the drug via IV push. As respondent's medical expert testified at trial, "by talking plungers and rigid needles, that's the way you do it, to push it with the plunger." *Id.,* at 53 (testimony of Dr. John Matthew). Moreover, Phenergan's 2000 label devoted almost a full page to discussing the "Tubex system," which, as noted above, is used only to administer the drug via IV push.

While Phenergan's label very clearly authorized the use of IV push, it also made clear that IV push is the delivery method of last resort. The label specified that "[t]he preferred parenteral route of administration is by deep intramuscular injection." *Id.,* at 390. If an intramuscular injection is ineffective, then "it is usually preferable to inject [Phenergan] through the tubing of an intravenous infusion set that is known to be functioning satisfactorily." *Ibid.* Finally, if for whatever reason a medical professional chooses to use IV push, he or she is on notice that "INADVERTENT INTRA-ARTERIAL INJECTION CAN RESULT IN GANGRENE OF THE AFFECTED EXTREMITY." *Id.,* at 391. . . .

Phenergan's label also directs medical practitioners to choose veins wisely when using IV push:

> "Due to the close proximity of arteries and veins in the areas most commonly used for intravenous injection, extreme care should be exercised to avoid perivascular extravasation or inadvertent intra-arterial injection. Reports compatible with inadvertent intra-arterial injection of Phenergan Injection, usually in conjunction with other drugs intended for intravenous use, suggest that pain, severe chemical irritation, severe spasm of distal vessels, and resultant gangrene requiring amputation are likely under such circumstances." *Ibid.*

Thus, it is demonstrably untrue that, as of 2000, Phenergan's "labeling did not contain a specific warning about the risks of IV-push administration." And whatever else might be said about the extensive medical authorities and case reports that the FDA cited in "support" of its approval of IV-push administration of Phenergan, it cannot be said that the FDA "paid no more than passing attention to" IV push; nor can it be said that the FDA failed to weigh its costs and benefits. . . .

. . . .

For her part, respondent does not dispute the FDA's conclusion that IV push has certain benefits. At trial, her medical practitioners testified that they used IV push in

---

11. See App. 311 (requiring Phenergan's label to warn that practitioners should "'[b]eware of the close proximity of arteries and veins at commonly used injection sites and consider the possibility of aberrant arteries'").

Clarence Thomas
D.C. Circuit Court of Appeals (1990-91)
U.S. Supreme Court (1991-present)

Sonia Sotomayor
District Court, Southern District of New York (1992-98)
Second Circuit Court of Appeals (1998-2009)
U.S. Supreme Court (2009-present)

3. *Congress or the FDA?* In *Wyeth*, Justice Stevens made an impassioned and detailed argument that preemption of products liability suits was never intended by Congress: not in the initial passing of the FDCA, not in the Act's revision in 1962, and not in any subsequent revisions. Justice Alito did not reply to this argument on its own terms, but he made a similarly sustained argument that the FDA and its committees took seriously the risks of Phenergan. The majority seemed to look more closely than the dissent did at legislative history, while the dissent seemed to focus more closely on the history of FDA's dealings with Wyeth over Phenergan. Which matters more? Why? Is it fair to say that Justice Stevens *ignored* the FDA's dealings with Wyeth or that Justice Alito *ignored* legislative history?

4. *From Brand-Name to Generic Drugs.* As indicated by the movement from *Medtronic, Inc. v. Lohr*, 518 U.S. 470 (1998) (denying preemptive effect to FDA approval of medical devices that were allowed on the market with minimal safety review) to *Riegel v. Medtronic, Inc.*, 552 U.S. 312 (2008) (giving preemptive effect to a more rigorous form of FDA approval of medical devices) and then to *Wyeth*, the Supreme Court has seesawed (perhaps appropriately) in its treatment of facially similar preemption arguments. The same pattern was displayed in the shift from *Geier* (preemption by federal automobile safety regulations of state-law design defect claims in light of the regulations' objective to provide manufacturers with discretion to choose among safety devices) to *Williamson* (no preemption of state tort law by federal automobile safety regulations with respect to the use of certain kinds of seat belts). Given this checkered doctrinal history, when *Wyeth* was handed down, a prudent lawyer for drug manufacturers would have been well-advised *not* to take it as the Supreme Court's last word on the preemption of failure-to-warn claims against drug manufacturers. And so it is not surprising to find that, soon after *Wyeth* was decided, Pliva, Inc., a manufacturer of generic pharmaceuticals, pressed before the Court a pro-preemption argument that on its face seemed to run strongly counter to *Wyeth*'s holding.

Pliva, Inc. v. Mensing

131 S. Ct. 2567 (2011)

Thomas, J.* These consolidated lawsuits involve state tort-law claims based on certain drug manufacturers' alleged failure to provide adequate warning labels for generic metoclopramide. The question presented is whether federal drug regulations applicable to generic drug manufacturers directly conflict with, and thus pre-empt, these state-law claims. We hold that they do.

---

* Justice Kennedy joins all but Part III–B–2 of this opinion.

I

Metoclopramide is a drug designed to speed the movement of food through the digestive system. The Food and Drug Administration (FDA) first approved metoclopramide tablets, under the brand name Reglan, in 1980. Five years later, generic manufacturers also began producing metoclopramide. The drug is commonly used to treat digestive tract problems such as diabetic gastroparesis and gastroesophageal reflux disorder.

Evidence has accumulated that long-term metoclopramide use can cause tardive dyskinesia, a severe neurological disorder. Studies have shown that up to 29% of patients who take metoclopramide for several years develop this condition.

Accordingly, warning labels for the drug have been strengthened and clarified several times. In 1985, the label was modified to warn that "tardive dyskinesia . . . may develop in patients treated with metoclopramide," and the drug's package insert added that "[t]herapy longer than 12 weeks has not been evaluated and cannot be recommended." Physician's Desk Reference 1635–1636 (41st ed.1987). . . . In 2004, the brand-name Reglan manufacturer requested, and the FDA approved, a label change to add that "[t]herapy should not exceed 12 weeks in duration." And in 2009, the FDA ordered a black box warning — its strongest — which states: "Treatment with metoclopramide can cause tardive dyskinesia, a serious movement disorder that is often irreversible. . . . Treatment with metoclopramide for longer than 12 weeks should be avoided in all but rare cases." See Physician's Desk Reference 2902 (65th ed.2011).

Gladys Mensing and Julie Demahy, the plaintiffs in these consolidated cases, were prescribed Reglan in 2001 and 2002, respectively. Both received generic metoclopramide from their pharmacists. After taking the drug as prescribed for several years, both women developed tardive dyskinesia.

In separate suits, Mensing and Demahy sued the generic drug manufacturers that produced the metoclopramide they took (Manufacturers). Each alleged, as relevant here, that long-term metoclopramide use caused her tardive dyskinesia and that the Manufacturers were liable under state tort law (specifically, that of Minnesota and Louisiana) for failing to provide adequate warning labels. They claimed that "despite mounting evidence that long term metoclopramide use carries a risk of tardive dyskinesia far greater than that indicated on the label," none of the Manufacturers had changed their labels to adequately warn of that danger.

In both suits, the Manufacturers urged that federal law pre-empted the state tort claims. According to the Manufacturers, federal statutes and FDA regulations required them to use the same safety and efficacy labeling as their brand-name counterparts. This means, they argued, that it was impossible to simultaneously comply with both federal law and any state tort-law duty that required them to use a different label.

The Courts of Appeals for the Fifth and Eighth Circuits rejected the Manufacturers' arguments and held that Mensing and Demahy's claims were not pre-empted. . . .

II

Pre-emption analysis requires us to compare federal and state law. We therefore begin by identifying the state tort duties and federal labeling requirements applicable to the Manufacturers.

brand-name manufacturer to create a new label for both the brand-name and generic drug.

The agency traces this duty to 21 U.S.C. § 352(f)(2), which provides that a drug is "misbranded . . . [u]nless its labeling bears . . . adequate warnings against . . . unsafe dosage or methods or duration of administration or application, in such manner and form, as are necessary for the protection of users." By regulation, the FDA has interpreted that statute to require that "labeling shall be revised to include a warning as soon as there is reasonable evidence of an association of a serious hazard with a drug." 21 CFR § 201.57(e).

According to the FDA, these requirements apply to generic drugs. As it explains, a "'central premise of federal drug regulation is that the manufacturer bears responsibility for the content of its label at all times.'" U.S. Brief 12–13 (quoting *Wyeth,* 555 U.S., at 570–571). The FDA reconciles this duty to have adequate and accurate labeling with the duty of sameness in the following way: Generic drug manufacturers that become aware of safety problems must ask the agency to work toward strengthening the label that applies to both the generic and brand-name equivalent drug.

The Manufacturers and the FDA disagree over whether this alleged duty to request a strengthened label actually existed. The FDA argues that it explained this duty in the preamble to its 1992 regulations implementing the Hatch–Waxman Amendments. The Manufacturers claim that the FDA's 19–year–old statement did not create a duty, and that there is no evidence of any generic drug manufacturer ever acting pursuant to any such duty. Because we ultimately find pre-emption even assuming such a duty existed, we do not resolve the matter.

C

To summarize, the relevant state and federal requirements are these: State tort law places a duty directly on all drug manufacturers to adequately and safely label their products. Taking Mensing and Demahy's allegations as true, this duty required the Manufacturers to use a different, stronger label than the label they actually used. Federal drug regulations, as interpreted by the FDA, prevented the Manufacturers from independently changing their generic drugs' safety labels. But, we assume, federal law also required the Manufacturers to ask for FDA assistance in convincing the brand-name manufacturer to adopt a stronger label, so that all corresponding generic drug manufacturers could do so as well. We turn now to the question of pre-emption.

III

The Supremacy Clause establishes that federal law "shall be the supreme Law of the Land . . . any Thing in the Constitution or Laws of any State to the Contrary notwithstanding." U.S. Const., Art. VI, cl. 2. Where state and federal law "directly conflict," state law must give way. *Wyeth, supra,* at 583, (Thomas, J., concurring in judgment). . . .[5]

5. The Hatch–Waxman Amendments contain no provision expressly pre-empting state tort claims. Nor do they contain any saving clause to expressly preserve state tort claims. Although an express statement on pre-emption is always preferable, the lack of such a statement does not end our

We find impossibility here. It was not lawful under federal law for the Manufacturers to do what state law required of them. And even if they had fulfilled their federal duty to ask for FDA assistance, they would not have satisfied the requirements of state law.

If the Manufacturers had independently changed their labels to satisfy their state-law duty, they would have violated federal law. Taking Mensing and Demahy's allegations as true, state law imposed on the Manufacturers a duty to attach a safer label to their generic metoclopramide. Federal law, however, demanded that generic drug labels be the same at all times as the corresponding brand-name drug labels. Thus, it was impossible for the Manufacturers to comply with both their state-law duty to change the label and their federal law duty to keep the label the same.

The federal duty to ask the FDA for help in strengthening the corresponding brand-name label, assuming such a duty exists, does not change this analysis. Although requesting FDA assistance would have satisfied the Manufacturers' federal duty, it would not have satisfied their state tort-law duty to provide adequate labeling. State law demanded a safer label; it did not instruct the Manufacturers to communicate with the FDA about the possibility of a safer label. Indeed, Mensing and Demahy deny that their state tort claims are based on the Manufacturers' alleged failure to ask the FDA for assistance in changing the labels.

B

1

Mensing and Demahy contend that, while their state-law claims do not turn on whether the Manufacturers asked the FDA for assistance in changing their labels, the Manufacturers' federal affirmative defense of pre-emption does. Mensing and Demahy argue that if the Manufacturers had asked the FDA for help in changing the corresponding brand-name label, they might eventually have been able to accomplish under federal law what state law requires. That is true enough. The Manufacturers "freely concede" that they could have asked the FDA for help. If they had done so, and if the FDA decided there was sufficient supporting information, and if the FDA undertook negotiations with the brand-name manufacturer, and if adequate label changes were decided on and implemented, then the Manufacturers would have started a Mouse Trap game that eventually led to a better label on generic metoclopramide.

This raises the novel question whether conflict pre-emption should take into account these possible actions by the FDA and the brand-name manufacturer. Here, what federal law permitted the Manufacturers to do could have changed, even absent a change in the law itself, depending on the actions of the FDA and the brand-name manufacturer. Federal law does not dictate the text of each generic drug's label, but rather ties those labels to their brand-name counterparts. Thus, federal law would permit the Manufacturers to comply with the state labeling requirements if,

---

inquiry. Contrary to the dissent's suggestion, the absence of express pre-emption is not a reason to find no *conflict* pre-emption.

and only if, the FDA and the brand-name manufacturer changed the brand-name label to do so.

Mensing and Demahy assert that when a private party's ability to comply with state law depends on approval and assistance from the FDA, proving pre-emption requires that party to demonstrate that the FDA would not have allowed compliance with state law. Here, they argue, the Manufacturers cannot bear their burden of proving impossibility because they did not even *try* to start the process that might ultimately have allowed them to use a safer label. This is a fair argument, but we reject it.

The question for "impossibility" is whether the private party could independently do under federal law what state law requires of it. Accepting Mensing and Demahy's argument would render conflict pre-emption largely meaningless because it would make most conflicts between state and federal law illusory. We can often imagine that a third party or the Federal Government *might* do something that makes it lawful for a private party to accomplish under federal law what state law requires of it. In these cases, it is certainly possible that, had the Manufacturers asked the FDA for help, they might have eventually been able to strengthen their warning label. Of course, it is also *possible* that the Manufacturers could have convinced the FDA to reinterpret its regulations in a manner that would have opened the CBE process to them. Following Mensing and Demahy's argument to its logical conclusion, it is also *possible* that, by asking, the Manufacturers could have persuaded the FDA to rewrite its generic drug regulations entirely or talked Congress into amending the Hatch–Waxman Amendments.

If these conjectures suffice to prevent federal and state law from conflicting for Supremacy Clause purposes, it is unclear when, outside of express pre-emption, the Supremacy Clause would have any force. We do not read the Supremacy Clause to permit an approach to pre-emption that renders conflict pre-emption all but meaningless. The Supremacy Clause, on its face, makes federal law "the supreme Law of the Land" even absent an express statement by Congress.

2

Moreover, the text of the Clause — that federal law shall be supreme, "any Thing in the Constitution or Laws of any State to the Contrary notwithstanding" — plainly contemplates conflict pre-emption by describing federal law as effectively repealing contrary state law. *Ibid.;* see Nelson, Preemption, 86 Va. L. Rev. 225, 234 (2000). . . . The phrase "any [state law] to the Contrary notwithstanding" is a *non obstante* provision. *Id.*, at 238–240, nn. 43–45. Eighteenth-century legislatures used *non obstante* provisions to specify the degree to which a new statute was meant to repeal older, potentially conflicting statutes in the same field. *Id.*, at 238–240 (citing dozens of statutes from the 1770's and 1780's with similar provisions). A *non obstante* provision "in a new statute acknowledged that the statute might contradict prior law and instructed courts not to apply the general presumption against implied repeals." *Id.*, at 241–242. . . . The *non obstante* provision in the Supremacy Clause therefore suggests that federal law should be understood to impliedly repeal conflicting state law.

Further, the provision suggests that courts should not strain to find ways to reconcile federal law with seemingly conflicting state law. Traditionally, courts went to great lengths attempting to harmonize conflicting statutes, in order to avoid implied repeals. A *non obstante* provision thus was a useful way for legislatures to specify that they did not want courts distorting the new law to accommodate the old. . . . The *non obstante* provision of the Supremacy Clause indicates that a court need look no further than "the ordinary meanin[g]" of federal law, and should not distort federal law to accommodate conflicting state law.

To consider in our pre-emption analysis the contingencies inherent in these cases — in which the Manufacturers' ability to comply with state law depended on uncertain federal agency and third-party decisions — would be inconsistent with the *non obstante* provision of the Supremacy Clause. The Manufacturers would be required continually to prove the counterfactual conduct of the FDA and brand-name manufacturer in order to establish the supremacy of federal law. We do not think the Supremacy Clause contemplates that sort of contingent supremacy. The *non obstante* provision suggests that pre-emption analysis should not involve speculation about ways in which federal agency and third-party actions could potentially reconcile federal duties with conflicting state duties. When the "ordinary meaning" of federal law blocks a private party from independently accomplishing what state law requires, that party has established pre-emption.

3

. . . . To decide these cases, it is enough to hold that when a party cannot satisfy its state duties without the Federal Government's special permission and assistance, which is dependent on the exercise of judgment by a federal agency, that party cannot independently satisfy those state duties for pre-emption purposes.

. . . .

C

Wyeth is not to the contrary. In that case, as here, the plaintiff contended that a drug manufacturer had breached a state tort-law duty to provide an adequate warning label. The Court held that the lawsuit was not pre-empted because it was possible for Wyeth, a brand-name drug manufacturer, to comply with both state and federal law. Specifically, the CBE regulation, 21 CFR § 314.70(c)(6)(iii), permitted a brand-name drug manufacturer like Wyeth "to unilaterally strengthen its warning" without prior FDA approval. 555 U.S., at 573. . . . Thus, the federal regulations applicable to Wyeth allowed the company, of its own volition, to strengthen its label in compliance with its state tort duty.

That analysis is consistent with our holding today. The Court in *Wyeth* asked what the drug manufacturer could independently do under federal law, and in the absence of clear evidence that Wyeth could not have accomplished what state law required of it, found no pre-emption. The *Wyeth* Court held that, because federal law accommodated state law duties, "the possibility of impossibility" was "not enough." But here, "existing" federal law directly conflicts with state law. The question in these cases is not whether the possibility of *impossibility* establishes pre-emption, but rather whether the possibility of *possibility* defeats pre-emption.

We recognize that from the perspective of Mensing and Demahy, finding pre-emption here but not in *Wyeth* makes little sense. Had Mensing and Demahy taken

Reglan, the brand-name drug prescribed by their doctors, *Wyeth* would control and their lawsuits would not be pre-empted. But because pharmacists, acting in full accord with state law, substituted generic metoclopramide instead, federal law pre-empts these lawsuits. We acknowledge the unfortunate hand that federal drug regulation has dealt Mensing, Demahy, and others similarly situated.[9]

But "it is not this Court's task to decide whether the statutory scheme established by Congress is unusual or even bizarre." *Cuomo v. Clearing House Assn., L.L.C.*, 557 U.S. ____, ____, 129 S.Ct. 2710, 2733 (Thomas, J., concurring in part and dissenting in part) (internal quotation marks and brackets omitted). It is beyond dispute that the federal statutes and regulations that apply to brand-name drug manufacturers are meaningfully different than those that apply to generic drug manufacturers. Indeed, it is the special, and different, regulation of generic drugs that allowed the generic drug market to expand, bringing more drugs more quickly and cheaply to the public. But different federal statutes and regulations may, as here, lead to different pre-emption results. We will not distort the Supremacy Clause in order to create similar pre-emption across a dissimilar statutory scheme. As always, Congress and the FDA retain the authority to change the law and regulations if they so desire.

* * *

The judgments of the Fifth and Eighth Circuits are reversed, and the cases are remanded for further proceedings consistent with this opinion.

It is so ordered.

SOTOMAYOR, J. (joined by Ginsburg, Breyer and Kagan, JJ.) (dissenting). The Court today invokes the doctrine of impossibility pre-emption to hold that federal law immunizes generic-drug manufacturers from all state-law failure-to-warn claims because they cannot unilaterally change their labels. I cannot agree. We have traditionally held defendants claiming impossibility to a demanding standard: Until today, the mere possibility of impossibility had not been enough to establish pre-emption.

The Food and Drug Administration (FDA) permits — and, the Court assumes, requires — generic-drug manufacturers to propose a label change to the FDA when they believe that their labels are inadequate. If it agrees that the labels are inadequate, the FDA can initiate a change to the brand-name label, triggering a corresponding change to the generic labels. Once that occurs, a generic manufacturer is in full compliance with both federal law and a state-law duty to warn. Although generic manufacturers may be able to show impossibility in some cases, petitioners, generic

---

9. That said, the dissent overstates what it characterizes as the "many absurd consequences" of our holding. First, the FDA informs us that "[a]s a practical matter, genuinely new information about drugs in long use (as generic drugs typically are) appears infrequently." U.S. Brief 34–35. That is because patent protections ordinarily prevent generic drugs from arriving on the market for a number of years after the brand-name drug appears. Indeed, situations like the one alleged here are apparently so rare that the FDA has no "formal regulation" establishing generic drug manufacturers' duty to initiate a label change, nor does it have any regulation setting out that label-change process. Second, the dissent admits that, even under its approach, generic drug manufacturers could establish pre-emption in a number of scenarios.

manufacturers of metoclopramide (Manufacturers), have shown only that they *might* have been unable to comply with both federal law and their state-law duties to warn respondents Gladys Mensing and Julie Demahy. This, I would hold, is insufficient to sustain their burden.

The Court strains to reach the opposite conclusion. It invents new principles of pre-emption law out of thin air to justify its dilution of the impossibility standard. It effectively rewrites our decision in *Wyeth v. Levine,* 555 U.S. 555 (2009), which holds that federal law does not pre-empt failure-to-warn claims against brand-name drug manufacturers. And a plurality of the Court tosses aside our repeated admonition that courts should hesitate to conclude that Congress intended to pre-empt state laws governing health and safety. As a result of today's decision, whether a consumer harmed by inadequate warnings can obtain relief turns solely on the happenstance of whether her pharmacist filled her prescription with a brand-name or generic drug. The Court gets one thing right: This outcome "makes little sense."

I

A

Today's decision affects 75 percent of all prescription drugs dispensed in this country. The dominant position of generic drugs in the prescription drug market is the result of a series of legislative measures, both federal and state.

. . . .

. . . [L]egislative efforts to expand production and consumption of generic drugs have proved wildly successful. It is estimated that in 1984, when the Hatch–Waxman Amendments were enacted, generic drugs constituted 19 percent of drugs sold in this country. Today, they dominate the market. Ninety percent of drugs for which a generic version is available are now filled with generics. In many cases, once generic versions of a drug enter the market, the brand-name manufacturer stops selling the brand-name drug altogether. Reflecting the success of their products, many generic manufacturers, including the Manufacturers and their *amici,* are huge, multinational companies. In total, generic drug manufacturers sold an estimated $66 billion of drugs in this country in 2009.

B

As noted, to obtain FDA approval a generic manufacturer must generally show that its drug is the same as an approved brand-name drug. It need not conduct clinical trials to prove the safety and efficacy of the drug. This does not mean, however, that a generic manufacturer has no duty under federal law to ensure the safety of its products. The FDA has limited resources to conduct postapproval monitoring of drug safety. See *Wyeth,* 555 U.S., at 578. Manufacturers, we have recognized, "have superior access to information about their drugs, especially in the postmarketing phase as new risks emerge." *Id.,* at 578–579. Federal law thus obliges drug manufacturers — both brand-name and generic — to monitor the safety of their products.

Under federal law, generic manufacturers must "develop written procedures for the surveillance, receipt, evaluation, and reporting of postmarketing adverse drug experiences" to the FDA. 21 CFR § 314.80(b); see also § 314.98 (making § 314.80 applicable to generic manufacturers); Brief for United States as *Amicus Curiae* 6, and n. 2 (hereinafter U.S. Brief). They must review all reports of adverse drug experiences received from "any source." § 314.80(b). . . .

Generic manufacturers, the majority assumes, also bear responsibility under federal law for monitoring the adequacy of their warnings. I agree with the majority's conclusion that generic manufacturers are not permitted unilaterally to change their labels through the "changes-being-effected" (CBE) process or to issue additional warnings through "Dear Doctor" letters. According to the FDA, however, that generic manufacturers cannot disseminate additional warnings on their own does not mean that federal law permits them to remain idle when they conclude that their labeling is inadequate. FDA regulations require that labeling "be revised to include a warning as soon as there is reasonable evidence of an association of a serious hazard with a drug." 21 CFR § 201.57(e) (2006), currently codified at 21 CFR § 201.80(e) (2010). . . . The FDA construes this regulation to oblige generic manufacturers "to seek to revise their labeling and provide FDA with supporting information about risks" when they believe that additional warnings are necessary. U.S. Brief 20.

. . . .

II

This brings me to the Manufacturers' pre-emption defense. . . .

A

Two principles guide all pre-emption analysis. First, "'the purpose of Congress is the ultimate touchstone in every pre-emption case.'" *Wyeth,* 555 U.S., at 565 (quoting *Medtronic, Inc. v. Lohr,* 518 U.S. 470, 485 (1996)). Second, "'[i]n all pre-emption cases, and particularly in those in which Congress has legislated . . . in a field which the States have traditionally occupied, . . . we start with the assumption that the historic police powers of the States were not to be superseded by the Federal Act unless that was the clear and manifest purpose of Congress.'" *Wyeth,* 555 U.S., at 565 (quoting *Lohr,* 518 U.S., at 485; some internal quotation marks omitted; alterations in original).

These principles find particular resonance in these cases. The States have traditionally regulated health and safety matters. Notwithstanding Congress' "certain awareness of the prevalence of state tort litigation" against drug manufacturers, *Wyeth,* 555 U.S., at 575, Congress has not expressly pre-empted state-law tort actions against prescription drug manufacturers, whether brand-name or generic. To the contrary, when Congress amended the FDCA in 1962 to "enlarg[e] the FDA's powers to 'protect the public health' and 'assure the safety, effectiveness, and reliability of drugs,' [it] took care to preserve state law." *Id.,* at 567 (quoting 76 Stat. 780). . . . Notably, although Congress enacted an express pre-emption provision for medical devices in 1976, it included no such provision in the Hatch–Waxman Amendments eight years later. Cf. *Wyeth,* 555 U.S., at 567, 574–575. Congress' "silence on the issue . . . is powerful evidence that [it] did not intend FDA oversight to be the exclusive means of ensuring drug safety and effectiveness." *Id.,* at 575.

B

Federal law impliedly pre-empts state law when state and federal law "conflict"— *i.e.*, when "it is impossible for a private party to comply with both state and federal law" or when state law "stands as an obstacle to the accomplishment and execution of the full purposes and objectives of Congress." *Crosby v. National Foreign Trade Council*, 530 U.S. 363, 372–373 (2000) (internal quotation marks omitted). The Manufacturers rely solely on the former ground of pre-emption.

Impossibility pre-emption, we have emphasized, "is a demanding defense." *Wyeth*, 555 U.S., at 573. Because pre-emption is an affirmative defense, a defendant seeking to set aside state law bears the burden to prove impossibility. To prevail on this defense, a defendant must demonstrate that "compliance with both federal and state [law] is a physical impossibility." *Florida Lime & Avocado Growers, Inc. v. Paul*, 373 U.S. 132, 142–143 (1963). . . . In other words, there must be an "inevitable collision" between federal and state law. *Florida Lime*, 373 U.S., at 143. "The existence of a hypothetical or potential conflict is insufficient to warrant" pre-emption of state law. *Rice v. Norman Williams Co.*, 458 U.S. 654, 659 (1982). . . . In other words, the mere possibility of impossibility is not enough.

The Manufacturers contend that it was impossible for them to provide additional warnings to respondents Mensing and Demahy because federal law prohibited them from changing their labels unilaterally. They concede, however, that they could have asked the FDA to initiate a label change. If the FDA agreed that a label change was required, it could have asked, and indeed pressured, the brand-name manufacturer to change its label, triggering a corresponding change to the Manufacturers' generic labels. Thus, had the Manufacturers invoked the available mechanism for initiating label changes, they may well have been able to change their labels in sufficient time to warn respondents. Having failed to do so, the Manufacturers cannot sustain their burden (at least not without further factual development) to demonstrate that it was impossible for them to comply with both federal and state law. At most, they have demonstrated only "a hypothetical or potential conflict." *Rice*, 458 U.S., at 659.

Like the majority, the Manufacturers focus on the fact that they cannot change their labels unilaterally—which distinguishes them from the brand-name-manufacturer defendant in *Wyeth*. They correctly point out that in *Wyeth* we concluded that the FDA's CBE regulation authorized the defendant to strengthen its warnings before receiving agency approval of its supplemental application describing the label change. 555 U.S., at 568–571. . . . But the defendant's label change was contingent on FDA acceptance, as the FDA retained "authority to reject labeling changes made pursuant to the CBE regulation." *Wyeth*, 555 U.S., at 571. Thus, in the long run, a brand-name manufacturer's compliance with a state-law duty to warn required action by two actors: The brand-name manufacturer had to change the label and the FDA, upon reviewing the supplemental application, had to agree with the change. The need for FDA approval of the label change did not make compliance with federal and state law impossible in every case. Instead, because the defendant bore the burden to show impossibility, we required it to produce "clear evidence that the FDA would not have approved a change to [the] label." *Ibid.*

I would apply the same approach in these cases. . . . Just like the brand-name manufacturer in *Wyeth,* the Manufacturers had available to them a mechanism for attempting to comply with their state-law duty to warn. Federal law thus "accommodated" the Manufacturers' state-law duties. It was not necessarily impossible for the Manufacturers to comply with both federal and state law because, had they approached the FDA, the FDA may well have agreed that a label change was necessary. Accordingly, as in *Wyeth,* I would require the Manufacturers to show that the FDA would not have approved a proposed label change. They have not made such a showing: They do "not argue that [they] attempted to give the kind of warning required by [state law] but [were] prohibited from doing so by the FDA." *Wyeth,* 555 U.S., at 572.

This is not to say that generic manufacturers could never show impossibility. If a generic-manufacturer defendant proposed a label change to the FDA but the FDA rejected the proposal, it would be impossible for that defendant to comply with a state-law duty to warn. Likewise, impossibility would be established if the FDA had not yet responded to a generic manufacturer's request for a label change at the time a plaintiff's injuries arose. A generic manufacturer might also show that the FDA had itself considered whether to request enhanced warnings in light of the evidence on which a plaintiff's claim rests but had decided to leave the warnings as is. But these are questions of fact to be established through discovery. Because the burden of proving impossibility falls on the defendant, I would hold that federal law does not render it impossible for generic manufacturers to comply with a state-law duty to warn as a categorical matter.

. . . .

C

The majority concedes that the Manufacturers might have been able to accomplish under federal law what state law requires. To reach the conclusion that the Manufacturers have nonetheless satisfied their burden to show impossibility, the majority invents a new pre-emption rule: "The question for 'impossibility' is whether the private party could *independently* do under federal law what state law requires of it." *Ante* (emphasis added). Because the Manufacturers could not have changed their labels without the exercise of judgment by the FDA, the majority holds, compliance with both state and federal law was impossible in these cases.

. . . .

With so little support in our case law, the majority understandably turns to other rationales. None of the rationales that it offers, however, makes any sense. First, it offers a *reductio ad absurdum:* If the possibility of FDA approval of a label change is sufficient to avoid conflict in these cases, it warns, as a "logical conclusion" so too would be the possibility that the FDA might rewrite its regulations or that Congress might amend the Hatch–Waxman Amendments. The logic of this conclusion escapes me. Conflict analysis necessarily turns on existing law. It thus would be ridiculous to conclude that federal and state law do not conflict on the ground that the defendant could have asked a federal agency or Congress to change the law. Here, by contrast, the Manufacturers' compliance with their state-law duty to warn did not require them to ask for a change in federal law, as the majority itself recognizes. The FDA already afforded them a mechanism for attempting to comply with their state-law duties. Indeed, the majority assumes that FDA regulations *required* the Manufacturers to request a label change when they had "reasonable evidence of an association of a serious hazard with a drug." 21 CFR § 201.57(e).

Second, the majority suggests that any other approach would render conflict pre-emption "illusory" and "meaningless." It expresses concern that, without a robust view of what constitutes conflict, the Supremacy Clause would not have "any force" except in cases of express pre-emption. To the extent the majority's purported concern is driven by its *reductio ad absurdum*, that concern is itself illusory, for the reasons just stated. To the extent the majority is concerned that our traditionally narrow view of what constitutes impossibility somehow renders conflict pre-emption as a whole meaningless, that concern simply makes no sense: We have repeatedly recognized that conflict pre-emption may be found, even absent impossibility, where state law "stands as an obstacle to the accomplishment and execution of the full purposes and objectives of Congress." The majority's expansive view of impossibility is thus unnecessary to prevent conflict pre-emption from losing all meaning.[13]

Third, a plurality of the Court adopts the novel theory that the Framers intended for the Supremacy Clause to operate as a so-called *non obstante* provision. According to the plurality, *non obstante* provisions in statutes "instruc[t] courts not to apply the general presumption against implied repeals." From this understanding of the Supremacy Clause, the plurality extrapolates the principle that "courts should not strain to find ways to reconcile federal law with seemingly conflicting state law."

This principle would have been news to the Congress that enacted the Hatch–Waxman Amendments in 1984: Our precedents hold just the opposite. For more than half a century, we have directed courts to presume that congressional action does *not* supersede "the historic police powers of the States . . . unless that was the clear and manifest purpose of Congress." *Rice v. Santa Fe Elevator Corp.*, 331 U.S. 218, 230 (1947). . . . We apply this presumption against pre-emption both where Congress has spoken to the pre-emption question and where it has not. . . .

The plurality's new theory of the Supremacy Clause is a direct assault on these precedents.[4] Whereas we have long presumed that federal law does not pre-empt, or repeal, state law, the plurality today reads the Supremacy Clause to operate as a provision instructing courts "*not* to apply the general presumption against implied repeals." And whereas we have long required evidence of a "clear and manifest" purpose to pre-empt, *Rice*, 331 U.S., at 230, the plurality now instructs courts to

13. Justice Thomas . . . has previously expressed the view that obstacle pre-emption is inconsistent with the Constitution. That position, however, has not been accepted by this Court, and it thus should not justify the majority's novel expansion of impossibility pre-emption.

4. The author of the law review article proposing this theory of the Supremacy Clause acknowledges as much. See Nelson, Preemption, 86 Va. L.Rev. 225, 304 (2000) ("The *non obstante* provision rejects an artificial presumption that Congress did not intend to contradict any state laws and that federal statutes must therefore be harmonized with state law"). The plurality, on the other hand, carefully avoids discussing the ramifications of its new theory for the longstanding presumption against pre-emption.

4. *From Failure to Warn to Design Defect: Bartlett.* In *Mutual Pharmaceutical Co. v. Bartlett*, 133 S.Ct. 2466 (2013), the plaintiff suffered permanent disabilities and horrific disfigurements after taking an FDA-approved generic pain reliever. The drug's federally approved label did not include a warning as to the risk of these side effects. In the lower federal courts, plaintiff prevailed on a claim of design defect. Specifically, the First Circuit Court of Appeals held that the product's greater risks relative to other similarly effective pain relievers, as well as its lack of adequate labeling, rendered the product defectively designed under New Hampshire's risk-utility test for design defect.

In a 5-4 decision authored by Justice Alito, the Supreme Court held that Bartlett's design defect claim was preempted. Federal law, the Court reasoned, barred Mutual Pharmaceutical from unilaterally taking the very actions necessary to enable it to comply with New Hampshire products liability law: namely, changing the drug's chemical composition or its warning label. The Court conceded that, as a practical matter, Mutual Pharmaceutical could also comply with state law either by pulling its drug from the market or by continuing to sell the drug while paying damages to persons injured by its defects. However, it concluded that a recognition of either of these modes of compliance would undermine the purpose of preemption doctrine, which is to enable product sellers who comply with federal safety requirements to sell their products without facing liability.

Justice Breyer's dissent, joined by Justice Kagan, endorsed the First Circuit's conclusion that the manufacturer could comply with both bodies of law by ceasing to sell the drug or by incurring liability. Neither result, he reasoned, would "seriously undercut" the purposes of Congress's scheme for approving and labeling drugs. Justice Sotomayor, joined by Justice Ginsburg, likewise argued that New Hampshire products liability law did not, strictly speaking, require Mutual Pharmaceutical to do anything but rather imposed on it a duty to compensate persons injured by the drug's defects for so long as Mutual chose to sell the drug.

5. *Fraud on a Federal Agency.* In *Buckman Co. v. Plaintiffs' Legal Committee*, 531 U.S 341 (2001), a class of patients sued the manufacturer of allegedly defective screws used in surgery and the consultant (Buckman Co.) who assisted the manufacturer in filing and pursuing its application to the FDA for approval to market the screws. The plaintiffs alleged that the manufacturer, with Buckman's help, had obtained that approval by submitting false documentation to the agency. A majority of seven held that the patients could not recover against Buckman on the theory that the consultant's defrauding of the FDA was tortious as to the patients. Permitting the recognition of a "fraud-on-the-agency" tort, the Court reasoned, would upset the carefully constructed administrative process established by Congress for approving medical devices.

6. *State Regulatory Compliance Statutes: Desiano, Garcia, and Kent.* A number of states — most prominently, Michigan, Texas, and New Jersey — have passed legislation that, *as a matter of state law*, forecloses or limits failure-to-warn claims against pharmaceutical companies whose warning labels comply with FDA standards. Although such statutes might appear to sidestep federalism issues by accomplishing their objective through state tort law alone, matters are not so simple.

A relatively narrow but important pharmaceutical preemption issue was presented in *Desiano v. Warner-Lambert & Co.*, 467 F.3d 85 (2d Cir. 2006), *cert. granted sub nom.* Warner-Lambert Co., LLC. V. Kent, 551 U.S. 1190 (2007). *Desiano* involved a Michigan regulatory compliance statute that immunizes pharmaceutical manufacturers from liability if their product is FDA-approved, but creates an exception to the immunity when a plaintiff is able to prove that the company intentionally submitted false information to the FDA or intentionally withheld legally required information from the FDA. (The plaintiff must also prove that the FDA would have made a different regulatory decision if the required information had been submitted). Warner-Lambert argued that, under *Buckman*, the foregoing exception to Michigan's regulatory compliance defense is preempted. Writing for a panel of the Second Circuit, Judge Calabresi disagreed, distinguishing *Buckman*. For example, he reasoned that the presumption against preemption applied to Desiano's action, because—unlike the federal regulatory-based claim in *Buckman*—it was a traditional state common law tort claim, which the Michigan legislature had chosen to preserve in the event that the FDA's decision was based on false submissions by the pharmaceutical company.

Because the Second Circuit's resolution of this issue conflicted with that of the Sixth Circuit in *Garcia v. Wyeth-Ayerst Labs.*, 385 F.3d 961 (6th Cir. 2004), the Supreme Court granted certiorari. Notwithstanding their desire to settle the circuit split, however, the Justices were unable to do so, dividing 4-4 (with Chief Justice Roberts not participating). Warner-Lambert Co., LLC. v. Kent, 552 U.S. 440 (2008) (per curiam). The Second Circuit's decision in *Desiano*—and the circuit split—remain intact, and subsequent decisions in federal and state courts have come down on both sides of the issue. *Compare, e.g.*, Lofton v. McNeil Consumer & Specialty Pharms., 672 F.3d 372 (5th Cir. 2012) (following *Garcia*) *with* Yocham v. Novartis Pharm. Corp., 736 F. Supp. 2d 875, 885 (D.N.J. 2010) (following *Desiano*).

7. ERISA Preemption. The Employment Retirement Income Security Act (ERISA) sets federal standards for how companies must set up and fund retirement and benefit plans for their employees. Overwhelmingly, employee healthcare plans, including many of those operated through managed care organizations (MCOs), are organized under ERISA. During the 1990s and early 2000s, patients who believed they were injured because of a healthcare plan's wrongful denial of coverage for the cost of a medical procedure or course of treatment frequently sued their MCO and/or healthcare plan. These defendants responded by asserting that ERISA preempted such suits. Their argument was that ERISA expressly supersedes state laws that "relate to any employment benefit plan" governed by the statute. 29 U.S.C. § 1144. After several years of splits among lower federal courts, the U.S. Supreme Court ruled that ERISA preempts state-law "wrongful denial of medical coverage" claims brought against an ERISA-governed plan or MCO. Aetna Health Inc. v. Davila, 542 U.S. 200 (2004). Lower courts have read *Davila*'s preemptive sweep broadly. *See, e.g.*, Lind v. Aetna Health, Inc., 466 F.3d 1195 (10th Cir. 2006) (*Davila* meant to leave no room for state-law wrongful denial of coverage claims); Mayeaux v. Louisiana Health Services and Indemnity Co., 376 F.3d 420 (5th Cir. 2004) (same).

REFERENCES/FURTHER READING

Daubert and Science in the Courts

Marcia Angell, *Science on Trial: The Clash of Medical Evidence and the Law in the Breast Implant Case* (1996).

Erica Beecher-Monas, *The Heuristics of Intellectual Due Process: A Primer for Triers of Science*, 75 N.Y.U. L. Rev. 1563 (2000).

David E. Bernstein, Frye, Frye *Again: The Past, Present, and Future of the General Acceptance Test*, 41 Jurimetrics J. 385 (2001).

David S. Caudill, *Give Me a Line in a U.S. Supreme Court Opinion or in Official Commentary to the Rules of Evidence for Admissibility of Experts in Court, and I Will Move the [Legal] World*, 39 Hous. L. Rev. 437 (2002).

Michael D. Green, *Bendectin and Birth Defects: The Challenges of Mass Toxic Substances Litigation* (1996).

Edward J. Imwinkelried, *Should the Courts Incorporate a Best Evidence Ruling into the Standard Determining the Admissibility of Scientific Testimony?: Enough Is Enough Even When It Is Not the Best*, 50 Case W. Res. L. Rev. 19 (1999).

Sheila Jasanoff, *Science at the Bar* (1995).

Gore, Williams, and Punitive Damages (with notes on Tobacco Litigation)*

Theodore Eisenberg & Martin T. Wells, *The Predictability of Punitive Damages Awards in Published Opinions, The Impact of* BMW v. Gore *on Punitive Damages Awards, and Forecasting Which Punitive Awards Will Be Reduced*, 7 S. Ct. Econ. Rev. 59 (1999).

Mark Geistfeld, *Constitutional Tort-Reform*. 38 Loy. L.A. L. Rev. 1095 (2005).

John C. Jeffries, Jr., *A Comment on the Constitutionality of Punitive Damages*, 72 Va. L. Rev. 139 (1986).

Lisa Litwiller, *Has the Supreme Court Sounded the Death Knell for Jury-Assessed Punitive Damages? A Critical Re-Examination of the American Jury*, 36 U.S.F. L. Rev. 411 (2002).

Colleen P. Murphy, *Judgment as a Matter of Law on Punitive Damages*, 75 Tul. L. Rev. 459 (2000).

Richard W. Murphy, *Punitive Damages, Explanatory Verdicts, and the Hard Look*, 76 Wash. L. Rev. 995 (2001).

Robert A. Rabin, *The Tobacco Litigation: A Tentative Assessment*, 51 DePaul L. Rev. 331 (2001).

Doug Rendleman, *Common Law Restitution in the Mississippi Tobacco Settlement: Did the Smoke Get in Their Eyes?* 33 Ga. L. Rev. 847 (1999).

Victor E. Schwartz, Mark A. Behrens & Rochelle M. Tedesco, *Selective Due Process: The United States Supreme Court Has Said That Punitive Damages Awards Must Be Reviewed for Excessiveness, But Many Courts Are Failing to Follow the Letter and Spirit of the Law*, 82 Or. L. Rev. 33 (2003).

Anthony J. Sebok, *After* Philip Morris v. Williams*: What Is Left of the "Single Digit" Ratio?*, 2 Charleston L. Rev. 287(2008).

Benjamin C. Zipursky, *A Theory of Punitive Damages*, 84 Tex. L. Rev. 105 (2006).

---

* For additional analyses of *Gore* and punitive damages, see the References/Further Reading section at the end of Chapter 8.

Buckley and Fear of Disease

Kenneth Abraham, *Liability for Medical Monitoring and the Problem of Limits*, 88 Va. L. Rev. 1975 (2002).

Mark Geistfeld, *The Analytics of Duty: Medical Monitoring and Related Forms of Economic Loss*, 88 Va. L. Rev. 1921 (2002).

John C.P. Goldberg & Benjamin C. Zipursky, *Unrealized Torts*, 88 Va. L. Rev. 1625 (2002).

James A. Henderson, Jr. & Aaron D. Twerski, *Asbestos Litigation Gone Mad: Exposure-Based Recovery for Increased Risk, Mental Distress, and Medical Monitoring*, 53 S.C. L. Rev. 815 (2002).

Andrew R. Klein, *Fear of Disease and the Puzzle of Future Cases in Tort*, 35 U.C. Davis L. Rev. 965 (2002).

Wyeth, Pliva, and Preemption

Mary J. Davis, *Unmasking the Presumption in Favor of Preemption*, 53 S.C. L. Rev. 967 (2002).

Steven Gardbaum, *The Nature of Preemption*, 79 Cornell L. Rev. 767 (1994).

Roderick M. Hills, Jr., *Against Preemption: How Federalism Can Improve the National Legislative Process*, 82 N.Y.U. L. Rev. 1 (2007).

Keith N. Hylton, *An Economic Perspective on Preemption*, 53 B.C.L. Rev. 203 (2012).

Keith N. Hylton, *Preemption and Products Liability: A Positive Theory* 16 S. Ct. Econ. Rev. 205 (2008).

Russell Korobkin, *The Failed Jurisprudence of Managed Care and How to Fix It: Reinterpreting ERISA Preemption*, 51 UCLA L. Rev. 457 (2003).

Richard A. Nagareda, *FDA Preemption: When Tort Law Meets the Administrative State*, 1 Journal of Tort Law (No. 1) (2006).

Caleb Nelson, *Preemption*, 86 Va. L. Rev. 225 (2000).

Ronen Perry, *Differential Preemption*, 72 Ohio St. L.J. 821 (2011).

Robert L. Rabin, *Territorial Claims in the Domain of Accidental Harm: Conflicting Conceptions of Tort Preemption*, 74 Brook. L. Rev. 987 (2009).

Catherine M. Sharkey, *Inside Agency Preemption*, 110 Mich. L. Rev. 521 (2012).

Catherine M. Sharkey, *Products Liability Preemption: An Institutional Approach*, 76 Geo. Wash. L. Rev. 449 (2008).

Catherine M. Sharkey, *Preemption by Preamble: Federal Agencies and the Federalization of Tort Law*, 56 DePaul L. Rev. 227 (2007).

Catherine M. Sharkey, *Federalism in Action: FDA Regulatory Preemption in Pharmaceutical Cases in State Versus Federal Courts*, 15 Brook. J.L. & Pol'y 1013 (2007).

Benjamin C. Zipursky, Palsgraf, *Punitive Damages, and Preemption*, 125 Harv. L. Rev. 1757 (2012).

APPENDIX

MATERIALS CONCERNING WALTER v. WAL-MART STORES, INC.

I. **Plaintiff's Complaint**

II. **Defendant's Answer**

III. **Requests for Documents and Interrogatories**

IV. **Notice of Deposition of Antoinette Walter**

V. **Jury Verdict Form**

VI. **Consent Agreement: *In re: Henry Lovin, III***

VII. **Supplemental Notes and Questions**

Sections I-VI of this appendix reproduce documents referenced in the discussion of *Walter v. Wal-Mart* in Chapter 1. Section VII provides further information about the litigation and discusses additional procedural, substantive, and tactical issues it posed. The authors gratefully acknowledge the assistance of Steven Silin, Esq. and Mark Franco, Esq. in assembling these materials.

I. PLAINTIFF'S COMPLAINT

STATE OF MAINE
KNOX, SS.

SUPERIOR COURT
CIVIL ACTION
DOCKET NO.

ANTOINETTE WALTER, *
*
Plaintiff, *
*
vs. *
*
*
WAL-MART STORES, INC., #1797, *
an Arkansas Corporation with a place of *
business located in Rockland, Maine, *
*
Defendant, *

COMPLAINT AND DEMAND FOR JURY TRIAL

1. At all times pertinent hereto the Plaintiff was a resident of Rockland, County of Knox and State of Maine.

2. That at all times relevant hereto the Defendant was an Arkansas corporation doing business in Rockland, County of Knox and State of Maine and did operate a pharmacy at that location.

3. That on or about May 7, 1997, Plaintiff's physician, Dr. Stephen Ross, wrote Plaintiff a prescription for Chlorambucil (2 mg.).

4. That on or about that date the Defendant by or through one of its employees or agents, did undertake to fill that prescription and did fill that prescription in a negligent, careless and reckless manner, specifically included but not limited to substituting a different drug, Melthalan, for the drug prescribed by Dr. Ross.

5. That as a result of the Defendant's actions as aforesaid the Plaintiff did suffer severe, painful and permanent, physical and emotional injuries, including an extended hospitalization because of the adverse reaction that the inappropriately filled medication caused.

6. Because of the Defendant's actions as aforesaid the Plaintiff did incur and will continue to incur great expenses in an effort to heal the said injuries.

7. The Plaintiff does hereby make a demand for trial by jury.

WHEREFORE, Plaintiff demands judgment against this Defendant in an amount which will fairly and reasonably compensate her together with interest and costs.

DATED at Lewiston, Maine this 12th day of May, 1998.

____

Steven D. Silin, Esquire -- Bar Roll #2686
Attorney for Plaintiff

II. DEFENDANT'S ANSWER

STATE OF MAINE **KNOX, SS.**	**SUPERIOR COURT** **CIVIL ACTION** **DOCKET NO: CV-98-035**

ANTOINETTE WALTER	)	
	)	
Plaintiff	)	
	)	**ANSWER TO PLAINTIFF'S COMPLAINT AND DEMAND FOR JURY TRIAL**
vs.	)	
	)	
WAL-MART STORES, INC.	)	
	)	
Defendant	)	

NOW COMES Defendant Wal-Mart Stores, Inc. (hereinafter referred to as "Wal-Mart") and answers Plaintiff's Complaint and Demand for Jury Trial as follows:

1. Defendant Wal-Mart admits the allegations contained in Paragraph 1 of Plaintiff's Complaint.

2. Defendant Wal-Mart admits the allegations contained in Paragraph 2 of Plaintiff's Complaint.

3. Defendant Wal-Mart has insufficient information with which to form a belief as to the truth of the allegations contained in Paragraph 3 of Plaintiff's Complaint and, therefore, denies same.

4. Defendant Wal-Mart denies the allegations contained in Paragraph 4 of Plaintiff's Complaint.

5. Defendant Wal-Mart denies the allegations contained in Paragraph 5 of Plaintiff's Complaint.

6. Defendant Wal-Mart denies the allegations contained in Paragraph 6 of Plaintiff's Complaint.

7. Defendant Wal-Mart admits the allegations contained in Paragraph 7 of Plaintiff's Complaint.

WHEREFORE, Defendant Wal-Mart respectfully requests that Plaintiff's Complaint be dismissed and for its costs and for such other relief the Court deems just and appropriate.

AFFIRMATIVE DEFENSES

1. The Plaintiff's Complaint fails to state a claim upon which relief may be granted.

2. The negligence of the Plaintiff was equal to or greater than the alleged negligence of the Defendant.

3. The Plaintiff's claim is barred by the doctrine of mitigation of damages.

Dated at Portland, Maine, this 28th day of May, 1998.

Mark V. Franco, Esq.
Attorney for Defendant Wal-Mart Stores, Inc.

THOMPSON & BOWIE
Three Canal Plaza
P. O. Box 4630
Portland, ME 04112
(207) 774-2500

STATE OF MAINE
KNOX, SS.

SUPERIOR COURT
CIVIL ACTION
DOCKET NO: CV-98-035

ANTOINETTE WALTER)
)
Plaintiff)
)
vs.)
)
WAL-MART STORES, INC.)
)
Defendant)

REQUEST FOR PRODUCTION OF DOCUMENTS PROPOUNDED TO PLAINTIFF

NOW COMES Defendant, Wal-Mart Stores, Inc., and requests, pursuant to Rule 34 of the Maine Rules of Civil Procedure, that Plaintiff, Antoinette Walter, produce for inspection and copying by the Defendant at the offices of Thompson & Bowie, Three Canal Plaza, Portland, Maine, within thirty (30) days, the following documents:

1. A certified, legible copy of any memoranda, notes, correspondence, reports including pharmacology reports, or other documents of any kind, of any hospital, laboratory, clinic or other medical or health facility, by or at which the Plaintiff has been examined. treated, or tested within the last ten years;

2. Legible copies of any and all reports, correspondence, memoranda, notes including office notes or other documents of any kind whatsoever reflecting the examination, testing, or treatment provided by any physician, technician, physical therapist, or other practitioner of the healing arts, or psychologist, psychiatrist, marriage and/or sex counselor, or other treating individual, relative to the Plaintiff within ten years prior to this request;

3. Legible copies of any report, list, memoranda, graph, correspondence or other documents of any kind, reflecting in any way test or treatment or examination performed on or with the Plaintiff, within the ten years prior to the date of this request;

4. Each and every statement, bill, check or other document of any kind reflecting any medical expenses on the part of the Plaintiff, related to the occurrence of which the Plaintiff s complained in this action;

5. Each and every document of any kind which relates in any way to the damages which are not of a medical nature which the Plaintiff claims to have suffered or incurred in relation to the subject matter of this action;

6. Any and all notes, memoranda, correspondence, reports, or other documents of any kind, reflecting treatment, examination, testing, or consultation for each and every psychologist, psychiatrist, psychotherapist, or similar health professional, relating to injuries allegedly sustained by the Plaintiff relative to the occurrence which forms the subject matter of this suit;

7. Each and every document in the nature of a report or otherwise reflecting any of the Plaintiff's expert's opinions concerning the subject matter of this action,

Dated at Portland, Maine, this 26th day of June, 1998.

Mark V. Franco, Esq.
Attorney for Defendant Wal-Mart Stores, Inc.
Bar Roll No: 2967

THOMPSON & BOWIE
Three Canal Plaza
P. O. Box 4630
Portland, ME 04112
(207) 774-2500

F. The term "the incident" as used in these Interrogatories shall mean the incident which occurred on or about the date, which allegedly caused the damage, as set forth in your Complaint.

G. When referring to non-natural persons, to "identify" means to state the full name, form (e.g., corporation, partnership, Professional Association, etc.), state the origin and principal place of business.

H. When referring to objects or things (other than documents), to identify means to describe the object or thing by stating its approximate size (dimensions) and weight, color, function, purpose, the materials of which it is (or was) composed, and any and all serial numbers or other identifying numbers, letters, or marks. When the request to identify objects or things refers to a group or class, the identifying marks, letters or numbers of a series, so long as all items in the series are substantially identical.

INTERROGATORIES

1. Please identify yourself by stating your full name, present address, present employment position, if any, date of birth, the full name and present address of your spouse, if you are married, your height and weight as of the time of the incident referred to in the Complaint, color of hair, color of eyes, Social Security number, and the names, ages and addresses of your children, if any.

2. Please state each of the addresses at which you have lived during the past ten (10) years, together with the inclusive dates for each such residence address.

3. Please state the full names, current addresses, employment positions and employers of each and every person who, to your knowledge or to that of your agents, attorneys or employees have knowledge of any of the facts concerning the incident referred to in the Complaint. Identify all documents which relate to each of these persons and the incident.

4. State the full name, current address and employment position of each person who investigated on your behalf the matters which are the subject of this suit. Identify each and every document which relates in any way to this Interrogatory answer.

5. Set forth in full the substance of any admission by a party or by an alleged agent of a party, and include within your answer the name of the person making each such admission, the date and time of the admission, and the name and address of all

persons present at the time of the admission. Identify each and every document which relates in any way to each such admission.

6. Please itemize in complete and exhaustive detail each and every element of damage which you claim or contend is associated with the incident. Identify all documents presently in your possession, or of which you, your agents, servants, employees or attorneys are aware, which in any way substantiates these damages.

7. Do you claim or contend that you incurred any other damages as a result of the incident? If so, please itemize in complete and exhaustive detail each and every element of damage, other than that referred to in the previous Interrogatory, which you claim or contend resulted from the incident. Identify all documents presently in your possession, or of which you, your agents, servants, employees or attorneys are aware, which in any way substantiates these damages.

8. If you, or anyone on your behalf, has obtained any statements concerning the accident which is the subject matter of this lawsuit, describe separately each such statement by setting forth the name and address of the person who gave it, the name, address and employment position of the person who took it, the date it was taken, whether it was written or recorded, whether it was reduced to writing, whether it was signed and the present location of all notes, recordings, transcripts or other writings of any kind pertaining to each statement.

9. If you have made an insurance claim or have been reimbursed by any insurer for any of the losses or damages claimed in this suit, state with respect to each such claim or reimbursement the name and address of the insurer, the policy number under which the claim or reimbursement was made, the nature of insurance coverage provided, the amount claimed, and the amount of each reimbursement made. Identify all documents which relate in any way to the claim or reimbursement.

10. Please identify and itemize by source, date and amount all expenses, including medical expenses, which you claim in this lawsuit as having resulted from the incident.

11. Please identify each and every physician, technician, physical therapist, hospital, laboratory, clinic or other medical person or facility by whom or at which you have been examined, tested or treated during the ten (10) year period immediately preceding the date of the incident. Include within your answer the inclusive dates during which each such exam, test or treatment occurred, together with the name, type and/or description of <u>each</u> such examination, test or treatment and the reason therefore.

12. Please identify each and every physician, technician, physical therapist, hospital, laboratory, clinic or other medical person or facility by whom or at which you have been examined, tested or treated from the date of the incident up to and including the present date; and include within your answer the dates of each exam, test or treatment, and the name, type and/or description of each such examination, test or treatment, and the reason therefore.

13. If you have had physical complaints of any kind since the incident, set forth in complete and exhaustive detail the nature of each such complaint, including the dates and times of each complaint; and describe the frequency, intensity and duration of each complaint.

14. Please describe in detail each and every diagnosis you have received from each and every doctor you have consulted to date concerning injuries you may have suffered as a result of the incident.

15. If you were at any time confined as a result of injuries sustained in this accident, please describe in detail:

a. The period of time you were confined in any hospital;
b. The period of time you were confined to bed; and,
c. The period of time you were confined to your home.

16. Please describe in complete and exhaustive detail your symptoms at the present time, including the sites and intensities of any pain.

17. Please describe in complete and exhaustive detail any and all injuries, painful symptoms, and/or congenital defects you had suffered before the incident, and further indicate how recently before the incident you had been treated for such difficulties, by date.

18. Please describe in detail each and every occupational activity which you were able to perform before the incident that you were unable to perform to any extent as a consequence of the incident.

19. Please describe in detail each and every activity, other than activities referred to in the preceding Interrogatory, which you were able to perform before the incident which you claim you cannot perform now as a result of the incident.

20. Do you claim or contend that you are entitled to damages for pain and suffering?

21. If so, please list in precise detail each and every occurrence, symptom or other factor which in any way supports this claim or contention.

22. State how the occurrence which is the subject of this suit took place setting forth, in detail, the events in the order in which they occurred.

23. Identify each expert witness you will call by stating his name, address, employment position and a summary of his qualifications as an expert; state the subject matter of which he is expected to testify, the substance of all facts and opinions to which he is expected to testify, and a summary of the grounds for each opinion he will give.

Dated at Portland, Maine, this 26th day of June, 1998.

Mark V. Franco, Esq.
Attorney for Defendant Wal-Mart Stores, Inc.
Bar Roll No: 2967

THOMPSON & BOWIE
Three Canal Plaza
P. O. Box 4630
Portland, ME 04112
(207) 774-2500

STATE OF MAINE
KNOX, SS.

SUPERIOR COURT
CIVIL ACTION
DOCKET NO: 98-035

ANTOINETTE WALTER, *
*
*
*
Plaintiff *
*
WAL-MART STORES, INC. #1797 *
*
*
Defendant *

PLAINTIFF'S REQUEST FOR PRODUCTION OF DOCUMENTS PROPOUNDED TO DEFENDANT

In accordance with the provisions of Rule 34, M.R.Civ.P., the Plaintiff requests the Defendant, to produce for inspection and copying in the offices of Plaintiff's Attorney, 129 Lisbon Street, Lewiston, Maine on or before August 14, 1998 the following:

1. All documents relating in any way to the filling of the prescription for the Plaintiff on or about May 7, 1997, that is the prescription which underlies this complaint, specifically included but not limited to all prescription slips, invoices, incident reports, subsequent directives pertaining to any policies with respect to filling of prescriptions or substituting of prescriptions, or any other documents of any kind relating in any way to the filling of the prescription which is the basis of the complaint in this case.

2. Any and all guidelines, manuals, policies or regulations or any other related documents which relate generally to the filling of prescriptions or substituting of prescriptions used, referred to, made available to, or relied upon by pharmacy employees of the Defendant with respect to the filling or substituting of prescriptions as of May 7, 1997 or at any point subsequent.

3. Any and all documents supporting, or anything relied upon by any employee of the Defendant with respect to, the appropriateness of substituting Chlorambucil (Leukeran) with Melphalan (Alkeran).

4. All literature within the Defendant's possession, custody or control pertaining to Chlorambucil (Leukeran) and Melphalan (Alkeran), derived from medical texts or other medical literature, manuals, guidelines, manufacturer's literature or from any other source, specifically including but not limited to information on dosage and administration, clinical pharmacology, indications and usage, precautions, adverse reactions, contraindications, warnings, substitution with other drugs, or possible anticipated adverse reactions.

DATED: July 14, 1998

Steven D. Silin, Esquire -- Bar Roll #2686
ATTORNEY FOR PLAINTIFF

STATE OF MAINE
KNOX, SS.

SUPERIOR COURT
CIVIL ACTION
DOCKET NO. 98-035

ANTOINETTE WALTER, *
*
Plaintiff, *
*
vs. *
*
*
WAL-MART STORES, INC., #1797, *
*
Defendant, *

PLAINTIFF'S INTERROGATORIES PROPOUNDED TO DEFENDANT

Plaintiff, by and though counsel, requests that the Plaintiff answer, under oath, the following Interrogatories and Request for Production of Documents within thirty days of service upon them in accordance with Rules 33 and 34 of the Maine Rules of Civil Procedure. The Defendant is further requested to provide supplemental information to Plaintiff as it becomes available to them so that the answers may remain true and accurate until this matter is finally adjudicated.

1. Please state the name, address, age, social security number, telephone number, height, weight, name and address of present employer and present occupation or position of each and every person answering these Interrogatories.

2. Have any statements been taken from you or anyone else, by you or anyone acting on your behalf relating to the occurrence which is the subject matter of this lawsuit? If so, for each statement, please state the following:

   a. The name of the person who gave the statement;
   b. The substance of said statement;
   c. The date upon which said statement was taken;
   d. The name of the person who took the statement;
   e. Whether or not the statement was reduced to writing;
   f. The present location of the statement and the name and address of the person who is now in possession of it; and
   g. If you will do so without a formal Notice to Produce, please attach a copy of all statements described in your answer to this Interrogatory if they are in your or your attorney's possession.

3. Please describe in detail the substance of any admission by a party or agent of a party with respect to the facts which give rise to this action, including within your answer the names and addresses of the person or persons making each admission, the substance of each admission, date and time of each admission and the names and addresses of any person present at the time of each admission.

4. State the full name and last known address of each and every person known to you, your agents, servants, employees or attorneys who has or may have information with regard to the subject matter of this lawsuit and summarize what you understand this information to be.

5. Please state the full name and complete address of each and every person you intend to call upon on your behalf as an expert witness in this matter, and, as to each such person, please state:

   a. In what field this witness is an expert, and a resume of his/her education and experience and qualifications in such field;
   b. The date, place and form of each occasion when he/ she has been offered as an expert witness and, with respect to each such occasion, the subject matter upon which he/she was called to testify, whether he/she did in fact qualify as an expert, and a detailed description of the technical area, if any, in which he/she is qualified as an expert;
   c. The name of each organization with which he/she is affiliated and with respect to his/her testimony, the full name and complete address of each person, firm or corporation with whom he/she has consulted concerning his/her testimony;
   d. The date of publication, publisher, or any text, textbook, article or other published material which was authored by said expert;
   e. The subject matter in which the expert is expected to testify;
   f. The substance of all facts and opinions to which the expert is expected to testify and a summary of the grounds for each such opinion; and
   g. A description of any reports, memoranda, correspondence, notes or writings of any kind in any way related to his/her anticipated testimony and the date, author, addressee and substance of each.

6. Please state the name and current address of each and every person who you intend to call as a witness and who will testify to the facts.

7. The name of the pharmacist and/or pharmacy technician or assistant involved in the filling or execution of the prescription for Plaintiff Antoinette Walter at the Rockland Wal-Mart Store on or about May 7, 1997 for Chlorambucil -- as prescribed by Dr. Stephen Ross, and the following information:

a. Current address;
b. Current employment status;
c. Position as of May 7, 1997 and as of this date;
d. License status as of May 7, 1997 and as of this date;
3. Educational training and employment background prior to May 7, 1997.

8. With respect to any pharmacist or pharmacy technicians, not included in the previous interrogatory answer, that were on duty at the Rockland Wal-Mart Store on May 7, 1997 please provide the following information:

a. Name;
b. Current address;
c. Current employment status;
d. Employment position as of May 7, 1997;
e. License status as of May 7, 1997 and as of this date;
f. Educational training and employment background prior to May 7, 1997.

9. The name and current employment position of any and all Wal-Mart personnel or any other individuals who investigated or made inquiry into the specific prescription practices which underlies the Complaint in this case, including but not limited to any state or other governmental regulatory or oversight board or personnel. With respect to any such individuals please provide their address and position.

DATED: July 14, 1998

Steven D. Silin, Esquire -- Bar Roll #2686
ATTORNEY FOR PLAINTIFF

C:\FILES\CLIENTS\WALTER\WALINTE3.DIS

IV. NOTICE OF DEPOSITION OF ANTOINETTE WALTER

V. JURY VERDICT FORM

STATE OF MAINE
KNOX, SS.

SUPERIOR COURT
CIVIL ACTION
DOCKET NO. 98-035

ANTOINETTE WALTER, *
*
Plaintiff, *
*
* JURY VERDICT FORM
vs. *
*
*
WAL-MART STORES, INC., #1797, *
*
Defendant, *

1. What are Antoinette Walter's total damages?

$ 550,000.00

Number of Jurors concurring in verdict 8

Number of Jurors not concurring in verdict 0

DATED: 2-23-99

Robert Lee Bradstreet
FOREPERSON

VI. CONSENT AGREEMENT: *IN RE: HENRY LOVIN, III*

STATE OF MAINE
BOARD OF PHARMACY

In re:	)	CONSENT
Henry Lovin, III, R.Ph.	)	AGREEMENT
Complaint No. PHR–148	)	

PARTIES

This document is a Consent Agreement regarding disciplinary action against Henry Lovin, III's license to practice pharmacy in the State of Maine. The parties to this Consent Agreement are: Henry Lovin, III, R.Ph. ("Mr. Lovin"), the State of Maine Board of Pharmacy ("the Board") and the Maine Department of the Attorney General ("the Attorney General"). This Consent Agreement is entered into pursuant to 32 M.R.S.A. § 13741(2) and 10 M.R.S.A. § 8003(5).

FACTS

1. Mr. Lovin is a licensee of the Board.

2. On or about February 13, 1998, the Board received a complaint from State Pharmacy Inspector Tonya Dickey, a copy of which is annexed hereto and made a part hereof as Exhibit A and which the Board docketed as Complaint No. PHR–148.

3. On June 9, 1998, the Board voted to offer Mr. Lovin this Consent Agreement, in order to resolve Complaint No. PHR–148.

COVENANTS

4. Mr. Lovin admits violations alleged in Complaint No. PHR–148.

5. As discipline for conduct admitted in ¶ 4 above, Mr. Lovin shall, no later

than thirty (30) days after the date of the last signature hereto, pay the Board a monetary penalty of Five Hundred Dollars ($500.00), which payment is to be made to "Treasurer, State of Maine" and remitted to Kelly B. Webster, Complaints & Investigations Clerk, Maine Department of Professional and Financial Regulation, 35 State House Station, Augusta, Maine 04333. Further, effective April 1, 1999, Mr. Lovin's license shall be SUSPENDED for fourteen (14) consecutive days.

6. In his regular application for license renewal, Mr. Lovin shall submit to the Board proof of fifteen (15) extra hours of continuing professional education on a topic relevant to Complaint No. PHR–148.

7. This Consent Agreement is not appealable and is effective until modified or rescinded by the parties hereto.

8. The Board and the Department of the Attorney General may communicate and cooperate regarding any matter related to this Consent Agreement.

9. This Consent Agreement is a public record within the meaning of 1 M.R.S.A. § 402 and will be available for inspection and copying by the public pursuant to 1 M.R.S.A. § 408.

10. Nothing in this Consent Agreement shall be construed to affect any right or interest of any person not a party hereto.

11. Mr. Lovin acknowledges by his signature hereto that he has read this Consent Agreement, that he has had an opportunity to consult with an attorney before executing this Consent Agreement, that he executed this Consent Agreement

- 3 -

of his own free will and that he agrees to abide by all terms and conditions set forth herein.

DATED: 3/6/99 HENRY LOVIN, III, R.Ph.

DATED: 3/9/99 President
Maine Board of Pharmacy

DATED: 3/9/99 JAMES M. BOWIE
Assistant Attorney General

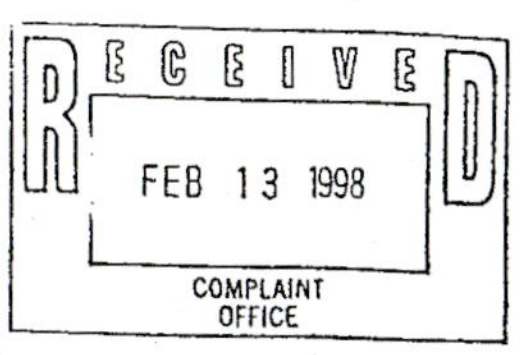

STATE OF MAINE
DEPARTMENT OF PROFESSIONAL
AND FINANCIAL REGULATION
OFFICE OF LICENSING AND REGISTRATION
BOARD OF COMMISSIONERS OF THE PROFESSION OF PHARMACY
35 STATE HOUSE STATION
AUGUSTA, MAINE
04333-0035

ANGUS S. KING, JR.
GOVERNOR

S. CATHERINE LONGLEY
COMMISSIONER
ANNE L. HEAD
DIRECTOR

February 5, 1998

To: Kelly Webster

EXHIBIT A

Please file a complaint against the following license: Henry Lovin III RPh
25 Wadsworth St.
Thomaston, ME 04861
License No. 2960

The statutes and regulation being cited for violation are:

Title 32: Section 13784 (1) Patient Information Regulation
Section 13794 Labeling of Prescriptions
Board Rules, Chapter 16 (1)(B) Patient Counseling Requirements

The above violations are being cited for the error in dispensing caused by Henry Lovin III RPh on a prescription for Antoinette Walter dated 5/7/97.

Sincerely,

Tonya Dickey RPh
Pharmacy Inspector

PHONE: (207)624-8603 (Voice)
INSPECTOR VOICE MAIL: (207)624-8604
PRINTED ON RECYCLED PAPER
(207) 624-8563 (TDD)
FAX: (207)624-8637

VII. SUPPLEMENTAL NOTES AND QUESTIONS

Section II of Chapter 1 discussed some of the basic procedural and substantive issues associated with Antoinette Walter's negligence action against Wal-Mart. The notes that follow provide additional information about the suit and pose additional questions raised by it.

1. *What Went Wrong?* Recall that the trial judge, Judge Marsano, entered judgment as a matter of law for the plaintiff, ruling that a reasonable jury would have to find that Wal-Mart breached the duty of reasonable care it owed to Walter so as to cause her injury. The evidence presented at trial pertaining to Wal-Mart's breach of duty—i.e., its carelessness—was minimal: it consisted entirely of brief testimony from Henry Lovin, the pharmacist employed by Wal-Mart. That testimony came under direct examination from Mr. Silin, the plaintiff's attorney:

MR. SILIN: . . . As I understand it, what you did when you saw [Walter's] prescription receipt, in your mind you thought Alkeran is the brand . . . name for Chlorambucil. Is that what you did?

MR. LOVIN: Yes, unfortunately. . . .

MR. SILIN: You went ahead and filled the prescription with the Alkeran drug instead of the Chlorambucil or the Leukeran drug prescribed by Dr. Ross?

MR. LOVIN: Yes.

MR. SILIN: You would agree with me, would you not, that that was a serious error?

MR. LOVIN: Definitely.

MR. SILIN: That was not the kind of substitution [that] . . . you intentionally or purposely or knowingly [would] make if you were even remotely trying to satisfy the proper standard of care for a pharmacist?

MR. LOVIN: No. . . .

MR. SILIN: This wasn't a purposeful substitution you made because you thought it would be appropriate for the prescription that was written?

MR. LOVIN: No.

MR. SILIN: This simply was an error that you made, a mistake, a serious mistake that resulted in the wrong drug being given to Antoinette Walter?

MR. LOVIN: Yes.

MR. SILIN: As I understand it, at the time this prescription was filled there were various protocols in place at Wal-Mart, and I assume at every other pharmacy on the face of this planet, certainly in this part of the country to help prevent this very thing from ever occurring . . . [and] in the literature [from Wal-Mart] it talks about a four-point step process to double check, triple check that under no circumstances is a wrong drug prescribed for a patient; is that correct?

MR. LOVIN: Right. . . .

MR. SILIN: [To follow this protocol,] . . . what you need to do is to check the stock bottle against the doctor's prescription to make sure . . . [they match]?

MR. LOVIN: True.

MR. SILIN: So would you agree with me that would have been the second error that you did in this case. The first being mixing up the brand names. . . . Then the second mistake was failing to check the stock bottle against the written prescription provided by the doctor?

MR. LOVIN: Yes.

MR. SILIN: That's something that is incumbent upon you as a pharmacist practicing safe pharmacy, complying with the standard of pharmacy care to check the stock bottle against the prescription?

MR. LOVIN: That's correct.

MR. SILIN: If you had, you would have, don't you agree, discovered the mistake that you had made?

MR. LOVIN: Yes. . . .

MR. SILIN: An additional check in your process . . . is for you to . . . counsel the patient, showing her the drug that is prescribed, discussing what it's used for and discussing that in the context of the doctor's specific prescription?

MR. LOVIN: Yes.

MR. SILIN: Would you agree with me that . . . if you had done that, that yet once again your error would have been detected?

MR. LOVIN: It very definitely could have been. . . .

MR. SILIN: There were three chances to find out about [the mistake] and correct it. All three of those checkpoints were missed by you; would you agree with that?

MR. LOVIN: Yes.

On cross-examination conducted by the defense attorney, Mr. Franco, the jury learned that Henry Lovin's father had been a pharmacist, and that Lovin, age 51 at the time of trial, had worked in, and eventually taken over, his father's store before moving to Maine and joining Wal-Mart. Lovin further testified that he had wanted to be a pharmacist since he was a teenager. He professed horror at what had happened to Ms. Walter: "Obviously I [have] been in this career all my life. I went into it to help people, not to cause anybody harm."

The trial transcript does not shed any more light on the explanation for Lovin's error. For example, no evidence was introduced concerning Lovin's general practices as a pharmacist, his record for safety prior to this incident, or the performance evaluations that he had received from his superiors at Wal-Mart. One may perhaps infer from the absence of such evidence that Lovin's mistake was a one-off lapse that came about through an unfortunate sequence of errors. Assuming that this was the case, does it affect your assessment of Lovin's conduct? Is it plausible to argue that a jury was at least permitted to conclude that, although Lovin made a mistake, it was *not* a careless mistake?

2. *A Reasonable Mistake?* In fact, attorney Franco made exactly this argument in opposition to plaintiff's motion for judgment as a matter of law (obviously without success):

> *MR. FRANCO:* With respect to the plaintiff's . . . motion [for judgment as a matter of law], the defendant objects. [It would] be unusual for a trial court to take the issue of negligence away from the jury in a case such as this. . . .
>
> The uncontroverted facts of the case are Mr. Lovin dispensed the wrong medication to Ms. Walter. The law is clear that the fact that somebody makes a mistake in the exercise of their duties, whatever it may be, it doesn't have to be just a pharmacist, it could be in the exercise of driving an automobile, it could be in the exercise of maintaining . . . premises. . . .
>
> There are human factors involved in the law that have to be recognized. Mistakes are made everyday. That doesn't mean that a mistake translates into negligence as a matter of law. If that were the case . . . we might as well just rid the system of the law of negligence. A mistake equals negligence basically means strict liability.
>
> We are not here to talk about strict liability. Whether or not this was an acceptable mistake, whether or not this is a mistake that falls within what a jury would consider to be . . . a reasonable mistake under the circumstances, is up for them to decide, not for this Court to decide as a matter of law. . . .

Franco's observation that mistakes are made every day is surely correct. But how does it support his contention that the jury was entitled to conclude that Lovin acted with reasonable care for Ms. Walter's well-being? What does he have in mind when he says that the jury could have found that Lovin made an "acceptable" or "reasonable" mistake?* What does the trial and appellate courts' rejection of this argument tell you about negligence law's conception of what it means to be act with reasonable care?

3. *How Do We Know How Pharmacists and Pharmacies Should Conduct Themselves?* As indicated in Section II of Chapter 1, attorney Franco also argued that Judge Marsano should grant judgment as a matter of law in favor of Wal-Mart. Among other things, Franco argued that the plaintiff had failed to produce an expert to establish a

---

* For a decision endorsing the idea that the commission of a mistake does not necessarily entail a finding of carelessness, see Myers v. Beem, 712 P.2d 1092 (Colo. 1985). There, the defendant attorney admitted that he "screwed up" in representing his client, yet the state Supreme Court held that the client was not entitled to a directed verdict on a subsequent claim against the attorney for legal malpractice because a reasonable jury could find that the lawyer's mistake was not a careless mistake. To note the ruling in *Myers* is not to suggest that the Maine Supreme Court erred in reaching the opposite conclusion in *Walter.* As indicated in Chapter 1, even superficially similar precedents are often distinguishable. Certainly *Walter* does not suggest that *all* instances of error constitute instances of carelessness. Rather it holds only that the evidence pertaining to Lovin's errors conclusively established that he was careless.

standard or benchmark against which to assess the reasonableness of Lovin's conduct. Here is part of that argument, which was made to the judge without the jury present:

> *MR. FRANCO:* Your Honor, at this point the defendant would also move for [judgment as a matter of law]. This is what is called a professional tort or an allegation of professional tort. A professional tort . . . requires testimony of an expert witness as to the appropriate standard of care attributable to the defendant.
>
> The [Maine Supreme] Court has made it clear in every case in which they have spoken on this subject that expert testimony is necessary as a matter of law to prove malpractice. What we are talking about is malpractice. We can dance around various terms all we want. But we are talking about [a] professional dispensing a medication. . . .
>
> In the case of a . . . medical professional or a quasi-medical professional, it's the burden of the plaintiff to prove negligence, that is the failure of reasonable care. Reasonable care is that degree of care which a reasonably careful pharmacist would use under similar or like circumstances.
>
> In order to prove the elements . . . of negligence, the plaintiff is required at the outset to establish what the standard of practice is applicable to pharmacists and the pharmacy profession. The record contains no evidence of the standard applicable to Mr. Lovin in this case. The only evidence in this case that was discussed in the context of the standard of practice is the standard of practice that is exercised by Wal-Mart. That is their own practice — their own prescription drug check . . . the four-point check.
>
> There has been an acknowledgement on the part of Mr. Lovin that he made a mistake. There is no question about that. There has never been a question that a mistake was made in the four-point check, in adhering or failing to adhere to the Wal-Mart standard of practice. That Wal-Mart standard of practice doesn't necessarily mean that that's the standard of practice in the pharmacy industry. In fact, there has been no evidence of that. . . .
>
> . . . Mr. Lovin . . . was not here as an expert witness.

Does Franco have a point in noting the absence of any evidence indicating whether other national or local pharmacies follow a protocol like Wal-Mart's? Suppose most of them don't have such a protocol. Would this fact affect your judgment about Wal-Mart's responsibility for Walter's injury?

Obviously, the Maine Supreme Court agreed with Judge Marsano that Franco's objections were off-base, and that the plaintiff was not required to produce an expert to testify whether other pharmacies have in place protocols such as Wal-Mart's, or whether other pharmacists routinely follow those protocols. Its ground for doing so was that certain instances of professional malpractice are so straightforward as to be identifiable by judges and juries without the help of expert testimony as to how prudent members of the profession ordinarily conduct themselves. (It is perhaps also worth noting that, as stated in the Consent Agreement reached between Lovin and the Maine Board of Pharmacy, Lovin's conduct violated Maine regulations as to the proper methods for dispensing prescription medication. The role of regulations in setting standards of care for tort law is discussed in Chapter 6.)

4. *Respondeat Superior Revisited.* As explained briefly in Section II of Chapter 1, the doctrine of *respondeat superior* holds even employers with reasonable hiring and supervision policies and procedures are held responsible for injuries to customers and others caused by an employee's careless performance of his job. Is it fair to say that Franco's arguments in favor of judgment as a matter of law for Wal-Mart, and against entry of judgment for Walter, are really arguments against the application of that well-established doctrine? Do they collapse the issue of whether Lovin behaved reasonably in this instance with the issue of whether Wal-Mart had adopted reasonable policies for the dispensation of prescription medications?

5. *Accepting Responsibility?* As indicated in footnote 1 of the Maine Supreme Court's opinion, attorney Franco opened by telling the jury that "Wal-Mart has never denied responsibility for this incident," and that the major issue it would need to decide is how much compensation was owed to Walter. How could he take that position and then proceed to argue that Wal-Mart was entitled to judgment as a matter of law on the issue of breach, and to contest the entry of judgment as a matter of law for Walter? In a concurring opinion, omitted from the excerpt of *Walter v. Wal-Mart* in Chapter 1, three Justices of the Maine Supreme Court indicated displeasure with the defense's approach:

> WATHEN, C.J. (concurring) (joined by Rudman and Dana, JJ.).
>
> [¶40] I concur in the result, but I reach that result on different grounds. . . . In my judgment, defense counsel in this case admitted liability in his opening statement when he told the jury that Wal-Mart had never denied liability and that the only issue concerned the amount of fair and just compensation. Having made that statement, he then sought to try the issue of liability behind the jurors' backs. To countenance such a strategy would be to ignore the requirement of the Maine Bar Rules that trial counsel employ "such means only as are consistent with truth, and shall not seek to mislead the . . . jury . . . by any artifice or false statement of fact or law." M. Bar R. 3.7(e)(1)(i). . . .

6. *Trial Tactics: Stipulating and Blaming.* Judge Marsano ruled that a reasonable jury not only *could* conclude that Lovin breached the legal standard of reasonable care, but that it *would have to* reach that conclusion. Yet attorney Silin could hardly have been certain at the outset that the judge would issue such a ruling, or that the Supreme Court would uphold any such ruling. Nonetheless, prior to trial, Silin never retained the services of an expert who could testify that Lovin failed to act as would an average qualified pharmacist. Indeed, Silin never even deposed Lovin. What might explain these tactical decisions? Was Silin being cavalier? Was he attempting to minimize the costs of preparing for trial? Or was he justifiably confident that, even if he could not obtain a directed verdict, he could convince a jury that Lovin's error was negligence?

The answer seems to reside in the fact that Silin had obtained through discovery a copy of a letter that Lovin had written in response to an inquiry from the Maine Board of Pharmacy.* In that letter, Lovin apparently expressly acknowledged his mistakes and expressed great remorse over them. In light of this "smoking gun," and conversations between himself and Franco, Silin expected until just before trial that Wal-Mart would *stipulate to liability*, i.e., formally concede at the outset of trial that Lovin had acted unreasonably so as to cause injury to Walter. Even if no stipulation was reached, however, he believed that the letter provided more than enough information to establish that Lovin had acted unreasonably so as to breach a duty owed to Walter.

Consider the following portion of the trial transcript, which reflects a conversation that was held outside of the jury's hearing at the commencement of the trial. Ask yourself whether the issue of stipulating to Lovin's negligence was something the two lawyers had adequately discussed with one another before the trial.

MR. SILIN: I've . . . thought until probably . . . last week . . . that we were going to stipulate to liability. I still don't know how liability is an issue. They want it both ways, to admit to liability but to still have the jury somehow give them an out. I now realize because they are not stipulating to anything that I have to [sic]. I didn't intend until I thought about [it] last week . . . to call Mr. Lovin to establish the elements of negligence in this case. I have no reason to think he's not going to admit everything in there. I have the [letter] to keep him honest. . . .

MR. FRANCO: Your Honor, at this point I'm not prepared to stipulate to liability simply because it's my understanding from speaking to Steve [Silin] that if I had done that, he would fight me tooth and nail over Mr. Lovin testifying at all. I think it's an important part of my case for Mr. Lovin to testify.

THE COURT: I understand that quite often logic yield[s] to tactics; that's where we are at.

Franco's stated reason for refusing to stipulate to liability—to guarantee that Lovin would be able to testify at trial—was in one respect well-taken. Rules of evidence bar the introduction of superfluous or irrelevant testimony. Thus, if the only issues left after stipulation as to liability were the issues of the extent of Walter's damages and whether she failed to mitigate them, the judge might well have ruled that Lovin could not testify because Lovin had nothing to say about those issues. Still, why do you suppose that Franco was so anxious to ensure that Lovin would testify at trial? (Here it may be helpful to recall from Note 1 the nature of the testimony from Lovin elicited by Franco.)

Is there any other explanation for the failure of Silin and Franco to stipulate to liability? Keep in mind that lawyers are ultimately answerable to their clients, and that decisions about litigation strategy, although usually made by trial counsel in consultation with their clients, are sometimes insisted upon by the client, particularly when

* The Board's inquiry ultimately led to the Consent Agreement reproduced in Part VI of this appendix.

the client is a sophisticated business with in-house lawyers of its own. Thus, it is quite possible that Wal-Mart instructed Franco not to stipulate to liability. In hindsight, would Franco and/or Wal-Mart have been well-advised to stipulate that Wal-Mart was liable to Walter for at least some damages? Suppose the jury had never heard Lovin testify to his mistakes, and suppose Silin was not able to harp on Wal-Mart's refusal to "accept responsibility" in his opening and closing statements. Would the jury have returned a damage award of the same magnitude?

7. *Settlement.* Stipulation is a method by which the parties can agree to set aside uncontested issues so as to limit the issues submitted to the jury at trial. Settlement agreements, by contrast, provide a method for resolving all the issues in a case, including damages, and for doing so prior to trial, if possible.

Today, most tort suits are resolved by settlements reached at some point after the filing of the complaint and prior to trial. Such agreements offer various advantages to the parties, including, most importantly, the promise of a prompt disposition of the dispute, and the avoidance of often substantial litigation expenses. The latter is of particular value to defendants, but also provides incentives to settle for plaintiffs. A plaintiff's attorney operating under a contingent fee agreement will often stand to recover a fixed percentage of the plaintiff's recovery, regardless of whether it is received as a settlement payment or a jury award. Still, as the litigation progresses, the plaintiff's lawyer will be required to invest additional hours of work in the litigation. Thus, unless there is reason to believe that the jury will render an award substantially larger than a figure at which the defendant might settle, the plaintiff's attorney's rate of compensation (per hour devoted to the case) will decrease over time.

The typical tort settlement agreement consists of a document, signed by both parties, in which the defendant disavows responsibility or liability for the plaintiff's injury, but nonetheless agrees to pay a certain amount to the plaintiff in order to avoid the trouble and expense of fully litigating the dispute. Often such agreements include confidentiality provisions that forbid either side from disclosing the nature of the lawsuit or the terms of the settlement. This practice is controversial, with critics arguing that such provisions withhold from the public important information about dangers facing the general populace. (For example, imagine that a driver is injured when his car rolls over as he swerves to avoid an obstacle. Now suppose that he sues the car's manufacturer, claiming that it was negligent in producing a car that was prone to roll over under normal driving conditions. If that suit is resolved by a confidential settlement, it cannot serve as a warning to thousands of other drivers who might be at risk of injury through roll-overs.) Some courts have recently promulgated so-called "sunshine" rules that mandate that settlement agreements be publicly available.

Given that tort suits often result in settlement, it is worth pondering why no settlement was reached in *Walter.* Indeed, the failure of the lawyers to come to terms prior to trial is in some respects quite surprising. The issues in the case were not complex by the standards of ordinary tort litigation. Thus, while attorney Silin could not be certain that a jury would find for his client, nor could he predict exactly what they would award her, he had plenty of reason for optimism. Likewise, the defendant's lawyer, Franco, certainly had grounds to worry that the jury would find for Walter and that they would award her a substantial sum. So why couldn't they resolve the matter with a negotiated settlement? Silin's first offer of settlement sought an amount in the neighborhood of $250,000. However, Franco apparently was authorized to offer only about $100,000. Despite further conversations during the course of litigation, the two attorneys could not get any closer to settlement. Does the following excerpt offer insight into the settlement dynamics of the case?

Wal-Mart Shifting Litigation Strategy
The Retailer Settles Cases, Prompting Lawyers To Ask, "What's Happening?"

Catherine Aman & Gary Young
The National Law Journal
September 30, 2002

In late July, Wal-Mart Stores Inc. settled a suit brought by Robert McClung, whose wife was abducted from the parking lot at a Memphis, Tenn., store in 1990 and murdered.

For any other company, resolving a horrific case like this would be routine, but Wal-Mart has a long history of refusing to negotiate with plaintiffs. Indeed, for more than a decade the retailing colossus fought tooth-and-nail against McClung and his lawyer, Bruce Kramer of Borod & Kramer in Memphis. When Wal-Mart first proposed mediation this past May, Kramer said he was "more than skeptical." . . .

The shift in litigation strategy is just one of several significant changes in the company's law department during the past year. . . .

With 4,300 stores worldwide and 100 million shoppers a week, Wal-Mart has more exposure than a Playboy centerfold. According to spokesman William Wertz, the company is sued roughly 5,000 times a year, and, typically, has about 10,000 pending cases. Until recently, Wal-Mart routinely reacted to these challenges by playing judicial hardball.

"They absolutely would not consider settling anything," said Mary Jo O'Neill, acting regional attorney for the Equal Employment Opportunity Commission in Phoenix. Her agency has brought dozens of employment suits against the company in the past decade. "It was part of the corporate culture." Several factors probably forced Wal-Mart to rethink its legal strategy. Among these are a string of embarrassing and expensive court losses in the late 1990s; widespread negative publicity for its hard-nosed litigation style; a threatened $18 million sanction for discovery abuse in 1999; and the 2000 appointment of a new chief executive officer, H. Lee Scott, who appears to back the changes in the law department.

"Wal-Mart has probably recognized that, based on the litigation strategy they chose in the past, they've created a horrible reputation for themselves among judges and lawyers," said Gilbert Adams III, an associate in the Beaumont, Texas, practice of his father, Gilbert T. Adams. The younger Adams, who has brought several suits against the company, added, "That horrible reputation is causing them difficulty litigating cases." . . .

Wal-Mart has also dropped a long-standing policy of retaining only those outside counsel who would work for a flat, per-case fee. Wertz said that the change was prompted by a desire to hire the most qualified attorneys, many of whom insist on hourly compensation. But the change may also reflect a reconsideration of the company's hardball tactics. Critics have long charged that flat-fee arrangements added to Wal-Mart's intransigence, since the company did not have to pay the price for stalling, rejecting settlement offers and insisting on trial. Wertz would not comment on whether Wal-Mart was now settling more cases than in the past. . . .

8. *Summing Up.* What is your impression of tort law in light of the foregoing account of *Walter v. Wal-Mart*? What were the procedural and substantive aspects of the tort system able or unable to accomplish in this instance? Perhaps it will be helpful to break these questions down into other, slightly more manageable questions.

First, and most obviously, one can ask about the desirability of the result: a verdict of $550,000 for the plaintiff, upheld by the trial judge and the Maine Supreme Court. Attorney Silin argued to the jury that Ms. Walter — already 80 at the time — incurred about $70,000 in medical expenses.* Thus, so far as the jury was concerned, the vast bulk of the award — $480,000 — compensated her for the distress, suffering, and lost quality of life associated with illness she was caused to suffer by Wal-Mart's carelessness. Does this figure seem appropriate, excessive, or inadequate? As measured against what criteria or scales? What does this sum represent or accomplish?

Second, one might ask what was accomplished in terms of process. Clearly, both sides were given the ability to discover and present a lot of information to the jury, even though, as it turned out, the jury was permitted to decide only a small portion of the case. Thus, the trial judge and the jury heard from Lovin himself about how the error was caused. They also heard from Walter and a friend of hers about what she did and didn't do after the error occurred, and how it adversely affected her life. And they heard from two doctors — Walter's doctor and an expert hired by Wal-Mart — about the medical effects of the error. In this respect, the procedures of tort law seemed to permit a relatively complete investigation into what went wrong as a predicate to the judge's and the jury's assignation of responsibility. Could similarly complete information have

---

* Fixing the amount of Walter's medical expenses at $70,000 turns out to involve something more than simple arithmetic. Silin based that figure on the total amount billed by medical providers for the services rendered to Walter during and after her hospitalization. As explained in Chapter 1, Section III.A.3, Walter herself did not actually pay the full amount of these bills: at least 80 percent of the charges were probably covered by Medicare — federally-funded health insurance for senior citizens. However, the jury was not told of this fact because of the *collateral source rule*, a doctrine that specifies that jurors are not allowed to consider other sources of compensation to a tort victim in determining damages. The collateral source rule thus dictated that the jury was to be presented with a figure representing Walter's "expenses" even though she didn't pay most of them. Even so, there remained a question as to what that figure should be. This is because the amount of reimbursement paid by the government to providers of medical services to Medicare patients is *not* determined by the amount the providers charge, but rather by schedules set by the government that are invariably lower than those charges. Indeed, in this case, the government's schedules dictated payment to Walter's providers of about $34,000 — roughly half the amount nominally charged by Walter's healthcare providers. Franco argued to the trial judge that the jury should thus have been instructed that Walter's medical "expenses" were $34,000 (what was actually paid) not $70,000 (what the providers billed). Obviously, the judge was unpersuaded.

been obtained by other means? Is there any potential downside to a system that is geared to permit litigants to explore in great depth all the different facets of a dispute?

Another aspect of tort law revealed by *Walter* is that tort suits tend to place the alleged victim and injurer in a starkly adversarial posture, one that can easily block potentially sensible resolutions of disputes even if the key actors — the attorneys and the trial judge — are proceeding in good faith. Moreover, it may at times induce some of these actors to behave in a manner that might strike you as less than ideal. These observations in turn suggest that the proper functioning of tort law cannot help but depend in part on the exercise of good judgment by the professionals who make up the tort bar and bench.

Table of Cases

Italics indicate principal cases.

Index